P9-DTE-808

FOURTH EDITION

Foundations of Physiological Psychology

Neil R. Carlson

University of Massachusetts, Amherst

ALLYN AND BACON

BOSTON • LONDON • TORONTO • SYDNEY • TOKYO • SINGAPORE

Vice-President and Editor-in-Chief, Social Sciences: *Sean W. Wakely*
Senior Editor: *Carolyn Merrill*
Series Editorial Assistant: *Amy Goldmacher*
Marketing Manager: *Joyce Nilsen*
Composition and Prepress Buyer: *Linda Cox*
Manufacturing Buyer: *Megan Cochran*
Cover Administrator: *Linda Knowles*
Photo Researcher: *Helane Prottas*
Production Administrator: *Mary Beth Finch*
Editorial-Production Service: *Barbara Gracia*
Text Designer: *Carol Somberg for Omegatype Typography, Inc.*
Illustrator: *Jay Alexander*

Copyright © 1999, 1995, 1992, 1988 by Allyn and Bacon
A Viacom Company
Needham Heights, MA 02494

Internet: www.abacon.com

All rights reserved. No part of the material protected by this copyright notice may be
reproduced or utilized in any form or by any means, electronic or mechanical, including photocopying, recording, or by any information storage and retrieval system, without written permission from the copyright owner.

Library of Congress Cataloging-in-Publication Data

Carlson, Neil R.
    Foundations of physiological psychology / Neil R. Carson. — 4th
      ed. p.   cm.
    Includes bibliographical references and index.
    ISBN 0–205–28311–X
    1. Psychophysiology.   I. Title.
QP360.C352   1999
612.8—dc21   98–38532
                                          CIP

Photo Credits: p. 3, Tom Bean/© Tony Stone Images; p. 7,
© R. Crandall/The Image Works; p. 15, Bruce Ayres/
© Tony Stone Images; p. 35, © K. Preuss/The Image Works;
p. 36, © Clay Wiseman/Animals Animals; p. 48, © R. Kuiter/
Animals Animals; p. 70, © John Eastcott/YVA Momatiuk/
The Image Works; p. 75, © Dion Ogust/The Image Works;
p. 77, © David Wells/The Image Works; p. 100, © Leonard
Lee Rue, III/Earth Scenes; p. 102, © Topham/The Image
Works; p. 132 © Anupl Manoj Shah/Animals Animals; p. 134,
Paul Grebliunas/© Tony Stone Images; p.137, © Michael
Schwarz/The Image Works; p. 144, © Carson Baldwin, Jr./
Animals Animals; p. 156, © Richard Kolar/Animals Animals;
p. 168, Amwell/© Tony Stone Images; p. 185, Robert E.
Daemmrich/© Tony Stone Images; p. 193, Mark Williams/
© Tony Stone Images; p. 202, Dratch/The Image Works;
p. 215, © Scott Johnson/Animals Animals; p. 241,
© M. Antman/The Image Works; p. 258, David Joel/© Tony
Stone Images; p. 290, Will Hart; p. 297, © Gerard Lacz/
Animals Animals; p. 300, © B. Daemmrich/The Image
Works; p. 318, Lawrence Migdale/© Tony Stone Images;
p. 334, Richard Clintsman/© Tony Stone Images; p. 353,
Will Hart; p. 359, Howard Grey/© Tony Stone Images;
p. 370, Frank Siteman/© Tony Stone Images; p. 385,
© Esbin-Anderson/The Image Works; p. 398, Will Hart;
p. 405, © Cameramann/The Image Works; p. 421,
© J. Griffin/The Image Works; p. 424, © Nancy Rich-
mond/The Image Works; p. 425, © Ellen Senisi/The Image
Works; p. 445, © Rob Crandall/The Image Works; p. 450,
© B. Daemmrich/The Image Works; p. 457, Rosanne Olson/
© Tony Stone Images; p. 469, © B. Daemmrich/The Image
Works; p. 477, Paul Merideth/© Tony Stone Images; p. 491,
© Lee Snider/The Image Works; p. 492, Timothy Shonnard/
© Tony Stone Images.

Printed in the United States of America
10 9 8 7 6 5 4 3 2   03 02 01 00 99

BRIEF CONTENTS

CONTENTS

CHAPTER 4

Psychopharmacology   86

CHAPTER 5

Methods and Strategies of Research   113

CHAPTER 6

Vision   141

CHAPTER **7**

Audition, the Body Senses, and the Chemical Senses   175

CHAPTER **8**

Sleep and Biological Rhythms   209

CHAPTER 11
Ingestive Behavior   306

CHAPTER 12
Learning and
Memory   339

PREFACE

All my life I have wanted to know how things work. When I was a boy I took apart alarm clocks, radios, my mother's sewing machine, and other interesting gadgets, to see what was inside. Much to my parents' relief, I outgrew that habit (or at least got better at putting things back together), but my curiosity is still with me. Since my college days, I have been trying to find out all I can about the workings of the most intricate piece of machinery that we know of: the human brain.

The field of neuroscience research is a very busy and productive one today. A large number of scientists are trying to understand the physiology of behavior, using more and more advanced methods, yielding more and more interesting results. Their findings provide me with much to write about. I admire their dedication and hard work, and I thank them for giving me something to say. Without their efforts I could not have written this book.

I wrote the first edition of this book at the request of my colleagues who teach the course, and who wanted a briefer version of *Physiology of Behavior* with more emphasis on research related to humans. The first part of this book is concerned with foundations: the history of the field, the structure and functions of neurons, neuroanatomy, psychopharmacology, and methods of research. The second part is concerned with inputs: the sensory systems. The third part deals with what might be called "motivated" behavior: sleep, reproduction, emotion, and ingestion. The fourth part deals with learning and with verbal communication. The final part deals with neurological and mental disorders.

There are some important differences between this book and *Physiology of Behavior*. The text of this book is not simply a shorter and denser version of its predecessor. I kept the illustrative examples, especially those dealing with human disorders, and added explanations of phenomena to be sure that students without much background in biology could understand what I was saying. Although I have simplified some of the detailed explanations I have retained the important principles.

STRATEGIES FOR LEARNING

This theme, which runs throughout the book, was created to help apply physiological psychology to daily life. You will find a *Strategies for Learning* heading in Chapter 1, and a chapter entitled *Methods and Strategies of Research*. This chapter does not contain a bewildering list of research methods; instead, the reader are led through a set of hypothetical investigations organized the way that a research project might proceed. Each step illustrates a particular procedure in the context in which it would be applied in an ongoing program.

Strategies for Learning Features

- Each chapter begins with a list of *Learning Objectives*, which also serve as the framework for the study guide that accompanies this text.
- A *Prologue*, which contains the description of an episode involving a neurological disorder or an issue in neuroscience, opens each chapter.
- An *Epilogue* at the end of the chapter resolves the issues raised in the prologue, discussing them in terms of what the reader has learned in the chapter, or introduces a related topic.

- *Interim Summaries* follow each major section of the book. They not only provide useful reviews, but also break each chapter into manageable chunks.
- *Thought Questions* follow most interim summaries, and provide an opportunity to think about what has been learned in the previous section.
- *Definitions of Key Terms* are printed in the margin near the places where the terms are first discussed. *Pronunciation Guides* for terms that might be difficult to pronounce are also found there.

Each chapter ends with *Key Concepts,* which provide a quick review, and a list of *Suggested Readings* that provide more information about the topics discussed in the chapter.

CONTENT CHANGES

This edition contains a new chapter, *Psychopharmacology.* Psychopharmacological methods have become increasingly important in recent years, and the identification of specific classes of receptors and drugs that interact with them have contributed much to our understanding of neural mechanisms of behavior.

Of course, all chapters have been revised. My colleagues keep me busy by providing me with interesting research results to describe in my book. The problem is always to include the interesting new material without letting the length of the book get out of hand. Like the previous editions, this edition contains a chapter entitled *Neurological Disorders,* which is not found in *Physiology of Behavior.*

REVISED FULL-COLOR ART

The book looks different from its predecessors: Most of the illustrations are new, prepared by Jay Alexander, of I-Hua Graphics. Jay also works in the Psychology Department at the University of Massachusetts, and he and I have been working together on my books for several years. I think the result of our collaboration is a set of clear, consistent, and attractive illustrations.

STRATEGIES FOR LEARNING SUPPLEMENTS

I have prepared a revised set of *Animations Disks.* The animations demonstrate some of the most important principles of neuroscience through movement and interactions. The full-color electronic art, coordinated with the text, provides yet another strategy for learning physiological psychology.

A *Study Guide,* which my wife and I wrote, is also available. This workbook provides a framework for guiding study behavior. It promotes a thorough understanding of the principles of physiological psychology through active participation in the learning process. The study guide contains a set of *Concept Cards.* An important part of learning about physiological psychology is acquiring a new vocabulary, and the concept cards will help with this task. Terms are printed on one side of these cards, and definitions are printed on the other.

A diskette containing an interactive *Computerized Self Test,* a set of *Terms and Definitions* for review, and a *Neuroanatomy Review* accompanies each study guide. The self tests and list of terms and definitions present questions and keeps track of the student's progress, presenting missed items until they are correctly answered. The neuroanatomy review presents full-color pictures of the nervous system (along with figures from other chapters) and prompts the student to identify the parts.

IN CONCLUSION

Trying to keep up with the rapid progress being made in neuroscience research poses a challenge for teachers and textbook writers. If a student simply memorizes what we believe at the time to be facts, he or she is left with knowledge that quickly becomes obsolete. In this book I have tried to provide enough background material and enough knowledge of basic physiological processes so that the reader can revise what he or she has learned when research provides us with new information.

I designed this text to be interesting and informative. I have endeavored to provide a solid foundation for further study. Students who will not take subsequent courses in this or related fields should receive the satisfaction of a much better understanding of their own behavior. Also, they will have a greater appreciation for the forthcoming advances in medical practices related to disorders that affect a person's perception, mood, or behavior. I hope that people who carefully read this book will henceforth perceive human behavior in a new light.

ACKNOWLEDGEMENTS

Although I must accept the blame for any shortcomings of the book, I want to thank colleagues who helped me. I thank Paul Wellman for his work on the instructor's manual, and Linda I. Siegel-Stelzer, who wrote the test bank. I want to thank colleagues who helped me with the present edition of this book and the latest edition of *Physiology of Behavior* by sending reprints of their work, suggesting topics that I should cover, sending photographs that have been reproduced in this book, and pointing out deficiencies in the previous edition. I thank:

Peter Arnett, Gary Aston-Jones, Deborah Baldwin, Jeffrey Blaustein, Gemma Calvert, Edna Cohen, Geert DeVries, David Diamond, Nina Dronkers, Guinevere Eden, Owen Floody, Mark George, Eugenia Gurevich, Leonard Hamilton, Marc Hauser, A.J. Hudspeth, Sarah Leibowitz, Deborah Mash, Julian Mercer, Jerrold Meyer, Shiro Minami, Mitchell Nobler, Steven Reppert, Randall Sakai, Dennis Selkoe, Dick Swaab, Simon Thornton, and Joe Tsien.

Several colleagues reviewed the manuscript of parts of this book and of *Physiology of Behavior* and made suggestions for improving the final drafts. I thank:

Anne Powell Anderson, Lisa Baker, Robin Bowers, Joshua E. Blustein, John Broida, David Gilliam, Jeffrey W. Grimm, Ivan Lorentzen, Karen Luh, Eric Nisenbaum, Linda M. Noble, Antonio Nunez, B. Glenn Stanley, Frank Webbe, Meg Waraczynski, and Nancy Woolf

I want to thank the people at Allyn and Bacon. Carolyn Merrill, senior editor, provided assistance, support, and encouragement and helped gather comments and suggestions from colleagues who have read the book. Marilyn Freedman, freelance developmental editor, carefully read my first drafts of many of the chapters and suggested changes that improved the book's clarity. Mary Beth Finch, production editor, got things organized and kept them running smoothly. Barbara Gracia, of Woodstock Publishers' Services, managed the book's production and somehow managed to remain calm and collected (at least when I spoke with her) despite an extremely tight production schedule. Barbara Willette was my copy editor. Her attention to detail uncovered inconsistencies in my terminology, awkwardness in my prose, and disjunctions in my logical discourse and gave me a chance to fix them before anyone else saw them in print.

I must also thank my wife Mary for her support. Writing is a lonely pursuit, because one must be alone with one's thoughts for many hours of the day. I thank her for giving me the time to read, reflect, and write without feeling that I was neglecting her too much.

TO THE READER

I hope that in reading this book you will come not only to learn more about the brain but also to appreciate it for the marvelous organ it is. The brain is wonderfully complex, and perhaps the most remarkable thing is that we are able to use it in our attempt to understand it.

While working on this book, I imagined myself talking with students, telling them interesting stories about the findings of clinicians and research scientists. Imagining your presence made the task of writing a little less lonely. I hope that the dialogue will continue. Please write to me and tell me what you like and dislike about the book. My address is: Department of Psychology, Tobin Hall, University of Massachusetts, Amherst, Massachusetts 01003. My e-mail address is *nrc@psych.umass.edu*. If you write to me (or send me an e-mail), we can make the conversation a two-way exchange.

1

Origins of Physiological Psychology

LEARNING OBJECTIVES

1. Describe the behavior of people with split brains, and explain what this phenomenon contributes to our understanding of self-awareness.

2. Describe the goals of scientific research.

3. Describe the biological roots of physiological psychology.

4. Describe the role of natural selection in the evolution of behavioral traits.

5. Discuss the value of research with animals and ethical issues concerning their care.

6. Describe career opportunities in neuroscience.

René's Inspiration

René, a lonely and intelligent young man of eighteen years, had secluded himself in Saint-Germain, a village to the west of Paris. He had recently suffered a nervous breakdown and chose the retreat to recover. Even before coming to Saint-Germain, he had heard of the fabulous royal gardens built for Henri IV and Marie de Médicis, and one sunny day he decided to visit them. The guard stopped him at the gate, but when he identified himself as a student at the King's School at La Flèche, he was permitted to enter. The gardens consisted of a series of six large terraces overlooking the Seine, planted in the symmetrical, orderly fashion so loved by the French. Grottoes were cut into the limestone hillside at the end of each terrace; René entered one of them. He heard eerie music accompanied by the gurgling of water but at first could see nothing in the darkness. As his eyes became accustomed to the gloom, he could make out a figure illuminated by a flickering torch. He approached the figure, which he soon recognized as that of a young woman. As he drew closer, he saw that she was actually a bronze statue of Diana, bathing in a pool of water. Suddenly, the Greek goddess fled and hid behind a bronze rose bush. As René pursued her, an imposing statue of Neptune rose in front of him, barring the way with his trident.

René was delighted. He had heard about the hydraulically operated mechanical organs and the moving statues, but he had not expected such realism. As he walked back toward the entrance to the grotto, he saw the plates buried in the ground that controlled the valves operating the machinery. He spent the rest of the afternoon wandering through the grottoes, listening to the music and being entertained by the statues.

During his stay in Saint-Germain, René visited the royal gardens again and again. He had been thinking about the relation between the movements of animate and inanimate objects, which had concerned philosophers for some time. He thought he saw in the apparently purposeful, but obviously inanimate, movements of the statues an answer to some important questions about the relation between the mind and the body. Even after he left Saint-Germain, he revisited the grottoes in his memory; and he went so far as to name his daughter Francine after their designers, the Francini brothers of Florence.

The last frontier in this world—and perhaps the greatest one—lies within us. The human nervous system makes possible all that we can do, all that we can know, and all that we can experience. Its complexity is immense, and the task of studying it and understanding it dwarfs all previous explorations our species has undertaken.

One of the most universal of all human characteristics is curiosity. We want to explain what makes things happen. In ancient times, people believed that natural phenomena were caused by animating spirits. All moving objects—animals, the wind and tides, the sun, moon, and stars—were assumed to have spirits that caused them to move. For example, stones fell when they were dropped because their animating spirits wanted to be reunited with Mother Earth. As our ancestors became more sophisticated and learned more about nature, they abandoned this approach (which we call *animism*) in favor of physical explanations for inanimate moving objects. But they still used spirits to explain human behavior.

From the earliest historical times, people have believed that they possessed something intangible that animated them—a mind, a soul, or a spirit. This belief stems from the fact that each of us is aware of his or her own existence. When we think or act, we feel as though something inside us is thinking or deciding to act. But what is the nature of the human mind? We have physical bodies, with muscles that move it and sensory organs such as eyes and ears that perceive information about the world around us. Within our bodies the nervous system plays a central role, receiving information from the sensory organs and controlling the movements of the muscles. But what is the mind, and what role does it play? Does it *control* the nervous system? Is it a *part of* the nervous system? Is it physical and tangible, like the rest of the body, or is it a spirit that will always remain hidden?

Physiological psychologists take an empirical and practical approach to the study of human nature. Most of us believe that the mind is a phenomenon produced by

Most physiological psychologists believe that by understanding the workings of the nervous system we eventually will understand how we think, remember, and act—and will even understand the nature of our own self-awareness.

the workings of the nervous system. We believe that once we understand the workings of the human body—in particular, the workings of the nervous system—we will be able to explain how we perceive, how we think, how we remember, and how we act. We will even be able to explain the nature of our own self-awareness. Of course, we are far from understanding the workings of the nervous system, so only time will tell whether this belief is justified.

◼ UNDERSTANDING HUMAN CONSCIOUSNESS: A PHYSIOLOGICAL APPROACH

How can physiological psychologists study human consciousness? First, let's define our terms. The word *consciousness* can be used to refer to a variety of concepts, including simple wakefulness. Thus, a researcher may write about an experiment using "conscious rats," referring to the fact that the rats were awake and not anesthetized. By *consciousness,* I am referring to something else: the fact that we humans are aware of—and can tell others about—our thoughts, perceptions, memories, and feelings.

We know that brain damage or drugs can profoundly affect consciousness. Because consciousness can be altered by changes in the structure or chemistry of the brain, we may hypothesize that consciousness is a physiological function, just like behavior. We can even speculate about the origins of this self-awareness. Consciousness and the ability to communicate seem to go hand in hand. Our species, with its complex social structure and enormous capacity for learning, is well served by our ability to communicate: to express intentions to one another and to make requests of one another. Verbal communication makes cooperation possible and permits us to establish customs and laws of behavior. Perhaps the evolution of this ability is what has given rise to the phenomenon of consciousness. That is, our ability to send and receive messages with other people enables us to send and receive our own messages—in other words, to think and to be aware of our own existence. (See *Figure 1.1.*)

VIVITVR IN-
GENIO.
CÆTERA MOR-
TIS ERPNT.

FIGURE 1.1

Will the human brain ever completely understand its own workings? A sixteenth-century woodcut from the first edition of *De humani corporis fabrica (On the Workings of the Human Body)* by Andreas Vesalius.

[Courtesy of National Library of Medicine.]

Split Brains

Studies of humans who have undergone a particular surgical procedure demonstrate dramatically how disconnecting parts of the brain that are involved with perceptions from parts involved with verbal behavior also disconnects them from consciousness. These results suggest that the parts of the brain involved in verbal behavior may be the ones responsible for consciousness.

The surgical procedure is one that has been used for people with very severe epilepsy that cannot be controlled by drugs. In these people, nerve cells in one side of the brain become overactive, and the overactivity is transmitted to the other side of the brain by a structure called the corpus callosum. The **corpus callosum** is a large bundle of nerve fibers that connect corresponding parts of one side of the brain with those of the other. Both sides of the brain then engage in wild activity and stimulate each other, causing a generalized epileptic seizure. These seizures can occur many times each day, preventing the person from leading a normal life. Neurosurgeons discovered that cutting the corpus callosum (the **split-brain operation**) greatly reduced the frequency of the epileptic seizures.

Figure 1.2 shows a drawing of the split-brain operation. We see the brain being sliced down the middle, from front to back, dividing it into its two symmetrical halves. A "window" has been opened in the left side of the brain so that we can see the corpus callosum being cut by the neurosurgeon's special knife. (See *Figure 1.2*.)

Sperry (1966) and Gazzaniga and his associates (Gazzaniga, 1970; Gazzaniga and LeDoux, 1978) have studied these patients extensively. The largest part of the brain consists of two symmetrical parts, called the **cerebral hemispheres,** which receive sensory information from the opposite sides of the body. They also control movements of the opposite sides. The corpus callosum enables the two hemispheres to share information so that each side knows what the other side is perceiving and doing. After the split-brain operation is performed, the two hemispheres are disconnected and operate independently. Their sensory mechanisms, memories, and motor systems can no longer exchange information. The effects of these disconnections are not obvious to the casual observer, for the simple reason that only one hemisphere—in most people, the left—controls speech. The right hemisphere of an epileptic person with a split brain appears to be able to understand verbal instructions reasonably well, but it is totally incapable of producing speech.

Because only one side of the brain can talk about what it is experiencing, people who speak with a person with a split brain are conversing with only one hemisphere—the left. The operations of the right hemisphere are more difficult to detect. Even the patient's left hemisphere has to learn about the independent existence of the right hemisphere. One of the first things that these patients say they notice after the operation is that their left hand seems to have a "mind of its own." For example, patients may find themselves putting down a book held in the left hand, even if they have been reading it with great interest. This conflict occurs because the right hemisphere, which controls the left hand, cannot read and therefore finds the book boring. At other times, these patients surprise themselves by making obscene gestures (with the left hand) when they had not intended to. A psychologist once reported that a man with a split brain attempted to beat his wife with one hand and protect her with the other. Did he *really* want to hurt her? Yes and no, I guess.

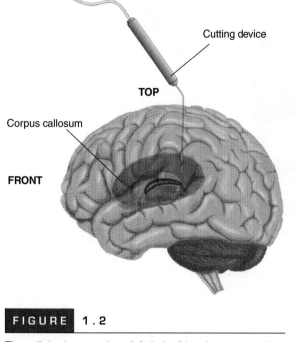

Cutting device

TOP

Corpus callosum

FRONT

FIGURE 1.2

The split-brain operation. A "window" has been opened in the side of the brain so that we can see the corpus callosum being cut at the midline of the brain.

Corpus callosum (*core pus ka low* sum) A large bundle of nerve fibers that connect corresponding parts of one side of the brain with those of the other

Split-brain operation Brain surgery occasionally performed to treat a form of epilepsy; surgeon cuts the corpus callosum, which connects the two hemispheres of the brain.

Cerebral hemispheres The two symmetrical halves of the brain; constitute the major part of the brain.

FIGURE 1.3

Identification of an object in response to an olfactory stimulus by a person with a split brain.

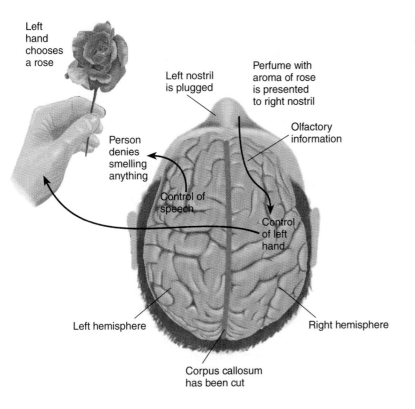

Left hand chooses a rose

Left nostril is plugged

Perfume with aroma of rose is presented to right nostril

Olfactory information

Person denies smelling anything

Control of speech

Control of left hand

Left hemisphere

Right hemisphere

Corpus callosum has been cut

One exception to the crossed representation of sensory information is the olfactory system. That is, when a person sniffs a flower through the left nostril, only the left brain receives a sensation of the odor. Thus, if the right nostril of a patient with a split brain is closed, leaving only the left nostril open, the patient will be able to tell us what the odors are (Gordon and Sperry, 1969). However, if the odor enters the right nostril, the patient will say that he or she smells nothing. But, in fact, the right brain *has* perceived the odor and *can* identify it. To show that this is so, we ask the patient to smell an odor with the right nostril and then reach for some objects that are hidden from view by a partition. If asked to use the left hand, controlled by the hemisphere that detected the smell, the patient will select the object that corresponds to the odor—a plastic flower for a floral odor, a toy fish for a fishy odor, a model tree for the odor of pine, and so forth. But if asked to use the right hand, the patient fails the test because the right hand is connected to the left hemisphere, which did not smell the odor. (See ***Figure 1.3.***)

The effects of cutting the corpus callosum reinforce the conclusion that we become conscious of something only if information about it is able to reach the parts of the brain responsible for verbal communication, which are located in the left hemisphere. If the information does not reach these parts of the brain, then that information does not reach the consciousness associated with these mechanisms. We still know very little about the physiology of consciousness, but studies of people with brain damage are beginning to provide us with some useful insights. This issue is discussed in later chapters.

INTERIM SUMMARY

The concept of the mind has been with us for a long time—probably from the earliest history of our species. Modern science has adopted a belief that the world consists of matter and energy and that what we call the mind can be explained by the same laws that govern all other natural phenomena. Studies of the functions of the human nervous system tend to support this position, as the specific example of the split brain shows. Brain damage, by disconnecting brain functions from the speech mechanisms in the left hemisphere, reveals that the mind does not have direct access to all brain functions.

When sensory information about a particular object is presented to the right hemisphere of a person who has had a split-brain operation, the person is not aware of the object but can, nevertheless, indicate by movements of the left hand that the object has been perceived. This phenomenon suggests that consciousness involves operations of the verbal mechanisms of the left hemisphere. Indeed, consciousness may be, in large part, a matter of our "talking to ourselves." Thus, once we understand the language functions of the brain, we may have gone a long way to understanding how the brain can be conscious of its own existence.

■ THOUGHT QUESTIONS

1. How can you tell whether another person is aware of himself or herself? Could a sufficiently large and complex computer ever be programmed to be aware of itself? Suppose that someone someday claims to have done just that. What kind of evidence would you need to prove or disprove this claim?
2. Clearly, the left hemisphere of a person with a split brain is conscious of the information it receives and of its own thoughts. It is *not* conscious of the mental processes of the right hemisphere. But is it possible that the right hemisphere is conscious, too, but is just unable to talk to us? How could we possibly find out whether it is? Do you see some similarities between this issue and the one raised in the first question?

■ THE NATURE OF PHYSIOLOGICAL PSYCHOLOGY

The modern history of physiological psychology has been written by psychologists who have combined the experimental methods of psychology with those of physiology and have applied them to the issues that concern all psychologists. Thus, we have studied perceptual processes, control of movement, sleep and waking, reproductive behaviors, ingestive behaviors, emotional behaviors, learning, and language. In recent years we have begun to study the physiology of human pathological conditions, such as addictions and mental disorders.

The Goals of Research

The goal of all scientists is to explain the phenomena they study. But what do we mean by *explain?* Scientific explanation takes two forms: generalization and reduction. Most psychologists deal with **generalization.** They explain particular instances of behavior as examples of general laws, which they deduce from their experiments. For instance, most psychologists would explain a pathologically strong fear of dogs as an example of a particular form of learning called *classical conditioning.* Presumably, the person was frightened earlier in life by a dog. An unpleasant stimulus was paired with the sight of the animal (perhaps the person was knocked down by an exuberant dog or was attacked by a vicious one), and the subsequent sight of dogs evokes the earlier response: fear.

Most physiologists deal with **reduction.** They explain complex phenomena in terms of simpler ones. For example, they may explain the movement of a muscle in terms of the changes in the membranes of muscle cells, the entry of particular chem-

Generalization Type of scientific explanation; a general conclusion based on many observations of similar phenomena.

Reduction Type of scientific explanation; a phenomenon is described in terms of the more elementary processes that underlie it.

icals, and the interactions among protein molecules within these cells. By contrast, a molecular biologist would explain these events in terms of forces that bind various molecules together and cause various parts of the molecules to be attracted to one another. In turn, the job of an atomic physicist is to describe matter and energy themselves and to account for the various forces found in nature. Practitioners of each branch of science use reduction to call on sets of more elementary generalizations to explain the phenomena they study.

The task of the physiological psychologist is to explain behavior in physiological terms. But physiological psychologists cannot simply be reductionists. It is not enough to observe behaviors and correlate them with physiological events that occur at the same time. Identical behaviors may occur for different reasons and thus may be initiated by different physiological mechanisms. Therefore, we must understand "psychologically" why a particular behavior occurs before we can understand what physiological events made it occur.

Let me provide a specific example: Mice, like many other mammals, often build nests. Behavioral observations show that mice will build nests under two conditions: when the air temperature is low and when the animal is pregnant. A nonpregnant mouse will build a nest only if the weather is cool, whereas a pregnant mouse will build one regardless of the temperature. The same behavior occurs for different reasons. In fact, nest-building behavior is controlled by two different physiological mechanisms. Nest building can be studied as a behavior related to the process of temperature regulation, or it can be studied in the context of parental behavior.

Sometimes, physiological mechanisms can tell us something about psychological processes. This relationship is particularly true of complex phenomena such as language, memory, and mood, which are poorly understood psychologically. For example, damage to a specific part of the brain can cause very specific impairments in a person's language abilities. The nature of these impairments suggests how these abilities are organized. When the damage involves a brain region that is important in analyzing speech sounds, it also produces deficits in spelling. This finding suggests that the ability to recognize a spoken word and the ability to spell it call on related brain mechanisms. Damage to another region of the brain can produce extreme difficulty in reading unfamiliar words by sounding them out, but it does not impair the person's ability to read words with which he or she is already familiar. This finding suggests that

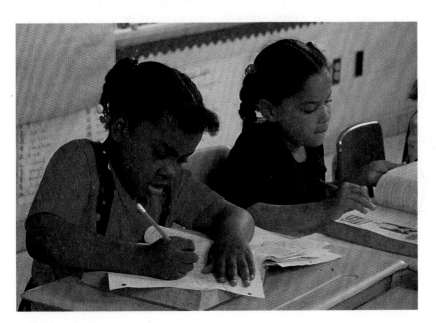

Studies of people with brain damage have given us insights into the brain mechanisms involved in reading and writing.

reading comprehension can take two routes: one that is related to speech sounds and another that is primarily a matter of visual recognition of whole words.

In practice, the research efforts of physiological psychologists involve both forms of explanation—generalization and reduction. Ideas for experiments are stimulated by the investigator's knowledge both of psychological generalizations about behavior and of physiological mechanisms. A good physiological psychologist must therefore be both a good psychologist *and* a good physiologist.

Biological Roots of Physiological Psychology

René Descartes, a seventeenth-century French philosopher and mathematician, has been called the father of modern philosophy. Although he was not a biologist, his speculations about the roles of the mind and brain in the control of behavior provide a good starting point in the history of physiological psychology. Descartes assumed that the world was a purely mechanical entity that, once having been set in motion by God, ran its course without divine interference. Thus, to understand the world, one had only to understand how it was constructed. To Descartes, animals were mechanical devices; their behavior was controlled by environmental stimuli. His view of the human body was much the same: It was a machine. As Descartes observed, some movements of the human body were automatic and involuntary. For example, if a person's finger touched a hot object, the arm would immediately withdraw from the source of stimulation. Reactions like this did not require participation of the mind; they occurred automatically. Descartes called these actions **reflexes** (from the Latin *reflectere,* "to bend back upon itself"). Energy coming from the outside source would be reflected back through the nervous system to the muscles, which would contract. The term is still in use today, but, of course, we explain the operation of a reflex differently. (See *Figure 1.4.*)

Like most philosophers of his time, Descartes was a dualist; he believed that each person possesses a mind—a uniquely human attribute that is not subject to the laws of the universe. But his thinking differed from that of his predecessors in one important way: He was the first to suggest that a link exists between the human mind and its purely physical housing, the brain. He believed that the mind controls the movements of the body, while the body, through its sense organs, supplies the mind with information about what is happening in the environment. In particular, he hypothesized that this interaction takes place in the pineal body, a small organ situated on top of the brain stem, buried beneath the cerebral hemispheres. He noted that the brain contains hollow chambers (the *ventricles*) that are filled with fluid, and he hypothesized that this fluid is under pressure. In his theory, when the mind decides to perform an action, it tilts the pineal body in a particular direction like a little joystick, causing fluid to flow from the brain into the appropriate set of nerves. This flow of fluid causes the same muscles to inflate and move. (See *Figure 1.5.*)

As we saw in the Prologue, the young René Descartes was greatly impressed by the moving statues in the royal gardens (Jaynes, 1970). These devices served as models for Descartes in theorizing about how the body worked. The pressurized water of the moving statues was replaced by pressurized fluid in the ventricles; the pipes were replaced by nerves; the cylinders by muscles; and finally, the hidden valves by the pineal body. This story illustrates one of the first times that a technological device was used as a model for explaining how the nervous system works. In science, a **model** is a relatively simple system that works on known principles and is able to do at least some of the things that

Reflex An automatic, stereotyped movement produced as the direct result of a stimulus.

Model A mathematical or physical analogy for a physiological process; for example, computers have been used as models for various functions of the brain.

FIGURE 1.4

Descartes's explanation of a reflex action to a painful stimulus.

[Stock Montage]

FIGURE 1.5

A woodcut from *De homine* by René Descartes, published in 1662. Descartes believed that the "soul" (what we would today call the *mind*) controls the movements of the muscles through its influence on the pineal body. His explanation is modeled on the mechanism that animated statues in the Royal Gardens. According to his theory, the eyes sent visual information to the brain, where it could be examined by the soul. When the soul decided to act, it would tilt the pineal body (labeled H in the diagram), which would divert pressurized fluid through nerves to the appropriate muscles.

a more complex system can do. For example, when scientists discovered that elements of the nervous system communicate by means of electrical impulses, researchers developed models of the brain based upon telephone switchboards and, more recently, computers. Abstract models, which are completely mathematical in their properties, have also been developed.

Descartes's model was useful because, unlike purely philosophical speculations, it could be tested experimentally. In fact, it did not take long for biologists to prove that Descartes was wrong. For example, Luigi Galvani, a seventeenth-century Italian physiologist, found that electrical stimulation of a frog's nerve caused contraction of the muscle to which it was attached. Contraction occurred even when the nerve and muscle were detached from the rest of the body, so the ability of the muscle to contract and the ability of the nerve to send a message to the muscle were characteristics of these tissues themselves. Thus, the brain did not inflate muscles by directing pressurized fluid through the nerve. Galvani's experiment prompted others to study the nature of the message transmitted by the nerve and the means by which muscles contracted. The results of these efforts gave rise to an accumulation of knowledge about the physiology of behavior.

One of the most important figures in the development of experimental physiology was Johannes Müller, a nineteenth-century German physiologist. (See *Figure 1.6.*) Müller was a forceful advocate of the application of experimental techniques

FIGURE 1.6

Johannes Müller (1801–1858).
(Courtesy of National Library of Medicine.)

to physiology. Previously, the activities of most natural scientists were limited to observation and classification. Although these activities are essential, Müller insisted that major advances in our understanding of the workings of the body would be achieved only by experimentally removing or isolating animals' organs, testing their responses to various chemicals, and otherwise altering the environment to see how the organs responded. His most important contribution to the study of the physiology of behavior was his **doctrine of specific nerve energies.** Müller observed that although all nerves carry the same basic message—an electrical impulse—we perceive the messages of different nerves in different ways. For example, messages carried by the optic nerves produce sensations of visual images, and those carried by the auditory nerves produce sensations of sounds. How can different sensations arise from the same basic message?

The answer is that the messages occur in different channels. The portion of the brain that receives messages from the optic nerves interprets the activity as visual stimulation, even if the nerves are actually stimulated mechanically. (For example, when we rub our eyes, we see flashes of light.) Because different parts of the brain receive messages from different nerves, the brain must be functionally divided: Some parts perform some functions, while other parts perform others.

Müller's advocacy of experimentation and the logical deductions from his doctrine of specific nerve energies set the stage for performing experiments directly on the brain. Indeed, Pierre Flourens, a nineteenth-century French physiologist, did just that. Flourens removed various parts of animals' brains and observed their behavior. By seeing what the animal could no longer do, he could infer the function of the missing portion of the brain. This method is called **experimental ablation** (from the Latin *ablatus*, "carried away"). Flourens claimed to have discovered the regions of the brain that control heart rate and breathing, purposeful movements, and visual and auditory reflexes.

Soon after Flourens performed his experiments, Paul Broca, a French surgeon, applied the principle of experimental ablation to the human brain. Of course, he did not intentionally remove parts of human brains to see how they worked. Instead, he observed the behavior of people whose brains had been damaged by strokes. In 1861 he performed an autopsy on the brain of a man who had had a stroke that resulted in the loss of the ability to speak. Broca's observations led him to conclude that a portion of the cerebral cortex on the left side of the brain performs functions necessary for speech. (See *Figure 1.7.*) Other physicians soon obtained evidence supporting his conclusions. As you will learn in Chapter 13, the control of speech is not localized in a particular region of the brain. Indeed, speech requires many different functions, which are organized throughout the brain. Nonetheless, the method of experimental ablation remains important to our understanding of the brains of both humans and laboratory animals.

As I mentioned earlier, Luigi Galvani used electricity to demonstrate that muscles contain the source of the energy that powers their contractions. In 1870, German physiologists Gustav Fritsch and Eduard Hitzig used electrical stimulation as a tool for understanding the physiology of the brain. They applied weak electrical current to the exposed surface of a dog's brain and observed the effects of the stimulation. They found that stimulation of different portions of a specific region of the brain caused contraction of specific muscles on the opposite side of the body. We now refer to this region as the *primary motor cortex,* and we know that nerve cells there

Doctrine of specific nerve energies Müller's conclusion that because all nerve fibers carry the same type of message, sensory information must be specified by the particular nerve fibers that are active.

Experimental ablation The research method in which the function of a part of the brain is inferred by observing the behaviors an animal can no longer perform after that part is damaged.

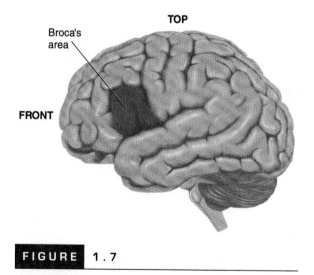

Broca's area

TOP

FRONT

FIGURE 1.7

Broca's area, a region of the brain named for French surgeon Paul Broca. Broca discovered that damage to a part of the left side of the brain disrupted a person's ability to speak.

communicate directly with those that cause muscular contractions. We also know that other regions of the brain communicate with the primary motor cortex and thus control behaviors. For example, the region that Broca found necessary for speech communicates with, and controls, the portion of the primary motor cortex that controls the muscles of the lips, tongue, and throat, which we use to speak.

One of the most brilliant contributors to nineteenth-century science was the German physicist and physiologist Hermann von Helmholtz. Helmholtz devised a mathematical formulation of the law of conservation of energy, invented the ophthalmoscope (used to examine the retina of the eye), devised an important and influential theory of color vision and color blindness, and studied audition, music, and many physiological processes. Although Helmholtz had studied under Müller, he opposed Müller's belief that human organs are endowed with a vital nonmaterial force that coordinates their operations. Helmholtz believed that all aspects of physiology are mechanistic, subject to experimental investigation.

Helmholtz was also the first scientist to attempt to measure the speed of conduction through nerves. Scientists had previously believed that such conduction was identical to the conduction that occurs in wires, traveling at approximately the speed of light. But Helmholtz found that neural conduction was much slower—only about 90 feet per second. This measurement proved that neural conduction was more than a simple electrical message, as we will see in Chapter 2.

Twentieth-century developments in experimental physiology include many important inventions, such as sensitive amplifiers to detect weak electrical signals, neurochemical techniques to analyze chemical changes within and between cells, and histological techniques to see cells and their constituents. Because these developments belong to the modern era, they are discussed in detail in subsequent chapters.

Functionalism: Natural Selection and Evolution

Müller's insistence that biology must be an experimental science provided the starting point for an important tradition. However, other biologists continued to observe, classify, and think about what they saw, and some of them arrived at valuable conclusions. The most important of these biologists was Charles Darwin. (See *Figure 1.8.*) Darwin formulated the principles of *evolution* and *natural selection*, which revolutionized biology. He noted that across succeeding generations, individual members of a species spontaneously undergo structural changes. If these changes produce favorable effects that permit the individual to reproduce more successfully, some of the individual's offspring will inherit the favorable characteristics and will themselves produce more offspring.

Darwin's theory emphasized that all of an organism's characteristics—its structure, its coloration, its behavior—have functional significance. For example, the strong talons and sharp beaks that eagles possess permit the birds to catch and eat prey. Caterpillars that eat green leaves are themselves green, and their color makes it difficult for birds to see them against their usual background. Mother mice construct nests, which keep their offspring warm and out of harm's

 1.8

Charles Darwin (1809–1882). His theory of evolution revolutionized biology and strongly influenced early psychologists.

(North Wind Picture Archives.)

FIGURE 1.9

Bones of the forelimb: (a) human, (b) bat, (c) whale, (d) dog. Through the process of natural selection, these bones have been adapted to suit many different functions.

way. Obviously, the behavior itself is not inherited—how can it be? What *is* inherited is a brain that causes the behavior to occur. Thus, Darwin's theory gave rise to **functionalism,** a belief that characteristics of living organisms perform useful functions. So, to understand the physiological basis of various behaviors, we must first understand what these behaviors accomplish. We must therefore understand something about the natural history of the species being studied so that the behaviors can be seen in context.

To understand the workings of a living organism, we should know what its functions are. For example, the forelimbs shown in Figure 1.9 evolved from those of common ancestors that lived long ago. The differences in their structures are explained by the particular functions they perform. (See *Figure 1.9.*)

A good example of the functional analysis of an adaptive trait was demonstrated in an experiment by Blest (1957). Certain species of moths and butterflies have spots on their wings that resemble eyes—particularly the eyes of predators such as owls. (See *Figure 1.10.*) These insects normally rely on camouflage for protection; the backs of their wings, when folded, are colored like the bark of a tree. However, when a bird approaches, the insect's wings flip open, and the hidden eyespots are suddenly displayed. The bird then tends to fly away rather than eat the insect. Blest performed an experiment to see whether the eyespots on a moth's or butterfly's wings really disturbed birds that saw them. He placed mealworms on different backgrounds and counted how many worms the birds ate. Indeed, when the worms were placed on a background that contained eyespots, the birds tended to avoid them.

Darwin formulated his theory of evolution in an attempt to explain the means by which species acquired their adaptive characteristics. The cornerstone of this theory is the principle of **natural selection.** Briefly, here is how the process works: Every sexually reproducing multicellular organism consists of a large number of cells, each of which contains chromosomes. Chromosomes are large, complex molecules that contain the recipes for producing the proteins that cells need to grow and to perform their functions. In essence, the chromosomes contain the blueprints for the construction (that is, the embryological development) of a particular member of a particular species. If the plans are altered, a different organism is produced.

FIGURE 1.10

The owl butterfly. This butterfly displays its eyespots when approached by a bird. The bird usually will fly away.

(A. Cosmos Blank/Photo Researchers Inc.)

The plans do get altered; mutations occur from time to time. **Mutations** are accidental changes in the chromosomes of sperms or eggs that join together and develop into new organisms. For example, cosmic radiation might strike a chromosome in a cell of an animal's testis or ovary, thus producing a mutation that affects that animal's offspring. Most mutations are deleterious; the offspring either fails to survive or survives with some sort of deficit. (See *Figure 1.11*.) However, a small percentage of mutations are beneficial and confer a **selective advantage** to the organism that possesses them. That is, the animal is more likely than other members of its species to live long enough to reproduce and hence to pass on its chromosomes to its own offspring. Many different kinds of traits can confer a selective advantage: resistance to a particular disease, the ability to digest new kinds of food, more effective weapons for defense or for procurement of prey, and even a more attractive appearance to members of the opposite sex (after all, one must reproduce to pass on one's chromosomes).

Naturally, the traits that can be altered by mutations are physical ones; chromosomes make proteins, which affect the structure and chemistry of cells. But the *effects* of these physical alterations can be seen in an animal's behavior. Thus, the process of natural selection can act on behavior indirectly. For example, if a particular mutation results in changes in the brain that cause a small animal to stop moving and freeze when it perceives a novel stimulus, that animal is more likely to escape undetected when a predator passes nearby. This tendency makes the animal more likely to survive and produce offspring, thus passing on its genes to future generations.

Other mutations are not immediately favorable, but because they do not put their possessors at a disadvantage, they are inherited by at least some members of the species. As a result of thousands of such mutations, the members of a particular species possess a variety of genes and are all at least somewhat different from one another. Variety is a definite advantage for a species. Different environments provide optimal habitats for different kinds of organisms. When the environment changes, species must adapt or run the risk of becoming extinct. If some members of the species possess assortments of genes that provide characteristics permitting them to adapt to the new environment, their offspring will survive, and the species will continue.

When I ask my students what they think the ultimate function of the brain is, they often say "thinking," or "logical reasoning," or "perceiving," or "remembering things." Certainly, the nervous system performs these functions, but they support the primary one: control of movement. The basic function of perception is to inform us of what is happening in our environment so that our behaviors will be adaptive and useful: Perception without the ability to act would be useless. Of course, once perceptual abilities have evolved, they can be used for purposes other than guiding behavior. For example, we can enjoy a beautiful sunset or a great work of art without the perception causing us to do anything in particular. And thinking can often take place without causing any overt behavior. However, the *ability to think* evolved because it has a useful function: It permits us to perform complex behaviors that accomplish useful goals. And whereas reminiscing about things that happened in our past can be an enjoyable pastime, the ability to learn and remember evolved—again—because it permitted our ancestors to profit from experience and perform behaviors that were useful to them.

FIGURE 1.11

An example of a maladaptive trait. Most mutations do not produce selective advantages, but those that do are passed on to future generations.

(J.H. Robinson/Animals Animals.)

Functionalism The principle that the best way to understand a biological phenomenon (a behavior or a physiological structure) is to try to understand its useful functions for the organism.

Natural selection The process by which inherited traits that confer a selective advantage (increase an animal's likelihood to live and reproduce) become more prevalent in the population.

Mutation A change in the genetic information contained in the chromosomes of sperms or eggs, which can be passed on to an organism's offspring; provides genetic variability.

Selective advantage A characteristic of an organism that permits it to produce more than the average number of offspring of its species.

An understanding of the principle of natural selection plays some role in the thinking of every person who undertakes research in physiological psychology. Some researchers explicitly consider the genetic mechanisms of various behaviors and the physiological processes upon which these behaviors depend. Others are concerned with comparative aspects of behavior and its physiological basis; they compare the nervous systems of animals from a variety of species to make hypotheses about the evolution of brain structure and the behavioral capacities that correspond to this evolutionary development. But even though many researchers are not directly involved with the problem of evolution, the principle of natural selection guides the thinking of physiological psychologists. We ask ourselves what the selective advantage of a particular trait might be. We think about how nature might have used a physiological mechanism that already existed in order to perform more complex functions in more complex organisms. When we entertain hypotheses, we ask ourselves whether a particular explanation makes sense from an evolutionary perspective.

INTERIM SUMMARY

All scientists hope to explain natural phenomena. In this context, the term *explanation* has two basic meanings: generalization and reduction. Generalization refers to the classification of phenomena according to their essential features so that general laws can be formulated. For example, observing that gravitational attraction is related to the mass of two bodies and to the distance between them helps to explain the movement of planets. Reduction refers to the description of phenomena in terms of more basic physical processes. For example, gravitation can be explained in terms of forces and subatomic particles.

Physiological psychologists use both generalization and reduction to explain behavior. In large part, generalizations use the traditional methods of psychology. Reduction explains behaviors in terms of physiological events within the body—primarily within the nervous system. Thus, physiological psychology builds on the tradition of both experimental psychology and experimental physiology.

The physiological psychology of today is rooted in important developments of the past. René Descartes proposed a model of the brain based on hydraulically activated statues. His model stimulated observations that produced important discoveries. The results of Galvani's experiments eventually led to an understanding of the nature of the message transmitted by nerves between the brain and the sensory organs and the muscles. Müller's doctrine of specific nerve energies paved the way for study of the functions of specific parts of the brain through the methods of experimental ablation and electrical stimulation.

Darwin's theory of evolution, which was based on the concept of natural selection, provided an important contribution to modern physiological psychology. The theory asserts that we must understand the functions performed by an organ, a body part, or a behavior. Through random mutations, changes in an individual's genetic material cause different proteins to be produced, which results in the alteration of some physical characteristics. If the changes confer a selective advantage on the individual, the new genes will be transmitted to more and more members of the species. Even behaviors can evolve, through the selective advantage of alterations in the structure of the nervous system.

THOUGHT QUESTIONS

What useful functions are provided by the fact that a human can be self-aware? How was this trait selected for during the evolution of our species? Is ours the only species that can be self-aware? How could you prove whether an animal of another species was self-aware? How could you prove that another *person* was self-aware?

Ethical Issues in Research with Animals

Most of the research described in this book involves experimentation on living animals. Any time we use another species of animals for our own purposes, we should be sure that what we are doing is both humane and worthwhile. I believe that a good case can be made that research on the physiology of behavior qualifies on both counts. Humane treatment is a matter of procedure. We know how to maintain laboratory animals in good health in comfortable, sanitary conditions. We know how to administer anesthetics and analgesics so that animals do not suffer during or after surgery, and we know how to prevent infections with proper surgical procedures and the use of antibiotics. Most industrially developed societies have very strict regulations about the care of animals and require approval of the experimental procedures used on them. There is no excuse for mistreating animals in our care. In fact, the vast majority of laboratory animals *are* treated humanely.

We use animals for many purposes. We eat their meat and eggs, and we drink their milk; we turn their hides into leather; we extract insulin and other hormones from their organs to treat people's diseases; we train them to do useful work on farms or to entertain us. Even having a pet is a form of exploitation; it is we—not they—who decide that they will live in our homes. The fact is, we have been using other animals throughout the history of our species.

Pet-owning causes much more suffering among animals than scientific research does. As Miller (1983) notes, pet owners are not required to receive permission from a board of experts that includes a veterinarian to house their pets, nor are they subject to periodic inspections to be sure that their homes are clean and sanitary, that their pets have enough space to exercise properly, or that their pets' diets are appropriate. Scientific researchers are. Miller also notes that fifty times more dogs and cats are killed by humane societies each year because they have been abandoned by former pet owners than are used in scientific research.

If a person believes that it is wrong to use another animal in any way, regardless of the benefits to humans, there is nothing anyone can say to convince him or her of the value of scientific research with animals. For this person, the issue is closed from the very beginning. Moral absolutes cannot be settled logically; like religious beliefs, they can be accepted or rejected, but they cannot be proved or disproved. My arguments in support of scientific research with animals are based on an evaluation of the benefits the research has to humans. (We should also remember that research with animals often helps *other animals;* procedures used by veterinarians, as well as those used by physicians, come from such research.)

Before describing the advantages of research with animals, let me point out that the use of animals in research and teaching is a special target of animal rights activists. Nicholl and Russell (1990) examined twenty-one books written by such activists and counted the number of pages devoted to concern for different uses of animals. Next, they compared the relative concern the authors showed for these uses to the numbers of animals actually involved in each of these categories. The results indicate that the authors showed relatively little concern for animals used for food, hunting, or furs, or for those killed in pounds.

Unlike pet owners, scientists who use animals in their research must follow stringent regulations designed to ensure that the animals are properly cared for.

In contrast, although only 0.3 percent of the animals are used for research and education, 63.3 percent of the pages were devoted to criticizing this use. In terms of pages per million animals used, the authors devoted 0.08 to food, 0.23 to hunting, 1.27 to furs, 1.44 to killing in pounds—and 53.2 to research and education. The authors showed 665 times more concern for research and education than for food and 231 times more than for hunting. Even the use of animals for furs (which consumes two-thirds as many animals as research and education) attracted 41.9 times less attention per animal.

The disproportionate amount of concern that animal rights activists show toward the use of animals in research and education is puzzling, particularly because this is the one *indispensable* use of animals. We *can* survive without eating animals, we *can* live without hunting, we *can* do without furs. But without using animals for research and for training future researchers, we *cannot* make progress in understanding and treating diseases. In not too many years, our scientists will probably have developed a vaccine that will prevent the further spread of AIDS. Some animal rights activists believe that preventing the deaths of laboratory animals in the pursuit of such a vaccine is a more worthy goal than preventing the deaths of millions of humans that will occur as a result of the disease if a vaccine is not found. Even diseases that we have already conquered would take new victims if drug companies could no longer use animals. If they were deprived of animals, these companies could no longer extract hormones used to treat human diseases, and they could not prepare many of the vaccines that we now use to prevent them.

Our species is beset by medical, mental, and behavioral problems, many of which can be solved only through biological research. Let us consider some of the major neurological disorders. Strokes, caused by bleeding or occlusion of a blood vessel within the brain, often leave people partly paralyzed, unable to read, write, or converse with their friends and family. Basic research on the means by which nerve cells communicate with each other has led to important discoveries about the causes of the death of brain cells. This research was not directed toward a specific practical goal; the potential benefits actually came as a surprise to the investigators.

Experiments based on these results have shown that if a blood vessel leading to the brain is blocked for a few minutes, the part of the brain that is nourished by that vessel will die. However, the brain damage can be prevented by first administering a drug that interferes with a particular kind of neural communication. This research is important, because it may lead to medical treatments that can help to reduce the brain damage caused by strokes. But it involves operating on a laboratory animal such as a rat and pinching off a blood vessel. (The animals are anesthetized, of course.) Some of the animals will sustain brain damage, and all will be killed so that their brains can be examined. However, you will probably agree that research like this is just as legitimate as using animals for food.

As you will learn later in this book, research with laboratory animals has produced important discoveries about the possible causes or potential treatments of neurological and mental disorders, including Parkinson's disease, schizophrenia, manic-depressive illness, anxiety disorders, obsessive-compulsive disorders, anorexia nervosa, obesity, and drug addictions. Although much progress has been made, these problems are still with us, and they cause much human suffering. Unless we continue our research with laboratory animals, the problems will not be solved. Some people have suggested that instead of using laboratory animals in our research, we could use tissue cultures or computers. Unfortunately, neither tissue cultures nor computers are substitutes for living organisms. We have no way to study behavioral problems such as addictions in tissue cultures, nor can we program a computer to simulate the workings of an animal's nervous system. (If we could, that would mean we already had all the answers.)

This book will discuss some of the many important discoveries that have helped to reduce human suffering. For example, the discovery of a vaccine for polio, a serious disease of the nervous system, involved the use of rhesus monkeys. As you will learn in Chapter 4, Parkinson's disease, an incurable, progressive neurological disorder, has been treated for years with a drug called L-DOPA, discovered through animal research. Now, because of research with rats, mice, rabbits, and monkeys, stimulated by the accidental poisoning of several young people with a contaminated batch of synthetic heroin, patients are being treated with a drug that may actually slow down the rate of brain degeneration. Researchers have hopes that a drug will be found to prevent the brain degeneration altogether.

The easiest way to justify research with animals is to point to actual and potential benefits to human health, as I have just done. However, we can also justify this research with a less practical, but perhaps equally important, argument. One of the things that characterize our species is a quest for an understanding of our world. For example, astronomers study the universe and try to uncover its mysteries. Even if their discoveries never lead to practical benefits such as better drugs or faster methods of transportation, the fact that they enrich our understanding of the beginning and the fate of our universe justifies their efforts. The pursuit of knowledge is itself a worthwhile endeavor. Surely, the attempt to understand the universe within us—our nervous system, which is responsible for all that we are or can be—is also valuable.

CAREERS IN NEUROSCIENCE

What is physiological psychology, and what do physiological psychologists do? By the time you finish this book, you will have as complete an answer as I can give to these questions, but perhaps it is worthwhile for me to describe the field and careers that are open to those who specialize in it before we begin our study in earnest.

Physiological psychologists study all behavioral phenomena that can be observed in nonhuman animals. They attempt to understand the physiology of behavior: the role of the nervous system, interacting with the rest of the body (especially the endocrine system, which secretes hormones), in controlling behavior. They study such topics as sensory processes, sleep, emotional behavior, ingestive behavior, aggressive behavior, sexual behavior, parental behavior, and learning and memory. They also study animal models of disorders that afflict humans, such as anxiety, depression, obsessions and compulsions, phobias, psychosomatic illnesses, and schizophrenia.

Although physiological psychology is the original name for this field, several other terms are now in general use, such as *biological psychology, biopsychology, psychobiology,* and *behavioral neuroscience.* Most professional physiological psychologists have received a Ph.D. from a graduate program in psychology or from an interdisciplinary program. (My own university awards a Ph.D. in Neuroscience and Behavior. The program includes faculty members from the departments of psychology, biology, biochemistry, and computer science.)

Physiological psychology belongs to the larger field of *neuroscience.* Neuroscientists concern themselves with all aspects of the nervous system: its anatomy, chemistry, physiology, development, and functioning. The research of neuroscientists ranges from the study of molecular genetics to the study of social behavior. The field has grown enormously in the last few years; the most recent meeting of the Society for Neuroscience was attended by over twenty thousand members and graduate students.

Most professional physiological psychologists are employed by colleges and universities, where they are engaged in teaching and research. Others are employed by institutions devoted to research—for example, laboratories owned and operated by national governments or by private philanthropic organizations. A few work in industry, usually for pharmaceutical companies that are interested in assessing the

Physiological psychologist
A scientist who studies the physiology of behavior, primarily by performing physiological and behavioral experiments with laboratory animals.

effects of drugs on behavior. To become a professor or independent researcher, one must receive a doctorate—usually a Ph.D., although some people turn to research after receiving an M.D. Nowadays, most physiological psychologists spend two years in a temporary postdoctoral position, working in the laboratory of a senior scientist to gain more research experience. During this time, they write articles describing their research findings and submit them for publication in scientific journals. These publications are an important factor in obtaining a permanent position.

Two other fields often overlap with that of physiological psychology: *neurology* and *experimental neuropsychology*. Neurologists are physicians involved in the diagnosis and treatment of diseases of the nervous system. Most neurologists are solely involved in the practice of medicine, but a few engage in research devoted to advancing our understanding of the physiology of behavior. They study the behavior of people whose brains have been damaged by natural causes, using advanced brain-scanning devices to study the activity of various regions of the brain as a subject participates in various behaviors. This research is also carried out by experimental neuropsychologists—scientists with a Ph.D. in psychology and specialized training in the principles and procedures of neurology.

Not all people who are engaged in neuroscience research have doctoral degrees. Many research technicians perform essential—and intellectually rewarding—services for the scientists with whom they work. Some of these technicians gain enough experience and education on the job to enable them to collaborate with their employers on their research projects rather than simply work for them.

INTERIM SUMMARY

Research on the physiology of behavior necessarily involves the use of laboratory animals. It is incumbent on all scientists using these animals to see that they are housed comfortably and treated humanely, and laws have been enacted to ensure that they are. Such research has already produced many benefits to humankind and promises to continue to do so.

Physiological psychology (also called biological psychology, biopsychology, psychobiology, and behavioral neuroscience) is a field devoted to our understanding of the physiology of behavior. Physiological psychologists are allied with other scientists in the broader field of neuroscience. To pursue a career in physiological psychology (or in the sister field of experimental neuropsychology), one must obtain a graduate degree and (usually) serve two years or more as a "postdoc"—a scientist pursuing further training.

THOUGHT QUESTIONS

Why do you think some people are apparently more upset about using animals for research and teaching than for other purposes?

STRATEGIES FOR LEARNING

The brain is a complicated organ. After all, it is responsible for all our abilities and all our complexities. Scientists have been studying this organ for a good many years and (especially in recent years) have been learning a lot about how it works. It is impossible to summarize this progress in a few simple sentences; therefore, this book contains a lot of information. I have tried to organize this information logically, telling you what you need to know in the order you need to know it. (After all, to understand some things, you sometimes need to understand other things first.) I have also tried to write as clearly as possible, making my examples as simple and as vivid as I can. Still, you cannot expect to master the information in this book by simply giving it a passive read; you will have to do some work.

Learning about the physiology of behavior involves much more than memorizing facts. Of course, there *are* facts to be memorized: names of parts of the nervous system, names of chemicals and drugs, scientific terms for particular phenomena and procedures used to investigate them, and so on. But the quest for information is nowhere near completed; we know only a small fraction of what we have to learn. And almost certainly, many of the "facts" that we now accept will someday be shown to be incorrect. If all you do is learn facts, where will you be when these facts are revised?

The antidote to obsolescence is knowledge of the process by which facts are obtained. In science, facts are the conclusions scientists make about their observations. If you learn only the conclusions, obsolescence is almost guaranteed. You will have to remember which conclusions are overturned and what the new conclusions are, and that kind of rote learning is hard to do. But if you learn about the research strategies the scientists use, the observations they make, and the reasoning that leads to the conclusions, you will develop an understanding that is easily revised when new observations (and new "facts") emerge. If you understand what lies behind the conclusions, then you can incorporate new information into what you already know and revise these conclusions yourself.

In recognition of these realities about learning, knowledge, and the scientific method, this book presents not just a collection of facts, but a description of the procedures, experiments, and logical reasoning that scientists have used in their attempt to understand the physiology of behavior. If, in the interest of expediency, you focus on the conclusions and ignore the process that leads to them, you run the risk of acquiring information that will quickly become obsolete. On the other hand, if you try to understand the experiments and see how the conclusions follow from the results, you will acquire knowledge that lives and grows.

Now let me offer some practical advice about studying. You have been studying throughout your academic career, and you have undoubtedly learned some useful strategies along the way. Even if you have developed efficient and effective study skills, at least consider the possibility that there might be some ways to improve them.

If possible, the first reading of the assignment should be as uninterrupted as you can make it; that is, read the chapter without worrying much about remembering details. Next, after the first class meeting devoted to the topic, read the assignment again in earnest. Use a pen or pencil as you go, making notes. *Don't use a highlighter.* Sweeping the felt tip of a highlighter across some words on a page provides some instant gratification; you can even imagine that the highlighted words are somehow being transferred to your knowledge base. You have selected what is important, and when you review the reading assignment you have only to read the highlighted words. But this is an illusion.

Be active, not passive. Force yourself to write down whole words and phrases. The act of putting the information into your own words will not only give you something to study shortly before the next exam but also put something into your head (which is helpful at exam time). Using a highlighter puts off the learning until a later date; rephrasing the information in your own words starts the learning process *right then*.

A good way to get yourself to put the information into your own words (and thus into your own brain) is to answer the questions in the study guide. If you cannot answer a question, look up the answer in the book, *close the book*, and write the answer down. The phrase *close the book* is important. If you *copy* the answer, you will get very little out of the exercise. However, if you make yourself remember the information long enough to write it down, you have a good chance of remembering it later. The importance of the study guide is *not* to have a set of short answers in your own handwriting that you can study before the quiz. The behaviors that lead to long-term learning are doing enough thinking about the material to summarize it in your own words, then going through the mechanics of writing those words down.

Before you begin reading the first chapter, let me say a few things about the design of the book that may help you with your studies. The text and illustrations are integrated as closely as possible. In my experience, one of the most annoying aspects of reading some books is not knowing when to look at an illustration. Therefore, in this book you will find figure references in boldfaced italics (like this: ***Figure 5.6***), which means "stop reading and look at the figure." These references appear in locations I think will be optimal. If you look away from the text then, you will be assured that you will not be interrupting a line of reasoning in a crucial place and will not have to reread several sentences to get going again. You will find sections like this: "Figure 3.1 shows an alligator and a human. This alligator is certainly laid out in a linear fashion; we can draw a straight line that starts between its eyes and continues down the center of its spinal cord. (See ***Figure 3.1.***)" This particular example is a trivial one and will give you no problems no matter when you look at the figure. But in other cases the material is more complex, and you will have less trouble if you know what to look for before you stop reading and examine the illustration.

You will notice that some words in the text are *italicized* and others are printed in **boldface.** Italics mean one of two things: Either the word is being stressed for emphasis and is not a new term, or I am pointing out a new term that is not necessary for you to learn. On the other hand, a word in boldface is a new term that you should try to learn. Most of the boldfaced terms in the text are part of the vocabulary of the physiological psychologist. Often, they will be used again in a later chapter. As an aid to your studying, definitions of these terms are printed in the margin of the page, along with pronunciation guides for those terms whose pronunciation is not obvious. In addition, a comprehensive index at the end of the book provides a list of terms and topics, with page references.

At the end of each major section (there are usually three to five of them in a chapter) you will find an *Interim Summary*, which provides a place for you to stop and think again about what you have just read to make sure that you understand the direction in which the discussion has gone. Many interim summaries are followed by some thought questions, which may serve to stimulate your thoughts about what you have learned and apply them to questions that have not yet been answered. Taken together, these sections provide a detailed summary of the information introduced in the chapter. My students tell me that they review the interim summaries just before taking a test.

Okay, the preliminaries are over. The next chapter starts with something you can sink your (metaphorical) teeth into: the structure and functions of neurons, the most important elements of the nervous system.

EPILOGUE

Models of Brain Functions

René Descartes had no way to study the operations of the nervous system. He did, however, understand how the statues in the Royal Gardens at Saint-Germain were powered and controlled, which led him to view the body as a complicated piece of plumbing. Many scientists have followed Descartes's example, using technological devices that were fashionable at the time to explain how the brain worked.

What motivates people to use artificial devices to explain the workings of the brain? The most important reason, I suppose, is that the brain is enormously complicated. Even the most complex human inventions are many times simpler than the brain, and because they have been designed and made by people, people can understand them. If an artificial device can do some of the things that the brain does, then perhaps both the brain and the device accomplish their tasks in the same way.

Most models of brain function developed in the last half of this century have been based on the modern, general-purpose digital computer. Actually, they have been based not on the computers themselves but on computer *programs*. Computers can be programmed to store any kind of information that can be coded in numbers or words, can solve any logical problem that can be explicitly described, and can compute any mathematical equations that can be written. Therefore in principle at least, they can be programmed to do the things we do: perceive, remember, make deductions, solve problems.

The construction of computer programs that simulate human brain functions can help to clarify the nature of these functions. For instance, to construct a program and simulate, say, perception and classification of certain types of patterns, the investigator is forced to specify precisely what is required by the task of pattern perception. If the program fails to recognize the patterns, then the investigator knows that something is wrong with the model or with the way it has been implemented in the program. The investigator revises the model, tries again, and keeps working until it finally works (or until he or she gives up the task as being too ambitious).

Ideally, this task tells the investigator the kinds of processes the brain must perform. However, there is usually more than one way to accomplish a particular goal; critics of computer

modeling have pointed out that it is possible to write a program that performs a task that the human brain performs and comes up with exactly the same results but does the task in an entirely different way. In fact, some say, given the way that computers work and what we know about the structure of the human brain, the computer program is *guaranteed* to work differently.

When we base a model of brain functions on a physical device with which we are familiar, we enjoy the advantage of being able to think concretely about something that is difficult to observe. However, if the brain does not work like a computer, then our models will not tell us very much about the brain. Such models are *constrained* ("restricted") by the computer metaphor; they will be able to do things only the way that computers can do them. If the brain can actually do some different sorts of things that computers cannot do, the models will never contain these features.

In fact, computers and brains are fundamentally different. Modern computers are *serial devices;* they work one step at a time. (*Serial*, from the Latin *serere*, "to join," refers to events that occur in order, one after the other.) Programs consist of a set of instructions stored in the computer's memory. The computer follows these instructions, one at a time. Because each of these steps takes time, a complicated program will take more time to execute. But we do some things extremely quickly that computers take a very long time to do. The best example is visual perception. We can recognize a complex figure about as quickly as a simple one; for example, it takes about the same amount of time to recognize a friend's face as it does to identify a simple triangle. The same is not true at all for a serial computer. A com-

puter must "examine" the scene through an input device something like a television camera. Information about the brightness of each point of the picture must be converted into a number and stored in a memory location. Then the program examines each memory location, one at a time, and does calculations that determine the locations of lines, edges, textures, and shapes; finally, it tries to determine what these shapes represent. Recognizing a face takes *much* longer than recognizing a triangle. In fact, even the best computer programs do a terrible job in recognizing faces.

Unlike serial computers, the brain is a *parallel processor*, in which many different modules (collections of circuits of neurons) work simultaneously at different tasks. A complex task is broken down into many smaller ones, and separate modules work on each of them. Because the brain consists of many billions of neurons, it can afford to devote different clusters of neurons to different tasks. With so many things happening at the same time, the task gets done quickly.

Very recently, researchers have turned the tables and have begun developing models of *computers* that resemble the *nervous system*. The elements of these computers are based on nerve cells, and the rules that govern the way they interact are based on the rules you will learn about in Chapter 2. Furthermore, instead of programming these models to perform a function, researchers give them information that permits them to learn, just as a real brain does. Someday we may even see organic computers, using materials similar to those found in the body; scientists are developing polymers (special organic compounds) that can take over the functions of the silicon chips used in the integrated circuits that make up present-day computers.

KEY CONCEPTS

UNDERSTANDING HUMAN CONSCIOUSNESS: A PHYSIOLOGICAL APPROACH

1. Physiological psychologists believe that the mind is a function performed by the brain.
2. Study of human brain functions has helped us gain some insight into the nature of human consciousness, which appears to be related to the language functions of the brain. This chapter described one example, the effects of the split-brain operation.

THE NATURE OF PHYSIOLOGICAL PSYCHOLOGY

3. Scientists attempt to explain natural phenomena by means of generalization and reduction. Because physiological psychologists use the methods of psychology and physiology, they employ both types of explanations.
4. Descartes developed the first model to explain how the brain controls movement, based on the animated statues in the Royal Gardens. Subsequently, investigators tested their ideas with scientific experiments.

5. Darwin's theory of evolution, with its emphasis on function, helps physiological psychologists discover the relations between brain mechanisms, behaviors, and an organism's adaptation to its environment.

ETHICAL ISSUES IN RESEARCH WITH ANIMALS

6. Scientific research with animals has taught us most of what we know about the functions of the body, including that of the nervous system. This knowledge is essential in developing ways to prevent and treat neurological and mental disorders.

CAREERS IN NEUROSCIENCE

7. Physiological psychologists study the physiology of behavior by performing research with animals. They use the research methods and findings of other neuroscientists in pursuit of their particular interests.

SUGGESTED READINGS

Butterfield, H. *The Origins of Modern Science: 1300–1800.* New York: Macmillan, 1959.

Damasio, A.R. *Descartes' Error: Emotion, Reason, and the Human Brain.* New York: G.P. Putnam, 1994.

Sacks, O. *The Man Who Mistook His Wife for a Hat and Other Clinical Tales.* New York: Harper & Row, 1987.

Schultz, D., and Schultz, S.E. *A History of Modern Psychology,* 4th ed. New York: Academic Press, 1987.

2

Structure and Functions of Cells of the Nervous System

LEARNING OBJECTIVES

1. Name and describe the parts of a neuron and explain their functions.

2. Briefly describe the neural circuitry responsible for a withdrawal reflex and its inhibition by brain mechanisms.

3. Describe the supporting cells of the central and peripheral nervous systems, and describe and explain the importance of the blood-brain barrier.

4. Describe the measurement of the action potential, and explain how the balance between the forces of diffusion and electrostatic pressure is responsible for the membrane potential.

5. Describe the role of ion channels in action potentials, and explain the all-or-none law and the rate law.

6. Describe the structure of synapses, the release of neurotransmitter, and the activation of postsynaptic receptors.

7. Describe postsynaptic potentials: the ionic movements that cause them, the processes that terminate them, and their integration.

8. Describe the role of autoreceptors and axoaxonic synapses in synaptic communication, and describe the role of neuromodulators and hormones in nonsynaptic communication.

Unresponsive Muscles

Kathryn D. was getting desperate. All her life she had been healthy and active, eating wisely and keeping fit with sports and regular exercise. She went to her health club almost every day for a session of low-impact aerobics, followed by a swim. But several months ago, she began having trouble keeping up with her usual schedule. At first, she found herself getting tired toward the end of her aerobics class. Her arms, particularly, seemed to get heavy. Then when she entered the pool and started swimming, she found that it was hard to lift her arms over her head; she abandoned the crawl and the backstroke and did the sidestroke and breaststroke instead. She did not have any flulike symptoms, so she told herself that she needed more sleep and perhaps she should eat a little more.

Over the next few weeks, however, things only got worse. Aerobics classes were becoming an ordeal. Her instructor became concerned and suggested that Kathryn see her doctor. She did so, but he could find nothing wrong with her. She was not anemic, showed no signs of an infection, and seemed to be well nourished. He asked how things were going at work.

"Well, lately I've been under some pressure," she said. "The head of my department quit a few weeks ago, and I've taken over his job temporarily. I think I have a chance of getting the job permanently, but I feel as if my bosses are watching me to see whether I'm good enough for the job." Kathryn and her physician agreed that increased stress could be the cause of her problem. "I'd prefer not to give you any medication at this time," he said, "but if you don't feel better soon we'll have a closer look at you."

She *did* feel better for a while, but then all of a sudden her symptoms got worse. She quit going to the health club and found that she even had difficulty finishing a day's work. She was certain that people were noticing that she was no longer her lively self, and she was afraid that her chances for the promotion were slipping away. One afternoon she tried to look up at the clock on the wall and realized that she could hardly see—her eyelids were drooping, and her head felt as if it weighed a hundred pounds. Just then, one of her supervisors came over to her desk, sat down, and asked her to fill him in on the progress she had been making on a new project. As she talked, she found herself getting weaker and weaker. Her jaw was getting tired, even her tongue was getting tired, and her voice was getting

weaker. With a sudden feeling of fright she realized that the act of breathing seemed to take a lot of effort. She managed to finish the interview, but immediately afterward, she packed up her briefcase and left for home, saying she had a bad headache.

She telephoned her physician, who immediately arranged for her to go to the hospital to be seen by Dr. T., a neurologist. Dr. T. listened to a description of her symptoms and examined her briefly. She said to Kathryn, "I think I know what may be causing your symptoms, Miss D. I'd like to give you an injection and watch your reaction." She gave some orders to the nurse, who left the room and came back with a syringe. Dr. T. took it, swabbed Kathryn's arm, and injected the drug. She started questioning Kathryn about her job. Kathryn answered slowly, her voice almost a whisper. As the questions continued, she realized that it was getting easier and easier to talk. She straightened her back and took a deep breath. Yes, she was sure. Her strength was returning! She stood up and raised her arms above her head. "Look," she said, her excitement growing. "I can do this again. I've got my strength back! What was that you gave me? Am I cured?"

The brain is the organ that moves the muscles. That may sound simplistic, but ultimately, movement—or more accurately, behavior—is the primary function of the nervous system. To make useful movements, the brain must know what is happening outside, in the environment. Thus, the body contains cells that are specialized for detecting environmental events and other cells that are specialized for producing movements. Of course, complex animals such as we do not react automatically to events in our environment; our brains are flexible enough so that we behave in different ways, according to present circumstances and those we experienced in the past. Besides perceiving and acting, we can remember and decide. All these abilities are made possible by the billions of cells found in the nervous system.

This chapter describes the structure and functions of the most important cells of the nervous system. Specialized cells called **sensory neurons** gather information

Sensory neuron A neuron that detects changes in the external or internal environment and sends information about these changes to the central nervous system.

from the environment in the form of light, sound waves, odors, tastes, or contact with objects. **Motor neurons** accomplish movements through the contraction of muscles, which they control. (The term *motor* is used here in its original sense to refer to movement, not to a mechanical engine.) And in between sensory neurons and motor neurons come the **interneurons**—neurons that lie entirely within the central nervous system. Circuits of interneurons (primarily those in the brain) are responsible for perceiving, learning, remembering, deciding, and controlling complex behaviors. How many neurons are there in the human nervous system? I have seen estimates of between 100 billion and 1000 billion—but no one has counted them yet.

To understand how the nervous system controls behavior, we must first understand its parts—the cells that compose it. Because this chapter deals with cells, you do not need to be familiar with the structure of the nervous system, which is presented in Chapter 3. However, you need to know that the nervous system consists of two basic divisions, the central nervous system and the peripheral nervous system. The **central nervous system (CNS)** consists of the parts that are encased by the bones of the skull and spinal column: the brain and the spinal cord. The **peripheral nervous system (PNS)** is found outside these bones and consists of the nerves and some of the sensory organs.

CELLS OF THE NERVOUS SYSTEM

The first part of this chapter describes the most important cells of the nervous system—neurons and their supporting cells—and the blood-brain barrier, which provides cells in the central nervous system with chemical isolation from the rest of the body.

Neurons

Basic Structure

The neuron (nerve cell) is the information-processing and information-transmitting element of the nervous system. Neurons come in many shapes and varieties, according to the specialized jobs they perform. Neurons usually have, in one form or another, four structures or regions: (1) cell body, or soma; (2) dendrites; (3) axon; and (4) terminal buttons.

Soma.   The **soma** (cell body) contains the nucleus and much of the machinery that provides for the life processes of the cell. (See *Figure 2.1.*) Its shape varies considerably in different kinds of neurons.

Dendrites.   *Dendron* is the Greek word for tree, and the **dendrites** of the neuron look very much like trees. (See *Figure 2.1.*) Neurons "converse" with one another, and dendrites serve as important recipients of these messages.

The messages that pass from neuron to neuron are transmitted across the **synapse,** a junction between the terminal buttons (described soon) of the sending cell and a portion of the somatic or dendritic membrane of the receiving cell. (The word *synapse* derives from the Greek *sunaptein*, "to join together.") Communication at a synapse proceeds in one direction: from the terminal button to the membrane of the other cell. (Like many general rules, this one has some exceptions. As we will see in Chapter 4, some synapses pass information in both directions.)

Axon.   The **axon** is a long, slender tube that carries information from the cell body to the terminal button. Axons are often covered by a *myelin sheath*—a layer of insulation. (The myelin sheath is described later.) The axon carries information from

Motor neuron A neuron located within the central nervous system that controls the contraction of a muscle.

Interneuron A neuron located entirely within the central nervous system.

Central nervous system (CNS) The brain and spinal cord.

Peripheral nervous system (PNS) That part of the nervous system outside the brain and spinal cord, including the nerves attached to the brain and spinal cord.

Soma The cell body of a neuron, which contains the nucleus.

Dendrite A branched, treelike structure attached to the soma of a neuron; receives information from the terminal buttons of other neurons.

Synapse A junction between the terminal button of an axon and the membrane of another neuron.

Axon The long, thin, cylindrical structure that conveys information from the soma of a neuron to its terminal buttons.

FIGURE 2.1

The principal parts of a multi-polar neuron.

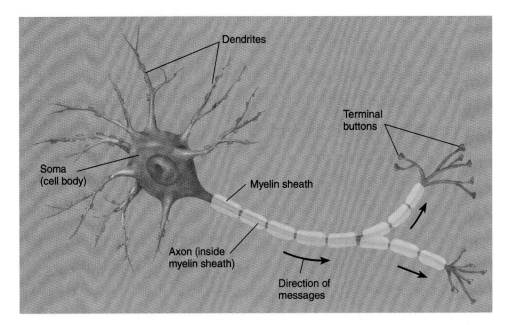

Dendrites

Terminal buttons

Soma (cell body)

Myelin sheath

Axon (inside myelin sheath)

Direction of messages

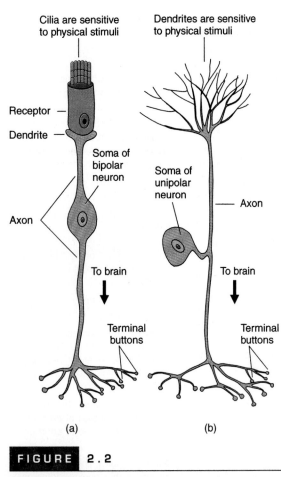

Cilia are sensitive to physical stimuli

Dendrites are sensitive to physical stimuli

Receptor

Dendrite

Soma of bipolar neuron

Soma of unipolar neuron

Axon

Axon

To brain

To brain

Terminal buttons

Terminal buttons

(a)

(b)

FIGURE 2.2

Neurons. (a) A bipolar neuron, found primarily in sensory systems (for example, vision and hearing). (b) A unipolar neuron, found in the somatosensory system (touch, pain, and the like).

the cell body to the terminal buttons. (See *Figure 2.1.*) The basic message an axon carries is called an *action potential.* This function is an important one and will be described in more detail later in the chapter. For now, it's enough to say that it is a brief electrical/chemical event that starts at the end of the axon next to the cell body and travels toward the terminal buttons.

Dendrites, axons, and their branches come in different shapes. In fact, the three principal types of neurons are classified according to the way in which their axons and dendrites leave the soma. The neuron depicted in Figure 2.1 is the most common type found in the central nervous system; it is a multipolar neuron. In a **multipolar neuron** the somatic membrane gives rise to one axon but to the trunks of many dendritic trees.

Bipolar neurons give rise to one axon and one dendritic tree, at opposite ends of the soma. (See *Figure 2.2a.*) Bipolar neurons are usually sensory; that is, their dendrites detect events occurring in the environment and communicate information about these events to the central nervous system.

The third type of nerve cell is the **unipolar neuron.** It has only one stalk—an axon that leaves the soma and divides into two branches a short distance away. (See *Figure 2.2b.*) Unipolar neurons, like bipolar neurons, transmit sensory information from the environment to the CNS. The treelike branches on the end of the axon away from the CNS are dendrites that detect sensory information. The branches on the end of the axon within the CNS end in terminal buttons. The dendrites of most unipolar neurons detect touch, temperature changes, and other sensory events that affect the skin. Other unipolar neurons detect events in our joints, muscles, and internal organs.

The central nervous system communicates with the rest of the body through nerves attached to the brain and to the spinal cord. Nerves are bundles of many thousands of individual axons, all wrapped in a tough, protective membrane. Under a microscope, nerves look something like telephone cables, with

FIGURE 2.3

A photograph from a scanning electron microscope, showing a cross section of a nerve. A nerve consists of a sheath of tissue that encases a bundle of individual nerve fibers (also known as axons). BV = blood vessel; A = individual axons.

(From Tissues and Organs: A Text-Atlas of Scanning Electron Microscopy, *by Richard G. Kessel and Randy H. Kardon. Copyright © 1979 by W.H. Freeman and Co. Reprinted by permission.)*

their bundles of wires. (See *Figure 2.3.*) Like the individual wires in a telephone cable, axons transmit messages through the nerve, from a sense organ to the brain or from the brain to a muscle or gland.

Terminal Buttons.   Most axons divide and branch many times. At the ends of the twigs are found little knobs called **terminal buttons.** (Some neuroscientists prefer the original French word *bouton.*) Terminal buttons have a very special function: When an action potential traveling down the axon reaches them, they secrete a chemical called a **neurotransmitter,** also known as a **transmitter substance.** This chemical (there are many different ones in the CNS) either excites or inhibits the receiving cell and thus helps to determine whether an action potential occurs in the axon of the receiving cell. Details of this process will be described later in this chapter.

An individual neuron receives information from the terminal buttons of axons of other neurons—and the terminal buttons of *its* axons form synapses with other neurons. A single neuron may receive information from dozens or even hundreds of other neurons, each of which can form a large number of synaptic connections with it. Figure 2.4 illustrates the nature of these connections. As you can see, terminal buttons can form synapses on the membrane of the dendrites or the soma. (See *Figure 2.4.*)

Internal Structure

Figure 2.5 illustrates the internal structure of a typical multipolar neuron. (See *Figure 2.5.*) The **membrane** defines the boundary of the cell. It consists of a double layer of lipid (fatlike) molecules. Floating in the membrane are a variety of protein molecules that have special functions. Some proteins detect substances outside the cell (such as hormones) and pass information about the presence of these substances to the interior of the cell. Other proteins control access to the interior of the cell, permitting some substances to enter but barring others. Still other proteins act as transporters, actively carrying certain molecules into or out of the cell. Because the membrane of the neuron is especially important in the transmission of information, its characteristics will be discussed in more detail later in this chapter.

The cell is filled with **cytoplasm**, a jellylike substance that contains small specialized structures, just as the body contains specialized organs. Among these structures are **mitochondria**, which break down nutrients such as glucose and provide the cell

Multipolar neuron A neuron with one axon and many dendrites attached to its soma.

Bipolar neuron A neuron with one axon and one dendrite attached to its soma.

Unipolar neuron A neuron with one axon attached to its soma; the axon divides, with one branch receiving sensory information and the other sending the information into the central nervous system.

Terminal button The bud at the end of a branch of an axon; forms synapses with another neuron; sends information to that neuron.

Neurotransmitter/transmitter substance A chemical that is released by a terminal button; has an excitatory or inhibitory effect on another neuron.

Membrane A structure consisting principally of lipid (fatlike) molecules that defines the outer boundaries of a cell and also constitutes many of the cell organelles.

Cytoplasm The viscous, semiliquid substance contained in the interior of a cell.

Mitochondrion An organelle responsible for extracting energy from nutrients.

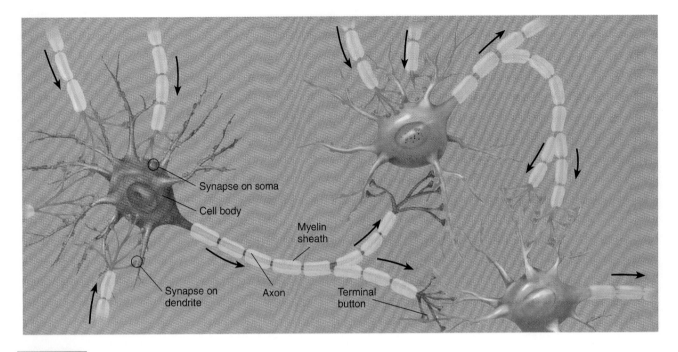

FIGURE 2.4

An overview of the synaptic connections among neurons. The arrows represent the directions of the flow of information.

Adenosine triphosphate (ATP)
(*ah den o seen*) A molecule of prime importance to cellular energy metabolism; its breakdown provides energy.

Nucleus A structure in the central region of a cell, containing the chromosomes.

Chromosome A strand of DNA, with associated proteins, found in the nucleus; carries genetic information.

Deoxyribonucleic acid (DNA)
(*dee ox ee ry bo new clay ik*) A long, complex macromolecule consisting of two interconnected helical strands; along with associated proteins, strands of DNA constitute the chromosomes.

Gene The functional unit of the chromosome, which directs synthesis of one or more proteins.

Cytoskeleton Formed of strands of proteins linked to each other and forming a cohesive mass that gives a cell its shape.

Enzyme A molecule that controls a chemical reaction, combining substances or breaking a substance into parts.

with energy to perform its functions. Mitochondria produce a chemical called **adenosine triphosphate (ATP),** which can be used throughout the cell as an energy source. Many eons ago mitochondria were free-living organisms that came to "infect" larger cells. Because the mitochondria could extract energy more efficiently than their hosts, they became useful to them and eventually became a permanent part of them. Mitochondria still contain their own genetic information and multiply independently of the cells in which they live. We inherit our mitochondria from our mothers; fathers' sperms do not contribute any mitochondria to the ova they fertilize.

Deep inside the cell is the **nucleus** (from the Greek word for "nut"). The nucleus contains the chromosomes. **Chromosomes**, as you have probably already learned, consist of long strands of **deoxyribonucleic acid (DNA).** The chromosomes have an important function: They contain the recipes for making proteins. Portions of the chromosomes, called **genes**, contain the recipes for individual proteins.

Proteins are important in cell functions. If a neuron grown in a tissue culture is exposed to a detergent, the lipid membrane and much of the interior of the cell dissolve away, leaving a matrix of insoluble strands of protein. This matrix, called the **cytoskeleton,** gives the neuron its shape. The cytoskeleton is made of various kinds of protein strands, linked to each other and forming a cohesive mass.

Besides providing structure, proteins serve as enzymes. **Enzymes** are the cell's marriage brokers or divorce judges: They cause particular molecules to join together or split apart. Thus, enzymes determine what gets made from the raw materials contained in the cell, and they determine which molecules remain intact.

Proteins are also involved in transporting substances within the cell. Axons can be extremely long, relative to their diameter and the size of the soma. For example, the longest axon in a human stretches from the foot to a region located in the base of the brain. Because terminal buttons need some items that can be produced only in the soma, there must be a system that can transport these items rapidly and efficiently through the axoplasm (that is, the cytoplasm of the axon). This system,

Dendritic spines

Dendrite

Cytoplasm

Nucleus

Membrane

Microtubules

Mitochondria

Myelin sheath

FIGURE 2.5

The principal internal structures of a multipolar neuron.

axoplasmic transport, is an active process that propels substances from one end of the axon to the other. This transport is accomplished by long protein strands called **microtubules,** bundles of thirteen filaments arranged around a hollow core. Microtubules serve as railroad tracks, guiding the progress of the substances being transported. Movement from the soma to the terminal buttons is called *anterograde* axoplasmic transport. (*Antero-* means "toward the front.") *Retrograde* axoplasmic transport carries substances from the terminal buttons back to the soma. (*Retro-* means "toward the back.") Anterograde axoplasmic transport is remarkably fast: up to 500 mm per day. Retrograde axoplasmic transport is about half as fast. Energy for both forms of transport is supplied by ATP, produced by the mitochondria.

Neural Communication: An Overview

Now that we know something about the structure of neurons and the synapses that connect them, let's look at a simple circuit of neurons that serves a useful function—automatically pulling our hand back when we touch a hot object.

We begin by examining a simple assembly of three neurons and a muscle that control a *withdrawal reflex.* In the next two figures (and in subsequent figures that illustrate simple neural circuits), neurons are depicted in short-hand fashion as several-sided stars. The points of these stars represent dendrites, and only one or two terminal buttons are shown at the end of the axon. The sensory neuron in this example detects painful stimuli. When its dendrites are stimulated by a noxious stim-

Axoplasmic transport An active process by which substances are propelled along microtubules that run the length of the axon. *Anterograde axoplasmic transport* travels from the cell body toward the terminal buttons; *retrograde axoplasmic transport* travels in the opposite direction.

Microtubule (*my kro **too** bule*) A long strand of bundles of protein filaments arranged around a hollow core; part of the cytoskeleton and involved in transporting substances from place to place within the cell.

Brain

Spinal cord

This interneuron excites motor neuron, causing muscular contraction

Motor neuron

Cross section of spinal cord

This muscle causes withdrawal from source of pain

Axon of sensory neuron (pain)

FIGURE 2.6

A withdrawal reflex, a simple example of a useful function of the nervous system. The painful stimulus causes the hand to pull away from the hot iron.

ulus (such as contact with a hot object), it sends messages down the axon to the terminal buttons, which are located in the spinal cord. (You may recognize this cell as a unipolar neuron; see *Figure 2.6.*) The terminal buttons of the sensory neuron release a neurotransmitter that excites the interneuron, causing it to send messages down its axon. The terminal buttons of the interneuron release a neurotransmitter that excites the motor neuron, which sends messages down its axon. The axon of the motor neuron joins a nerve and travels to a muscle. When the terminal buttons of the motor neuron release their neurotransmitter, the muscle cells contract, causing the hand to move away from the hot object. (See *Figure 2.6.*)

So far, all of the synapses have had excitatory effects. Now let's complicate matters a bit to see the effect of *inhibitory* synapses. Suppose you have removed a hot casserole from the oven. As you start over to the table to put it down, the heat begins to penetrate the rather thin pot holders you are using. The pain caused by the hot casserole triggers a withdrawal reflex that tends to make you drop it. Yet you manage to keep hold of it long enough to get to the table and put it down. What prevented your withdrawal reflex from making you drop the casserole on the floor?

The pain from the hot casserole increases the activity of excitatory synapses on the motor neurons, which tends to cause the hand to pull away from the casserole. However, this excitation is counteracted by *inhibition,* supplied by another source—the brain. The brain contains neural circuits that recognize what a disaster it would be if you dropped the casserole on the floor. These neural circuits send information to the spinal cord that prevents the withdrawal reflex from making you drop the dish.

Figure 2.7 shows how this information reaches the spinal cord. As you can see, an axon from a neuron in the brain reaches the spinal cord, where its terminal buttons form synapses with an inhibitory interneuron. When the neuron in the brain becomes active, it excites this inhibitory interneuron. The interneuron releases an inhibitory neurotransmitter, which *decreases* the activity of the motor neuron, blocking the withdrawal reflex. This circuit provides an example of a contest between two competing tendencies: to drop the casserole and to hold on to it. (See *Figure 2.7.*)

Of course, reflexes are more complicated than this description, and the mechanisms that inhibit them are even more so. And thousands of neurons are involved in this process. The five neurons shown in Figure 2.7 represent many others: Dozens of sensory neurons detect the hot object, hundreds of interneurons are stimulated by their activity, hundreds of motor neurons produce the contraction—and thousands of neurons in the brain must become active if the reflex is to be inhibited. Yet this simple model provides an overview of the process of neural communication, which is described in more detail later in this chapter.

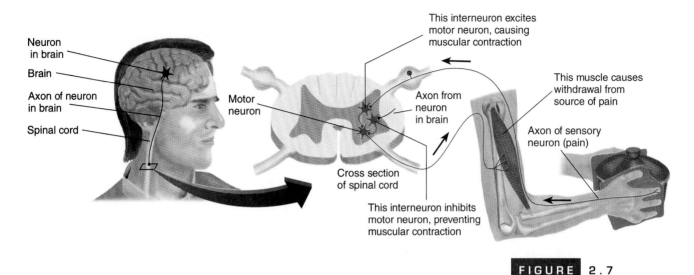

Neuron
in brain

Brain

Axon of neuron
in brain

Spinal cord

Motor
neuron

Cross section
of spinal cord

This interneuron excites
motor neuron, causing
muscular contraction

Axon from
neuron
in brain

This muscle causes
withdrawal from
source of pain

Axon of sensory
neuron (pain)

This interneuron inhibits
motor neuron, preventing
muscular contraction

FIGURE 2.7

The role of inhibition. Inhibitory signals arising from the brain can prevent the withdrawal reflex from causing the person to drop the casserole.

Supporting Cells

Neurons constitute only about half the volume of the CNS. The rest consists of a variety of supporting cells. Because neurons have a very high rate of metabolism but have no means of storing nutrients, they must constantly be supplied with nutrients and oxygen or they will quickly die. Unlike most other cells of the body, neurons cannot be replaced when they die. Thus, the role played by the cells that support and protect neurons is very important to our existence.

Glia

The most important supporting cells of the central nervous system are the *neuroglia,* or "nerve glue." **Glia** (also called *glial cells*) do indeed glue the CNS together, but they do much more than that. Glial cells provide physical and chemical buffers that isolate neurons from the rest of the body, providing neurons with a sheltered existence. Glial cells surround neurons and hold them in place, controlling their supply of some of the chemicals they need to exchange messages with other neurons; they insulate neurons from one another so that neural messages do not get scrambled; and they even act as housekeepers, destroying and removing the carcasses of neurons that are killed by injury or that die as a result of old age.

There are several types of glial cells, each of which plays a special role in the CNS. The two most important types are *astrocytes* and *oligodendrocytes.* **Astrocyte** means "star cell," and this name accurately describes the shape of these cells. Astrocytes (or *astroglia*) provide physical support to neurons and clean up debris within the brain. They produce some chemicals that neurons need to fulfill their functions. They help control the chemical composition of the fluid surrounding neurons by actively taking up or releasing substances whose concentrations must be kept within critical levels. Finally, astrocytes are involved in providing nourishment to neurons.

Some of the astrocyte's processes (the arms of the star) are wrapped around blood vessels. Other processes are wrapped around parts of neurons, so the somatic and dendritic membranes of neurons are largely surrounded by astrocytes. Recent evidence suggests that astrocytes receive nutrients from the capillaries, store them, and release them to neurons when needed (Tsacopoulos and Magistretti, 1996). Besides having a role in transporting chemicals to neurons, astrocytes serve as the matrix that holds neurons in place. These cells also surround and isolate synapses, limiting the dispersion of neurotransmitters that are released by the terminal buttons. (See *Figure 2.8.*)

Glia (*glee ah*) The supporting cells of the central nervous system.

Astrocyte A glial cell that provides support for neurons of the central nervous system, provides nutrients and other substances, and regulates the chemical composition of the extracellular fluid.

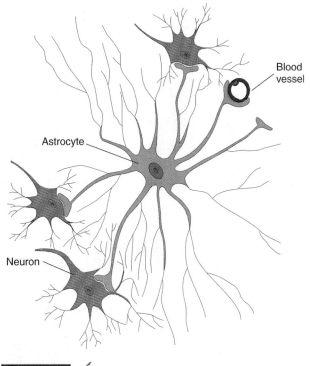

Blood vessel

Astrocyte

Neuron

FIGURE 2.8

Structure and location of astrocytes, whose processes surround capillaries and neurons of the central nervous system.

Myelinated axons

Node of Ranvier

Soma of oligodendrocyte

Microtubule

Mitochondrion in axoplasm

Node of Ranvier

FIGURE 2.9

An oligodendrocyte, which forms the myelin that surrounds many axons in the central nervous system. Each cell forms one segment of myelin for several adjacent axons.

Neurons occasionally die for unknown reasons or are killed by head injury or stroke. Certain kinds of astrocytes then take up the task of cleaning away the debris. These cells are able to travel around the CNS; they extend and retract their processes (*pseudopodia,* or "false feet") and glide about the way amoebas do. When these astrocytes contact a piece of debris from a dead neuron, they push themselves against it, finally engulfing and digesting it. We call this process **phagocytosis** (*phagein,* "to eat"; *kutos,* "cell"). If there is considerable injured tissue to be cleaned up, astrocytes will divide and produce enough new cells to do the task. Once the dead tissue is broken down, a framework of astrocytes will be left to fill in the vacant area, and a specialized kind of astrocyte will form scar tissue, walling off the area.

Oligodendrocytes are residents of the CNS, and their principal function is to provide support to axons and to produce the myelin sheath. The **myelin sheath** insulates most axons from one another. (Some axons are not myelinated and lack this sheath.) Myelin, 80 percent lipid and 20 percent protein, is produced by the oligodendrocytes in the form of a tube surrounding the axon. This tube does not form a continuous sheath. Rather, it consists of a series of segments, each approximately 1 mm long, with a small (1–2 μm) portion of uncoated axon between the segments. (A *micrometer,* abbreviated μm, is one-millionth of a meter, or one-thousandth of a millimeter.) The bare portion of axon is called a **node of Ranvier,** after its discoverer. The myelinated axon, then, resembles a string of elongated beads. (Actually, the beads are *very much* elongated—their length is approximately 80 times their width.)

A given oligodendrocyte produces several segments of myelin. During the development of the CNS, oligodendrocytes form processes shaped something like canoe paddles. Each of these paddle-shaped processes then wraps itself many times around a segment of an axon and, while doing so, produces layers of myelin. Each paddle thus becomes a segment of an axon's myelin sheath. (See *Figure 2.9.*)

As their name indicates, **microglia** are the smallest of the glial cells. Like some types of astrocytes, they act as phagocytes, engulfing and breaking down dead and dying neurons. But in addition, they serve as one of the representatives of the immune system in the brain, protecting the brain from invading microorganisms. They are primarily responsible for the inflammatory reaction in response to brain damage.

Schwann Cells

In the CNS the oligodendrocytes support axons and produce myelin. In the PNS the **Schwann cells** perform the same functions. Most axons in the PNS are myelinated. The myelin sheath occurs in segments, as it does in the CNS; each segment consists of a single Schwann cell, wrapped many times around the axon. In the CNS the oligodendrocytes grow a number of paddle-shaped processes that wrap around a number of axons. In the PNS

FIGURE 2.10

Formation of myelin. During development, a process of an oligodendrocyte or an entire Schwann cell tightly wraps itself many times around an individual axon and forms one segment of the myelin sheath. (a) Oligodendrocyte. (b) Schwann cell.

a Schwann cell provides myelin for only one axon, and the entire Schwann cell—not merely a part of it—surrounds the axon. (See *Figure 2.10.*)

Schwann cells also differ from their CNS counterparts, the oligodendrocytes, in an important way. As we saw, a nerve consists of a bundle of many myelinated axons, all covered in a sheath of tough, elastic connective tissue. If damage occurs to such a nerve, Schwann cells aid in the digestion of the dead and dying axons. Then the Schwann cells arrange themselves in a series of cylinders that act as guides for regrowth of the axons. The distal portions of the severed axons die, but the stump of each severed axon grows sprouts, which then spread in all directions. If one of these sprouts encounters a cylinder provided by a Schwann cell, the sprout will grow through the tube quickly (at a rate of up to 3–4 mm a day), while the other, nonproductive sprouts wither away. If the cut ends of the nerve are still located close enough to each other, the axons will reestablish connections with the muscles and sense organs they previously served.

Unfortunately, the glial cells of the CNS are not as cooperative as the supporting cells of the PNS. If axons in the brain or spinal cord are damaged, new sprouts will form, as in the PNS. However, the budding axons encounter scar tissue produced by the astrocytes, and they penetrate this barrier with great difficulty. Even if some sprouts get through, the axons need guidance to reestablish their original connections, which the glial cells in the mature central nervous system do not provide. Although researchers have reported a few cases in which axons reestablished some of their connections after they had been severed in the brains of laboratory animals, such cases are rare (Farris et al., 1993).

The Blood-Brain Barrier

Over one hundred years ago, Paul Ehrlich discovered that if a blue dye is injected into an animal's bloodstream, all tissues except the brain and spinal cord will be tinted blue. However, if the same dye is injected into the ventricles of the brain, the blue color will spread throughout the CNS (Bradbury, 1979). This experiment demonstrates that a barrier exists between the blood and the fluid that surrounds the cells of the brain—the **blood-brain barrier.**

Some substances can cross the blood-brain barrier; others cannot. Thus, it is *selectively permeable* (*per*, "through"; *meare*, "to pass"). In most of the body the cells that line the capillaries do not fit together absolutely tightly. Small gaps are found between them that permit the free exchange of most substances between the blood plasma and the fluid outside the blood vessels that surrounds the cells. In the central nervous system the capillaries lack these gaps, and therefore many substances cannot leave the blood. Some substances, such as glucose (the primary fuel of the central nervous system), must be actively transported through the capillary walls, carried by special proteins. (See *Figure 2.11.*)

What is the function of the blood-brain barrier? The messages conveyed from place to place in the nervous system involve movements of substances through the

Phagocytosis (*fagg o sy toe sis*) The process by which cells engulf and digest other cells or debris caused by cellular degeneration.

Oligodendrocyte (*oh li go den droh site*) A type of glial cell in the central nervous system that forms myelin sheaths.

Myelin sheath (*my a lin*) A sheath that surrounds axons and insulates them, preventing messages from spreading between adjacent axons.

Node of Ranvier (*raw vee ay*) A naked portion of a myelinated axon, between adjacent oligodendrocytes or Schwann cells.

Microglia The smallest of glial cells; act as phagocytes and protect the brain from invading microorganisms.

Schwann cell A cell in the peripheral nervous system that is wrapped around a myelinated axon, providing one segment of its myelin sheath.

Blood-brain barrier A semipermeable barrier produced by the cells in the walls of the capillaries in the brain.

FIGURE 2.11

The blood-brain barrier. (a) The cells that form the walls of the capillaries in the body outside the brain have gaps that permit the free passage of substances into and out of the blood. (b) The cells that form the walls of the capillaries in the brain are tightly joined, with no gaps, to form the blood-brain barrier.

Gaps that permit the free flow of substances into and out of the blood

Capillary in all of body except brain

Capillary in brain

(a)   (b)

membranes of neurons. If the composition of the fluid that bathes neurons is changed even slightly, the transmission of these messages will be disrupted. Thus, if this fluid is not closely regulated, the brain cannot function normally. The blood-brain barrier makes it easier to regulate the composition of this fluid.

The blood-brain barrier is not uniform throughout the nervous system. In several places the barrier is relatively permeable, allowing substances that are excluded elsewhere to cross freely. For example, the **area postrema** is a part of the brain that controls vomiting. The blood-brain barrier is much weaker there, permitting neurons in this region to detect the presence of toxic substances in the blood. A poison that enters the circulatory system from the stomach can thus stimulate this area to initiate vomiting. If the organism is lucky, the poison can be expelled from the stomach before it causes too much damage.

INTERIM SUMMARY

Neurons are the most important cells of the nervous system. The central nervous system (CNS) includes the brain and spinal cord; the peripheral nervous system (PNS) includes nerves and some sensory organs.

Neurons have four principal parts: soma (cell body), dendrites, axon, and terminal buttons. They communicate by means of synapses, located at the ends of the axons. When an action potential travels down an axon, the terminal buttons secrete a chemical that has either an excitatory or an inhibitory effect on the neuron with which it communicates. The interactions of circuits of neurons, with their excitatory and inhibitory synapses, are responsible for all of our perceptions, memories, thoughts, and behavior.

Neurons contain a quantity of clear cytoplasm, enclosed in a membrane. Embedded in the membrane are protein molecules that have special functions, such as the transport of particular substances into and out of the cell. The cytoplasm contains the nucleus, which contains the genetic information; the ribosomes, which serve as sites of protein synthesis; microtubules and other protein filaments, which compose the cytoskeleton and help to transport chemicals from place to place; and the mitochondria, which serve as the location for most of the chemical reactions through which the cell extracts energy from nutrients.

The withdrawal reflex illustrates how neurons can be connected to accomplish useful behaviors. The circuit responsible for this reflex consists of three sets of neurons: sensory neurons, interneurons, and motor neurons. The reflex can be suppressed when neurons in the brain activate inhibitory interneurons that form synapses with the motor neurons.

Area postrema (*poss **tree** ma*) A region of the medulla where the blood-brain barrier is weak; poisons can be detected there and can initiate vomiting.

Touch, temperature changes, and other sensory events that affect the skin are detected by the dendrites of unipolar neurons.

Neurons in the central nervous system are supported by glial cells. Within the CNS, astrocytes provide the primary support and also remove debris and form scar tissue in the event of tissue damage. Oligodendrocytes form myelin, the substance that insulates axons, and also support unmyelinated axons. Microglia are phagocytes that serve as the representatives of the immune system. Within the PNS, support and myelin are provided by the Schwann cells.

In most organs, molecules freely move between the blood within the capillaries that serve them and the extracellular fluid that bathes their cells. The molecules pass through gaps between the cells that line the capillaries. The walls of the capillaries of the CNS lack these gaps and thus form a barrier between the blood and the brain. As a consequence, fewer substances can enter or leave the brain across the blood-brain barrier.

THOUGHT QUESTIONS

The fact that the mitochondria in our cells were originally microorganisms that infected our very remote ancestors points out that evolution can involve interactions between two or more species. Many species have other organisms living inside them; in fact, the bacteria in our intestines are necessary for our good health. Some microorganisms can exchange genetic information, so adaptive mutations developed in one species can be adopted by another. Is it possible that some of the features of the cells of our nervous system were bequeathed to our ancestors from other species?

COMMUNICATION WITHIN A NEURON

This section describes the nature of communication *within* a neuron—the way an action potential is sent from the cell body down the axon to the terminal buttons, informing them to release some neurotransmitter. The details of synaptic transmission—the communication between neurons—will be described in the next section. As we will see in this section, an action potential consists of a series of alterations in the membrane of the axon that permit various chemicals to move between the interior of the axon and the fluid surrounding it. These exchanges produce electrical currents.

Measuring Electrical Potentials of Axons

Let's examine the nature of the message that is conducted along the axon. To do so, we need an axon that is large enough to work with. Fortunately, nature has provided the neuroscientist with the giant squid axon (the giant axon of a squid, not the axon of a giant squid!). This axon is about 0.5 mm in diameter—hundreds of times larger than the largest mammalian axon. (This large axon controls an emergency response: sudden contraction of the mantle, which squirts water through a jet and propels the squid away from a source of danger.) To study the axon, we place it in a dish of seawater, in which it can exist for a day or two.

To measure the electrical charges generated by an axon, we will need to use a pair of electrodes. **Electrodes** are electrical conductors that provide a path for electricity to enter or leave a medium. One of the electrodes is a simple wire that we place in the seawater. The other one, which we use to record the message from the axon, has to be special. Because even a giant squid axon is rather small, we must use a tiny electrode that will record the membrane potential without damaging the axon. To do so, we use a microelectrode.

A **microelectrode** is simply a very small electrode, which can be made of metal or glass. In this case we will use one made of thin glass tubing, which is heated and drawn down to an exceedingly fine point, less than a thousandth of a millimeter in diameter. Because glass will not conduct electricity, the glass microelectrode is filled with a liquid that conducts electricity, such as a solution of potassium chloride.

Electrode A conductive medium that can be used to apply electrical stimulation or to record electrical potentials.

Microelectrode A very fine electrode, generally used to record activity of individual neurons.

Using the giant axon of the squid, researchers discovered the nature of the message carried by axons.

We place the wire electrode in the seawater and insert the microelectrode into the axon. (See *Figure 2.12a.*) As soon as we do so, we discover that the inside of the axon is negatively charged with respect to the outside—the difference in charge being 70 mV (millivolts, or thousandths of a volt). Thus, the inside of the membrane is –70 mV. This electrical charge is called the **membrane potential.** The term *potential* refers to a stored-up source of energy—in this case, electrical energy. For example, a flashlight battery that is not connected to an electrical circuit has a *potential* charge of 1.5 V between its terminals. If we connect a light bulb to the terminals, the potential energy is tapped and converted into radiant energy (light). (See *Figure 2.12b.*) Similarly, if we connect our electrodes—one inside the axon and one outside it—to a very sensitive voltmeter, we will convert the potential energy to movement of the meter's needle. Of course, the potential electrical energy of the axonal membrane is very weak in comparison with that of a flashlight battery.

As we will see, the message that is conducted down the axon consists of a brief change in the membrane potential. However, this change occurs very rapidly—too rapidly for us to see if we were using a voltmeter. Thus, to study the message, we will use an oscilloscope. Like a voltmeter, an **oscilloscope** measures voltages, but it also produces a record of these voltages, graphing them as a function of time. These graphs are displayed on a screen, much like the one found in a television. The vertical axis represents voltage, and the horizontal axis represents time, going from left to right.

Once we insert our microelectrode into the axon, the oscilloscope draws a straight horizontal line at –70 mV, as long as the axon is not disturbed. This electrical charge across the membrane is called the **resting potential**—the membrane potential measured while the membrane is at rest.

Now let's disturb the resting potential and see what happens. To do so, we will use another device—an electrical stimulator that allows us to alter the membrane potential at a specific location. (See *Figure 2.13.*) The stimulator can pass current through another microelectrode that we have inserted into the axon. Because the inside of the axon is negative, a positive charge applied to the inside of the membrane produces a **depolarization.** That is, it takes away some of the electrical charge across the membrane near the electrode, reducing the membrane potential.

Let's see what happens to an axon when we artificially change the membrane potential at one point. Figure 2.14 shows a graph drawn by an oscilloscope that has been monitoring the effects of brief depolarizing stimuli. The graphs of the effects of these separate stimuli are superimposed on the same drawing so that we can compare them. We deliver a series of depolarizing stimuli, starting with a very weak stimulus (number 1) and gradually increasing its strength. Each stimulus briefly depolarizes the membrane potential a little more. Finally, after we present depolarization number 4, the membrane potential suddenly reverses itself, so that the inside becomes *positive* (and the outside becomes negative). The membrane potential quickly returns to normal, but first it overshoots the resting potential, becoming **hyperpolarized**—more polarized than normal—for a short time. The whole process takes about 2 msec (milliseconds, or thousandths of a second). (See *Figure 2.14.*)

This phenomenon, a very rapid reversal of the membrane potential, is called the **action potential.** It constitutes the message carried by the axon from the cell body to

FIGURE 2.12

Measuring electrical charge. (a) A voltmeter detecting the charge across a membrane of an axon. (b) A light bulb detecting the charge across the terminals of a battery.

Membrane potential The electrical charge across a cell membrane; the difference in electrical potential inside and outside the cell.

Oscilloscope A laboratory instrument capable of displaying a graph of voltage as a function of time on the face of a cathode ray tube.

Resting potential The membrane potential of a neuron when it is not being altered by excitatory or inhibitory postsynaptic potentials; approximately –70 mV in the giant squid axon.

Depolarization Reduction (toward zero) of the membrane potential of a cell from its normal resting potential.

Hyperpolarization An increase in the membrane potential of a cell, relative to the normal resting potential.

Action potential The brief electrical impulse that provides the basis for conduction of information along an axon.

FIGURE 2.13

The means by which an axon can be stimulated while its membrane potential is being recorded.

Electrical stimulator

Oscilloscope

Stimulator

FREQUENCY   MODE

Records of changes in membrane potential displayed here

Wire electrode placed in seawater

Glass micro-electrodes

Giant squid axon

the terminal buttons. The voltage level that triggers an action potential—which was achieved only by depolarizing shock number 4—is called the **threshold of excitation.**

The Membrane Potential: Balance of Two Forces

To understand what causes the action potential to occur, we must first understand the reasons for the existence of the membrane potential. As we will see, this electrical charge is the result of a balance between two forces: diffusion and electrostatic pressure.

The Force of Diffusion

When a spoonful of sugar is carefully poured into a container of water, it settles to the bottom. After a time the sugar dissolves, but it remains close to the bottom of the container. After a much longer time (probably several days) the molecules of sugar distribute themselves evenly throughout the water, even if no one stirs the liquid. The process whereby molecules distribute themselves evenly throughout the medium in which they are dissolved is called **diffusion.**

When there are no forces or barriers to prevent diffusion, molecules diffuse from regions of high concentration to regions of low concentration. Molecules are constantly in motion, and their rate of movement is proportional to the temperature. Only at absolute zero [0 K (kelvin) = −273.15° C = −459.7° F] do molecules cease their random movement. At all other temperatures they move about, colliding and veering off in different directions, thus pushing one another away. The result of these collisions in the example of sugar and water is to force sugar molecules upward (and to force water molecules downward), away from the regions in which they are most concentrated.

The Force of Electrostatic Pressure

When some substances are dissolved in water, they split into two parts, each with an opposing electrical charge. Substances with this property are called **electrolytes.** The charged particles into which they decompose are called **ions.** Ions are of two basic types: *Cations* have a positive charge, and *anions* have a negative charge. For example, when sodium chloride (NaCl, table salt) is dissolved in water, many of the molecules split into sodium cations (Na^+) and chloride anions (Cl^-). (I find that the easiest way to keep the terms *cation* and *anion* straight is to think of the

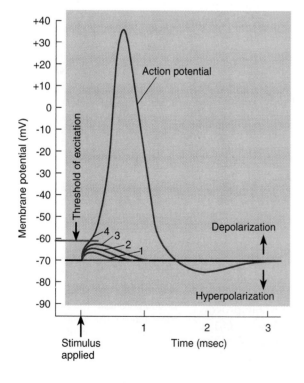

FIGURE 2.14

A graph of an action potential. These results would be seen on an oscilloscope screen if depolarizing stimuli of varying intensities were delivered to the axon shown in Figure 2.13.

cation's plus sign as a cross and remember the superstition of a black *cat* crossing your path.)

As you have undoubtedly learned, particles with the same kind of charge repel each other (+ repels +, and − repels −), but particles with different charges attract each other (+ and − attract). Thus, anions repel anions, cations repel cations, but anions and cations attract each other. The force exerted by this attraction or repulsion is called **electrostatic pressure.** Just as the force of diffusion moves molecules from regions of high concentration to regions of low concentration, electrostatic pressure moves ions from place to place: Cations are pushed away from regions with an excess of cations, and anions are pushed away from regions with an excess of anions.

Ions in the Extracellular and Intracellular Fluid

The fluid within cells (**intracellular fluid**) and the fluid surrounding them (**extracellular fluid**) contain different ions. The forces of diffusion and electrostatic pressure contributed by these ions give rise to the membrane potential. Because the membrane potential is produced by a balance between the forces of diffusion and electrostatic pressures, understanding what produces this potential requires that we know the concentration of the various ions in the extracellular and intracellular fluids.

There are several important ions in these fluids. I will discuss four of them here: organic anions (symbolized by A⁻), chloride ions (Cl⁻), sodium ions (Na⁺), and potassium ions (K⁺). The Latin words for sodium and potassium are *natrium* and *kalium;* hence, they are abbreviated *Na* and *K,* respectively. Organic anions—negatively charged proteins and intermediate products of the cell's metabolic processes—are found only in the intracellular fluid. Although the other three ions are found in both the intracellular and extracellular fluids, K⁺ is found predominantly in the intracellular fluid, whereas Na⁺ and Cl⁻ are found predominantly in the extracellular fluid. The sizes of the boxes in Figure 2.15 indicate the relative concentrations of these four ions. (See *Figure 2.15.*) The easiest way to remember which ion is found where is to recall that the fluid that surrounds our cells is similar to seawater, which is predominantly a solution of salt, NaCl. The primitive ancestors of our cells lived in the ocean; thus, the seawater was their extracellular fluid. Our extracellular fluid thus resembles seawater, produced and maintained by regulatory mechanisms that are described in Chapter 11.

Threshold of excitation The value of the membrane potential that must be reached to produce an action potential.

Diffusion Movement of molecules from regions of high concentration to regions of low concentration.

Electrolyte A water-based solution of a material that ionizes—namely, a soluble acid, base, or salt.

Ion A charged molecule. *Cations* are positively charged, and *anions* are negatively charged.

Electrostatic pressure The attractive force between atomic particles charged with opposite signs or the repulsive force between atomic particles charged with the same sign.

Intracellular fluid The fluid contained within cells.

Extracellular fluid Body fluids located outside of cells.

FIGURE 2.15

The relative concentration of some important ions inside and outside the neuron and the forces acting on them.

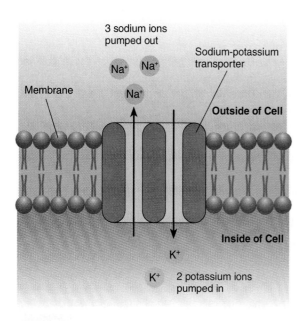

FIGURE 2.16

A sodium-potassium transporter, situated in the cell membrane.

Sodium-potassium transporter
A protein found in the membrane of all cells that transports sodium ions out of the cell and transports potassium ions into the cell.

Ion channel A specialized protein molecule that permits specific ions to enter or leave cells.

Voltage-dependent ion channel An ion channel that opens or closes according to the value of the membrane potential.

Let's consider the ions in Figure 2.15 and examine the forces of diffusion and electrostatic pressure exerted on each, which determine why each ion in located where it is. A^-, the organic anion, is unable to pass through the membrane of the axon; therefore, although the presence of this ion within the cell affects the other ions, we need not consider what forces act on it.

The potassium ion K^+ is concentrated within the axon; thus, the force of diffusion tends to push it out of the cell. (Remember, particles tend to be pushed away from regions where they are highly concentrated.) However, the outside of the cell is charged positively with respect to the inside, so electrostatic pressure tends to force K^+ inside. Thus, the two opposing forces balance. (See *Figure 2.15.*)

The chloride ion Cl^- is in greatest concentration outside the axon. The force of diffusion pushes this ion inward. However, because the inside of the axon is negatively charged, electrostatic pressure pushes the anion outward. Again, two opposing forces balance each other. (See *Figure 2.15.*)

The sodium ion Na^+ is also in greatest concentration outside the axon, so it, like Cl^-, is pushed into the cell by the force of diffusion. But unlike chloride, the sodium ion is *positively* charged. Therefore, electrostatic pressure does *not* prevent Na^+ from entering the cell; indeed, the negative charge inside the axon *attracts* Na^+. (See *Figure 2.15.*)

How can Na^+ remain in greatest concentration in the extracellular fluid, despite the fact that both forces (diffusion and electrostatic pressure) tend to push it inside? The simplest explanation would be that the membrane is impermeable to Na^+, as it is to A^-, the organic anion. However, experiments have shown that the membrane does allow some Na^+ to leak through. But at the same time, another force, provided by the *sodium-potassium pump,* continuously pumps Na^+ out of the axon. The sodium-potassium pump consists of a large number of individual protein molecules situated in the membrane, driven by energy provided by the mitochondria as they metabolize the cell's nutrients. These molecules, known as **sodium-potassium transporters,** exchange Na^+ for K^+, pushing three sodium ions out for every two potassium ions they push in. (See *Figure 2.16.*)

Because the membrane is not very permeable to Na^+, sodium-potassium transporters very effectively keep the intracellular concentration of Na^+ low. By transporting K^+ into the cell, they also increase the intracellular concentration of K^+ somewhat. The membrane is approximately 100 times more permeable to K^+ than to Na^+, so the increase is slight; but as we will see when we study the process of neural inhibition later in this chapter, it is very important. The transporters that make up the sodium-potassium pump use considerable energy: Up to 40 percent of a neuron's metabolic resources are used to operate them. Neurons, muscle cells, glia—in fact, most cells of the body—have sodium-potassium transporters in their membranes.

The Action Potential

As we saw, the forces of both diffusion and electrostatic pressure tend to push Na^+ into the cell. However, the membrane is not very permeable to this ion, and sodium-potassium transporters continuously pump out Na^+, keeping the intracellular level of Na^+ low. But imagine what would happen if the membrane suddenly became permeable to Na^+. The forces of diffusion and electrostatic pressure would cause Na^+ to rush into the cell. This sudden inflow of positively charged ions would drastically change the membrane potential. Indeed, experiments have shown that this mechanism is precisely what causes the action potential: A brief drop in the membrane resistance to Na^+ (allowing these ions to rush into the cell) is immediately followed by a transient drop in the membrane resistance to K+ (allowing these ions to rush out of the cell).

I said earlier that the membrane consists of a double layer of lipid molecules in which are floating many different kinds of protein molecules. One class of protein molecules provides a way for ions to enter or leave the cells. These molecules constitute **ion channels,** which contain passages ("pores") that can open or close. When an ion channel is open, a particular type of ion can flow through the pore and thus can enter or leave the cell. (See *Figure 2.17.*) Neural membranes contain many thousands of ion channels. For example, the giant squid axon contains from 100 to 600 sodium channels in each square micrometer of membrane. (There are one million square micrometers in a square millimeter; thus, a patch of axonal membrane the size of a lowercase letter "o" in this book would contain several hundred million sodium channels.) Each open sodium channel can admit up to 100 million ions per second. The permeability of a membrane to a particular ion at a given moment is determined by the number of ion channels that are open. (By the way, cell biologists have discovered approximately 75 different types of ion channels, and more will undoubtedly be discovered.)

The following numbered paragraphs describe the movements of ions through the membrane during the action potential. The numbers on Figure 2.18 correspond to the numbers of the paragraphs. (See *Figure 2.18.*)

1. As soon as the threshold of excitation is reached, the sodium channels in the membrane open and Na+ rushes in, propelled by the forces of diffusion and electrostatic pressure. The opening of these channels is triggered by the depolarization of the membrane potential; they open at the threshold of excitation. Because these channels are opened by changes in the membrane potential, they are called **voltage-dependent ion channels.** The inflow of positively charged sodium ions produces a rapid change in the membrane potential, from −70 to +40 mV.

2. The membrane of the axon contains voltage-dependent potassium channels, but these channels are less sensitive than voltage-dependent sodium channels. That is, they require a greater level of depolarization before they begin to open. Thus, they begin to open later than the sodium channels.

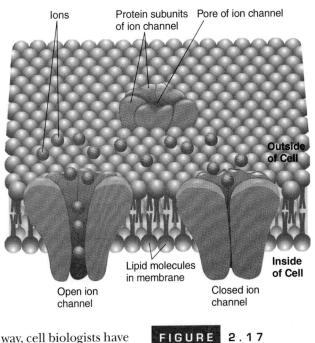

Ions   Protein subunits of ion channel   Pore of ion channel

Outside of Cell

Lipid molecules in membrane   **Inside of Cell**

Open ion channel   Closed ion channel

FIGURE 2.17

Ion channels. When they are open, ions can pass through them, entering or leaving the cell.

FIGURE 2.18

The movements of ions during the action potential. The shaded box at the top shows the opening of sodium channels at the threshold of excitation, their refractory condition at the peak of the action potential, and their resetting when the membrane potential returns to normal.

3. At about the time the action potential reaches its peak (in approximately 1 msec), the sodium channels become *refractory*—they cannot open again until the membrane once more reaches the resting potential. At this time, then, no more Na⁺ can enter the cell.

4. By now, the voltage-dependent potassium channels in the membrane are open, letting K⁺ ions move freely through the membrane. At this time, the inside of the axon is now *positively* charged, so K⁺ is driven out of the cell by diffusion and by electrostatic pressure. This outflow of cations causes the membrane potential to return toward its normal value. As it does so, the potassium channels begin to close again.

5. As the membrane potential returns to normal, the potassium channels close, and no more potassium leaves the cell.

6. The membrane actually overshoots its resting value (–70 mV) and only gradually returns to normal. The accumulation of K⁺ ions outside the membrane causes it to become temporarily hyperpolarized. These extra ions soon diffuse away, and the membrane potential returns to –70 mV. Eventually, sodium-potassium transporters remove the Na⁺ that leaked in and retrieve the K⁺ that leaked out.

Figure 2.19 summarizes the changes in permeability of the membrane to sodium and potassium ions during the action potential. (See *Figure 2.19.*)

How much ionic flow is there? The drop in membrane resistance to Na⁺ is brief, and diffusion over any appreciable distance takes some time. Thus, when I say "Na⁺ rushes in," I do not mean that the axoplasm becomes flooded with Na⁺. At the peak of the action potential a very thin layer of fluid immediately inside the axon becomes full of newly arrived Na⁺ ions; this amount is indeed enough to reverse the membrane potential. However, not enough time has elapsed for these ions to fill the entire axon. Before that event can take place, the Na⁺ channels close and K⁺ starts flowing out.

Experiments have shown that an action potential temporarily increases the number of Na⁺ ions inside the giant squid axon by 0.0003 percent. Although the concentration just inside the membrane is high, the total number of ions entering the cell is very small relative to the number already there. On a short-term basis, sodium-potassium transporters are not very important. The few Na⁺ ions that manage to leak in diffuse into the rest of the axoplasm, and the slight increase in Na⁺ concentration is hardly noticeable. However, sodium-potassium transporters are important on a long-term basis, because in many axons, action potentials occur at a very high rate. Without the activity of sodium-potassium transporters, the concentration of sodium ions in the axoplasm would increase enough that the axon would no longer be able to function.

FIGURE 2.19

Changes in the permeability of the membrane to Na⁺ and K⁺ during the action potential.

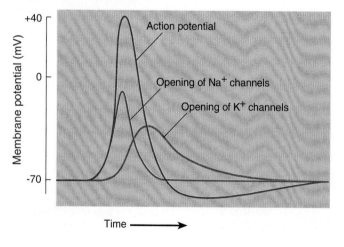

Conduction of the Action Potential

Now that we have a basic understanding of the resting membrane potential and the production of the action potential, we can consider the movement of the message down the axon, or *conduction of the action potential.* To study this phenomenon, we again make use of the giant squid axon. We attach an electrical stimulator to an electrode at one end of the axon and place recording electrodes, attached to oscilloscopes, at different distances from the stimulating electrode. Then we apply a depolarizing stimulus to the end of the axon and trigger an action potential. We record the action potential from each of the electrodes, one after the other. Thus, we see that the action potential is conducted down the axon. As the action potential travels, it remains constant in size. (See *Figure 2.20.*)

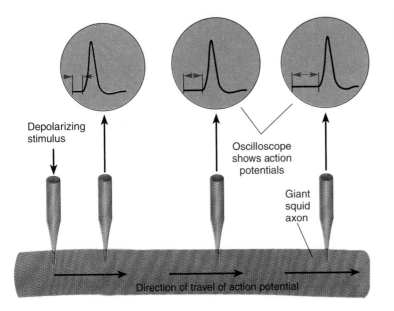

FIGURE 2.20

Conduction of the action potential. When an action potential is triggered, its size remains undiminished as it travels down the axon. The speed of conduction can be calculated from the delay between time of the stimulus and arrival of the action potential at a particular point.

This experiment establishes a basic law of axonal conduction: the **all-or-none law.** This law states that an action potential either occurs or does not occur; once triggered, it is transmitted down the axon to its end. An action potential always remains the same size, without growing or diminishing. In fact, the axon will transmit an action potential in either direction, or even in both directions, if it is started in the middle of the axon's length. However, because action potentials in living animals always start at the end attached to the soma, axons normally carry one-way traffic.

As you know, the strength of a muscular contraction can vary from very weak to very forceful, and the strength of a stimulus can vary from barely detectable to very intense. We know that the occurrence of action potentials in axons controls the strength of muscular contractions and represents the intensity of a physical stimulus. But if the action potential is an all-or-none event, how can it represent information that can vary in a continuous fashion? The answer is simple: A single action potential is not the basic element of information; rather, variable information is represented by an axon's *rate of firing*. (In this context, *firing* refers to the production of action potentials.) A high rate of firing causes a strong muscular contraction, and a strong stimulus (such as a bright light) causes a high rate of firing in axons that serve the eyes. Thus, the all-or-none law is supplemented by the **rate law.** (See *Figure 2.21.*)

Recall that all but the smallest axons in mammalian nervous systems are myelinated; segments of the axons are covered by a myelin sheath produced by the oligodendrocytes of the CNS or the Schwann cells of the PNS. These segments are separated by portions of naked axon, the nodes of Ranvier. Conduction of an action potential in a myelinated axon is somewhat different from conduction in an unmyelinated axon.

Schwann cells and the oligodendrocytes of the CNS wrap tightly around the axon, leaving no measurable extracellular fluid between them and the axon. The only place where a myelinated axon comes into contact with the extracellular fluid is at a node of Ranvier, where the axon is naked. In the myelinated areas there can be no inward flow of Na^+ when the sodium channels open, because there *is* no extracellular sodium. The

All-or-none law The principle that once an action potential is triggered in an axon, it is transmitted, without decreasing in size, to the end of the fiber.

Rate law The principle that variations in the intensity of a stimulus or other information being transmitted in an axon are represented by variations in the rate at which that axon fires.

FIGURE 2.21

The rate law. The strength of a stimulus is represented by the rate of firing of an axon. The size of each action potential is always constant.

FIGURE 2.22

Saltatory conduction, showing propagation of an action potential down a myelinated axon.

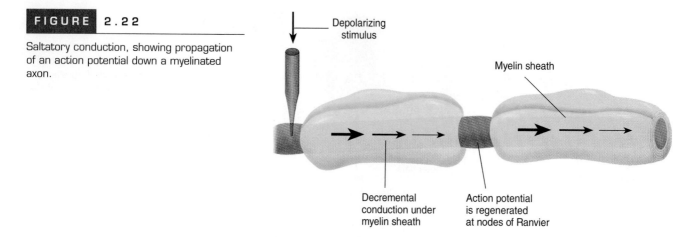

axon conducts the electrical disturbance from the action potential to the next node of Ranvier. The disturbance is conducted passively, the way an electrical signal is conducted through an insulated cable. The disturbance gets smaller as it passes down the axon, but it is still large enough to trigger a new action potential at the next node. The action potential gets retriggered, or repeated, at each node of Ranvier, and the electrical disturbance that results is conducted along the myelinated area to the next node. Such conduction, hopping from node to node, is called **saltatory conduction,** from the Latin *saltare,* "to dance." (See *Figure 2.22.*)

Saltatory conduction confers two advantages. The first is economic. Sodium-potassium transporters must expend energy to get rid of the excess Na^+ that enters the axon during the action potential. Sodium-potassium transporters must be located along an unmyelinated axon because Na^+ enters everywhere. However, because Na^+ can enter a myelinated axon only at the nodes of Ranvier, much less gets in and, consequently, much less has to be pumped out again. Therefore, a myelinated axon expends much less energy to maintain its sodium balance.

The second advantage to myelin is speed. Conduction of an action potential is faster in a myelinated axon because the transmission between the nodes is very fast. Increased speed enables an animal to react faster and (undoubtedly) to think faster. One of the ways to increase the speed of conduction is to increase size. Because it is so large, the unmyelinated squid axon, with a diameter of 500 μm, achieves a conduction velocity of approximately 35 m/sec (meters per second). However, a myelinated cat axon achieves the same speed with a diameter of a mere 6 μm. The fastest myelinated axon, 20 μm in diameter, can conduct action potentials at a speedy 120 m/sec, or 432 km/h. At that speed a signal can get from one end of an axon to the other without much delay.

INTERIM SUMMARY

The message conducted down an axon is called an action potential. The resting membrane potential occurs because various ions are located in different concentrations in the fluid inside and outside the cell. The extracellular fluid (like seawater) is rich in Na^+ and Cl^-, and the intracellular fluid is rich in K^+ and various organic anions, designated as A^-.

The cell membrane is freely permeable to water, but its permeability to various ions—in particular, Na^+ and K^+—is regulated by ion channels. When the membrane potential is at its resting value (–70 mV), the gates of the voltage-dependent sodium and potassium channels are closed. A small amount of Na^+ continuously leaks into the axon but is promptly forced out of the cell again by the sodium-potassium transporters (which also pump potassium *into* the axon). When an electrical stimulator

Saltatory conduction Conduction of action potentials by myelinated axons. The action potential "jumps" from one node of Ranvier to the next.

depolarizes the membrane potential of the axon so that it reaches the threshold of excitation, voltage-dependent sodium channels open and Na^+ rushes into the cell, driven by the force of diffusion and by electrostatic pressure. The entry of the positively charged ions further reduces the membrane potential and, indeed, causes it to reverse, so that the inside becomes positive. The opening of the sodium channels is temporary; they soon close again. The depolarization of the membrane potential caused by the inflow of Na^+ activates voltage-dependent potassium channels, and K^+ leaves the axon, traveling down its concentration gradient. This outflow of K^+ quickly brings the membrane potential back to its resting value.

Because an action potential of a given axon is an all-or-none phenomenon, neurons represent intensity by their rate of firing. The action potential normally begins at one end of the axon, where the axon attaches to the soma. The action potential travels continuously down unmyelinated axons, remaining constant in size, until it reaches the terminal buttons. (When the axon divides, the action potential continues down each branch.) In myelinated axons, ions can flow through the membrane only at the nodes of Ranvier, because the axons are covered everywhere else with myelin, which isolates them from the extracellular fluid. Thus, the action potential is conducted passively from one node of Ranvier to the next. When the electrical message reaches a node, voltage-dependent sodium channels open, and the action potential reaches full strength again. This mechanism saves a considerable amount of energy because sodium-potassium transporters are not needed along the myelinated portions of the axon. Saltatory conduction is also faster than conduction of action potentials in unmyelinated axons.

■ THOUGHT QUESTIONS

The evolution of the human brain, with all its complexity, depended on many apparently trivial mechanisms. For example, what if cells had not developed the ability to manufacture myelin? Unmyelinated axons must be very large if they are to transmit action potentials rapidly. How big would the human brain have to be if oligodendrocytes did not produce myelin? *Could* the human brain as we know it have evolved without myelin?

■ COMMUNICATION BETWEEN NEURONS

Now that you know about the basic structure of neurons and the nature of the action potential, it is time to describe the ways in which neurons can communicate with each other. These communications make it possible for circuits of neurons to gather sensory information, make plans, and initiate behaviors.

The primary means of communication between neurons is *synaptic transmission*—the transmission of messages from one neuron to another through a synapse. As we saw, these messages are carried by neurotransmitters, released by terminal buttons. These chemicals diffuse across the fluid-filled gap between the terminal buttons and the membranes of the neurons with which they form synapses. As we will see in this section, neurotransmitters produce **postsynaptic potentials**—brief depolarizations or hyperpolarizations—that increase or decrease the rate of firing of the axon of the postsynaptic neuron.

Neurotransmitters exert their effects on cells by attaching to a particular region of a receptor molecule called the **binding site.** A molecule of the chemical fits into the binding site the way a key fits into a lock: The shape of the binding site and the shape of the molecule of the neurotransmitter are complementary. A chemical that attaches to a binding site is called a **ligand,** from *ligare,* "to bind." Neurotransmitters are natural ligands, produced and released by neurons. But other chemicals found

Postsynaptic potential Alterations in the membrane potential of a postsynaptic neuron, produced by release of neurotransmitter at the synapse.

Binding site The location on a receptor protein to which a ligand binds.

Ligand (*lye* gand or *ligg* and) A chemical that binds with the binding site of a receptor.

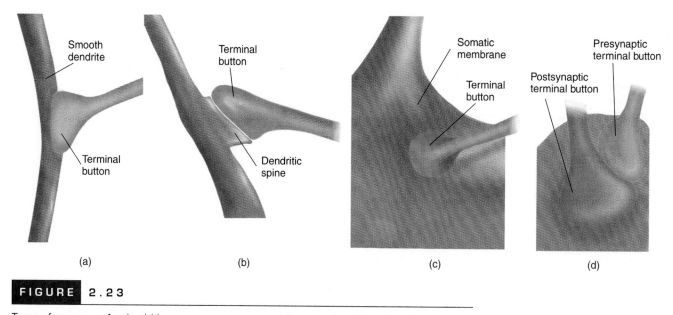

FIGURE 2.23

Types of synapses. Axodendritic synapses can occur on the smooth surface of a dendrite (a) or on dendritic spines (b). Axosomatic synapses occur on somatic membrane (c). Axoaxonic synapses consist of synapses between two terminal buttons (d).

in nature (primarily in plants or in the poisonous venoms of animals) can serve as ligands, too. In addition, artificial ligands can be produced in the laboratory. These chemicals are discussed in Chapter 4, which deals with drugs and their effects.

Structure of Synapses

Dendritic spine A small bud on the surface of a dendrite, with which a terminal button from another neuron forms a synapse.

Presynaptic membrane The membrane of a terminal button that lies adjacent to the postsynaptic membrane.

Postsynaptic membrane The cell membrane opposite the terminal button in a synapse; the membrane of the cell that receives the message.

Synaptic cleft The space between the presynaptic membrane and the postsynaptic membrane.

Synaptic vesicle (*vess* i *kul*) A small, hollow, beadlike structure found in terminal buttons; contains molecules of a neurotransmitter.

Release zone A region of the interior of the presynaptic membrane to which synaptic vesicles attach and release their neurotransmitter into the synaptic cleft.

As you have already learned, synapses are junctions between the terminal buttons at the ends of the axonal branches of one neuron and the membrane of another. Synapses can occur in three places: on dendrites, on the soma, and on other axons. These synapses are referred to as *axodendritic, axosomatic,* and *axoaxonic.* Axodendritic synapses can occur on the smooth surface of a dendrite or on **dendritic spines**—small protrusions that stud the dendrites of several types of large neurons in the brain. (See *Figure 2.23.*)

Figure 2.24 illustrates a synapse. The **presynaptic membrane,** located at the end of the terminal button, faces the **postsynaptic membrane,** located on the neuron that receives the message (the *postsynaptic* neuron). These two membranes face each other across the **synaptic cleft,** a gap that varies in size from synapse to synapse but is usually around 20 nm wide. (A nanometer, nm, is one billionth of a meter.) The synaptic cleft contains extracellular fluid, through which the neurotransmitter diffuses. (See *Figure 2.24.*)

As you may have noticed in Figure 2.24, the cytoplasm of the terminal button contains **synaptic vesicles,** small, rounded objects in the shape of spheres or ovoids. (The term *vesicle* means "little bladder.") These vesicles are found in greatest numbers around the part of the presynaptic membrane that faces the synaptic cleft—next to the **release zone,** the region from which neurotransmitter is released. Synaptic vesicles are produced in the soma and are carried by fast axoplasmic transport to the terminal button. (See *Figure 2.24.*)

In an electron micrograph the postsynaptic membrane under the terminal button appears somewhat thicker and more dense than the membrane elsewhere. This postsynaptic density is caused by the presence of receptors—specialized protein molecules that detect the presence of neurotransmitters in the synaptic cleft. (See *Figure 2.24.*)

Detail of Synapse

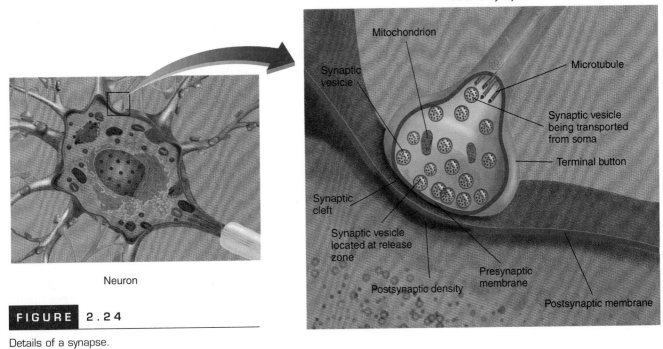

Neuron

FIGURE 2.24

Details of a synapse.

Release of a Neurotransmitter

When action potentials are conducted down an axon (and down all of its branches), something happens inside all of the terminal buttons: Several synaptic vesicles located just inside the presynaptic membrane fuse with the membrane and then break open, spilling their contents into the synaptic cleft.

Heuser and colleagues (Heuser, 1977; Heuser et al., 1979) obtained photomicrographs that illustrate this process. Because the release of a neurotransmitter is a very rapid event, taking only a few milliseconds to occur, special procedures are needed to stop the action so that the details can be studied. The experimenters electrically stimulated the nerve attached to an isolated frog muscle and then dropped the muscle against a block of pure copper that had been cooled to 4° K (approximately −453° F). Contact with the supercooled metal froze the outer layer of tissue in 2 msec or less. The ice held the components of the terminal buttons in place until they could be chemically stabilized and examined with an electron microscope. Figure 2.25 shows a portion of the synapse in cross section. Note the vesicles that appear to be fused with the presynaptic membrane, forming the shape of an omega (Ω). (See *Figure 2.25.*)

FIGURE 2.25

A photograph from an electron microscope, showing a cross section of a synapse. The omega-shaped figures are synaptic vesicles fusing with the presynaptic membranes of terminal buttons that form synapses with frog muscle.

[From Heuser, J.E., in Society for Neuroscience Symposia, Vol. II, edited by W.M. Cowan and J.A. Ferrendelli. Bethesda, MD: Society for Neuroscience, 1977. Micrograph produced by Dr. John E. Heuser of Washington University School of Medicine, St. Louis, Mo.]

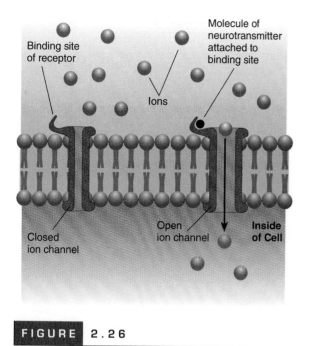

Binding site
of receptor

Molecule of
neurotransmitter
attached to
binding site

Ions

Closed
ion channel

Open
ion channel

Inside
of Cell

FIGURE 2.26

Ionotropic receptors. The ion channel opens when a molecule of neurotransmitter attaches to the binding site. For purposes of clarity, the drawing is schematic; molecules of neurotransmitter are actually much larger than individual ions.

Activation of Receptors

How do molecules of the neurotransmitter produce a depolarization or hyperpolarization in the postsynaptic membrane? They do so by diffusing across the fluid that fills the synaptic cleft. Once they reach the other side of the synaptic cleft, they attach to the binding sites of the **postsynaptic receptors,** special protein molecules embedded in the postsynaptic membrane. Once binding occurs, the postsynaptic receptors open **neurotransmitter-dependent ion channels,** which permit the passage of specific ions into or out of the cell. Thus, the presence of the neurotransmitter in the synaptic cleft allows particular ions to pass through the membrane, changing the local membrane potential.

Neurotransmitters open ion channels by at least two different methods, direct and indirect. The direct method is simpler, so I shall describe it first. Figure 2.26 illustrates a neurotransmitter-dependent ion channel that is equipped with its own binding site. When a molecule of the appropriate neurotransmitter attaches to it, the ion channel opens. The formal name for this combination receptor/ion channel is an **ionotropic receptor.** (See *Figure 2.26.*)

The ionotropic receptor was first discovered in the organ that produces electrical current in the electric ray, *Torpedo,* where it occurs in great number. (The electric ray is a fish that generates a powerful electrical current, not some kind of Star Wars weapon.) These receptors, which are sensitive to a neurotransmitter called *acetylcholine,* contain sodium channels. When these channels are open, sodium ions enter the cell.

The indirect method is more complicated. Most receptors do not open ion channels directly but instead start a chain of chemical events. These receptors are called **metabotropic receptors** because they involve steps that require that the cell expend energy. Metabotropic receptors are located in close proximity to another protein attached to the membrane—a **G protein.** When a molecule of the neurotransmitter binds with the receptor, the receptor activates a G protein situated nearby. When acti-

The skin of *Torpedo,* the electric ray, contains large numbers of ionotropic receptors with sodium channels. The flow of sodium through these channels produces an electric current.

Molecule of neurotransmitter

Surface of membrane

Metabotropic receptor

Open ion channel

Molecule of neurotransmitter attached to binding site of metabotropic receptor

Closed ion channel

FIGURE 2.27

Metabotropic receptors.

vated, the G protein activates an enzyme and stimulates the production of a chemical called a **second messenger.** (The neurotransmitter is the first messenger.) Molecules of the second messenger travel through the cytoplasm, attach themselves to nearby ion channels, and cause them to open. Compared with postsynaptic potentials produced by ionotropic receptors, those produced by metabotropic receptors take longer to begin and last longer. (See *Figure 2.27.*)

The first second messenger to be discovered was *cyclic AMP,* a chemical that is synthesized from ATP. Since then, several other second messengers have been discovered. As you will see in later chapters, second messengers play an important role in both synaptic and nonsynaptic communication. And they can do more than open ion channels. For example, they can travel to the nucleus or other regions of the neuron and initiate biochemical changes that affect the functions of the cell.

Postsynaptic Potentials

Postsynaptic potentials can be either depolarizing (excitatory) or hyperpolarizing (inhibitory). What determines the nature of the postsynaptic potential at a particular synapse? It is not the neurotransmitter itself. Instead, it is determined by the characteristics of the postsynaptic receptors—in particular, *by the particular type of ion channel they open.* A particular neurotransmitter may bind with different types of ion channels, each of which may have a different effects. (By analogy, a particular key might open several different doors, which open up to very different types of rooms.)

As Figure 2.28 shows, there are three major types of neurotransmitter-dependent ion channels found in the postsynaptic membrane: sodium (Na^+), potassium (K^+), and chloride (Cl^-). Although the figure depicts only directly activated (ionotropic) ion channels, you should realize that many ion channels are activated indirectly, by metabotropic receptors coupled to G proteins.

The neurotransmitter-dependent sodium channel is the most important source of excitatory postsynaptic potentials. As we saw, sodium-potassium transporters keep sodium outside the cell, waiting for the forces of diffusion and electrostatic pressure

Postsynaptic receptor A receptor molecule in the postsynaptic membrane that contains a binding site for a neurotransmitter.

Neurotransmitter-dependent ion channel An ion channel that opens when a molecule of a neurotransmitter binds with a postsynaptic receptor.

Ionotropic receptor (*eye on oh trow* pik) A receptor that contains a binding site for a neurotransmitter and an ion channel that opens when a molecule of the neurotransmitter attaches to the binding site.

Metabotropic receptor (*meh tab oh trow* pik) A receptor that contains a binding site for a neurotransmitter; activates an enzyme that begins a series of events that opens an ion channel elsewhere in the membrane of the cell when a molecule of the neurotransmitter attaches to the binding site.

G protein A protein coupled to a metabotropic receptor; conveys messages to other molecules when a ligand binds with and activates the receptor.

Second messenger A chemical produced when a G protein activates an enzyme; carries a signal that results in the opening of the ion channel or causes other events to occur in the cell.

FIGURE 2.28

Ionic movements during postsynaptic potentials.

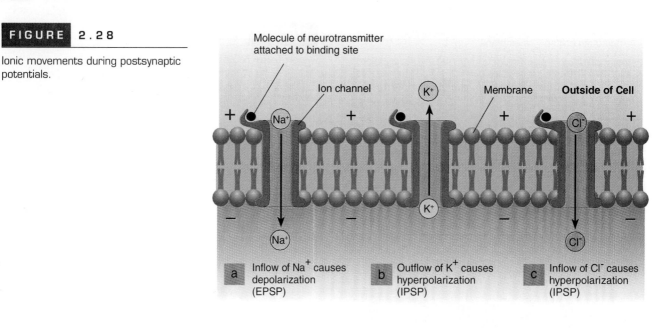

to push it in. When sodium channels are opened, sodium rushes in and causes a depolarization—an **excitatory postsynaptic potential (EPSP).** (See *Figure 2.28a.*)

Earlier we saw that sodium-potassium transporters maintain a small surplus of potassium ions inside the cell. If potassium channels open, some of these cations will follow this gradient and leave the cell. Because K^+ is positively charged, its outflow will hyperpolarize the membrane, producing an **inhibitory postsynaptic potential (IPSP).** (See *Figure 2.28b.*)

At many synapses, inhibitory neurotransmitters open the chloride channels, instead of (or in addition to) potassium channels. The effect of opening chloride channels depends on the membrane potential of the neuron. If the membrane is at the resting potential, nothing happens, because (as we saw earlier) the forces of diffusion and electrostatic pressure balance perfectly for the chloride ion. However, if the membrane potential has already been depolarized by the activity of excitatory synapses located nearby, then the opening of chloride channels will permit Cl^- to enter the cell. The inflow of anions will bring the membrane potential back to its normal resting condition. Thus, the opening of chloride channels serves to neutralize EPSPs. (See *Figure 2.28c.*)

Termination of Postsynaptic Potentials

Postsynaptic potentials are brief depolarizations or hyperpolarizations caused by the activation of postsynaptic receptors with molecules of a neurotransmitter. Two mechanisms keep them brief: reuptake and enzymatic deactivation.

The postsynaptic potentials produced by almost all neurotransmitters are terminated by reuptake. **Reuptake** is simply an extremely rapid removal of neurotransmitter from the synaptic cleft by the terminal button. The neurotransmitter does not return in the vesicles that get pinched off the membrane of the terminal button. Instead, the membrane contains special transporter molecules that draw on the cell's energy reserves to force molecules of the neurotransmitter from the synaptic cleft directly into the cytoplasm—just as sodium-potassium transporters move Na^+ and K^+ across the membrane. When an action potential arrives, the terminal button releases a small amount of neurotransmitter into the synaptic cleft and then takes it back, giving the postsynaptic receptors only a brief exposure to the neurotransmitter. (See *Figure 2.29.*)

Excitatory postsynaptic potential (EPSP) An excitatory depolarization of the postsynaptic membrane of a synapse caused by the liberation of a neurotransmitter by the terminal button.

Inhibitory postsynaptic potential (IPSP) An inhibitory hyperpolarization of the postsynaptic membrane of a synapse caused by the liberation of a neurotransmitter by the terminal button.

Reuptake The reentry of a neurotransmitter just released by a terminal button back through its membrane, thus terminating the postsynaptic potential.

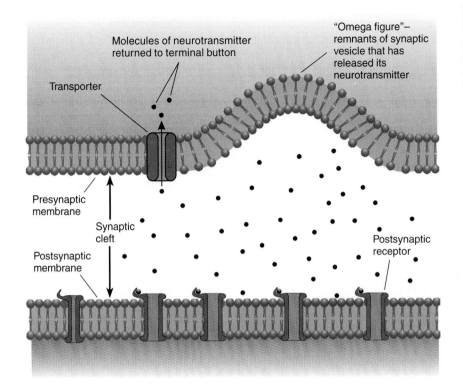

Transporter

Molecules of neurotransmitter returned to terminal button

"Omega figure"—remnants of synaptic vesicle that has released its neurotransmitter

Presynaptic membrane

Synaptic cleft

Postsynaptic membrane

Postsynaptic receptor

FIGURE 2.29

Reuptake. Molecules of a neurotransmitter that has been released into the synaptic cleft are transported back into the terminal button.

Enzymatic deactivation is accomplished by an enzyme that destroys the transmitter molecule. As far as we know, postsynaptic potentials are terminated in this way for only one neurotransmitter—**acetylcholine (ACh)**. Transmission at synapses on muscle fibers and at some synapses between neurons is mediated by ACh. Postsynaptic potentials produced by ACh are short-lived because the postsynaptic membrane at these synapses contains an enzyme called **acetylcholinesterase (AChE)**. AChE destroys ACh by breaking it into its constituents—choline and acetate. Because neither of these substances is capable of activating postsynaptic receptors, the postsynaptic potential is terminated once the molecules of ACh are broken apart. AChE is an extremely energetic destroyer of ACh; one molecule of AChE will chop apart more that five thousand molecules of ACh each second.

Effects of Postsynaptic Potentials: Neural Integration

We have seen how neurons are interconnected by means of synapses, how action potentials trigger the release of neurotransmitters, and how these chemicals initiate excitatory or inhibitory postsynaptic potentials. Excitatory postsynaptic potentials increase the likelihood that the postsynaptic neuron will fire; inhibitory postsynaptic potentials decrease this likelihood. (In this context, "firing" refers to the occurrence of an action potential.) Thus, the rate at which an axon fires is determined by the relative activity of the excitatory and inhibitory synapses on the soma and dendrites of that cell.

Let's look at the elements of this process. The interaction of the effects of excitatory and inhibitory synapses on a particular neuron is called **neural integration.** (*Integration* means "to make whole," in the sense of combining two or more functions.) Figure 2.30 illustrates the effects of excitatory and inhibitory synapses. The top panel shows what happens when several excitatory synapses become active. The

Enzymatic deactivation The destruction of a neurotransmitter by an enzyme after its release—for example, the destruction of acetylcholine by acetylcholinesterase.

Acetylcholine (ACh) (*a see tul koh leen*) A neurotransmitter found in the brain, spinal cord, and parts of the peripheral nervous system; responsible for muscular contraction.

Acetylcholinesterase (AChE) (*a see tul koh lin **ess** ter ace*) The enzyme that destroys acetylcholine soon after it is released by the terminal buttons, thus terminating the postsynaptic potential.

Neural integration The process by which inhibitory and excitatory postsynaptic potentials summate and control the rate of firing of a neuron.

Activity of inhibitory synapses produces IPSPs (blue) in postsynaptic neuron

Activity of excitatory synapses produces EPSPs (red) in postsynaptic neuron

Axon hillock reaches threshold of excitation; action potential is triggered in axon

IPSPs counteract EPSPs; action potential is not triggered in axon

(a) (b)

FIGURE 2.30

Neural integration. (a) If several excitatory synapses are active at the same time, the EPSPs they produce (shown in red) summate as they travel toward the axon, and the axon fires. (b) If several inhibitory synapses are active at the same time, the IPSPs they produce (shown in blue) diminish the size of the EPSPs and prevent the axon from firing.

release of the neurotransmitter produces depolarizing EPSPs in the dendrites of a neuron. These EPSPs (represented in red) are then transmitted down the dendrites, across the soma, to the base of the axon. If the depolarization is still strong enough when it reaches this point, the axon will fire. (See *Figure 2.30a.*)

Now let's consider what would happen if, at the same time, inhibitory synapses also become active. Inhibitory postsynaptic potentials are hyperpolarizing—they bring the membrane potential away from the threshold of excitation. Thus, they tend to cancel the effects of excitatory postsynaptic potentials. (See *Figure 2.30b.*)

The rate at which a neuron fires is controlled by the relative activity of the excitatory and inhibitory synapses on its dendrites and soma. If the activity of excitatory synapses goes up, the rate of firing will go up. If the rate of inhibitory synapses goes up, the rate of firing will go down.

Autoreceptors

Postsynaptic receptors detect the presence of a neurotransmitter in the synaptic cleft and initiate excitatory or inhibitory postsynaptic potentials. But the postsynaptic membrane is not the only location of receptors that respond to neurotransmitters. Many neurons also possess receptors that respond to the neurotransmitter that *they* release, called **autoreceptors.**

Autoreceptors can be located on the membrane of any part of the cell, but in this discussion we will consider those located on the terminal button. As far as we know, autoreceptors do not control ion channels. Thus, when stimulated by a molecule of the appropriate neurotransmitter, autoreceptors do not produce changes in the membrane potential. Instead, they regulate internal processes, including the synthesis and release of the neurotransmitter. (As you may have guessed, autoreceptors are metabotropic; the control they exert on these processes is accomplished through G

Autoreceptor A receptor molecule located on a neuron that responds to the neurotransmitter released by that neuron.

proteins and second messengers.) In most cases the effects of autoreceptor activation are inhibitory; that is, the presence of the neurotransmitter in the extracellular fluid in the vicinity of the neuron causes a decrease in the rate of synthesis or release of the neurotransmitter. Autoreceptors are part of a regulatory system that controls the amount of neurotransmitter released. If too much is released, the autoreceptors inhibit both production and release; if not enough is released, the rates of production and release go up.

Communication at Axoaxonic Synapses

So far, the discussion of synaptic activity has referred only to the effects of postsynaptic excitation or inhibition. These effects occur at axosomatic or axodendritic synapses. Axoaxonic synapses work differently. Axoaxonic synapses do not contribute directly to neural integration. Instead, axoaxonic synapses alter the amount of a neurotransmitter released by the terminal buttons of the postsynaptic axon. They can produce presynaptic modulation: presynaptic inhibition or presynaptic facilitation.

As you know, the release of a neurotransmitter by a terminal button is initiated by an action potential. Normally, a particular terminal button releases a fixed amount of neurotransmitter each time an action potential arrives. However, the release of a neurotransmitter can be modulated by the activity of axoaxonic synapses. If the activity of the axoaxonic synapse decreases the release of the neurotransmitter, the effect is called **presynaptic inhibition.** If it increases the release, it is called **presynaptic facilitation.** (See *Figure 2.31.*)

Nonsynaptic Communication: Neuromodulators and Hormones

Neurotransmitters are released by terminal buttons of neurons and are detected by receptors in the membrane of another cell located a very short distance away. The communication at each synapse is private. Neuromodulators are chemicals released by neurons that travel farther and are dispersed more widely than are neurotransmitters. **Neuromodulators** are secreted in larger amounts and diffuse for longer distances, modulating the activity of many neurons in a particular part of the brain. For example, neuromodulators affect general behavioral states such as vigilance, fearfulness, and sensitivity to pain. Most neuromodulators are composed of proteinlike molecules called *peptides*, which are described in Chapter 4.

Most **hormones** are produced in cells located in the **endocrine glands** (from the Greek *endo-*, "within," and *krinein*, "to secrete"). Others are produced by specialized cells located in various organs, such as the stomach, the intestines, the kidneys, and the brain. Cells that secrete hormones release these chemicals into the extracellular fluid. The hormones are then distributed to the rest of the body through the bloodstream. Hormones affect the activity of cells (including neurons) that contain specialized receptors located either on the surface of their membrane or deep within their nuclei. Cells that contain receptors for a particular hormone are referred to as **target cells** for that hormone; only these cells respond to its presence. Many neurons contain hormone receptors, and hormones are able to affect behavior by stimulating the receptors and changing the activity of these neurons. For example, a sex hormone, testosterone, increases the aggressiveness of most male mammals.

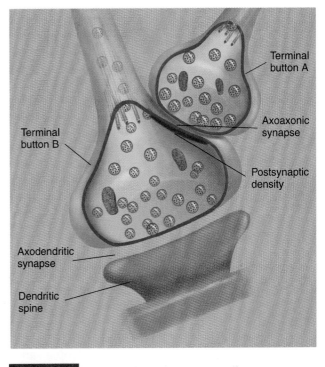

FIGURE   2.31

An axoaxonic synapse. The activity of terminal button A can increase the amount of neurotransmitter released by terminal button B, causing presynaptic facilitation, or decrease it, causing presynaptic inhibition.

Presynaptic inhibition The action of a presynaptic terminal button in an axoaxonic synapse; reduces the amount of neurotransmitter released by the postsynaptic terminal button.

Presynaptic facilitation The action of a presynaptic terminal button in an axoaxonic synapse; increases the amount of neurotransmitter released by the postsynaptic terminal button.

Neuromodulator A naturally secreted substance that acts like a neurotransmitter except that it is not restricted to the synaptic cleft but diffuses through the extracellular fluid.

Hormone A chemical substance that is released by an endocrine gland and that has effects on target cells in other organs.

Endocrine gland A gland that releases its secretions into the extracellular fluid around capillaries and hence into the bloodstream.

Target cell The type of cell that is directly affected by a hormone or nerve fiber.

INTERIM SUMMARY

Synapses consist of junctions between the terminal buttons of one neuron and the membrane—usually the somatic or dendritic membrane—of another. When an action potential is transmitted down an axon, the terminal buttons at the end release a neurotransmitter, a chemical that produces either depolarizations (EPSPs) or hyperpolarizations (IPSPs) of the postsynaptic membrane. The rate of firing of the axon of the postsynaptic cell is determined by the relative activity of the excitatory and inhibitory synapses on the membrane of its dendrites and soma—a phenomenon known as *neural integration.*

Chemical communication takes place between a cell that secretes a chemical and one that contains receptors for that chemical. The communication can involve neurotransmitters, neuromodulators, or hormones; the distance varies from the space that separates the presynaptic and postsynaptic membrane to the space that separates cells at different locations in the body. Neurotransmitters, neuromodulators, and hormones act on cells by attaching to the binding sites of receptors and initiating chemical changes in these cells.

Terminal buttons contains synaptic vesicles, mostly clustered around the release zone of the presynaptic membrane. When an action potential reaches a terminal button, it causes the release of the neurotransmitter: Synaptic vesicles that are located at the release zone fuse with the presynaptic membrane of the terminal button, break open, and release their neurotransmitter into the synaptic cleft.

The activation of postsynaptic receptors by molecules of a neurotransmitter causes neurotransmitter-dependent ion channels to open, resulting in postsynaptic potentials. Ionotropic receptors contain ion channels, which are directly opened when a ligand attaches to the binding site. Metabotropic receptors are linked to G proteins, which, when activated, open ion channels by producing a chemical called a second messenger.

The nature of the postsynaptic potential depends on the type of ion channel that is opened by the postsynaptic receptors at a particular synapse. Excitatory postsynaptic potentials occur when Na^+ enters the cell. Inhibitory postsynaptic potentials are produced by the opening of K^+ channels or Cl^- channels.

Postsynaptic potentials normally are brief. They are terminated by two means. The most common mechanism is reuptake: retrieval of molecules of the neurotransmitter from the synaptic cleft by means of transporters located in the presynaptic membrane, which transport the molecules back into the cytoplasm. Acetylcholine is deactivated by the enzyme acetylcholinesterase.

The presynaptic membrane, as well as the postsynaptic membrane, contains receptors that detect the presence of a neurotransmitter. Presynaptic receptors, also called autoreceptors, monitor the quantity of neurotransmitter that a neuron releases and, apparently, regulate the amount that is synthesized or released.

Axosomatic and axodendritic synapses are not the only kinds found in the nervous system. Axoaxonic synapses produce presynaptic inhibition or presynaptic facilitation, reducing or enhancing the amount of neurotransmitter that is released.

THOUGHT QUESTIONS

Why does synaptic transmission involve the release of chemicals? Direct electrical coupling of neurons is far simpler, so why do we not use it more extensively? (A tiny percentage of synaptic connections in the human brain do use electrical coupling.) Normally, nature uses the simplest means possible to a given end, so there must be some advantages to chemical transmission. What do you think they are? Consider the control of the withdrawal reflex illustrated in Figure 2.7. Could you design a circuit using electrical synapses that would accomplish the same tasks?

Myasthenia Gravis

"Am I cured?" asked Kathryn.

Dr. T. smiled ruefully. "I wish it were so simple!" she said. "No, I'm afraid you aren't cured, but now we know what is causing your weakness. There *is* a treatment," she hastened to add, seeing Kathryn's disappointment. "You have a condition called *myasthenia gravis*. The injection I gave you lasts only for a few minutes, but I can give you some pills that have effects that last much longer." Indeed, as she was talking, Kathryn felt herself weakening, and she sat down again.

Myasthenia gravis was first described in 1672 by Thomas Willis, an English physician. The term literally means "grave muscle weakness." It is not a very common disorder, but most experts believe that many cases—much milder than Kathryn's, of course—go undiagnosed. Kathryn's disease involved her face, neck, arm, and trunk muscles, but sometimes only the eye muscles are involved. Before the 1930s, Kathryn would have become bedridden, and almost certainly, she would have died within a few years, probably of pneumonia resulting from difficulty in breathing and coughing. But fortunately, Kathryn's future is not so bleak. The cause of myasthenia gravis is well understood, and it can be treated, if not cured.

The hallmark of myasthenia gravis is *fatigability*. That is, a patient has reasonable strength when rested but becomes very weak after moving for a little while. For many years, researchers have realized that the weakness occurs in the synapses on the muscles, not in the nervous system or the muscles themselves. In the late nineteenth century, a physician placed electrodes on the skin of a person with myasthenia gravis and electrically stimulated a nerve leading to a muscle. The muscle contracted each time he stimulated the nerve, but the contractions became progressively weaker. However, when he placed the electrodes above the muscle and stimulated it directly, the contractions showed no signs of fatigue. Later, with the development of techniques of electrical recording, researchers found that the action potentials in the nerves of people with myasthenia gravis were completely normal. If nerve conduction and muscular contraction were normal, then the problem had to lie in the synapses.

In 1934, Dr. Mary Walker remarked that the symptoms of myasthenia gravis resembled the effects of curare, a poison that blocks neural transmission at the synapses on muscles. The antidote for curare poisoning was a drug called *physostigmine*, which deactivates acetylcholinesterase (AChE). As you learned in this chapter, AChE is an enzyme that destroys the neurotransmitter acetylcholine (ACh) and terminates the postsynaptic potentials it produces. By deactivating AChE, physostigmine greatly increases and prolongs the effects of ACh on the postsynaptic membrane. Thus, it increases the strength of synaptic transmission at the synapses on muscles and reverses the effects of curare. (Chapter 4 will say more about both curare and physostigmine.)

Dr. Walker reasoned that if physostigmine reversed the effects of curare poisoning, perhaps it would also reverse the symptoms of myasthenia gravis. She tried it, and it did within a matter of a few minutes. Subsequently, pharmaceutical companies discovered drugs that could be taken orally and that produced longer-lasting effects. Nowadays, an injectable drug is used to make the diagnosis and an oral drug is used to treat it.

Researchers turned their efforts to understanding the cause of myasthenia gravis (MG). They made several interesting observations. First, people with MG usually had tumors or other abnormalities in their thymus gland; if the gland was removed, their symptoms often got better. (Kathryn's neurologist may recommend that this step be taken.) Second, microscopic examination of tissue taken from the muscles of MG patients showed damage localized to the region around the synapses, and this region showed an infiltration of white blood cells. These two facts suggested that the immune system was involved; white blood cells are responsible for the immune reaction, and the thymus gland is one of the sources of these cells.

In fact, MG is an *autoimmune disease*. Normally, the immune system protects us from infections by being alert for proteins that are present on invading microorganisms. The immune system produces antibodies that attack these foreign proteins, and the microorganisms are killed. However, sometimes the immune system makes a mistake and becomes sensitized against one of the proteins normally present in our bodies. As researchers have found, the blood of patients with MG contains antibodies against the protein that makes up acetylcholine receptors. Thus, myasthenia gravis is an autoimmune disease in which the immune system attacks and destroys many of the person's ACh receptors, which are necessary for synaptic transmission.

Recently, researchers have succeeded in developing an animal model of MG. An *animal model* is a disease that can be produced in laboratory animals and that closely resembles a human disease. The course of the disease can then be studied, and possible treatments or cures can be tested. In this case, the disease is produced by extracting ACh-receptor protein from electric rays (*Torpedo*) and injecting it into laboratory animals. The

(continued)

EPILOGUE *(continued)*

animals' immune systems become sensitized to the protein and develop antibodies that attack their own ACh receptors. The animals exhibit the same muscular fatigability shown by people with MG, and they become stronger after receiving an injection of a drug such as physostigmine.

One promising result that has emerged from studies with the animal model of MG is the finding that an animal's immune system can be *desensitized* so that it will not produce antibodies that destroy ACh recep-

tors. If ACh-receptor proteins are modified and then injected into laboratory animals, their immune systems develop an antibody against the altered protein. This antibody does not attack the animals' own ACh receptors. Later, if they are given the pure ACh-receptor protein, they do *not* develop MG. Apparently, the pure protein is so similar to the one to which the animals were previously sensitized that the immune system does not bother to produce another antibody. Perhaps a vaccine can be developed

that can be used to arrest MG in its early stages by inducing the person's immune system to produce the harmless antibody rather than the one that attacks acetylcholine receptors.

Even with the drugs available to physicians today, myasthenia gravis remains a serious disease. The drugs do not restore a person's strength to normal, and they can have serious side effects. But the progress made in the laboratory in recent years gives us hope for a brighter future for people like Kathryn.

KEY CONCEPTS

CELLS OF THE NERVOUS SYSTEM

1. Neurons have a soma, dendrites, an axon, and terminal buttons. Circuits of interconnected neurons are responsible for the functions performed by the nervous system. Neurons are supported by glia and by Schwann cells, which provide myelin sheaths, housekeeping services, and physical support. The blood-brain barrier helps to regulate the chemicals that reach the brain.

COMMUNICATION WITHIN A NEURON

2. The action potential occurs when the membrane potential of an axon reaches the threshold of excitation. Although the action potential is electrical, it is caused by the flow of sodium and potassium ions through voltage-dependent ion channels in the membrane. Saltatory conduction, which takes place in myelinated axons, is faster and more efficient than conduction in unmyelinated axons.

COMMUNICATION BETWEEN NEURONS

3. Neurons communicate by means of synapses, which enable the presynaptic neuron to produce excitatory or inhibitory effects on the postsynaptic neuron. These effects increase or decrease the rate at which

the axon of the postsynaptic neuron sends action potentials down to its terminal buttons.

4. When an action potential reaches the end of an axon, it causes some synaptic vesicles to release a neurotransmitter into the synaptic cleft. Molecules of the neurotransmitter attach themselves to receptors in the postsynaptic membrane.

5. When they become activated by molecules of the neurotransmitters, postsynaptic receptors produce either excitatory or inhibitory postsynaptic potentials by opening voltage-controlled sodium, potassium, or chloride ion channels.

6. The postsynaptic potential is terminated by the destruction of the neurotransmitter or by its reuptake into the terminal button.

7. Autoreceptors help to regulate the amount of neurotransmitter that is released.

8. Axoaxonic synapses consist of junctions between two terminal buttons. Release of neurotransmitter by the first terminal button increases or decreases the amount of neurotransmitter released by the second.

9. Neuromodulators and hormones have actions similar to those of neurotransmitters: They bind with and activate receptors on their target cells.

SUGGESTED READINGS

Hall, A. *An Introduction to Molecular Neurobiology.* Sunderland, MA: Sinauer, 1992.

Kandel, E.R., Schwartz, J.H., and Jessell, T.M. *Principles of Neural Science,* 3rd ed. Norwalk, CT: Appleton & Lange, 1992.

Nicholls, J.G., Martin, A.R., Wallace, B.G., and Kuffler, S.W. *From Neuron to Brain,* 3rd ed. Sunderland, MA: Sinauer, 1992.

3

Structure of the Nervous System

LEARNING OBJECTIVES

1. Describe the appearance of the brain, and identify the terms used to indicate directions and planes of section.

2. Describe the divisions of the nervous system, the meninges, the ventricular system, and the flow of cerebrospinal fluid through the brain and its production.

3. Outline the development of the central nervous system.

4. Describe the telencephalon—one of the two major structures of the forebrain.

5. Describe the two major structures of the diencephalon.

6. Describe the major structures of the midbrain, the hindbrain, and the spinal cord.

7. Describe the peripheral nervous system, including the two divisions of the autonomic nervous system.

The Left is Gone

Miss S. was a sixty-year-old woman with a history of high blood pressure, which was not responding well to the medication she was taking. One evening she was sitting in her reclining chair reading the newspaper when the phone rang. She got out of her chair and walked to the phone. As she did, she began feeling giddy and stopped to hold onto the kitchen table. She has no memory of what happened after that.

The next morning, a neighbor, who usually stopped by to have coffee with her, found her lying on the floor, mumbling incoherently. She called an ambulance, which took Miss S. to a hospital.

Two days after her admission, I visited her in her room, along with a group of people being led by the chief of neurology. We had already been told by the neurological resident in charge of her case that she had had a stroke in the back part of the right side of the brain. He had attached a CT scan to an illuminated viewer mounted on the wall and had showed us a white spot caused by the accumulation of blood in a particular region of her brain. (You can look at the scan yourself, if you like; it is shown in Figure 5.15.)

About a dozen of us entered Miss S.'s room. She was awake but seemed a little confused. The resident greeted her and asked how she was feeling. "Fine, I guess," she said. "I still don't know why I'm here."

"Can you see the other people in the room?"

"Why, sure."

"How many are there?"

She turned her head to the right and began counting. She stopped when she had counted the people at the foot of her bed. "Seven," she reported. "What about us?" asked a voice from the left of her bed. "What?" she said, looking at the people she had already counted. "Here, to your left. No, toward your left!" the voice repeated. Slowly, rather reluctantly, she began turning her head to the left. The voice kept insisting, and finally, she saw who was talking. "Oh," she said, "I guess there are more of you."

The resident approached the left side of her bed and touched her left arm. "What is this?" he asked. "Where?" she said. "Here," he answered, holding up her arm and moving it gently in front of her face.

"Oh, that's an arm."

"An arm? Whose arm?"

"I don't know. . . . I guess it must be yours."

"No, it's yours. Look, it's a part of you." He traced with his fingers from her arm to her shoulder.

"Well, if you say so," she said, still sounding unconvinced.

When we returned to the residents' lounge, the chief of neurology said that we had seen a classic example of unilateral neglect, caused by damage to a particular part of the brain. "I've seen many cases like this," he explained. "People can still perceive sensations from the left side of their body, but they just don't pay attention to them. A woman will put makeup on only the right side of her face, and a man will shave only half of his beard. When they put on a shirt or a coat, they will use their left hand to slip it over their right arm and shoulder, but then they'll just forget about their left arm and let the garment hang from one shoulder. They also don't look at things located toward the left or even the left halves of things. Once I saw a man who had just finished eating breakfast. He was sitting in his bed, with a tray in front of him. There was half of a pancake on his plate. 'Are you all done?' I asked. 'Sure,' he said. I turned the plate around so that the uneaten part was on his right. He gave a startled look and said, 'Where the hell did that come from?'"

The goal of neuroscience is to understand how the brain works, and the rest of this book will describe what researchers have learned so far. To understand what they have learned, you must be acquainted with the basic structure of the nervous system. The number of terms introduced in this chapter is kept to a minimum (but as you will see, the minimum is still a rather large number). With the framework you will receive from this chapter, you should have no trouble understanding what I have to say in the rest of the book.

BASIC FEATURES OF THE NERVOUS SYSTEM

Before beginning a description of the nervous system, I want to discuss the terms used to describe it. The gross anatomy of the brain was described long ago, and

Neuraxis An imaginary line drawn through the center of the length of the central nervous system, from the bottom of the spinal cord to the front of the forebrain.

Anterior With respect to the central nervous system, located near or toward the head.

Posterior With respect to the central nervous system, located near or toward the tail.

everything that could be seen without the aid of a microscope was given a name. Early anatomists named most brain structures according to their similarity to commonplace objects: amygdala, or "almond-shaped object"; hippocampus, or "sea horse"; genu, or "knee"; cortex, or "bark"; pons, or "bridge"; uncus, or "hook," to give a few examples. Throughout this book I will translate the names of anatomical terms as I introduce them, because the translation makes the terms more memorable. For example, knowing that *cortex* means "bark" (like the bark of a tree) will help you remember that the cortex is the outer layer of the brain.

When describing features of a structure as complex as the brain, we need to use terms denoting directions. Directions in the nervous system are normally described relative to the **neuraxis,** an imaginary line drawn through the spinal cord up to the front of the brain. For simplicity's sake, let us consider an animal with a straight neuraxis. Figure 3.1 shows an alligator and a human. This alligator is certainly laid out in a linear fashion; we can draw a straight line that starts between its eyes and continues down the center of its spinal cord. (See *Figure 3.1.*) The front end is **anterior,** and the tail is **posterior.** The terms **rostral** (toward the beak) and **caudal** (toward the tail) are also used, especially when referring specifically to the brain. The top of the head and

Rostral "Toward the beak"; with respect to the central nervous system, in a direction along the neuraxis toward the front of the face.

Caudal "Toward the tail"; with respect to the central nervous system, in a direction along the neuraxis away from the front of the face.

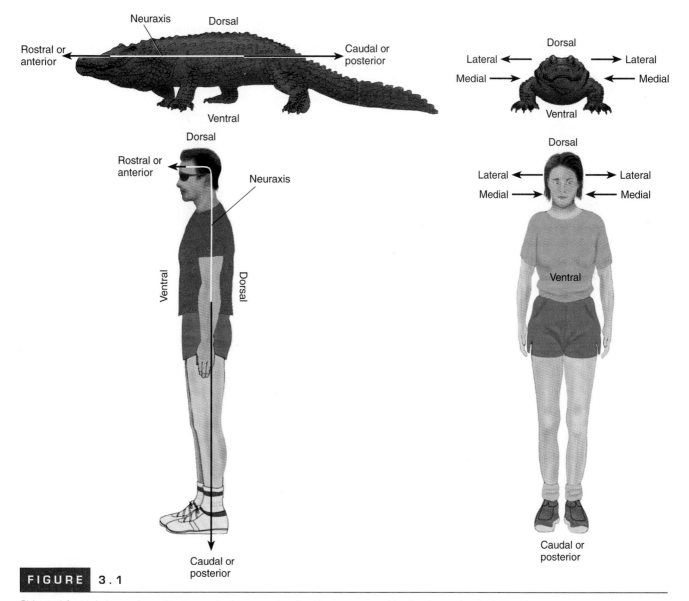

FIGURE 3.1

Side and frontal views of an alligator and a human, showing the terms used to denote anatomical directions.

Dorsal "Toward the back"; with respect to the central nervous system, in a direction perpendicular to the neuraxis toward the top of the head or the back.

Ventral "Toward the belly"; with respect to the central nervous system, in a direction perpendicular to the neuraxis toward the bottom of the skull or the front surface of the body.

Lateral Toward the side of the body, in a direction at right angles with the neuraxis and away from it.

Medial Toward the neuraxis, away from the side of the body.

Ipsilateral Located on the same side of the body.

Contralateral Located on the opposite side of the body.

Cross section With respect to the central nervous system, a slice taken at right angles to the neuraxis.

the back are part of the **dorsal** surface, while the **ventral** (front) surface faces the ground. These directions are somewhat more complicated in the human; because we stand upright, our neuraxis bends, so that the top of the head is perpendicular to the back. The frontal views of the alligator and the human illustrate the terms **lateral** and **medial,** toward the side and toward the midline, respectively. (See *Figure 3.1.*)

Two other useful terms are *ipsilateral* and *contralateral*. **Ipsilateral** (from the Latin *ipse,* "same") refers to structures on the same side of the body. Thus, if we say that the olfactory bulb sends axons to the *ipsilateral* hemisphere, we mean that the left olfactory bulb sends axons to the left hemisphere and the right olfactory bulb sends axons to the right hemisphere. **Contralateral** (from the Latin *contra,* "against") refers to structures on opposite sides of the body. If we say that a particular region of the left cerebral cortex controls movements of the *contralateral* hand, we mean that the region controls movements of the right hand.

To see what is in the nervous system, we have to cut it open. To be able to convey information about what we find, we slice it in a standard way. Figure 3.2 shows a human brain and part of the spinal cord. We can slice the central nervous system in three ways:

1. Transversely, like a salami, giving us **cross sections** (also known as **frontal sections,** referring to the brain)
2. Parallel to the ground, giving us **horizontal sections**
3. Perpendicular to the ground and parallel to the neuraxis, giving us **sagittal sections.** The **midsagittal plane** divides the brain into two symmetrical halves. The sagittal section in Figure 3.2 lies in the midsagittal plane.

FIGURE 3.2

Standard slices of the human central nervous system.

Note that because of our upright posture, cross sections of the spinal cord are actually parallel to the ground. (See *Figure 3.2.*)

An Overview

The nervous system consists of the brain and spinal cord, which make up the **central nervous system (CNS),** and the cranial nerves, spinal nerves, and peripheral ganglia, which make up the **peripheral nervous system (PNS).** The CNS is encased in bone: The brain is covered by the skull, and the spinal cord is encased by the vertebral column.

Figure 3.3 illustrates the relation of the brain and spinal cord to the rest of the body. Do not be concerned with unfamiliar labels on this figure; these structures will be described later. (See *Figure 3.3.*) The brain is a large mass of neurons, glia, and other supporting cells. It is the most protected organ of the body, encased in a tough, bony skull and floating in a pool of cerebrospinal fluid. The brain receives a copious supply of blood and is chemically guarded by the blood-brain barrier.

Meninges

The entire nervous system—brain, spinal cord, cranial and spinal nerves, and peripheral ganglia—is covered by tough connective tissue. The protective sheaths around the brain and spinal cord are called the **meninges** (singular: *meninx*). The meninges consist of three layers, which are shown in Figure 3.3. The outer layer is thick, tough, and flexible but unstretchable; its name, **dura mater,** means "hard mother." The middle layer of the meninges, the **arachnoid membrane,** gets its name from the weblike appearance of the *arachnoid trabeculae* that protrude from it (from the Greek *arachne,* meaning "spider"; *trabecula* means "track"). The arachnoid membrane, soft and spongy, lies beneath the dura mater. Closely attached to the brain and spinal cord, and following every surface convolution, is the **pia mater** ("pious mother"). The smaller surface blood vessels of the brain and spinal cord are contained within this layer. Between the pia mater and arachnoid membrane is a gap called the **subarachnoid space.** This space is filled with a liquid called **cerebrospinal fluid (CSF).** (See *Figure 3.3.*)

The peripheral nervous system (PNS) is covered with only two layers of meninges: the dura mater and the pia mater. The middle layer (arachnoid membrane), with its associated pool of CSF, covers only the brain and spinal cord. Outside the central nervous system, the outer and inner layers (dura mater and pia mater) fuse and form a sheath that covers the spinal and cranial nerves and the peripheral ganglia.

The Ventricular System and Production of Cerebrospinal Fluid

The brain is very soft and jellylike. The considerable weight of a human brain (approximately 1400 g), along with its delicate construction, necessitates that it be protected from shock. A human brain cannot even support its own weight well; it is difficult to remove and handle a fresh brain from a recently deceased human without damaging it.

Fortunately, the intact brain within a living human is well protected. It floats in a bath of CSF contained within the subarachnoid space. Because the brain is completely immersed in liquid, its net weight is reduced to approximately 80 g; thus, pressure on the base of the brain is considerably diminished. The CSF surrounding the brain and spinal cord also reduces the shock to the central nervous system that would be caused by sudden head movement.

Frontal section A slice through the brain parallel to the forehead.

Horizontal section A slice through the brain parallel to the ground.

Sagittal section (*sadj i tul*) A slice through the brain parallel to the neuraxis and perpendicular to the ground.

Midsagittal plane The plane through the neuraxis perpendicular to the ground; divides the brain into two symmetrical halves.

Central nervous system (CNS) The brain and spinal cord.

Peripheral nervous system (PNS) The nerves and ganglia located outside the central nervous system.

Meninges (singular: **meninx**) (*men in jees*) The three layers of tissue that encase the central nervous system: the dura mater, arachnoid membrane, and pia mater.

Dura mater The outermost of the meninges; tough, flexible, unstretchable.

Arachnoid membrane (*a rak noyd*) The middle layer of the meninges, between the outer dura mater and inner pia mater. The subarachnoid space beneath the arachnoid membrane is filled with cerebrospinal fluid, which cushions the brain.

Pia mater The layer of the meninges adjacent to the surface of the brain.

Subarachnoid space The fluid-filled space between the arachnoid membrane and the pia mater.

Cerebrospinal fluid (CSF) A clear fluid, similar to blood plasma, that fills the ventricular system of the brain and the subarachnoid space surrounding the brain and spinal cord.

Meninges

Opening in meninges to show brain

Central Nervous System:

Brain

Spinal cord

Cranial nerves

Ribs

Spinal nerves

Edge of dura mater (cut open)

Spinal nerves

Lung

Kidney

Cauda equina

(a)

Dura mater

Arachnoid membrane

Layers of meninges

Subarachnoid space (filled with cerebrospinal fluid)

Arachnoid trabeculae

Pia mater

(b)

Surface of brain

Spinal cord

Cauda equina

Edge of dura mater (cut open)

(c)

FIGURE 3.3

(a) The relation of the nervous system to the rest of the body. (b) Detail of the meninges that cover the central nervous system. (c) A closer view of the lower spinal cord and cauda equina.

Ventricle (*ven trik ul*) One of the hollow spaces within the brain, filled with cerebrospinal fluid.

Lateral ventricle One of the two ventricles located in the center of the telencephalon.

The brain contains a series of hollow, interconnected chambers called **ventricles,** which are filled with CSF. (See *Figure 3.4.*) The largest chambers are the **lateral ventricles,** which are connected to the **third ventricle.** The third ventricle is located at the midline of the brain; its walls divide the surrounding part of the brain into symmetrical halves. A bridge of neural tissue called the *massa intermedia* crosses through the middle of the third ventricle and serves as a convenient reference point. The **cerebral aqueduct,** a long tube, connects the third ventricle to the **fourth ventricle.** The lateral ventricles are actually the first and second ventricles, but they are never referred to as such. (See *Figure 3.4.*)

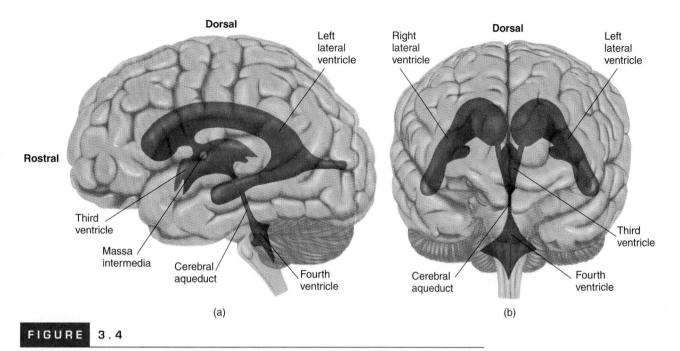

FIGURE 3.4

The ventricular system of the brain. (a) Lateral view of the left side of the brain. (b) Frontal view.

Cerebrospinal fluid is extracted from the blood and resembles blood plasma in its composition. It is manufactured by a special structure that is rich in blood vessels called the **choroid plexus,** which protrudes into all four of the ventricles. Circulation of CSF begins in the lateral ventricles, flows into the third ventricle, then flows through the cerebral aqueduct into the fourth ventricle. From there, it flows through a set of openings into the subarachnoid space, which encases the entire central nervous system. Finally, the fluid is reabsorbed into the blood supply. The total volume of CSF is approximately 125 milliliters (ml), and the half-life (the time it takes for half of the CSF to be replaced by fresh fluid) is about 3 hours. Therefore, several times this amount is produced by the choroid plexus each day.

Occasionally, the flow of CSF is interrupted at some point in its route of passage. For example, a brain tumor growing in the midbrain may push against the cerebral aqueduct, blocking its flow, or an infant may be born with a cerebral aqueduct that is too small to accommodate a normal flow of CSF. This occlusion results in greatly increased pressure within the ventricles, because the choroid plexus continues to produce CSF. The walls of the ventricles then expand and produce a condition known as **obstructive hydrocephalus** (*hydrocephalus* literally means "water-head"). If the obstruction remains, and if nothing is done to reverse the increased intracerebral pressure, blood vessels will be squeezed shut and permanent—perhaps fatal—brain damage will occur. Fortunately, a surgeon can usually operate on the person, drilling a hole through the skull and inserting a plastic tube into one of the ventricles. The tube is then placed beneath the skin and connected to a pressure relief valve that is implanted in the abdominal cavity. When the pressure in the ventricles becomes excessive, the valve permits the CSF to escape into the abdomen, where it is eventually reabsorbed into the blood supply. (See *Figure 3.5.*)

INTERIM SUMMARY

Anatomists have adopted a set of terms to describe the locations of parts of the body. *Anterior* is toward the head, *posterior* is toward the tail, *lateral* is toward the side, *medial* is toward the middle, *dorsal* is toward the back, and *ventral* is toward the front surface of the body. In the special case of the nervous system, *rostral*

Third ventricle The ventricle located in the center of the diencephalon.

Cerebral aqueduct A narrow tube interconnecting the third and fourth ventricles of the brain, located in the center of the mesencephalon.

Fourth ventricle The ventricle located between the cerebellum and the dorsal pons, in the center of the metencephalon.

Choroid plexus The highly vascular tissue that protrudes into the ventricles and produces cerebrospinal fluid.

Obstructive hydrocephalus A condition in which all or some of the brain's ventricles are enlarged; caused by an obstruction that impedes the normal flow of CSF.

Valve to regulate pressure

Tube inserted into lateral ventricle

Tube to abdominal cavity

FIGURE 3.5

Hydrocephalus in an infant. A surgeon places a shunt in a lateral ventricle, which permits cerebrospinal fluid to escape to the abdominal cavity, where it is absorbed into the blood supply. A pressure valve regulates the flow of CSF through the shunt.

means toward the beak (or nose) and *caudal* means toward the tail. *Ipsilateral* means same side, and *contralateral* means other side. A cross section (or, in the case of the brain, a frontal section) slices the nervous system at right angles to the neuraxis. A horizontal section slices the brain parallel to the ground. A sagittal section slices it perpendicular to the ground and parallel to the neuraxis.

The central nervous system consists of the brain and spinal cord, and the peripheral nervous system consists of the spinal and cranial nerves and peripheral ganglia. The CNS is covered with the meninges: dura mater, arachnoid membrane, and pia mater. The space under the arachnoid membrane is filled with cerebrospinal fluid, in which the brain floats. The PNS is covered with only the dura mater and pia mater. Cerebrospinal fluid is produced in the choroid plexus of the lateral, third, and fourth ventricles. It flows from the two lateral ventricles into the third ventricle, through the cerebral aqueduct into the fourth ventricle, then into the subarachnoid space, and finally back into the blood supply. If the flow of CSF is blocked by a tumor or other obstruction, the result is hydrocephalus: enlargement of the ventricles and subsequent brain damage.

THE CENTRAL NERVOUS SYSTEM

Although the brain is exceedingly complicated, an understanding of the basic features of brain development makes it easier to learn and remember the location of the most important structures. With that end in mind, I introduce these features here in the context of development of the central nervous system.

Development of the Central Nervous System

The central nervous system begins its existence early in embryonic life as a hollow tube, and it maintains this basic shape even after it is fully developed. During development, parts of the tube elongate, pockets and folds form, and the tissue around the tube thickens. The cells that give rise to neurons are found on the inner surface of the tube. These cells divide and produce neurons, which then migrate in a radial direction, away from the center. Their final location is guided by both physical and chemical factors. Physical guidance is provided by radially oriented glial cells; the newly born neurons migrate along the processes of these cells. Chemical guidance attracts particular types of neurons to particular locations, where they come to rest. (See *Figure 3.6*.)

Early in development, the central nervous system contains three interconnected chambers. These chambers become ventricles, and the tissue that surrounds them becomes the three major parts of the brain: the forebrain, the midbrain, and the hindbrain. (See *Figures 3.7a* and *3.7c*.) As development progresses, the rostral chamber divides into three separate chambers, which become the two lateral ventricles

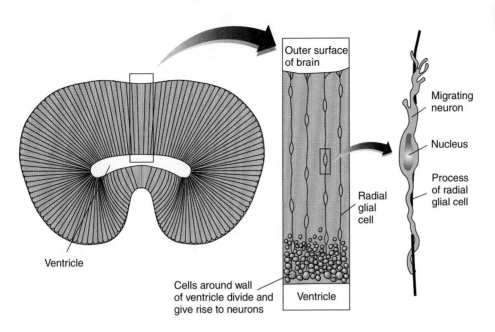

FIGURE 3.6

A cross section through the nervous system early in its development. Radially oriented glial cells help to guide the migration of newly formed neurons.

(Adapted from Bloom, F.E., and Lazerson, A. Brain, Mind, and Behavior, *2nd ed. New York: W.H. Freeman, 1988.)*

and the third ventricle. The region around the lateral ventricles becomes the telencephalon ("end brain"), and the region around the third ventricle becomes the diencephalon ("interbrain"). (See **Figures 3.7b** and **3.7d.**) In its final form the chamber inside the midbrain (mesencephalon) becomes narrow, forming the cerebral aqueduct, and two structures develop in the hindbrain: the metencephalon ("afterbrain") and the myelencephalon ("marrowbrain"). (See **Figure 3.7e.**)

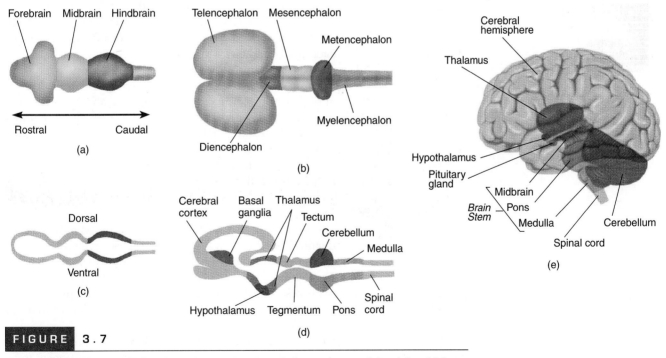

FIGURE 3.7

A schematic outline of brain development, showing its relation to the ventricles. (a) and (c) Early in development. (b) and (d) Later in development. (e) A lateral view of the left side of a semitransparent human brain, showing the brain stem "ghosted in." The colors of all figures denote corresponding regions.

TABLE 3.1	Anatomical Subdivisions of the Brain		
Major Division	**Ventricle**	**Subdivision**	**Principal Structures**
Forebrain	Lateral	Telencephalon	Cerebral cortex
			Basal ganglia
			Limbic system
	Third	Diencephalon	Thalamus
			Hypothalamus
Midbrain	Cerebral aqueduct	Mesencephalon	Tectum Tegmentum
Hindbrain	Fourth	Metencephalon	Cerebellum
			Pons
		Myelencephalon	Medulla oblongata

Table 3.1 summarizes the terms I have introduced here and mentions some of the major structures found in each part of the brain. The colors in the table match those in Figure 3.7. These structures will be described in the remainder of the chapter. (See *Table 3.1.*)

Once neurons have migrated to their final locations, where they collect in groups, they begin forming connections with other groups of neurons. They grow dendrites, which receive the terminal buttons from the axons of other neurons, and they grow axons of their own. Like neural migration, axonal growth is guided by physical and chemical factors. Apparently, different types of cells secrete different chemicals, which attract different types of axons. Once the growing ends of the axons (the *growth cones*) reach their targets, they form numerous branches. Each of these branches finds a vacant place on the membrane of the appropriate type of postsynaptic cell, grows a terminal button, and establishes a synaptic connection. Of course, the establishment of a synaptic connection also requires efforts on the part of the postsynaptic cell; this cell must contribute its parts of the synapse, including the postsynaptic receptors. The chemical signals that the cells exchange to tell one another to establish these connections are not yet known.

The layer of cells surrounding the neural tube gives rise to many more neurons than are needed. In fact, the neurons that are produced must compete in order to survive. The axons of approximately 50 percent of these neurons do not find vacant postsynaptic cells of the right type with which to form synaptic connections, so they die. This phenomenon, too, involves a chemical signal; when a presynaptic neuron establishes synaptic connections, it receives a signal from the postsynaptic cell that permits it to survive. Neurons that come too late do not find any available space and thus do not receive this life-sustaining signal. This scheme may seem wasteful, but apparently the evolutionary process found that the safest strategy was to produce too many neurons and let them fight to establish synaptic connections, rather than try to produce exactly the right number of each type of neuron.

During development, thousands of different pathways develop in the brain. These pathways—groups of axons that connect one brain region with another—seem to be specified genetically. And within many of these pathways, the connections are orderly and systematic. For example, the axons of sensory neurons from the skin form orderly connections in the brain; axons from the little finger form synapses in one region, those of the ring finger form synapses in a neighboring region, and so on. In fact, the surface of the body is "mapped" on the surface of the brain. Similarly, the surface of the retina of the eye is "mapped" on another region of the surface of the brain.

The Forebrain

As we saw, the **forebrain** surrounds the rostral end of the neural tube. Its two major components are the telencephalon and the diencephalon.

Telencephalon

The telencephalon includes most of the two symmetrical **cerebral hemispheres** that make up the cerebrum. The cerebral hemispheres are covered by the cerebral cortex and contain the limbic system and the basal ganglia. The limbic system and the basal ganglia are primarily in the **subcortical regions** of the brain—those located deep within it, beneath the cerebral cortex.

Cerebral Cortex.   As we saw, *cortex* means "bark," and the **cerebral cortex** surrounds the cerebral hemispheres like the bark of a tree. In humans the cerebral cortex is greatly convoluted. These convolutions, consisting of **sulci** (small grooves), **fissures** (large grooves), and **gyri** (bulges between adjacent sulci or fissures), greatly enlarge the surface area of the cortex, compared with a smooth brain of the same size. In fact, two-thirds of the surface of the cortex is hidden in the grooves; thus, the presence of gyri and sulci triples the area of the cerebral cortex. The total surface area is approximately 2360 cm^2 (2.5 ft^2), and the thickness is approximately 3 mm.

The cerebral cortex consists mostly of glia and the cell bodies, dendrites, and interconnecting axons of neurons. Because cells predominate, the cerebral cortex has a grayish brown appearance, and it is called *gray matter*. (See **Figure 3.8**.) Millions of axons run beneath the cerebral cortex and connect its neurons with those located elsewhere in the brain. The large concentration of myelin around these axons gives this tissue an opaque white appearance—hence the term *white matter*.

Different regions of the cerebral cortex perform different functions. Three regions receive information from the sensory organs. The **primary visual cortex,** which

Forebrain The most rostral of the three major divisions of the brain; includes the telencephalon and diencephalon.

Cerebral hemisphere (*sa ree brul*) One of the two major portions of the forebrain, covered by the cerebral cortex.

Subcortical region The region located within the brain, beneath the cortical surface.

Cerebral cortex The outermost layer of gray matter of the cerebral hemispheres.

Sulcus (plural: sulci) (*sul kus, sul sigh*) A groove in the surface of the cerebral hemisphere, smaller than a fissure.

Fissure A major groove in the surface of the brain, larger than a sulcus.

Gyrus (plural: gyri) (*jye russ, jye rye*) A convolution of the cortex of the cerebral hemispheres, separated by sulci or fissures.

Primary visual cortex The region of the cerebral cortex whose primary input is from the visual system.

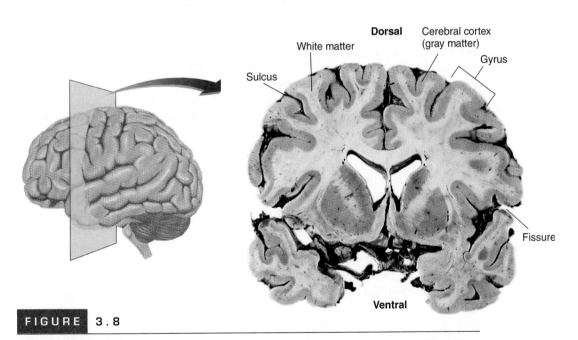

FIGURE **3.8**

A slice of a human brain showing fissures and gyri and the layer of cerebral cortex that follows these convolutions.

Primary auditory cortex

Portion of Left Hemisphere

Primary motor cortex

Central sulcus

Primary somatosensory cortex

Right Hemisphere

Calcarine fissure

Feet Feet
Trunk Trunk
Hands Hands
Fingers Fingers
Face Face
Lips Lips

Primary visual cortex

Lateral fissure

Primary auditory cortex

Left Hemisphere

FIGURE 3.9

A lateral view of the left side of a human brain and part of the inner surface of the right side. The inset shows a cutaway of part of the frontal lobe of the left hemisphere, permitting us to see the primary auditory cortex on the dorsal surface of the temporal lobe.

Calcarine fissure (*kal ka rine*) A fissure located in the occipital lobe on the medial surface of the brain; contains most of the primary visual cortex.

Primary auditory cortex The region of the cerebral cortex whose primary input is from the auditory system.

Lateral fissure The fissure that separates the temporal lobe from the overlying frontal and parietal lobes.

Primary somatosensory cortex The region of the cerebral cortex whose primary input is from the somatosensory system.

Central sulcus (*sul kus*) The sulcus that separates the frontal lobe from the parietal lobe.

Primary motor cortex The region of the cerebral cortex that contains neurons that control movements of skeletal muscles.

Frontal lobe The anterior portion of the cerebral cortex, rostral to the parietal lobe and dorsal to the temporal lobe.

Parietal lobe (*pa rye i tul*) The region of the cerebral cortex caudal to the frontal lobe and dorsal to the temporal lobe.

Temporal lobe (*tem por ul*) The region of the cerebral cortex rostral to the occipital lobe and ventral to the parietal and frontal lobes.

Occipital lobe (*ok sip i tul*) The region of the cerebral cortex caudal to the parietal and temporal lobes.

Sensory association cortex Those regions of the cerebral cortex that receive information from the regions of the primary sensory cortex.

receives visual information, is located at the back of the brain, on the inner surfaces of the cerebral hemispheres—primarily, on the upper and lower banks of the **calcarine fissure.** (*Calcarine* means "spur-shaped." See *Figure 3.9.*) The **primary auditory cortex,** which receives auditory information, is located on the upper surface of a deep fissure in the side of the brain—the **lateral fissure.** (See inset, *Figure 3.9.*) The **primary somatosensory cortex,** a vertical strip of cortex just caudal to the **central sulcus,** receives information from the body senses. As Figure 3.9 shows, different regions of the primary somatosensory cortex receive information from different regions of the body. In addition, the base of the somatosensory cortex receives information concerning taste. (See *Figure 3.9.*)

With the exception of olfaction, sensory information from the body or the environment is sent to the primary sensory cortex of the contralateral hemisphere. Thus, the primary somatosensory cortex of the left hemisphere learns what the right hand is holding, the left primary visual cortex learns what is happening toward the person's right, and so on.

The region of the cerebral cortex most directly involved in the control of movement is the **primary motor cortex,** located just in front of the primary somatosensory cortex. Neurons in different parts of the primary motor cortex are connected to muscles in different parts of the body. The connections, like those of the sensory regions of the cerebral cortex, are contralateral; the left primary motor cortex controls the right side of the body and vice versa. Thus, if a surgeon places an electrode on the surface of the left primary motor cortex and stimulates the neurons there with a weak electrical current, the result will be movement of a particular part of the right side of the body. Moving the electrode to a different spot will cause a different part of the right side of the body to move. (See *Figure 3.9.*) I like to think of the strip of primary motor cortex as the keyboard of a piano, with each key controlling a different movement. (We will see shortly who the "player" of this piano is.)

The regions of primary sensory and motor cortex occupy only a small part of the cerebral cortex. The rest of the cerebral cortex accomplishes what is done between sensation and action: perceiving, learning and remembering, planning, and acting. These processes take place in the *association areas* of the cerebral cortex. The central sulcus provides an important dividing line between the anterior and posterior regions of the cerebral cortex. (See *Figure 3.9.*) The anterior region is involved in movement-related activities, such as planning and executing behaviors. The posterior part is involved in perceiving and learning.

Discussing the various regions of the cerebral cortex is easier if we have names for them. In fact, the cerebral cortex is divided into four areas, or *lobes,* named for the bones of the skull that cover them: the frontal lobe, parietal lobe, temporal lobe, and occipital lobe. Of course, the brain contains two of each lobe, one in each hemisphere. The **frontal lobe** (the "front") includes everything in front of the central fissure. The **parietal lobe** (the "wall") is located on the side of the cerebral hemisphere, just behind the central sulcus, caudal to the frontal lobe. The **temporal lobe** (the "temple") juts forward from the base of the brain, ventral to the frontal and parietal lobes. The **occipital lobe** (*ob,* "in back of"; *caput,* "head") lies at the very back of the brain, caudal to the parietal and temporal lobes. Figure 3.10 shows these lobes in three views of the cerebral hemispheres: a ventral view (a view from the bottom), a midsagittal view (a view of the inner surface of the right hemisphere after the left hemisphere has been removed), and a lateral view. (See *Figure 3.10.*)

Each primary sensory area of the cerebral cortex sends information to adjacent regions, called the **sensory association cortex.** Circuits of neurons in the sensory association cortex analyze the information received from the primary sensory cortex; perception takes place there, and memories are stored there. The regions of the sensory association cortex located closest to the primary sensory areas receive information from only one sensory system. For example, the region closest to the primary visual cortex analyzes visual information and stores visual memories. Regions of the sensory association cortex located far from the primary sensory areas receive information from more than one sensory system; thus, they are involved in several kinds of perceptions and memories. These regions make it possible to integrate information from more than one sensory system.

FIGURE 3.10

The four lobes of the cerebral cortex, the primary sensory and motor cortex, and the association cortex. (a) Ventral view, from the base of the brain. (b) Midsagittal view, with the cerebellum and brain stem removed. (c) Lateral view.

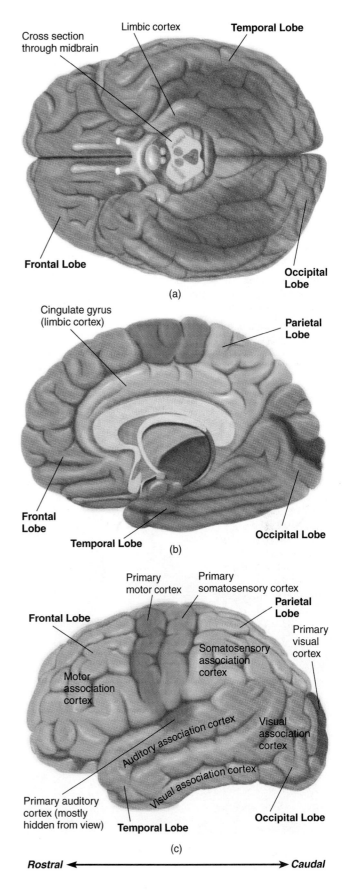

Cross section through midbrain
Limbic cortex
Temporal Lobe
Frontal Lobe
Occipital Lobe
(a)

Cingulate gyrus (limbic cortex)
Parietal Lobe
Frontal Lobe
Temporal Lobe
Occipital Lobe
(b)

Primary motor cortex
Primary somatosensory cortex
Parietal Lobe
Frontal Lobe
Primary visual cortex
Somatosensory association cortex
Motor association cortex
Auditory association cortex
Visual association cortex
Visual association cortex
Primary auditory cortex (mostly hidden from view)
Temporal Lobe
Occipital Lobe
(c)

Rostral ◄———————————► *Caudal*

For example, we can learn the connection between the sight of a particular face and the sound of a particular voice. (See *Figure 3.10.*)

If people sustain damage to the somatosensory association cortex, their deficits are related to somatosensation and to the environment in general; for example, they may have difficulty perceiving the shapes of objects that they can touch but not see, they may be unable to name parts of their bodies, or they may have trouble drawing maps or following them. Destruction of the primary visual cortex causes blindness. People who sustain damage to the visual association cortex will not become blind, although they may be unable to recognize objects by sight. People who sustain damage to the auditory association cortex may have difficulty perceiving speech or even producing meaningful speech of their own. People who sustain damage to regions of the association cortex at the junction of the three posterior lobes, where the somatosensory, visual, and auditory functions overlap, may have difficulty reading or writing.

Just as regions of the sensory association cortex are involved in perceiving and remembering, the **motor association cortex,** located just rostral to the primary motor cortex, is involved in the planning and execution of movements. This region controls the primary motor cortex; thus, it directly controls behavior. If the primary motor cortex is the keyboard of the piano, then the motor association cortex is the piano player. The rest of the frontal lobe, rostral to the motor association cortex, is known as the **prefrontal cortex.** This region of the brain is less involved with the control of movement and more involved in formulating plans and strategies.

Although the two cerebral hemispheres cooperate with each other, they do not perform identical functions. Some functions are **lateralized**—located primarily in one side of the brain. In general, the left hemisphere participates in the *analysis* of information—the extraction of the elements that make up the whole of an experience. This ability makes the left hemisphere particularly good at recognizing *serial events*—events whose elements occur one after the other. The left hemisphere is also involved in controlling serial behaviors. The serial functions performed by the left hemisphere include verbal activities, such as talking, understanding the speech of other people, reading, and writing. These abilities are disrupted by damage to the various regions of the left hemisphere. (I will say more about language and the brain in Chapter 13.)

In contrast, the right hemisphere is specialized for *synthesis;* it is particularly good at putting isolated elements together to perceive things as a whole. For example, our ability to draw sketches (especially of three-dimensional objects), read maps, and construct complex objects out of smaller elements depends heavily on circuits of neurons located in the right hemisphere. Damage to the right hemisphere disrupts these abilities. (In a few people the functions of the left and right hemispheres are reversed.)

We are not aware of the fact that each hemisphere perceives the world differently. Although the two cerebral hemispheres perform somewhat different functions, our perceptions and our memories are unified. This unity is accomplished by the **corpus callosum,** a large band of axons that connects the two cerebral hemispheres. The corpus callosum connects corresponding parts of the left and right hemispheres: The left and right temporal lobes are connected, the left and right parietal lobes are connected, and so on. Because of the corpus callosum, each region of the association cortex knows what is happening in the corresponding region of the opposite side of the brain.

Motor association cortex The region of the frontal lobe rostral to the primary motor cortex.

Prefrontal cortex The region of the frontal lobe rostral to the motor association cortex.

Lateralized Said of a function that is primarily controlled by neural circuits located in only one side of the brain.

Corpus callosum (*ka loh sum*) The largest commissure of the brain, interconnecting the areas of neocortex on each side of the brain.

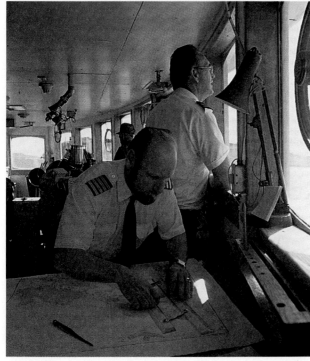

The ability to navigate depends heavily on circuits of neurons in the parietal lobe.

FIGURE 3.11

A midsagittal view of the brain and part of the spinal cord.

Neocortex The phylogenetically newest cortex, including the primary sensory cortex, primary motor cortex, and association cortex.

Limbic cortex Phylogenetically old cortex, located at the edge ("limbus") of the cerebral hemispheres; part of the limbic system.

Cingulate gyrus (*sing* yew lett) A strip of limbic cortex lying along the lateral walls of the groove separating the cerebral hemispheres, just above the corpus callosum.

Commissure (*kahm* i sher) A fiber bundle that interconnects corresponding regions on each side of the brain.

Limbic system A group of brain regions including the amygdala, hippocampus, limbic cortex, and parts of the hypothalamus, as well as their interconnecting fiber bundles.

Hippocampus A forebrain structure of the temporal lobe, constituting an important part of the limbic system; includes the hippocampus proper (Ammon's horn), dentate gyrus, and subiculum.

Amygdala (*a mig da la*) A structure in the interior of the rostral temporal lobe, containing a set of nuclei; part of the limbic system.

Fornix A fiber bundle that connects the hippocampus with other parts of the brain, including the mammillary bodies of the hypothalamus.

Mammillary bodies (*mam i lair ee*) A protrusion of the bottom of the brain at the posterior end of the hypothalamus, containing some hypothalamic nuclei.

Figure 3.11 shows a *midsagittal* view of the brain. The brain (and part of the spinal cord) has been sliced down the middle, dividing it into its two symmetrical halves. The left half has been removed, so we see the inner surface of the right half. The cerebral cortex that covers most of the surface of the cerebral hemispheres (including the frontal, parietal, occipital, and temporal lobes) is called the **neocortex** ("new" cortex, because it is of relatively recent evolutionary origin). Another form of cerebral cortex, the **limbic cortex,** is located around the medial edge of the cerebral hemispheres (*limbus* means "border"). The **cingulate gyrus,** an important region of the limbic cortex, can be seen in this figure. (See *Figure 3.11.*) In addition, if you look back at the top two drawings of Figure 3.10, you will see that the limbic cortex occupies the regions that have not been colored in. (Refer to *Figure 3.10.*)

Figure 3.11 also shows the corpus callosum, the largest **commissure** (cross-hemisphere connection) in the brain. To slice the brain into its two symmetrical halves, one must slice through the middle of the corpus callosum. (Recall that I described the split-brain operation, in which the corpus callosum is severed, in Chapter 1.) (See *Figure 3.11.*)

Limbic System. A neuroanatomist, Papez (1937), suggested that a set of interconnected brain structures formed a circuit whose primary function was motivation and emotion. This system included several regions of the limbic cortex and a set of interconnected structures surrounding the core of the forebrain. A physiologist, MacLean (1949), expanded the system to include other structures and coined the term **limbic system.** Besides the limbic cortex, the most important parts of the limbic system are the **hippocampus** ("sea horse") and the **amygdala** ("almond"), located next to the lateral ventricle in the temporal lobe. The **fornix** is a bundle of axons that connects the hippocampus with other regions of the brain, including the **mammillary bodies,** protrusions on the base of the brain that contain parts of the hypothalamus (described later). (See *Figure 3.12.*)

MacLean noted that the evolution of this system, which includes the first and simplest form of cerebral cortex, appears to have coincided with the development of emotional responses. As you will see in Chapter 12, we now know that parts of the

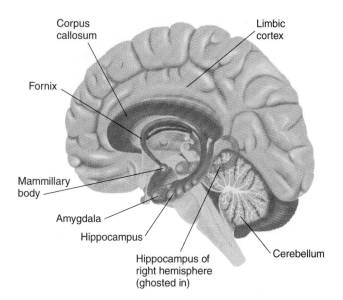

Corpus callosum

Limbic cortex

Fornix

Mammillary body

Amygdala

Hippocampus

Hippocampus of right hemisphere (ghosted in)

Cerebellum

Basal ganglia A group of subcortical nuclei in the telencephalon, the caudate nucleus, the globus pallidus, and the putamen; important parts of the motor system.

Nucleus (plural: nuclei) An identifiable group of neural cell bodies in the central nervous system.

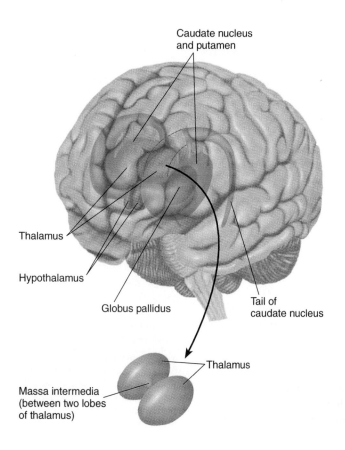

Caudate nucleus and putamen

Thalamus

Hypothalamus

Globus pallidus

Tail of caudate nucleus

Thalamus

Massa intermedia (between two lobes of thalamus)

FIGURE 3.12

The major components of the limbic system. All of the left hemisphere except for the limbic system has been removed.

limbic system (notably, the hippocampal formation and the region of limbic cortex that surrounds it) are involved in learning and memory rather than emotional behavior. Only part of the limbic system—the amygdala—is specifically involved in emotions.

Basal Ganglia. The **basal ganglia** are collections of nuclei located deep within the forebrain, beneath the anterior portion of the lateral ventricles. **Nuclei** are groups of neurons of similar shape. (The word *nucleus,* from the Greek "nut," can refer to the inner portion of an atom, to the structure of a cell that contains the chromosomes, and—as in this case—to a collection of neurons located within the brain.) The major parts of the basal ganglia are the *caudate nucleus* (the "nucleus with a tail"), the *putamen* (the "shell"), and the *globus pallidus* (the "pale globe"). (See **Figure 3.13.**) The basal ganglia are involved in the control of movement. For example, Parkinson's disease is caused by degeneration of certain neurons located in the midbrain that send axons to the caudate nucleus and the putamen. This disease consists of weakness, tremors, rigidity of the limbs, poor balance, and difficulty in initiating movements. As we will see in Chapter 14, one of the treatments for Parkinson's disease is surgical destruction of part of the globus pallidus.

Diencephalon

The second major division of the forebrain, the **diencephalon,** is situated between the telencephalon and the mesencephalon; it surrounds the third ventricle. Its two most important structures are the thalamus and the hypothalamus. (See **Figure 3.13.**)

Thalamus. The **thalamus** (from the Greek *thalamos,* "inner chamber") comprises the dorsal part of the diencephalon. It is situated near the middle of the cerebral hemispheres, immediately medial and caudal to the basal ganglia. The thalamus has two lobes, connected by a bridge of gray matter called the *massa intermedia,* which pierces the middle of the third ventricle. (See **Figure 3.13.**)

Most neural input to the cerebral cortex is received from the thalamus; indeed, much of the cortical surface can be divided into regions that receive projections from specific parts of the thalamus. **Projection axons** are sets of axons that arise from cell bodies located in one region of the brain and synapse on neurons located within another region (that is, they *project to* these regions).

FIGURE 3.13

The location of the basal ganglia and diencephalon, "ghosted in" to a semitransparent brain.

The thalamus is divided into several nuclei. Some thalamic nuclei receive sensory information from the sensory systems. The neurons in these nuclei then relay the sensory information to specific sensory projection areas of the cerebral cortex. For example, the **lateral geniculate nucleus** receives information from the eye and sends axons to the primary visual cortex, and the **medial geniculate nucleus** receives information from the inner ear and sends axons to the primary auditory cortex. Other thalamic nuclei project to specific regions of the cerebral cortex, but they do not relay sensory information. For example, the **ventrolateral nucleus** receives information from the cerebellum and projects it to the primary motor cortex. And as we will see in Chapter 8, several nuclei are involved in controlling the general excitability of the cerebral cortex. To accomplish this task, these nuclei have widespread projections to all cortical regions.

Hypothalamus.   As its name implies, the **hypothalamus** lies at the base of the brain, under the thalamus. It is situated on both sides of the lower part of the third ventricle. Although the hypothalamus is a relatively small structure, it is an important one. It controls the autonomic nervous system and the endocrine system and organizes behaviors related to survival of the species, such as fighting, feeding, fleeing, and mating.

The hypothalamus is a complex structure, containing many nuclei and fiber tracts. Figure 3.14 indicates its location and size. Note that the pituitary gland is attached to the base of the hypothalamus via the pituitary stalk. Just in front of the pituitary stalk is the **optic chiasm,** where half of the axons in the optic nerves (from the eyes) cross from one side of the brain to the other. (See *Figure 3.14.*) The role of the hypothalamus in the control of behavior will be considered in several chapters later in this book.

Much of the endocrine system is controlled by hormones produced by cells in the hypothalamus. A special system of blood vessels directly connects the hypo-

Diencephalon (*dy en **seff** a lahn*) A region of the forebrain surrounding the third ventricle; includes the thalamus and the hypothalamus.

Thalamus The largest portion of the diencephalon, located above the hypothalamus; contains nuclei that project information to specific regions of the cerebral cortex and receive information from it.

Projection fiber An axon of a neuron in one region of the brain whose terminals form synapses with neurons in another region.

Lateral geniculate nucleus A group of cell bodies within the lateral geniculate body of the thalamus that receives axons from the retina and projects axons to the primary visual cortex.

Medial geniculate nucleus A group of cell bodies within the medial geniculate body of the thalamus; receives axons from the auditory system and projects axons to the primary auditory cortex.

Corpus callosum   Fornix   Massa intermedia   Wall of third ventricle

Hypothalamic nuclei   Optic chiasm   Pituitary gland   Mammillary body

FIGURE 3.14

A midsagittal view of part of the brain, showing some of the nuclei of the hypothalamus. The nuclei are situated on the far side of the wall of the third ventricle, inside the right hemisphere.

Neurosecretory Cells in Hypothalamus
For posterior pituitary gland   For anterior pituitary gland

Mammillary body

Capillary bed around terminals
of neurosecretory cells;
hypothalamic hormones
released here

Artery

Artery

Pituitary stalk

Anterior pituitary gland

Posterior pituitary gland

Secretory cells; release
anterior pituitary hormones

Terminals release posterior
pituitary hormones

FIGURE 3.15

The pituitary gland. Hormones released by the neurosecretory cells in the hypothalamus enter capillaries and are conveyed to the anterior pituitary gland, where they control its secretion of hormones. The hormones of the posterior pituitary gland are produced in the hypothalamus and carried there in vesicles by means of axoplasmic transport.

Ventrolateral nucleus A nucleus of the thalamus that receives inputs from the cerebellum and sends axons to the primary motor cortex.

Hypothalamus The group of nuclei of the diencephalon situated beneath the thalamus; involved in regulation of the autonomic nervous system, control of the anterior and posterior pituitary glands, and integration of species-typical behaviors.

Optic chiasm (*kye az'm*) A cross-shaped connection between the optic nerves, located below the base of the brain, just anterior to the pituitary gland.

Anterior pituitary gland The anterior part of the pituitary gland; an endocrine gland whose secretions are controlled by the hypothalamic hormones.

Neurosecretory cell A neuron that secretes a hormone or hormonelike substance.

Posterior pituitary gland The posterior part of the pituitary gland; an endocrine gland that contains hormone-secreting terminal buttons of axons whose cell bodies lie within the hypothalamus.

thalamus with an important endocrine gland, the **anterior pituitary gland.** (See *Figure 3.15.*) The hormones produced by the hypothalamus are secreted by specialized neurons called **neurosecretory cells,** located near the base of the pituitary stalk. These hormones stimulate the anterior pituitary gland to secrete its hormones. For example, the *gonadotropin-releasing hormone* causes the anterior pituitary gland to secrete the *gonadotropic hormones,* which play a role in reproductive physiology and behavior.

Most of the hormones secreted by the anterior pituitary gland control other endocrine glands. Because of this function, the anterior pituitary gland has been called the body's "master gland." For example, the gonadotropic hormones stimulate the gonads (ovaries and testes) to release male or female sex hormones. These hormones affect cells throughout the body, including some in the brain. Two other anterior pituitary hormones—prolactin and somatotropic hormone (growth hormone)—do not control other glands but act as the final messenger. The behavioral effects of many of the anterior pituitary hormones are discussed in later chapters.

The **posterior pituitary gland** is in many ways an extension of the hypothalamus. The hypothalamus produces the posterior pituitary hormones and directly controls their secretion. These hormones include oxytocin, which stimulates ejection of milk and uterine contractions at the time of childbirth, and vasopressin, which regulates urine output by the kidneys. They are produced by two different sets of neurons in the hypothalamus whose axons travel down the pituitary stalk and terminate in the posterior pituitary gland. The hormones are carried in vesicles through the axo-

Prolactin, a hormone produced by the anterior pituitary gland, stimulates milk production in a nursing mother. Oxytocin, a hormone released by the posterior pituitary gland, stimulates the ejection of milk when the baby sucks on a nipple.

plasm of these neurons and collect in the terminal buttons in the posterior pituitary gland. When these axons fire, the hormone contained within their terminal buttons is liberated and enters the circulatory system.

The Midbrain

The **midbrain** (also called the **mesencephalon**) surrounds the cerebral aqueduct and consists of two major parts: the tectum and the tegmentum.

Tectum

The **tectum** ("roof") is located in the dorsal portion of the midbrain. Its principal structures are the **superior colliculi** and **inferior colliculi,** which appear as four bumps on the surface of the **brain stem.** The brain stem includes the diencephalon, midbrain, and hindbrain, and it is so called because it looks just like that—a stem. Figure 3.16 shows several views of the brain stem: lateral and posterior views of the brain stem inside a semitransparent brain, an enlarged view of the brain stem with part of the cerebellum cut away to reveal the inside of the fourth ventricle, and a cross section through the midbrain. (See *Figure 3.16.*) The inferior colliculi are a part of the auditory system. The superior colliculi are part of the visual system. In mammals they are involved primarily in visual reflexes and reactions to moving stimuli.

Tegmentum

The **tegmentum** ("covering") consists of the portion of the midbrain beneath the tectum. It includes the rostral end of the reticular formation, several nuclei that control eye movements, the periaqueductal gray matter, the red nucleus, the substantia nigra, and the ventral tegmental area. (See *Figure 3.16d.*)

The **reticular formation** is a structure consisting of many individual nuclei. It is also characterized by a diffuse, interconnected network of neurons with complex dendritic and axonal processes. (Indeed, *reticulum* means "little net"; early anatomists were struck by the netlike appearance of the reticular formation.) The reticular formation occupies the core of the brain stem, from the lower border of the medulla to the upper border of the midbrain. (See *Figure 3.16d.*) The reticular formation receives sensory information by means of various pathways and projects ax-

Midbrain The mesencephalon; the central of the three major divisions of the brain.

Mesencephalon (*mezz en **seff** a lahn*) The midbrain; a region of the brain that surrounds the cerebral aqueduct; includes the tectum and the tegmentum.

Tectum The dorsal part of the midbrain; includes the superior and inferior colliculi.

Superior colliculi (*ka lik yew lee*) Protrusions on top of the midbrain; part of the visual system.

Inferior colliculi Protrusions on top of the midbrain; part of the auditory system.

Brain stem The "stem" of the brain, from the medulla to the diencephalon, excluding the cerebellum.

Tegmentum The ventral part of the midbrain; includes the periaqueductal gray matter, reticular formation, red nucleus, and substantia nigra.

Reticular formation A large network of neural tissue located in the central region of the brain stem, from the medulla to the diencephalon.

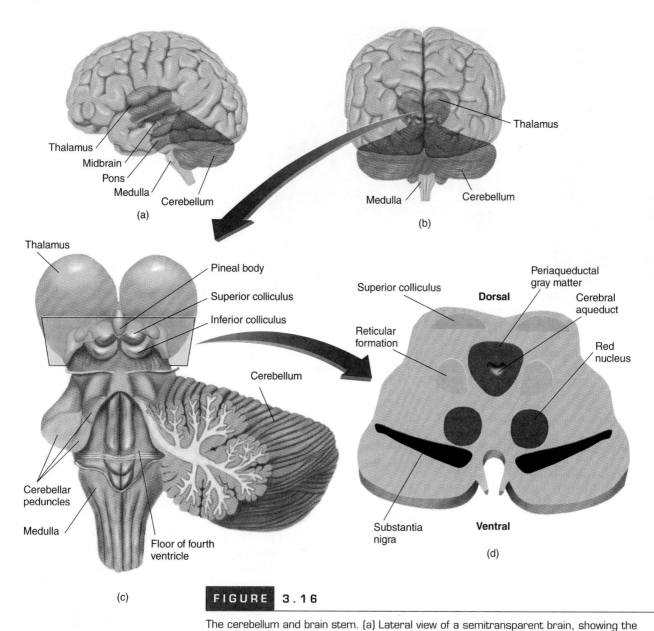

Thalamus
Midbrain
Pons
Medulla
Cerebellum
(a)

Thalamus
Medulla
Cerebellum
(b)

Thalamus
Pineal body
Superior colliculus
Inferior colliculus
Cerebellum
Cerebellar peduncles
Medulla
Floor of fourth ventricle
(c)

Superior colliculus
Reticular formation
Substantia nigra
Dorsal
Periaqueductal gray matter
Cerebral aqueduct
Red nucleus
Ventral
(d)

FIGURE 3.16

The cerebellum and brain stem. (a) Lateral view of a semitransparent brain, showing the cerebellum and brain stem "ghosted in." (b) View from the back of the brain. (c) A dorsal view of the brain stem. The left hemisphere of the cerebellum and part of the right hemisphere have been removed to show the inside of the fourth ventricle and the cerebellar peduncles. (d) A cross section of the midbrain.

Periaqueductal gray matter The region of the midbrain surrounding the cerebral aqueduct; contains neural circuits involved in species-typical behaviors.

Red nucleus A large nucleus of the midbrain that receives inputs from the cerebellum and motor cortex and sends axons to motor neurons in the spinal cord.

Substantia nigra A darkly stained region of the tegmentum that contains neurons that communicate with the caudate nucleus and putamen in the basal ganglia.

ons to the cerebral cortex, thalamus, and spinal cord. It plays a role in sleep and arousal, attention, muscle tonus, movement, and various vital reflexes. Its functions will be described more fully in later chapters.

The **periaqueductal gray matter** is so called because it consists mostly of cell bodies of neurons ("gray matter," as contrasted with the "white matter" of axon bundles) that surround the cerebral aqueduct as it travels from the third to the fourth ventricle. The periaqueductal gray matter contains neural circuits that control sequences of movements seen in some species-typical behaviors, such as fighting and mating. As we will see in Chapter 7, opiates such as morphine decrease an organism's sensitivity to pain by stimulating receptors on neurons located in this region.

The **red nucleus** and **substantia nigra** ("black substance") are important components of the motor system. A bundle of axons that arises from the red nucleus makes up one of the two major fiber systems that bring motor information from the cerebral cortex and cerebellum to the spinal cord. I mentioned earlier that Parkinson's disease is caused by degeneration of certain neurons located in the midbrain that send axons to the caudate nucleus and the putamen. These neurons are located in the substantia nigra.

The Hindbrain

The **hindbrain,** which surrounds the fourth ventricle, consists of two major divisions: the metencephalon and the myelencephalon.

Metencephalon

The metencephalon consists of the pons and the cerebellum.

Cerebellum.   The **cerebellum** ("little brain"), with its two hemispheres, resembles a miniature version of the cerebrum. It is covered by the **cerebellar cortex** and has a set of **deep cerebellar nuclei.** These nuclei receive projections from the cerebellar cortex and themselves send projections out of the cerebellum to other parts of the brain. Each hemisphere of the cerebellum is attached to the dorsal surface of the pons by bundles of axons: the superior, middle, and inferior **cerebellar peduncles** ("little feet"). (See *Figure 3.16c.*)

Damage to the cerebellum impairs standing, walking, or performance of coordinated movements. A virtuoso pianist or other performing musician owes much to his or her cerebellum. The cerebellum receives visual, auditory, vestibular, and somatosensory information, and it also receives information about individual muscle movements being directed by the brain. The cerebellum integrates this information and modifies the motor outflow, exerting a coordinating and smoothing effect on the movements. Cerebellar damage results in jerky, poorly coordinated, exaggerated movements; extensive cerebellar damage makes it impossible even to stand.

Pons.   The **pons,** a large bulge in the brain stem, lies between the mesencephalon and medulla oblongata, immediately ventral to the cerebellum. *Pons* means "bridge," but it does not really look like one. (Refer to *Figures 3.11* and *3.16a.*) The pons contains, in its core, a portion of the reticular formation, including some nuclei that appear to be important in sleep and arousal. It also contains a large nucleus that relays information from the cerebral cortex to the cerebellum.

Myelencephalon

The myelencephalon contains one major structure, the **medulla oblongata** (literally, "oblong marrow"), usually just called the *medulla.* This structure is the most caudal portion of the brain stem; its lower border is the rostral end of the spinal cord. (Refer to *Figures 3.11* and *3.16a.*) The medulla contains part of the reticular formation, including nuclei that control vital functions such as regulation of the cardiovascular system, respiration, and skeletal muscle tonus.

Hindbrain The most caudal of the three major divisions of the brain; includes the metencephalon and myelencephalon.

Cerebellum (*sair a bell um*) A major part of the brain located dorsal to the pons, containing the two cerebellar hemispheres, covered with the cerebellar cortex; an important component of the motor system.

Cerebellar cortex The cortex that covers the surface of the cerebellum.

Deep cerebellar nuclei Nuclei located within the cerebellar hemispheres; receive projections from the cerebellar cortex and send projections out of the cerebellum to other parts of the brain.

Cerebellar peduncle (*pee dun kul*) One of three bundles of axons that attach each cerebellar hemisphere to the dorsal pons.

Pons The region of the metencephalon rostral to the medulla, caudal to the midbrain, and ventral to the cerebellum.

Medulla oblongata (*me doo la*) The most caudal portion of the brain; located in the myelencephalon, immediately rostral to the spinal cord.

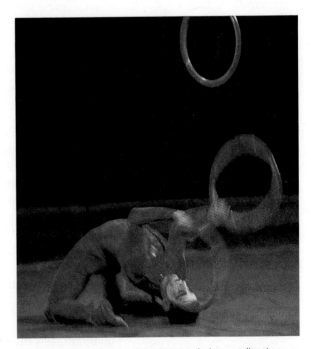

The cerebellum plays an important role in coordinating skilled movements.

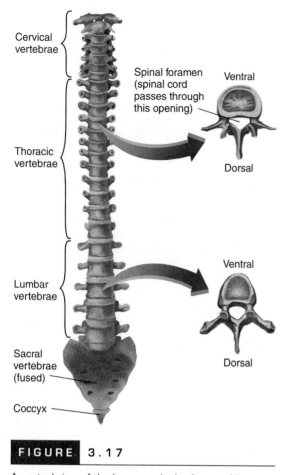

Cervical vertebrae

Spinal foramen (spinal cord passes through this opening)

Ventral

Dorsal

Thoracic vertebrae

Ventral

Lumbar vertebrae

Dorsal

Sacral vertebrae (fused)

Coccyx

FIGURE 3.17

A ventral view of the human spinal column, with details showing the anatomy of the vertebrae.

Spinal cord The cord of nervous tissue that extends caudally from the medulla.

Spinal root A bundle of axons surrounded by connective tissue that occurs in pairs, which fuse and form a spinal nerve.

Cauda equina (*ee kwye na*) A bundle of spinal roots located caudal to the end of the spinal cord.

Caudal block The anesthesia and paralysis of the lower part of the body produced by injection of a local anesthetic into the cerebrospinal fluid surrounding the cauda equina.

Dorsal root The spinal root that contains incoming (afferent) sensory axons.

Ventral root The spinal root that contains outgoing (efferent) motor axons.

The Spinal Cord

The **spinal cord** is a long, conical structure, approximately as thick as our little finger. The principal function of the spinal cord is to distribute motor axons to the effector organs of the body (glands and muscles) and to collect somatosensory information to be passed on to the brain. The spinal cord also has a certain degree of autonomy from the brain; various reflexive control circuits are located there.

The spinal cord is protected by the vertebral column, which is composed of twenty-four individual vertebrae of the *cervical* (neck), *thoracic* (chest), and *lumbar* (lower back) regions, and the fused vertebrae making up the *sacral* and *coccygeal* portions of the column (located in the pelvic region). The spinal cord passes through a hole in each of the vertebrae (the *spinal foramens*). Figure 3.17 illustrates the divisions and structures of the spinal cord and vertebral column. (See *Figure 3.17.*) The spinal cord is only about two-thirds as long as the vertebral column; the rest of the space is filled by a mass of **spinal roots** composing the **cauda equina** ("horse's tail"). (Refer to *Figure 3.3c.*)

Early in embryological development the vertebral column and spinal cord are the same length. As development progresses, the vertebral column grows faster than the spinal cord. This differential growth rate causes the spinal roots to be displaced downward; the most caudal roots travel the farthest before they emerge through openings between the vertebrae and thus compose the cauda equina. To produce the **caudal block** that is sometimes used in pelvic surgery, a local anesthetic can be injected into the CSF contained within the sac of dura mater surrounding the cauda equina. The drug blocks conduction in the axons of the cauda equina, which produces temporary anesthesia (and paralysis) of the lower part of the body.

Figure 3.18(a) shows a portion of the spinal cord, with the layers of the meninges that wrap it. Small bundles of axons emerge from each side of the spinal cord in two straight lines along its dorsolateral and ventrolateral surfaces. Groups of these bundles fuse together and become the thirty-one paired sets of **dorsal roots** and **ventral roots.** The dorsal and ventral roots join together as they pass through gaps between the vertebrae and become spinal nerves. (See *Figure 3.18a.*)

Figure 3.18(b) shows a cross section of the spinal cord. Like the brain, the spinal cord consists of white matter and gray matter. However, the arrangement is opposite that found in the brain: In the spinal cord, the white matter is on the outside and the gray matter is on the inside. The white matter consists of ascending and descending bundles of myelinated axons, and the gray matter consists mostly of neural cell bodies and short, unmyelinated axons. In Figure 3.18(b), ascending tracts in the white matter are indicated in blue; descending tracts are indicated in red. (See *Figure 3.18b.*)

INTERIM SUMMARY

The brain consists of three major divisions, organized around the three chambers of the tube that develops early in embryonic life: the forebrain, the midbrain, and the hindbrain. The development of the CNS is illustrated in Figure 3.7, and Table 3.1 outlines the major divisions and subdivisions of the brain.

The forebrain, which surrounds the lateral and third ventricles, consists of the telencephalon and diencephalon. The telencephalon contains the cerebral cortex,

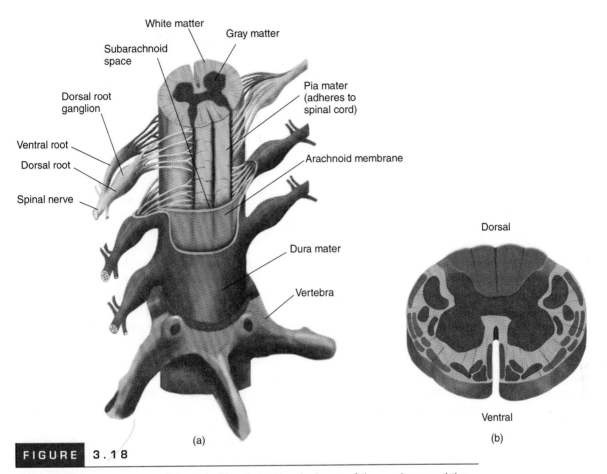

White matter
Gray matter
Subarachnoid space
Dorsal root ganglion
Ventral root
Dorsal root
Spinal nerve
Pia mater (adheres to spinal cord)
Arachnoid membrane
Dura mater
Vertebra
Dorsal
Ventral
(a)
(b)

FIGURE 3.18

The spinal cord. (a) A portion of the spinal cord, showing the layers of the meninges and the relation of the spinal cord to the vertebral column. (b) A cross section through the spinal cord. Ascending tracts are shown in blue; descending tracts are shown in red.

the limbic system, and the basal ganglia. The cerebral cortex is organized into the frontal, parietal, temporal, and occipital lobes. The central sulcus divides the frontal lobe, which deals specifically with movement and the planning of movement, from the other three lobes, which deal primarily with perceiving and learning. The limbic system, which includes the limbic cortex, the hippocampus, and the amygdala, is involved in emotion, motivation, and learning. The basal ganglia participate in the control of movement. The diencephalon consists of the thalamus, which directs information to and from the cerebral cortex, and the hypothalamus, which controls the endocrine system and modulates species-typical behaviors.

The midbrain, which surrounds the cerebral aqueduct, consists of the tectum and tegmentum. The tectum is involved in hearing and the control of visual reflexes and reactions to moving stimuli. The tegmentum contains the reticular formation, which is important in sleep, arousal, and movement; the periaqueductal gray matter, which controls various species-typical behaviors; and the red nucleus and the substantia nigra, both parts of the motor system. The hindbrain, which surrounds the fourth ventricle, contains the cerebellum, the pons, and the medulla. The cerebellum plays an important role in integrating and coordinating movements. The pons contains some nuclei that are important in sleep and arousal. The medulla oblongata, too, is involved in sleep and arousal, but it also plays a role in control of movement and in control of vital functions such as heart rate, breathing, and blood pressure.

The outer part of the spinal cord consists of white matter: axons conveying information up or down, to or from the brain. The central gray matter contains cell bodies.

◻ THE PERIPHERAL NERVOUS SYSTEM

The brain and spinal cord communicate with the rest of the body via the cranial nerves and spinal nerves. These nerves are part of the peripheral nervous system, which conveys sensory information to the central nervous system and conveys messages from the central nervous system to the body's muscles and glands.

Spinal Nerves

The **spinal nerves** begin at the junction of the dorsal and ventral roots of the spinal cord. The nerves leave the vertebral column and travel to the muscles or sensory receptors they innervate, branching repeatedly as they go. Branches of spinal nerves often follow blood vessels, especially those branches that innervate skeletal muscles. (Refer to *Figure 3.3.*)

Now let us consider the pathways by which sensory information enters the spinal cord and motor information leaves it. The cell bodies of all axons that bring sensory information into the brain and spinal cord are located outside the CNS. (The sole exception is the visual system; the retina of the eye is actually a part of the brain.) These incoming axons are referred to as **afferent axons** because they "bear toward" the CNS. The cell bodies that give rise to the axons that bring somatosensory information to the spinal cord reside in the **dorsal root ganglia,** rounded swellings of the dorsal root. (See *Figure 3.19.*) These neurons are of the unipolar type (described in Chapter 2). The axonal stalk divides close to the cell body, sending one limb into the spinal cord and the other limb out to the sensory organ. Note that all of the axons in the dorsal root convey somatosensory information.

Cell bodies that give rise to the ventral root are located within the gray matter of the spinal cord. The axons of these multipolar neurons leave the spinal cord via a ventral root, which joins a dorsal root to make a spinal nerve. The axons that leave the spinal cord through the ventral roots control muscles and glands. They are referred to as **efferent axons** because they "bear away from" the CNS. (See *Figure 3.19.*)

Spinal nerve A peripheral nerve attached to the spinal cord.

Afferent axon An axon directed toward the central nervous system, conveying sensory information.

Dorsal root ganglion A nodule on a dorsal root that contains cell bodies of afferent spinal nerve neurons.

Efferent axon (*eff ur ent*) An axon directed away from the central nervous system, conveying motor commands to muscles and glands.

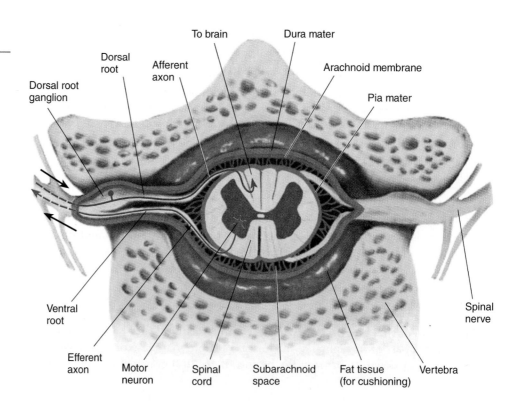

FIGURE 3.19

A cross section of the spinal cord, showing the route taken by afferent and efferent axons through the dorsal and ventral roots.

Cranial Nerves

Twelve pairs of **cranial nerves** leave the ventral surface of the brain. Most of these nerves serve sensory and motor functions of the head and neck region. One of them, the *tenth*, or **vagus nerve**, regulates the functions of organs in the thoracic and abdominal cavities. It is called the *vagus* ("wandering") nerve because its branches wander throughout the thoracic and abdominal cavities. (The word *vagabond* has the same root.) Figure 3.20 presents a view of the base of the brain and illustrates the cranial nerves and the structures they serve. Note that efferent (motor) axons are drawn in red and that afferent (sensory) axons are drawn in blue. (See *Figure 3.20.*)

Several forms of sensory information are received through cranial nerves. These nerves convey somatosensory information from the head and neck region, information concerning taste from the tongue, auditory information and information concerning balance from the ears, visual information from the eyes, and information concerning smell from the nose. Sensory mechanisms are described in more detail in Chapters 6 and 7.

Cranial nerve A peripheral nerve attached directly to the brain.

Vagus nerve The largest of the cranial nerves, conveying efferent axons of the parasympathetic division of the autonomic nervous system to organs of the thoracic and abdominal cavities.

FIGURE 3.20

The twelve pairs of cranial nerves and the regions and functions they serve. Red lines denote axons that control muscles or glands; blue lines denote sensory axons.

The Autonomic Nervous System

The part of the peripheral nervous system that I have discussed so far—which receives sensory information from the sensory organs and that controls movements of the skeletal muscles—is called the **somatic nervous system.** The other branch of the peripheral nervous system—the **autonomic nervous system (ANS)**—is concerned with regulation of smooth muscle, cardiac muscle, and glands. (*Autonomic* means "self-governing.") Smooth muscle is found in the skin (associated with hair follicles), in blood vessels, in the eyes (controlling pupil size and accommodation of the lens), and in the walls and sphincters of the gut, gallbladder, and urinary bladder. Thus, the autonomic nervous system is involved in controlling blood pressure, body temperature, digestive functions, and other physiological functions.

The ANS consists of two anatomically separate systems, the *sympathetic division* and the *parasympathetic division*. With few exceptions, organs of the body are innervated by both of these subdivisions, and each has a different effect. For example, the sympathetic division speeds the heart rate, whereas the parasympathetic division slows it.

Sympathetic Division of the ANS

The **sympathetic division** is most involved in activities associated with expenditure of energy from reserves that are stored in the body. For example, when an organism is excited, the sympathetic nervous system increases blood flow to skeletal muscles, stimulates the secretion of epinephrine (a hormone that increases heart rate and raises blood sugar level), and causes piloerection—erection of fur in mammals that have it and production of "goose bumps" in humans.

The cell bodies of sympathetic motor neurons are located in the gray matter of the thoracic and lumbar regions of the spinal cord (hence the sympathetic nervous system is also known as the *thoracolumbar system*). The axons of these neurons exit via the ventral roots. After joining the spinal nerves, the axons branch off and pass into **spinal sympathetic ganglia** (not to be confused with the dorsal root ganglia). Figure 3.21 shows the relation of these ganglia to the spinal cord. Note that the various spinal sympathetic ganglia are connected to the neighboring ganglia above and below, thus forming the **sympathetic ganglion chain.** (See *Figure 3.21*.)

The axons that leave the spinal cord through the ventral root are part of the **preganglionic neurons.** With one exception, all sympathetic preganglionic axons enter the ganglia of the sympathetic chain, but not all of them form synapses there. (The exception is the medulla of the adrenal gland, described in Chapter 10.) Some axons leave and travel to one of the other sympathetic ganglia, located among the internal organs. All sympathetic preganglionic axons form synapses with neurons located in one of the ganglia. The neurons with which they form synapses are called **postganglionic neurons.** In turn, the postganglionic neurons send axons to the target organs, such as the intestines, stomach, kidneys, or sweat glands. (See *Figure 3.21*.)

Parasympathetic Division of the ANS

The **parasympathetic division** of the autonomic nervous system supports activities that are involved with increases in the body's supply of stored energy. These activities include salivation, gastric and intestinal motility, secretion of digestive juices, and increased blood flow to the gastrointestinal system.

Cell bodies that give rise to preganglionic axons in the parasympathetic nervous system are located in two regions: the nuclei of some of the cranial nerves (especially the vagus nerve) and the gray matter in the sacral region of the spinal cord. Thus, the parasympathetic division of the ANS has often been referred to as the *craniosacral system*. Parasympathetic ganglia are located in the immediate vicinity of the target or-

Somatic nervous system The part of the peripheral nervous system that controls the movement of skeletal muscles or transmits somatosensory information to the central nervous system.

Autonomic nervous system (ANS) The portion of the peripheral nervous system that controls the body's vegetative functions.

Sympathetic division The portion of the autonomic nervous system that controls functions that accompany arousal and expenditure of energy.

Spinal sympathetic ganglia Sympathetic ganglia either adjacent to the spinal cord in the sympathetic chain or located in the abdominal cavity.

Sympathetic ganglion chain One of a pair of groups of sympathetic ganglia that lie ventrolateral to the vertebral column.

Preganglionic neuron The efferent neuron of the autonomic nervous system whose cell body is located in a cranial nerve nucleus or in the intermediate horn of the spinal gray matter and whose terminal buttons synapse upon postganglionic neurons in the autonomic ganglia.

Postganglionic neuron Neurons of the autonomic nervous system that form synapses directly with their target organ.

Parasympathetic division The portion of the autonomic nervous system that controls functions that occur during a relaxed state.

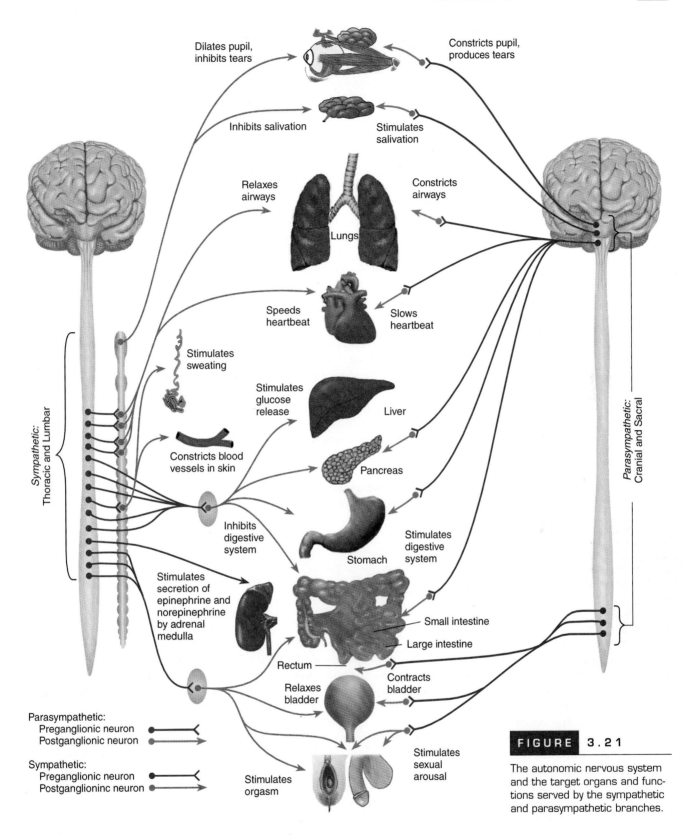

Dilates pupil, inhibits tears

Constricts pupil, produces tears

Inhibits salivation

Stimulates salivation

Relaxes airways

Constricts airways

Lungs

Speeds heartbeat

Slows heartbeat

Stimulates sweating

Stimulates glucose release

Liver

Constricts blood vessels in skin

Pancreas

Inhibits digestive system

Stimulates digestive system

Stomach

Stimulates secretion of epinephrine and norepinephrine by adrenal medulla

Small intestine

Large intestine

Rectum

Relaxes bladder

Contracts bladder

Parasympathetic:
Preganglionic neuron
Postganglionic neuron

Sympathetic:
Preganglionic neuron
Postganglioninc neuron

Stimulates orgasm

Stimulates sexual arousal

Sympathetic:
Thoracic and Lumbar

Parasympathetic:
Cranial and Sacral

FIGURE 3.21

The autonomic nervous system and the target organs and functions served by the sympathetic and parasympathetic branches.

gans; the postganglionic axons are therefore relatively short. The terminal buttons of both preganglionic and postganglionic neurons in the parasympathetic nervous system secrete acetylcholine.

Table 3.2 summarizes the major divisions of the peripheral nervous system.

TABLE 3.2	The Major Divisions of the Peripheral Nervous System
Somatic Nervous System	**Autonomic Nervous System (ANS)**
SPINAL NERVES	SYMPATHETIC BRANCH
Afferents from sense organs	Spinal nerves (from thoracic and lumbar regions)
Efferents to muscles	Sympathetic ganglia
CRANIAL NERVES	PARASYMPATHETIC BRANCH
Afferents from sense organs	Cranial nerves (3rd, 7th, 9th, and 10th)
Efferents to muscles	Spinal nerves (from sacral region)
	Parasympathetic ganglia (adjacent to organs)

INTERIM SUMMARY

The spinal nerves and the cranial nerves convey sensory axons into the central nervous system and motor axons out from it. Spinal nerves are formed by the junctions of the dorsal roots, which contain incoming (afferent) axons, and the ventral roots, which contain outgoing (efferent) axons. The autonomic nervous system consists of two divisions: the sympathetic division, which controls activities that occur during excitement or exertion, such as increased heart rate; and the parasympathetic division, which controls activities that occur during relaxation, such as decreased heart rate and increased activity of the digestive system. The pathways of the autonomic nervous system contain preganglionic axons, from the brain or spinal cord to the sympathetic or parasympathetic ganglia, and postganglionic axons, from the ganglia to the target organ.

EPILOGUE

Unilateral Neglect

When we see people like Miss S., the woman with unilateral neglect, we realize that perception and attention are somewhat independent. The perceptual mechanisms of our brain provide the information, and the mechanisms involved in attention determine whether we become conscious of this information.

Unilateral neglect occurs when the right parietal lobe is damaged. The parietal lobe contains the primary somatosensory cortex. It receives information from the skin, the muscles, the joints, the internal organs, and the part of the inner ear that is concerned with balance. Thus, it is concerned with the body and its position.

But that is not all; the association cortex of the parietal lobe also receives auditory and visual information from the association cortex of the occipital and temporal lobes. Its most important function seems to be to put together information about the movements and location of the parts of the body with the locations of objects in space around us. The right and left parietal lobes each handle somewhat different tasks; the left concerns itself with the position of the parts of the body, and the right concerns itself with the three-dimensional space around the body and the contents of that space. (The left parietal lobe is also involved in language

abilities, but they will be discussed later, in Chapter 13.)

If unilateral neglect simply consisted of blindness in the left side of the visual field and anesthesia of the left side of the body, it would not be nearly so interesting. Individuals with pure unilateral neglect are neither half blind nor half numb. Under the proper circumstances, they *can* see things located to their left and they *can* tell when someone touches the left side of their bodies. But normally, they ignore such stimuli and act as if the left side of the world and of their bodies did not exist.

Volpe, LeDoux, and Gazzaniga (1979) presented pairs of visual stimuli to people with unilateral neglect—one stimulus in the left visual field, and one stimulus in the right. Invariably, the people reported seeing only the right-hand stimulus. But when the investigators asked the people to say whether or not the two stimuli were identical, they answered correctly, *even though they said that they were unaware of the left-hand stimulus.*

If you think about the story that the chief of neurology told about the man who ate only the right half of a pancake, you will realize that people with unilateral neglect *must* be able to perceive more than the right visual field. Remember that people with unilateral neglect fail to notice not only things to their left but also the *left halves* of things. But to distinguish between the left and right halves of an object, you first have to perceive the entire object; otherwise, how would you know where the middle was?

People with unilateral neglect also demonstrate their unawareness of the left half of things when they draw pictures. For example, when asked to draw a clock, they almost always successfully draw a circle; but then when they fill in the numbers, they scrunch them all in on the right side. Sometimes they simply stop after reaching 6 or 7, and sometimes they write the rest of the numbers underneath the circle. When asked to draw a daisy, they begin with a stem and a leaf or two and then draw all the petals to the right. When asked to draw a bicycle, they draw wheels and then put in spokes, but only to the right.

Bisiach and Luzzatti (1978) demonstrated a similar phenomenon, which suggests that unilateral neglect extends even to a person's own visual imagery. The investigators asked two patients with unilateral neglect to describe the Piazza del Duomo, a well-known landmark in Milan, the city in which they and the patients lived. They asked them to imagine that they were standing at the north end of the piazza and to tell them what they saw.

The patients duly named the buildings, but only those on the west to their right. Then the investigators asked them to imagine themselves at the south end of the piazza. This time, they named the buildings on the east—again, to their right. Obviously, they knew about *all* of the buildings and their locations, but they visualized them only when the buildings were located in the right side of their (imaginary) visual field.

You might wonder whether damage to the *left* parietal lobe causes unilateral *right* neglect The answer is yes, but it is very slight, it is difficult to detect, and it seems to be temporary. For all practical purposes, then, there is no right neglect. But why not? The answer is still a mystery. To be sure, people have suggested some possible explanations, but they are still quite speculative. Not until we know a lot more about the brain mechanisms of attention will we be able to understand this discrepancy.

KEY CONCEPTS

BASIC FEATURES OF THE NERVOUS SYSTEM

1. The central nervous system consists of the brain and spinal cord; it is covered with the meninges and floats in cerebrospinal fluid.

THE CENTRAL NERVOUS SYSTEM

2. The nervous system develops first as a tube, which thickens and forms pockets and folds as cells are produced. The tube becomes the ventricular system.
3. The forebrain, surrounding the lateral and third ventricles, consists of the telencephalon (cerebral cortex, limbic system, and basal ganglia) and diencephalon (thalamus and hypothalamus).

4. The midbrain, which surrounds the cerebral aqueduct, consists of the tectum and tegmentum.
5. The hindbrain, which surrounds the fourth ventricle, contains the cerebellum, the pons, and the medulla.

THE PERIPHERAL NERVOUS SYSTEM

6. The spinal and cranial nerves connect the central nervous system with the rest of the body. The autonomic nervous system consists of two divisions, sympathetic and parasympathetic.

SUGGESTED READINGS

Diamond, M.C., Scheibel, A.B., and Elson, L.M. *The Human Brain Coloring Book.* New York: Barnes & Noble, 1985.

Gluhbegovic, N., and Williams, T.H. *The Human Brain: A Photographic Guide.* New York: Harper & Row, 1980.

Heimer, L. *The Human Brain and Spinal Cord: Functional Neuroanatomy and Dissection Guide,* 2nd ed. New York: Springer-Verlag, 1995.

Nauta, W.J.H., and Feirtag, M. *Fundamental Neuroanatomy.* New York: W.H. Freeman, 1986.

Netter, F.H. *The CIBA Collection of Medical Illustrations. Vol. 1: Nervous System. Part 1: Anatomy and Physiology.* Summit, NJ: CIBA Pharmaceutical Products Co., 1983.

4

Psycho-pharmacology

LEARNING OBJECTIVES

1. Describe the routes of administration of drugs and their distribution within the body.

2. Describe drug effectiveness, the effects of repeated administration of drugs, and the placebo effect.

3. Describe the effects of drugs on synaptic activity.

4. Review the general role of neurotransmitters and neuromodulators, and describe the acetylcholinergic pathways in the brain and the drugs that affect these neurons.

5. Describe the monoaminergic pathways in the brain and the drugs that affect these neurons.

6. Review the role of neurons that release amino acid neurotransmitters, and describe drugs that affect these neurons.

7. Describe the effects of peptides, lipids, nucleosides, and soluble gases released by neurons.

A Contaminated Drug

In July 1982, some people in northern California began showing up at neurology clinics displaying dramatic, severe symptoms (Langston, Ballard, Tetrud, and Irwin, 1983). The most severely affected patients were almost totally paralyzed. They were unable to speak intelligibly, they drooled constantly, and their eyes were open with a fixed stare. Others, less severely affected, walked with a slow, shuffling gait and moved slowly and with great difficulty. The symptoms looked like those of Parkinson's disease, but that disorder has a very gradual onset. In addition, it rarely strikes people before late middle age, and the patients were all in their twenties or early thirties.

The common factor linking these patients was intravenous drug use; all of them had been taking a "new heroin," a synthetic opiate related to meperidine (Demerol). Because the symptoms looked like those of Parkinson's disease, the patients were given L-DOPA, the drug used to treat this disease, and they all showed significant improvement in their symptoms. But even with this treatment the symptoms were debilitating. In normal cases of Parkinson's disease, L-DOPA therapy works for a time, but as the degeneration of dopamine-secreting neurons continues, the drug loses its effectiveness. Early indications suggest that this fate is likely for the young patients (Langston and Ballard, 1984).

Some detective work revealed that the chemical that caused the neurological symptoms was not the synthetic opiate itself but another chemical with which it was contaminated. According to researcher William Langston, the mini-epidemic appears to have started "when a young man in Silicon Valley was sloppy in his synthesis of synthetic heroin. That sloppiness led to the presence of MPTP, which by an extraordinary trick of fate is highly toxic to the very same neurons that are lost in Parkinson's disease" (Lewin, 1989, p. 467). Because of the research that followed up on that "trick of fate," patients with Parkinson's disease are now receiving a drug that slows the rate of degeneration of their dopamine-secreting neurons. There is hope that new drugs may even halt the degeneration, giving patients many more years of useful, productive lives and preventing others from ever developing the disease. And maybe—just maybe—researchers have stumbled on a drug that will retard the aging process.

Chapter 2 introduced you to the cells of the nervous system, and Chapter 3 described its basic structure. Now it is time to build on this information by introducing the field of psychopharmacology. **Psychopharmacology** is the study of the effects of drugs on the nervous system and (of course) on behavior. (*Pharmakon* is the Greek word for "drug.")

But what *is* a drug? Like many words, this one has several different meanings. In one context, it refers to a medication that we would obtain from a druggist—a chemical that has a therapeutic effect on a disease or its symptoms. In another context, the word refers to a chemical that people are likely to abuse, such as heroin or cocaine. The meaning that will be used in this book (and the one generally accepted by pharmacologists) is "an exogenous chemical not necessary for normal cellular functioning that significantly alters the functions of certain cells of the body when taken in relatively low doses." Because the topic of this chapter is *psycho*pharmacology, we will concern ourselves here only with chemicals that alter the functions of cells within the nervous system. The word *exogenous* rules out chemical messengers produced by the body, such as neurotransmitters, neuromodulators, or hormones. (*Exogenous* means produced from without—that is, from outside the body.) Chemical messengers produced by the body are not drugs, although synthetic chemicals that mimic their effects are classified as drugs. The definition of a drug also rules out essential nutrients, such as proteins, fats, carbohydrates, minerals, and vitamins that are a necessary constituent of a healthy diet. Finally, it states that drugs are effective in low doses. This qualification is important, because large quantities of almost any substance—even common ones such as table salt—will alter the functions of cells.

As we will see in this chapter, drugs have *effects* and *sites of action*. **Drug effects** are the changes we can observe in an organism's physiological processes and behavior.

Psychopharmacology The study of the effects of drugs on the nervous system and on behavior.

Drug effect The changes a drug produces in an organism's physiological processes and behavior.

For example, the effects of morphine, heroin, and other opiates include decreased sensitivity to pain, slowing of the digestive system, sedation, muscular relaxation, constriction of the pupils, and euphoria. The **sites of action** of drugs are the points at which molecules of drugs interact with molecules located on or in cells of the body, thus affecting some biochemical processes of these cells. For example, the sites of action of the opiates are specialized receptors situated in the membrane of certain neurons. When molecules of opiates attach to and activate these receptors, the drugs alter the activity of these neurons and produce their effects. This chapter considers both the effects of drugs and their sites of action.

Psychopharmacology is an important field of neuroscience. It has been responsible for the development of psychotherapeutic drugs, which are used to treat psychological and behavioral disorders. It has also provided tools that have enabled other investigators to study the functions of cells of the nervous system and the behaviors that are controlled by particular neural pathways.

This chapter begins with a description of the basic principles of psychopharmacology: the routes of administration of drugs and their fate in the body. The second section discusses the sites of drug actions. The final section discusses specific neurotransmitters and neuromodulators and the physiological and behavioral effects of specific drugs that interact with them. This chapter does not contain all this book has to say about the subject of psychopharmacology. Throughout the book you will learn about the use of drugs to investigate the nature of neural circuits involved in the control of perception, memory, and behavior. In addition, Chapters 15 and 16 discuss the physiology of drug abuse and the use of drugs to study and treat mental disorders such as schizophrenia, depression, and the anxiety disorders.

PRINCIPLES OF PSYCHOPHARMACOLOGY

Although drugs can affect the nervous system in a variety of ways, some common principles apply to all of them.

Pharmacokinetics

To be effective, a drug must reach its sites of action. To do so, molecules of the drug must enter the body and then enter the bloodstream so that they can be carried to the organ (or organs) they act on. Once there, they must leave the bloodstream and come into contact with the molecules with which they interact. For almost all of the drugs we are interested in, the molecules of the drug must enter the central nervous system.

Molecules of drugs must cross several barriers to enter the body and find their way to their sites of action. Some molecules pass through these barriers easily and quickly; others do so very slowly. And once molecules of drugs enter the body, they begin to be metabolized—broken down by enzymes—or excreted in the urine (or both). In time, the molecules either disappear or are transformed into inactive fragments. The process by which drugs are absorbed, distributed within the body, metabolized, and excreted is called **pharmacokinetics** ("movements of drugs").

Routes of Administration

First, let's consider the routes by which drugs can be administered. For laboratory animals, the most common route is injection. The drug is dissolved in a liquid (or, in some cases, suspended in a liquid in the form of fine particles) and injected through a hypodermic needle. The fastest route is **intravenous (IV) injection**—injection into a vein. The drug immediately enters the bloodstream, and it reaches the brain within a few seconds. The disadvantages of IV injections are the increased care

---

Sites of action The locations at which molecules of drugs interact with molecules located on or in cells of the body, thus affecting some biochemical processes of these cells.

Pharmacokinetics The process by which drugs are absorbed, distributed within the body, metabolized, and excreted.

Intravenous (IV) injection Injection of a substance directly into a vein.

and skill they require in comparison to other forms of injection and the fact that the entire dose reaches the bloodstream at once. If an organism is especially sensitive to the drug, there may be little time to administer another drug to counteract its effects.

An **intraperitoneal (IP) injection** is rapid, but not as rapid as an IV injection. The drug is injected through the abdominal wall into the *peritoneal cavity*—the space that surrounds the stomach, intestines, liver, and other abdominal organs. IP injections are the most common route for administering drugs to small laboratory animals. An **intramuscular (IM) injection** is made directly into a large muscle, such as one found in the upper arm, thigh, or buttocks. The drug is absorbed into the bloodstream through the capillaries that supply the muscle. If very slow absorption is desirable, the drug can be mixed with another drug (such as ephedrine) that constricts blood vessels and retards the flow of blood through the muscle.

A drug can also be injected into the space beneath the skin, by means of a **subcutaneous (SC) injection.** A subcutaneous injection is useful only if small amounts of drug need to be administered, because large amounts would be painful. Some fat-soluble drugs can be dissolved in vegetable oil and administered subcutaneously. In this case, molecules of the drug will slowly leave the deposit of oil over a period of several days. If *very* slow and prolonged absorption of a drug is desirable, the drug can be formed into a dry pellet or placed in a sealed silicone rubber capsule and implanted beneath the skin.

Oral administration is the most common form of administering medicinal drugs to humans. Because of the difficulty getting laboratory animals to eat something that does not taste good to them, researchers seldom use this route. Some substances cannot be administered orally because they will be destroyed by stomach acid or digestive enzymes or because they are not absorbed from the digestive system into the bloodstream. For example, insulin, a peptide hormone, must be injected. **Sublingual administration** of certain drugs can be accomplished by placing them beneath the tongue. The drug is absorbed into the bloodstream by the capillaries that supply the mucous membrane that lines the mouth. (Obviously, this method works only with humans, who will cooperate and leave the capsule beneath their tongue.) Nitroglycerine, a drug that causes blood vessels to dilate, is taken sublingually by people who suffer the pains of angina pectoris, caused by obstructions in the coronary arteries.

Drugs can also be administered at the opposite end of the digestive tract, in the form of suppositories. **Intrarectal administration** is rarely used to give drugs to experimental animals. For obvious reasons, this process would be difficult with a small animal. In addition, when agitated, small animals such as rats tend to defecate, which would mean that the drug would not remain in place long enough to be absorbed. And I'm not sure I would want to try to administer a rectal suppository to a large animal. Rectal suppositories are most commonly used to administer drugs that might upset a person's stomach.

The lungs provide another route for drug administration: **inhalation.** Nicotine, freebase cocaine, and marijuana are usually smoked. In addition, drugs that are used to treat lung disorders are often inhaled in the form of a vapor or fine mist. The route from the lungs to the brain is very short, and drugs administered this way have very rapid effects.

Some drugs can be absorbed directly through the skin, so they can be given by means of **topical administration.** Natural or artificial steroid hormones can be administered this way, as can nicotine (as a treatment to make it easier for a person to stop smoking). The mucous membrane lining the nasal passages also provides a route for topical administration. Commonly abused drugs such as cocaine hydrochloride are often sniffed so that they come in contact with the nasal mucosa. This route delivers the drug to the brain very rapidly. (The technical, rarely used name for this route is *insufflation.*)

Finally, drugs can be administered directly into the brain. As we saw in Chapter 2, the blood-brain barrier prevents certain chemicals from leaving capillaries and

Intraperitoneal (IP) injection [*in tra pair i toe nee ul*] Injection of a substance into the peritoneal cavity—the space that surrounds the stomach, intestines, liver, and other abdominal organs.

Intramuscular (IM) injection Injection of a substance into a muscle.

Subcutaneous (SC) injection Injection of a substance into the space beneath the skin.

Oral administration Administration of a substance into the mouth, so that it is swallowed.

Sublingual administration [*sub ling wul*] Administration of a substance by placing it beneath the tongue.

Intrarectal administration Administration of a substance into the rectum.

Inhalation Administration of a vaporous substance into the lungs.

Topical administration Administration of a substance directly onto the skin or mucous membrane.

FIGURE 4.1

The concentration of cocaine in blood plasma after intravenous injection, inhalation, sniffing, and oral administration.

[Adapted from Feldman, Meyer, and Quenzer, 1997; after Jones, 1990.]

entering the brain. Some drugs cannot cross the blood-brain barrier. If these drugs are to reach the brain, they must be injected directly into the brain or into the cerebrospinal fluid in the brain's ventricular system. To study the effects of a drug in a specific region of the brain (for example, in a particular nucleus of the hypothalamus), a researcher will inject a very small amount of the drug directly into the brain. This procedure, known as **intracerebral administration,** is described in more detail in Chapter 5. To achieve a widespread distribution of a drug in the brain, a researcher will get past the blood-brain barrier by injecting the drug into a cerebral ventricle. The drug is then absorbed into the brain tissue, where it can exert its effects. This route, **intracerebroventricular (ICV) administration,** is used very rarely in humans—primarily to deliver antibiotics directly to the brain to treat certain types of infections.

Figure 4.1 shows the time course of blood levels of a commonly abused drug, cocaine, after intravenous injection, inhalation, sniffing, and oral administration. The amounts received were not identical, but the graph illustrates the relative rapidity with which the drug reaches the blood. (See *Figure 4.1.*)

Distribution of Drugs Within the Body

As we saw, drugs exert their effects only when they reach their sites of action. In the case of drugs that affect behavior, most of these sites are located on or in particular cells in the central nervous system. The previous section described the routes by which drugs can be introduced into the body. With the exception of intracerebral or intracerebroventricular administration, the differences in the routes of drug administration vary only in the rate at which a drug reaches the blood plasma (that is, the liquid part of the blood). But what happens next? All the sites of action of drugs that are of interest to psychopharmacologists lie outside the blood vessels.

Several factors determine the rate at which a drug that is present in the bloodstream reaches sites of action within the brain. The first is lipid solubility. The blood-brain barrier is a barrier only for water-soluble molecules. Molecules that are soluble in lipids (fats) pass through the cells that line the capillaries in the central nervous system, and they distribute themselves rapidly throughout the brain. For example, diacetylmorphine (more commonly known as heroin) is more lipid soluble than morphine. Thus, an intravenous injection of heroin produces more rapid effects than one of morphine. Even though the molecules of the two drugs are equally effective when they reach their sites of action in the brain, the fact that heroin molecules get there faster means that they produce a more intense "rush" and thus explains why drug addicts prefer heroin to morphine.

Inactivation and Excretion

Drugs do not remain in the body indefinitely. Many are deactivated by enzymes, and all are eventually excreted—primarily by the kidneys. The liver plays an especially active role in enzymatic deactivation of drugs, but some deactivating enzymes are also found in the blood. The brain also contains enzymes that destroy some drugs. In some cases, enzymes transform molecules of a drug into other forms that themselves are biologically active. Occasionally, the transformed molecule is even more active than the one that is administered. In such cases, the effects of a drug can have a very long duration.

Intracerebral administration Administration of a substance directly into the brain.

Intracerebroventricular (ICV) administration Administration of a substance into one of the cerebral ventricles.

Drug Effectiveness

Drugs vary widely in their effectiveness. A small dose of a relatively effective drug can equal or exceed the effects of larger amounts of a relatively ineffective drug. The best way to measure the effectiveness of a drug is to plot a **dose-response curve.** To do this, subjects are given various doses of a drug, usually defined as milligrams of drug per kilogram of a subject's body weight, and the effects of the drug are plotted. Because the molecules of most drugs distribute themselves throughout the blood and then throughout the rest of the body, a heavier subject will require a larger quantity of a drug to achieve the same concentration as a smaller subject. As Figure 4.2 shows, increasingly stronger doses of a drug cause increasingly larger effects, until the point of maximum effect is reached. At this point, increasing the dose of the drug does not produce any more effect. (See *Figure 4.2.*)

Most drugs have more than one effect. Opiates such as morphine and codeine produce analgesia (reduction in sensitivity to pain), but they also depress the activity of neurons in the medulla that control heart rate and respiration. A physician who prescribes an opiate to relieve a patient's pain wants to administer a dose that is large enough to produce analgesia but not enough to depress heart rate and respiration—effects that could be fatal. Figure 4.3 shows two dose-response curves, one for the analgesic effects of a painkiller and one for the drug's depressant effects on respiration. The difference between these curves indicates the drug's margin of safety. Obviously, the most desirable drugs have a large margin of safety. (See *Figure 4.3.*)

One measure of a drug's margin of safety is its **therapeutic index.** This measure is obtained by administering varying doses of the drug to a group of laboratory animals such as mice. Two numbers are obtained: the dose that produces the desired effects in 50 percent of the animals and the dose that produces toxic effects in 50 percent of the animals. The therapeutic index is the ratio of these two numbers. For example, if the toxic dose is five times higher than the effective dose, then the therapeutic index is 5.0. The lower the therapeutic index, the more care must be taken in prescribing the drug. For example, barbiturates have relatively low therapeutic indexes—as low as 2 or 3. In contrast, tranquilizers such as Librium or Valium have therapeutic indexes of well over 100. As a consequence, an accidental overdose of a barbiturate is much more likely to have tragic effects than a similar overdose of Librium or Valium.

Why do drugs vary in their effectiveness? There are two reasons. First, different drugs—even those with the same behavioral effects—may have different sites of action. For example, both morphine and aspirin have analgesic effects, but morphine suppresses the activity of neurons in the spinal cord and brain that are involved in pain perception, whereas aspirin reduces the production of a

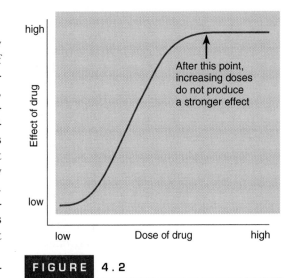

FIGURE 4.2

A dose-response curve. Increasingly stronger doses of the drug produce increasingly larger effects until the maximum effect is reached. After that point, increments in the dose do not produce any increments in the drug's effect. However, the risk of adverse side effects increases.

Dose-response curve A graph of the magnitude of an effect of a drug as a function of the amount of drug administered.

Therapeutic index The ratio between the dose that produces the desired effect in 50 percent of the animals and the dose that produces toxic effects in 50 percent of the animals.

FIGURE 4.3

Dose-response curves for the analgesic effect of morphine and for the drug's adverse side effect, its depressant effect on respiration. A drug's margin of safety is reflected by the difference between the dose-response curve for its therapeutic effects and its adverse side effects.

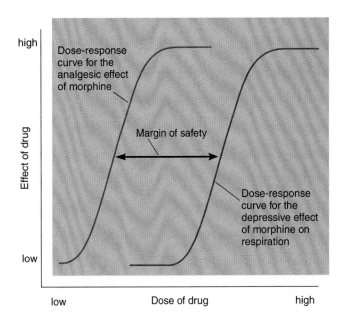

chemical involved in transmitting information from damaged tissue to pain-sensitive neurons. Because the drugs act very differently, a given dose of morphine (expressed in terms of milligrams of drug per kilogram of body weight) produces much more pain reduction than the same dose of aspirin.

The second reason that drugs vary in their effectiveness has to do with the affinity of the drug with its site of action. As we will see in the next major section of this chapter, most drugs of interest to psychopharmacologists exert their effects by binding with other molecules located in the central nervous system—with presynaptic or postsynaptic receptors, with transporter molecules, or with enzymes involved in the production or deactivation of neurotransmitters. Drugs vary widely in their **affinity** for the molecules to which they attach—the readiness with which the two molecules join together. A drug with a high affinity will produce effects at a relatively low concentration, whereas one with a low affinity must be administered in relatively high doses. Thus, even two drugs with identical sites of action can vary widely in their effectiveness if they have different affinities for their binding sites. In addition, because most drugs have multiple effects, a drug can have high affinities for some of its sites of action and low affinities for others. The most desirable drug has a high affinity for sites of action that produce therapeutic effects and a low affinity for sites of action that produce toxic side effects. One of the goals of research by drug companies is to find chemicals with just this pattern of effects.

Effects of Repeated Administration

Often, when a drug is administered repeatedly, its effects will not remain constant. In most cases, its effects will diminish—a phenomenon known as **tolerance.** In other cases, a drug becomes more and more effective—a phenomenon known as **sensitization.**

Let's consider tolerance first. Tolerance is seen in many drugs that are commonly abused. For example, a regular user of heroin must take larger and larger amounts of the drug for it to be effective. And once a person has taken an opiate regularly enough to develop tolerance, that individual will suffer **withdrawal symptoms** if he or she suddenly stops taking the drug. Withdrawal symptoms are primarily the opposite of the effects of the drug itself. For example, heroin produces euphoria; withdrawal from it produces *dysphoria*—a feeling of anxious misery. (*Euphoria* and *dysphoria* mean "easy to bear" and "hard to bear," respectively.) Heroin produces constipation; withdrawal from it produces nausea and cramping. Heroin produces relaxation; withdrawal from it produces agitation.

Withdrawal symptoms are caused by the same mechanisms that are responsible for tolerance. Tolerance is the result of the body's attempt to compensate for the effects of the drug. That is, most systems of the body, including those controlled by the brain, are regulated so that they stay at an optimal value. When the effects of a drug alter these systems for a prolonged time, compensatory mechanisms begin to produce the opposite reaction, at least partially compensating for the disturbance from the optimal value. These mechanisms account for the fact that more and more of the drug must be taken to achieve a given level of effects. Then, when the person stops taking the drug, the compensatory mechanisms make themselves felt, unopposed by the action of the drug.

Research suggests that there are several types of compensatory mechanisms. As we will see, many drugs that affect the brain do so by binding with receptors. The first compensatory mechanism involves a decrease in the effectiveness of such binding. Either the receptors become less sensitive to the drug (that is, their affinity for the drug decreases) or the receptors decrease in number. The second compensatory mechanism involves the process that couples the receptors to ion channels in the membrane or to the production of second messengers. After prolonged stimulation

Affinity The readiness with which two molecules join together.

Tolerance A decrease in the effectiveness of a drug that is administered repeatedly.

Sensitization An increase in the effectiveness of a drug that is administered repeatedly.

Withdrawal symptom The appearance of symptoms opposite to those produced by a drug when the drug is administered repeatedly and then suddenly no longer taken.

of the receptors, one or more steps in the coupling process become less effective. (Of course, *both* effects can occur.)

Many drugs have several different sites of action and thus produce several different effects. As a consequence, some of the effects of a drug may show tolerance but others may not. For example, barbiturates cause sedation and also depress neurons that control respiration. The sedative effects show tolerance, but the respiratory depression does not. This means that if larger and larger doses of a barbiturate are taken to achieve the same level of sedation, the person begins to run the risk of taking a dangerously large dose of the drug.

Sensitization is, of course, the exact opposite of tolerance: Repeated doses of a drug produce larger and larger effects. Because homeostatic mechanisms tend to correct for deviations away from the optimal values of physiological processes, sensitization is less common than tolerance. And some of the effects of a drug may show sensitization while others show tolerance. For example, repeated injections of cocaine become more and more likely to produce movement disorders and convulsions, whereas the euphoric effects of the drug do not show sensitization—and may even show tolerance.

Placebo Effects

A **placebo** is an innocuous substance without a specific physiological effect. The word comes from the Latin *placere,* "to please." A physician may sometimes give a placebo to anxious patients to placate them. (You can see that *placate* also has the same root.) But although placebos have no *specific* physiological effect, it is incorrect to say that they have *no* effect. If a person thinks that a placebo has a physiological effect, then administration of the placebo may actually produce that effect. And I do not mean that the patient will *imagine* the effect; it will actually occur.

Consider the following experiment. Levine, Gordon, and Fields (1979) measured people's sensitivity to pain. Next, they gave the people an injection of a painkiller— or so they said. Actually, they administered a placebo. When the experimenters again applied some painful stimuli, they found that the subjects were less sensitive to them. Clearly, they had demonstrated a placebo effect. Next, the experimenters administered another injection—some more painkiller, they said. Actually, the injection contained a drug that blocked the brain's opiate receptors. (This drug, naloxone, is described later in this chapter.) The drug abolished the placebo effect; the subjects regained their original sensitivity to pain. Thus, the subjects' belief that they had received a painkiller seems to have been responsible for a real, physiological event: the secretion of an endogenous opiatelike chemical in the brain. (See ***Figure 4.4.***)

Clearly, when experimenters want to investigate the behavioral effects of drugs in humans, they must use control groups whose members receive placebos, or they cannot be sure that the behavioral effects they observe were caused by specific effects of the drug. Studies with laboratory animals must also use placebos, even though we

Placebo (*pla see boh*) An inert substance given to an organism in lieu of a physiologically active drug; used experimentally to control for the effects of mere administration of a drug.

FIGURE 4 . 4

An explanation of the results of the study of the analgesic effects of a placebo by Levine, Gordon, and Fields (1979).

This effect blocked by naloxone

need not worry about the animals' "beliefs" about the effects of the drugs we give them. Consider what you must do to give a rat an intraperitoneal injection of a drug. You reach into the animal's cage, pick it up, hold it in such a way that its abdomen is exposed and its head is positioned to prevent it from biting you, insert a hypodermic needle through its abdominal wall, press the plunger of the syringe, and replace the animal in its cage, being sure to let go of it quickly so that it cannot turn and bite you. Even if the substance you inject is innocuous, the experience of receiving the injection will activate the animal's autonomic nervous system, cause the secretion of stress hormones, and have other physiological effects. If we want to know what the behavioral effects of a drug are, we must compare the drug-treated animals with other animals who receive a placebo, administered in exactly the same way as the drug. (By the way, a skilled and experienced researcher can handle a rat so gently that it shows very little reaction to a hypodermic injection.)

INTERIM SUMMARY

Psychopharmacology is the study of the effects of drugs on the nervous system and behavior. Drugs are exogenous chemicals not necessary for normal cellular functioning that significantly alter the functions of certain cells of the body when taken in relatively low doses. Drugs have *effects,* physiological and behavioral, and they have *sites of action*—molecules with which they interact to produce these effects.

Pharmacokinetics is the fate of a drug as it is absorbed into the body, circulates throughout the body, and reaches its sites of action. Drugs may be administered by intravenous, intraperitoneal, intramuscular, and subcutaneous injection; they may be administered orally, sublingually, intrarectally, by inhalation, and topically; and they may be injected intracerebrally or intracerebroventricularly. Lipid-soluble drugs easily pass through the blood-brain barrier, whereas others pass this barrier slowly or not at all.

With the exception of intravenous injection directly into the bloodstream, the time courses of the various routes of drug administration are different. Eventually, drugs disappear from the body. Some are deactivated by enzymes, especially in the liver, and others are simply excreted.

The dose-response curve represents a drug's effectiveness; it relates the amount administered (usually in mg/kg of the subject's body weight) to the resulting effect.

Most drugs have more than one site of action and thus more than one effect. The safety of a drug is measured by the difference between doses that produce desirable effects and those that produce adverse side effects. Drugs vary in their effectiveness because of the nature of their sites of actions and the affinity between molecules of the drug and these sites of action.

Repeated administration of a drug can cause either tolerance, often resulting in withdrawal symptoms, or sensitization. Tolerance can be caused by decreased affinity of a drug with its receptors, by decreased numbers of receptors, or by decreased coupling of receptors with the biochemical steps it controls. Some of the effects of a drug may show tolerance, while others may not—or may even show sensitization.

SITES OF DRUG ACTION

Throughout the history of our species, people have discovered that plants—and a few animals—produce chemicals that act on synapses. (Of course, the people who discovered these chemicals knew nothing about neurons and synapses.) Some of these chemicals have been used for their pleasurable effects; others have been used to treat illness, reduce pain, or poison other animals (or enemies). More recently, scientists have learned to produce completely artificial drugs, some with potencies far greater than the naturally occurring ones. The traditional uses of drugs remain, but in addition, they can be used in research laboratories to investigate the operations of the nervous system. Most drugs that affect behavior do so by affecting synaptic transmission. Drugs that affect synaptic transmission are classified into two general categories. Those that block or inhibit the postsynaptic effects are called **antagonists.** Those that facilitate them are called **agonists.** (The Greek word *agon* means "contest." Thus, an *agonist* is one who takes part in the contest.)

This section will describe the basic effects of drugs on synaptic activity. Recall from Chapter 2 that the sequence of synaptic activity goes like this: Neurotransmitters are synthesized and stored in synaptic vesicles. The synaptic vesicles travel to the presynaptic membrane. When an axon fires, the neurotransmitter is released into the synaptic cleft. Molecules of the neurotransmitter bind with postsynaptic receptors, causing particular ion channels to open, which produces excitatory or inhibitory postsynaptic potentials. The effects of the neurotransmitter are kept relatively brief by their reuptake by transporter molecules in the presynaptic membrane or by their destruction by enzymes. In addition, the stimulation of presynaptic autoreceptors regulates the synthesis and release of the neurotransmitter. The discussion of the effects of drugs in this section follows the same basic sequence. All of the effects I will describe are summarized in Figure 4.5, with some details shown in additional figures. Some of the effects are complex, so the discussion that follows bears careful reading.

Effects on Production of Neurotransmitters

The first step in the sequence of synaptic activity is the synthesis of the neurotransmitter from its precursors. In some cases the rate of synthesis and release of a neurotransmitter is increased when a precursor is administered; in these cases the precursor itself serves as an agonist. (See step 1 in *Figure 4.5.*)

The steps in the synthesis of neurotransmitters are controlled by enzymes. Therefore, if a drug inactivates one of these enzymes, it will prevent the neurotransmitter from being produced. Such a drug serves as an antagonist. (See step 2 in *Figure 4.5.*)

Effects on Storage and Release of Neurotransmitters

Neurotransmitters are stored in synaptic vesicles, which are transported to the presynaptic membrane, where the chemicals are released. The storage of neurotransmitters in vesicles is accomplished by the same kind of transporter molecules that are responsible for reuptake of a neurotransmitter into a terminal button. The transporter molecules are situated in the membrane of synaptic vesicles, and their action is to pump molecules of the neurotransmitter across the membrane, filling the vesicles. Some of the transporter molecules that fill synaptic vesicles are capable of being blocked by a drug. Molecules of the drug bind with a particular site on the transporter and inactivate it. Because the synaptic vesicles remain empty, nothing is released when the vesicles eventually rupture against the presynaptic membrane. The drug serves as an antagonist. (See step 3 in *Figure 4.5.*)

Some drugs act as antagonists by preventing the release of neurotransmitters from the terminal button. They do so by deactivating the proteins that cause docked synaptic vesicles to fuse with the presynaptic membrane and expel their contents into the synaptic cleft. Other drugs have just the opposite effect: They act as agonists by binding with these proteins and directly triggering release of the neurotransmitter. (See steps 4 and 5 in *Figure 4.5.*)

Antagonist A drug that opposes or inhibits the effects of a particular neurotransmitter on the postsynaptic cell.

Agonist A drug that facilitates the effects of a particular neurotransmitter on the postsynaptic cell.

1 Drug serves as precursor
AGO

2 Drug inactivates synthetic enzyme;
inhibits synthesis of NT
ANT

3 Drug prevents storage of NT in vesicles
ANT

4 Drug stimulates release of NT
AGO

8 Drug stimulates autoreceptors;
inhibits synthesis/release of NT
ANT

5 Drug inhibits release of NT
ANT

9 Drug blocks autoreceptors;
increases synthesis/release of NT
AGO

6 Drug stimulates
postsynaptic receptors
AGO

10 Drug blocks reuptake
AGO

7 Drug blocks
postsynaptic receptors
ANT

11 Drug inactivates
acetylcholinesterase
AGO

Precursor

Enzyme

Transmitter
substance

Inhibition

Choline
+
acetate

ACh AChE

Molecules of
drugs

FIGURE 4.5

A summary of the ways that drugs can affect the synaptic transmission (AGO = agonist;
ANT = antagonist; NT = neurotransmitter). Drugs that act as agonists are marked
in blue; drugs that act as antagonists are marked in red.

Effects on Receptors

The most important—and most complex—site of action of drugs in the nervous system is on receptors, both presynaptic and postsynaptic. Let's consider postsynaptic receptors first. (Here is where the careful reading should begin.) Once a neurotransmitter is released, it must stimulate the postsynaptic receptors. Some drugs bind with these receptors, just as the neurotransmitter does. Once a drug has bound with the receptor, it can serve as either an agonist or an antagonist.

A drug that mimics the effects of a neurotransmitter acts as a **direct agonist.** Molecules of the drug attach to the binding site to which the neurotransmitter normally attaches. This binding causes ion channels controlled by the receptor to open, just as they do when the neurotransmitter is present. Ions then pass through these channels and produce postsynaptic potentials. (See step 6 in *Figure 4.5*.)

Drugs that bind with postsynaptic receptors can also serve as antagonists. Molecules of such drugs bind with the receptors but *prevent* the ion channels from opening. These drugs are called **receptor blockers,** or **direct antagonists.** (See step 7 in *Figure 4.5*.)

Some postsynaptic receptors have multiple binding sites, to which different ligands can attach. Molecules of the neurotransmitter bind with one site, and other substances (such as neuromodulators and various drugs) bind with the others. Binding of a molecule with one of these alternative sites can either facilitate or inhibit the action of the neurotransmitter on the primary binding site; thus, they can serve as either agonists or antagonists.

As we saw in Chapter 2, the presynaptic membranes of some neurons contain autoreceptors that regulate the amount of neurotransmitter that is released. Because

Direct agonist A drug that binds with and activates a receptor.

Receptor blocker A drug that binds with a receptor but does not activate it; prevents the natural ligand from binding with the receptor.

Direct antagonist A synonym for *receptor blocker.*

stimulation of these receptors causes less neurotransmitter to be released, drugs that selectively activate them but do not activate the postsynaptic receptors act as antagonists. Drugs that *block* presynaptic autoreceptors have the opposite effect: They *increase* the release of the neurotransmitter, acting as agonists. (See steps 8 and 9 in *Figure 4.5.*)

Effects on Reuptake or Destruction of Neurotransmitters

The next step after stimulation of the postsynaptic receptor is termination of the postsynaptic potential. Two processes accomplish that task: Molecules of the neurotransmitter are taken back into the terminal button through the process of reuptake, or they are destroyed by an enzyme. Drugs can interfere with either of these processes. In the first case, molecules of the drug attach to the transporter molecules responsible for reuptake and inactivate them, thus blocking reuptake. In the second case, molecules of the drug bind with the enzyme that normally destroys the neurotransmitter, which prevents the enzyme from working. The most important example of such an enzyme is acetylcholinesterase, which destroys acetylcholine. Because both types of drugs prolong the presence of the neurotransmitter in the synaptic cleft (where they can stimulate postsynaptic receptors), they serve as *agonists*. (See steps 10 and 11 in *Figure 4.5.*)

INTERIM SUMMARY

The process of synaptic transmission entails the synthesis of the neurotransmitter, its storage in synaptic vesicles, its release into the synaptic cleft, its interaction with postsynaptic receptors, and the consequent opening of ion channels in the postsynaptic membrane. The effects of the neurotransmitter are then terminated by reuptake into the terminal button, or by enzymatic deactivation.

Each of the steps necessary for synaptic transmission can be interfered with by drugs that serve as *antagonists,* and a few of these steps can be stimulated by drugs that serve as *agonists.* In particular, drugs can increase the pool of available precursor, block a biosynthetic enzyme, prevent the storage of neurotransmitter in the synaptic vesicles, stimulate or block the release of the neurotransmitter, stimulate or block presynaptic or postsynaptic receptors, retard reuptake, or deactivate enzymes that destroy the neurotransmitter postsynaptically or presynaptically. A drug that activates postsynaptic receptors serves as an agonist, whereas one that activates presynaptic autoreceptors serves as an antagonist. A drug that blocks postsynaptic receptors serves as an antagonist, whereas one that blocks autoreceptors serves as an agonist.

NEUROTRANSMITTERS AND NEUROMODULATORS

Because neurotransmitters have two general effects on postsynaptic membranes—depolarization (EPSP) and hyperpolarization (IPSP)—one might expect that there would be two neurotransmitters, one excitatory and one inhibitory. Instead, there are many different kinds—several dozen, at least. In the brain, most synaptic communication is accomplished by two neurotransmitters: one with excitatory effects (glutamate) and one with inhibitory effects (GABA). (Another inhibitory neurotransmitter, glycine, is found in the spinal cord and lower brain stem.) Most of the activity of local circuits of neurons involves balances between the excitatory and inhibitory effects of these chemicals, which are responsible for most of the information transmitted from place to place within the brain. In fact, there are probably no neurons in the brain that do not receive excitatory input from glutamate-secreting terminal buttons and inhibitory input from neurons that secrete either GABA or glycine. And with the exception of neurons that detect painful stimuli, all sensory organs transmit information to the brain through axons whose terminals release glutamate. (Pain-detecting neurons secrete a peptide.)

What do all the other neurotransmitters do? In general, they have modulating effects rather than information-transmitting effects. That is, the release of neurotransmitters other than glutamate and GABA tends to activate or inhibit entire circuits of neurons that are involved in particular brain functions. For example, secretion of acetylcholine activates the cerebral cortex and facilitates learning, but the information that is learned and remembered is transmitted by neurons that secrete glutamate and GABA. Secretion of norepinephrine increases vigilance and enhances readiness to act when a signal is detected. Secretion of serotonin suppresses certain categories of behaviors and reduces the likelihood that an animal acts impulsively. Secretion of dopamine in some regions of the brain generally activates voluntary movements but does not specify which movements will occur. In other regions, secretion of dopamine reinforces ongoing behaviors and makes them more likely to occur at a later time. Because particular drugs can selectively affect neurons that secrete particular neurotransmitters, they can have specific effects on behavior.

This section introduces the most important neurotransmitters, discusses some of their behavioral functions, and describes a few of the most important drugs that interact with them. Those whose effects I describe in some detail are more important than those I mention in passing or simply indicate in a figure or a table. If you want to learn more details about these drugs (and many others), you should consult an up-to-date psychopharmacology text. I particularly recommend the one by Feldman, Meyer, and Quenzer (1997).

Acetylcholine

Acetylcholine (ACh) is the primary neurotransmitter secreted by efferent axons of the central nervous system. All muscular movement is accomplished by the release of acetylcholine, and ACh is also found in the ganglia of the autonomic nervous system and at the target organs of the parasympathetic branch of the ANS. Because ACh is found outside the central nervous system in locations that are easy to study, this neurotransmitter was the first to be discovered, and it has received much attention from neuroscientists. Some terminology: These synapses are said to be *acetylcholinergic*. *Ergon* is the Greek word for "work." Thus, *acetylcholinergic* synapses release acetylcholine, *dopaminergic* synapses release dopamine, *serotonergic* synapses release serotonin, and so on. (The suffix *-ergic* is pronounced **ur** *jik*.)

The axons and terminal buttons of acetylcholinergic neurons are distributed widely throughout the brain. Three systems have received the most attention from neuroscientists: the systems originating in the dorsolateral pons, the basal forebrain, and the medial septum (a part of the limbic system). The behavioral effects of ACh release in the brain are, for the most part, excitatory. The acetylcholinergic neurons located in the dorsolateral pons are responsible for triggering most of the characteristics of REM sleep (the phase of sleep during which dreaming occurs). Those located in the basal forebrain are involved in activating the cerebral cortex and facilitating learning, especially perceptual learning. Those located in the medial septum control the electrical rhythms of the hippocampus and modulate its functions, which include the formation of particular kinds of memories. These functions of acetylcholinergic neurons are described in more detail in Chapters 8 and 12.

ACh is composed of two components: *choline*, a substance derived from the breakdown of lipids, and *acetate*, the anion found in vinegar, also called acetic acid. Acetate

---

Acetyl-CoA (*a see* tul) A cofactor that supplies acetate for the synthesis of acetylcholine.

Choline acetyltransferase (ChAT) (*koh leen a see tul trans fer ace*) The enzyme that transfers the acetate ion from acetyl coenzyme A to choline, producing the neurotransmitter acetylcholine.

Botulinum toxin (*bot you lin um*) An acetylcholine antagonist: prevents release by terminal buttons.

Black widow spider venom A poison produced by the black widow spider that triggers the release of acetylcholine.

cannot be attached directly to choline; instead, it is transferred from a molecule of *acetyl-CoA*. CoA is produced by the mitochondria, and it takes part in many reactions in the body. **Acetyl-CoA** is simply CoA with an acetate ion attached to it. ACh is produced by the following reaction: In the presence of the enzyme **choline acetyltransferase (ChAT),** the acetate ion is transferred from the acetyl-CoA molecule to the choline molecule, yielding a molecule of ACh and one of ordinary CoA. (See *Figure 4.6.*)

A simple analogy will illustrate the role of coenzymes in chemical reactions. Think of acetate as a hot dog and choline as a bun. The task of the person (enzyme) who operates the hot dog vending stand is to put a hot dog into the bun (make acetylcholine). To do so, the vendor needs a fork (coenzyme) to remove the hot dog from the boiling water. The vendor inserts the fork into the hot dog (attaches acetate to CoA) and transfers the hot dog from fork to bun.

Two drugs, botulinum toxin and the venom of the black widow spider, affect the release of acetylcholine. **Botulinum toxin** is produced by *Clostridium botulinum,* a bacterium that can grow in improperly canned food. This drug, which prevents the release of ACh, is an extremely potent poison. Someone once calculated that a teaspoonful of pure botulinum toxin could kill the world's entire human population. **Black widow spider venom** has the opposite effect: It stimulates the release of ACh. Although the effects of black widow spider venom can also be fatal, the venom is much less toxic than botulinum toxin. In fact, it would take several bites to kill a healthy adult, but infants or frail, elderly people would be more susceptible.

You will recall from Chapter 2 that after being released by the terminal button, ACh is deactivated by the enzyme acetylcholinesterase (AChE), which is present in the postsynaptic membrane. (See *Figure 4.7.*)

Drugs that deactivate or inhibit AChE are used for several purposes. Some are used as insecticides. These drugs readily kill insects but not humans and other mammals, because our blood contains enzymes that destroy them. Insects lack the enzyme. Other AChE inhibitors are used medically. As we saw in the prologue and epilogue to Chapter 2, a hereditary disorder called *myasthenia gravis* is caused by an attack of a person's immune system against acetylcholine receptors located on skeletal muscles. The person becomes weaker and weaker as the muscles become less responsive to the neurotransmitter. If the person is given an AChE inhibitor such as **physostigmine,** the person will regain some strength, because the acetylcholine that is released has a more prolonged effect on the remaining receptors. (Because physostigmine cannot cross the blood-brain barrier, it does not affect the AChE found in the central nervous system.)

There are two different types of ACh receptors, which were identified when investigators discovered that different drugs activated or inhibited them. One of these receptors is stimulated by nicotine, a drug found in tobacco leaves; the other is stimulated by muscarine, a drug found in the poison mushroom *Amanita muscaria.* Consequently, these two ACh receptors are referred to as **nicotinic receptors** and **muscarinic receptors,** respectively.

Just as two different drugs stimulate the two classes of acetylcholine receptors, two different drugs *block* them. Both drugs were discovered in nature long ago. The first, **atropine,** blocks muscarinic receptors. The drug is named after *Atropos,*

FIGURE 4.6

The biosynthesis of acetylcholine.

Physostigmine (*fy zo **stig** meen*) A drug that inhibits the activity of acetylcholinesterase.

Nicotinic receptor An ionotropic acetylcholine receptor that is stimulated by nicotine and blocked by curare.

Muscarinic receptor (*muss ka rin ic*) A metabotropic acetylcholine receptor that is stimulated by muscarine and blocked by atropine.

Atropine (*a tro peen*) A drug that blocks muscarinic acetylcholine receptors.

FIGURE 4.7

The destruction of acetylcholine by acetylcholinesterase.

Amanita muscaria, a colorful mushroom, is the source of muscarine, a drug that stimulates muscarinic acetylcholine receptors.

the Greek fate who cut the thread of life (which a sufficient dose of atropine will certainly do). Atropine is one of several *belladonna alkaloids* extracted from a plant called the "deadly nightshade," and therein lies a tale. Many years ago, women who wanted to increase their attractiveness to men put drops containing belladonna alkaloids into their eyes. In fact, *belladonna* means "pretty lady." Why was the drug used this way? One of the unconscious responses that occurs when we are interested in something is dilation of our pupils. By blocking the effects of acetylcholine on the pupil, belladonna alkaloids such as atropine make the pupils dilate. This change makes a woman appear more interested in a man when she looks at him, and, of course, this apparent sign of interest makes him regard her as more attractive.

Another drug, **curare,** blocks nicotinic receptors. Because these receptors are the ones found on muscles, curare, like botulinum toxin, causes paralysis. However, the effects of curare are much faster. The drug is extracted from several different species of plants found in South America, where it was discovered long ago by people who used it to coat the tips of arrows and darts. Within minutes of being struck by one of these poisoned points, an animal collapses, ceases breathing, and dies. Nowadays, curare (and other drugs with the same site of action) are used to paralyze patients who are to undergo surgery so that their muscles will relax completely and not contract when they are cut with a scalpel. An anesthetic must also be used, because a person who receives only curare will remain perfectly conscious and sensitive to pain, even though paralyzed. And, of course, a respirator must be used to supply air to the lungs.

The most important drugs that affect acetylcholinergic synapses are summarized in *Table 4.1.*

The Monoamines

Curare (*kew rahr ee*) A drug that blocks nicotinic acetylcholine receptors.

Monoamine (*mahn o a meen*) A class of amines that includes indolamines such as serotonin and catecholamines such as dopamine, norepinephrine, and epinephrine.

Catecholamine (*cat a kohl a meen*) A class of amines that includes the neurotransmitters dopamine, norepinephrine, and epinephrine.

Dopamine (DA) (*dope a meen*) A neurotransmitter; one of the catecholamines.

L-DOPA (*ell dope a*) The biologically active form of DOPA; the precursor of the catecholamines; often used to treat Parkinson's disease because of its effect as a dopamine agonist.

Epinephrine, norepinephrine, dopamine, and serotonin are four chemicals that belong to a family of compounds called **monoamines.** Because the molecular structures of these substances are similar, some drugs affect the activity of all of them, to some

TABLE 4.1	Some Drugs That Affect Acetylcholinergic Synapses	
Effect of Drug	**Name of Drug**	**Effect on Synaptic Transmission**
Block release of ACh	Botulinum toxin	Antagonist
Stimulate release of ACh	Black widow spider venom	Agonist
Stimulate nicotinic receptors	Nicotine	Agonist
Block nicotinic receptors	Curare	Antagonist
Stimulate muscarinic receptors	Muscarine	Agonist
Block muscarinic receptors	Atropine	Antagonist
Inhibit cholinesterase	Physostigmine	Agonist
Inhibit reuptake of choline	Hemicholinium	Antagonist

degree. The first three—epinephrine, norepinephrine, and dopamine—belong to a subclass of monoamines called **catecholamines.** The fourth, serotonin, is an *indolamine.* It is worthwhile learning the terms in Table 4.2, because they will be used many times throughout the rest of this book. (See *Table 4.2.*)

The monoamines are produced by several systems of neurons in the brain. Most of these systems consist of a relatively small number of cell bodies located in the brain stem, whose axons branch repeatedly and give rise to an enormous number of terminal buttons distributed throughout many regions of the brain. Monoaminergic neurons thus serve to modulate the function of widespread regions of the brain, increasing or decreasing the activities of particular brain functions.

TABLE 4.2	Classification of the Monoamine Neurotransmitters
Catecholamines	**Indolamines**
Dopamine	Serotonin
Norepinephrine	
Epinephrine	

Dopamine

The first catecholamine, **dopamine (DA),** produces both excitatory and inhibitory postsynaptic potentials, depending on the postsynaptic receptor. Dopamine is one of the more interesting neurotransmitters because it has been implicated in several important functions, including movement, attention, learning, and the reinforcing effects of drugs that people tend to abuse; thus, it is discussed in several chapters later in this book.

The synthesis of the catecholamines is somewhat more complicated than that of ACh, but each step is a simple one. The precursor molecule is modified slightly, step by step, until it achieves its final shape. Each step is controlled by a different enzyme, which causes a small part to be added or taken off. The precursor for the two major catecholamine neurotransmitters (dopamine and norepinephrine) is *tyrosine,* an essential amino acid that we must obtain from our diet. An enzyme converts tyrosine into **L-DOPA.** Another enzyme converts L-DOPA into dopamine. In dopaminergic neurons, that conversion is the last step, but in noradrenergic neurons, dopamine is converted into norepinephrine. These reactions are shown in *Figure 4.8.*

The brain contains several systems of dopaminergic neurons. The three most important of these originate in the midbrain. The cell bodies of neurons of the **nigrostriatal system** are located in the substantia nigra and project their axons to the neostriatum: the caudate nucleus and the putamen. The neostriatum is an important part of the basal ganglia, involved in the control of movement. The cell bodies of neurons of the **mesolimbic system** are located in the ventral tegmental area and project their axons to several parts of the limbic system, including the nucleus accumbens, amygdala, and hippocampus. (The term *meso-* refers to the midbrain, or mesencephalon.) The nucleus accumbens plays an important role in the reinforcing (rewarding) effects of certain categories of stimuli, including those of drugs that people abuse. The cell bodies of neurons of the **mesocortical system** are also located in the ventral tegmental area. Their axons project to the prefrontal cortex. These neurons have an excitatory effect on the frontal cortex and thus affect such functions as formation of short-term memories, planning, and strategy preparation for problem solving. (See *Table 4.3.*)

Degeneration of dopaminergic neurons that connect the substantia nigra with the caudate nucleus causes **Parkinson's disease,** a movement disorder characterized by tremors, rigidity of the limbs, poor balance, and difficulty in initiating movements. The cell bodies of these neurons are located in a region of the brain called the *substantia nigra* ("black substance"). This region is normally stained black with melanin, the substance that gives color to skin. This compound is produced by the breakdown of dopamine. (The brain damage that causes Parkinson's disease was discovered by pathologists who observed that the substantia nigra of a deceased person who had had this disorder was pale rather than black.) People with Parkinson's disease are treated with L-DOPA, the precursor to dopamine. Although dopamine can-

Nigrostriatal system (*nigh grow stry ay tul*) A system of neurons originating in the substantia nigra and terminating in the neostriatum (caudate nucleus and putamen).

Mesolimbic system (*mee zo lim bik*) A system of dopaminergic neurons originating in the ventral tegmental area and terminating in the nucleus accumbens, amygdala, and hippocampus.

Mesocortical system (*mee zo kor ti kul*) A system of dopaminergic neurons originating in the ventral tegmental area and terminating in the prefrontal cortex.

Parkinson's disease A neurological disease characterized by tremors, rigidity of the limbs, poor balance, and difficulty in initiating movements; caused by degeneration of the nigrostriatal system.

FIGURE 4.8

Biosynthesis of the catecholamines.

Name	Origin (Location of Cell Bodies)	Location of Terminal Buttons	Behavioral Effects
Nigrostriatal system	Substantia nigra	Neostriatum (caudate nucleus and putamen)	Control of movement
Mesolimbic system	Ventral tegmental area	Nucleus accumbens and amygdala	Reinforcement, effects of addictive drug
Mesocortical system	Ventral tegmental area	Prefrontal cortex	Short-term memories, planning, strategies for problem solving

TABLE 4.3   The Three Major Dopaminergic Pathways

AMPT A drug that blocks the activity of tyrosine hydroxylase and thus interferes with the synthesis of the catecholamines.

Reserpine (*ree sur peen*) A drug that interferes with the storage of monoamines in synaptic vesicles.

Methylphenidate (*meth ul fen i date*) A drug that inhibits the reuptake of dopamine.

Monoamine oxidase (MAO) (*mahn o a meen*) A class of enzymes that destroy the monoamines: dopamine, norepinephrine, and serotonin.

Deprenyl (*depp ra nil*) A drug that blocks the activity of MAO-B; acts as a dopamine agonist.

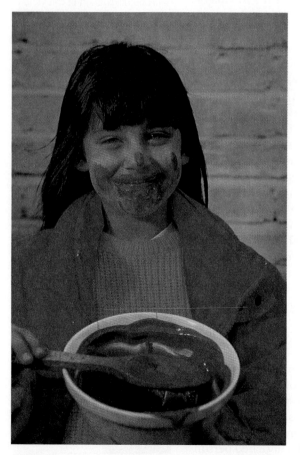

Amines found in chocolate would be toxic, but they are deactivated by the monoamine oxidase found in the blood.

not cross the blood-brain barrier, L-DOPA can. Once L-DOPA reaches the brain, it is taken up by dopaminergic neurons and is converted to dopamine. The increased synthesis of dopamine causes more dopamine to be released by the surviving dopaminergic neurons in patients with Parkinson's disease. As a consequence, the patients' symptoms are alleviated.

As you can see, L-DOPA serves as a dopaminergic agonist. A drug called **AMPT** binds with—and inactivates—the enzyme that converts tyrosine to L-DOPA. As a consequence, this drug blocks the synthesis of dopamine and thus serves as a dopaminergic antagonist. (As you can see by looking at Figure 4.8, it blocks the synthesis of norepinephrine, too.)

The drug **reserpine** prevents the storage of all the monoamines (DA, NE, and 5-HT) in synaptic vesicles by blocking the transporters in the membrane that pump monoamines into the vesicles. Because the synaptic vesicles remain empty, no neurotransmitter is released when an action potential reaches the terminal button. Reserpine, then, is a monoamine antagonist. The drug, which comes from the root of a shrub, was discovered over three thousand years ago in India, where it was found to be useful in treating snakebite and seemed to have a calming effect. Pieces of the root are still sold in markets in rural areas of India. In Western medicine, reserpine was previously used to treat high blood pressure, but it has been replaced by drugs with fewer side effects.

Several drugs inhibit the reuptake of dopamine, thus serving as potent dopamine agonists. The best known of these drugs are amphetamine, cocaine, and methylphenidate. The effects of amphetamine are complex. Besides inhibiting dopamine reuptake, amphetamine causes the release of dopamine from the terminal buttons by causing dopamine transporters to run in reverse, propelling DA into the synaptic cleft. Because cocaine also blocks voltage-dependent sodium channels, it is sometimes used as a topical anesthetic, especially in the form of eyedrops for eye surgery. **Methylphenidate** (Ritalin) is used to treat children with attention deficit disorder.

The production of the catecholamines is regulated by an enzyme called **monoamine oxidase (MAO).** This enzyme is found within monoaminergic terminal buttons, where it destroys excessive amounts of neurotransmitter. A drug called **deprenyl** destroys the particular form of monoamine oxidase (MAO-B) that is found in dopaminergic terminal buttons. (As

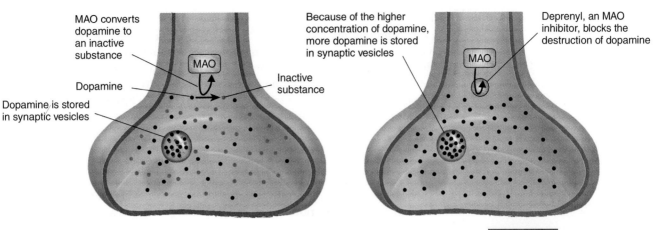

MAO converts dopamine to an inactive substance

Dopamine

Dopamine is stored in synaptic vesicles

MAO

Inactive substance

Because of the higher concentration of dopamine, more dopamine is stored in synaptic vesicles

Deprenyl, an MAO inhibitor, blocks the destruction of dopamine

MAO

FIGURE 4.9

The role of monoamine oxidase in dopaminergic terminal buttons and the action of deprenyl.

you will see in the epilogue to this chapter, the case of the young people poisoned by MPTP led to the discovery of a therapeutic use of deprenyl.) Because deprenyl prevents the destruction of dopamine, more dopamine is released when an action potential reaches the terminal button. Thus, deprenyl serves as a dopamine agonist. (See *Figure 4.9*.)

MAO is also found in the blood, where it deactivates amines that are present in foods such as chocolate and cheese; without such deactivation these amines could cause dangerous increases in blood pressure.

At least five types of dopamine receptors have been identified. Of these, two are the most common: D_1 *dopamine receptors* and D_2 *dopamine receptors*. It appears that D_1 receptors are exclusively postsynaptic, whereas D_2 receptors are found both presynaptically and postsynaptically in the brain. Several drugs stimulate or block specific types of dopamine receptors.

Dopamine has been implicated as a neurotransmitter that might be involved in schizophrenia, a serious mental disorder whose symptoms include hallucinations, delusions, and disruption of normal, logical thought processes. Drugs such as **chlorpromazine,** which block D_2 dopamine receptors, alleviate these symptoms. Hence, investigators have speculated that schizophrenia is produced by overactivity of dopaminergic neurons. More recently discovered drugs, such as **clozapine,** may exert their therapeutic effects by blocking D_4 receptors. The physiology of schizophrenia is discussed in Chapter 15.

Some of the more important drugs that affect dopaminergic synapses are shown in *Table 4.4*.

TABLE 4.4	Some Drugs That Affect Dopaminergic Synapses	
Effect of Drug	**Name of Drug**	**Effect on Synaptic Transmission**
Facilitate synthesis of DA	L-DOPA	Agonist
Inhibit synthesis of DA	AMPT	Antagonist
Inhibit storage of DA in synaptic vesicles	Reserpine	Antagonist
Block D_2 receptors	Chlorpromazine	Antagonist
Block D_4 receptors	Clozapine	Antagonist
Block dopamine reuptake	Cocaine	Agonist
Block MAO-B	Deprenyl	Agonist

Chlorpromazine (*klor proh ma zeen*) A drug that reduces the symptoms of schizophrenia by blocking dopamine D_2 receptors.

Clozapine (*kloz a peen*) A drug that reduces the symptoms of schizophrenia, apparently by blocking dopamine D_4 receptors.

Norepinephrine

Because **norepinephrine (NE),** like ACh, is found in neurons in the autonomic nervous system, this neurotransmitter has also received much experimental attention. Note that *adrenaline* and *epinephrine* are synonymous, as are *noradrenaline* and *norepinephrine*. **Epinephrine** is a hormone produced by the adrenal medulla, the central core of the adrenal glands, located just above the kidneys. Epinephrine also serves as a neurotransmitter in the brain, but it is of minor importance compared with norepinephrine. *Ad renal* is Latin for "toward kidney." In Greek, one would say *epi nephron* ("upon the kidney"), hence the term *epinephrine*. The latter term has been adopted by pharmacologists, probably because the word *Adrenalin* was appropriated by a drug company as a proprietary name; therefore, to be consistent with general usage, I will refer to the neurotransmitter as *norepinephrine*. The accepted adjectival form is *noradrenergic;* I suppose that *norepinephrinergic* never caught on because it takes so long to pronounce.

We have already seen the biosynthetic pathway for norepinephrine in Figure 4.8. The drug **fusaric acid,** which prevents the conversion of dopamine to norepinephrine, blocks the production of NE.

Almost every region of the brain receives input from noradrenergic neurons. The cell bodies of most of these neurons are located in seven regions of the pons and medulla and one region of the thalamus. The cell bodies of the most important noradrenergic system begin in the **locus coeruleus,** a nucleus located in the dorsal pons. The axons of these neurons project to widespread regions of the brain. As we will see in Chapter 8, one effect of activation of these neurons is an increase in vigilance—attentiveness to events in the environment.

Most neurons that release norepinephrine do not do so through terminal buttons on the ends of axonal branches. Instead, they usually release them through **axonal varicosities,** beadlike swellings of the axonal branches. These varicosities give the axonal branches of catecholaminergic neurons the appearance of beaded chains.

There are several types of noradrenergic receptors, identified by their differing sensitivities to various drugs. Actually, these receptors are usually called *adrenergic* receptors rather than *noradrenergic* receptors, because they are sensitive to epinephrine (Adrenalin) as well as norepinephrine. Neurons in the central nervous system contain β_1- and β_2-*adrenergic receptors* and α_1- and α_2-*adrenergic receptors*. All four kinds of receptors are also found in various organs of the body besides the brain and are responsible for the effects of the catecholamines when they act as hormones outside the central nervous system.

Some of the more important drugs that affect noradrenergic synapses are listed in *Table 4.5*.

Norepinephrine (NE) (*nor epp i neff rin*) One of the catecholamines; a neurotransmitter found in the brain and in the sympathetic division of the autonomic nervous system.

Epinephrine (*epp i neff rin*) One of the catecholamines; a hormone secreted by the adrenal medulla; serves also as a neurotransmitter in the brain.

Fusaric acid (*few sahr ik*) A drug that inhibits the activity of the enzyme that converts dopamine to norepinephrine and thus blocks the production of norepinephrine.

Locus coeruleus (*sur oo lee us*) A dark-colored group of noradrenergic cell bodies located in the pons near the rostral end of the floor of the fourth ventricle.

Axonal varicosities Enlarged regions along the length of an axon that contain synaptic vesicles and release a neurotransmitter or neuromodulator.

TABLE 4.5	Some Drugs That Affect Noradrenergic Synapses	
Effect of Drug	**Name of Drug**	**Effect on Synaptic Transmission**
Inhibit synthesis of NE	Fusaric acid	Antagonist
Inhibit storage of NE in synaptic vesicles	Reserpine	Antagonist
Stimulate α_1 receptors	Phenylephrine	Agonist
Stimulate α_2 receptors	Clonidine	Agonist
Block α_2 receptors	Yohimbine	Antagonist
Inhibit reuptake of NE	Desipramine	Agonist

Serotonin

The third monoamine neurotransmitter, **serotonin** (also called **5-HT,** or 5-hydroxy-tryptamine), has also received much experimental attention. Its behavioral effects are complex. Serotonin plays a role in the regulation of mood; in the control of eating, sleep, and arousal; and in the regulation of pain. Serotonergic neurons are involved somehow in the control of dreaming.

The precursor for serotonin is the amino acid *tryptophan*. An enzyme converts tryptophan to *5-HTP* (5-hydroxytryptophan). Another enzyme converts 5-HTP to 5-HT (serotonin). (See *Figure 4.10.*) The drug **PCPA** (*p*-chlorophenylalanine) blocks the conversion of tyrosine to 5-HTP and thus serves as a serotonergic antagonist.

The cell bodies of serotonergic neurons are found in nine clusters, most of which are located in the raphe nuclei of the midbrain, pons, and medulla. The two most important clusters are found in the dorsal and medial raphe nuclei, and I will restrict my discussion to these clusters. The word *raphe* means "seam," or "crease," and refers to the fact that most of the raphe nuclei are found at or near the midline of the brain stem. Both the dorsal and median raphe nuclei project axons to the cerebral cortex. In addition, neurons in the dorsal raphe innervate the basal ganglia, and those in the median raphe innervate the dentate gyrus, a part of the hippocampal formation.

Like norepinephrine, 5-HT is released from varicosities rather than terminal buttons. Investigators have identified at least nine different types of serotonin receptors. Pharmacologists have discovered drugs that serve as agonists or antagonists for some, but not all, of the types of 5-HT receptors.

Drugs that inhibit the reuptake of serotonin have found a very important place in the treatment of mental disorders. The most popular of these, **fluoxetine** (Prozac), is used to treat depression, some forms of anxiety disorders, and obsessive-compulsive disorder. These disorders—and their treatment—are discussed in Chapter 15. Another drug, **fenfluramine,** which causes the release of serotonin as well as inhibits its reuptake, has been used as an appetite suppressant in the treatment of obesity. Fenfluramine is usually prescribed in combination with phentermine, a drug that acts on catecholamines. This drug has appetite suppressing effects of its own and also counteracts the drowsiness caused by fenfluramine. (Because of questions about possible serious side-effects, the U.S. Food and Drug Administration took fenfluramine off the market.) Chapter 11 discusses the topic of obesity.

Several hallucinogenic drugs appear to produce their effects by interacting with serotonergic transmission. **LSD** (lysergic acid diethylamide) produces distortions of visual perceptions that some people find awesome and fascinating but that simply frighten other people. This drug, which is effective in extremely small doses, has many sites of action in the brain. For years, researchers thought that its behavioral effects were produced by the stimulation of 5-HT autoreceptors located on somatic and dendritic membranes in the raphe nuclei. In this role, LSD acts as a serotonin antagonist. However, more recent studies have concluded that LSD is also a direct agonist for a particular postsynaptic 5-HT receptor found in the forebrain (the 5-HT$_{2A}$ receptor) and that this action is responsible for the behavioral effects of the drug. Other drugs that act as 5-HT$_{2A}$ agonists also have hallucinogenic effects.

Some of the more important drugs that affect serotonergic synapses are listed in *Table 4.6.*

Amino Acids

So far, all of the neurotransmitters I have described are synthesized within neurons: acetylcholine from choline, the catecholamines from the amino acid tyrosine, and serotonin from the amino acid tryptophan. In addition, some neurons secrete simple amino acids as neurotransmitters. Because amino acids are used for protein synthesis by all cells of the brain, it is difficult to prove that a particular amino acid is a

Tryptophan

Enzyme

5-hydroxytryptophan (5-HTP)

Enzyme

5-hydroxytryptamine (5-HT, or serotonin)

FIGURE 4.10

Biosynthesis of serotonin (5-hydroxytryptamine, or 5-HT).

Serotonin (5-HT) (*sair a toe nin*) An indolamine neurotransmitter; also called 5-hydroxytryptamine.

PCPA A drug that inhibits the activity of tryptophan hydroxylase and thus interferes with the synthesis of 5-HT.

Fluoxetine (*floo ox i teen*) A drug that inhibits the reuptake of 5-HT.

Fenfluramine (*fen floor i meen*) A drug that stimulates the release of 5-HT.

LSD A drug that stimulates 5-HT$_{2A}$ receptors.

TABLE 4.6	Some Drugs That Affect Serotonergic Synapses		
Effect of Drug		**Name of Drug**	**Effect on Synaptic Transmission**
Inhibit synthesis of 5-HT		PCPA	Antagonist
Inhibit storage of 5-HT in synaptic vesicles		Reserpine	Antagonist
Stimulate release of 5-HT		Fenfluramine	Agonist
Inhibit reuptake of 5-HT		Fluoxetine	Agonist

neurotransmitter. However, investigators suspect that at least eight amino acids may serve as neurotransmitters in the mammalian central nervous system (CNS). As we saw in the introduction to this section, three of them are especially important because they are the most common neurotransmitters in the CNS: glutamate, gamma-aminobutyric acid (GABA), and glycine.

Glutamate

Because **glutamate** (also called *glutamic acid*) and gamma-aminobutyric acid (GABA) are found in very simple organisms, many investigators believe that these neurotransmitters are the first to have evolved. Besides producing postsynaptic potentials by activating postsynaptic receptors, they also have direct excitatory effects (glutamic acid) and inhibitory effects (GABA) on axons; they raise or lower the threshold of excitation, thus affecting the rate at which action potentials occur. These direct effects suggest that these substances had a general modulating role even before the evolutionary development of specific receptor molecules.

Glutamate is the principal excitatory neurotransmitter in the brain and spinal cord. It is produced in abundance by the cells' metabolic processes. There is no effective way to prevent its synthesis without disrupting other activities of the cell.

Investigators have discovered four types of glutamate receptors. Three of these receptors are ionotropic and are named after the artificial ligands that stimulate them: the **NMDA receptor,** the **AMPA receptor,** and the **kainate receptor.** The other glutamate receptor—the **metabotropic receptor**—is (obviously!) metabotropic. Actually, there appear to be at least seven different metabotropic receptors, but little is known about their functions except that some of them serve as presynaptic autoreceptors. The AMPA receptor is the most common glutamate receptor. It controls a sodium channel, so when glutamate attaches to the binding site, it produces EPSPs. The kainate receptor has similar effects.

The NMDA receptor has some special—and very important—characteristics. It contains at least six different binding sites, four located on the exterior of the receptor, and two located deep within the ion channel. When it is open, the ion channel controlled by the NMDA receptor permits both sodium and calcium ions to enter the cell. The influx of both of these ions causes a depolarization, of course, but the entry of calcium (Ca^{2+}) is especially important. Calcium serves as a second messenger, binding with—and activating—various enzymes within the cell. These enzymes have profound effects on the biochemical and structural properties of the cell. As we shall see, one important result is alteration in the characteristics of the synapse that provide one of the building blocks of a newly formed memory. These effects of NMDA receptors will be discussed in much more detail in Chapter 12.

One of the six binding sites on the NMDA receptor is sensitive to alcohol. In fact, as we will see in Chapter 14, researchers believe that this binding site is responsible

Glutamate An amino acid; the most important excitatory neurotransmitter in the brain.

NMDA receptor A specialized ionotropic glutamate receptor that controls a calcium channel that is normally blocked by Mg^{2+} ions; has several other binding sites.

AMPA receptor An ionotropic glutamate receptor that controls a sodium channel; stimulated by AMPA.

Kainate receptor (*kay in ate*) An ionotropic glutamate receptor that controls a sodium channel; stimulated by kainic acid.

Metabotropic receptor (*meh tab a troh pik*) A metabotropic glutamate receptor.

for the dangerous convulsions that can be caused by sudden withdrawal from heavy, long-term alcohol abuse. Another binding site is sensitive to a hallucinogenic drug, **PCP** (phencyclidine, also known as "angel dust"). When PCP attaches to its binding site, calcium ions cannot pass through the ion channel; thus, PCP serves as an antagonist. PCP is a synthetic drug and is not produced by the brain. Thus, it is not the natural ligand of the PCP binding site. What that ligand is and what useful functions it serves are not yet known.

Several drugs affect glutamatergic synapses. As you already know, NMDA, AMPA, and kainate serve as direct agonists at the receptors named after them.

GABA

GABA (gamma-aminobutyric acid) is produced from glutamic acid by the action of an enzyme. GABA is an inhibitory neurotransmitter, and it appears to have a widespread distribution throughout the brain and spinal cord. Two GABA receptors have been identified: $GABA_A$ and $GABA_B$. The $GABA_A$ receptor is ionotropic and controls a chloride channel; the $GABA_B$ receptor is metabotropic and controls a potassium channel.

As you know, neurons in the brain are greatly interconnected. Without the activity of inhibitory synapses these interconnections would make the brain unstable. That is, through excitatory synapses, neurons would excite their neighbors, which would then excite *their* neighbors, which would then excite the originally active neurons, and so on, until most of the neurons in the brain would be firing uncontrollably. In fact, this event does sometimes occur, and we refer to it as a *seizure. Epilepsy* is a neurological disorder characterized by the presence of seizures. Normally, an inhibitory influence is supplied by GABA-secreting neurons, which are present in large numbers in the brain. Some investigators believe that one of the causes of epilepsy is an abnormality in the biochemistry of GABA-secreting neurons or in GABA receptors.

Like NMDA receptors, $GABA_A$ receptors are complex; they contain at least five different binding sites. The primary binding site is, of course, for GABA. A second site on the $GABA_A$ receptor binds with a class of tranquilizing drugs called the **benzodiazepines.** These drugs include diazepam (Valium) and chlordiazepoxide (Librium), which are used to reduce anxiety, promote sleep, reduce seizure activity, and produce muscle relaxation. The third site binds with barbiturates. The fourth site binds with various steroids, including some steroids used to produce general anesthesia. The fifth site binds with picrotoxin, a poison found in an East Indian shrub. In addition, alcohol binds with one of these sites—probably the benzodiazepine binding site. (See *Figure 4.11.*)

Barbiturates, drugs that bind to the steroid site, and benzodiazepines all promote the activity of the $GABA_A$ receptor; thus, all these drugs serve as agonists. The benzodiazepines are very effective **anxiolytics,** or "anxiety-dissolving" drugs. They are often used to treat people with anxiety disorders. In addition, some benzodiazepines serve as effective sleep medications, and others are used to treat some types of seizure disorder.

In low doses, barbiturates have a calming effect. In progressively higher doses they produce difficulty in walking and talking, unconsciousness, coma, and death. Although veterinarians sometimes use barbiturates to produce anesthesia for surgery, the therapeutic index—the ratio between a dose that produces anesthesia and

PCP Phencyclidine; a drug that binds with the PCP binding site of the NMDA receptor and serves as an antagonist.

GABA Gamma-aminobutyric acid, an amino acid; the most important inhibitory neurotransmitter in the brain.

Benzodiazepine [*ben zoe dy azz a peen*] A category of anxiolytic drugs; an indirect agonist for the $GABA_A$ receptor.

Anxiolytic [*angz ee oh lit ik*] An anxiety-reducing effect.

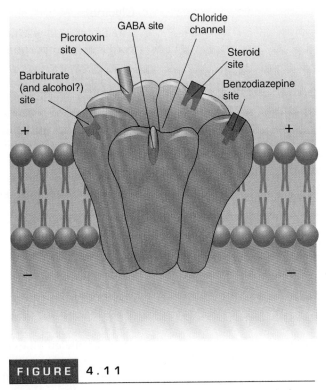

FIGURE 4.11

A schematic illustration of a $GABA_A$ receptor, with its binding sites.

one that causes fatal depression of the respiratory centers of the brain—is small. As a consequence, these drugs are rarely used by themselves to produce surgical anesthesia in humans.

Picrotoxin has effects opposite to those of benzodiazepines and barbiturates: It *inhibits* the activity of the GABA$_A$ receptor. In high enough doses, this drug causes convulsions.

Various steroid hormones are normally produced in the body, and some hormones related to progesterone (the principal pregnancy hormone) act on the steroid binding site of the GABA$_A$ receptor, producing a sedative effect. However, the brain does not produce Valium, barbiturates, or picrotoxin. What are the natural ligands for these binding sites? So far, most research has concentrated on the benzodiazepine binding site. These binding sites are more complex than the others. They can be activated by drugs such as the benzodiazepines, which promote the activity of the receptor and thus serve as agonists. They can also be activated by other drugs that have the opposite effect—that inhibit the activity of the receptor, thus serving as antagonists.

There is good evidence that a chemical produced by the brain, **β-CCM,** serves as a natural ligand for the benzodiazepine binding site. β-CCM (known by chemists as methyl-β-carboline-3-carboxylate) acts as an antagonist. Thus, its behavioral effects are fear, tension, and anxiety, which are just the opposite of those of the benzodiazepines. Perhaps, some investigators believe, β-CCM or other neuromodulators are released in times of danger and motivate an animal to perform behaviors that will permit it to escape or defend itself. Whether the brain also produces chemicals that act as indirect agonists, as the benzodiazepines do, is not yet known.

What about the GABA$_B$ receptor? This metabotropic receptor serves as both a postsynaptic receptor and a presynaptic autoreceptor. A GABA$_B$ agonist, baclofen, serves as a muscle relaxant. The activation of GABA$_B$ receptors opens potassium channels, producing hyperpolarizing inhibitory postsynaptic potentials.

Glycine

The amino acid **glycine** appears to be the inhibitory neurotransmitter in the spinal cord and lower portions of the brain. Little is known about its biosynthetic pathway; there are several possible routes, but not enough is known to decide how neurons produce glycine. The bacteria that cause tetanus (lockjaw) release a chemical that prevents the release of glycine (and GABA as well). The removal of the inhibitory effect of these synapses causes muscles to contract continuously.

The glycine receptor is ionotropic, and it controls a chloride channel. Thus, when it is active, it produces inhibitory postsynaptic potentials. The drug **strychnine,** an alkaloid found in the seeds of the *Strychnos nux vomica,* a tree found in India, serves as a glycine agonist. Strychnine is very toxic, and even relatively small doses cause convulsions and death. No drugs have yet been found that serve as specific glycine antagonists.

Peptides

Recent studies have discovered that the neurons of the central nervous system release a large variety of peptides. Peptides consist of two or more amino acids, linked together by peptide bonds. All the peptides that have been studied so far are produced from precursor molecules. These precursors are large polypeptides that are broken into pieces by special enzymes. A neuron manufactures both the polypeptides and the enzymes that it needs to break them apart in the right places. The appropriate sections are retained, and the other ones are destroyed. Because the synthesis of peptides takes place in the soma, vesicles containing these chemicals must be delivered to the terminal buttons by axoplasmic transport.

Peptides are released from all parts of the terminal button, not just from the active zone; thus, only a portion of the molecules are released into the synaptic cleft.

β-CCM A direct agonist for the benzodiazepine binding site of the GABA$_A$ receptor.

Glycine (*gly seen*) An amino acid; an important inhibitory neurotransmitter in the lower brain stem and spinal cord.

Strychnine (*strik neen*) A direct agonist for the glycine receptor.

The rest presumably act on receptors belonging to other cells in the vicinity. Once released, peptides are deactivated by enzymes. There is no mechanism for reuptake and recycling of peptides.

Several different peptides are released by neurons. Although most peptides appear to serve as neuromodulators, some act as neurotransmitters. One of the most important families of peptides is the **endogenous opioids.** (*Endogenous* means "produced from within"; *opioid* means "like opium.") Several years ago it became clear that opiates (drugs such as opium, morphine, and heroin) reduce pain because they have direct effects on the brain. (Please note that the term *opioid* refers to endogenous chemicals, and *opiate* refers to drugs.) Pert, Snowman, and Snyder (1974) discovered that neurons in a localized region of the brain contain specialized receptors that respond to opiates. Then, soon after the discovery of the opiate receptor, other neuroscientists discovered the natural ligands for these receptors (Terenius and Wahlström, 1975; Hughes et al., 1975), which they called **enkephalins** (from the Greek word *enkephalos*, "in the head"). We now know that the enkephalins are members of a family of endogenous opioid peptides, all of which are synthesized from one of three large peptides that serve as precursors. In addition, we know that there are at least three different types of opiate receptors: μ (mu), δ (delta), and κ (kappa).

Several different neural systems are activated when opiate receptors are stimulated. One type produces analgesia, another inhibits species-typical defensive responses such as fleeing and hiding, and another stimulates a system of neurons involved in reinforcement ("reward"). The last effect explains why opiates are often abused. The situations that cause neurons to secrete endogenous opioids are discussed in Chapter 7, and the brain mechanisms of opiate addiction are discussed in Chapter 16.

So far, pharmacologists have developed only two types of drugs that affect neural communication by means of opioids: direct agonists and antagonists. Many synthetic opiates, including heroin (dihydromorphine) and Percodan (levorphanol), have been developed and are used clinically as analgesics. Several drugs that block opiate receptors have also been developed. One of them, **naloxone,** is used clinically to reverse opiate intoxication. This drug has saved the lives of many drug abusers who would otherwise have died of an overdose of heroin. And as we saw earlier in this chapter, naloxone was used to demonstrate that the administration of a placebo can cause analgesia by triggering the release of endogenous opioids.

Several peptide hormones are also found in the brain, where they serve as neurotransmitters or neuromodulators. In some cases, the peripheral and the central peptides perform related functions (Panksepp, 1991). For example, outside the nervous system the hormone angiotensin acts directly on the kidneys and blood vessels to produce effects that help the body cope with the loss of fluid. Inside the nervous system, circuits of neurons that use angiotensin as a neurotransmitter perform similar functions, including the activation of neural circuits that produce thirst.

Lipids

Various substances derived from lipids can serve to transmit messages within or between cells. One of them appears to be the natural ligand for the THC receptor, which is responsible for the physiological effects of the active ingredient in marijuana. Matsuda et al. (1990) discovered that THC (tetrahydrocannibinol, the active ingredient of marijuana) stimulates specific receptors in specific regions of the brain. (See *Figure 4.12.*) THC produces analgesia and sedation, stimulates appetite, reduces nausea caused by drugs used to treat cancer, relieves asthma attacks, decreases pressure within the eyes in patients with glaucoma, and reduces the symptoms of certain motor disorders. On the other hand, THC interferes with concentration and memory, alters visual and auditory perception, and distorts perceptions of the pas-

Endogenous opioid (*en **dodge** en us **oh** pee oyd*) A class of peptides secreted by the brain that act as opiates.

Enkephalin (*en **keff** a lin*) One of the endogenous opioids.

Naloxone (*na **lox** own*) A drug that blocks opiate receptors.

FIGURE 4.12

An autoradiogram of a sagittal section of a rat brain that has been incubated in a solution containing a radioactive ligand for THC receptors. The receptors are indicated by dark areas. (Autoradiography is described in Chapter 5.) (Br St = brain stem, Cer = cerebellum, CP = caudate nucleus/putamen, Cx = cortex, EP = entopeduncular nucleus, GP = globus pallidus, Hipp = hippocampus, SNr = substantia nigra.)

(Courtesy of Miles Herkenham, National Institute of Mental Health, Bethesda, MD.)

Anandamide (*a nan da mide*) A lipid; the endogenous ligand for receptors that bind with THC, the active ingredient of marijuana.

Adenosine (*a den oh seen*) A nucleoside; a combination of ribose and adenine; serves as a neuromodulator in the brain.

Caffeine A drug that blocks adenosine receptors.

Nitric oxide (NO) A gas produced by cells in the nervous system; used as a means of communication between cells.

sage of time. Devane et al. (1992) discovered what appears to be the natural ligand for the THC receptor: a lipidlike substance that they named **anandamide,** from the Sanskrit word *ananda,* or "bliss." Researchers have not yet found how it is released or what physiological functions it performs.

Nucleosides

A nucleoside is a compound that consists of a sugar molecule bound with a purine or pyrimidine base. One of these compounds, **adenosine** (a combination of ribose and adenine), serves as a neuromodulator in the brain.

Adenosine is known to be released, apparently by glial cells as well as neurons, when cells are short of fuel or oxygen. The release of adenosine activates receptors on nearby blood vessels and causes them to dilate, increasing the flow of blood and helping bring more fuel and oxygen to the region. Adenosine also acts as a neuromodulator, through its action on at least three different types of adenosine receptors. Adenosine receptors are metabotropic, and the effect of their activation is to open potassium channels, producing inhibitory postsynaptic potentials. Because adenosine is present in all cells, investigators have not yet succeeded in distinguishing neurons that release this chemical as a neuromodulator. Thus, circuits of adenosinergic neurons have not yet been identified.

Because adenosine receptors suppress neural activity, adenosine and other adenosine receptor agonists have generally inhibitory effects on behavior. In fact, as we will see in Chapter 8, some investigators believe that adenosine receptors may be involved in the control of sleep. A very common drug, **caffeine,** blocks adenosine receptors and hence produces excitatory effects. Caffeine is a bitter-tasting alkaloid found in coffee, tea, cocoa beans, and other plants. In much of the world, a majority of the adult population ingests caffeine every day—without apparent harm.

Prolonged use of caffeine leads to a moderate amount of tolerance, and people who suddenly stop taking caffeine complain of withdrawal symptoms, which include headaches, drowsiness, and difficulty in concentrating. If the person continues to abstain, the symptoms disappear within a few days. Caffeine does not produce the compulsive drug-taking behavior often seen in people who abuse amphetamine, cocaine, or the opiates. In addition, laboratory animals do not readily self-administer caffeine, as they do drugs that are commonly abused by humans.

Soluble Gases

Recently, investigators have discovered that neurons use at least two simple, soluble gases—nitric oxide and carbon monoxide—to communicate with one another. One of these, **nitric oxide (NO),** has received the most attention. Nitric oxide (not to be confused with nitrous oxide, or laughing gas) is a soluble gas that is produced by the activity of an enzyme found in certain neurons. Researchers have found that NO is used as a messenger in many parts of the body. For example, it is involved in the control of the muscles in the wall of the intestines, it dilates blood vessels in regions of the brain that become metabolically active, and it stimulates the changes in blood vessels that produce penile erections (Culotta and Koshland, 1992). As we will see in Chapter 12, it may also play a role in the establishment of neural changes that are produced by learning. And as we will see in Chapter 14, nitric oxide has also been implicated in the brain degeneration that accompanies Huntington's chorea, a hereditary disorder.

All of the neurotransmitters and neuromodulators discussed so far (with the exception of anandamide and, perhaps, adenosine) are stored in synaptic vesicles and released by terminal buttons. In contrast, nitric oxide is produced in several regions of a nerve cell—including dendrites—and is released as soon as it is produced. More accurately, it diffuses out of the cell as soon as it is produced. It does not activate membrane-bound receptors but enters neighboring cells, where it activates an enzyme responsible for the production of a second messenger, cyclic GMP. Within a few seconds of being produced, nitric oxide is converted into biologically inactive compounds.

INTERIM SUMMARY

The nervous system contains a variety of neurotransmitters, each of which interacts with a specialized receptor. Those that have received the most study are acetylcholine and the monoamines: dopamine, norepinephrine, and 5-hydroxytryptamine (serotonin). The synthesis of these neurotransmitters is controlled by a series of enzymes. Several amino acids also serve as neurotransmitters, the most important of which are glutamate (glutamic acid), GABA, and glycine. Glutamate serves as an excitatory neurotransmitter; the others serve as inhibitory neurotransmitters.

Peptide neurotransmitters consist of chains of amino acids. The best known class of peptides in the nervous system includes the endogenous opioids, whose effects are mimicked by drugs such as opium and heroin. One lipid appears to serve as a chemical messenger: anandamide, the endogenous ligand for the THC (marijuana) receptor. Adenosine, a nucleoside that has inhibitory effects on synaptic transmission, is released by neurons and glial cells in the brain. In addition, two soluble gases—nitric oxide and carbon monoxide—can diffuse out of the cell in which they are produced and trigger the production of a second messenger in adjacent cells.

EPILOGUE Helpful Hints from a Tragedy

The discovery that MPTP damages the brain and causes the symptoms of Parkinson's disease galvanized researchers interested in the disease. The first step was to find out whether the drug would have the same effect in laboratory animals so that the details of the process could be studied. It did; Langston et al. (1984) found that injections of MPTP produced parkinsonian symptoms in squirrel monkeys and that these symptoms could be reduced by L-DOPA therapy. And just as the investigators had hoped, examination of the animals' brains showed a selective loss of dopamine-secreting neurons in the substantia nigra.

It turns out that MPTP itself does not cause neural damage; instead, the drug is converted by an enzyme present in glial cells into another substance, MPP+. *That* chemical is taken up by dopamine-secreting neurons, by means of the reuptake mechanism that normally retrieves dopamine that is released by terminal buttons. MPP+ accumulates in mitochondria in these cells and blocks their ability to metabolize nutrients, thus killing the cells (Maret et al., 1990). The enzyme that converts MPTP into MPP+ is none other than monoamine oxidase (MAO), which, as you already know, is responsible for deactivating excess amounts of monoamines present in terminal buttons. Because pharmacologists had already developed MAO inhibitors, Langston and his colleagues decided to see whether one of these drugs (pargyline) would protect squirrel monkeys from the toxic effects of MPTP by preventing its conversion into MPP+ (Langston et al., 1984). It worked; when MAO was inhibited by pargyline, MPTP injections had no effects.

These results made researchers wonder whether MAO inhibitors might possibly protect against the degeneration of dopamine-secreting neurons in patients with Parkinson's disease. No one thought that Parkinson's disease was caused by MPP+, but perhaps some other toxins were involved. Epidemiologists have found that Parkinson's disease is more common in highly industrialized countries, which suggests that environmental toxins produced in these societies may be responsible for the brain damage (Tanner, 1989). Fortunately, several MAO inhibitors have

(continued)

EPILOGUE *(continued)*

been tested and approved for use in humans. One of them, deprenyl, is a specific blocker of the form of MAO responsible for the conversion of MPTP into MPP⁺. (It is normally used to treat high blood pressure.) In a controlled, double-blind study of fifty-four patients with Parkinson's disease, Tetrud and Langston (1989) found that deprenyl slowed down the progression of neurological symptoms by up to 83 percent. No adverse side effects were seen.

As a result of this study, many neurologists are now treating their Parkinson's patients with deprenyl, as well as with L-DOPA. The benefits of this treatment have probably already paid for all of the research that led to this discovery; in the United States alone, each week that patients with Parkin-

son's disease can continue working saves $10 million dollars in taxes and disability payments (Lewin, 1989).

Deprenyl is the first drug that has been found to retard the progress of a degenerative disease. Many researchers believe that Parkinson's disease is not the only one that will respond to such treatment; other degenerative neurological diseases such as amyotrophic lateral sclerosis may involve an accumulation of toxic chemicals that are similar in their action to MPP⁺. Even normal aging may involve such accumulation; if so, there is hope of finding ways to slow down the ravages of time on our brains. And the story gets better yet. Knoll, Dallo, and Yen (1989) found that deprenyl increases rats' longevity. Rats that received injections of deprenyl three

times a week lived about 45 weeks longer, on the average, than rats that received control injections of saline. (Rats have a normal life span of about 3.5 years, so an increase of 45 weeks is quite substantial.) In addition, unlike the control animals, the deprenyl-treated rats continued to be sexually active in their old age.

These findings have been replicated and have been extended to hamsters (Stoll et al., 1994; Knoll, 1997; Bickford et al., 1997). We do not yet know why the animals lived longer, and, of course, we cannot conclude that similar results will be obtained with humans. Still, I have no doubt that other researchers will find such results sufficiently interesting to follow up on them. Who among us is not hoping that they will succeed?

KEY CONCEPTS

PRINCIPLES OF PSYCHOPHARMACOLOGY

1. Pharmacokinetics is the process by which drugs are absorbed, distributed within the body, metabolized, and excreted.
2. Drugs can act at several different sites and have several different effects. The effectiveness of a drug is the magnitude of the effects of a given quantity of the drug.
3. A drug's therapeutic index is its margin of safety: the difference between an effective dose and a dose that produces toxic side effects.
4. When a drug is administered repeatedly, it often produces tolerance, and withdrawal effects often occur when the drug is discontinued. Sometimes, repeated administration of a drug causes sensitization.
5. Placebo effects of inert substances actually involve physiological changes in the brain.

SITES OF DRUG ACTION

6. Each of the steps involved in synaptic transmission can be interfered with by drugs, and some can be facilitated. These steps include synthesis of the neurotransmitter, storage in synaptic vesicles, release, activation of postsynaptic and presynaptic receptors, and termination of postsynaptic potentials through reuptake or enzymatic deactivation.

NEUROTRANSMITTERS AND NEUROMODULATORS

7. Neurons use a variety of chemicals as neurotransmitters, including acetylcholine, the monoamines (dopamine, norepinephrine, and 5-HT), the amino acids (glutamic acid, GABA, and glycine), various peptides, lipids, nucleosides, and soluble gases.

SUGGESTED READINGS

Cooper, J.R., Bloom, F.E., and Roth, R.H. *The Biochemical Basis of Neuropharmacology*, 7th ed. New York: Oxford University Press, 1996.

Feldman, R.S., Meyer, J.S., and Quenzer, L.F. *Principles of Neuropsychopharmacology*. Sunderland, MA: Sinauer Associates, 1997.

Grilly, D.M. *Drugs and Human Behavior*. Boston: Allyn and Bacon, 1994.

5

Methods and Strategies of Research

LEARNING OBJECTIVES

1. Discuss the research method of experimental ablation: the rationale, the evaluation of behavioral effects resulting from brain damage, and the production of brain lesions.

2. Describe stereotaxic surgery.

3. Describe research methods for preserving, sectioning, and staining the brain and for studying its parts and interconnections.

4. Describe research methods for tracing efferent and afferent axons and for studying the living human brain.

5. Describe how the neural activity of the brain is measured and recorded, both electrically and chemically.

6. Describe how neural activity in the brain is stimulated, both electrically and chemically.

7. Describe research methods for locating particular neurochemicals, the neurons that produce them, and the receptors that respond to them.

8. Discuss research techniques to identify genetic factors that may influence behavior.

Heart Repaired, Brain Damaged

All her life, Mrs. H. had been active. She had never been particularly athletic, but she and her husband often went hiking and camping with their children when they were young, and they continued to hike and go for bicycle rides after their children left home. Her husband died when she was 60, and even though she no longer rode her bicycle, she enjoyed gardening and walking around the neighborhood with her friends.

A few years later, Mrs. H. was digging in her garden when a sudden pain gripped her chest. She felt as if a hand were squeezing her heart. She gasped and dropped her spade. The pain crept toward her left shoulder and then traveled down her left arm. The sensation was terrifying; she was sure that she was having a heart attack and was going to die. But after a few minutes the pain melted away, and she walked slowly back to her house.

Her physician examined her and performed some tests and later told her that she had not had a heart attack. Her pain was that of angina pectoris, caused by insufficient flow of blood to the heart. Some of her coronary arteries had become partially obstructed with atherosclerotic plaque—cholesterol-containing deposits on the walls of the blood vessels. Her efforts in her garden had increased her heart rate, and as a consequence, the metabolic activity of her heart muscle had also increased. Her clogged coronary arteries simply could not keep up with the demand, and the accumulation of metabolic byproducts caused intense pain. Her physician cautioned her to avoid unnecessary exertion and prescribed nitroglycerine tablets to place under her tongue if another attack occurred.

Mrs. H. stopped working in her garden but continued to walk around the neighborhood with her friends. Then one evening, while climbing the stairs to get ready for bed, she felt another attack grip her heart. With difficulty, she made her way to her bathroom cabinet, where she found her nitroglycerine tablets. Fumbling with the childproof cap, she extracted a tablet and placed it under her tongue. As the tablet dissolved and the nitroglycerine entered her bloodstream, she felt the tightness in her chest loosen, and she stumbled to her bed.

Over the next year the frequency and intensity of Mrs. H.'s attacks increased. Finally, the specialist to whom her physician had referred her recommended that she consider having a coronary artery bypass performed. She readily agreed. The surgeon, Dr. G., replaced two of her coronary arteries with sections of vein that he had removed from her leg. During the procedure, an artificial heart took over the pumping of her blood so that the surgeon could cut out the diseased section of the arteries and delicately sew in the replacements.

Several days later, Dr. G. visited Mrs. H. in her hospital room. "How are you feeling, Mrs. H?"

"I'm feeling fine," she said, "but I'm having trouble with my vision. Everything looks so confusing, and I feel disoriented. I can't . . . "

"Don't worry," he cut in. "It's normal to feel confused after such serious surgery. Your tests look fine, and we don't expect a recurrence of your angina. You should be good for many years!" He flashed a broad smile at her and left the room.

But Mrs. H.'s visual problems and her confusion did not get better. Although the surgeon's notes indicated a successful outcome, her family physician saw that something was wrong and asked Dr. J., a neuropsychologist, to evaluate her. Dr. J.'s report confirmed his fears Mrs. H. had Balint's syndrome. She could still see, but she could not control her eye movements. The world confused her because she saw only fleeting, fragmentary images. She could no longer read, and she could no longer locate and grasp objects in front of her. In short, her vision was almost useless. Her heart was fine, but she would henceforth have to live in a nursing home, where others could care for her.

Study of the physiology of behavior involves the efforts of scientists in many disciplines, including physiology, neuroanatomy, biochemistry, psychology, endocrinology, and histology. Pursuing a research project in physiological psychology requires competence in many experimental techniques. Because different procedures often produce contradictory results, investigators must be familiar with the advantages and limitations of the methods they employ. Scientific investigation entails a process of asking questions of nature. The research method that is used frames the question. Often we receive a puzzling answer, only to realize later that we were not asking the question we thought we were. As we will see, the best conclusions about the physiology of behavior are made not by any single experiment, but by a program of research that enables us to compare the results of studies that approach the problem with a variety of research methods.

An enormous—and bewildering—array of research methods is available to the investigator. If I merely presented a catalog of them, it would not be surprising if you got lost or simply lost interest. Instead, I will present only the most important and commonly used procedures, organized around a few problems that researchers have studied. This way, it should be easier to see the types of information that various research methods provide and to understand their advantages and disadvantages. It will also permit me to describe the strategies that researchers use as they follow up the results of one experiment by designing and executing another one.

EXPERIMENTAL ABLATION

One of the most common research methods used to investigate brain functions involves destroying part of an animal's brain and evaluating the animal's subsequent behavior. This method is called **experimental ablation** (from the Latin word *ablatus,* a "carrying away"). In most cases the researcher does not actually remove brain tissue; instead, he or she destroys some tissue and leaves it in place.

Evaluating the Behavioral Effects of Brain Damage

The term *lesion* literally refers to a wound or injury, and a researcher who destroys part of the brain usually refers to the damage as a *brain lesion.* Experiments in which part of the brain is damaged and the animal's behavior is subsequently observed are called **lesion studies.** The logic behind lesion studies is that the function of an area of the brain can be inferred from the behaviors that the animal can no longer perform after the area is damaged. For example, if, after part of the brain is destroyed, an animal can no longer perform tasks that require vision, we can conclude that the animal is blind—and that the damaged area plays some role in vision.

We must be very careful in interpreting the effects of brain lesions. For example, how do we know that the animal is blind? Does it bump into objects, or fail to run through a maze toward a light that signals the location of food, or no longer constrict its pupils in response to light? An animal could bump into objects because of deficits in motor coordination, it could have lost its appetite for food (and thus its motivation to run through the maze), or it could see quite well but could have lost its visual reflexes. Researchers can often be fooled. Years ago, they thought that the albino rat was blind. (It isn't.) Think about it: How would you test whether a rat can see? Remember that rats have whiskers that can be used to detect a wall before bumping into it or the edge of a table before walking off it. They can also find their way around a room by following odor trails.

Just what can we learn from lesion studies? Our goal is to discover what functions are performed by different regions of the brain and then to understand how these functions are combined to accomplish particular behaviors. The distinction between *brain function* and *behavior* is an important one. Circuits of neurons in the brain perform functions, not behaviors. No one brain region or neural circuit is solely responsible for a behavior; each region performs a function (or set of functions) that contributes to performance of the behavior. For example, the act of reading involves functions required for controlling eye movements, focusing the lens of the eye, perceiving and recognizing words and letters, comprehending the meaning of the words, and so on. Some of these functions also participate in other behaviors; for example, controlling eye movement and focusing are required for any task that involves looking, and brain mechanisms used for comprehending the meanings of

Experimental ablation The removal or destruction of a portion of the brain of a laboratory animal; presumably, the functions that can no longer be performed are the ones the region previously controlled.

Lesion study An experimental study in which the behavior of animals with brain lesions is studied.

FIGURE **5.1**

Radio frequency lesion. The arrows point to very
small lesions produced by passing radio frequency
current through the tips of stainless steel electrodes placed in the medial preoptic nucleus of a
rat brain. (Frontal section, cell-body stain.)

*(From Turkenburg, J.L., Swaab, D.F., Endert, E.,
Louwerse, A.L., and van de Poll, N.E. Brain Research
Bulletin, 1988, 21, 215–224.)*

RF lesion A brain lesion produced by passing radio frequency (RF) current through a
fine wire inserted into the brain.

Excitotoxic lesion [ek sigh tow
tok sik] A brain lesion produced
by intracerebral injection of an
excitatory amino acid, such as
kainic acid.

Sham lesion A "placebo" procedure that duplicates all the steps
of producing a brain lesion except for the one that actually
causes the brain damage.

Stereotaxic surgery [*stair ee oh
tak* sik] Brain surgery using a
stereotaxic apparatus to position
an electrode or cannula in a
specified position of the brain.

Bregma The junction of the
sagittal and coronal sutures of
the skull; often used as a reference point for stereotaxic brain
surgery.

Stereotaxic atlas A collection of
drawings of sections of the brain
of a particular animal with measurements that provide coordinates for stereotaxic surgery.

words also participate in comprehending speech. The task of the researcher is to understand the functions that are required for performing a particular behavior and to determine what circuits of
neurons in the brain are responsible for each of these functions.

Producing Brain Lesions

How do we produce brain lesions? To destroy parts of the brain immediately beneath the skull, we anesthetize the animal, cut its scalp,
remove part of its skull, and cut through the dura mater, bringing
the cortex into view. Then we can use a suction device to aspirate the
brain tissue. To accomplish this tissue removal, we place a glass
pipette on the surface of the brain and suck away brain tissue with a
vacuum pump attached to the pipette by a flexible tube.

More often, we want to destroy regions that are hidden away in
the depths of the brain. Brain lesions of subcortical regions (regions
located beneath the cortex) are usually produced by passing electrical current through a stainless steel wire that is coated with an insulating varnish except for the very tip. We guide the wire to the
proper location with a special device described in the next subsection. Then we turn on a lesion-making device, which produces radio
frequency (RF) current—alternating current of a very high frequency. The passage of the current through the brain tissue produces heat that kills cells in the region surrounding the tip of the
electrode. The result is an **RF lesion.** (See *Figure 5.1.*)

Lesions produced by these means destroy everything in the vicinity of the electrode tip, including neural cell bodies and the axons of
neurons that pass through the region. A more selective method of
producing brain lesions employs an excitatory amino acid such as *kainic acid,* which
kills neurons by stimulating them to death. (As we saw in Chapter 4, kainic acid stimulates glutamate receptors.) Lesions produced this way are referred to as **excitotoxic
lesions.** When an excitatory amino acid is injected through a *cannula* (a fine metal
tube) into a region of the brain, the chemical destroys neural cell bodies in the vicinity but spares axons that belong to different neurons that happen to pass nearby.

The selectivity of excitotoxic lesions permits the investigator to determine
whether the behavioral effects of destroying a particular brain structure are caused
by the death of neurons located there or by the destruction of axons that pass nearby.
For example, some researchers discovered that RF lesions of a particular region in
the brain stem abolished REM sleep. (REM sleep is the stage of sleep during which
dreaming occurs.) Thus, they believed that this region was involved in the production of this stage of sleep. But later studies showed that when kainic acid was used to
destroy the neurons located there, the animals' sleep was *not* affected. Thus, the RF
lesions must have altered sleep by destroying the axons that pass through the area.

Note that when we produce subcortical lesions by passing RF current through an
electrode or infusing a chemical through a cannula, we always cause additional damage to the brain. When we pass an electrode or a cannula through the brain to get to
our target, we inevitably cause a small amount of damage even before turning on the
lesion maker or starting the infusion. Thus, we cannot simply compare the behavior
of brain-lesioned animals with that of unoperated control animals; the incidental
damage to the brain regions above the lesion may actually be responsible for some of
the behavioral deficits we see. Instead, we operate on a group of animals and produce
sham lesions. To do so, we anesthetize each animal, cut open the scalp, drill the holes,
insert the electrode or cannula, and lower it to the proper depth. In other words, we
do everything we would do to produce the lesion except turn on the lesion maker or
start the infusion. This group of animals serves as a control group. If the behavior of

the animals with brain lesions is different from that of the sham-operated control animals, we can conclude that the lesions caused the behavioral deficits. (As you can see, a sham lesion serves the same purpose as a placebo does in a pharmacology study.)

Most of the time, investigators produce permanent brain lesions, but sometimes it is advantageous to disrupt the activity of a particular region of the brain temporarily. The easiest way to do so is to inject a local anesthetic into the appropriate part of the brain. The anesthetic blocks action potentials in axons entering or leaving that region, thus effectively producing a temporary lesion, usually called a *reversible* brain lesion.

Stereotaxic Surgery

So how do we get the tip of an electrode or cannula to a precise location in the depths of an animal's brain? The answer is **stereotaxic surgery.** *Stereotaxis* literally means "solid arrangement"; more specifically, it refers to the ability to locate objects in space. A *stereotaxic apparatus* contains a holder that fixes the animal's head in a standard position and a carrier that moves an electrode or a cannula through measured distances in all three axes of space. However, to perform stereotaxic surgery, one must first study a *stereotaxic atlas.*

The Stereotaxic Atlas

No two brains of animals of a given species are completely identical, but there is enough similarity among individuals to predict the location of particular brain structures relative to external features of the head. For instance, a subcortical nucleus of a rat might be so many millimeters ventral, anterior, and lateral to a point formed by the junction of several bones of the skull. Figure 5.2 shows two views of a rat skull: a drawing of the dorsal surface and, beneath it, a midsagittal view. (See *Figure 5.2.*)

The skull is composed of several bones that grow together and form *sutures* (seams). The heads of newborn babies contain a soft spot at the junction of the coronal and sagittal sutures called the *fontanelle.* Once this gap closes, the junction is called **bregma,** from the Greek word meaning "front of head." We can find bregma on a rat's skull, too, and it serves as a convenient reference point. If the animal's skull is oriented as shown in the illustration, a particular region of the brain is found in a fairly constant position, relative to bregma.

A **stereotaxic atlas** contains photographs or drawings that correspond to frontal sections taken at various distances rostral and caudal to bregma. For example, the page shown in Figure 5.3 is a drawing of a slice of the brain that contains a brain structure (shown in red) that we are interested in. If we wanted to place the tip of a wire in this structure (the fornix), we would have to drill a hole through the skull immediately above it. (See *Figure 5.3.*) Each page of the stereotaxic atlas is labeled according to the distance of the section anterior or posterior to bregma. The grid on each page indicates distances of brain structures ventral to the top of the skull and lateral to the midline. To place the tip of a wire in

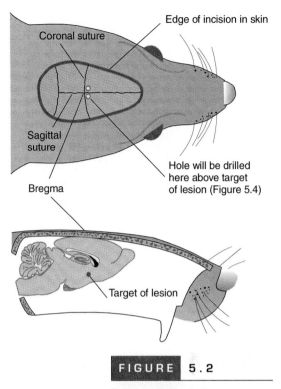

FIGURE 5.2

Relation of the skull sutures to a rat's brain, and the location of a target for an electrode placement. *Top:* Dorsal view. *Bottom:* Midsagittal view.

FIGURE 5.3

A sample page from a stereotaxic atlas of the rat brain. The target (the fornix) is indicated in red. Labels have been removed for the sake of clarity.

[Adapted from Swanson, L.W. Brain Maps: Structure of the Rat Brain. New York: Elsevier, 1992.]

Adjusting knobs

Skull

Electrode in brain

FIGURE 5.4

A stereotaxic apparatus for performing brain surgery on rats.

the fornix, we would drill a hole above the target and then lower the electrode through the hole until the tip was at the correct depth, relative to the skull height at bregma. (See *Figures 5.2* and *5.3.*) Thus, by finding a neural structure (which we cannot see in our animal) on one of the pages of a stereotaxic atlas, we can determine the structure's location relative to bregma (which we can see). Note that, because of variations in different strains and ages of animals, the atlas gives only an approximate location. We always have to try out a new set of coordinates, slice and stain the animal's brain, see the actual location of the lesion, correct the numbers, and try again. (Slicing and staining of brains are described later.)

The Stereotaxic Apparatus

A **stereotaxic apparatus** operates on simple principles. The device includes a head holder, which maintains the animal's skull in the proper orientation, a holder for the electrode, and a calibrated mechanism that moves the electrode holder in measured distances along the three axes: anterior-posterior, dorsal-ventral, and lateral-medial. Figure 5.4 illustrates a stereotaxic apparatus designed for small animals; various head holders can be used to outfit this device for such diverse species as rats, mice, hamsters, pigeons, and turtles. (See *Figure 5.4.*)

Once we obtain the coordinates from a stereotaxic atlas, we anesthetize the animal, place it in the apparatus, and cut the scalp open. We locate bregma, dial in the appropriate numbers on the stereotaxic apparatus, drill a hole through the skull, and lower the device into the brain by the correct amount. Now the tip of the cannula or electrode is where we want it to be, and we are ready to produce the lesion.

Of course, stereotaxic surgery may be used for purposes other than lesion production. Wires placed in the brain may be used to stimulate neurons as well as destroy them, and drugs can be injected that stimulate neurons or block specific receptors. We can attach cannulas or wires permanently by following a procedure that will be described later in this chapter. In all cases, once surgery is complete, the wound is sewed together, and the animal is taken out of the stereotaxic apparatus and allowed to recover from the anesthetic.

Stereotaxic apparatuses are also made for humans, by the way. Sometimes a neurosurgeon produces subcortical lesions—for example, to reduce severe tremors caused by Parkinson's disease. Usually, the surgeon uses multiple landmarks and verifies the location of the wire (or other device) inserted into the brain by taking MRI scans before producing a brain lesion.

Histological Methods

After producing a brain lesion and observing its effects on an animal's behavior, we must slice and stain the brain so that we can observe it under the microscope and see the actual location of the lesion. Brain lesions often miss the mark, so we have to verify the precise location of the brain damage after testing the animal behaviorally. To do so, we must fix, slice, stain, and examine the brain. Together, these procedures are referred to as *histological methods.* (The prefix *histo-* refers to body tissue.)

Fixation and Sectioning

If we hope to study the tissue in the form it had at the time of the organism's death, we must destroy the autolytic enzymes (*autolytic* means "self-dissolving"), which will

Stereotaxic apparatus A device that permits a surgeon to position an electrode or cannula into a specific part of the brain.

otherwise turn the tissue into shapeless mush. The tissue must also be preserved to prevent its decomposition by bacteria or molds. To achieve both of these objectives, we place the neural tissue in a **fixative.** The most commonly used fixative is **formalin,** an aqueous solution of formaldehyde, a gas. Formalin halts autolysis, hardens the very soft and fragile brain, and kills any microorganisms that might destroy it.

Once the brain has been fixed, we must slice it into thin sections and stain various cellular structures to see anatomical details. Slicing is done with a **microtome** (literally, "that which slices small"). (See *Figure 5.5.*) Slices prepared for examination under a light microscope are typically 10 to 80 μm in thickness; those prepared for the electron microscope are generally cut at less than 1 μm. (A μm, or *micrometer*, is one-millionth of a meter, or one-thousandth of a millimeter.) For some reason, slices of brain tissue are usually referred to as *sections.*

After the tissue is cut, we attach the slices to glass microscope slides. We can then stain the tissue by putting the entire slide into various chemical solutions. Finally, we cover the stained sections with a small amount of a transparent liquid known as a *mounting medium* and place a very thin glass coverslip over the sections. The mounting medium keeps the coverslip in position.

Staining

If you looked at an unstained section of brain tissue under a microscope, you would be able to see the outlines of some large cellular masses and the more prominent fiber bundles. However, no fine details would be revealed. For this reason, the study of microscopic neuroanatomy requires special histological stains. Researchers have developed many different stains to identify specific substances within and outside of cells. For verifying the location of a brain lesion, we use one of the simplest: a cell-body stain.

In the late nineteenth century, Franz Nissl, a German neurologist, discovered that a dye known as methylene blue would stain the cell bodies of brain tissue. The material that takes up the dye, known as the *Nissl substance,* consists of RNA, DNA, and associated proteins located in the nucleus and scattered, in the form of granules, in the cytoplasm. Many other dyes besides methylene blue can be used to stain cell bodies found in slices of the brain, but the most frequently used is cresyl violet. Incidentally, the dyes were not developed specifically for histological purposes but were originally formulated for use in dyeing cloth.

The discovery of cell-body stains made it possible to identify nuclear masses in the brain. Figure 5.6 shows a frontal section of a cat brain stained with cresyl violet. Note that you can observe fiber bundles by their lighter appearance; they do not take up the stain. (See *Figure 5.6.*) The stain is not selective for *neural* cell bodies; all cells are stained, neurons and glia alike. It is up to the investigator to determine which is which—by size, shape, and location.

Electron Microscopy

The light microscope is limited in its ability to resolve extremely small details. Because of the nature of light itself, magnification of more than approximately 1500 times does not add any detail. To see such small anatomical structures as synaptic vesicles and details of cell or-

FIGURE 5.5

A microtome.

Fixative A chemical such as formalin; used to prepare and preserve body tissue.

Formalin (*for ma lin*) The aqueous solution of formaldehyde gas; the most commonly used tissue fixative.

Microtome (*my krow tome*) An instrument that produces very thin slices of body tissues.

FIGURE 5.6

A frontal section of a cat brain, stained with cresyl violet, a cell-body stain. The arrowheads point to *nuclei,* or groups of cell bodies.

(Histological material courtesy of Mary Carlson.)

FIGURE 5.7

An electron photomicrograph of a section through an axodendritic synapse. Two synaptic regions are indicated by arrows, and a circle points out a region of pinocytosis in an adjacent terminal button, presumably representing recycling of vesicular membrane. T = terminal button; f = microfilaments; M = mitochondrion.

(From Rockel, A.J., and Jones, E.G. Journal of Comparative Neurology, 1973, 147, 61–92.)

ganelles, investigators must use an electron microscope. A beam of electrons is passed through the tissue to be examined. A shadow of the tissue is then cast on a sheet of photographic film, which is exposed by the electrons. Electron photomicrographs produced in this way can provide information about structural details on the order of a few nanometers. (See *Figure 5.7.*)

A **scanning electron microscope** provides less magnification than a standard transmission electron microscope, which transmits the electron beam through the tissue. However, it shows objects in three dimensions. The microscope scans the tissue with a moving beam of electrons. The information received from the reflection of the beam is used to produce a remarkably detailed three-dimensional view. (See *Figure 5.8.*)

Tracing Neural Connections

Let's suppose that we were interested in discovering the neural mechanisms responsible for reproductive behavior. To start out, we decided to study the physiology of sexual behavior of female rats. On the basis of some hints we received by reading reports of experiments by other researchers published in scientific journals, we performed stereotaxic surgery on two groups of female rats. We made a lesion in the ventromedial nucleus of the hypothalamus (VMH) of the rats in the experimental group and performed sham surgery on the rats in the control group. After a few days' recovery, we placed the animals (individually, of course) with male rats. The females in the control group responded positively to the males' attention; they engaged in courting behavior followed by copulation. However, the females with the VMH lesions rejected the males' attention and refused to copulate with them. We confirmed with histology that the VMH was, indeed, destroyed in the brains of the experimental animals. (One rat did copulate, but we found that we had missed the VMH in that animal, so we discarded the data from that subject.)

The results of our experiment indicate that neurons in the VMH appear to play a role in functions required for copulatory behavior in females. (By the way, it turns out that such lesions do not affect copulatory behavior in males.) So where do we go from here? What is the next step? In fact, there are many questions that we could pursue. One question concerns the system of brain structures that participate in female copulatory behavior. Certainly, the VMH does not stand alone; it receives inputs from other structures and sends outputs to still others. Copulation requires integration of visual, tactile, and olfactory perceptions and organization of patterns of movements in response to those of the partner. In addition, the entire network requires activation by the appropriate sex hormones. What is the precise role of the VMH in this complicated system?

Before we can hope to answer this question, we must know more about the connections of the VMH with the rest of the brain. What structures send their axons to the VMH, and to what structures does the VMH, in turn, send its axons? Once we know what the connections are, we can investigate the role of these structures and the nature of their interactions. (See *Figure 5.9.*)

How do we investigate the connections of the VMH? The question cannot be answered by means of histological procedures that stain all neurons, such as cell-body stains. If we look closely at a brain that has been prepared by these means, we see only a tangled mass of neurons. But in recent years, researchers have developed very pre-

Neuron   Terminal buttons forming synapses with neuron

FIGURE 5.8

A scanning-electron micrograph of neurons and glia.

(From Kessel, R.G., and Kardon, R.H. Tissues and Organs: A Text-Atlas of Scanning Electron Microscopy. San Francisco: W.H. Freeman, 1979. By permission of the authors.)

cise methods that make specific neurons stand out from all of the others.

Tracing Efferent Axons

Because neurons in VMH are not directly connected to muscles, they cannot affect behavior directly. Neurons in the VMH must send axons to parts of the brain that contain neurons that are responsible for muscular movements. The pathway is probably not direct; more likely, neurons in the VMH affect neurons in other structures, which influence those in yet other structures, until, eventually, the appropriate motor neurons are stimulated. To discover this system, we want to be able to identify the paths followed by axons leaving the VMH. In other words, we want to trace the *efferent axons* of this structure.

We will use an **anterograde labeling method** to trace these axons. (*Anterograde* means "moving forward.") Anterograde labeling methods employ chemicals that are taken up by dendrites or cell bodies and are then transported through the axons toward the terminal buttons.

Over the years, neuroscientists have developed several different methods for tracing the pathways followed by efferent axons. A recently developed method is replacing earlier ones, so we will use this new method. Cell biologists have discovered that a family of proteins produced by plants binds with specific complex molecules present in cells of the immune system. These proteins, called *lectins*, have also found a use in tracing neural pathways. A particular lectin produced by the kidney bean, **PHA-L** (*phaseolus vulgaris leukoagglutinin,* if you really want to know), is used to identify efferent axons.

To discover the destination of the efferent axons of neurons located within the VMH, we inject a minute quantity of PHA-L into that nucleus. (We use a stereotaxic apparatus to do so, of course.) The molecules of PHA-L are taken up by dendrites and are transported through the soma to the axon, where they travel by means of fast axoplasmic transport to the terminal buttons. Within a few days, the cells are filled in their entirety with molecules of PHA-L: dendrites, soma, axons and all their branches, and terminal buttons. Then we kill the animal, slice the brain, and mount the sections on microscope slides. A special staining method is used to make the molecules of PHA-L visible, and the slides are examined under a microscope. (See *Figure 5.10.*)

FIGURE 5.9

Once we know that a particular brain region is involved in a particular function, we may ask what structures provide inputs to the region and what structures receive outputs from it.

Scanning electron microscope
A microscope that provides three-dimensional information about the shape of the surface of a small object.

Anterograde labeling method
(*ann ter oh grade*) A histological method that labels the axons and terminal buttons of neurons whose cell bodies are located in a particular region.

PHA-L Phaseolus vulgaris leukoagglutinin; a protein derived from kidney beans used as an anterograde tracer; taken up by dendrites and cell bodies and carried to the ends of the axons.

FIGURE 5.10

The rationale for the use of PHA-L to trace efferent axons.

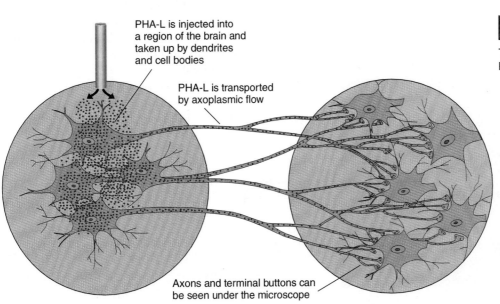

PHA-L is injected into a region of the brain and taken up by dendrites and cell bodies

PHA-L is transported by axoplasmic flow

Axons and terminal buttons can be seen under the microscope

FIGURE 5.11

An anterograde labeling method. PHA-L was injected into the ventromedial nucleus of the hypothalamus (VMH), where it was taken up by dendrites and carried through the cells' axons to their terminal buttons. Labeled axons and terminal buttons are found in the periaqueductal gray matter (PAG).

(Courtesy of Kirsten Nielsen Ricciardi and Jeffrey Blaustein, University of Massachusetts.)

Retrograde labeling method
A histological method that labels cell bodies that give rise to the terminal buttons that form synapses with cells in a particular region.

Fluorogold (*flew* roh gold) A dye that serves as a retrograde label; taken up by terminal buttons and carried back to the cell bodies.

Figure 5.11 shows how PHA-L can be used to identify the efferents of a particular region of the brain. Molecules of this chemical were injected into the VMH. Two days later, after the PHA-L had been taken up by the neurons in this region and transported to the ends of their axons, the animal was killed. Slices of the brain were treated with a chemical procedure that stains the tissue containing molecules of PHA-L a brown color. Figure 5.11 shows a photomicrograph of the periaqueductal gray matter (PAG). As you can see, this region contains some axons and terminal buttons labeled by the PHA-L, which proves that some of the efferent axons of the VMH terminate in the PAG. (See *Figure 5.11.*)

To continue our study of the role of the VMH in female sexual behavior, we would find the structures that receive information from neurons in the VMH (such as the PAG) and see what happens when each of them is destroyed. Let's suppose that damage to some of these structures also impairs female sexual behavior. We will inject these structures with PHA-L and see where *their* axons go. Eventually, we will discover the relevant pathways from the VMH to the motor neurons whose activity is necessary for copulatory behavior. (In fact, researchers have done so, and some of their results are presented in Chapter 9.)

Tracing Afferent Axons

Tracing efferent axons from the VMH will tell us only part of the story about the neural circuitry involved in female sexual behavior: the part between the VMH and the motor neurons. What about the circuits *before* the VMH? Is the VMH somehow involved in the analysis of sensory information (such as the sight, odor, or touch of the male)? Or perhaps the activating effect of a female's sex hormones on her behavior act through the VMH or through neurons whose axons form synapses there. To discover the parts of the brain that are involved in the "upstream" components of the neural circuitry, we need to find the inputs of the VMH—its afferent connections. To do so, we will employ a **retrograde labeling method.**

Retrograde means "moving backward." Retrograde labeling methods employ chemicals that are taken up by terminal buttons and carried back through the axons toward the cell bodies. The method for identifying the afferent inputs to a particular region of the brain is similar to the method used for identifying its efferents. First, we will inject a small quantity of a chemical called **fluorogold** into the VMH. The chemical is taken up by terminal buttons and is transported back by means of retrograde axoplasmic transport to the cell bodies. A few days later, we kill the animal, slice its brain, and examine the tissue under light of the appropriate wavelength. The molecules of fluorogold fluoresce under this light. We discover that the medial amygdala is one of the regions that provides input to the VMH. (See *Figure 5.12.*)

FIGURE 5.12

A retrograde tracing method. Fluorogold was injected in the VMH, where it was taken up by terminal buttons and transported back through the axons to their cell bodies. The photograph shows these cell bodies, located in the medial amygdala.

(Courtesy of Yvon Delville, University of Massachusetts Medical School.)

Together, anterograde and retrograde labeling methods enable us to discover the connections of a particular part of the brain (in this case, the VMH) with other parts of the brain. Thus, these methods help to provide us with a "wiring diagram" of the brain. (See *Figure 5.13*.) Armed with other research methods (including some to be described later in this chapter), we can try to discover the functions of each component of this circuit.

Study of the Living Human Brain

There are many good reasons to investigate the functions of brains of animals other than humans. For one thing, we can compare the results of studies made with different species in order to make some inferences about the evolution of various neural systems. Even if our primary interest is in the functions of the human brain, we certainly cannot ask people to submit to brain surgery for the purposes of research. But diseases and accidents do occasionally damage the human brain, and if we know where the damage occurs, we can study the people's behavior and try to make the same sorts of inferences we make with deliberately produced brain lesions in laboratory animals. The problem is, how do we locate the lesion?

In past years, a researcher might have studied the behavior of a person with brain damage and never found out exactly where the lesion was located. The only way to be sure was to obtain the patient's brain when he or she died and examine slices of it under a microscope. But this was often impossible to do so. Sometimes the patient outlived the researcher. Sometimes the patient moved out of town. Sometimes (often, perhaps) the family refused permission for an autopsy. Because of these practical problems, study of the behavioral effects of damage to specific parts of the human brain made rather slow progress.

Recent advances in X-ray techniques and computers have led to the development of several methods for studying the anatomy of the living brain. These advances permit researchers to study the location and extent of brain damage while the patient is still living. The first method to be developed is called **computerized tomography (CT)** (from the Greek for *tomos*, "cut"; *graphein*, "to write"). This procedure, usually referred to as a *CT scan*, works as follows: The patient's head is placed in a large doughnut-shaped ring. The ring contains an X-ray tube and, directly opposite it (on the other side of the patient's head), an X-ray detector. The X-ray beam passes through the patient's head, and the detector measures the amount of radioactivity that gets through it. The beam scans the head from all angles, and a computer translates the numbers it receives from the detector into pictures of the skull and its contents. (See *Figure 5.14*.)

Figure 5.15 shows a series of these CT scans taken through the head of a patient who sustained a stroke. The stroke damaged a part of the brain involved in bodily

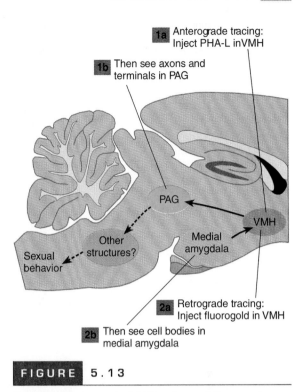

1a Anterograde tracing: Inject PHA-L inVMH
1b Then see axons and terminals in PAG
PAG
Other structures?
Sexual behavior
Medial amygdala
VMH
2a Retrograde tracing: Inject fluorogold in VMH
2b Then see cell bodies in medial amygdala

FIGURE 5.13

One of the inputs to the VMH and one of the outputs, as revealed by anterograde and retrograde labeling methods.

Computerized tomography (CT) The use of a device that employs a computer to analyze data obtained by a scanning beam of X-rays to produce a two-dimensional picture of a "slice" through the body.

FIGURE 5.14

A computerized tomography (CT) scanner.

(Larry Mulvehill/Rainbow)

FIGURE 5.15

A series of CT scans from a patient with a lesion in the right occipital-parietal area (scan 5). The lesion appears white because it was accompanied by bleeding; blood absorbs more radiation than the surrounding brain tissue. Rostral is up, caudal is down; left and right are reversed. Scan 1 shows a section through the eyes and the base of the brain.

[Courtesy of J.McA. Jones, Good Samaritan Hospital, Portland, Oregon.]

(1)   (2)   (3)

(4)   (5)   (6)

awareness and perception of space. The patient lost her awareness of the left side of her body and of items located on her left. You can see the damage as a white spot in the lower left corner of scan 5. (See *Figure 5.15.*)

An even more detailed picture of what is inside a person's head is provided by a process called **magnetic resonance imaging (MRI).** The MRI scanner resembles a CT scanner, but it does not use X-rays. Instead, it passes an extremely strong magnetic field through the patient's head. When a person's body is placed in a strong magnetic field, the nuclei of some atoms in molecules in the body spin with a particular orientation. If a radio frequency wave is then passed through the body, these nuclei emit radio waves of their own. Different molecules emit energy at different frequencies. The MRI scanner is tuned to detect the radiation from hydrogen molecules. Because these molecules are present in different concentrations in different tissues, the scanner can use the information to prepare pictures of slices of the brain. Unlike CT scans, which are generally limited to the horizontal plane, MRI scans can be taken in the sagittal or frontal planes, as well. (See *Figure 5.16.*)

Magnetic resonance imaging (MRI) A technique whereby the interior of the body can be accurately imaged; involves the interaction between radio waves and a strong magnetic field.

FIGURE 5.16

A midsagittal MRI scan of a human brain.

[Photo courtesy of Philips Medical Systems.]

INTERIM SUMMARY

The goal of research in physiological psychology is to understand the brain functions required for the performance of a particular behavior and then to learn the location of the neural circuits that perform these functions. The lesion method is the oldest one employed in such research, and it remains one of the most useful. A subcortical lesion is made under the guidance of a stereotaxic apparatus. The coordinates are obtained from a stereotaxic atlas, and the tip of an electrode or cannula is placed at the target. A lesion is made by passing RF current through the electrode or infusing an excitatory amino acid through the cannula, producing an excitotoxic lesion. The advantage of excitotoxic lesions is that they affect only neural cell bodies; axons passing through the region are not damaged.

The location of a lesion must be determined after the animal's behavior is observed. The animal is killed by humane means, and the brain is removed and placed in a fixative such as formalin. A microtome is used to slice the brain, which is usually frozen to make it hard enough to cut into thin sections. These sections are mounted on glass slides, stained with a cell-body stain, and examined under a microscope.

Light microscopes enable us to see cells and their larger organelles, but an electron microscope is needed to see small details, such as individual mitochondria and synaptic vesicles. Scanning electron microscopes provide a three-dimensional view of tissue, but at a lower magnification than transmission electron microscopes.

The next step in a research program often requires the investigator to discover the afferent and efferent connections of the region of interest with the rest of the brain. Efferent connections (those that carry information from the region in question to other parts of the brain) are revealed with anterograde tracing methods, such as the one that uses PHA-L. Afferent connections (those that bring information to the region in question from other parts of the brain) are revealed with retrograde tracing methods, such as the one that uses fluorogold.

Although brain lesions are not deliberately made in the human brain for the purposes of research, diseases and accidents can cause brain damage, and if we know where the damage is located, we can study people's behavior and make inferences about the location of the neural circuits that perform relevant functions. If the patient dies and the brain is available for examination, ordinary histological methods can be used. Otherwise, the living brain can be examined with CT scanners and MRI scanners.

Table 5.1 summarizes the research methods presented in this section.

TABLE 5.1	Research Methods: Part I	
Goal of Method	**Method**	**Remarks**
Destroy or inactivate specific brain region	Radio frequency lesion	Destroys all brain tissue near tip of electrode
	Excitotoxic lesion	Destroys only cell bodies near tip of cannula; spares axons passing through region
	Infusion of local anesthetic	Temporarily inactivates specific brain region; animal can serve as its own control
Place electrode or cannula in specific region within brain	Stereotaxic surgery	Consult stereotaxic atlas for coordinates
Find location of lesion	Fix brain; slice brain; stain sections	
Identify axons leaving a particular region and the terminal buttons of these axons	Anterograde tracing method, such as PHA-L	
Identify location of neurons whose axons terminate in a particular region	Retrograde tracing method, such as fluorogold	
Find location of lesion in living human brain	Computerized tomography (CT scanner)	Shows "slice" of brain
	Magnetic resonance imaging (MRI scanner)	Shows "slice" of brain; better detail than CT scan

■ **THOUGHT QUESTIONS**

Suppose that a man's brain is injured in an automobile accident. This man, who was formerly polite, restrained, and tactful, now becomes irresponsible and tactless. He talks excessively, interrupting other people without seeming to notice their annoyance. He cracks coarse, tasteless jokes and often directs crude sexual comments to women he finds attractive. How can we explain the fact that the man's brain damage caused the appearance of behaviors that were not previously seen?

■ RECORDING AND STIMULATING NEURAL ACTIVITY

The first section of this chapter dealt with the anatomy of the brain and the effects of damage to particular regions. This section considers a different approach: studying the brain by recording or stimulating the activity of particular regions. Brain functions involve activity of circuits of neurons; thus, different perceptions and behavioral responses involve different patterns of activity in the brain. Researchers have devised methods to record these patterns of activity or artificially produce them.

Recording Neural Activity

Axons produce action potentials, and terminal buttons elicit postsynaptic potentials in the membrane of the cells with which they form synapses. We can record these electrical events (as we saw in Chapter 2), and we can use changes in the electrical activity of a particular region to determine whether that region plays a role in various behaviors. For example, we can make recordings during stimulus presentations, decision making, or motor activities.

Recordings can be made *chronically,* over an extended period of time after an animal recovers from surgery, or *acutely,* for a relatively short period of time during which an animal is kept anesthetized. Acute recordings, made while an animal is anesthetized, are usually restricted to studies of sensory pathways. Acute recordings seldom involve behavioral observations, since the behavioral capacity of an anesthetized animal is limited, to say the least.

Recordings with Microelectrodes

Drugs that affect serotonergic and noradrenergic neurons also affect REM sleep. Suppose that, knowing this fact, we wondered whether the activity of serotonergic and noradrenergic neurons would vary during different stages of sleep. To find out, we would record the activity of these neurons with microelectrodes. **Microelectrodes** have a very fine tip, small enough to record the electrical activity of individual neurons. This technique is usually called **single-unit recording** (a unit refers to an individual neuron).

For accurate readings, we can use glass micropipettes, as described in Chapter 2. However, if we want to record the activity of single neurons over a long period of time in unanesthetized animals, we need to use more durable electrodes. Therefore, we will make them from fine tungsten wires, sharpened at the tip and insulated with a special varnish. We implant the electrodes in the brains of animals through stereotaxic surgery. We attach them to miniaturized electrical sockets and bond the sockets to the animals' skull, using plastics that were originally developed for the dental profession. Then, after recovery from surgery, the animal can be "plugged in" to the

Microelectrode A very fine electrode, generally used to record activity of individual neurons.

Single-unit recording Recording of the electrical activity of a single neuron.

recording system. Laboratory animals pay no heed to the electrical sockets on their skulls and behave quite normally. (See *Figure 5.17.*)

The electrical signals detected by microelectrodes are quite small and must be amplified. Amplifiers used for this purpose work just like the amplifiers in a stereo system, converting the weak signals recorded at the brain into stronger ones. These signals can be displayed on an oscilloscope and stored in the memory of a computer for analysis at a later time.

What about our results? As you will learn in Chapter 8, if we record the activity of noradrenergic and serotonergic neurons during various stages of sleep, we will find that the firing rate of these neurons falls almost to zero during REM sleep. This observation suggests that these neurons have an *inhibitory* effect on REM sleep. That is, REM sleep cannot occur until these neurons stop firing.

Recordings with Macroelectrodes

Sometimes, we want to record the activity of a region of the brain as a whole, not the activity of individual neurons located there. To do this we would use macroelectrodes. **Macroelectrodes** do not detect the activity of individual neurons; rather, the records obtained with these devices represent the postsynaptic potentials of many thousands—or millions—of cells in the area of the electrode. These electrodes can consist of unsharpened wires inserted into the brain, screws attached to the skull, or even metal disks attached to the human scalp with a special paste that conducts electricity. Recordings taken from the scalp, especially, represent the activity of an enormous number of neurons, whose electrical signals pass through the meninges, skull, and scalp before reaching the electrodes.

Occasionally, neurosurgeons implant macroelectrodes directly into the human brain. The reason for doing so is to detect the source of abnormal electrical activity that is giving rise to frequent seizures. Once the source is determined, the surgeon can open the skull and remove the source of the seizures—usually scar tissue caused by brain damage that occurred earlier in life. Most often, the electrical activity of a human brain is recorded through electrodes attached to the scalp and displayed on an *ink-writing oscillograph,* commonly called a *polygraph.*

A polygraph contains a mechanism that moves a very long strip of paper past a series of pens. These pens are essentially the pointers of large voltmeters, moving up and down in response to the electrical signal sent to them by the biological amplifiers. Figure 5.18 illustrates a record of electrical activity recorded from macroelectrodes attached to various locations on a person's scalp. (See *Figure 5.18.*) Such records are called **electroencephalograms (EEGs),** or "writings of electricity from the head." They can be used to diagnose epilepsy or brain tumors, or to study the stages of sleep and wakefulness, which are associated with characteristic patterns of electrical activity.

Recording the Brain's Metabolic and Synaptic Activity

Electrical signals are not the only signs of neural activity. If the neural activity of a particular region of the brain increases, the

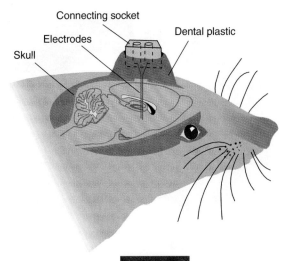

Connecting socket
Electrodes
Dental plastic
Skull

FIGURE 5.17

A permanently attached set of electrodes, with a connecting socket cemented to the skull.

Macroelectrode An electrode used to record the electrical activity of large numbers of neurons in a particular region of the brain; much larger than a microelectrode.

Electroencephalogram (EEG) An electrical brain potential recorded by placing electrodes on the scalp.

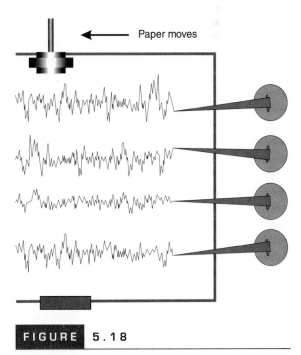

Paper moves

FIGURE 5.18

A record from an ink-writing oscillograph.

FIGURE 5.19

A 2-DG autoradiogram of a rat brain (frontal section, dorsal is at top), showing especially high regions of activity in the pair of nuclei in the hypothalamus, at the base of the brain.

(From Schwartz, W.J., and Gainer, H. Science, 1977, 197, 1089–1091. Copyright 1977 by the American Association for the Advancement of Science)

2-deoxyglucose (2-DG) (*dee ox ee gloo kohss*) A sugar that enters cells along with glucose but is not metabolized.

Autoradiography A procedure that locates radioactive substances in a slice of tissue; the radiation exposes a photographic emulsion or a piece of film that covers the tissue.

Fos (*fahs*) A protein produced in the nucleus of a neuron in response to synaptic stimulation.

---

metabolic rate of this region increases, too, largely as a result of increased operation of ion pumps in the membrane of the cells. This increased metabolic rate can be measured. The experimenter injects radioactive **2-deoxyglucose (2-DG)** into the animal. Because this chemical resembles glucose (the principal food for the brain), it is taken into cells. Thus, the most active cells, which use glucose at the highest rate, will take up the highest concentrations of radioactive 2-DG. But unlike normal glucose, 2-DG cannot be metabolized, so it stays in the cell. The experimenter then kills the animal, removes the brain, slices it, and prepares it for *autoradiography*.

Autoradiography can be translated roughly as "writing with one's own radiation." Sections of the brain are mounted on microscope slides. The slides are then taken into a darkroom, where they are coated with a photographic emulsion (the substance found on photographic film). Sometime later, the slides, with their coatings of emulsion, are developed, just like photographic film. The molecules of radioactive 2-DG show themselves as spots of silver grains in the developed emulsion because the radioactivity exposes the emulsion, just as X-rays or light will do.

The most active regions of the brain contain the most radioactivity, showing this radioactivity in the form of dark spots in the developed emulsion. Figure 5.19 shows an autoradiograph of a slice of a rat brain; the dark spots at the bottom (indicated by the arrow) are nuclei of the hypothalamus with an especially high metabolic rate. Chapter 8 describes these nuclei and their function. (See *Figure 5.19.*)

Another method of identifying active regions of the brain capitalizes on the fact that when neurons are activated (for example, by the terminal buttons that form synapses with them), particular genes in the nucleus are turned on and particular proteins are produced. These proteins then bind with the chromosomes in the nucleus; exactly what they do is not yet known. For our purposes, the important fact is their presence indicates that the cell has just been activated.

One of the nuclear proteins produced during neural activation is called **Fos.** You will remember that we already did some research on the neural circuitry involved in the sexual behavior of female rats. Suppose we want to use the Fos method in this research project. We place female rats with males and permit the animals to copulate. Then we remove the rats' brains, slice them, and follow a procedure that stains Fos protein. Figure 5.20 shows the results: Neurons in the medial amygdala of a female rat that has just mated show the presence of dark spots, indicating the presence of Fos protein. These neurons appear to be activated by some aspect of copulatory activity.

As you will recall, when we injected a retrograde tracer (fluorogold) into the VMH, we found that this region receives input from the medial amygdala. (See *Figure 5.20.*)

The metabolic activity of specific brain regions can be measured in human brains, too, using a method known as

FIGURE 5.20

Localization of Fos protein. The photomicrograph shows a frontal section of the brain of a female rat, taken through the medial amygdala. The dark spots indicate the presence of Fos protein, localized by means of immunocytochemistry. The synthesis of Fos protein was stimulated by permitting the animal to engage in copulatory behavior.

(Courtesy of Marc Tetel, University of Massachusetts.)

Relaxed condition

Right fist clenched and unclenched

0   12   24   36   48   60

FIGURE 5.21

PET scans of a human brain (horizontal sections). The top row shows three scans from a person at rest. The bottom row shows three scans from the same person while he clenched and unclenched his right fist. The scans show increased uptake of radioactive 2-deoxyglucose in regions of the brain that are devoted to the control of movement, which indicates increased metabolic rate in these areas. Different computer-generated colors indicate different rates of uptake of 2-DG, as shown in the scale below .

(Courtesy of the Brookhaven National Laboratory and the State University of New York, Stony Brook.)

positron emission tomography, or PET. First, the patient receives an injection of radioactive 2-DG. (Eventually, the chemical is broken down and leaves the cells. The dose given to humans is harmless.) The person's head is placed in a machine similar to a CT scanner. When the radioactive molecules of 2-DG decay, they emit subatomic particles called positrons, which are detected by the scanner. The computer determines which regions of the brain have taken up the radioactive substance, and it produces a picture of a slice of the brain, showing the activity level of various regions in that slice. (See *Figure 5.21*.)

One of the disadvantages of PET scanners is their operating cost. For reasons of safety, the radioactive chemicals that are administered have very short half-lives; that is, they decay and lose their radioactivity very quickly. Because these chemicals decay so quickly, they must be produced on site, in an atomic particle accelerator called a *cyclotron.* The cost of the cyclotron and the salaries of the personnel who operate it must be added to the cost of the PET scanner.

The most recent development in brain imaging is **functional MRI (fMRI).** Engineers have devised modifications to existing MRI scanners that acquire images very rapidly and permit the measurement of regional metabolism. Functional MRI scans have a higher resolution than PET scans, so they reveal more detailed information about the activity of particular brain regions. (See *Figure 5.22*.)

Measuring the Brain's Secretions

Sometimes we are interested not in the general metabolic activity of particular regions of the brain, but in the secretion of specific neurotransmitters or neuromodulators in these regions. For example, suppose we know that acetylcholinergic neurons in the brain stem participate in the control of REM sleep. (The experiments that provided this knowledge are described in the next section of this chapter.) One of the characteristics of REM

Positron emission tomography (PET) The use of a device that reveals the localization of a radioactive tracer in a living brain.

Functional MRI (fMRI) A modification of the MRI procedure that permits the measurement of regional metabolism in the brain.

FIGURE 5.22

A functional MRI scan of a human brain. Localized increases in neural activity of males (left) and females (right) while judging whether pairs of written words rhymed.

(Reprinted with permission from Shaywitz, B.A., et al., Nature, 1995, 373, 607–609. Copyright 1995 Macmillan Magazines Limited.)

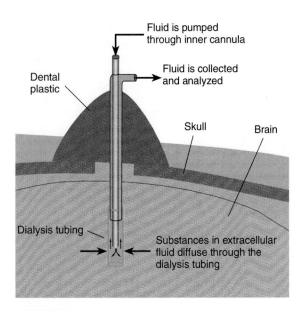

Fluid is pumped through inner cannula

Fluid is collected and analyzed

Dental plastic

Skull

Brain

Dialysis tubing

Substances in extracellular fluid diffuse through the dialysis tubing

FIGURE 5.23

Microdialysis. A salt solution is slowly infused into the microdialysis tube, where it picks up molecules that diffuse in from the extracellular fluid. The fluid is then analyzed by high-performance liquid chromatography (HPLC).

(Adapted from Hernandez, L., Stanley, B.G., and Hoebel, B.G. Life Sciences, 1986, 39, 2629–2637.)

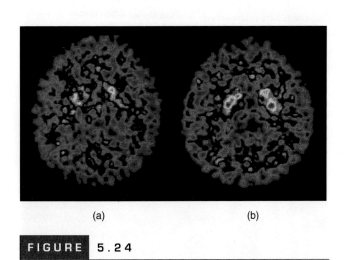

(a)   (b)

FIGURE 5.24

PET scans showing uptake of radioactive L-DOPA in the basal ganglia of a patient with parkinsonian symptoms induced by a toxic chemical before and after receiving a transplant of fetal dopaminergic neurons. (a) Preoperative scan. (b) Scan taken 13 months postoperatively. The increased uptake of L-DOPA indicates that the fetal transplant was secreting dopamine.

(Adapted from Widner, H., Tetrud, J., Rehncrona, S., Snow, B., Brundin, P., Gustavii, B., Björklund, A., Lindvall, O., and Langston, J.W. New England Journal of Medicine, 1992, 327, 1556–1563. Scans reprinted with permission.)

sleep is muscular paralysis, which prevents us from getting out of bed and acting out our dreams. We decide to measure the secretion of acetylcholine in a region of the medulla that is known to contain neurons that inhibit motor neurons in the spinal cord. To do so, we use a procedure called **microdialysis.**

Dialysis is a process in which substances are separated by means of an artificial membrane that is permeable to some molecules but not others. A microdialysis probe consists of a small metal tube that introduces a solution into a section of dialysis tubing—a piece of artificial membrane shaped in the form of a cylinder, sealed at the bottom. Another small metal tube leads the solution away after it has circulated through the pouch. A drawing of such a probe is shown in *Figure 5.23.*

We use stereotaxic surgery to place a microdialysis probe in a rat's brain so that the tip of the probe is located in the region we are interested in. We pump a small amount of a solution similar to extracellular fluid through one of the small metal tubes into the dialysis tubing. The fluid circulates through the dialysis tubing and passes through the second metal tube, from which it is taken for analysis. As the fluid passes through the dialysis tubing, it collects molecules from the extracellular fluid of the brain, which are pushed across the membrane by the force of diffusion.

We analyze the contents of the fluid that has passed through the dialysis tubing by an extremely sensitive analytical method known as *high-performance liquid chromatography.* This method is so sensitive that it can detect neurotransmitters (and their breakdown products) that have been released by the terminal buttons and have escaped from the synaptic cleft into the rest of the extracellular fluid. The results show that the amount of acetylcholine present in the extracellular fluid of the nucleus in the medulla *does* increase during REM sleep.

What about measuring neurochemicals in the human brain? Although microdialysis probes work in the human brain as well as they do in the brains of laboratory animals, a noninvasive procedure has been developed to accomplish the same goal. PET scanners may be very expensive machines, but they are also very versatile. They can be used to localize *any* radioactive substance that emits positrons.

As we saw in the prologue to Chapter 4, several years ago, several people injected themselves with an illicit drug that was contaminated with a chemical that destroyed their dopaminergic neurons. As a result, they suffered from severe parkinsonism. Recently, neurosurgeons used stereotaxic procedures to transplant fetal dopaminergic neurons into the basal ganglia of some of these patients. Figure 5.24 shows PET scans of the brain of one of them. The patient was given an injection of radioactive L-DOPA one hour before each scan was made. As you learned in Chapter 4, L-DOPA is taken up by the terminals of dopaminergic neurons, where it is converted to dopamine; thus, the radioactivity shown in the scans indicates the presence of dopamine-secreting terminals in the basal ganglia. The scans show the amount of radioactivity before (part a) and after (part b) the patient received the transplant, which greatly diminished his symptoms. (See *Figure 5.24.*)

Stimulating Neural Activity

So far, this section has been concerned with research methods that measure the activity of specific regions of the brain. But sometimes we may want to artificially change the activity of these regions to see what effects these changes have on the animal's behavior. For example, female rats will copulate with males only if certain female sex hormones are present. If we remove the rats' ovaries, the loss of these hormones will abolish their sexual behavior. We found in our earlier studies that VMH lesions disrupt this behavior. Perhaps if we *activate* the VMH, we will make up for the lack of female sex hormones and the rats will copulate again.

How do we activate neurons? We can do so by electrical or chemical stimulation. Electrical stimulation simply involves passing an electrical current through a wire inserted into the brain, as you saw in Figure 5.19. Chemical stimulation is usually accomplished by injecting a small amount of an excitatory amino acid, such as kainic acid or glutamic acid, into the brain. As you learned in Chapter 4, the principal excitatory neurotransmitter in the brain is glutamic acid (glutamate), and both of these substances stimulate glutamate receptors, thus activating the neurons on which these receptors are located.

Injections of chemicals into the brain can be done through an apparatus permanently attached to the skull so that the animal's behavior can be observed several times. We place a metal cannula (a guide cannula) in an animal's brain and cement its top to the skull. At a later date, we place a smaller cannula of measured length inside the guide cannula and then inject a chemical into the brain. Because the animal is free to move about, we can observe the effects of the injection on its behavior. (See *Figure 5.25*.)

The principal disadvantage of chemical stimulation is that it is slightly more complicated than electrical stimulation. Chemical stimulation requires cannulas, tubes, special pumps or syringes, and sterile solutions of excitatory amino acids. However, it has a distinct advantage over electrical stimulation: It activates cell bodies but not axons. Because only cell bodies (and their dendrites, of course) contain glutamate receptors, we can be assured that an injection of an excitatory amino acid into a particular region of the brain excites the cells there, but not the axons of other neurons that happen to pass through the region. Thus, the effects of chemical stimulation are more localized than the effects of electrical stimulation.

You may have noticed that I just said that kainic acid, which I described earlier as a neurotoxin, can be used to stimulate neurons. These two uses are not really contradictory. Kainic acid produces excitotoxic lesions by stimulating neurons to death. Whereas large doses of a concentrated solution kill neurons, small doses of a dilute solution simply stimulate them.

Microdialysis A procedure for analyzing chemicals present in the interstitial fluid through a small piece of tubing made of a semipermeable membrane that is implanted in the brain.

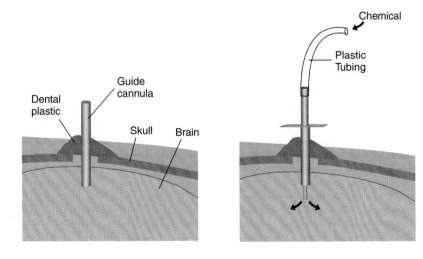

FIGURE 5.25

An intracranial cannula. A guide cannula is permanently attached to the skull, and at a later time a thinner cannula can be inserted through the guide cannula into the brain. Chemicals can be infused into the brain through this device.

Several species-typical behaviors, such as eating, drinking, or grooming, can be triggered by electrical stimulation of particular regions of the brain.

What about the results of our experiment? In fact, (as we shall see in Chapter 9), VMH stimulation *does* substitute for female sex hormones. Perhaps, then, the female sex hormones exert their effects in this nucleus. We will see how to test this hypothesis in the final section of this chapter.

INTERIM SUMMARY

When circuits of neurons participate in their normal functions, their electrical activity, metabolic activity, and chemical secretions increase. By observing these processes as an animal perceives various stimuli or engages in various behaviors, we can make some inferences about the functions performed by various regions of the brain. Microelectrodes can be used to record the electrical activity of individual neurons. Long-term recordings require that the electrode be attached to an electrical socket, which is fastened to the skull with a plastic adhesive. Macroelectrodes record the activity of large groups of neurons. In rare cases, macroelectrodes are placed in the depths of the human brain, but most often they are placed on the scalp and their activity is recorded on a polygraph.

Metabolic activity can be measured by giving an animal an injection of radioactive 2-DG, which accumulates in metabolically active neurons. The presence of the radioactivity is revealed through autoradiography: Slices of the brain are placed on microscope slides, covered with a photographic emulsion, left to sit a while, and then developed like photographic negatives. When neurons are stimulated, they synthesize the nuclear protein Fos. The presence of Fos, revealed by a special staining method, provides another way to discover active regions of the brain. Using a PET scanner, the metabolic activity of various regions of the living human brain can be revealed by the 2-DG method. A functional MRI scanner can accomplish the same purpose without the use of radioactive chemicals.

The secretions of neurotransmitters and neuromodulators can be measured by implanting the tip of a microdialysis probe in a particular region of the brain. A PET scanner can be used to perform similar observations of the human brain.

Researchers can stimulate various regions of the brain by implanting a macroelectrode and applying mild electrical stimulation. Alternatively, they can implant a guide cannula in the brain; after the animal has recovered from the surgery, they insert a smaller cannula and inject a weak solution of an excitatory amino acid into the brain. The advantage of this procedure is that only neurons whose cell bodies are located nearby will be stimulated; axons passing through the region will not be affected.

Table 5.2 summarizes the research methods presented in this section.

TABLE 5.2	Research Methods: Part II	
Goal of Method	**Method**	**Remarks**
Record electrical activity of single neurons	Glass or metal microelectrodes	Metal microelectrodes can be implanted permanently to record neural activity as animal moves
Record electrical activity of regions of brain	Metal macroelectrodes	In humans, usually attached to the scalp with a special paste
Record metabolic activity of regions of brain	2-DG autoradiography	Measures local glucose utilization
	Measurement of Fos protein	Identifies neurons that have recently been stimulated
	2-DG PET scan	Measures regional metabolic activity of human brain
	Functional MRI	Measures regional metabolic activity of human brain
Measure neurotransmitters and neuromodulators released by neurons	Microdialysis	A wide variety of substances can be analyzed
	PET scan	Can localize any radioactive substance in the human brain
Stimulate neural activity	Electrical stimulation	Stimulates neurons near the tip of the electrode and axons passing through region
	Chemical stimulation with excitatory amino acid	Stimulates only neurons near the tip of the cannula, not axons passing through region

■ THOUGHT QUESTIONS

1. What do you think happens to the activity of neurons in your brain while you sleep? Do all your neurons simply shut down? Are there changes in neural activity while you are dreaming? If so, in which parts of the brain would you expect to find changes in activity? How could you study these changes without using a procedure that would damage your brain?

2. What procedures could you use to study the neural activity in various regions of the brains of laboratory animals during sleep? Do animals other than humans dream while they sleep? How could we try to answer this question?

■ NEUROCHEMICAL METHODS

I have already described some neurochemical methods in the context of damaging or stimulating the brain or measuring neural activity. This section describes several other neurochemical methods that are useful in studying the physiology of behavior.

Finding Neurons That Produce Particular Neurochemicals

Suppose we learn that a particular drug affects behavior. How would we go about discovering the neural circuits responsible for the drug's effects? To answer this

Physicians discovered that exposure to insecticides that contained acetylcholinesterase inhibitors could cause intense, bizarre dreams and waking hallucinations.

question, let's take a specific example. Physicians discovered several years ago that farm workers who were exposed to certain types of insecticides (the organophosphates) had particularly intense and bizarre dreams and even reported having hallucinations while awake. A plausible explanation for these symptoms is that the drug stimulates the neural circuits responsible for dreaming. (After all, dreams are hallucinations that we have while sleeping.) Alternatively, the drug could disrupt inhibitory mechanisms that *prevent* dreaming while we are awake. Other evidence (which will not be described here) indicates that the former hypothesis is true: Organophosphate insecticides directly activate the neural circuits responsible for dreaming. (Other drugs, such as LSD, produce hallucinations by disrupting inhibitory mechanisms.)

The first question to ask relates to how the organophosphate insecticides work. Pharmacologists have the answer: These drugs are acetylcholinesterase inhibitors. As you learned in Chapter 4, acetylcholinesterase inhibitors are potent acetylcholine agonists. By inhibiting AChE, the drugs prevent the rapid destruction of ACh after it is released by terminal buttons and thus prolong the postsynaptic potentials at acetylcholinergic synapses.

Now that we understand the action of the insecticides, we know that these drugs act at acetylcholinergic synapses. What neurochemical methods should we use to discover the location of acetylcholine-secreting neurons in the brain? So far, neurochemists have not discovered a staining method that identifies acetylcholine itself. However, we can identify neurons that produce acetylcholine *indirectly*, by staining for the presence of choline acetyl transferase (ChAT), the enzyme responsible for the production of acetylcholine. As you know, enzymes are proteins, and proteins (and peptides, which are shorter chains of amino acids) can be detected by means of immunocytochemical methods.

Immunocytochemical methods take advantage of the immune reaction. The body's immune system has the ability to produce antibodies in response to antigens. *Antigens* are proteins (or peptides), such as those found on the surface of bacteria or viruses. *Antibodies*, which are also proteins, are produced by white blood cells to destroy invading microorganisms. Particular antibodies contain receptors that bind with particular antigens, the first step in identifying and destroying an invading microorganism.

Cell biologists have developed methods for producing antibodies to any peptide or protein. The antibody molecules are attached to various types of dye molecules—

Immunocytochemical method
A histological method that uses radioactive antibodies or antibodies bound with a dye molecule to indicate the presence of particular proteins or peptides.

most often, a fluorescent dye that glows when it is exposed to light of a particular wavelength. To determine where a peptide or protein (the antigen) is located in the brain, the investigator places fresh slices of brain tissue in a solution that contains the antibody/dye molecules. The antibodies attach themselves to their antigen. When the investigator examines the slices with a microscope under light of the appropriate wavelength, he or she can see which parts of the brain—even which individual neurons—contain the antigen.

In this case, we are interested in finding neurons that produce acetylcholine. To do so, we place sections of brain tissue in a solution that contains an antibody to ChAT, linked to a fluorescent dye. Then we rinse the sections, mount them on a microscope slide, and examine them under a microscope, using light of the correct wavelength. Figure 5.26 shows acetylcholinergic neurons in the pons that have been identified by means of immunocytochemistry. The brain tissue was exposed to an antibody to ChAT attached to a fluorescent dye. As we will see in Chapter 8, these neurons are, indeed, involved in the control of REM sleep. (See *Figure 5.26.*)

Localizing Particular Receptors

FIGURE 5.26

Localization of an enzyme responsible for the synthesis of a neurotransmitter, revealed by immunocytochemistry. The photomicrograph shows a section through the pons. The orange neurons contain choline acetyltransferase, which implies that they produce (and thus secrete) acetylcholine.

(Courtesy of David A. Morilak and Roland Ciaranello, Nancy Pritzker Laboratory of Developmental and Molecular Neurobiology, Department of Psychiatry and Behavioral Sciences, Stanford University School of Medicine.)

We have just seen how to identify the location of acetylcholine-secreting neurons. Is there a way to identify neurons that receive input from these neurons? Of course, we could use an anterograde labeling method, such as PHA-L, to trace the pathway of axons from the acetylcholine-secreting neurons in the pons. But we can also directly identify the location of acetylcholine receptors, which will provide us with similar information. In fact, there are two methods that accomplish this task.

The first method uses autoradiography, a procedure described earlier in this chapter. We expose slices of brain tissue to a solution containing a radioactive ligand for the acetylcholine receptor. Next, we rinse the slices so that the only radioactivity remaining in them is that of the molecules of the ligand bound to their receptors. Finally, we use autoradiographic methods to localize the radioactive ligand—and thus, the receptors.

The second method uses immunocytochemistry. Receptors are proteins; thus, we can produce antibodies against them. We expose slices of brain tissue to the appropriate antibody (labeled with a fluorescent dye) and look at the slices with a microscope under light of a particular wavelength.

Let's apply the method for localizing receptors to another line of investigation we considered earlier in this chapter: the role of the ventromedial hypothalamus (VMH) in the sexual behavior of female rats. As we saw, lesions of the VMH abolish sexual behavior. We also saw that the behavior does not occur if the rat's ovaries are removed, but it can be activated by stimulation of the VMH with electricity or an excitatory amino acid. These results suggest that the sex hormones produced by the ovaries act on neurons in the VMH.

This hypothesis suggests two experiments. First, we could use the procedure shown in Figure 5.25 to place a small amount of the appropriate sex hormone directly into the VMH of female rats whose ovaries we had previously removed. As we shall see in Chapter 9, this procedure works; the hormone *does* reactivate the animals' sexual behavior. The second experiment would use autoradiography to look for the receptors for the sex hormone. We would expose slices of rat brain to the radioactive hormone, rinse them, and perform autoradiography. If we did so, we would indeed find radioactivity in the VMH. (And if we compared slices from the brains of female and male rats, we would find evidence of more hormone receptors in the female brains.) We could also use immunocytochemistry to localize the hormone receptors, and we would obtain the same results.

INTERIM SUMMARY

Neurochemical methods can be used to determine the location of an enormous variety of substances in the brain. They can identify neurons that secrete a particular neurotransmitter or neuromodulator and those that possess receptors that respond to the presence of these substances. Peptides and proteins can be directly localized, through immunocytochemical methods. To do so, the tissue is exposed to an antibody that is linked to a molecule that fluoresces under light of a particular wavelength. Other substances can be detected by immunocytochemical localization of an enzyme required for their synthesis.

Receptors for neurochemicals can be localized by two means. The first method uses autoradiography to reveal the distribution of a radioactive ligand to which the tissue has been exposed. The second method uses immunocytochemistry to detect the presence of the receptors themselves, which are proteins.

Table 5.3 summarizes the research methods presented in this section.

GENETIC METHODS

All behavior is determined by interactions between an individual's brain and his or her environment. Many behavioral characteristics—such as talents, personality variables, and mental disorders—seem to run in families. This fact suggests that genetic factors may play a role in the development of physiological differences that are ultimately responsible for these characteristics. In some cases, the genetic link is very clear: A defective gene interferes with brain development and a neurological abnormality causes behavioral deficits. In other cases, the links between heredity and behavior are much more subtle, and special genetic methods must be used to reveal them.

TABLE 5.3	Research Methods: Part III		
Goal of Method	**Method**		**Remarks**
Identify neurons producing a particular neurotransmitter or neuromodulator	Immunocytochemical localization of peptide or protein		Requires a specific antibody
	Immunocytochemical localization of enzyme responsible for synthesis of substance		Useful if substance is not a peptide or protein
Identify neurons that contain a particular type of receptor	Autoradiographic localization of radioactive ligand		
	Immunocytochemical localization of receptor		Requires a specific antibody

Twin Studies

A powerful method for estimating the influence of heredity on a particular trait is to compare the *concordance rate* for this trait in pairs of monozygotic and dizygotic twins. Monozygotic twins (identical twins) have identical genotypes—that is, their chromosomes, and the genes they contain, are identical. In contrast, the genetic similarity between dizygotic twins (fraternal twins) is, on the average, 50 percent. Investigators study records to identify pairs of twins in which at least one member has the trait—for example, a diagnosis of a particular mental disorder. If both twins have been diagnosed with this disorder, they are said to be *concordant*. If only one has received this diagnosis, the twins are said to be *discordant*. Thus, if a disorder has a genetic basis, the percentage of monozygotic twins who are concordant for the diagnosis will be higher than that for dizygotic twins. For example, as we will see in Chapter 15, the concordance rate for schizophrenia in twins is at least four times higher in monozygotic twins than for dizygotic twins, a finding that provides strong evidence that schizophrenia is a heritable trait. Twin studies have found that many individual characteristics, including personality traits, prevalence of obesity, incidence of alcoholism, and a wide variety of mental disorders are influenced by genetic factors.

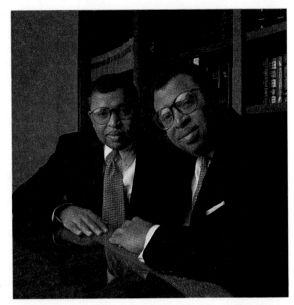

Twin studies provide a powerful method for estimating the relative roles of heredity and environment in the development of particular behavioral traits.

Adoption Studies

Another method for estimating the heritability of a particular behavioral trait is to compare people who were adopted early in life with their biological and adoptive parents. All behavioral traits are affected to some degree by hereditary factors, environmental factors, and an interaction between hereditary and environmental factors. Environmental factors are both social and biological in nature. For example, the mother's health, nutrition, and drug-taking behavior during pregnancy are prenatal environmental factors, and the child's diet, medical care, and social environment (both inside and outside the home) are postnatal environmental factors. If a child is adopted soon after birth, many of the postnatal environmental factors will be associated with the adoptive parents, while all of the genetic factors will be associated with the biological parents and the prenatal environmental factors with the biological mother.

Adoption studies require that the investigator knows the identity of the parents of the people being studied and is able to measure the behavioral trait in the biological and adoptive parents. If the people being studied strongly resemble their biological parents, we conclude that the trait is probably influenced by genetic factors. To be certain, we will have to rule out possible differences in the prenatal environment of the adopted children. If, instead, the people resemble their adoptive parents, we conclude that the trait is influenced by environmental factors. (It would take further study to determine just what these environmental factors might be.) Of course, it is possible that both hereditary and environmental factors play a role, in which case the people being studied will resemble both their biological and adoptive parents.

Targeted Mutations

A recently developed method has put a powerful tool in the hands of neuroscientists. **Targeted mutations** are mutated genes produced in the laboratory and inserted into the chromosomes of mice. These mutated genes (also called "knockout" genes) are defective—they fail to produce a functional protein. In many cases, the target of the

Targeted mutation Mutated genes that are produced in a laboratory and inserted into the chromosomes of mice.

mutation is an enzyme that controls a particular chemical reaction. For example, we will see in Chapter 12 that lack of a particular enzyme interferes with learning. This result suggests that the enzyme is partly responsible for changes in the structure of synapses required for learning to occur. In other cases, the target of the mutation is a protein that itself serves useful functions in the cell. For example, we will see in Chapter 16 that a particular type of opiate receptor is involved in the reinforcing and analgesic effects of opiates.

INTERIM SUMMARY

Because genes direct an organism's development, genetic methods are very useful in studies of the physiology of behavior. Twin studies compare the concordance rates of monozygotic (identical) and dizygotic (fraternal) twins for a particular trait. A higher concordance rate for monozygotic twins provides evidence that the trait is influenced by heredity. Adoption studies compare people who were adopted during infancy with their biological and adoptive parents. If the people resemble their biological parents, evidence is seen for genetic factors. If the people resemble their adoptive parents, evidence is seen for a role of factors in the family environment.

Targeted mutations permit neuroscientists to study the effects of a lack of a particular protein—for example, an enzyme, structural protein, or receptor—on the physiological and behavioral characteristics of an animal.

THOUGHT QUESTIONS

1. You have probably read news reports about studies of the genetics of human behavioral traits or seen them on television. What does it really mean when a laboratory reports the discovery of, say, a "gene for shyness"?
2. Most rats do not appear to like the taste of alcohol, but researchers have bred some rats that will drink alcohol in large quantities. Can you think of ways to use these animals to investigate the possible role of genetic factors in alcoholism in humans?

EPILOGUE

Watch the Brain Waves

What went wrong? Why did Mrs. H.'s "successful" surgery cause a neurological problem? And can anything be done for her?

First, let's consider the cause of the problem. As you will recall, a machine circulated Mrs. H.'s blood while the surgeon was removing two of her coronary arteries and replacing them with veins taken from her leg. The output of the machine is adjustable; that is, the person operating it can control the patient's blood pressure. The surgeon tries to keep the blood pressure just high enough to sustain the patient but not so high as to interfere with the delicate surgery on the coronary arteries. Unfortunately, Mrs. H.'s coronary arteries were not the only blood vessels to be partially blocked; the arteries in her brain, too, contained atherosclerotic plaque.

When the machine took over the circulation of her blood, some parts of her brain received an inadequate blood flow, and the cells in these regions were damaged.

If Mrs. H.'s blood pressure had been maintained at a slightly higher level during the surgery, her brain damage might have been prevented. For most patients, the blood pressure would have been sufficient, but in her case it was not. Mrs. H.'s brain damage is irreversible, but are there steps that can be taken to prevent others from sharing her fate?

The answer is yes. The solution is to use a method described in this chapter: electroencephalography. What we need is a warning system to tell the surgeon that the brain is not receiving a sufficient blood flow so that he or she can adjust the machine and increase the patient's blood pressure. That warning can be provided by an EEG. For many years, clinical electroencephalographers (specialists who perform EEGs to diagnose neurological disorders) have known that diffuse, widespread brain damage caused by various poisons, anoxia, or extremely low levels of blood glucose produce slowing of the regular rhythmic pattern of the EEG. Fortunately, this pattern begins right away, as soon as the damage commences. Thus, if EEG leads are attached to a patient undergoing cardiac surgery, an electroencephalographer can watch the record coming off the polygraph and warn the surgeon if the record shows slowing. If it does, the patient's blood flow can be increased until the EEG reverts to normal, and brain damage can be averted.

Mrs. H. was operated on over 15 years ago, at a time when only a few cardiac surgeons had their patients' brain waves monitored. Today, the practice is common, and it is used during other surgical procedures that may reduce blood flow to the brain. For example, when the carotid arteries (the vessels that provide most of the brain's blood supply) become obstructed by atherosclerotic plaque, a surgeon can cut open the arteries and remove the plaque. During this procedure, called *carotid endarterectomy*, clamps must be placed on the carotid artery, completely stopping the blood flow. Some patients can tolerate the temporary clamping of one carotid artery without damage; others cannot. If the EEG record shows no slowing while the artery is clamped, the surgeon can proceed. If it does, the surgeon must place the ends of a plastic tube into the artery above and below the clamped region to maintain a constant blood flow. This procedure introduces a certain amount of risk to the patient, so most surgeons would prefer to do it only if necessary. The EEG provides the essential information.

By the way, Balint's syndrome is described in more detail in Chapter 6, and Chapter 14 discusses the causes of strokes.

KEY CONCEPTS

EXPERIMENTAL ABLATION

1. Neuroscientists produce brain lesions to try to infer the functions of the damaged region from changes in the animals' behavior.
2. Brain lesions may be produced in the depths of the brain by passing electrical current through an electrode placed in the brain or by infusing an excitatory amino acid; the latter method kills cells but spares axons that pass through the region.
3. The behavior of animals with brain lesions must be compared with that of a control group consisting of animals with sham lesions.
4. A stereotaxic apparatus is used to place electrodes or cannulas in particular locations in the brain. The coordinates are obtained from a stereotaxic atlas.
5. The location of a lesion is verified by means of histological methods, which include fixation, slicing, staining, and examination of the tissue under a microscope.
6. Special histological methods have been devised to trace the afferent and efferent connections of a particular brain region.
7. The structure of the living human brain can be revealed through CT scans or MRI scans.

RECORDING AND STIMULATING NEURAL ACTIVITY

8. The electrical activity of single neurons can be recorded with microelectrodes, and that of regions of the brain can be recorded with macroelectrodes. EEGs are recorded on polygraphs and recorded from macroelectrodes pasted on a person's scalp.
9. Metabolic activity of particular parts of animals' brains can be assessed by means of 2-DG autoradiography or by measurement of the production of Fos protein. The metabolic activity of specific regions of the human brain can be revealed through PET scans or functional MRI scans.
10. Microdialysis permits a researcher to measure the secretion of particular chemicals in specific regions of the brain.
11. Neurons can be stimulated electrically, through electrodes, or chemically, by infusing dilute solutions of excitatory amino acids through cannulas.

NEUROCHEMICAL METHODS

12. Immunocytochemical methods can be used to localize peptides in the brain or localize the enzymes that produce substances other than peptides.

13. Receptors can be localized by exposing the brain tissue to radioactive ligands and assessing the results with autoradiography or immunocytochemistry.

GENETIC METHODS

14. Twin studies and adoption studies enable investigators to estimate the role of hereditary factors in a particular physiological characteristic or behavior.

15. Targeted mutations are artificially produced mutations that interfere with the action of one or more genes. They enable investigators to study the effects of the lack of a particular gene product.

SUGGESTED READINGS

LABORATORY MANUAL

Wellman, P. *Laboratory Exercises in Physiological Psychology.* Boston: Allyn and Bacon, 1994.

STEREOTAXIC ATLASES

Paxinos, G., and Watson, C. *The Rat Brain in Stereotaxic Coordinates,* 2nd ed. Sydney: Academic Press, 1986.

Slotnick, B.M., and Leonard, C.M. *A Stereotaxic Atlas of the Albino Mouse Forebrain.* Rockville, MD: Public Health Service, 1975. (U.S. Government Printing Office Stock Number 017–024–00491–0)

Snider, R.S., and Niemer, W.T. *A Stereotaxic Atlas of the Cat Brain.* Chicago: University of Chicago Press, 1961.

Swanson, L.W. *Brain Maps: Structure of the Rat Brain.* Amsterdam: Elsevier, 1992.

HISTOLOGICAL METHODS

Heimer, L., and Záborsky, L. *Neuroanatomical Tract-Tracing Methods 2: Recent Progress.* New York: Plenum Press, 1989.

6

Vision

LEARNING OBJECTIVES

1. Describe the characteristics of light and color, outline the anatomy of the eye and its connections with the brain, and describe the process of transduction of visual information.

2. Describe the coding of visual information by photoreceptors and ganglion cells in the retina.

3. Describe the striate cortex and discuss how its neurons respond to orientation, movement, and spatial frequency.

4. Discuss how neurons in the striate cortex respond to retinal disparity and color, and explain the modular organization of striate cortex and the phenomenon of blindsight.

5. Describe the anatomy of the visual association cortex and discuss the location and functions of the two streams of visual analysis that take place there.

6. Discuss the perception of color and the analysis of form by neurons in the ventral stream.

7. Describe the two basic forms of visual agnosia: apperceptive visual agnosia and associative visual agnosia.

8. Describe how neurons in extrastriate cortex respond to movement and location, and discuss the effects of brain damage on perception of these features.

Seeing with His Hands

One Sunday morning, a colleague called me and asked if I would like to meet him at a nearby hospital to interview a patient with an interesting disorder. I joined him there and met a pleasant man in his mid-thirties. Mr. M. had sustained brain damage from an inflammatory disease that affected the blood vessels in his brain. His speech appeared to be normal, but he had great difficulty recognizing objects or pictures of them. We went through a book of pictures that is ordinarily used to test children's vocabularies, and we found that he was unable to say what many of them were. However, he sometimes made unintentional gestures when he was studying a picture that gave him enough of a clue to identify it. For example, on one occasion while he was puzzling over a picture of a cow, he held his fists together and started making alternating up-and-down movements with them. Unmistakably, he was acting as if he were milking a cow. He looked at his hands and said, "Oh, a cow!" He laughed. "I live on a farm, you know."

We later learned that his tendency to make movements that helped him "see" things was first discovered by a speech therapist. The brain damage had destroyed his ability to read as well as to recognize objects, and she was trying to help him regain this ability. She wanted to capitalize on the potential of his visual perceptions to trigger automatic hand movements, even though he could not describe those perceptions in words. Therefore, she decided to try to teach him the manual alphabet used by deaf people, in which letters are represented by particular hand and finger movements. (This system is commonly called *finger spelling*.) She showed Mr. M. a letter and asked him to say what it was. He was unable to do so. Then she held his fingers and moved them into the position that "spelled" the letter. Over several sessions she was able to teach him to make the proper movements, which he could do even though he was unable to say what each letter was. Once his fingers moved, he could feel their position and say what the letter must be. He was able to use this ability to read whole words; he looked at individual letters of a word, made the appropriate movements, observed the sequence of letters that he spelled, and recognized the word. The process was slow, but it worked.

As we saw in Chapter 3, the brain performs two major functions: It controls the movements of the muscles, producing useful behaviors, and it regulates the body's internal environment. To perform both these tasks, the brain must be informed about what is happening both in the external environment and within the body. Such information is received by the sensory systems. This chapter and the next are devoted to a discussion of the ways in which sensory organs detect changes in the environment and the ways in which the brain interprets neural signals from these organs.

We receive information about the environment from **sensory receptors**—specialized neurons that detect a variety of physical events. (Do not confuse *sensory receptors* with receptors for neurotransmitters, neuromodulators, and hormones. Sensory receptors are specialized neurons, and the other types of receptors are specialized proteins that bind with certain molecules.) Stimuli interact with the receptors and alter their membrane potentials. This process is known as **sensory transduction** because sensory events are *transduced* ("transferred") into changes in the cells' membrane potential. These electrical changes are called **receptor potentials.** Receptor potentials affect the release of neurotransmitters and hence modify the pattern of firing in neurons with which these cells form synapses. Ultimately, the information reaches the brain.

People often say that we have five senses: sight, hearing, smell, taste, and touch. Actually, we have more than five, but even experts disagree about how the lines between the various categories should be drawn. Certainly, we should add the *vestibular senses*. As well as providing us with auditory information, the inner ear supplies information about head orientation and movement. The sense of touch (or, more accurately, *somatosensation*) detects changes in pressure, warmth, cold, vibration, limb position, and events that damage tissue (that is, produce pain). Everyone agrees that we can detect these stimuli; the issue is whether they are detected by separate senses.

Sensory receptor A specialized neuron that detects a particular category of physical events.

Sensory transduction The process by which sensory stimuli are transduced into slow, graded receptor potentials.

Receptor potential A slow, graded electrical potential produced by a receptor cell in response to a physical stimulus.

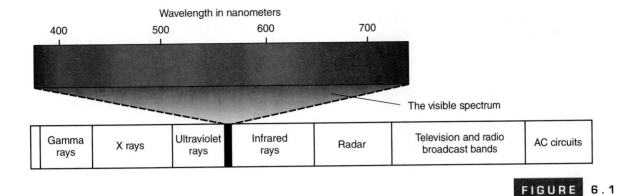

Wavelength in nanometers

400　　　500　　　600　　　700

The visible spectrum

| Gamma rays | X rays | Ultraviolet rays | Infrared rays | Radar | Television and radio broadcast bands | AC circuits |

FIGURE 6.1

The electromagnetic spectrum.

This chapter considers vision, the sensory modality that receives the most attention from psychologists, anatomists, and physiologists. One reason for this attention comes from the fascinating complexity of the sensory organs of vision and the relatively large proportion of the brain that is devoted to the analysis of visual information. Another reason, I am sure, is that vision is so important to us as individuals. A natural fascination with such a rich source of information about the world leads to curiosity about how this sensory modality works. Chapter 7 deals with the other sensory modalities: hearing, the vestibular senses, the somatosenses, taste, and smell.

 THE STIMULUS

As we all know, our eyes detect the presence of light. For humans, light is a narrow band of the spectrum of electromagnetic radiation. Electromagnetic radiation with a wavelength between 380 and 760 nm (a nanometer, nm, is one-billionth of a meter) is visible to us. (See *Figure 6.1*.) Other animals can detect different ranges of electromagnetic radiation. For example, honeybees can detect differences in ultraviolet radiation reflected by flowers that appear white to us. The range of wavelengths that we call *light* is not qualitatively different from the rest of the electromagnetic spectrum; it is simply the part of the continuum that we humans can see.

The perceived color of light is determined by three dimensions: *hue, saturation,* and *brightness.* Wavelength determines the first of the three perceptual dimensions of light: **hue.** The visible spectrum displays the range of hues that our eyes can detect.

Light can also vary in intensity, which corresponds to the second perceptual dimension of light: **brightness.** If the intensity of the electromagnetic radiation is increased, the apparent brightness increases, too. The third dimension, **saturation,** refers to the relative purity of the light that is being perceived. If all the radiation is of one wavelength, the perceived color is pure, or fully saturated. Conversely, if the radiation contains all wavelengths, it produces no sensation of hue—it appears white. Colors with intermediate amounts of saturation consist of different mixtures of wavelengths. Figure 6.2 shows some color samples, all with the same hue but with different levels of brightness and saturation. (See *Figure 6.2*.)

Hue One of the perceptual dimensions of color; the dominant wavelength.

Brightness One of the perceptual dimensions of color; intensity.

Saturation One of the perceptual dimensions of color; purity.

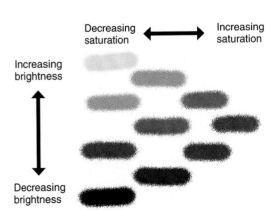

Decreasing saturation ⟷ Increasing saturation

Increasing brightness

Decreasing brightness

FIGURE 6.2

Examples of colors with the same dominant wavelength (hue) but different levels of saturation or brightness.

Some animals, such as this honeybee, can detect wavelengths of electromagnetic radiation that are invisible to us.

ANATOMY OF THE VISUAL SYSTEM

For an individual to see, an image must be focused on the retina, the inner lining of the eye. This image causes changes in the electrical activity of millions of neurons in the retina, which results in messages being sent through the optic nerves to the rest of the brain. (I said "the rest" because the retina and the optic nerve are actually part of the brain. This section describes the anatomy of the eyes, the photoreceptors in the retina that detect the presence of light, and the connections between the retina and the brain.

The Eyes

The eyes are suspended in the *orbits,* bony pockets in the front of the skull. They are held in place and moved by six *extraocular* muscles attached to the tough, white outer coat of the eye called the *sclera.* Normally, we cannot look behind our eyeballs and see these muscles, because their attachments to the eyes are hidden by the *conjunctiva.* These mucous membranes line the eyelid and fold back to attach to the eye (thus preventing a contact lens that has slipped off the cornea from "falling behind the eye"). Figure 6.3 illustrates the external and internal anatomy of the eye. (See *Figure 6.3.*)

The outer layer of most of the eye, the sclera, is opaque and does not permit entry of light. However, the cornea, the outer layer at the front of the eye, is transparent and admits light. The amount of light that enters is regulated by the size of the pupil, which is an opening in the iris, the pigmented ring of muscles situated behind the cornea. The lens, situated immediately behind the iris, consists of a series of transparent, onionlike layers. Its shape can be altered by contraction of the ciliary

FIGURE 6.3

The human eye.

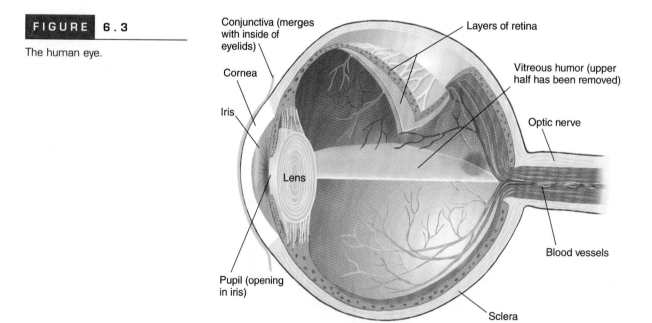

TABLE 6.1	Locations and Response Characteristics of Photoreceptors	
Cones	**Rods**	
Most prevalent in the central retina; found in the fovea	Most prevalent in the peripheral retina; not found in the fovea	
Sensitive to moderate-to-high levels of light	Sensitive to low levels of light	
Provide information about hue	Provide only monochromatic information	
Provide excellent acuity	Provide poor acuity	

Accommodation Changes in the thickness of the lens of the eye, accomplished by the ciliary muscles, that focus images of near or distant objects on the retina.

Retina The neural tissue and photoreceptive cells located on the inner surface of the posterior portion of the eye.

Rod One of the receptor cells of the retina; sensitive to light of low intensity.

Cone One of the receptor cells of the retina; maximally sensitive to one of three different wavelengths of light and hence encodes color vision.

Photoreceptor One of the receptor cells of the retina; transduces photic energy into electrical potentials.

Fovea (*foe vee a*) The region of the retina that mediates the most acute vision of birds and higher mammals. Color-sensitive cones constitute the only type of photoreceptor found in the fovea.

Optic disk The location of the exit point from the retina of the fibers of the ganglion cells that form the optic nerve; responsible for the blind spot.

muscles. These changes in shape permit the eye to focus images of near or distant objects on the retina—a process called **accommodation.**

After passing through the lens, light passes through the main part of the eye, which contains the *vitreous humor* ("glassy liquid"), a clear, gelatinous substance. After passing through the vitreous humor, light falls on the **retina,** the interior lining of the back of the eye. In the retina are located the receptor cells, the **rods** and **cones** (named for their shapes), collectively known as **photoreceptors.** The human retina contains approximately 120 million rods and 6 million cones. Although they are greatly outnumbered by rods, cones provide us with most of the information about our environment. In particular, they are responsible for our daytime vision. They provide us with information about small features in the environment and thus are the source of vision of the highest sharpness, or *acuity* (from *acus,* "needle"). The **fovea,** or central region of the retina, which mediates our most acute vision, contains only cones. Cones are also responsible for color vision—our ability to discriminate light of different wavelengths. Although rods do not detect different colors and provide vision of poor acuity, they are more sensitive to light. In a very dimly lighted environment we use our rod vision; therefore, in dim light we are color-blind and lack foveal vision. (See *Table 6.1.*)

Another feature of the retina is the **optic disk,** where the axons conveying visual information gather together and leave the eye through the optic nerve. The optic disk produces a *blind spot* because no receptors are located there. We do not normally perceive our blind spots, but their presence can be demonstrated. If you have not found yours, you may want to try the exercise described in *Figure 6.4.*

Close examination of the retina shows that it consists of several layers of neuron cell bodies, their axons and dendrites, and the photoreceptors. Figure 6.5 illustrates

FIGURE 6.4

A test for the blind spot. With your left eye closed, look at the + with your right eye and move the page nearer to and farther from you. When the page is about 20 cm from your face, the green circle disappears, because its image falls on the blind spot of your right eye.

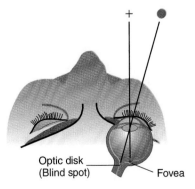

Optic disk (Blind spot) Fovea

+

FIGURE 6.5

Details of retinal circuitry.

[Adapted from Dowling, J.E., and Boycott, B.B. Proceedings of the Royal Society of London, B., 1966, 166, 80–111.]

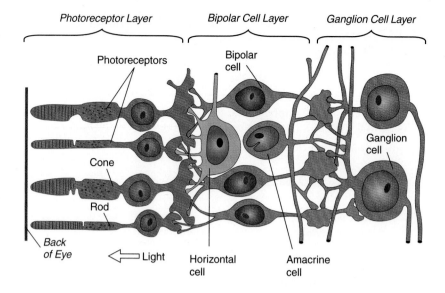

Bipolar cell A bipolar neuron located in the middle layer of the retina, conveying information from the photoreceptors to the ganglion cells.

Ganglion cell A neuron located in the retina that receives visual information from bipolar cells; its axons give rise to the optic nerve.

Horizontal cell A neuron in the retina that interconnects adjacent photoreceptors and the outer processes of the bipolar cells.

Amacrine cell (*amm a krin*) A neuron in the retina that interconnects adjacent ganglion cells and the inner processes of the bipolar cells.

Lamella A layer of membrane containing photopigments; found in rods and cones of the retina.

Photopigment A protein dye bonded to retinal, a substance derived from vitamin A; responsible for transduction of visual information.

a cross section through the primate retina, which is divided into three main layers: the photoreceptive layer, the bipolar cell layer, and the ganglion cell layer. Note that the photoreceptors are at the *back* of the retina; light must pass through the overlying layers to get to them. Fortunately, these layers are transparent. (See ***Figure 6.5.***)

The photoreceptors form synapses with **bipolar cells,** neurons whose two arms connect the shallowest and deepest layers of the retina. In turn, these neurons form synapses with the **ganglion cells,** neurons whose axons travel through the optic nerves (the second cranial nerves) and carry visual information into the brain. In addition, the retina contains **horizontal cells** and **amacrine cells,** both of which transmit information in a direction parallel to the surface of the retina and thus combine messages from adjacent photoreceptors. (See ***Figure 6.5.***)

Photoreceptors

Figure 6.6 shows a drawing of two rods and a cone. Note that each photoreceptor consists of an outer segment connected by a cilium to the inner segment, which contains the nucleus. (See ***Figure 6.6.***) The outer segment contains several hundred **lamellae,** or thin plates of membrane. (*Lamella* is the diminutive form of *lamina,* "thin layer.")

Let's consider the nature of transduction of visual information. The first step in the chain of events that leads to visual perception involves a special chemical called a photopigment. **Photopigments** are special molecules embedded in the membrane of the lamellae; a single human rod contains approximately 10 million of them. The molecules consist of two parts: an **opsin** (a protein) and **retinal** (a lipid). There are several forms of opsin; for example, the photopigment of human rods, **rhodopsin,** consists of *rod opsin* plus retinal. (*Rhod-* refers to the Greek *rhodon,* "rose," not to *rod.* Before it is bleached by the action of light, rhodopsin has a pinkish hue.) Retinal is synthesized from vitamin A, which explains why carrots, rich in this vitamin, are said to be good for your eyesight.

When a molecule of rhodopsin is exposed to light, it breaks into its two constituents, rod opsin

FIGURE 6.6

Photoreceptors.

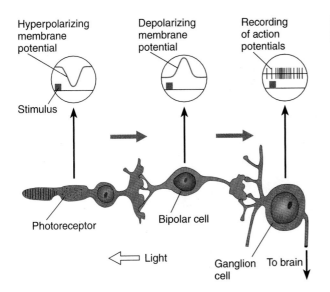

Hyperpolarizing membrane potential

Depolarizing membrane potential

Recording of action potentials

Stimulus

Photoreceptor

Bipolar cell

Light

Ganglion cell

To brain

FIGURE 6.7

Neural circuitry in the retina. Light striking a photoreceptor produces a hyperpolarization, so the photoreceptor releases *less* neurotransmitter. Because the neurotransmitter normally hyperpolarizes the membrane of the bipolar cell, the reduction causes a *depolarization*. This depolarization causes the bipolar cell to release *more* neurotransmitter, which excites the ganglion cell.

(Adapted from Dowling, J.E., in The Neurosciences: Fourth Study Program, *edited by F.O. Schmitt and F.G. Worden. Cambridge Mass.: MIT Press, 1979.)*

and retinal. When that happens, the rod opsin changes from its rosy color to a pale yellow; hence, we say that the light *bleaches* the photopigment. The splitting of the photopigment causes a change in the membrane potential of the photoreceptor (the receptor potential), which changes the rate at which the photoreceptor releases its neurotransmitter, glutamate.

In the vertebrate retina, photoreceptors provide input to both bipolar cells and horizontal cells. Figure 6.7 shows the neural circuitry from a photoreceptor to a ganglion cell. The circuitry is much simplified and omits the horizontal cells and amacrine cells. The first two types of cells in the circuit—photoreceptors and bipolar cells—do not produce action potentials. Instead, their release of neurotransmitter is regulated by the value of their membrane potential; depolarizations increase the release, and hyperpolarizations decrease it. The circles indicate what would be seen on an oscilloscope screen recording changes in the cells' membrane potentials in response to a spot of light shining on the photoreceptor.

The hyperpolarizing effect of light on the membranes of photoreceptors is shown in the left graph. The hyperpolarization *reduces* the release of neurotransmitter by the photoreceptor. Because the neurotransmitter normally hyperpolarizes the dendrites of the bipolar cell, a *reduction* in its release causes the membrane of the bipolar cell to *depolarize*. Thus, light hyperpolarizes the photoreceptor and depolarizes the bipolar cell. (See *Figure 6.7.*) The depolarization causes the bipolar cell to release more neurotransmitter, which depolarizes the membrane of the ganglion cell, causing it to increase its rate of firing. Thus, light shining on the photoreceptor causes excitation of the ganglion cell.

The circuit shown in Figure 6.7 illustrates a ganglion cell whose firing rate increases in response to light. As we will see, other ganglion cells *decrease* their firing rate in response to light. These neurons are connected to bipolar cells that form different types of synapses with the photoreceptors. The functions of these two types of circuits are discussed in a later section, Coding of Visual Information in the Retina.

Connections Between Eye and Brain

The axons of the retinal ganglion cells bring information to the rest of the brain. They ascend through the optic nerves and reach the **dorsal lateral geniculate nucleus** of the thalamus. This nucleus receives its name from its resemblance to a bent knee (*genu* means "knee"). It contains six layers of neurons, each of which receives input from only one eye. The neurons in the two inner layers contain cell bodies that are

Opsin (*opp* sin) A class of protein that, together with retinal, constitutes the photopigments.

Retinal (*rett* i nahl) A chemical synthesized from vitamin A; joins with an opsin to form a photopigment.

Rhodopsin (roh *dopp* sin) A particular opsin found in rods.

Dorsal lateral geniculate nucleus A group of cell bodies within the lateral geniculate body of the thalamus; receives inputs from the retina and projects to the primary visual cortex.

FIGURE 6.8

A photomicrograph of a section through the right lateral geniculate nucleus of a rhesus monkey (cresyl violet stain). Layers 1, 4, and 6 receive input from the contralateral (left) eye, and layers 2, 3, and 5 receive input from the ipsilateral (right) eye. Layers 1 and 2 are the magnocellular layers; layers 3–6 are the parvocellular layers. The receptive fields of all six layers are in almost perfect registration; cells located along the line of the unlabeled arrow have receptive fields centered on the same point.

(From Hubel, D.H., Wiesel, T.N., and Le Vay, S. Philosophical Transactions of the Royal Society of London, B., 1977, 278, 131–163.)

FIGURE 6.9

The primary visual pathway.

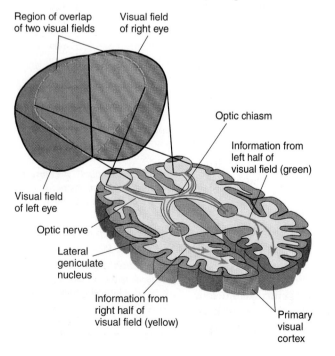

larger than those in the outer four layers. For this reason, the inner two layers are called the **magnocellular layers** and the outer four layers are called the **parvocellular layers** (*parvo*- refers to the small size of the cells). As we will see later, these two sets of layers belong to different systems, which are responsible for the analysis of different types of visual information. They receive input from different types of retinal ganglion cells. (See *Figure 6.8.*)

The neurons in the dorsal lateral geniculate nucleus send their axons to the primary visual cortex—the region surrounding the **calcarine fissure** (*calcarine* means "spur-shaped"), a horizontal fissure located in the medial and posterior occipital lobe. The primary visual cortex is often called the **striate cortex** because it contains a dark-staining layer *(striation)* of cells.

Figure 6.9 shows a diagrammatical view of a horizontal section of the human brain. The optic nerves join together at the base of the brain to form the X-shaped **optic chiasm** (*khiasma* means "cross" in Greek). There, axons from ganglion cells serving the inner halves of the retina (the nasal sides) cross through the chiasm and ascend to the dorsal lateral geniculate nucleus of the opposite side of the brain. The axons from the outer halves of the retina (the temporal sides) remain on the same side of the brain. (See *Figure 6.9.*) The lens inverts the image of the world projected on the retina (and similarly reverses left and right). Therefore, because the axons from the nasal halves of the retinas cross to the other side of the brain, each hemisphere receives information from the contralateral half (opposite side) of the visual scene. That is, if a person looks straight ahead, the right hemisphere receives information from the left half of the visual field, and the left hemisphere receives information from the right. (See *Figure 6.9.*)

Besides the primary retino-geniculo-cortical pathway, several other pathways are taken by fibers from the retina. For example, one pathway to the hypothalamus synchronizes an animal's activity cycles to the 24-hour rhythms of day and night. (We will study this system in Chapter 8.) Other pathways, especially those that travel to the optic tectum and the pretectal nuclei, coordinate eye movements, control the muscles of the iris (and thus, the size of the pupil) and the ciliary muscles (which control the lens), and help to direct our attention to sudden movements in the periphery of our visual field.

INTERIM SUMMARY

Light consists of electromagnetic radiation, similar to radio waves but of a different frequency and wavelength. Color can vary in three perceptual dimensions: hue, brightness, and saturation, which correspond, respectively, to the physical dimensions of wavelength, intensity, and purity.

The photoreceptors in the retina—the rods and the cones—detect light. Muscles move the eyes so that images of the environment fall on the retina. Accommodation is accomplished by the ciliary muscles, which change the shape of the lens. Photoreceptors communicate through synapses with bipolar cells, which communicate through synapses with ganglion cells. In addition, horizontal cells and amacrine cells combine messages from adjacent photoreceptors.

When light strikes a molecule of photopigment in a photoreceptor, the retinal molecule detaches from the opsin molecule, a process known as bleaching. This event causes the membrane potential to become more polarized. The change in the membrane potential decreases the release of glutamate and informs the bipolar cell with which the photoreceptors communicate that light has just been detected. As a result of this process, the rate of firing of the ganglion cell changes, and a message is sent through the axons of the optic nerves.

Visual information from the retina reaches the striate cortex surrounding the calcarine fissure after being relayed through the magnocellular and parvocellular layers of the dorsal lateral geniculate nuclei. Several other regions of the brain, including the hypothalamus and the tectum, also receive visual information. These regions help to regulate activity during the day–night cycle, coordinate eye and head movements, control attention to visual stimuli, and regulate the size of the pupils.

THOUGHT QUESTIONS

People who try to see faint, distant lights at night are often advised to look just to the side of the location where they expect to see the lights. Can you explain the reason for this advice?

CODING OF VISUAL INFORMATION IN THE RETINA

This section describes the way in which cells of the retina encode information they receive from the photoreceptors.

Magnocellular layer One of the inner two layers of cells in the dorsal lateral geniculate nucleus; transmits information necessary for the perception of form, movement, depth, and small differences in brightness.

Parvocellular layer One of the four outer layers of cells in the dorsal lateral geniculate nucleus; transmits information necessary for perception of color and fine details.

Calcarine fissure (*kal ka rine*) A horizontal fissure on the inner surface of the posterior cerebral cortex; the location of the primary visual cortex.

Striate cortex (*stry ate*) The primary visual cortex.

Optic chiasm A cross-shaped connection between the optic nerves, located below the base of the brain, just anterior to the pituitary gland.

Receptive field in center
of retina (fovea)

Photoreceptors

Bipolar
cells

Ganglion
cells

Receptive field in
periphery of retina

FIGURE 6.10

Central versus peripheral acuity. Ganglion cells in the fovea receive input from a smaller number of photoreceptors than in the periphery and hence provide more acute visual information.

Receptive field The portion of the visual field in which the presentation of visual stimuli will produce an alteration in the firing rate of a particular neuron.

Coding of Light and Dark

One of the most important methods for studying the physiology of the visual system is the use of microelectrodes to record the electrical activity of single neurons. As we saw in the previous section, some ganglion cells become excited when light falls on the photoreceptors with which they communicate. The **receptive field** of a neuron in the visual system is the part of the visual field that neuron "sees"—that is, the part in which light must fall for the neuron to be stimulated. Obviously, the location of the receptive field of a particular neuron depends on the location of the photoreceptors that provide it with visual information. If a neuron receives information from photoreceptors located in the fovea, its receptive field will be at the fixation point—the point at which the eye is looking. If the neuron receives information from photoreceptors located in the periphery of the retina, its receptive field will be located off to one side.

At the periphery of the retina, many individual receptors converge on a single ganglion cell, bringing information from a relatively large area of the retina—and hence a relatively large area of the visual field. However, foveal vision is more direct, with approximately equal numbers of ganglion cells and cones. These receptor-to-axon relationships explain the fact that our foveal (central) vision is very acute but our peripheral vision is much less precise. (See *Figure 6.10.*)

Over sixty years ago, Hartline (1938) discovered that the frog retina contained three types of ganglion cells. ON cells responded with an excitatory burst when the retina was illuminated, OFF cells responded when the light was turned off, and ON/OFF cells responded briefly when the light went on and again when it went off. Kuffler (1952, 1953), recording from ganglion cells in the retina of the cat, discovered that their receptive field consists of a roughly circular center, surrounded by a ring. Stimulation of the center or surrounding fields had contrary effects: ON cells were excited by light falling in the central field (*center*) and were inhibited by light falling in the surrounding field (*surround*), whereas OFF cells responded in the opposite manner. ON/OFF ganglion cells were briefly excited when light was turned on or off. In the primate retina, these ON/OFF cells project primarily to the superior colliculus (Schiller and Malpeli, 1977); thus, they do not appear to play a direct role in form perception. (See *Figure 6.11.*)

The two major categories of ganglion cells (ON and OFF) and the organization of their receptive fields into contrasting center and surround provide useful information to the rest of the visual system. Let us consider the two types of ganglion cells first. As Schiller (1992) notes, ganglion cells normally fire at a relatively low rate. Then, when the level of illumination in the center of their receptive field increases or decreases (for example, when an object moves or the eye moves), they signal the change. In particular, ON cells signal increases and OFF cells signal decreases—but both signal them by an increased rate of firing. Such a system is particularly efficient. Theoretically, a single type of ganglion cell could fire at an intermediate rate and signal changes in the level of illumination by increases or decreases in rate of firing. However, in this case the average rate of firing of the one million axons in each optic nerve would have to be much higher.

Several studies have shown that ON cells and OFF cells do, indeed, signal different kinds of information. Schiller, Sandell, and Maunsell (1986) injected monkeys

FIGURE 6.11

Responses of ON and OFF ganglion cells to stimuli presented in the center or the surround of the receptive field.

(Adapted from Kuffler, S.W. Cold Spring Harbor Symposium for Quantitative Biology, 1952, 17, 281–292.)

with APB (2-amino-4-phosphonobutyrate), a drug that selectively blocks synaptic transmission in ON bipolar cells. They found that the animals were less able to detect spots that were made brighter than the background but had no difficulty detecting spots that were slightly darker than the background. In addition, Dolan and Schiller (1989) found that an injection of APB completely blocked vision in very dim light, which is normally mediated by rods. Thus, rod bipolar cells must all be of the ON type. (If you think about it, that arrangement makes sense; in very dim light we are more likely to see brighter objects against a dark background than dark objects against a light background.)

The second characteristic of the receptive fields of ganglion cells—their center-surround organization—enhances our ability to detect the outlines of objects even when the contrast between the object and the background is low. Figure 6.12 illustrates this phenomenon. This figure shows six gray squares, arranged in order of brightness. The right side of each square looks lighter than the left side, which makes the borders between the squares stand out. But these exaggerated borders do not exist in the illustration; they are added by our visual system because of the center-surround organization of the receptive fields of the retinal ganglion cells. (See *Figure 6.12.*)

Figure 6.13 explains how this phenomenon works. We see the centers and surrounds of the receptive fields of several ganglion cells. (In reality, these receptive fields would be overlapping, but the simplified arrangement is easier to understand. This example also includes only ON cells—again, for the sake of simplicity.) The image of the transi-

FIGURE 6.12

Enhancement of contrast. Although each gray square is of uniform darkness, the right edge of each square looks somewhat lighter and the left edge looks somewhat darker. This effect appears to be caused by the opponent center-surround arrangement of the receptive fields of the retinal ganglion cells.

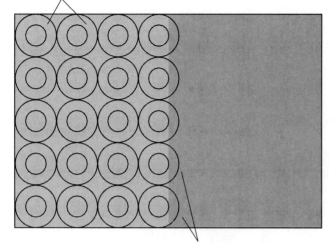

All of the surrounds of the ON cells whose receptive fields fall within the lighter gray are evenly illuminated; this illumination partially inhibits the firing of these cells.

A portion of the inhibitory surrounds of the ON cells near the border receives less illumination; thus, these cells have the highest rate of firing.

FIGURE 6.13

A schematic explanation of the phenomenon shown in Figure 6.12. Only ON cells are shown; OFF cells are responsible for the darker appearance of the left side of the darker square.

tion between lighter and darker regions falls across some of these receptive fields. The cells whose centers are located in the brighter region but whose surrounds are located at least partially in the darker region will have the highest rate of firing. (See *Figure 6.13.*)

Coding of Color

So far, we have been examining the monochromatic properties of ganglion cells—that is, their responses to light and dark. But, of course, objects in our environment selectively absorb some wavelengths of light and reflect others, which, to our eyes, gives them different colors. Although monochromatic (black-and-white) vision is perfectly adequate for most purposes, color vision gives us, for example, the ability to distinguish ripe fruit from unripe fruit and makes it more difficult for other animals to hide themselves by means of camouflage (Mollon, 1989). The retinas of humans, Old World monkeys, and apes contain three different types of cones, which provide them with the most elaborate form of color vision (Jacobs, 1996).

Color Mixing

Various theories of color vision have been proposed for many years—long before it was possible to disprove or validate them by physiological means. In 1802, Thomas Young, a British physicist and physician, proposed that the eye detected different colors because it contained three types of receptors, each sensitive to a single hue. His theory was referred to as the *trichromatic* (three-color) *theory*. It was suggested by the fact that for a human observer any color can be reproduced by mixing various quantities of three colors judiciously selected from different points along the spectrum.

I must emphasize that *color mixing* is different from *pigment mixing*. If we combine yellow and blue pigments (as when we mix paints), the resulting mixture is green. Color mixing refers to the addition of two or more light sources. If we shine a beam of red light and a beam of bluish green light together on a white screen, we will see yellow light. If we mix yellow and blue light, we get white light. When white appears on a color television screen or computer monitor, it actually consists of tiny dots of red, blue, and green light. The visual system uses the process of color mixing, not pigment mixing. (See *Figure 6.14.*)

Another fact of color perception suggested to a German physiologist, Ewald Hering (1905/1965), that hue might be represented in the visual system as *opponent colors*. Humans have long regarded yellow, blue, red, and green as primary colors. (Black and white are primary, too, but we perceive them as colorless.) All other colors can be described as mixtures of these primary colors. The trichromatic system cannot explain why *yellow* is included in this group. In addition, some colors appear to blend, whereas others do not. For example, one can speak of a bluish green or a yellowish green, and orange appears to have both red and yellow qualities. Purple resembles both red and blue. But try to imagine a reddish green or a bluish yellow. It is impossible; these colors seem to be opposite to each other. Again, these facts are not explained by the trichromatic theory. As we shall see in the following section, the visual system uses both trichromatic and opponent-color systems to encode information related to color.

FIGURE 6.14

Additive color mixing and paint mixing. When blue, red, and green light of the proper intensity are all shone together, the result is white light. When red, blue, and yellow paints are mixed together, the result is a dark gray.

Protanopia [*pro tan **owe** pee a*] An inherited form of defective color vision in which red and green hues are confused; "red" cones are filled with "green" cone opsin.

Deuteranopia [*dew ter an **owe** pee a*] An inherited form of defective color vision in which red and green hues are confused; "green" cones are filled with "red" cone opsin.

FIGURE 6.15

Relative absorbance of light of various wavelengths by rods and the three types of cones in the human retina.

(From Dartnall, H.J.A., Bowmaker, J.K., and Mollon, J.D. Human visual pigments: Microspectrophotometric results from the eyes of seven persons. Proceedings of the Royal Society of London, B., 1983, 220, 115–130.)

Photoreceptors: Trichromatic Coding

Physiological investigations of retinal photoreceptors in higher primates have found that Young was right: Three different types of photoreceptors (three different types of cones) are responsible for color vision. Investigators have studied how well light of different wavelengths is absorbed by individual photoreceptors, determining the amount of light of different wavelengths that is absorbed by the photopigments. These characteristics are controlled by the particular opsin a photoreceptor contains; different opsins absorb particular wavelengths more readily. Figure 6.15 shows the absorption characteristics of the four types of photoreceptors in the human retina: rods and the three types of cones. (See *Figure 6.15.*)

The peak sensitivities of the three types of cones are approximately 420 nm (blue-violet), 530 nm (green), and 560 nm (yellow-green). For convenience, the short-, medium-, and long-wavelength cones are traditionally called "blue," "green," and "red" cones, respectively. The retina contains approximately equal numbers of "red" and "green" cones but a much smaller number of "blue" cones (approximately 8 percent of the total).

Genetic defects in color vision appear to result from anomalies in one or more of the three types of cones (Boynton, 1979; Nathans et al., 1986). The first two kinds of defective color vision described here involve genes on the X chromosome; thus, because males have only one X chromosome, they are much more likely to have this disorder. (Females are likely to have a normal gene on one of their X chromosomes, which compensates for the defective one.) People with **protanopia** ("first-color defect") confuse red and green. They see the world in shades of yellow and blue; both red and green look yellowish to them. Their visual acuity is normal, which suggests that their retinas do not lack "red" or "green" cones. This fact, and their sensitivity to lights of different wavelengths, suggests that their "red" cones are filled with "green" cone opsin. People with **deuteranopia** ("second-color defect") also confuse red and green and also have normal visual acuity. Their "green" cones appear to be filled with "red" cone opsin.

| Yellow on, blue off | Blue on, yellow off | Red on, green off | Green on, red off |

FIGURE 6.16

Receptive fields of color-sensitive ganglion cells. When a portion of the receptive field is illuminated with the color shown, the cell's rate of firing increases. When a portion is illuminated with the complementary color, the cell's rate of firing decreases.

Tritanopia ("third-color defect") is rare, affecting fewer than 1 in 10,000 people. This disorder involves a faulty gene that is not located on an X chromosome; thus, it is equally prevalent in males and females. People with tritanopia have difficulty with hues of short wavelengths and see the world in greens and reds. To them, a clear blue sky is a bright green, and yellow looks pink. Their retinas appear to lack "blue" cones. Because the retina contains so few of these cones, their absence does not noticeably affect visual acuity.

Retinal Ganglion Cells: Opponent-Process Coding

At the level of the retinal ganglion cell, the three-color code gets translated into an opponent-color system. Daw (1968) and Gouras (1968) found that these neurons respond specifically to pairs of primary colors, with red opposing green and blue opposing yellow. Thus, the retina contains two kinds of color-sensitive ganglion cells: *red-green* and *yellow-blue*. Some color-sensitive ganglion cells respond in a center-surround fashion. For example, a cell might be excited by red and inhibited by green in the center of their receptive field, while showing the opposite response in the surrounding ring. (See *Figure 6.16*.) Other ganglion cells that receive input from cones do not respond differentially to different wavelengths but simply encode relative brightness in the center and surround. These cells serve as "black-and-white" detectors.

The response characteristics of retinal ganglion cells to light of different wavelengths are obviously determined by the particular circuits that connect the three types of cones with the two types of ganglion cells. These circuits involve different types of bipolar cells, amacrine cells, and horizontal cells.

Figure 6.17 helps to explain how particular hues are detected by the "red," "green," and "blue" cones and translated into excitation or inhibition of the red-green and yellow-blue ganglion cells. The diagram does not show the actual neural circuitry, which includes the retinal neurons that connect the cones with the ganglion cells. Although some progress is being made (Dacey, 1996; Dacey et al., 1996), the retinal circuitry responsible for color coding in ganglion cells is still largely unknown. The arrows in Figure 6.17 refer merely to the *effects* of the light falling on the retina.

Detection and coding of pure red, green, or blue light is the easiest to understand. For example, red light excites "red" cones, which causes the excitation of red-green ganglion cells. (See *Figure 6.17a*.) Green light excites "green" cones, which causes the *inhibition* of red-green cells. (See *Figure 6.17b*.) But consider the effect of yellow light. Because the wavelength that produces the sensation of yellow is intermediate between red and green, it will stimulate both "red" and "green" cones about equally. Yellow-blue ganglion cells are excited by both "red" and "green" cones, so their rate of firing increases. However, red-green ganglion cells are excited by red and inhibited by green, so their firing rate does not change. The brain detects an increased firing rate from the axons of yellow-blue ganglion cells, which it interprets as yellow. (See *Figure 6.17c*.) Blue light simply inhibits the activity of yellow-blue ganglion cells. (See *Figure 6.17d*.)

The opponent-color system employed by the ganglion cells explains why we cannot perceive a reddish green or a bluish yellow: An axon that signals red or green (or yellow or blue) can either increase or decrease its rate of firing; it cannot do both at the same time. A reddish green would have to be signaled by a ganglion cell firing slowly and rapidly at the same time, which is obviously impossible.

Tritanopia (*try tan **owe** pee a*) An inherited form of defective color vision in which hues with short wavelengths are confused; "blue" cones are either lacking or faulty.

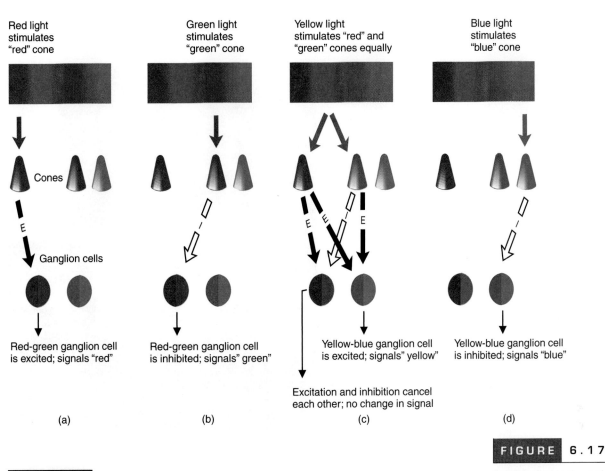

| Red light stimulates "red" cone | Green light stimulates "green" cone | Yellow light stimulates "red" and "green" cones equally | Blue light stimulates "blue" cone |

Cones

E

Ganglion cells

| Red-green ganglion cell is excited; signals "red" | Red-green ganglion cell is inhibited; signals" green" | Yellow-blue ganglion cell is excited; signals" yellow" | Yellow-blue ganglion cell is inhibited; signals "blue" |

Excitation and inhibition cancel each other; no change in signal

(a)   (b)   (c)   (d)

FIGURE 6.17

Color coding in the retina.
(a) Red light stimulating a "red" cone, which causes excitation of a red-green ganglion cell. (b) Green light stimulating a "green" cone, which causes inhibition of a red-green ganglion cell. (c) Yellow light stimulating "red" and "green" cones equally but not affecting "blue" cones. The stimulation of "red" and "green" cones causes excitation of a yellow-blue ganglion cell. (d) Blue light stimulating a "blue" cone, which causes inhibition of a yellow-blue ganglion cell. The arrows labeled E and I represent neural circuitry within the retina that translates excitation of a cone into excitation or inhibition of a ganglion cell. For clarity, only some of the circuits are shown.

INTERIM SUMMARY

Recordings of the electrical activity of single neurons in the retina indicate that each ganglion cell receives information from photoreceptors—just one in the fovea and many more in the periphery. The receptive field of most retinal ganglion cells consists of two concentric circles, with the cells becoming excited when light falls in one region and becoming inhibited when it falls in the other. This arrangement enhances the ability of the nervous system to detect contrasts in brightness. ON cells are excited by light in the center, and OFF cells are excited by light in the surround. ON cells detect light objects against dark backgrounds; OFF cells detect dark objects against light backgrounds.

Color vision occurs as a result of information provided by three types of cones, each of which is sensitive to light of a certain wavelength: long, medium, or short. The absorption characteristics of the cones are determined by the particular opsin that their photopigment contains. Most forms of defective color vision appear to be caused by alterations in cone opsins. The "red" cones of people with protanopia are filled with "green" cone opsin, and the "green" cones of people with deuteranopia are filled with "red" cone opsin. The retinas of people with tritanopia appear to lack "blue" cones.

Most color-sensitive ganglion cells respond in an opposing center-surround fashion to the pairs of primary colors: red and green, and blue and yellow. The responses of these neurons are determined by the retinal circuitry connecting them with the photoreceptors.

THOUGHT QUESTIONS

Why is color vision useful? Birds, some fish, and some primates have full, three-cone color vision. Considering our own species, what other benefits (besides the ability to recognize ripe fruit, which I mentioned in the previous section) might come from the evolution of color vision?

Birds have full, three-cone color vision; thus, this red breast can be perceived by rival males of this great frigate bird.

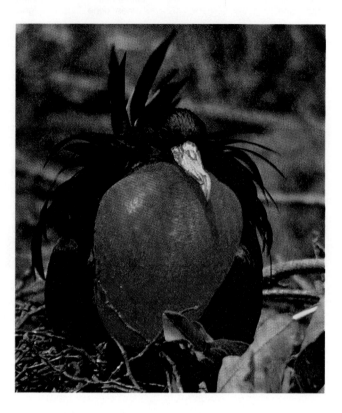

A photomicrograph of a small section of striate cortex, showing the six principal layers. The letter W refers to the white matter that underlies the visual cortex; beneath the white matter is layer VI of the striate cortex on the opposite side of the gyrus.

(From Hubel, D.H., and Wiesel, T.N. Proceedings of the Royal Society of London, B., 1977, 198, 1–59. Reprinted with permission.)

FIGURE 6.18

ANALYSIS OF VISUAL INFORMATION: ROLE OF THE STRIATE CORTEX

The retinal ganglion cells encode information about the relative amounts of light falling on the center and surround regions of their receptive field and, in many cases, about the wavelength of that light. The striate cortex performs additional processing of this information, which it then transmits to the visual association cortex.

Anatomy of the Striate Cortex

The striate cortex consists of six principal layers (and several sublayers), arranged in bands parallel to the surface. These layers contain the nuclei of cell bodies and dendritic trees that show up as bands of light or dark in sections of tissue that have been dyed with a cell-body stain. (See *Figure 6.18.*)

In primates, information from the dorsal lateral geniculate nucleus enters the middle layer (layer IV_c) of the striate cortex. From there, it is relayed upward and downward, to be analyzed by circuits of neurons in different layers.

If we consider the striate cortex as a whole—if we imagine that we remove it and spread it out on a flat surface—we find that it contains a map of the contralateral half of the visual field. (Remember that each side of the brain sees the opposite side of the visual field.) The map is distorted; approximately 25 percent of the striate cortex is devoted to the analysis of information from the fovea, which represents a small part of the visual field. (The area of the visual field seen by the fovea is approximately the size of a large grape held at arm's length.)

The pioneering studies of David Hubel and Torsten Wiesel at Harvard University during the 1960s began a revolution in the study of the physiology of visual perception (see Hubel and Wiesel, 1977, 1979). Hubel and Wiesel discovered that neurons in the visual cortex did not simply respond to spots of light; they selectively responded to specific *features* of the visual world. That is, the neural circuitry within the visual cortex combines information from several sources (for example, from axons carrying information received from several different ganglion cells) in such a way as to detect features that are larger than the receptive field of a single ganglion cell. The following subsections describe the visual characteristics that researchers have studied so far: orientation and movement, spatial frequency, retinal disparity, and color.

Orientation and Movement

Most neurons in the striate cortex are sensitive to *orientation*. That is, if a line is positioned in the cell's receptive field and rotated around its center, the cell will respond only when the line is in a particular position—a particular orientation. (See *Figure 6.19*.) Some neurons respond best to a vertical line, some to a horizontal line, and some to a line oriented somewhere in between.

Some orientation-sensitive neurons have receptive fields organized in an opponent fashion. Hubel and Wiesel referred to them as **simple cells.** For example, a line of a particular orientation (say, a dark 45-degree line against a white background) might excite a cell if placed in the center of the receptive field but inhibit it if moved away from the center. (See *Figure 6.20a*.) Another type of neuron, which the researchers referred to as a **complex cell,** also responded best to a line of a particular orientation but did not show an inhibitory surround; that is, it continued to respond while the line was moved within the receptive field. In fact, many complex cells increased their rate of firing when the line was moved perpendicular to its angle of orientation; thus, they also served as movement detectors. In addition, complex cells responded equally well to white lines against black backgrounds and black lines against white backgrounds. (See *Figure 6.20b*.)

Spatial Frequency

Although the early studies by Hubel and Wiesel suggested that neurons in the primary visual cortex detected lines and edges, subsequent research found that they actually responded best to sine-wave gratings (De Valois, Albrecht, and Thorell, 1978).

 FIGURE 6.19

Orientation sensitivity. An orientation-sensitive neuron in the striate cortex will become active only when a line of a particular orientation appears within its receptive field. For example, the neuron might respond to the black bar but not to either of the gray bars.

Simple cell An orientation-sensitive neuron in the striate cortex whose receptive field is organized in an opponent fashion.

Complex cell A neuron in the visual cortex that responds to the presence of a line segment with a particular orientation located within its receptive field, especially when the line moves perpendicularly to its orientation.

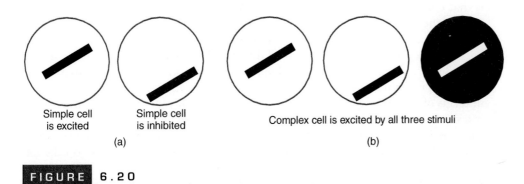

Simple cell is excited   Simple cell is inhibited   Complex cell is excited by all three stimuli

(a)   (b)

FIGURE 6.20

Response characteristics of neurons to orientation in the primary visual cortex. (a) Simple cell. (b) Complex cell.

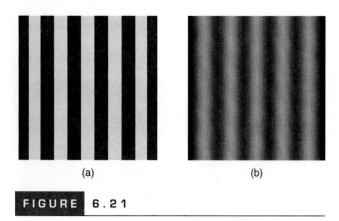

FIGURE 6.21

Parallel gratings. (a) Square-wave grating. (b) Sine-wave grating.

Visual angle

FIGURE 6.22

The concepts of visual angle and spatial frequency. Angles are drawn between the sine waves, with the apex at the viewer's eye. The *visual angle* between adjacent sine waves is smaller when the waves are closer together.

Sine-wave grating A series of straight parallel bands varying continuously in brightness according to a sine-wave function, along a line perpendicular to their lengths.

Spatial frequency The relative width of the bands in a sine-wave grating, measured in cycles per degree of visual angle.

Figure 6.21 compares a sine-wave grating with a more familiar square-wave grating. A square-wave grating consists of a simple set of rectangular bars that vary in brightness; the brightness along the length of a line perpendicular to them would vary in a stepwise (square-wave) fashion. (See *Figure 6.21a.*) A **sine-wave grating** looks like a series of fuzzy, unfocused parallel bars. Along any line perpendicular to the long axis of the grating, the brightness varies according to a sine-wave function. (See *Figure 6.21b.*)

A sine-wave grating is designated by its spatial frequency. We are accustomed to the expression of frequencies (for example, of sound waves or radio waves) in terms of time or distance (such as cycles per second or cycles per meter). But because the image of a stimulus on the retina varies in size according to how close it is to the eye, the visual angle is generally used instead of the physical distance between adjacent cycles. Thus, the **spatial frequency** of a sine-wave grating is its variation in brightness measured in cycles per degree of visual angle. (See *Figure 6.22.*)

Most neurons in the striate cortex respond best when a sine-wave grating of a particular spatial frequency is placed in the appropriate part of the visual field. Different neurons detect different spatial frequencies. For orientation-sensitive neurons the grating must be aligned at the appropriate angle of orientation.

What is the point of having neural circuits that analyze spatial frequency? A complete answer requires some rather complicated mathematics, so I will give a simplified one here. (If you are interested, you can consult De Valois and De Valois, 1988.) Consider the types of information provided by high and low spatial frequencies. Small objects, details within a large object, and large objects with sharp edges provide a signal that is rich in high frequencies, whereas large areas of light and dark are represented by low frequencies. An image that is deficient in high-frequency information looks fuzzy and out of focus, like the image seen by a nearsighted person who is not wearing corrective lenses. This image still provides much information about forms and objects in the environment; thus, the most important visual information is that contained in *low spatial frequencies.* When low-frequency information is removed, the shapes of images are very difficult to perceive. (As we will see, the more primitive magnocellular system provides low-frequency information.)

Many experiments have confirmed that the concept of spatial frequency plays a central role in visual perception, and mathematical models have shown that the information present in a scene can be represented very efficiently if it is first encoded in terms of spatial frequency. Thus, the brain probably represents the information in a similar way. Here I will describe just one example to help show the validity of the concept. Look at the two pictures in *Figure 6.23.* You can see that the picture on the right looks much more like the face of Abraham Lincoln than the one on the left does. Yet both pictures contain the same information. The creators of the pictures, Harmon and Julesz (1973), used a computer to construct the figure on the left, which consists of a series of squares, each representing the average brightness of a portion of a picture of Lincoln. The one on the right is simply a transformation of the first one in which high frequencies have been removed. Sharp edges contain high spatial frequencies, so the transformation eliminates them. In the case of the picture on the left, these frequencies have nothing to do with the information contained in the original picture; thus, they can be seen as visual "noise." The filtration process (accomplished by a computer) removes this noise—and makes the image much clearer to the human visual system. Presumably, the high frequencies produced by the edges of the squares in the left figure stimulate neurons in the striate cortex that are tuned to high spatial frequencies. When the visual association cortex receives this noisy information, it has difficulty perceiving the underlying form.

If you want to watch the effect of filtering the extraneous high-frequency noise, try the following demonstration. Put the book down and look at the pictures in Figure 6.23 from across the room. The distance "erases" the high frequencies, because they exceed the resolving power of the eye, and the two pictures look identical. Now walk toward the book, focusing on the left figure. As you get closer, the higher frequencies reappear and this face gets harder and harder to recognize. (See *Figure 6.23.*)

FIGURE 6.23

Spatial filtering. Both pictures contain the same amount of low-frequency information, but extraneous high-frequency information has been filtered from the picture on the right. If you look at the pictures from across the room, they look identical.

(From Harmon, L.D., and Julesz, B. Science, 1973, 180, 1191–1197. Copyright 1973 by the American Association for the Advancement of Science.)

Retinal Disparity

We perceive depth by many means, most of which involve cues that can be detected monocularly, by one eye alone. For example, perspective, relative retinal size, loss of detail through the effects of atmospheric haze, and relative apparent movement of retinal images as we move our heads all contribute to depth perception and do not require binocular vision. However, binocular vision provides a vivid perception of depth through the process of stereoscopic vision, or *stereopsis*. If you have used a stereoscope (such as a View Master) or have seen a "three-dimensional" movie, you know what I mean. Stereopsis is particularly important in the visual guidance of fine movements of the hands and fingers, such as we use when we thread a needle.

Most neurons in the striate cortex are *binocular*—that is, they respond to visual stimulation of either eye. Many of these binocular cells, especially those found in a layer that receives information from the magnocellular system, appear to contribute to the perception of depth (Poggio and Poggio, 1984). In most cases the cells respond most vigorously when each eye sees a stimulus in a slightly *different* location. That is, the neurons respond to **retinal disparity,** a stimulus that produces images on slightly different parts of the retina of each eye. This is exactly the information that is needed for stereopsis; each eye sees a three-dimensional scene slightly differently, and the presence of retinal disparity indicates differences in the distance of objects from the observer.

Color

In the striate cortex, information from color-sensitive ganglion cells is transmitted, through the parvocellular layers of the dorsal lateral geniculate nucleus, to special cells grouped together in **cytochrome oxidase (CO) blobs.** CO blobs were discovered by Wong-Riley (1978), who found that a stain for cytochrome oxidase, an enzyme present in mitochondria, showed a patchy distribution. Subsequent research with the stain (Horton and Hubel, 1980; Humphrey and Hendrickson, 1980) revealed the presence of a polka-dot pattern of dark columns extending through layers 2 and 3 and (more faintly) layers 5 and 6. The columns are oval in cross section, approximately 150 × 200 μm in diameter and spaced at 0.5-mm intervals (Fitzpatrick, Itoh, and Diamond, 1983; Livingstone and Hubel, 1987).

Retinal disparity The fact that points on objects located at different distances from the observer will fall on slightly different locations on the two retinas; provides the basis for stereopsis.

Cytochrome oxidase (CO) blob The central region of a module of the primary visual cortex, revealed by a stain for cytochrome oxidase; contains wavelength-sensitive neurons; part of the parvocellular system.

FIGURE 6.24

A photomicrograph of a slice through the primary visual cortex of a macaque monkey, parallel to the surface. The dark spots are the blobs, colored by a stain for cytochrome oxidase.

(From Hubel, D.H., and Livingstone, M.S. Journal of Neuroscience, 1989, 7, 3378–3415. Reprinted by permission of the Journal of Neuroscience.)

Figure 6.24 shows a photomicrograph of a slice through a macaque monkey visual cortex that has been flattened out and stained for the mitochondrial enzyme. You can clearly see the CO blobs within the striate cortex. Because the curvature of the cortex prevents it from being perfectly flattened, some of the tissue is missing in the center of the slice. (See *Figure 6.24*.)

To summarize, neurons in the striate cortex respond to several different features of a visual stimulus, including orientation, movement, spatial frequency, retinal disparity, and color. Now let us turn our attention to the way this information is organized within the striate cortex.

Modular Organization of the Striate Cortex

Most investigators believe that the brain is organized in modules, which probably range in size from a hundred thousand to a few million neurons. Each module receives information from other modules, performs some calculations, and then passes the results to other modules. In recent years investigators have been learning the characteristics of the modules that are found in the visual cortex (De Valois and De Valois, 1988; Livingstone and Hubel, 1988).

The striate cortex is divided into approximately 2500 modules, each approximately 0.5×0.7 mm and containing approximately 150,000 neurons. The neurons in each module are devoted to the analysis of various features contained in one very small portion of the visual field. Collectively, these modules receive information from the entire visual field, the individual modules serving like the tiles in a mosaic mural or pixels on the screen of a computer monitor. Input from the parvocellular and magnocellular layers of the dorsal lateral geniculate nucleus is received by different sublayers of the striate cortex: The parvocellular input is received by layer 4Cβ, whereas the magnocellular input is received by layer 4Cα.

The modules actually consist of two segments, each surrounding a CO blob. Neurons located within the blobs have a special function: They are sensitive to color and to low spatial frequencies but are relatively insensitive to other visual features. Outside the CO blob, neurons show sensitivity to orientation, movement, spatial frequency, texture, and binocular disparity—but most do not respond to color (Livingstone and Hubel, 1984; Born and Tootell, 1991; Edwards, Purpura, and Kaplan, 1995). Each half of the module receives input from only one eye, but the circuitry within the module combines the information from both eyes, which means that most of the neurons are binocular. Depending on their locations within the module, neurons receive varying percentages of input from each of the eyes.

If we record from neurons anywhere within a single module, we will find that all of their receptive fields overlap. Thus, all the neurons in a module analyze information from the same region of the visual field. Furthermore, if we insert a microelectrode straight down into an interblob region of the striate cortex (that is, in a location outside one of the CO blobs), we will find both simple and complex cells, but all of the orientation-sensitive cells will respond to lines of the same orientation. In addition, they will all share the same **ocular dominance**—that is, the same percentage of input from each of the eyes. If we move our electrode around the module, we will find that these two characteristics—orientation sensitivity and ocular dominance—vary systematically and are arranged at right angles to each other. (See *Figure 6.25*.)

How does spatial frequency fit into this organization? Edwards, Purpura, and Kaplan (1995) found that neurons within the CO blobs responded to low spatial frequencies but were sensitive to small differences in brightness. Outside the blobs, sensitivity to spatial frequency varied with the distance from the center of the nearest blob. Higher frequencies were associated with greater distances. However, neurons

Ocular dominance The extent to which a particular neuron receives more input from one eye than from the other.

outside the blobs were less sensitive to contrast; the difference between the bright and dark areas of the sine-wave grating had to be greater for these neurons than for neurons within the blobs.

Blindsight

Visual perception depends on the integrity of the connections between the retina and the striate cortex. Thus, damage to the eyes, optic nerves, optic tracts, lateral geniculate nucleus, axons that connect the lateral geniculate nucleus with the primary visual cortex, or primary visual cortex itself results in loss of vision in particular portions of the visual field or in complete blindness if the damage is total. However, an interesting phenomenon is seen in people with damage to the optic radiations or primary visual cortex.

It has long been recognized that damage to the optic radiations or primary visual cortex on one side of the brain causes blindness in the contralateral visual field. That is, if the right side of the brain is damaged, the patient will be blind to everything located to the left when he or she looks straight ahead. However, Weiskrantz and his colleagues (Weiskrantz et al., 1974; Weiskrantz, 1987) found that if an object is placed in the patient's blind field and the patient is asked to reach for it, he or she will be able to do so rather accurately. The patients are surprised to find their hands repeatedly coming into contact with an object in what appears to them as darkness; they say that they see nothing there. The patient is also sensitive to movement and, to a certain extent, the orientation of objects in the blind field.

This phenomenon, which Weiskrantz called **blindsight,** may depend on the connections that the visual association cortex receives from the superior colliculus and from the dorsal lateral geniculate nucleus (Cowey and Stoerig, 1991). The role of these connections in the intact brain is not known. Most of the inputs to the visual association cortex come directly from the striate cortex, and these connections are obviously necessary for normal visual perception.

Besides telling us something about the functions of the various parts of the visual system, the phenomenon of blindsight also shows that visual information can control behavior without producing a conscious sensation. Although the superior colliculi send visual information to parts of the brain that guide hand movements, they do not appear to send them to parts of the brain responsible for conscious awareness. Perhaps that connection is a more recent evolutionary development. I will have more to say about this topic in Chapters 12 and 13, which discuss memory and communication.

FIGURE   6.25

One of the modules of the primary visual cortex.

INTERIM SUMMARY

The striate cortex consists of six layers and several sublayers. Visual information is received from the magnocellular and parvocellular layers of the dorsal lateral geniculate nucleus. The magnocellular system is more primitive, color-blind, and sensitive to movement, depth, and small differences in brightness; the parvocellular system is more recent, color-sensitive, and able to discriminate finer details.

Blindsight The ability of a person to reach for objects located in his or her "blind" field; occurs after damage restricted to the primary visual cortex.

The striate cortex is organized into modules, each surrounding a pair of CO blobs, which are revealed by a stain for cytochrome oxidase, an enzyme found in mitochondria. Each half of a module receives information from one eye; but because information is shared, most of the neurons respond to input from both eyes. The neurons in the CO blobs are sensitive to color and to low-frequency sine-wave gratings, whereas those between the blobs are sensitive to sine-wave gratings of higher spatial frequencies, orientation, retinal disparity, and movement.

Damage to the visual system up to the striate cortex produces blindness in all or part of the visual field. However, damage that is limited to the striate cortex or to the optic radiations leading to them produces a syndrome called blindsight. People with blindsight deny seeing anything in the blind part of their visual field but can nevertheless point to objects located there and discriminate their size and orientation. They are also sensitive to movement. But although their behavior can be affected by objects in their blind field, they have no conscious awareness of the presence of these objects. Their ability to respond to visual stimuli apparently depends on connections from the superior colliculus and the lateral geniculate nucleus to the visual association cortex.

THOUGHT QUESTIONS

Chapter 1 discussed the behavior of people with split brains. Do you see any similarities between the consciousness of people with split brains and of people with blindsight?

ANALYSIS OF VISUAL INFORMATION: ROLE OF THE VISUAL ASSOCIATION CORTEX

Although the striate cortex plays an essential role in visual perception, perception of objects and of the totality of the visual scene does not take place there. Each module of the striate cortex sees only what is happening in one tiny part of the visual field. Thus, for us to perceive objects and entire visual scenes, the information from these individual modules must be combined. That combination takes place in the visual association cortex.

Two Streams of Visual Analysis

Visual information received from the striate cortex is analyzed in the visual association cortex. On the basis of their own research and a review of the literature, Ungerleider and Mishkin (1982) concluded that the visual association cortex contains two streams of analysis—dorsal and ventral. Subsequent anatomical studies have confirmed this conclusion (Baizer, Ungerleider, and Desimone, 1991). Both streams begin in the striate cortex, but they begin to diverge in the extrastriate cortex. One stream turns downward, ending in the cortex of the inferior temporal lobe. The other turns upward, ending in the cortex of the posterior parietal lobe. The ventral stream recognizes *what* an object is, and the dorsal stream recognizes *where* the object is located. (See *Figure 6.26.*)

FIGURE 6.26

The human visual system, from the eye to the two streams of visual association cortex.

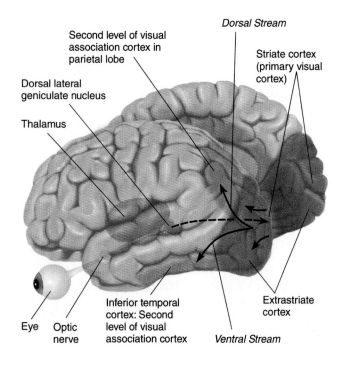

Dorsal Stream

Second level of visual association cortex in parietal lobe

Striate cortex (primary visual cortex)

Dorsal lateral geniculate nucleus

Thalamus

Inferior temporal cortex: Second level of visual association cortex

Extrastriate cortex

Eye   Optic nerve

Ventral Stream

TABLE 6.2	Properties of the Magnocellular and Parvocellular Divisions of the Visual System	
Property	**Magnocellular Division**	**Parvocellular Division**
Color	No	Yes
Sensitivity to contrast	High	Low
Spatial resolution	Low	High
Temporal resolution	Fast (transient response)	Slow (sustained response)

Source: Adapted from Livingston, M.S., and Hubel, D.H. *Journal of Neuroscience,* 1987, 7, 3416–3468.

The parvocellular and magnocellular systems provide different kinds of information (Livingstone and Hubel, 1987). The magnocellular system is found in all mammals, whereas the parvocellular system is found only in primates. These two systems receive information from different types of ganglion cells, which are connected to different types of bipolar cells and photoreceptors. Only the cells in the parvocellular system receive information about wavelength from cones; thus, this system analyzes information concerning color. Cells in this system also show high spatial resolution and low temporal resolution; that is, they are able to detect very fine details, but their response is slow and prolonged. In contrast, neurons in the magnocellular system are color-blind, are not able to detect fine details, and respond very briefly to a visual stimulus. And although they appear to be responsible for vision of lower acuity, these neurons are able to detect smaller contrasts between light and dark. Finally, they are especially sensitive to movement. (See *Table 6.2.*)

At one time, researchers believed that the dorsal stream received its information from the magnocellular system and the ventral stream received its information from the parvocellular system. But more recent research has shown that both systems contribute information to both streams (Maunsell, 1992). The dorsal stream receives mostly magnocellular input, but the ventral stream receives approximately equal input from both systems.

Neurons in the striate cortex send axons to the **extrastriate cortex,** the region of the visual association cortex that surrounds the striate cortex (Zeki and Shipp, 1988). The primate extrastriate cortex (sometimes called the prestriate cortex or circumstriate cortex) consists of several regions, each of which contains one or more independent maps of the visual field. Each region is specialized, containing neurons that respond to a particular feature of visual information, such as orientation, movement, spatial frequency, retinal disparity, or color. So far, investigators have identified twenty-five distinct regions and subregions of the visual cortex of the rhesus monkey. These regions are arranged hierarchically, beginning with the striate cortex (Van Essen, Anderson, and Felleman, 1992). Most of the information passes up the hierarchy; each region receives information from regions located beneath it in the hierarchy, analyzes the information, and passes the results on to "higher" regions for further analysis. Some information is also transmitted in the opposite direction, but axons that descend the hierarchy are much less numerous than those that ascend it. Unfortunately, we know much more about the anatomical details of the subdivisions of the visual cortex than we do about the functions performed by these regions.

Perception of Color

As we saw earlier, neurons within the CO blobs in the striate cortex respond to colors. Like the ganglion cells in the retina (and the parvocellular neurons in the dorsal

Extrastriate cortex A region of visual association cortex; receives fibers from the striate cortex and from the superior colliculi and projects to the inferior temporal cortex.

lateral geniculate nucleus), these neurons respond in opponent fashion. This information is analyzed by the regions of the visual association cortex that constitute the ventral stream.

Studies with Laboratory Animals

In the monkey brain, neurons in the CO blobs send information about color to a specific subarea of the extrastriate cortex. Zeki (1980) found that neurons in this subarea (called *V4*) also respond selectively to colors, but their response characteristics are much more complex. Unlike the neurons we have encountered so far, these neurons respond to a variety of wavelengths, not just those that correspond to red, green, yellow, and blue.

The appearance of the colors of objects remains much the same whether we observe them under artificial light, under an overcast sky, or at noon on a cloudless day. This phenomenon is known as **color constancy.** The visual system does not simply respond according to the wavelength of the light reflected by objects in each part of the visual field. Instead, it compensates for the source of the light. Walsh et al. (1993) found that damage to area V4 disrupts color constancy. The investigators observed that although monkeys could still discriminate between different colors after area V4 had been damaged, their performance was impaired when the color of the overall illumination was changed. But the fact that the monkeys could still perform a simple color discrimination task under constant illumination means that some region besides area V4 must be involved in color vision.

A study by Heywood, Gaffan, and Cowey (1995) appears to have found that region: a portion of the temporal cortex just anterior to area V4. The investigators destroyed this region, leaving area V4 intact, and observed severe impairment in color discrimination. Thus, this region may be even more important than V4 for color perception.

Studies with Humans

Lesions of a restricted region of the human extrastriate cortex in the medial occipital lobe can cause loss of color vision without disruption of visual acuity. The patients describe their vision as resembling a black-and-white film (Damasio et al., 1980; Kennard et al., 1995). The condition is known as **achromatopsia** ("vision without color"). If the brain damage is unilateral, people will lose color vision in only half of the visual field. In addition, they cannot even imagine colors or remember the colors or objects they saw before their brain damage occurred. As we just saw, Heywood, Gaffan, and Cowey (1995) found a region of the rhesus monkey brain whose damage disrupted the ability to make color discriminations. It will be interesting to see whether the regions are analogous in these two species.

Several PET or functional MRI studies confirm the studies of people with brain lesions. For example, Zeki et al. (1991) used a PET scanner to measure regional cerebral blood flow in normal human subjects. At the same time, they showed the subjects a plain gray stimulus or a multicolored pattern made up of rectangles of different sizes. They found that both stimuli increased the metabolic activity of the striate cortex and the region of the extrastriate cortex that surrounds it (region V2). The colored stimulus activated a specific region of the extrastriate cortex: the lingual and fusiform gyri, located in the occipital cortex on the medial surface of the brain.

Of course, perception of colors is useless in itself. The function of our ability to perceive different colors is to help us perceive different objects in our environment. Thus, to perceive and understand what is in front of us, we must have information about color combined with other forms of information. Some people with brain damage lose the ability to perceive shapes but can still perceive colors (Zeki, 1992). They can identify the colors of objects in their visual field, but they cannot say what these objects are.

Color constancy The relatively constant appearance of the colors of objects viewed under varying lighting conditions.

Achromatopsia (*ay krohm a top see a*) Inability to discriminate among different hues; caused by damage to the visual association cortex.

Analysis of Form

The analysis of form by the visual cortex begins with neurons in the striate cortex that are sensitive to orientation and spatial frequency. These neurons send information to the extrastriate cortex, which consists of several subregions. These subregions analyze the information and send it along the ventral stream toward the temporal neocortex.

Studies with Laboratory Animals

In primates the recognition of visual patterns and identification of particular objects takes place in the **inferior temporal cortex,** located on the ventral part of the temporal lobe. This region of visual association cortex is located at the end of the ventral stream. It is here that analyses of form and color are put together and perceptions of three-dimensional objects and backgrounds are achieved. The inferior temporal cortex consists of two major regions, areas TE and TEO. Damage to this region causes severe deficits in visual discrimination (Mishkin, 1966; Gross, 1973; Dean, 1976). (See *Figure 6.27.*)

Neurons in the inferior temporal cortex respond best to three-dimensional objects (or photographs of them). They respond poorly to simple stimuli such as spots, lines, or sine-wave gratings. Most of them continue to respond even when these stimuli are moved to a different location, are changed in size, are placed against a different background, or are partially occluded by another object (Rolls and Baylis, 1986; Kovács, Vogels, and Orban, 1995). Thus, they appear to participate in the recognition of objects rather than the analysis of specific features.

Like other regions of the visual cortex, the inferior temporal cortex is arranged in columns. Neurons in adjacent regions usually respond to slightly different versions of the same stimuli. For example, several studies (for example, Desimone et al., 1984) have found neurons in the temporal lobe that are specifically excited by the sight of another face—either that of another monkey or that of a human. Some of these neurons respond to full-face views, and others respond to profiles.

A study by Wang, Tanaka, and Tanifuji (1996) used an optical recording technique to study the functional organization of the inferior temporal cortex in monkeys. They placed transparent "windows" over the surface of the cortex that permitted them to monitor the surface of the brain. They used a special computer-driven video camera to record changes in the appearance of the cortex caused by changes in the oxidation level of hemoglobin in the cortical capillaries—changes that correlate with neural activity. Figure 6.28 shows the response to different views of a doll's head as it rotated. As you can see from the movement of the dark spot (arrows) from frame to frame, adjacent clusters of neurons were activated by different views of the head. (See *Figure 6.28.*)

Clearly, neurons in the primate inferior temporal cortex respond to very complex shapes, including things the animals have already seen, such as faces. The complexity and the specific nature of these features suggest that the development of the circuits responsible for detecting them must involve learning. And, indeed, that seems to be the case. For example, several studies have found neurons in the inferior temporal cortex that respond specifically to objects that the monkeys have already seen many times but not to unfamiliar objects (Kobatake, Tanaka, and Tamori, 1992; Logothetis, Pauls, and Poggio, 1995). Such studies will be discussed in more detail in Chapter 12.

FIGURE 6.27

Areas of visual cortex in the rhesus monkey brain.

(Adapted from Zeki, S.M. Journal of Physiology, *1978, 277, 227–244.)*

Inferior temporal cortex In primates, the highest level of the ventral stream of the visual association cortex; located on the inferior portion of the temporal lobe.

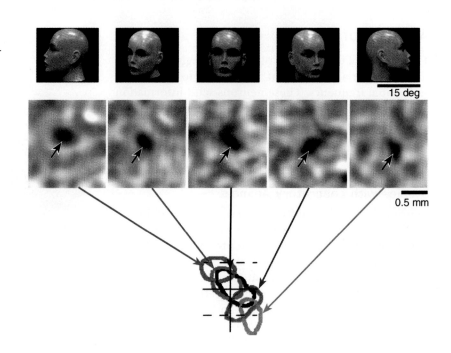

FIGURE 6.28

Results of the study by Wang, Tanaka, and Tanifuji (1996). *Top row:* Views of the doll's head shown to the monkey. *Middle row:* Computer-generated images of the surface of the inferior temporal cortex. The arrows point to dark spots indicating a cluster of activated neurons. *Bottom:* Superimposed drawings of the outline of the clusters of activated neurons.

(Reprinted with permission from Wang, G., Tanaka, K., and Tanifuji, M. Science, 1996, 272, 1665–1668. Copyright 1996 American Association for the Advancement of Science.)

Visual agnosia (*ag no zha*)
Deficits in visual perception in the absence of blindness; caused by brain damage.

Apperceptive visual agnosia
Failure to perceive objects, even though visual acuity is relatively normal.

Prosopagnosia (*prah soh pag no zha*) Failure to recognize particular people by the sight of their faces.

Studies with Humans

Damage to the human visual association cortex can cause a category of deficits known as **visual agnosia.** *Agnosia* ("failure to know") refers to an inability to perceive or identify a stimulus by means of a particular sensory modality, even though its details can be detected by means of that modality and the person retains relatively normal intellectual capacity. *Apperceptive* visual agnosias are failures in high-level perception, whereas *associative* visual agnosias are disconnections between these perceptions and verbal systems. The distinction will be described in more detail later in this section.

People with visual agnosia cannot identify common objects by sight, even though they have relatively normal visual acuity (Warrington and James, 1988). In some cases they can read small print but fail to recognize a common object, such as a wristwatch. However, if they are permitted to hold the object (say, the wristwatch), they can immediately recognize it by touch and say what it is. Thus, they have not lost their memory for the object or forgotten how to say its name.

Apperceptive Visual Agnosia. People with **apperceptive visual agnosia** may have normal visual acuity, but they cannot successfully recognize objects visually by their shape. For example, a brain-damaged patient studied by Benson and Greenberg (1969) was initially believed to be blind but was subsequently observed to navigate his wheelchair around the halls of the hospital. Testing revealed that his visual fields were full (there were no blind spots other than ones we all have) and that he could pick up threads placed on a sheet of white paper. He could discriminate among stimuli that differed in size, brightness, or hue but could not distinguish those that differed only in shape.

A common symptom of apperceptive visual agnosia is **prosopagnosia,** an inability to recognize particular faces (*prosopon* means "face"). That is, the patients can recognize that they are looking at a face, but they cannot say whose face it is—even if it belongs to a relative or close friend. They still remember who these people are and will usually recognize them when they hear their voice. Prosopagnosia is a subtle deficit that can occur even when a person has no apparent difficulty recognizing common objects visually. Some investigators have speculated that facial recognition is mediated by special circuits in the brain that are devoted to the specific analysis of facial features. Others argue that the distinction between prosopagnosia and visual agnosia for common objects is quantitative, not qualitative; that is, visual agnosia for common objects is simply a more severe deficit, caused by more extensive damage to the relevant parts of the visual association cortex. Alexander and Albert (1983) note that although prosopagnosia can occur without visual-object agnosia, all patients with visual-object agnosia also have prosopagnosia.

Damasio, Damasio, and Van Hoesen (1982) described three patients with prosopagnosia who could recognize common objects but had difficulty discriminating between particular objects of the same class. For example, none of them could recognize their own car, although they could tell a car from other types of motorized vehicles. One of them could find her own car in a parking lot only by reading all the license plates until she found her own. Another patient, a farmer, could no longer recognize his cows (Bornstein, Stroka, and Munitz, 1969). Sergent and Signoret (1990) studied three patients with prosopagnosia who could recognize drawings of objects presented as we normally see them but who could not recognize them when they were presented from unusual viewpoints. For example, they could recognize a drawing of a side view of a coffee cup but could not recognize a drawing of a coffee cup viewed from above. These results suggest that prosopagnosia is simply a relatively mild form of visual agnosia; faces are particularly complex stimuli, and even a mild agnosia will make it difficult for a person to recognize them.

Lesion studies also suggest that the right hemisphere may be more important than the left in the perception of faces. Although most cases of prosopagnosia involve bilateral damage, some cases have resulted from right-hemisphere damage (Sergent and Villemure, 1989; De Renzi et al., 1994; Evans et al., 1995). However, no cases of prosopagnosia that include only left-hemisphere damage have been reported in right-handed people.

Associative Visual Agnosia.   A person with apperceptive agnosia who cannot recognize common objects also cannot draw them or copy other people's drawings; thus, we properly speak of a deficit in perception. However, people with an **associative visual agnosia** appear to be able to perceive normally but cannot name what they have seen. In fact, they seem to be *unaware* of these perceptions. For example, a patient studied by Ratcliff and Newcombe (1982) could copy a drawing of an anchor (better than I could have done). Thus, he could perceive the shape of the anchor. However, he could not recognize either the sample or the copy that he had just drawn. When asked on another occasion to draw (not copy) a picture of an anchor, he could not do so. Even though he could copy a real image of an anchor, the word *anchor* failed to produce a mental image of one. (See *Figure 6.29.*) When asked (on yet another occasion) to define *anchor,* he said, "a brake for ships," so we can conclude that he knew what the word meant.

Associative agnosia also extends to prosopagnosia. For example, Sergent and Signoret (1992) reported the case of a patient who could match photos of different views of the same face but could not identify the faces—even when they were pictures of the patient herself. The lesion seems to have affected the ability to identify faces without severely damaging perceptual analysis.

Associative visual agnosia appears to involve a deficit in the ability to transfer information between the visual association cortex and brain mechanisms involved in language. That is, the person perceives the object well enough to draw it, but his or her verbal mechanisms do not receive the necessary information to produce the appropriate word or to

Associative visual agnosia
Inability to identify objects that are perceived visually, even though the form of the perceived object can be drawn or matched with similar objects.

FIGURE   6.29

Associative visual agnosia. The patient successfully copied an anchor (*top*) but failed on two attempts to comply with a request to "draw an anchor" (*bottom*).

(From Ratcliff, G., and Newcombe, F., in Normality and Pathology in Cognitive Functions, *edited by A.W. Ellis. London: Academic Press, 1982.)*

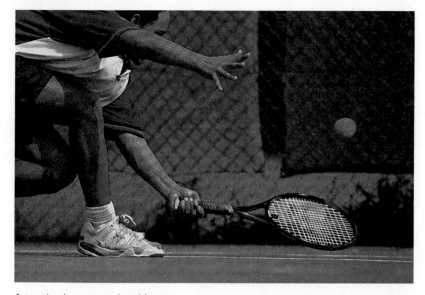

A tennis player must be able to perceive the direction and velocity of a tennis ball to predict its trajectory and intercept it with his racket. Perception of motion is disrupted by damage to a particular region of the extrastriate cortex.

think about what the object is. In the prologue to this chapter I described a Mr. M., man who was unable to recognize a picture of a cow until he observed himself making milking movements with his hands. We might speculate that his perceptual mechanisms in the visual association cortex were relatively normal but that connections between these mechanisms and the speech mechanisms of the left hemisphere were disrupted. However, the connections between the perceptual mechanisms and the motor mechanisms of the frontal lobe were spared, permitting him to make appropriate movements when looking at some pictures.

Recent studies suggest that associative visual agnosia is best explained as a disruption of connections between the ventral stream of the visual cortex from the brain's verbal mechanisms without damage to the connections between these mechanisms and the dorsal stream. I will say more about these studies in the next subsection.

Perception of Movement

We need not only to know what things are, but also where they are and where they are going. Without the ability to perceive the direction and velocity of movement of objects, we would have no way to predict where they will be. We would be unable to catch them (or avoid letting them catch us). This section examines the perception of movement; the final section examines the perception of location.

One of the regions of the extrastriate cortex—area V5, also known as area MT—contains neurons that respond to movement. Damage to this region severely disrupts a monkey's ability to perceive moving stimuli (Siegel and Andersen, 1986). Area V5 receives input directly from the striate cortex and from several regions of the extrastriate cortex. It also receives input from the superior colliculus—directly and from projections relayed through the thalamus.

Bilateral damage to parts of the visual association cortex of the human brain can produce an agnosia for movement. For example, Zihl et al. (1991) reported the case of a woman with bilateral lesions of the lateral occipital cortex and middle temporal gyrus and the underlying white matter. The woman had an almost total loss of movement perception. She was unable to cross a street without traffic lights, because she could not judge the speed at which cars were moving. Although she could tell when objects were moving, she found moving objects very unpleasant to look at. For example, while talking with another person, she avoided looking at the person's mouth because she found its movements very disturbing. When the investigators asked her to try to detect movements of a visual target in the laboratory, she said, "First the target is completely at rest. Then it suddenly jumps upwards and downwards" (p. 2244). She was able to see that the target was constantly changing its position, but she was unaware of any sensation of movement.

Several PET and functional MRI studies suggest that the region of the human brain most directly involved in perception of movement is located near the junction of the lateral occipital and temporal lobes. For example, Malach et al. (1995) showed people two types of stimuli: pictures of objects, faces, and textures, and moving random patterns of dots. As Figure 6.30 shows, these stimuli activated different regions of extrastriate cortex. The red region was activated by objects, faces, and textures, and the green region (presumably, corresponding to area V5) was activated by movement. (See *Figure 6.30.*)

Perception of movement can even help us to perceive three-dimensional forms. Johansson (1973) demonstrated just how much information we can derive from movement. He dressed actors in black and attached small lights to several points on their bodies, such as their wrists, elbows, shoulders, hips, knees, and feet. He made movies of the actors in a darkened room while they were performing various behaviors, such as walking, running, jumping, limping, doing push-ups, and dancing with a partner who was also equipped with lights. Even though observers who watched the films could see only a pattern of moving lights against a dark background, they could readily perceive the pattern as belonging to a moving human and could identify the behavior the actor was performing. Subsequent studies (Kozlowski and Cutting, 1977; Barclay, Cutting, and Kozlowski, 1978) showed that people could even tell, with reasonable accuracy, the sex of the actor wearing the lights. The cues appeared to be supplied by the relative amounts of movement of the shoulders and hips as the person walked.

Often, people with visual agnosia can still perceive *actions* (such as someone pretending to stir something in a bowl or deal out some playing cards) even though they cannot recognize objects by sight. They may be able to recognize friends by the way they walk, even though they cannot recognize their faces. Presumably, their lesions damage the ventral stream of the visual association cortex but leave intact area V5 and its connections with the rest of the brain.

Perception of Location

As we just saw, all subareas of the extrastriate cortex send information to the inferior temporal cortex, the region in which object perception appears to take place. In addition, three subareas of the extrastriate cortex—those involved with color, orientation, and movement—send information through area V5 to the parietal cortex. The parietal lobe is involved in spatial perception, and it is through these connections that it receives its visual input. Damage to the parietal lobes disrupts performance on a variety of tasks that require perceiving and remembering the locations of objects (Ungerleider and Mishkin, 1982).

Haxby et al. (1994) had human subjects perform two different discrimination tasks: one for form (human faces) and the other for spatial location (human faces and random patterns). In both cases, the subjects saw a display showing a face or a pattern, followed by a second display. In the form discrimination task, the subjects had to ignore the location of the faces but decide whether the second display contained the same face as the first. In the spatial location task, they had to ignore the nature of the forms but decide whether the form shown in the second display was in the same *location* as the one shown in the first display. While the subjects were performing the discrimination tasks, the investigators used a PET scanner to record their regional cerebral blood flow. They found that performance of both tasks increased the metabolic activity of much of the extrastriate cortex. However, only the form discrimination task activated the ventral stream, and only the location discrimination task activated the dorsal stream. (See *Figure 6.31.*)

A particularly interesting phenomenon called **Balint's syndrome** occurs in people with bilateral damage to the parieto-occipital region—the region bordering the parietal lobe and occipital lobe (Balint, 1909; Damasio, 1985). In the prologue to

Objects,
faces,
and textures   Movement

FIGURE 6.30

Responses to shapes and movement. Averaged PET images of activation in the occipital lobe produced by pictures of objects, faces, and textures (red) and moving random patterns of dots (green).

(From Malach, R., Reppas, J.B., Benson, R.R., Kwong, K.K., Jiang, H., Kennedy, W.A., Ledden, P.J., Brady, T.J., Rosen, B.R., and Tootell, R.B.H. Proceedings of the National Academy of Sciences, USA, 1995, 92, 8135–8139. Copyright 1995 National Academy of Science, USA.)

Balint's syndrome A syndrome caused by bilateral damage to the parieto-occipital region; includes optic ataxia, ocular apraxia, and simultanagnosia.

Left hemisphere   Right hemisphere

■ Form
■ Form and location
■ Location

FIGURE 6.31

Responses to objects and location. Averaged PET images of cortical activation produced by performing an object discrimination (human faces and random patterns) or a spatial location discrimination of the same stimuli.

(Adapted from Haxby, J.V., Horwitz, B., Ungerleider, L.G., Maisog, J.M., Pietrini, P., and Grady, C.L. Journal of Neuroscience, 1994, 14, *6336–6353.)*

Optic ataxia (*ay **tack** see a*) Difficulty in reaching for objects under visual guidance.

Ocular apraxia (*ay **prak** see a*) Difficulty in visual scanning.

Simultanagnosia (*sime ul tane ag **no** zha*) Difficulty in perceiving more than one object at a time.

Chapter 5 we encountered the case of Mrs. H., who developed Balint's syndrome when her brain was damaged by an inadequate flow of blood during heart surgery. Balint's syndrome consists of three major symptoms: optic ataxia, ocular apraxia, and simultanagnosia. All three symptoms are related to spatial perception.

Optic ataxia is a deficit in reaching for objects under visual guidance (*ataxia* comes from the Greek word for "disorderly"). A person with Balint's syndrome might be able to perceive and recognize a particular object, but when he or she tries to reach for it, the movement is often misdirected. **Ocular apraxia** (literally "without visual action") is a deficit of visual scanning. If a person with Balint's syndrome looks around a room filled with objects, he or she will see an occasional item and will be able to perceive it normally. However, the patient will not be able to maintain fixation; his or her eyes will begin to wander, and another object will come into view for a time. The person is unable to make a systematic scan of the contents of the room and will not be able to perceive the location of the objects he or she sees. If an object moves, or if a light flashes, the person may report seeing something but will not be able to make an eye movement that directs the gaze toward the target.

Simultanagnosia is the most interesting of the three symptoms (Rizzo and Robin, 1990). As I just mentioned, if the gaze of a person with Balint's syndrome happens to fall on an object, he or she will perceive it. But *only one object* will be perceived at a time. For example, if an examiner holds either a comb or a pen in front of a patient's eyes, the patient will recognize the object. But if the examiner holds a pen and a comb together (for example, so that they form the legs of an X), the patient will see either the comb or the pen, but not both. The existence of simultanagnosia means that perception of separate objects takes place at least somewhat independently, even when the outlines of the objects overlap in the visual field.

Goodale and his colleagues (Goodale and Milner, 1992; Goodale et al., 1994) suggested that the primary function of the dorsal stream of the visual cortex is to guide actions rather than simply to perceive spatial locations. As Ungerleider and Mishkin (1982) originally put it, the ventral and dorsal streams tell us "what" and "where." Goodale and his colleagues suggested that the better terms are "what" and *"how."* First, they noted that the visual cortex of the parietal lobe is extensively connected to regions of the frontal lobe involved in controlling eye movements, reaching movements of the limbs, and grasping movements of the hands and fingers (Cavada and Goldman-Rakic, 1989; Gentilucci and Rizzolatti, 1990; Broussaud, di Pellegrino, and Wise, 1996). Second, they noted that the optic ataxia and ocular apraxia of Balint's syndrome, which are caused by bilateral damage to the dorsal stream, are deficits in visually guided movements. They cited the case of a person with such lesions who had no difficulty recognizing line drawings (that is, the ventral stream was intact) but who had trouble picking up objects (Jakobson et al., 1991). The patient could easily perceive the difference in the size of wooden blocks set out before her, but she failed to adjust the distance between her thumb and forefinger to the size of the block she was about to pick up. In contrast, a patient with profound visual agnosia could not distinguish between wooden blocks of different sizes, but *could* adjust the distance between her thumb and forefinger when she picked them up. She made this adjustment by means of vision, before she actually touched them (Milner et al., 1991; Goodale et al., 1994).

The suggestion by Goodale and his colleagues seems a reasonable one. Of course, the dorsal stream is involved in perception of the location of an object's space—but then, if its primary role is to direct movements, it *must* be involved in location of these objects, or else how could it direct movements toward them? In addition, it must contain information about the size and shape of objects, or else how could it control the distance between thumb and forefinger?

I mentioned earlier that I would attempt to explain associative visual agnosia as a disruption of the connections between the ventral stream and the brain's verbal mechanisms. As we saw, people with associative agnosia cannot verbally identify visually presented objects or pictures of them, but they can copy them and sometimes they can make hand movements that enable them to guess what the object is. Sirigu, Duhamel, and Poncet (1991) reported the case of a patient with bilateral lesions of the anterior temporal cortex who was able to copy drawings of objects but was unable to name them. However, he was able to say or demonstrate *what to do* with these objects. For example, he said, "You open on one side, stick something on it, close it, and it stays in. I can tell you how it works, but I don't see its exact use" (p. 2555). And what had the investigators shown him? A safety pin. When they showed him a picture of a jackhammer, he acted as if he were holding one and made shaking movements. What was it for? "Probably to make holes . . . in the wall . . . when you want to hang a picture" (p. 2566).

It is important to realize that the patient recognized *what to do* with objects he saw, not *what they were used for.* He was able to describe or mime behaviors, not functions. Certainly, one would not use a jackhammer to hang a picture on the wall. Consider what he said when shown a pair of pliers: "It is used manually, when you pull apart here [points to handle] it opens up at the other end." So far, so good. But then he went on to say, "Perhaps to hold several pieces of paper together" (p. 2566). When shown an iron, he said "You hold it in one hand, and move it back and forth horizontally." He then mimed the action, as if he were pressing some clothes on an ironing board. "Maybe you can spread glue evenly with it" (p. 2566).

Even though the patient could not identify most objects visually, he accurately answered questions about their physical properties, such as "Which one would feel the heaviest?" "Which one is the softest?" or "Which one would feel the coldest?" The fact that he could answer these questions (and could mime what to do with them) indicates that the circuits responsible for visual form perception (those in the ventral stream) were relatively intact but that they were no longer connected to the circuits responsible for speech (and for consciousness). His dorsal stream and its connections with speech mechanisms were undamaged, and it was apparently through these connections that he was able to describe how to use the objects. This interpretation is consistent with Goodale and Milner's conclusion that the dorsal stream is primarily occupied with controlling movements, not simply perceiving the location of objects.

INTERIM SUMMARY

The visual cortex consists of the striate cortex, the extrastriate cortex (also called the prestriate or circumstriate cortex), and the visual association cortex of the inferior temporal lobe and the posterior parietal lobe. The visual cortex has at least twenty-five different subregions, arranged in a hierarchical fashion. The extrastriate cortex receives information from the striate cortex and from the superior colliculus. The color-sensitive cells in the CO blobs in the striate cortex send information to area V4 of the extrastriate cortex. Damage to the human extrastriate cortex (presumably, damage to area V4) can cause achromatopsia, a loss of color vision.

The visual cortex is organized into two streams. The ventral stream, which ends with the inferior temporal cortex, is involved with perception of objects. Lesions of this region disrupt visual object perception. Also, single neurons in the inferior temporal cortex respond best to complex stimuli and continue to do so even if the object is moved to a different location, changed in size, placed against a different background, or partially hidden. The dorsal stream, which ends with the posterior parietal cortex, is involved with perception of location, movement, and control of eye and hand movements. Damage to area V5 or to the posterior parietal cortex disrupts an animal's ability to perceive movement or the spatial location of objects.

PET studies indicate that specific regions of the cortex are involved in perception of form, movement, and color, and these studies will undoubtedly enable us to discover the correspondences between the anatomy of the human visual system and that of laboratory animals. Studies with humans who have sustained damage to the visual association cortex have discovered two basic forms of visual agnosia. Apperceptive visual agnosia involves difficulty in perceiving the shapes of objects, even though the fine details can often be detected. Prosopagnosia, failure to recognize faces, has traditionally been regarded as a separate disorder, but it probably represents a mild form of apperceptive visual agnosia. The second basic form of visual agnosia, associative visual agnosia, is characterized by relatively good object perception (shown by the fact that the patients can copy drawings of objects) but the inability to recognize what is perceived. This disorder is probably caused by damage to axons that connect the visual association cortex with regions of the brain that are important for verbalization and thinking in words. Some patients with this disorder can describe or mime actions appropriate to the objects that they see but cannot recognize.

Damage to the human visual association cortex corresponding to area V5 disrupts perception of movement. Sometimes people with visual agnosia caused by damage to the ventral system can still perceive the meanings of actions or recognize friends by the way they walk, which indicates that the dorsal stream of their visual cortex is largely intact. Balint's syndrome, which is caused by bilateral damage to the parieto-occipital region (the dorsal stream), includes the symptoms of optic ataxia, ocular apraxia, and simultanagnosia.

■ THOUGHT QUESTIONS

1. Some psychologists are interested in "top-down" processes in visual perception, that is, the effects of context on perceiving ambiguous stimuli. For example, if you are in a dimly lighted kitchen and see a shape that could be either a loaf of bread or a country mailbox, you will be more likely to perceive the object as a loaf of bread. Where in the brain might contextual information affect perception?

2. A neurologist friend once told me about a patient he saw who had such severe prosopagnosia that he could not even recognize his wife by sight. One day, while my friend was examining the patient, the patient's wife entered the hospital room. "Can you tell me who that is?" he asked, wanting to determine whether the patient's symptoms had improved. "I don't know," he said, "but it certainly can't be my dear Lucie." But it was. What type of prosopagnosia did the man have, apperceptive or associative? How might we explain his behavior?

EPILOGUE Case Studies

The discussion of Mr. M. in the prologue raises an issue about research that I'd like to address: the issue of making generalizations from the study of an individual patient. Some researchers have argued that because no two people are alike, we cannot make generalizations from a single individual like Mr. M. They say that valid inferences can be made only from studies that involve *groups* of people, so that individual differences can be accounted for statistically. Is this criticism valid?

The careful, detailed investigation of the abilities and disabilities of a single person is called a *case study*. In my opinion, case studies of people with brain damage can provide very useful information. In the first place, even if we were not able to make firm conclusions from the study of one person, a careful analysis of the pattern of deficits shown by an individual patient might give us some useful ideas for further research, and sources of good ideas for research should not be neglected. But under some circumstances we *can* draw conclusions from a single case.

Before describing what kinds of inferences we can and cannot make from case studies, let me review what we hope to accomplish by studying the behavior of people with brain damage. The brain seems to be organized in modules. A given module receives information from other modules, performs some kinds of analysis, and sends the results on to other modules with which it communicates. In some cases, the wiring of the module may change. That is, synaptic connections may be modified so that in the future the module will respond differently to its inputs. (As you will see in Chapter 12, the ability of modules to modify their synaptic connections serves as the basis for the ability to learn and remember.)

If we want to understand how the brain works, we have to know what the individual modules do. A particular module is not *responsible* for a behavior; instead, it performs one of the many functions that are necessary for a set of behaviors. For example, as I sit here typing this epilogue, I am using modules that perform functions related to posture and balance, to the control of eye movements, to memories related to the topic I am writing about, to memories of English words and their spellings, to control of finger movements . . . well, you get the idea. We would rarely try to analyze such a complex task as sitting and writing an epilogue; but we might try to analyze how we spell a familiar English word. Possibly, we use modules that perform functions normally related to hearing: We use these modules to "hear" the word in our head and then use other modules to convert the sounds into the appropriate patterns of letters. Alternatively, we may picture the word we want to spell, which would use modules that perform functions related to vision. I do not want to go into the details of spelling and writing here (they will be covered in Chapter 13), but I do want you to see why it is important to try to understand the functions performed by groups of modules located in particular parts of the brain. In practice, this means studying and analyzing the pattern of deficits shown by people with brain damage.

What kinds of conclusions can we make by studying a single individual? We *cannot* conclude that because two behaviors are impaired, the deficit is caused by damage to a set of common modules needed for both behaviors. Instead, it could be that behavior X is impaired by damage to module A and behavior Y is impaired by damage to module B and it just happens that modules A and B were both damaged by the brain lesion. However, we *can* conclude that if a brain lesion causes a loss of behavior X but not of behavior Y, then the functions performed by the damaged modules are not required to perform behavior Y. The study of a single patient permits us to make this conclusion.

The conclusion might seem rather modest, but it can advance our understanding of the types of brain functions involved in particular behaviors.

For example, Mr. M. could not tell us that a picture he was looking at showed a cow, but he could make hand movements that a person would make only with respect to a cow. Therefore, we can conclude with certainty that brain damage that prevents a person from verbally identifying a particular visual image will not necessarily prevent the person from making hand movements appropriate to that image. Perhaps the brain has two perceptual systems, each with an independent set of modules devoted to analyzing visual images: one perceptual system connected to verbal mechanisms and the other connected to mechanisms involved with hand movements. Although we cannot rule out this possibility, it seems unlikely that the organization of the brain is so wasteful of resources. Instead, it seems more likely that a single set of modules is devoted to analyzing visual images, and the information analyzed there is sent to several different parts of the brain. Possibly, then, Mr. M.'s brain lesion disrupted the pathway bringing visual information to modules involved in verbal mechanisms but did not disrupt the pathway bringing it to modules involved in control of hand movements. (If this conclusion were true, we would say that associative visual agnosia is a *disconnection syndrome*—a syndrome caused by a disconnection between particular sets of modules.) Of course, to confirm this hypothesis, we need to make further observations on other patients.

You can see that although case studies do not permit us to make sweeping conclusions, under the right circumstances we can properly draw firm if modest conclusions that help us to understand the organization of the brain and suggest hypotheses to test with further research.

KEY CONCEPTS

THE STIMULUS

1. Light, a form of electromagnetic radiation, can vary in wavelength, intensity, and purity; it can thus give rise to differences in perceptions of hue, brightness, and saturation.

ANATOMY OF THE VISUAL SYSTEM

2. The eyes are complex sensory organs that focus an image of the environment on the retina. The retina consists of three layers: the photoreceptor layer (rods and cones), the bipolar cell layer, and the ganglion cell layer.

3. Information from the eye is sent to the parvocellular and magnocellular layers of the dorsal lateral geniculate nucleus and then to the primary visual cortex (striate cortex).

CODING OF VISUAL INFORMATION IN THE RETINA

4. When light strikes a molecule of photopigment in a photoreceptor, the molecule splits and initiates a receptor potential.

5. Ganglion cells of the retina respond in an opposing center/surround fashion.

6. Colors are detected by three types of cones, and the code is changed into an opponent-process system by the time it reaches the retinal ganglion cells.

ANALYSIS OF VISUAL INFORMATION: ROLE OF THE STRIATE CORTEX

7. Neurons in the striate cortex are organized in modules, each containing two blobs. Neurons within the blobs respond to color; those outside the blobs respond to orientation, spatial frequency, movement, and retinal disparity.

8. Visual information is processed by two parallel systems, the magnocellular system and the parvocellular system.

ANALYSIS OF VISUAL INFORMATION: ROLE OF THE VISUAL ASSOCIATION CORTEX

9. Specific regions of the prestriate cortex receive information about specific features of the visual scene from the striate cortex, analyze it, and send their information on to higher levels of association cortex.

10. The association cortex of the inferior temporal gyrus (ventral stream) recognizes the shape of objects, whereas the parietal cortex (dorsal stream) recognizes their location.

11. Damage to the visual association cortex can produce apperceptive or associative visual agnosia in humans. Damage to a region located in the medial occipital lobe can produce achromatopsia. Damage to the region corresponding to area V5 disrupts perception of movement. Balint's syndrome is caused by bilateral damage to the parieto-occipital region.

SUGGESTED READINGS

De Valois, R.L., and De Valois, K.K. *Spatial Vision.* New York: Oxford University Press, 1988.

Land, M.F., and Fernald, R.D. The evolution of eyes. *Annual Review of Neuroscience,* 1992, *15,* 1–30.

Merigan, W.H., and Maunsell, J.H.R. How parallel are the primate visual pathways? *Annual Review of Neuroscience,* 1993, *16,* 369–402.

Miyashita, Y. Inferior temporal cortex: Where visual perception meets memory. *Annual Review of Neuroscience,* 1993, *16,* 245–264.

Tanaka, K. Inferotemporal cortex and object vision. *Annual Review of Neuroscience,* 1996, *19,* 100–139.

Valberg, A., and Lee, B.B. *From Pigments to Perception.* New York: Plenum Press, 1991.

Wandell, B.A. *Foundations of Vision.* Sunderland, MA: Sinauer Associates, 1995.

Zeki, S. *A Vision of the Brain.* Oxford: Blackwell Scientific Publications, 1992.

7

Audition, the Body Senses, and the Chemical Senses

LEARNING OBJECTIVES

1. Describe the parts of the ear and the auditory pathway.

2. Describe the detection of pitch, timbre, and the location of the source of a sound.

3. Describe the structures and functions of the vestibular system.

4. Describe the cutaneous senses and their response to touch, temperature, and pain.

5. Describe the somatosensory pathways and the perception of pain.

6. Describe the four taste qualities, the anatomy of the taste buds and how they detect taste, and the gustatory pathway and neural coding of taste.

7. Describe the major structures of the olfactory system, explain how odors are detected, and describe the patterns of neural activity produced by these stimuli.

All in Her Head?

Melissa, a junior at the state university, had volunteered to be a subject in an experiment at the dental school. She had been told that she might feel a little pain but that everything was under medical supervision and no harm would come to her. She didn't particularly like the idea of pain, but she would be well paid; and she saw in the experience an opportunity to live up to her own self-image as being as brave as anyone.

She entered the reception room, where she signed consent forms saying that she agreed to participate in the experiment and knew that a physician would be giving her a drug and that her reaction to pain would be measured. The experimenter greeted her, led her to a room, and asked her to be seated in a dental chair. He inserted a needle attached to a plastic tube into a vein in her right arm so that he could inject drugs.

"First," he said, "we want to find out how sensitive you are to pain." He showed her a device that looked something like an electric toothbrush with a metal probe on the end. "This device will stimulate nerves in the pulp of your tooth. Do you have some fillings?" She nodded. "Have you ever bitten on some aluminum foil?" She winced and nodded again. "Good, then you will know what to expect." He adjusted a dial on the stimulator, touched the tip of it to a tooth, and pressed the button. No response. He turned the dial

and stimulated the tooth again. Still no response. He turned the dial again, and this time, the stimulation made her gasp and wince. He recorded the voltage setting in his notebook.

"Okay, now we know how sensitive this tooth is to pain. Now I'm going to give you a drug we are testing. It should decrease the pain quite a bit." He injected the drug and after a short while said, "Let's try the tooth again." The drug apparently worked; he had to increase the voltage considerably before she felt any pain.

"Now," he said, "I want to give you some more of the drug to see if we can make you feel even less pain." He gave another injection and, after a little wait, tested her again. But the drug had not further decreased her pain sensitivity; instead, it had *increased* it; she was now as sensitive as she had been before the first injection.

After the experiment was over, the experimenter walked with Melissa into a lounge. "I want to tell you about the experiment you were in, but I'd like to ask you not to talk about it with other people who might also serve as subjects." She nodded her head in agreement.

"Actually, you did not receive a painkiller. The first injection was pure salt water."

"It was? But I thought it made me less sensitive to pain."

"It did. When an innocuous substance such as an injection of salt

water or a sugar pill has an effect like that, we call it a placebo effect."

"You mean that it was all in my mind? That I only *thought* that the shock hurt less?"

"No. Well, that is, it was necessary for you to think that you had received a painkiller. But the effect was a physiological one. We know that, because the second injection contained a drug that counteracts the effects of opiates."

"Opiates? You mean like morphine or heroin?"

"Yes." He saw her start to protest, shook his head, and said, "No, I'm sure you don't take drugs. But your brain makes them. For reasons we still do not understand, your believing that you had received a painkiller caused some cells in your brain to release a chemical that acts the way opiates do. The chemical acts on other neurons in your brain and decreases your sensitivity to pain. When I gave you the second injection—the drug that counteracts opiates—your sensitivity to pain came back."

"But then, did my mind or my brain make the placebo effect happen?"

"Well, think about it. Your mind and your brain are not really separate. Experiences can change the way your brain functions, and these changes can alter your experiences. Mind and brain have to be studied together, not separately."

One chapter was devoted to vision, but the rest of the sensory modalities must share a chapter. This unequal allocation of space reflects the relative importance of vision to our species and the relative amount of research that has been devoted to it.

This chapter is divided into five major sections, which discuss audition, the vestibular system, the somatosenses, gustation, and olfaction.

AUDITION

For most people, audition is the second most important sense. The value of verbal communication makes it even more important than vision in some respects; for example, a blind person can join others in conversation far more easily than a deaf person can. Acoustic stimuli also provide information about things that are hidden from view, and our ears work just as well in the dark. This section describes the nature of the stimulus, the sensory receptors, the brain mechanisms devoted to audition, and some of the details of the physiology of auditory perception.

The Stimulus

We hear sounds, which are produced by objects that vibrate and set molecules of air into motion. When an object vibrates, its movements cause the air surrounding it alternately to condense and rarefy (pull apart), producing waves that travel away from the object at approximately 700 miles per hour. If the vibration ranges between approximately 30 and 20,000 times per second, these waves will stimulate receptive cells in our ears and will be perceived as sounds. (See *Figure 7.1*.)

In Chapter 6 we saw that light has three perceptual dimensions—hue, brightness, and saturation—that correspond to three physical dimensions. Similarly, sounds vary in their pitch, loudness, and timbre. The perceived **pitch** of an auditory stimulus is determined by the frequency of vibration, which is measured in **hertz (Hz),** or cycles per second. (The term honors Heinrich Hertz, a nineteenth-century German physicist.) **Loudness** is a function of intensity—the degree to which the condensations and rarefactions of air differ from each other. More vigorous vibrations of an object produce more intense sound waves and hence louder ones. **Timbre** provides information about the nature of the particular sound—for example, the sound of an oboe or a train whistle. Most natural acoustic stimuli are complex, consisting of several different frequencies of vibration. The particular mixture determines the sound's timbre. (See *Figure 7.2*.)

The eye is a *synthetic* organ (literally, "a putting together"). When two different wavelengths of light are mixed, we perceive a single color. For example, when we see a mixture of red and bluish green light, we perceive pure yellow light and cannot detect either of the two constituents. In contrast, the ear is an *analytical* organ (from the Greek *analuein,* "to undo"). When two different frequencies of sound waves are mixed, we do not perceive an intermediate tone; instead, we hear both original tones. As we will see, the ability of our auditory system to detect the individual component frequencies of a complex tone gives us the capacity to identify the nature of particular sounds, such as those of different musical instruments.

Anatomy of the Ear

Figure 7.3 shows a section through the ear and auditory canal and illustrates the apparatus of the middle and inner ear. (See *Figure 7.3*.) Sound is funneled via the *pinna* (external ear) through the ear canal to the **tympanic membrane** (eardrum), which vibrates with the sound. We are not very good at moving our ears, but by orienting our heads we can modify the sound that finally reaches the receptors.

The *middle ear* consists of a hollow region behind the tympanic membrane, approximately 2 ml in volume. It contains the bones of the middle ear, called the **ossicles,** which are set into vibration by the tympanic membrane. The **malleus** (hammer) connects with the tympanic

FIGURE 7.1

Sound waves. Changes in air pressure from sound waves move the eardrum in and out. Air molecules are closer together in regions of higher pressure and farther apart in regions of lower pressure.

Pitch A perceptual dimension of sound; corresponds to the fundamental frequency.

Hertz (Hz) Cycles per second.

Loudness A perceptual dimension of sound; corresponds to intensity.

Timbre (*tim* ber or *tamm* ber) A perceptual dimension of sound; corresponds to complexity.

Tympanic membrane The eardrum.

Ossicle (*ahss* i kul) One of the three bones of the middle ear.

Malleus The "hammer"; the first of the three ossicles.

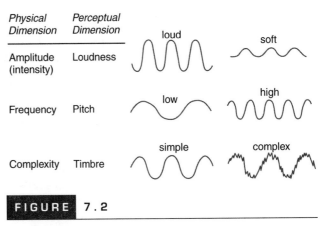

FIGURE 7.2

The physical and perceptual dimensions of sound waves.

FIGURE 7.3

The auditory apparatus.

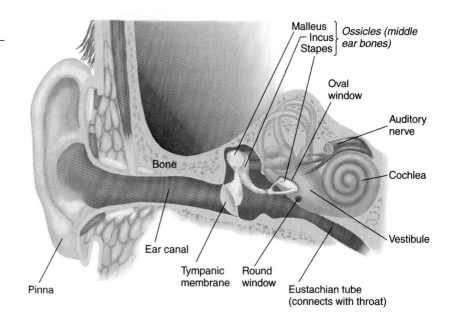

Ossicles (middle ear bones): Malleus, Incus, Stapes

Oval window

Auditory nerve

Cochlea

Vestibule

Bone

Pinna

Ear canal

Tympanic membrane

Round window

Eustachian tube (connects with throat)

Incus The "anvil"; the second of the three ossicles.

Stapes (*stay peez*) The "stirrup"; the last of the three ossicles.

Cochlea (*cock lee uh*) The snail-shaped structure of the inner ear that contains the auditory transducing mechanisms.

Oval window An opening in the bone surrounding the cochlea that reveals a membrane, against which the baseplate of the stapes presses, transmitting sound vibrations into the fluid within the cochlea.

Organ of Corti The sensory organ on the basilar membrane that contains the auditory hair cells.

Hair cell The receptive cell of the auditory apparatus.

Basilar membrane (*bazz i ler*) A membrane in the cochlea of the inner ear; contains the organ of Corti.

Tectorial membrane (*tek torr ee ul*) A membrane located above the basilar membrane; serves as a shelf against which the cilia of the auditory hair cells move.

Round window An opening in the bone surrounding the cochlea of the inner ear that permits vibrations to be transmitted, via the oval window, into the fluid in the cochlea.

membrane and transmits vibrations via the **incus** (anvil) and **stapes** (stirrup) to the **cochlea,** the structure that contains the receptors. The baseplate of the stapes presses against the membrane behind the **oval window,** the opening in the bony process surrounding the cochlea. (See *Figure 7.3.*)

The cochlea is part of the *inner ear.* It is filled with fluid; therefore, sounds transmitted through the air must be transferred into a liquid medium. This process normally is very inefficient—99.9 percent of the energy of airborne sound would be reflected away if the air impinged directly against the oval window of the cochlea. (If you have ever swum underwater, you have probably noted how quiet it is there; most of the sound arising in the air is reflected off the surface of the water.) The chain of ossicles serves as an extremely efficient means of energy transmission. The bones provide a mechanical advantage, with the baseplate of the stapes making smaller but more forceful excursions against the oval window than the tympanic membrane makes against the malleus.

The name *cochlea* comes from the Greek word *kokhlos,* or "land snail." It is indeed snail-shaped, consisting of two and three-quarters turns of a gradually tapering cylinder, 35 mm (1.37 in.) long. The cochlea is divided longitudinally into three sections, as shown in Figure 7.4. The receptive organ, known as the **organ of Corti,** consists of the *basilar membrane,* the *hair cells,* and the *tectorial membrane.* The auditory receptor cells are called **hair cells,** and they are anchored, via rodlike supporting cells (*Deiters's cells*), to the **basilar membrane.** The cilia of the hair cells pass through the *reticular membrane,* and the ends of some of them attach to the fairly rigid **tectorial membrane,** which projects overhead like a shelf. (See *Figure 7.4.*) Sound waves cause the basilar membrane to move relative to the tectorial membrane, which bends the cilia of the hair cells. This bending produces receptor potentials.

Georg von Békésy—in a lifetime of brilliant studies on the cochleas of various animals, from human cadavers to elephants—found that the vibratory energy exerted on the oval window causes the basilar membrane to bend (von Békésy, 1960). Because of the physical characteristics of the basilar membrane, the portion that bends the most is determined by the frequency of the sound: High-frequency sounds cause the end nearest the oval window to bend.

Figure 7.5 shows this process in a cochlea that has been partially straightened. If the cochlea were a closed system, no vibration would be transmitted through the oval window, because liquids are essentially incompressible. However, there is a membrane-covered opening, the **round window,** that allows the fluid inside the cochlea

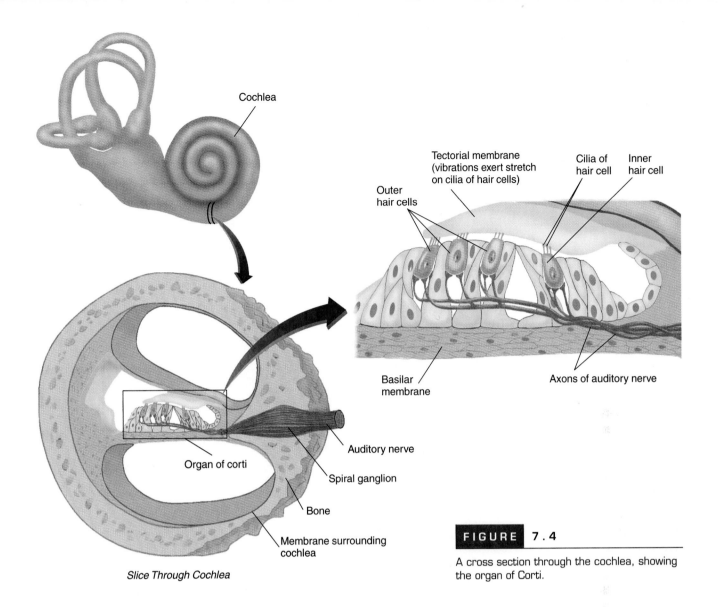

Cochlea

Tectorial membrane
(vibrations exert stretch
on cilia of hair cells)

Cilia of
hair cell

Inner
hair cell

Outer
hair cells

Basilar
membrane

Axons of auditory nerve

Organ of corti

Auditory nerve

Spiral ganglion

Bone

Membrane surrounding
cochlea

Slice Through Cochlea

FIGURE 7.4

A cross section through the cochlea, showing
the organ of Corti.

to move back and forth. The baseplate of the stapes vibrates against the membrane behind the oval window and introduces sound waves of high or low frequency into the cochlea. The vibrations cause part of the basilar membrane to flex back and forth. Pressure changes in the fluid underneath the basilar membrane are transmitted to the membrane of the round window, which moves in and out in a manner opposite to the movements of the oval window. That is, when the baseplate of the stapes pushes in, the membrane behind the round window bulges out. As we will see in a later subsection, different frequencies of sound vibrations cause different portions of the basilar membrane to flex. (See *Figure 7.5*.)

Some people suffer from a middle ear disease that causes the bone to grow over the round window. Because their basilar membrane cannot easily flex back and forth, these people have a severe hearing loss. However, their hearing can be restored by a surgical procedure called *fenestration* ("window making"), in which a tiny hole is drilled in the bone where the round window should be.

Auditory Hair Cells and the Transduction of Auditory Information

Two types of auditory receptors, *inner* and *outer* auditory hair cells, lie on the inside and outside of the cochlear coils, respectively. Hair cells contain **cilia** ("eyelashes"),

Cilium A hairlike appendage of a cell involved in movement or in transducing sensory information; found on the receptors in the auditory and vestibular system.

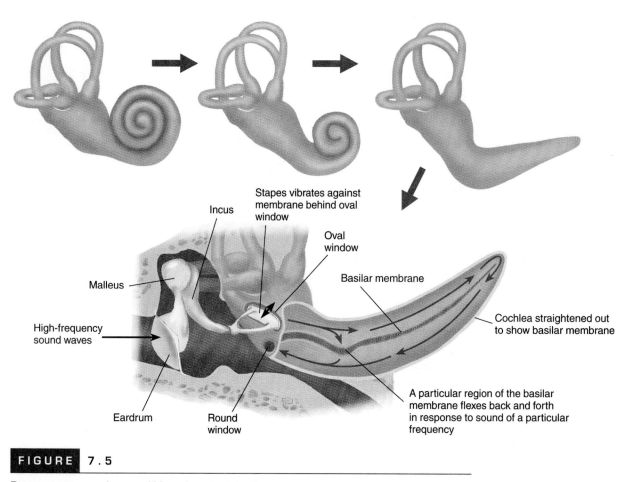

FIGURE 7.5

Responses to sound waves. When the stapes pushes against the membrane behind the oval window, the membrane behind the round window bulges outward. Different high-frequency and medium-frequency sound vibrations cause flexing of different portions of the basilar membrane. In contrast, low-frequency sound vibrations cause the tip of the basilar membrane to flex in synchrony with the vibrations.

Tip link Elastic filaments that attach the tip of one cilium to the side of the adjacent cilium.

Insertional plaque The point of attachment of a tip link to a cilium.

fine hairlike appendages, arranged in rows, according to height. The human cochlea contains 3500 inner hair cells and 12,000 outer hair cells. The hair cells form synapses with dendrites of bipolar neurons whose axons bring auditory information to the brain. (Refer to *Figure 7.4.*)

Sound waves cause both the basilar membrane and the tectorial membrane to flex up and down. These movements bend the cilia of the hair cells in one direction or the other. The tips of the cilia of outer hair cells are attached directly to the tectorial membrane. The cilia of the inner hair cells do not touch the overlying tectorial membrane, but the relative movement of the two membranes causes the fluid within the cochlea to flow past them, making them bend back and forth, too.

Cilia contain actin filaments, which make them stiff and rigid (Flock, 1977). Adjacent cilia are linked to each other by elastic filaments known as **tip links.** Each tip link is attached to the end of one cilium and to the side of an adjacent cilium. The points of attachment, known as **insertional plaques,** look dark under an electron microscope. As we will see, receptor potentials are triggered at the insertional plaques. (See *Figure 7.6.*)

Normally, tip links are slightly stretched, which means that they are under a small amount of tension. Thus, movement of the bundle of cilia in the direction of the tallest of them further stretches these linking fibers, whereas movement in the opposite direction relaxes them. The bending of the bundle of cilia causes receptor potentials (Pickles and Corey, 1992; Hudspeth and Gillespie, 1994; Gillespie, 1995;

Jaramillo, 1995). Each insertional plaque contains a single cation channel. When the bundle of hair cells is straight, the probability of an individual ion channel being open is approximately 10 percent. This means that a small amount of positively charged cations can diffuse into the cilium. When the bundle moves toward the tallest one, the increased tension on the tip links opens all the ion channels, the flow of cations into the cilium increases, and the membrane depolarizes. As a result, the release of neurotransmitter by the hair cell increases. When the bundle moves in the opposite direction, toward the shortest cilium, the relaxation of the tip links allows the opened ion channels to close. The influx of cations ceases, the membrane hyperpolarizes, and the release of neurotransmitter decreases. (See *Figure 7.7*.)

Exactly how does stretching a tip link cause an ion channel to open? Most researchers believe that the tip links are attached directly to the ion channels, and when there is a sufficient amount of tension on them, the pores of the ion channels are pulled open. In fact, Preyer et al. (1995) found that when tip links were dissolved by a special enzyme, displacement of the bundle of cilia no longer produced receptor potentials. Thus, tension on the tip links, and not simple movement of the cilia, is what opens the ion channels.

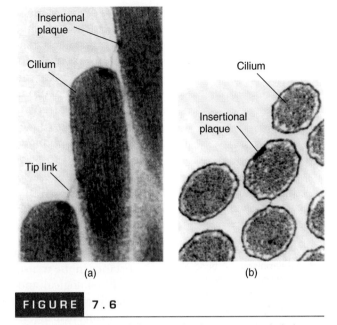

(a)   (b)

FIGURE 7.6

Electron micrographs of the transduction apparatus in hair cells. (a) Longitudinal section through three adjacent cilia. Tip links, elastic filaments attached to insertional plaques, link adjacent cilia. (b) A cross section through several cilia, showing an insertional plaque.

(From Hudspeth, A.J., and Gillespie, P.G. Neuron, 1994, 12, 1–9. Copyright 1994 Cell Press. Reprinted by permission.)

The Auditory Pathway

Connections with the Cochlear Nerve

The organ of Corti sends auditory information to the brain by means of the **cochlear nerve,** a branch of the auditory nerve (eighth cranial nerve). The neurons that give rise to the afferent axons that travel through this nerve are of the bipolar type. Their cell bodies reside in the *cochlear nerve ganglion.* (This ganglion is also called the *spiral ganglion,* because it consists of clumps of cell bodies arranged in a spiral caused

Cochlear nerve The branch of the auditory nerve that transmits auditory information from the cochlea to the brain.

FIGURE 7.7

Transduction in hair cells of the inner ear. Movement of the bundle of cilia toward the tallest one increases tension on the tip links, which opens ion channels and increases the inflow of positively charged cations. This influx increases the firing rate of the cochlear nerve axon attached to the hair cell. Movement of the bundle of cilia away from the tallest one has the opposite effects: ion channels close and the firing rate of the axon decreases.

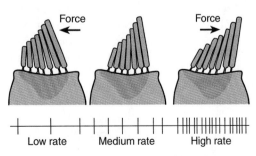

Low rate   Medium rate   High rate

Action Potentials in Cochlear Nerve Axon

by the curling of the cochlea.) These neurons have axonal processes, capable of sustaining action potentials, that protrude from both ends of the soma. The end of one process acts like a dendrite, responding with excitatory postsynaptic potentials when the transmitter substance is released by the auditory hair cells. The excitatory postsynaptic potentials trigger action potentials in the auditory nerve axons, which form synapses with neurons in the medulla. (Refer to *Figure 7.4.*)

Each cochlear nerve contains approximately 50,000 afferent axons. The dendrites of approximately 95 percent of these axons form synapses with the inner hair cells. Most afferent fibers make contact with only one inner hair cell, but each inner hair cell forms synapses with approximately twenty fibers (Dallos, 1992). The axons that receive information from the inner hair cells are thick and myelinated. The other 5 percent of the sensory fibers in the cochlear nerve form synapses with the much more numerous outer hair cells, at a ratio of approximately one fiber per thirty outer hair cells. In addition, these axons are thin and unmyelinated. Thus, although the inner hair cells represent only 29 percent of the total number of receptive cells, their connections with auditory nerves suggest that they are of primary importance in the transmission of auditory information to the central nervous system.

Physiological and behavioral studies confirm the inferences made from the synaptic connections of the two types of hair cells: The inner hair cells are necessary for normal hearing. In fact, Deol and Glueckschn-Waelsch (1979) found that a mutant strain of mice whose cochleas contain *only* outer hair cells apparently cannot hear at all. Most investigators currently believe that the outer hair cells are primarily *effector* cells, involved in altering the mechanical characteristics of the basilar membrane and thus influencing the effects of sound vibrations on the inner hair cells. I will discuss this possibility in the section on place coding of pitch.

The Central Auditory System

The anatomy of the auditory system is more complicated than that of the visual system. Rather than give a detailed verbal description of the pathways, I will refer you to *Figure 7.8*. Note that axons enter the **cochlear nucleus** of the medulla and synapse there. Most of the neurons in the cochlear nucleus send axons to the **superior olivary complex,** also located in the medulla. Neurons there project axons through a large bundle of axons called the **lateral lemniscus** to the inferior colliculus, located in the dorsal midbrain. Neurons there project to the medial geniculate nucleus of the thalamus, which sends axons to the auditory cortex of the temporal lobe. As you can see, there are many synapses along the way to complicate the story. Each hemisphere receives information from both ears but primarily from the contralateral one. And auditory information is relayed to the cerebellum and reticular formation as well.

If we unrolled the basilar membrane into a flat strip and followed afferent axons serving successive points along its length, we would reach successive points in the nuclei of the auditory system and ultimately successive points along the surface of the primary auditory cortex. The *basal* end of the basi-

Cochlear nucleus One of a group of nuclei in the medulla that receive auditory information from the cochlea.

Superior olivary complex A group of nuclei in the medulla; involved with auditory functions, including localization of the source of sounds.

Lateral lemniscus A band of fibers running rostrally through the medulla and pons; carries fibers of the auditory system.

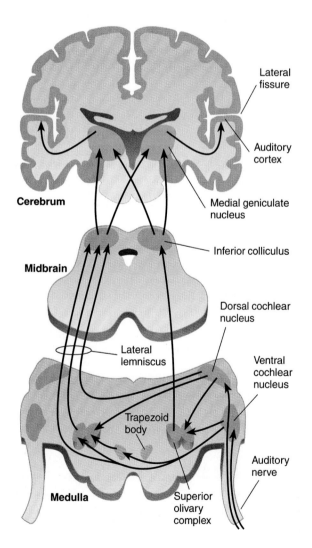

FIGURE 7.8

The pathway of the auditory system.

lar membrane (the end toward the oval window) is represented most medially in the auditory cortex, and the *apical* end is represented most laterally there. Because, as we will see, different parts of the basilar membrane respond best to different frequencies of sound, this relationship between cortex and basilar membrane is referred to as **tonotopic representation** (*tonos* means "tone" and *topos* means "place").

Neurons in the primary auditory cortex send axons to the auditory association cortex. In Chapter 4 we saw that the primary auditory cortex lies hidden on the inside of the lateral fissure and that the auditory association cortex lies on the superior part of the temporal lobe.

Detection of Pitch

As we have seen, the perceptual dimension of pitch corresponds to the physical dimension of frequency. The cochlea detects frequency by two means: moderate to high frequencies by place coding and low frequencies by rate coding.

Place Coding

The work of von Békésy has shown us that because of the mechanical construction of the cochlea and basilar membrane, acoustic stimuli of different frequencies cause different parts of the basilar membrane to flex back and forth. Figure 7.9 illustrates the amount of deformation along the length of the basilar membrane produced by stimulation with tones of various frequencies. Note that higher frequencies produce more displacement at the basal end of the membrane (the end closest to the stapes). (See *Figure 7.9.*)

These results suggest that at least some frequencies of sound waves are detected by means of a **place code.** In this context a code represents a means by which neurons can represent information. Thus, if neurons at one end of the basilar membrane are excited by higher frequencies and those at the other end by lower frequencies, we can say that the frequency of the sound is *coded* by the particular neurons that are active. In turn, the firing of particular axons in the cochlear nerve tells the brain about the presence of particular frequencies of sound.

Evidence for place coding of pitch comes from several sources. Perhaps the best evidence for place coding of pitch (at least in humans) comes from the effectiveness of cochlear implants. **Cochlear implants** are devices used to restore hearing in people with deafness caused by damage to the hair cells. The external part of a cochlear implant consists of a microphone and a miniaturized electronic signal processor. The internal part contains a very thin, flexible array of electrodes, which the surgeon carefully inserts into the cochlea in such a way that it follows the snail-like curl and ends up resting along the entire length of the basilar membrane. Each electrode in the array stimulates a different part of the basilar membrane. Information from the signal processor is passed to the electrodes by means of flat coils of wire, implanted under the skin.

The primary purpose of a cochlear implant is to restore a person's ability to understand speech. Because most of the important acoustical information in speech is contained in higher frequencies, the multichannel electrode was developed in an attempt to duplicate the place coding of higher frequencies on the basilar membrane (Loeb, 1990). The signal processor in the external device analyzes the sounds detected by the microphone and sends separate signals to the appropriate portions of the basilar membrane. The fact that this device can work so well—some people with cochlear implants can understand speech well enough to use a telephone—indicates the importance of place coding.

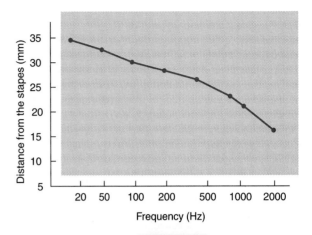

FIGURE 7.9

Anatomical coding of pitch. Stimuli of different frequencies maximally deform different regions of the basilar membrane.

(From von Békésy, G. Journal of the Acoustical Society of America, *1949, 21, 233–245.)*

Tonotopic representation [*tonn oh* **top** *ik*] A topographically organized mapping of different frequencies of sound that are represented in a particular region of the brain.

Place code The system by which information about different frequencies is coded by different locations on the basilar membrane.

Cochlear implant An electronic device surgically implanted in the inner ear that can enable some deaf people to hear.

Rate Coding

We have seen that the frequency of a sound can be detected by place coding. However, the lowest frequencies do not appear to be accounted for in this manner. Kiang (1965) was unable to find any cells that responded best to frequencies less than 200 Hz. How, then, can animals distinguish low frequencies? It appears that lower frequencies are detected by neurons that fire in synchrony with the movements of the apical end of the basilar membrane. Thus, lower frequencies are detected by means of **rate coding.**

The most convincing evidence of rate coding of pitch comes from studies of people with cochlear implants. Pijl and Schwartz (1995a, 1995b) found that stimulation of a single electrode with pulses of electricity produced sensations of pitch that were proportional to the frequency of the stimulation. In fact, the subjects could even recognize familiar tunes produced by modulating the pulse frequency. (The subjects had become deaf later in life, after already having learned to recognize the tunes.) As we would expect, the subjects' perceptions were best when the tip of the basilar membrane was stimulated, and only low frequencies could be distinguished by this method.

Detection of Timbre

Although laboratory investigations of the auditory system often employ pure sine waves as stimuli, these waves are seldom encountered outside the laboratory. Instead, we hear sounds with a rich mixture of frequencies—sounds of complex timbre. For example, consider the sound of a clarinet playing a particular note. If we hear it, we can easily say that it is a clarinet and not a flute or a violin. The reason we can do so is that these three instruments produce sounds of different timbre, which our auditory system can distinguish.

Figure 7.10 shows the waveform from a clarinet playing a steady note (*top*). The shape of the waveform repeats itself regularly at the **fundamental frequency,** which corresponds to the perceived pitch of the note. An analysis of the waveform shows that it actually consists of a series of sine waves that includes the fundamental frequency and many **overtones,** multiples of the fundamental frequency. Different instruments produce overtones with different intensities. (See *Figure 7.10.*) Electronic synthesizers simulate the sounds of real instruments by producing a series of overtones of the proper intensities, mixing them, and passing them through a loudspeaker.

When the basilar membrane is stimulated by the sound of a clarinet, different portions respond to each of the overtones. This response produces a unique anatomically coded pattern of activity in the cochlear nerve, which is subsequently identified by the auditory system of the brain. Just how this analysis is done is not known and probably will not be known for many years. When you consider that we can listen to an orchestra and identify several instruments that are playing simultaneously, you can appreciate the complexity of the analysis performed by the auditory system.

Rate code The system by which information about different frequencies is coded by the rate of firing of neurons in the auditory system.

Fundamental frequency The lowest, and usually most intense, frequency of a complex sound; most often perceived as the sound's basic pitch.

Overtone The frequency of complex tones that occurs at multiples of the fundamental frequency.

FIGURE 7.10

The shape of a sound wave from a clarinet (*top*) and the individual frequencies into which it can be analyzed.

[*Reprinted from* Stereo Review, *copyright © 1977 by Diamandis Communications Inc.*]

Detection of timbre, one of the perceptual dimensions of sound, enables us to distinguish between the sounds of various musical instruments.

Feature Detection in the Auditory System

So far, I have discussed the characteristics of pitch, loudness, and timbre only (the last of which is actually a complex frequency analysis). The auditory system also responds to other qualities of acoustic stimuli. For example, our ears are very good at determining whether the source of a sound is to the right or left of us. (To discriminate front from back, we merely turn our heads, transforming the discrimination into a left-right decision.) Two separate physiological mechanisms detect the location of sound sources: We use phase differences for low frequencies (less than approximately 3000 Hz) and intensity differences for high frequencies. Stevens and Newman (1936) found that localization is poorest at approximately 3000 Hz, presumably because both mechanisms are rather inefficient at that frequency.

Localization by Means of Arrival Time and Phase Differences

If we are blindfolded, we can still determine with rather good accuracy the location of a stimulus that emits a click. We do so because neurons respond selectively to different *arrival times* of the sound waves at the left and right ears. If the source of the click is to the right or left of the midline, the sound pressure wave will reach one ear sooner and initiate action potentials there first. Only if the stimulus is straight ahead will the ears be stimulated simultaneously. Many neurons in the auditory system respond to sounds presented to either ear. Some of these neurons, especially those in the superior olivary complex of the medulla, respond according to the difference in arrival times of sound waves produced by clicks presented *binaurally* (that is, to both ears). Their response rates reflect differences as small as a fraction of a millisecond.

Of course, we can hear continuous sounds as well as clicks, and we can also perceive the location of their source. We detect the source of continuous low-pitched sounds by means of phase differences. **Phase differences** refer to the simultaneous arrival, at each ear, of different portions (phases) of the oscillating sound wave. For example, if we assume that sound travels at 700 miles per hour through the air, adjacent cycles of a 1000-Hz tone are 12.3 inches apart. Thus, if the source of the sound is located to one side of the head, one eardrum is pulled out while the other is pushed in. The movement of the eardrums will reverse, or be 180° *out of phase*. If the source were located directly in front of the head, the movements would be perfectly in phase (0° out of phase). (See *Figure 7.11.*) Because some auditory neurons respond only

Phase difference The difference in arrival times of sound waves at each of the eardrums.

FIGURE 7.11

Localizing the source of medium-frequency and high-frequency sounds through phase differences. (a) Source of a 1000-Hz tone to the right. The pressure waves on each eardrum are out of phase; one eardrum is pushed in while the other is pushed out. (b) Source of a sound directly in front. The vibrations of the eardrums are synchronized (in phase).

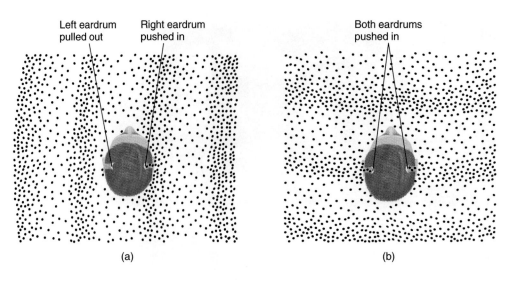

(a)

(b)

when the eardrums (and thus the bending of the basilar membrane) are at least somewhat out of phase, neurons in the superior olivary complex in the brain are able to use the information they provide to detect the source of a continuous sound.

Localization by Means of Intensity Differences

The auditory system cannot readily detect binaural phase differences of high-frequency stimuli; the differences in phases of such rapid sine waves are just too short to be measured by the neurons. However, high-frequency stimuli that occur to the right or left of the midline stimulate the ears unequally. The head absorbs high frequencies, producing a "sonic shadow," so that the ear closest to the source of the sound receives the most intense stimulation. Some neurons in the auditory system respond differentially to binaural stimuli of different intensity in each ear, which means that they provide information that can be used to detect the source of tones of high frequency.

The neurons that detect binaural differences in loudness are located in the superior olivary complex. But whereas neurons that detect binaural differences in phase or arrival time are located in the *medial* superior olivary complex, these neurons are located in the *lateral* superior olivary complex. Information from both sets of neurons is sent to other levels of the auditory system.

Behavioral Functions of the Auditory System

Hearing has three primary functions: to detect sounds, to determine the location of their sources, and to recognize the identity of these sources—and thus their meaning and relevance to us (Heffner and Heffner, 1990; Yost, 1991). Let us consider the third function, recognizing the identity of a sound source. Unless you are in a completely silent location, pay attention to what you can hear. Right now, I am sitting in an office and can hear the sound of a fan in a computer, the tapping of the keys as I write this, the footsteps of someone passing outside the door, and the voices of some people talking in the hallway. How can I recognize these sources? The axons in my cochlear nerve contain a constantly changing pattern of activity corresponding to the constantly changing mixtures of frequencies that strike my eardrums. Somehow, the auditory system of my brain recognizes particular patterns that belong to particular sources, and I perceive each of them as independent entities.

The task of the auditory system in identifying sound sources, then, is one of *pattern recognition*. The auditory system must recognize that particular patterns of constantly changing activity belong to different sound sources. And few patterns are simple mixtures of fixed frequencies. For example, when a clarinet plays notes of different pitches, different patterns of activity are produced in our cochlear nerve—yet we recognize each of the notes as belonging to a clarinet. Needless to say, we are far from understanding how this pattern recognition works.

Although the subcortical components of the auditory system are often referred to as "relay nuclei," it is clear that these nuclei do much more than passively transmit information from the cochlear nerve to the auditory cortex. For example, as we saw earlier in this chapter, the superior olivary complex contains circuits that analyze the location of sound sources according to arrival time (or phase differences) and intensity differences.

Pattern recognition, however, appears to be accomplished by circuits of neurons in the neocortex. We know a little bit about the types of analyses that the auditory cortex accomplishes. Various studies (Whitfield and Evans, 1965; Saitoh, Maruyama, and Kudoh, 1981) have found neurons in the auditory cortex that respond only to the onset or cessation of a sound (or to both), to changes in pitch or intensity (sometimes only to changes in one direction), or to complex stimuli that contain a variety of frequencies. Winter and Funkenstein (1971) found neurons in the auditory cortex of the squirrel monkey that responded specifically to the vocalizations made by members of this species. McKenna, Weinberger, and Diamond (1989) found that when they presented a series of different tones, some neurons in the primary auditory cortex responded to a particular frequency only in a particular context; for example, they would respond if the tone were the last in a series but not if it were the first. Rauschecker, Tian, and Hauser (1995) found that neurons in the auditory association cortex of rhesus monkeys responded much better to sound mixtures than to pure tones. Thus, neurons in the auditory cortex encode rather complex features. Because data are scanty so far, we have no real conception of the coding mechanism that the brain uses for these changes or even of precisely what features are coded.

Bilateral lesions of the auditory cortex in monkeys cause an almost total hearing loss, which eventually shows some recovery (Heffner and Heffner, 1990). The animals' ability to localize sounds is severely disrupted; they can eventually learn to discriminate a sound coming from the left or right from one coming from the center, but they are unable to walk toward the source of the sound. Thus, their sound localizing ability does not translate into useful behavior (Heffner and Heffner, 1990). In addition, lesions of the left auditory cortex disrupt the animals' ability to discriminate the vocalizations made by other members of this species.

As we saw in the Chapter 6, lesions of the visual association cortex in humans can produce visual agnosias—the inability to recognize objects even though the visual acuity may be good. Similarly, lesions of the auditory association cortex can produce auditory agnosias, the inability to comprehend the meaning of sounds even though the individuals are not deaf. If the lesion occurs in the left hemisphere, the person will sustain a particular form of language disorder. If it occurs in the right hemisphere, the person will be unable to recognize the nature or location of nonspeech sounds. Because of the importance of audition to language, these topics are discussed in much more detail in Chapter 13.

INTERIM SUMMARY

The receptive organ for audition is the organ of Corti, located on the basilar membrane. When sound strikes the tympanic membrane, it sets the ossicles into motion, and the baseplate of the stapes pushes against the membrane behind the oval window. Pressure changes thus applied to the fluid within the cochlea cause a portion of the basilar membrane to flex, causing the basilar membrane to move laterally with respect to the tectorial membrane that overhangs it. This movement pulls directly on the cilia of the outer hair cells and causes movements in the fluid within the cochlea, which, in turn, causes the cilia of the inner hair cells to wave back and forth. These mechanical forces open ion channels in the tips of the hair cells and thus produce receptor potentials.

The hair cells form synapses with the dendrites of the bipolar neurons whose axons give rise to the cochlear branch of the eighth cranial nerve. The central auditory system involves several brain stem nuclei, including the cochlear nuclei, superior olivary complexes, and inferior colliculi. The medial geniculate nucleus relays auditory information to the primary auditory cortex on the medial surface of the temporal lobe.

Pitch is encoded by two means. High-frequency sounds cause the base of the basilar membrane (near the oval window) to flex; low-frequency sounds cause the apex (opposite end) to flex. Because high and low frequencies thus stimulate different groups of auditory hair cells, frequency is encoded anatomically. The lowest frequencies cause the apex of the basilar membrane to flex back and forth in time with the acoustic vibrations. The outer hair cells act as motive elements rather than as sensory transducers, contracting in response to activity of the efferent axons and modifying the mechanical properties of the basilar membrane.

The auditory system is analytical in its operation. That is, it can discriminate between sounds with different timbres by detecting the individual overtones that constitute the sounds and producing unique patterns of neural firing in the auditory system.

Left-right localization is performed by analyzing binaural differences in arrival time, in phase relations, and in intensity. The location of sources of brief sounds (such as clicks) and sounds of frequencies below approximately 3000 Hz is detected by neurons in the medial superior olivary complex, which respond most vigorously when one ear receives the click first or when the phase of a sine wave received by one ear leads that received by the other. The location of sources of high-frequency sounds is detected by neurons in the lateral superior olivary complex, which respond most vigorously when one organ of Corti is stimulated more intensely than the other.

To recognize the source of sounds, the auditory system must recognize the constantly changing patterns of activity received from the axons in the cochlear nerve. Studies have found neurons in the auditory cortex that respond to complex stimuli, such as ascending or descending pitches, series of tones, combinations of two or more tones, or even species-specific vocalizations. Bilateral lesions of the auditory cortex of monkeys produce severe impairments in hearing, and lesions of the left auditory cortex impair the ability to discriminate the vocalizations of other monkeys.

■ THOUGHT QUESTIONS

A naturalist once noted that when a male bird stakes out his territory, he sings with a very sharp, staccato song that says, in effect, "Here I am, and stay away!" In contrast, if a predator appears in the vicinity, many birds will emit alarm calls that consist of steady whistles that start and end slowly. Knowing what you do about the two means of localizing sounds, why do these two types of calls have different characteristics?

■ VESTIBULAR SYSTEM

Vestibular sac One of a set of two receptor organs in each inner ear that detect changes in the tilt of the head.

Semicircular canal One of the three ringlike structures of the vestibular apparatus that detect changes in head rotation.

The vestibular system has two components: the vestibular sacs and the semicircular canals. They represent the second and third components of the *labyrinths* of the inner ear. (We just studied the first component, the cochlea.) The **vestibular sacs** respond to the force of gravity and inform the brain about the head's orientation. The **semicircular canals** respond to angular acceleration—changes in the rotation of the head—but not to steady rotation. They also respond (but rather weakly) to changes in position or to linear acceleration.

The functions of the vestibular system include balance, maintenance of the head in an upright position, and adjustment of eye movement to compensate for head movements. Vestibular stimulation does not produce any readily definable sensation; certain low-frequency stimulation of the vestibular sacs can produce nausea, and stimulation of the semicircular canals can produce dizziness and rhythmic eye movements (*nystagmus*). However, we are not directly aware of the information received from these organs. This section describes the vestibular system: the vestibular apparatus, the receptor cells, and the vestibular pathway in the brain.

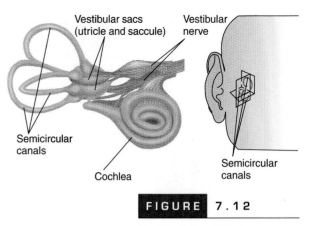

FIGURE 7.12

The labyrinths of the inner ear.

Anatomy of the Vestibular Apparatus

Figure 7.12 shows the labyrinths of the inner ear, which include the cochlea, the semicircular canals, and the two vestibular sacs: the **utricle** ("little pouch") and the **saccule** ("little sack"). (See *Figure 7.12.*) The semicircular canals approximate the three major planes of the head: sagittal, transverse, and horizontal. Receptors in each canal are activated by changes in rotation of the head in one plane. Figure 7.13 shows cross sections through one semicircular canal. The semicircular canal consists of a membranous canal floating within a bony one; the membranous canal contains a fluid called *endolymph* and floats within a fluid called *perilymph*. An enlargement called the **ampulla** contains the organ in which the sensory receptors reside. The sensory receptors are hair cells similar to those found in the cochlea. Their cilia are embedded in a gelatinous mass called the **cupula,** which blocks part of the ampulla. When the head suddenly turns, inertia causes the endolymph to move relative to the cupula, and the bending of the cupula exerts a shearing force on the cilia of the hair cells. (See *Figure 7.13.*)

The vestibular sacs (the utricle and saccule) work very differently. These organs are roughly circular, and each contains a patch of receptive tissue. The receptive tissue is located on the "floor" of the utricle and on the "wall" of the saccule when the head is in an upright position. The receptive tissue, like that of the semicircular canals and cochlea, contains hair cells. The cilia of these receptors are embedded in an overlying gelatinous mass, which contains something rather unusual: *otoconia,* which are small crystals of calcium carbonate. The weight of the crystals causes the

Utricle (*you* trih kul) One of the vestibular sacs.

Saccule (*sak* yule) One of the vestibular sacs.

Ampulla (*am pull uh*) An enlargement in a semicircular canal; contains the cupula and the crista.

Cupula (*kew pew luh*) A gelatinous mass found in the ampulla of the semicircular canals; moves in response to the flow of the fluid in the canals.

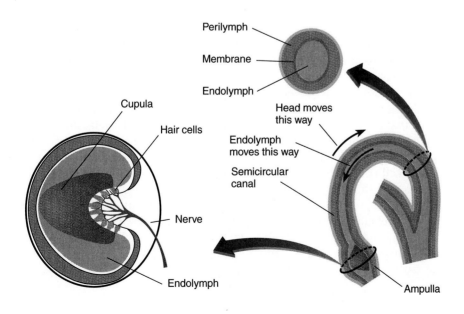

FIGURE 7.13

Cross sections through one semicircular canal.

(a)

(b)

FIGURE 7.14

(a) Oblique view of a normal bundle of vestibular hair cells. (b) Top view of a bundle of hair cells from which the longest has been detached.

(From Hudspeth, A.J., and Jacobs, R. Proceedings of the National Academy of Sciences, USA, 1979, 76, 1506–1509.)

gelatinous mass to shift in position as the orientation of the head changes. Thus, movement produces a shearing force on the cilia of the receptive hair cells.

The Receptor Cells

The hair cells of the semicircular canal and vestibular sacs are similar in appearance. Each hair cell contains several cilia, graduated in length from short to long. Figure 7.14 shows two views of a hair cell of a bullfrog saccule made by a scanning electron microscope. (See *Figure 7.14*.)

The Vestibular Pathway

The vestibular and cochlear nerves constitute the two branches of the eighth cranial nerve (auditory nerve). The bipolar cell bodies that give rise to the afferent axons of the vestibular nerve are located in the **vestibular ganglion,** which appears as a nodule on the vestibular nerve.

Most of the axons of the vestibular nerve synapse within the vestibular nuclei in the medulla, but some axons travel directly to the cerebellum. Neurons of the vestibular nuclei send their axons to the cerebellum, spinal cord, medulla, and pons. There also appear to be vestibular projections to the temporal cortex, but the precise pathways have not been determined. Most investigators believe that the cortical projections are responsible for feelings of dizziness; the activity of projections to the lower brain stem can produce the nausea and vomiting that accompany motion sickness. Projections to brain stem nuclei controlling neck muscles are clearly involved in maintaining an upright position of the head.

Perhaps the most interesting connections are those to the cranial nerve nuclei (third, fourth, and sixth) that control the eye muscles. As we walk or (especially) run, the head is jarred quite a bit. The vestibular system exerts direct control on eye movement, to compensate for the sudden head movements. This process, called the *vestibulo-ocular reflex,* maintains a fairly steady retinal image. Test this reflex yourself: Look at a distant object and hit yourself (gently) on the side of the head. Note that your image of the world jumps a bit, but not too much. People who have suffered vestibular damage, and who lack the vestibulo-ocular reflex, have difficulty seeing anything while walking or running. Everything becomes a blur of movement.

INTERIM SUMMARY

The semicircular canals are filled with fluid. When the head begins rotating or comes to rest after rotation, inertia causes the fluid to push the cupula to one side or the other. This movement exerts a shearing force on the cupula, the organ containing the vestibular hair cells. The vestibular sacs contain a patch of receptive tissue that contains hair cells whose cilia are embedded in a gelatinous mass. The weight of the otoconia in the gelatinous mass shifts when the head tilts, causing a shearing force on some of the cilia of the hair cells.

Each hair cell contains one long cilium and several shorter ones. These cells form synapses with dendrites of bipolar neurons whose axons travel through the vestibular nerve. The receptors also receive efferent terminal buttons from neurons located in the cerebellum and medulla, but the function of these connections is not known. Vestibular information is received by the vestibular nuclei in the medulla, which relay it on to the cerebellum, spinal cord, medulla, pons, and temporal cortex. These pathways are responsible for control of posture, head movements, eye movements, and the puzzling phenomenon of motion sickness.

Vestibular ganglion A nodule on the vestibular nerve that contains the cell bodies of the bipolar neurons that convey vestibular information to the brain.

■ **THOUGHT QUESTIONS**

Why can slow, repetitive vestibular stimulation cause nausea and vomiting? Obviously, there are connections between the vestibular system and the area postrema, which (as you learned in Chapter 2) controls vomiting. Can you think of any useful functions that might be served by these connections?

◼ SOMATOSENSES

The somatosenses provide information about what is happening on the surface of our body and inside it. The **cutaneous senses** (skin senses) include several submodalities commonly referred to as *touch*. **Kinesthesia** provides information about body position and movement and arises from receptors in joints, tendons, and muscles. The **organic senses** arise from receptors in and around the internal organs, providing us with unpleasant sensations, such as stomachaches or gallbladder attacks, or pleasurable ones, such as those provided by a warm drink on a cold winter day. Because the cutaneous senses are the most studied of the somatosenses, both perceptually and physiologically, I will devote most of my discussion to them.

The Stimuli

The cutaneous senses respond to several different types of stimuli: pressure, vibration, heating, cooling, and events that cause tissue damage (and hence, pain). Feelings of pressure are caused by mechanical deformation of the skin. Vibration is produced in the laboratory or clinic by tuning forks or mechanical devices, but it more commonly occurs when we move our fingers across a rough surface. Thus, we use vibration sensitivity to judge an object's roughness. Obviously, sensations of warmth and coolness are produced by objects that change skin temperature from normal. Sensations of pain can be caused by many different types of stimuli, but it appears that most cause at least some tissue damage.

Kinesthesia is provided by stretch receptors in skeletal muscles that report changes in muscle length to the central nervous system and by stretch receptors in tendons that measure the force being exerted by the muscles. Receptors within joints between adjacent bones respond to the magnitude and direction of limb movement. The muscle length detectors (sensory endings on the *intrafusal muscle fibers*) do not give rise to conscious sensations; their information is used to control movement.

Organic sensitivity is provided by receptors in the linings of muscles, outer layers of the gastrointestinal system and other internal organs, and linings of the abdominal and thoracic cavities. Many of these tissues are sensitive only to stretch and do not report sensations when cut, burned, or crushed. In addition, the stomach and esophagus are responsive to heat and cold and to some chemicals.

Anatomy of the Skin and Its Receptive Organs

The skin is a complex and vital organ of the body—one that we tend to take for granted. We cannot survive without it; extensive skin burns are fatal. Our cells, which must be bathed by a warm fluid, are protected from the hostile environment by the skin's outer layers. The skin participates in thermoregulation by producing sweat, thus cooling the body, or by restricting its circulation of blood, thus conserving heat. Its appearance varies widely across the body, from mucous membrane to hairy skin to the smooth, hairless skin of the palms and the soles of the feet.

Skin consists of subcutaneous tissue, dermis, and epidermis and contains various receptors scattered throughout these layers. Figure 7.15 shows cross sections

Cutaneous sense [*kew tane ee us*] One of the somatosenses; includes sensitivity to stimuli that involve the skin.

Kinesthesia Perception of the body's own movements.

Organic sense A sense modality that arises from receptors located within the inner organs of the body.

FIGURE 7.15

Sensory receptors. (a) In hairy skin. (b) In glabrous (hairless) skin.

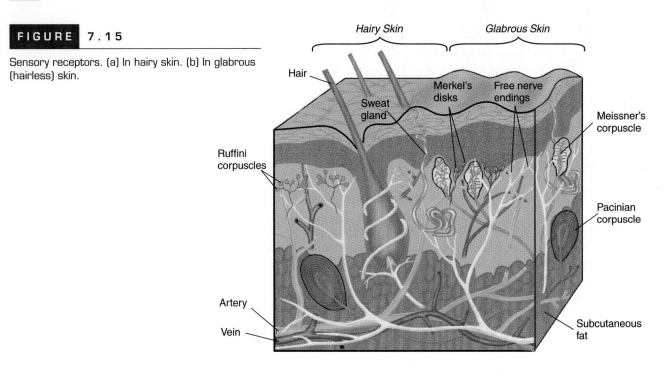

Glabrous skin (*glab russ*) Skin that does not contain hair; found on the palms and soles of the feet.

Ruffini corpuscle A vibration-sensitive organ located in hairy skin.

Pacinian corpuscle (*pa chin ee un*) A specialized, encapsulated somatosensory nerve ending that detects mechanical stimuli, especially vibrations.

Meissner's corpuscle The touch-sensitive end organs located in the papillae, small elevations of the dermis that project up into the epidermis.

Merkel's disk The touch-sensitive end organs found at the base of the epidermis, adjacent to sweat ducts.

through hairy skin and **glabrous skin** (hairless skin, such as we have on our fingertips and palms). Hairy skin contains unencapsulated (free) nerve endings and **Ruffini corpuscles,** which respond to low-frequency vibration. Free nerve endings are found just below the surface of the skin, in a basketwork around the base of hair follicles and around the emergence of hair shafts from the skin. (See *Figure 7.15.*)

Glabrous skin contains a more complex mixture of free nerve endings and axons that terminate within specialized end organs (Iggo and Andres, 1982). The increased complexity probably reflects the fact that we use the palms of our hands and the inside surfaces of our fingers to explore the environment actively: We use them to hold and touch objects. In contrast, the rest of our body most often contacts the environment passively; that is, other things come into contact with it.

Pacinian corpuscles are the largest sensory end organs in the body. Their size, approximately 0.5 × 1.0 mm, makes them visible to the naked eye. They are found in glabrous skin and in the external genitalia, mammary glands, and various internal organs. These receptors consist of up to seventy onionlike layers wrapped around the terminal button of a single myelinated axon. They are sensitive to touch, particularly to high-frequency vibration. **Meissner's corpuscles** are found in *papillae* ("nipples"), small elevations of the dermis that project up into the epidermis. These end organs are innervated by two to six axons. They respond to low-frequency vibration. **Merkel's disks,** which also respond to indentation of the skin, are found at the base of the epidermis, in the same general locations as Meissner's corpuscles, adjacent to sweat ducts. (See *Figure 7.15.*)

Detection of Cutaneous Stimulation

The three most important qualities of cutaneous stimulation are touch, temperature, and pain. These qualities are described in the sections that follow.

Touch

Sensitivity to pressure and vibration is caused by movement of the skin. The best-studied receptor is the Pacinian corpuscle, which primarily detects vibration. When the corpuscle is bent relative to the axon, the membrane becomes depolarized. If the threshold of excitation is exceeded, an action potential is produced at the first node of Ranvier. Loewenstein and Mendelson (1965) have shown that the layers of the corpuscle alter the mechanical characteristics of the organ, so the axon responds briefly when the intact organ is bent and again when it is released. Thus, this receptor is sensitive to vibration but not to steady pressure.

The bending of the tip of the nerve ending in a Pacinian corpuscle appears to produce a receptor potential by opening ion channels in the membrane. These channels appear to be anchored to protein filaments beneath the membrane and have long carbohydrate chains attached to them. When a mechanical stimulus changes the shape of the nerve ending, tension is exerted on the carbohydrate chains, pulling the channel open. (See *Figure 7.16*.) Most investigators believe that the encapsulated endings serve only to modify the physical stimulus transduced by the axons that enter them.

FIGURE **7.16**

A hypothetical explanation of transduction of somatosensory information. Mechanical force on carbohydrate chains linked to ion channels opens the channels, permitting the entry of cations, which depolarizes the membrane potential.

Adaptation. Investigators have known for a long time that a moderate, constant stimulus applied to the skin fails to produce any sensation after it has been present for a while. For example, we not only ignore the pressure of a wristwatch, but we cannot feel it at all if we keep our arm still (assuming that the band is not painfully tight). Physiological studies have shown that the reason for the lack of sensation is the absence of receptor firing; the receptors adapt to a constant stimulus.

This adaptation is not caused by "fatigue" of physical or chemical processes within the receptor. Instead, adaptation occurs because of the physical construction of the skin and the cutaneous sensory organs. Nafe and Wagoner (1941) recorded the sensations reported by human subjects as a stimulus weight gradually moved downward, deforming the skin. Pressure was reported until the weight finally stopped moving. When the weight was increased, pressure was reported until downward movement stopped again. Pressure sensations were also briefly recorded when the weight was removed, while the surface of the skin regained its normal shape. (You may have noticed that when you first take your hat off, you feel for a few moments as if you were still wearing it.)

Responsiveness to Moving Stimuli. A moderate, constant, nondamaging stimulus is rarely of any importance to an organism, so this adaptation mechanism is useful. Our cutaneous senses are used much more often to analyze shapes and textures of stimulus objects moving with respect to the surface of the skin. Sometimes, the object itself moves; but more often, we do the moving ourselves.

If I placed an object in your palm and asked you to keep your hand still, you would have a great deal of difficulty recognizing the object by touch alone. If I said you could now move your hand, you would manipulate the object, letting its surface slide across your palm and the pads of your fingers. You would be able to describe its three-dimensional shape, hardness, texture, slipperiness, and so on. Obviously, your motor system must cooperate, and you need kinesthetic sensation from your muscles and joints, besides the cutaneous information. If you squeeze the object and

After wearing a wristwatch for several minutes, this man can no longer feel it unless it moves on his wrist.

feel a lot of well-localized pressure in return, it is hard. If you feel a less intense, more diffuse pressure in return, it is soft. If it produces vibrations as it moves over the ridges on your fingers, it is rough. If very little effort is needed to move the object while pressing it against your skin, it is slippery. If it does not produce vibrations as it moves across your skin, but moves in a jerky fashion, and if it takes effort to remove your fingers from its surface, it is sticky. Thus, our somatosenses work dynamically with the motor system to provide useful information about the nature of objects that come into contact with our skin.

Temperature

Feelings of warmth and coolness are relative, not absolute (except at the extremes). There is a temperature level that, for a particular region of skin, will produce a sensation of temperature neutrality—neither warmth nor coolness. This neutral point is not an absolute value but depends on the prior history of thermal stimulation of that area. If the temperature of a region of skin is raised by a few degrees, the initial feeling of warmth is replaced by one of neutrality. If the skin temperature is lowered to its initial value, it now feels cool. Thus, increases in temperature lower the sensitivity of warmth receptors and raise the sensitivity of cold receptors. The converse holds for decreases in skin temperature. This adaptation to ambient temperature can be demonstrated easily by placing one hand in a bucket of warm water and the other in a bucket of cool water until some adaptation has taken place. If you then simultaneously immerse both hands in water at room temperature, it will feel warm to one hand and cool to the other.

Thermal receptors are difficult to study, because changes in temperature alter the metabolic activity, and also the rate of axonal firing, of a variety of cells. For example, a receptor that responds to pressure might produce varying amounts of activity in response to the same mechanical stimulus, depending on the temperature. Nevertheless, most investigators agree that changes in temperature are detected by free nerve endings and that warmth and coolness are detected by different populations of receptors (Sinclair, 1981). The transduction of temperature changes into the rate of axonal firing has not yet been explained.

Pain

Most investigators identify pain reception with the networks of free nerve endings in the skin. Pain appears to be produced by a variety of procedures. Intense mechanical stimulation activates a class of high-threshold receptors that produce a sensation of pain. However, most painful stimuli cause tissue damage, suggesting that pain is also caused by the release of a chemical by injured cells (Besson et al., 1982). When cells are damaged, they very rapidly synthesize a **prostaglandin,** a category of hormones that was first discovered in the prostate gland. This chemical sensitizes free nerve endings to another chemical, histamine, which is also released by damaged cells. (The analgesic effect of aspirin occurs by virtue of the fact that it interferes with the synthesis of prostaglandins.)

The Somatosensory Pathways

Prostaglandin A member of a family of fatty acid derivatives that serve as hormones; first discovered in the prostate gland; involved in many physiological processes, including pain perception.

Somatosensory axons from the skin, muscles, or internal organs enter the central nervous system via spinal nerves. Those located in the face and head primarily enter through the trigeminal nerve (fifth cranial nerve). The cell bodies of the unipolar neurons are located in the dorsal root ganglia and cranial nerve ganglia. Axons that convey precisely localized information, such as fine touch, ascend through the *dorsal columns* in the white matter of the spinal cord to nuclei in the lower medulla. From there, axons cross the brain and ascend through the *medial lemniscus* to the *ven-*

tral posterior nuclei of the thalamus, the relay nuclei for somato-sensation. Axons from the thalamus project to the primary somatosensory cortex, which in turn sends axons to the secondary somatosensory cortex. In contrast, axons that convey poorly localized information, such as pain or temperature, form synapses with other neurons as soon as they enter the spinal cord. The axons of these neurons cross to the other side of the spinal cord and ascend through the *spinothalamic tract* to the ventral posterior nuclei of the thalamus. (See *Figure 7.17.*)

As you learned in Chapter 6, the extrastriate cortex consists of several subareas, each of which contains an independent representation of the visual field. For example, one area responds specifically to color and form, and another responds to movement. The somatosensory cortex appears to follow a similar scheme: Each cortical map of the body contains neurons that respond to a specific submodality of stimulation. Undoubtedly, further investigations will provide more accurate functional maps of the cortical subareas of both of these sensory systems.

Perception of Pain

Pain is a curious phenomenon. It is more than a mere sensation; it can be defined only by some sort of withdrawal reaction or, in humans, by verbal report. Pain can be modified by opiates, by hypnosis, by the administration of pharmacologically inert sugar pills, by emotions, and even by other forms of stimulation, such as acupuncture. Recent research efforts have made remarkable progress in discovering the physiological bases of these phenomena.

We might reasonably ask *why* we experience pain. In most cases, pain serves a constructive role. For example, people who have congenital insensitivity to pain suffer an abnormally large number of injuries, such as cuts and burns. One woman did not make the shifts in posture that we normally do when our joints start to ache. As a consequence, she suffered damage to the spine that ultimately resulted in death. Other people have died from ruptured appendixes and ensuing abdominal infections that they did not feel (Sternbach, 1968). I am sure that a person who is passing a kidney stone would not find much comfort in the fact that pain does more good than ill; but pain is, nevertheless, very important to our existence.

Some environmental events diminish the perception of pain. For example, Beecher (1959) noted that wounded American soldiers back from the battle at Anzio, Italy, during World War II reported that they felt no pain from their wounds—they did not even want medication. It would appear that their perception of pain was diminished by the relief they felt from surviving such an ordeal. There are other instances in which people still report the perception of pain but are not bothered by it. Some tranquilizers have this effect.

A particularly interesting form of pain sensation occurs after a limb has been amputated. After the limb is gone, up to 70 percent of amputees report that they feel as though the missing limb still existed and that it often hurts. This phenomenon is referred to as the **phantom limb** (Melzak, 1992). People with phantom limbs report

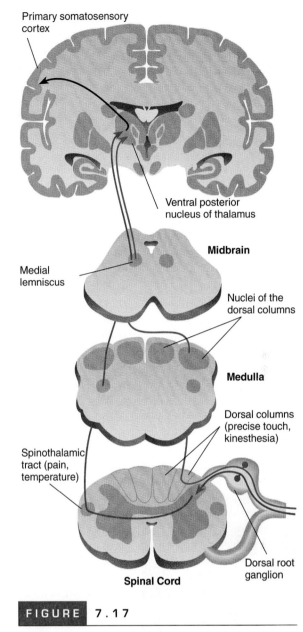

FIGURE 7.17

The somatosensory pathways from the spinal cord to the somatosensory cortex. Note that precisely localized information (such as fine touch) and imprecisely localized information (such as pain and temperature) are transmitted by different pathways.

Phantom limb Sensations that appear to originate in a limb that has been amputated.

that the limb feels very real, and they often say that if they try to reach out with it, it feels as though it were responding. Sometimes, they perceive it as sticking out, and they may feel compelled to avoid knocking it against the side of a doorframe or sleeping in a position that would make it come between them and the mattress. People have reported all sorts of sensations in phantom limbs, including pain, pressure, warmth, cold, wetness, itching, sweatiness, and prickliness.

The classic explanation for phantom limbs has been activity of the sensory axons belonging to the amputated limb. Presumably, this activity is interpreted by the nervous system as coming from the missing limb. When nerves are cut and connections cannot be reestablished between the proximal and distal portions, the cut ends of the proximal portions form nodules known as *neuromas*. The treatment for phantom pain has been to cut the nerves above these neuromas, to cut the dorsal roots that bring the afferent information from these nerves into the spinal cord, or to make lesions in somatosensory pathways in the spinal cord, thalamus, or cerebral cortex. Sometimes these procedures work for a while, but often the pain returns.

Melzak suggested that the phantom limb sensation is inherent in the organization of the parietal cortex. As we saw in Chapter 3, the parietal cortex is involved in our awareness of our own bodies. Indeed, people with lesions of the parietal lobe (especially in the right hemisphere) have been known to push their own leg out of bed, believing that it actually belongs to someone else. Melzak reports that some people who were born with missing limbs nevertheless experience phantom limb sensations, which would suggest that our brains are genetically programmed to provide sensations for all four limbs.

For many years, investigators have known that perception of pain can be modified by environmental stimuli. Recent work, beginning in the 1970s, has revealed the existence of neural circuits whose activity can produce analgesia. A variety of environmental stimuli can activate these analgesia-producing circuits. Most of these stimuli cause the release of the endogenous opioids, which were described in Chapter 4.

Electrical stimulation of particular locations within the brain can cause analgesia, which can even be profound enough to serve as an anesthetic for surgery in rats (Reynolds, 1969). The most effective locations appear to be within the periaqueductal gray matter and in the rostroventral medulla. For example, Mayer and Liebeskind (1974) reported that electrical stimulation of the periaqueductal gray matter produced analgesia in rats equivalent to that produced by at least 10 milligrams (mg) of morphine per kilogram of body weight, which is a large dose. The technique has even found an application in reducing severe, chronic pain in humans: Fine wires are surgically implanted in parts of the central nervous system and attached to a radio-controlled device that permits the patient to administer electrical stimulation when necessary (Kumar, Wyant, and Nath, 1990). (See *Figure 7.18.*)

Analgesic brain stimulation apparently triggers the neural mechanisms that reduce pain, primarily by causing endogenous opioids to be released. Basbaum and Fields (1978, 1984), who summarized their work and that of others, proposed a neural circuit that mediates opiate-induced analgesia. Basically, they proposed the following: Endogenous opioids (released by environmental stimuli or administered as a drug) stimulate opiate receptors on neurons in the periaqueductal gray matter. Because the effect of opiates appears to be inhibitory (Nicoll, Alger, and Nicoll, 1980), Basbaum and Fields proposed that the neurons that contain opiate receptors are themselves inhibitory interneurons. Thus, the administration of opiates activates the neurons on which these interneurons synapse. (See *Figure 7.19.*)

Neurons in the periaqueductal gray matter send axons to the **nucleus raphe magnus,** located in the medulla. The neurons in this nucleus send axons to the dorsal horn of the spinal cord gray matter; destruction of these axons eliminates analgesia induced by an injection of morphine. The inhibitory effects of these neurons apparently involve one or two interneurons in the spinal cord. (See *Figure 7.19.*)

Nucleus raphe magnus A nucleus of the raphe that contains serotonin-secreting neurons that project to the dorsal gray matter of the spinal cord and is involved in analgesia produced by opiates.

FIGURE 7.18

A person who suffers from chronic pain, holding a device that permits him to stimulate the periaqueductal gray matter of his brain through implanted electrodes, thus producing analgesia.

(Dan McCoy/Rainbow.)

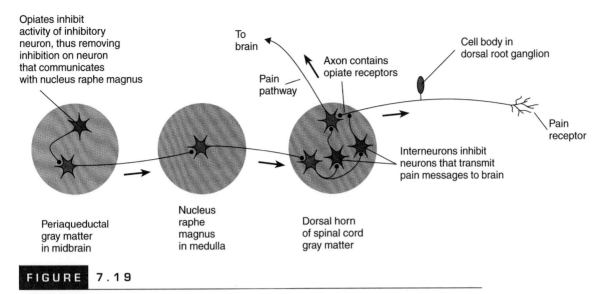

Opiates inhibit activity of inhibitory neuron, thus removing inhibition on neuron that communicates with nucleus raphe magnus

To brain

Pain pathway

Axon contains opiate receptors

Cell body in dorsal root ganglion

Pain receptor

Interneurons inhibit neurons that transmit pain messages to brain

Periaqueductal gray matter in midbrain

Nucleus raphe magnus in medulla

Dorsal horn of spinal cord gray matter

FIGURE 7.19

The neural circuit that mediates opiate-induced analgesia, as hypothesized by Basbaum and Fields (1978).

INTERIM SUMMARY

Cutaneous sensory information is provided by specialized receptors in the skin. Pacinian corpuscles provide information about vibration. Ruffini corpuscles, similar to Pacinian corpuscles but considerably smaller, respond to low-frequency vibration, usually referred to as "flutter." Meissner's corpuscles, found in papillae and innervated by several axons, respond to mechanical stimuli. Merkel's disks, also found in papillae, consist of single, flattened dendritic endings next to specialized epithelial cells. These receptors respond to mechanical stimulation. Painful stimuli are detected primarily by free nerve endings.

Our somatosensory system is most sensitive to changes in mechanical stimuli. Unless the skin is moving, we do not detect nonpainful stimuli, because the receptors adapt to constant mechanical pressure. Temperature receptors also adapt; moderate changes in skin temperature are soon perceived as "neutral," and deviations above or below this temperature are perceived as warmth or coolness.

Precise, well-localized somatosensory information is conveyed by a pathway through the dorsal columns and their nuclei and the medial lemniscus, connecting the dorsal column nuclei with the ventral posterior nuclei of the thalamus. This nucleus projects to the primary somatosensory cortex. Information about pain and temperature ascends the spinal cord through the spinothalamic system. Organic sensibility reaches the central nervous system by means of axons that travel through nerves of the autonomic nervous systems.

Pain perception is not a simple function of stimulation of pain receptors; it is a complex phenomenon that can be modified by experience and the immediate environment. The phantom limb phenomenon, which often is accompanied by phantom pain, appears to be inherent in the organization of the parietal lobe.

Just as we have mechanisms to perceive pain, we have mechanisms to reduce it—to produce analgesia. Under the appropriate circumstances, neurons in the periaqueductal gray matter are stimulated through synaptic connections with the frontal cortex, amygdala, and hypothalamus. In addition, some neurosecretory cells in the brain release enkephalins, a class of endogenous opioids. These neuromodulators activate receptors on neurons in the periaqueductal gray matter and provide additional stimulation of neurons in this region. Connections from the periaqueductal gray matter to the nucleus raphe magnus of the medulla activate serotonergic neurons located there. These neurons send axons to the dorsal horn of the spinal cord gray matter, where they inhibit the transmission of pain information to the brain. In humans, chronic pain is sometimes treated by implanting electrodes in the periaqueductal gray matter or the thalamus and permitting the patients to stimulate the brain through these electrodes when the pain becomes severe.

■ THOUGHT QUESTIONS

Our fingertips and our lips are the most sensitive parts of our bodies; relatively large amounts of the primary somatosensory cortex are devoted to analyzing information from these parts of the body. It is easy to understand why are fingertips are so sensitive: We use them to explore object by touch. But why are our lips so sensitive? Does it have something to do with eating?

■ GUSTATION

The stimuli we have encountered so far produce receptor potentials by imparting physical energy: thermal, photic (involving light), or kinetic. However, the stimuli received by the last two senses to be studied, gustation and olfaction, interact with their receptors chemically. This section discusses the first of them: gustation.

The Stimuli

Gustation is clearly related to eating; this sense modality helps us determine the nature of things we put in our mouths. For a substance to be tasted, molecules of it must dissolve in the saliva and stimulate the taste receptors on the tongue. Tastes of different substances vary, but much less than we generally realize. There are only four qualities of taste: *bitterness, sourness, sweetness,* and *saltiness.* (As we will see later, researchers have suggested that at least some species can detect two other taste qualities.) Flavor, as opposed to taste, is a composite of olfaction and gustation. Much of the flavor of a steak depends on its odor; to an *anosmic* person (one who lacks the sense of smell) or to a person whose nostrils are stopped up, an onion tastes like an apple, and a steak tastes like salty cardboard.

Most vertebrates possess gustatory systems that respond to all four taste qualities. (An exception is the cat family; lions, tigers, leopards, and house cats do not detect sweetness.) Clearly, sweetness receptors are food detectors. Most sweet-tasting foods, such as fruits and some vegetables, are safe to eat (Ramirez, 1990). Saltiness receptors detect the presence of sodium chloride. In some environments, inadequate amounts of this mineral are obtained from the usual source of food, so sodium chloride detectors help the animal to detect its presence. Injuries that cause bleeding deplete an organism of its supply of sodium rapidly, so the ability to find it quickly can be critical.

Most species of animals will readily ingest substances that taste sweet or somewhat salty. However, they will tend to avoid substances that taste sour or bitter. Because of bacterial activity, many foods become acidic when they spoil. The acidity tastes sour and causes an avoidance reaction. (Of course, we have learned to make highly preferred mixtures of sweet and sour, such as lemonade.) Bitterness is almost universally avoided and cannot easily be improved by adding some sweetness. Many plants produce poisonous alkaloids, which protect them from being eaten by animals. Alkaloids taste bitter; thus, the bitterness receptor undoubtedly serves to warn animals away from these chemicals.

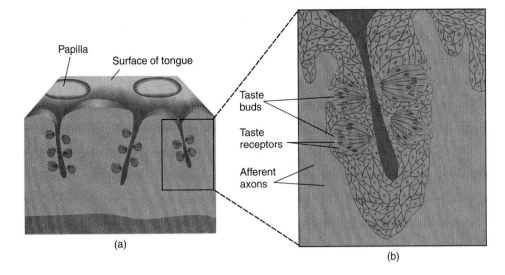

Papilla

Surface of tongue

Taste buds

Taste receptors

Afferent axons

(a)

(b)

FIGURE 7.20

The tongue. (a) Papillae on the surface of the tongue. (b) Taste buds.

Anatomy of the Taste Buds and Gustatory Cells

The tongue, palate, pharynx, and larynx contain approximately 10,000 taste buds. Most of these receptive organs are arranged around *papillae,* small protuberances of the tongue. Taste buds consist of groups of twenty to fifty receptor cells, arranged somewhat like the segments of an orange. Cilia are located at the end of each cell and project through the opening of the taste bud (the pore) into the saliva that coats the tongue. Figure 7.20 shows the appearance of a papilla; a cross section through the surrounding trench contains a taste bud. (See *Figure 7.20.*)

Taste buds that respond to the different taste qualities have different distributions on the tongue. The tip of the tongue is most sensitive to sweetness and saltiness, the sides are most sensitive to sourness, and the back of the tongue, throat, and soft palate are most sensitive to bitterness. This distribution explains why saccharin, an artificial sweetener, tastes both sweet and bitter to some people, producing a sensation of sweetness on the front of the tongue when it is first tasted and then a sensation of bitterness in the back of the mouth when it is swallowed. (See *Figure 7.21.*)

Taste receptors form synapses with dendrites of sensory neurons that convey gustatory information to the brain. The receptors have a life span of only ten days. They quickly wear out, being directly exposed to a rather hostile environment. As they degenerate, they are replaced by newly developed cells; the afferent dendrite is passed on to the new cell (Beidler, 1970).

Detection of Gustatory Information

Transduction of taste is similar to the chemical transmission that takes place at synapses: The tasted molecule binds with the receptor and produces changes in membrane permeability that cause receptor potentials. Different substances bind with different types of receptors, producing different taste sensations.

To taste salty, a substance must ionize. Although the best stimulus for saltiness receptors is sodium chloride (NaCl), a variety of salts containing metallic cations (such as Na^+, K^+, and Li^+) with a halogen or other small anion (such as Cl^-, Br^-, SO_4^{2-}, or NO_3^-) taste salty. The receptor for saltiness seems to be a simple sodium channel. When present in the saliva, sodium enters the taste cell and depolarizes it, triggering action potentials that cause the cell to release transmitter substance

Bitter

Sour

Salty

Sweet

FIGURE 7.21

Sensitivity of different regions of the tongue to different tastes.

(Avenet and Lindemann, 1989; Kinnamon and Cummings, 1992). The best evidence that sodium channels are involved is the fact that amiloride, a drug that is known to block sodium channels, prevents sodium chloride from activating taste cells and blocks sensations of saltiness (Schiffman, Lockhead, and Maes, 1983).

Sourness receptors appear to respond to the hydrogen ions present in acidic solutions. Kinnamon, Dionne, and Beam (1988) suggest that sourness is detected by sites on potassium channels in the membrane of taste cell cilia. These channels are normally open, permitting K^+ to flow out of the cell. Hydrogen ions bind with these sites and close the channels. Their closure prevents this outward current and depolarizes the membrane, producing action potentials.

Bitter and sweet substances are more difficult to characterize. The typical stimulus for bitterness is a plant alkaloid such as quinine; for sweetness it is a sugar such as glucose or fructose. The fact that some molecules elicit both sensations suggests that bitterness and sweetness receptors may be similar. For example, the Seville orange rind contains a glycoside (complex sugar) that tastes extremely bitter; the addition of a hydrogen ion to the molecule makes it taste intensely sweet (Horowitz and Gentili, 1974). Some amino acids taste sweet. Indeed, the commercial sweetener aspartame consists simply of two amino acids: aspartate and phenylalanine.

The structure of molecules that taste bitter appears to include a hydrophobic residue—that is, a region that is repelled by the presence of water. Especially bitter substances also have a region with a positive charge (Kurihara et al., 1994). Most molecules that taste sweet have a hydrogen ion situated 0.3 nm from a site that will accept a hydrogen ion. Presumably, the sweetness receptor has sites that match these.

Researchers have proposed two other taste qualities: umami and carbohydrates. **Umami,** a Japanese word that means "good taste," refers to the taste of monosodium glutamate (MSG), a substance that is often used as a flavor enhancer in Asian cuisine (Kurihara, 1987; Scott and Plata-Salaman, 1991). MSG is present in meats, cheeses, and some vegetables. There is good evidence that the umami receptor exists in several species, but the existence of this taste quality is still not universally accepted in humans. Chaudhari et al. (1996) suggest that a specialized metabotropic glutamate receptor (mGluR4) may be responsible for detecting the taste of glutamate. The investigators found this receptor in taste buds but not in other parts of the tongue. They also reported that rats did not distinguish the taste of MSG from that of a ligand for this receptor, L-AP4. Some studies suggest that monkeys and rodents can also taste complex carbohydrates (Feigin, Sclafani, and Sunday, 1987; Sunderland and Sclafani, 1988), but further research is needed to be certain.

Table 7.1 summarizes the transduction of taste qualities. (See *Table 7.1.*)

The Gustatory Pathway

Gustatory information is transmitted through cranial nerves 7, 9, and 10. Information from the anterior part of the tongue travels through the **chorda tympani,** a branch of the seventh cranial nerve (facial nerve). Taste receptors in the posterior part of the tongue send information through the lingual (tongue) branch of the ninth cranial nerve (glossopharyngeal nerve); the tenth cranial nerve (vagus nerve) carries information from receptors of the palate and epiglottis. The chorda tympani gets its name because it passes through the middle ear just beneath the tympanic membrane. Be-

Umami (*oo mah mee*) The taste sensation produced by glutamate.

Chorda tympani A branch of the facial nerve that passes beneath the eardrum; conveys taste information from the anterior part of the tongue and controls the secretion of some salivary glands.

TABLE 7.1	Detection of Gustatory Information
Taste Quality	**Nature of Detection**
Saltiness	Sodium ions enter sodium channels, depolarize taste cell
Sourness	Hydrogen ions bind with sites on potassium channels and close them, blocking outflow of potassium ions; depolarizes taste cell
Sweetness	Molecule with hydrogen ion 0.3 nm away from a site that will accept a hydrogen ion binds with unknown receptor
Bitterness	Molecule with hydrophobic residue (and often a region with a positive charge) binds with unknown receptor
Umami (glutamate)	Glutamate ion binds with a metabotropic glutamate receptor (mGluR4)
Carbohydrates (possible)	Unknown

cause of its convenient location, it is accessible to a recording or stimulating electrode. Investigators have even recorded from this nerve during the course of human ear operations.

The first relay station for taste is the **nucleus of the solitary tract,** located in the medulla. In primates the taste-sensitive neurons of this nucleus send their axons to the ventral posteromedial thalamic nucleus, a nucleus that also receives somatosensory information received from the trigeminal nerve (Beckstead, Morse, and Norgren, 1980). Thalamic taste-sensitive neurons send their axons to the primary gustatory cortex, which is located in the insular and opercular regions of the frontal lobe (Pritchard et al., 1986). Neurons in this region project to the secondary gustatory cortex, located in the caudolateral orbitofrontal cortex (Rolls, Yaxley, and Sienkiewicz, 1990). Unlike most other sense modalities, taste is ipsilaterally represented in the brain. (See *Figure 7.22.*)

Gustatory information also reaches the amygdala and the hypothalamus and adjacent basal forebrain (Nauta, 1964; Russchen, Amaral, and Price, 1986). Many investigators believe that the hypothalamic pathway plays a role in mediating the reinforcing effects of sweet and salty tastes. In fact, some neurons in the hypothalamus respond to sweet stimuli only when the animal is hungry (Rolls et al., 1986). I will discuss this phenomenon in more detail in Chapter 12.

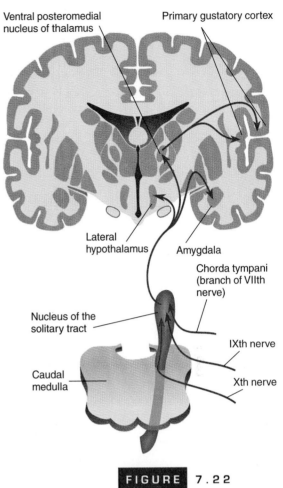

FIGURE 7.22

Neural pathways of the gustatory system.

INTERIM SUMMARY

Taste receptors detect only four sensory qualities: bitterness, sourness, sweetness, and saltiness. Bitter foods often contain plant alkaloids, many of which are poisonous. Sour foods have usually undergone bacterial fermentation, which can produce toxins. On the other hand, sweet foods (such as fruits) are usually nutritious and safe to eat, and salty foods contain an essential cation, sodium. The fact that people in affluent cultures today tend to ingest excessive amounts of sweet and salty foods suggests that these taste qualities are naturally reinforcing.

Saltiness receptors appear to be simple sodium channels. Sourness receptors appear to detect the presence of hydrogen ions, which closes potassium channels located on the cilia and depolarizes the membrane of the cell. The structure of molecules that taste bitter appears to include a hydrophobic residue, and some also have a region with a positive charge. Most molecules that taste sweet have a hydrogen ion situated 0.3 nm from a site that will accept a hydrogen ion. The taste of glutamate (umami) is—at least, in some species—detected by a particular metabolic glutamate receptor (mGluR4). Some animals may also be able to taste complex carbohydrates.

Gustatory information from the anterior part of the tongue travels through the chorda tympani, a branch of the facial nerve that passes beneath the eardrum on its way to the brain. The posterior part of the tongue sends gustatory information through the glossopharyngeal nerve, and the palate and epiglottis send gustatory information through the vagus nerve. Gustatory information is received by the nucleus of the solitary tract (located in the medulla) and is relayed by the ventral posteromedial thalamus to the primary gustatory cortex in the opercular and insular regions of the frontal lobes. The caudolateral orbitofrontal cortex contains the secondary gustatory cortex. Gustatory information is also sent to the amygdala, hypothalamus, and basal forebrain.

Nucleus of the solitary tract (NST) A nucleus of the medulla that receives information from visceral organs and from the gustatory system.

■ **THOUGHT QUESTIONS**

Bees and birds can taste sweet substances, but cats and alligators cannot. Obviously, the ability to taste particular substances is related to the range of foods a species eats. If, through the process of evolution, a species develops a greater range of foods, what do you think comes first: the food or the receptor? Would a species start eating something with a new taste (say, something sweet) and later develop the appropriate taste receptors, or would the taste receptors evolve first and then lead the animal to a new taste?

▇ OLFACTION

Olfaction, the second chemical sense, helps us to identify food and avoid food that has spoiled and is unfit to eat. It helps the members of many species to track prey or detect predators and to identify friends, foes, and receptive mates. For humans, olfaction is the most enigmatic of all sensory modalities. Odors have a peculiar ability to evoke memories, often vague ones that seem to have occurred in the distant past—a phenomenon that Marcel Proust vividly described in his book *Remembrance of Things Past*. Although people can discriminate among many thousands of different odors, we lack a good vocabulary to describe them. It is relatively easy to describe sights we have seen or sounds we have heard, but the description of an odor is difficult. At best, we can say that it smells like something else. Thus, the olfactory system appears to be specialized for *identifying things,* not for analyzing particular qualities.

The Stimulus

The stimulus for odor consists of volatile substances having a molecular weight in the range of approximately 15 to 300. Almost all odorous compounds are lipid soluble and of organic origin. However, many substances that meet these criteria have no odor at all.

Olfactory epithelium The epithelial tissue of the nasal sinus that covers the cribriform plate; contains the cilia of the olfactory receptors.

Anatomy of the Olfactory Apparatus

Our 50 million olfactory receptor cells reside within two patches of mucous membrane (the **olfactory epithelium**), each having an area of about 1 square inch. The

Particular odors that we experience when we are young often have the ability to evoke poignant memories later in life.

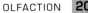
FIGURE 7.23

The olfactory system.

olfactory epithelium is located at the top of the nasal cavity, as shown in *Figure 7.23*. Less than 10 percent of the air that enters the nostrils reaches the olfactory epithelium; a sniff is needed to sweep air upward into the nasal cavity so that it reaches the olfactory receptors.

The inset in Figure 7.23 illustrates a group of olfactory receptor cells, along with their supporting cells. (See *inset, Figure 7.23*.) Olfactory receptor cells are bipolar neurons whose cell bodies lie within the olfactory mucosa that lines the *cribriform plate,* a bone at the base of the rostral part of the brain. There is a constant turnover of olfactory receptor cells, as there is of gustatory receptor cells; their life cycle is approximately 60 days. The cells send a process toward the surface of the mucosa, which divides into ten to twenty cilia that penetrate the layer of mucus. Odorous molecules must dissolve in the mucus and stimulate receptor molecules on the olfactory cilia. The axons of olfactory receptor cells enter the skull through small holes in the cribriform ("perforated") plate. The olfactory mucosa also contains free nerve endings of trigeminal nerve axons; these nerve endings presumably mediate sensations of pain that can be produced by sniffing some irritating chemicals, such as ammonia.

The **olfactory bulbs** lie at the base of the brain on the ends of the stalklike olfactory tracts. Each olfactory receptor cell sends a single axon into the olfactory bulb, where it forms synapses with dendrites of **mitral cells** (named for their resemblance to a bishop's miter). These synapses take place in the complex axonal and dendritic arborizations called **olfactory glomeruli** (from *glomus,* "ball"). There are approximately 10,000 glomeruli, each of which receives input from a bundle of approximately 2000 axons. The axons of the mitral cells travel to the rest of the brain through the olfactory tracts. Some of these axons terminate in the brain; others cross the brain, enter the other olfactory nerve, and terminate in the contralateral olfactory bulb.

Olfactory bulb The protrusion at the end of the olfactory tract; receives input from the olfactory receptors.

Mitral cell A neuron located in the olfactory bulb that receives information from olfactory receptors; axons of mitral cells bring information to the rest of the brain.

Olfactory glomerulus (*glow mare you luss*) A bundle of dendrites of mitral cells and the associated terminal buttons of the axons of olfactory receptors.

Olfactory tract axons project directly to the amygdala and to two regions of the limbic cortex: the pyriform cortex and the entorhinal cortex. (See *Figure 7.23*.) The amygdala sends olfactory information to the hypothalamus, the entorhinal cortex sends it to the hippocampus, and the pyriform cortex sends it to the hypothalamus and to the orbitofrontal cortex, via the dorsomedial nucleus of the thalamus (Buck, 1996; Shipley and Ennis, 1996). As you may recall, the orbitofrontal cortex also receives gustatory information; thus, it may be involved in the combining of taste and olfaction into flavor. The hypothalamus also receives a considerable amount of olfactory information, which is probably important for the acceptance or rejection of food and for the olfactory control of reproductive processes seen in many species of mammals.

Most mammals have another organ that responds to olfactory stimuli: the *vomeronasal organ*. Because it plays an important role in animals' responses to odors that affect reproductive physiology and behavior, its structure and function are described in Chapter 9.

Transduction of Olfactory Information

Olfactory cilia contain receptors that are stimulated by odor molecules. Jones and Reed (1989) discovered a protein, which they called G_{olf}, which was able to activate an enzyme that can open sodium channels and depolarize the membrane of the olfactory cell (Nakamura and Gold, 1987; Firestein, Zufall, and Shepherd, 1991; Menco et al., 1992).

Buck and Axel (1991) used molecular genetics techniques and discovered a family of genes that code for the olfactory receptor protein. There appear to be between 500 and 1000 different receptors in humans and rodents, each sensitive to different odorants (Ressler, Sullivan, and Buck, 1994a).

Detection of Specific Odors

For many years, recognition of specific odors has been an enigma. Humans can recognize up to 10,000 different odorants, and other animals can probably recognize even more (Shepherd, 1994). Even if we have 1000 different olfactory receptors, that leaves many odors unaccounted for. And every year, chemists synthesize new chemicals, many with odors unlike those that anyone has previously detected. How can we use a relatively small number of receptors to detect so many different odorants?

Before I answer this question, we should look more closely at the relation between receptors, olfactory neurons, and the glomeruli to which the axons of these neurons project. First, the cilia of each olfactory neuron contain only one type of receptor (Nef et al., 1992; Vassar, Ngai, and Axel, 1993). As we saw, each glomerulus receives information from approximately 2000 different olfactory receptor cells. Using neurochemical methods to identify particular receptor proteins in individual cells, Ressler, Sullivan, and Buck (1994) discovered that although a given glomerulus receives information from approximately 2000 different olfactory receptor cells, each of these cells contains the same type of receptor molecule. Thus, there are as many types of glomeruli as there are types of receptor molecules. Furthermore, the location of particular types of glomeruli (defined by the type of receptor that sends information to them) appears to be the same in each of the olfactory bulbs in a given animal and may even be the same from one animal to another. (See *Figure 7.24*.)

Now let's get back to the question I just posed: How can we use a relatively small number of receptors to detect so many different odorants? The answer is that a particular odorant binds to more than one receptor. Moreover, it binds to some of these receptors better than to others. Thus, because a given glomerulus receives information from only one type of receptor, different odorants produce different *patterns* of activity in different glomeruli. Recognizing a particular odor, then, is a matter of recognizing a particular pattern of activity in the glomeruli. The task of chemical recognition is transformed into a task of spatial recognition.

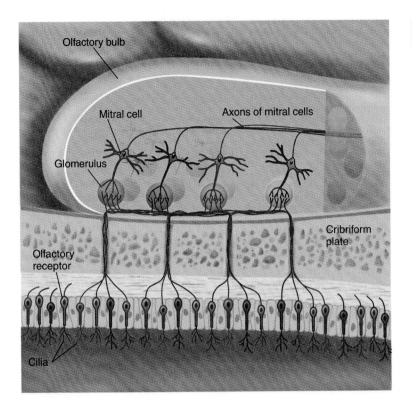

FIGURE 7.24

Details of the connections of olfactory receptor cells with the glomeruli of the olfactory bulb. Each glomerulus receives information from only one type of receptor cell. Olfactory receptor cells of different colors contain different types of receptor molecules.

Just how the brain recognizes these patterns is not yet known. The task is obviously complex. Cain (1988) noted that although most odors are produced by mixtures of many different chemicals, we identify odors as belonging to particular objects. For example, the smells of coffee, fried bacon, and cigarette smoke that you might encounter at a breakfast counter are each made of up to several hundred different types of molecules. Although each of these odors is a mixture, we recognize them as being unique—we do not detect the individual components. However, if the smells of coffee, fried bacon, and cigarette smoke are mixed together, we still recognize all three odors, even though each one of them is itself a mixture!

Recordings in more central levels of the olfactory system show that neural responses tend to be finely tuned to particular odors. For example, Tanabe et al. (1974) and Tanabe, Iino, and Takagi (1975) found that neurons in the olfactory area of the orbitofrontal cortex of monkeys were rather selective. Of the forty cells from which they recorded, half responded to only one odor, and decreasing numbers responded to two, three, or four different odors. None responded to more than five odors. The nature of the coding system in the olfactory cortex is unknown.

INTERIM SUMMARY

The olfactory receptors consist of bipolar neurons located in the olfactory epithelium that lines the roof of the nasal sinuses, on the bone that underlies the frontal lobes. The receptors send processes toward the surface of the mucosa, which divide into cilia. The membranes of these cilia contain receptors that detect aromatic molecules dissolved in the air that sweeps past the olfactory mucosa. The axons of the olfactory receptors pass through the perforations of the cribriform plate into the olfactory bulbs, where they form synapses in the glomeruli with the dendrites of the mitral cells. These neurons send axons through the olfactory tracts to the brain, principally to the amygdala, the pyriform cortex, and the entorhinal cortex. The hippocampus, hypothalamus, and orbitofrontal cortex receive olfactory information indirectly.

Aromatic molecules produce membrane potentials by interacting with a newly discovered family of receptor molecules, which may number up to 1000. These receptors are coupled to a special protein, G_{olf}. This protein activates an enzyme that opens sodium channels and depolarizes the membrane. Each glomerulus receives information from only one type of olfactory receptor. This means that the task of detecting different odors is a spatial one; the brain recognizes odors by means of the patterns of activity created in the glomeruli.

THOUGHT QUESTIONS

As I mentioned in the preceding section, odors have a peculiar ability to evoke memories, a phenomenon that Marcel Proust vividly described in his book *Remembrance of Things Past*. Have you ever encountered an odor that you knew was somehow familiar, but you couldn't say exactly why? Can you think of any explanations? Might this phenomenon have something to do with the fact that the sense of olfaction developed very early in our evolutionary history?

EPILOGUE
Natural Analgesia

As we have seen, the brain contains an elaborate system through which certain types of stimuli can produce analgesia primarily through the release of the endogenous opiates. What functions does this system perform? Most researchers believe that it prevents pain from disrupting animals' behavior in situations in which pain is unavoidable and in which the damaging effects of the painful stimuli are less important than the goals of the animals' behavior. This explanation accounts for several types of situations that produce analgesia, but not all of them; some mysteries still remain.

When an animal encounters a noxious stimulus, it usually stops what it is doing and engages in withdrawal or escape behaviors. Obviously, these responses are quite appropriate. However, they are sometimes counterproductive. For example, if an animal sustains a wound that causes chronic pain, a tendency to engage in withdrawal responses will interfere with its performance of everyday activities, such as obtaining food. Thus, the in-

hibitory effects of chronic, unavoidable pain would best be diminished.

Another useful function of analgesia is the suppression of pain during important behaviors such as fighting or mating. For example, males fighting for access to females during mating season will fail to pass on their genes if pain elicits withdrawal responses that interfere with fighting. As you will see, these conditions (fighting or mating) *do* diminish pain.

Let us consider the effects of unavoidable pain. Several experiments have shown that analgesia can be produced by the application of painful stimuli or even by the presence of nonpainful stimuli that have been paired with painful ones. For example, Maier, Drugan, and Grau (1982) administered inescapable shocks to rats' tails or administered shocks that the animals could learn to escape by making a response. Although both groups of animals received the same amount of shock, only those that received *inescapable* shocks showed analgesia. That is, when their pain sensitivity was tested, it was found to be lower than

that of control subjects. The analgesia was abolished by administration of naloxone, which indicates that it was mediated by the release of endogenous opiates. (*Naloxone* is a drug that blocks opiate receptors. The experimenter in the Prologue used this drug when he blocked the analgesic effect of Melissa's own endogenous opiates.) The results make good sense, biologically. If pain is escapable, it serves to motivate the animal to make appropriate responses. If it occurs no matter what the animal does, then a reduction in pain sensitivity is in the animal's best interest.

There is evidence that engaging in behaviors that are important to survival also reduces sensitivity to pain. For example, Komisaruk and Larsson (1971) found that genital stimulation produced analgesia. They gently probed the cervix of female rats with a glass rod and found that the procedure diminished the animals' sensitivity to pain. It also increased the activity of neurons in the periaqueductal gray matter and decreased the pain response in the thalamus

[Komisaruk and Steinman, 1987]. The phenomenon also occurs in humans; Whipple and Komisaruk (1988) found that self-administered vaginal stimulation reduces women's sensitivity to painful stimuli but not to neutral tactile stimuli. Presumably, copulation also triggers analgesic mechanisms. The adaptive significance of this phenomenon is clear: Painful stimuli that are encountered during the course of copulation are less likely to cause the behavior to be interrupted; thus, the chances of pregnancy are increased. (As you will recall, passing on one's genes is the ultimate criterion of the adaptive significance of a trait.)

As we saw in the Prologue, pain can also be reduced at least in some people by administering a *placebo*, a pharmacologically inert substance. (The term *placebo* comes from the Latin *placere*, which means "to please." The physician pleases an anxious patient by giving him or her an innocuous substance.) The pain reduction seems to be mediated by the release of endogenous opiates, because it is blocked by naloxone (Levine, Gordon, and Fields, 1979). Thus, *believing* that pain is going to diminish is a self-fulfilling prophecy. *Why* this particular phenomenon occurs is still a mystery.

Pain can be also reduced by stimulating regions other than those that hurt. For example, people often rub or scratch the area around a wound in an apparent attempt to diminish the severity of the pain. And as you know, acupuncturists insert needles into various parts of the body to reduce pain. The needle is usually then rotated, thus stimulating axons and nerve endings in the vicinity. Often, the region that is stimulated is far removed from the region that becomes less sensitive to pain.

Several experimental studies have shown that acupuncture can produce analgesia. Mayer, Price, Rafii, and Barber (1976) reported that the analgesic effects of acupuncture could be blocked by naloxone. However, when pain was reduced by hypnotic suggestion, naloxone had no effect. Thus, acupuncture, but not hypnosis, appears to cause analgesia through the release of endogenous opiates.

The endogenous opiates were first discovered by scientists who were investigating the perception of pain; thus, many of the studies using these peptides have examined their role in mechanisms of analgesia. However, their role in other functions may be even more important. As you will see in subsequent chapters, the endogenous opiates may even be involved in learning, especially in mechanisms of reinforcement. This connection should not come as a surprise; as you know, many people have found injections of opiates like morphine or heroin to be extremely pleasurable.

KEY CONCEPTS

AUDITION

1. The bones of the middle ear transmit sound vibrations from the eardrum to the cochlea, which contains the auditory receptors the hair cells.
2. The hair cells send information through the eighth cranial nerve to nuclei in the brain stem; it is then relayed to the medial geniculate nucleus and finally to the primary auditory cortex.
3. The ear is analytical; it detects individual frequencies by means of place coding and rate coding. Left-right localization is also accomplished by two means: arrival time (phase differences) and binaural differences in intensity.

VESTIBULAR SYSTEM

4. The vestibular system helps us to maintain our balance and makes compensatory eye movements to help us maintain fixation when our head moves. The semicircular canals detect head rotations and the vestibular sacs detect changes in the tilt of the head.

SOMATOSENSES

5. Cutaneous receptors in the skin provide information about touch, pressure, vibration, changes in temperature, and stimuli that cause tissue damage.
6. Pain perception helps protect us from harmful stimuli. Sensitivity to pain is modulated by the release of the endogenous opiates by cells in the brain.

GUSTATION

7. Taste receptors on the tongue respond to bitterness, sourness, sweetness, and saltiness and, together with olfactory information, provide us with information about complex flavors.

OLFACTION

8. The olfactory system detects the presence of aromatic molecules. The discovery of a family of receptors coupled to a special G protein (G_{olf}) suggests that several hundred different receptors may be involved in olfactory discrimination.

SUGGESTED READINGS

AUDITION

Ashmore, J.F. The electrophysiology of hair cells. *Annual Review of Physiology*, 1991, *53*, 465–476.

Corwin, J.T., and Warchol, M.E. Auditory hair cells: Structure, function, development, and regeneration. *Annual Review of Neuroscience*, 1991, *14*, 301–333.

Ehret, G., and Romand, R. *The Central Auditory System.* New York: Oxford University Press, 1997.

Moore, B.C.J. *Hearing: Handbook of Perception and Cognition,* 2nd ed. San Diego: Academic Press, 1995.

Yost, W.A. *Fundamentals of Hearing: An Introduction,* 3rd ed. San Diego: Academic Press, 1994.

VESTIBULAR SYSTEM

Cohen, B., Tomko, D.L., and Guedry, F.E. *Sensing and Controlling Motion: Vestibular and Sensorimotor Function.* New York: New York Academy of Sciences, 1992.

SOMATOSENSES

Bromm, B., and Desmedt, J.E. *Pain and the Brain: From Nociception to Cognition.* New York: Raven Press, 1995.

García-Añoveros, J., and Corey, D.P. The molecules of mechanosensation. *Annual Review of Neuroscience*, 1997, *20*, 567–594.

Kruger, L. *Pain and Touch: Handbook of Perception and Cognition,* 2nd ed. San Diego: Academic Press, 1996.

Melzak, R. Phantom limbs. *Scientific American*, 1992, *266*(4), 120–126.

OLFACTION AND GUSTATION

Buck, L.B. Information coding in the vertebrate olfactory system. *Annual Review of Neuroscience*, 1996, *19*, 517–544.

Getchell, T.V. *Smell and Taste in Health and Disease.* New York: Raven Press, 1991.

Hildebrand, J.G., and Shepherd, G.M. Mechanisms of olfactory discrimination: Converging evidence for common principles across phyla. *Annual Review of Neuroscience*, 1997, *20*, 595–632.

Kinnamon, S.C., and Cummings, T.A. Chemosensory transduction mechanisms in taste. *Annual Review of Physiology*, 1992, *54*, 715–731.

Laing, D.G., Doty, R.L., and Breipohl, W. *The Human Sense of Smell.* New York: Springer-Verlag, 1991.

8

Sleep and Biological Rhythms

LEARNING OBJECTIVES

1. Describe the course of a night's sleep: its stages and their characteristics.

2. Review the hypothesis that sleep is an adaptive response.

3. Review the hypothesis that sleep serves as a period of restoration by discussing the effects of sleep deprivation, exercise, and mental activity.

4. Discuss the functions of REM sleep.

5. Evaluate evidence that the onset and amount of sleep is chemically controlled, and describe the neural control of arousal.

6. Discuss the neural control of slow-wave and REM sleep.

7. Discuss insomnia, sleeping medications, and sleep apnea.

8. Discuss problems associated with REM and slow-wave sleep.

9. Describe circadian rhythms, and discuss research on the neural and physiological bases of biological clocks.

Waking Nightmares

Lately, Michael felt almost afraid of going to bed because of the unpleasant experiences he had been having. His dreams seemed to have become more intense, in a rather disturbing way. Several times in the past few months, he felt as if he were paralyzed as he lay in bed, waiting for sleep to come. It was a strange feeling; was he *really* paralyzed, or was he just not trying hard enough to move? He always fell asleep before he was able to decide. A couple of times he woke up just before it was time for his alarm to go off and felt unable to move. Then the alarm would ring, and he would quickly shut it off. That meant that he really wasn't paralyzed, didn't it? Was he going crazy?

Last night brought the worst experience of all. As he was falling asleep, he felt again as if he were paralyzed. Then he saw his old roommate enter his bedroom. But that wasn't possible! Since the time he graduated from college, he had lived alone, and he always locked the door. He tried to say something, but he couldn't. His roommate was holding a hammer. He walked up to his bed, stood over Michael, and suddenly raised the hammer, as if to smash in his forehead. When he awoke in the morning, he shuddered with the remembrance. It had seemed so real! It must have been a dream, but he didn't think he was asleep. He was in bed. Can a person really dream that he is lying in bed, not yet asleep?

That day at the office he had trouble concentrating on his work. He forced himself to review his notes, because he had to present the details of the new project to the board of directors. This was his big chance; if the project were accepted, he would certainly be chosen to lead it, and that would mean a promotion and a substantial raise. Naturally, with so much at stake, he felt nervous when he entered the boardroom. His boss introduced Michael and asked him to begin. He glanced at his notes and opened his mouth to talk. Suddenly, he felt his knees buckle. All his strength seemed to slip away. He fell heavily to the floor. He could hear people running over and asking what had happened. He couldn't move anything except his eyes. His boss got down on his knees, looked into his face, and asked, "Michael, are you all right?" Michael looked at his boss and tried to answer, but he couldn't say a thing. A few seconds later, he felt his strength coming back. He opened his mouth and said, "I'm okay." He struggled to his knees and then sat in a chair, feeling weak and frightened.

"You undoubtedly have a condition known as narcolepsy," said the doctor whom Michael visited. "It's a problem that concerns the way your brain controls sleep. I'll have you spend a night in the sleep clinic and get some recordings done to confirm my diagnosis, but I'm sure that I'll be proved correct. You told me that lately you've been taking short naps during the day. What were these naps like? Were you suddenly struck by an urge to sleep?" Michael nodded. "I just had to put my head on the desk, even though I was afraid that my boss might see me. But I don't think I slept more than five minutes or so." "Did you still feel sleepy when you woke?" "No," he replied, "I felt fine again." The doctor nodded. "All the symptoms you have reported—the sleep attacks, the paralysis you experienced before sleeping and after waking up, the spell you had today—they all fit together. Fortunately, we can usually control narcolepsy with medication. I'm sure we'll have you back to normal, and there is no reason why you can't continue with your job. If you'd like, I can talk with your boss and reassure him, too."

Why do we sleep? Why do we spend at least one-third of our lives doing something that provides most of us with only a few fleeting memories? I will attempt to answer this question in several ways. In the first two parts of this chapter I will describe what is known about the phenomenon of sleep: How much do we sleep? What do we do while asleep? What happens if we do not get enough sleep? Does sleep perform a restorative function? In the third part of the chapter I will describe the search for the chemicals and the neural circuits that control sleep and wakefulness. In the fourth section I will explore whether sleeping medications are effective and what we know about narcolepsy, sleepwalking, and other sleep-related disorders. In the final part of the chapter I will discuss the brain's biological clock—the mechanism that controls daily rhythms of sleep and activity.

A PHYSIOLOGICAL AND BEHAVIORAL DESCRIPTION

Sleep is a behavior. That statement may seem peculiar, because we usually think of behaviors as activities that involve movements, such as walking or talking. Except for the rapid eye movements that accompany a particular stage, sleep is not distinguished by movement. What characterizes sleep is that the insistent urge of sleepiness forces us to seek out a quiet, comfortable place, lie down, and remain there for several hours. Because we remember very little about what happens while we sleep, we tend to think of sleep more as a state of consciousness than as a behavior. The change in consciousness is undeniable, but it should not prevent us from noticing the behavioral changes.

The best research on human sleep is conducted in a sleep laboratory. A sleep laboratory, usually located at a university or medical center, consists of one or several small bedrooms adjacent to an observation room, where the experimenter spends the night (trying to stay awake). The experimenter prepares the sleeper for electrophysiological measurements by attaching electrodes to the scalp to monitor the electroencephalogram (EEG) and to the chin to monitor muscle activity, recorded as the **electromyogram (EMG).** Electrodes attached around the eyes monitor eye movements, recorded as the **electro-oculogram (EOG).** In addition, other electrodes and transducing devices can be used to monitor autonomic measures such as heart rate, respiration, and skin conductance. Wires from the electrodes are bundled together in a "ponytail," which is then plugged into a junction box at the head of the bed. (See *Figure 8.1.*)

During wakefulness the EEG of a normal person shows two basic patterns of activity: *alpha activity* and *beta activity*. **Alpha activity** consists of regular, medium-frequency waves of 8–12 Hz. The brain produces this activity when a person is resting quietly, not particularly aroused or excited and not engaged in strenuous mental activity (such as problem solving). Although alpha waves sometimes occur when a person's eyes are open, they are much more prevalent when the eyes are closed. The other type of waking EEG pattern, **beta activity,** consists of irregular, mostly low-amplitude waves of 13–30 Hz. This activity occurs when a person is alert and attentive to events in the environment or is thinking actively. (See *Figure 8.2.*)

Let us look at a typical night's sleep of a female college student on her third night in the laboratory. (Of course, we would obtain similar results from a male, with one exception, which is noted later.) The experimenter attaches the electrodes, turns the lights off, and closes the door. Our subject becomes drowsy and soon enters stage 1 sleep, marked by the presence of some **theta activity** (3.5–7.5 Hz). (See *Figure 8.2.*) This stage is actually a transition between sleep and wakefulness; if we watch our volunteer's eyelids, we will see that from time to time they slowly open and close and that her eyes roll upward and downward. About 10 minutes later she enters stage 2 sleep. The EEG during this stage is generally irregular but contains periods of theta activity, *sleep spindles,* and *K complexes.* Sleep spindles are short bursts of waves of 12–14 Hz that occur between two and five times a minute during stages 1–4 of sleep. Some investigators believe that sleep spindles represent the activity of a mechanism that decreases the brain's sensitivity to sensory input—disconnects the

FIGURE 8.1

A subject prepared for a night's sleep in a sleep laboratory.
(Philippe Platilly/Science Photo Library/Photo Researchers Inc.)

Electromyogram (EMG) (*my oh gram*) An electrical potential recorded from an electrode placed on or in a muscle.

Electro-oculogram (EOG) (*ah kew loh gram*) An electrical potential from the eyes, recorded by means of electrodes placed on the skin around them; detects eye movements.

Alpha activity Smooth electrical activity of 8–12 Hz recorded from the brain; generally associated with a state of relaxation.

Beta activity Irregular electrical activity of 13–30 Hz recorded from the brain; generally associated with a state of arousal.

Theta activity EEG activity of 3.5–7.5 Hz that occurs intermittently during early stages of slow-wave sleep and REM sleep.

Awake

Alpha activity   Beta activity

Stage 1 sleep

Theta activity

Stage 2 sleep

Sleep
spindle   K complex   Seconds

Stage 3 sleep

Delta activity

Stage 4 sleep

Delta activity

REM sleep

Theta activity   Beta activity

FIGURE 8.2

An EEG recording of the stages of sleep.

[From Horne, J.A. Why We Sleep: The Functions of Sleep in Humans and Other Mammals. Oxford, England: Oxford University Press, 1988. Copyright 1988 Oxford University Press. By permission of the Oxford University Press.]

Delta activity Regular, synchronous electrical activity of less than 3.5 Hz recorded from the brain; occurs during the deepest stages of slow-wave sleep.

REM sleep A period of desynchronized EEG activity during sleep, at which time dreaming, rapid eye movements, and muscular paralysis occur; also called *paradoxical sleep.*

brain from the outside world, so to speak—and thus permits the person to enter deeper stages of sleep (Bowersox, Kaitin, and Dement, 1985; Steriade, 1992). The sleep of older people contains fewer sleep spindles and is generally accompanied by more awakenings during the night. K complexes are sudden, sharp waveforms, which, unlike sleep spindles, are usually found only during stage 2 sleep. They spontaneously occur at the rate of approximately one per minute but often can be triggered by noises—especially unexpected noises (Niiyama et al., 1995, 1996). Some investigators believe that they, too, represent mechanisms involved in keeping the person asleep (Wauquier, Aloe, and Declerck, 1995). (See *Figure 8.2.*)

The subject is sleeping soundly now; but if awakened, she might report that she has not been asleep. This phenomenon is often reported by nurses who awaken loudly snoring patients early in the night (probably to give them a sleeping pill) and find that the patients insist they were lying there awake all the time. About 15 minutes later, the subject enters stage 3 sleep, signaled by the occurrence of high-amplitude **delta activity** (less than 3.5 Hz). (See *Figure 8.2.*) The distinction between stage 3 and stage 4 is not clearcut; stage 3 contains 20–50 percent delta activity, and stage 4 contains more than 50 percent delta activity. (See *Figure 8.2.*)

About 90 minutes after the beginning of sleep (and about 45 minutes after the onset of stage 4 sleep), we notice an abrupt change in a number of physiological measures recorded from our subject. The EEG suddenly becomes mostly desynchronized, with a sprinkling of theta waves, very similar to the record obtained during stage 1 sleep. (See *Figure 8.2.*) We also note that her eyes are rapidly darting back and forth beneath her closed eyelids. We can see this activity in the EOG, recorded from electrodes attached to the skin around her eyes, or we can observe the eye movements directly—the cornea produces a bulge in the closed eyelids that can be seen to move about. We also see that the EMG becomes silent; there is a profound loss of muscle tonus. In fact, physiological studies have shown that, aside from occasional twitching, a person actually becomes paralyzed during REM sleep.

This peculiar stage of sleep is quite distinct from the quiet sleep we saw earlier. It is usually referred to as **REM sleep** (for the **r**apid **e**ye **m**ovements that characterize it). It has also been called *paradoxical sleep*, because of the presence of beta activity, which is usually seen during wakefulness or stage 1 sleep. The term *paradoxical* merely reflects people's surprise at observing an unexpected phenomenon, but the years since its first discovery (reported by Aserinsky and Kleitman in 1955) have blunted the surprise value.

At this point, I should introduce some terminology. Stages 1–4 are usually referred to as **non-REM sleep.** Stages 3 and 4 are referred to as **slow-wave sleep,** because of the presence of delta activity. As we will see, research has focused on the role of REM sleep and of slow-wave sleep; most investigators believe that the other stages of non-REM sleep, stages 1 and 2, are less important than the others. (As we shall see, when people are sleep deprived, they make up most of their slow-wave sleep and REM sleep, but not their stage 1 and stage 2 sleep.) By some criteria, stage 4 is the deepest stage of sleep; only loud noises will cause a person to awaken, and when awakened, the person acts groggy and confused. During REM sleep a person may not react to noises, but he or she is easily aroused by meaningful stimuli, such as the sound of his or her name. Also, when awakened from REM sleep, a person appears alert and attentive.

If we arouse our volunteer during REM sleep and ask her what was going on, she will almost certainly report that she had been dreaming. The dreams of REM sleep tend to be narrative in form; there is a storylike progression of events. If we wake her during slow-wave sleep and ask, "Were you dreaming?" she will most likely say, "No." However, if we question her more carefully, she might report the presence of a thought, an image, or some emotion. I will return to this issue later.

During the rest of the night our subject's sleep alternates between periods of REM and non-REM sleep. Each cycle is approximately 90 minutes long, containing a 20- to 30-minute bout of REM sleep. Thus, an 8-hour sleep will contain four or five periods of REM sleep. Figure 8.3 shows a graph of a typical night's sleep. The *y*-axis indicates the EEG activity that is being recorded; thus REM sleep and stage 1 sleep are placed on the same line because similar patterns of EEG activity occur at these times. Note that most slow-wave sleep (stages 3 and 4) occurs during the first half of night. Subsequent bouts of non-REM sleep contain more and more stage 2 sleep, and bouts of REM sleep (indicated by the horizontal bars) become more prolonged. (See *Figure 8.3*.)

The fact that REM sleep occurs at regular 90-minute intervals suggests that a brain mechanism alternately causes REM and slow-wave sleep. Normally, a period of slow-wave sleep must precede REM sleep. In addition, there seems to be a refractory period after each occurrence of REM sleep, during which time REM sleep cannot take place again. In fact, the cyclical nature of REM sleep appears to be controlled by a "clock" in the brain that also controls an activity cycle that continues through waking. The first suggestion that a 90-minute activity cycle occurs throughout the day came from the observation that infants who are fed on demand show regular feeding patterns (Kleitman, 1961). Later studies found 90-minute cycles of rest and activity, including such activities as eating, drinking, smoking, heart rate, oxygen consumption, stomach motility, urine production, and performance on various tasks that make demands upon a person's ability to pay attention. Kleitman termed this phenomenon the **basic rest-activity cycle (BRAC).** (See Kleitman, 1982, for a review.) As we will see later in this chapter, an internal "clock," probably located in the medulla, causes regular changes in activity and alertness during the day and controls periods of slow-wave and REM sleep at night.

As we saw, during REM sleep we become paralyzed; most of our spinal and cranial motor neurons are strongly inhibited. (Obviously, the ones that control respiration and eye movements are spared.) At the same time, the brain is very active. Cerebral blood flow and oxygen consumption are accelerated. In addition, a male's penis will become at least partially erect, and a female's vaginal secretions will increase. However, Fisher, Gross, and Zuch (1965) found that in males, genital changes do not signify that the person is experiencing a dream with sexual content. (Of course, people can have dreams with frank sexual content. In males some dreams culminate in ejaculation—the so-called nocturnal emissions, or "wet dreams." Females, too, sometimes experience orgasm during sleep.)

The fact that penile erections occur during REM sleep, independent of sexual arousal, has been used clinically to assess the causes of impotence (Karacan, Salis, and Williams, 1978; Singer and Weiner, 1996). A subject sleeps in the laboratory with a device attached to his penis that measures its circumference. If penile enlargement occurs during REM sleep, then his failure to obtain an erection during attempts at intercourse is not caused by physiological problems such as nerve damage or a circulatory disorder. (A neurologist told me that there is a less expensive way to gather the same data. The patient obtains a strip of postage stamps, moistens them, and ap-

FIGURE 8.3

A typical pattern of the stages of sleep during a single night. The dark blue shading indicates REM sleep.

Non-REM sleep All stages of sleep except REM sleep.

Slow-wave sleep Non-REM sleep, characterized by synchronized EEG activity during its deeper stages.

Basic rest-activity cycle (BRAC) A 90-minute cycle (in humans) of waxing and waning alertness, controlled by a biological clock in the caudal brain stem; controls cycles of REM sleep and slow-wave sleep.

TABLE 8.1	Principal Characteristics of REM and Slow-Wave Sleep
REM Sleep	**Slow-Wave Sleep**
EEG desynchrony (rapid, irregular waves)	EEG synchrony (slow waves)
Lack of muscle tonus	Moderate muscle tonus
Rapid eye movements	Slow or absent eye movements
Penile erection or vaginal secretion	Lack of genital activity
Dreams	

plies them around his penis before going to bed. In the morning he checks to see whether the perforations are broken.)

The important differences between REM and slow-wave sleep are listed in *Table 8.1*.

INTERIM SUMMARY

Sleep is generally regarded as a state, but it is, nevertheless, a behavior. As we will see later in this chapter, we do not sleep because our brains "run down"; instead, active brain mechanisms cause us to engage in the behavior of sleep. The stages of non-REM sleep, stages 1–4, are defined by EEG activity. Slow-wave sleep (stages 3 and 4) comprises the two deepest stages. Alertness consists of desynchronized beta activity (13–30 Hz); relaxation and drowsiness consist of alpha activity (8–12 Hz); stage 1 sleep consists of alternating periods of alpha activity, irregular fast activity, and theta activity (3.5–7.5 Hz); the EEG of stage 2 sleep lacks alpha activity but contains sleep spindles (short periods of 12–14 Hz activity) and occasional K complexes; stage 3 sleep consists of 20–50 percent delta activity (less than 3.5 Hz); and stage 4 sleep consists of more than 50 percent delta activity. About 90 minutes after the beginning of sleep, people enter REM sleep. Cycles of REM and slow-wave sleep alternate in periods of approximately 90 minutes.

REM sleep consists of rapid eye movements, a desynchronized EEG, sensitivity to external stimulation, muscular paralysis, genital activity, and dreaming.

THOUGHT QUESTIONS

1. What is accomplished by dreaming? Some researchers believe that the subject matter of a dream does not matter; it is the REM sleep itself that is important. Others believe that the subject matter *does* count. Some researchers believe that if we remember a dream, then the dream failed to accomplish all of its functions; others say that remembering dreams is useful, because it can give us some insights into our problems. What do you think of these controversies?

2. Some people report that they are "in control" of some of their dreams, that they feel as if they determine what comes next and are not simply swept along passively. Have you ever had this experience? And have you ever had a "lucid dream," in which you were aware of the fact that you were dreaming?

WHY DO WE SLEEP?

We all know how insistent the urge to sleep can be and how uncomfortable we feel when we have to resist it and stay awake. With the exception of the effects of severe pain and the need to breathe, sleepiness is probably the most insistent drive. People can commit suicide by refusing to eat or drink, but even the most stoical person cannot indefinitely defy the urge to sleep. Sleep will come, sooner or later, no matter how hard a person tries to stay awake. However, despite the insistent nature of sleepiness, researchers have not yet found a simple answer to the question posed in the title of this section. The two major hypotheses that have been proposed are discussed next.

Sleep as an Adaptive Response

Sleep is a universal phenomenon among vertebrates. As far as we know, all mammals and birds sleep (Durie, 1981). Reptiles also sleep, and fish and amphibians enter periods of quiescence that probably can be called sleep. However, only warm-blooded vertebrates (mammals and birds) exhibit unequivocal REM sleep, with a desynchronized EEG and rapid eye movements. (Obviously, birds such as flamingos, which sleep while perched on one leg, do not lose tone in the muscles they use to remain standing.) This special form of sleep will be discussed separately, in a later section.

Some investigators believe that the best way to understand sleep is to see it as a useful behavior that we have inherited from our ancestors. For example, Webb (1975, 1982) suggested that sleep might not have special restorative properties but might simply be a behavior that keeps an animal out of harm's way when there is nothing important to do. We can imagine that our primitive ancestors benefited from irresistible periods of sleep that kept them from stumbling around in the dark, when predators were harder to see, when food was difficult to find, and when injuries were more likely to occur.

Many animals obtain food during only part of the day–night cycle. These animals profit from a period of inactivity, during which less energy is expended. In fact, animals that have safe hiding places (such as rabbits) sleep a lot, unless they are very small and need to eat much of the time (such as shrews). Large predators such as lions can sleep safely wherever and whenever they choose, and indeed, they sleep many hours of the day. In contrast, large animals that are preyed upon and have no place to hide (such as cattle) sleep very little. Presumably, they must remain awake to be alert for predators.

An argument *against* the suggestion that sleep serves merely as an adaptive response is the fact that sleep is found in some species of mammals that would seem to be better off without it. For example, the Indus dolphin *(Platanista indi)* lives in the muddy waters of the Indus estuary in Pakistan (Pilleri, 1979). Over the years it has become blind, presumably because vision is not useful in the animal's environment. (It has an excellent sonar system, which it uses to navigate and find prey.) However, despite the dangers caused by sleeping, sleep has not disappeared. The Indus dolphin never stops swimming; doing so would result in injury, because of the dangerous currents and the vast quantities of debris carried by the river during the monsoon season. Pilleri captured two dolphins and studied their habits. He found that they slept a total of 7 hours a day, in brief naps of 4–60 seconds each. If sleep were simply an adaptive response, why was it not eliminated (as vision was) through the process of natural selection?

Some other species of marine mammals have developed an extraordinary pattern of sleep: The cerebral hemispheres take turns sleeping, presumably because that strategy always permits at least one hemisphere to be alert. The bottlenose dolphin *(Tursiops truncatus)* and the porpoise *(Phocoena phocoena)* both sleep this way

The two cerebral hemispheres of some species of porpoises take turns sleeping—although probably not when the animals are as active as they are shown here.

FIGURE 8.4

Sleep in a dolphin. The two hemispheres sleep at different times, presumably so that the animal remains behaviorally alert.

(Adapted from Mukhametov, L.M., in Sleep Mechanisms, *edited by A.A. Borbély and J.L. Valatx. Munich: Springer-Verlag, 1984.)*

(Mukhametov, 1984). Figure 8.4 shows the EEG recordings from the two hemispheres; note that slow-wave sleep occurs alternately in the left and right hemispheres. (See *Figure 8.4*.)

Undoubtedly, sleep *does* serve as a useful behavior. The fact that sleeping time varies with environmental factors suggests that the amount of sleep an organism engages in is somewhat flexible. But its presence in all species of mammals and birds suggests that at least a certain amount of sleep is necessary.

Sleep as a Restorative Process

Most investigators believe that sleep accomplishes some sort of restoration from the effects of wear and tear that occur during wakefulness. However, until recently, evidence for this hypothesis was very thin, indeed. In fact, sleep does not seem to be related to physical exercise; thus, its most important role is probably not rest and recuperation of the body. However, it *does* appear to be needed to keep the brain functioning normally. (For convenience, I will talk about the "body" and the "brain" in the following section, even though we both know that the brain is a part of the body.)

Effects of Sleep Deprivation

When we are forced to miss a night's sleep, we become very sleepy. The fact that sleepiness is so motivating suggests that sleep is a necessity of life. If so, it should be possible to deprive people or laboratory animals of sleep and see what functions are disrupted. We should then be able to infer the role that sleep plays. However, the results of sleep deprivation studies have not revealed as much as investigators had originally hoped.

Studies with Humans. Deprivation studies have not obtained persuasive evidence that sleep is needed to keep the body functioning normally. Horne (1978) reviewed over fifty experiments in which humans had been deprived of sleep. He reported that most of them found that sleep deprivation did not interfere with people's ability to perform physical exercise. In addition, the studies found no evidence of a physiological stress response to sleep deprivation. If people encounter stressful situations that cause illness or damage to various organ systems, changes can be seen in such physiological measures as blood levels of cortisol and epinephrine. (The physiology of stress is described in more detail in Chapter 16.) Generally, these changes did not occur with sleep deprivation.

What happens to sleep-deprived subjects after they are permitted to sleep again? Most of them sleep longer the next night or two, but they never regain all of the sleep they lost. In one remarkable case a seventeen-year-old boy stayed awake for 264 hours so that he could obtain a place in the *Guinness Book of World Records* (Gulevich, Dement, and Johnson, 1966). After his ordeal the boy slept for a little less than 15 hours and awoke feeling fine. He slept slightly more than 10 hours the second night and just under 9 hours the third. Almost 67 hours were never made up. However, percentages of recovery were not equal for all stages of sleep. Only 7 percent of stages 1 and 2 were made up, but 68 percent of stage 4 slow-wave sleep and 53 percent of REM sleep were made up. Other studies (for example, Kales et al., 1970) have found similar results, which suggest that stage 4 sleep and REM sleep are more important than the other stages.

As I mentioned earlier, REM sleep will be discussed later. But what do we know about the possible functions of slow-wave sleep? What happens then that is so important? Both cerebral metabolic rate and cerebral blood flow decline during slow-wave sleep, falling to about 75 percent of the waking level during stage 4 sleep (Sakai et al., 1979; Buchsbaum et al., 1989; Maquet, 1995). In particular, the regions that have the highest levels of activity during waking show the highest levels of delta waves—and the lowest levels of activity—during slow-wave sleep. Thus, the presence of delta activity in a particular region of the brain appears to indicate that that region is resting. As we know from behavioral observation, people are unreactive to all but intense stimuli during slow-wave sleep and, if awakened, act groggy and confused—as if their cerebral cortex has been shut down and has not yet resumed its functioning. These observations suggest that during stage 4 sleep the brain is, indeed, resting.

An inherited neurological disorder called **fatal familial insomnia** results in damage to portions of the thalamus (Sforza et al., 1995; Gallassi et al., 1996). The symptoms of this disease include deficits in attention and memory, followed by a dreamlike, confused state; loss of control of the autonomic nervous system and the endocrine system; and insomnia. The first signs of sleep disturbances are reductions in sleep spindles and K complexes. As the disease progresses, slow-wave sleep completely disappears and only brief episodes of REM sleep (without the accompanying paralysis) remain. As the name indicates, the disease is fatal. Whether the insomnia, caused by the brain damage, contributes to the other symptoms and to the patient's death is not known. In any case, as we shall see in the next section, when laboratory animals are kept awake indefinitely, they, too, will die.

Studies with Laboratory Animals.   Until recently, sleep deprivation studies with animals have provided us with little insight into the role of sleep. Because animals cannot be "persuaded" to stay awake, it is especially difficult to separate the effects of sleep deprivation from those caused by the method used to keep the animals awake. We can ask a human volunteer to try to stay awake and can expect some cooperation. He or she will say, "I'm getting sleepy—help me to stay awake." However, animals are interested only in getting to sleep and must constantly be stimulated—and hence stressed. Rechtschaffen and his colleagues (Rechtschaffen et al., 1983, 1989; Rechtschaffen and Bergmann, 1995) devised a procedure to control for the effects of forced exercise that are necessary to keep an animal from sleeping. They constructed a circular platform on which two rats lived, each restrained in a plastic cage. When the platform was rotated by an electrical motor, the rats were forced to walk to avoid falling into a pool of water. (See *Figure 8.5.*)

Fatal familial insomnia A fatal inherited disorder characterized by progressive insomnia.

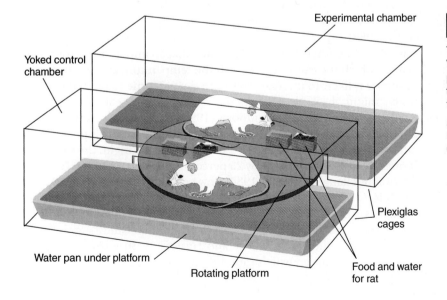

Yoked control chamber

Experimental chamber

Plexiglas cages

Water pan under platform

Rotating platform

Food and water for rat

FIGURE 8 . 5

The apparatus used to deprive rats of sleep. Whenever one of the pair of rats in the experimental chambers fell asleep, the turntable was rotated until the animal was awake for 6 seconds.

(Redrawn from Rechtschaffen, A., Gilliland, M.A., Bergmann, B.M., and Winter, J.B. Science, 1983, 221, 182–184.)

The investigators employed a *yoked-control* procedure to deprive one rat of sleep but force both members of the pair to exercise an equal amount of time. (The term is used for any experiment in which two animals receive the same treatment at the same time, like two oxen fastened together with a yoke.) A computer recorded the EEGs and EMGs of both rats and detected both slow-wave and REM sleep. One rat served as the experimental (sleep-deprived) animal, and the other served as the yoked control. As soon as the EEG recording indicated that the experimental animal was falling asleep, the computer turned on the motor that rotated the disk, forcing both animals to exercise. Because the platform rotated whenever the experimental animal started to sleep, the procedure reduced the experimental animal's total sleep time by 87 percent. However, the sleep time of the yoked-control rat was reduced by only 31 percent.

Sleep deprivation had serious effects. The control animals remained in perfect health. However, the experimental animals looked sick and stopped grooming their fur. They became weak and uncoordinated and lost their ability to regulate their body temperature. (As we will see later, neurons involved in sleep also appear to be involved in thermoregulation.) Although they began eating much more food than normal, their metabolic rates became so high that they continued to lose weight.

As we saw, the effects of sleep deprivation are less drastic in humans than in rats. Perhaps human sleep deprivation studies have just not continued long enough to cause serious harm. The human body is much larger than that of a rat, and changes in metabolic rate would take much longer to affect body weight—and prolonged sleep deprivation of human subjects would clearly be unethical.

Effects of Exercise on Sleep

Sleep deprivation studies with humans suggest that the brain may need slow-wave sleep in order to recover from the day's activities but that the rest of the body does not. Another way to determine whether sleep is needed for restoration of physiological functioning is to look at the effects of daytime activity on nighttime sleep. If the function of sleep is to repair the effects of activity during waking hours, then we should expect that sleep and exercise are related. That is, we should sleep more after a day of vigorous exercise than after a day spent quietly at an office desk.

However, the relation between sleep and exercise is not very compelling. For example, Ryback and Lewis (1971) found no changes in slow-wave or REM sleep of healthy subjects who spent six weeks resting in bed. If sleep repairs wear and tear, we would expect these people to sleep less. Adey, Bors, and Porter (1968) studied the sleep of *completely* immobile quadriplegics and paraplegics and found only a small decrease in slow-wave sleep as compared with uninjured people.

Horne (1981, 1988) reported that some studies have found that exercise increases slow-wave sleep but others have not. He noted that an important factor seems to be the climate in which the exercise occurs. If the temperature and the humidity are high, the exercise is likely to increase slow-wave sleep. Horne suggested that the important variable might be whether the exercise succeeded in heating the body.

To test this hypothesis, Horne and Moore (1985) had subjects exercise on a treadmill. Some subjects were cooled by electric fans, and their skin was periodically sprayed with water. Their body temperature rose only 1° C. That night, the slow-wave sleep of the "hot exercised" subjects rose by 25 percent, whereas that of the "cool exercised" subjects was unchanged. Horne (1988) now believes that the increased body temperature itself is not the significant factor but that an increase in brain temperature is. Perhaps, he said, an increase in brain temperature raises its metabolic rate and hence its demand for more slow-wave sleep. A preliminary study suggests that this hypothesis may have some merit. Horne and Harley (1989) warmed subjects' heads and faces with a hair dryer, which raised their brain temperature by an estimated 1° C. Four of the six subjects showed an increase in slow-wave sleep the next night. Clearly, further research is needed.

Effects of Mental Activity on Sleep

If the primary function of slow-wave sleep is to permit the brain to rest and recover from its daily activity, then we might expect that a person would spend more time in slow-wave sleep after a day of intense cerebral activity. Indeed, as we just saw, that is precisely the way that Horne interpreted the effects of increased body temperature. First of all, tasks that demand alertness and mental activity *do* increase glucose metabolism in the brain, as measured by a PET scanner (Roland, 1984). The most significant increases are seen in the frontal lobes, where delta activity is most intense during slow-wave sleep. In an experiment that supports this interpretation, Kattler, Dijk, and Borbély (1994) stimulated a person's hand with a vibrator, which activated the contralateral somatosensory cortex. The next night, a recording of the subject's EEG showed more delta activity in that region of the brain. Presumably, the increased activity of the cortical neurons called for more rest during the following night's sleep.

In an ingenious study, Horne and Minard (1985) found a way to increase mental activity without affecting physical activity and without causing stress. The investigators told subjects to show up for an experiment in which they were supposed to take some tests designed to measure reading skills. When the subjects turned up, however, they were told that the plans had been changed. They were invited for a day out, at the expense of the experimenters. (Not surprisingly, the subjects willingly accepted.) They spent the day visiting an art exhibition, a shopping center, a museum, an amusement park, a zoo, and an interesting mansion. After a scenic drive through the countryside they watched a movie in a local theater. They were driven from place to place and certainly did not become overheated by exercise. After the movie they returned to the sleep laboratory. They said they were tired, and they readily fell asleep. Their sleep duration was normal, and they awoke feeling refreshed. However, their slow-wave sleep—particularly stage 4 sleep—was increased.

The Functions of REM Sleep

Clearly, REM sleep is a time of intense physiological activity. The eyes dart about rapidly, the heart rate shows sudden accelerations and decelerations, breathing becomes irregular, and the brain becomes more active. It would be unreasonable to expect that REM sleep has the same functions as slow-wave sleep. An early report on the effects of REM sleep deprivation (Dement, 1960) observed that as the deprivation progressed, subjects had to be awakened from REM sleep more frequently; the "pressure" to enter REM sleep built up. Furthermore, after several days of REM sleep deprivation, subjects would show a **rebound phenomenon** when permitted to sleep normally; they spent a much greater-than-normal percentage of the recovery night in REM sleep. This rebound suggests that there is a need for a certain amount of REM sleep—that REM sleep is controlled by a regulatory mechanism. If selective deprivation causes a deficiency in REM sleep, the deficiency is made up later, when uninterrupted sleep is permitted.

How have investigators explained the occurrence of REM sleep? The similarities between REM sleep and waking have led some to suggest that REM sleep permits an animal to become more sensitive to its environment and avoid being surprised by predators (Snyder, 1966). (You will recall that during REM sleep, humans are more sensitive to meaningful stimuli, such as the sound of their name.) Of course, given that an animal spends only a portion of its total sleep time in REM sleep, a predator would have to come by at just the right time for its potential prey to hear it coming.

Other investigators have suggested that REM sleep has a special role in learning. Some investigators suggest that memories of events of the previous day—especially those dealing with emotionally related information—are consolidated and integrated with existing memories (Greenberg and Pearlman, 1974); others have suggested that this time is utilized to accomplish the opposite function: to flush useless information from memory, to prevent the storage of useless clutter (Crick and

Rebound phenomenon The increased frequency or intensity of a phenomenon after it has been temporarily suppressed; for example, the increase in REM sleep seen after a period of REM sleep deprivation.

Mitchison, 1983, 1995). Another investigator (Jouvet, 1980) has suggested that REM sleep helps to integrate learned and instinctive behaviors—it provides a time to modify the neural circuits controlling species-typical behaviors according to the experience gained in the past day. The fact that the sleep of infants consists mainly of REM sleep has suggested to others that this stage is associated with brain development (Roffwarg, Muzio, and Dement, 1966). The association could go either way; brain development could cause REM sleep (perhaps to tidy up after spurts of neural growth), or REM sleep could be setting the stage for brain growth to occur.

As you can see, many hypotheses have been advanced to explain the rather puzzling phenomenon of REM sleep. In the previous two paragraphs I mentioned four categories: *vigilance, learning* (either consolidation or flushing), *species-typical reprogramming,* and *brain development.* It is probably safe to say that when there are so many hypothetical explanations for a phenomenon, we do not know very much about its causes. So far, none of the hypotheses have been either unambiguously supported or proved wrong.

The developmental hypothesis is supported by the fact that infant animals born with well-developed brains (such as guinea pigs) spend proportionally less time in REM sleep than do infant animals born with less-developed brains (such as rats, cats, or humans). Researchers have long been struck by the fact that the highest proportion of REM sleep is seen during the most active phase of brain development. Perhaps, then, REM sleep plays a role in this process. Studies of human fetuses and infants born prematurely indicate that REM sleep begins to appear 30 weeks after conception and peaks at around 40 weeks (Roffwarg, Muzio, and Dement, 1966; Petre-Quadens and De Lee, 1974; Inoue et al., 1986). Approximately 70 percent of a newborn infant's sleep is REM sleep. By six months of age, this proportion has declined to approximately 30 percent. By eight years of age, it has fallen to approximately 22 percent, and by late adulthood, it is less than 15 percent.

But if the function of REM sleep is to promote brain development, why do adults have REM sleep? One possibility is that REM sleep facilitates the massive changes in the brain that occur during development but also the more modest changes responsible for learning that occur later in life. Studies with laboratory animals suggest that REM sleep performs functions that facilitate learning. Investigators have carried out two types of experiments. In the first, they train animals in a learning task and then deprive them of REM sleep for a period of time. If REM sleep facilitates learning—perhaps by promoting changes in the brain that store the information just acquired—then animals that are deprived of the opportunity to engage in REM sleep after the training session should not learn as well as control subjects. In the second type of experiment, investigators train animals in a learning task and then monitor their sleep for several hours. An increase in REM sleep suggests that learning increases the need for this stage of sleep.

Experiments of both types have obtained positive results. For example, when animals are deprived of REM sleep after participating in a training session, they learn the task more slowly; thus, REM sleep deprivation retards memory formation (Smith, 1996). In an example of the second type of experiment, Bloch, Hennevin, and Leconte (1977) gave rats daily training trials in a complex maze. They found that the experience enhanced subsequent REM sleep. Moreover, daily performance was related to subsequent REM sleep. The lower curve in Figure 8.6 shows REM sleep as a percentage of total sleep. The upper curve illustrates the animals' performance in the maze. You can see that the largest increase in running speed (possibly representing the largest increase in learning) was accompanied by the largest amount of REM sleep. Also note that once the task was well learned (after day 6), REM sleep declined to baseline levels. (See *Figure 8.6.*)

A particularly interesting case of brain damage suggests that whatever the functions of REM sleep may be, they do not appear to be necessary for survival. Lavie et al. (1984) reported that a 33-year-old man whose head was injured by shrapnel at age

20 engaged in almost no REM sleep. In the sleep laboratory the man slept an average of 4.5 hours. On three of eight nights he engaged in no REM sleep; the average on the other five nights was approximately 6 minutes. The pieces of metal damaged the pons, left temporal lobe, and left thalamus. As we shall see later in this chapter, the pons seems to be the part of the brain that controls REM sleep. The almost complete lack of REM sleep did not appear to cause serious side effects. After receiving his injury, the man completed high school, attended law school, and began practicing law. (I have a feeling that I could work in a lawyer joke here, but I think I'll refrain.)

INTERIM SUMMARY

The two principal explanations for sleep are that sleep serves as an adaptive response or that it provides a period of restoration. The fact that a species' degree of safety and rate of metabolism are related to the amount of sleep it engages in supports the adaptive hypothesis, but the fact that all vertebrates sleep, including some that would seem to be better off without it, does not.

Deep slow-wave sleep appears to be the most important stage, and perhaps its function is to permit the brain (but not necessarily the rest of the body) to recuperate. Animals that are sleep-deprived for an extended period of time look sick, stop grooming, lose their ability to regulate their body temperature, and, although they eat voraciously, lose weight. Fatal familial insomnia is an inherited disease that results in degeneration of parts of the thalamus, deficits in attention and memory, a dreamlike state, loss of control of the autonomic nervous system and the endocrine system, insomnia, and death.

Exercise can increase the amount of slow-wave sleep a person receives, but only if the brain temperature rises; the effect can be abolished by cooling the person's head and face. Perhaps, then, the most important function of slow-wave sleep is to lower the brain's metabolism and permit it to rest. In support of this hypothesis, research has shown that increased mental activity can cause an increase in slow-wave sleep the next night.

The functions of REM sleep are even less understood than those of slow-wave sleep. REM sleep may promote vigilance, learning, species-typical reprogramming, or brain development. So far, the evidence is inconclusive, although several studies have shown a moderate relation between REM sleep and learning. Whatever functions REM sleep performs, its absence, unlike that of slow-wave sleep, is not fatal.

THOUGHT QUESTIONS

The evidence presented in this section suggests that the primary function of sleep is to permit the brain to rest. But could sleep also have some other functions? For example, could sleep serve as an adaptive response, keeping animals out of harm's way *as well as* provide some cerebral repose? Sleep researcher William Dement pointed out that one of the functions of the lungs is communication. Obviously, the *primary* function of our lungs is to provide oxygen and rid the body of carbon dioxide, and this function explains the evolution of the respiratory system. But we can also use our lungs to vibrate our vocal cords and provide sounds used to talk, so they play a role in communication, too. Other functions of our lungs are to warm our cold hands (by breathing on them), to kindle fires by blowing on hot coals, or to blow out candles. With this perspective in mind, can you think of some other useful functions of sleep?

FIGURE 8.6

Percentage of sleep time spent in REM sleep (*lower curve*) as a function of maze-learning performance (*upper curve*).

(From Bloch, V., Hennevin, E., and Leconte, P., in Neurobiology of Sleep and Memory, edited by R.R. Drucker-Colin and J.L. McGaugh. New York: Academic Press, 1978.)

PHYSIOLOGICAL MECHANISMS OF SLEEP AND WAKING

So far, I have discussed the nature of sleep, its functions, problems associated with it, and the control of biological rhythms. Now it is time to examine what researchers have discovered about the physiological mechanisms that are responsible for the behavior of sleep and for its counterpart, alert wakefulness. But before doing so, I must emphasize that sleep does not occur simply because neurons get tired and begin to fire more slowly. Like other behaviors, sleep occurs when certain neural circuits become *active*.

Chemical Control of Sleep

As we have seen, sleep is *regulated;* that is, if an organism is deprived of slow-wave sleep or REM sleep, the organism will make up at least part of the missed sleep when permitted to do so. In addition, the amount of slow-wave sleep that a person obtains during a daytime nap is deducted from the amount of slow-wave sleep he or she obtains the next night (Karacan et al., 1970). These facts suggest that some physiological mechanism monitors the amount of sleep that an organism receives. What might this mechanism be? Perhaps prolonged wakefulness produces a *sleep-promoting substance* or sleep produces a *wakefullness-promoting substance.*

Where might these substances be located? They do not appear to be found in the general circulation of the body. As we saw earlier, the cerebral hemispheres of the bottlenose dolphin sleep at different times (Mukhametov, 1984). If sleep were controlled by *blood-borne* chemicals, the hemispheres should sleep at the same time. This observation suggests that if sleep is controlled by chemicals, these chemicals are produced within the brain and act there. Several different categories of chemicals affect sleep and wakefulness, but we cannot yet conclude that they are responsible for the insistent urge to sleep that inevitably comes after a long period of wakefulness.

An important category of drugs, the benzodiazepines, promotes sleep. In fact, they are widely used to treat insomnia. As we saw in Chapter 4, these drugs act on the benzodiazepine binding site located at the GABA$_A$ receptor. The existence of a special receptor suggests the existence of at least one endogenous ligand for this receptor, and this ligand could be involved in the control of sleep. However, no one has yet discovered a benzodiazepinelike substance whose concentration in the brain varies as a function of sleepiness.

A second category of drugs affects both sleep and body temperature. For example, anti-inflammatory drugs such as aspirin and ibuprofen reduce body temperature and interfere with sleep (Murphy et al., 1994), and a class of chemicals known as cytokines increases body temperature and produces drowsiness (Knefati et al., 1995; Krueger and Majde, 1995). As we will see later, sleep and thermoregulation are closely related functions. It is possible that the anti-inflammatory drugs and the cytokines affect sleep indirectly, through their effects on body temperature.

As we saw earlier in this chapter, evidence seems to support the hypothesis that slow-wave sleep serves as a period of rest and recuperation for the brain. Presumably, increased mental activity makes the brain become "tired," and the brain displays more delta activity the following night. But what, exactly, does it mean for the brain to become "tired"? The answer is that we do not yet know for certain, but Benington, Kodali, and Heller (1995) suggested the following hypothesis: The primary nutrient of the brain is glucose, carried to it by the blood. The blood supply usually delivers an adequate amount of glucose, but if some regions of the brain become especially active, the cells located there consume the glucose faster than it can be supplied. In such cases, extra nutrients are supplied by astrocytes (Swanson, 1992;

Swanson et al., 1992.). Astrocytes maintain a small stock of nutrients in the form of glycogen, an insoluble carbohydrate that is also stocked by the liver and the muscles. The metabolism of glycogen causes an increase in the levels of **adenosine,** a neuromodulator that has inhibitory effects. Benington and his colleagues suggested that this accumulation of adenosine increases the amount of delta activity during the next night's sleep. The cells in that region rest, and the astrocytes renew their stock of glycogen. In support of this hypothesis, the investigators found that when they administered a drug that stimulates adenosine receptors, they saw increases in delta activity during the animals' slow-wave sleep.

Neural Control of Arousal

As we have seen, sleep is not a unitary condition but consists of several different stages with very different characteristics. Wakefulness, too, is nonuniform; sometimes we are alert and attentive, and sometimes we fail to notice much about what is happening around us. Of course, sleepiness has an effect on wakefulness; if we are fighting to stay awake, the struggle might impair our ability to concentrate on other things. But everyday observations suggest that even when we are not sleepy, our alertness can vary. For example, when we observe something very interesting (or frightening, or simply surprising), we feel ourselves become more activated and aware of our surroundings.

Experimental evidence suggests that the brain stem contains circuits of neurons that can increase an animal's level of alertness and activation—what is commonly referred to as *arousal.* In 1949, Moruzzi and Magoun found that electrical stimulation of the brain stem reticular formation produced arousal. The reticular formation, which occupies the central core of the brain stem, receives collateral axons from ascending sensory pathways. Presumably, sensory input, the event that normally produces arousal, activates the reticular formation by means of these collateral axons. The activated reticular formation then arouses the cerebral cortex by means of two pathways (Jones, 1990). The dorsal pathway projects to the medial and intralaminar nuclei of the thalamus, which in turn projects to the cerebral cortex; and the ventral pathway projects to the lateral hypothalamus, basal ganglia, and basal forebrain region. One part of the basal forebrain region projects extensively to the cerebral cortex, and another part projects to the hippocampus. (See *Figure 8.7.*)

At least three different systems of neurons play a role in some aspect of arousal and wakefulness: noradrenergic, acetylcholinergic, and serotonergic (Marrocco, Witte, and Davidson, 1994). Investigators have long known that catecholamine agonists such as amphetamine produce arousal and sleeplessness. These effects appear to be mediated primarily by the noradrenergic system of the **locus coeruleus,** located in the dorsal pons. Neurons of the locus coeruleus send axons that branch widely, releasing norepinephrine (from axonal varicosities) throughout the neocortex, hippocampus, thalamus, cerebellar cortex, pons, and medulla; thus, they potentially affect widespread and important regions of the brain. (See *Figure 8.8.*)

Aston-Jones and Bloom (1981a) recorded from noradrenergic neurons of the locus coeruleus (LC) across the sleep–waking cycle in unrestrained rats. As Figure 8.9 shows, the activity of these neurons exhibited a close relation to behavioral arousal. Note the decline in firing rate before and during sleep and the abrupt increase when the animal wakes. The rate of firing of neurons in the locus coeruleus falls almost to zero during REM sleep and increases dramatically when the animal wakes. As we shall see later in this chapter, these facts suggest that these neurons (along with serotonergic neurons) play a role in controlling REM sleep. (See *Figure 8.9.*)

Adenosine A chemical produced when increased neural activity requires the breakdown of glycogen stored in astrocytes; may increase delta activity during the next night's sleep and thus enable the region to recover from its energy expenditure.

Locus coeruleus [*sa roo lee us*] A dark-colored group of noradrenergic cell bodies located in the pons near the rostral end of the floor of the fourth ventricle; involved in arousal and vigilance.

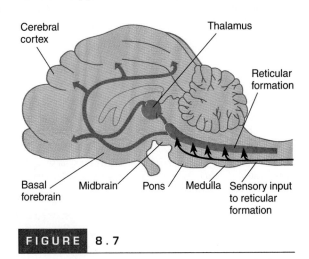

FIGURE 8.7

A midsagittal view of a cat brain, showing the reticular formation and its hypothesized role in arousal.

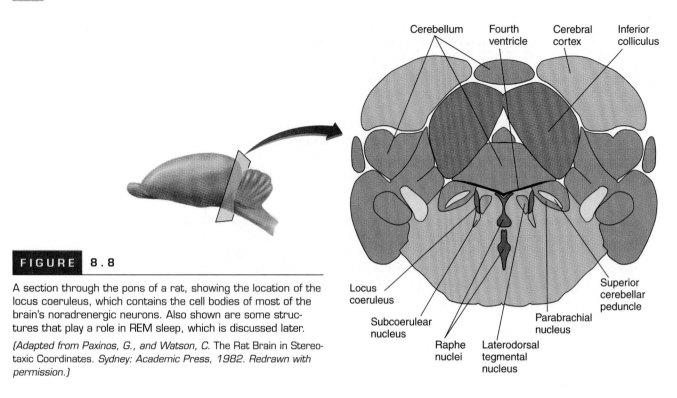

FIGURE 8.8

A section through the pons of a rat, showing the location of the locus coeruleus, which contains the cell bodies of most of the brain's noradrenergic neurons. Also shown are some structures that play a role in REM sleep, which is discussed later.

(Adapted from Paxinos, G., and Watson, C. The Rat Brain in Stereotaxic Coordinates. Sydney: Academic Press, 1982. Redrawn with permission.)

The second neurotransmitter involved in arousal is acetylcholine. Two groups of acetylcholinergic neurons, one in the pons and one located in the basal forebrain, produce activation and cortical desynchrony when they are stimulated (Jones, 1990; Steriade, 1996). Researchers have long known that acetylcholinergic antagonists decrease EEG signs of cortical arousal and that acetylcholinergic agonists increase them (Vanderwolf, 1992). Day, Damsma, and Fibiger (1991) used microdialysis probes to measure the release of acetylcholine in the striatum, hippocampus, and frontal cortex—three regions whose activity is closely related to an animal's alertness and behavioral arousal. They found that the levels of ACh in these regions were closely related to the animals' level of activity. In addition, Rasmusson, Clow, and Szerb (1994) electrically stimulated a region of the pontine reticular formation and found that the stimulation activated the cerebral cortex and increased the release of acetylcholine there by 350 percent (as measured by microdialysis probes).

A third neurotransmitter, serotonin (5-HT), also appears to play a role in activating behavior. Almost all of the brain's serotonergic neurons are found in the **raphe nuclei,** which are located in the medullary and pontine regions of the retic-

Raphe nuclei (*ruh fay*) A group of nuclei located in the reticular formation of the medulla, pons, and midbrain, situated along the midline; contain serotonergic neurons.

FIGURE 8.9

Activity of noradrenergic neurons in the locus coeruleus of freely moving rats during various stages of sleep and waking.

(From Aston-Jones, G., and Bloom, F.E. The Journal of Neuroscience, 1981, 1, 876–886. Copyright 1981, The Society for Neuroscience.)

ular formation. (See *Figure 8.10.*) The axons of these neurons project to many parts of the brain, including the thalamus, hypothalamus, basal ganglia, hippocampus, and neocortex. Stimulation of the raphe nuclei causes locomotion and cortical arousal (as measured by the EEG), whereas PCPA, a drug that prevents the synthesis of serotonin, reduces cortical arousal (Peck and Vanderwolf, 1991).

Figure 8.11 shows the activity of serotonergic neurons, recorded by Trulson and Jacobs (1979). As you can see, these neurons, like the noradrenergic neurons studied by Aston-Jones and Bloom (1981a), were most active during waking. Their firing rate declined during slow-wave sleep and became virtually zero during REM sleep. However, once the period of REM sleep ended, the neurons temporarily became very active again. (See *Figure 8.11.*)

Neural Control of Slow-Wave Sleep

Although sleep is a behavior that involves most of the brain, one region seems to be particularly important: the **basal forebrain region,** located just rostral to the hypothalamus. Nauta (1946) found that destruction of this area produced total insomnia in rats. The animals subsequently fell into a coma and died; the average survival time was only three days. McGinty and Sterman (1968) found that cats reacted somewhat differently; the animals did not become sleepless until several days after the lesion was made. Two of the cats, whose sleep was totally suppressed, died within ten days. Infusions of kainic acid into the basal forebrain region, which destroy cell bodies without damaging axons passing through the region, also suppress sleep (Szymusiak and McGinty, 1986b).

The effects of these lesion experiments are corroborated by the effects of electrical stimulation of the basal forebrain region. Sterman and Clemente (1962a,

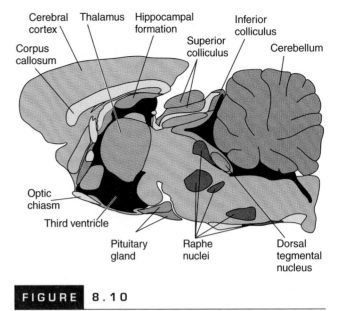

FIGURE 8.10

The raphe nuclei, the location of the cell bodies of most of the brain's serotonergic neurons.

[Adapted from Paxinos, G., and Watson, C. The Rat Brain in Stereotaxic Coordinates. Sydney: Academic Press, 1982.]

Basal forebrain region The region at the base of the forebrain rostral to the hypothalamus; involved in thermoregulation and control of sleep.

FIGURE 8.11

Activity of serotonergic (5-HT-secreting) neurons in the dorsal raphe nuclei of freely moving cats during various stages of sleep and waking.

[Adapted from Trulson, M.E., and Jacobs, B.L. Brain Research, 1979, 163, 135–150.]

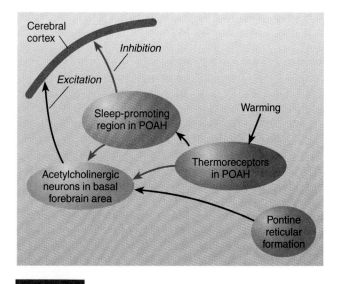

FIGURE 8.12

A schematic diagram of the role of the POAH in the sleep-promoting effects of warming and the wakefulness-promoting effects of the pontine reticular formation. The role of the thalamus is omitted for simplicity.

POAH The region of the preoptic area and the adjacent anterior hypothalamus, involved in thermoregulation and induction of slow-wave sleep.

PGO wave Bursts of phasic electrical activity originating in the pons, followed by activity in the lateral geniculate nucleus and visual cortex; a characteristic of REM sleep.

1962b) found that electrical stimulation of this region produced signs of drowsiness in the behavior and the EEG of unanesthetized, freely moving cats. The average latency period between the stimulation and the changes in the EEG was 30 seconds, but sometimes the effect was immediate. The animals often subsequently fell asleep.

A considerable amount of evidence suggests that forebrain mechanisms involved in sleep are closely linked to those involved in thermoregulation—an animal's ability to regulate its body temperature. Part of the basal forebrain, the preoptic area and the adjacent anterior hypothalamus (often referred to as the **POAH**), contains neurons involved in thermoregulation. Some of these neurons are directly sensitive to changes in brain temperature, and some receive information from thermosensors located in the skin. Warming of the POAH, like electrical stimulation, induces slow-wave sleep (McGinty, Szymusiak, and Thomson, 1994). Thus, a more "natural" stimulation mimics the effects of electrical stimulation. In addition, many neurons in the POAH increase their rate of firing when the animal falls asleep, and most of them also do so in response to increases in body temperature (Scammell, Price, and Sagar, 1993; Alam et al., 1995a, 1995b). The excessive sleepiness that accompanies a fever may be produced by this mechanism. And perhaps the connections between the thermosensors in the skin and the POAH account for the drowsiness and lassitude we feel on a hot day. (See *Figure 8.12.*)

As we saw earlier in this chapter, the most likely function of slow-wave sleep is to permit the brain to rest. As Horne and his colleagues showed, when people's brains are warmed during the day, they engage in more sleep the following night. And sleep appears to reduce brain temperature. You will recall that the cerebral hemispheres of dolphins take turns sleeping. Kolvalzon and Mukhametov (1982) found that the temperature of the sleeping hemisphere was always lower than that of the awake one. Furthermore, the injection of prostaglandins into the preoptic area raises body temperature and increases slow-wave sleep (Hayaishi, 1988), whereas drugs that inhibit the synthesis of prostaglandins (such as aspirin or ibuprofen) lower body temperature and reduce slow-wave sleep (Naito et al., 1988; Murphy et al., 1994).

Neural Control of REM Sleep

As we saw earlier in this chapter, REM sleep consists of desynchronized EEG activity, muscular paralysis, rapid eye movements, and (in humans, at least) increased genital activity. The rate of cerebral metabolism is as high as it is during waking (Maquet et al., 1990), and were it not for the state of paralysis, the level of *physical* activity would also be high. In laboratory animals, REM sleep also includes *PGO waves*. **PGO waves** (for **p**ons, **g**eniculate, and **o**ccipital) are the first manifestation of REM sleep. They consist of brief, phasic bursts of electrical activity that originate in the pons and are propagated to the lateral geniculate nuclei and then to the primary visual (occipital) cortex. They can be seen only when electrodes are placed directly into the brain, so they have not been recorded in humans. It seems likely, however, that they occur in our species, too. Figure 8.13 shows the typical onset of REM sleep, recorded in a cat. The first sign of an impending bout of REM sleep is the presence of PGO waves—in this case, recorded from electrodes implanted in the lateral geniculate nucleus. Next, the EEG becomes desynchronized, and then muscular activity ceases and rapid eye movements commence. (See *Figure 8.13.*)

As we shall see, REM sleep is controlled by mechanisms located within the pons. The executive mechanism (that is, the one whose activity turns on the various components of REM sleep) consists of a group of neurons that secrete acetylcholine.

FIGURE 8.13

Onset of REM sleep in a cat. The arrows indicate the onset of PGO waves, EEG desynchrony (beta activity), loss of muscular activity, and rapid eye movements. LG = lateral geniculate nucleus; EOG = electro-oculogram (eye movements).

[Adapted from Steriade, M., Paré, D., Bouhassira, D., Deschênes, M., and Oakson, G. Journal of Neuroscience, 1989, 9, 2215–2229.]

During waking and slow-wave sleep, REM sleep is inhibited by the serotonergic neurons of the raphe nuclei and the noradrenergic neurons of the locus coeruleus.

The Executive Mechanism

Researchers have long known that acetylcholinergic agonists facilitate REM sleep. Stoyva and Metcalf (1968) found that people who have been exposed to organophosphate insecticides, which act as acetylcholine agonists, spend an increased time in REM sleep. In a controlled experiment with human subjects, Sitaram, Moore, and Gillin (1978) found that an ACh agonist (arecoline) shortened the interval between periods of REM sleep and that a cholinergic antagonist (scopolamine) lengthened it.

Jasper and Tessier (1969) analyzed the levels of acetylcholine that had been released by terminal buttons in the cat cerebral cortex. They found that the levels of ACh were highest during waking and REM sleep and were lowest during slow-wave sleep. Using 2-DG autoradiography in cats, Lydic et al. (1991) found that the rate of glucose metabolism was elevated in those regions of the brain that contain ACh-secreting neurons or that receive input from the axons of these neurons. As we saw earlier in this chapter, acetylcholinergic neurons play an important role in cerebral activation during alert wakefulness. The findings I just cited suggest that these neurons are also responsible for the cerebral activation that is seen during REM sleep.

The brain contains several groups of acetylcholinergic neurons. The ones that play the most central role in triggering the onset of REM sleep are found in the dorsolateral pons, primarily in the *pedunculopontine tegmental nucleus* (PPT) and *laterodorsal tegmental nucleus* (LDT) (Jones and Beaudet, 1987). Most investigators now refer to this region as the **peribrachial area,** because it is located in the region of the brachium conjunctivum. Figure 8.14 contains two drawings through the brain stem of a cat, prepared by Jones and Beaudet (1987). The locations of acetylcholinergic cell bodies (identified by a stain for choline acetyltransferase) are shown by colored circles. As you can see, these neurons surround the brachium conjunctivum (bc). (See *Figure 8.14.*)

Peribrachial area (*pair ee bray kee ul*) The region around the brachium conjunctivum, located in the dorsolateral pons; contains acetylcholinergic neurons involved in the initiation of REM sleep.

FIGURE 8.14

Acetylcholinergic neurons (colored circles) in the peribrachial area of the cat, as revealed by a stain for choline acetyltransferase. LDT = laterodorsal tegmental nucleus; PPT = pedunculopontine tegmental nucleus; bc = brachium conjunctivum, IC = inferior colliculus.

[Adapted from Jones, B.E., and Beaudet, A. Journal of Comparative Neurology, 1987, 261, 15–32. Reprinted with permission.]

(a)

10 sec

(b)

FIGURE 8.15

Firing pattern of an acetylcholinergic REM-ON cell in the peribrachial area of the pons. (a) Action potentials during 60-sec intervals during waking, slow-wave sleep, and REM sleep. (b) Rate of firing just before and after the transition from slow-wave sleep to REM sleep. The increase in activity begins approximately 80 sec before the onset of REM sleep.

[Adapted from El Mansari, M., Sakai, K., and Jouvet, M. *Experimental Brain Research*, *1989, 76, 519–529.*]

Several studies (for example, El Mansari, Sakai, and Jouvet, 1989; Steriade et al., 1990; Kayama, Ohta, and Jodo, 1992) have shown that the activity of single neurons in the peribrachial area is related to the sleep cycle. Most of these neurons fire at a high rate during REM sleep or during both REM sleep and active wakefulness. Figure 8.15 shows the activity of a so-called *REM-ON* cell, which fires at a high rate only during REM sleep. As you can see, this neuron increased its activity approximately 80 sec before the onset of REM sleep. The increase in the activity of these acetylcholinergic cells may be the event that initiates a bout of REM sleep. (See *Figure 8.15.*)

Webster and Jones (1988) made lesions of the peribrachial area by infusing kainic acid into this region. They found that REM sleep was drastically reduced. The amount of REM sleep that remained was directly related to the number of cholinergic neurons that were spared.

Where do the acetylcholinergic neurons of the peribrachial area exert their effects? The axons of these neurons project to the medial pontine reticular formation; to several regions of the forebrain, including the thalamus, basal ganglia, preoptic area, hippocampus, hypothalamus, and cingulate cortex; and to several brain stem regions involved with the control of eye movements (Cornwall, Cooper, and Phillipson, 1990; Bolton, Cornwall, and Phillipson, 1993).

Let us examine the role of these connections. If a small amount of **carbachol,** a drug that stimulates acetylcholine receptors, is infused into the **medial pontine reticular formation (MPRF)**, the animal will display some or all of the components of REM sleep (Katayama et al., 1986; Callaway et al., 1987). Carbachol is effective when infused into the MPRF because it stimulates postsynaptic acetylcholine receptors of neurons that receive projections from the ACh cells of the peribrachial area (Quattrochi et al., 1989). For this reason, this region is often referred to as the *cholinoceptive* region of the MPRF (because it is *receptive* to ACh). As you might expect, lesions of the MPRF, like those of the peribrachial area, reduce or abolish REM sleep (Siegel, 1989). (See *Figure 8.16.*)

If the acetylcholinergic neurons in the peribrachial area of the pons are responsible for the onset of REM sleep, how do they control each of its components: cortical arousal, PGO waves, rapid eye movements, and muscular paralysis? As we saw, the acetylcholinergic neurons of the pons comprise an integral part of the reticular activating system. They send axons directly to regions of the thalamus that are involved in the control of cortical arousal. In addition, these neurons send

Peribrachial area contains ACh-secreting neurons. Lesions disrupt REM sleep.

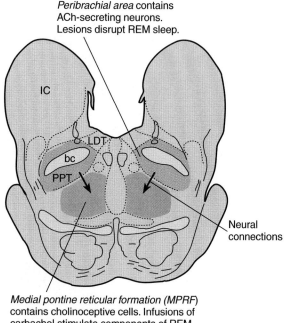

Neural connections

Medial pontine reticular formation (MPRF) contains cholinoceptive cells. Infusions of carbachol stimulate components of REM sleep. Lesions disrupt REM sleep.

FIGURE 8.16

A cross section through the pons of a cat, showing the locations of the peribrachial area and the medial pontine reticular formation (MPRF), regions involved in the control of REM sleep.

axons to glutamatergic neurons in the mesopontine reticular formation, which, in turn, send axons to the acetylcholinergic neurons of the basal forebrain. Activation of the forebrain neurons produces arousal and cortical desynchrony. PGO waves appear to be controlled by direct connections between the peribrachial area and the lateral geniculate nucleus (Sakai and Jouvet, 1980; Steriade, Paré, Datta, Oakson, and Curró Dossi, 1990). The control of rapid eye movements appears to be achieved by projections from the peribrachial area to the tectum (Webster and Jones, 1988).

A recent PET study with human volunteers (Braun et al., 1998) obtained some interesting results that may be related to dreaming. They found that during REM sleep, neural activity increased significantly in the ventral stream of the visual association cortex—the region of the brain involved in analysis of visual shapes. However, neural activity in the primary visual cortex—the region of the brain that receives visual information from the eyes—was suppressed. These findings are what we might predict would occur when a person is having a visual hallucination—perceptual activity without actual visual input.

The last of the REM-related phenomenon, muscular paralysis, is particularly interesting. As we will see, some patients with lesions in the brain stem fail to become paralyzed during REM sleep and thus act out their dreams. (This phenomenon is called *REM without atonia.*) The same thing happens to cats—that is, assuming that they dream—when a lesion is placed just caudal to the peribrachial area of the pons. Jouvet (1972) described this phenomenon:

> To a naive observer, the cat, which is standing, looks awake since it may attack unknown enemies, play with an absent mouse, or display flight behavior. There are orienting movements of the head or eyes toward imaginary stimuli, although the animal does not respond to visual or auditory stimuli. These extraordinary episodes . . . are a good argument that "dreaming" occurs during [REM sleep] in the cat. (Jouvet, 1972, pp. 236–237)

Jouvet's lesions destroyed a set of neurons responsible for the muscular paralysis that occurs during REM sleep. These neurons, which are activated by nonacetylcholinergic neurons, are located just ventral to the locus coeruleus—in the subcoerulear region. Their axons travel caudally to the **magnocellular nucleus,** located in the medial medulla (Sakai, 1980). Neurons in the magnocellular nucleus send axons to the spinal cord, where they form inhibitory synapses with motor neurons (Morales, Boxer, and Chase, 1987). (See *Figure 8.17.*)

The fact that our brains contain an elaborate mechanism whose sole function is to keep us paralyzed while we dream—that is, to prevent us from acting out our dreams—suggests that the motor components of dreams are as important as the sensory components. Perhaps the practice our motor system gets during REM sleep helps us improve our performance of behaviors we have learned that day. The inhibition of the motor neurons in the spinal cord prevents the movements being practiced from actually occurring, with the exception of a few harmless twitches of the hands and feet.

As you will certainly appreciate, the neural circuitry controlling REM sleep is rather complicated. Figure 8.18 summarizes the evidence I have just reviewed. The first event preceding a bout of REM sleep appears to be activation of acetylcholinergic neurons in the peribrachial area of the dorsolateral pons. These neurons directly activate brain stem mechanisms responsible for rapid eye movements and trigger PGO waves through their connections with the lateral geniculate nucleus of the thalamus. They also activate neurons in the subcoerulear area that, through their connections

Carbachol (*car ba call*) A drug that stimulates acetylcholine receptors.

Medial pontine reticular formation (MPRF) A region that contains neurons involved in the initiation of REM sleep; activated by acetylcholinergic neurons of the peribrachial area.

Magnocellular nucleus A nucleus in the medulla; involved in the atonia (muscular paralysis) that accompanies REM sleep.

FIGURE   8.17

The neural pathway responsible for the muscular paralysis that occurs during REM sleep.

Pons

Neuron in subcoerulear nucleus

Medulla

Inhibitory neuron in magnocellular nucleus

Motor neuron

Muscle

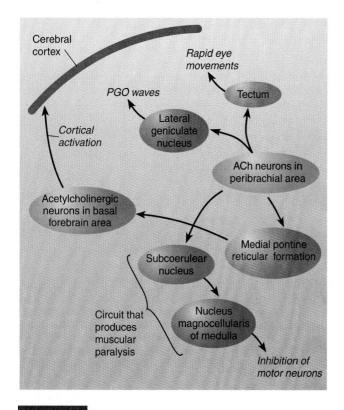

FIGURE 8.18

A summary of the neural circuitry thought to be responsible for REM sleep. The dashed arrow represents a connection from the MPRF to the peribrachial area that appears to be responsible for some of the phenomena of REM sleep produced by infusion of carbachol into the MPRF.

FIGURE 8.19

Interactions between serotonergic, noradrenergic, and acetylcholinergic neurons in the control of REM sleep.

with the nucleus magnocellularis of the medulla, produce atonia. Finally, these neurons activate neurons in the MPRF that, in turn, activate acetylcholinergic neurons of the basal forebrain responsible for the cortical activation that accompanies REM sleep. (See *Figure 8.18.*)

One of the factors (but certainly not the only one) that stimulates REM sleep is temperature. As we saw, brain temperature falls during slow-wave sleep; in fact, this fall in temperature (reflecting a decrease in metabolic activity of the brain) may even be one of the major functions of this phase of sleep. The fall in temperature appears to stimulate neurons responsible for REM sleep (Jouvet, 1975). The increased brain activity that occurs during REM sleep causes a rise in brain temperature, which then falls again during the subsequent period of slow-wave sleep.

Inhibitory Effects of Serotonin and Norepinephrine

As you will learn in a discussion of sleep disorders later in this chapter, serotonergic and noradrenergic agonists have inhibitory effects on REM sleep. In addition, the rate of activity in the serotonergic neurons of the raphe nuclei and that of the noradrenergic neurons of the locus coeruleus are at their very lowest levels during REM sleep. The patterns of firing of noradrenergic neurons of the locus coeruleus and the serotonergic neurons of the raphe nuclei were presented in Figures 8.9 and 8.11.

Evidence suggests that the activity of neurons in the locus coeruleus and the dorsal raphe nucleus normally inhibits REM sleep and that a reduction in the rate of firing of these neurons is the event that triggers a bout of REM sleep. Acetylcholinergic neurons in the peribrachial area receive both serotonergic and noradrenergic inputs (Honda and Semba, 1994; Leonard et al., 1995), and infusion of inhibitors of norepinephrine or serotonin into the pons causes an increase in REM sleep (Bier and McCarley, 1994; Portas et al., 1996).

Several unanswered questions await further research. What makes the neurons of the locus coeruleus and the dorsal raphe nuclei become silent? Is there an excitatory input to the peribrachial area as well as the inhibitory ones whose activity *increases* at the beginning of REM sleep? Where is the pacemaker that controls the regular cycles of REM and slow-wave sleep, and how is this pacemaker connected to the REM sleep mechanisms in the pons? Finally, are rises and falls in brain temperature partly responsible for these cycles? (See *Figure 8.19.*)

INTERIM SUMMARY

The fact that the amount of sleep is regulated suggests that sleep-promoting substances (produced during wakefulness) or wakefulness-promoting substances (produced during sleep) may exist. The sleeping pattern of the dolphin brain suggests that such substances do not accumulate in the blood. They may accumulate in the brain, but so far, attempts to find them have not been successful. One hypothesis suggests that adenosine, released when neurons are obliged to utilize the supply of glycogen stored in astrocytes, serves as the link between increased brain metabolism and the necessity of sleep.

Three systems of neurons appear to be important for alert, active wakefulness: the noradrenergic system of the locus coeruleus, the acetylcholinergic system of the peribrachial area of the pons and the basal forebrain, and the serotonergic system of the raphe nuclei.

Slow-wave sleep occurs when neurons in the basal forebrain become active. These neurons are also sensitive to changes in temperature, leading some investigators to suggest that an important function of slow-wave sleep is to lower brain temperature (and permit the brain to rest). REM sleep occurs when the activity of acetylcholinergic neurons in the peribrachial area increases. These neurons initiate PGO waves and cortical arousal through their connections with the thalamus, and they activate neurons in the MPRF whose axons travel to the acetylcholinergic neurons of the basal forebrain. The peribrachial neurons also produce rapid eye movements. Atonia (muscular paralysis that prevents our acting out our dreams) is produced by a group of acetylcholinergic neurons located in the subcoerulear nucleus that activate other neurons located in the magnocellular nucleus of the medulla, which in turn produce inhibition of motor neurons in the spinal cord. REM sleep, too, is related to temperature; it occurs only after the brain temperature has been lowered by a period of slow-wave sleep.

The noradrenergic neurons of the locus coeruleus and the serotonergic neurons of the raphe nuclei have inhibitory effects on pontine neurons responsible for REM sleep. Bouts of REM sleep begin only after the activity of the noradrenergic and serotonergic neurons ceases; whether this event is the only one to trigger REM sleep or whether direct excitation of acetylcholinergic neurons also occurs is not yet known.

■ THOUGHT QUESTIONS

Have you ever been lying in bed, almost asleep, when you suddenly thought of something important you had forgotten to do? Did you then suddenly become fully awake and alert? If so, neurons in your reticular formation undoubtedly became active, which aroused your cerebral cortex. What do you think the source of this activation was? What activated your reticular formation? How would you go about answering this question? What research methods described in Chapter 5 would be helpful?

■ DISORDERS OF SLEEP

Insomnia

Insomnia is a problem that is said to affect at least 20 percent of the population at some time (Raybin and Detre, 1969). At the outset I must emphasize that there is no single definition of insomnia that can apply to all people. The amount of sleep that individuals require is quite variable. A short sleeper may feel fine with 5 hours; a long sleeper may still feel unrefreshed after 10 hours of sleep. Insomnia must be defined in relation to a person's particular sleep needs. Some short sleepers have sought medical assistance because they thought that they were supposed to get more sleep, even though they felt fine. These people should be reassured that whatever amount of sleep seems to be enough *is* enough. Meddis, Pearson, and Langford (1973) reported the case of a 70-year-old woman who slept approximately 1 hour each day (documented by sessions in a sleep laboratory). She felt fine and was of the opinion that most people "wasted much time" in bed.

Ironically, one of the most important causes of insomnia seems to be sleeping medication. Insomnia is not a disease that can be corrected with a medicine, in the way that diabetes can be treated with insulin. Insomnia is a symptom. If it is caused by pain or discomfort, the physical ailment that leads to the sleeplessness should be treated. If it is secondary to personal problems or psychological disorders, these problems should be dealt with directly. Patients who receive a sleeping medication develop a tolerance to the drug and suffer rebound symptoms if it is withdrawn (Weitzman, 1981). That is, the drug loses its effectiveness, so the patient requests larger doses from the physician. If the patient attempts to sleep without the accustomed medication or even takes a smaller dose one night, he or she is likely to experience a withdrawal effect: a severe disturbance of sleep. The patient becomes convinced that the insomnia is even worse than before and turns to more medication for relief. This common syndrome is called **drug dependency insomnia.** Kales et al. (1979) found that withdrawal of some sleeping medications produced a rebound insomnia after the drugs were used for as few as three nights.

Most patients who receive a prescription for a sleeping medication are given one on the basis of their own description of their symptoms. That is, they tell their physician that they sleep very little at night, and the drug is prescribed on the basis of this testimony. Very few patients are observed during a night's sleep in a sleep laboratory; thus, insomnia is one of the few medical problems that physicians treat without having direct clinical evidence for its existence. But studies on the sleep of people who complain of insomnia show that most of them grossly underestimate the amount of time they actually sleep. The U.S. Institute of Medicine (1979) found that most insomniacs, even without sleeping medication, fall asleep in less than 30 minutes and sleep for at least 6 hours. *With* sleeping medication they obtained less than a 15-minute reduction in falling asleep, and their sleep length was increased by only about 30 minutes. Given the unfortunate side effects, sleeping medication does not seem to be worthwhile, except perhaps on a short-term basis.

For many years, the goal of sleeping medication was to help people fall asleep, and when drug companies evaluated potential medications, they concentrated on that property. However, if we think about the ultimate goal of sleeping medication, it is to make the person feel more refreshed the next day. If a medication puts people to sleep right away but produces a hangover of grogginess and difficulty concentrating the next day, it is worse than useless. In fact, many drugs that traditionally were used to treat insomnia had just this effect. More recently, researchers have recognized that the true evaluation of a sleeping medication must be made the following day, and "hangover-free" drugs are finally being developed (Hajak et al., 1995).

A particular form of insomnia is caused by the inability to sleep and breathe at the same time. Patients with this disorder, called **sleep apnea,** fall asleep and then cease to breathe. (Nearly all people, especially people who snore, have occasional episodes of sleep apnea, but not to the extent that it interferes with sleep.) During a period of sleep apnea the level of carbon dioxide in the blood stimulates chemoreceptors (neurons that detect the presence of certain chemicals), and the person wakes up, gasping for air. The oxygen level of the blood returns to normal, the person falls asleep, and the whole cycle begins again. Fortunately, many cases of sleep apnea are caused by an obstruction of the airway that can be corrected surgically or relieved by a device that attaches to the sleeper's face and provides pressurized air that keeps the airway open (Sher, 1990; Westbrook, 1990).

Problems Associated with REM Sleep

Narcolepsy (*narke* means "numbness," and *lepsis* means "seizure") is a neurological disorder characterized by sleep (or some of its components) at inappropriate times. The symptoms can be described in terms of what we know about the phenomena of sleep. The primary symptom of narcolepsy is the **sleep attack.** The narcoleptic sleep

---

Drug dependency insomnia An insomnia caused by the side effects of ever-increasing doses of sleeping medications.

Sleep apnea (*app nee a*) Cessation of breathing while sleeping.

Narcolepsy (*nahr ko lep see*) A sleep disorder characterized by periods of irresistible sleep, attacks of cataplexy, sleep paralysis, and hypnagogic hallucinations.

Sleep attack A symptom of narcolepsy; an irresistible urge to sleep during the day, after which the person awakes feeling refreshed.

attack is an overwhelming urge to sleep that can happen at any time but occurs most often under monotonous, boring conditions. Sleep (which appears to be entirely normal) generally lasts for 2–5 minutes. The person usually wakes up feeling refreshed.

Another symptom of narcolepsy—in fact, the most striking one—is **cataplexy** (from *kata,* "down," and *plexis,* "stroke"). During a cataplectic attack, a person will suddenly wilt and fall like a sack of flour. The person will lie there, *fully conscious,* for a few seconds to several minutes. What apparently happens is that one of the phenomena of REM sleep—muscular paralysis—occurs at an inappropriate time. As we saw, this loss of tonus is caused by massive inhibition of motor neurons in the spinal cord. When this happens during waking, the victim of a cataplectic attack falls as suddenly as if a switch had been thrown.

Cataplexy is quite different from a narcoleptic sleep attack; cataplexy is usually precipitated by strong emotion or by sudden physical effort, especially if the patient is caught unawares. Laughter, anger, or an effort to catch a suddenly thrown object can trigger a cataplectic attack. In fact, as Guilleminault, Wilson, and Dement (1974) noted, even people who do not have cataplexy sometimes lose muscle strength after a bout of intense laughter. (Perhaps that is why we say that a person can become "weak from laughter.") Common situations that bring on cataplexy are attempting to discipline one's children or making love (an awkward time to become paralyzed!). Michael, the man described in the Prologue, had his first cataplectic attack when he was addressing the board of directors.

REM sleep paralysis sometimes intrudes into waking, but at a time that does not present any physical danger—just before or just after normal sleep, when a person is already lying down. This symptom of narcolepsy is referred to as **sleep paralysis,** an inability to move just before the onset of sleep or upon waking in the morning. A person can be snapped out of sleep paralysis by being touched or by hearing someone call his or her name. Sometimes, the mental components of REM sleep intrude into sleep paralysis; that is, the person dreams while lying awake, paralyzed. These episodes, called **hypnagogic hallucinations,** are often alarming or even terrifying. (The term *hypnagogic* comes from the Greek words *hupnos,* "sleep," and *agogos,* "leading.")

Almost certainly, narcolepsy is produced by a brain abnormality that causes the neural mechanisms responsible for various aspects of REM sleep to become active at inappropriate times. Indeed, Rechtschaffen et al. (1963) found that narcoleptic patients generally skip the slow-wave sleep that normally begins a night's sleep; instead, they go directly into REM sleep from waking. This finding suggests that in the brains of narcoleptics, the neural mechanisms that produce REM sleep are poorly controlled.

Narcolepsy is primarily a genetic disorder, caused by one of two different mutations (Aldrich, 1992). Occasionally, the disorder can also be caused by brain damage (D'Cruz et al., 1994). Researchers have even successfully bred dogs that are afflicted with narcolepsy. (See *Figure 8.20.*) Slices of the dogs' brains do not show any obvious abnormalities in brain structure, but Nishino et al. (1994, 1995) found that acetyl-

Cataplexy [*kat a plex ee*] A symptom of narcolepsy; complete paralysis that occurs during waking.

Sleep paralysis A symptom of narcolepsy; paralysis occurring just before a person falls asleep.

Hypnagogic hallucination [*hip na gah jik*] A symptom of narcolepsy; vivid dreams that occur just before a person falls asleep; accompanied by sleep paralysis.

FIGURE 8.20

A dog undergoing a cataplectic attack triggered by its excitement at finding some food on the floor. (a) Sniffing the food. (b) Muscles beginning to relax. (c) Dog is temporarily paralyzed, as it would be during REM sleep.

(Photos courtesy of the Sleep Disorders Foundation, Stanford University.)

(a)　　　　　　　　　(b)　　　　　　　　　(c)

cholinergic neurons involved in control of REM sleep in these animals were more excitable than those in normal brains. Another study (Nitz et al., 1995) found that the brains of narcoleptic dogs contained a larger number of these neurons.

The symptoms of narcolepsy can be successfully treated with drugs. As we saw, both noradrenergic and serotonergic neurons exert inhibitory control over the acetylcholinergic neurons in the peribrachial area. Sleep attacks are diminished by stimulants such as amphetamine, a catecholamine agonist. The REM sleep phenomena (cataplexy, sleep paralysis, and hypnagogic hallucinations) can be alleviated by antidepressant drugs, which facilitate both serotonergic and noradrenergic activity (Mitler, 1994; Hublin, 1996). Often, the drugs are given together.

Schenck et al. (1986) reported the existence of an interesting disorder. The formal name is *REM sleep behavior disorder,* but a better name is **REM without atonia.** (*Atonia* refers to the lack of muscular activity seen during paralysis.) As you now know, REM sleep is accompanied by paralysis. Despite the fact that the motor cortex and subcortical motor systems are extremely active (McCarley and Hobson, 1979), people are unable to move at this time. The fact that they are dreaming suggests the possibility that but for the paralysis, they would act out their dreams. Indeed, they would. The behavior of people who exhibit REM without atonia corresponds with the contents of their dreams. Consider the following case:

> I was a halfback playing football, and after the quarterback received the ball from the center he lateraled it sideways to me and I'm supposed to go around end and cut back over tackle and—this is very vivid—as I cut back over tackle there is this big 280-pound tackle waiting, so I, according to football rules, was to give him my shoulder and bounce him out of the way . . . when I came to I was standing in front of our dresser and I had [gotten up out of bed and run and] knocked lamps, mirrors and everything off the dresser, hit my head against the wall and my knee against the dresser. (Schenck et al., 1986, p. 294)

Like narcolepsy, REM without atonia appears to be an inherited disorder (Schenck et al., 1996). In addition, it can be caused by brain damage—apparently, to the pathway between the subcoerulear region and the magnocellular nucleus (Culebras and Moore, 1989). The symptoms of REM without atonia are the opposite of those of cataplexy; that is, rather than exhibiting paralysis outside REM sleep, patients with REM without atonia *fail* to exhibit paralysis *during* REM sleep. As you might expect, the drugs used to treat the symptoms of cataplexy will aggravate the symptoms of REM without atonia (Schenck and Mahowald, 1992). REM without atonia is usually treated by clonazepam, a benzodiazepine (Schenck, Hurwitz, and Mahowald, 1993).

Problems Associated with Slow-Wave Sleep

Some maladaptive behaviors occur during slow-wave sleep, especially during its deepest phase, stage 4. *Sleepwalking* can be as simple as getting out of bed and right back in again or as complicated as walking out of a house and climbing into a car. (Fortunately, sleepwalkers apparently do not try to drive.) We know that sleepwalking is not the acting out of a dream because it occurs during stage 4 of slow-wave sleep, when the EEG shows high-amplitude slow waves and the person's mental state generally involves a static situation, not a narrative. Sleepwalkers are difficult to awaken; once awakened, they are often confused and disoriented. However, contrary to popular belief, it is perfectly safe to wake them up.

Sleepwalking is *not* a manifestation of some deep-seated emotional problem. Most sleepwalkers are children, who almost invariably outgrow this behavior. The worst thing to do, according to sleep researchers, is to try to get them treated for it. Of course, a house inhabited by a sleepwalker should be made as safe as possible, and the doors should be kept locked at night. For some reason sleepwalking runs in families; Dement (1974) tells of a family whose grown members were reunited for a hol-

REM without atonia (*ay tone ee a*) A neurological disorder in which the person does not become paralyzed during REM sleep and thus acts out dreams.

iday celebration. In the middle of the night they awoke to find that they had all gathered in the living room—during their sleep.

Sleeptalking sometimes occurs as part of a REM sleep dream, but it more usually occurs during other stages of sleep. Often, one can carry on a conversation with the sleeptalker, indicating that the person is very near the boundary between sleep and waking. During this state, sleeptalkers are sometimes very suggestible. So-called truth serums are used in an attempt to duplicate this condition, so that the person being questioned is not on guard against giving away secrets and is not functioning well enough to tell elaborate lies. Unfortunately for the interrogators (and fortunately for the rest of the population), there are no foolproof, reliable truth serums.

Night terrors, like sleepwalking, occur most often in children. In this disorder, the child awakes, screaming with terror. When questioned, the child does not report a dream and often seems confused. Usually, the child falls asleep quickly without showing any aftereffects and seldom remembers the event the next day. Night terrors are not the same as nightmares, which are simply frightening dreams from which one happens to awaken. Apparently, night terrors are caused by sudden awakenings from the depths of stage 4 sleep. The sudden, dramatic change in consciousness is a frightening experience for the child. The treatment for night terrors, like that for sleepwalking, is no treatment at all.

The final disorder of slow-wave sleep, *enuresis,* or "bed-wetting," is fairly common in young children. Most children outgrow it, just as they outgrow sleepwalking or night terrors. Emotional problems can trigger enuresis, but bed-wetting does not itself indicate that a child is psychologically unwell. The problem with enuresis is that, unlike the other stage 4 phenomena, there are aftereffects that must be cleaned up. Parents dislike having their sleep disturbed and get tired of frequently changing and laundering sheets. The resulting tension in family relationships can make the child feel anxious and guilty and can thus unnecessarily prolong the disorder.

Fortunately, a simple training method often cures enuresis. A moisture-sensitive device is placed under the bed sheet; when it gets wet, it causes a bell to ring. Because a child releases only a few drops of urine before the bladder begins to empty in earnest, the bell wakes the child in time to run to the bathroom. In about a week, most children learn to prevent their bladders from emptying and manage to wait until morning. Perhaps what they really learn is not to enter such a deep level of stage 4 sleep in which the mechanism that keeps the bladder from emptying seems to break down.

INTERIM SUMMARY

Although many people believe that they have insomnia—that they do not obtain as much sleep as they would like—insomnia is not a disease. Insomnia can be caused by depression, pain, illness, or even excited anticipation of a pleasurable event. Far too many people receive sleeping medications, which often lead to a condition called drug dependency insomnia. Sometimes, insomnia is caused by sleep apnea, which can often be corrected surgically or treated by wearing a mask that delivers pressurized air.

Narcolepsy is characterized by four symptoms. *Sleep attacks* consist of overwhelming urges to sleep for a few minutes. *Cataplexy* is sudden paralysis, during which the person remains conscious. *Sleep paralysis* is similar to cataplexy, but it occurs just before sleep or on waking. *Hypnagogic hallucinations* are dreams that occur during periods of sleep paralysis, just before a night's sleep. Sleep attacks are treated with stimulants such as amphetamine, and the other symptoms are treated with serotonin agonists. Studies with narcoleptic dogs suggest that the disorder may involve biochemical abnormalities in the brain. Another disorder associated with REM sleep, REM without atonia, is a genetic disorder that can also be produced by damage to brain stem mechanisms that produce paralysis during REM sleep.

During slow-wave sleep, especially during stage 4, some people are afflicted by bed-wetting (nocturnal enuresis), sleepwalking (somnambulism), or night terrors. These problems are most common in children, who usually outgrow them. Only if they occur in adults do they suggest the existence of a physical or psychological disorder.

▋THOUGHT QUESTIONS

1. Recall the case of Michael, the man described in the Prologue. What medication do you think his physician prescribed to treat his narcolepsy? How does this drug work?
2. Suppose you spent the night at a friend's house and, hearing a strange noise during the night, got out of bed and found your friend walking around, still asleep. How would you tell whether your friend was sleepwalking or had REM without atonia (REM sleep behavior disorder)?

▋ BIOLOGICAL CLOCKS

Much of our behavior follows regular rhythms. For example, we saw that the stages of sleep are organized around a 90-minute cycle of REM and slow-wave sleep. The same rhythm continues during the day as the basic rest-activity cycle (BRAC). And, of course, our daily pattern of sleep and waking follows a 24-hour cycle. Finally, many animals display seasonal breeding rhythms in which reproductive behaviors and hormone levels show yearly fluctuations. In recent years, investigators have learned much about the neural mechanisms that are responsible for these rhythms.

Circadian rhythm (*sur **kay** dee un* or *sur ka **dee** un*) A daily rhythmical change in behavior or physiological process.

FIGURE 8.21

Wheel-running activity of a rat. Note that the animal's activity occurs at "night" (that is, during the 12 hours the light is off) and that the active period is reset when the light period is changed. When the animal is maintained in constant dim illumination, it displays a free-running activity cycle of approximately 25 hours.

(From Groblewski, T.A., Nuñez, A., and Gold, R.M. Paper presented at the meeting of the Eastern Psychological Association, April 1980.)

Circadian Rhythms and Zeitgebers

Daily rhythms in behavior and physiological processes are found throughout the plant and animal world. These cycles are generally called **circadian rhythms.** (*Circa* means "about," and *dies* means "day"; therefore, a circadian rhythm is one that varies on a cycle of approximately 24 hours.) Some of these rhythms are passive responses to changes in illumination. However, other rhythms are controlled by mechanisms within the organism—by "internal clocks." For example, Figure 8.21 shows the activity of a rat during various conditions of illumination. Each horizontal line represents 24 hours. Vertical tick marks represent the animal's activity in a running wheel. The upper portion of the figure shows the activity of the rat during a normal day–night cycle, with alternating 12-hour periods of light and dark. Notice that the animal is active during the night, which is normal for a rat. (See *Figure 8.21.*)

Next, the dark–light cycle was shifted by 6 hours; the animal's activity cycle quickly followed the change. (See *Figure 8.21.*) Finally, dim lights were left on continuously. The cyclical pattern in the rat's activity remained. Because there were no cycles of light and dark in the rat's environment, the source of rhythmicity must be located within the animal; that is, the animal must possess an internal, biological clock. You can see that the rat's clock was not set precisely to 24 hours; when the illumination was held constant, the clock ran a bit slow. The animal began its bout of activity almost one hour later each day. (See *Figure 8.21.*)

The phenomenon illustrated in Figure 8.21 is typical of the circadian rhythms shown by many species. A free-running clock, with a cycle a little longer than 24 hours, controls some biological functions—in this case, motor activity. Regular daily variation in the level of illumination (that is, sunlight and darkness) normally keeps the clock adjusted to 24 hours. Light serves as a **zeitgeber** (German for "time giver"); it synchronizes the endogenous rhythm. Studies with many species of animals have shown that if they are maintained in constant darkness (or constant dim light), a brief period of bright light will reset their internal clock, advancing or retarding it, depending upon when the light flash occurs (Aschoff, 1979). For example, if an animal is exposed to bright light soon after dusk, the biological clock is set back to an earlier time—as if dusk had not yet arrived. On the other hand, if the light occurs late at night, the biological clock is set ahead to a later time—as if dawn had already come.

Like other animals, humans exhibit circadian rhythms. Our normal period of inactivity begins several hours after the start of the dark portion of the day–night cycle and persists for a variable amount of time into the light portion. Without the benefits of modern civilization we would probably go to sleep earlier and get up earlier than we do; we use artificial lights to delay our bedtime and window shades to extend our time for sleep. Under constant illumination our biological clocks will run free, gaining or losing time like a watch that runs too slow or too fast. Different people have different cycle lengths, but most people in that situation will begin to live a "day" that is approximately 25 hours long. This works out quite well, because the morning light, acting as a zeitgeber, simply resets the clock.

Role of the Suprachiasmatic Nucleus

Researchers working independently in two laboratories (Moore and Eichler, 1972; Stephan and Zucker, 1972) discovered that the primary biological clock of the rat is located in the **suprachiasmatic nucleus (SCN)** of the hypothalamus; they found that lesions disrupted circadian rhythms of wheel running, drinking, and hormonal secretion. The SCN also provides the primary control over the timing of sleep cycles. Rats are nocturnal animals; they sleep during the day and forage and feed at night. Lesions of the SCN abolish this pattern; sleep occurs in bouts that are randomly dispersed throughout both day and night (Ibuka and Kawamura, 1975; Stephan and Nuñez, 1977). However, rats with SCN lesions still obtain the same amount of sleep that normal animals do. The lesions disrupt the circadian pattern but do not affect the total amount of sleep.

Anatomy and Connections

Figure 8.22 shows the suprachiasmatic nuclei in a cross section through the hypothalamus of a rat; they appear as two clusters of dark-staining neurons at the base of the brain, just above the optic chiasm. (See *Figure 8.22.*) The suprachiasmatic nuclei of the rat consist of approximately 10,000 small neurons, tightly packed into a volume of between 0.1 and 0.3 mm³ (Meijer and Rietveld, 1989). The dendrites of these neurons form synapses with one another—a phenomenon that is found only in this part of the hypothalamus and that probably relates to the special function of these nuclei. A group of neurons is found clustered around the capillaries that serve the SCN. These neurons contain a large amount of rough en-

Zeitgeber (*tsite* gay ber) A stimulus (usually the light of dawn) that resets the biological clock responsible for circadian rhythms.

Suprachiasmatic nucleus (SCN) (*soo pra ky az* **mat** ik) A nucleus situated atop the optic chiasm. It contains a biological clock responsible for organizing many of the body's circadian rhythms.

FIGURE 8.22

A cross section through a rat brain, showing the location and appearance of the suprachiasmatic nuclei. Cresyl violet stain.

(Courtesy of Geert DeVries, University of Massachusetts.)

doplasmic reticulum, which suggests that they may be neurosecretory cells (Card, Riley, and Moore, 1980; Moore, Card, and Riley, 1980). Thus, some of the control that the SCN exerts over other parts of the brain may be accomplished by the secretion of neuromodulators.

Because light is the primary zeitgeber for most mammals' activity cycles, we would expect that the SCN receives fibers from the visual system. Indeed, anatomical studies have revealed a direct projection of fibers from the retina to the SCN: the *retinohypothalamic pathway* (Hendrickson, Wagoner, and Cowan, 1972; Aronson et al., 1993). If you look carefully at Figure 8.22, you can see small dark spots within the optic chiasm, just ventral and medial to the base of the SCN; these are cell bodies of oligodendrocytes that serve axons that enter the SCN and provide information from the retina. (See *Figure 8.22*.)

Pulses of light that reset an animal's circadian rhythm trigger the production of Fos protein in the SCN, which indicates that the light initiates a period of neural activity in this nucleus (Rusak et al., 1990, 1992). (The significance of the Fos protein as an indicator of neural activation was discussed in Chapter 5.)

How does the SCN control drinking, eating, sleep cycles, and hormone secretion? Although neurons of the SCN project to several parts of the brain, transplantation studies suggest that the SCN controls some functions by releasing chemical signals. Lehman et al. (1987) destroyed the SCN and then transplanted in their place a new set of suprachiasmatic nuclei obtained from donor animals. The grafts succeeded in reestablishing circadian rhythms, even though very few efferent connections were observed between the graft and the recipient's brain. Even more convincing evidence comes from a transplantation study by Silver et al. (1996). Silver and her colleagues first destroyed the SCN in a group of hamsters, abolishing their circadian rhythms. Then, a few weeks later, they removed SCN tissue from donor animals and placed it in very small semipermeable capsules, which they then implanted in the animals' third ventricles. Nutrients and other chemicals could pass through the walls of the capsules, keeping the SCN tissue alive, but the neurons inside the capsules were not able to establish synaptic connections with the surrounding tissue. Nevertheless, the transplants reestablished circadian rhythms in the recipient animals.

The Nature of the Clock

All clocks must have a time base. Mechanical clocks use flywheels or pendulums; electronic clocks use quartz crystals. The SCN, too, must contain a physiological mechanism that parses time into units. After years of research, investigators are finally beginning to discover the nature of the biological clock in the SCN.

Several studies have demonstrated daily activity rhythms in the SCN, which indicates that the circadian clock is located there. A study by Schwartz and Gainer (1977) nicely demonstrated day–night fluctuations in the activity of the SCN. These investigators injected rats with radioactive 2-deoxyglucose (2-DG). As you will recall from Chapter 5, this chemical is structurally similar to ordinary glucose; thus, it is taken up by cells that are metabolically active. However, it cannot be utilized, nor can it leave the cell. Therefore, metabolically active cells will accumulate radioactivity.

Schwartz and Gainer injected some rats with radioactive 2-DG during the day and injected others at night. The animals were then killed, and autoradiographs of cross sections through the brain were prepared. Figure 8.23 shows photographs of two of these cross sections. Note the evidence of radioactivity (and hence a high metabolic rate) in the SCN of the brain that was injected during the day (*left*). (See *Figure 8.23*.)

The "ticking" of the biological clock within the SCN could involve interactions of circuits of neurons, or it could be intrinsic to individual neurons themselves. Evidence suggests the latter—that each neuron contains a clock. For example, Welsh et al. (1995) removed tissue

---

FIGURE 8.23

Autoradiographs of cross sections through the brains of rats that had been injected with carbon-14-labeled 2-deoxyglucose during the day (*left*) and the night (*right*). The dark region at the base of the brain (*arrows*) indicates increased metabolic activity of the suprachiasmatic nuclei.

[From Schwartz, W.J., and Gainer, H. Science, 1977, 197, 1089–1091. Reprinted with permission. Copyright 1977 by the American Association for the Advancement of Science.]

from the rat SCN and dissolved the connections between the cells with papain, an enzyme that is sometimes used as a meat tenderizer. They kept the cells alive in a culture medium. Recordings from an array of microelectrodes showed that the neurons displayed individual, independent circadian rhythms in activity. Figure 8.24 shows the activity cycles of four neurons. As you can see, all showed circadian rhythms, but their periods of peak activity occurred at different times of day. (In an intact brain, of course, something synchronizes the activity of the SCN neurons.) (See *Figure 8.24.*)

What causes SCN neurons to "tick"? Researchers have uncovered some of the details of one mechanism so far—that of the circadian clock of *Drosophila melanogaster,* the common fruit fly (Hunterensor, Ousley, and Sehgal, 1996; Lee et al., 1996; Myers et al., 1996; Zeng et al., 1996). It appears that in this species, circadian rhythms are produced by the production of two proteins, PER and TIM, that inhibit their own production when they reach a certain level in the cell. As a result, the levels of the proteins decline, which removes the inhibition and starts the production cycle again. One of these proteins, TIM, may be involved in mediating the effects of a zeitgeber.

What about the mammalian clock? Is this mechanism peculiar to insects, or do cells in the SCN work this way, too? Although it is too early to say, it does appear that a PER-like protein is produced in the rat SCN (Rosewell, Siwicki, and Wise, 1994). We will have to await the results of further research.

Control of Seasonal Rhythms: The Pineal Gland and Melatonin

Although the SCN has an intrinsic rhythm of approximately 24 hours, it plays a role in much longer rhythms. (We could say that it is involved in a biological calendar as well as a biological clock.) Male hamsters show annual rhythms of testosterone secretion, which appear to be based on the amount of light that occurs each day. Their breeding season begins as the day length increases and ends when it decreases. Lesions of the SCN abolish these annual breeding cycles; the animals' testes then secrete testosterone all year (Rusak and Morin, 1976). Possibly, the lesions disrupt these annual cycles because they destroy the 24-hour clock against which the daily light period is measured to determine the season. That is, if the light period is considerably shorter than 12 hours, the season is winter; if it is considerably longer than 12 hours, the season is summer.

The control of seasonal rhythms involves another part of the brain: the **pineal gland** (Bartness et al., 1993; Moore, 1995). This structure sits on top of the midbrain, just in front of the cerebellum. (See *Figure 8.25.*) The pineal gland secretes a hormone called **melatonin,** so named because it has the ability in certain animals (primarily fish, reptiles, and amphibians) to turn the skin temporarily dark. (The dark color is produced by a chemical known as *melanin.*) In mammals, melatonin controls seasonal rhythms. Neurons in the SCN make synaptic connections with neurons in the *paraventricular nucleus of the hypothalamus* (the PVN). The axons of these neurons travel all the way to the spinal cord, where they form synapses with preganglionic neurons of the sympathetic nervous system. The postganglionic neurons innervate the pineal gland and control the secretion of melatonin.

In response to input from the SCN, the pineal gland secretes melatonin during the night. This melatonin acts back on various structures in the brain (including the SCN, whose cells contain melatonin receptors) and controls hormones, physiological processes, and behaviors that show seasonal variations. During long nights a large amount of melatonin is secreted, and the animals go into the winter phase of their cycle. Lesions of the SCN, the paraventricular nucleus (PVN), or the pineal gland

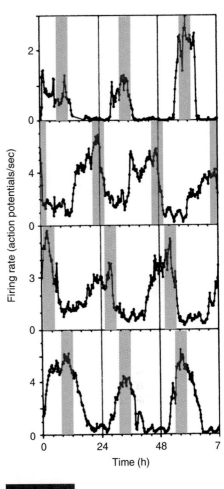

FIGURE 8.24

Firing rate of individual SCN neurons in a tissue culture. Color bars have been added to emphasize the daily peaks. Note that although each neuron has a period of approximately one day, their activity cycles are not synchronized.

(From Welsh, D.K., Logothetis, D.E., Meister, M., and Reppert, S.M. Neuron, 1995, 14, 697–706. Copyright 1995 Cell Press. Reprinted by permission.)

Pineal gland [*py nee ul*] A gland attached to the dorsal tectum; produces melatonin and plays a role in circadian and seasonal rhythms.

Melatonin [*mell a tone in*] A hormone secreted during the night by the pineal body; plays a role in circadian and seasonal rhythms.

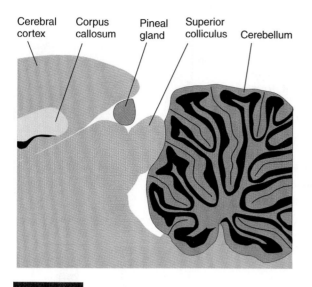

Cerebral cortex | Corpus callosum | Pineal gland | Superior colliculus | Cerebellum

FIGURE 8.25

The pineal gland, located on the dorsal surface of the midbrain.

(Adapted from Paxinos, G., and Watson, C. The Rat Brain in Stereotaxic Coordinates. Sydney: Academic Press, 1982.)

disrupt seasonal rhythms that are controlled by day length—and so do knife cuts that interrupt the neural connection between the SCN and the PVN, which indicates that this is one function of the SCN that is mediated through its neural connections with another structure. Furthermore, although transplants of fetal suprachiasmatic nuclei will restore circadian rhythms, they will not restore seasonal rhythms, because the transplanted tissue does not establish neural connections with the PVN (Ralph and Lehman, 1991).

Changes in Circadian Rhythms: Shift Work and Jet Lag

When people abruptly change their daily rhythms of activity, their internal circadian rhythms, controlled by the SCN, become desynchronized with those in the external environment. For example, if a person who normally works on the day shift begins working on a night shift or if someone travels east or west across several time zones, his or her SCN will signal the rest of the brain that it is time to sleep during the work shift (or the middle of the day, in the case of jet travel). This disparity between internal rhythms and the external environment results in sleep disturbances and mood changes and interferes with people's ability to function during waking hours.

Jet lag is a temporary phenomenon; after several days, people who have crossed several time zones find it easier to fall asleep at the appropriate time, and their daytime alertness improves. Shift work can present a more enduring problem when people are required to change shifts frequently. Obviously, the solution to jet lag and to the problems caused by shift work is to get the internal clock synchronized with the external environment as quickly as possible. The most obvious way to start is to try to provide strong zeitgebers at the appropriate time. If a person is exposed to bright light before the low point in the daily rhythm of body temperature (which occurs an hour or two before the person usually awakens), the person's circadian rhythm is delayed. If the exposure to bright light occurs after the low point, the circadian rhythm is advanced (Dijk et al., 1995). In fact, several studies have shown that exposure to bright lights at the appropriate time helps to ease the transition (Boulos et al., 1995). Houpt, Boulos, and Moore-Ede (1996) have even developed a computer program that helps to determine the optimal pattern of light exposure to minimize the effects of jet travel between various parts of the world. Similarly, people adapt to shift work more rapidly if artificial light is kept at a brighter level and if their bedroom is kept as dark as possible (Eastman et al., 1995).

As we saw in the previous subsection, the role of melatonin in seasonal rhythms is well established. Studies in recent years suggest that melatonin may also be involved in circadian rhythms. As we saw, melatonin is secreted during the night, which, for diurnal mammals such as ourselves, is the period during which we sleep. But although our species lacks strong seasonal rhythms, the daily rhythm of melatonin secretion persists. Thus, melatonin must have some functions besides regulation of seasonal rhythms.

Recent studies have found that melatonin, acting on receptors in the SCN, can affect the sensitivity of SCN neurons to zeitgebers and can itself alter circadian rhythms (Gillette and McArthur, 1995; Starkey et al., 1995). Researchers do not yet understand exactly what role melatonin plays in the control of circadian rhythms, but they have already discovered practical applications. Melatonin secretion normally reaches its highest levels early in the night, at around bedtime. Investigators have found that the administration of melatonin at the appropriate time (in most cases, just before going to bed) significantly reduces the adverse effects of both jet lag and shifts in work sched-

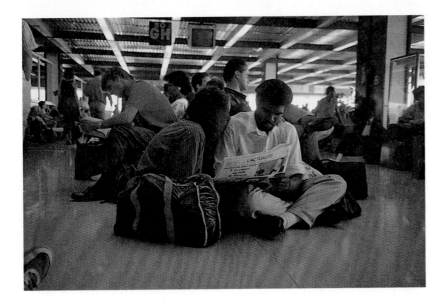

Researchers are beginning to understand the role of the suprachiasmatic nucleus and the pineal gland in phenomena such as jet lag.

ules (Arendt et al., 1995; Deacon and Arendt, 1996). Bedtime melatonin has even helped to synchronize circadian rhythms and improved the sleep of blind people for whom light cannot serve as a zeitgeber (Skene, Deacon, and Arendt, 1996).

INTERIM SUMMARY

Our daily lives are characterized by cycles in physical activity, sleep, body temperature, secretion of hormones, and many other physiological changes. Circadian rhythms—those with a period of approximately one day—are controlled by biological clocks in the brain. The principal biological clock appears to be located in the suprachiasmatic nuclei of the hypothalamus; lesions of these nuclei disrupt most circadian rhythms, and the activity of neurons located there correlates with the day–night cycle. Light serves as a zeitgeber for most circadian rhythms. That is, the biological clocks tend to run a bit slow, with a period of approximately 25 hours. The sight of sunlight in the morning is conveyed from the retina to the SCN—directly and via the IGL of the lateral geniculate nucleus. The effect of the light is to reset the clock to the start of a new cycle.

Individual neurons, rather than circuits of neurons, are responsible for the "ticks." Studies with tissue cultures suggest that synchronization of the firing patterns of individual neurons is accomplished by means of chemical communication between cells, perhaps involving astrocytes. In the fruit fly, two genes, *tim* and *per,* are responsible for circadian rhythms. These genes' proteins (TIM and PER) bind, travel to the nucleus, and inhibit further protein synthesis until they disintegrate and the cycle begins again.

The SCN and the pineal gland control annual rhythms. During the night the SCN signals the pineal gland to secrete melatonin. Prolonged melatonin secretion, which occurs during winter, causes the animals to enter the winter phase of their annual cycle. Melatonin also appears to be involved in synchronizing circadian rhythms: The hormone can help people to adjust to the effects of shift work or jet lag and even synchronize the daily rhythms of blind people for whom light cannot serve as a zeitgeber.

THOUGHT QUESTIONS

Until recently (in terms of the evolution of our species), our ancestors tended to go to sleep when the sun set and wake up when it rose. Once our ancestors learned how to control fire, they undoubtedly stayed up somewhat later, sitting in front of a fire. But it was only with the development of cheap, effective lighting that many members of our species adopted the habit of staying up late and waking several hours after sunrise. Considering that our biological clock and the neural mechanisms it controls evolved long ago, do you think the changes in our daily rhythms impair any of our physical and intellectual abilities?

Functions of Dreams

Even though we are still not sure why REM sleep occurs, the elaborate neural circuitry involved with its control indicates that it must be important. Nature would probably not invent this circuitry if it did not do something useful. Michael's attacks of sleep paralysis, hypnagogic hallucinations, and cataplexy, described in the Prologue, occurred when two of the aspects of REM sleep (paralysis and dreaming) occurred at inappropriate times. Normally, the brain mechanisms responsible for these phenomena are inhibited during waking; perhaps this inhibition is too weak in Michael's case.

As we saw, researchers have proposed four categories of hypothetical explanations for REM sleep: vigilance, learning, species-typical reprogramming, and brain development. Each of these explanations has some support, and possibly, REM sleep performs more than one function. But what about the subjective aspect of REM sleep dreaming? Is there some special purpose served by those vivid, storylike hallucinations we have while we sleep, or are dreams just irrelevant side effects of more important things going on in the brain?

Since ancient times, people have regarded dreams as important, using them to prophesy the future, decide whether to go to war, or determine the guilt or innocence of a person accused of a crime. In this century, Sigmund Freud proposed a very influential theory about dreaming. He said that dreams arise out of inner con-

flicts between unconscious desires (primarily sexual ones) and prohibitions against acting out these desires, which we learn from society. According to Freud, although all dreams represent unfulfilled wishes, their contents are disguised. The *latent content* of the dream (from the Latin word for "hidden") is transformed into the *manifest content* (the actual story line or plot). Taken at face value, the manifest content is innocuous, but a knowledgeable psychoanalyst can recognize unconscious desires disguised as symbols in the dream. For example, climbing a set of stairs might represent sexual intercourse. The problem with Freud's theory is that it is not disprovable; even if it is wrong, a psychoanalyst can always provide a plausible interpretation of a dream that reveals hidden conflicts, disguised in obscure symbols.

Many sleep researchers—especially those who are interested in the biological aspects of dreaming—disagree with Freud and suggest alternative explanations. For example, Hobson (1988) suggests that the brain activation that occurs during REM sleep leads to hallucinations that we try to make sense of by creating a more or less plausible story. As you learned in this chapter, REM sleep occurs when a circuit of acetylcholinergic neurons in the peribrachial region becomes active, stimulating rapid eye movements and cortical arousal. The visual system is especially active. So is the motor system—in fact, we have

a mechanism that paralyzes and prevents the activity of the motor system from causing us to get out of bed and doing something that might harm us. (As we saw, people who suffer from REM without atonia actually *do* act out their dreams and sometimes injure themselves. On occasion, they have even attacked their spouses while dreaming that they were fighting with someone.)

Research indicates that the two systems of the brain that are most active, the visual system and the motor system, account for most of the sensations that occur during dreams. Many dreams are silent, but almost all are full of visual images. In addition, many dreams contain sensations of movements, which are probably caused by feedback from the activity of the motor system. Very few dreamers report tactile sensations, smells, or tastes. Hobson, a wine lover, reported that although he has drunk wine in his dreams, he has never experienced any taste or smell. (He reported this fact rather wistfully; I suspect that he would have appreciated the opportunity to taste a fine wine without having to open one of his own bottles.) Why are these sensations absent? Is it because our "hidden desires" involve only sight and movement, or is it because the neural activation that occurs during REM sleep simply does not involve other systems to a very great extent? Hobson suggests the latter, and I agree with him.

◪ KEY CONCEPTS

A PHYSIOLOGICAL AND BEHAVIORAL DESCRIPTION

1. Sleep consists of slow-wave sleep divided into four stages, and REM sleep. Dreaming occurs during REM sleep.

WHY DO WE SLEEP?

2. Slow-wave sleep appears to permit the cerebral cortex to rest. It may also have adaptive value as a behavior that conserves energy and keeps the animal out of harm's way.

3. REM sleep may be important in brain development, and it appears to be somehow involved in learning.

PHYSIOLOGICAL MECHANISMS OF SLEEP AND WAKING

4. Adenosine, a neuromodulator that is produced as a by-product of cerebral metabolism, may play a role in initiating sleep.

5. The brain stem contains an arousal mechanism with three major components: the acetylcholinergic system of the dorsolateral pons and basal forebrain, the noradrenergic system originating in the locus coeruleus, and the serotonergic system originating

in the raphe nuclei. The basal forebrain region contains a mechanism that appears to be necessary for sleep.

6. REM sleep is produced by the activity of acetylcholinergic neurons in the dorsolateral pons, which are normally inhibited by both noradrenergic and serotonergic synapses. The circuit responsible for the muscular paralysis that accompanies REM sleep has been located, and damage to it is responsible for REM without atonia.

DISORDERS OF SLEEP

7. People sometimes suffer from such sleep disorders as insomnia, sleep apnea, narcolepsy, REM without atonia, bedwetting, sleepwalking, or night terrors. Three symptoms of narcolepsy (cataplexy, sleep paralysis, and hypnagogic hallucinations) can be understood as components of REM sleep occurring at inappropriate times.

BIOLOGICAL CLOCKS

8. Circadian rhythms are largely under the control of a mechanism located in the suprachiasmatic nucleus. They are synchronized by the day–night light cycle.

◪ SUGGESTED READINGS

Cohen, D.B. *Sleep and Dreaming: Origins, Nature and Functions.* Oxford: Pergamon Press, 1979.

Hastings, J.W., Rusak, B., and Boulos, Z. Circadian rhythms: The physiology of biological timing. In *Neural and Integrative Animal Physiology,* edited by C.L. Prosser. New York: Wiley-Liss, 1991.

Horne, J. *Why We Sleep: The Functions of Sleep in Humans and Other Mammals.* Oxford: Oxford University Press, 1988.

Kryger, M.H., Roth, T., and Dement, W.C. *Principles and Practices of Sleep Disorders in Medicine.* New York: W.B. Saunders, 1989.

Mancia, M., and Marini, G. *The Diencephalon and Sleep.* New York: Raven Press, 1990.

Webb, W. *Sleep: The Gentle Tyrant,* 2nd ed. Bolton, MA: Anker, 1992.

9

Reproductive Behavior

LEARNING OBJECTIVES

1. Describe mammalian sexual development and explain the factors that control it.

2. Describe the hormonal control of the female reproductive cycle and of male and female sexual behavior.

3. Describe the role of pheromones in reproductive physiology and sexual behavior.

4. Discuss the activational effects of gonadal hormones on the sexual behavior of women and men.

5. Discuss sexual orientation, the prenatal androgenization of genetic females, and the failure of androgenization of genetic males.

6. Discuss the neural control of male sexual behavior.

7. Discuss the neural control of female sexual behavior.

8. Describe the maternal behavior of rodents and explain how it is elicited and maintained.

9. Explain the hormonal and neural mechanisms that control maternal behavior and the neural control of paternal behavior.

The Smell of Success

Mr. D. owned a small company that supplied essences to cosmetics companies. Some of his customers diluted these essences with alcohol and bottled and sold them under their own names as perfumes or eaux de cologne; others used the essences to provide a pleasant odor to their shampoos, hand lotions, deodorants, and other beauty products.

Mr. D. was a shrewd entrepreneur who was quick to spot and exploit business opportunities. He had an engaging personality that inspired confidence in his company and its products. But his most important asset, the one that enabled his company to survive in a market dominated by companies owned by conglomerates, was his nose. His heredity had endowed him with an extraordinary olfactory system, which he had diligently trained while working for one of the large perfume makers. After a long apprenticeship, and with some help from his and his wife's families, he quit his job and started his own company. After the slow start that is common to most small businesses during their infancy, he landed a series of lucrative contracts that established him firmly in his niche.

But the recent recession was starting to hurt. His customers had been paying their bills later and later, orders were being scaled back, and new business had almost dried up. Some of his larger competitors, who had previously ignored small orders that he counted on for the bulk of his business, were now bidding against him. His loyalty to his employees, many of whom had been through the early, lean days with him, made him reluctant even to think about laying anyone off to save money. But if he did not do so, could his business survive until times got better?

It was with such unhappy thoughts that Mr. D. sat in his easy chair in the living room one evening, long after the rest of the family had gone to bed. He had been sitting there for several hours, trying to think of ways to find new business or cut expenses without cutting his payroll, and now the mental effort was beginning to tell. He let his mind wander and began fantasizing a more pleasant outlook than the one he was currently facing . . .

While reading an article in a scientific journal devoted to the chemical senses olfaction and gustation, he came across a report of the discovery of a sex attractant pheromone that had been discovered by researchers working in the Mid-Atlantic Regional Primate Center. He called Dr. T., the author of the article, and arranged to meet her the next day. The scientist was not a chemist, but her analysis gave him enough information to guess what the molecular structure of the pheromone was. He smelled a sample of the extract she had produced and found that it had only a faint, slightly musky odor. But he thought the odor was surprisingly pleasant. He sniffed it again, comparing the odor to the thousands of memories he had locked up in his brain. He felt lightheaded, almost euphoric. When engaged in the task of smelling essences, he was always serious and professional, but he felt the same surge of joy that he remembered from his adolescence. He turned to Dr. T. and felt his heart give a lurch. It was with great effort that he told himself that he was a married man and Dr. T. was undoubtedly married, too. Why had he not noticed her beauty when he shook hands with her? He hastily stammered his thanks and rushed out of the laboratory.

Once he was home, recovered from his sudden infatuation, he became even more excited as he realized the significance of his experience. He called a meeting with his laboratory personnel, and within a month they managed to synthesize a novel chemical that seemed to have the effects of the one he had smelled in Dr. T.'s lab. He enlisted the assistance of Dr. V., a psychology professor at the University of X., who confirmed his suspicions and reported, with obvious awe, the effect that the new perfume had on interpersonal attraction. "I couldn't believe it!" he said. "What was in that stuff?"

Mr. D. acted quickly. He did not want his competition to learn what he was doing, so he obtained a mortgage on his business and a second mortgage on his home. He bought new laboratory equipment and set up a production facility to synthesize the new chemical. Meanwhile, he hired an attorney to apply for a patent on the molecule. Armed with a prepublication manuscript of Dr. V.'s research and a sample of his perfume, he met with the director of the largest, most prestigious cosmetics company.

Reproductive behaviors constitute the most important category of social behaviors, because without them, most species would not survive. These behaviors—which include courting, mating, parental behavior, and most forms of aggressive behaviors—are the most striking categories of **sexually dimorphic behaviors,** that is, behaviors that differ in males and females (*di* + *morphous,* "two forms"). As you will see, hormones that are present both before and after birth play a very special role in the development and control of sexually dimorphic behaviors.

Sexually dimorphic behavior
A behavior that has different forms or that occurs with different probabilities or under different circumstances in males and females.

This chapter describes male and female sexual development and then discusses the neural and hormonal control of two sexually dimorphic behaviors that are most important to reproduction: sexual behavior and maternal behavior.

SEXUAL DEVELOPMENT

A person's chromosomal sex is determined at the time of fertilization. However, this event is merely the first in a series of steps that culminate in the development of a male or a female. This section considers the major features of sexual development.

Production of Gametes and Fertilization

All cells of the human body (other than sperms or ova) contain twenty-three pairs of chromosomes. The genetic information that programs the development of a human is contained in the DNA that constitutes these chromosomes. We pride ourselves on our ability to miniaturize computer circuits on silicon chips, but that accomplishment looks primitive when we consider that the blueprint for a human being is too small to be seen by the naked eye.

The production of **gametes** (ova and sperms; *gamein* means "to marry" in Greek) entails a special form of cell division. This process produces cells that contain one member of each of the twenty-three pairs of chromosomes. The development of a human begins at the time of fertilization, when a single sperm and ovum join, sharing their twenty-three single chromosomes to reconstitute the twenty-three pairs.

A person's genetic sex is determined at the time of fertilization by the father's sperm. Twenty-two of the twenty-three pairs of chromosomes determine the organism's physical development independent of its sex. The last pair consists of two **sex chromosomes,** which determine whether the offspring will be a boy or a girl.

There are two types of sex chromosomes: X chromosomes and Y chromosomes. Females have two X chromosomes (XX); thus, all the ova that a woman produces will contain an X chromosome. Males have an X and a Y chromosome (XY). When a man's sex chromosomes divide, half the sperms contain an X chromosome and the other half contain a Y chromosome. A Y-bearing sperm produces an XY-fertilized ovum and therefore a male. An X-bearing sperm produces an XX-fertilized ovum and therefore a female. (See *Figure 9.1.*)

Development of the Sex Organs

Men and women differ in many ways: Their bodies are different, parts of their brains are different, and their reproductive behaviors are different. Are all these differences encoded on the tiny Y chromosome, the sole piece of genetic material that distinguishes males from females? The answer is no. The X chromosome and the twenty-two nonsex chromosomes found in the cells of both males and females contain all the information needed to develop the bodies of either sex. Exposure to sex hormones, both before and after birth, is responsible for our sexual dimorphism. What the Y chromosome does control is the development of the glands that produce the male sex hormones.

Gonads

There are three general categories of sex organs: the gonads, the internal sex organs, and the external genitalia. The **gonads**—testes or ovaries—are the first to develop. Gonads (from the Greek *gonos,* "procreation") have a dual function: They produce ova or sperms, and they secrete hormones. Through the fourth week of prenatal development, male and female fetuses are identical. Both sexes have a pair of identical undifferentiated gonads, which have the potential of developing into either testes or ovaries. The factor that con-

Gamete (*gamm eet*) A mature reproductive cell; a sperm or ovum.

Sex chromosome The X and Y chromosomes, which determine an organism's gender. Normally, XX individuals are female, and XY individuals are male.

Gonad (rhymes with *moan ad*) An ovary or testis.

FIGURE 9.1

Determination of gender. The gender of the offspring depends on whether the sperm cell that fertilizes the ovum carries an X or a Y chromosome.

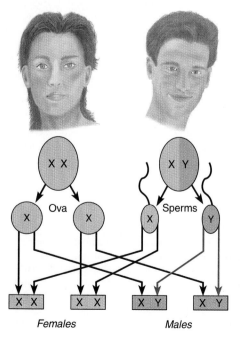

trols their development appears to be a single gene on the Y chromosome called *SRY*. This gene produces an enzyme called *testis-determining factor*, which causes the undifferentiated gonads to become testes. If the gene is not present, they become ovaries (Smith, 1994). In fact, if this gene is inserted into one of the X chromosomes of a female (XX) embryonic mouse, the animal will develop as a male (Koopman et al., 1991).

Once the gonads have developed, a series of events is set into action that determines the individual's gender. These events are directed by hormones, which affect sexual development in two ways. During prenatal development these hormones have **organizational effects,** which influence the development of a person's sex organs and brain. These effects are permanent; once a particular path is followed in the course of development, there is no going back. The second role of sex hormones is their **activational effect.** These effects occur later in life, after the sex organs have developed. For example, hormones activate the production of sperms, make erection and ejaculation possible, and induce ovulation. Because the bodies of adult males and females have been organized differently, sex hormones will have different activational effects in the two sexes.

Internal Sex Organs

Early in embryonic development, the internal sex organs are *bisexual;* that is, all embryos contain the precursors for both female and male sex organs. However, during the third month of gestation, only one of these precursors develops; the other withers away. The precursor of the internal female sex organs, which develops into the *fimbriae* and *Fallopian tubes*, the *uterus*, and the *inner two-thirds of the vagina*, is called the **Müllerian system.** The precursor of the internal male sex organs, which develops into the *epididymis, vas deferens, seminal vesicles,* and *prostate*, is called the **Wolffian system.** (These systems were named after their discoverers, Müller and Wolff. See *Figure 9.2.*)

Organizational effect (of hormone) The effect of a hormone on tissue differentiation and development.

Activational effect (of hormone) The effect of a hormone that occurs in the fully developed organism; may depend on the organism's prior exposure to the organizational effects of hormones.

Müllerian system The embryonic precursors of the female internal sex organs.

Wolffian system The embryonic precursors of the male internal sex organs.

FIGURE 9.2

Development of the internal sex organs.

Early in Fetal Development

Adult Female

Adult Male

Anti-Müllerian hormone A peptide secreted by the fetal testes that inhibits the development of the Müllerian system, which would otherwise become the female internal sex organs.

Defeminizing effect An organizational effect of a hormone that reduces or prevents the later development of anatomical or behavioral characteristics typical of females.

Androgen (*an dro jen*) A male sex steroid hormone. Testosterone is the principal mammalian androgen.

Masculinizing effect An organizational effect of a hormone that promotes the later development of anatomical or behavioral characteristics typical of males.

The gender of the internal sex organs of a fetus is determined by the presence or absence of hormones secreted by the testes. If these hormones are present, the Wolffian system develops. If they are not, the Müllerian system develops. The Müllerian (female) system needs no hormonal stimulus from the gonads to develop; it just normally does so. In contrast, the cells of the Wolffian (male) system do not develop unless they are stimulated to do so by a hormone. Thus, testes secrete two types of hormones. The first, a peptide hormone called **anti-Müllerian hormone,** does exactly what its name says: It prevents the Müllerian (female) system from developing. It therefore has a **defeminizing effect.** The second, a set of steroid hormones called **androgens,** stimulates the development of the Wolffian system. (This class of hormone is also aptly named: *andros* means "man," and *gennan* means "to produce.") Androgens have a **masculinizing effect.** The primary androgen, **testosterone,** is secreted by the testes—and gets its name from these glands.

As you will recall from Chapter 2, hormones exert their effects on target cells by stimulating the appropriate hormone receptor. Thus, the precursor of the male internal sex organs—the Wolffian system—contains androgen receptors that are coupled to cellular mechanisms that promote growth and division. When molecules of androgens bind with these receptors, the epididymis, vas deferens, and prostate develop and grow. In contrast, the cells of the Müllerian system contain receptors for anti-Müllerian hormone that *prevent* growth and division. Thus, anti-Müllerian hormone prevents the development of the female internal sex organs.

The fact that the internal sex organs of the human embryo are bisexual and could potentially develop as either male or female is dramatically illustrated by two genetic disorders: *androgen insensitivity syndrome* and *persistent Müllerian duct syndrome.* Some people are insensitive to androgens; they have **androgen insensitivity syndrome,** one of the more aptly named disorders (Money and Ehrhardt, 1972; MacLean, Warne, and Zajac, 1995). The cause of androgen insensitivity syndrome is a genetic mutation that prevents the formation of functioning androgen receptors. (The gene for the androgen receptor is located on the X chromosome.) The primitive gonads of a genetic male fetus with androgen insensitivity syndrome become testes and secrete both anti-Müllerian hormone and androgens. The lack of androgen receptors prevents the androgens from having a masculinizing effect; thus, the epididymis, vas deferens, seminal vesicles, and prostate fail to develop. However, the anti-Müllerian hormone still has its defeminizing effect, preventing the female internal sex organs from developing. The uterus, fimbriae, and Fallopian tubes fail to develop, and the vagina is shallow. Their external genitalia are female, and at puberty they develop a woman's body. Of course, lacking a uterus and ovaries, these people cannot have children. (See *Figure 9.3.*)

The second genetic disorder, **persistent Müllerian duct syndrome,** is caused by defective receptors for Müllerian inhibiting hormone (Behringer, 1995; Imbeaud et al., 1995). When this syndrome occurs in genetic males, androgens have their masculinizing effect but not their defeminizing effect. Thus, the person is born with *both* sets of internal sex organs, male and female. The presence of the additional female sex organs usually interferes with normal functioning of the male sex organs.

FIGURE 9.3

An XY female displaying androgen insensitivity syndrome.

(From Money, J., and Ehrhardt, A.A. Man & Woman, Boy & Girl. Copyright 1973 by The Johns Hopkins University Press, Baltimore, Maryland. By permission.)

So far, I have been discussing only male sex hormones. What about prenatal sexual development in females? A genetic anomaly indicates that female sex organs are not needed for development of the Müllerian system. This fact has led to the dictum "Nature's impulse is to create a female." People with **Turner's syndrome** have only one sex chromosome: an X chromosome. (Thus, instead of having XX cells, they have X0 cells—0 indicating a missing sex chromosome.) In most cases the existing X chromosome comes from the mother, which means that the cause of the disorder lies with a defective sperm (Knebelmann et al., 1991). Because a Y chromosome is not present, testes do not develop. In addition, because two X chromosomes are needed to produce ovaries, these glands are not produced, either. But even though people with Turner's syndrome have no gonads at all, they develop into females, with normal female internal sex organs and external genitalia—which proves that fetuses do not need ovaries or the hormones they produce to develop as females. Of course, they cannot bear children, because without ovaries they cannot produce ova.

External Genitalia

The external genitalia are the visible sex organs, including the penis and scrotum in males and the labia, clitoris, and outer part of the vagina in females. (See *Figure 9.4.*) As we just saw, the external genitalia do not need to be stimulated by female sex hormones to become female; they just naturally develop that way. However, masculine development requires the presence of androgens—in particular, the presence of dihydrotestosterone (Josso et al., 1991). Thus, the gender of a person's external genitalia

Testosterone (*tess **tahss** ter own*) The principal androgen found in males.

Androgen insensitivity syndrome A condition caused by a congenital lack of functioning androgen receptors; in a person with XY sex chromosomes, causes the development of a female with testes but no internal sex organs.

Persistent Müllerian duct syndrome A condition caused by a congenital lack of functioning anti-Müllerian hormone receptors; in a male, causes development of both male and female internal sex organs.

Turner's syndrome The presence of only one sex chromosome (an X chromosome); characterized by lack of ovaries but otherwise normal female sex organs and genitalia.

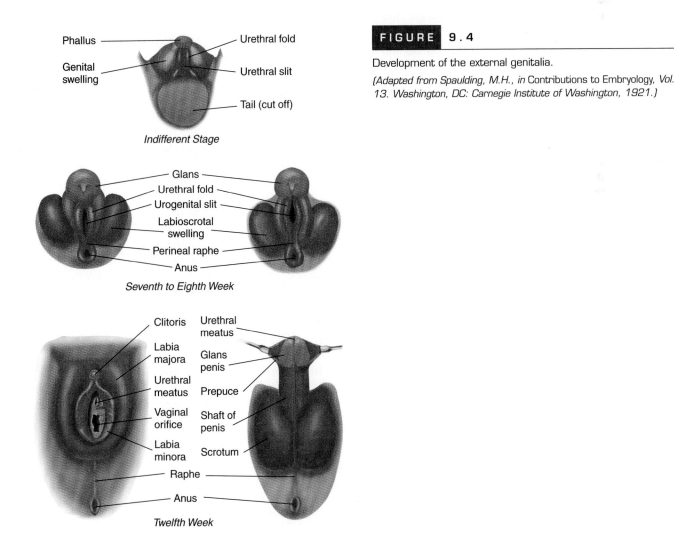

FIGURE 9.4

Development of the external genitalia.

(Adapted from Spaulding, M.H., in Contributions to Embryology, *Vol. 13. Washington, DC: Carnegie Institute of Washington, 1921.)*

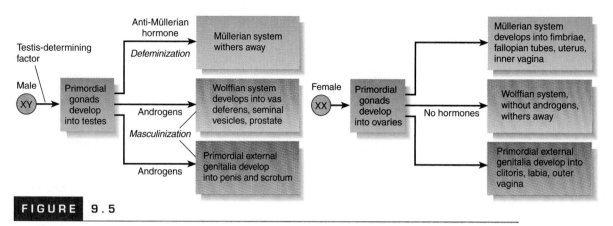

FIGURE 9.5

Hormonal control of masculinization and defeminization of the internal sex organs and external genitalia.

Gonadotropin-releasing hormone (*go nad oh* **trow** *pin*) A hypothalamic hormone that stimulates the anterior pituitary gland to secrete gonadotropic hormone.

Gonadotropic hormone A hormone of the anterior pituitary gland that has a stimulating effect on cells of the gonads.

Follicle-stimulating hormone (FSH) The hormone of the anterior pituitary gland that causes development of an ovarian follicle and the maturation of its oocyte into an ovum.

Luteinizing hormone (LH) (*lew tee a nize ing*) A hormone of the anterior pituitary gland that causes ovulation and development of the ovarian follicle into a corpus luteum.

Estradiol (*ess tra* **dye** *ahl*) The principal estrogen of many mammals, including humans.

is determined by the presence or absence of testes—or, more precisely, by the presence or absence of the androgens they secrete. This fact explains why people with Turner's syndrome have female external genitalia even though they lack ovaries.

Figure 9.5 summarizes the factors that control the development of the gonads, internal sex organs, and genitalia. (See **Figure 9.5.**)

Sexual Maturation

The *primary* sex characteristics include the gonads, internal sex organs, and external genitalia. These organs are present at birth. The *secondary* sex characteristics, such as enlarged breasts and widened hips or a beard and deep voice, do not appear until puberty. Without seeing genitals, we must guess the sex of a prepubescent child from his or her haircut and clothing; the bodies of young boys and girls are rather similar. However, at puberty the gonads are stimulated to produce their hormones, and these hormones cause the person to mature sexually. The onset of puberty occurs when cells in the hypothalamus secrete **gonadotropin-releasing hormones** (GnRH), which stimulate the production and release of two **gonadotropic hormones** by the anterior pituitary gland. The gonadotropic ("gonad-turning") hormones stimulate the gonads to produce *their* hormones, which are ultimately responsible for sexual maturation. (See **Figure 9.6.**)

The two gonadotropic hormones are **follicle-stimulating hormone (FSH)** and **luteinizing hormone (LH),** named for the effects they produce in the female (production of a *follicle* and its subsequent *luteinization,* to be described in the next section of this chapter). However, the same hormones are produced in the male, where they stimulate the testes to produce sperms and to secrete testosterone. If male and female pituitary glands are exchanged in rats, the ovaries and testes respond perfectly to the hormones secreted by the new glands (Harris and Jacobsohn, 1951–1952).

In response to the gonadotropic hormones (usually called *gonadotropins*) the gonads secrete steroid sex hormones. The ovaries produce **estradiol,** one of a class of

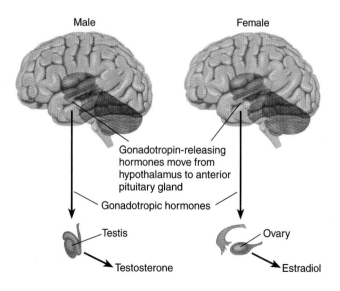

Gonadotropin-releasing hormones move from hypothalamus to anterior pituitary gland

Gonadotropic hormones

FIGURE 9.6

Sexual maturation. Puberty is initiated when the hypothalamus secretes gonadotropin-releasing hormones.

TABLE 9.1   Classification of Sex Steroid Hormones

Class	Principal Hormone in Humans (Where Produced)	Examples of Effects
Androgens	Testosterone (testes)	Development of Wolffian system; production of sperms; growth of facial, pubic, and axillary hair; muscular development; enlargement of larynx; inhibition of bone growth; sex drive in men (and women?)
	Androstenedione (adrenal glands)	In women, growth of pubic and axillary hair; less important than testosterone in men
Estrogens	Estradiol (ovaries)	Maturation of female genitalia; growth of breasts; alterations in fat deposits; growth of uterine lining; inhibition of bone growth; sex drive in women (?)
Gestagens	Progesterone (ovaries)	Maintenance of uterine lining
Hypothalamic hormones	Gonadotropin-releasing hormone (hypothalamus)	Secretion of gonadotropins
Gonadotropins	Follicle-stimulating hormone (anterior pituitary)	Development of ovarian follicle
	Luteinizing hormone (anterior pituitary)	Ovulation; development of corpus luteum

hormones known as **estrogens.** As we saw, the testes produce testosterone, an androgen. Both types of glands also produce a small amount of the hormones of the other sex. The gonadal steroids affect many parts of the body. Both estradiol and testosterone initiate closure of the growing portions of the bones and thus halt skeletal growth. Estradiol also causes breast development, growth of the lining of the uterus, changes in the deposition of body fat, and maturation of the female genitalia. Testosterone stimulates growth of facial, axillary (underarm), and pubic hair; lowers the voice; alters the hairline on the head (often causing baldness later in life); stimulates muscular development; and causes genital growth. This description leaves out two of the female secondary characteristics: axillary and pubic hair. These characteristics are produced not by estradiol but rather by androgens secreted by the cortex of the adrenal glands. Even a male who is castrated before puberty (whose testes are removed) will grow axillary and pubic hair, stimulated by his own adrenal androgens. A list of the principal sex hormones and examples of their effects are presented in Table 9.1. Note that some of these effects are discussed later in this chapter. (See *Table 9.1.*)

The bipotentiality of some of the secondary sex characteristics remains throughout life. If a man is treated with an estrogen (for example, to control an androgen-dependent tumor), he will grow breasts, and his facial hair will become finer and softer. However, his voice will remain low, because the enlargement of the larynx is permanent. Conversely, a woman who receives high levels of an androgen (usually, from a tumor that secretes androgens) will grow a beard, and her voice will become lower.

INTERIM SUMMARY

Gender is determined by the sex chromosomes: XX produces a female, and XY produces a male. Males are produced by the action of the SRY gene on the Y chromosome, which contains the code for the production of the testis-determining protein, which in turn causes the primitive gonads to become testes. The testes secrete two kinds of hormones that cause a male to develop. Testosterone (an

Estrogen (*ess trow jen*) A class of sex hormones that cause maturation of the female genitalia, growth of breast tissue, and development of other physical features characteristic of females.

androgen) stimulates the development of the Wolffian system (masculinization), and anti-Müllerian hormone suppresses the development of the Müllerian system (defeminization). Androgen insensitivity syndrome results from a hereditary defect in androgen receptors, and persistent Müllerian duct syndrome results from a hereditary defect in anti-Müllerian hormone receptors.

By default, the body is female ("Nature's impulse . . . "); only by the actions of testicular hormones does it become male. Masculinization and defeminization are referred to as *organizational* effects of hormones; *activational* effects occur after development is complete. A person with Turner's syndrome (X0) fails to develop gonads but nevertheless develops female internal sex organs and external genitalia. The external genitalia develop from common precursors. In the absence of gonadal hormones, the precursors develop the female form; in the presence of androgens, they develop the male form (masculinization).

Sexual maturity occurs when the hypothalamus begins secreting gonadotropin-releasing hormone, which stimulates the secretion of follicle-stimulating hormone and luteinizing hormone by the anterior pituitary gland. These hormones stimulate the gonads to secrete their hormones, thus causing the genitals to mature and the body to develop the secondary sex characteristics (activational effects).

■ THOUGHT QUESTIONS

1. Suppose that people could determine the sex of their child, say, by having one of the would-be parents take a drug before conceiving the baby. What would the consequences be?
2. With appropriate hormonal treatment, the uterus of a postmenopausal woman can be made ready for the implantation of another woman's ovum, fertilized in vitro, and she can become a mother. In fact, several women in their fifties and sixties have done so. What do you think about this procedure? Should decisions about using it be left to couples and their physicians, or does the rest of society (represented by their legislators) have an interest?

■ HORMONAL CONTROL OF SEXUAL BEHAVIOR

We have seen that hormones are responsible for sexual dimorphism in the structure of the body and its organs. Hormones have organizational and activational effects on the internal sex organs, genitals, and secondary sex characteristics. Naturally, all of these effects influence a person's behavior. Simply having the physique and genitals of a man or a woman exerts a powerful effect. But hormones do more than give us masculine or feminine bodies; they also affect behavior by interacting directly with the nervous system. Androgens present during prenatal development affect the development of the nervous system. In addition, both male and female sex hormones have activational effects on the adult nervous system that influence both physiological processes and behavior. This section considers some of these hormonal effects.

Hormonal Control of Female Reproductive Cycles

Menstrual cycle (*men strew al*) The female reproductive cycle of most primates, including humans; characterized by growth of the lining of the uterus, ovulation, development of a corpus luteum, and (if pregnancy does not occur), menstruation.

Estrous cycle The female reproductive cycle of mammals other than primates.

The reproductive cycle of female primates is called a **menstrual cycle** (from *mensis,* meaning "month"). Females of other species of mammals also have reproductive cycles, called **estrous cycles.** *Estrus* means "gadfly"; when a female rat is in estrus, her hormonal condition goads her to act differently than she does at other times. (For that matter, it goads male rats to act differently, too.) The primary feature of menstrual cycles that distinguishes them from estrous cycles is the monthly growth and loss of the lining of the uterus. The other features are approximately the same—except that the estrous cycle of rats takes four days. Also, the sexual behavior of female mammals with estrous cycles is linked with ovulation, whereas most female primates can mate at any time during their menstrual cycle.

Menstrual cycles and estrous cycles consist of a sequence of events that are controlled by hormonal secretions of the pituitary gland and ovaries. These glands interact, the secretions of one affecting those of the other. A cycle begins with the secretion of gonadotropins by the anterior pituitary gland. These hormones (especially FSH) stimulate the growth of **ovarian follicles,** small spheres of epithelial cells surrounding each ovum. Women normally produce one ovarian follicle each month; if two are produced and fertilized, dizygotic (fraternal) twins will develop. As ovarian follicles mature, they secrete estradiol, which causes the growth of the lining of the uterus in preparation for implantation of the ovum, should it be fertilized by a sperm. Feedback from the increasing level of estradiol eventually triggers the release of a surge of LH by the anterior pituitary gland. (See *Figure 9.7.*)

The LH surge causes *ovulation:* The ovarian follicle ruptures, releasing the ovum. Under the continued influence of LH the ruptured ovarian follicle becomes a **corpus luteum** ("yellow body"), which produces estradiol and **progesterone.** (See *Figure 9.7.*) The latter hormone promotes pregnancy *(gestation).* It maintains the lining of the uterus, and it inhibits the ovaries from producing another follicle. Meanwhile, the ovum enters one of the Fallopian tubes and begins its progress toward the uterus. If it meets sperm cells during its travel down the Fallopian tube and becomes fertilized, it begins to divide, and several days later it attaches itself to the uterine wall.

If the ovum is not fertilized, or if it is fertilized too late to develop sufficiently by the time it gets to the uterus, the corpus luteum will stop producing estradiol and progesterone, and then the lining of the walls of the uterus will slough off. At this point, menstruation will commence.

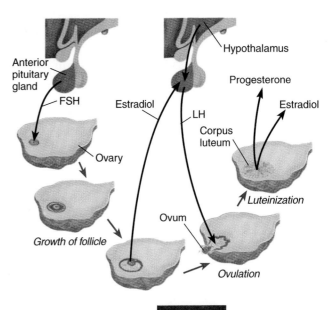

FIGURE 9.7

Neuroendocrine control of the menstrual cycle.

Hormonal Control of Sexual Behavior of Laboratory Animals

The interactions between sex hormones and the human brain are difficult to study. We must turn to two sources of information: experiments with animals and various developmental disorders in humans, which serve as nature's own "experiments." Let us first consider the evidence gathered from research with laboratory animals.

Males

Male sexual behavior is quite varied, although the essential features of *intromission* (entry of the penis into the female's vagina), *pelvic thrusting* (rhythmic movement of the hindquarters, causing genital friction), and *ejaculation* (discharge of semen) are characteristic of all male mammals. Humans, of course, have invented all kinds of copulatory and noncopulatory sexual behavior. For example, the pelvic movements leading to ejaculation may be performed by the woman, and sex play can lead to orgasm without intromission.

The sexual behavior of rats has been studied more than that of any other laboratory animal. When a male rat encounters a receptive female, he will spend some time nuzzling her and sniffing and licking her genitals, mount her, and engage in pelvic thrusting. He will mount her several times, achieving intromission on most of the mountings. After eight to fifteen intromissions approximately 1 minute apart (each lasting only about one-quarter of a second), the male will ejaculate.

Ovarian follicle A cluster of epithelial cells surrounding an oocyte, which develops into an ovum.

Corpus luteum (*lew* tee um) A cluster of cells that develops from the ovarian follicle after ovulation; secretes estradiol and progesterone.

Progesterone (pro *jess* ter own) A steroid hormone produced by the ovary that maintains the endometrial lining of the uterus during the later part of the menstrual cycle and during pregnancy; along with estradiol, it promotes receptivity in female mammals with estrous cycles.

After ejaculating, the male refrains from sexual activity for a period of time (minutes, in the rat). Most mammals will return to copulate again and again, showing a longer pause, called a **refractory period,** after each ejaculation. (The term comes from the Latin *refringere,* "to break off.")

Sexual behavior of male rodents depends on testosterone, a fact that has long been recognized (Bermant and Davidson, 1974). If a male rat is castrated (that is, if his testes are removed), his sexual activity eventually ceases. However, the behavior can be reinstated by injections of testosterone. I will describe the neural basis of this activational effect later in this chapter.

Females

The mammalian female has been described as the passive participant in copulation. It is true that in some species the female's role during the act of copulation is merely to assume a posture that exposes her genitals to the male. This behavior is called the **lordosis** response (from the Greek *lordos,* meaning "bent backward"). The female will also move her tail away (if she has one) and stand rigidly enough to support the weight of the male.

The behavior of a female rodent in *initiating* copulation is often very active, however. Certainly, if a male attempts to copulate with a nonestrous rodent, the female will either actively flee or rebuff him. But when the female is in a receptive state, she will often approach the male, nuzzle him, sniff his genitals, and show behaviors characteristic of her species. For example, a female rat will exhibit quick, short, hopping movements and rapid ear wiggling, which most male rats find irresistible (McClintock and Adler, 1978).

Sexual behavior of female rodents depends on the gonadal hormones that are present during estrus: estradiol and progesterone. In rats, estradiol increases about 40 hours before the female becomes receptive; just before receptivity occurs, the corpus luteum begins secreting large quantities of progesterone (Feder, 1981). Ovariectomized rats (rats whose ovaries have been removed) are not sexually receptive. Although sexual receptivity can be produced in ovariectomized rodents by administering large doses of estradiol alone, the most effective treatment duplicates the normal sequence of hormones: a small amount of estradiol, followed by progesterone. Progesterone alone is ineffective; thus, the estradiol "primes" its effectiveness. Priming with estradiol takes about 16–24 hours, after which an injection of progesterone produces receptive behaviors within an hour (Takahashi, 1990).

The sequence of estradiol followed by progesterone has three effects on female rats: It increases their receptivity, their proceptivity, and their attractiveness. *Receptivity* refers to their ability and willingness to copulate—to accept the advances of a male by holding still and displaying lordosis when he attempts to mount. *Proceptivity* refers to a female's eagerness to copulate, as shown by the fact that she seeks out a male and engages in behaviors that tend to arouse his sexual interest. *Attractiveness* refers to physiological and behavioral changes that affect the male. The male rat (along with many other male mammals) is most responsive to females who are in estrus ("in heat"). Males will ignore a female whose ovaries have been removed, but injections of estradiol and progesterone will restore her attractiveness (and also change her behavior toward the male). The stimuli that arouse a male rat's sexual interest include her odor and her behavior. In some species, visible changes, such as the swollen sex skin in the genital region of a female monkey, also affect sex appeal.

Organizational Effects of Androgens on Behavior: Masculinization and Defeminization

The dictum "Nature's impulse is to create a female" applies to sexual behavior as well as to sex organs. That is, if a rodent's brain is *not* exposed to androgens during

Refractory period (*ree frak to ree*) A period of time after a particular action (for example, an ejaculation by a male) during which that action cannot occur again.

Lordosis A spinal sexual reflex seen in many four-legged female mammals; arching of the back in response to approach of a male or to touching the flanks, which elevates the hindquarters.

a critical period of development, the animal will engage in female sexual behavior as an adult (if then given estradiol and progesterone). Fortunately for experimenters, this critical time comes shortly after birth for rats and for several other species of rodents that are born in a rather immature condition. Thus, if a male rat is castrated immediately after birth, permitted to grow to adulthood, and then given injections of estradiol and progesterone, it will respond to the presence of another male by arching its back and presenting its hindquarters. In other words, it will act as if it were a female (Blaustein and Olster, 1989).

In contrast, if a rodent brain is exposed to androgens during development, two phenomena occur: behavioral defeminization and behavioral masculinization. *Behavioral defeminization* refers to the organizational effect of androgens that prevents the animal from displaying female sexual behavior in adulthood. As we shall see later, this effect is accomplished by suppressing the development of neural circuits controlling female sexual behavior. For example, if a female rodent is ovariectomized and given an injection of testosterone immediately after birth, she will *not* respond to a male rat when, as an adult, she is given injections of estradiol and progesterone. *Behavioral masculinization* refers to the organizational effect of androgens that enables animals to engage in male sexual behavior in adulthood. This effect is accomplished by stimulating the development of neural circuits controlling male sexual behavior. For example, if the female rodent in my previous example is given testosterone in adulthood, rather than estradiol and progesterone, she will mount and attempt to copulate with a receptive female. (See Breedlove, 1992, and Carter, 1992, for references to specific studies.) (See *Figure 9.8*.)

Research by Moore and her colleagues (reviewed by Moore, 1986) indicates that some of the masculinizing and defeminizing effects of androgens are even more indirect. As we will see in a later section in this chapter, female rats spend a considerable amount of time licking the genital region of their offspring. This behavior is very useful, because it stimulates urination and permits the mother to ingest the water and minerals that are released so that they can be recycled in her milk.

Moore and her colleagues discovered that mothers spent much more time licking their male offspring and wondered whether this licking could have any effects on the sexual behavior of these offspring later in life. Indeed, it did. First, the experimenters found that androgens caused the secretion of an odorous chemical in the male pups' urine, which was attractive to the mothers. Next, they found that if they destroyed the mothers' ability to smell the odor, the mothers failed to give the males special attention—and that these males showed decreases in their sexual behavior in adulthood. But if the experimenters stroked the genitals of the male pups with a small brush each day, the animals showed a greater level of sexual behavior when they grew up. Thus, at least some of the organizational effects of androgens are accomplished through an intermediary—the infant's mother.

Effects of Pheromones

Hormones transmit messages from one part of the body (the secreting gland) to another (the target tissue). Another class of chemicals, called **pheromones,** carries messages from one animal to another. Some of these chemicals, like hormones, affect reproductive behavior. Karlson and Luscher (1959) coined the term, from the Greek *pherein,* "to carry," and *horman,* "to excite." Pheromones are released by one animal

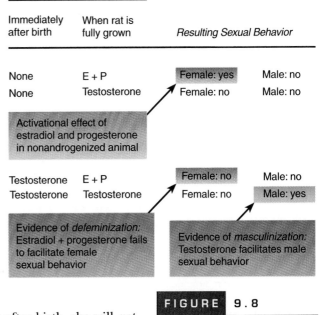

Hormone Treatment

Immediately after birth	When rat is fully grown	Resulting Sexual Behavior	
None	E + P	Female: yes	Male: no
None	Testosterone	Female: no	Male: no

Activational effect of estradiol and progesterone in nonandrogenized animal

| Testosterone | E + P | Female: no | Male: no |
| Testosterone | Testosterone | Female: no | Male: yes |

Evidence of *defeminization:* Estradiol + progesterone fails to facilitate female sexual behavior

Evidence of *masculinization:* Testosterone facilitates male sexual behavior

FIGURE 9.8

Organizational effects of testosterone. Around the time of birth, testosterone masculinizes and defeminizes rodents' sexual behavior.

Pheromone [*fair* oh *moan*]
A chemical released by one animal that affects the behavior or physiology of another animal; usually smelled or tasted.

Lee-Boot effect The increased incidence of false pregnancies seen in female animals that are housed together; caused by a pheromone in the animals' urine; first observed in mice.

Whitten effect The synchronization of the menstrual or estrous cycles of a group of females, which occurs only in the presence of a pheromone in a male's urine.

Vandenbergh effect The earlier onset of puberty seen in female animals that are housed with males; caused by a pheromone in the male's urine; first observed in mice.

Bruce effect Termination of pregnancy caused by the odor of a pheromone in the urine of a male other than the one that impregnated the female; first identified in mice.

Vomeronasal organ [*voe mer oh nay zul*] A sensory organ that detects the presence of certain chemicals, especially when a liquid is actively sniffed; mediates the effects of some pheromones.

Accessory olfactory bulb A neural structure located in the main olfactory bulb that receives information from the vomeronasal organ.

Medial nucleus of the amygdala [*a mig da la*] A nucleus that receives olfactory information from the olfactory bulb and accessory olfactory bulb; involved in the effects of odors and pheromones on reproductive behavior.

and directly affect the physiology or behavior of another. In mammalian species, most pheromones are detected by means of olfaction.

Pheromones can affect reproductive physiology or behavior. First, let us consider the effects on reproductive physiology. When groups of female mice are housed together, their estrous cycles slow down and eventually stop. This phenomenon is known as the **Lee-Boot effect** (van der Lee and Boot, 1955). If groups of females are exposed to the odor of a male (or of his urine), they begin cycling again, and their cycles tend to be synchronized. This phenomenon is known as the **Whitten effect** (Whitten, 1959). The **Vandenbergh effect** (Vandenbergh, Whitsett, and Lombardi, 1975) is the acceleration of the onset of puberty in a female rodent caused by the odor of a male. Both the Whitten effect and the Vandenbergh effect are caused by a pheromone that is present only in the urine of intact adult males; the urine of a juvenile or castrated male has no effect. Thus, the production of the pheromone requires the presence of testosterone.

The **Bruce effect** (Bruce, 1960a, 1960b) is a particularly interesting phenomenon: When a recently impregnated female mouse encounters a normal male mouse other than the one with which she mated, the pregnancy is very likely to fail. This effect, too, is caused by a substance secreted in the urine of intact males—but not of males that have been castrated. Thus, a male mouse that encounters a pregnant female is able to prevent the birth of infants carrying another male's genes and subsequently impregnate the female himself. This phenomenon is advantageous even from the female's point of view. The fact that the new male has managed to take over the old male's territory indicates that he is probably healthier and more vigorous—and therefore his genes will contribute to the formation of offspring that are more likely to survive.

As you learned in Chapter 7, detection of odors is accomplished by the olfactory bulbs, which constitute the primary olfactory system. However, the four effects that pheromones have on reproductive cycles appear to be mediated by another organ—the **vomeronasal organ**—which consists of a small group of sensory receptors arranged around a pouch connected by a duct to the nasal passage. The vomeronasal organ, which is present in all orders of mammals except for cetaceans (whales and dolphins), projects to the **accessory olfactory bulb,** located immediately behind the olfactory bulb (Wysocki, 1979). (See *Figure 9.9.*) The vomeronasal organ probably does not detect airborne molecules, as the olfactory bulbs do, but instead is sensitive to nonvolatile compounds found in urine or other substances. In fact, stimulation of a nerve that serves the nasal region of the hamster causes fluid to be pumped into the vomeronasal organ, which exposes the receptors to any substances that may be present (Meredith and O'Connell, 1979). This pump is activated whenever the animal encounters a novel stimulus (Meredith, 1994).

Removal of the accessory olfactory bulb disrupts the Lee-Boot effect, the Whitten effect, the Vandenbergh effect, and the Bruce effect; thus, this organ is essential for these phenomena (Halpern, 1987). The accessory olfactory bulb sends axons to the **medial nucleus of the amygdala,** which in turn projects to the preoptic area and anterior hypothalamus and to the ventromedial nucleus of the hypothalamus. (As you learned in Chapter 7, so

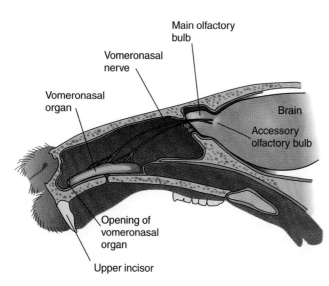

Main olfactory bulb

Vomeronasal nerve

Vomeronasal organ

Brain

Accessory olfactory bulb

Opening of vomeronasal organ

Upper incisor

FIGURE   9.9

The rodent accessory olfactory system.

[Adapted from Wysocki, C.J. Neuroscience & Biobehavioral Reviews, *1979, 3, 301–341.]*

does the main olfactory bulb.) Thus, the neural circuit responsible for the effects of these pheromones appears to involve these regions. As we shall see, the preoptic area, the medial amygdala, and the ventromedial nucleus of the hypothalamus all play important roles in reproductive behavior. (See *Figure 9.10.*)

The Bruce effect involves learning; the female obviously learns to recognize the odor of the male with which she mates, because his odor will not cause her to abort if she encounters it later. This learning appears to require the activity of a set of noradrenergic axons that enter the olfactory bulbs and form synapses with neurons in both the main and accessory olfactory bulbs. Keverne and de la Riva (1982) found that after these axons had been destroyed with infusions of 6-hydroxydopamine (6-HD), a female mouse would not learn to recognize the odor of the male that mated with her; even *his* odor would cause her to abort.

It is possible that the stimuli associated with copulation trigger the noradrenergic mechanism and "imprint" the odor of the male on the female, ensuring that she will not abort if she later encounters his odor. Indeed, Rosser and Keverne (1985) found that vaginal stimulation increases the activity in the noradrenergic axons that serve the olfactory bulbs. As other studies have shown (Gray, Freeman, and Skinner, 1986; Leon, 1987), the release of norepinephrine in the olfactory bulbs is necessary for olfactory learning.

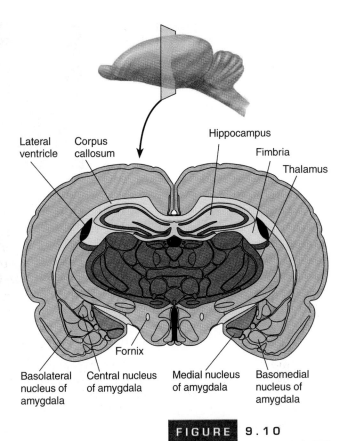

FIGURE 9.10

A cross section through the rat brain showing the location of the amygdala.

[Adapted from Swanson, L. W. Brain Maps: Structure of the Rat Brain. New York: Elsevier, 1992.]

Besides having effects on reproductive physiology, some pheromones directly affect behavior. For example, pheromones present in the vaginal secretions of female hamsters stimulate sexual behavior in males. Males are attracted to the secretions of females, and they sniff and lick the female's genitals before copulating. In fact, there may be two categories of pheromones, one detected by the vomeronasal organ and another detected by the olfactory epithelium; mating behavior of male hamsters is disrupted only if *both* systems are interrupted (Powers and Winans, 1975; Winans and Powers, 1977). As we saw, both the primary and accessory olfactory systems send fibers to the medial nucleus of the amygdala. Lehman and Winans (1982) found that lesions of the medial amygdala abolished the sexual behavior of male hamsters. Thus, the amygdala is part of the system that mediates the effects of pheromones on the sexual behavior of male hamsters.

It appears that at least some pheromone-related phenomena occur in humans. McClintock (1971) studied the menstrual cycles of women attending an all-female college. She found that women who spent a large amount of time together tended to have synchronized cycles—their menstrual periods began within a day or two of one another. In addition, women who regularly spent some time in the presence of men tended to have shorter cycles than those who rarely spent time with (smelled?) men.

Russell, Switz, and Thompson (1977) obtained direct evidence that olfactory stimuli can synchronize women's menstrual cycles. The investigators collected daily samples of a woman's underarm sweat. They dissolved the samples in alcohol and swabbed them on the upper lips of a group of women three times each week, in the order in which they were originally taken. The cycles of the women who received the extract (but not those of control subjects whose lips were swabbed with pure alcohol) began to synchronize with the cycle of the odor donor. Are there any sex-attractant pheromones that affect human behavior? Is the scenario described in the Prologue a plausible one? I will discuss this issue in the Epilogue at the end of the chapter.

The presence of pheromone-related phenomena in humans was confirmed by the discovery that women who regularly spend time together tend to have synchronized menstrual cycles.

Human Sexual Behavior

Human sexual behavior, like that of other mammals, is influenced by activational effects of gonadal hormones and, almost certainly, organizational effects as well. But as we will see in the following subsections, the effects of these hormones are different in our species—especially in women.

If hormones have organizational effects on human sexual behavior, they must exert these effects by altering the development of the brain. Although there is good evidence that prenatal exposure to androgens affects development of the human brain, we cannot yet be certain that this exposure has long-lasting behavioral effects. The evidence pertaining to these issues is discussed later, in a section on sexual orientation.

Activational Effects of Sex Hormones in Women

As we saw, the sexual behavior of most female mammals other than higher primates is controlled by the ovarian hormones estradiol and progesterone. (In some species, such as cats and rabbits, only estradiol is necessary.) As Wallen (1990) pointed out, the ovarian hormones control not only the *willingness* (or even eagerness) of an estrous female to mate but also her *ability* to mate. That is, a male rat cannot copulate with a female rat that is not in estrus. Even if he were to overpower her and mount her, her lordosis response would not occur, and he would be unable to achieve intromission. (The neural control of the lordosis response and the effects of ovarian hormones on it are described later in this chapter.)

In higher primates (including our own species) the ability to mate is not controlled by ovarian hormones. There are no physical barriers to sexual intercourse during any part of the menstrual cycle. If a woman or other female primate consents to sexual activity at any time (or is forced to submit by a male), intercourse can certainly take place.

This difference between females with estrous cycles and those with menstrual cycles has obscured the effects of ovarian hormones on the sexual behavior of female primates. Most studies have reported that fluctuations in the level of the ovarian hormones have only a minor effect on women's sexual interest (Adams, Gold, and Burt, 1978; Morris et al., 1987). However, as Wallen (1990) pointed out, these studies have almost all involved married women who live with their husbands. In stable, monogamous relationships in which the partners are together on a daily basis, sexual activity can be instigated by either of them. Normally, a husband does not force his wife to have intercourse with him, but even if she is not interested in engaging in sexual activity at that moment, she may find that she wants to do so because of her affection for him. In fact, a study of lesbian couples (whose menstrual cycles are likely to be synchronized) found a significant increase in sexual interest and activity during the middle portions of the women's cycles (Matteo and Rissman, 1984).

Several studies have found that the sexual behavior of female monkeys is only poorly related to their menstrual cycles. However, most of these studies were carried out with small numbers of monkeys living in small cages. Thus, intercourse was as likely to be instigated by a male as by the female. Wallen et al. (1986) observed female monkeys that were housed in large groups in large cages, in a situation in which a female could seek out a sex partner if she wanted one but could avoid sexual contact if she preferred. Figure 9.11 contrasts the results of these two types of studies; note that the sexual activity of females housed in large-group situations closely corresponded with their cycles of ovarian hormones. (See *Figure 9.11.*)

These results pose an interesting question. If all of a woman's sexual encounters were initiated by her, without regard to her partner's desires, would we find as strong an effect of ovarian hormones as Wallen and his colleagues found in monkeys? As Alexander et al. (1990) showed, women taking oral contraceptives (which prevent the normal cycles in secretion of ovarian hormones) were less likely to show fluctuations in sexual interest during the menstrual cycle. In any event, the results with monkeys indicate that the possibility remains that ovarian hormones *do* have a significant effect on a woman's sexual desire.

Where higher primates and animals with estrous cycles differ is in their reaction to androgens. In mammals other than primates, androgens stimulate only male sexual behavior. Persky et al. (1978) studied the sexual activity and blood levels of various hormones in married couples over a period of three menstrual cycles. They found that the frequency of intercourse over the entire cycle was at least moderately correlated with the wife's peak testosterone level, which occurs around the time of ovulation. In addition, the wives reported more sexual gratification when their testosterone levels were high. A follow-up study by Morris et al. (1987) found similar results. And in a study of women using oral contraceptives, Alexander and Sherwin (1993) found that plasma testosterone levels were correlated with the women's "sexual desire, sexual thoughts, and anticipation of sexual activity."

In a carefully controlled study, Sherwin, Gelfand, and Brender (1985) investigated the effects of testosterone on sexual interest in women who had undergone hysterectomies and ovariectomies. They found the hormone increased the intensity of the women's sexual desire and the frequency of sexual fantasies. As Sherwin (1994) concluded in a review of the relevant literature, "it would now seem that testosterone is the hormone most crucially implicated in the maintenance of . . . sexual desire, in women just as it is in men" (p. 423).

Activational Effects of Sex Hormones in Men

Although women and mammals with estrous cycles differ in their behavioral responsiveness to sex hormones, men resemble other mammals in their behavioral responsiveness to testosterone. With normal levels they can be potent and fertile; without testosterone, sperm production ceases and, sooner or later, so does sexual potency. Some investigators have said that the sexual activity of humans is "emancipated" from the effects of hormones. In one sense this is true. Many men who have been castrated (for medical reasons) do report a continuing interest in sexual activity with their wives. Even if sexual activity no longer takes the form of intercourse, other types of sexual contact can occur.

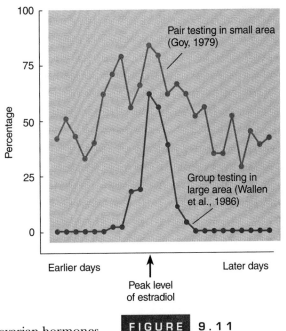

FIGURE 9.11

Percentage of tests in which ejaculations occurred in the course of a female monkey's menstrual cycle.

[Adapted from Wallen, K. Neuroscience and Biobehavioral Reviews, 1990, 14, 233–241; after Goy, 1979 and Wallen et al., 1986.]

The decline of sexual activity after castration is quite variable. As reported by Money and Ehrhardt (1972), some men lose potency immediately, whereas others show a slow, gradual decline over several years. Perhaps at least some of the variability is a function of prior experience; practice not only may "make perfect" but may also forestall a decline in function. Although there is no direct evidence with respect to this possibility in humans, Rosenblatt and Aronson (1958a, 1958b) found that male cats that had engaged in high levels of sexual activity remained potent for a longer time after they were castrated. Also, there are other sources of androgens besides the testes that may supply at least small amounts of male sex hormones: the adrenal glands, the prostate gland, and even fat tissue (Carter, 1992).

Testosterone not only affects sexual activity but also is affected by it—or even by thinking about it. A scientist stationed on a remote island (Anonymous, 1970) removed his beard with an electrical shaver each day and weighed the clippings. Just before he left for visits to the mainland (and to the company of a female companion), his beard began growing faster. Because rate of beard growth is related to androgen levels, the effect indicates that his anticipation of sexual activity stimulated testosterone production. Confirming these results, Hellhammer, Hubert, and Schurmeyer (1985) found that watching an erotic film increased men's testosterone level.

Sexual Orientation

What controls a person's sexual orientation—the gender of the preferred sex partner? Some people (especially males) who are essentially heterosexual engage in homosexual episodes sometime during their lives. Although many animals occasionally engage in sexual activity with a member of the same sex, *exclusive* homosexuality appears to occur only in humans (Ehrhardt and Meyer-Bahlburg, 1981). Animals of other species, if they are not exclusively heterosexual, are likely to be bisexual, engaging in sexual activity with members of both sexes. In contrast, the number of men and women who describe themselves as exclusively homosexual exceeds the number who describe themselves as bisexual.

Some investigators believe that homosexuality is a result of childhood experiences, especially interactions between the child and parents. A large-scale study of several hundred male and female homosexuals reported by Bell, Weinberg, and Hammersmith (1981) attempted to assess the effects of these factors. The researchers found no evidence that homosexuals had been raised by domineering mothers or submissive fathers, as some clinicians had suggested. The best predictor of adult homosexuality was a self-report of homosexual feelings, which usually preceded homosexual activity by three years. The investigators concluded that their data did not support social explanations for homosexuality but were consistent with the possibility that homosexuality is at least partly biologically determined.

If homosexuality does have a physiological cause, it certainly is not variations in the levels of sex hormones during adulthood. Many studies have examined the levels of sex steroids in male homosexuals (Meyer-Bahlburg, 1984), and the vast majority of them found these levels to be similar to those of heterosexuals. A few studies suggest that about 30 percent of female homosexuals have elevated levels of testosterone (but still lower than those found in men). Whether these differences are related to a biological cause of lesbianism or whether differences in lifestyles may increase the secretion of testosterone is not yet known.

A more likely biological cause of homosexuality is a subtle difference in brain structure caused by differences in the amount of prenatal exposure to androgens. Perhaps, then, the brains of male homosexuals are neither masculinized nor defeminized, those of female homosexuals are masculinized and defeminized, and those of bisexuals are masculinized but not defeminized. Of course, these are *speculations* that so far cannot be supported by human data; they are not *conclusions*. They should be regarded as suggestions to guide future research.

Prenatal Androgenization of Genetic Females

Evidence suggests that prenatal androgens can affect human social behavior and sexual orientation, as well as anatomy. In a disorder known as **congenital adrenal hyperplasia (CAH),** the adrenal glands secrete abnormal amounts of androgens. (*Hyperplasia* means "excessive formation.") The secretion of androgens begins prenatally; thus, the syndrome causes prenatal masculinization. Boys born with CAH develop normally; the extra androgen does not seem to have significant effects. However, a girl with CAH will be born with an enlarged clitoris, and her labia may be partly fused together. (As Figure 9.4 shows, the scrotum and labia develop from the same tissue in the fetus.) If the masculinization of the genitals is pronounced, surgery can be performed to correct them. In any event, once the syndrome is identified, the person can be given a synthetic hormone that suppresses the abnormal secretion of androgens.

Money, Schwartz, and Lewis (1984) studied thirty young women with a history of CAH. They had all been born with enlarged clitorises and partly fused labia, which led to the diagnosis. (A few mild cases were not diagnosed for several years.) Once the diagnosis was made, they were treated with drugs that suppress the secretion of adrenal androgens, and, if necessary, genital surgery was performed. Money and his colleagues asked the young women to describe their sexual orientation. Thirty-seven percent of the women described themselves as bisexual or homosexual, 40 percent said they were exclusively heterosexual, and 23 percent refused to talk about their sex lives. If the noncommittal women are excluded from the sample, the percentage of homosexuality or bisexuality rises to 48 percent.

The Kinsey report on sexuality in women (Kinsey et al., 1943) reported that approximately 10 percent of American women had had some sexual contact with another woman by the age of 20; in the sample of women exposed prenatally to androgens the percentage was at least four times as high. The results suggest that the exposure of a female fetus to an abnormally high level of androgens does affect sexual orientation. A plausible explanation is that the effect takes place in the brain, but we must remember that the androgens also affect the genitals; possibly, the changes in the genitals played a role in shaping the development of the girls' sexual orientation. If the differences seen in sexual orientation *were* caused by effects of the prenatal androgens on brain development, then we could reasonably conclude that androgens have this effect in males, too. That is, these results support the hypothesis that male sexual orientation is at least partly determined by masculinizing (and defeminizing) effects of androgens on the human brain.

Because controlled experiments cannot be performed on humans, some investigators have turned to our close relatives to see whether exposure to prenatal androgens has enduring behavioral effects. Goy, Bercovitch, and McBrair (1988) administered injections of testosterone to pregnant monkeys. The testosterone entered the blood supply of the fetuses and masculinized them. Female infants that had been exposed to androgens during early fetal development were born with masculinized genitals; the genitals of those that had been exposed to androgens later were normal. *Both* groups showed differences in their sociosexual interactions with peers, displaying a higher proportion of malelike behavior than normal females did. For example, even as young adults, the androgen-exposed females with normal genitals continued to mount their peers significantly more than normal females did. The results suggest that genital changes cannot account for all the behavioral effects of prenatal exposure to androgens in primates. Whether *human* primates share these characteristics is, of course, another question.

Failure of Androgenization of Genetic Males

As we saw, genetic males with androgen insensitivity syndrome develop as females, with female external genitalia—but also with testes and without uterus or Fallopian tubes. If an individual with this syndrome is raised as a girl, all is well. Normally, the

Congenital adrenal hyperplasia (CAH) (*hy per play zha*) A condition characterized by hypersecretion of androgens by the adrenal cortex; in females, causes masculinization of the external genitalia.

testes are removed because they often become cancerous; but if they are not, the body will mature into that of a woman at the time of puberty through the effects of the small amounts of estradiol produced by the testes. (If the testes are removed, the person will be given estradiol to accomplish the same result.) At adulthood the individual will function sexually as a woman, although surgical lengthening of the vagina may be necessary. Women with this syndrome report average sex drives, including normal frequency of orgasm in intercourse. Most marry and lead normal sex lives.

Studies of the social behavior of people with androgen insensitivity syndrome indicate that they tend to be very "feminine" (Money and Ehrhardt, 1972). There is no indication of sexual orientation toward women. Thus, the lack of androgen receptors appears to prevent both the masculinizing and defeminizing effects of androgens on a person's sexual interest. Of course, it is also possible that rearing a child as a girl plays an important role in that person's sexual orientation.

Sexual Orientation and the Brain

The human brain is a sexually dimorphic organ. This fact has long been suspected, even before confirmation was received from anatomical studies and studies of regional cerebral metabolism using PET and functional MRI. For example, neurologists discovered that the two hemispheres of a woman's brain appear to share functions more than those of a man's brain do. If a man sustains a stroke that damages the left side of the brain, he is more likely to show impairments in language than is a woman with similar damage. Presumably, the woman's right hemisphere shares language functions with the left, so that damage to one hemisphere is less devastating than it is in men. Also, men's brains are, on the average, somewhat larger—apparently because men's bodies are generally larger than those of women. In addition, the sizes of some specific regions of the telencephalon and diencephalon are different in males and females, and the shape of the corpus callosum may also be sexually dimorphic. (See Breedlove, 1994, and Swaab, Gooren, and Hofman, 1995, for specific references.)

Most investigators believe that the sexual dimorphism of the human brain is a result of differential exposure to androgens prenatally and during early postnatal life. Of course, additional changes could occur at the time of puberty, when another surge in androgens occurs. The differences could even be a result of differences in the social environments of males and females. We cannot manipulate the hormone levels of humans before and after birth as we can with laboratory animals, so it may be a long time before enough evidence is gathered to permit us to make definite conclusions.

Several studies have examined the brains of deceased heterosexual and homosexual men and heterosexual women. So far, these studies have found differences in the size of three different subregions of the brain: the suprachiasmatic nucleus, a sexually dimorphic nucleus of the hypothalamus, and the anterior commissure (Swaab and Hofman, 1990; LeVay, 1991; Allen and Gorski, 1992). You are already familiar with the suprachiasmatic nucleus from Chapter 8; the anterior commissure is a fiber bundle that interconnects parts of the left and right temporal lobes. The suprachiasmatic nucleus was found to be larger in homosexual men and smaller in heterosexual men and women; a sexually dimorphic nucleus of the hypothalamus (the *third interstitial nucleus of the anterior hypothalamus,* or *INAH-3*) was found to be larger in heterosexual men and smaller in homosexual men and heterosexual women; and the anterior commissure was found to be larger in homosexual men and heterosexual women and smaller in heterosexual men. Obviously, the differences did not follow a simple pattern.

Although this section has been considering sexual orientation—the sex of a person to whom an individual is sexually and romantically attracted—another sexual characteristic is related to structural differences in the brain. Zhou et al. (1995) found that the size of a particular region of the forebrain, the central subdivision of the *bed nucleus of the stria terminalis (BNST)*, is larger in males than in females. They also found that in male transsexuals, this nucleus is as small as it is in females. The size of this nucleus was as large in male homosexuals as in male heterosexuals. Thus, its size was related to sexual *identity*, not to sexual *orientation*. (See *Figure 9.12*.) Male transsexuals are men who regard themselves as females trapped in male bodies. Some go so far as to seek medical assistance to obtain female sex hormones and sex-change operations. (Most male homosexuals have male sexual identities; although they are romantically and sexually oriented toward other men, they do not regard themselves as women, nor do they wish to be.) Whether the BNST actually plays a role in a person's sexual identity will have to be determined by further research.

We cannot necessarily conclude that any of the brain regions I just mentioned are directly involved in people's sexual orientation (or sexual identity), but the results do suggest the following: The brains of heterosexual women, heterosexual men, and homosexual men may have been exposed to different patterns of hormones prenatally. The *real* differences—if indeed sexual orientation is determined by prenatal exposure to androgens—may lie elsewhere in the brain, but at least we have an indication that differences do exist. There remains also the possibility that a person's lifestyle may affect the structure of parts of his or her brain; thus, the differences mentioned in this section could be the *result* of people's sexual orientation rather than the cause. In any event, more research must be done on this subject.

Heredity and Sexual Orientation

Another factor that may play a role in sexual orientation is heredity. Twin studies take advantage of the fact that identical twins have identical genes, whereas the genetic similarity between fraternal twins is, on the average, 50 percent. Bailey and Pillard (1991) studied pairs of male twins in which at least one member identified himself as homosexual. If both twins are homosexual, they are said to be *concordant* for this trait. If only one is homosexual, the twins are said to be *discordant*. Thus, if homosexuality has a genetic basis, the percentage of monozygotic twins concordant for homosexuality should be higher than that for dizygotic twins. And this is exactly what Bailey and Pillard found: The concordance rate was 52 percent for identical twins and only 22 percent for fraternal twins.

Genetic factors also appear to affect female homosexuality. Bailey et al. (1993) found that the concordance of female monozygotic twins for homosexuality was 48 percent, while that of dizygotic twins was 16 percent. Another study, by Pattatucci and Hamer (1995), found an increased incidence of homosexuality and bisexuality in sisters, daughters, nieces, and female cousins (through a paternal uncle) of homosexual women.

To summarize, evidence suggests that two biological factors—prenatal hormonal exposure and heredity—may affect a person's sexual orientation. These research findings certainly contradict the suggestion that a person's sexual orientation is a moral issue. It appears that homosexuals are no more responsible for their sexual orientation than heterosexuals are. Ernulf, Innala, and Whitam (1989) found that people who believed that homosexuals were "born that way" expressed more positive attitudes toward them than did people who believed that homosexuals "chose to be" or "learned to be" that way. Thus, we can hope that research on the origins of homosexuality will reduce prejudice based on a person's sexual orientation. The question, "Why does someone become homosexual?" will probably be answered when we find out why someone becomes *heterosexual*.

Heterosexual man   Heterosexual woman   Homosexual man   Transexual male-to-female

FIGURE 9.12

Photomicrographs of slices of the human brain containing the central subdivision of the bed nucleus of the stria terminalis (BNST). (a) From a heterosexual man. (b) From a heterosexual woman. (c) From a homosexual man. (d) From a male-to-female transsexual. (BSTc = central subdivision of the bed nucleus of the stria terminalis.)

(Reprinted with permission from Zhou, J.-N., Hofman, M.A., Gooren, L.J.G., and Swaab, D.F. Nature, 1995, 378, 68–70. Copyright 1995 Macmillan Magazines Limited.)

INTERIM SUMMARY

Sexual behaviors are controlled by the organizational and activational effects of hormones. The female reproductive cycle (menstrual cycle or estrous cycle) begins with the maturation of one or more ovarian follicles, which occurs in response to the secretion of FSH by the anterior pituitary gland. As the ovarian follicle matures, it secretes estradiol, which causes the lining of the uterus to develop. When estradiol reaches a critical level, it causes the pituitary gland to secrete a surge of LH, triggering ovulation. The empty ovarian follicle becomes a corpus luteum, under the continued influence of LH, and secretes estradiol and progesterone. If pregnancy does not occur, the corpus luteum dies and stops producing hormones, and menstruation begins.

The sexual behavior of males of all mammalian species appears to depend on the presence of androgens. The proceptivity, receptivity, and attractiveness of female mammals other than primates depend primarily on estradiol and progesterone. In particular, estradiol has a priming effect on the subsequent appearance of progesterone.

In most mammals, female sexual behavior is the norm, just as the female body and female sex organs are the norm. That is, unless prenatal androgens masculinize and defeminize the animal's brain, its sexual behavior will be feminine. Behavioral masculinization refers to the androgen-stimulated development of neural circuits that respond to testosterone in adulthood, producing male sexual behavior. Behavioral defeminization refers to the inhibitory effects of androgens on the development of neural circuits that respond to estradiol and progesterone in adulthood, producing female sexual behavior.

Some organizational effects of androgens are indirect. Androgens cause the secretion of a chemical into the urine of male rat pups that makes it more attractive to their mothers, which spend more time licking the male pups' anogenital regions than those of female pups. This tactile stimulation contributes to their behavioral masculinization.

Pheromones can affect sexual physiology and behavior. Odorants present in the urine of female mice affect their estrous cycles, lengthening and eventually stopping them (Lee-Boot effect). Odorants present in the urine of male mice abolish these effects and cause the females' cycles to become synchronized (Whitten effect). (Phenomena similar to the Lee-Boot effect and the Whitten effect also occur in women.) Odorants can also accelerate the onset of puberty in females (Vandenbergh effect). In addition, the odor of the urine from a male other than the one that impregnated a female mouse will cause her to abort (Bruce effect). The Bruce effect involves learning the odor of the male that impregnates the female, and the activity of a noradrenergic input to the olfactory bulb (triggered by vaginal stimulation) is involved in this learning.

In the hamster the attractiveness of an estrous female to the male derives in part from chemicals present in her vaginal secretions, detected by the olfactory epithelium and vomeronasal organ. Connections between the olfactory system and the amygdala appear to be important in stimulating male sexual behavior.

The behavioral effects of prenatal exposure to androgens in humans, if any, are not well understood. Studies of prenatally androgenized girls suggest that organizational effects may well influence the development of sexual orientation; androgenization appears to increase the incidence of homosexuality. If androgens cannot act (as they cannot in cases of androgen insensitivity syndrome), then the person's anatomy and behavior are feminine. Testosterone has an activational effect on the sexual behavior of men, just as it does on the behavior of other male mammals. Women do not require estradiol or progesterone to experience sexual interest or to engage in sexual behavior. These hormones may affect the quality and intensity of their sex drive, and studies comparing the sexual behavior of female monkeys housed in small groups with those housed in large groups in large cages suggest that the sexual proceptivity may be related to ovarian hormones, even in higher primates. However, the strongest hormonal effect on women's sex drives appears to come from androgens.

Sexual orientation (that is, heterosexuality or homosexuality) may be influenced by prenatal exposure to androgens. So far, researchers have obtained evidence that suggests that the sizes of three brain regions are related to a man's sexual orientation, and studies with rats have shown that events that cause stress during pregnancy can interfere with defeminization of the sexual behavior of the male offspring. The size of another part of the brain has been found to be related to sexual identity in males. In addition, twin studies suggest that heredity may play a role in sexual orientation in both men and women.

■ THOUGHT QUESTIONS

Whatever the relative roles played by biological and environmental factors may be, most investigators believe that a person's sexual orientation is not a matter of choice. Why do you think so many people consider sexual orientation to be a moral issue?

■ NEURAL CONTROL OF SEXUAL BEHAVIOR

The control of sexual behavior—at least in laboratory animals—involves different brain mechanisms in males and females. This section describes these mechanisms.

Males

The **medial preoptic area (MPA),** located just rostral to the hypothalamus, is the forebrain region most critical for male sexual behavior. (As we will see later in this chapter and in Chapter 10, it is also critical for other sexually dimorphic behavior, including maternal behavior and territorial aggression.) Electrical stimulation of this region elicits male copulatory behavior (Malsbury, 1971), and sexual activity increases the firing rate of single neurons in the MPA (Shimura, Yamamoto, and Shimokochi, 1994; Mas, 1995). In addition, the act of copulation increases the metabolic activity of the MPA and induces the production of Fos protein (Oaknin et al., 1989; Robertson et al., 1991; Wood and Newman, 1993). (The significance of the Fos protein as an indicator of neural activation was discussed in Chapter 5.) Finally, destruction of the MPA permanently abolishes male sexual behavior (Heimer and Larsson, 1966/1967).

Of course, the MPA does not stand alone. It receives chemosensory input from the vomeronasal organ through connections with the medial amygdala and the bed nucleus of the stria terminalis (BNST). (You will recall that in humans, the BNST is sexually dimorphic and that it is smaller in transsexual males.) The MPA also receives somatosensory information from the genitals through connections with the midbrain reticular formation and the medial amygdala. (See *Figure 9.13.*)

The organizational effects of androgens are responsible for sexual dimorphisms in brain structure. Gorski et al. (1978) discovered a nucleus within the MPA of the rat that is three to seven times larger in males than in females. This area is called (appropriately enough) the **sexually dimorphic nucleus (SDN)** of the preoptic area. The size of this nucleus is controlled by the amount of androgens present during fetal development. According to Rhees, Shryne, and Gorski (1990a, 1990b), the critical period for masculinization of the SDN appears to start on the eighteenth day of gestation and end once the animals are five days old. (Normally, rats are born on the twenty-second day of gestation.)

Androgens exert their activational effects on neurons in the medial preoptic area. If a male rodent is castrated in adulthood, its sexual behavior will cease. How-

Medial preoptic area (MPA)
An area of cell bodies just rostral to the hypothalamus; plays an essential role in male sexual behavior.

Sexually dimorphic nucleus (SDN) A nucleus in the preoptic area that is much larger in males than in females; first observed in rats; plays a role in male sexual behavior.

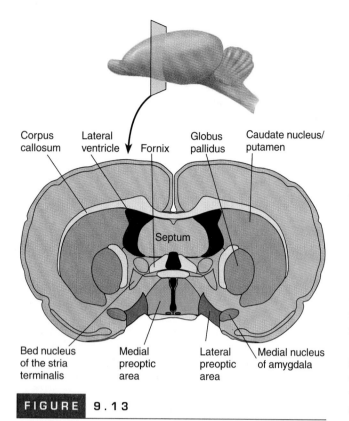

Corpus callosum | Lateral ventricle | Fornix | Globus pallidus | Caudate nucleus/putamen

Septum

Bed nucleus of the stria terminalis | Medial preoptic area | Lateral preoptic area | Medial nucleus of amygdala

FIGURE   9.13

Cross sections through the rat brain showing the location of the medial preoptic area (MPA), the medial amygdala, and the bed nucleus of the stria terminalis (BNST).

[Adapted from Swanson, L.W. Brain Maps: Structure of the Rat Brain. New York: Elsevier, 1992.]

ever, the behavior can be reinstated by implanting a small amount of testosterone directly into the medial preoptic area (Davidson, 1980; Nyby, Matochik, and Barfield, 1992). This region has been shown to contain a high concentration of androgen receptors in the male rat brain—more than five times as many as are found in females (Roselli, Handa, and Resko, 1989).

Neurons in the medial preoptic area send axons to the lateral tegmental field of the midbrain (just dorsal and medial to the substantia nigra), and destruction of these axons disrupts male sexual behavior (Brackett and Edwards, 1984). In addition, Shimura and Shimokochi (1990) recorded from single neurons in the lateral tegmental field and found that the activity of virtually all neurons increased during various aspects of copulatory behavior. For example, some increased their firing rate only when the male achieved intromission. These results suggest that the medial preoptic area exerts its effect on male sexual behavior by activating motor mechanisms in the midbrain.

In humans, temporal lobe dysfunctions are often correlated with decreased sex drives. (The temporal lobes contain the amygdala, but the hippocampus and the temporal neocortex may also be involved.) For example, seizures that originate from localized, irritative lesions of the temporal lobes are often associated with lack of interest in sexual activity (Blumer and Walker, 1975; Morrell, 1991). Morrell et al. (1994) found that men with temporal lobe epilepsy were much less likely than other men to have penile erections while watching an erotic film. Usually, if the seizures are successfully treated by medication or by surgical removal of the affected tissue, the person attains normal sexual interest.

Figure 9.14 summarizes the evidence I have presented in this section. (See *Figure 9.14*.)

FIGURE   9.14

A possible explanation of the interacting excitatory effects of pheromones, genital stimulation, and testosterone on male sexual behavior.

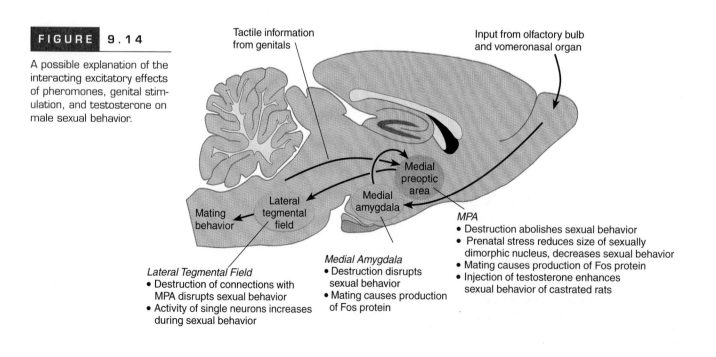

Tactile information from genitals

Input from olfactory bulb and vomeronasal organ

Medial preoptic area

Medial amygdala

Mating behavior | Lateral tegmental field

Lateral Tegmental Field
• Destruction of connections with MPA disrupts sexual behavior
• Activity of single neurons increases during sexual behavior

Medial Amygdala
• Destruction disrupts sexual behavior
• Mating causes production of Fos protein

MPA
• Destruction abolishes sexual behavior
• Prenatal stress reduces size of sexually dimorphic nucleus, decreases sexual behavior
• Mating causes production of Fos protein
• Injection of testosterone enhances sexual behavior of castrated rats

Females

Just as the MPA plays an essential role in male sex behavior, another region in the ventral forebrain plays a similar role in female sexual behavior: the **ventromedial nucleus of the hypothalamus (VMH)**. A female rat with bilateral lesions of the ventromedial nuclei will not display lordosis, even if she is treated with estradiol and progesterone. Conversely, electrical stimulation of the ventromedial nucleus facilitates female sexual behavior (Pfaff and Sakuma, 1979). (See *Figure 9.15*.)

As we saw in the previous section, the medial amygdala of males receives chemosensory information from the vomeronasal system and somatosensory information from the genitals, and it sends efferent axons to the medial preoptic area. These connections are found in females as well. In addition, neurons in the medial amygdala also send efferent axons to the VMH. In fact, copulation or mechanical stimulation of the genitals or flanks increases the production of Fos protein in both the medial amygdala and the VMH (Pfaus et al., 1993; Tetel, Getzinger, and Blaustein, 1993).

As we saw earlier, sexual behavior of female rats is activated by a priming dose of estradiol, followed by progesterone. The estrogen sets the stage, so to speak, and the progesterone stimulates the sexual behavior. Injections of these hormones directly into the VMH will stimulate sexual behavior even in females whose ovaries have been removed (Rubin and Barfield, 1980; Pleim and Barfield, 1988). And if a chemical that blocks the production of progesterone receptors is injected into the VMH, the animal's sexual behavior is disrupted (Ogawa et al., 1994). Thus, estradiol and progesterone exert their effects on female sexual behavior by activating neurons in this nucleus.

Rose (1990) recorded from single neurons in the ventromedial hypothalamus of freely moving female hamsters and found that injections of progesterone (following estradiol pretreatment) increased the activity level of these neurons, particularly when the animals were displaying lordosis. In a double-labeling study, Tetel, Celentano, and Blaustein (1994) found that neurons in both the VMH and the medial amygdala that showed increased Fos production when the animal's genitals were stimulated also contained estrogen receptors. Thus, the stimulating effects of estradiol and genital stimulation converge on the same neurons.

The neurons of the ventromedial nucleus send axons to the **periaqueductal gray matter (PAG)** of the midbrain, which surrounds the cerebral aqueduct. This region, too, has been implicated in female sexual behavior; Sakuma and Pfaff (1979a, 1979b) found that electrical stimulation of the PAG facilitates lordosis in female rats and that lesions there disrupt it. In addition, Hennessey et al. (1990) found that lesions that disconnect the VMH from the PAG abolish female sexual behavior. Finally, Sakuma and Pfaff (1980a, 1980b) found that estradiol treatment or electrical stimulation of the ventromedial nuclei increased the firing rate of neurons in the PAG. (The PAG contains both estrogen and progesterone receptors.)

The neurons of the periaqueductal gray matter send axons to the reticular formation of the medulla, and cells there send axons to the spinal cord. It seems likely that this pathway is the final link between the hormone-sensitive neurons in the ventromedial nucleus of the hypothalamus and the muscles that are responsible for the lordosis response.

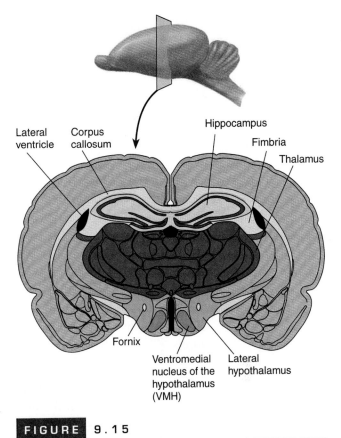

Lateral ventricle · Corpus callosum · Hippocampus · Fimbria · Thalamus · Fornix · Ventromedial nucleus of the hypothalamus (VMH) · Lateral hypothalamus

FIGURE 9.15

A cross section through the rat brain showing the location of the ventromedial nucleus of the hypothalamus.

[Adapted from Swanson, L. W. Brain Maps: Structure of the Rat Brain. New York: Elsevier, 1992.]

Ventromedial nucleus of the hypothalamus (VMH) A large nucleus of the hypothalamus located near the walls of the third ventricle; plays an essential role in female sexual behavior.

Periaqueductal gray matter (PAG) The region of the midbrain that surrounds the cerebral aqueduct; plays an essential role in various species-typical behaviors, including female sexual behavior.

INTERIM SUMMARY

In laboratory animals, different brain mechanisms control male and female sexual behavior. The medial preoptic area is the forebrain region most critical for male sexual behavior. Stimulating this area produces copulatory behavior; destroying it permanently abolishes the behavior. The sexually dimorphic nucleus, located in the medial preoptic area, develops only if an animal is exposed to androgens early in life. This nucleus is found in humans as well.

Neurons in the MPA contain androgen receptors. Copulatory activity causes an increase in the activity of neurons in this region. Implantation of testosterone directly into the MPA reinstates copulatory behavior that was previously abolished by castration in adulthood. Neurons in the MPA send their axons to various regions, including the lateral tegmental field, where lesions also disrupt male sexual behavior.

The temporal lobes also appear to play a role in sexual interest; damage to the medial amygdala (which receives input from both the main and accessory olfactory systems) disrupts male sexual behavior. In humans, sexual dysfunctions are associated with seizure activity originating in the temporal lobes.

The most important forebrain region for female sexual behavior is the ventromedial nucleus of the hypothalamus (VMH). Its destruction abolishes copulatory behavior, and its stimulation facilitates this behavior. Both estradiol and progesterone exert their facilitating effects on female sexual behavior in this region, and studies have confirmed the existence of progesterone and estrogen receptors there. The steroid-sensitive neurons of the VMH send axons to the periaqueductal gray matter (PAG) of the midbrain; presumably, neurons in the midbrain, through their connections with the medullary reticular formation, control the particular responses that constitute female sexual behavior.

PARENTAL BEHAVIOR

In most mammalian species, reproductive behavior takes place after the offspring are born as well as at the time they are conceived. This section examines the role of hormones in the initiation and maintenance of maternal behavior and the role of the neural circuits that are responsible for their expression. Most of the research has involved rodents; less is known about the neural and endocrine bases of maternal behavior in primates.

Although most research on the physiology of parental behavior has focused on maternal behavior, some researchers are now studying paternal behavior shown by the males of some species of rodents. It goes without saying that the human paternal behavior is very important for the offspring of our species, but the physiological basis of this behavior has not yet been studied.

Maternal Behavior of Rodents

The final test of the fitness of an animal's genes is the number of offspring that survive to a reproductive age. Just as the process of natural selection favors reproductively competent animals, it favors those that care adequately for their young (if their young in fact require care). Rat and mouse pups certainly do; they cannot survive without a mother to attend to their needs.

At birth, rats and mice resemble fetuses. The infants are blind (their eyes are still shut), and they can only helplessly wriggle. They are poikilothermous ("cold-blooded"); their brain is not yet developed enough to regulate body temperature. They even lack the ability to release their own urine and feces spontaneously and must be helped to do so by their mother. As we will see shortly, this phenomenon actually serves a useful function.

During gestation, female rats and mice build nests. The form this structure takes depends on the material available for its construction. In the laboratory the animals are usually given strips of paper or lengths of rope or twine. A good *brood nest,* as it is called, is shown in Figure 9.16. This nest is made of hemp rope; a piece of the rope is shown below the nest. The mouse laboriously shredded the rope and then wove an enclosed nest, with a small hole for access to the interior. (See *Figure 9.16.*)

At the time of **parturition** (delivery of offspring) the female begins to groom and lick the area around the vagina. As a pup begins to emerge, she assists the uterine contractions by pulling the pup out with her teeth. She then eats the placenta and umbilical cord and cleans off the fetal membranes—a quite delicate operation. (A newborn pup looks like it is sealed in very thin plastic wrap.) After all the pups are born and cleaned up, the mother will probably nurse them. Milk is usually present in the mammary glands very near the time of birth.

Periodically, the mother licks the pups' anogenital region, stimulating reflexive urination and defecation. Friedman and Bruno (1976) have shown the utility of this mechanism. They noted that a lactating female rat produces approximately 48 grams of milk on the tenth day of lactation. This milk contains approximately 35 milliliters (ml) of water. The experimenters injected some of the pups with tritiated (radioactive) water and later found radioactivity in the mother and in the littermates. They calculated that a lactating rat normally consumes 21 ml of water in the urine of her young, thus recycling approximately two-thirds of the water she gives to the pups in the form of milk. The water, traded back and forth between mother and young, serves as a vehicle for the nutrients—fats, protein, and sugar—contained in milk. Because each day the milk production of a lactating rat is approximately 14 percent of her body weight (for a human weighing 120 lb, that would be around 2 gal), the recycling is extremely useful, especially when the availability of water is a problem.

Besides cleaning, nursing, and purging her offspring, a female rodent will retrieve pups if they leave or are removed from the nest. The mother will even construct another nest in a new location and move her litter there, should the conditions at the old site become unfavorable (for example, when an inconsiderate experimenter puts a heat lamp over it). The way a female rodent picks up her pup is quite consistent: She gingerly grasps the animal by the back, managing not to injure it with her very sharp teeth. (I can personally attest to the ease with which these teeth can penetrate skin.) She then carries the pup with a characteristic prancing walk, her head held high. (See *Figure 9.17.*) The pup is brought back to the nest and is left there. The female then leaves the nest again to search for another pup. She continues to retrieve pups until she finds no more; she does not count her pups and

FIGURE 9.16

A mouse's brood nest. Beside it is a length of the kind of rope the mouse used to construct it.

Parturition (*par tew ri shun*)
The act of giving birth.

FIGURE 9.17

A female mouse carrying one of her pups.

stop retrieving when they are all back. A mouse or rat will usually accept all the pups she is offered, if they are young enough. I once observed two lactating female mice with nests in corners of the same cage, diagonally opposite each other. I disturbed their nests, which triggered a long bout of retrieving, during which each mother stole youngsters from the other's nest. The mothers kept up their exchange for a long time, passing each other in the middle of the cage.

Stimuli That Elicit and Maintain Maternal Behavior

As we saw earlier in this chapter, most sexually dimorphic behaviors are controlled by the organizational and activational effects of sex hormones. Maternal behavior is somewhat different in this respect. First, there is no evidence that organizational effects of hormones play a role; as we will see, under the proper conditions, even males will take care of infants. (Obviously, they cannot provide them with milk.) Second, although maternal behavior is affected by hormones, it is not *controlled* by them.

Most virgin female rats will begin to retrieve and care for young pups after having infants placed with them for several days (Wiesner and Sheard, 1933). And once the rats are sensitized, they will thereafter take care of pups as soon as they encounter them; sensitization lasts for a lifetime.

Olfaction plays an important role in sensitization—at least, in species such as the rat. A virgin female rat does not normally approach a rat pup; in fact, when she encounters one, she retreats from the pup as if she were repelled by the pup's odor. Fleming and Rosenblatt (1974) confirmed that the avoidance is, indeed, based on smell. They rinsed the olfactory mucosa of virgin female rats with zinc sulfate, which temporarily eliminates olfactory sensitivity. The treatment abolished the animals' natural aversion to the pups, and soon they started taking care of them. Thus, sensitization involves overcoming a natural aversion to the odor of pups.

Fleming et al. (1979) found that cutting the vomeronasal nerve, which disrupts the accessory olfactory system, also facilitates the responsiveness of virgin females to pups. Thus, both the primary and the accessory olfactory systems play a role in olfactory control of maternal behavior. You will recall that both the primary and accessory olfactory systems project to the medial amygdala. Fleming, Vaccarino, and Luebke (1980) found that lesions of the medial amygdala also facilitated responsiveness, as did lesions of the **stria terminalis,** a fiber bundle that connects the medial amygdala with various forebrain regions, including the medial preoptic area. As we will see, the medial preoptic area is essential for maternal behavior. (Refer to *Figure 9.10.*) Note that lesions of the amygdala or stria terminalis do not abolish the sense of smell; they only abolish the animals' aversion to the smell of pups.

The most important sense modalities in the *initiation* of maternal behavior in rodents appear to be olfaction and somatosensation. However, other sense modalities are involved in its control. For example, mouse, rat, and hamster pups emit at least two different kinds of ultrasonic calls (Noirot, 1972; Hofer and Shair, 1993; Ihnat, White, and Barfield, 1995). These sounds cannot be heard by humans; they have to be translated into lower frequencies by a special device (a "bat detector") to be perceived by the experimenter. Of course, the mother can hear these calls. When a pup gets cold (as it would if it were removed from the nest), it emits a characteristic call that brings the mother out of her nest. The sound is so effective that female mice have been observed to chew the cover off a loudspeaker that is transmitting a recording of this call. Once out of the nest, the female uses olfactory cues as well as auditory ones to find the pups; she can find a buried, anesthetized baby mouse that is unable to make any noise. The second call is made in response to rough handling. When a mother hears this sound, she stops what she is doing. Typically, it is she that is administering the rough handling, and the distress call makes her stop. This mechanism undoubtedly plays an important role in training mother mice to handle pups properly.

Stria terminalis (*stree a ter mi nal is*) A long fiber bundle that connects portions of the amygdala with the hypothalamus.

Hormonal Control of Maternal Behavior

As we have just seen, hormones are not essential for the activation of maternal behavior; mere exposure to pups will accomplish that. (Of course, hormones are necessary for milk production.) However, many aspects of maternal behavior are facilitated by hormones. Nest-building behavior is facilitated by progesterone, the principal hormone of pregnancy. Lisk, Pretlow, and Friedman (1969) found that nonpregnant female mice built brood nests after a pellet of progesterone was implanted under the skin. The pellet slowly dissolved, maintaining a continuously high level of progesterone. The enhanced nest building was suppressed by the administration of estradiol. After parturition, mothers continue to maintain their nests, and they construct new nests if necessary, even though their blood level of progesterone is very low then. Voci and Carlson (1973) found that hypothalamic implants of prolactin as well as progesterone facilitated nest building in mice. Presumably, nest building can be facilitated by either hormone: progesterone during pregnancy and prolactin after parturition. (Prolactin, produced by the anterior pituitary gland, is responsible for milk production.)

Although pregnant female rats will not immediately care for foster pups that are given to them during pregnancy, they will do so as soon as their pups are born. A female rodent's responsiveness to her offspring appears to be triggered by the hormones that are present during pregnancy. Figure 9.18 shows the levels of the three hormones that have been implicated in maternal behavior: estradiol, progesterone, and prolactin. Note that just before parturition the level of estradiol begins rising, then the level of progesterone falls dramatically, followed by a sharp increase in prolactin. (See *Figure 9.18.*) If ovariectomized virgin female rats are given estradiol and progesterone in a pattern that duplicates this sequence, the time it takes to sensitize their maternal behavior is drastically reduced (Moltz, Lubin, Leon, and Numan, 1970; Bridges, 1984). Prolactin is not necessary.

Fleming et al. (1989) found that the administration of progesterone and estradiol produced effects similar to those of sensitization. First, the hormone-treated rats became less timid in a strange environment that contained novel odors. Second, the animals spent more time near a jar containing some bedding material removed from a nest containing a lactating female and her pups. These effects may be the ones that occur during sensitization: The animal is no longer repelled by (frightened by?) the strange odor of pups and, indeed, comes to prefer the smell. In addition, Fleming and Sarker (1990) found that sensitization produces stronger long-term effects if the animal is first primed with estradiol and progesterone.

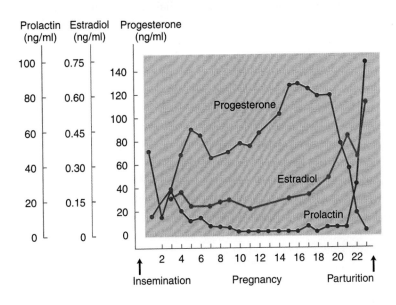

FIGURE 9.18

Blood levels of progesterone, estradiol, and prolactin in pregnant rats.

(From Rosenblatt, J.S., Siegel, H.I., and Mayer, A.D. Advances in the Study of Behavior, 1979, 10, 225–310.)

Another hormone that is present during lactation—prolactin—may also have stimulating effects on maternal behavior; and its effects, like those of estradiol, may be exerted in the medial preoptic area. Bridges et al. (1990) infused minute quantities of prolactin into the lateral ventricles or directly into the MPA of virgin female rats. They found that the animals quickly began taking care of pups. The effect occurred only if the animals were first given a series of injections of progesterone and estradiol; thus, the maternal behavior of normal females may depend on an interaction between several hormones.

Neural Control of Maternal Behavior

The medial preoptic area, the region of the forebrain that plays the most critical role in male sexual behavior, appears to play a similar role in maternal behavior. Numan (1974) found that lesions of the MPA disrupted both nest building and pup care. The mothers simply ignored their offspring. However, female sexual behavior was unaffected by these lesions.

As you learned earlier, in the discussion of the neural basis of male sexual behavior, the MPA sends axons to the midbrain. Numan and his colleagues found that the pathway critical for maternal behavior runs from the MPA to the **ventral tegmental area (VTA)** of the midbrain. Numan and Smith (1984) found that lesions that interrupted this pathway disrupted maternal behavior. A later study (Numan and Numan, 1991) found that lesions of the ventral tegmental area made by injecting an excitatory amino acid (which kills cell bodies but spares axons that are passing through the region) did not disrupt maternal behavior. However, knife cuts caudal to the VTA did; thus, the critical axons pass through the VTA and form synapses with neurons farther back in the brain stem. Where they do so is not yet known.

The medial preoptic area appears to be the place where estradiol affects maternal behavior. The MPA contains estrogen receptors (Pfaff and Keiner, 1973). Giordano et al. (1989) found that the concentration of estrogen receptors in the MPA increases during pregnancy and appears to reflect the priming effect produced by the sequence of hormones that occurs during pregnancy. In addition, direct implants of estradiol in the MPA facilitate maternal behavior (Numan, Rosenblatt, and Komisaruk, 1977) and injections of an antiestrogen into the MPA block it (Adieh, Mayer, and Rosenblatt, 1987).

Ventral tegmental area A nucleus in the ventral midbrain; plays an essential role in maternal behavior.

As we just saw, zinc sulfate treatment (which abolishes olfactory sensitivity), lesions of the medial amygdala, or lesions of the stria terminalis (which connects the medial amygdala with the medial preoptic area) all facilitate maternal behavior in virgin female rats by eliminating the inhibitory effects caused by the odor of pups. Perhaps the stimulating effect of estradiol on the medial preoptic area works in a similar fashion, removing the inhibitory influence of the amygdala. (See *Figure 9.19*.)

FIGURE 9.19

A possible explanation of the facilitating effects of estradiol on maternal behavior.

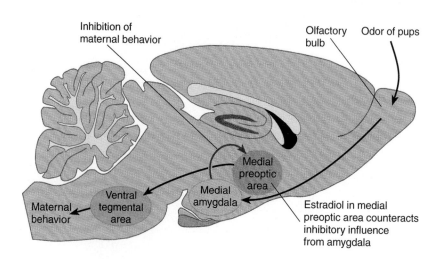

Neural Control of Paternal Behavior

Newborn infants of most species of mammals are cared for by their mother, and it is, of course, their mother that feeds them. However, males of a few species of rodents share the task of infant care with the mothers, and the brains of these nurturing fathers show some interesting differences compared with those of nonpaternal fathers of other species.

Several laboratories have been investigating parental behavior in some closely related species of voles (small rodents that are often mistaken for mice). Prairie voles are monogamous; males and females form pair bonds after mating, and the fathers help to care for the pups. Montane voles are promiscuous; after mating, the male leaves, and the mother cares for the pups by herself. The size of the MPA, which plays an essential role in maternal behavior, shows less sexual dimorphism in monogamous prairie voles than in promiscuous montane voles (Shapiro et al., 1991).

Kirkpatrick, Kim, and Insel (1994) found that when male prairie voles were exposed to a pup, Fos production increased in the MPA (and also several other regions of the forebrain). In addition, electrolytic or excitotoxic lesions of the MPA produce severe deficits in paternal behavior of male rats (Rosenblatt, Hazelwood, and Poole, 1996; Sturgis and Bridges, 1997). Thus, the MPA appears to play an essential role in parental behavior of both males and females.

INTERIM SUMMARY

Many species must care for their offspring. Among most rodents, this duty falls to the mother, who must build a nest, deliver her own pups, clean them, keep them warm, nurse them, and retrieve them if they are moved out of the nest. They must even induce their pups' urination and defecation, and their ingestion of the urine recycles water, which is often a scarce commodity.

Exposure to young pups stimulates maternal behavior within a few days. Apparently, the odor of pups elicits handling and licking, whereas the sound of their distress calls elicits nest building. Unsensitized virgin female rats appear to be repelled by the odor of pups, but temporary deactivation of the olfactory system with zinc sulfate abolishes this aversion and causes the animals to begin caring for pups more quickly. The inhibitory effect of the odor of pups may be mediated by the accessory olfactory system; cutting the vomeronasal nerve facilitates maternal behavior. Both components of the olfactory system project to the medial amygdala. Lesions of the medial amygdala or the stria terminalis also facilitate maternal responsiveness. Therefore, the inhibitory effects of olfaction on maternal behavior may be mediated by the pathway from the olfactory system to the medial amygdala to the medial preoptic area, via the stria terminalis.

Nest building appears to be facilitated by progesterone during pregnancy and by prolactin during the lactation period. Injections of progesterone and estradiol that duplicate the sequence that occurs during pregnancy facilitate maternal behavior, as does injection of prolactin directly into the brain.

The medial preoptic area is the most important forebrain structure for maternal behavior, and the ventral tegmental area of the midbrain is the most important brain stem structure. Neurons in the medial preoptic area send axons caudally through the ventral tegmental area toward more caudal regions of the brain stem. If these connections are interrupted bilaterally, rats cease providing maternal care.

Paternal behavior is relatively rare in mammalian species, but research indicates that sexual dimorphism of the MPA is less pronounced in monogamous species of voles (prairie voles), in which both the male and the female care for the offspring. When male prairie voles are exposed to pups, the activity of the MPA (as measured by Fos production) is increased. In addition, lesions of the MPA disrupt paternal behavior of male rats.

■ THOUGHT QUESTIONS

As you saw, both male sexual behavior and maternal behavior are disrupted by lesions of the medial preoptic area; thus, the MPA performs some functions necessary for both behaviors. Do you think that the functions are common to both categories of behavior, or do you think that different functions are involved? If you think the former possibility is true, what might these functions be? Can you think of any common elements of male sexual behavior and maternal behavior?

EPILOGUE

Human Sex Attractants

At the beginning of the chapter I described a perfume maker's fantasy: discovering a sex attractant pheromone that works for humans. An exclusive patent on such a chemical would certainly bring fabulous wealth. Think of how much money people spend on perfumes, makeup, shampoos, styling mousse, acne cream, and other beauty aids. Think of how much more money people would be willing to spend on a chemical that would go right from the nose to the brain and arouse romantic ardor.

Unfortunately for perfume makers, there is no evidence that human sex attractant pheromones exist. For a while, researchers believed that they had discovered one in monkeys that provided at least some hope for finding them in humans, but subsequent studies found that the effect was produced by something altogether different. In the original studies, the experimenters found that extracts obtained from the vaginal fluid of a female monkey during the middle of her menstrual cycle (when she is most attractive to males) served as a sex attractant pheromone. If this chemical were swabbed onto the vagina of another female during an early or late part of her cycle, a male would find her more attractive. It turned out, however, that something other than pheromones was responsible for the phenomenon. In some cases the treatment simply provided a novel odor, which made the male notice the female. In other cases the smell apparently reminded the male of the odor of one of his favorite partners.

Cowley and Brooksbank (1991) obtained some interesting evidence that suggests that pheromones may affect the social behavior of humans. They asked male and female college students to wear necklaces overnight and to keep a record of their social interactions the following day. Some of the necklaces contained *androstenol*, a substance found in human underarm sweat, especially that of males. Other necklaces contained an inert control substance. The investigators found that the androstenol had no effect on the social interactions of male subjects but that female subjects engaged in more social exchanges with men. Thus, exposure to a substance that is normally produced by men has at least a small effect on women's tendency to engage in social interactions with men. The phenomenon is probably mediated by the main olfactory bulbs, because activation of the vomeronasal organ appears to require direct contact with chemicals dissolved in liquids.

Odors of a particular person—a loved one, for example—can affect sexual arousal, just as the sight of that person or the sound of his or her voice can do. We are not generally conscious of the fact, but we can learn to recognize other people by their odor. For example, a study by Russell (1976) found that people were able to distinguish by odor between T-shirts that they had worn and those previously worn by other people. They could also tell whether the unknown owner of a T-shirt was male or female. Thus, it is likely that men and women can *learn* to be attracted by their partners' characteristic odors. However, this phenomenon is different from the responses produced by pheromones, which apparently need not be learned.

Learning to recognize sex partners (primarily by their odor) is important for species in which a male controls a herd of females and impregnates all of them. In many species of mammals, if a male is presented with a single female, he will copulate with her several times but will eventually appear to be exhausted. However, if the male is presented with a new female, he will begin to respond again. If he is introduced to a series of new females, his performance will continue for prolonged periods of time. If one of the original females is reintroduced, the male will *not* respond.

In one of the most unusual studies I have read about, Beamer, Bermant, and Clegg (1969) tested the ability of a ram (male sheep) to recognize ewes with which he had mated. A ram that is given a new ewe each time will quickly begin copulating and will ejaculate within two minutes. (In one study, a ram kept up this performance with twelve ewes. The experimenters finally got tired of shuffling sheep around; the ram was still ready to go.) Beamer and his colleagues tried to fool rams by putting trench coats and Halloween face masks on females with which the rams had mated. (No, I'm not making this up.) The males were not fooled by the disguise; they apparently recognized their former partners by their odor and were no longer interested in them.

The rejuvenating effect of a new female, also seen in roosters, is usually called the *Coolidge effect*. The following story is reputed to be true, but I cannot vouch for that fact. (If it is not true, it ought to be.) The late U.S. President Calvin Coolidge and his wife were touring a farm when Mrs. Coolidge pointedly asked the farmer whether the continuous and vigorous sexual activity among the flock of hens was the work of just one rooster. The reply was yes. She smiled and said, "You might point that out to Mr. Coolidge." The president looked thoughtfully at the birds and then asked the farmer whether a different hen was involved each time. Again, the answer was yes. "You might point *that* out to Mrs. Coolidge," he said dryly.

KEY CONCEPTS

SEXUAL DEVELOPMENT

1. Gender is determined by the sex chromosomes, which control development of the gonads. Two hormones secreted by the testes, testosterone and anti-Müllerian hormone, cause masculinization and defeminization, respectively; otherwise, the organism will be female.
2. Sexual maturation occurs when the anterior pituitary gland secretes gonadotropic hormones, which instruct the gonads to secrete sex steroid hormones.

HORMONAL CONTROL OF SEXUAL BEHAVIOR

3. Female reproductive cycles are caused by interactions between the ovaries and the anterior pituitary gland.
4. Androgens cause behavioral masculinization and defeminization by affecting brain development.
5. In mammals other than primates, estradiol and progesterone activate female sexual behavior. Testosterone activates male sexual behavior in all mammalian species.
6. Pheromones, detected by the vomeronasal organ or by the olfactory receptors, permit animals to affect the reproductive status or sexual interest of other members of their species by their mere presence.

7. In humans, organizational effects of androgens may manifest themselves in sexual preference. Androgens appear to have the most important activational effects for both men and women.

NEURAL CONTROL OF SEXUAL BEHAVIOR

8. In laboratory animals, the sexually dimorphic nucleus of the medial preoptic area is critical for male sexual behavior, and the ventromedial nucleus of the hypothalamus is critical for female sexual behavior. In addition, sex hormones exert their behavioral effects on neurons in these brain regions, and on those in the medial amygdala, which receive pheromone-related information.

PARENTAL BEHAVIOR

9. Maternal behavior is influenced by hormones—primarily estradiol and prolactin—but depends also on the stimuli provided by the female's offspring. Some of the neural circuitry that controls the behaviors involves a pathway from the medial preoptic area to the ventral tegmental area. The medial preoptic area also appears to be involved in paternal behavior.

SUGGESTED READINGS

Becker, J.B., Breedlove, S.M., and Crews, D. *Behavioral Endocrinology.* Cambridge, MA: MIT Press, 1992.

Bornstein, M.H. *Handbook of Parenting. Vol. 2: Biology and Ecology of Parenting.* Mahwah, NJ: Lawrence Erlbaum Associates, 1995.

Gerall, A.A., Moltz, H., and Ward, I.I. *Handbook of Behavioral Neurobiology. Vol. 11: Sexual Differentiation.* New York: Plenum Press, 1992.

Knobil, E., and Neill, J. *The Physiology of Reproduction.* New York: Raven Press, 1988.

Krasnegor, N.A., and Bridges, R.S. *Mammalian Parenting: Biochemical, Neurobiological, and Behavioral Determinants.* New York: Oxford University Press, 1990.

Rosen, R.C., and Beck, J.G. *Patterns of Sexual Arousal.* New York: Guilford Press, 1988.

10

Emotion

LEARNING OBJECTIVES

1. Discuss the behavioral, autonomic, and hormonal components of an emotional response and the role of the amygdala in controlling them.

2. Discuss the role of the orbitofrontal cortex in the analysis of social situations and the effects of damage to this region, including those produced by psychosurgery.

3. Discuss cross-cultural studies on the expression and comprehension of emotions.

4. Discuss the neural control of the recognition of emotional expression in normal people and people with brain damage.

5. Discuss the neural control of emotional expression in normal people and people with brain damage.

6. Discuss the James-Lange theory of feelings of emotion and evaluate relevant research.

7. Discuss the nature, functions, and neural control of aggressive behavior.

8. Discuss the hormonal control of intermale aggression, interfemale aggression, and maternal aggression.

9. Discuss the effects of androgens on human aggressive behavior.

Intellect and Emotion

Several years ago, while I was on a sabbatical leave, a colleague stopped by my office and asked whether I would like to see an interesting patient. The patient, a 72-year-old man, had suffered a massive stroke in his right hemisphere that had paralyzed the left side of his body. Three of us went to see him: Dr. W.; Lisa, an undergraduate psychology student who was on a summer internship; and I.

Mr. V. was seated in a wheelchair equipped with a large tray on which his right arm was resting; his left arm was immobilized in a sling, to keep it out of the way. He greeted us politely, almost formally, articulating his words carefully with a slight European accent.

Mr. V. seemed intelligent, and this impression was confirmed when we gave him some of the subtests of the Wechsler Adult Intelligence Test. He could define rather obscure words, provide the meanings of proverbs, supply information, and do mental arithmetic. In fact, his verbal intelligence appeared to be in the upper 5 percent of the population. The fact that English was not his native language made his performance even more remarkable. But as we expected, he did poorly on simple tasks that required him to deal with shapes and geometry. He failed to solve even the sample problem for the block design subtest, in which colored blocks must be put together to duplicate a pattern shown in a drawing.

The most interesting aspect of Mr. V.'s behavior after his stroke was his lack of reaction to his symptoms. After we had finished with the testing, we asked him to tell us a little about himself and his lifestyle. What, for example, was his favorite pastime?

"I like to walk," he said. "I walk at least two hours each day around the city, but mostly I like to walk in the woods. I have maps of most of the national forests in the state on the walls of my study, and I mark all of the trails I've taken. I figure that in about six months I will have walked all of the trails that are short enough to do in a day. I'm too old to camp out in the woods."

"You're going to finish up those trails in the next six months?" asked Dr. W.

"Yes, and then I'll start over again!" he replied.

"Mr. V., are you having any trouble?" asked Dr. W.

"Trouble? What do you mean?"

"I mean physical difficulty."

"No." Mr. V. gave him a slightly puzzled look.

"Well, what are you sitting in?"

Mr. V. gave him a look that indicated he thought that the question was rather stupid—or perhaps insulting. "A wheelchair, of course," he answered.

"Why are you in a wheelchair?"

Now Mr. V. looked frankly exasperated; he obviously did not like to answer foolish questions. "Because my left leg is paralyzed!" he snapped.

The word *emotion* can mean several things. Most of the time, it refers to positive or negative feelings that are produced by particular situations. For example, being treated unfairly makes us angry, seeing someone suffer makes us sad, and being close to a loved one makes us feel happy. Emotions consist of patterns of physiological responses and species-typical behaviors. In humans these responses are accompanied by feelings. In fact, most of us use the word *emotion* to refer to the feelings, not to the behaviors. But it is behavior, not private experience, that has consequences for survival and reproduction. Thus, the useful purposes that emotional behaviors serve are what guided the evolution of our brain. The feelings that accompany these behaviors came rather late in the game.

This chapter is divided into four major sections. The first considers the patterns of behavioral and physiological responses that constitute emotions. It describes the nature of these response patterns, their neural control, and the perception of situations that give rise to emotions; and it includes a discussion of prefrontal lobotomy and other types of psychosurgery. The second section describes the communication of emotions—their expression and recognition. The third section examines the nature of the feelings that accompany emotions. Finally, the fourth section considers the neural and hormonal control of aggressive and defensive behaviors.

EMOTIONS AS RESPONSE PATTERNS

An emotional response consists of three types of components: behavioral, autonomic, and hormonal. The *behavioral* component consists of muscular movements that are appropriate to the situation that elicits them. For example, a dog defending its territory against an intruder first adopts an aggressive posture, growls, and shows its teeth. If the intruder does not leave, the defender runs toward the intruder and attacks. *Autonomic* responses facilitate the behaviors and provide quick mobilization of energy for vigorous movement. In this example the activity of the sympathetic branch of the autonomic nervous system increases while that of the parasympathetic branch decreases. As a consequence, the dog's heart rate increases, and changes in the size of blood vessels shunt the circulation of blood away from the digestive organs toward the muscles. *Hormonal* responses reinforce the autonomic responses. The hormones secreted by the adrenal medulla—epinephrine and norepinephrine—further increase blood flow to the muscles and cause nutrients stored in the muscles to be converted into glucose. In addition, the adrenal cortex secretes steroid hormones, which also help to make glucose available to the muscles.

This section discusses research on the control of overt emotional behaviors and the autonomic and hormonal responses that accompany them. Special behaviors that serve to communicate emotional states to other animals, such as the threat gestures that precede an actual attack and the smiles and frowns used by humans, will be discussed in the second section of the chapter. As you will see, negative emotions receive much more attention than positive ones. Most of the research on the physiology of emotions has been confined to fear and anxiety—emotions associated with situations in which we must defend ourselves or our loved ones. The physiology of behaviors associated with positive emotions—such as those associated with lovemaking, caring for one's offspring, enjoying a good meal or a cool drink of water (or an alcoholic beverage)—is described in other chapters but not in the specific context of emotions. And Chapter 16 discusses the long-term consequences of situations that evoke negative emotions—stress.

Neural Control of Emotional Response Patterns: Role of the Amygdala

As we will see, stimulation of various parts of the brain can induce an animal to attack another one or can cause it to make vigorous attempts to escape. In other words, the stimulation can produce the behaviors associated with anger or fear. The overt behaviors, the autonomic responses, and the hormonal secretions associated with these emotional reactions are controlled by separate neural systems. The *integration* of these responses appears to be controlled by the amygdala.

Anatomy of the Amygdala

The amygdala plays a special role in physiological and behavioral reactions to objects and situations that have special biological significance, such as those that warn of pain or other unpleasant consequences or signify the presence of food, water, salt, potential mates or rivals, or infants in need of care. Researchers in several different laboratories have shown that single neurons in various nuclei of the amygdala become active when emotionally relevant stimuli are presented. For example, these neurons are excited by such stimuli as the sight of a device that has been used to squirt either a bad-tasting or a sweet solution into the animal's mouth, the sound of another animal's vocalization, the sound of the opening of the laboratory door, the smell of smoke, or the sight of another animal's face (O'Keefe and Bouma, 1969; Jacobs and McGinty, 1972; Rolls, 1982; Leonard et al., 1985). And as we have already seen in Chapter 9, the amygdala is involved in the effects of pheromones on reproductive physiology and behavior (including maternal behavior). This section describes research on the role of the amygdala in organizing emotional responses produced by aversive stimuli.

The amygdala (or more precisely, the *amygdaloid complex*) is located within the temporal lobes. It consists of several groups of nuclei, each with different inputs and outputs—and with different functions (Canteras, Simerly, and Swanson, 1995; Pitkaenen et al., 1995; Savander et al., 1995). The major parts of the amygdala are the *medial nucleus*, the *lateral/basolateral nuclei*, the *central nucleus*, and the *basal nucleus*. The **medial nucleus** consists of several subnuclei that receive sensory input (including information about the presence of odors and pheromones from the main and accessory olfactory bulbs) and relay the information to the medial basal forebrain and to the hypothalamus. Reproductive functions of the medial nucleus were discussed in Chapter 9. The **lateral/basolateral nuclei** receive sensory information from the primary sensory cortex, association cortex, thalamus, and hippocampal formation. These nuclei project to the ventral striatum (a region involved in the effects of reinforcing stimuli on learning) and to the dorsomedial nucleus of the thalamus, whose projection region is the prefrontal cortex. They also provide sensory input to the **central nucleus,** which is the part of the amygdala that will most concern us in this chapter. The central nucleus projects to regions of the hypothalamus, midbrain, pons, and medulla that are responsible for the expression of the various components of emotional responses. The **basal nucleus** consists of several subnuclei that, like the central nucleus, receive sensory input from the lateral and basolateral nuclei and relay information to other amygdaloid nuclei and to the periaqueductal gray matter of the midbrain. (See *Figure 10.1*.)

The central nucleus of the amygdala is the single most important part of the brain for the expression of emotional responses provoked by aversive stimuli. When threatening stimuli are presented, both the neural activity of the central nucleus and the production of Fos protein increase (Pascoe and Kapp, 1985; Campeau et al., 1991). Damage to the central nucleus (or to the lateral/basolateral nuclei, which provide it with sensory information) reduces or abolishes a wide range of emotional behaviors and physiological responses. After the central nucleus has been destroyed, animals no longer show signs of fear when confronted with stimuli that have been paired with aversive events. They also act more tamely when handled by humans, their blood levels of stress hormones are lower, and they are less likely to develop ulcers or other forms of stress-induced illnesses (Coover, Murison, and Jellestad, 1992; Davis, 1992b; LeDoux, 1992). In contrast, when the central amygdala is stimulated by means of electricity or by an injection of an excitatory amino acid, the animal shows physiological and behavioral signs of fear and agitation (Davis, 1992b), and long-term stimulation of the central nucleus produces stress-induced illnesses such as gastric ulcers (Henke, 1982). These observations suggest that the autonomic and endocrine responses controlled by the central nucleus are among those responsible for the harmful effects of long-term stress, which are discussed in Chapter 16.

Conditioned Emotional Responses

The central amygdala is particularly important for aversive emotional learning. A few stimuli automatically produce fear reactions—for example, loud unexpected noises, the approach of large animals, heights, or (for

Medial nucleus A group of subnuclei of the amygdala that receives sensory input, including information about the presence of odors and pheromones, and relays it to the medial basal forebrain and hypothalamus.

Lateral/basolateral nuclei Nuclei of the amygdala that receive sensory information from the neocortex, thalamus, and hippocampus and send projections to the ventral striatum, dorsomedial nucleus of the thalamus, and central nucleus.

Central nucleus The region of the amygdala that receives information from the basolateral division and sends projections to a wide variety of regions in the brain; involved in emotional responses.

Basal nucleus A group of subnuclei of the amygdala that receives sensory input from the lateral and basolateral nuclei and relays information to other amygdaloid nuclei and to the periaqueductal gray matter.

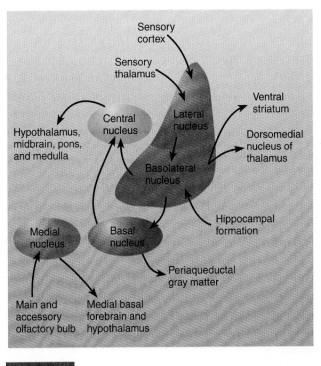

FIGURE 10.1

A much-simplified diagram of the major divisions and connections of the amygdala.

some species) specific sounds or odors. Even more important, however, is the fact that we can *learn* that a particular situation is dangerous or threatening. Once the learning has taken place, we will become frightened when we encounter that situation. Our heart rate and blood pressure will increase, our muscles will become more tense, our adrenal glands will secrete epinephrine, and we will proceed cautiously, alert and ready to respond.

Let's examine a specific (if somewhat contrived) example. A **conditioned emotional response** is produced by a neutral stimulus that has been paired with an emotion-producing stimulus. For example, suppose you are helping a friend prepare a meal. You pick up an electric mixer to mix some batter for a cake. Before you can turn the mixer on, the device makes a sputtering noise and then gives you a painful electrical shock. Your first response would be a defensive reflex: You would let go of the mixer, which would end the shock. This response is *specific;* it is aimed at terminating the painful stimulus. In addition, the painful stimulus would elicit *nonspecific* responses controlled by your autonomic nervous system: Your pupils would dilate, your heart rate and blood pressure would increase, you would breathe faster, and so on. The painful stimulus would also trigger the secretion of some stress-related hormones, another nonspecific response.

Suppose that a while later you visit your friend again and once more agree to make a cake. Your friend tells you that the electric mixer is perfectly safe—it has been fixed. Just seeing the mixer and thinking of holding it again make you a little nervous, but you accept your friend's assurance and pick it up. Just then, it makes the same sputtering noise that it did when it shocked you. What would your response be? Almost certainly, you would drop the mixer again, even if it did not give you a shock. And your pupils would dilate, your heart rate and blood pressure would increase, and your endocrine glands would secrete some stress-related hormones. In other words, the sputtering sound would trigger a conditioned emotional response.

The word *conditioned* refers to the process of *classical conditioning*, which is described in more detail in Chapter 12. Briefly, classical conditioning occurs when a neutral stimulus is regularly followed by a stimulus that automatically evokes a response. For example, if a dog regularly hears a bell ring just before it receives some food that makes it salivate, it will begin salivating as soon as it hears the sound of the bell. (You probably already know that this phenomenon was discovered by Ivan Pavlov.)

If an organism learns to make a specific response that avoids contact with the aversive stimulus (or at least minimizes its painful effect), most of the nonspecific "emotional" responses will eventually disappear. That is, if the organism learns a successful **coping response**—a response that terminates, avoids, or minimizes an aversive stimulus—the emotional responses will no longer occur. For example, suppose you suspect that your friend's electric mixer is still defective but you are determined to make the cake anyway. You get your gloves from the pocket of your overcoat and put them on. Now you can safely handle the mixer; the gloves provide electrical insulation for your hands. This time the sputtering noise does not bother you because you are protected from electrical shocks. The noise does not activate your autonomic nervous system (at least, not very much), nor does it cause your glands to secrete stress-related hormones.

Several laboratories have investigated the role of the central nucleus of the amygdala in the development of classically conditioned emotional responses. For example, LeDoux and his colleagues have studied these responses in rats by pairing an auditory stimulus with a brief electrical shock delivered to the feet (reviewed by LeDoux, 1995). In their studies they presented an 800-Hz tone for 10 sec, and then they delivered a brief (0.5-sec) shock to the floor on which the animals were standing. (See *Figure 10.2*.) By itself, the shock produces an *unconditional* emotional response: The animal jumps into the

Conditioned emotional response A classically conditioned response that develops when a neutral stimulus is repeatedly followed by an aversive stimulus; usually includes autonomic, behavioral, and endocrine components such as changes in heart rate, freezing, and secretion of stress-related hormones.

Coping response A response through which an organism can avoid, escape from, or minimize an aversive stimulus; reduces the stressful effects of an aversive stimulus.

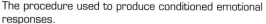

FIGURE 10.2

The procedure used to produce conditioned emotional responses.

air, its heart rate and blood pressure increase, its breathing becomes more rapid, and its adrenal glands secrete catecholamines and steroid stress hormones. The experimenters presented several pairings of the two stimuli, which established classical conditioning.

The investigators tested conditioned emotional responses the next day by presenting the 800-Hz tone several times and measuring the animals' blood pressure and heart rate and observing their behavior. (This time, they did not present the shock.) Upon hearing the tone, the rats showed the same type of physiological responses as when they were shocked the previous day. In addition, they showed behavioral arrest—a species-typical defensive response called *freezing*. That is, the animals acted as if they were expecting to receive a shock.

LeDoux and his colleagues have shown that the central nucleus is necessary for the development of a conditioned emotional response (LeDoux, 1987). If this nucleus is destroyed, conditioning does not take place. In addition, LeDoux et al. (1988) destroyed two regions that receive projections from the central nucleus: the lateral hypothalamus and the caudal periaqueductal gray matter. They found that lesions of the lateral hypothalamus interfered with the change in blood pressure, whereas lesions of the periaqueductal gray matter interfered with the freezing response. Thus, two different mechanisms, both under the control of the central nucleus of the amygdala, are responsible for the autonomic and behavioral components of conditioned emotional responses. (Activation of the central nucleus produces many other responses, such as changes in heart rate, sweating, or trembling, but not all of them have been studied in this situation.)

Research on the details of the physical changes responsible for classical conditioning—including the role of the central nucleus of the amygdala—has provided some interesting information about the physiology of learning and memory. This research will be discussed in more detail in Chapter 12.

Some of the effects of anxiolytic (anxiety-reducing) drugs appear to be produced through the central nucleus. The amygdala contains a high concentration of benzodiazepine receptors—especially the basolateral nucleus, which projects to the central nucleus—and the central nucleus itself contains a high concentration of opiate receptors. The infusion of either opiates or benzodiazepine tranquilizers into the amygdala decreases both the learning and the expression of conditioned emotional responses (Kapp et al., 1982; Davis, 1992a). In addition, Sanders and Shekhar (1995) found that an injection of a benzodiazepine antagonist into the basolateral nucleus blocked the anxiolytic effects of an intraperitoneal injection of chlordiazepoxide (Librium). Thus, tranquilizers appear to exert their anxiolytic effect in the basolateral amygdala. It is possible that some other regions are also involved in this effect; Yadin et al. (1991) found that even after the amygdala is destroyed, benzodiazepines still have some anxiolytic effect. And as we will see in Chapter 16, opiates have effects on many different parts of the brain.

As we will see in Chapter 15, some evidence suggests that increased activity of the neural mechanisms described in this section are associated with a fairly common category of psychological disorders: the *anxiety disorders*. Some investigators have suggested that anxiety disorders are caused by hyperactivity of the central nucleus of the amygdala, perhaps as a result of increased secretion of endogenous anxiety-producing ligands for the $GABA_A$ receptor, of which the benzodiazepine receptor is a part. Whether the primary cause of the increased anxiety lies within these circuits or elsewhere in the brain (or in people's environments and past histories) has yet to be determined.

We will see in Chapter 11 that the amygdala is involved in behaviors associated with another negative emotion—disgust. When an animal (including a member of our own species) becomes nauseated as a result of eating tainted food (or receiving an injection of a nausea-inducing drug), the animal develops an aversion to the flavor of the last thing it ate or drank before the nausea. This form of learning is abolished by lesions of the basolateral amygdala.

Research with Humans

A considerable amount of evidence indicates that the amygdala is involved in emotional responses in humans. One of the earliest studies observed the reactions of people who were being evaluated for surgical removal of parts of the brain to treat severe seizure disorders. These studies found that stimulation of parts of the brain (for example, the hypothalamus) produced autonomic responses that are often associated with fear and anxiety but that only when the amygdala was stimulated did people also report that they actually felt afraid (White, 1940; Halgren et al., 1978; Gloor et al., 1982).

Lesions of the amygdala decrease people's emotional responses. Two studies (LaBar et al., 1995; Bechara et al., 1995) found that people with lesions of the amygdala showed impaired acquisition of a conditioned emotional response, just as rats do. Angrilli et al. (1996) found that the startle response of a man with a localized lesion of the right amygdala was not increased by the presence of an unpleasant emotion. Normally, a person's startle response, elicited by a sudden noise, is larger when the person looks at unpleasant photos than when he or she looks at neutral ones. Presumably, the increased response is produced by the negative emotion caused by the unpleasant scene. Angrilli and his colleagues did not observe this effect in their patient; the man showed the same startle response regardless of the nature of the photographs.

Damage to the amygdala interferes with the effects of emotions on memory. Normally, when people encounter events that produce a strong emotional response, they are more likely to remember these events. Cahill et al. (1995) studied a patient with bilateral degeneration of the amygdala. The investigators narrated a story about a young boy walking with his mother on his way to visit his father at work. To accompany the story, they showed a series of slides. During one part of the story, the boy was injured in a traffic accident, and gruesome slides illustrated his injuries. When this slide show is presented to normal subjects, they remember more details from the emotion-laden part of the story. However, a patient with amygdala damage showed no such increase in memory.

Several imaging studies have shown that the human amygdala participates in emotional responses. For example, Cahill et al. (1996) had people watch both neutral and emotionally arousing films (such as scenes of violent crimes). Later, the experimenters placed the subjects in a PET scanner and asked them to recall the films. The activity of the right amygdala increased while the subjects recalled the emotionally arousing films but not when they recalled the neutral ones. Schneider et al. (1996) had people attempt to solve anagrams (rearrangements of scrambled words into sentences). Some of the anagrams could be solved relatively easily, but others were actually impossible to solve. When well motivated people work on such tasks, they tend to become tense and unhappy and usually report feelings of frustration. A PET scanner showed that the blood flow in the amygdala increased while the subjects were working on the unsolvable anagrams but not when working on the solvable ones.

Social Judgments and Emotions: Role of the Orbitofrontal Cortex

We humans are capable of reacting emotionally to very complex situations, especially those involving other people. Perceiving the meaning of social situations is obviously more complex than perceiving individual stimuli. The analysis of social situations involves much more than sensory analysis; it involves experiences and memories, inferences and judgments. In fact, the skills that are involved include some of the most complex ones we possess. These skills are not localized in any one part of the cerebral cortex, although research does suggest that the right hemisphere is more important than the left. But one region of the brain—the orbitofrontal cortex—plays a special role.

The **orbitofrontal cortex** is located at the base of the frontal lobes. It covers the part of the brain just above the *orbits*—the bones that form the eye sockets—hence the term *orbitofrontal*. (See *Figure 10.3*.) The orbitofrontal cortex receives direct inputs from the dorsomedial thalamus, temporal cortex, ventral tegmental area, olfactory system, and amygdala. Its outputs go to several brain regions, including the cingulate cortex, hippocampal formation, temporal cortex, lateral hypothalamus, and amygdala. Finally, it communicates with other regions of the frontal cortex. Thus, its inputs provide it with information about what is happening in the environment and what plans are being made by the rest of the frontal lobes, and its outputs permit it to affect a variety of behaviors and physiological responses, including emotional responses organized by the amygdala.

The fact that the orbitofrontal cortex plays an important role in emotional behavior is shown by the effects of damage to this region. The first—and most famous—case comes from the mid-1800s. Phineas Gage, a dynamite worker, was using a steel rod to ram a charge of dynamite into a hole drilled in solid rock. Suddenly, the charge exploded and sent the rod into his cheek, through his brain, and out the top of his head. (See *Figure 10.4*.) He survived, but he was a different man. Before his injury he was serious, industrious, and energetic. Afterward, he became childish, irresponsible, and thoughtless of others. He was unable to make or carry out plans, and his actions appeared to be capricious and whimsical. His accident largely destroyed the orbitofrontal cortex (Damasio et al., 1994).

Over the succeeding years, physicians reported several cases similar to that of Phineas Gage. In general, damage to the orbitofrontal cortex reduced people's inhibitions and self-concern; they became indifferent to the consequences of their actions. In addition, although they remained sensitive to noxious stimuli, the pain no longer bothered them—it no longer produced an emotional reaction. Then in 1935 the report of an experiment with a chimpanzee triggered events whose repercussions are still felt today.

Jacobsen, Wolf, and Jackson (1935) tested some chimpanzees on a behavioral task that requires the animal to remain quiet and remember the location of food that the experimenter has placed behind a screen. One animal, Becky, displayed a violent emotional reaction whenever she made an error while performing this task. "[When] the experimenter lowered . . . the opaque door to exclude the animal's view of the cups, she immediately flew into a temper tantrum, rolled on the floor, defecated, and urinated. After a few such reactions during the training period, the animal would make no further responses." After the chimpanzee's frontal lobes were removed, it became a model of good comportment. It "offered its usual friendly greeting, and eagerly ran from its living quarters to the transfer cage, and in turn went properly to the experimental cage. . . . If the animal made a mistake, it showed no evidence of emotional disturbance but quietly awaited the loading of the cups for the next trial" (Jacobsen, Wolf, and Jackson, 1935, pp. 9–10).

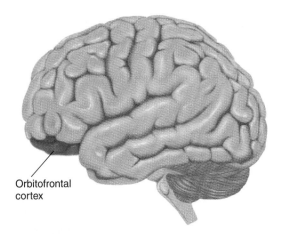

FIGURE 10.3

The orbitofrontal cortex.

Orbitofrontal cortex The region of the prefrontal cortex at the base of the anterior frontal lobes.

FIGURE 10.4

A bust and skull of Phineas Gage. The steel rod entered his left cheek and exited through his left forehead.

(From Warren Museum, Harvard Medical School. Reprinted with permission.)

These findings were reported at a scientific meeting in 1935, which was attended by Egas Moniz, a Portuguese neuropsychiatrist. He heard the report by Jacobsen and his colleagues and also one by Brickner (1936), which indicated that radical removal of the frontal lobes in a human patient (performed because of a tumor) did not appear to produce intellectual impairment—thus, people could presumably get along without their frontal lobes. These two reports suggested to Moniz that "if frontal-lobe removal . . . eliminates frustrational behavior, why would it not be feasible to relieve anxiety states in man by surgical means?" (Fulton, 1949, pp. 63–64). In fact, Moniz persuaded a neurosurgeon to do so, and approximately one hundred operations were eventually performed under his supervision. (In 1949 Moniz received the Nobel Prize for the development of this procedure.)

Three paragraphs ago, I wrote that the repercussions of the 1935 meeting are still felt today. Since that time, tens of thousands of people have received prefrontal lobotomies, primarily to reduce symptoms of emotional distress, and many of these people are still alive. At first, the procedure was welcomed by the medical community because it provided their patients with relief from emotional anguish. Only after many years were careful studies performed on the side effects of the procedure. These studies showed that although patients did perform well on standard tests of intellectual ability, they showed serious changes in personality, becoming irresponsible and childish. They also lost the ability to carry out plans, and most were unemployable. And although pathological emotional reactions were eliminated, so were normal ones. Because of these findings, and because of the discovery of drugs and therapeutic methods that relieve the patients' symptoms without producing such drastic side effects, neurosurgeons eventually abandoned the prefrontal lobotomy procedure (Valenstein, 1986).

I should point out that the prefrontal lobotomies performed under Moniz's supervision, and by the neurosurgeons who followed, were not as drastic as the surgery performed by Jacobsen and his colleagues on Becky, the chimpanzee. In fact, no brain tissue was removed. Instead, the surgeons introduced various kinds of cutting devices into the frontal lobes and severed white matter (bundles of axons). One rather gruesome procedure did not even require an operating room; it could be performed in a physician's office. A *transorbital leucotome,* shaped like an ice pick, was introduced into the brain by passing it beneath the upper eyelid until the point reached the orbital bone above the eye. The instrument was hit with a mallet, driving it through the bone into the brain. The end was then swept back and forth so that it cut through the white matter. The patient often left the office within an hour. (See *Figure 10.5.*)

Many physicians objected to the "ice pick" procedure because it was done blind (that is, the surgeon could not see just where the blade of the leucotome was located) and because it produced more damage than was necessary. Also, the fact that it was so easy and left no external signs other than a pair of black eyes may have tempted its practitioners to perform it too casually. In fact, at least 2500 patients received this form of surgery (Valenstein, 1986).

What we know today about the effects of prefrontal lobotomy—whether done transorbitally or by more conventional means—tells us that such radical surgery should never have been performed. For too long the harmful side effects were ignored. (As we will see in Chapter 15, neurosurgeons eventually developed a much restricted version of this surgery, which reduces the symptoms without producing the harmful side effects.) But the fact remains that the surgery *did* reduce people's emotional suffering, or it would never have become so popu-

FIGURE 10.5

"Ice pick" prefrontal lobotomy. The sharp metal rod is inserted under the eyelid and just above the eye so that it pierces the skull and enters the base of the frontal lobe.

(Adapted from Freeman, W. Proceedings of the Royal Society of Medicine, 1949, 42(suppl.), 8–12.)

lar. Primarily, the surgery reduced anxiety, obsessions, and compulsions. People's groundless fears disappeared, and they no longer felt compelled to perform rituals to ward off some (imaginary) disastrous events. Before the surgery the world was a threatening place, and their emotional responses and behavior caused them anguish and made shambles of their lives. After surgery their cares disappeared.

All types of prefrontal lobotomies disrupted the functions of the frontal lobes (primarily the orbitofrontal cortex) by severing connections between this area and the rest of the brain. Some procedures approached the frontal lobes from the base of the brain, primarily cutting their connections with the diencephalon and temporal lobes. Other procedures approached the frontal lobes from above and disconnected the orbitofrontal cortex from the cingulate gyrus. In either case the patients' emotional distress was usually reduced.

What, exactly, does the orbitofrontal cortex do? One possibility is that it is involved in assessing the personal consequences of what is currently happening. However, this analysis does not appear to be correct. People whose orbitofrontal cortex has been damaged by disease or accident are still able to accurately assess the significance of particular situations, but only in a *theoretical* sense. For example, Eslinger and Damasio (1985) found that a patient with bilateral damage of the orbitofrontal cortex (produced by a benign tumor, which was successfully removed) displayed excellent social judgment. When he was given hypothetical situations that required him to make decisions about what the people involved should do—situations involving moral, ethical, or practical dilemmas—he always gave sensible answers and justified them with carefully reasoned logic. However, his own life was a different matter. He frittered away his life's savings on investments that his family and friends pointed out were bound to fail. He lost one job after another because of his irresponsibility. He became unable to distinguish between trivial decisions and important ones, spending hours trying to decide where to have dinner but failing to use good judgment in situations that concerned his occupation and family life. (His wife finally left him and sued for divorce.) As the authors noted, "He had learned and used normal patterns of social behavior before his brain lesion, and although he could recall such patterns when he was questioned about their applicability, *real-life situations failed to evoke them*" (p. 1737). Thus, it appears that the orbitofrontal cortex is not directly involved in making judgments and conclusions about events (these occur elsewhere in the brain) but has a role in translating these judgments into appropriate feelings and behaviors.

INTERIM SUMMARY

The word *emotion* refers to behaviors, physiological responses, and feelings. This section has discussed emotional response patterns, which consist of behaviors that deal with particular situations and physiological responses (both autonomic and hormonal) that support the behaviors. The amygdala organizes behavioral, autonomic, and hormonal responses to a variety of situations, including those that produce fear, anger, or disgust. In addition, it is involved in the effects of odors and pheromones on sexual and maternal behavior. It receives inputs from the olfactory system, the association cortex of the temporal lobe, the frontal cortex, and the rest of the limbic system. Its outputs go to the frontal cortex, hypothalamus, hippocampal formation, and brain stem nuclei that control autonomic functions and some species-typical behaviors. Damage to specific brain regions that receive these outputs will abolish particular components of emotional response patterns. Electrical recordings of single neurons in the amygdala indicate that some of them respond when the animal perceives particular stimuli with emotional significance. Stimulation of the amygdala leads to emotional responses, and its destruction disrupts them. Receptors in the amygdala are largely responsible for the anxiolytic effects of the benzodiazepine tranquilizers and the opiates. Studies of people with amygdala lesions and PET and functional MRI studies with humans indicate that the amygdala is involved in emotional reactions in our species, too.

The orbitofrontal cortex plays an important role in emotional reactions. People with orbitofrontal lesions are able to explain the implications of complex social situations but are unable to respond appropriately when these situations concern *them*. Thus, this region does not appear to be necessary for making judgments about the personal significance of social situations, but it does appear to be necessary for translating these judgments into actions and emotional responses. The orbitofrontal cortex receives information from other regions of the frontal lobes, from the temporal pole, and from the amygdala and other parts of the limbic system via the mediodorsal nucleus of the thalamus. It produces emotional reactions through its connections with the amygdala and the cingulate gyrus.

Between the late 1930s and the late 1950s many people received prefrontal lobotomies, which involved cutting the white matter in the ventromedial frontal lobes. Although the operations affected many parts of the frontal lobes, the most important region was probably the orbitofrontal cortex. The surgery did often relieve emotional anguish and the suffering caused by pain, but it also made people become largely indifferent to the social consequences of their own behavior and to the feelings of others, and it interfered with their ability to make and execute plans. Prefrontal lobotomies are no longer performed.

EXPRESSION AND RECOGNITION OF EMOTIONS

The previous section described emotions as organized responses (behavioral, autonomic, and hormonal) that prepare an animal to deal with existing situations in the environment, such as events that pose a threat to the organism. For our earliest premammalian ancestors that is undoubtedly all there was to emotions. But over time, other responses, with new functions, evolved. Many species of animals (including our own) communicate their emotions to others by means of postural changes, facial expressions, and nonverbal sounds (such as sighs, moans, and growls). These expressions serve useful social functions; they tell other individuals how we feel and—more to the point—what we are likely to do. For example, they warn a rival that we are angry or tell friends that we are sad and would like some comfort and reassurance. In many species they indicate that a danger may be present or that something interesting seems to be happening. This section examines such expression and communication of emotions.

Facial Expression of Emotions: Innate Responses

Charles Darwin (1872/1965) suggested that human expressions of emotion have evolved from similar expressions in other animals. He said that emotional expressions are innate, unlearned responses consisting of a complex set of movements, principally of the facial muscles. Thus, a human's sneer and a wolf's snarl are biologically determined response patterns, both controlled by innate brain mechanisms, just as coughing and sneezing are. (Of course, humans can sneer and wolves can snarl for quite different reasons.) Some of these movements resemble the behaviors themselves and may have evolved from them. For example, a snarl shows one's teeth and can be seen as an anticipation of biting.

Darwin obtained evidence for his conclusion that emotional expressions were innate by observing his own children and by corresponding with people living in various isolated cultures around the world. He reasoned that if people all over the world, no matter how isolated, show the same facial expressions of emotion, then these expressions must be inherited instead of learned. The logical argument goes like this: When groups of people are isolated for many years, they develop different languages. Thus, we can say that the words people use are arbitrary; there is no biological basis for using particular words to represent particular concepts. However, if facial expressions are inherited, then they should take approximately the same form in people from all cultures, despite their isolation from one another. And Darwin did, indeed, find that people in different cultures used the same patterns of movement of facial muscles to express a particular emotional state.

Research by Ekman and his colleagues (Ekman and Friesen, 1971; Ekman, 1980) tends to confirm Darwin's hypothesis that facial expression of emotion uses an innate, species-typical repertoire of movements of facial muscles (Darwin, 1872/1965). For example, Ekman and Friesen (1971) studied the ability of members of an isolated tribe in New Guinea to recognize facial expressions of emotion produced by Westerners. They had no trouble doing so and themselves produced facial expressions that Westerners readily recognized. Figure 10.6 shows four photographs taken from videotapes of a man from this tribe reacting to stories designed to evoke facial expressions of sadness, disgust, happiness, and anger. I am sure that you will have no trouble recognizing which is which. (See *Figure 10.6*.)

Because the same facial expressions were used by people who had not previously been exposed to each other, Ekman and Friesen concluded that the expressions were unlearned behavior patterns. In contrast, different cultures use different words to express particular concepts; production of these words does not involve innate responses but must be learned.

Other researchers have compared the facial expressions of blind and normally sighted children. They reasoned that if the facial expressions of both groups are similar, then the expressions are natural for our species and do not require learning by imitation. (Studies of blind adults would not be conclusive, because adults would have heard enough descriptions of facial expressions to be able to pose them.) In fact, the facial expressions of young blind and sighted children are very similar (Woodworth and Schlosberg, 1954; Izard, 1971). Thus, both the cross-cultural studies and the investigations with blind children confirm the naturalness of these expressions.

Researchers have not yet determined whether other means of communicating emotions, such as tone of voice or changes in body posture, are learned or are at least partly innate. However, as we will see, some progress has been made in studying the neuroanatomical basis of expressing and recognizing emotions.

Neural Basis of the Communication of Emotions: Recognition

Effective communication is a two-way process. That is, the ability to display one's emotional state by changes in expression is useful only if other people are able to recognize them. In fact, Kraut and Johnston (1979) unobtrusively observed people in circumstances that would be likely to make them happy. They found that happy situations (such as making a strike while bowling, seeing the home team score, or experiencing a beautiful day) produced only small signs of happiness when the people were alone. However, when the people were interacting socially with other people, they were much more likely to smile. For example, bowlers who made a strike usu-

(a) (b)

(c) (d)

FIGURE 10.6

A member of an isolated New Guinea tribe, studied by Ekman and Friesen, making faces when told stories. (a) "Your friend has come and you are happy." (b) "Your child had died." (c) "You are angry and about to fight." (d) "You see a dead pig that has been lying there a long time."

(From Ekman, P., The Face of Man: Expressions of Universal Emotions in a New Guinea Village. New York: Garland STPM Press, 1980. Reprinted with permission.)

ally did not smile when the ball hit the pins, but when they turned around to face their companions, they often smiled. Jones et al. (1991) found that even ten-month-old children showed this tendency.

We recognize other people's feelings by means of vision and audition—seeing their facial expressions and hearing their tone of voice and choice of words. Many studies have found that the right hemisphere plays a more important role than the left hemisphere in comprehension of emotion. For example, many investigators have found a left-ear and a left-visual-field advantage in recognition of emotionally related stimuli. The rationale for these studies is that each hemisphere directly receives information from the contralateral part of the environment. For example, when a person looks directly ahead, visual stimuli to the left of the fixation point (seen with *both* eyes) are transmitted to the right hemisphere, and stimuli to the right are transmitted to the left hemisphere. Of course, the hemispheres exchange information by means of the corpus callosum, but it appears that this transcommissural information is not as precise and detailed as information that is directly received. Similarly, although each hemisphere receives auditory information from both ears, the contralateral projections are richer than the ipsilateral ones. Thus, when stimuli are presented to the left visual field or left ear, the right hemisphere receives more specific information than the left hemisphere does.

In studies of hemispherical differences in visual recognition, stimuli are usually presented to the left or right visual field so rapidly that the subject does not have time to move his or her eyes. Many studies (reviewed by Bryden and Ley, 1983) have shown that the left hemisphere is better than the right at recognizing words or letter strings but that the right hemisphere is better at detecting differences in facial expressions of emotion. Similarly, subjects can more easily understand the verbal content of a message presented to the left hemisphere but can more accurately detect the emotional tone of the voice presented to the right hemisphere. These results suggest that when a message is heard, the right hemisphere assesses the emotional expression of the voice while the left hemisphere assesses the meaning of the words.

Blonder, Bowers, and Heilman (1991) found that patients with right hemisphere lesions had no difficulty making emotional judgments about particular situations but were severely impaired in judging the emotions conveyed by facial expressions or hand gestures. For example, they had no difficulty deciding what emotion would be evoked by the situations described in sentences like *After you drink the water, you see the sign* (fear) or *Your house seems empty without her* (sadness). However, these patients had difficulty recognizing the emotions depicted by sentences like *He scowled, Tears fell from her eyes,* or *He shook his fist.* In addition, Bowers et al. (1991) found that patients with right hemisphere damage had difficulty producing or describing mental images of facial expressions of emotions. Subjects were asked to imagine the face of someone who was very happy (or very sad, angry, or afraid). Then they were asked questions about the facial expression—for example, *Do the eyes look twinkly? Is the brow raised? Are the corners of the lips raised up?* People with right hemisphere damage had trouble answering these questions but could easily answer questions about non-emotional images, such as *What's higher off the ground, a horse's knee or the top of its tail?* or *What number from one to ten does a peanut look like?* or *What's bigger, a thimble or a pencil eraser?*

Several PET studies have confirmed these results. For example, George et al. (1996) measured subjects' regional cerebral blood flow with a PET scanner while they listened to some sentences and identified their emotional content. In one condition the subjects listened to the meaning of the words and said whether they described a situation in which someone would be happy, sad, angry, or neutral. In another condition they judged the emotional state from the tone of the voice. In a control condition they simply repeated the second word they heard from each sentence. The investigators found that comprehension of emotion from word meaning increased the activity of both frontal lobes, the left more than the right. Compre-

FIGURE 10.7

PET scans indicating brain regions activated by listening to emotions expressed by tone of voice (green) or meanings of words (red).

[From George, M.S., Parekh, P.I., Rosinsky, N., Ketter, T.A., Kimbrell, T.A., Heilman, K.M., Herscovitch, P., and Post, R.M., Archives of Neurology, 1996, 53, 665–670.]

Right   Left

● Meanings of words
● Tone of voice
● Both

Frontal section

hension of emotion from tone of voice increased the activity of only the right prefrontal cortex. (See *Figure 10.7*.)

Observations of people with brain damage are consistent with the studies with normal subjects. Heilman, Scholes, and Watson (1975) had patients with unilateral lesions of the temporal-parietal region listen to sentences with neutral content (such as *The boy went to the store*) said in a happy, sad, angry, or indifferent tone of voice. Patients with right hemisphere damage judged the emotion being expressed less accurately. Heilman, Watson, and Bowers (1983) recorded a particularly interesting case of a man with a disorder called *pure word deafness* (described in Chapter 13). The man could not comprehend the meaning of speech but had no difficulty identifying the emotion being expressed by its intonation. This case, like the study by George et al., indicates that comprehension of words and recognition of tone of voice are independent functions.

As we saw in Chapter 6, damage to the visual association cortex can cause *prosopagnosia*—inability to recognize particular faces. Just as recognition of the meaning of words and the emotion expressed by tone of voice are accomplished by different brain functions, so are recognition of particular faces and facial expressions of emotions. Some patients can recognize faces but not the emotions they express; others can recognize the emotions but not the faces (Bowers and Heilman, 1981; Humphreys, Donnelly, and Riddoch, 1993). In addition, most patients who cannot recognize facial expressions can easily recognize emotions from tone of voice.

As we saw in the previous section, the amygdala plays a special role in emotional responses. It may play a role in emotional recognition as well. For example, several studies have found that lesions of the amygdala (the result of degenerative diseases or surgery for severe seizure disorders) impairs people's ability to recognize facial expressions of emotion—especially expressions of fear (Adolphs et al., 1994, 1995; Young et al., 1995; Calder et al., 1996). Scott et al. (1997) report the case of a woman with bilateral amygdala lesions who had normal hearing but had difficulty recognizing emotions—particularly fear and anger—expressed in a person's tone of voice. Finally, Morris et al. (1996) found a large increase in the activity of the amygdala (measured by PET) when people viewed photographs of faces expressing fear but only a small increase when they looked at photographs of happy faces.

Neural Basis of the Communication of Emotions: Expression

Facial expressions of emotion are automatic and involuntary. It is not easy to produce a realistic facial expression of emotion when we do not really feel that way. In fact, Ekman and Davidson have confirmed an early observation by a nineteenth-century neurologist, Guillaume-Benjamin Duchenne de Boulogne, that genuinely happy smiles, in contrast to false smiles or smiles people make when they greet someone else, involve contraction of a muscle near the eyes, the lateral part of the orbicularis oculi—now sometimes referred to as Duchenne's muscle (Ekman, 1992; Ekman and Davidson, 1993). As Duchenne put it, "The first [zygomatic major muscle] obeys the will but the second [orbicularis oculi] is only put in play by the sweet

Although a skilled actor or model can learn to produce realistic facial expressions, genuine smiles are controlled by neural circuits that we cannot voluntarily activate.

Volitional facial paresis Difficulty in moving the facial muscles voluntarily; caused by damage to the face region of the primary motor cortex or its subcortical connections.

Emotional facial paresis Lack of movement of facial muscles in response to emotions in people who have no difficulty moving these muscles voluntarily; caused by damage to the insular prefrontal cortex, subcortical white matter of the frontal lobe, or parts of the thalamus.

emotions of the soul; the . . . fake joy, the deceitful laugh, cannot provoke the contraction of this latter muscle" (Duchenne, 1862/1990, p. 72). The difficulty actors have in voluntarily producing a convincing facial expression of emotion is one of the reasons that led Konstantin Stanislavsky to develop his system of *method acting*, in which actors attempt to imagine themselves in a situation that would lead to the desired emotion. Once the emotion is evoked, the facial expressions follow naturally.

This observation is confirmed by two neurological disorders with complementary symptoms (Hopf et al., 1992). The first, **volitional facial paresis,** is caused by damage to the face region of the primary motor cortex or to the fibers connecting this region with the motor nucleus of the facial nerve, which controls the muscles responsible for movement of the facial muscles. (*Paresis*, from the Greek "to let go," refers to a partial paralysis.) The interesting thing about volitional facial paresis is that the patient cannot voluntarily move the facial muscles but will express a genuine emotion with those muscles. For example, Figure 10.8(a) shows a woman trying to pull her lips apart and show her teeth. Because of the lesion in the face region of her right primary motor cortex, she could not move the left side of her face. However, when she laughed (Figure 10.8b), both sides of her face moved normally. (See *Figure 10.8a* and *10.8b*.)

In contrast, **emotional facial paresis** is caused by damage to the insular region of the prefrontal cortex, to the white matter of the frontal lobe, or to parts of the

(a)   (b)

(c)   (d)

FIGURE   10.8

Emotional and volitional paresis. (a) A woman with volitional facial paresis caused by a right hemisphere lesion trying to pull her lips apart and show her teeth. Only the right side of her face responds. (b) The same woman showing a genuine smile. (c) A man with emotional facial paresis caused by a left-hemisphere lesion showing his teeth. (d) The same man smiling. Only the left side of his face responds.

(From Hopf, H.C., Mueller-Forell, W., and Hopf, N.J., Neurology, 1992, 42, 1918–1923. Reprinted with permission.)

(a) (b) (c)

FIGURE 10.9

An example of a stimulus used by Sackheim and Gur (1978). (a) Original photo. (b) Composite of the right side of the man's face. (c) Composite of the left side of the man's face.

[Reprinted with permission from Neuropsychologia, *16, H.A. Sackheim and R.C. Gur,* Lateral asymmetry in intensity of emotional expression. *Copyright 1978, Pergamon Press.]*

thalamus. People with this disorder can move their face muscles voluntarily but do not express emotions on the affected side of the face. Figure 10.8(c) shows a man pulling his lips apart to show his teeth, which he had no trouble doing. Figure 10.8(d) shows him smiling; as you can see, only the left side of his mouth is raised. He had a stroke that damaged the white matter of the left frontal lobe. (See *Figure 10.8c* and *10.8d.*) These two syndromes clearly indicate that different brain mechanisms are responsible for voluntary movements of the facial muscles and automatic, involuntary expression of emotions involving the same muscles.

As we saw in the previous subsection, the right hemisphere plays a more significant role in recognizing emotions in the voice or facial expressions of other people—especially negative emotions. The same hemispheric specialization appears to be true for expressing emotions. When people show emotions with their facial muscles, the left side of the face usually makes a more intense expression. For example, Sackheim and Gur (1978) cut photographs of people who were posing emotions into right and left halves, prepared mirror images of each of them, and pasted them together, producing so-called *chimerical faces* (from the mythical Chimera, a fire-breathing monster, part goat, part lion, and part serpent). They found that the left halves were more expressive than the right ones. (See *Figure 10.9.*) Because motor control is contralateral, the results suggest that the right hemisphere is more expressive than the left.

Moscovitch and Olds (1982) made more natural observations of people in restaurants and parks and found that the left side of their faces appeared to make stronger expressions of emotions. They confirmed these results in the laboratory by analyzing videotapes of people telling sad or humorous stories.

Using the chimerical faces technique, Hauser (1993) found that rhesus monkeys, like humans, express emotions more strongly in the left sides of their faces. Analysis of videotapes further showed that emotional expressions also begin sooner in the left side of the face. These findings suggest that hemispherical specialization for emotional expression appeared before the emergence of our own species. Figure 10.10 shows six videotape frames of a monkey's fear grimace expressed during the course of an interaction with a more dominant monkey. (See *Figure 10.10.*)

Left hemisphere lesions do not usually impair vocal expressions of emotion. For example, people with Wernicke's aphasia (described in Chapter 13) usually modulate their voice according to mood, even though the words they say make no sense. In contrast, right-hemisphere lesions do impair expression of emotion, both facially and by tone of voice.

FIGURE 10.10

Successive frames from a videotape of a rhesus monkey showing a fear grimace in response to an interaction with a more dominant monkey.

[Reprinted with permission from Hauser, M.D., Science, *1993, 261, 475–477. Copyright 1993 American Association for the Advancement of Science.]*

Interesting information about hemispherical specialization in the expression of emotion has been obtained during the Wada test. The **Wada test** (named after its developer) is performed before a person receives surgery for removal of a seizure focus. Ross, Homan, and Buck (1994) asked people who were about to be evaluated for seizure surgery about experiences they had had that caused an intense emotion. The subjects narrated their experiences and described their feelings at the time. Then, while the right hemisphere was anesthetized with a fast-acting barbiturate injected into the right carotid artery, the subjects were asked about these experiences again. This time, most of the subjects described less intense emotions. For example, one subject described an accident in which he had wrecked his car. Before the injection, he said, "I was scared, scared to death. I could have run off the road and killed myself or someone else . . . I was really scared." During the right hemisphere anesthesia he said that after the accident he felt "silly . . . silly." Another patient described an accident with a truck as the scariest situation he had ever experienced. While his right hemisphere was anesthetized, he said he was "sort of scared" but denied that the accident was the scariest event in his life. Another patient said he was very angry when he learned that his wife was having an affair and threw a phone across the room. During the anesthesia he said that he had become "a little angry" and "kind'a tossed the phone."

Ross and his colleagues suggest that the right hemisphere plays a role in what they call *primary* emotions, most of which are negative. The left hemisphere, they believe, is involved in modulating emotional displays controlled by the right hemisphere and organizing social displays of positive emotions, such as the quick smile we flash when we meet someone we know. These social displays are different from the expressions of genuine emotions—for example, the social smile does not involve the contraction of Duchenne's muscle. Unfortunately, it is not possible to query people about their emotional responses while the left hemisphere is anesthetized, because the anesthesia of the speech mechanisms in the left hemisphere prevents them from speaking or understanding the speech of other people.

INTERIM SUMMARY

We (and members of other species) communicate our emotions primarily through facial gestures. Darwin believed that such expressions of emotion were innate—that these muscular movements were inherited behavioral patterns. Ekman and his colleagues performed cross-cultural studies with members of an isolated tribe in New Guinea. Their results supported Darwin's hypothesis.

Recognition of other people's emotional expressions involves the right hemisphere more than the left. Studies with normal people have shown that people can judge facial expressions or tone of voice better when the information is presented to the right hemisphere than when it is presented to the left hemisphere. PET scans made while people judge the emotions of voices show that such judgments activate the right hemisphere more than the left. Studies of people with left or right hemisphere brain damage corroborate these findings. In addition, they show that recognition of particular faces involves neural circuits different from those needed to recognize facial expressions of emotions. Finally, the amygdala plays a role in recognition in emotions; lesions of the amygdala disrupt this ability, and PET scans show increased activity of the amygdala while engaging in this task.

Facial expression of emotions (and other stereotypical behaviors such as laughing and crying) are almost impossible to simulate. For example, only a genuine smile of pleasure causes the contraction of the lateral part of the orbicularis oculi (Duchenne's muscle). Genuine expressions of emotion are controlled by special neural circuits. The best evidence for this assertion comes from the complementary syndromes of emotional and volitional facial paresis. People with emotional facial paresis can move their facial muscles voluntarily but not in response to an emotion,

Wada test A test often performed before brain surgery; verifies the functions of one hemisphere by testing patients while the other hemisphere is anesthetized.

whereas people with volitional facial paresis show the opposite symptoms. In addition, the left halves of people's faces—and the faces of monkeys—tend to be more expressive than the right halves. While the right hemisphere is anesthetized during the Wada test, the emotional feelings that accompany people's recollection of memories generally become less intense.

FEELINGS OF EMOTIONS

So far, we have examined two aspects of emotions: the organization of patterns of responses that deal with the situation that provokes the emotion, and the communication of emotional states with other members of the species. The final aspect of emotion to be examined in this chapter is the subjective component: feelings of emotion.

The James-Lange Theory

William James (1842–1910), an American psychologist, and Carl Lange (1834–1900), a Danish physiologist, independently suggested similar explanations for emotion, which most people refer to collectively as the **James-Lange theory** (James, 1884; Lange, 1887). Basically, the theory states that emotion-producing situations elicit an appropriate set of physiological responses, such as trembling, sweating, and increased heart rate. The situations also elicit behaviors, such as clenching of the fists or fighting. The brain receives sensory feedback from the muscles and from the organs that produce these responses; it is this feedback that constitutes our feeling of emotion.

James says that our own emotional feelings are based on what we find ourselves doing and on the sensory feedback we receive from the activity of our muscles and internal organs. Thus, when we find ourselves trembling and feel queasy, we experience fear. Where feelings of emotions are concerned, we are self-observers. Thus, the two aspects of emotions reported in the first two sections of this chapter (patterns of emotional responses and expressions of emotions) give rise to the third: feelings. (See *Figure 10.11.*)

James's description of the process of emotion might strike you as being at odds with your own experience. Many people think that they experience emotions directly, internally. They consider the outward manifestations of emotions to be secondary events. But have you ever found yourself in an unpleasant confrontation with someone else and discovered that you were trembling, even though you did not think that you were so bothered by the encounter? Or did you ever find yourself blushing in response to some public remark that was made about you? Or did you ever find tears coming to your eyes while watching a film that you did not think was affecting you? What would you conclude about your emotional states in situations like these? Would you ignore the evidence from your own physiological reactions?

A well-known physiologist, Walter Cannon, criticized James's theory. He said that the internal organs were relatively insensitive and that they could not respond very quickly, so feedback from them could not account for our feelings of emotions. In addition, he observed that cutting the nerves that provide feedback from the internal organs to the brain did not alter emotional behavior (Cannon, 1927). However, subsequent research indicated that Cannon's criticisms are not relevant. For example, although the viscera are

James-Lange theory A theory of emotion that suggests that behaviors and physiological responses are directly elicited by situations and that feelings of emotions are produced by feedback from these behaviors and responses.

FIGURE 10.11

A diagrammatic representation of the James-Lange theory of emotion. An event in the environment triggers behavioral, autonomic, and endocrine responses. Feedback from these responses produces feelings of emotions.

not sensitive to some kinds of stimuli, such as cutting and burning, they provide much better feedback than Cannon suspected. Moreover, many changes in the viscera can occur rapidly enough that they could be the causes of feelings of emotion.

Cannon cited the fact that cutting the sensory nerves between the internal organs and the central nervous system does not abolish emotional behavior in laboratory animals. However, this observation misses the point. It does not prove that feelings of emotion survive this surgical disruption—only that emotional *behaviors* do. We do not know how the animals feel; we know only that they will snarl and attempt to bite if threatened. In any case, James did not attribute all feelings of emotion to the internal organs; he also said that feedback from muscles was important. The threat might make the animal snarl and bite, and the feedback from the facial and neck muscles might constitute a "feeling" of anger, even if feedback from the internal organs was cut off. But we have no way to ask the animal how it felt.

James's theory is difficult to verify experimentally because it attempts to explain *feelings* of emotion, not the causes of emotional responses—and feelings are private events. Some anecdotal evidence supports the theory. For example, Sweet (1966) reported the case of a man in whom some sympathetic nerves were severed on one side of the body to treat a cardiovascular disorder. The man—a music lover—reported that the shivering sensation he felt while listening to music now occurred only on the unoperated side of his body. He still enjoyed listening to music, but the surgery altered his emotional reaction.

In one of the few tests of James's theory, Hohman (1966) collected data from people with spinal cord damage. He asked these people about the intensity of their emotional feelings. If feedback is important, one would expect that emotional feelings would be less intense if the injury were high (that is, close to the brain) than if it were low, because a high spinal cord injury would make the person become insensitive to a larger part of the body. In fact, this result is precisely what Hohman found: The higher the injury, the less intense the feeling was. As one of Hohman's subjects said:

> I sit around and build things up in my mind, and I worry a lot, but it's not much but the power of thought. I was at home alone in bed one day and dropped a cigarette where I couldn't reach it. I finally managed to scrounge around and put it out. I could have burned up right there, but the funny thing is, I didn't get all shook up about it. I just didn't feel afraid at all, like you would suppose. (Hohman, 1966, pp. 150–151)

Another subject showed that angry behavior (an emotional response) does not appear to depend on *feelings* of emotion. Instead, the behavior is evoked by the situation (and by the person's evaluation of it) even if the spinal cord damage has reduced the intensity of the person's emotional feelings.

> Now, I don't get a feeling of physical animation, it's sort of cold anger. Sometimes I act angry when I see some injustice. I yell and cuss and raise hell, because if you don't do it sometimes, I've learned people will take advantage of you, but it doesn't have the heat to it that it used to. It's a mental kind of anger. (Hohman, 1966, pp. 150–151)

INTERIM SUMMARY

From the earliest times, people recognized that emotions were accompanied by feelings that seemed to come from inside the body, which probably provided the impetus for developing physiological theories of emotion. James and Lange suggested that emotions were primarily responses to situations. Feedback from the physiological and behavioral reactions to emotion-producing situations gave rise to the feelings of emotion; thus, feelings are the *results*, not the *causes*, of emotional reactions. Hohman's study of people with spinal cord damage supported the James-Lange theory; people who could no longer feel the reactions from most of their body reported that they no longer experienced intense emotional states.

AGGRESSIVE BEHAVIOR

Almost all species of animals engage in aggressive behaviors, which involve threatening gestures or actual attack directed toward another animal. Aggressive behaviors are species-typical; that is, the patterns of movements (for example, posturing, biting, striking, and hissing) are organized by neural circuits whose development is largely programmed by an animal's genes. Many aggressive behaviors are related to reproduction. For example, aggressive behaviors that gain access to mates, defend territory needed to attract mates or to provide a site for building a nest, or defend offspring against intruders can all be regarded as reproductive behaviors. Other aggressive behaviors are related to self-defense, such as that of an animal threatened by a predator.

Aggressive behaviors can consist of actual attacks, or they may simply involve **threat behaviors,** which consist of postures or gestures that warn the adversary to leave or it will become the target of an attack. The threatened animal might show **defensive behaviors**—threat behaviors or an actual attack against the animal threatening it—or it might show **submissive behaviors**—behaviors that indicate that it accepts defeat and will not challenge the other animal. In the natural environment most animals display far more threats than actual attacks. Threat behaviors are useful in reinforcing social hierarchies in organized groups of animals or in warning intruders away from an animal's territory. They have the advantage of not involving actual fighting, which can harm one or both of the combatants.

Predation is the attack of a member of one species on that of another, usually because the latter serves as food for the former. While engaged in attacking a member of the same species or defending oneself against the attack, an animal appears to be extremely aroused and excited, and the activity of the sympathetic branch of its autonomic nervous system is high. In contrast, the attack of a predator is much more "cold-blooded"; it is generally efficient and not accompanied by a high level of sympathetic activation.

Neural Control of Aggressive Behavior

The neural control of aggressive behavior is hierarchical. That is, the particular muscular movements an animal makes in attacking or defending itself are programmed by neural circuits in the brain stem. Whether an animal attacks depends on many factors, including the nature of the eliciting stimuli in the environment and the animal's previous experience. The activity of the brain stem circuits appears to be controlled by the hypothalamus and the amygdala, which also influence many other species-typical behaviors. And, of course, the activity of the hypothalamus and amygdala is controlled by perceptual systems that detect the status of the environment, including the presence of other animals.

Both defensive behavior and predation can be elicited by stimulating the periaqueductal gray matter (PAG) of a cat's midbrain. During a defensive display, a cat turns sideways and arches its back, and its fur stands on end; this behavior makes the animal look larger. It also retracts its ears, unsheathes its claws, and growls and hisses. A predatory attack is directed against a small animal such as a rat. Predation is not accompanied by a strong display of rage. A cat stalks a rat and suddenly pounces on it, directing powerful bites to the head and neck region. The cat does not growl or scream, and it stops attacking once the rat ceases to move. Although a cat looks excited when it pounces on a rat and bites it, it does not show signs of "rage." The attack appears cold-blooded and ruthless.

As we all know, a cat will often stalk and kill rodents and birds even when it is not hungry; it seems to enjoy this activity independent of its food-getting utility. In contrast, animals that are fighting do not act as if they are enjoying themselves. Panksepp (1971) observed a significant difference in rats' preference for receiving electrical

Defensive behavior A species-typical behavior by which an animal defends itself against the threat of another animal.

Threat behavior A stereotypical species-typical behavior that warns another animal that it may be attacked if it does not flee or show a submissive behavior.

Submissive behavior A stereotyped behavior shown by an animal in response to threat behavior by another animal; serves to prevent an attack.

Predation Attack of one animal directed at an individual of another species on which the attacking animal normally preys.

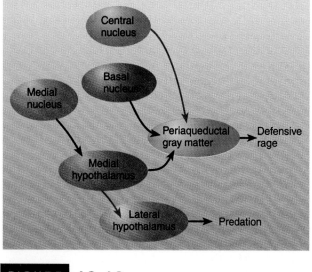

FIGURE 10.12

Results of the studies by Shaikh, Siegel, and their colleagues. The diagram shows interconnections of parts of the amygdala, hypothalamus, and periaqueductal gray matter and their effects on defensive rage and predation in cats. Black arrows indicate excitation; red arrows indicate inhibition.

brain stimulation that elicits predatory attack or defensive attack. If he turned on the stimulation that produced defensive attack but permitted the rats to press a lever to turn it off, they quickly learned to do so. Thus, brain stimulation that elicits defensive attack appears to be aversive. In contrast, rats quickly learned to press a lever that turned *on* stimulation that elicited predatory attack. Thus, stimulation of the brain regions involved in the elicitation of predatory attack is reinforcing.

A series of studies by Shaikh, Siegel, and their colleagues (see Han, Shaikh, and Siegel, 1996a, 1996b for references) investigated the neural circuitry involved in defensive behavior and predation in cats. The investigators placed electrodes in various regions of the brain and observed the effects of electrical stimulation of these regions on the animals' behavior. In some cases the electrode was actually a stainless-steel cannula, coated with an insulating material except for the tip. These devices (called *cannula electrodes*) could be used to infuse chemicals into the brain as well as to stimulate it. The investigators found that defensive behavior and predation can be elicited by stimulation of different parts of the PAG and that the hypothalamus and the amygdala influence these behaviors through excitatory and inhibitory connections with the PAG. They found that the three principal regions of the amygdala and two regions of the hypothalamus affect defensive rage and predation, both of which appear to be organized by the PAG. (They assessed predation by presenting the cats with an anesthetized rat, so no pain was inflicted.) A possible connection between the lateral hypothalamus and the ventral PAG has not yet been verified. Rather than list the connections and their effects, I will direct you to *Figure 10.12.*

Of course, brain regions other than the amygdala, hypothalamus, and periaqueductal gray matter are involved in aggressive behavior. In general, increased activity of serotonergic synapses inhibits aggression. For this reason some clinicians have used serotonergic drugs to treat violent behavior in humans. Destruction of serotonergic axons in the forebrain facilitates aggressive attack, presumably by removing an inhibitory effect (Vergnes et al., 1988).

A group of researchers has studied the relation between serotonergic activity and aggressiveness in a free-ranging colony of rhesus monkeys (Mehlman et al., 1995; Higley et al., 1996a, 1996b). They assessed serotonergic activity by capturing the monkeys and removing a sample of cerebrospinal fluid and analyzing it for 5-HIAA, a metabolite of serotonin (5-HT). When 5-HT is released, most of the neurotransmitter is taken back into the terminal buttons by means of reuptake, but some escapes and is broken down to 5-HIAA, which finds its way into the cerebrospinal fluid. Thus, high levels of 5-HIAA in the CSF indicates an elevated level of serotonergic activity. The investigators found that young male monkeys with the lowest levels of 5-HIAA showed a pattern of risk-taking behavior, including high levels of aggression directed toward animals that were older and much larger than themselves. They were much more likely to take dangerous, unprovoked long leaps from tree to tree at a height of more than 7 m (27.6 ft). They were also more likely to pick fights that they could not possibly win. Of 49 preadolescent male monkeys that the investigators followed for four years, 46 percent of those with the lowest 5-HIAA levels died, while all of the monkeys with the highest levels survived. (See *Figure 10.13.*) Most of the monkeys were killed by other monkeys. In fact, the first monkey to be killed had the lowest level of 5-HIAA and was seen attacking two mature males the night before his death.

It is clear that serotonin does not simply inhibit aggression; rather, it exerts a controlling influence on risky behavior, which includes aggression. Raleigh et al. (1991) removed the dominant male from each of several groups of vervet monkeys and treated the top two remaining males with serotonergic drugs: One received an agonist, and the other received an antagonist. The monkeys who received the serotonin agonist became dominant, while the status of those who received the antagonist declined. You might think that removing some inhibitory control over aggressiveness would increase a monkey's dominance. However, dominance and aggression are not synonymous. Certainly, a dominant animal will use aggression if it is overtly challenged by a rival. However, becoming the dominant animal in a group of monkeys requires good social skills. As Mehlman et al. (1995) noted in their naturalistic study, the monkeys with low levels of serotonergic activity showed the lowest levels of social competency.

Several studies have found that serotonergic neurons play an inhibitory role in human aggression. (See Coccaro, 1996, for a review.) For example, Brown et al. (1979, 1982) found that a history of aggressiveness and psychological test scores indicating antisocial tendencies was related to low levels of CSF 5-HIAA in a group of naval recruits. Coccaro et al. (1994) studied a group of men with personality disorders (including a history of impulsive aggression). They found that the men with the lowest serotonergic activity were more likely to have close relatives with a history of similar behavior problems. The study did not collect evidence needed to determine whether the association was genetic or environmental (or both).

CSF-5HIAA Concentration Quartile

FIGURE   10.13

Percentage of young male monkeys alive or dead as a function of 5-HIAA level in the CSF, measured four years previously.

(Adapted from Higley, J.D., Mehlman, P.T., Higley, S.B., Fernald, B., Vickers, J., Lindell, S.G., Taub, D.M., Suomi, S.J., and Linnoila, M., Archives of General Psychiatry, 1996, 53, 537–543.)

Hormonal Control of Aggressive Behavior

As we saw, many instances of aggressive behavior are in some way related to reproduction. For example, males of some species establish territories that attract females during the breeding season. To do so, they must defend them against the intrusion of other males. Even in species in which breeding does not depend on the establishment of a territory, males may compete for access to females, which also involves aggressive behavior. Females, too, often compete with other females for space in

Studies of groups of vervet monkeys confirm the role of serotonin in control of aggression.

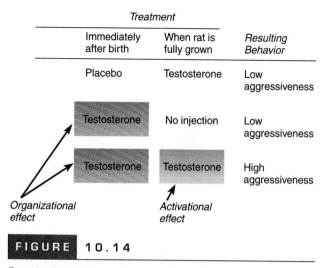

FIGURE 10.14

Organizational and activational effects of testosterone on social aggression.

which to build nests or dens in which to rear their offspring, and they will defend their offspring against the intrusion of other animals. As you learned in Chapter 9, most reproductive behaviors are controlled by the organizational and activational effects of hormones; thus, we should not be surprised that many forms of aggressive behavior are, like mating, affected by hormones.

Aggression in Males

Adult males of many species fight for territory or access to females. In laboratory rodents, androgen secretion occurs prenatally, decreases, and then increases again at the time of puberty. Intermale aggressiveness also begins around the time of puberty, which suggests that the behavior is controlled by neural circuits that are stimulated by androgens. Indeed, many years ago, Beeman (1947) found that castration reduced aggressiveness and that injections of testosterone reinstated it.

In Chapter 9 we saw that early androgenization has an *organizational effect*. The secretion of androgens early in development modifies the developing brain, making neural circuits that control male sexual behavior become more responsive to testosterone. Similarly, early androgenization has an organizational effect that stimulates the development of testosterone-sensitive neural circuits that facilitate intermale aggression. (See *Figure 10.14*.)

The organizational effect of androgens on intermale aggression (aggressive displays or actual fights between two males of the same species) is important, but it is not an all-or-none phenomenon. Prolonged administration of testosterone will eventually induce intermale aggression even in rodents that were castrated immediately after birth. Data reviewed by vom Saal (1983) show that exposure to androgens early in life decreases the amount of exposure that is necessary to activate aggressive behavior later in life. Thus, early androgenization *sensitizes* the neural circuits to the activational effects of testosterone—the earlier the androgenization, the more effective the sensitization.

We also saw in Chapter 9 that androgens stimulate male sexual behavior by interacting with androgen receptors in neurons located in the medial preoptic area (MPA). This region also appears to be important in mediating the effects of androgens on intermale aggression. Bean and Conner (1978) found that implanting testosterone in the MPA reinstated intermale aggression in castrated male rats. Presumably, the testosterone directly activated the behavior by stimulating the androgen-sensitive neurons located there. The medial preoptic area, then, appears to be involved in several behaviors related to reproduction: male sexual behavior, maternal behavior, and intermale aggression.

FIGURE 10.15

Effects of estradiol and testosterone on interfemale aggression in rats.

(Adapted from van de Poll, N.E., Taminiau, M.S., Endert, E., and Louwerse, A.L., International Journal of Neuroscience, 1988, 41, 271–286.)

Aggression in Females

Two adult female rodents that meet in a neutral territory are less likely than males to fight. But aggression between females, like aggression between males, appears to be facilitated by testosterone. Van de Poll et al. (1988) ovariectomized female rats and then gave them daily injections of testosterone, estradiol, or a placebo for fourteen days. The animals were then placed in a test cage, and an unfamiliar female was introduced. As Figure 10.15 shows, testosterone increased aggressiveness, whereas estradiol had no effect. (See *Figure 10.15*.)

Androgens have an organizational effect on the aggressiveness of females, and a certain amount of prenatal androgenization appears to occur naturally. Most rodent fetuses share their mother's uterus with brothers and sisters, arranged in a row like peas in a pod. A female mouse may have zero, one, or two brothers adjacent to her. Researchers refer to these females as 0M, 1M, or 2M, respectively. (See ***Figure 10.16.***) Being next to a male fetus has an effect on a female's blood levels of androgens prenatally. Vom Saal and Bronson (1980) found that females located between two males had significantly higher levels of testosterone in their blood than females located between two females (or between a female and the end of the uterus). When they are tested as adults, 2M females are more likely to exhibit interfemale aggressiveness.

Females of some primate species (for example, rhesus monkeys and baboons) are more likely to engage in fights around the time of ovulation (Carpenter, 1942; Saayman, 1971). This phenomenon is probably caused by their increased sexual interest and consequent proximity to males. As Carpenter noted, "She actively approaches males and must overcome their usual resistance to close association, hence she becomes an object of attacks by them" (p. 136). Another period of fighting occurs just before menstruation (Sassenrath, Powell, and Hendrickx, 1973; Mallow, 1979). During this time, females tend to attack other females.

Researchers have studied the possibility that irritability and aggressiveness may increase in women just before the time of menstruation, as it does in some other primate species. Floody (1983) reviewed the literature on the so-called *premenstrual syndrome* (PMS). Almost all studies that observed actual aggressiveness, primarily of women in institutions, found decreases around the time of ovulation and increases just before menstruation. Clearly, the changes in irritability are not universal; some women experience little or no mood shift before menstruation. And even if changes in mood occur, most women do not actually become aggressive. Although women with a history of criminal behavior (such as those in prison) may indeed exhibit premenstrual aggressiveness, emotionally stable women may fail to show even a small increase in aggressiveness (Persky, 1974). Depending on their history and temperament, different people respond differently to similar physiological changes.

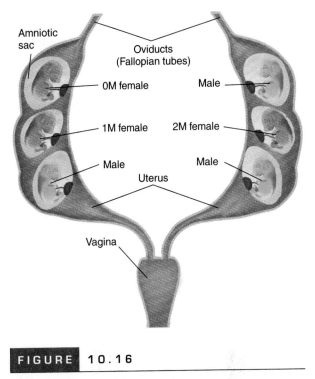

FIGURE **10.16**

OM, 1M, and 2M female mouse fetuses.

[Adapted from vom Saal, F.S., in Hormones and Aggressive Behavior, *edited by B.B. Svare. New York: Plenum Press, 1983.]*

Maternal Aggression

Most parents who actively raise their offspring will vigorously defend them against intruders. In laboratory rodents the responsible parent is the female, so the most commonly studied form of parental defense is maternal aggression. Female mice very effectively defend their young, driving away intruding adults of either sex. Counterattacks by the intruder are rare (Svare, Betteridge, Katz, and Samuels, 1981). Whereas strange males who encounter each other engage in mutual investigation for a minute or two before fighting begins, the attack of a lactating female on an intruder is immediate (Svare, 1983).

Maternal aggressiveness actually begins during pregnancy. Like maternal nest building, it appears to be stimulated by progesterone. The onset of aggressiveness in pregnant mice occurs when progesterone levels begin to rise significantly (Mann, Konen, and Svare, 1984). Immediately after birth, for a period of approximately 48 hours, female mice become completely docile; they do not attack intruders (Ghiraldi and Svare, 1989). As Svare (1989) noted, it is at this time that female mice typically mate again; thus, the fact that they do not attack a male is biologically significant. This phenomenon is probably caused by the high level of estradiol that is present at that time. Ghiraldi and Svare found that removing a female mouse's ovaries just before parturition shortened the period of docility by 24 hours, and administering estradiol restored it.

The tendency for a lactating female mouse to attack a stranger is induced by stimuli provided by her offspring. If the newborn mice are removed, the mother fails to become aggressive. The important activating stimulus appears to be the tactile stimulation produced by suckling. Normally, maternal aggressiveness begins after the mother has suckled her young for 48 hours. If the mother's nipples are surgically removed, she does not become aggressive, even if pups are present (Svare and Gandelman, 1976; Gandelman and Simon, 1980). These effects do not depend on the presence of ovarian or pituitary hormones (Svare et al., 1982.)

Prenatal exposure to androgens appears to have an organizational effect on maternal aggression. As we saw in the previous section, female mice who were located between two males in the uterus (2M females) are more likely to attack other females and are more responsive to the activating effects of androgens in adulthood. Vom Saal and Bronson (1980a) also found that 2M females are more maternally aggressive than 0M females. Kinsley, Konen, Miele, Ghiraldi, and Svare (1986) found that they were also more likely to exhibit aggressiveness during pregnancy.

Effects of Androgens on Human Aggressive Behavior

Boys are generally more aggressive than girls. Clearly, Western society tolerates assertiveness and aggressive behavior from boys more than from girls. Without doubt, the way we treat boys and girls and the models we expose them to play important roles in sex differences in aggressiveness in our species. The question is not whether socialization has an effect (certainly, it does) but whether biological influences, such as exposure to androgens, have an effect, too.

Prenatal androgenization increases aggressive behavior in all species that have been studied, including primates. Therefore, if androgens did not affect aggressive behavior in humans, our species would be exceptional. After puberty, androgens also begin to have activational effects. Boys' testosterone levels begin to increase during the early teens, at which time aggressive behavior and intermale fighting also increase (Mazur, 1983). Of course, boys' social status changes during puberty, and their

Aggressive behavior can be seen at all ages and in both sexes, but its frequency generally increases in males after puberty.

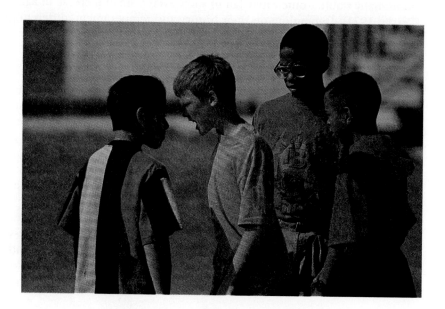

testosterone affects their muscles as well as their brains; so we cannot be sure that the effect is hormonally produced or, if it is, that it is mediated by the brain.

Scientifically rigorous evidence that androgens increase aggression in humans is difficult to obtain. Obviously, we cannot randomly castrate some men to see whether their aggressiveness declines. In the past, authorities have attempted to suppress sex-related aggression by castrating convicted male sex offenders. Investigators have reported that both heterosexual and homosexual aggressive attacks disappear, along with the offender's sex drive (Hawke, 1951; Sturup, 1961; Laschet, 1973). However, the studies typically lack appropriate control groups and usually do not measure aggressive behavior directly.

Some cases of aggressiveness, especially sexual assault, have been treated with synthetic steroids that inhibit the production of androgens by the testes. Clearly, treatment with drugs is preferable to castration, because the effects are not irreversible. However, the efficacy of treatment with antiandrogens has yet to be established conclusively. According to Walker and Meyer (1981), these drugs decrease sex-related aggression but have no effect on other forms of aggression. In fact, Zumpe et al. (1993) found that one of these drugs decreased sexual activity and aggression toward females when administered to male monkeys but that it actually *increased* intermale aggression.

Another way to determine whether androgens affect aggressiveness in humans is to examine the testosterone levels of people who exhibit varying levels of aggressive behavior. However, even though this approach poses fewer ethical problems, it presents methodological ones. First, let me review some evidence. In a review of the literature, Archer (1994) found that most studies found a positive relation between men's testosterone levels and their level of aggressiveness. For example, Dabbs and Morris (1990) studied 4462 U.S. military veterans. The men with the highest testosterone levels had records of more antisocial activities, including assaults on other adults and histories of more trouble with parents, teachers, and classmates during adolescence. The largest effects were seen in men of lower socioeconomic status. Dabbs et al. (1987) measured the testosterone levels of male prison inmates and found a significant correlation with several measures of violence, including the nature of the crime for which they were convicted, infractions of prison rules, and ratings of "toughness" by their peers. These relations are also seen in female prison inmates; Dabbs et al. (1988) found that women prisoners who showed unprovoked violence and had several prior convictions also showed higher levels of testosterone. (As we saw earlier, testosterone increases interfemale aggression in laboratory animals as well.)

But we must remember that *correlation* does not necessarily indicate *causation*. A person's environment can affect his or her testosterone level. For example, losing a tennis match or a wrestling competition causes a fall in blood levels of testosterone (Mazur and Lamb, 1980; Elias, 1981). Even winning or losing a simple game of chance carried out in a psychology laboratory can affect participants' testosterone levels: Winners feel better afterward and have a higher level of testosterone (McCaul, Gladue, and Joppa, 1992). In a very elaborate study, Jeffcoate et al. (1986) found that the blood levels of a group of five men confined on a boat for fourteen days changed as they established a dominance ranking among themselves. The higher the rank a person eventually achieved, the higher his testosterone level. Thus, we cannot be sure in any correlational study that high testosterone levels *cause* people to become dominant or aggressive; perhaps their success in establishing a position of dominance increases their testosterone levels relative to those of the people they dominate.

A few studies have looked at the behavioral effects of administering androgens. Because of ethical concerns, people cannot be given androgen supplements for any length of time merely to see whether they become more aggressive—excessive amounts of androgens have deleterious effects on a person's health. Thus, the only evidence we have of the effects of long-term administration comes from case studies in which people with abnormally low levels of testosterone (the *hypogonadal syn-*

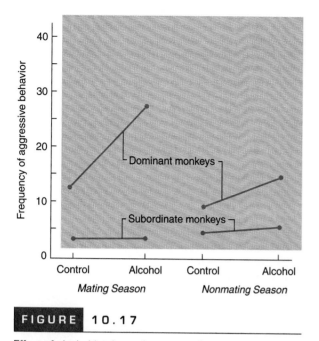

FIGURE **10.17**

Effect of alcohol intake on frequency of aggressive behavior of dominant and subordinate male squirrel monkeys during the mating season and the nonmating season.

(Based on data from Winslow, J.T., and Miczek, J.A., Psychopharmacologia, 1988, 95, 92–98.)

drome) are given an androgen to replace what would normally be present. In general, such people feel happier and their sexual activity increases, but they do not usually show more aggressiveness (Skakkebaek et al., 1981; O'Carroll, Shapiro, and Bancroft, 1985). One double-blind study (Su et al., 1993) did administer testosterone for several days to a group of normal volunteers, men aged 18 to 42 years. Those receiving the highest doses reported more euphoria and sexual arousal but also more irritability and feelings of hostility. However, the effects were small, and the investigators did not observe behaviors, only self-reports of feelings.

As everyone knows, some athletes take anabolic steroids to increase their muscle mass and strength and, supposedly, to increase their competitiveness. Anabolic steroids include natural androgens and synthetic hormones with androgenic effects. Thus, we might expect that these hormones would increase aggressiveness. Indeed, several studies have found exactly that. For example, Yates, Perry, and Murray (1992) found male weight lifters who were taking anabolic steroids to be more aggressive and hostile than those who were not. But as the authors note, we cannot be certain that the steroid is responsible for the increased aggressiveness; it could simply be that the men who were already more competitive and aggressive were the ones who chose to take the steroids.

An interesting set of experiments with another species of primates may have some relevance to human aggression. As you undoubtedly know, alcohol intake is often associated with aggression in humans. Alcohol increases intermale aggression in dominant male squirrel monkeys, but only during the mating season, when their blood level of testosterone is two to three times higher than during the nonmating season (Winslow and Miczek, 1985). Alcohol does *not* increase the aggressive behavior of subordinate monkeys at any time of the year. These studies suggest that the effects of alcohol interact with both social status and testosterone. (See *Figure 10.17*.) This suggestion was confirmed by Winslow, Ellingoe, and Miczek (1988), who tested monkeys during the nonmating season. They found that alcohol increased the aggressive behavior of dominant monkeys if they were also given injections of testosterone. However, these treatments were ineffective in subordinate monkeys, who had presumably learned not to be aggressive. The next step will be to find the neural mechanisms that are responsible for these interactions.

INTERIM SUMMARY

Aggressive behaviors are species-typical and serve useful functions most of the time. In addition, animals may exhibit threat or submissive behaviors, which may avoid an actual fight.

The periaqueductal gray matter appears to be involved in defensive behavior and predation. These mechanisms are modulated by the hypothalamus and amygdala. Activation of the central nucleus inhibits defensive aggression, while stimulation of the basal or medial amygdala stimulates it. Stimulation of the medial hypothalamus also facilitates defensive aggression but, through inhibitory connections with the lateral hypothalamus, inhibits predation.

Because many aggressive behaviors are related to reproduction, they are influenced by hormones, especially sex steroid hormones. Androgens primarily affect offensive attack; they are not necessary for defensive behaviors, which are shown by females as well as males. In males, androgens have organizational and activational effects on offensive attack, just as they have on male sexual behavior. The effects of androgens on intermale aggression appear to be mediated by the medial preoptic area.

Females rodents will fight when they meet in neutral territory, but less often than males. Female rodents who have been slightly androgenized (2M females) are more likely to attack other females. Female primates are most likely to fight around the time of ovulation, perhaps because their increased sexual interest brings them closer to males. Although some women report irritability just before menstruation, the phenomenon is not universal.

Maternal aggression is a very swift and effective behavior. It begins during pregnancy, apparently triggered by the secretion of progesterone. After parturition, maternal aggression is stimulated by the tactile feedback from suckling. Prenatal androgens have an organizational effect on maternal aggression; 2M females are more likely than 0M females to display maternal aggression.

Androgens apparently promote aggressive behavior in humans, but this topic is more difficult to study in our species than in laboratory animals. Differences in testosterone levels have been observed in criminals with a history of violence, but we cannot be sure whether higher androgen levels promote violence or whether successful aggression increases androgen levels. Studies with monkeys suggest that testosterone and alcohol have synergistic effects, particularly in dominant animals. (*Synergy*, from a Greek word meaning "working together," refers to combinations of factors that are more effective than the sum of their individual actions.) Perhaps these effects are related to our observations that some men with a history of violent behavior become more aggressive when they drink.

EPILOGUE

Mr. V. Revisited

After our visit to Mr. V. (described in the Prologue), we were discussing the case. Lisa, the student, asked why Mr. V. talked about continuing his walking schedule when he obviously knew that he couldn't walk. Did he think that he would recover soon?

"No, that's not it," said Dr. W. "He *knows* what his problem is, but he doesn't really *understand* it. The people at the rehab center are having trouble with him because he keeps trying to go outside for a walk. The first time, he managed to wheel his chair to the top of the stairs, but someone caught him just in time. Now they have a chain across the doorframe of his room so that he can't get into the hall without an attendant.

"Mr. V.'s problem is not that he can't verbally recognize what's going on; it's that he just can't grasp its significance. The right hemisphere is specialized in seeing many things at once: in seeing all the parts of a geometric shape and grasping its form, or in seeing all the elements of a situation and understanding what they mean. That's what's wrong. He can tell you about his paralyzed leg, about the fact that he is in a wheelchair, and so on, but he can't put these facts together and realize that his days of walking are over.

"As you could see, Mr. V. can still express emotions." We all smiled at the thought of the contemptuous look on Mr. V.'s face. "But the right hemisphere is especially important in as-

sessing the significance of a situation and making conclusions that lead to our being happy or sad or whatever. People with certain right-hemisphere lesions are not bothered at all by their conditions. They can *tell* you about their problems, so I guess they verbally understand it, but their problems just don't affect them emotionally."

He turned to me. "Neil, do you remember Mr. P.?" I nodded. "Mr. P. had a left-hemisphere lesion. He had a severe aphasia and could hardly say a word. We showed him a picture of some objects and asked him to try to name them. He looked at them and started crying. Although he couldn't talk, he knew that he had a serious problem and that things would never be the same for him. His right hemi-

(continued)

sphere was still working. It could assess the situation and give rise to feelings of sadness and despair.".

Dr. W. suggested that the right hemisphere's special role in emotional processes is related to its ability to deal with perception and evaluation of patterns of stimuli that occur simultaneously. His suggestion is plausible, but we still do not know enough about hemispheric differences to be sure that it is correct. In any event, many studies have shown that the right hemisphere does play a special role in evaluating the emotional significance of a situation. I described some of these studies in the chapter, but let's look at a few more examples. Bear and Fedio (1977) reported that people with seizures that primarily involve the left hemisphere tend to have thought disorders, whereas those with right-hemisphere seizures tend to have emotional disorders. Mesulam (1985) reported that people with damage to the right temporal lobe (but not the left temporal lobe) are likely to lose their sensitivity to social cues. Obviously, this observation is meaningful only for patients who were sensitive to social cues before the brain damage; if someone is socially insensitive *before* having a stroke, we can hardly blame the behavior on brain damage. In particular, people with right temporal lobe lesions tend to show bad manners. They talk when they feel like it and do not yield the floor to someone else who has something to say; they sim-

ply ignore the social cues that polite people observe and follow. They also adopt a familiar conversational style with people to whom they would normally be deferential (usually, the physician who is treating them and writes up a report of their behavior).

Perhaps my favorite example of possible hemispheric specialization is hypnosis. Sackheim (1982) reported that when people are hypnotized, the left side of their body is more responsive to hypnotic suggestion than the right side. Because the left side of the body is controlled by the right hemisphere, this observation indicates that the right hemisphere may be more susceptible to hypnotic suggestion. In addition, Sackheim, Paulus, and Weiman (1979) found that students who are easily hypnotized tend to sit on the right side of the classroom. In this position they see most of the front of the room (including the teacher) with their right hemispheres, so perhaps their choice represents a preference for right-hemisphere involvement in watching another person.

One of the reasons I enjoy writing these epilogues is that I can permit myself to be more speculative than I am in the text of the chapter itself. Why might the right hemisphere be more involved in hypnosis? One explanation of hypnosis, which I find appealing, is that it derives from our ability to get emotionally involved in a story—to get wrapped up in what is happening to the characters in a film or a novel (Barber, 1975). When we

become involved in a story, we experience genuine feelings of emotion: happiness, sadness, fear, or anger. We laugh, cry, and show the same sorts of physiological changes that we would if the story were really happening to us. Similarly, according to Barber, we become involved in the "story" that the hypnotist is creating for us, and we suspend our belief and act it out. According to this explanation, hypnosis is related to our susceptibility to social situations and to our ability to empathize with others. In fact, people with the ability to produce vivid mental images, a high capacity for becoming involved in imaginative activities, and a rich, vivid imagination are those most likely to be susceptible to hypnosis (Kihlstrom, 1985).

As we saw in this chapter, the right hemisphere appears to play a special role in assessing social situations and appreciating their emotional significance. If Barber's explanation of hypnosis is correct, then we can see why the right hemisphere might play a special role in hypnosis, too. Perhaps researchers interested in hypnosis will begin studying patients with right- or left-hemisphere damage, and neuropsychologists already studying these people will start investigating hypnosis and its possible relation to social and emotional variables and either confirm or disprove these speculations.

▮ KEY CONCEPTS

EMOTIONS AS RESPONSE PATTERNS

1. Emotional responses consist of three components: behavioral, autonomic, and hormonal.
2. The amygdala plays a central role in coordinating all three components in response to threatening or aversive stimuli. In particular, the central nucleus is involved in conditioned emotional responses.

3. The orbitofrontal cortex plays a special role in control of emotional responses to social situations.
4. Prefrontal lobotomy, surgery that disrupts the connections of the orbitofrontal cortex with the limbic system or cingulate gyrus, can reduce severe abnormal emotional reactions, but because of adverse side effects, the procedure has been abandoned.

EXPRESSION AND RECOGNITION OF EMOTIONS

5. Facial expressions of emotions appear to be species-typical responses, even in humans.

6. Expression and recognition of emotions is largely accomplished by neural mechanisms located in the right hemisphere.

FEELINGS OF EMOTION

7. The James-Lange theory suggests that we experience our own emotions through feedback from the expression of the physiological and behavioral components. Evidence from people with spinal cord injuries supports this theory.

AGGRESSIVE BEHAVIOR

8. Species-typical forms of aggression include offensive and defensive behavior and predation. These be-haviors are controlled by neural circuits in the periaqueductal gray matter and the ventral tegmental area, which are modulated by the circuits in the hypothalamus and the amygdala.

9. Androgens have both organizational and activational effects on aggression in males and females. Females of many species will attack intruders, and most will defend their offspring.

10. Androgens may be at least partly responsible for the increased level of aggression seen in males of our species, but ethical considerations make it difficult to be certain. Antiandrogens have been used in an attempt to control sex-related violence.

SUGGESTED READINGS

Aggleton, J. (ed.). *The Amygdala: Neurobiological Aspects of Emotion, Memory, and Mental Dysfunction.* New York: Wiley-Liss, 1992.

Damasio, A.R. *Decartes' Error: Emotion, Reason, and the Human Brain.* New York: G.P. Putnam, 1994.

LeDoux, J.E. *The Emotional Brain: The Mysterious Underpinnings of the Emotional Life.* New York: Simon and Schuster, 1996.

McNaughton, Neil. *Biology and Emotion.* Cambridge, England: Cambridge University Press, 1989.

Stein, N.L., Leventhal, B., and Trabasso, T. (eds.). *Psychological and Biological Approaches to Emotion.* Hillsdale, NJ: Lawrence Erlbaum Associates, 1990.

11

Ingestive Behavior

LEARNING OBJECTIVES

1. Explain the characteristics of a regulatory mechanism.

2. Describe the fluid compartments of the body.

3. Explain the control of osmometric thirst and volumetric thirst and the role of angiotensin.

4. Describe the neural control of thirst.

5. Describe characteristics of the two nutrient reservoirs and the absorptive and fasting phases of metabolism.

6. Discuss social and environmental factors that begin a meal.

7. Discuss the head, gastric, and intestinal factors responsible for stopping a meal.

8. Describe research on the role of the brain stem and hypothalamus in hunger and satiety.

9. Discuss the physiological factors that may contribute to obesity.

10. Discuss the physiological factors that may contribute to anorexia nervosa and bulimia nervosa.

Not Her Fault?

Emily and her younger brother, Jonathan, prided themselves on their lack of racial and religious prejudice. Jonathan was a self-proclaimed feminist and enjoyed telling his friends how well his sister was doing in her engineering courses at a prestigious university. He and his sister shared a contempt for intolerance and chauvinism and believed that if other people were more like themselves, the world would be a better place in which to live. The few times that acquaintances had told jokes in their presence that stereotyped other cultures or racial groups, Emily and Jonathan immediately pounced on them and chided them for their bigotry.

Just before the end of Emily's first year of college, she saw a notice asking for students to provide living accommodations for foreign students who could not afford to return home during summer vacation. She called her parents, who readily agreed to put someone up at their house. The whole family felt that they would enjoy getting to know a foreign student really well and looked forward to showing how nice a North American family could be.

When Emily met her guest at a party that was held to introduce the students to their hosts, she was dismayed. The girl, Norella, was fat! Well, not grossly obese, but certainly far heavier than she should be. Her face was pretty, and she was intelligent and witty; why didn't she pay attention to her diet?

Emily and her brother exchanged a significant glance when she introduced Norella to her family. However, within a few days Norella had fit right into the family routine, and they almost forgot that she was fat. She helped to prepare the meals and do the dishes afterward; she charmed the whole family with her stories of her own country and delighted them with her astute observations of life in their country.

Three weeks after Norella had come to live with them, Emily and Jonathan began talking about a topic they previously had studiously ignored.

"You know," Jonathan said, "I just realized this evening that Norella eats less than you do."

Emily looked startled, then said, "You're right! I hadn't thought about that! How can that be?"

"I don't know," he said. "Does she eat between meals?"

"No," answered Emily, "I don't think I've ever seen her do that." She paused, looking pensive, then shook her head. "No. I'm positive that I've never seen her eat between meals. When we've gone out shopping together, I always buy something to eat, but Norella never does. I've offered her some of mine, but she's always said, 'No.'"

Emily and Jonathan sat together in silence. "You know," Jonathan said, "I've never really liked fat people, because it seems like they don't have enough self-respect to keep from overeating. I've always thought that they ate like pigs. But Norella doesn't even eat as much as you do, and she's fat! Maybe it's not her fault."

As the French physiologist Claude Bernard (1813–1878) said, "The constancy of the internal milieu is a necessary condition for a free life." This famous quotation says succinctly what organisms must do to be able to exist in environments that are hostile to the living cells that compose them (that is, to live a "free life"): They must regulate the nature of the internal fluid that bathes their cells.

The physiological characteristics of the cells that constitute our bodies evolved long ago, when these cells floated freely in the ocean. In essence, what the evolutionary process has accomplished is the ability to make our own seawater for bathing our cells, to add to this seawater the oxygen and nutrients that our cells need, and to remove from it waste products that would otherwise poison them. To perform these functions, we have digestive, respiratory, circulatory, and excretory systems. We also have the behaviors necessary for finding and ingesting food and water.

Regulation of the fluid that bathes our cells is part of a process called **homeostasis** ("similar standing"). This chapter discusses the means by which we mammals achieve homeostatic control of the vital characteristics of our extracellular fluid through our **ingestive behavior:** intake of food, water, and minerals such as sodium. First, we will examine the general nature of regulatory mechanisms; then we will consider drinking and eating and the neural mechanisms responsible for these behaviors. Finally, we will look at some research on the eating disorders.

Homeostasis (*home ee oh stay sis*) The process by which the body's substances and characteristics (such as temperature and glucose level) are maintained at their optimal level.

Ingestive behavior (*in jess tiv*) Eating or drinking.

FIGURE **11.1**

An example of a regulatory system.

System variable A variable that is controlled by a regulatory mechanism; for example, temperature in a heating system.

Set point The optimal value of the system variable in a regulatory mechanism.

Detector In a regulatory process, a mechanism that signals when the system variable deviates from its set point.

Correctional mechanism In a regulatory process, the mechanism that is capable of changing the value of the system variable.

Negative feedback A process whereby the effect produced by an action serves to diminish or terminate that action; a characteristic of regulatory systems.

Satiety mechanism A brain mechanism that causes cessation of hunger or thirst, produced by adequate and available supplies of nutrients or water.

Intracellular fluid The fluid contained within cells.

Extracellular fluid All body fluids outside cells: interstitial fluid, blood plasma, and cerebrospinal fluid.

PHYSIOLOGICAL REGULATORY MECHANISMS

A physiological regulatory mechanism is one that maintains the constancy of some internal characteristic of the organism in the face of external variability—for example, keeping body temperature constant despite changes in the ambient temperature. A regulatory mechanism contains four essential features: the **system variable** (the characteristic to be regulated), a **set point** (the optimal value of the system variable), a **detector** that monitors the value of the system variable, and a **correctional mechanism** that restores the system variable to the set point.

An example of a regulatory system is a room whose temperature is regulated by a thermostatically controlled heater. The system variable is the air temperature of the room, and the detector for this variable is a thermostat. This device can be adjusted so that contacts of a switch will be closed when the temperature falls below a preset value (the set point). Closure of the contacts turns on the correctional mechanism—the coils of the heater. (See *Figure 11.1.*)

If the room cools below the set point of the thermostat, the thermostat turns the heater on, and the heater warms the room. The rise in room temperature causes the thermostat to turn the heater off. Because the activity of the correctional mechanism (heat production) feeds back to the thermostat and causes it to turn the heater off, this process is called **negative feedback.** Negative feedback is an essential characteristic of all regulatory systems.

This chapter considers regulatory systems that involve ingestive behaviors: drinking and eating. These behaviors are correctional mechanisms that replenish the body's depleted stores of water or nutrients. Because of the delay between ingestion and replenishment of the depleted stores, ingestive behaviors are controlled by **satiety mechanisms** as well as by detectors that monitor the system variables. Satiety mechanisms are required because of the physiology of our digestive system. For example, suppose you spend some time in a hot, dry environment and lose body water. The loss of water causes internal detectors to initiate the correctional mechanism—drinking. You quickly drink a glass or two of water and then stop. What stops your ingestive behavior? The water is still in your digestive system, not yet in the fluid surrounding your cells, where it is needed. Therefore, although drinking was initiated by detectors that measure your body's need for water, *it was stopped by other means.* There must be a satiety mechanism that says, in effect, "Stop—this water, when absorbed by the digestive system into the blood, will eventually replenish the body's need." Satiety mechanisms monitor the activity of the correctional mechanism (in this case, drinking), not the system variables themselves. When a sufficient amount of drinking occurs, the satiety mechanisms stop further drinking *in anticipation* of the replenishment that will occur later. (See *Figure 11.2.*)

FIGURE **11.2**

An outline of the system that controls drinking.

DRINKING

To maintain our internal milieu at its optimal state, we have to drink some water from time to time. This section describes the control of this form of ingestive behavior.

Some Facts about Fluid Balance

Before you can understand the physiological control of drinking, you must know something about the fluid compartments of the body and their relations with each other. The body contains four major fluid compartments: one compartment of intracellular fluid and three compartments of extracellular fluid. Approximately two-thirds of the body's water is contained in the **intracellular fluid,** the fluid portion of the cytoplasm of cells. The rest is **extracellular fluid,** which includes the **intravascular fluid** (the blood plasma), the cerebrospinal fluid, and the **interstitial fluid.** *Interstitial* means "standing between"; indeed, the interstitial fluid stands between our cells—it is the "seawater" that bathes them. For the purposes of this chapter we will ignore the cerebrospinal fluid and concentrate on the other three compartments. (See *Figure 11.3.*)

Two of the fluid compartments of the body must be kept within precise limits: the intracellular fluid and the intravascular fluid. The intracellular fluid is controlled by the concentration of solutes in the interstitial fluid. (*Solutes* are the substances dissolved in a solution.) Normally, the interstitial fluid is **isotonic** (from *isos,* "equal," and *tonos,* "tension") with the intracellular fluid. That is, the concentration of solutes in the cells and in the interstitial fluid that bathes them is balanced, so that water does not tend to move into or out of the cells. If the interstitial fluid loses water (becomes more concentrated, or **hypertonic**), water will move out of the cells through osmosis. On the other hand, if the interstitial fluid gains water (becomes more dilute, or **hypotonic**), water will move into the cells. Either condition endangers cells; a loss of water deprives them of the ability to perform many chemical reactions, and a gain of water can cause their membranes to rupture. Therefore, the concentration of the interstitial fluid must be closely regulated. (See *Figure 11.4.*)

The volume of the blood plasma must be closely regulated because of the mechanics of the operation of the heart. If the blood volume falls too low, the heart can no longer pump the blood effectively; if the volume is not restored, heart failure will result. This condition is called **hypovolemia,** literally "low volume of the blood" (*-emia* comes from the Greek *haima,* "blood"). The vascular system of the body can make some adjustments for loss of blood volume by contracting the muscles in smaller veins and arteries, thereby presenting a smaller space for the blood to fill, but this correctional mechanism has definite limits.

As you will see, the two important characteristics of the body fluids—the solute concentration of the intracellular fluid and the volume of the blood—are monitored by two different sets of receptors. A single set of receptors would not work, because it is possible for one of these fluid compartments to be changed without affecting the other. For example, a loss of blood obviously reduces the volume of the intravascular fluid, but it has no effect on the volume of the

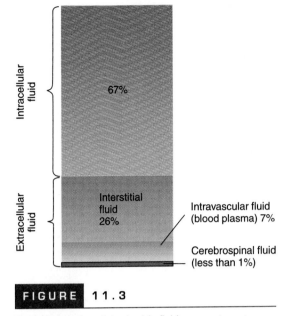

FIGURE 1 1 . 3

The relative size of the body's fluid compartments.

Intravascular fluid The fluid found within the blood vessels.

Interstitial fluid The fluid that bathes the cells, filling the space between the cells of the body (the "interstices").

Isotonic Equal in osmotic pressure to the contents of a cell. A cell placed in an isotonic solution neither gains nor loses water.

Hypertonic The characteristic of a solution that contains enough solute that it will draw water out of a cell placed in it, through the process of osmosis.

Hypotonic The characteristic of a solution that contains so little solute that a cell placed in it will absorb water, through the process of osmosis.

Hypovolemia (*hy poh voh lee mee a*) Reduction in the volume of the intravascular fluid.

FIGURE 1 1 . 4

Effects of differences in solute concentration on the movement of water molecules.

Solution A is hypertonic to solution B; water is drawn out of solution B

Solution C is hypotonic to solution B; water is drawn into solution B

Solution A   Solution B   Solution C

intracellular fluid. On the other hand, a salty meal will increase the solute concentration of the interstitial fluid, drawing water out of the cells, but it will not cause hypovolemia. Thus, the body needs two sets of receptors, one measuring blood volume and another measuring cell volume.

Two Types of Thirst

As you just saw, for our bodies to function properly, the volume of two fluid compartments—intracellular and intravascular—must be regulated. Most of the time, we ingest more water and sodium than we need and the kidneys excrete the excess. However, if the levels of water or sodium fall too low, correctional mechanisms—drinking water or ingesting sodium—are activated. Everyone is familiar with the sensation of thirst, which occurs when we need to ingest water. However, a salt appetite is much more rare, because it is difficult for people *not* to get enough sodium in their diet, even if they do not put extra salt on their food. Nevertheless, the mechanisms to increase sodium intake exist, even though they are seldom called upon in members of our species.

Because loss of water from either the intracellular or intravascular fluid compartments stimulates drinking, researchers have adopted the terms *osmometric thirst* and *volumetric thirst* to describe them. The term *volumetric* is clear; it refers to the metering (measuring) of the volume of the blood plasma. The term *osmometric* requires more explanation, which will be provided in the next section. The term *thirst* means different things in different circumstances. Its original definition referred to a sensation that people say they have when they are dehydrated. Here I use it in a descriptive sense. Because we do not know how other animals feel, *thirst* simply means a tendency to seek water and to ingest it.

Our bodies lose water continuously, primarily through evaporation. Each breath exposes the moist inner surfaces of the respiratory system to the air; thus, each breath causes the loss of a small amount of water. In addition, our skin is not completely waterproof; some water finds its way through the layers of the skin and evaporates from the surface. The moisture that is lost through evaporation is, of course, pure distilled water. (Sweating loses water, too; but because it loses salt along with the water, it produces a need for sodium as well as for water.) Figure 11.5 illustrates how the loss of water through evaporation depletes both the intracellular fluid and intravascular fluid compartments. For the sake of simplicity, only a few cells are shown, and the volume of the interstitial fluid is greatly exaggerated. Water is lost directly from the interstitial fluid, which becomes slightly more concentrated than either the intracellular or the intravascular fluid. Thus, water is drawn from both the cells and the blood plasma. Eventually, the loss of water from the cells and the blood plasma will be great enough that both osmometric thirst and volumetric thirst will be produced. (See *Figure 11.5*.)

Osmometric thirst Thirst produced by an increase in the osmotic pressure of the interstitial fluid relative to the intracellular fluid, thus producing cellular dehydration.

Osmoreceptor A neuron that detects changes in the solute concentration of the interstitial fluid that surrounds it.

Osmometric Thirst

Osmometric thirst occurs when the tonicity (solute concentration) of the interstitial fluid increases. This increase draws water out of the cells, and they shrink in volume. The term *osmometric* refers to the fact that the detectors are actually responding to (metering) changes in the concentration of the interstitial fluid that surrounds them. *Osmosis* is the movement of water through a semipermeable membrane from a region of low solute concentration to one of high solute concentration.

The existence of neurons that respond to changes in the solute concentration of the interstitial fluid was first hypothesized by Verney (1947). Verney suggested that these detectors, which he called **osmoreceptors,** were neu-

Skin

1 Water is lost through evaporation

2 Concentration of interstitial fluid increases

3a Capillaries lose water by osmosis

3b Cells lose water by osmosis

FIGURE 11.5

The loss of water through evaporation.

rons whose firing rate was affected by their level of hydration. That is, if the interstitial fluid surrounding them became more concentrated, they would lose water through osmosis. The shrinkage would cause them to alter their firing rate, which would send signals to other parts of the brain. (See *Figure 11.6.*)

When we eat a salty meal, we incur a pure osmometric thirst. The salt is absorbed from the digestive system into the blood plasma; hence the blood plasma becomes hypertonic. This condition draws water from the interstitial fluid, which makes this compartment become hypertonic, too, and thus causes water to leave the cells. As the blood plasma increases in volume, the kidneys begin excreting large amounts of both sodium and water. Eventually, the excess sodium is excreted, along with the water that was taken from the interstitial and intracellular fluid. The net result is a loss of water from the cells. *At no time does the volume of the blood plasma fall.*

Most researchers now believe that osmoreceptors responsible for osmometric thirst are located in the region of the anterior hypothalamus that borders the anteroventral tip of the third ventricle (the *AV3V*). Buggy et al. (1979) found that injections of hypertonic saline directly into the AV3V produced drinking, whereas injections into the lateral preoptic area did not. In some species (such as the dog) the osmoreceptors may be located in a specialized *circumventricular organ* located just rostral to the AV3V. The brain contains several circumventricular organs, specialized regions with rich blood supplies located along the ventricular system. You are already familiar with one of these: the area postrema, discussed in Chapter 2. You will learn about two more in this chapter: the OVLT and the SFO. (Refer to *Figure 11.8.*)

The **OVLT** (if you really want to know, that stands for the *organum vasculosum of the lamina terminalis*), like the other circumventricular organs, is located on the *blood* side of the blood-brain barrier. That means that substances dissolved in the blood pass easily into the interstitial fluid within this organ. Thrasher and Keil (1987) found that after the OVLT was destroyed, dogs that were given injections of hypertonic saline no longer drank.

Volumetric Thirst

Volumetric thirst occurs when the volume of the blood plasma—the intravascular volume—decreases. As we saw earlier, when we lose water through evaporation, we lose it from all three fluid compartments: intracellular, interstitial, and intravascular. Thus, evaporation produces both volumetric thirst and osmometric thirst. In addition, loss of blood, vomiting, and diarrhea all cause loss of blood volume (hypovolemia) without depleting the intracellular fluid.

Loss of blood is the most obvious cause of pure volumetric thirst. From the earliest recorded history, reports of battles note that the wounded survivors called out for water. Should damage occur to the osmometric system, volumetric thirst provides a second line of defense against a loss of water, and it provides the means for the loss of isotonic fluid to instigate drinking. In addition, because hypovolemia involves a loss of sodium as well as water (that is, the sodium that was contained in the isotonic fluid that was lost), volumetric thirst leads to a salt appetite.

What detectors are responsible for initiating volumetric thirst and a salt appetite? There are two sets of receptors that accomplish this dual function: one set in the kidneys, which controls the secretion of angiotensin, and one set in the heart and large blood vessels (atrial baroreceptors).

The Role of Angiotensin. The kidneys contain cells that are able to detect decreases in the flow of blood to the kidneys. The usual cause of a reduced flow of blood is a loss of blood volume; thus, these cells detect the presence of hypovolemia. When the

FIGURE 11.6

A hypothetical explanation of the workings of an osmoreceptor.

OVLT (organum vasculosum of the lamina terminalis) A circumventricular organ located anterior to the anteroventral portion of the third ventricle; served by fenestrated capillaries and thus lacks a blood-brain barrier.

Volumetric thirst Thirst produced by hypovolemia.

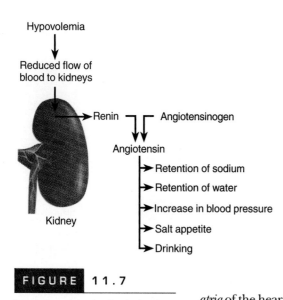

Hypovolemia

Reduced flow of blood to kidneys

Renin

Angiotensinogen

Angiotensin

→ Retention of sodium

→ Retention of water

→ Increase in blood pressure

→ Salt appetite

→ Drinking

Kidney

FIGURE 11.7

Detection of hypovolemia by the kidney and the renin-angiotensin system.

Renin [*ree nin*] A hormone secreted by the kidneys that causes the conversion of angiotensinogen in the blood into angiotensin.

Angiotensin [*ann gee oh ten sin*] A peptide hormone that constricts blood vessels, causes the retention of sodium and water, and produces thirst and a salt appetite.

Nucleus of the solitary tract A nucleus of the medulla that receives information from visceral organs and from the gustatory system.

Subfornical organ (SFO) A small organ located in the confluence of the lateral ventricles, attached to the underside of the fornix; contains neurons that detect the presence of angiotensin in the blood and excite neural circuits that initiate drinking.

flow of blood to the kidneys decreases, these cells secrete an enzyme called **renin**. Renin enters the blood, where it catalyzes the conversion of a protein called *angiotensinogen* into a hormone called **angiotensin**.

Angiotensin has several physiological effects: It stimulates the secretion of hormones by the posterior pituitary gland and the adrenal cortex that cause the kidneys to conserve water and sodium, and it increases blood pressure by causing muscles in the small arteries to contract. In addition, it has two behavioral effects: It initiates both drinking and a salt appetite. Therefore, a reduction in the flow of blood to the kidneys causes water and sodium to be retained by the body, helps to compensate for their loss by reducing the size of the blood vessels, and encourages the animal to find and ingest both water and salt. (See *Figure 11.7*.)

Atrial Baroreceptors. The second set of receptors for volumetric thirst lies within the heart. Physiologists had long known that the *atria* of the heart (the parts that receive blood from the veins) contain sensory neurons that detect stretch. (The term *baro-* comes from the Greek *baros*, "heavy," and refers to weight or pressure.) The atria are passively filled with blood being returned from the body by the veins. The more blood that is present, the fuller the atria become just before each contraction of the heart. Thus, when the volume of the blood plasma falls, the atria become less full, and the stretch receptors within them will detect this change.

Fitzsimons and Moore-Gillon (1980) showed that information from these receptors can stimulate thirst. They operated on dogs and placed a small balloon in the inferior vena cava, the vein that brings blood from most of the body (excluding the head and arms) to the heart. When the balloon was inflated, it reduced the flow of blood to the heart and thus lowered the amount of blood that entered the right atrium. Within 30 minutes the dogs began to drink. Quillen, Keil, and Reid (1990) confirmed these results. They found that when the nerves connecting the atrial baroreceptors with the brain were cut, animals drank much less water when the blood flow to their heart was temporarily reduced.

Neural Mechanisms of Thirst

As you have already learned, the osmoreceptors that initiate drinking are located in the OVLT and (in some species, at least) in the brain tissue around the AV3V. The entire region around the anterior third ventricle—dorsal as well as ventral—seems to be the part of the brain where osmometric and volumetric signals are integrated to control drinking. The AV3V also appears to receive information that can stimulate volumetric thirst. Sensory information from the baroreceptors located in the atria of the heart is sent to a nucleus in the medulla: the **nucleus of the solitary tract.** This nucleus sends efferent axons to many parts of the brain, including the region around the AV3V (see Johnson and Edwards, 1990).

The second signal for volumetric thirst is provided by angiotensin. Because this peptide does not cross the blood-brain barrier, it cannot directly affect neurons in the brain except for those located in one of the circumventricular organs. In fact, research indicates that one of these organs, the **subfornical organ (SFO),** is the site at which blood angiotensin acts to produce thirst. This structure gets its name from its location, just below the commissure of the ventral fornix. (See *Figure 11.8*.)

Simpson, Epstein, and Camardo (1978) found that very low doses of angiotensin injected directly into the SFO caused drinking and that destruction of the SFO or injection of a drug that blocks angiotensin receptors abolished the drinking that normally occurs when angiotensin is injected into the blood. In addition, Phillips and Felix (1976) found that injections of minute quantities of angiotensin into the

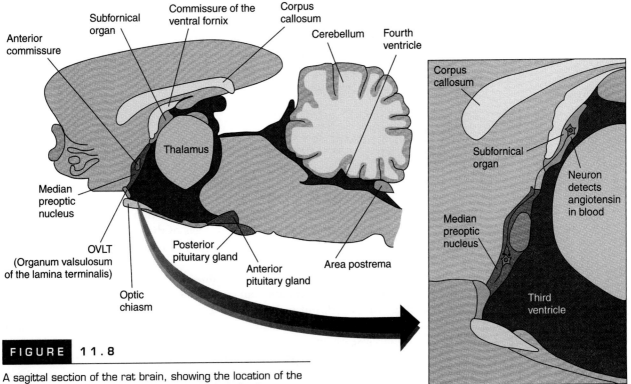

FIGURE 11.8

A sagittal section of the rat brain, showing the location of the circumventricular organs. Inset: A hypothetical circuit connecting the subfornical organ with the median preoptic nucleus.

SFO increased the firing rate of single neurons located there; evidently, these neurons contain angiotensin receptors.

Neurons in the subfornical organ send their axons to the **median preoptic nucleus** (not to be confused with the *medial* preoptic nucleus), a small nucleus wrapped around the front of the anterior commissure, a fiber bundle that connects the amygdala and anterior temporal lobe. (See the inset in ***Figure 11.8.***)

On the basis of these findings, Thrasher and his colleagues (see Thrasher, 1989) suggested that the region in front of the third ventricle acts as an integrating system for most or all of the stimuli for osmometric and volumetric thirst. As you just saw, the median preoptic nucleus receives information from angiotensin-sensitive neurons in the SFO. In addition, this nucleus receives information from the OVLT (which contains osmoreceptors) and from the nucleus of the solitary tract (which receives information from the atrial baroreceptors). According to Thrasher and his colleagues, the median preoptic nucleus integrates the information it receives and, through its efferent connections with other parts of the brain, controls drinking. (See ***Figure 11.9.***)

Median preoptic nucleus
A small nucleus situated around the decussation of the anterior commissure; plays a role in thirst stimulated by angiotensin.

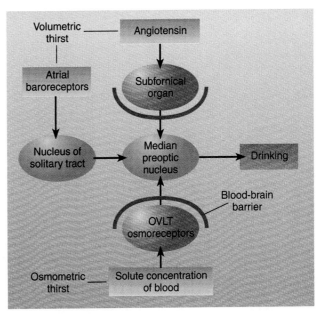

FIGURE 11.9

Neural circuitry concerned with the control of drinking. Not all connections are shown, and some connections may be indirect. PVN = paraventricular nucleus; SON = supraoptic nucleus.

[Adapted from Thrasher, T.N. Acta Physiologica Scandanivica, 1989, 136, 141–150.]

The region of the AV3V seems to play a critical role in fluid regulation in humans as well. For example, McIver et al. (1991) report that brain damage that includes this region can cause both diabetes insipidus and *adipsia*—lack of drinking. The patients report no sensation of thirst, even after they are given an injection of hypertonic saline. To survive, they must deliberately drink water at regular intervals each day, even though they feel no need to do so.

INTERIM SUMMARY

A regulatory system contains four features: a system variable (the variable that is regulated), a set point (the optimal value of the system variable), a detector to measure the system variable, and a correctional mechanism to change it. Physiological regulatory systems, such as control of body fluids and nutrients, require a satiety mechanism to anticipate the effects of the correctional mechanism, because the changes brought about by eating and drinking occur only after a considerable period of time.

The body contains three major fluid compartments: intracellular, interstitial, and intravascular. Sodium and water can easily pass between the intravascular fluid and the interstitial fluid, but sodium cannot penetrate the cell membrane. The solute concentration of the interstitial fluid must be closely regulated. If it becomes hypertonic, cells lose water; if it becomes hypotonic, they gain water. The volume of the intravascular fluid (blood plasma) must also be kept within bounds.

Osmometric thirst occurs when the interstitial fluid becomes hypertonic, drawing water out of cells. This event, which can be caused by evaporation of water from the body or by ingestion of a salty meal, is detected by osmoreceptors in the region of the anteroventral third ventricle (the AV3V). The receptors are located both in the OVLT, a circumventricular organ, and in adjacent regions of the brain. Activation of the osmoreceptors stimulates drinking.

Volumetric thirst occurs along with osmometric thirst when the body loses fluid through evaporation. Pure volumetric thirst is caused by blood loss, vomiting, and diarrhea. One stimulus for volumetric thirst is provided by a fall in blood flow to the kidneys. This event triggers the secretion of renin, which converts plasma angiotensinogen to angiotensin. Angiotensin acts on neurons in the brain and stimulates thirst. The hormone also increases blood pressure and stimulates the secretion of pituitary and adrenal hormones that inhibit the secretion of water and sodium by the kidneys and induce a sodium appetite. (Sodium is needed to help restore the plasma volume.) Volumetric drinking can also be stimulated by a set of baroreceptors in the atria of the heart that detect decreased blood volume and send this information to the brain.

The region of the AV3V detects and integrates signals that produce both osmometric and volumetric thirst. Volumetric thirst stimulated by angiotensin involves another circumventricular organ: the subfornical organ. Volumetric thirst stimulated by the atrial stretch receptor system reaches the AV3V region via a relay in the nucleus of the solitary tract. Neurons in the SFO, the AV3V region, and the OVLT (which, you will remember, contains osmoreceptors) all send axons to the median preoptic nucleus. Neurons in this nucleus stimulate drinking through their connections with other parts of the brain.

THOUGHT QUESTIONS

How do we know that we are thirsty? What does thirst feel like? It cannot simply be a dry mouth or throat, because a real thirst is not quenched by taking a small sip of water, which moistens the mouth and throat as well as a big drink does.

EATING AND METABOLISM

Clearly, eating is one of the most important things we do—and it can also be one of the most pleasurable. Much of what an animal learns to do is motivated by the constant struggle to obtain food; thus, the need to ingest undoubtedly shaped the evolutionary development of our own species. After having read the first section of this chapter, in which you saw that the signals that cause thirst are well understood, you may be surprised to learn that researchers are only now discovering what the system variables for hunger are. Control of ingestive behavior is even more complicated than the control of drinking and sodium intake. We can achieve water balance by the intake of two ingredients: water and sodium chloride. When we eat, we must obtain adequate amounts of carbohydrates, fats, amino acids, vitamins, and minerals other than sodium. Thus, our food-ingestive behaviors are more complex, as are the physiological mechanisms that control them.

To stay alive, our cells must be supplied with fuel and oxygen. Obviously, fuel comes from the digestive tract, and its presence there is a result of eating. But the digestive tract is sometimes empty; in fact, most of us wake up in the morning in that condition. So there has to be a reservoir that stores nutrients to keep the cells of the body nourished when the gut is empty. Indeed, there are two reservoirs—one short-term and the other long-term. The short-term reservoir stores carbohydrates, and the long-term reservoir stores fats.

The short-term reservoir is located in the cells of the liver and the muscles, and it is filled with a complex, insoluble carbohydrate called **glycogen.** I will consider only the most important of these locations: the liver. Cells in the liver convert glucose (a simple, soluble carbohydrate) into glycogen and store the glycogen. They are stimulated to do so by the presence of **insulin,** a peptide hormone produced by the pancreas. Thus, when glucose and insulin are present in the blood, some of the glucose is used as a fuel and some of it is stored as glycogen. Later, when all of the food has been absorbed from the digestive tract, the level of glucose in the blood begins to fall.

The fall in glucose is detected by cells in the brain, which cause an increase in the activity of sympathetic axons that innervate the pancreas. This activity inhibits the secretion of insulin and causes another set of cells of the pancreas to begin secreting a different peptide hormone, **glucagon.** The effect of glucagon is opposite that of insulin: It stimulates the conversion of glycogen into glucose. (Unfortunately, the terms *glucose, glycogen,* and *glucagon* are similar enough that it is easy to confuse them. Even worse, you will soon encounter another one, *glycerol.*) (See *Figure 11.10.*) Thus, the liver soaks up excess glucose and stores it as glycogen when plenty of glucose is available, and it releases glucose from its reservoir when the digestive tract becomes empty and the level of glucose in the blood begins to fall.

The carbohydrate reservoir in the liver is reserved primarily for the central nervous system. When you wake in the morning, your brain is being fed by your liver, which is in the process of converting glycogen to glucose and releasing it into the blood. The glucose reaches the CNS, where it is absorbed and metabolized by the neurons and the glia. This process can continue for a few hours, until all of the carbohydrate reservoir in the liver is used up. (The average liver holds approximately 300 calories of carbohydrate.) Usually, we eat some food before this reservoir gets depleted, which permits us to refill it. But if we do not eat, the CNS has to start living on the products of the long-term reservoir.

Our long-term reservoir consists of adipose tissue (fat tissue). This reservoir is filled with fats, or, more precisely, with **triglycerides.** Triglycerides are complex molecules that contain **glycerol** (a soluble carbohydrate, also called *glycerine*) combined with three **fatty acids** (stearic acid, oleic acid, and

Glycogen (*gly ko jen*) A polysaccharide often referred to as *animal starch;* stored in liver and muscle; constitutes the short-term store of nutrients.

Insulin A pancreatic hormone that facilitates entry of glucose and amino acids into the cell, conversion of glucose into glycogen, and transport of fats into adipose tissue.

Glucagon (*gloo ka gahn*) A pancreatic hormone that promotes the conversion of liver glycogen into glucose.

Triglyceride (*try gliss er ide*) The form of fat storage in adipose cells; consists of a molecule of glycerol joined with three fatty acids.

Glycerol (*gliss er all*) A substance (also called glycerine) derived from the breakdown of triglycerides, along with fatty acids; can be converted by the liver into glucose.

Fatty acid A substance derived from the breakdown of triglycerides, along with glycerol; can be metabolized by most cells of the body except for the brain.

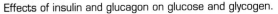

FIGURE 11.10

Effects of insulin and glucagon on glucose and glycogen.

palmitic acid). Adipose tissue is found beneath the skin and in various locations in the abdominal cavity. It consists of cells that are capable of absorbing nutrients from the blood, converting them to triglycerides, and storing them. These cells can expand enormously in size; in fact, the primary physical difference between an obese person and a person of normal weight is the size of their fat cells, which is determined by the amount of triglycerides that these cells contain.

The long-term fat reservoir is obviously what keeps us alive when we are fasting. As we begin to use the contents of our short-term carbohydrate reservoir, fat cells start converting triglycerides into fuels that the cells can use and releasing these fuels into the bloodstream. As we just saw, when we wake in the morning with an empty digestive tract, our brain (in fact, all of the central nervous system) is living on glucose released by the liver. But what about the other cells of the body? They are living on fatty acids, sparing the glucose for the brain. As you will recall from Chapter 3, the sympathetic nervous system is primarily involved in the breakdown and utilization of stored nutrients. When the digestive system is empty, there is an increase in the activity of the sympathetic axons that innervate adipose tissue, the pancreas, and the adrenal medulla. All three effects (direct neural stimulation, secretion of glucagon, and secretion of catecholamines) cause triglycerides in the long-term fat reservoir to be broken down into glycerol and fatty acids. The fatty acids can be directly metabolized by cells in all of the body *except the brain,* which needs glucose. That leaves glycerol. The liver takes up glycerol and converts it to glucose. That glucose, too, is available to the brain.

You may be asking *why* the cells of the rest of the body treat the brain so kindly, letting it consume almost all the glucose that the liver releases from its carbohydrate reservoir and constructs from glycerol. The answer is simple: Insulin has several other functions besides causing glucose to be converted to glycogen. One of these functions is the control of the entry of glucose into cells. Glucose easily dissolves in water, but it will not dissolve in fats. Cell membranes are made of lipids (fatlike substances); therefore, glucose cannot directly pass through them. To be taken into a cell, glucose must be transported there by *glucose transporters*—protein molecules that are situated in the membrane and are similar to those responsible for the reuptake of transmitter substances. Glucose transporters contain insulin receptors, which control their activity; only when insulin binds with these receptors can glucose be transported into the cell. But the cells of the nervous system are an exception to this rule. Their glucose transporters do not contain insulin receptors; thus, these cells can absorb glucose *even when insulin is not present.*

Figure 11.11 reviews what I have said so far about the metabolism that takes place while the digestive tract is empty, which physiologists refer to as the **fasting phase** of metabolism. A fall in the blood glucose level causes the pancreas to stop secreting insulin and to start secreting glucagon. The absence of insulin means that most of the cells of the body can no longer use glucose; thus, all the glucose present in the blood is reserved for the central nervous system. The presence of glucagon instructs the liver to start drawing on the short-term carbohydrate reservoir—to start converting its glycogen into glucose. The presence of glucagon, along with increased activity of the sympathetic nervous system, also instructs fat cells to start drawing on the long-term fat reservoir—to start breaking down triglycerides into fatty acids and glycerol. Most of the body lives on the fatty acids; the glycerol, which is converted into glucose by the liver, gets used by the brain. If fasting is prolonged, proteins (especially protein found in muscle) will be broken down to amino acids, which can be metabolized by all of the body except for the central nervous system. (See *Figure 11.11.*)

The phase of metabolism that occurs when food is present in the digestive tract is called the **absorptive phase.** Now that you understand the fasting phase, this one is simple. Suppose that you eat a balanced meal of carbohydrates, proteins, and fats. The carbohydrates are broken down into glucose and the proteins are broken down

Fasting phase The phase of metabolism during which nutrients are not available from the digestive system; glucose, amino acids, and fatty acids are derived from glycogen, protein, and adipose tissue during this phase.

Absorptive phase The phase of metabolism during which nutrients are absorbed from the digestive system; glucose and amino acids constitute the principal source of energy for cells during this phase, and excess nutrients are stored in adipose tissue in the form of triglycerides.

FIGURE 11.11

Metabolic pathways during the fasting phase and absorptive phase of metabolism.

into amino acids. The fats basically remain as fats. Let us consider each of these three nutrients.

1. As we start absorbing the nutrients, the level of glucose in the blood rises. This rise is detected by cells in the brain, which causes the activity of the sympathetic nervous system to decrease and the activity of the parasympathetic nervous system to increase. This change tells the pancreas to stop secreting glucagon and to begin secreting insulin. The insulin permits all the cells of the body to use glucose as a fuel. Extra glucose is converted into glycogen, which fills the short-term carbohydrate reservoir. If some glucose is left over, fat cells absorb it and convert it to triglycerides.

2. A small proportion of the amino acids received from the digestive tract are used as building blocks to construct proteins and peptides; the rest are converted to fats and stored in adipose tissue.

3. Fats are not used at this time; they are simply stored in adipose tissue. (See *Figure 11.11.*)

INTERIM SUMMARY

Metabolism consists of two phases. During the absorptive phase we receive glucose, amino acids, and fats from the intestines. The blood level of insulin is high, permitting all cells to metabolize glucose. In addition, the liver and the muscles convert glucose to glycogen, which replenishes the short-term reservoir. Excess carbohydrates and amino acids are converted to fats, and fats are placed into the long-term reservoir in the adipose tissue.

During the fasting phase the activity of the parasympathetic nervous system falls, and the activity of the sympathetic nervous system increases. In response, the level of insulin falls, and the level of glucagon and the adrenal catecholamines rises. These events cause liver glycogen to be converted to glucose and triglycerides to be broken down into glycerol and fatty acids. In the absence of insulin, only the central nervous system can use the glucose available in the blood; the rest of the body lives on fatty acids. Glycerol is converted to glucose by the liver, and the glucose is metabolized by the brain.

WHAT STARTS A MEAL?

The heading to this section is a very simple question, but the answer is complex. The short answer, I suppose, is that we still are not sure, but that will not stop me from writing more. In fact, many factors start a meal, including the presence of appetizing food, the company of people who are eating, or the words "It's time to eat!" More fundamentally, there must be some sort of signal that tells the brain that the supply of nutrients has gotten low and that it is time to begin looking for, and ingesting, some food. This section considers all of these factors.

Before I begin, I will point out that the physiological signals that cause a meal to begin are different from the ones that cause it to end. As I said in the discussion of regulatory systems at the beginning of this chapter, there is a considerable delay between the act of eating (the correctional mechanism) and a change in the system variable. We may start eating because the supply of nutrients has fallen below a certain level, but we certainly do not stop eating because the level of those nutrients has been restored to normal. In fact, we stop eating long before that happens, because digestion takes several hours. Thus, the signals for hunger and satiety are sure to be different.

Social and Environmental Factors

Most people, if they were asked why they eat, would say that they do so because they get hungry. By that, they probably mean that something happens inside their body that provides a sensation that makes them want to eat. In other words, we tend to think of eating as something provoked by physiological factors. But often we eat because of

Social factors, and not just physiological ones, affect when and how much we eat.

habit or because of some stimuli present in our environment. These stimuli include a clock indicating that it is time to eat, the sight of a plate of food, the smell of food cooking in the kitchen, or the presence of other people sitting around the table.

One of the most important variables affecting appetite is the meal schedule. We tend to take our meals at fixed times: soon after waking, at midday, and in the evening. This custom makes it difficult for us to adjust the timing of our meals, as other animals can do. What we do instead is adjust the *size* of our meals. If we have eaten recently or if the previous meal was large, we tend to eat a smaller meal (Jiang and Hunt, 1983; de Castro et al., 1986).

The presence of other people is yet another factor that strongly affects our eating behavior. De Castro and de Castro (1989) asked people to keep diaries that listed all the food they ate during a seven-day period and the number of other people who were present while they were eating. The investigators found that the amount of food eaten was directly related to the number of other people who were present—the more people who were present, the more the subjects ate. In addition, the correlation that is normally seen between the time since the previous meal and the size of the present meal was observed only when the subjects ate alone; when other people were present, the correlation was abolished. Thus, social factors can overcome the effects of metabolic factors.

Physiological Hunger Signals

Most of the time, we begin a meal because it is time to eat. The amount of food we eat during that meal depends on several factors, including the amount and variety of food available to us, how good the food tastes to us, and (as we just saw) the presence of other people. But the amount of food we eat also depends on metabolic factors. If we skip several meals, we get hungrier and hungrier, presumably because of physiological signals indicating that we have been withdrawing nutrients from our long-term reservoir. All other things being equal, the hungrier we are, the more we will eat. This observation suggests that the amount of food we eat is inversely related to the amount of nutrients left over from previous meals.

What happens to the level of nutrients in our body as time passes after a meal? As you learned earlier in this chapter, during the absorptive phase of metabolism we live on food that is being absorbed from the digestive tract. After that, we start drawing on our nutrient reservoirs: The brain lives on glucose and the rest of the body lives on fatty acids. Although the metabolic needs of the cells of the body are being met, we are taking fuel out of our long-term reservoir—making withdrawals rather than deposits. Clearly, this is the time to start thinking about our next meal.

A fall in blood glucose level (a condition known as *hypoglycemia*) is a potent stimulus for hunger. Hypoglycemia can be produced experimentally by injecting an animal with 2-deoxyglucose (2-DG). You are already familiar with this chemical, because I have described several experiments that used radioactive 2-DG in conjunction with PET scanners or autoradiography to study the metabolic rate of different parts of the brain. When (nonradioactive) 2-DG is given in large doses, it interferes with glucose metabolism by competing with glucose for access to the mechanism that transports glucose through the cell membrane and for access to the enzymes that metabolize glucose. (A similar chemical, *5-TG*, has the same effect.) Both hypoglycemia and 2-DG cause **glucoprivation;** that is, they deprive cells of glucose. And glucoprivation, whatever its cause, stimulates eating.

Hunger can also be produced by causing **lipoprivation**—depriving cells of lipids. More precisely, they are deprived of the ability to metabolize fatty acids through injection of one of two drugs, **methyl palmoxirate (MP)** or **mercaptoacetate (MA).**

What is the nature of the detectors that monitor the level of metabolic fuels, and where are they located? The evidence that has been gathered so far indicates that both the brain and the liver contain nutrient detectors. The detectors in the brain

Glucoprivation A dramatic fall in the level of glucose available to cells; can be caused by a fall in the blood level of glucose or by drugs that inhibit glucose metabolism.

Lipoprivation A dramatic fall in the level of fatty acids available to cells; usually caused by drugs that inhibit fatty-acid metabolism.

Methyl palmoxirate (MP) A drug that inhibits fatty-acid metabolism and produces lipoprivic hunger.

Mercaptoacetate (MA) A drug that inhibits fatty-acid metabolism and produces lipoprivic hunger.

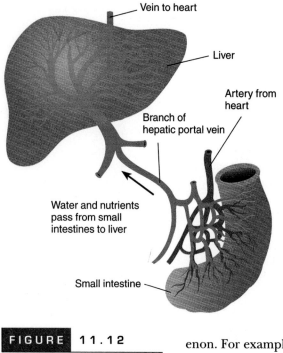

FIGURE 11.12

The hepatic portal blood supply. The liver receives water, minerals, and nutrients from the digestive system through this system.

Capsaicin (*kap say sin*) An ingredient in hot peppers that can destroy small, unmyelinated sensory axons that innervate the internal organs.

FIGURE 11.13

Effects of capsaicin-induced damage to unmyelinated peripheral axons on lipoprivic hunger (MA treatment) and glucoprivic hunger (2-DG treatment). Only lipoprivic hunger is affected.

(Based on data from Ritter, S., and Taylor, J.S. American Journal of Physiology, 1989, 256, R1232–R1239.)

monitor the nutrients available on their side of the blood-brain barrier, and the detectors in the liver monitor the nutrients available to the rest of the body. Because the brain can use only glucose, its detectors are sensitive to glucoprivation, and because the rest of the body can use both glucose and fatty acids, the detectors in the liver are sensitive to both glucoprivation and lipoprivation.

Let's first review the evidence for the detectors in the liver. A study by Novin, VanderWeele, and Rezek (1973) suggested that receptors in the liver can stimulate glucoprivic hunger; when these neurons are deprived of nutrients, they cause eating. The investigators infused 2-DG into the hepatic portal vein. This vein brings blood from the intestines to the liver; thus, an injection of a drug into this vein delivers it directly to the liver. (See *Figure 11.12.*) The investigators found that the intraportal infusions of 2-DG caused immediate eating. When they cut the vagus nerve, which connects the liver with the brain, the infusions no longer stimulated eating. Thus, the brain receives the hunger signal through this connection.

What about liproprivic hunger? Several studies suggest that detectors in the liver are also responsible for this phenomenon. For example, Ritter and Taylor (1989) administered intraperitoneal (IP) injections of capsaicin to rats. **Capsaicin,** a neurotoxin found in hot peppers, destroys fine-diameter, unmyelinated sensory axons of the vagus nerve. The capsaicin blocked lipoprivic hunger but did not affect glucoprivic hunger. (See *Figure 11.13.*) Ritter and Taylor (1990) found that cutting the vagus nerve as it entered the abdominal cavity also abolished lipoprivic hunger. These results indicate that the signal for lipoprivation originates in the internal organs (presumably in the liver).

Now let's look at some of the evidence that indicates that the brain has its own nutrient detectors. Because the brain can use only glucose, it would make sense that these detectors respond to glucoprivation—and, indeed, they do. Ritter, Slusser, and Stone (1981) injected some silicone grease into the cerebral aqueduct, which blocked communication between the third and fourth ventricles. Next, they injected 5-TG into either the third ventricle or the fourth ventricle. (5-TG, like 2-DG, produces glucoprivation.) Injections into the fourth ventricle stimulated eating, but injections into the third ventricle (located in the middle of the diencephalon) had no effect. Presumably, the 5-TG diffused out of the fourth ventricle into the surrounding brain tissue and inhibited glucose metabolism in neurons in the hindbrain.

The location of the hindbrain nutrient receptors is not yet known, but one possible location is the area postrema or the adjacent nucleus of the solitary tract, located in the medulla. Bird, Cardone, and Contreras (1983) found that after the area postrema had been destroyed, an injection of 5-TG into the ventricular system no longer stimulated food intake. Also, Yettefti, Orsini, and Perrin (1997) found that the firing rate of some neurons in the nucleus of the solitary tract changed when the investigators infused glucose into that region or injected glucose intravenously.

To summarize: The brain contains detectors that monitor the availability of glucose (its only fuel) inside the blood-brain barrier, and the liver contains detectors that monitor the availability of nutrients (glucose and fatty acids) outside the blood-brain barrier.

Before closing this section I should note that no single set of receptors is solely responsible for the information the brain uses to control eating. For example, Tordoff, Hopfenbeck, and Novin (1982) found that cutting the hepatic branch of the vagus nerve, which prevents hunger signals originating in the liver from reaching the brain, had little effect on an animal's day-to-day eating. In addition, lesions of the area postrema and the nucleus of the solitary tract, which abolish both glucoprivic and lipoprivic signals, do not lead to long-term disturbances in the control of feeding (Ritter et al., 1992). Apparently, the control of metabolism and ingestive behavior is just too important to entrust to one mechanism.

INTERIM SUMMARY

Many stimuli, environmental and physiological, can initiate a meal. Stimuli associated with eating—such as clocks pointing to lunchtime or dinnertime, the smell or sight of food, or (especially) the taste of food—increase appetite. Most people eat at relatively fixed times but vary their intake according to how much (or when) they ate the previous meal. The presence of other people tends to increase our meal and removes the controlling effect of the previous meal.

Studies with inhibitors of the metabolism of glucose (2-DG or 5-TG) and fatty acids (MP or MA) indicate that low levels of both of these nutrients are involved in hunger; that is, animals will eat in response to both glucoprivation and lipoprivation. The effects of capsaicin and cutting the vagus nerve indicate that the signal for lipoprivic eating is detected by receptors in the liver and transmitted through unmyelinated sensory axons of the vagus nerve. Glucoprivic eating can also be stimulated by interfering with glucose metabolism in the region surrounding the fourth ventricle by injecting 5-TG into the fourth ventricle; thus, the brain stem contains its own glucose-sensitive detectors. Although the evidence is not yet conclusive, these detectors may lie in the area postrema/nucleus of the solitary tract, which also receives information from the detectors in the liver.

THOUGHT QUESTIONS

Do you find hunger unpleasant? I find that when I'm looking forward to a meal I particularly like, I don't mind being hungry, knowing that I'll enjoy the meal that much more.

WHAT STOPS A MEAL?

As we saw, the signals that stop a meal are different from those that start it. However, these two types of signals interact. If a meal is started when there is not much physiological need for nutrients (that is, when the nutrient reservoirs are well stocked), the meal will be a small one. But if a meal is started after a long fast, when the nutrient reservoirs are somewhat depleted, the meal will be a large one. In other words, if the hunger signal is moderate, a moderate satiety signal will stop the meal. If the hunger signal is strong, only a strong satiety signal will stop it.

There are two primary sources of satiety signals—the signals that stop a meal. Short-term satiety signals come from the immediate consequence of eating a particular meal. To search for these signals, we follow the pathway traveled by ingested food: the eyes, nose, and mouth; the stomach; the duodenum; and the liver. (The *duodenum* is the first part of the small intestine, attached directly to the stomach.) Each of these locations can potentially provide a signal to the brain that indicates that food has been ingested and is progressing on the way toward absorption. Long-term satiety signals arise in the adipose tissue, which contains the long-term nutrient reservoir. These signals do not control the beginning and end of a particular meal, but they do, in the long run, control the intake of calories by modulating the sensitivity of brain mechanisms involved in hunger.

Head Factors

The term *head factors* refers to several sets of receptors located in the head: the eyes, the nose, the tongue, and the throat. Information about the appearance, odor, taste, texture, and temperature of food has some automatic effects on food intake, but most of the effects involve learning. The mere act of eating does not produce long-lasting satiety; an animal with a gastric fistula (a tube placed in the stomach that drains food out of the stomach before it can be digested) will eat indefinitely.

Undoubtedly, the most important role of head factors in satiety is the fact that taste and odor of food can serve as stimuli that permit animals to learn about the caloric contents of different foods. Thus, animals can learn to adjust their intake according to the caloric value of what they are eating. For example, Mather, Nicolaïdis, and Booth (1978) found that rats learned to eat less of a food with a particular flavor when the eating of that food was accompanied by intravenous infusions of glucose, which supplied extra calories.

Gastric Factors

Although most people associate feelings of hunger with "hunger pangs" in the stomach and feelings of satiety with an impression of gastric fullness, the stomach is not necessary for feelings of hunger. Humans whose stomachs have been removed because of cancer or the presence of large ulcers still periodically get hungry (Ingelfinger, 1944). Of necessity, these people eat frequent, small meals; in fact, a large meal causes nausea and discomfort, apparently because the duodenum quickly fills up. (The duodenum is the part of the small intestine that attaches to the stomach.) However, although the stomach may not be especially important in producing hunger, it does appear to play an important role in satiety.

The stomach apparently contains receptors that can detect the presence of nutrients. Davis and Campbell (1973) allowed rats to eat their fill, and shortly thereafter, they removed food from the rats' stomachs through an implanted tube. When the rats were permitted to eat again, they ate almost exactly the same amount of food that had been taken out. This finding suggests that animals are able to monitor the amount of food in their stomachs.

Deutsch and Gonzalez (1980) confirmed and extended these findings. They operated on rats and attached an inflatable cuff around the pylorus—something that looked like a miniature blood pressure cuff. The cuff could be inflated by remote control, which would cause it to compress the pylorus, preventing the stomach from emptying. (The *pylorus* is located at the junction of the stomach and the duodenum and contains a sphincter that regulates the flow of nutrients out of the stomach.) With their device, Deutsch and Gonzalez could confine food to the stomach, eliminating the possible influence of receptors in the intestine or liver. After observations were made, the cuff could be deflated so that the stomach would empty normally.

Each day, the investigators inflated the pyloric cuff and gave the rats a 30-minute opportunity to drink a commercial high-calorie liquid diet. Because the rats had not eaten for 15 hours, they readily consumed the liquid diet. After the meal the investigators removed 5 ml of the stomach's contents through an implanted tube. On some days they replaced the contents with a saline solution, and on others they let the rats eat without intervention. The rats adjusted their food intake perfectly, compensating for the calories that were removed but ignoring the added nonnutritive saline solution. (See *Figure 11.14.*) The results indicate that animals can monitor the total amount of nutrients received by the stomach. They do not do so simply by measuring the volume of the food there, because they are not fooled by the infusion of a saline solution. And the detection takes place in the stomach, not the intestine, because the pyloric cuff keeps all the food in the stomach. Of course, this study proves only that the stomach contains nutrient receptors; it does not prove that there are not detectors in the intestines as well.

Intestinal Factors

Indeed, the intestines do contain nutrient detectors. Studies have shown that afferent axons arising from the duodenum are sensitive to the presence of glucose, amino acids, and fatty acids (Ritter et al., 1992). These axons may transmit a satiety signal to the brain. In fact, studies have replicated the findings of Deutsch and Gonzalez but have shown that the animals eat the same amount of food whether the pyloric cuff is open or closed (Rauhofer, Smith, and Gibbs, 1993; Seeley, Kaplan, and Grill, 1995).

Greenberg, Smith, and Gibbs (1990) showed that the entry of food into the duodenum suppresses food intake. They attached gastric fistulas to a group of rats so that when the animals drank a liquid diet, it would drain out of their stomachs. Under these conditions, animals will eat for a long time, because food does not accumulate in the digestive system. (This behavior is referred to as **sham feeding** because it is an imitation of the real thing.) The researchers infused Intralipid, a commercial mixture of lipids and fatty acids, into the rats' duodenums. The infusion inhibited the sham feeding, which indicates the presence of a duodenal satiety signal. When the researchers added a local anesthetic to the liquid diet, the infusion was much less effective in reducing sham feeding. Thus, the signal seems to arise from nutrient detectors located inside the duodenum—the local anesthetic prevented these detectors from sending a signal to the brain, and the animals continued to eat. In support of this conclusion, Greenberg et al. (1991) found that the satiating effect of an injection of radioactively labeled Intralipid into the duodenum occurred before radioactivity was seen in the blood of the hepatic portal vein. Thus, the satiating effect occurred before digestion had taken place.

After food reaches the stomach, it is mixed with hydrochloric acid and pepsin, an enzyme that breaks proteins into their constituent amino acids. As digestion proceeds, food is gradually introduced into the duodenum. There, the food is mixed with bile and pancreatic enzymes, which continue the digestive process. The duodenum controls the rate of stomach emptying by secreting a peptide hormone called **cholecystokinin (CCK)**. This hormone receives its name from the fact that it causes the gallbladder (cholecyst) to contract, injecting bile into the duodenum. (Bile breaks fats down into small particles so that they can be absorbed from the intestines.) CCK is secreted in response to the presence of fats, which are detected by receptors in the walls of the duodenum. In addition to stimulating contraction of the gallbladder, CCK causes the pylorus to constrict and inhibits gastric contractions, thus keeping the stomach from giving it more food.

Obviously, the blood level of CCK must be related to the amount of nutrients (particularly fats) that the duodenum receives from the stomach. Thus, this hormone could potentially provide a satiety signal to the brain, telling it that the duodenum was receiving food from the stomach. In fact, many studies have indeed found that injections of CCK suppress eating (Gibbs, Young, and Smith, 1973; Smith, Gibbs, and Kulkosky, 1982). Because CCK cannot cross the blood-brain barrier, its site of actions

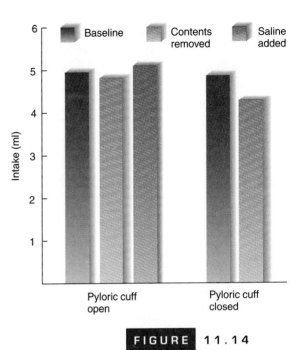

FIGURE 11.14

Evidence for a gastric satiety signal. Rats compensate for the removal of food from the stomach and ignore the addition of a saline solution. To permit direct comparisons, the amount drunk does not reflect the amount removed from the stomach.

(Based on data from Deutsch, J.A., and Gonzalez, M.F. Behavioral and Neural Biology, 1980, 31, 113–116.)

Sham feeding Feeding behavior of an animal with an open gastric or esophageal fistula that prevents food from remaining in the stomach.

Cholecystokinin (CCK) [*coal i sis toe ky nin*] A hormone secreted by the duodenum that regulates gastric motility and causes the gallbladder (cholecyst) to contract; appears to provide a satiety signal transmitted to the brain through the vagus nerve.

FIGURE 11.15

Effects of cholecystokinin (CCK) on the amount of glucose consumed by rats before and after removal of the pyloric region.

(Based on data from Moran, T.H., Shnayder, L., Hostetler, A.M., and McHugh, P.R. American Journal of Physiology, 1989, 255, R1059–R1063.)

must be either outside the central nervous system or in one of the circumventricular organs (like that of angiotensin).

In fact, CCK seems to act peripherally. Smith, Gibbs, and Kulkosky (1982) reported that the inhibitory effect of CCK on food intake was abolished by cutting the gastric branch of the vagus nerve, which disconnects the stomach from the brain. Evidence suggests that the pylorus, a region that is rich in CCK receptors, may be an important site of action. Moran et al. (1989) removed rats' pyloruses, attaching the stomach directly to the cut end of the duodenum. After the surgery the suppressive effect of CCK on the animals' eating was significantly decreased. However, by 2 to 3 months after the surgery the junction between the stomach and the duodenum had grown new CCK receptors, and the hormone again suppressed food intake. (See *Figure 11.15*.)

Liver Factors

Satiety produced by head factors and gastric factors is anticipatory; that is, these factors predict that the food in the digestive system will, when absorbed, eventually restore the system variables that cause hunger. Food in the mouth or stomach does not restore the body's store of nutrients. Not until nutrients are absorbed from the intestines are the internal system variables that cause hunger returned to normal. The last stage of satiety appears to occur in the liver, which is the first organ to learn that food is finally being received from the intestines.

Evidence for the role of the liver in satiety comes from several sources. For example, Tordoff and Friedman (1988) infused small amounts of two nutrients—glucose and fructose—into the hepatic portal vein. The infusions "fooled" the liver; both nutrients reduced the amount of food that the rats ate. Fructose cannot cross the blood-brain barrier and is metabolized very poorly by cells in the rest of the body; however, it can be readily metabolized by the liver. Therefore, the results strongly suggest that when the liver receives nutrients from the intestines, it sends a signal to the brain that produces satiety. (More accurately, the signal *continues* the satiety that was already started by head factors and gastric factors.)

Long-Term Satiety: Signals from Adipose Tissue

So far, I have discussed satiety factors arising from a meal. But as we saw in the first section of this chapter, total body fat appears to be regulated on a long-term basis. If an animal is force-fed so that it becomes fatter than normal, it will reduce its food intake once it is permitted to choose how much to eat (Wilson et al., 1990). (See *Figure 11.16*.) Similar studies have shown that an animal will adjust its food intake appropriately if it is given a high-calorie or low-calorie diet. And if an animal is put on a diet that reduces its body weight, gastric satiety factors become much less effective (Cabanac and Lafrance, 1991). Thus, signals arising from the long-term nutrient reservoir may either suppress hunger signals or augment satiety signals.

What exactly is the system variable that permits the body weight of most organisms to remain relatively sta-

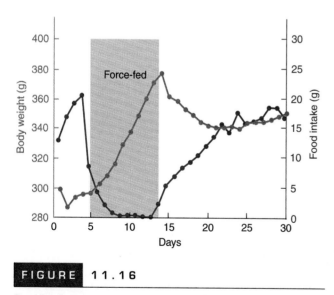

FIGURE 11.16

Food intake and body weight of rats that received an excess of their normal food intake through force-feeding. Their food intake fell during the period of force-feeding and recovered only when their body weight returned to normal.

(Adapted from Wilson, B.E., Meyer, G.E., Cleveland, J.C., and Weigle, D.S. American Journal of Physiology, 1990, 259, R1148–R1155.)

ble? It seems highly unlikely that body *weight* itself is regulated; this variable would have to be measured by detectors in the soles of our feet or (for those of us who are sedentary) in the skin of our buttocks. What is more likely is that some variable related to body fat is regulated.

For years, researchers have been trying to identify a signal from fat tissue that could tell the brain how well stocked the long-term reservoir was. Finally, they succeeded. The discovery came after years of study with a strain of genetically obese mice. The **ob mouse** (as this strain is called) has a low metabolism, overeats, and gets exceedingly fat. It also develops diabetes in adulthood, just as many obese people do. Researchers in several laboratories have discovered the cause of the obesity (Campfield et al., 1995; Halaas et al., 1995; Pelleymounter et al., 1995). A particular gene, called OB, normally produces a protein that has been given the name **leptin** (from the Greek word *leptos,* "thin"). Leptin is normally secreted by fat cells that contain a large amount of triglycerides. Because of a genetic mutation, the fat cells of ob mice are unable to produce leptin.

Leptin has profound effects on metabolism and eating, acting as an antiobesity hormone. If ob mice are given daily injections of leptin, their metabolic rate increases, their body temperature rises, they become more active, and they eat less. As a result, their weight returns to normal. Figure 11.17 shows a picture of an untreated ob mouse and an ob mouse that has received injections of leptin. (See *Figure 11.17*.)

The discovery of leptin has stimulated much interest among researchers interested in finding ways to treat human obesity. Because it is a natural hormone, it might provide a way to help people lose weight without the use of drugs with potentially harmful effects. The next section describes the brain mechanisms responsible for its effects on metabolism and behavior, and the final section explores the possibilities of its use in treating obesity.

FIGURE 11.17

The effects of leptin on obesity in mice of the ob (obese) strain. The ob mouse on the left is untreated; the one on the right received daily injections of leptin.

[Photo courtesy of Dr. J. Sholtis, The Rockefeller University. Copyright © 1995 Amgen, Inc.]

INTERIM SUMMARY

Because of the long delay between swallowing food and digesting it, the regulation of food intake requires a satiety mechanism; without it, we would overeat and damage our stomachs. The feedback produced by tasting, smelling, and swallowing food provides the first satiety signal, but unless this signal is followed by feedback from the stomach indicating that food has arrived there, the animal will eat again. The stomach contains nutrient detectors that tell the brain how much food has been received. If some food is removed from the stomach, the animal eats enough to replace it, even if the experimenter tries to fool the animal by injecting an equal volume of a saline solution.

Signals originating in the intestines may also produce satiety. Several investigators have suggested that cholecystokinin, released by the duodenum when it receives fat-rich food from the stomach, provides a satiety signal. The inhibitory effect of CCK on eating appears to be mediated by receptors in the pylorus and transmitted to the brain via the vagus nerve. The duodenum also appears to contain nutrient detectors that send a satiety signal to the brain; infusion of a mixture of lipids and fatty acids suppresses sham feeding.

Another satiety signal comes from the liver, which detects nutrients being received from the intestines. Infusion of glucose or fructose (which do not cross the blood-brain barrier) directly into the hepatic portal vein suppresses food intake of hungry animals.

Signals arising from nutrient reservoirs affect food intake on a long-term basis. Force-feeding facilitates satiety, and starvation inhibits it. Studies of the ob mouse led

Ob mouse A strain of mice whose obesity and low metabolic rate are caused by a mutation that prevents the production of leptin.

Leptin A hormone secreted by adipose tissue; decreases food intake and increases metabolic rate, primarily by inhibiting NPY-secreting neurons in the arcuate nucleus.

to the discovery of leptin, a peptide hormone secreted by well-nourished adipose tissue that increases an animal's metabolic rate and decreases food intake.

■ THOUGHT QUESTIONS

The drive-reduction hypothesis of motivation and reinforcement says that drives are aversive and satiety is pleasurable. Clearly, *satisfying* hunger is pleasurable, but what about *satiety?* Which do you prefer, eating a meal while you are hungry or feeling full afterward?

■ BRAIN MECHANISMS

Although hunger and satiety signals originate in the digestive system and in the body's nutrient reservoirs, the target of these signals is the brain. This section looks at some of the research on brain mechanisms of food intake and metabolism.

Brain Stem

Ingestive behaviors are phylogenetically ancient; obviously, all our ancestors ate and drank or died. Thus, we should expect that the basic ingestive behaviors of chewing and swallowing are programmed by phylogenetically ancient brain circuits. Indeed, studies have shown that these behaviors can be performed by decerebrate rats, whose brains were transected between the diencephalon and the midbrain (Norgren and Grill, 1982; Grill and Kaplan, 1990). Decerebration disconnects the motor neurons of the brain stem and spinal cord from the neural circuits of the cerebral hemispheres (such as the cerebral cortex and basal ganglia) that normally control them. The only behaviors that decerebrate animals can display are those that are directly controlled by neural circuits located within the brain stem. A decerebrate rat cannot approach and eat food; the experimenters must place food, in liquid form, into their mouths. Decerebrate rats can distinguish between different tastes; they drink and swallow sweet or slightly salty liquids and spit out bitter ones. They even respond to hunger and satiety signals. They drink more sucrose after having been deprived of food for 24 hours, and they drink less of it if some sucrose is first injected directly into their stomachs.

The area postrema and the nucleus of the solitary tract (henceforth referred to as the AP/NST) receive taste information from the tongue and a variety of sensory information from the internal organs—including hunger signals from detectors in the liver. In addition, we saw that this region appears to contain a set of detectors that are sensitive to the brain's own fuel, glucose. All this information is transmitted to regions of the forebrain more directly involved in control of eating and metabolism.

Several kinds of evidence indicate the importance of the AP/NST to hunger. Ritter, Dinh, and Friedman (1994) found that injections of 2,5-AM (which disrupt liver metabolism and produce hunger) stimulated Fos production in the AP/NST. (The presence of Fos protein is a sign of neural activation.) They found that both eating and Fos production were abolished by cutting the branch of the vagus nerve that connects the liver to the brain. In addition, Ritter and Taylor (1990) found that lesions of the NST and the area postrema (AP/NST) abolished both glucoprivic and lipoprivic feeding. (See *Figure 11.18.*)

Information from the tongue and internal organs received by the AP/NST is relayed to the **lateral parabrachial nucleus** of

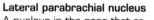

Lateral parabrachial nucleus
A nucleus in the pons that receives gustatory information and information from the liver and digestive system and relays it to the forebrain.

FIGURE 11.18

Effects of lesions of the nucleus of the solitary tract and adjacent area postrema on glucoprivic hunger (MA treatment) and lipoprivic hunger (2-DG treatment).

(Based on data from Ritter, S., and Taylor, J.S. American Journal of Physiology, 1990, 258, R1395–R1401.)

FIGURE 11.19

Effects of parabrachial lesions on glucoprivic hunger signaled by detectors in the liver (2,5-AM treatment) or in the brain stem (2-DG treatment).

(Adapted from Grill, H.J., Friedman, M.I., Norgren, R., Scalera, G., and Seeley, R. American Journal of Physiology, 1995, 268, R676–R682.)

the pons. Lesions of the lateral parabrachial nucleus eliminate the effects of hunger signals detected by the liver; they disrupt both lipoprivic feeding and feeding elicited by 2,5-AM (Calingasan and Ritter, 1993; Grill et al., 1995). These lesions do *not* disrupt feeding produced by 2-DG, which indicates that information from the brain's own glucose-sensitive detectors reaches the forebrain by a different pathway. The route that these neurons take is not yet known. (See *Figure 11.19.*)

Hypothalamus

Discoveries made in the 1940s and 1950s focused the attention of researchers interested in ingestive behavior on two regions of the hypothalamus: the lateral area and the ventromedial nucleus. (See *Figure 11.20.*) For many years, investigators believed

FIGURE 11.20

Cross sections through the rat brain, showing the location of regions of the hypothalamus that play a role in the control of eating and metabolism.

(Adapted from Swanson, L.W. Brain Maps: Structure of the Rat Brain. New York: Elsevier, 1992.)

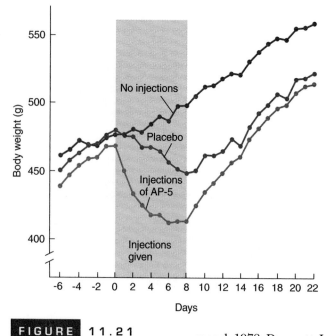

FIGURE 11.21

Body weight of rats that received twice-daily injections of a gluta-mate antagonist (AP-5) into the lateral hypothalamus.

(Adapted from Stanley, B.G., Willett, V.L., Donias, H.W., Dee, M.G., and Duva, M.A. American Journal of Physiology: Regulatory, Integrative and Comparative Physiology, 1996, 270, R443–R449.)

Neuropeptide Y (NPY) A peptide neurotransmitter whose release stimulates feeding, insulin and glucocorticoid secretion, decreased breakdown of triglycerides, and a decrease in body temperature.

Arcuate nucleus [*are kew ett*] A nucleus in the base of the hypothalamus that controls secretions of the anterior pituitary gland; contains NPY-secreting neurons involved in feeding and control of metabolism.

that these two regions controlled hunger and satiety, respectively; one was the accelerator, and the other was the brake. The basic findings were these: After the lateral hypothalamus was destroyed, animals stopped eating or drinking (Anand and Brobeck, 1951; Teitelbaum and Stellar, 1954). Electrical stimulation of the same region would produce eating, drinking, or both behaviors. Conversely, lesions of the ventromedial hypothalamus produced overeating that led to gross obesity, whereas electrical stimulation suppressed eating (Hetherington and Ranson, 1942). The story was too simple, of course. Although both the lateral and ventromedial hypothalamus participate in the control of food intake, both regions appear to play both excitatory and inhibitory roles.

Role in Hunger

Neurotoxic lesions of the lateral hypothalamus made with ibotenic acid, which kills cells while sparing axons passing through the region, produce a long-lasting decrease in food intake and body weight (Stricker, Swerdloff, and Zigmond, 1978; Dunnett, Lane, and Winn, 1985). In addition, stimulation of the lateral hypothalamus with direct injections of excitatory amino acids produces eating (Stanley et al., 1993a), and injections of a glutamate antagonist in this region decrease food intake (Stanley et al., 1996). These studies indicate that the lateral hypothalamus plays an excitatory role in the control of eating. (See *Figure 11.21.*)

A neurotransmitter released in the hypothalamus is an extremely potent stimulator of food intake). Infusion of **neuropeptide Y** into the hypothalamus produces ravenous, almost frantic eating (Clark et al., 1984; Stanley et al., 1993b). Rats that receive an infusion of this peptide will work very hard, pressing a lever many times for each morsel of food; they will eat food made bitter with quinine; and they will continue to drink milk even when doing so means that they receive an electric shock to their tongue (Flood and Morley, 1991; Jewett et al., 1992). The potency of this peptide suggests that it plays an important role in the control of food intake.

Neuropeptide Y affects metabolism as well as behavior. When infused into the paraventricular nucleus, located in the medial hypothalamus around the dorsal part of the third ventricle, it produces metabolic effects, including insulin and glucocorticoid secretion, decreased breakdown of triglycerides, and a decrease in body temperature (Wahlestedt et al., 1987; Abe, Saito, and Shimazu, 1989; Currie and Coscina, 1996). (Refer to *Figure 11.20.*)

Neuropeptide Y is found in neurons that project from regions of the brain stem to the hypothalamus (Sawchenko et al., 1985). Levels of neuropeptide Y are affected by hunger and satiety signals; Sahu, Kalra, and Kalra (1988) found that depriving an animal of food raises hypothalamic levels of NPY and eating lowers them. In addition, Myers et al. (1995) found that hypothalamic injections of a drug that blocks neuropeptide Y receptors suppress eating caused by food deprivation or by hypothalamic injections of NPY. This last finding, in particular, provides strong evidence that normal food intake is at least partially stimulated by neuropeptide Y.

The neurons that secrete NPY are found in the **arcuate nucleus**, located in the hypothalamus at the base of the third ventricle. The arcuate nucleus also contains neurosecretory cells whose hormones control the secretions of the anterior pituitary gland. (Refer to *Figure 11.20.*) The NPY-containing neurons send a dense projection of axons to the paraventricular nucleus—the region where infusions of NPY affect metabolic functions (Bai et al., 1985). They also send a lighter projection elsewhere in the hypothalamus. Presumably, the latter set of projections is responsible for the direct effects of NPY on eating.

Minami et al. (1995) found that glucoprivation produced by injection of 2-DG into the cerebral ventricles activates NPY-secreting neurons in the arcuate nucleus. In a double-labeling study, they showed that glucoprivation induced the production of Fos protein in arcuate neurons that produced neuropeptide Y. The glucoprivation also increased Fos production in neurons in the paraventricular nucleus, which receive projections from the NPY neurons in the arcuate nucleus. (See *Figure 11.22.*)

Another peptide, **galanin,** is released by terminal buttons in the hypothalamus (Melander et al., 1987). Infusion of galanin into the PVN produces eating. In particular, when rats that receive such an infusion are permitted to choose among carbohydrates, fats, and proteins, they choose to eat fats (Tempel, Leibowitz, and Leibowitz, 1988). Akabayashi et al. (1994) found that rats that show a natural preference for a high-fat diet have higher levels of galanin in the PVN than rats that prefer a diet lower in fat. A neuroanatomical study by Horvath et al. (1996) found that NPY-secreting terminals appear to form synapses with galanin-secreting neurons. Otherwise, little is known about the control of galanin secretion.

Role in Satiety

As we saw in the previous subsection, the release of NPY in the lateral hypothalamus increases food intake. The release of another transmitter substance, 5-HT, has the opposite effect: It *inhibits* the eating of carbohydrates. The inhibitory effects of 5-HT are not precisely localized; Leibowitz, Weiss, and Suh (1990) found that injections of 5-HT into the PVN, VMH, and suprachiasmatic nucleus (SCN) all suppressed carbohydrate intake. This effect occurred only if the neurotransmitter was injected early in the dark part of the day–night cycle, when rats normally eat a high-carbohydrate meal (their breakfast, so to speak). Perhaps, the authors suggested, the 5-HT interferes with a signal that originates in the SCN, which (as you learned in Chapter 8) serves as the circadian pacemaker.

Drugs that destroy serotonergic neurons, inhibit the synthesis of 5-HT, or block 5-HT receptors have an effect opposite that of 5-HT: They *increase* food intake, especially carbohydrates (Breisch, Zemlan, and Hoebel, 1976; Saller and Stricker, 1976; Stallone and Nicolaïdis, 1989). Dryden et al. (1995) found that an IP injection of methysergide, a 5-HT antagonist, increased the secretion of NPY in the hypothalamus and (as you might expect) increased food intake. This finding suggests that 5-HT somehow inhibits the activity of NPY neurons.

As we will see later, a 5-HT agonist, **fenfluramine (FEN),** has been used to suppress appetite in obese people who are trying to lose weight. The appetite-suppressing effects of FEN do not take place in the PVN; Fletcher et al. (1993) found that IP injections of the drug still decreased food intake after the PVN had been destroyed. At least one site of action of FEN could be in the brain stem; Li, Spector, and Rowland (1994) found that the appetite-suppressing effect of the drug was reduced after destruction of the lateral parabrachial nucleus.

As we saw, leptin, a hormone secreted by well-fed adipose tissue, has an inhibitory effect on eating. The interaction of this long-term satiety signal with neural circuits involved in hunger are now being discovered. Leptin appears to produce its effects by binding with receptors in the brain. Schwartz et al. (1996) found that in-

2-DG   Placebo

Paraventricular nuclei

Arcuate nuclei

FIGURE   11.22

The effects of glucoprivic hunger induced by intracerebroventricular injection of 2-DG in expression of c-*Fos* messenger RNA. The treatment activated neurons in the arcuate nucleus and the paraventricular nucleus of the hypothalamus.

(Photograph courtesy of Dr. S. Minami, Nippon Medical School, Tokyo.)

Galanin [*gal a nin*] A peptide neurotransmitter whose release stimulates ingestion of fats.

Fenfluramine (FEN) A drug that causes the release of serotonin and inhibits eating.

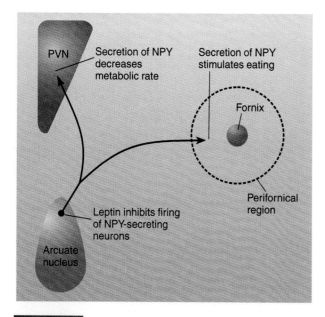

FIGURE 11.23

A schematic diagram of the interactions between leptin and NPY-secreting neurons.

fusions of leptin into the cerebral ventricles, which inhibit eating, also inhibit the production of neuropeptide Y in the arcuate nucleus. As you will recall, the arcuate nucleus contains the largest concentration of NPY-secreting neurons, and the axons of these neurons project to the PVN and to other regions of the hypothalamus that are involved in hunger and the control of metabolism. Two double-labeling studies (Hakansson et al., 1996; Mercer et al., 1996) found that neuropeptide Y-secreting neurons in the PVN contain leptin receptors.

Glaum et al. (1996) obtained direct evidence that activation of leptin receptors on NPY-secreting neurons in the arcuate nucleus has an inhibitory effect. They used micropipettes to record postsynaptic potentials from these neurons while infusing small amounts of chemicals by means of iontophoresis. They found that infusion of glutamate produced excitatory postsynaptic potentials and that infusion of leptin decreased the magnitude of these potentials. These findings suggest that glutamatergic input to the arcuate nucleus excites NPY-secreting cells, resulting in hunger and metabolic changes associated with the fasting phase of metabolism, and that leptin inhibits these effects. (See *Figure 11.23*.)

Erickson, Hollopeter, and Palmiter (1996) prepared a targeted mutation of the gene responsible for production of NPY in ob mice. Thus, the mice had two mutations: a natural one that prevented them from producing leptin, and a genetically engineered one preventing them from producing NPY. If the only effect of leptin were to inhibit the release of NPY, we would expect these mice to be thin. But Erickson et al. found that their body weight was about midway between that of a normal mouse and an ob mouse without the targeted mutation. These findings indicate that leptin must have other effects beside inhibition of NPY release. They also suggest that NPY is not the only appetite-promoting neurotransmitter.

INTERIM SUMMARY

The brain stem contains neural circuits that are able to control acceptance or rejection of sweet or bitter foods and can even be modulated by satiation or physiological hunger signals, such as a decrease in glucose metabolism or the presence of food in the digestive system. The area postrema and nucleus of the solitary tract (AP/NST) receive signals from the tongue, stomach, small intestine, and liver and send the information on to the lateral parabrachial nucleus of the pons, which passes the information on to many regions of the forebrain. These signals interact and help to control food intake. Lesions of the AP/NST disrupt both glucoprivic and lipoprivic eating, whereas lesions of the lateral parabrachial nucleus disrupt only liproprivic eating.

Stimulation of the lateral hypothalamus with electricity or excitatory amino acids produces eating, while lesions or infusion of glutamate antagonists decrease eating. The release of neuropeptide Y in the lateral hypothalamus induces ravenous eating. When NPY is infused in the paraventricular nucleus, it decreases metabolic rate. The cell bodies of most NPY-secreting neurons are located in the arcuate nucleus, the region that controls the secretion of the anterior pituitary gland. Glucoprivation caused by injection of 2-DG into the cerebral ventricles increases the activity of NPY-secreting neurons. Secretion of another peptide, galanin, increases the intake of fats.

Lesions of the ventromedial hypothalamus produce overeating and obesity, and electrical or chemical stimulation of this area inhibits eating. However, this region is not a simple "satiety center." The injection of 5-HT into the PVN has an inhibitory effect on eating. Fenfluramine, an appetite suppressant, is a 5-HT agonist, but its behavioral effects seem to be exerted in the brain stem, not in the hypothalamus.

Leptin, the long-term satiety hormone secreted by well-stocked adipose tissue, desensitizes the brain to hunger signals. It binds with receptors in the arcuate nucleus of the hypothalamus, where it inhibits NPY-secreting neurons, increasing metabolic rate and suppressing eating.

EATING DISORDERS

Unfortunately, some people are susceptible to the development of eating disorders. Some people grow obese, even though our society regards this condition as unattractive and even though obese people tend to have more health problems—and to die sooner—than people of normal weight. Other people (especially young women) can become obsessed with losing weight, eating little and increasing their activity level until their body weight becomes extremely low—sometimes fatally so. Others manage to keep from losing or gaining weight but often lose control of intake, eating enormous amounts of food and then taking strong laxatives or forcing themselves to vomit. Has what we have learned about the physiology of appetite helped us to understand these conditions?

Obesity

Obesity is a widespread problem that can have serious medical consequences. In the United States, approximately 34 million people are overweight, 12.5 million of them severely so (Kuczmarski, 1992). The known health hazards include hypertension, diabetes, and cardiovascular disease (Pi-Sunyer, 1991). The economic costs from obesity-related diseases in the United States alone have been estimated at over $39 billion per year (Colditz, 1992).

There are undoubtedly many causes of obesity, including learning and innate or acquired differences in metabolism. The behavior of eating, like most other behaviors, is subject to modification through learning. Unfortunately, many aspects of modern, industrialized societies tend to weaken physiological controls over eating. For example, as children we learn to eat what is put on our plates; indeed, many children are praised for eating all they have been given and punished for failing to do so. As we get older, our metabolic requirements decrease; and if we continue to eat as we did when we were younger, we tend to accumulate fat. The inhibitory signals associated with food consumption are certainly not absolute; they can be overridden by habit or by the simple pleasure of ingesting good-tasting food.

One reason that many people have so much difficulty losing weight is that metabolic factors appear to play an important role in obesity. In fact, a good case can be made that obesity is most often not an *eating disorder* (despite the title of this section), but a *metabolic disorder.* Just as cars differ in their fuel efficiency, so do people. Rose and Williams (1961) studied pairs of people who were matched for weight, height, age, and activity. Some of these matched pairs differed by a factor of 2 in the number of calories they ate each day. People with an efficient metabolism have calories left over to deposit in the long-term nutrient reservoir; thus, they have difficulty keeping this reservoir from growing. In contrast, people with an inefficient metabolism can eat large meals without getting fat. Thus, whereas a fuel-efficient automobile is desirable, a fuel-efficient body runs the risk of becoming obese.

Differences in body weight (perhaps reflecting differences in metabolism) appear to have a hereditary basis. Twin studies suggest that between 40 and 85 percent of the variability in body fat is due to genetic differences (Price and Gottesman, 1991; De Castro, 1993; Allison et al., 1996). Bouchard (1989, 1991) concluded that heredity probably plays a role in people's resting metabolic rate, in the amount of heat produced by the body after a meal, in the energy expended during exercise, and in the likelihood that ingested calories will be stored as fat. And the family environment in which people are raised apparently has no significant effect on their body weight as adults; Stunkard et al. (1986) found that the body weight of a sample of people who had been adopted as infants was highly correlated with their *biological* parents but not with their *adoptive* parents.

Why are there genetic differences in metabolic efficiency? James and Trayhurn (1981) suggested that under some environmental conditions, metabolic efficiency is advantageous. That is, in places where food is only intermittently available in sufficient quantities, being able to stay alive on small amounts of food and to store up extra nutrients in the form of fat when food becomes available for a while is a highly adaptive trait. When the famine comes, it is the people with efficient metabolisms and adequate supplies of fat—and their genes—who survive. Therefore, people's metabolic rates may reflect the nature of the environment experienced by their ancestors.

James and Trayhurn's hypothesis has received support from epidemiological studies. The tiny island of Nauru, comprising only eight square miles of territory, contains a stock of seabird guano, which is now mined for its rich source of phosphate by companies that sell fertilizer. The average per capita income of Nauru suddenly went from very low to one of the highest in the world (Gibbs, 1996). With this wealth came a much less active lifestyle and the ability to buy expensive, imported foods. In the course of a generation the Nauru islanders became some of the most obese people on earth. Ravussin et al. (1994) studied two groups of Pima Indians, who live in the southwestern United States and northwestern Mexico. Members of both groups appear to have the same genetic background; they share the same language and share common historical traditions. The two groups separated 700–1000 years ago and now live under very different environmental conditions. The Pima Indians in the southwestern United States eat a high-fat American diet and weigh an average of 90 kg (198 lb), men and women combined. In contrast, the lifestyle of the Mexican Pimas is probably similar to that of their ancestors. They spend long hours working at subsistence farming and eat a low-fat diet—and weigh an average of 64 kg (141 lb). The cholesterol level of the American Pimas is much higher than that of the Mexican Pimas, and their rate of diabetes is more than five times higher. These findings show that genes that promote an efficient metabolism are of benefit to people who must work hard for their calories but that these same genes turn into a liability when people live in an environment where the physical demands are low and high-calorie food is cheap and plentiful.

As we saw earlier, study of the ob mouse led to the discovery of leptin, the hormone secreted by well-nourished adipose tissue. The explanation of obesity in the ob mouse was simple: The animals could not produce leptin. Following this discovery, researchers have been trying to determine whether understanding the role of leptin can help us to understand at least some of the causes of obesity in humans.

So far, no studies have found evidence that obesity in humans is caused by a deficiency in secretion of leptin. Schwartz et al. (1996) found that plasma levels of leptin were related to total body fat in lean and obese people. It is possible, of course, that a small number of obese people owe their condition to a mutation of the gene responsible for leptin production, just like the mutation that produces the ob mouse. Most investigators believe that if leptin plays a role in human obesity, the likely mechanism is reduced *sensitivity* to the hormone, not decreased secretion. Leptin is a peptide, and peptides normally cannot cross the blood-brain barrier. However, an active mechanism transports molecules of leptin across this barrier so that it can exert its behavioral and metabolic effects (Banks et al., 1996; Golden, Maccagnan, and Pardridge, 1997). Caro et al. (1996) suggested that differences in the effectiveness of this transport system may be one cause of obesity. If not much leptin gets across the blood-brain barrier, the leptin signal in the brain will be weaker than it should be. Another possible cause of leptin insensitivity is a mutation of the gene responsible for production of the leptin receptor. In fact, three strains of obese rodents—the *db mouse,* the *corpulent rat,* and the *Zucker rat*—all have mutations of the leptin receptor gene (Gura, 1997). So far, there is no evidence that obese humans have mutations of this gene.

Obesity is extremely difficult to treat; the enormous financial success of diet books, fat farms, and weight reduction programs attests to the trouble people have losing weight. More precisely, many programs help people to lose weight initially, but then the weight is quickly regained. Kramer et al. (1989) reported that four to five years after participating in a fifteen-week behavioral weight loss program, fewer than 3 percent of the participants managed to maintain the weight loss they had achieved during the program. Some experts have suggested that given the extremely low long-term success rate, perhaps we should stop treating people for obesity until our treatments are more successful. As Wooley and Garner (1994) said:

> We should stop offering ineffective treatments aimed at weight loss. Researchers who think they have invented a better mousetrap should test it in controlled research before setting out their bait for the entire population. Only by admitting that our treatments do not work—and showing that we mean it by refraining from offering them—can we begin to undo a century of recruiting fat people for failure. (p. 656)

Drug treatment for obesity shows some promise. As we saw earlier in this chapter, the stimulation of 5-HT receptors in the brain suppresses eating. A review by Bray (1992) concluded that serotonin agonists can be of benefit in weight loss programs. The use of fenfluramine, a drug that directly stimulates the release of 5-HT, was recently approved by the U.S. Food and Drug Administration. (The drug has been in use for several years in other countries.) However, even more recently, the drug was taken off the market again because of questions about possible serious side effects. Figure 11.24 shows the effects of this drug on the body weight of a group of 176 patients. As you can see, the patients showed a stable weight loss during the twelve months they took the drug but then largely regained their weight after they discontinued it. (See *Figure 11.24.*) More recent studies (for example, O'Connor et al., 1995) have obtained similar results; patients regain their weight after the drug is discontinued, even if they remain in weight-loss programs.

Does the discovery of the antiobesity effects of leptin hold any promise for the treatment of obesity? Is there any possibility that researchers will find drugs that will stimulate leptin receptors—or perhaps block neuropeptide Y receptors—thus decreasing people's appetite and increasing the rate at which they metabolize fats? Unfortunately, there is no immediate prospect of such medications. As we saw, the level of leptin is high in most obese people, so increasing it would probably not be of benefit. If the reason for their leptin insensitivity is an inefficient transport mechanism of leptin molecules through the blood-brain barrier, then perhaps pharmacologists will be able to discover a leptin receptor agonist that will pass through this barrier, bypassing the transport system. In a review of recent research on obesity, Gibbs (1996) noted that drug companies are currently developing several different types of antiobesity drugs. Researchers are targeting both behavioral and metabolic variables controlled by the brain, the digestive system, fat tissues, and muscles.

Anorexia Nervosa/Bulimia Nervosa

Most people, if they have an eating problem, tend to overeat. However, some people, especially young adolescent women, have the opposite problem: They eat too little, even to the

FIGURE **11.24**

Mean weight change during twelve months of treatment with fenfluramine.

[Adapted from Bray, 1992; after Hudson, K.D. Journal of the Royal College of General Practitioners, 1977, 27, 497–501.]

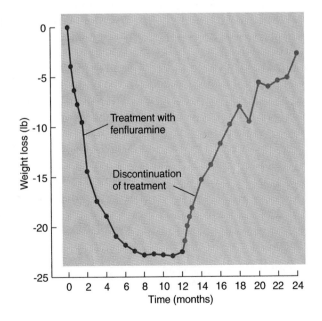

Anorexia nervosa most often occurs in young women. An especially high incidence of this eating disorder is seen in ballet dancers, who must be both athletic and thin.

point of starvation. This disorder is called **anorexia nervosa.** Another eating disorder, **bulimia nervosa,** is characterized by a loss of control of food intake. (The term *bulimia* comes from the Greek *bous*, "ox," and *limos*, "hunger.") People with bulimia nervosa periodically gorge themselves with food, especially dessert or snack food and especially in the afternoon or evening. These binges are usually followed by self-induced vomiting or the use of laxatives, along with feelings of depression and guilt (Mawson, 1974; Halmi, 1978). With this combination of binging and purging, the net nutrient intake (and consequently, the body weight) of bulimics can vary; Weltzin et al. (1991) reported that 19 percent of bulimics undereat, 37 percent eat a normal amount, and 44 percent overeat. Episodes of bulimia are seen in some patients with anorexia nervosa.

The literal meaning of the word *anorexia* suggests a loss of appetite, but people with this disorder are usually interested in—even preoccupied with—food. They may enjoy preparing meals for others to consume, collect recipes, and even hoard food that they do not eat. Although anorexics may not be oblivious to the effects of food, they express an intense fear of becoming obese, which continues even if they become dangerously thin. Many exercise by cycling, running, or almost constant walking and pacing. Studies with animals suggest that the increased activity may be a result of the fasting. When rats are deprived of food, they will spend more and more time running in a wheel if one is available, even though doing so means that the animals will lose weight faster (Routtenberg, 1968). Some investigators believe that the exercise stimulates the breakdown of lipids into fatty acids and glycerol and thus actually reduces feelings of hunger. Wilckens, Schweiger, and Pirke (1992) found that deprivation-induced wheel running can be inhibited by drugs that stimulate 5-HT$_{1C}$ receptors.

The fact that anorexia nervosa is seen primarily in young women has prompted both biological and social explanations. Most psychologists favor the latter, concluding that the emphasis our society places on slimness—especially in women—is responsible for this disorder. However, the success of therapy is not especially encouraging; Ratnasuriya et al. (1991) reported that twenty years later, only 29 percent of a group of patients treated for anorexia nervosa showed a good recovery. Almost 15 percent of the patients had died of suicide or complications of the disease. Many anorexics suffer from osteoporosis, and bone fractures are common. When the weight loss becomes severe enough, they cease menstruating.

There is good evidence, primarily from twin studies, that hereditary factors play an important role in the development of anorexia (Russell and Treasure, 1989; Wal-

Anorexia nervosa A disorder that most frequently afflicts young women; exaggerated concern with overweight that leads to excessive dieting and often compulsive exercising; can lead to starvation.

Bulimia nervosa Bouts of excessive hunger and eating, often followed by forced vomiting or purging with laxatives; sometimes seen in people with anorexia nervosa.

ters and Kendler, 1995). The existence of hereditary factors suggests that abnormalities in physiological mechanisms may be involved. As you might suspect, many investigators have suggested that anorexia and bulimia may be caused by biochemical or structural abnormalities in the brain mechanisms that control metabolism or eating. In a review of the literature, Fava et al. (1989) reported that studies have found evidence for changes in NE, 5-HT, and opioids in people with anorexia nervosa and changes in NE and 5-HT in people with bulimia nervosa. Many studies have reported changes in endocrine levels of anorexic patients, but these changes are probably effects of the disorder, not causes. In most cases, when a patient recovers, the endocrine system returns to normal.

Some investigators have suggested that neuropeptide Y may play a role in anorexia (Kaye et al., 1990; Kaye, 1996). Kaye and his colleagues found elevated levels of NPY in the cerebrospinal fluid of severely underweight anorexics. However, once the patients regained their normal weights, the levels of the peptide returned to normal. The investigators suggested that the increased level of NPY is a response to the loss of weight and at least partly accounts for the obsession with food that is typical in anorexia.

We cannot rule out the possibility that some biochemical disturbance in brain functions related to metabolism or food intake underlie anorexia nervosa. Measurement of neurotransmitters, neuromodulators, and their metabolites in the cerebrospinal fluid is a crude and indirect indication of the release and activity of these substances in the brain. Unfortunately, we do not have a good animal model of anorexia to study in the laboratory.

Researchers have tried to treat anorexia nervosa with many drugs that increase appetite in nonanorexics or in laboratory animals—for example, antipsychotic medications, drugs that stimulate adrenergic α_2 receptors, L-DOPA, and THC (the active ingredient in marijuana). Unfortunately, none of these drugs have shown themselves to be helpful (Mitchell, 1989). One study (Halmi et al., 1986) found that cyproheptadine, an antihistaminergic drug that also has an antiserotonergic effect, may speed the recovery of anorexics. The drug aided only patients who did not exhibit bulimia; the drug actually interfered with the recovery of those who did exhibit bulimia. These results have not yet been confirmed by other investigators. In any event, the fact that anorexics are often obsessed with food (and show high levels of neuropeptide Y in their CSF) suggests that the disorder is not caused by the absence of hunger. Researchers have had better luck with bulimia nervosa; several studies suggest that serotonin agonists such as fenfluramine (also used to treat obesity) and fluoxetine (an antidepressant drug that is best known as Prozac) may aid in the treatment of this disorder (Kennedy and Goldbloom, 1991; Advokat and Kutlesic, 1995).

Anorexia nervosa is a serious condition; understanding its causes is more than an academic matter. We can hope that research on the biological and social control of feeding and metabolism will help us understand this puzzling and dangerous disorder.

INTERIM SUMMARY

Two sets of eating disorders—obesity and anorexia/bulimia nervosa—present serious health problems. Although environmental effects, such as learning to eat everything on the plate and arranging food in appetizing courses, may contribute to overeating, the most important cause appears to be an efficient metabolism, which permits fat to accumulate easily. Metabolic rates are controlled by hereditary and environmental factors. Adoption studies find no evidence that a person's early family environment has a significant effect on his or her body weight in adulthood. But other environmental factors do play an important role in the development of obesity. A high percentage of Pima Indians who live in the United States and consume a high-fat diet become obese and, as a consequence, develop diabetes. In contrast, Mexican Pima Indians, who work hard at subsistence farming and eat a low-fat diet, remain thin and have a low incidence of obesity.

So far, there is little evidence that obesity in humans is related to a deficient secretion of leptin, as it is in ob mice; in general, obese people have very high levels of leptin in their blood. Nor is there good evidence that obese people have faulty leptin receptors, as do db mice and Zucker rats. One possible reason for insensitivity to leptin in obese people might be inefficient transport of leptin through the blood-brain barrier.

Anorexia nervosa is a serious—even life-threatening—disorder. Although anorexic patients avoid eating, they often remain preoccupied with food, and their insulin level rises when they are presented with an appetizing stimulus. Bulimia nervosa (sometimes associated with anorexia) consists of periodic binging and purging.

Researchers are beginning to study possible abnormalities in the regulation of transmitter substances and neuropeptides that seem to play a role in normal control of feeding to see whether medical treatments for anorexia and bulimia can be discovered. So far, no useful drugs have been found to treat anorexia nervosa; but fenfluramine—a serotonin agonist that is also used to treat obesity—and fluoxetine—a serotonin agonist that is used to treat depression—may help to suppress episodes of bulimia.

THOUGHT QUESTIONS

1. One of the last prejudices that people admit to publicly is a dislike of fat people. Is this fair, given that genetic differences in metabolism are such an important cause of obesity?
2. Undoubtedly, anorexia has both environmental and physiological causes. Do you think that sex differences in the incidence of this disorder (that is, the fact that almost all anorexics are female) is entirely caused by social factors (such as the emphasis on thinness in our society) or do you think that biological factors (such as hormonal differences) also play a role?

EPILOGUE

Scalpels and Devices

As Emily and Jonathan, the students discussed at the beginning of the chapter, came to realize, some people become fat without eating enormous quantities of food. Heredity has given them efficient metabolisms that, in societies where food is plentiful, make weight gain easy and weight loss difficult. Of course, some fat people *do* eat enormous amounts of food; they may be addicted to eating the way some people are addicted to drugs.

Whatever the cause of obesity, the metabolic fact of life is this: If calories in exceed calories out, then body fat will increase. Because it is difficult to increase the "calories out" side of the equation enough to bring an obese

person's weight back to normal, most treatments for obesity attempt to reduce the "calories in." The extraordinary difficulty that obese people have in reducing caloric intake for a sustained period of time (that is, for the rest of their lives) has led to the development of some extraordinary means. The rest of this discussion will describe mechanical and surgical methods that have been devised to make obese people eat less.

To eat, we must open our mouths. This obvious fact led to the development of jaw wiring, a procedure in which wires are attached to a person's teeth to keep the jaw from opening. The patient is not left to starve;

he or she is given a liquid diet to sip through a straw. Of course, there is no guarantee that a person will ingest fewer calories each day simply because he or she is deprived of the opportunity to chew. In fact, Munro et al. (1987) reported that some of their patients managed to *gain* weight on a liquid diet. However, many patients do manage to lose weight. Unfortunately, almost all of them regain it once the wires are removed, and many become even more obese than they were when they started out.

To reduce the recidivism rate, some therapists have fastened a nylon cord around the waist of their patients after they had lost weight through a jaw-wiring procedure. The ends of the cord were fused together so that the cord could not be removed without cutting it. Unfortunately, about half of the patients did just that.

Surgeons have also become involved in trying to help obese people lose weight. The procedures they have developed either reduce the amount of food that can be eaten during a meal or interfere with absorption of calories from the intestines. Surgery has been aimed at the stomach, the small intestine, or both.

The most common surgical procedure for reducing food intake has been to make the person's stomach smaller. Early procedures actually removed some of the stomach, but more recent methods have stapled part of it shut or have put bands around it so that it can expand only a limited amount, a procedure known as *gastroplasty* (literally, "a reshaping of the stomach"). Ideally, gastroplasty should result in a feeling of satiety after the ingestion of a small amount of food. But in fact, the surgery usually produces *nimiety*, or an aversive feeling of overfullness (from the Latin *nimius*, "excessive"). The meal stops not because the patients feel satisfied but because they feel so uncomfortable that they cannot go on.

Surgeons have developed several procedures that reduce the absorption of food from the intestines. All of

these procedures rearrange the intestines so that food takes a shorter path to the large intestine, leaving less time for nutrients to be absorbed. The unabsorbed nutrients are evacuated from the body, of course, so it should come as no surprise that diarrhea and flatulence (excessive intestinal gas) are commonly associated with these procedure. Many types of intestinal bypass operations do not simply interfere with absorption; they also reduce food intake by producing nimiety. After some surgical procedures, relatively undigested food is dumped into regions of the intestines that normally receive only well-digested food, and the result is a feeling of discomfort.

Besides producing diarrhea and flatulence, intestinal bypass surgery can produce undesirable side effects such as bacterial overgrowth and production of toxins in a bypassed segment of intestine; deficiencies of iron, vitamin B_{12}, vitamin B_1, or protein; and abnormalities in calcium metabolism. A severe vitamin B_1 (thiamine) deficiency can damage the nervous system; as you will learn in Chapter 12, the result can be a permanent memory loss. Of course, if, after the surgery, a patient's condition is carefully monitored by a physician, these complications can be avoided or corrected; but not all patients cooperate with their physicians for postsurgical care.

To avoid the necessity of surgery, some therapists have tried putting balloons in people's stomachs and inflating them to reduce the amount of food they will hold. The results have not been entirely successful; as Kral (1989) noted, "After a brief period of extraordinary financial success for the gastroenterologists placing the balloons, the 'Gastric Bubble' has been taken off the market in the United States, largely because of proven lack of efficacy and the realization that chronic balloon placement is not tolerated by the gastric mucosa" (p. 254).

The variety of methods—surgical, mechanical, behavioral, and pharmacological—that therapists and surgeons have developed to treat obesity attests to the tenacity of the problem. The basic difficulty, beyond that caused by having an efficient metabolism, is that eating is pleasurable and satiety signals are easy to ignore or override. Despite the fact that relatively little success has been seen until now, I am personally optimistic about what the future may hold. I think that if we learn more about the physiology of hunger signals, satiety signals, and the reinforcement provided by eating, we will be able to develop drugs that attenuate the signals that encourage us to eat and strengthen those that encourage us to stop eating.

KEY CONCEPTS

PHYSIOLOGICAL REGULATORY SYSTEMS

1. Regulatory systems include four essential features: a system variable, a set point, a detector, and a correctional mechanism. Because of the time it takes for substances to be absorbed from the digestive system, eating and drinking behaviors are also controlled by satiety mechanisms.

DRINKING

2. The body's water is located in the intracellular and extracellular compartments; the latter consist of the interstitial fluid and the blood plasma.
3. Normal loss of water depletes both major compartments and produces both osmometric and volumetric thirst.

4. Osmometric thirst is detected by neurons in the OVLT and surrounding parts of the anterior hypothalamus; volumetric thirst is detected by the kidney, which secretes an enzyme that produces angiotensin, and by baroreceptors in the atria of the heart, which communicate directly with the brain.

EATING AND METABOLISM

5. The body has two nutrient reservoirs: a short-term reservoir containing glycogen (a carbohydrate) and a long-term reservoir containing fats.
6. Metabolism is divided into the absorptive and fasting phases, controlled primarily by the hormones insulin and glucagon.

WHAT STARTS A MEAL?

7. Hunger is affected by social and environmental factors, such as time of day and the presence of other people.
8. The most important physiological signal for hunger occurs when receptors located in the liver and the brain signal a low availability of nutrients.

WHAT STOPS A MEAL?

9. Satiety is controlled by receptors in several locations. Nutrient receptors in the stomach send signals to the brain. The release of CCK by the duodenum may decrease food intake by its effects on neurons serving the pyloric region. Receptors in the small intestines and in the liver detect the presence of nutrients of a meal that is being digested and absorbed into the body.

NEURAL MECHANISMS

10. Neural mechanisms in the brain stem are able to control acceptance or rejection of food, even when they are isolated from the forebrain. The area postrema and the nucleus of the solitary tract (AP/NST) appear to be particularly important.
11. The hypothalamus in involved in the control of eating. Damage to the lateral hypothalamus decreases food intake, and release of neuropeptide Y in this region causes ravenous eating. The release of galanin stimulates an appetite for fats.
12. Well-fed adipose tissue releases a hormone, leptin, that suppresses eating by binding with leptin receptors on neuropeptide Y–secreting neurons in the paraventricular nucleus of the hypothalamus, inhibiting them.

EATING DISORDERS

13. An important cause of obesity is an efficient metabolism, which may have a genetic basis.
14. Drugs that activate leptin receptors, inhibit the release of neuropeptide Y, or block neuropeptide Y receptors may be helpful in treating obesity.
15. Some investigators believe that physiological mechanisms such as misregulation of the release of 5-HT or neuropeptide Y in the hypothalamus may play a role in anorexia nervosa, but so far evidence is lacking.

SUGGESTED READINGS

Bouchard, C., and Bray, G.A. *Regulation of Body Weight: Biological and Behavioral Mechanisms.* New York: John Wiley & Sons, 1996.

Brownell, K.D., and Fairburn, C.G. *Eating Disorders and Obesity: A Comprehensive Handbook.* New York: Guilford Press, 1995.

Capaldi, E.D. *Why We Eat What We Eat: The Psychology of Eating.* Washington, DC: American Psychological Association, 1996.

Johnson, A.K., and Edwards, G.L. The neuroendocrinology of thirst: Afferent signaling and mechanisms of central integration. *Current Topics in Neuroendocrinology,* 1990, *10,* 149–190.

Legg, C.R., and Booth, D.A. *Appetite: Neural and Behavioural Bases.* Oxford: Oxford University Press, 1994.

Le Magnen, J. *Neurobiology of Feeding and Nutrition.* San Diego: Academic Press, 1992.

Stricker, E.M. *Handbook of Behavioral Neurobiology. Vol. 10: Neurobiology of Food and Fluid Intake.* New York: Plenum Press, 1990.

Ritter, S., Ritter, R.C., and Barnes, C.D. *Neuroanatomy and Physiology of Abdominal Vagal Afferents.* Boca Raton, FL: CRC Press, 1992.

12

Learning and Memory

LEARNING OBJECTIVES

1. Describe each of four basic forms of learning: perceptual learning, stimulus–response learning, motor learning, and relational learning.
2. Describe the anatomy of the hippocampus, describe the establishment of long-term potentiation, and discuss the role of NMDA receptors in this phenomenon.
3. Discuss research on the physiological basis of synaptic plasticity during long-term potentiation.
4. Describe research on the role of the inferior temporal cortex in visual perceptual learning.
5. Discuss the physiology of the classically conditioned emotional response to aversive stimuli.
6. Describe the role of the basal ganglia in instrumental conditioning and motor learning.
7. Describe the role of dopamine in reinforcing brain stimulation, and discuss the effects of systemic administration of dopamine antagonists and agonists.
8. Discuss how the reinforcement system may detect reinforcing stimuli and strengthen synaptic connections.
9. Describe the nature of human anterograde amnesia and explain what it suggests about the organization of learning.
10. Describe the role of the hippocampus in relational learning, including spatial learning, and discuss the function of hippocampal place cells.
11. Outline a possible explanation for the role of the hippocampal formation in learning and memory.

Coming Back for More

In 1954, James Olds, a young assistant professor, designed an experiment to determine whether the reticular formation might play a role in learning. Recent studies had suggested that the reticular formation was involved in arousal; when it was active, it would apparently increase an animal's attention and vigilance. Olds decided to place an electrode in the brains of rats to electrically stimulate the reticular formation. Perhaps the stimulation would increase the rats' attention to their environment and facilitate their learning a maze. If the stimulated animals learned the task faster than those that were not stimulated, his hypothesis would have strong support.

Olds enlisted the aid of Peter Milner, a graduate student who had experience with the surgical procedure needed to implant the electrodes in the brain. Because the procedure had only recently been developed and was not very accurate, one of the electrodes wound up in the wrong place—near the opposite end of the brain, in fact. This accident was a lucky one for the investigators, because they discovered a phenomenon that they would not have seen if the electrode had been located where they had intended it to be.

Olds and Milner had heard a talk by another physiological psychologist, Neal Miller, who reported that he had discovered that electrical stimulation of some parts of the brain could be aversive; the animals would work to avoid having the current turned on. The investigators decided that before they began their study, they would make sure that aversive stimulation was not occurring, because it might interfere with the animals' performance in the maze. The behavior of most of the animals was unremarkable, but here is Olds's report of what happened when he tested the rat with the misplaced electrode:

> I applied a brief train of 60-cycle sine-wave electrical current whenever the animal entered one corner of the enclosure. The animal did not stay away from that corner, but rather came back quickly after a brief sortie which followed the first stimulation and came back even more quickly after a briefer sortie which followed the second stimulation. By the time the third electrical stimulus had been applied the animal seemed indubitably to be "coming back for more." (Olds, 1973, p. 81)

Realizing that they had just seen something very important, Olds and Milner put more electrodes in rats' brains and allowed the rats to press a switch that controlled the current to the brain. The rats quickly learned to press the switch at a rate of over seven hundred times per hour. Subsequent studies obtained response rates of several thousand presses per hour. It turned out that the reinforcing effect of the electrical brain stimulation was very potent; when given a choice between pressing the lever and eating, drinking, or copulating, animals would choose the lever.

Olds and Milner's discovery probably had more impact on psychology than any other experiment performed by physiological psychologists. Articles in the popular press speculated on the nature of the "pleasure centers" in the brain. Some writers warned that a totalitarian society might one day control its population by putting electrodes in their brains and providing rewarding stimulation when they did what they were supposed to and withholding it when they did not. Such speculations prompted Eliot Valenstein to write a book demystifying the phenomenon, putting it in perspective (Valenstein, 1973).

The interest in reinforcing brain stimulation has peaked, but because the circuits discovered by Olds and Milner are responsible for the powerful addictive potential of drugs such as cocaine, the research they began is still continuing. Many investigators are trying to understand the function these circuits play and how they relate to the effects of addictive drugs and the effectiveness of natural reinforcers. (By the way, it turns out that electrical stimulation of the reticular formation does *not* facilitate learning, but that is another story.)

Experiences change us; encounters with our environment alter our behavior by modifying our nervous system. As many investigators have said, an understanding of the physiology of memory is the ultimate challenge to neuroscience research. The brain is complex, and so are learning and remembering. Although the individual changes that occur within the cells of the brain may be relatively simple, the brain consists of many billions of neurons. Therefore, isolating and identifying the particular changes that are responsible for a particular memory are exceedingly difficult. Similarly, although the elements of a particular learning task may be simple, its implications for an organism may be complex. The behavior that the investigator observes and measures may be only one of many that change as a result of an experience. However, despite the difficulties, the long years of work finally seem to be paying off. New approaches and new methods have evolved from old ones, and real progress has been made in understanding the anatomy and physiology of learning and remembering.

■ THE NATURE OF LEARNING

Learning refers to the process by which experiences change our nervous system and hence our behavior. We refer to these changes as *memories*. Although it is convenient to describe memories as if they were notes placed in filing cabinets, this is certainly not the way experiences are reflected within the brain. Experiences are not "stored"; rather, they change the way we perceive, perform, think, and plan. They do so by physically changing the structure of the nervous system, altering neural circuits that participate in perceiving, performing, thinking, and planning.

Learning can take at least four basic forms: perceptual learning, stimulus–response learning, motor learning, and relational learning. **Perceptual learning** is the ability to learn to recognize stimuli that have been perceived before. The primary function of this type of learning is the ability to identify and categorize objects (including other members of our own species) and situations. Unless we have learned to recognize something, we cannot learn how we should behave with respect to it— we will not profit from our experiences with it, and profiting from experience is what learning is all about.

Each of our sensory systems is capable of perceptual learning. We can learn to recognize objects by their visual appearance, the sounds they make, how they feel, or how they smell. We can recognize people by the shape of their faces, the movements they make when they walk, or the sound of their voices. When we hear people talk, we can recognize the words they are saying and perhaps their emotional state. As we shall see, perceptual learning appears to be accomplished primarily by changes in the sensory association cortex. That is, learning to recognize complex visual stimuli involves changes in the visual association cortex, learning to recognize complex auditory stimuli involves changes in the auditory association cortex, and so on.

Stimulus–response learning is the ability to learn to perform a particular behavior when a particular stimulus is present. Thus, it involves the establishment of connections between circuits involved in perception and those involved in movement. The behavior could be an automatic response such as a defensive reflex, or it could be a complicated sequence of movements that was learned previously. Stimulus–response learning includes two major categories of learning that psychologists have studied extensively: *classical conditioning* and *instrumental conditioning*.

Classical conditioning is a form of learning in which an unimportant stimulus acquires the properties of an important one. It involves an *association between two stimuli*. A stimulus that previously had little effect on behavior becomes able to evoke a reflexive, species-typical behavior. For example, a defensive eyeblink response can be conditioned to a tone. If we direct a brief puff of air toward a rabbit's eye, the eye will automatically blink. The response is called an **unconditional response (UR)** because it occurs unconditionally, without any special training. The stimulus that produces it (the puff of air) is called an **unconditional stimulus (US).** Now we begin the training. We present a series of brief 1000-Hz tones, each followed 500 ms later by a puff of air. After several trials, the rabbit's eye begins to close even before the puff of air occurs. Classical conditioning has occurred; the **conditional stimulus (CS**—the 1000-Hz tone) now elicits the **conditional response (CR**—the eye blink). (See *Figure 12.1*.)

When classical conditioning takes place, what kinds of changes occur in the brain? Figure 12.1 shows a simplified neural circuit that could account for this type of learn-

Perceptual learning Learning to recognize a particular stimulus.

Stimulus–response learning Learning to automatically make a particular response in the presence of a particular stimulus; includes classical and instrumental conditioning.

Classical conditioning A learning procedure; when a stimulus that initially produces no particular response is followed several times by an **unconditional stimulus (US)** that produces a defensive or appetitive response (the **unconditional response, UR**), the first stimulus (now called a **conditional stimulus, CS**) itself evokes the response (now called a **conditional response, CR**).

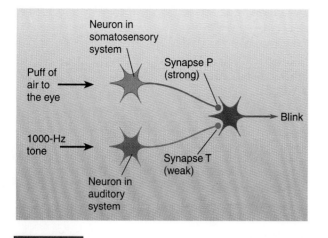

FIGURE 12.1

A simple neural model of classical conditioning. When the 1000-Hz tone is presented just before the puff of air to the eye, synapse T is strengthened.

Hebb rule The hypothesis proposed by Donald Hebb that the cellular basis of learning involves strengthening of a synapse that is repeatedly active when the postsynaptic neuron fires.

Instrumental conditioning A learning procedure whereby the effects of a particular behavior in a particular situation increase (reinforce) or decrease (punish) the probability of the behavior; also called *operant conditioning.*

Reinforcing stimulus An appetitive stimulus that follows a particular behavior and thus makes the behavior become more frequent.

Punishing stimulus An aversive stimulus that follows a particular behavior and thus makes the behavior become less frequent.

ing. For the sake of simplicity, we will assume that the US (the puff of air) is detected by a single neuron in the somatosensory system, and the CS (the 1000-Hz tone) is detected by a single neuron in the auditory system. We will also assume that the response—the eyeblink—is controlled by a single neuron in the motor system. (See *Figure 12.1.*)

Now let's see how the circuits work. If we present a 1000-Hz tone, we find that the animal makes no reaction, because the synapse connecting the tone-sensitive neuron with the neuron in the motor system is weak. However, if we present a puff of air to the eye, the eye blinks. This reaction occurs because nature has provided the animal with a strong synapse between the somatosensory neuron and the motor neuron that causes a blink (synapse P, for "puff"). To establish classical conditioning, we first present the 1000-Hz tone and then almost immediately follow it with a puff of air. After we repeat these pairs of stimuli several times, we find that we can dispense with the air puff; the 1000-Hz tone produces the blink all by itself.

Over forty years ago, Donald Hebb proposed a rule that might explain how neurons are changed by experience in a way that would cause changes in behavior (Hebb, 1949). The **Hebb rule** says that if a synapse repeatedly becomes active at about the same time that the postsynaptic neuron fires, changes will take place in the structure or chemistry of the synapse that will strengthen it. How would the Hebb rule apply to our circuit? If the 1000-Hz tone is presented first, then weak synapse T (for "tone") becomes active. If the puff is presented immediately afterward, then strong synapse P becomes active and makes the motor neuron fire. The act of firing then strengthens any synapse with the motor neuron *that has just been active.* Of course, this means synapse T. After several pairings of the two stimuli, and after several increments of strengthening, synapse T becomes strong enough to cause the motor neuron to fire by itself. Learning has occurred. (See *Figure 12.1.*)

When Hebb formulated his rule, he was unable to determine whether it was true or false. Now, finally, enough progress has been made in laboratory techniques that the strength of individual synapses can be determined, and investigators are studying the physiological bases of learning. We will see the results of some of these approaches in the next section of this chapter.

The second major class of stimulus–response learning is **instrumental conditioning** (also called *operant conditioning*). Whereas classical conditioning involves automatic, species-typical responses, instrumental conditioning involves behaviors that have been learned. And whereas classical conditioning involves an association between two stimuli, instrumental conditioning involves an *association between a response and a stimulus.* Instrumental conditioning is a more flexible form of learning. It permits an organism to adjust its behavior according to the consequences of that behavior. That is, when a behavior is followed by favorable consequences, the behavior tends to occur more frequently; when it is followed by unfavorable consequences, it tends to occur less frequently. Collectively, "favorable consequences" are referred to as **reinforcing stimuli,** and "unfavorable consequences" are referred to as **punishing stimuli.** For example, a response that enables a hungry organism to find food will be reinforced, and a response that causes pain will be punished. (Psychologists often refer to these terms as *reinforcers* and *punishers.*)

Let's consider the process of reinforcement. Briefly stated, reinforcement causes changes in an animal's nervous system that increase the likelihood that a particular stimulus will elicit a particular response. For example, when a hungry rat is first put in an operant chamber (a "Skinner box"), it is not very likely to press the lever mounted on a wall. However, if it does press the lever, and if it receives a piece of food immediately afterward, the likelihood of making another response increases. Put an-

FIGURE 12.2

A simple neural model of instrumental conditioning.

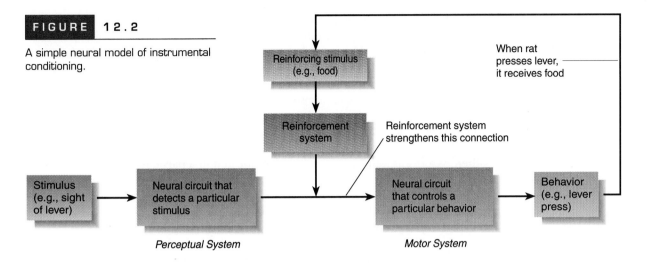

other way, reinforcement causes the sight of the lever to serve as the stimulus that elicits the lever-pressing response. It is not accurate to say simply that a particular behavior becomes more frequent. If no lever is present, a rat that has learned to press one will not wave its paw around in the air. The *sight of a lever* is needed to produce the response. Thus, the process of reinforcement strengthens a connection between neural circuits involved in perception (the sight of the lever) and those involved in movement (the act of lever pressing). As we will see later in this chapter, the brain contains reinforcement mechanisms that control this process. (See ***Figure 12.2.***)

The third major category of learning, **motor learning,** is actually a component of stimulus–response learning. For simplicity's sake, we can think of perceptual learning as the establishment of changes within the sensory systems of the brain, stimulus–response learning as the establishment of connections between sensory systems and motor systems, and motor learning as the establishment of changes within motor systems. But, in fact, motor learning cannot occur without sensory guidance from the environment. For example, most skilled movements involve interactions with objects: bicycles, pinball machines, knitting needles, and so on. Even skilled movements that we make by ourselves, such as solitary dance steps, involve feedback from the joints, muscles, vestibular apparatus, eyes, and contact between the feet and the floor. Motor learning differs from other forms of learning primarily in the degree to which new forms of behavior are learned; the more novel the behavior, the more the neural circuits in the motor systems of the brain must be modified. (See ***Figure 12.3.***)

A particular learning situation can involve varying amounts of all three types of learning that I have described so far: perceptual, stimulus–response, and motor. For example, if we teach an animal to make a new response whenever we present a stimulus it has never seen before, it must learn to recognize the stimulus (perceptual learning) and make the response (motor learning), and a connection must be established between these two new memories (stimulus–response learning). If we

Motor learning Learning to make a new response.

FIGURE 12.3

An overview of perceptual, stimulus–response (S–R), and motor learning.

teach it to make a response that it has already learned whenever we present a new stimulus, only perceptual learning and stimulus–response learning will take place.

The three forms of learning I have described so far consist primarily of changes in one sensory system, between one sensory system and the motor system, or in the motor system. But obviously, learning is usually more complex than that. The fourth form of learning, **relational learning,** involves learning the *relations* among individual stimuli. For example, consider what we must learn to become familiar with the contents of a room. First, we must learn to recognize each of the objects. But then, in addition, we must learn the relative locations of the objects with respect to each other. As a result, when we find ourselves located in a particular place in the room, our perceptions of these objects and their locations relative to us tell us exactly where we are. Thus, spatial learning is a form of relational learning.

Other types of relational learning are even more complex. *Episodic learning*—remembering sequences of events (episodes) that we witness—requires us to keep track not only of individual stimuli but also of the order in which they occur. *Observational learning*—learning by watching and imitating other people—requires us to remember what someone else does, the situation in which the behavior is performed, and the relation between the other person's movements and our own. As we will see in the last section of this chapter, a special system that involves the hippocampus and associated structures appears to perform coordinating functions that are necessary for many types of learning that go beyond single regions of the cerebral cortex.

INTERIM SUMMARY

Learning produces changes in the way we perceive, act, think, and feel. It does so by producing changes in the nervous system in the circuits responsible for perception, in those responsible for the control of movement, and in connections between the two.

Perceptual learning consists primarily of changes in perceptual systems that make it possible for us to recognize stimuli so that we can respond to them appropriately. Stimulus–response learning consists of connections between perceptual and motor systems. The most important forms are classical and instrumental conditioning. Classical conditioning occurs when a neutral stimulus is followed by an unconditional stimulus (US) that naturally elicits an unconditional response (UR). After this pairing, the neutral stimulus becomes a conditional stimulus (CS); it now elicits the conditional response (CR) by itself.

Instrumental conditioning occurs when a response is followed by a reinforcing stimulus, such as a drink of water for a thirsty animal. The reinforcing stimulus increases the likelihood that the other stimuli that are present when the response was made will evoke the response. Both forms of stimulus–response learning may occur as a result of strengthened synaptic connections, as described by the Hebb rule.

Motor learning, although it may primarily involve changes within neural circuits that control movement, is guided by sensory stimuli; thus, it is actually a form of stimulus–response learning. Relational learning, the most complex form of learning, is described later in this chapter. It includes the ability to recognize objects through more than one sensory modality, to recognize the relative location of objects in the environment, and to remember the sequence in which events occurred during particular episodes.

Relational learning A complex form of learning that involves the relations among individual stimuli; includes spatial learning, episodic learning, and observational learning.

THOUGHT QUESTIONS

Can you think of specific examples of each of the categories of learning described in this section? Can you think of some examples that include more than one category?

LEARNING AND SYNAPTIC PLASTICITY

On theoretical considerations alone, it would appear that learning must involve synaptic plasticity—changes in the structure or biochemistry of synapses that alter their effects on postsynaptic neurons. But what might trigger these changes? As we saw in the first section of this chapter, the Hebb rule states that if a synapse is active at about the same time that the postsynaptic neuron is active, that synapse will be strengthened. Research on a phenomenon that was originally discovered in the hippocampal formation has discovered at least one way that the Hebb rule may operate.

Induction of Long-Term Potentiation

Electrical stimulation of circuits within the hippocampal formation can lead to long-term synaptic changes that seem to be among those responsible for learning. Lømo (1966) discovered that intense electrical stimulation of axons leading from the entorhinal cortex to the dentate gyrus caused a long-term increase in the magnitude of excitatory postsynaptic potentials in the postsynaptic cells; this increase has come to be called **long-term potentiation.** (The word *potentiate* means "to strengthen, to make more potent.")

First, let's review some anatomy. The **hippocampal formation** is a specialized region of the limbic cortex located in the temporal lobe. (Its location in a human brain is shown in Figure 3.12.) Because the hippocampal formation is folded in one dimension and then curved in another, it has a complex, three-dimensional shape. Thus, it is difficult to show what it looks like with a diagram on a two-dimensional sheet of paper. Fortunately, the structure of the hippocampal formation is orderly; a slice taken anywhere contains the same set of circuits.

Figure 12.4 shows a slice of the hippocampal formation, illustrating a typical procedure for producing long-term potentiation. The primary input to the hippocampal formation comes from the entorhinal cortex. The axons of neurons in the entorhinal cortex pass through the *perforant path* and form synapses with the granule cells of the *dentate gyrus.* A stimulating electrode is placed in the perforant path, and a recording electrode is placed in the dentate gyrus, near the granule cells. (See *Figure 12.4.*) First, a single pulse of electrical stimulation is delivered to the perforant

Long-term potentiation A long-term increase in the excitability of a neuron to a particular synaptic input caused by repeated high-frequency activity of that input.

Hippocampal formation A forebrain structure of the temporal lobe, constituting an important part of the limbic system; includes the hippocampus proper (Ammon's horn), dentate gyrus, and subiculum.

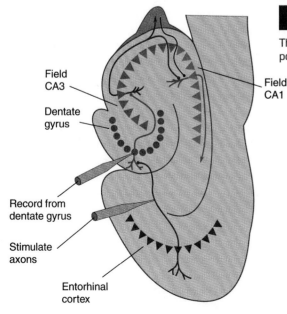

FIGURE 12.4

The procedure for producing long-term potentiation.

Before long-term potentiation

After long-term potentiation

Population EPSP

1 hour

24 hours

48 hours

72 hours

96 hours

FIGURE 12.5

Population EPSPs recorded from the dentate gyrus before and after electrical stimulation that led to long-term potentiation.

(From Berger, T.W. Science, 1984, 224, 627–630. Copyright 1984 by the American Association for the Advancement of Science.)

Population EPSP An evoked potential that represents the EPSPs of a population of neurons.

Associative long-term potentiation A long-term potentiation in which concurrent stimulation of weak and strong synapses to a given neuron strengthens the weak ones.

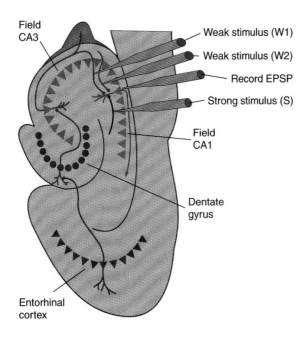

path, and then the resulting population EPSP is recorded in the dentate gyrus. The **population EPSP** is an extracellular measurement of the excitatory postsynaptic potentials (EPSP) produced by the synapses of the perforant path axons with the dentate granule cells. The size of the first population EPSP indicates the strength of the synaptic connections before long-term potentiation has taken place. Long-term potentiation can be induced by stimulating the axons in the perforant path with a burst of approximately one hundred pulses of electrical stimulation, delivered within a few seconds. Evidence that long-term potentiation has occurred is obtained by periodically delivering single pulses to the perforant path and recording the response in the dentate gyrus. If the response is greater than it was before the burst of pulses was delivered, long-term potentiation has occurred. (See *Figure 12.5.*)

Long-term potentiation can be produced in other regions of the hippocampal formation and, as we shall see, in other places in the brain. It can last for several months (Bliss and Lømo, 1973). It can be produced in isolated slices of the hippocampal formation as well as in the brains of living animals, which allows researchers to stimulate and record from individual neurons and to analyze biochemical changes. The brain is removed from the skull, the hippocampal complex is dissected, and slices are placed in a temperature-controlled chamber filled with liquid that resembles interstitial fluid.

Many experiments have demonstrated that long-term potentiation in hippocampal slices can follow the Hebb rule. That is, when weak and strong synapses to a single neuron are stimulated at approximately the same time, the weak synapse becomes strengthened. This phenomenon is called **associative long-term potentiation,** because it is produced by the association (in time) between the activity of the two sets of synapses. Kelso and Brown (1986) stimulated two different weak inputs (W1 and W2) and one strong input (S) to pyramidal cells in the CA1 field. (See *Figure 12.6.*) In some cases they paired W1 with S; in others they paired W2 with S. They found that only the synapses that were stimulated at the same time as the strong input were strengthened. (See *Figure 12.7.*) These results are particularly important because they indicate that the pairing did not simply make the CA1 pyramidal cells become more sensitive to *all* its inputs. Thus, the strengthening occurs in *specific synapses.*

Role of NMDA Receptors

Long-term potentiation requires some sort of additive effect. That is, a series of pulses delivered at a high rate all in one burst will produce long-term potentiation, but the same number of pulses given at a slow rate will not. The reason for this phenomenon is now clear. Several experiments have shown that synaptic strengthening occurs when molecules of the neuro-

FIGURE 12.6

The procedure used by Kelso and Brown (1986) to demonstrate associative long-term potentiation.

transmitter bind with postsynaptic receptors located in a dendritic spine that is already depolarized. Kelso, Ganong, and Brown (1986) found that if they artificially depolarized CA1 neurons and then stimulated the axons that formed synapses with them, the synapses became stronger. However, if the stimulation of the synapses and the depolarization of the neuron occurred at different times, no effect was seen; thus, the two events had to occur together. (See *Figure 12.8*.)

Experiments such as the ones I just described indicate that long-term potentiation requires two events: activation of synapses and depolarization of the postsynaptic neuron. The explanation for this phenomenon, at least in some parts of the brain, lies in the characteristics of a very special receptor. As we saw in Chapter 4, the most important excitatory neurotransmitter in the brain is glutamic acid (usually referred to as *glutamate*). We also saw that the postsynaptic effects of glutamate are mediated by several different types of receptors. One of them, the NMDA receptor (short for *N*-methyl-D-aspartate), plays a critical role in long-term potentiation.

The **NMDA receptor** has some unusual properties. It is found in the hippocampal formation, especially in field CA1. The NMDA receptor controls a calcium ion channel. However, this channel is normally blocked by a magnesium ion (Mg^{2+}), which prevents calcium ions from entering the cell, even when the receptor is stimulated by glutamate. But if the postsynaptic membrane is depolarized, the Mg^{2+} is ejected from the ion channel, and the channel is free to admit Ca^{2+} ions. Thus, calcium ions enter the cells through the channels controlled by NMDA receptors only when glutamate is present *and* when the postsynaptic membrane is already depolarized. That means that the ion channel

FIGURE **12.7**

Differential associative long-term potentiation.

(Data from Kelso, S.R., and Brown, T.H. Science, 1986, 232, 85–87.)

NMDA receptor A specialized ionotropic glutamate receptor that controls a calcium channel that is normally blocked by Mg^{2+} ions; involved in long-term potentiation.

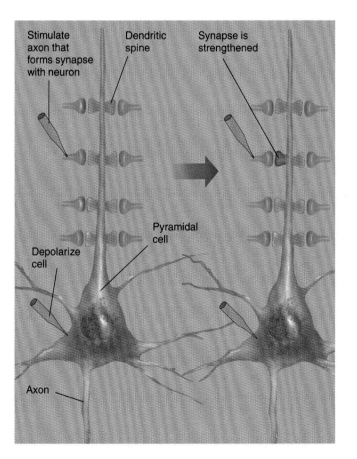

FIGURE **12.8**

Long-term potentiation. Synaptic strengthening occurs when synapses are active while the membrane of the postsynaptic cell is depolarized.

Molecule of glutamate

Before priming:
If a molecule of glutamate binds with NMDA receptor, calcium channel cannot open, because magnesium ion blocks channel

(a)

Priming:
An EPSP arrives from nearby synapses; depolarization evicts magnesium ion

(b)

Activation:
A molecule of glutamate binds with NMDA receptor, opens calcium channel

Because membrane is still depolarized, magnesium ion is still gone; calcium ion enters cell, initiates changes responsible for long-term potentiation

(c)

Ca²⁺ NMDA receptor Mg²⁺

FIGURE 12.9

The NMDA receptor. (a) Before priming. (b) Priming. Depolarization from nearby non-NMDA glutamate receptors evicts the magnesium ion. (c) Activation. When glutamate attaches to the binding site, the ion channel opens, allowing calcium ions to enter the dendritic spine.

AP5 2-amino-5-phosphonopentanoate; a drug that blocks NMDA receptors.

Dendritic spike An action potential that occurs in the dendrite of some types of pyramidal cells.

controlled by the NMDA receptor is a neurotransmitter- *and* voltage-dependent channel. (See *Figure 12.9.*)

The strongest evidence implicating NMDA receptors in long-term potentiation comes from research with drugs that block NMDA receptors, such as **AP5** (2-amino-5-phosphonopentanoate). AP5 prevents the establishment of long-term potentiation in field CA1 and the dentate gyrus.

Cell biologists have discovered that the calcium ion is used by many cells as a second messenger. The entry of calcium ions through the ion channels controlled by NMDA receptors is an essential step in long-term potentiation. Lynch et al. (1984) demonstrated this fact by injecting EGTA directly into hippocampal pyramidal cells. This chemical binds with calcium and makes it insoluble, destroying its biological activity. The EGTA blocked the establishment of long-term potentiation in the injected cells; their excitability was not increased by high-frequency stimulation of axons that formed synapses with them. However, neighboring cells, which were not injected with EGTA, showed long-term potentiation.

In Chapter 2 you learned that only axons are capable of producing action potentials. Actually, they can also occur in dendrites of some types of pyramidal cells, including those in field CA1 of the hippocampal formation. The threshold of excitation for **dendritic spikes** (as these action potentials are called) is rather high. As far as we know, they occur only when an action potential is triggered in the axon of the pyramidal cell. The backwash of depolarization across the cell body triggers a dendritic spike, which is propagated up the trunk of the dendrite. This means that whenever a pyramidal cell fires, all of its dendritic spines become depolarized for a brief time.

I think that considering what you already know about associative long-term potentiation, you can anticipate the role that NMDA receptors play in its establishment. If weak synapses are active by themselves, nothing happens, because the membrane of the dendritic spine does not depolarize sufficiently for the calcium channels controlled by the NMDA receptors to open. (Remember that for these channels to open, the postsynaptic membrane must depolarize and displace the Mg²⁺ ions that normally block them.) However, if the activity of strong synapses located elsewhere on the postsynaptic cell have caused the cell to fire, then a dendritic spike will depolarize the postsynaptic membrane enough for calcium to enter the ion channels controlled by the NMDA receptors. Thus, the special properties of NMDA receptors account not only for the existence of long-term potentiation but also for its associative nature. (See *Figure 12.10.*)

Long-term potentiation was discovered in the hippocampal formation and has been studied more in this region than in others, but it also occurs elsewhere in the brain. So far, it has been demonstrated in the prefrontal cortex, piriform cortex, entorhinal cortex, motor cortex, visual cortex, thalamus, and amygdala (Gerren and Weinberger, 1983; Clugnet and LeDoux, 1990; Aroniadou and Teyler, 1991; Baranyi, Szente, and Woody, 1991; Lynch et al., 1991). It has even been demonstrated in slices of human neocortex, removed during surgery to treat seizure disorders (Chen et al., 1996). NMDA receptors are probably involved in the potentiation that takes place in the piriform and entorhinal cortex and in the amygdala, but research on the role of these receptors in the other regions has not yet been reported. At least one form of

Action potential reaches terminal button of strong synapse; produces strong EPSP (depolarization) in pyramidal cell

Dendritic spine

Dendritic spike washes back along dendrite; primes NMDA receptors in dendritic spines

Action potential reaches terminal button; glutamate is released

Long-term potentiation: synapse is strengthened

Strong synapse

Dendrite of pyramidal cell

Dendritic spike

Depolarization is sufficient to trigger action potential in axon of pyramidal cell

Axon

Action potential in axon

FIGURE 12.10

Associative long-term potentiation. If the activity of strong synapses is sufficient to trigger an action potential in the neuron, the dendritic spike will depolarize the membrane of dendritic spines, priming NMDA receptors so that any weak synapses active at that time will become strengthened.

long-term potentiation that takes place in the visual cortex does not involve NMDA receptors (Aroniadou and Teyler, 1991). Thus, these receptors do not appear to be responsible for all forms of learning.

Mechanisms of Synaptic Plasticity

What is responsible for the increases in synaptic strength that occur during long-term potentiation? These increases could be caused by several different means. They could be produced presynaptically, through increased release of transmitter substance; or they could be produced postsynaptically, through an increased number of receptors or an increased ability of the receptors to activate changes in the permeability of the postsynaptic membrane. They could also be produced by an increased number of synapses, which would involve both presynaptic and postsynaptic changes. As we shall see, evidence indicates that there are postsynaptic changes, and probably presynaptic changes as well.

Several studies have found that NMDA-mediated long-term potentiation increases the number of postsynaptic **AMPA** receptors—that is, *non*-NMDA glutamate receptors. For example, Liao, Hessler, and Malinow (1995) recorded postsynaptic potentials produced by the activity of single synapses on dendritic spines of CA1 pyramidal cells. Initially, they found that the spines of many of the synapses contained only NMDA receptors. But after inducing long-term potentiation in the inputs to the cells, they found that the spines now contained AMPA receptors as well. Thus, one of the effects of long-term potentiation appears to be insertion of new AMPA receptors in the postsynaptic membrane. This increase in postsynaptic AMPA receptors makes the

AMPA receptor An ionotropic glutamate receptor that controls a sodium channel; when open, produces EPSPs.

postsynaptic membrane of the dendritic spine more sensitive to the release of glutamate by the presynaptic terminal button, strengthening the synapse.

Researchers agree that long-term potentiation produced by the activation of NMDA receptors is initiated postsynaptically, by the entry of calcium ions. Most also agree that the entry of calcium activates some special calcium-dependent enzymes known as **protein kinases.** Protein kinases are inactive until a calcium ion binds with them; when activated, they add phosphate groups (PO_4) to particular protein molecules, causing some part of the protein to move, changing its properties. In fact, two studies using mice with targeted mutations against two different protein kinases found that the absence of these enzymes interfered with long-term potentiation in field CA1 (Grant et al., 1992; Silva et al., 1992).

Several studies have found evidence that long-term potentiation causes structural changes in synapses. One of the most compelling studies was performed by Hosokawa et al. (1995), who used a confocal microscope to observe individual dendritic spines of CA1 pyramidal cells before and after long-term potentiation. A confocal microscope uses special optics to examine an extremely thin "slice" of tissue located beneath the surface of a specimen, screening out all elements that are out of focus. What they saw indicated that a subpopulation of small spines grew in length and changed their orientation toward the shaft of the dendrite away from the perpendicular. Figure 12.11 shows a drawing of hypothetical changes in a dendritic spine that are consistent with the observed changes. As you can see, as the dendritic spine and terminal button elongate, two active zones appear. (See *Figure 12.11.*)

What about the possibility of presynaptic changes? How could a process that occurs postsynaptically, in the dendritic spines, cause presynaptic changes? A possible answer comes from the discovery that a simple molecule, nitric oxide, can communicate messages from one cell to another. As we saw in Chapter 4, nitric oxide is a soluble gas produced by the activity of an enzyme known as **nitric oxide synthase.** Researchers have found that nitric oxide (NO) is used as a messenger in many parts of the body; for example, it is involved in the control of the muscles in the wall of the intestines, it dilates blood vessels in regions of the brain that become metabolically active, and it stimulates the changes in blood vessels that produce penile erections (Culotta and Koshland, 1992). Once produced, NO lasts only a short time before it is destroyed. Thus, if it were produced in dendritic spines in the hippocampal formation, it could diffuse only as far as the nearby terminal buttons, where it might produce changes related to the induction of long-term potentiation.

Several experiments suggest that NO may, indeed, be a retrograde messenger involved in long-term potentiation. (*Retrograde* means "moving backward"; in this con-

Protein kinase An enzyme that attaches a phosphate (PO_4) to a protein and thereby causes it to change its shape.

Nitric oxide synthase An enzyme responsible for the production of nitric oxide.

FIGURE 12.11

Hypothetical changes in the structure of synapses on dendritic spines produced by long-term potentiation.

[Adapted from Hosokawa, T., Rusakov, D.A., Bliss, T.V.P., and Fine, A. Journal of Neuroscience, 1995, 15, 5560–5573.]

Before long-term potentiation

After long-term potentiation

text it refers to messages sent from the dendritic spine back to the terminal button.) Several studies (for example, O'Dell et al., 1991; Bon et al., 1992) have found that drugs that block nitric oxide synthase prevented the establishment of long-term potentiation in hippocampal slices. Endoh, Maiese, and Wagner (1994) found that a calcium-activated NO synthase is located in several regions of the brain, including the dentate gyrus and fields CA1 and CA3 of the hippocampus. Zhang and Wong-Riley (1996) found that most cells that contain NO synthase also contain NMDA receptors.

Figure 12.12 summarizes the biochemistry discussed in this subsection. I suspect that you may feel overwhelmed by all the new terms I have introduced here, and I hope that the figure will help to clarify things. The evidence we have seen so far indicates that the entry of calcium ions through channels controlled by NMDA receptors activates at least two calcium-dependent protein kinases. These enzymes may activate biochemical processes that produce postsynaptic changes that cause the insertion of AMPA receptors into the postsynaptic membrane and change the physical structure of the synapse. (See *Figure 12.12.*) In addition, the entry of calcium activates a calcium-dependent NO synthase, and the newly produced NO then presumably diffuses out of the dendritic spine, back to the terminal button, where it induces presynaptic changes. (See *Figure 12.12.*)

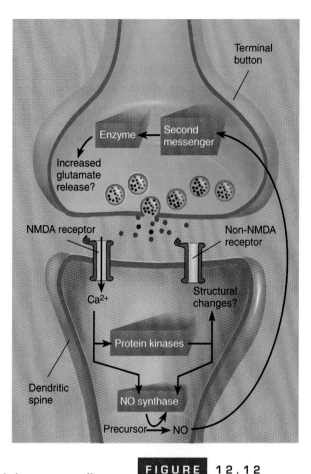

FIGURE 12.12

A summary of the chemical reactions triggered by the entry of an adequate amount of calcium into the dendritic spine.

Long-Term Depression

I mentioned earlier that low-frequency stimulation of the synaptic inputs to a cell can *decrease* rather than increase their strength. This phenomenon, known as **long-term depression,** also plays a role in learning. After all, although the number of synapses in the brain is very large, it is still finite, and animals can continue to learn throughout their lives. Thus, it seems unlikely that once a synapse is strengthened, it must remain that way forever.

Stanton and Sejnowski (1989) demonstrated associative long-term depression in field CA1. They found that when a weak input was paired with a strong input, long-term potentiation was produced. However, when the two inputs were stimulated at different times, long-term *depression* was produced. Other studies have shown that long-term depression is produced when synaptic inputs are activated at the same time that the postsynaptic membrane is either weakly depolarized or hyperpolarized (Debanne, Gähwiler, and Thompson, 1994; Thiels et al., 1996). Thus, at least at some synapses the Hebb rule appears to work in both directions: Inputs correlated with strong inputs (or with activation of the postsynaptic neuron) are strengthened, whereas inputs *not* correlated with strong inputs (or correlated with *nonactivation* of the postsynaptic neuron) are weakened. This mechanism could conceivably allow for the reversal of previously established synaptic changes when the contingencies in the environment change.

Long-term depression A long-term decrease in the excitability of a neuron to a particular synaptic input caused by stimulation of the terminal button while the postsynaptic membrane is hyperpolarized or only slightly depolarized.

INTERIM SUMMARY

The study of long-term potentiation in the hippocampal formation has suggested a mechanism that might be responsible for at least some of the synaptic changes that occur during learning. A circuit of neurons passes through the hippocampal formation, from the entorhinal cortex to the dentate gyrus, to field CA3, to field CA1, to the subiculum. High-frequency stimulation of the axons in this circuit strengthens synapses; it leads to an increase in the size of the EPSPs in the dendritic spines of the postsynaptic neurons. Associative long-term potentiation can also occur, in which weak synapses are strengthened by the action of strong ones. In fact, the only requirement for long-term potentiation is that the postsynaptic membrane be depolarized at the same time that the synapses are active.

In field CA1 and in the dentate gyrus, NMDA receptors play a special role in long-term potentiation. These receptors, sensitive to glutamate, control calcium channels but can open them only if the membrane is already depolarized. Thus, the combination of membrane depolarization (for example, from a dendritic spike produced by the activity of strong synapses) and activation of a NMDA receptor causes the entry of calcium ions. The increase in calcium activates several calcium-dependent enzymes. Inhibition of these enzymes disrupts long-term potentiation; presumably, they cause the insertion of AMPA receptors into the membrane of the dendritic spine, increasing its sensitivity to glutamate released by the terminal button. This change is accompanied by structural alterations in the shape of the dendritic spine, including the appearance of an additional release zone. The enzymes may also produce presynaptic changes, through the activation of NO synthase, an enzyme responsible for the production of nitric oxide. This soluble gas may diffuse into nearby terminal buttons where it induces presynaptic changes. Long-term potentiation takes place in many regions of the brain, but it does not always involve NMDA receptors.

Once a synapse has been strengthened, it can still undergo further changes, which permits further learning (or unlearning) to take place. Long-term depression occurs when a synapse is activated at the time that the postsynaptic membrane is hyperpolarized or only slightly depolarized.

■ THOUGHT QUESTIONS

The brain is the most complex organ in the body, and it is also the most malleable. Every experience leaves at least a small trace, in the form of altered synapses. When we tell something to someone or participate in an encounter that the other person will remember, we are (literally) changing connections in the person's brain. How many synapses change each day? What prevents individual memories from becoming confused?

■ PERCEPTUAL LEARNING

Learning enables us to adapt to our environment and to respond to changes in it. In particular, it provides us with the ability to perform an appropriate behavior in an appropriate situation. Situations can be as simple as the sound of a buzzer or as complex as the social interactions of a group of people. The first part of learning involves learning to perceive.

Perceptual learning involves learning *about* things, not *what to do* when they are present. (Learning what to do is discussed in the subsequent sections of this chapter.) Perceptual learning can involve learning to recognize entirely new stimuli, or it can involve learning to recognize changes or variations in familiar stimuli. For example, if a friend gets a new hairstyle or replaces glasses with contact lenses, our visual memory of that person changes. We also learn that particular stimuli are found in particular locations or contexts or in the presence of other stimuli. We can even learn and remember particular *episodes:* sequences of events taking place at a particular time and place. The more complex forms of perceptual learning will be discussed in the last section of this chapter, which is devoted to relational learning.

Learning to Recognize Visual Stimuli

In mammals with large and complex brains, objects are recognized visually by circuits of neurons in the visual association cortex. As we saw in Chapter 6, the primary visual cortex receives information from the lateral geniculate nucleus of the thalamus. Within the primary visual cortex, individual modules of neurons analyze information from restricted regions of the visual scene that pertain to movement, orientation, color, binocular disparity, and spatial frequency. Information about each of these attributes is collected in subregions of the extrastriate cortex, which surrounds the primary visual cortex (striate cortex). For example, specific regions are devoted to the analysis of form, color, and movement. After analyzing particular attributes of the visual scene, the subregions of the extrastriate cortex send the results of their analysis to the next level of the visual association cortex. As we saw in Chapter 6, the second level of the visual association cortex is divided into two "streams." The *ventral stream*, which is involved with object recognition, begins in the extrastriate cortex and continues ventrally into the inferior temporal cortex. The *dorsal stream*, which is involved with perception of the location of objects, also begins in the extrastriate cortex of the occipital lobe, but it continues dorsally into the posterior parietal cortex. As some investigators have said, the ventral stream is involved with the *what* of visual perception; the dorsal stream is involved with the *where*.

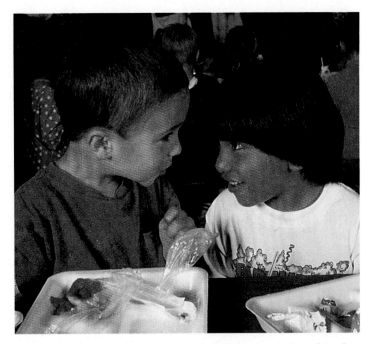

Learning to recognize a friend's face is an important form of perceptual learning.

Let's first consider the ventral stream. Many studies have shown that lesions that damage the inferior temporal cortex disrupt the ability to discriminate between different visual stimuli (Mishkin 1966). Presumably, learning to recognize a particular visual stimulus is accomplished by changes in synaptic connections in the inferior temporal cortex that establish new neural circuits—changes such as the ones described in the previous section of this chapter. At a later time, when the animal sees the same stimulus again and the same pattern of activity is transmitted to the inferior temporal cortex, these circuits become active again. This activity constitutes the recognition of the stimulus—the "readout" of the visual memory, so to speak.

As we saw in Chapter 6, some neurons in the inferior temporal cortex show remarkable specificity in their response characteristics, which suggests that they are part of circuits that detect the presence of specific stimuli. For example, neurons located near the superior temporal sulcus become active when the animal is shown pictures of faces. Baylis, Rolls, and Leonard (1985) found that most of these neurons are sensitive to *particular* faces. Rolls and Baylis (1986) found that the responses of some of these neurons remain constant even if the picture is blurred or changed in color, size, or distance. Thus, these neurons belong to circuits of neurons that recognize the *identities* of particular faces, not simply a specific view.

Two recent studies using PET scanners (Moscovitch et al., 1995; Owen et al., 1996) have found that the recall of perceptual memories of the identities and locations of objects in the human brain involve activity in the ventral and dorsal streams, respectively. Let's consider just one of these studies. Moscovitch and his colleagues measured the activity of the human brain during the recall of the identity and location of visual stimuli—in other words, the retrieval of perceptual memories of objects and their locations. First, they had people study and memorize 28 different visual displays such as the ones illustrated in Figure 12.13. Each display contained a set of

FIGURE 12.13

Examples of the types of stimuli used in the PET-scanning study by Moscovitch et al., 1995. (a) One of the stimuli to be memorized. (b) The object-memory retrieval task. One of the objects in the right-hand figure is incorrect. (c) The spatial-memory retrieval task. One of the objects in the right-hand figure is located in the wrong place.

[Adapted from Moscovitch, M., Kapur, S., Koehler, S., and Houle, S. Proceedings of the National Academy of Sciences, 1995, 92, 3721–3725.]

three objects placed in specific locations on the screen. Later, the subjects were shown a pair of displays, one that they had seen before and one that they had never seen, and were asked to indicate which was which. The displays differed in one of two ways. During the *object-memory retrieval task,* one of the objects from the familiar display was replaced with a new object. During the *spatial-memory retrieval task,* all three objects were the same, but one of them was shown in a new location. The PET scanner recorded the subjects' regional cerebral blood flow while they were performing these tasks. (See *Figure 12.13.*)

The results of the experiment are shown in Figure 12.14. As you can see, both tasks produced activity in the visual association cortex of the occipital, temporal, and parietal lobes, as well as a region of the frontal cortex. (See *Figure 12.14a.*) The two scans at the bottom show the differences between the upper two scans. As you can see, the object-memory retrieval task activated the ventral stream in the inferior temporal cortex, while the spatial-memory retrieval task activated the dorsal stream in the posterior parietal cortex. (See *Figure 12.14b.*)

Visual Short-Term Memory

So far, all the studies I have mentioned involved simple recognition of visual stimuli, either particular objects or their locations. What neural circuits are involved not only in recognizing stimuli but in remembering them for a period of time? As we will see, **short-term memory**—memory of information that has just been presented—involves the prefrontal cortex as well as the sensory association cortex.

Most studies of short-term memory employ a **delayed matching-to-sample task,** which requires an animal to remember a particular stimulus for a period of time. For example, Fuster and Jervey (1981) trained monkeys on such a task. They turned on a colored light (yellow, green, red, or blue) behind a translucent disk (the *sample stimulus*), turned it off, and, after a delay interval, turned on yellow, green, red, and blue lights behind four other disks (the *test stimuli*). (See *Figure 12.15.*) If the monkey pressed the disk whose color matched the one it had just seen, it received a piece of food.

FIGURE 12.14

The results of PET scans from the task shown in Figure 12.13.

[From Moscovitch, M., Kapur, S., Koehler, S., and Houle, S. Proceedings of the National Academy of Sciences, 1995, 92, 3721–3725. Copyright 1995 National Academy of Sciences, USA.]

While the monkeys were performing this task, the experimenters recorded the activity of single neurons in the inferior temporal cortex. Some neurons responded selectively to color: to yellow, red, green, or blue. Presumably, they became active because the *circuits* of neurons of which they were a part became active. It is these circuits, not individual neurons, that recognize particular stimuli. In addition, many of these neurons remained active during the delay interval. Under normal conditions a stimulus causes a neuron to respond briefly. Thus, the sustained response during the delay interval suggests that the neuron was part of a circuit involved in a particular visual short-term memory: remembering that a red light was presented. Similar experiments have shown that neurons in the posterior parietal lobe—in the dorsal stream—retain information about the location of a visual stimulus that has just been perceived (Constantinidis and Steinmetz, 1996).

Visual short-term memory appears to *require* the activity of neurons in the inferior temporal cortex throughout the delay interval. Kovner and Stamm (1972) implanted electrodes in the inferior temporal cortex of monkeys and trained them on a visual delayed matching-to-sample task. Once the monkeys had learned the task, they electrically stimulated the cortex through the electrodes from time to time while the animals were performing. When they administered the stimulation during the delay interval, just before they showed the monkeys the test stimuli, the animals performed poorly on that trial. It was as if the stimulation had disrupted the normal activity in the cortex and erased the memory of the stimulus the monkeys had just seen.

A similar experiment suggests that short-term memory of the location of objects requires neural activity of the posterior parietal lobe. Oyachi and Ohtsuka (1995) temporarily disrupted the activity of the human posterior parietal cortex by means of **transcranial magnetic stimulation.** When alternating current is passed through an electromagnetic coil placed against the skull, the magnetic field temporarily disrupts the activity of the neural circuits in the brain located beneath the coil. The investigators found that disruption of the right posterior parietal cortex disrupted performance of a delayed matching-to-sample task that required people to move their eyes toward the location of a stimulus that had been presented two seconds earlier.

Although the neural circuits responsible for visual memories appear to reside in the visual association cortex, short-term memory involves other brain regions, as well—especially the prefrontal cortex. Both major regions of the visual association cortex—the ventral stream of the inferior temporal cortex and the dorsal stream of the posterior parietal cortex—have direct connections with the dorsolateral prefrontal cortex. Each of these regions of visual association cortex is individually connected with a particular region of the prefrontal cortex (Wilson, Scalaidhe, and Goldman-Rakic, 1993). In fact, the dorsolateral prefrontal cortex is involved in short-term memory for all sense modalities. Damage to this region or temporary deactivation by cooling the cortex disrupts performance on a variety of delayed matching-to-sample tasks using visual, tactile, or auditory stimuli (Passingham, 1975; Bauer and Fuster, 1976; Shindy, Posley, and Fuster, 1994; Bodner, Kroger, and Fuster, 1996).

Sample stimulus

Delay interval

Matching stimuli

FIGURE 12.15

The delayed matching-to-sample procedure used by Fuster and Jervey (1981).

Short-term memory Memory for a stimulus that has just been perceived.

Delayed matching-to-sample task A task that requires the subject to indicate which of several stimuli has just been perceived.

Transcranial magnetic stimulation Stimulation of the cortex by the magnetic field produced by alternating current passing through a coil placed against the skull; disrupts normal activity of the affected brain region.

INTERIM **SUMMARY**

Perceptual learning occurs as a result of changes in synaptic connections within the sensory association cortex. Damage to a monkey's inferior temporal cortex—the highest level of visual association cortex—disrupts visual discriminations. Electrical recording studies have shown that some neurons respond preferentially to particular complex stimuli, including faces of individual monkeys. PET studies with humans have shown that retrieval of visual memories of objects activates the inferior temporal cortex and that retrieval of memories of locations activates the posterior parietal cortex.

Visual short-term memory involves the activation of neurons in the visual association cortex. Electrical-recording studies have shown that some neurons in the inferior temporal cortex encode the information presented during the sample period of a delayed matching-to-sample task and continue to fire during the delay interval. Electrical stimulation of the inferior temporal cortex during the delay interval of this task disrupts performance, as if the memory of the stimulus had been erased. Erasure of visual short-term memories can also be produced in human subjects by transcranial magnetic stimulation. The dorsolateral prefrontal cortex is also involved in short-term memory. Lesions or temporary deactivation of this brain region disrupts performance on delayed matching-to-sample tasks using a variety of different sense modalities.

■ THOUGHT QUESTIONS

How many perceptual memories does your brain hold? How many images, sounds, and odors can you recognize, and how many objects and surfaces can you recognize by touch? Is there any way we could estimate these quantities?

■ CLASSICAL CONDITIONING

Neuroscientists have studied the anatomy and physiology of classical conditioning using many models, such as the gill withdrawal reflex in *Aplysia* (a marine invertebrate) or the eyeblink reflex in the rabbit (Carew, 1989; Lavond, Kim, and Thompson, 1993). I have chosen to describe a simple mammalian model of classical conditioning—the conditioned emotional response—to illustrate the results of such investigations.

The central nucleus of the amygdala plays an important role in organizing a pattern of emotional responses that are provoked by aversive stimuli, both learned and unlearned. As we saw in Chapter 10, when this nucleus is activated, its efferent connections with other regions of the brain trigger several behavioral, autonomic, and endocrine responses that are elicited by aversive stimuli. Most stimuli that cause an aversive emotional response are not intrinsically aversive; we have to *learn* to fear them. The central nucleus of the amygdala is part of an important system involved in a particular form of stimulus–response (S–R) learning: the classically conditioned emotional responses.

A conditioned emotional response to a very simple auditory stimulus can occur in the absence of the auditory cortex (LeDoux et al., 1984); therefore, I will confine my discussion to the subcortical components of this process. Information about the CS (the tone) reaches a part of the thalamus known as the **MGm** (the medial division of the medial geniculate nucleus) and is then relayed to the basolateral amygdala. Information about the US (the foot shock) reaches both the MGm and the basolateral amygdala. Thus, there is convergence of information about the CS and the US in two regions: the MGm and the basolateral amygdala. Synaptic changes responsible for learning could take place in either (or both) of these locations.

A hypothetical neural circuit is shown in Figure 12.16. When a rat encounters a painful stimulus, strong synapses in the MGm and the basolateral amygdala are activated; as a result, neurons in the central nucleus begin firing, evoking an unlearned (unconditioned) emotional response. If a tone is paired with the painful stimulus,

MGm The medial division of the medial geniculate nucleus; transmits auditory and somatosensory information to the lateral nucleus of the amygdala.

the weak synapses in the MGm and the basolateral amygdala are strengthened, through the action of the Hebb rule. (See *Figure 12.16.*)

This hypothesis has a considerable amount of support. Lesions of the MGm, basolateral amygdala, or central nucleus disrupt conditioned emotional responses that involve a simple auditory stimulus as a CS and a shock to the feet as a US (Iwata et al., 1986; LeDoux et al., 1986, 1990; Sananes and Davis, 1992). Thus, the synaptic changes responsible for this learning appear to take place within this circuit.

There is evidence for synaptic changes in both the MGm and the basolateral amygdala. A single-unit-recording study by Weinberger and his colleagues (reported by Weinberger, 1982) showed that neurons in the MGm increased their responsiveness to the auditory CS after this stimulus was paired with an aversive US.

Quirk, Repa, and LeDoux (1995) found similar changes in the lateral amygdala. They recorded the activity of neurons in the lateral amygdala in freely moving rats before, during, and after pairing of a tone with footshock. Within a few trials, neurons became more responsive to the tone, and many neurons that had not previously responded to the tone began doing so. (See *Figure 12.17.*)

Seeing that it is likely that the synaptic changes responsible for classically conditioned emotional responses take place in two particular locations, we can ask whether these changes may be produced by a phenomenon we already know something about: long-term potentiation. Indeed, studies have shown that long-term potentiation can take place in the synaptic connections in both the MGm and the basolateral amygdala. Even more significantly, Rogan and LeDoux (1995) found that these changes could, indeed, be responsible for classical conditioning: When they produced long-term potentiation in the lateral nucleus of the amygdala, neurons there became more responsive to auditory stimuli.

As we saw, long-term potentiation in at least some parts of the brain is accomplished through the activation of NMDA receptors. Several experiments suggest that these receptors also participate in the synaptic plasticity that occurs in the amygdala. When AP5 (a drug that blocks NMDA receptors) is injected directly into the basolateral amygdala, rats no longer learned a conditioned emotional response. However, if the AP5 is injected *after* a classically conditioned emotional response has been established, the drug had no effect (Campeau, Miserendino, and Davis, 1992; Fanselow and Kim, 1994). Thus, it seems that AP5 can disrupt the establishment of learning by blocking synaptic plasticity in the basolateral amygdala, but the drug does not affect synaptic changes that have already taken place.

INTERIM SUMMARY

You have already encountered the conditioned emotional response in Chapter 10 and in the previous section of this chapter, where I discussed perceptual learning. When an auditory stimulus (CS) is paired with a foot shock (US), the two types of information converge in the medial division of the me-

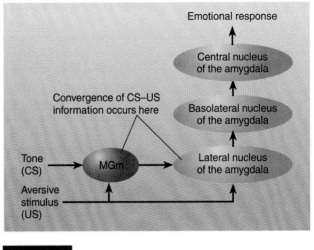

FIGURE 12.16

The probable location of the changes in synaptic strength produced by the classically conditioned emotional response that results from pairing a tone with a foot shock.

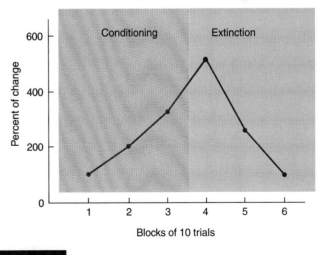

FIGURE 12.17

Change in rate of firing of neurons in the lateral amygdala in response to the tone, relative to baseline levels.

[Adapted from Quirk, G.J., Repa, J.C., and LeDoux, J.E. Neuron, 1995, 15, 1029–1039.]

dial geniculate nucleus (MGm) and again in the lateral amygdala. The lateral amygdala is connected, via the basolateral nucleus, with the central nucleus, which is responsible for the various components of the emotional response. Lesions anywhere in this circuit disrupt the response.

Recordings of single neurons in both the MGm and the lateral nucleus of the amygdala indicate that classical conditioning changes the response of neurons to the CS. The mechanism of synaptic plasticity in this system appears to be NMDA-mediated long-term potentiation. High-frequency electrical stimulation of the inputs to both the MGm and the lateral amygdala produces long-term potentiation, and long-term potentiation in the lateral nucleus increases the responses of neurons there to auditory stimuli. The establishment of long-term potentiation in the basolateral amygdala increases the sensitivity of neurons there to auditory stimuli. In addition, the injection of AP5 into the lateral amygdala prevents classical conditioning from taking place but has no effect on conditioning that was established earlier.

INSTRUMENTAL CONDITIONING AND MOTOR LEARNING

Instrumental (operant) conditioning is the means by which we (and other animals) profit from experience. If, in a particular situation, we make a response that has favorable outcomes, we will tend to make the response again. Sometimes the response is one we already know how to perform, which means that all that needs to occur is a strengthening of connections between neural circuits that detect the relevant stimuli and those that control the relevant response. However, if the response is one we have not made before, our performance is likely to be slow and awkward. As we continue to practice the response, our behavior becomes faster, smoother, and more automatic. In other words, motor learning takes place as well. This section first describes the neural pathways involved in instrumental conditioning and its close relative, motor learning, and then discusses the neural basis of reinforcement.

Basal Ganglia

As we saw earlier in this chapter, instrumental conditioning entails the strengthening of connections between neural circuits that detect a particular stimulus and neural circuits that produce a particular response. Clearly, the circuits responsible for instrumental conditioning begin in various regions of the sensory association cortex, where perception takes place, and end in the motor association cortex of the frontal lobe, which controls movements. But what pathways are responsible for these connections, and where do the synaptic changes responsible for the learning take place?

There are two major pathways between the sensory association cortex and the motor association cortex: direct transcortical connections and connections via the basal ganglia and thalamus. (A third pathway, involving the cerebellum and thalamus, also exists, but the role of this pathway in instrumental conditioning has, until very recently, received little attention from neuroscientists.) Both of these pathways appear to be involved in instrumental conditioning, but they play different roles.

The direct connections between the sensory association cortex and the motor association cortex are, as we saw earlier, involved in short-term memory. In conjunction with the hippocampal formation, they are also involved in the acquisition of episodic memories—complex perceptual memories of sequences of events that we witness or are described to us. (The acquisition of these types of memories is discussed later in this chapter.) The transcortical connections are also involved in the acquisition of complex behaviors that involve deliberation or instruction. For ex-

When we are first learning a complex skill such as driving a car, we must give it our full attention. Eventually, we can drive without thinking and can easily carry on a conversation with passengers at the same time.

ample, a person learning to drive a car with a manual transmission might say, "Let's see, push in the clutch, move the shift lever to the left and then away from me—there, it's in gear—now let the clutch come up—oh! It died—I should have given it more gas. Let's see, clutch down, turn the key. . . ." A memorized set of rules (or an instructor sitting next to us) provides a script for us to follow. Of course, this process does not have to be audible or even involve actual movements of the speech muscles; a person can think in words with neural activity that does not result in overt behavior. (Animals that cannot communicate by means of language can acquire complex responses by observing and imitating the behavior of other animals.)

At first, performing a behavior through observation or by following a set of rules is slow and awkward. And because so much of the brain's resources are involved with recalling the rules and applying them to our behavior, we cannot respond to other stimuli in the environment—we must ignore events that might distract us. But then, with practice, the behavior becomes much more fluid. Eventually, we perform it without thinking and can easily do other things at the same time, such as carry on a conversation with passengers as we drive our car.

Evidence suggests that as learned behaviors become automatic and routine, they are "transferred" to the basal ganglia. The process seems to work like this. As we deliberately perform a complex behavior, the basal ganglia receive information about the stimuli that are present and the responses we are making. At first, the basal ganglia are passive "observers" of the situation, but as the behaviors are repeated again and again, they begin to learn what to do. Eventually, they take over most of the details of the process, leaving the transcortical circuits free to do something else. We need no longer think about what we are doing.

The basal ganglia receive sensory information from all regions of the cerebral cortex. They also receive information from the frontal lobes about movements that are planned or are actually in progress. (So as you can see, the basal ganglia have all the information they need to monitor the progress of someone learning to drive a car.) The outputs of the basal ganglia are sent to the frontal cortex—to the premotor and supplementary motor cortex, where plans for movements are made, and to the primary motor cortex, where they are executed.

Now let's review some evidence that supports the assertion that the basal ganglia are involved in learning. Studies with laboratory animals have found that lesions of the basal ganglia disrupt instrumental conditioning but do not affect other forms of learning (Divac, Rosvold, and Szcwarcbart, 1967; McDonald and White, 1993).

FIGURE **12.18**

The probability learning task used by Knowlton, Mangels, and Squire.

[Adapted from Knowlton, B.J., Mangels, J.A., and Squire, L.R. Science, 1996, 273, 1399–1402.]

Studies with humans also indicate that the basal ganglia play an important role in automatic, nondeliberate learning. Investigators have studied people with Parkinson's disease, a neurological disorder that affects the basal ganglia. The symptoms of Parkinson's disease have been described as "motor deficits." However, some of them can be seen as failures of automated memories. For example, although people with Parkinson's disease have sufficient muscular strength, they have difficulty performing many everyday tasks, such as getting out of a chair. Also, if someone bumps into them while they are standing, they are likely to fall—and they will not put their hands out in front of them to catch themselves. These symptoms can, of course, be viewed as motor deficits. But we can also regard them as failure to remember how to do something. We do not think of rising from a chair as a learned behavior, but it surely must be. It involves leaning forward to bring our center of gravity over our feet before beginning to contract the extensor muscles of our legs. Unless the disease is well advanced, people with Parkinson's disease can eventually stand up from a chair, but it takes them some time, as if they to have to think about how to do it. Similarly, we do not think of putting our hands out in front of us to break a fall as a learned response, but perhaps it is.

Knowlton, Mangels, and Squire (1996) found that patients with Parkinson's disease did poorly on a probability learning task. The task required them to predict the weather. On each trial the subjects were shown one to three cards, each of which contained a particular pattern. Each pattern predicted either sunshine or rain, with a probability ranging from 25 percent to 75 percent. (See *Figure 12.18.*) Normal subjects gradually get better and better at this task, but most of them remain unaware of what they have learned—they are unable to state explicitly the rules they use to predict the weather. Knowlton and her colleagues found that the patients with Parkinson's disease failed to learn this task. Clearly, the results cannot be attributed to a motor deficit. (See *Figure 12.19.*)

Reinforcement

As we saw, learning provides a means for us to profit from experience—to make responses that provide favorable outcomes. When good things happen (that is, when reinforcing stimuli occur), reinforcement mechanisms in the brain become active, and the establishment of synaptic changes is facilitated.

Neural Circuits Involved in Reinforcement

As you read in the Prologue, an animal's behavior can be reinforced by electrical stimulation of the brain. Subsequent research has found that stimulation of many parts of the brain—including the olfactory bulb, prefrontal cortex, nucleus accumbens, caudate nucleus, putamen, various thalamic nuclei, reticular formation, amygdala, ventral tegmental area, substantia nigra, and locus coeruleus—is

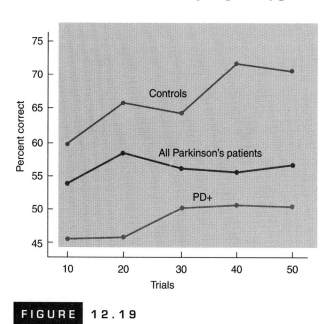

FIGURE **12.19**

Results of subjects on the task illustrated in Figure 12.18. The curve labeled PD+ refers to those patients with Parkinson's disease who exhibited the worst motor symptoms.

[Adapted from Knowlton, B.J., Mangels, J.A., and Squire, L.R. Science, 1996, 273, 1399–1402.]

reinforcing (Olds and Fobes, 1981). Undoubtedly, this means that there is more than one reinforcement mechanism. The best and most reliable location is the **medial forebrain bundle (MFB),** a bundle of axons that travel in a rostral–caudal axis from the midbrain to the rostral basal forebrain. The MFB passes through the lateral hypothalamus, and it is in this region that most investigators place the tips of their electrodes. The MFB contains long ascending and descending axons that interconnect forebrain and midbrain structures and short axons that connect adjacent regions. It also contains ascending dopaminergic, noradrenergic, and serotonergic axons on their way from the brain stem to their projection areas in the forebrain. As we will see, the activity of dopaminergic neurons plays a particularly important role in this phenomenon.

The **mesolimbic system** begins in the ventral tegmental area (located in the midbrain—mesencephalon—just adjacent to the substantia nigra) and projects through the medial forebrain bundle to the amygdala, the lateral septum, the bed nucleus of the stria terminalis, the hippocampus, and the nucleus accumbens. Much of the research on the physiology of reinforcement has focused on the last of these structures. The **nucleus accumbens** is located in the basal forebrain rostral to the preoptic area and immediately adjacent to the septum. (In fact, the full name of this region is the *nucleus accumbens septi,* or "nucleus leaning against the septum.") (See *Figure 12.20.*)

Another system of dopaminergic axons, the **mesocortical system,** also plays a role in reinforcement. This system also begins in the ventral tegmental area. In rats, the neurons project to the prefrontal neocortex, limbic cortex (entorhinal, suprarhinal, and anterior cingulate cortex), and hippocampus. In primates, the mesocortical projections are much more widespread; in addition to the regions just listed, all of the frontal lobes and all regions of association cortex in the parietal and temporal lobes receive dopaminergic innervation (Berger, Gaspar, and Verney, 1991).

A large body of experimental evidence indicates that the mesolimbic pathway—particularly the branch that terminates in the nucleus accumbens—is at least partly responsible for the reinforcing effects of electrical stimulation of the medial forebrain bundle. It also plays an important role in the reinforcing effects of amphetamine and cocaine and other addictive drugs. (This role is discussed in more detail in Chapter 16.) Treatments that stimulate dopamine receptors in the nucleus accumbens will reinforce behaviors; thus, animals will press a lever that causes electri-

Medial forebrain bundle (MFB) A fiber bundle that runs in a rostral–caudal direction through the basal forebrain and lateral hypothalamus; electrical stimulation of these axons is reinforcing.

Mesolimbic system A system of dopaminergic neurons whose cell bodies are located in the ventral tegmental area and whose terminal buttons are located in the nucleus accumbens, amygdala, lateral septum, hippocampus, and bed nucleus of the stria terminalis.

Nucleus accumbens A nucleus of the basal forebrain near the septum; receives dopamine-secreting terminal buttons from neurons of the ventral tegmental area and is thought to be involved in reinforcement and attention.

Mesocortical system A system of dopaminergic neurons whose cell bodies are located in the ventral tegmental area and whose terminal buttons are located in the cerebral cortex and hippocampus.

FIGURE 12.20

Sections through a rat brain showing the location of the ventral tegmental area and the nucleus accumbens.

[Adapted from Swanson, L.W. Brain Maps: Structure of the Rat Brain. New York: Elsevier, 1992.]

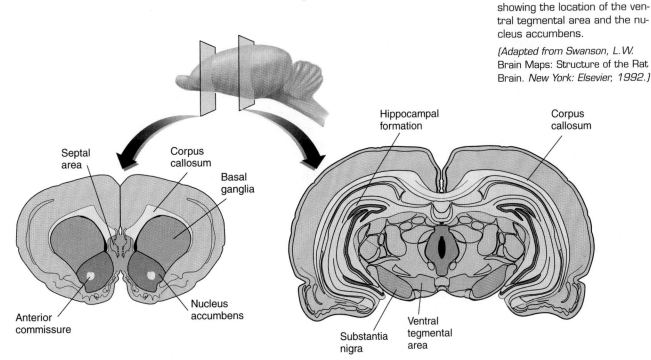

Electrode delivers
electrical stimulation to
medial forebrain bundle

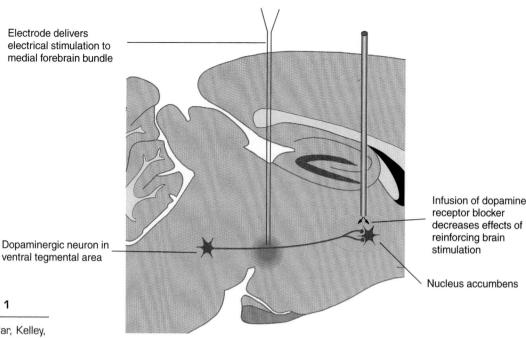

Infusion of dopamine
receptor blocker
decreases effects of
reinforcing brain
stimulation

Dopaminergic neuron in
ventral tegmental area

Nucleus accumbens

FIGURE 12.21

The experiment by Stellar, Kelley, and Corbett (1983). Blocking dopamine receptors in the nucleus accumbens reduces the reinforcing effects of electrical stimulation of the medial forebrain bundle.

cal stimulation of the ventral tegmental area, medial forebrain bundle, or nucleus accumbens itself (Routtenberg and Malsbury, 1969; Crow, 1972; Olds and Fobes, 1981). They will also press a lever that delivers direct injections of very small amounts of dopamine or amphetamine directly into the nucleus accumbens (Hoebel et al., 1983; Guerin et al., 1984).

If the activation of dopamine receptors in the nucleus accumbens is one of the events responsible for reinforcement, then we would expect that the injection of drugs that block these receptors would interfere with reinforcement. And it does. Stellar, Kelley, and Corbett (1983) trained rats to travel through a runway to receive electrical stimulation of the medial forebrain bundle. They found that when they injected a dopamine receptor blocker into the nucleus accumbens, they had to turn up the current level of the stimulator to get the animals to run. That is, the drug reduced the reinforcing value of the electrical brain stimulation. (See ***Figure 12.21.***)

Chapter 5 described a research technique called *microdialysis*, which enables an investigator to analyze the contents of the interstitial fluid within a specific region of the brain. Researchers using this method have shown that reinforcing electrical stimulation of the medial forebrain bundle or the ventral tegmental area, or the administration of cocaine or amphetamine, causes the release of dopamine in the nucleus accumbens (Moghaddam and Bunney, 1989; Nakahara et al., 1989; Phillips et al., 1992). (See ***Figure 12.22.***) Microdialysis studies have also found that the presence of natural reinforcers, such as water, food, or a sex partner, stimulate the release of dopamine in the nucleus accumbens. Thus, the effects of reinforcing brain stimulation seem to be similar in many ways to those of natural reinforcers.

I should note that microdialysis studies have found that aversive stimuli, as well as reinforcing stimuli, can cause the release of dopamine in various parts of the brain—including the

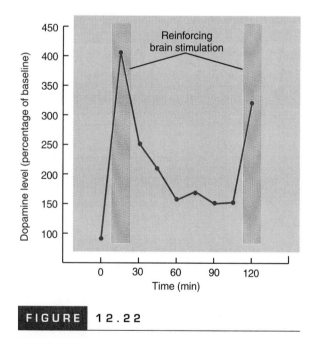

FIGURE 12.22

Release of dopamine in the nucleus accumbens, measured by microdialysis, produced when a rat pressed a lever that delivered electrical stimulation to the ventral tegmental area.

(Adapted from Phillips, A.G., Coury, A., Fiorino, D., LePiane, F.G., Brown, E., and Fibiger, H.C. Annals of the New York Academy of Sciences, 1992, 654, 199–206.)

nucleus accumbens (Salamone, 1992). Thus, it is clear that reinforcement is not the sole function of dopaminergic neurons; these neurons appear to be involved in stress, as well. Also, because the stimulation of so many regions of the brain is reinforcing, the mesolimbic system is only one of several reinforcement systems. The mesolimbic system is the one that has received by far the most attention, so little is known about other possible mechanisms.

Functions of the Reinforcement System

What does reinforcing brain stimulation tell us about the brain mechanisms involved in instrumental conditioning? Almost all investigators believe that electrical stimulation of some parts of the brain is reinforcing because it activates the same systems that are activated by natural reinforcers, such as food, water, or sexual contact. A reinforcement system must perform two functions: detect the presence of a reinforcing stimulus and strengthen the connections between the neurons that detect the discriminative stimulus (such as the sight of a lever) and the neurons that produce the instrumental response (a lever press).

Reinforcement occurs when neural circuits detect a reinforcing stimulus and cause the activation of dopaminergic neurons in the ventral tegmental area. Detection of a reinforcing stimulus is not a simple matter; a stimulus that serves as a reinforcer on one occasion may fail to do so on another. For example, the presence of food will reinforce the behavior of a hungry organism but not one that has just eaten. Thus, the reinforcement system is not automatically activated when particular stimuli are present; its activation also depends on the state of the organism.

What neural circuits are responsible for detecting the presence of a reinforcing stimulus and then activating dopaminergic neurons in this region? The ventral tegmental area receives inputs from many regions of the brain. Although we still know very little about how reinforcing stimuli are detected, the three inputs that probably play the most important role in reinforcement are the amygdala, the lateral hypothalamus, and the prefrontal cortex.

As we saw in Chapter 10 and again in this chapter, the amygdala is involved in classically conditioned emotional responses. Several studies suggest that it is also involved in reinforcement. For example, destruction of the amygdala or its disconnection from the visual system has no effect on monkeys' ability to recognize particular visual stimuli by sight, but it does disrupt their ability to remember which of them has been paired with food (Spiegler and Mishkin, 1981; Gaffan, Gaffan, and Harrison, 1988). In addition, Cador, Robbins, and Everitt (1989) and Everitt, Cador, and Robbins (1989) found that neurotoxic lesions of the basolateral amygdala reduced the reinforcing value of stimuli that had been paired with natural reinforcers: water (in thirsty rats) and sexual contact. The experimenters paired the reinforcing stimuli with a flashing light and found that later, the animals would press a lever that turned on the flashing light. Thus, the flashing light had become a conditioned reinforcer. The lesions of the amygdala severely depressed the animals' rate of responding for the flashing light without otherwise affecting their motor performance.

The inputs to the ventral tegmental area from the lateral hypothalamus may also play a role in the detection of reinforcing stimuli. Burton, Rolls, and Mora (1976) studied the response characteristics of single neurons in the lateral hypothalamus and substantia innominata (a nearby region in the basal forebrain). They found that some neurons located there respond to either the sight or taste of food, but they do so *only if the animal is hungry.*

Rolls et al. (1986) found that the firing rate of these neurons was related to an animal's willingness to eat a particular type of food. For example, one neuron showed a high rate of firing when the monkey was shown a peanut, a banana, an orange, or a syringe that was used to squirt a glucose solution into its mouth. The animal was then given repeated drinks of the glucose solution. At first it drank the solution enthusiastically, but after a while, acceptance turned to rejection. At the

FIGURE 12.23

Sensory-specific satiety. The graph plots the firing rate of a single neuron in a monkey's lateral hypothalamus when the animal is shown various foods. The smaller graph indicates ratings of the monkey's acceptance or rejection of the glucose solution, presented nine times.

(Adapted from Rolls, E.T., Murzi, E., Yaxley, S., Thorpe, S.J., and Simpson, S.J. Brain Research, 1986, 368, 79–86.)

same time the neuron responded less and less when the monkey was shown the syringe. However, the neuron still responded to the sight of a peanut, an orange, or a banana. The monkey was then allowed to eat all the bananas it wanted. The neuron stopped responding to the sight of the banana, but it still responded to the sight of the peanut. It pretty much stopped responding to the sight of an orange, too, but perhaps after drinking 440 milliliters of a glucose solution and eating all the bananas one wants, an orange provides less of a flavor contrast than a peanut does. Thus, the connections between the lateral hypothalamus and the ventral tegmental area may convey information about the presence of reinforcing stimuli. (See *Figure 12.23*.)

The prefrontal cortex also provides an important input to the ventral tegmental area. The terminal buttons of the axons connecting these two areas secrete glutamate, an excitatory transmitter substance, and the activity of these synapses makes dopaminergic neurons in the ventral tegmental area fire in a bursting pattern, greatly increasing the amount of dopamine they secrete in the nucleus accumbens (Gariano and Groves, 1988). The prefrontal cortex is generally involved in devising strategies, making plans, evaluating progress made toward goals, judging the appropriateness of one's own behavior, and so on (Mesulam, 1986). Perhaps the prefrontal cortex turns on the reinforcement mechanism when it determines that the ongoing behavior is bringing the organism nearer to its goals—that the present strategy is working.

The prefrontal and premotor cortex are *targets* of dopaminergic neurons as well as a source of their control. Evidence suggests that the dopaminergic system of the frontal cortex is involved in reinforcement. For example, Stein and Belluzzi (1989) found that rats will press a lever that produces an injection of a dopamine agonist into this region. Duvauchelle and Ettenberg (1991) found that if a rat's prefrontal cortex is electrically stimulated while the animal is in a particular location, it will learn to prefer that location to others where the stimulation did not take place. This effect appears to involve the release of dopamine, because it is blocked by injections of a drug that blocks dopamine receptors. And in a microdialysis study, Hernandez and Hoebel (1990) found that when rats were performing a food-reinforced lever-pressing task, the levels of dopamine in the prefrontal cortex increased.

INTERIM **SUMMARY**

Instrumental conditioning entails the strengthening of connections between neural circuits that detect stimuli and neural circuits that produce responses. One of the locations of these changes appears to be the basal ganglia—especially the changes responsible for learning of automated and routine behaviors. The basal ganglia receive sensory information and information about plans for movement from the neocortex. Damage to the basal ganglia disrupts instrumental conditioning in laboratory animals, and Parkinson's disease disrupts automatic motor responses (as opposed to deliberate ones) and even impairs learning of some tasks that do not involve learning particular movements.

Although several neurotransmitters may play a role in reinforcement, one is particularly important: dopamine. The cell bodies of the most important system of dopaminergic neurons are located in the ventral tegmental area, and their axons project to the nucleus accumbens, prefrontal cortex, and amygdala.

Infusions of dopamine agonists directly into the nucleus accumbens will reinforce an animal's behavior. Both laboratory animals and humans will self-administer dopamine agonists such as amphetamine or cocaine; laboratory animals will press a lever to have amphetamine injected directly into the nucleus accumbens. Microdialysis studies have also shown that natural and artificial reinforcers stimulate the release of dopamine in the nucleus accumbens. The system of neurons that detect reinforcing stimuli and activate the dopaminergic neurons in the mesolimbic and mesocortical systems probably involves the amygdala and lateral hypothalamus; these neurons fire in response to food-related stimuli capable of reinforcing an animal's behavior. Damage to the amygdala disrupts the reinforcing value of stimuli that have been paired with reinforcement. The frontal cortex may play a role in reinforcement that occurs when our own behavior brings us nearer to a goal.

The location of synaptic changes responsible for instrumental conditioning may be the nucleus accumbens, basal ganglia, and frontal cortex. Microdialysis studies suggest that the release of dopamine in the prefrontal cortex may also be important. The release of dopamine in the prefrontal cortex is reinforcing.

■ THOUGHT QUESTIONS

Have you ever been working hard on a problem and suddenly thought of a possible solution? Did the thought make you feel excited and happy? What would we find if we had a microdialysis probe in your nucleus accumbens?

■ RELATIONAL LEARNING

So far, I have discussed relatively simple forms of learning, which can be understood as changes in circuits of neurons that detect the presence of particular stimuli or as strengthened connections between neurons that convey sensory information and those that produce responses. But most forms of learning are more complex; most memories of real objects and events are related to other memories. Seeing a photograph of an old friend may remind you of the sound of the person's name and of the movements you have to make to pronounce it. You may also be reminded of things you have done with your friend: places you have visited, conversations you have had, experiences you have shared. Each of these memories can contain a series of events, complete with sights and sounds, which you will be able to recall in the proper sequence. Obviously, the neural circuits in the inferior temporal cortex that recognize your friend's face are connected to circuits in many other parts of the brain, and these circuits are connected to many others. This section discusses research on relational learning, which includes the establishment and retrieval of memories of events and episodes.

Human Anterograde Amnesia

One of the most dramatic and intriguing phenomena caused by brain damage is *anterograde amnesia,* which, at first glance, appears to be the inability to learn new information. However, when we examine the phenomenon more carefully, we find that the

FIGURE 12.24

A schematic definition of retrograde amnesia and anterograde amnesia.

Anterograde amnesia Amnesia for events that occur after some disturbance to the brain, such as head injury or certain degenerative brain diseases.

Retrograde amnesia Amnesia for events that preceded some disturbance to the brain, such as a head injury or electroconvulsive shock.

Korsakoff's syndrome Permanent anterograde amnesia caused by brain damage resulting from chronic alcoholism or malnutrition.

basic abilities of perceptual learning, stimulus–response learning, and motor learning are intact but that complex relational learning, of the type I just described, is gone. This section discusses the nature of anterograde amnesia in humans and its anatomical basis. The section that follows discusses related research with laboratory animals.

The term **anterograde amnesia** refers to difficulty in learning new information. A person with pure anterograde amnesia can remember events that occurred in the past, during the time before the brain damage occurred, but cannot retain information he or she encounters *after* the damage. In contrast, **retrograde amnesia** refers to the inability to remember events that happened *before* the brain damage occurred. (See *Figure 12.24*.) As we will see, pure anterograde amnesia is rare; usually, there is also a retrograde amnesia for events that occurred for a period of time before the brain damage occurred.

In 1889, Sergei Korsakoff, a Russian physician, first described a severe memory impairment caused by brain damage, and the disorder was given his name. The most profound symptom of **Korsakoff's syndrome** is a severe anterograde amnesia: The patients appear to be unable to form new memories, although they can still remember old ones. They can converse normally and can remember events that happened long before their brain damage occurred, but they cannot remember events that happened afterward.

Korsakoff's syndrome is usually (but not always) a result of brain damage produced by chronic alcoholism. The disorder actually results from a thiamine (vitamin B_1) deficiency caused by the alcoholism (Adams, 1969; Haas, 1988). Because alcoholics receive a substantial number of calories from the alcohol they ingest, they usually eat a poor diet, and their vitamin intake is consequently low. Furthermore, alcohol interferes with intestinal absorption of thiamine. The ensuing deficiency produces brain damage.

Anterograde amnesia can also be caused by damage to the temporal lobes. Scoville and Milner (1957) reported that bilateral removal of the medial temporal lobe produced a memory impairment in humans that was apparently identical to that seen in Korsakoff's syndrome. Thirty operations had been performed on psychotic patients in an attempt to alleviate their mental disorder, but it was not until this operation was performed on patient H.M. that the anterograde amnesia was discovered. The psychotic patients' behavior was already so disturbed that their amnesia was not detected. However, patient H.M. was reasonably intelligent and was not psychotic; therefore, his postoperative deficit was discovered immediately. He had received the surgery in an attempt to treat his very severe epilepsy, which could not be controlled even by high doses of anticonvulsant medication.

The surgery successfully treated H.M.'s seizure disorder, but it became apparent that the operation had produced a serious memory impairment. Subsequently, Scoville and Milner (1957) examined eight of the psychotic patients who were coherent enough to cooperate with them. Careful testing revealed that some of these patients also had anterograde amnesia; the deficit appeared to occur only when the hippocampus was removed. They concluded that the hippocampus was the critical structure destroyed by the surgery. Once it was discovered that bilateral medial temporal lobectomy causes anterograde amnesia, neurosurgeons stopped performing them and are now careful to operate on only one temporal lobe. (Unilateral temporal lobectomy may cause minor memory problems, but nothing like what occurs after bilateral operations.)

Basic Description

For you to understand more fully the nature of anterograde amnesia, I will discuss the case of patient H.M. in more detail (Milner, Corkin, and Teuber, 1968; Milner,

1970; Corkin et al., 1981). Patient H.M. has been extensively studied because his amnesia is relatively pure. His intellectual ability and his immediate verbal memory appear to be normal. He can repeat seven numbers forward and five numbers backward, and he can carry on conversations, rephrase sentences, and perform mental arithmetic. He has a retrograde amnesia for events that occurred during several years preceding the operation, but he can recall older memories very well. He showed no personality change after the operation, and he appears to be generally polite and good-natured.

However, since the operation, H.M. has been unable to learn anything new. He cannot identify by name people he has met since the operation (performed in 1953, when he was twenty-seven years old), nor can he find his way back home if he leaves his house. (His family moved to a new house after his operation, and he never learned how to get around in the new neighborhood. He now lives in a nursing home, where he can be cared for.) He is aware of his disorder and often says something like this:

> Every day is alone in itself, whatever enjoyment I've had, and whatever sorrow I've had . . . Right now, I'm wondering. Have I done or said anything amiss? You see, at this moment everything looks clear to me, but what happened just before? That's what worries me. It's like waking from a dream; I just don't remember. (Milner, 1970, p. 37)

H.M. is capable of remembering a small amount of verbal information as long as he is not distracted; constant rehearsal can keep information in his immediate memory for a long time. However, rehearsal does not appear to have any long-term effects; if he is distracted for a moment, he will completely forget whatever he had been rehearsing. He works very well at repetitive tasks. Indeed, because he so quickly forgets what previously happened, he does not easily become bored. He can endlessly reread the same magazine or laugh at the same jokes, finding them fresh and new each time. His time is typically spent solving crossword puzzles and watching television.

From these findings, Milner and her colleagues made the following conclusions:

1. *The hippocampus is not the location of long-term memories; nor is it necessary for the retrieval of long-term memories.* If it were, H.M. would not have been able to remember events from early in his life, he would not know how to talk, he would not know how to dress himself, and so on.

2. *The hippocampus is not the location of immediate (short-term) memories.* If it were, H.M. would not be able to carry on a conversation, because he would not remember what the other person said long enough to think of a reply.

3. *The hippocampus is involved in converting immediate (short-term) memories into long-term memories.* This conclusion is based on a particular hypothesis of memory function: that our immediate memory of an event is retained by neural activity and that long-term memories consist of relatively permanent biochemical or structural changes in neurons. The conclusion seems a reasonable explanation for the fact that when presented with new information, H.M. seems to understand it and remember it as long as he thinks about it but that a permanent record of the information is just never made.

As we will see, these three conclusions are too simple. Subsequent research on patients with anterograde amnesia indicates that the facts are more complicated—and more interesting—than they first appeared to be. But to appreciate the significance of the findings of more recent research, we must understand these three conclusions and remember the facts that led to them.

Many psychologists believe that learning consists of at least two stages: short-term memory and long-term memory. They conceive of short-term memory as a means of storing a limited amount of information temporarily and long-term memory as a means of storing an unlimited amount (or at least an enormously large

FIGURE 12.25

A simple model of the learning process.

Set I

Set II

Set III

Set IV

Set V

FIGURE 12.26

Examples of broken drawings.

(Reprinted with permission of author and publisher from Gollin, E.S. Developmental studies of visual recognition of incomplete objects. Perceptual and Motor Skills, 1960, 11, 289–298.)

amount) of information permanently. As we saw earlier in this chapter, short-term memory is an immediate memory for stimuli that have just been perceived. We can remember a new item of information (such as a telephone number) for as long as we want to by engaging in a particular behavior: rehearsal. However, once we stop rehearsing the information, we may or may not be able to remember it later; that is, the information may or may not get stored in **long-term memory.**

Short-term memory can hold only a limited amount of information. To demonstrate this fact, read the following numbers to yourself just once, and then close your eyes and recite them back.

1 4 9 2 3 0 7

You probably had no trouble remembering them. Now, try the following set of numbers, and go through them *only once* before you close your eyes.

7 2 5 2 3 9 1 6 5 8 4

Very few people can repeat eleven numbers; in fact, you may not have even bothered to try, once you saw how many numbers there were. Therefore, short-term memory has definite limits. But of course, if you wanted to, you could recite the numbers again and again until you had memorized them; that is, you could rehearse the information in short-term memory until it was eventually stored in long-term memory. Long-term memory has no known limits; and as its name suggests, it is relatively durable. Presumably, it is a result of changes in synaptic strength, such as the ones responsible for long-term potentiation. If we stop thinking about something we have just perceived (that is, something contained in short-term memory), we may or may not remember the information later. However, information in long-term memory need not be continuously rehearsed; once we have learned something, we can stop thinking about it until we need the information at a future time.

The simplest model of the memory process says that sensory information enters short-term memory, rehearsal keeps it there, and eventually, the information makes its way into long-term memory, where it is permanently stored. The conversion of short-term memories into long-term memories has been called **consolidation,** because the memories are "made solid," so to speak. (See *Figure 12.25.*)

Now you can understand the original conclusions of Milner and her colleagues: If H.M.'s short-term memory is intact and if he can remember events from before his operation, then the problem must be that consolidation does not take place. Thus, the role of the hippocampal formation in memory is consolidation—converting short-term memories to long-term memories.

Spared Learning Abilities

H.M.'s memory deficit is striking and dramatic. However, when he and other patients with anterograde amnesia are studied more carefully, it becomes apparent that the amnesia does not represent a total failure in learning ability. When the patients are appropriately trained and tested, we find that they are capable of three of the four major types of learning described in the first section of this chapter: perceptual learning, stimulus–response learning, and motor learning.

First, let's consider perceptual learning. Figure 12.26 shows two sample items from a test of the ability to recognize broken drawings; note how the drawings are successively more complete. (See *Figure 12.26.*) Subjects are first shown the least complete set (set I) of each of twenty different drawings. If they do not recognize a figure (and most people do not recognize set I), they are shown more complete sets until they identify it. One hour later, the subjects are tested again for retention, starting with set I. H.M. was given this test and, when retested an hour later, showed considerable improvement (Milner, 1970). When he was retested four months later, he *still* showed this improvement. His performance was not as good as that of normal control subjects, but he showed unmistakable evidence of long-term retention.

The incomplete drawing task is known as a **priming task.** *Priming* refers to the fact that when people perceive a particular stimulus, it becomes easier for them to perceive it again. As you will see, researchers have used several different types of priming tasks to investigate the nature of anterograde amnesia.

Johnson, Kim, and Risse (1985) found that patients with anterograde amnesia could learn to recognize faces and melodies. They played unfamiliar melodies from Korean songs to amnesic patients and found that when they were tested later, the patients preferred these melodies to ones they had not heard before. The experimenters also presented photographs of two men along with stories of their lives: One man was dishonest, mean, and vicious, and the other was nice enough to invite home to dinner. Twenty days later, the amnesic patients said they liked the picture of the "nice" man better than that of the "nasty" one.

Investigators have also succeeded in demonstrating stimulus–response learning by H.M. and other amnesic subjects. For example, Woodruff-Pak (1993) found that H.M. and another patient with anterograde amnesia could acquire a classically conditioned eyeblink response. H.M. even showed retention of the task two years later: He acquired the response again in one-tenth the number of trials that were needed previously. Sidman, Stoddard, and Mohr (1968) successfully trained patient H.M. on an instrumental conditioning task—a visual discrimination task in which pennies were given for correct responses.

Finally, Milner (1965) demonstrated motor learning. She and her colleagues presented H.M. with a mirror-drawing task. This procedure requires the subject to trace the outline of a figure (in this case, a star) with a pencil while looking at the figure in a mirror. (See *Figure 12.27*.) The task may seem simple, but it is actually rather difficult and requires some practice to perform well. With practice, H.M. became proficient at mirror drawing; his errors were reduced considerably during the first session, and his improvement was retained on subsequent days of testing. He also learned a pursuit rotor task, which required him to try to keep a pointer placed above a spot of light moving in a circular path. Thus, several different forms of long-term memory can certainly be established in patients with anterograde amnesia.

Declarative and Nondeclarative Memories

If amnesic patients can learn tasks like these, you might ask, why do we call them *amnesic*? The answer is this: Although the patients can learn to perform these tasks, they do not remember anything about having learned them. They do not remember the experimenters, the room in which the training took place, the apparatus that was used, or any events that occurred during the training. Although H.M. learned to recognize the broken drawings, he denied that he had ever seen them before. Although the amnesic patients in the study by Johnson, Kim, and Risse learned to like some melodies better, they did not recognize that they had heard them before; nor did they remember having seen the pictures of the two young men. Although H.M. successfully acquired a classically conditioned eyeblink response, he did not remember the experimenter, the apparatus, or the headband he wore that held the device that delivered a puff of air to his eye. Similarly, in the experiment by Sidman, Stoddard, and Mohr, although H.M. learned to make the correct response (press a

Long-term memory Relatively stable memory of events that occurred in the more distant past, as opposed to short-term memory.

Consolidation The process by which short-term memories are converted into long-term memories.

Priming task A phenomenon in which exposure to a particular stimulus automatically facilitates perception of that stimulus or related stimuli.

FIGURE 12.27

The mirror-drawing task.

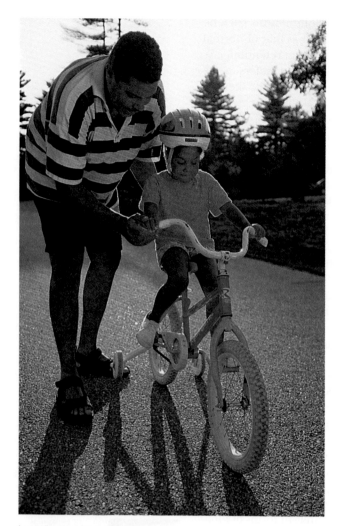

Learning to ride a bicycle is a combination of stimulus-response learning and motor learning, both of which are non-declarative in nature. Remembering when we learned to ride a bicycle is an episodic memory, a form of relational learning.

Declarative memory Memory that can be verbally expressed, such as memory for events in a person's past.

Nondeclarative memory Memory whose formation does not depend on the hippocampal formation; a collective term for perceptual, stimulus–response, and motor memory.

panel with a picture of a circle on it), he was unable to recall having done so. In fact, once H.M. had learned the task, the experimenters interrupted him, had him count his pennies (to distract him for a little while), and then asked him to say what he was supposed to do. He seemed puzzled by the question; he had absolutely no idea. But when they turned on the stimuli again, he immediately made the correct response.

The distinction between what people with anterograde amnesia can and cannot learn is obviously important, because it reflects the basic organization of the learning process. Clearly, there are at least two major categories of memories. Psychologists have given them several different names. For example, some investigators (Eichenbaum, Otto, and Cohen, 1992; Squire, 1992) suggest that patients with anterograde amnesia are unable to form **declarative memories,** which have been defined as those that are "explicitly available to conscious recollection as facts, events, or specific stimuli" (Squire, Shimamura, and Amaral, 1989, p. 218). The term *declarative* obviously comes from *declare*, which means "to proclaim; to announce." The term reflects the fact that patients with anterograde amnesia cannot talk about experiences that they have had since the time of their brain damage. And note that the definition refers specifically to *stimuli*. Thus, according to Squire and his colleagues, declarative memory is a form of *perceptual memory*—specifically, memory of events that we can think and talk about.

The other category of memories, often called **nondeclarative memories,** includes instances of perceptual, stimulus–response, and motor learning that we are not necessarily conscious of. (Some psychologists refer to these two categories as *explicit* and *implicit* memories, respectively.) Nondeclarative memories appear to operate automatically. They do not require deliberate attempts on the part of the learner to memorize something. They do not seem to include facts; instead, they control behaviors. For example, suppose we learn to ride a bicycle. We do so quite consciously and develop declarative memories about our attempts: who helped us learn, where we rode, how we felt, how many times we fell, and so on. But we also form nondeclarative stimulus–response and motor memories; *we learn to ride*. We learn to make automatic adjustments with our hands and bodies that keep our center of gravity above the wheels.

A particularly interesting experiment by Squire et al. (1992) showed that the priming task that I described earlier does not involve the hippocampus but that a test of declarative memory does. Normal subjects were given lists of words to study. Then they were placed in a PET scanner that recorded regional brain activation. They were shown the first three letters of the words and were asked either to say the first word that came to mind (*priming task*) or to use the letter sequences as cues and try to remember the words they had seen on the list (*declarative memory task*). Note that the stimuli were the same in both cases; only the instructions were different.

When the subjects performed the declarative memory task, increased activity was seen in the right hippocampus and right prefrontal cortex. When they performed the priming task, changes were seen in a region of the visual association cortex, but no changes were seen in the hippocampus. (See *Figure 12.28*.)

Table 12.1 lists the declarative and nondeclarative memory tasks that I have described so far. (See *Table 12.1*.)

Memory minus baseline

FIGURE 12.28

PET scan of regional cerebral blood flow. The image represents the difference between blood flow during the baseline condition and during performance of the memory task, averaged across fourteen normal subjects. The peak activity (white center ringed by red, yellow, green, and blue) is located in the region of the hippocampal formation and parahippocampal gyrus.

(From Squire, L.R., Ojemann, J.G., Miezin, F.M., Petersen, S.E., Videen, T.O., and Raichle, M.E. Proceedings of the National Academy of Sciences, 1992, 89, 1837–1841. Reprinted with permission.)

Anterograde Amnesia: Failure of Relational Learning

As we have seen, anterograde amnesia appears to be a loss of the ability to establish new declarative memories; the ability to establish new nondeclarative memories (perceptual, stimulus–response, or motor learning) is intact. What, exactly, are declarative memories? Are they *verbal* memories? Is it simply that people with anterograde amnesia cannot learn new verbal information?

The answer seems to be "no". Declarative memories are not necessarily verbal memories; they are recollections of things or events we have previously experienced. Let's consider the most complex forms of declarative memories: memories of particular episodes. Episodic memories consist of collections of perceptions of events organized in time and identified by a particular context. For example, consider my memory of this morning's breakfast. I put on my robe and slippers, walked downstairs, made coffee, drank some orange juice, made waffle batter, baked a waffle,

TABLE 12.1 Examples of Declarative and Nondeclarative Memory Tasks

DECLARATIVE MEMORY TASKS	
Remembering past experiences	
Learning new works	
Recalling words (DEF___)	

NONDECLARATIVE MEMORY TASKS	TYPE OF LEARNING
Broken drawings	Perceptual
Recognizing faces	Perceptual (and stimulus–response?)
Recognizing melodies	Perceptual
Classical conditioning (eyeblink)	Stimulus–response
Instrumental conditioning (choose circle)	Stimulus–response
Mirror drawing	Motor
Pursuit rotor	Motor
Word completion (DEF___)	Stimulus–response

and ate it at the table next to the window. If I wanted to (and if I thought you were interested), I could give you many more details. The point is that the memory contains many events, organized in time. But would we say that my memory is a *verbal* memory? Clearly not; what I remember about my experience this morning is perceptions of a series of *events,* not a series of *words.* I remember not words but perceptions: the sight of the snow falling outside, the feel of the cold floor replaced by the comfortable warmth of my slippers, the smell of the coffee beans as I opened the container, the rasping sound made by the coffee grinder, and so on.

Obviously, memories must be organized. If you asked me about this morning's breakfast, your words would bring to mind a *set* of perceptual memories—memories of events that occurred at a particular time and place. What does the hippocampal formation have to do with that ability? The most likely explanation is that during the original experience, it somehow ties together a series of perceptions in such a way that their memories, too, are linked. The hippocampal formation enables us to learn the *relation* between the stimuli that were present at the time—the *context* in which the episode occurred—and the events themselves. As we saw, people with anterograde amnesia can form perceptual memories. As the priming studies have shown, once they see something, they are more likely to recognize it later. But their perceptual memories are isolated; the memories of individual objects and events are not tied together or to the context in which they occurred. Thus, seeing a particular person does not remind them of other times they have seen that person or of the things they have done together. Anterograde amnesia appears to be a loss of the ability to learn about the relations among stimuli, including the time and place in which they occurred and the order of their occurrence.

Anatomy of Anterograde Amnesia

The phenomenon of anterograde amnesia and its implications for the nature of relational learning has led investigators to study this phenomenon in laboratory animals. But before I review this research (which has provided some very interesting results), we should examine the brain damage that produces anterograde amnesia. One fact is clear: Damage to the hippocampus, or to regions that supply its inputs and receive its outputs, causes anterograde amnesia.

As we saw earlier in this chapter, the most important input to the hippocampal formation comes from the entorhinal cortex. The entorhinal cortex receives its inputs from the cingulate cortex and all regions of the association cortex, either directly or via two adjacent regions of limbic cortex: the **perirhinal cortex** and the **parahippocampal cortex.** (See *Figure 12.29.*) It also receives information from the amygdala, which may be responsible for the role that emotions play in memories. The outputs of the hippocampal system are relayed back through the entorhinal, perirhinal, and parahippocampal to the same regions that provide inputs: the cingulate cortex and all regions of the association cortex.

The hippocampal formation also receives input from subcortical regions via the fornix. As far as we know, these inputs select and modulate the functions of the hippocampal formation, but they do not supply it with specific information. (An analogy may make this distinction clearer. An antenna supplies a radio with information that is being broadcast, whereas the on–off switch, the volume control, and the station selector control the radio's functions.) The fornix carries dopaminergic axons from the ventral tegmental area, noradrenergic axons from the locus coeruleus, serotonergic axons from the raphe nuclei, and acetylcholinergic axons from the medial septum.

The clearest evidence that damage to the hippocampal formation produces anterograde amnesia came from a case studied by Zola-Morgan, Squire, and Amaral (1986). Patient R.B., a 52-year-old man with a history of heart trouble, sustained a cardiac arrest. Although his heart was successfully restarted, the period of anoxia caused by the temporary halt in blood flow resulted in brain damage. The primary

Perirhinal cortex A region of limbic cortex adjacent to the hippocampal formation that, along with the parahippocampal cortex, relays information between the entorhinal cortex and other regions of the brain.

Parahippocampal cortex A region of limbic cortex adjacent to the hippocampal formation that, along with the perirhinal cortex, relays information between the entorhinal cortex and other regions of the brain.

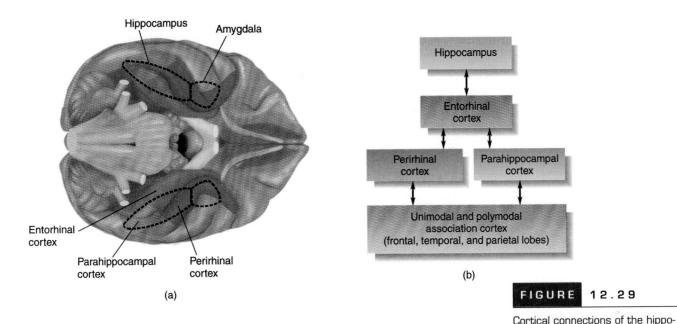

(a)

(b)

FIGURE 12.29

Cortical connections of the hippocampal formation. (a) A view of the base of a monkey's brain. (b) Connections with the cerebral cortex.

(Adapted from Squire, L.R. Psychological Review, 1992, 99, 195–231.)

symptom of this brain damage was a permanent anterograde amnesia, which Zola-Morgan and his colleagues carefully documented. Five years after the onset of the amnesia, R.B. died of heart failure. His family gave permission for histological examination of his brain.

The investigators discovered that field CA1 of the hippocampal formation was gone; its neurons had completely degenerated. Subsequent studies reported other patients with anterograde amnesia caused by CA1 damage (Victor and Agamonolis, 1990; Kartsounis, Rudge, and Stevens, 1995; Rempel-Clower et al., 1996). (See *Figure 12.30.*) In addition, several studies have found that a period of anoxia causes damage to field CA1 in monkeys and in rats and that the damage causes anterograde amnesia in these species, too (Auer, Jensen, and Whishaw, 1989; Zola-Morgan et al., 1992).

Relational Learning in Laboratory Animals

The discovery that hippocampal lesions produced anterograde amnesia in humans stimulated interest in the exact role that this structure plays in the learning process. To pursue this interest, many investigators turned to

(a)

(b)

FIGURE 12.30

Damage to field CA1 caused by anoxia. (a) Section through a normal hippocampus. (b) Section through the hippocampus of patient G.D. The pyramidal cells of field CA1 (between the two arrowheads) have degenerated. (DG = dentate gyrus; gl, ml, pl = layers of the dentate gyrus; PaS = parasubiculum; PrS = presubiculum; S = subiculum; F = fornix).

(From Rempel-Clower, N.L., Zola, S.M., Squire, L.R., and Amaral, D.G. Journal of Neuroscience, 1996, 16, 5233–5255. Reprinted with permission.)

studies with laboratory animals. After the discovery that lesions of the hippocampus caused anterograde amnesia, experimenters began making lesions of the hippocampal formation in animals and testing their learning ability. They quickly found that the animals remained capable of learning most tasks. At the time they were surprised, and some even thought that the hippocampal formation had different functions in humans than it had in other animals. We now realize that most of the learning tasks that the animals were given tested simple stimulus–response learning, and as we saw in the previous section, even humans with anterograde amnesia can do well on such tasks. People's anterograde amnesia becomes apparent only when we talk with them—which is something we cannot do with other animals. However, researchers have developed other tasks that require relational learning, and on such tasks, laboratory animals with hippocampal lesions show memory deficits, just as humans do.

Spatial Perception and Learning

Hippocampal lesions disrupt the ability to keep track of and remember spatial locations. As we saw, H.M. never learned to find his way home when his parents moved after his surgery. Laboratory animals show similar problems in navigation. Morris et al. (1982) developed a task that has been adopted by other researchers as a standard test of rodents' spatial abilities. The task requires rats to find a particular location in space solely by means of visual cues external to the apparatus. The "maze" consists of a circular pool, 1.3 meters in diameter, filled with a mixture of water and powdered milk. The milk mixture hides the location of a small platform, situated just beneath the surface of the liquid. The experimenters put the rats into the milky water and let them swim until they encountered the hidden platform and climbed onto it. They released the rats from a new position on each trial. After a few trials, normal rats learned to swim directly to the hidden platform from wherever they were released. However, rats with hippocampal lesions swam in what appeared to be an aimless fashion until they encountered the platform. Figure 12.31 shows the performance of three rats: a normal rat, one with a neocortical lesion (to control for the fact that removal of the hippocampus entails damage to the overlying neocortex), and one with a hippocampal lesion. The results speak for themselves. (See *Figure 12.31*.)

The Morris milk maze requires relational learning; to navigate around the maze, the animals get their bearings from the relative locations of stimuli located outside the maze. But the maze can be used for nonrelational, stimulus–response learning, too. If the platform is elevated just above the surface of the water so that the rats can see it, even those with hippocampal lesions quickly learn to swim directly toward it. Similarly, if the animals are always released at the same place, they learn to head in a particular direction—say, toward a particular landmark that they can see above the wall of the maze (Eichenbaum, Stewart, and Morris, 1990). I will say more later about why spatial learning is an example of relational learning.

FIGURE 12.31

Effects of hippocampal lesions and neocortical control lesions on performance in the circular "milk maze." The small circle marks the location of the submerged platform.

(Reprinted by permission from Morris, R.G.M., Garrud, P., Rawlins, J.N.P., and O'Keefe, J. Nature, 1982, 297, 681–683. Copyright © 1982, Macmillan Journals Limited.)

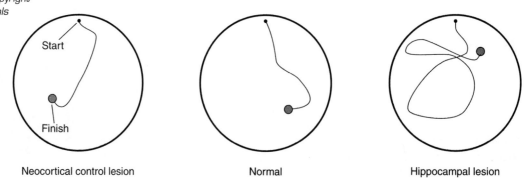

Neocortical control lesion   Normal   Hippocampal lesion

Many different types of studies have confirmed the importance of the hippocampus in spatial learning. For example, Bingman and Mench (1990) found that hippocampal lesions disrupted navigation in homing pigeons. The lesions did not seem to disrupt the birds' ability to get their initial bearing toward the home roost. Instead, the lesions disrupted their ability to keep track of where they were when they got near the end of their flight—at a time during which the birds begin to use familiar landmarks to determine where they are. In a review of the literature, Sherry, Jacobs, and Gaulin (1992) reported that the hippocampal formation of species of birds and rodents that normally store seeds in hidden caches and later retrieve them (and that have excellent memories for spatial locations) is larger than that of animals without this ability.

Place Cells in the Hippocampal Formation

One of the most intriguing discoveries about the hippocampal formation was made by O'Keefe and Dostrovsky (1971), who recorded the activity of individual pyramidal cells in the hippocampus as an animal moved around the environment. The experimenters found that some neurons fired at a high rate only when the rat was in a particular location. Different neurons had different *spatial receptive fields;* that is, they responded when the animals were in different locations. For obvious reasons these neurons were named **place cells.**

When a rat is placed in a symmetrical chamber, where there are few cues to distinguish one part of the apparatus from another, the animal must keep track of its location from objects it sees (or hears) in the environment outside the maze. Changes in these items affect the firing of the rats' place cells as well as their navigational ability. When experimenters move the stimuli as a group, maintaining their relative positions, the animals simply reorient their responses accordingly. However, when the experimenters interchange the stimuli so that they are arranged in a new order, the animals' performance (and the firing of their place cells) is disrupted. (Imagine how disoriented you might be if you entered a familiar room and found that the windows, doors, and furniture were in new positions.)

The fact that neurons in the hippocampal formation have spatial receptive fields does not mean that each neuron encodes a particular location. Instead, this information is undoubtedly represented by particular *patterns* of activity in circuits of neurons within the hippocampal formation. Most investigators believe that when animals encounter new environments, they learn their layout and establish "maps" in their hippocampus. (Presumably, these maps are formed through the process of synaptic strengthening that is responsible for long-term potentiation.) An animal's location within each environment (the animal's place on the map) is encoded by the pattern of firing of these neurons. Obviously, a useful map must remain stable over time. Indeed, Thompson and Best (1990) obtained evidence that the hippocampal maps *are* stable; they found that the receptive fields of hippocampal neurons remained unchanged for as long as they were able to record from them—up to 153 days in one case.

The hippocampal formations of monkeys, like those of rodents, also contain neurons that respond to location, but most of them encode information about what part of the environment the animal is *looking at* rather than where the animal is located. Rolls (1996) refers to these neurons as *spatial view cells* and suggests that their presence in the hippocampus of the monkey reflects the fact that vision is such an important sense modality for primates. The hippocampus of the monkey also contains place cells that respond the way they do in the hippocampus of the rat, but these cells are relatively less numerous (O'Mara et al., 1994).

Role of Long-Term Potentiation in Hippocampal Functioning

Earlier in this chapter we saw how synaptic connections could be quickly modified in the hippocampal formation, leading to long-term potentiation or long-term de-

Place cell A neuron of the hippocampus that becomes active when the animal is in a particular location in the environment.

(a)   (b)

FIGURE 12.32

Effects of a targeted mutation (knockout) of the NMDA receptor gene expressed only in field CA1 of the hippocampus. Photomicrographs of sections through the hippocampus showing in situ hybridization of messenger RNA responsible for the production of NMDA receptors. (a) Normal mouse. (b) Mouse with the targeted mutation (CA1 knockout). Ctx = neocortex, CA1 = hippocampal field CA1, DG = dentate gyrus.

(From Tsien, J.Z., Huerta, P.T., and Tonegawa, S. Cell, 1996, 87, 1327–1338. Reprinted with permission.)

pression. Are these changes in synaptic strength related to the role the hippocampus plays in learning?

The answer appears to be "yes." Recently, researchers have developed targeted mutations of the gene responsible for the production of NMDA receptors which, as we saw, are responsible for long-term potentiation in several parts of the hippocampal formation. Two studies from the same laboratory (McHugh et al., 1996; Tsien, Huerta, and Tonegawa, 1996) used a newly developed method to produce a targeted mutation of the NMDA receptor gene that affects only the CA1 pyramidal cells. NMDA receptors in these neurons failed to develop; in all other parts of the brain these receptors were normal. Figure 12.32 shows photomicrographs of slices through the hippocampus of a normal mouse and a "knockout" mouse, showing in situ hybridization of the messenger RNA for the NMDA receptor. As you can see, this chemical is missing in the CA1 field of the mouse with the targeted mutation. (See *Figure 12.32*.)

As you might expect, the experimenters found that the lack of NMDA receptors prevented the establishment of long-term potentiation in field CA1 in the mice with the targeted mutation. In addition, although the pyramidal cells of CA1 did show spatial receptive fields, these fields were larger and less focused than those shown by cells in normal animals. Finally, the knockout mice learned a Morris milk maze much more slowly than mice whose CA1 neurons contained NMDA receptors.

Theoretical Explanations of Hippocampal Functioning

As we saw earlier, people with anterograde amnesia can learn to recognize new stimuli, can learn new responses, and can learn to make a particular response when a particular stimulus is presented. What they cannot do is to talk about what they have learned. Anterograde amnesia appears to be a loss of the ability to learn about complex relations between many stimuli, including the order of their occurrence in time. How does research with laboratory animals help us to understand this process?

Many investigators have come to the conclusion that the deficit in spatial learning produced by hippocampal lesions is caused by a failure to learn complex relations among stimuli—patterns of stimuli rather than the individual stimuli themselves. For example, according to Wiener, Paul, and Eichenbaum (1989), "An emerging consensus . . . has indicated that the hippocampus is critical to learning and memory over a large range of information modalities that share a common demand for representing relationships among multiple independent percepts, but not for acquiring independent stimulus-reinforcement associations" (p. 2761). Sutherland and Rudy (Sutherland and Rudy, 1989; Rudy and Sutherland, 1995) present a "configural association theory," which suggests that the hippocampal system "combines the representations of elementary stimulus events to construct unique representations and allows for the formation of associations between these configural representations and other elementary representations" (Sutherland and Rudy, 1989, p. 129).

I think it is likely that the original function of the hippocampus was to help the animal learn to navigate in the environment. Later, the process of evolution gave the hippocampus the ability to detect other types of contexts also. Let's first consider the spatial functions. Suppose you are standing in an environment similar to the circular milk maze I described earlier: a large field covered with grass and surrounded by distinctive objects such as trees and buildings. You are familiar with the environment, having walked across it and played games on it many times. If someone blindfolds you and then picks you up and drops you somewhere on the field, you will recognize your location as soon as you remove the blindfold. Your location is defined by the *configuration* of objects you see—the *relation* they have with respect to each other. You will get a different view of these objects from each position on the field. Of course, if there are distinctive objects present on the field itself (trees, garbage cans, drinking fountains), the task will be even easier, because you can judge your position relative to nearby objects as well as distant ones.

How can we put all the information about the hippocampal complex together? As you will recall, the hippocampal complex receives information from all regions of the sensory association cortex and from the motor association cortex of the frontal lobe. It also receives information from the amygdala concerning odors and dangerous stimuli. Thus, the hippocampal complex knows what is going on in the environment, where the animal is located, and what responses it has just made. It also knows about the animal's emotional state: whether the animal is hungry, sexually aroused, frightened, and so on. Thus, when something happens, the hippocampal system has all the information necessary to put that event into the proper context.

What does context have to do with declarative memory deficits in humans? Let's go back to a study involving a human with hippocampal damage and consider why the person can learn a nondeclarative task but cannot recall anything about the experience later. Consider a normal person learning to press a panel with a picture of a circle on it, as patient H.M. did in the experiment by Sidman, Stoddard, and Mohr (1968). While the person is seated in front of the apparatus, his or her hippocampal formation receives information about the context in which the learning is taking place: the room, the other people present, the person's mood, and so on. These pieces of information are collected and are somehow attached to the patterns of activity in the association cortex in several different regions of the brain. Later, when the person is asked about the task, the question reactivates the pattern of activity in the hippocampus, which causes the retrieval of the memory of the episode, pieces of which are stored all over the brain. Patient H.M., lacking a functioning hippocampal system, is unable to accomplish this act.

How might the hippocampus recognize a particular context? Rolls (1989, 1996) presents a hypothetical model of the role of the hippocampal formation in learning and memory that may prove to be useful. Rolls suggests that the hippocampal formation contains neural networks that are capable of *pattern completion:* When they are presented with a fuzzy version of a pattern that the animal previously perceived—or simply a fragment of it—they supply the complete pattern in their output to the association areas of the neocortex. Let's go back to an example I described earlier: this morning's breakfast. When I got up, put on my slippers and robe, and went downstairs to have breakfast, my hippocampus received information from multiple sites in the neocortex about where I was, what time it was, how I was feeling, and so on. That is, it registered the context of that situation. As I went about preparing my breakfast, the memories of what was happening were being recorded in the form of synaptic changes in various regions of my sensory association cortex. The hippocampus communicated with these regions, somehow tying together these memories as they were being formed.

When you asked me about what I had for breakfast this morning, the words were recognized and understood by language mechanisms in my left temporal and parietal lobes (more about that in Chapter 13). Information about this recognition was sufficient for my hippocampal formation to recognize the context—to *complete the pattern.* The pattern was broadcast through outputs of the hippocampal formation to the locations in my neocortex that contain the individual components of the memory of the episode, and I told you about my breakfast.

This analysis is certainly speculative, but I think it is consistent with the experimental data I have presented in this chapter. Of course, it is vague about many parts of the process. For example, just how does asking someone a question activate the pattern of activity in the hippocampus? And how, exactly, are memories "tied together"? How are pieces of information collected and attached to sets of neural circuits? Obviously, we need to think about these questions, design clever experiments to obtain useful information, think about the questions in light of the new information, design more clever experiments . . .

INTERIM SUMMARY

Brain damage can produce anterograde amnesia, which consists of the inability to remember events that happen after the damage occurs, even though short-term memory (such as that needed to carry on a conversation) is largely intact. The patients also have a retrograde amnesia of several years' duration but can remember information from the distant past. Anterograde amnesia can be caused by the thiamine deficiency that sometimes accompanies chronic alcoholism (Korsakoff's syndrome), or it can be produced by bilateral removal of the medial temporal lobes.

The first explanation for anterograde amnesia was that the ability of the brain to consolidate short-term memories into long-term memories was damaged. However, ordinary perceptual, stimulus–response, and motor learning do not appear to be impaired; people can learn to recognize new stimuli, they are capable of instrumental and classical conditioning, and they can acquire motor memories. But they are not capable of *declarative learning*—of describing events that happen to them. The amnesia has also been called a deficit in explicit memory. An even more descriptive term—one that applies to laboratory animals as well as to humans—is *relational learning*.

Although other structures may be involved, researchers are now confident that the primary cause of anterograde amnesia is damage to the hippocampal formation or to its inputs and outputs. Temporary anoxia damages field CA1 and produces anterograde amnesia. The entorhinal cortex receives information from all regions of the association cortex, directly and through its connections with the perirhinal and parahippocampal cortex that surrounds it. The outputs of the hippocampal formation are relayed through these same regions. Subcortical inputs and outputs to the hippocampal formation pass through the fornix and modulate hippocampal functions.

Studies with laboratory animals indicate that damage to the hippocampal formation disrupts the ability to learn spatial relations and to distinguish events that have just occurred from those that have occurred at another time. For example, rats with hippocampal damage cannot learn the Morris milk maze unless they can see the platform or they are always released from the same place in the maze. The basic deficit appears to be an inability to distinguish among different contexts, which includes locations in space and in time.

The hippocampal formation contains neurons that respond when the animal is in a particular location, which implies that the hippocampus contains neural networks that keep track of the relations among stimuli in the environment that define the animal's location. Neurons in the hippocampal formation also respond to particular visual and tactual cues, such as those on the floors and walls of particular arms of a maze. Place cells in primates tend to respond according to the particular location the animal is looking at.

Long-term potentiation appears to be related to learning. A unique targeted mutation against the NMDA receptor gene in field CA1 disrupts long-term potentiation and the ability to learn the Morris milk maze.

The original role of the hippocampal formation may well have been to provide animals with the ability to orient in space, keeping track of the multiple stimuli that define spatial location; but it is clear that its role has expanded to learning relations among nonspatial stimuli and situations as well. More generally, the hippocampus is important in distinguishing one context from another. Presumably, people with anterograde amnesia can no longer learn about episodes in their lives because their inability to distinguish one context from another prevents the elements that make up an episode from being tied together.

■ THOUGHT QUESTIONS

Although we can only live in the present, our memories are an important aspect of our identities. Imagine having a memory deficit like H.M.'s. Imagine having no recollection of over 30 years of experiences. Imagine being surprised every time you see yourself in the mirror and discover someone who is more than 30 years older than you believe yourself to be.

EPILOGUE
Mnemonic Devices

Some things are exceedingly easy to remember. Suppose you are walking down the street and see someone fall from the roof of a building. You will not have to rehearse this information verbally to remember it; you see it so vividly that the scene remains with you always. But often we must remember information that does not fit in such a tidy package. When the information is hard to learn, we usually employ a special word to identify the process: *memorization*.

When we can imagine information vividly and concretely, and when it fits into the context of what we already know, it is easy to remember later. People have known this fact for millennia and have devised systems for remembering things to take advantage of it. All *mnemonic systems* (from the Greek *mneme*, meaning "memory") make use of information already stored in long-term memory to make memorization an easier task.

Mnemonic systems do not simplify information; in fact, they make it more elaborate. *More* information is stored, not less. However, the additional information makes the material easier to recall. Furthermore, mnemonic

systems organize new information into a cohesive whole so that retrieval of part of the information ensures retrieval of the rest of it. These facts suggest that the ease or difficulty with which we learn new information depends not on *how much* we must learn but on *how well it fits with what we already know*. The better it fits, the easier it is to retrieve.

In Greece before the sixth century B.C., few people knew how to write, and those who did had to use cumbersome clay tablets. Consequently, oratory skills and memory for long epic poems (running for several hours) were highly prized, and some people earned a living by using them. Because people could not carry around several hundred pounds of clay tablets, they had to keep important information in their heads. To do so, the Greeks devised the *method of loci*. (The word *locus* means "place"; the plural is *loci*.)

To use the method of loci, would-be mnemonists (memory artists) had to memorize the inside of a building. In Greece they would wander through public buildings, stopping to study and memorize various locations and ar-

ranging them in order, usually starting with the door of the building. After memorizing the locations, they could make the tour mentally, just as you could make a mental tour of your house to count the windows. To learn a list of words, they would visualize each word in a particular location in the memorized building and picture the association as vividly as possible. For example, for the word *love* they might imagine an embracing couple leaning against a particular column in a hall of the building. To recall the list, they would imagine each of the locations in sequence, "see" the word, and say it. To store a speech, they would group the words into concepts and place a "note" for each concept at a particular location in the sequence.

Mnemonists could use a single building as a "memory temple" to store many different sequences. Modern psychologists still cannot explain why sequences from different speeches or poems did not become confused with each other.

Another useful aid to memory is to organize information into a narrative. Bower and Clark (1969) showed that even inexperienced subjects can use

(continued)

EPILOGUE *(continued)*

this method. The investigators asked subjects to try to learn twelve lists of ten concrete nouns each. They gave some of the subjects the following advice:

> A good way to learn the list of items is to make up a story relating the items to one another. Specifically, start with the first item and put it in a setting which will allow other items to be added to it. Then, add the other items to the story in the same order as the items appear. Make each story meaningful to yourself. Then, when you are asked to recall the items, you can simply go through your story and pull out the proper items in their correct order. (Bower and Clark, 1969, p. 181)

A typical narrative, described by one of the subjects, was as follows (list words are italicized): "A *lumberjack darted* out of the forest, *skated* around a *hedge* past a *colony* of *ducks*. He tripped on some *furniture*, tearing his *stocking* while hastening to the *pillow* where his *mistress* lay."

Control subjects were merely asked to learn the lists and were given the same amount of time as the "narrative" subjects to study them.

Both groups could remember a particular list equally well immediately afterward. However, when all the lists had been learned, recall of all 120 words was far superior in the group that had constructed narrative stories.

Information is often easier to remember when it is organized by rhythm and rhyme (or both). For example, when most people learn the alphabet, they do so to the tune of a little song. Because of this, when they recite the alphabet they say: A, B, C, D, E, F, G (pause), H, I, J, K (now go twice as fast), L-M-N-O-P (pause) . . . and so on. Somehow, the structure of the rhythm and the melody of a song facilitate the learning of a list of verbal material.

Sometimes, information can be cast into the form of a poem, which people find easy to remember. Perhaps you learned a rhyme similar to the following one: "I before E except after C, or when sounded as A, as in neighbor or weigh." And if you need to remember how many days there in December, do you say to yourself, "Thirty days have September, April, June, and November . . . "?

Another use of rhythm and rhyme is to keep the initial letters of a list of words to be remembered and re-

place them with words that will fit into a verse. For example, to keep track of the order of the names of the twelve cranial nerves, students learn, "On old Olympus' towering tops, a Finn and German viewed some hops" (with the intention of making beer, I suppose). The initial letters stand for *olfactory, optic, occulomotor, trochlear, trigeminal, abducens, facial, auditory, glossopharyngeal, vagus, spinal accessory, hypoglossal*. If the students need help in remembering the order of the three nerves that begin with the letter O, they can remember that the second letters (L, P, and C) spell out "Lovers prefer caresses."

Obviously, mnemonic systems have their limitations. They are useful for memorizing information that can be reduced to a list of words, but not all information can easily be converted to such a form. For example, if you were preparing to take an examination on the information in this chapter, figuring out how to encode it into lists would probably take you more time than studying and learning it by more traditional methods, such as those suggested in Chapter 1, in the section titled "Strategies for Learning," and in the study guide.

KEY CONCEPTS

THE NATURE OF LEARNING

1. Learning takes many forms. The most important categories appear to be perceptual learning, stimulus–response learning, motor learning, and relational learning.

2. The Hebb rule describes the synaptic change that appears to be responsible for stimulus–response learning: If an initially weak synapse repeatedly fires at the same time that the postsynaptic neuron fires, the synapse will become strengthened.

LEARNING AND SYNAPTIC PLASTICITY

3. Long-term potentiation occurs when axons in the hippocampal formation are repeatedly stimulated.

4. Associative long-term potentiation appears to follow the Hebb rule and understanding it may help us understand the physiological basis of learning.

5. The special properties of NMDA receptors account for associative long-term potentiation.

PERCEPTUAL LEARNING

6. Learning to recognize complex stimuli involves changes in the association cortex of the appropriate sensory modality.

CLASSICAL CONDITIONING

7. Study of the role of the amygdala and associated structures in learning conditioned emotional re-

sponses has furthered our understanding of the physiological basis of classical conditioning.

INSTRUMENTAL CONDITIONING AND MOTOR LEARNING

8. The basal ganglia appear to be involved in the retention of learned behaviors that have become automatic and routine.
9. Electrical stimulation of several parts of the brain, especially the medial forebrain bundle, can reinforce an animal's behavior.
10. Reinforcing brain stimulation is effective because it causes the activation of neurons in the mesolimbic system, which releases dopamine in the nucleus accumbens.
11. Drugs that block dopaminergic transmission in the nucleus accumbens block the reinforcing effects of electrical stimulation of the brain.

RELATIONAL LEARNING

12. Damage to the hippocampal complex causes a syndrome of anterograde amnesia, in which people can learn to perform perceptual, S–R, or motor learning tasks but cannot describe episodes from their lives.
13. Studies with laboratory animals suggest that the hippocampal formation, which may originally have developed as part of a mechanism for spatial learning, now is also responsible for other forms of relational learning, recognizing contexts and coordinating learning that takes place in many parts of the brain.

◼ SUGGESTED READINGS

Cohen, N.J., and Eichenbaum, H. *Memory, Amnesia, and the Hippocampal System.* Cambridge, MA: MIT Press, 1993.

Graf, P., and Masson, M.E.J. *Implicit Memory: New Directions in Cognition, Development, and Neuropsychology.* Hillsdale, NJ: Erlbaum Associates, 1993.

McGaugh, J.L., Weinberger, N.M., and Lynch, G. *Brain and Memory: Modulation and Mediation of Neuroplasticity.* New York: Oxford University Press, 1995.

Ono, T., McNaughton, B.L., Molotchnikoff, S., Rolls, E.T., and Nishijo, H. *Perception, Memory and Emotion: Frontier in Neuroscience.* Amsterdam: Elsevier, 1996.

Schacter, D.L. *Searching for Memory: The Brain, the Mind, and the Past.* New York: Basic Books, 1996.

Squire, L.R., and Butters, N. *Neuropsychology of Memory.* New York: Guilford Press, 1992.

Thompson, R.F. Mammalian brain substrates of aversive classical conditioning. *Annual Review of Psychology,* 1993, *43,* 317–342.

13

Human Communication

LEARNING OBJECTIVES

1. Describe the use of subjects with brain damage in the study of language, and explain the concept of lateralization.

2. Describe Broca's aphasia and the three major speech deficits that result from damage to Broca's area: agrammatism, anomia, and articulation difficulties.

3. Describe the symptoms of Wernicke's aphasia, pure word deafness, and transcortical sensory aphasia, and explain how they are related.

4. Discuss the brain mechanisms that underlie our ability to understand the meaning of words and to express our own thoughts and perceptions in words.

5. Describe the symptoms of conduction aphasia and anomic aphasia, including aphasia in deaf people.

6. Describe pure alexia, and explain why this disorder is caused by damage to two specific parts of the brain.

7. Describe whole-word and phonetic reading, and discuss five categories of acquired dyslexias.

8. Explain the relation between speaking and writing, and describe the symptoms of phonological dysgraphia, orthographic dysgraphia, and semantic (direct) dysgraphia.

9. Describe research on the neurological basis of developmental dyslexias.

Can't Hear Words

Dr. D. presented the case. "Mr. S. had two strokes about ten years ago, which damaged both temporal lobes. His hearing, tested by an audiologist, is in the normal range. But as you will see, his speech comprehension is deficient."

Actually, as we soon saw, it was nonexistent. Mr. S. was ushered into the conference room and shown an empty chair at the head of the table, where we could all see and hear him. He looked calm and unworried; in fact, he seemed to be enjoying himself, and it occurred to me that this was probably not the first time he had been the center of attention. I had read about the syndrome I was about to see, and I knew that it was very rare.

"Mr. S., will you tell us how you are feeling?" asked Dr. D.

The patient turned his head at the sound of his voice and said, "Sorry, I can't understand you."

"How are you feeling?" he asked in a loud voice.

"Oh, I can hear you all right, I just can't understand you. Here," he said, handing Dr. D. a pencil and a small pad of paper.

Dr. D. took the pencil and paper and wrote something. He handed them back to Mr. S., who looked at it and said, "Fine. I'm just fine."

"Will you tell us about what you have been doing lately?" asked Dr. D. Mr. S. smiled, shook his head, and handed him the paper and pencil again.

"Oh sure," he said after reading the new question, and he proceeded to tell us about his garden and his other hobbies. "I don't get much from television unless there are a lot of close-ups, where I can read their lips. I like to listen to music on the radio, but, of course, the lyrics don't mean too much to me!" He laughed at his own joke, which had probably already seen some mileage.

"You mean that you can read lips?" someone asked.

Mr. S. immediately turned toward the sound of the voice and said, "What did you say? Say it slow, so I can try to read your lips." We all laughed, and Mr. S. joined us when the question was repeated slowly enough for him to decode. Another person tried to ask him a question, but apparently his Spanish accent made it impossible for Mr. S. to read his lips.

Suddenly, the phone rang. We all, including Mr. S., looked up at the wall where it was hanging. "Someone else had better get that," he said. "I'm not much good on the phone."

After Mr. S. had left the room, someone observed that although Mr. S.'s speech was easy to understand, it seemed a bit strange. "Yes," said a speech therapist, "he almost sounds like a deaf person who has learned to talk but doesn't get the pronunciation of the words just right."

Dr. D. nodded and played a tape for us. "This recording was made a few months after his strokes, ten years ago." We heard the same voice, but this time it sounded absolutely normal.

"Oh," said the speech therapist. "He has lost the ability to monitor his own speech, and over the years he has forgotten some of the details of how various words are pronounced."

"Exactly," said Dr. D. "The change has been a gradual one."

Verbal behaviors constitute one of the most important classes of human social behavior. Our cultural evolution has been possible because we can talk and listen, write and read. Language enables our discoveries to be cumulative; knowledge gained by one generation can be passed on to the next.

The basic function of verbal communication is seen in its effects on other people. When we talk to someone, we almost always expect our speech to induce the person to engage in some sort of behavior. Sometimes, the behavior is of obvious advantage to us, as when we ask for an object or for help in performing a task. At other times we are simply asking for a social exchange: some attention and perhaps some conversation. Even "idle" conversation is not idle, because it causes another person to look at us and say something in return.

This chapter discusses the neural basis of verbal behavior: talking, understanding speech, reading, and writing.

◼ SPEECH PRODUCTION AND COMPREHENSION: BRAIN MECHANISMS

Our knowledge of the physiology of language has been obtained primarily by observing the effects of brain lesions on people's verbal behavior. Although investigators have studied people who have undergone brain surgery or who have sustained head injuries, brain tumors, or infections, most of the observations have been made on people who have suffered strokes, or **cerebrovascular accidents.** The most common type of cerebrovascular accident is caused by obstruction of a blood vessel. The interruption in blood flow deprives a region of the brain of its blood supply, which causes cells in that region to die.

The most important category of speech disorders is **aphasia,** a primary disturbance in the comprehension or production of speech, caused by brain damage. Not all speech disturbances are aphasias; a patient must have difficulty comprehending, repeating, or producing meaningful speech, and this difficulty must not be caused by simple sensory or motor deficits or by lack of motivation. For example, inability to speak caused by deafness or paralysis of the speech muscles is not considered to be aphasia. In addition, the deficit must be relatively isolated; that is, the patient must appear to be aware of what is happening in his or her environment and to comprehend that others are attempting to communicate.

Lateralization

Verbal behavior is a *lateralized* function; most language disturbances occur after damage to the left side of the brain. The best way to determine which side of the brain is dominant for speech is to perform a *Wada test,* named after its inventor. A patient who is about to undergo surgery that might encroach on a speech area receives a short-acting anesthetic in one carotid artery and then, when the effects have worn off, in the other. This procedure anesthetizes first one cerebral hemisphere and then the other; thus, in a few minutes the involvement of each hemisphere in speech functions can be assessed. In over 95 percent of right-handed people the left hemisphere is dominant for speech. That is, when the left hemisphere is anesthetized, the person loses the ability to speak. However, when the right hemisphere is anesthetized, the person can still talk and carry on a conversation. The figure is somewhat lower in left-handed people: approximately 70 percent. Therefore, unless I say otherwise, you can assume that the brain damage described in this chapter is located in the left (speech-dominant) hemisphere.

Why is one hemisphere specialized for speech? The perceptual functions of the left hemisphere are more specialized for the analysis of sequences of stimuli, occurring one after the other. The perceptual functions of the right hemisphere are more specialized for the analysis of space and geometrical shapes and forms, the elements of which are all present at the same time. Speech is certainly sequential; it consists of sequences of words, which are composed of sequences of sounds. Therefore, it makes sense for the left hemisphere to have become specialized at perceiving speech. In addition, as we saw in Chapter 3, the left hemisphere is involved in the control of sequences of voluntary movements. Perhaps this fact accounts for the localization of neural circuits involved in speech production, as well as speech perception, in the left hemisphere.

Although the circuits that are *primarily* involved in speech comprehension and production are located in the left hemisphere, it would be a mistake to conclude that the right hemisphere plays no role in speech. Speech is not simply a matter of talking; it is also having something to say. Similarly, listening is not simply hearing and recognizing words; it is understanding the meaning of what has been said. When we

Cerebrovascular accident A "stroke"; brain damage caused by occlusion or rupture of a blood vessel in the brain.

Aphasia Difficulty in producing or comprehending speech not produced by deafness or a simple motor deficit; caused by brain damage.

hear and understand words, and when we talk about or think about our own perceptions or memories, we are using neural circuits besides those directly involved in speech. Thus, these circuits, too, play a role in verbal behavior. For example, damage to the right hemisphere makes it difficult for a person to read maps, perceive spatial relations, and recognize complex geometrical forms. People with such damage also have trouble talking about things like maps and complex geometrical forms or understanding what other people have to say about them. The right hemisphere also appears to be involved in organizing a narrative—selecting and assembling the elements of what we want to say (Gardner et al., 1983). As we saw in Chapter 10, the right hemisphere is involved in the expression and recognition of emotion in the tone of voice. Therefore, both hemispheres of the brain have a contribution to make to our language abilities.

Speech Production

Being able to talk—that is, to produce meaningful speech—requires several abilities. First, the person must have something to talk about. Let us consider what this means. We can talk about something that is currently happening or something that happened in the past. In the first case we are talking about our perceptions: things we are seeing, hearing, feeling, smelling, and so on. In the second case we are talking about our memories of what happened in the past. Both perceptions of current events and memories of events that occurred in the past involve brain mechanisms in the posterior part of the cerebral hemispheres (the occipital, temporal, and parietal lobes). Thus, this region is largely responsible for our having something to say.

Of course, we can also talk about something that *did not* happen. That is, we can use our imagination to make up a story (or to tell a lie). We know very little about the neural mechanisms that are responsible for imagination, but it seems likely that they involve the mechanisms responsible for perceptions and memories; after all, when we make up a story, we must base it on knowledge that we originally acquired through perception and have retained in our memory.

Given that a person has something to say, actually doing so requires some additional brain functions. As we shall see in this section, the conversion of perceptions, memories, and thoughts into speech makes use of neural mechanisms located in the frontal lobes.

Damage to a region of the inferior left frontal lobe (Broca's area) disrupts the ability to speak: It causes **Broca's aphasia.** This disorder is characterized by slow, laborious, and nonfluent speech. When trying to talk with patients who have Broca's aphasia, most people find it hard to resist supplying the words the patients are obviously groping for. But although they often mispronounce words, the ones they manage to come out with are usually meaningful. The posterior part of the cerebral hemispheres has something to say, but the damage to the frontal lobe makes it difficult for the patients to express these thoughts.

People with Broca's aphasia find it easier to say some types of words than others. They have great difficulty saying the little words with grammatical meaning, such as *a, the, some, in,* or *about.* These words are called **function words,** because they have important grammatical functions. The words that they do manage to say are almost entirely **content words**—words that convey meaning, including nouns, verbs, adjectives, and adverbs, such as

Broca's aphasia A form of aphasia characterized by agrammatism, anomia, and extreme difficulty in speech articulation.

Function word A preposition, article, or other word that conveys little of the meaning of a sentence but is important in specifying its grammatical structure.

Content word A noun, verb, adjective, or adverb that conveys meaning.

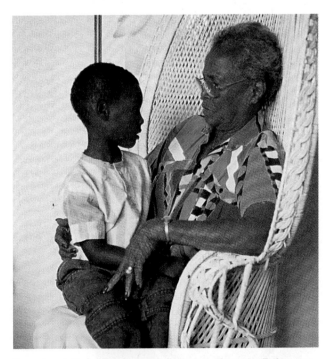

Speech entails more than the production of words: Before we can communicate, we must have something to say.

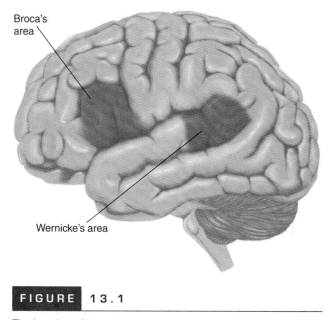

Broca's area

Wernicke's area

FIGURE 13.1

The location of the primary speech areas of the brain. (Wernicke's area will be described later.)

apple, house, throw, or heavy. Here is a sample of speech from a man with Broca's aphasia, who is telling the examiner why he has come to the hospital. As you will see, his words are meaningful, but what he says is certainly not grammatical. The dots indicate long pauses.

> Ah . . . Monday . . . ah Dad and Paul [patient's name] . . . and Dad . . . hospital. Two . . . ah doctors . . . , and ah . . . thirty minutes . . . and yes . . . ah . . . hospital. And, er Wednesday . . . nine o'clock. And er Thursday, ten o' clock . . . doctors. Two doctors . . . and ah . . . teeth. Yeah . . . fine. (Goodglass, 1976, p. 278)

People with Broca's aphasia can comprehend speech much better than they can produce it. In fact, some observers have said that their comprehension is unimpaired, but as we will see, this is not quite true. Broca (1861) suggested that this form of aphasia is produced by a lesion of the frontal association cortex, just anterior to the face region of the primary motor cortex. Subsequent research proved him to be essentially correct, and we now call the region **Broca's area.** (See *Figure 13.1.*)

Lesions that produce Broca's aphasia are certainly centered in the vicinity of Broca's area. However, damage that is restricted to the cortex of Broca's area does not appear to produce Broca's aphasia; the damage must extend to surrounding regions of the frontal lobe and to the underlying subcortical white matter (H. Damasio, 1989; Naeser et al., 1989). In addition, there is evidence that lesions of the basal ganglia—especially the head of the caudate nucleus—can also produce a Broca-like aphasia (Damasio, Eslinger, and Adams, 1984). Figure 13.2 shows the averaged plot of PET scans of regional blood flow from a group of subjects who were reading words aloud (Leblanc et al., 1992). As you can see, the task activated subcortical regions under Broca's area (including the head of the caudate nucleus) as well as the neocortex. (See *Figure 13.2.*)

What do the neural circuits in and around Broca's area do? Wernicke (1874) suggested that Broca's area contains motor memories—in particular, *memories of the sequences of muscular movements that are needed to articulate words.* Talking involves rapid movements of the tongue, lips, and jaw, and these movements must be coordinated with each other and with those of the vocal cords; thus, talking requires some very sophisticated motor control mechanisms. Obviously, circuits of neurons somewhere in our brain will, when properly activated, cause these sequences of movements to be executed. Because damage to the inferior caudal left frontal lobe (including Broca's area) disrupts the ability to articulate words, this region is the most likely candidate for the location of these "programs." The fact that this region is directly connected to the part of the primary motor cortex that controls the muscles used for speech certainly supports this conclusion.

Broca's area   A region of the frontal cortex, located just rostral to the base of the left primary motor cortex, that is necessary for normal speech production.

Percent change in blood flow

FIGURE 13.2

An averaged plot of PET scans of regional cerebral blood flow, superimposed on an MRI scan, taken while the subjects were reading words aloud. Note that the region of activation includes subcortical regions as well as the cerebral cortex of Broca's area. Also note that left and right are reversed.

(From Leblanc, R., Meyer, E., Bub, D., Zatorre, R.J., and Evans, A.C. Neurosurgery, 1992, 31, 369–373. Reprinted with permission.)

But the speech functions of the left frontal lobe include more than programming the movements that are used to speak. Broca's aphasia is much more than a deficit in pronouncing words. In general, three major speech deficits are produced by lesions in and around Broca's area: *agrammatism, anomia,* and *articulation difficulties.* Although most patients with Broca's aphasia will have all of these deficits to some degree, their severity can vary considerably from person to person—presumably, because their brain lesions differ.

Agrammatism refers to a patient's difficulty in using grammatical constructions. This disorder can appear all by itself, without any difficulty in pronouncing words (Nadeau, 1988). As we saw, people with Broca's aphasia rarely use function words. In addition, they rarely use grammatical markers such as *-ed* or auxiliaries such as *have* (as in *I have gone*). For some reason, they *do* often use *-ing*, perhaps because this ending converts a verb into a noun. A study by Saffran, Schwartz, and Marin (1980) illustrates this difficulty. The following quotations are from agrammatic patients attempting to describe pictures:

Picture of a boy being hit in the head by a baseball

The boy is catch . . . the boy is hitch . . . the boy is hit the ball. (Saffran, Schwartz, and Marin, 1980, p. 229)

Picture of a girl giving flowers to her teacher

Girl . . . wants to . . . flowers . . . flowers and wants to. . . . The woman . . . wants to. . . . The girl wants to . . . the flowers and the woman. (Saffran, Schwartz, and Marin, 1980, p. 234)

So far, I have described Broca's aphasia as a disorder in speech *production.* In an ordinary conversation, Broca's aphasics seem to understand everything that is said to them. They appear to be irritated and annoyed by their inability to express their thoughts well, and they often make gestures to supplement their scanty speech. The striking disparity between their speech and their comprehension often leads people to assume that their comprehension is normal. But it is not. Schwartz, Saffran, and Marin (1980) showed Broca's aphasics pairs of pictures in which agents and objects of the action were reversed: for example, a horse kicking a cow and a cow kicking a horse, a truck pulling a car and a car pulling a truck, and a dancer applauding a clown and a clown applauding a dancer. As they showed each pair of pictures, they read the subject a sentence; for example, *The horse kicks the cow.* The subjects' task was to point to the appropriate picture, indicating whether they understood the grammatical construction of the sentence. (See *Figure 13.3.*) They performed very poorly.

The correct picture in the study by Schwartz and her colleagues was specified by a particular aspect of grammar: word order. The agrammatism that accompanies Broca's aphasia appears to disrupt patients' ability to use grammatical information, including word order, to decode the meaning of a sentence. Thus, their deficit in comprehension parallels their deficit in production. If they heard a sentence such as *The man swats the mosquito,* they would understand that it concerns a man and a mosquito and the action of swatting. They would have no trouble figuring out who is doing what to whom. But a sentence such as *The horse kicks the cow* does not provide any extra cues; if the grammar is not understood, neither is the meaning of the sentence.

The second major speech deficit seen in Broca's aphasia is **anomia** ("without name"). Anomia refers to a word-finding

Agrammatism One of the usual symptoms of Broca's aphasia; a difficulty in comprehending or properly employing grammatical devices, such as verb endings and word order.

Anomia Difficulty in finding (remembering) the appropriate word to describe an object, action, or attribute; one of the symptoms of aphasia.

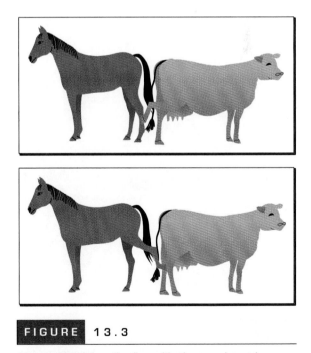

FIGURE 13.3

An example of the stimuli used in the experiment by Schwartz, Saffran, and Marin (1980).

difficulty; and because all aphasics omit words or use inappropriate ones, anomia is actually a primary symptom of *all* forms of aphasia. However, because the speech of Broca's aphasics lacks fluency, their anomia is especially apparent; their facial expression and frequent use of sounds such as "uh" make it obvious that they are groping for the correct words.

The third major characteristic of Broca's aphasia is *difficulty with articulation*. Patients mispronounce words, often altering the sequence of sounds. For example, *lipstick* might be pronounced "likstip." People with Broca's aphasia recognize that their pronunciation is erroneous, and they usually try to correct it.

These three deficits are seen in various combinations in different patients, depending on the exact location of the lesion and, to a certain extent, on their stage of recovery. We can think of these deficits as constituting a hierarchy. On the lowest, most elementary level is control of the sequence of movements of the muscles of speech; damage to this ability leads to articulation difficulties. The next higher level is selection of the particular "programs" for individual words; damage to this ability leads to anomia. Finally, the highest level is selection of grammatical structure, including word order, use of function words, and word endings; damage to this ability leads to agrammatism.

We might expect that the direct control of articulation would involve the face area of the primary motor cortex and portions of the basal ganglia, while the selection of words, word order, and grammatical markers would involve Broca's area and adjacent regions of the frontal association cortex. Some recent studies indicate that different categories of symptoms of Broca's aphasia do, indeed, involve different brain regions. Dronkers (1996) appears to have found a critical location for control of speech articulation: the left precentral gyrus of the insula. The insular cortex is located on the lateral wall of the cerebral hemisphere behind the anterior temporal lobe. Normally, this region is hidden and can be seen only when the temporal lobe is dissected away. (See *Figure 13.4*.) Dronkers discovered the apparent role of this region by plotting the lesions of patients with and without apraxia of speech who had strokes that damaged the same general area of the brain. (**Apraxia of speech** is an impairment in the ability to program movements of the tongue, lips, and throat that are required to produce the proper sequence of speech sounds.) Figure 13.5(a) shows the overlap of the lesions of twenty-five patients with apraxia of speech. As you can see, a region of 100 percent overlap, shown in yellow, falls on the left precentral gyrus of the insula. (See *Figure 13.5a*.) In contrast, *none* of the lesions of nineteen patients who did not show apraxia of speech included damage to this region. (See *Figure 13.5b*.)

The agrammatism and anomia of Broca's aphasia are normally caused by subcortical damage or damage to the neocortex of the inferior frontal lobe. These findings are supported by a PET study by Stromswold et al. (1996). Subjects listened to syntactically complex sentences and had to decide whether they made sense. For example, "The dog that the cat scratched chased the mouse" makes sense, while "The mouse that the cat scratched chased the dog" does not. Listening to such sentences and judging their plausibility certainly exercises neural circuits involved in comprehension of grammar—and the investigators found that doing so increased the activity of Broca's area, especially the part closest to the lateral fissure.

Experiments have shown that people with Broca's aphasia have difficulty carrying out a sequence of com-

Apraxia of speech Impairment in the ability to program movements of the tongue, lips, and throat required to produce the proper sequence of speech sounds.

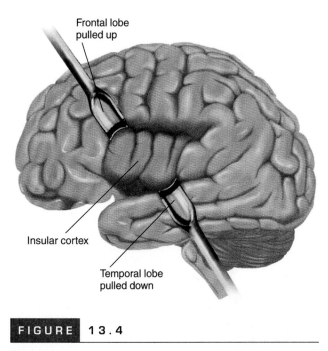

Frontal lobe pulled up

Insular cortex

Temporal lobe pulled down

FIGURE 13.4

The insular cortex, normally hidden behind the rostral temporal lobe.

mands such as "Pick up the red circle and touch the green square with it" (Boller and Dennis, 1979). This finding, along with the other symptoms I have described in this section, suggests that an important function of the left frontal lobe is sequencing—of movements of the muscles of speech (producing words) and of words (comprehending and producing grammatical speech).

One study has found that agrammatism can be caused by damage to the cerebellum. Traditionally, the cerebellum has been regarded as a computer involved in coordinating movements, especially those involving precise timing. Neurologists have long recognized the fact that damage to the cerebellum can disrupt motor control of speech, which is not surprising when we consider the role the cerebellum plays in all forms of rapid, skilled movements. The speech of patients who have cerebellar damage is slow and monotonous, syllables tend to be separated by brief pauses, and enunciation is imprecise (Adams and Victor, 1981). However, the advent of PET and functional MRI scanning has found that even when movement is controlled for, engaging in various types of verbal activity activates the cerebellum (Fiez, 1996). The cerebellum may even be involved in grammatical aspects of speech. Silveri, Leggio, and Molinari (1994) studied a patient with cerebellar damage with agrammatic speech, characterized by uninflected verb forms. The following quotation (a word-by-word translation from the original Italian) illustrates the agrammatic nature of this patient's speech:

FIGURE 13.5

Evidence for involvement of the insular cortex in speech articulation. Percentage overlap in the lesions of twenty-five patients (a) with apraxia of speech and (b) without apraxia of speech. The only region common to all lesions that produced apraxia of speech was the precentral gyrus of the insular cortex.

(Reprinted with permission from Dronkers, N.F. Nature, 1996, 384, 159–161. Copyright 1996 Macmillan Magazines Limited.)

> I was watching television. One moment after, immediately after, to feel one half not to go. To have an attack, to be unable to speak. Upstairs there was my wife sleeping because it was midnight. I suddenly to stand up suddenly to fall down. Not to do anything because there was the carpet. Not to speak then to vomit all night long. I to vomit. My son came, soon an injection he gives and the drips. I to wait that here at the Polyclinic is admitted that free the bed. To wait that here to be the bed free to give the bed free.

Speech Comprehension

Comprehension of speech obviously begins in the auditory system, which detects and analyzes sounds. But *recognizing* words is one thing; *comprehending* them—understanding their meaning—is another. Recognizing a spoken word is a complex perceptual task that relies on memories of sequences of sounds. This task appears to be accomplished by neural circuits in the middle and posterior portion of the superior temporal gyrus of the left hemisphere—a region that has come to be known as **Wernicke's area.** (Refer to *Figure 13.1.*)

Wernicke's Aphasia: Description

The primary characteristics of **Wernicke's aphasia** are poor speech comprehension and production of meaningless speech. Unlike Broca's aphasia, Wernicke's aphasia is fluent and unlabored; the person does not strain to articulate words and does not appear to be searching for them. The patient maintains a melodic line, with the voice rising and falling normally. When you listen to the speech of a person with Wernicke's aphasia, it appears to be grammatical. That is, the person uses function words such as *the* and *but* and employs complex verb tenses and subordinate clauses. However, the person uses few content words, and the words that he or she strings to-

Wernicke's area A region of auditory association cortex on the left temporal lobe of humans, which is important in the comprehension of words and the production of meaningful speech.

Wernicke's aphasia A form of aphasia characterized by poor speech comprehension and fluent but meaningless speech.

gether just do not make sense. In the extreme, speech deteriorates into a meaning-less jumble, illustrated by the following quotation:

Examiner: What kind of work did you do before you came into the hospital?

Patient: Never, now mista oyge I wanna tell you this happened when happened when he rent. His—his kell come down here and is—he got ren something. It happened. In thesse ropiers were with him for hi—is friend—like was. And it just happened so I don't know, he did not bring around anything. And he did not pay it. And he ro-den all o these arranjen from the pedis on from iss pescid. In these floors now and so. He hadn't had em round here. (Kertesz, 1981, p. 73)

Because of the speech deficit of people with Wernicke's aphasia, when we try to assess their ability to comprehend speech, we must ask them to use nonverbal re-sponses. That is, we cannot assume that they do not understand what other people say to them just because they do not give the proper answer. A commonly used test of comprehension assesses their ability to understand questions by pointing to ob-jects on a table in front of them. For example, they are asked to "Point to the one with ink." If they point to an object other than the pen, they have not understood the request. When tested this way, people with severe Wernicke's aphasia do indeed show poor comprehension.

A remarkable fact about people with Wernicke's aphasia is that they often seem unaware of their deficit. That is, they do not appear to recognize that their speech is faulty, nor do they recognize that they cannot understand the speech of others. They do not look puzzled when someone tells them something, even though they obviously cannot understand what they hear. Perhaps their comprehension deficit prevents them from realizing that what they say and hear makes no sense. They still follow social conventions, taking turns in conversation with the examiner, even though they do not understand what the examiner says and what they say in return makes little sense. They remain sensitive to the other person's facial expression and tone of voice and begin talking when he or she asks a question and pauses for an an-swer. One patient with Wernicke's aphasia made the following responses when asked to name ten common objects.

toothbrush → "stoktery"	*quarter* → "minkt"
cigarette → "cigarette"	*pen* → "spentee"
pen → "tankt"	*matches* → "senktr"
knife → "nike"	*key* → "seek"
fork → "fahk"	*comb* → "sahk"

He acted sure of himself and gave no indication that he recognized that most of his responses were meaningless. The responses he made were not simply new words that he had invented; he was asked several times to name the objects and gave different responses each time (except for *cigarette,* which he always named correctly).

Wernicke's Aphasia: Analysis

Because the superior temporal gyrus is a region of auditory association cortex, and because a comprehension deficit is so prominent in Wernicke's aphasia, this disor-der has been characterized as a *receptive* aphasia. Wernicke suggested that the region that now bears his name is the location of *memories of the sequences of sounds that con-stitute words.* This hypothesis is reasonable; it suggests that the auditory association cortex of the superior temporal gyrus recognizes the sounds of words, just as the vi-sual association cortex of the inferior temporal gyrus recognizes the sight of objects.

But why should damage to an area that is responsible for the ability to recognize spoken words disrupt people's ability to speak? In fact, it does not; Wernicke's apha-sia, like Broca's aphasia, actually appears to consist of several deficits. The abilities that are disrupted include *recognition of spoken words, comprehension of the meaning of words,* and the *ability to convert thoughts into words.* Let us consider each of these abilities in turn.

Recognition: Pure Word Deafness.   As I said in the introduction to this section, *recognizing* a word is not the same as *comprehending* it. If you hear a foreign word several times, you will learn to recognize it; but unless someone tells you what it means, you will not comprehend it. Recognition is a perceptual task; comprehension involves retrieval of additional information from memory.

Damage to the left temporal lobe can produce a disorder of auditory word recognition, uncontaminated by other problems. This syndrome is called **pure word deafness.** (Mr. S., the patient described in the Prologue, had this disorder.) Although people with pure word deafness are not deaf, they cannot understand speech. As one patient put it, "I can hear you talking, I just can't understand what you're saying." Another said, "It's as if there were a bypass somewhere, and my ears were not connected to my voice" (Saffran, Marin, and Yeni-Komshian, 1976, p. 211). These patients can recognize nonspeech sounds such as the barking of a dog, the sound of a doorbell, and the chirping of a bird. Often, they can recognize the emotion expressed by the intonation of speech even though they cannot understand what is being said. More significantly, their own speech is excellent. They can often understand what other people are saying by reading their lips. They can also read and write, and sometimes, they ask people to communicate with them in writing. Clearly, pure word deafness is not an inability to comprehend the meaning of words; if it were, people with this disorder would not be able to read people's lips or read words written on paper.

Functional imaging studies confirm that perception of speech sounds activates neurons in the auditory association cortex of the superior temporal gyrus. Binder et al. (1994) found that the sounds of real words (such as *barn* and *box*) and pseudowords containing speech sounds (such as *narb* and *skob*) activated this region better than noise did. The stimuli activated the left and right hemispheres equally.

Apparently, two types of brain injury can cause pure word deafness: disruption of auditory input to Wernicke's area or damage to Wernicke's area itself. Disruption of auditory input can be produced by bilateral damage to the primary auditory cortex, or it can be caused by damage to the white matter in the left temporal lobes that cuts axons bringing auditory information from the primary auditory cortex to Wernicke's area (Digiovanni et al., 1992; Kaga, Shindo, and Tanaka, 1997). Either type of damage—disruption of auditory input or damage to Wernicke's area—disturbs the analysis of the sounds of words and hence prevents people from recognizing other people's speech. (See *Figure 13.6.*)

Comprehension: Transcortical Sensory Aphasia.   The other symptoms of Wernicke's aphasia—failure to comprehend the meaning of words and inability to express thoughts in meaningful speech—appear to be produced by damage that extends beyond Wernicke's area into the region that surrounds the posterior part of the lateral fissure, near the junction of the temporal, occipital, and parietal lobes. For want of a better term, I will refer to this region as the *posterior language area.* (See *Figure 13.7.*) The posterior language area appears to serve as a place for interchanging information between the auditory representation of words and the meanings of these words, stored as memories in the rest of the sensory association cortex.

Pure word deafness The ability to hear, to speak, and (usually) to read and write without being able to comprehend the meaning of speech; caused by damage to Wernicke's area or disruption of auditory input to this region.

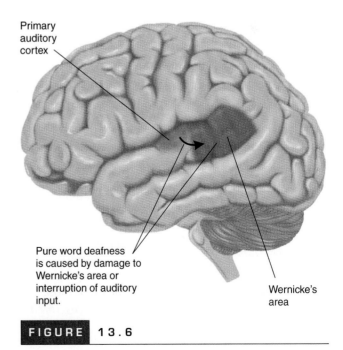

Primary auditory cortex

Pure word deafness is caused by damage to Wernicke's area or interruption of auditory input.

Wernicke's area

FIGURE   13.6

The brain damage that causes pure word deafness.

FIGURE 13.7

The location and interconnections of the posterior language area and an explanation of its role in transcortical sensory aphasia and Wernicke's aphasia.

Broca's area

A direct connection between Wernicke's area and Broca's area enables patients with transcortical sensory aphasia to repeat words that they cannot understand

Posterior language area

Primary auditory cortex

Wernicke's aphasia is caused by damage to both regions; patient can neither understand the meanings of words nor repeat them

Transcortical sensory aphasia is caused by damage to the posterior language area; patient cannot understand the meanings of words but can repeat them

Transcortical sensory aphasia A speech disorder in which a person has difficulty comprehending speech and producing meaningful spontaneous speech but can repeat speech; caused by damage to the region of the brain posterior to Wernicke's area.

Damage to the posterior language area alone, which isolates Wernicke's area from the rest of the posterior language area, produces a disorder known as **transcortical sensory aphasia.** (See *Figure 13.7.*) The difference between transcortical sensory aphasia and Wernicke's aphasia is that patients with this disorder *can repeat what other people say to them;* therefore, they can recognize words. However, *they cannot comprehend the meaning of what they hear and repeat; nor can they produce meaningful speech of their own.* How can these people repeat what they hear? Because the posterior language area is damaged, repetition does not involve this part of the brain. Obviously, there must be a direct connection between Wernicke's area and Broca's area that bypasses the posterior language area. (See *Figure 13.7.*)

The fact that recognition and comprehension of speech require separate brain functions is illustrated dramatically by a case reported by Geschwind, Quadfasel, and Segarra (1968). The patient sustained extensive brain damage from carbon monoxide produced by a faulty water heater. (The damage included considerably more brain tissue than occurs in most cases of transcortical sensory aphasia, but it illustrates the distinction between the recognition and comprehension of speech.) The patient spent several years in the hospital before she died, without ever saying anything meaningful on her own. She did not follow verbal commands or otherwise give signs of understanding them. However, she often repeated what was said to her. The repetition was not parrotlike; she did not imitate accents different from her own, and if someone made a grammatical error while saying something to her, she sometimes repeated correctly, without the error. She could also recite poems if someone started them. For example, when an examiner said "Roses are red, violets are blue," she continued with "Sugar is sweet and so are you." She could sing and would do so when someone started singing a song she knew. She even learned new songs from the radio while in the hospital. Remember, though, that she gave *no signs of understanding anything she heard or said.* This disorder, along with pure word deafness, clearly confirms the conclusion that *recognizing* spoken words and *comprehending* them involve different brain mechanisms.

In conclusion, transcortical sensory aphasia can be seen as Wernicke's aphasia without a repetition deficit. To put it another way, the symptoms of Wernicke's aphasia consist of those of pure word deafness plus those of transcortical sensory aphasia. (See *Figure 13.7.*)

What Is Meaning? As we have seen, Wernicke's area is involved in the analysis of speech sounds and thus in the recognition of words. Damage to the posterior language area does not disrupt people's ability to recognize words, but it does disrupt their ability to understand them or to produce meaningful speech of their own. But what, exactly, do we mean by the word *meaning*? And what types of brain mechanisms are involved?

Words refer to objects, actions, or relations in the world. Thus, the meaning of a word is defined by particular memories associated with it. For example, knowing the meaning of the word *tree* means being able to imagine the physical characteristics of trees: what they look like, what the wind sounds like blowing through their leaves, what the bark feels like, and so on. It also means knowing facts about trees: about their roots, buds, flowers, nuts, wood, and the chlorophyll in their leaves. These memories are stored not in the primary speech areas but in other parts of the brain, especially regions of the association cortex. Different categories of memories may be stored in particular regions of the brain, but they are somehow tied together, so that hearing the word *tree* activates all of them. (As we saw in Chapter 12, the hippocampal formation is involved in this process of tying related memories together.)

In thinking about the brain's verbal mechanisms involved in recognizing words and comprehending their meaning, I find that the concept of a dictionary serves as a useful analogy. Dictionaries contain entries (the words) and definitions (the meanings of the words). In the brain we have at least two types of entries: auditory and visual. That is, we can look up a word according to how it sounds or how it looks (in writing). Let us just consider just one type of entry: the sound of a word. (I will discuss reading and writing later in this chapter.) We hear a familiar word and understand its meaning. How do we do so?

First, we must recognize the sequence of sounds that constitute the word; we find the auditory entry for the word in our "dictionary." As we saw, this entry appears in Wernicke's area. Next, the memories that constitute the meaning of the word must be activated. Presumably, Wernicke's area is connected—through the posterior language area—with the neural circuits that contain these memories. (See *Figure 13.8.*)

The process works in reverse when we describe our thoughts or perceptions in words. Suppose we want to tell someone about a tree that we just planted in our yard. Thoughts about the tree (for example, a visual image of it) occur in our association cortex—the visual association cortex, in this example. Information about the activity of these circuits is sent first to the posterior language area and then to Broca's area, which causes the words to be set into a grammatical sentence and pronounced. (See *Figure 13.8.*)

Broca's area
(speech production)

Meanings
of words

Perceptions and memories

Primary
auditory
cortex

Wernicke's area
(word recognition)

Perceptions and memories

Posterior language area
(interface between Wernicke's area
and perceptions and memories)

FIGURE **1 3 . 8**

The "dictionary" in the brain. Wernicke's area contains the auditory entries of words; the meanings are contained as memories in the sensory association areas. Black arrows represent comprehension of words—the activation of memories that correspond to a word's meaning. Red arrows represent translation of thoughts or perceptions into words.

What evidence do we have that meanings of words are represented by neural circuits in various regions of the association cortex? The best evidence comes from the fact that damage to particular regions of the sensory association cortex can damage particular kinds of information and thus abolish particular kinds of meanings. For example, I met a patient who had recently had a stroke that damaged a part of her right parietal lobe that played a role in spatial perception. She was alert and intelligent and showed no signs of aphasia. However, she was confused about directions and other spatial relations. When asked to, she could point to the ceiling and the floor, but she could not say which was *over* the other. Her perception of other people appeared to be entirely normal, but she could not say whether a person's head was at the *top* or *bottom* of the body.

I wrote a set of multiple-choice questions to test her ability to use words denoting spatial relations. The results of the test indicated that she did not know the meaning of words such as *up, down,* and *under* when they referred to spatial relations, but she could use these words normally when they referred to nonspatial relations. For example, here are some of her incorrect responses when the words referred to spatial relations:

A tree's branches are *under* its roots.

The sky is *down.*

The ceiling is *under* the floor.

She made only ten correct responses on the sixteen-item test. In contrast, she got all eight items correct when the words referred to nonspatial relations like the following:

After exchanging pleasantries, they got *down* to business.

He got sick and threw *up.*

Damage to part of the association cortex of the *left* parietal lobe can produce an inability to name the body parts. The disorder is called **autotopagnosia,** or "poor knowledge of one's own topography." (A better name would have been *autotopanomia,* "poor naming of one's own topography.") People who can otherwise converse normally cannot reliably point to their elbow, knee, or cheek when asked to do so and cannot name body parts when the examiner points to them. However, they have no difficulty understanding the meaning of other words.

More widespread damage to the temporal and parietal lobes can cause a general loss in comprehension—and not simply naming—presumably because of damage to regions of the brain that contain specific memories. For example, Damasio and Tranel (1990) studied a patient who had sustained severe damage to the temporal lobes. Besides becoming amnesic (his hippocampal formation was destroyed bilaterally), he had lost a considerable amount of specific information. For example, he recognized that a raccoon was an animal but had no idea of where it lived, what it ate, or what its name was. Hodges et al. (1992) reported several similar cases, caused by progressive degeneration of the temporal lobes. One patient was asked, "Have you been to America?" She replied, "What's America?" When she was asked, "What is your favorite food?" she said, "Food, food, I wish I knew what that was" (p. 1786). Another patient was frightened when he found a snail in his garden and thought that a goat was a strange creature. Hodges and his colleagues suggest the term *semantic aphasia* to refer to this syndrome.

So far, most of the studies I have described have dealt with comprehension of simple concepts: spatial direction and orientation, body parts, animals, and other concrete objects. But speech also conveys abstract concepts, some of them quite subtle. What parts of the brain are responsible for comprehending the meaning behind proverbs such as "People who live in glass houses shouldn't throw stones" or the moral of stories such as the one about the race between the tortoise and the hare?

Autotopagnosia Inability to name body parts or to identify body parts that another person names.

Studies of brain-damaged patients suggest that comprehension of the more subtle, figurative aspects of speech involves the right hemisphere in particular (Brownell et al., 1983, 1990). Functional imaging studies confirm these observations. Bottini et al. (1994) had people listen to sentences and judge their plausibility. Some sentences were straightforward and factual. For example, "The old man has a branch as a walking stick" is plausible, whereas "The lady has a bucket as a walking stick" is not. Other sentences presented metaphors, the comprehension of which goes beyond the literal meaning of the words. For example, "The old man had a head full of dead leaves" is plausible, whereas "The old man had a head full of barn doors" is not. The investigators found that judging the metaphors activated parts of the right hemisphere, while judging factual sentences did not. Nichelli et al. (1995) found that judging the moral of Aesop's fables (as opposed to judging more superficial aspects of the stories) also activated additional regions of the right hemisphere.

R   L

FIGURE 13.9

MRI scans showing subcortical damage responsible for a case of conduction aphasia. This lesion damaged the arcuate fasciculus, a fiber bundle connecting Wernicke's area and Broca's area. Note that the left and right are reversed.

(From Arnett, P.A., Rao, S.M., Hussain, M., Swanson, S.J., and Hammeke, T.A. Neurology, 1996, 47, 576–578. Reprinted with permission.)

Repetition: Conduction Aphasia. As we saw earlier in this section, the fact that people with transcortical sensory aphasia can repeat what they hear suggests that there is a direct connection between Wernicke's area and Broca's area—and there is, the **arcuate fasciculus** ("arch-shaped bundle"). This bundle of axons appears to convey information about the *sounds* of words but not their *meanings*. The best evidence for this conclusion comes from a syndrome known as conduction aphasia, which is produced by damage to the inferior parietal lobe that extends into the subcortical white matter and damages the arcuate fasciculus (Damasio and Damasio, 1980). (See *Figure 13.9.*)

Conduction aphasia is characterized by meaningful, fluent speech; relatively good comprehension; but very poor repetition. For example, the spontaneous speech of patient L.B. (observed by Margolin and Walker, 1981) was excellent; he made very few errors and had no difficulty naming objects. But let us see how patient L.B. performed when he was asked to repeat words.

Examiner: bicycle
Patient: bicycle

Examiner: hippopotamus
Patient: hippopotamus

Examiner: blaynge
Patient: I didn't get it.

Examiner: Okay, some of these won't be real words, they'll just be sounds. Blaynge.
Patient: I'm not . . .

Examiner: blanch
Patient: blanch

Examiner: north
Patient: north

Examiner: rilld
Patient: Nope, I can't say.

You will notice that the patient can repeat individual words (all nouns, in this case) but utterly fails to repeat nonwords. People with conduction aphasia can repeat speech sounds that they hear *only if these sounds have meaning.*

Arcuate fasciculus A bundle of axons that connects Wernicke's area with Broca's area; damage causes conduction aphasia.

Conduction aphasia An aphasia characterized by inability to repeat words that are heard but normal speech and the ability to comprehend the speech of others.

Sometimes, when a person with conduction aphasia is asked to repeat a word, he or she says a word with the same meaning—or at least, one that is related. For example, if the examiner says *house,* the patient may say *home.* If the examiner says *chair,* the patient may say *sit.* One patient made the following response when asked to repeat an entire sentence:

Examiner: The auto's leaking gas tank soiled the roadway.
Patient: The car's tank leaked and made a mess on the street.

The symptoms that are seen in transcortical sensory aphasia and conduction aphasia lead to the conclusion that there are pathways connecting the speech mechanisms of the temporal lobe with those of the frontal lobe. The direct pathway through the arcuate fasciculus simply conveys speech sounds to the frontal lobes. We use this pathway to repeat unfamiliar words—for example, when we are learning a foreign language or a new word in our own language or when we are trying to repeat a nonword such as *blaynge.* The second pathway is indirect and is based on the *meaning* of words, not the sounds they make. When patients with conduction aphasia hear a word or a sentence, the meaning of what they hear evokes some sort of image related to that meaning. (The patient in the second example presumably imagined the sight of an automobile leaking fuel onto the pavement.) They are then able to describe that image, just as they would put their own thoughts into words. Of course, the words they choose may not be the same as the ones used by the person who spoke to them. (See *Figure 13.10.*)

Memory of Words: Anomic Aphasia

As I already noted, anomia, in one form or other, is a hallmark of aphasia. However, one category of aphasia consists of almost pure anomia, the other symptoms being inconsequential. Speech of patients with anomic aphasia is fluent and grammatical, and their comprehension is excellent, but they have difficulty finding the appropriate words. They often employ **circumlocutions** (literally, "speaking in a roundabout way") to get around missing words. Anomic aphasia is different from Wernicke's aphasia. People with anomic aphasia can understand what other people say, and what they say makes perfect sense, even if they often choose roundabout ways to say it.

The following quotation is from a patient that some colleagues and I studied (Margolin, Marcel, and Carlson, 1985). We asked her to describe the picture shown in *Figure 13.11.* Her pauses, which are marked with three dots, indicate word-finding difficulties. In some cases, when she could not find a word, she supplied a definition

Circumlocution A strategy by which people with anomia find alternative ways to say something when they are unable to think of the most appropriate word.

FIGURE 13.10

A hypothetical explanation of conduction aphasia. A lesion that damages the arcuate fasciculus disrupts transmission of auditory information, but not information related to meaning, to the frontal lobe.

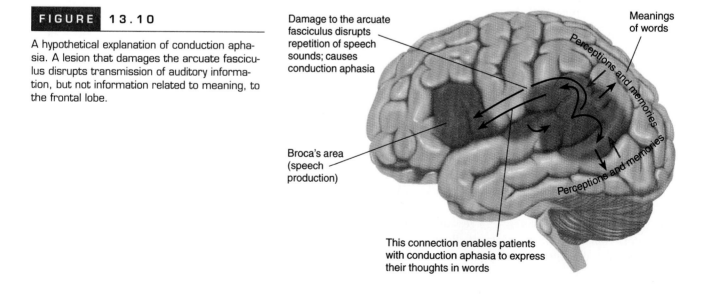

Damage to the arcuate fasciculus disrupts repetition of speech sounds; causes conduction aphasia

Meanings of words

Perceptions and memories

Perceptions and memories

Broca's area (speech production)

This connection enables patients with conduction aphasia to express their thoughts in words instead (a form of circumlocution) or went off on a new track. I have added the words in brackets that I think she intended to use.

> *Examiner:* Tell us about that picture.
> *Patient:* It's a woman who has two children, a son and a daughter, and her son is to get into the . . . cupboard in the kitchen to get out [*take*] some . . . cookies out of the [*cookie jar*] . . . that she possibly had made, and consequently he's slipping [*falling*] . . . the wrong direction [*backward*] . . . on the . . . what he's standing on [*stool*], heading to the . . . the cupboard [*floor*] and if he falls backwards he could have some problems [*get hurt*], because that [*the stool*] is off balance.

Anomia has been described as a partial amnesia for words. It can be produced by lesions in either the anterior or posterior region of the brain, but only posterior lesions produce a *fluent* anomia. The most likely location of lesions that produce anomia without the other symptoms of aphasia, such as comprehension deficits, agrammatism, or difficulties in articulation, is the left temporal or parietal lobe, usually sparing Wernicke's area. In the case of the woman described above, the damage included the middle and inferior temporal gyri, which includes an important region of the visual association cortex. (See *Figure 13.12*.)

When my colleagues and I were studying the anomic patient, I was struck by the fact that she seemed to have more difficulty finding nouns than other types of words. I informally tested her ability to name actions by asking her what people shown in a series of pictures were doing. She made almost no errors finding verbs. For example, although she could not say what a boy was holding in his hand, she had no trouble saying that he was *throwing* it. Similarly, she knew that a girl was *climbing* something but could not tell me the name of what she was climbing (a fence). In addition, she had no trouble finding nonvisual adjectives; for example, she could say that lemons tasted *sour,* that ice was *cold,* and that a cat's fur felt *soft.*

For several years I thought that our patient was unique. But more recently, similar patterns of deficits have been reported in the literature. For example, Manning and Campbell (1992) described a patient who had difficulty naming objects but not actions. Some patients have even more specific deficits; Semenza and Zettin (1989) described a patient who had great difficulty with proper nouns (names of people and places). Damasio et al. (1991) studied several patients with similar deficits and concluded that anomia for proper nouns is caused by damage to the temporal pole, whereas anomia for common nouns is caused by damage to the inferior temporal cortex. Damage to both regions causes anomia for both types of nouns. They suggest that the important distinction between the two types of words is that proper nouns are specific to particular individuals (people or places) whereas common nouns apply to *categories.* Presumably, the cortex of the temporal pole is specifically involved with recognition of individuals.

What about the ability to name actions? As we saw, the anomic patient my colleagues and I studied had no trouble with verbs. Neither did the anomic patients studied by Semenza and Zettin (1989), Manning and Campbell (1992), or Damasio et al. (1992). Several studies have found that anomia for verbs (more correctly called *averbia*) is caused by damage to the frontal cortex, in and around Broca's area (Damasio and Tranel, 1993; Daniele

FIGURE 13.11

The drawing of the kitchen story, part of the Boston Diagnostic Aphasia Test.

(From Goodglass, H., and Kaplan, E. The Assessment of Aphasia and Related Disorders, 2nd ed. Philadelphia: Lea & Febiger, 1983. Reprinted with permission.)

FIGURE 13.12

The location of the brain damage of patient R.F.

Lesion in left temporal lobe caused a fluent anomic aphasia

Low   High

Activity Level

FIGURE 13.13

A PET scan showing the regions of activation while people thought of verbs that depicted actions appropriate to nouns supplied by the experimenters.

(From Fiez, J.A., Raichle, M.E., Balota, D.A., Tallal, P., and Petersen, S.E. Cerebral Cortex, 1996, 6, 1–10.)

et al., 1994). If you think about it, that makes sense. The frontal lobes are devoted to planning, organizing, and executing actions, so it should not surprise us that they are involved in the task of remembering the names of actions.

Several functional imaging studies have confirmed the importance of Broca's area and the region surrounding it in production of verbs (Petersen et al., 1988; Wise et al., 1991; McCarthy et al., 1993; Fiez et al., 1996). In these studies, subjects either read or heard nouns and then had to say (or think to themselves) verbs describing actions appropriate to these nouns. For example, on reading or hearing the noun *hammer,* they might think of the verb *pound.* Figure 13.13 shows a PET scan from people who generated verbs in response to written nouns. The activity produced by simply reading nouns aloud has been subtracted out, leaving only the activity associated with the verb generation process. Presumably, the activity in the temporal lobe represents neural processes involved with comprehension of the nouns, while the activity in the frontal lobe represents the neural processes directly involved with thinking of appropriate actions and the associated verbs. (See *Figure 13.13.*)

The picture I have drawn so far suggests that comprehension of speech includes a flow of information from Wernicke's area to the posterior language area to the sensory association cortex. Production of spontaneous speech involves the flow of information concerning perceptions and memories from the posterior language area to Broca's area. This model is certainly an oversimplification, but it is a useful starting point in conceptualizing basic mental processes. For example, thinking in words probably involves two-way communication between the speech areas and surrounding association cortex (and subcortical regions such as the hippocampus, of course).

Aphasia in Deaf People

So far, I have restricted my discussion to brain mechanisms of spoken and written language. But communication among members of the Deaf community involves another medium: sign language. Sign language is expressed manually, by movements of the hands. Sign language is *not* English; nor is it French, or Spanish, or Chinese. The most common sign language in North America is ASL—American Sign Language. ASL is a full-fledged language, having signs for nouns, verbs, adjectives, adverbs, and all the other parts of speech contained in oral languages. People can converse rapidly and efficiently by means of sign language, can tell jokes, and can even make puns based on the similarity between signs. They can also use their language ability to think in words.

Sign language can express complex thoughts, just as spoken language can.

The grammar of ASL is based on its visual, spatial nature. For example, if a person makes the sign for *John* in one place and later makes the sign for *Mary* in another place, she can place her hand in the *John* location and move it toward the *Mary* location while making the sign for *love.* As you undoubtedly figured out for yourself, she is saying, "John loves Mary." Signers can also modify the meaning of signs through facial expressions or the speed and vigor with which they make a sign. Thus, many of the prepositions, adjectives, and adverbs found in spoken languages do not require specific words in ASL. The fact that signed languages are based on three-dimensional hand and arm movements accompanied by facial expressions means that their grammars are very different from those of spoken languages. Therefore, a word-for-word translation from a spoken language to a signed language (or vice versa) is impossible.

The fact that the grammar of ASL is spatial suggests that aphasic disorders in deaf people who use sign language might be caused by lesions of the right hemisphere, which is primarily involved in spatial perception and memory. However, all the cases of deaf people with aphasia for signs reported in the literature so far have involved lesions of the left hemisphere (Hickok, Bellugi, and Klima, 1996). Therefore, sign language, like auditory and written language, appears to rely primarily on the left hemisphere for comprehension and expression.

Lipreading

When deaf people communicate with hearing people who do not know sign language, they must do so in writing or by reading the hearing people's lips. What most people do not realize is that even hearing people sometimes use visual information about movements of a speaker's mouth to assist their comprehension of speech. Many studies have shown that in noisy environments, speech comprehension is much improved when the listener can watch the speaker's lips. People are not usually aware of this phenomenon, although they become acutely aware of a desynchronization between lip movements and speech sounds, such as that produced by a movie with a faulty sound track. Two recent studies have investigated the neural basis of lipreading. Campbell, De Gelder, and De Haan (1996) found that although the right hemisphere is more important in judging the identity of faces, the left hemisphere is more important in judging the positions that the lips take when a person is producing different vowel sounds. (For example, the lips describe a circle when we say /oo/, but the corners of the lips are drawn apart when we say /ee/.)

Calvert et al. (1997) obtained functional MRI scans from people who were watching a silent videotape of speakers slowly saying a list of numbers. The subjects had to repeat silently to themselves the numbers they saw being mouthed. The regions of the brain that were activated by performance of this lipreading task included parts of the visual association cortex (including area V5, which is devoted to the analysis of movement), the angular gyrus of the parietal lobe, and the primary auditory cortex and auditory association cortex of the temporal lobe—especially in the left hemisphere. (See *Figure 13.14*.) A similar pattern of activation was seen when subjects watched videotapes of people saying pronounceable pseudowords but not when they watched people making movements of their jaws and lower face with the lips closed.

- Auditory speech perception
- Silent lipreading
- Overlap of both

FIGURE 13.14

A PET scan showing regions of activation that accompanied auditory speech perception (blue), silent lipreading (magenta), and their overlap (yellow).

(Reprinted with permission from Calvert, G.A., Bullmore, E.T., Brammer, M.J., Campbell, R., Williams, S.C.R., McGuire, P.K., Woodruff, P.W.R., Iversen, S.D., and David, A.S. Science, 1997, 276, 593–596. Copyright 1997 American Association for the Advancement of Science.)

INTERIM SUMMARY

Two regions of the brain are especially important in understanding and producing speech. Broca's area, in the frontal lobe just rostral to the region of the primary motor cortex that controls the muscles of speech, is involved with speech production. This region contains memories of the sequences of muscular movements that produce words, each of which is connected with its auditory counterpart in the posterior part of the brain. Broca's aphasia—which is caused by damage to Broca's area, adjacent regions of the frontal cortex, and underlying white matter—consists of varying degrees of agrammatism, anomia, and articulation difficulties.

Wernicke's area, in the posterior superior temporal lobe, is involved with speech perception. The region just adjacent to Wernicke's area, which I have called the posterior language area, is necessary for speech comprehension and the translation of thoughts into words. Presumably, Wernicke's area contains memories of the sounds of words, each of which is connected through the posterior language area with memories about the properties of the things the words denote. Damage restricted to Wernicke's area causes pure word deafness—loss of the ability to understand speech but intact speech production, reading, and writing. Wernicke's aphasia, caused by damage to Wernicke's area and the posterior language area, consists of poor speech comprehension, poor repetition, and production of fluent, meaningless speech. Transcortical sensory aphasia, caused by damage to the posterior speech area, consists of poor speech comprehension and production, but the patients can repeat what they hear. Thus, the symptoms of Wernicke's area consist of those of transcortical sensory aphasia plus those of pure word deafness. The fact that people with transcortical sensory aphasia can repeat words they cannot understand suggests that there is a direct connection between Wernicke's area and Broca's area. Indeed, there is—the arcuate fasciculus. Damage to this bundle of axons produces conduction aphasia: disruption of the ability to repeat exactly what was heard without disruption of the ability to comprehend speech.

The meanings of words are our memories of objects, actions, and other concepts associated with them. These meanings are memories and are stored in the association cortex, not in the speech areas themselves. Pure anomia, caused by damage to the temporal or parietal lobes, consists of difficulty in word finding—particularly in naming objects. Some patients have a specific difficulty with proper nouns, while others have difficulty with common nouns; most patients have little difficulty with verbs. Damage to Broca's area and surrounding regions disrupts the ability to name actions—to think of appropriate verbs. Brain damage can also disrupt the "definitions" as well as the "entries" in the mental dictionary; damage to specific regions of the association cortex effectively erases some categories of the *meanings* of words.

Because so many terms and symptoms were described in this section, I have provided a table that summarizes them. (See ***Table 13.1***.)

TABLE 13.1	Aphasic Syndromes Produced by Brain Damage				
Disorder	Areas of Lesion	Spontaneous Speech	Comprehension	Repetition	Naming
Wernicke's aphasia	Posterior portion of superior temporal gyrus (Wernicke's area) and posterior language area	Fluent	Poor	Poor	Poor
Pure word deafness	Wernicke's area or its connection with primary auditory cortex	Fluent	Poor	Poor	Good
Broca's aphasia	Frontal cortex rostral to base of primary motor cortex (Broca's area)	Nonfluent	Good	Poor[a]	Good
Conduction aphasia	White matter beneath parietal lobe superior to lateral fissure (arcuate fasciculus)	Fluent	Good	Poor	Good
Anomic aphasia	Various parts of parietal and temporal lobes	Fluent	Good	Good	Poor
Transcortical sensory aphasia	Posterior language area	Fluent	Poor	Good	Poor

[a]May be better than spontaneous speech.

■ **THOUGHT QUESTIONS**

Suppose you were asked to determine the abilities and deficits of people with aphasia. What tasks would you include in your examination to test for the presence of particular deficits?

■ DISORDERS OF READING AND WRITING

Reading and writing are closely related to listening and talking; thus, oral and written language abilities have many brain mechanisms in common. This section discusses the neural basis of reading and writing disorders. As you will see, the study of these disorders has provided us with some useful and interesting information.

Pure Alexia

Dejerine (1892) described a remarkable syndrome, which we now call **pure alexia,** or sometimes *pure word blindness* or *alexia without agraphia.* His patient had a lesion in the visual cortex of the left occipital lobe and the posterior end of the corpus callosum. The patient could still write, although he had lost the ability to read. In fact, if he was shown some of his own writing, he could not read it.

> **Pure alexia** Loss of the ability to read without loss of the ability to write; produced by brain damage.

Several years ago, some colleagues and I studied a man with pure alexia who discovered his ability to write in an interesting way. A few months after he sustained a head injury that caused his brain damage, he and his wife were watching a service person repair their washing machine. The patient wanted to say something privately to his wife, so he picked up a pad of paper and jotted a note. As he was handing it to her, they suddenly realized with amazement that although he could not read, he was able to write. His wife brought the note to their neurologist, who asked the patient to read it. Although he remembered the gist of the message, he could not read the words. Unfortunately, I do not have that note, but Figure 13.15 shows the writing of another person with pure alexia. (See *Figure 13.15.*)

Although patients with pure alexia cannot read, they can recognize words that are spelled aloud to them; therefore, they have not lost their memories of the spellings of words. Pure alexia is obviously a perceptual disorder; it is similar to pure word deafness, except that the patient has difficulty with visual input, not auditory input. The disorder is caused by lesions that prevent visual information from reaching the extrastriate cortex of the left hemisphere (Damasio and Damasio, 1983, 1986). Figure 13.16 explains why Dejerine's original patient could not read. The first diagram shows the pathway that visual information would take if a person had damage *only to the left primary visual cortex.* In this case the person's right visual field would be blind; he or she would see nothing to the right of the fixation point. But people with this disorder can read. Their only problem is that they must look to the right of each word so that they can see all of it, which means that they read somewhat more slowly than someone with full vision.

FIGURE 13.15

A letter written to Dr. Elizabeth Warrington by a patient with pure alexia. The letter reads as follows: "Dear Dr. Warrington, Thank you for your letter of September the 16th. I shall be pleased to be at your office between 10 & 10:30 am on Friday 17th october. I still find it very odd to be able to write this letter but not to be able to read it back a few minutes later. I much appreciate the opportunity to see you. Yours sincerely, Harry X.

(From McCarthy, R.A., and Warrington, E.K. Cognitive Neuropsychology: A Clinical Introduction. San Diego: Academic Press, 1990. *Reprinted with permission.)*

Let us trace the flow of visual information for a person with this brain damage. Information from the left side of the visual field is transmitted to the right striate cortex (primary visual cortex) and then to the lingual and fusiform gyri—a region of extrastriate cortex involved in the recognition of written text. From there, the information crosses the posterior corpus callosum and is transmitted to the left extrastriate cortex and then to speech mechanisms located in the left frontal lobe. Thus, the person can read the words aloud. (See *Figure 13.16a.*)

The second diagram shows Dejerine's patient. Notice how the additional lesion of the corpus callosum prevents visual information concerning written text from reaching the posterior left hemisphere. Without this information, the patient cannot read. (See *Figure 13.16b.*)

I must note that the diagrams shown in Figure 13.16 are as simple and schematic as possible. They illustrate only the pathway involved in seeing a word and pronouncing it, and they ignore neural structures that would be involved in understanding its meaning. As we will see later in this chapter, evidence from patients with brain lesions indicates that seeing and pronouncing words can take place independently of understanding them. Thus, although the diagrams are simplified, they are not unreasonable, given what we know about the neural components of the reading process.

You will recall that writing is not the only form of visible language; deaf people can communicate by means of sign language just as well as hearing people can communicate by means of spoken language. Hickok et al. (1995) reported on a case of

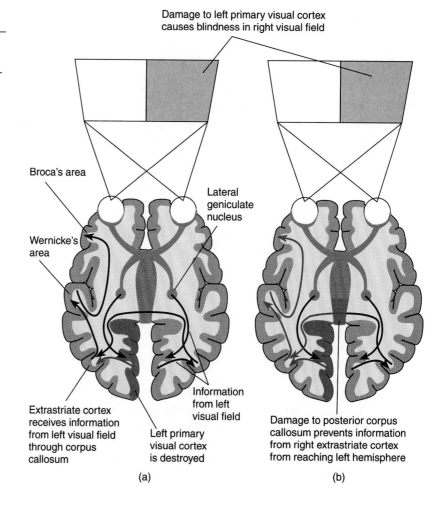

FIGURE 13.16

Pure alexia. Red arrows indicate the flow of information that has been interrupted by brain damage. (a) The route followed by information as a person with damage to the left primary visual cortex reads aloud. (b) Additional damage to the posterior corpus callosum interrupts the flow of information and produces pure alexia.

Damage to left primary visual cortex causes blindness in right visual field

Broca's area

Wernicke's area

Lateral geniculate nucleus

Information from left visual field

Extrastriate cortex receives information from left visual field through corpus callosum

Left primary visual cortex is destroyed

Damage to posterior corpus callosum prevents information from right extrastriate cortex from reaching left hemisphere

(a)

(b)

"sign blindness" caused by damage similar to that which causes pure alexia. The patient, a right-handed deaf woman, sustained a stroke that damaged her left occipital lobe and the posterior corpus callosum. The lesion did not impair her ability to sign in coherent sentences, so she did not have a Wernicke-like aphasia. However, she could no longer understand other people's sign language, and she lost her ability to read. She had some ability to comprehend single signs (corresponding to single words), but she could not comprehend signed sentences.

You will recall from Chapter 6 that visual agnosia is a perceptual deficit in which people with damage to the visual association cortex cannot recognize objects by sight. Patients with pure alexia do *not* have visual agnosia; they can recognize objects and supply their names. Similarly, people with visual agnosia can still read. Thus, the perceptual analysis of objects and words requires different mechanisms. I find this fact both interesting and puzzling. Certainly, the ability to read cannot have shaped the evolution of the human brain, because the invention of writing is only a few thousand years old, and until very recently, the vast majority of the world's population was illiterate. Thus, reading and object recognition use brain mechanisms that undoubtedly existed even before the invention of writing. What is the nature of these mechanisms? What features of the world around us require analysis similar to the analysis we use to recognize objects versus words?

(a)   (b)

TWEAL   BOARD

(c)   (d)

FIGURE 13.17

PET scans of the medial surface of the brains of subjects who read (a) letterlike forms, (b) strings of consonants, (c) pronounceable nonwords, or (d) real words.

(From Petersen, S.E., Fox, P.T., Snyder, A.Z., and Raichle, M.E. Science, 1990, 249, 1041–1044. Copyright 1990 by the American Association for the Advancement of Science.)

Although these questions have not yet been answered, a region of the extrastriate cortex that is essential for visual analysis of written text has been identified. Petersen et al. (1990) used a PET scanner to measure regional cerebral blood flow while presenting subjects with four types of visual stimuli: unfamiliar letterlike forms, strings of consonants, pronounceable nonwords, and real words. They found that one region of the extrastriate cortex was activated only by pronounceable nonwords or real words. Their finding suggests that this region plays a role in recognition of familiar combinations of letters. (See *Figure 13.17.*)

Toward an Understanding of Reading

Most investigators believe that reading involves at least two different processes: direct recognition of the word as a whole and sounding it out letter by letter. When we see a familiar word, we normally recognize it by its shape and pronounce it—a process known as **whole-word reading.** (With very long words we might instead perceive segments of several letters each.) The second method, which we use for unfamiliar words, requires recognition of individual letters and knowledge of the sounds they make. This process is known as **phonetic reading.**

Evidence for our ability to sound out words is easy to obtain. In fact, you can prove to yourself that phonetic reading exists by trying to read the following words:

glab   trisk   chint

Well, as you could see, they are not really words, but I doubt that you had trouble pronouncing them. Obviously, you did not *recognize* them, because you probably never saw them before. Therefore, you had to use what you know about the sounds that are represented by particular letters (or groups of letters, such as *ch*) to figure out how to pronounce the words.

Whole-word reading Reading by recognizing a word as a whole; "sight reading."

Phonetic reading Reading by decoding the phonetic significance of letter strings; "sound reading."

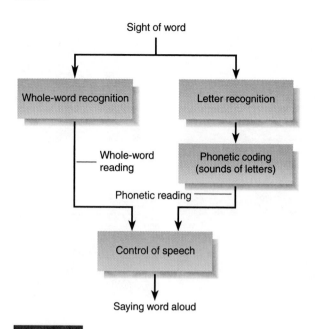

Sight of word

Whole-word recognition

Letter recognition

Whole-word reading

Phonetic coding (sounds of letters)

Phonetic reading

Control of speech

Saying word aloud

FIGURE 13.18

A simplified model of the reading process, showing whole-word and phonetic reading. Whole-word reading is used for most familiar words; phonetic reading is used for unfamiliar words and for nonwords such as *glab, trisk,* or *chint.*

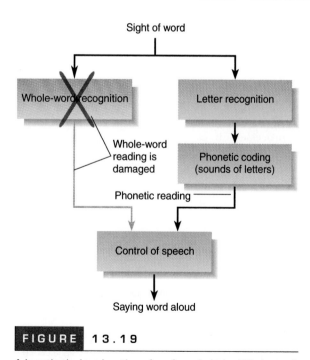

Sight of word

Whole-word recognition

Letter recognition

Whole-word reading is damaged

Phonetic coding (sounds of letters)

Phonetic reading

Control of speech

Saying word aloud

FIGURE 13.19

A hypothetical explanation of surface dyslexia. Whole-word reading is damaged; only phonetic reading remains.

The best evidence that proves that people can read words without sounding them out, using the whole-word method, comes from studies of patients with acquired dyslexias. *Dyslexia* means "faulty reading." *Acquired* dyslexias are those caused by damage to the brains of people who already know how to read. In contrast, *developmental* dyslexias refer to reading difficulties that become apparent when children are learning to read. Developmental dyslexias, which may involve anomalies in brain circuitry, are discussed in a later section.

Figure 13.18 illustrates some elements of the reading processes. The diagram is an oversimplification of a very complex process, but it helps to organize some of the facts that investigators have obtained. It considers only reading and pronouncing single words, not understanding the meaning of text. When we see a familiar word, we normally recognize it as a whole and pronounce it. If we see an unfamiliar word or a pronounceable nonword, we must try to read it phonetically. (See ***Figure 13.18.***)

Although investigators have reported several types of acquired dyslexias, I will mention five of them here. **Surface dyslexia** is a deficit in whole-word reading (Marshall and Newcombe, 1973; McCarthy and Warrington, 1990). The term *surface* reflects the fact that people with this disorder make errors related to the visual appearance of the words and to pronunciation rules, not to the meaning of the words, which is metaphorically "deeper" than the appearance. (See ***Figure 13.19.***)

Patients with **phonological dyslexia** have the opposite problem; they can read by the whole-word method but cannot sound words out. Thus, they can read words that they are already familiar with but have great difficulty figuring out how to read unfamiliar words or pronounceable nonwords (Beauvois and Dérouesné, 1979; Dérouesné and Beauvois, 1979). (In this context, *phonology*—loosely translated as "laws of sound"—refers to the relation between letters and the sounds they represent.) People with phonological dyslexia may be excellent readers if they had already acquired a good reading vocabulary before their brain damage occurred. (See ***Figure 13.20.***)

Phonological dyslexia provides further evidence that whole-word reading and phonological reading involve different brain mechanisms. Phonological reading, which is the only way we can read nonwords or words we have not yet learned, entails some sort of letter-to-sound decoding. Obviously, phonological reading of English requires more than decoding of the sounds produced by single letters, because, for example, some sounds are transcribed as two-letter sequences (such as *th* or *sh*) and the addition of the letter *e* to the end of a word lengthens an internal vowel (*can* becomes *cane*).

The Japanese language provides a particularly interesting distinction between phonetic and whole-word reading. The Japanese language makes use of two kinds of written symbols. *Kanji* symbols are pictographs, adopted from the Chinese language (although they are pronounced as Japanese words). Thus, they represent concepts by means of visual symbols but do not provide a guide to their pronunciation. Reading words expressed in kanji symbols is analogous, then, to whole-word reading. *Kana* symbols are phonetic representations of syllables; thus, they encode acoustical information. These symbols are used primarily to represent foreign words or Japanese

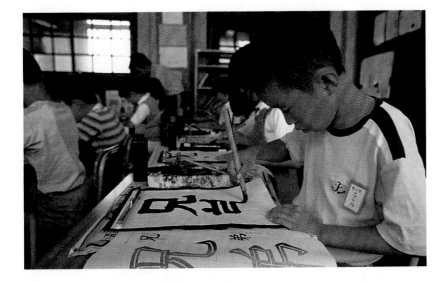

Japanese writing uses two forms of characters, which encode information phonetically or nonphonetically.

Surface dyslexia A reading disorder in which a person can read words phonetically but has difficulty reading irregularly spelled words by the whole-word method.

Phonological dyslexia A reading disorder in which a person can read familiar words but has difficulty reading unfamiliar words or pronounceable nonwords.

Word-form dyslexia A disorder in which a person can read a word only after spelling out the individual letters.

Spelling dyslexia An alternative name for word-form dyslexia.

Direct dyslexia A language disorder caused by brain damage in which the person can read words aloud without understanding them.

words that the average reader would be unlikely to recognize if they were represented by their kanji symbols. Reading words expressed in kana symbols is obviously phonetic.

Studies of Japanese people with localized brain damage have shown that the reading of kana and kanji symbols involves different brain mechanisms (Iwata, 1984; Sakurai et al., 1994). In general, dyslexia for kanji symbols is caused by damage to the left posterior inferior temporal lobe; the damage that causes dyslexia for kana symbols is less certain. Difficulty reading kanji symbols is analogous to surface dyslexia, whereas difficulty reading kana symbols is analogous to phonological dyslexia.

What would happen if individuals sustained brain damage that did not make them blind but destroyed their ability to read words either by the whole-word or phonetic methods? Would they be *completely* unable to read? The answer is no—not quite. They would have a disorder known as **word-form dyslexia** or **spelling dyslexia** (Warrington and Shallice, 1980). Although patients with word-form dyslexia cannot either recognize words as a whole or sound them out phonetically, they can still recognize individual letters and can read the words if they are permitted to name the letters, one at a time. Thus, they read very slowly, taking more time with longer words. As you might expect, patients with word-form dyslexia can identify words that someone else spells aloud, just as they can recognize their own oral spelling. Sometimes, the deficit is so severe that patients have difficulty identifying individual letters, in which case they make mistakes in spelling that prevent them from reading test words. For example, a patient studied by Patterson and Kay (1980) was shown the word *men* and said, "h, e, n, hen."

As we saw earlier in this chapter, recognizing a spoken word is different from understanding it. For example, patients with transcortical sensory aphasia can repeat what is said to them even though they show no signs of understanding what they hear or say. The same is true for reading. **Direct dyslexia** resembles transcortical sensory aphasia, except that the words in question are written, not spoken (Schwartz, Marin, and Saffran, 1979; Lytton and Brust, 1989). Patients with direct dyslexia are able to read aloud *even though they cannot understand the words they are saying*. After sustaining a stroke that damaged his left frontal and temporal lobes, Lytton and

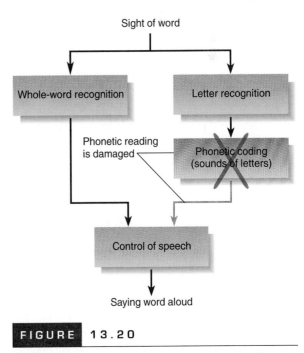

FIGURE 13.20

A hypothetical explanation of phonological dyslexia. Phonetic reading is damaged; only whole-word reading remains.

tree
flag
pole
flare

FIGURE 13.21

An item from a task given to patient R.F. Although she could not read, she could choose the word that went with the picture.

Brust's patient lost the ability to communicate verbally; his speech was meaningless, and he was unable to comprehend what other people said to him. However, he could read words with which he was already familiar. He could *not* read pronounceable nonwords; therefore, he had lost the ability to read phonetically. His comprehension deficit seemed complete; when the investigators presented him with a word and several pictures, one of which corresponded to the word, he read the word correctly but had no idea what picture went with it.

Several investigators have reported a deficit opposite to that of direct dyslexia. People with this unnamed disorder (we could call it *comprehension without reading*) show some comprehension of words that they cannot read (Margolin, Marcel, and Carlson, 1985). Our patient, R.F., sustained a head injury in an automobile accident that destroyed much of her left temporal lobe and part of the anterior occipital lobe. She had a classic case of anomic aphasia—in fact, I quoted her in the section on that topic earlier in this chapter. Although her speech was fluent and she could repeat whatever we said to her, she could not name most common objects, nor could she read most words. Nevertheless, she could match pictures of *objects she could not name* with *words she could not read*. For example, when we showed her the picture and words that appear in Figure 13.21, she immediately pointed to the correct word, *flag*, even though she could not name the object or read any of the words. (See *Figure 13.21*.)

Patient R.F. was utterly unable to read words phonetically. However, the fact that she could match words with pictures indicates that she could still *perceive* them by the whole-word method. This fact was made especially apparent one day when she was trying (without success) to read some words that I had typed. Suddenly, she said, "Hey! You spelled this one wrong." I looked at the word and realized that she was right; I had. But even though she saw that the word was misspelled, she still could not say what it was, even when she tried very hard to sound it out. That evening I made up a list of eighty pairs of words, one spelled correctly and the other incorrectly. The next day she was able to go through the list quickly and easily, correctly identifying 95 percent of the misspelled words. She was able to *read* only five of them.

Toward an Understanding of Writing

Writing depends on knowledge of the words that are to be used, along with the proper grammatical structure of the sentences they are to form. Thus, if a patient is unable to express himself or herself by speech, we should not be surprised to see a writing disturbance as well.

One type of writing disorder involves difficulties in motor control—in directing the movements of a pen or pencil to form letters and words. Investigators have reported surprisingly specific types of writing disorders that fall under this category. For example, some patients can write numbers but not letters, some can write uppercase letters but not lowercase letters, some can write consonants but not vowels, some can write cursively but not print uppercase letters, and others can write letters normally but have difficulty placing them in an orderly fashion on the page (Cubelli, 1991; Alexander et al., 1992; Margolin and Goodman-Schulman, 1992; Silveri, 1996).

The second type of writing disorder involves problems in the ability to spell words, as opposed to problems with making accurate movements of the fingers. I will devote the rest of this section to this type of disorder. Like reading, writing (or more specifically, spelling) involves more than one method. The first is related to audition. When children acquire language skills, they first learn the sounds of words, then learn to say them, then learn to read, and then learn to write. Undoubtedly, reading and writing depend heavily on the skills that are learned earlier. For example, to write most words, we must be able to "sound them out in our heads," that is, to hear them and to articulate them subvocally. If you want to demonstrate this to yourself, try to write a long word such as *antidisestablishmentarianism* from memory and see whether you can do it without saying the word to yourself. If you recite a poem or sing a song to yourself under your breath at the same time, you will see that the writing comes to a halt.

A second way of writing involves transcribing an image of what a particular word looks like—copying a visual mental image. Have you ever looked off into the distance to picture a word so that you can remember how to spell it? Some people are not very good at phonological spelling and have to write some words down to see whether they look correct. This method obviously involves *visual* memories, not acoustical ones.

Neurological evidence supports at least the first three of these speculations. Brain damage can impair the first of these methods: phonetic writing. This deficit is called **phonological dysgraphia** (Shallice, 1981). (*Dysgraphia* refers to a writing deficit just as *dyslexia* refers to a reading deficit.) People with this disorder are unable to sound out words and write them phonetically. Thus, they cannot write unfamiliar words or pronounceable nonwords, such as the ones I presented in the section on reading. They can, however, visually imagine familiar words and then write them. **Orthographic dysgraphia** is just the opposite—a disorder of visually based writing. People with orthographic dysgraphia can *only* sound words out; thus, they can spell regular words such as *care* or *tree,* and they can write pronounceable nonwords. However, they have difficulty spelling irregular words such as *half* or *busy* (Beauvois and Dérouesné, 1981); they may write *haff* or *bizzy.*

Japanese patients show writing deficits similar to those of patients whose languages use the Roman alphabet; some patients have difficulty writing kana symbols, whereas others have difficulty with kanji symbols (Iwata, 1984; Yokota et al., 1990). Kawamura, Hirayama, and Yamamoto (1989) reported a particularly interesting case of a man with damage to the middle part of the corpus callosum who could write kana symbols with both hands and could write kanji symbols with the right hand but not the left. He could *copy* kanji symbols with his left hand; he just could not write them down when the investigators dictated them to him. (See *Figure 13.22.*) Another patient, reported by Tei, Soma, and Maruyama (1994), had the opposite symptoms: very bad kana writing with the nondominant hand but better kanji writing.

These results have interesting implications. Writing appears to be organized in the speech-dominant hemisphere (normally, the left hemisphere). That is, the information needed to specify the shape of the symbols is provided by circuits in this hemi-

Phonological dysgraphia A writing disorder in which the person cannot sound out words and write them phonetically.

Orthographic dysgraphia A writing disorder in which the person can spell regularly spelled words but not irregularly spelled ones.

FIGURE **13.22**

The writing of a Japanese patient with damage to the middle part of the corpus callosum. He could write both kanji and kana characters with his right hand, but he could not write kanji characters with his left hand (color). He could, however, *copy* kanji characters with his left hand if he was given a model to look at.

(From Kawamura, M., Hirayama, K., and Yamamoto, H. Brain, 1989, 112, 1011–1018. Reprinted by permission of Oxford University Press.)

Task	Dictation			Copy
	Right hand	Left hand		Left hand
Kanji Kana	Kanji Kana	Kanji Kana		Kanji

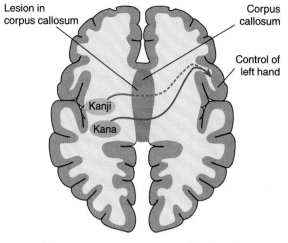

Lesion in corpus callosum

Corpus callosum

Control of left hand

Kanji

Kana

FIGURE 13.23

The role of the corpus callosum in Japanese writing. Information about kana and kanji characters apparently crosses different parts of the corpus callosum.

Developmental dyslexia A reading difficulty in a person of normal intelligence and perceptual ability; of genetic origin or caused by prenatal or perinatal factors.

sphere. When a person uses his or her left hand to write these symbols, the information must be sent across the corpus callosum to the motor cortex of the right hemisphere, which controls the left hand. Apparently, information about the two forms of Japanese symbols is transmitted through different parts of the corpus callosum; the brain damage of the patient studied by Kawamura and his colleagues disrupted one of these pathways but not the other. (See *Figure 13.23*.)

As we saw in the section on reading, some patients (those with direct dyslexia) can read aloud without being able to understand what they are reading. Similarly, some patients can write words that are dictated to them even though they cannot understand these words (Roeltgen, Rothi, and Heilman, 1986; Lesser, 1989). Of course, they cannot communicate by means of writing, because they cannot translate their thoughts into words. (In fact, because most of these patients have sustained extensive brain damage, their thought processes themselves are severely disturbed.) Some of these patients can even spell pronounceable nonwords, which indicates that their ability to spell phonetically is intact. Roeltgen et al. (1986) referred to this disorder as *semantic agraphia,* but perhaps the term *direct dysgraphia* would be more appropriate, because of the parallel with direct dyslexia.

Developmental Dyslexias

Some children have great difficulty learning to read and never become fluent readers, even though they are otherwise intelligent. Specific language learning disorders, called **developmental dyslexias,** tend to occur in families, a finding that suggests a genetic (and hence biological) component (Pennington et al., 1991; Wolff and Melngailis, 1994). Linkage studies suggest that the chromosomes 6 and 15 may contain genes responsible for different components of this disorder (Grigorenko et al., 1997). A study of fifty-six dyslexic boys in Sydney, Australia, found that two-thirds of them showed impairments in both phonological and word-form reading. Among the other third, 64 percent had difficulty only with phonological reading, and 46 percent had difficulty only with word-form reading (Castles and Coltheart, 1993). (You will recall that phonological difficulty is the primary symptom of phonological dyslexia, while word-form difficulty is the primary symptom of surface dyslexia.)

In a review of the literature, Filipek (1995) concluded that imaging studies have failed to find a "marker" for developmental dyslexia—that is, a reliable abnormality that is universally found in a particular location in the brains of dyslexics. Over the years, investigators have reported finding differences in the size or shape of the corpus callosum or various parts of the region around the posterior part of the lateral fissure, but follow-up studies have been equivocal.

One finding has been receiving a considerable amount of attention in recent years. Galaburda and Livingstone (1993) found evidence for a deficit in the magnocellular layers of the lateral geniculate nucleus of the thalamus. As we saw in Chapter 6, the visual system has two major components, named after two types of layers in the lateral geniculate nucleus, which relays information from the retina to the visual cortex. The *magnocellular system* is more ancient. It consists of two layers of neurons with large cell bodies that transmit information about movement, depth, and small differences in contrast. The *parvocellular system,* which evolved more recently, consists of four layers of neurons that transmit information about color and fine details. Galaburda and Livingstone studied the brains of deceased patients with developmental dyslexia and discovered that the magnocellular layers of these people were disorganized. The cell bodies in these layers were 27 percent smaller, and they were more variable in their size and shape. The parvocellular layers were normal.

Why should abnormalities in the magnocellular system impair people's ability to read? Stein and Walsh (1997) note that the primary target of the magnocellular system is the posterior parietal lobe, the endpoint of the dorsal stream of the visual system. As we saw in Chapter 6, this system is concerned with the "where" of vision, while the ventral stream, which terminates in the inferior temporal lobe, is concerned with the "what" of vision. But why should the "where" system be so important to reading? Stein and Walsh point out that dyslexics often have trouble with spatial perception and of movements in space. They often transpose letters (for example, reading *saw* as *was*), they are often clumsy and have difficulties with balance, their handwriting tends to be very poor, they learn to walk later than most other children and have trouble learning to ride a bike, they are slower to learn to tell time or learn the days of the week and months of the year, they have difficulty reading maps and distinguishing between left and right, and they tend not to establish strong handedness. Such problems are often associated with damage or developmental abnormalities in the posterior parietal lobe. Perhaps, Stein and Walsh suggest, abnormal input to the parietal lobe caused by an abnormal magnocellular system impairs the development of this region and causes a variety of symptoms, including dyslexia.

In support of their hypothesis, Stein and Walsh note that many dyslexics complain that when they try to read, letters move around, merge, and become blurry. Their gaze is often unsteady, and their ability to read is sometimes improved by providing them with text with larger type (Cornelissen et al., 1991). They also note that monkeys with lesions of the posterior parietal lobes have no trouble discriminating between different shapes but have trouble distinguishing between reversals of the same shape, such as < versus > or b versus d (Walsh and Butler, 1996).

Eden et al. (1996) performed a functional MRI study that provides further support for Stein and Walsh's hypothesis. They found that although no differences were seen in the activity of the primary visual cortex to stationary visual stimuli, there were differences in activation of visual area V5 by moving stimuli. Area V5 receives input from the magnocellular system and is involved in the perception of motion. As Figure 13.24 shows, looking at a pattern of black dots moving against a gray background activated area V5 in control subjects (white arrows), but such activation was not seen in the brains of subjects with developmental dyslexia. (See *Figure 13.24*.)

| Controls/Stationary pattern | Dyslexics/Stationary pattern | Controls/Motion | Dyslexics/Motion |

FIGURE 13.24

Functional MRI scans from dyslexics and control subjects looking at a stationary pattern (a plus sign against a gray background) or at a moving pattern (an array of black dots moving against a gray background). Note that viewing the moving pattern activated area V5 of the visual association cortex in control subjects (white arrows) but not in dyslexics.

(Reprinted with permission from Eden, G.F., VanMeter, J.W., Rumsey, J.M., Maisog, J.M., Woods, R.P., and Zeffiro, T.A. Nature, 1996, 382, 66–69. Copyright 1996 Macmillan Magazines Limited.)

Brain damage can produce reading and writing disorders. With few exceptions, aphasias are accompanied by writing deficits that parallel the speech production deficits and by reading deficits that parallel the speech comprehension deficits. Pure alexia is caused by lesions that produce blindness in the right visual field and that destroy fibers of the posterior corpus callosum. Damage that is restricted to the posterior corpus callosum produces alexia only in the left visual field.

Research in the past few decades has discovered that acquired reading disorders (dyslexias) can fall into one of several categories, and the study of these disorders has provided neuropsychologists and cognitive psychologists with thought-provoking information that has helped them understand how normal people read. Surface dyslexia is a loss of whole-word reading ability. Phonological dyslexia is loss of the ability to read phonetically. Word-form (spelling) dyslexia is caused by a deficit in both phonetic and whole-word reading; patients can still recognize individual letters and can read slowly by pronouncing each letter. Direct dyslexia is analogous to transcortical sensory aphasia; the patients can read words aloud but cannot understand what they are reading. Some dyslexia patients can at least partially comprehend written words without being able to pronounce them; they can match corresponding words and pictures and recognize misspelled words they cannot read.

Brain damage can disrupt writing ability by impairing people's ability to form letters—or even specific types of letters, such as uppercase or lowercase letters, or vowels. Other deficits involve the ability to spell words. We normally use at least two different strategies to spell words: phonetic (sounding the word out), and visual (remembering how it looks on paper). Two types of dysgraphia—phonological and orthographic—represent difficulties implementing phonetic and visual strategies, respectively. The existence of these two disorders indicates that several different brain mechanisms are involved in the process of writing. In addition, some patients have a deficit parallel to direct dyslexia; they can write words that they cannot understand. Developmental dyslexia may involve abnormal development of parts of the brain that play a role in language. Recent evidence suggests that abnormal development of the magnocellular system of the lateral geniculate nucleus, seen in people with developmental dyslexia, may impair normal development of the posterior parietal lobe. A better understanding of the components of reading and writing may help us to develop effective teaching methods that will permit people with dyslexia to take advantage of the abilities that they do have.

Table 13.2 summarizes the disorders described in this section.

TABLE 13.2	Reading and Writing Disorders Produced by Brain Damage		
Reading Disorder	**Whole-Word Reading**	**Phonetic Reading**	**Remarks**
Pure alexia	Poor	Poor	Can write
Surface dyslexia	Poor	Good	
Phonological dyslexia	Good	Poor	
Spelling dyslexia	Poor	Poor	Can read words letter-by-letter
Direct dyslexia	Good	Good	Cannot comprehend words
Comprehension without reading	Poor	Poor	Show some comprehension of words
Writing Disorder	**Whole-Word Writing**	**Phonetic Writing**	
Phonological dysgraphia	Good	Poor	
Orthographic dysgraphia	Poor	Good	

■ **THOUGHT QUESTIONS**

Suppose someone close to you received a head injury that caused phonological dyslexia. What would you do to try to help her read better? (It would probably be best to build on her remaining abilities.) Suppose she needed to learn to read some words she had never seen before. How would help her to do so?

EPILOGUE **Analysis of Speech Sounds**

Mr. S., the man described at the beginning of the chapter, had pure word deafness. As you learned in this chapter, pure word deafness is a perceptual deficit that does not affect people's general language abilities; nor does it affect their ability to recognize nonspeech sounds.

As you saw in this chapter, pure word deafness is caused by lesions that damage Wernicke's area or prevent it from receiving auditory input. Thus, Wernicke's area appears to contain the neural network responsible for analyzing speech sounds. The auditory association cortex of the right hemisphere is apparently involved in perception of nonspeech sounds and of the rhythmic elements of speech (such as those we use for emphasis or to express emotions). Many patients with pure word deafness can recognize the emotion expressed by the intonation of speech even though they cannot understand what is being said. In addition, perception of the melodic and harmonic structure of music is accomplished by the right hemisphere; damage to this hemisphere can result in *amusia*, or loss of musical ability.

Hemispheric specialization in auditory function is not limited to the human brain. Heffner and Heffner (1990) reviewed a series of experiments from their laboratory indicating that the auditory system of the left hemisphere in monkeys plays a special role in recognizing vocal communications. Although Japanese macaques obviously cannot talk, they do have a repertoire of vocal calls that they use to communicate with each other. Heffner and Heffner found that lesions of the left auditory cortex produce a much more severe impairment than right-hemisphere lesions.

Exactly what do we mean when we say that the auditory system of the left hemisphere is specialized for the analysis of speech sounds? First, the specialization is only for the discrimination of the sounds that distinguish one word from another, not the sounds related to the rhythmic aspects of speech. In general, the sounds that distinguish between words are very brief, whereas those that convey emphasis or emotion are of longer duration. Perhaps the auditory system of the left hemisphere is simply specialized for the recognition of acoustical events of short duration.

In a review of the literature, Phillips and Farmer (1990) suggest precisely this hypothesis. They note that careful studies of patients with pure word deafness have shown that the patients can distinguish between different vowels but not between different consonants—especially between different stop consonants, such as /t/, /d/, /k/, or /p/. (Linguists represent speech sounds by putting letters or special phonetic symbols between pairs of slashes.) Patients with pure word deafness *can* generally recognize consonants with a long duration, such as /s/, /z/, or /f/. (Say these consonants to yourself, and you will see how different they sound.)

Phillips and Farmer note that the important acoustical events in speech sounds fall within a time range of a few milliseconds to a few tens of milliseconds. Speech sounds are made by rapidly moving lips, tongue, and soft palate, which can produce acoustical events that can be distinguished only by a fine-grained analysis. In contrast, most environmental sounds do not contain such a fine temporal structure. The authors also note that "pure" word deafness is not absolutely pure. That is, when people with this disorder are tested carefully with recordings of a variety of environmental sounds, they have difficulty recognizing at least some of them. Although *most* environmental sounds do not contain a fine temporal structure, some do, and patients have difficulty recognizing them.

Several studies have found deficits in auditory perception that support Phillips and Farmer's "temporal grain" hypothesis of pure word deafness. For example, normal subjects can perceive a series of clicks as being separate events when they are separated by only 1–3 msec; in contrast, patients with pure word deafness require a separation of 15–30 msec. In addition, although normal subjects can count clicks that are presented at a rate of up to 9–11 per second, pa-

(continued)

tients with pure word deafness cannot count clicks presented faster than 2 per second. This perceptual difficulty shows up in recognition of non-speech sounds in which the timing of brief events is important; one study reported that a patient with pure word deafness could no longer understand

messages in Morse code, although he could still *send* messages that way. Thus, his deficit was perceptual, not motor.

Although more research needs to be done on hemispheric differences in the functions of the auditory system, the temporal grain hypothesis

appears to be quite reasonable and has considerable support. Most investigators have focused on the linguistic aspects of language deficits produced by brain damage; it is clear that study of the brain mechanisms involved in the perceptual aspects of speech deserves attention, too.

KEY CONCEPTS

SPEECH PRODUCTION AND COMPREHENSION: BRAIN MECHANISMS

1. Broca's area, located in the left frontal lobe, is important in articulating words and producing and understanding grammatical constructions.
2. Wernicke's area, located in the auditory association cortex of the left hemisphere, is important in recognizing the sounds of words.
3. Comprehension of speech involves connections between Wernicke's area and memories that define words. These memories are located in the sensory association cortex, and the connections are made via the posterior language area.
4. Conduction aphasia occurs when Wernicke's area and Broca's area can no longer communicate directly.

READING AND WRITING DISORDERS

5. Brain damage can produce a variety of reading and writing disorders. Study of these disorders is helping investigators discover the brain functions necessary for these behaviors.
6. Reading takes two forms: whole-word and phonetic. Writing can be based on memories of the sounds the words make or their visual shape.
7. Developmental dyslexia may be caused by abnormal development of the brain regions involved in language abilities. In particular, abnormal development of the magnocellular layers of the lateral geniculate nucleus of the thalamus may adversely affect development of the posterior parietal lobe.

SUGGESTED READINGS

Kolb, B., and Whishaw, I.Q. *Fundamentals of Human Neuropsychology*, 4th ed. New York: W.H. Freeman, 1996.

Margolin, D.I. *Cognitive Neuropsychology in Clinical Practice.* New York: Oxford University Press, 1992.

McCarthy, R.A., and Warrington, E.K. *Cognitive Neuropsychology: A Clinical Introduction.* San Diego: Academic Press, 1990.

Parkin, A.J. *Explorations in Cognitive Neuropsychology.* Oxford: Blackwell Publishers, 1996.

Posner, M.I., and Raichle, M.E. *Images of Mind.* New York: Scientific American Library, 1994.

14

Neurological Disorders

LEARNING OBJECTIVES

1. Discuss the causes, symptoms, and treatment of brain tumors, seizure disorders, and cerebrovascular accidents.

2. Discuss developmental disorders resulting from toxic chemicals, inherited metabolic disorders, and Down syndrome.

3. Discuss the causes and describe the neurological changes resulting from degeneration of the basal ganglia that occur in Parkinson's disease and Huntington's chorea.

4. Discuss the causes and describe the neurological changes resulting from Alzheimer's disease and multiple sclerosis.

5. Discuss the causes, symptoms, and available treatments for encephalitis, dementia caused by the AIDS virus, and meningitis.

It Started with Her Foot

Mrs. R., a divorced, fifty-year-old elementary school teacher, was sitting in her car, waiting for the traffic light to change. Suddenly, her right foot began to shake. Afraid that she would inadvertently press the accelerator and lurch forward into the intersection, she quickly grabbed the shift lever and switched the transmission into neutral. Now her lower leg was shaking; then her upper leg, as well. With horrified fascination she felt her body, then her arm, begin to shake in rhythm with her leg. The shaking slowed and finally stopped. By this time the light had changed to green, and the cars behind her began honking at her. She missed that green light, but by the time the light changed again, she had recovered enough to put the car in gear and drive home.

Mrs. R. was frightened by her experience and tried in vain to think what she might have done to cause it. The next evening, some close friends visited her apartment for dinner. She found it hard to concentrate on their conversation and thought of telling them about her spell, but she finally decided not to bring up the matter. After dinner, while she was clearing the dishes off the table, her right foot began shaking again. This time she was standing up, and the contractions—much more violent than before—caused her to fall. Her friends, seated in the living room, heard the noise and came running to see what had happened. They saw Mrs. R. lying on the floor, her legs and arms held out stiffly before her, vibrating uncontrollably. Her head was thrown back and she seemed not to hear their anxious questions. The convulsion soon ceased; less than a minute later, Mrs. R. regained consciousness but seemed dazed and confused.

Mrs. R. was brought by ambulance to a hospital. After learning about her first spell and hearing her friends describe the convulsion, the emergency room physician immediately called a neurologist, who ordered a CT scan. The scan showed a small, circular white spot right where the neurologist expected it, between the frontal lobes, above the corpus callosum. Two days later, a neurosurgeon removed a small benign tumor, and Mrs. R. made an uneventful recovery.

When my colleagues and I met Mrs. R., we saw a pleasant, intelligent woman, much relieved to know that her type of brain tumor rarely produces brain damage if it is removed in time. Indeed, although we tested her carefully, we found no signs of intellectual impairment.

Although the brain is the most protected organ, many pathological processes can damage it or disrupt its functioning. Because much of what we have learned about the functions of the human brain has been gained by studying people with brain damage, you have already encountered many neurological disorders in this book: movement disorders, such as Parkinson's disease and apraxia; perceptual disorders, such as visual agnosia and blindness caused by damage to the visual system; language disorders such as aphasia, alexia, and agraphia; and memory disorders, such as Korsakoff's syndrome. This chapter describes the major categories of the neuropathological conditions that the brain can sustain—tumors, seizure disorders, cerebrovascular accidents, disorders of development, degenerative disorders, and disorders caused by infectious diseases—and discusses the behavioral effects of these conditions and their treatments.

TUMORS

Malignant tumor A cancerous (literally, "harm-producing") tumor; lacks a distinct border and may metastasize.

Benign tumor (*bee nine*) A noncancerous (literally, "harmless") tumor; has a distinct border and cannot metastasize.

A tumor is a mass of cells whose growth is uncontrolled and that serves no useful function. Some are **malignant,** or cancerous, and others are **benign** ("harmless"). The major distinction between malignancy and benignancy is whether the tumor is *encapsulated*: whether there is a distinct border between the mass of tumor cells and the surrounding tissue. If there is such a border, the tumor is benign; the surgeon can cut it out, and it will not regrow. However, if the tumor grows by *infiltrating* the surrounding tissue, there will be no clear-cut border between the tumor and normal tissue. If the surgeon removes the tumor, some cells may be missed, and these cells will produce a new tumor. In addition, malignant tumors often give rise to **metastases.** A metastasizing tumor will shed cells, which then travel through the bloodstream, lodge in capillaries, and serve as seeds for the growth of new tumors in different locations in the body.

Tumors damage brain tissue by two means: compression and infiltration. Obviously, *any* tumor growing in the brain, malignant or benign, can produce neurological symptoms and threaten the patient's life. Even a benign tumor occupies space and thus pushes against the brain. The compression can directly destroy brain tissue, or it can do so indirectly by blocking the flow of cerebrospinal fluid and causing hydrocephalus. Even worse are malignant tumors, which cause both compression and infiltration. As a malignant tumor grows, it invades the surrounding region and destroys cells in its path. Figure 14.1 illustrates the compressive effect of a large nonmalignant tumor. As you can see, the tumor has displaced the lateral and third ventricles. (See *Figure 14.1*.)

Tumors do not arise from nerve cells, which are not capable of dividing. Instead, they arise from other cells found in the brain or from metastases originating elsewhere in the body. The most common types are listed in Table 14.1. (See *Table 14.1*.) The most serious types of tumors are metastases and the **gliomas** (derived from various types of glial cells), which are usually very malignant and fast growing. Figures 14.2 and 14.3 show gliomas located in the basal ganglia and the pons, respectively. (See *Figures 14.2* and *14.3*.) Figure 14.4 shows an ependymoma in the lateral ventricles. (See *Figure 14.4*.) Some tumors are sensitive to radiation and can be destroyed by a beam of radiation focused on them. Usually, a neurosurgeon first removes as much of the tumor as possible, and then the remaining cells are targeted by the radiation.

![Figure 14.1 brain slice]

FIGURE 14.1

A slice of a human brain, showing how a large nonmalignant tumor (a meningioma) has displaced the right side of the brain toward the left. (The dotted line indicates the location of the midline.) The right lateral ventricle is almost completely occluded.

(Courtesy of A. D'Agostino, Good Samaritan Hospital, Portland, Oregon.)

Metastasis [*meh **tass** ta sis*] The process by which cells break off of a tumor, travel through the vascular system, and grow elsewhere in the body.

Glioma [*glee oh mah*] A cancerous brain tumor composed of one of several types of glial cells.

TABLE 14.1	Types of Brain Tumors

GLIOMAS
Glioblastoma multiformae (poorly differentiated glial cells)
Astrocytoma (astrocytes)
Ependymoma (ependymal cells that line ventricles)
Medulloblastoma (cells in roof of the fourth ventricle)
Oligodendrocytoma (oligodendroglial cells)

MENINGIOMA (cells of the meninges)

PITUITARY ADENOMA (hormone-secreting cells of the pituitary gland)

NEURINOMA (Schwann cells or cells of connective tissue covering cranial nerves)

METASTATIC CARCINOMA (depends on nature of primary tumor)

ANGIOMA (cells of blood vessels)

PINEALOMA (cells of pineal gland)

FIGURE 14.2

A slice of a human brain, showing a large glioma located in the basal ganglia, which has invaded both the left and right lateral ventricles.

(Courtesy of A. D'Agostino, Good Samaritan Hospital, Portland, Oregon.)

FIGURE 14.3

A midsagittal view of a human brain, showing a glioma located in the dorsal pons (*arrowhead*).

(Courtesy of A. D'Agostino, Good Samaritan Hospital, Portland, Oregon.)

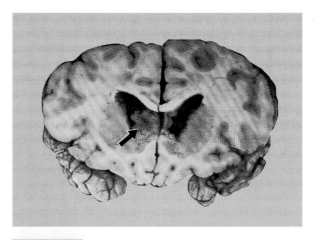

FIGURE 14.4

A slice of a human brain, showing an ependymoma of the left lateral ventricle (*arrowhead*).

(Courtesy of A. D'Agostino, Good Samaritan Hospital, Portland, Oregon.)

The Prologue described a woman whose sudden onset of seizures suggested the presence of a tumor near the top of the primary motor cortex. Indeed, she had a **meningioma,** an encapsulated, benign tumor consisting of cells that constitute the dura mater or arachnoid membrane. Such tumors tend to originate in the part of the dura mater that is found between the two cerebral hemispheres, or along the tentorium, the sheet of dura mater that lies between the occipital lobes and the cerebellum. (See *Figure 14.5*.)

SEIZURE DISORDERS

Because of negative connotations that were acquired in the past, most physicians prefer not to use the term *epilepsy*. Instead, they use the phrase **seizure disorder** to refer to a condition that has many causes. Seizure disorders constitute the second most important category of neurological disorders, following stroke. A *seizure* is a period of sudden, excessive activity of cerebral neurons. Sometimes, if neurons that comprise the

FIGURE 14.5

A CT scan of a brain, showing the presence of a meningioma (round white spot indicated by the arrow).

(Courtesy of J.McA. Jones, Good Samaritan Hospital, Portland, Oregon.)

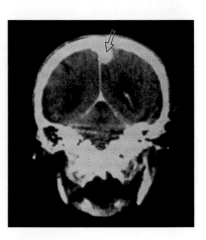

Meningioma (*men in jee oh ma*) A benign brain tumor composed of the cells that constitute the meninges.

Seizure disorder The preferred term for epilepsy.

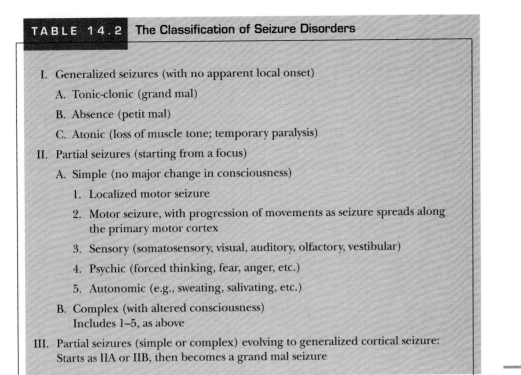

TABLE 14.2 The Classification of Seizure Disorders

I. Generalized seizures (with no apparent local onset)

    A. Tonic-clonic (grand mal)

    B. Absence (petit mal)

    C. Atonic (loss of muscle tone; temporary paralysis)

II. Partial seizures (starting from a focus)

    A. Simple (no major change in consciousness)

        1. Localized motor seizure

        2. Motor seizure, with progression of movements as seizure spreads along the primary motor cortex

        3. Sensory (somatosensory, visual, auditory, olfactory, vestibular)

        4. Psychic (forced thinking, fear, anger, etc.)

        5. Autonomic (e.g., sweating, salivating, etc.)

    B. Complex (with altered consciousness)
Includes 1–5, as above

III. Partial seizures (simple or complex) evolving to generalized cortical seizure: Starts as IIA or IIB, then becomes a grand mal seizure

---

motor system are involved, a seizure can cause a **convulsion,** which is wild, uncontrollable activity of the muscles. But not all seizures cause convulsions; in fact, most do not.

Table 14.2 presents a summary of the most important categories of seizure disorders. Two distinctions are important: *partial* versus *generalized* seizures and *simple* versus *complex* ones. **Partial seizures** have a definite *focus,* or source of irritation: typically, a scarred region caused by an old injury. The neurons that become involved in the seizure are restricted to a small part of the brain. **Generalized seizures** are widespread, involving most of the brain. In many cases they grow from a focus, but in some cases their origin is not discovered. Simple and complex seizures are two categories of partial seizures. **Simple partial seizures** often cause *changes* in consciousness but do not cause *loss* of consciousness. In contrast, because of their particular location and severity, **complex partial seizures** lead to loss of consciousness. (See *Table 14.2.*)

The most severe form of seizure is often referred to as **grand mal.** This seizure is generalized, and because it includes the motor systems of the brain, it is accompanied by convulsions. Often, before having a grand mal seizure, a person has warning symptoms, such as changes in mood or perhaps a few sudden jerks of muscular activity upon awakening. (Almost everyone sometimes experiences these jolts while falling asleep.) A few seconds before the seizure occurs, the person often experiences an **aura,** which is presumably caused by excitation of neurons surrounding a seizure focus. This excitation has effects similar to those that would be produced by electrical stimulation of the region. Obviously, the nature of an aura varies according to the location of the focus. For example, because structures in the temporal lobe are involved in the control of emotional behaviors, seizures that originate from a focus located there often begin with feelings of fear and dread or, occasionally, euphoria.

The beginning of a grand mal seizure is called the **tonic phase.** All the patient's muscles contract forcefully. The arms are rigidly outstretched, and he or she may make an involuntary cry as the tense muscles force air out of the lungs. (At this point the patient is completely unconscious.) The patient holds a rigid posture for about 15 seconds, and then the **clonic phase** begins. (*Clonic* means "agitated.") The muscles begin trembling, then start jerking convulsively—quickly at first, then more and more

Convulsion A violent sequence of uncontrollable muscular movements caused by a seizure.

Partial seizure A seizure that begins at a focus and remains localized, not generalizing to the rest of the brain.

Generalized seizure A seizure that involves most of the brain, as contrasted with a partial seizure, which remains localized.

Simple partial seizure A partial seizure, starting from a focus and remaining localized, that does not produce loss of consciousness.

Complex partial seizure A partial seizure, starting from a focus and remaining localized, that produces loss of consciousness.

Grand mal seizure A generalized, tonic-clonic seizure, which results in a convulsion.

Aura A sensation that precedes a seizure; its exact nature depends on the location of the seizure focus.

Tonic phase The first phase of a grand mal seizure, in which all of the patient's skeletal muscles are contracted.

Clonic phase The phase of a grand mal seizure in which the patient shows rhythmic jerking movements.

slowly. Meanwhile, the eyes roll, the patient's face is contorted with violent grimaces, and the tongue may be bitten. Intense activity of the autonomic nervous system manifests itself in sweating and salivation. After about 30 seconds, the patient's muscles relax; only then does breathing begin again. The patient falls into a stuporous, unresponsive sleep, which lasts for about 15 minutes. After that the patient may awaken briefly but usually falls back into an exhausted asleep that may last for a few hours.

Recordings made during grand mal seizures from electrodes implanted into patients' brains show that neural firing first begins in the focus at the time of the aura; it then spreads to other regions of the brain (Adams and Victor, 1981). The activity spreads to regions surrounding the focus and then to the contralateral cortex (through the corpus callosum), the basal ganglia, the thalamus, and various nuclei of the brain stem reticular formation. At this point the symptoms begin. The excited subcortical regions feed back more excitation to the cortex, amplifying the activity there. Neurons in the motor cortex begin firing continuously, producing the tonic phase. Next, diencephalic structures begin quenching the seizure by sending inhibitory messages to the cortex. At first the inhibition comes in brief bursts; this causes the jerking movements of the clonic phase, as the muscles repeatedly relax and then contract again. Then the bursts of inhibition become more and more prolonged, and the jerks occur more and more slowly. Finally, the inhibition wins, and the patient's muscles relax.

Other types of seizures are far less dramatic. Partial seizures involve relatively small portions of the brain. The symptoms can include sensory changes, motor activity, or both. For example, a simple partial seizure that begins in or near the motor cortex can involve jerking movements that begin in one place and spread throughout the body as the excitation spreads along the precentral gyrus. In the Prologue I described such a progression, caused by a seizure triggered by a meningioma. The tumor was pressing against the "foot" region of the left primary motor cortex. When the seizure began, it involved the foot; and as it spread, it began involving the other parts of the body. (See *Figure 14.6.*) Mrs. R.'s first spell was a simple partial seizure, but her second one—much more severe—would be classed as a complex partial seizure, because she lost consciousness. A seizure beginning in the occipital lobe may produce visual symptoms such as spots of color, flashes of light, or temporary blindness; one originating in the parietal lobe can evoke somatosensations, such as feelings of pins and needles, or heat and cold. Seizures in the temporal lobes may cause hallucinations that include old memories; presumably, neural circuits involved in these memories are activated by the spreading excitation. Depending on the location and extent of the seizure, the patient may or may not lose consciousness.

Children are especially susceptible to seizure disorders. Many of them do not have grand mal episodes but, instead, have very brief seizures that are referred to as spells of **absence.** During an absence seizure, which is a *generalized* seizure disorder, they stop what they are doing and stare off into the distance for a few seconds, often blinking their eyes repeatedly. (These spells are also sometimes referred to as *petit mal* seizures.) During this time they are unresponsive and usually do not notice their attacks. Because absence seizures can occur up to several hundred times each day, they can disrupt a child's performance in school. Unfortunately, many of these children are considered to be inattentive and unmotivated unless the disorder is diagnosed.

Absence A type of seizure disorder often seen in children; characterized by periods of inattention, which are not subsequently remembered; also called *petit mal seizure.*

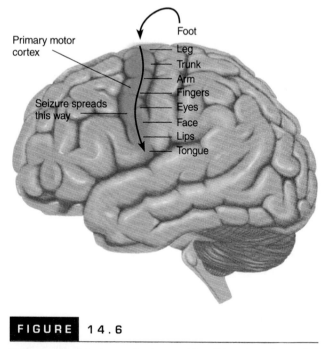

FIGURE 14.6

Primary motor cortex and seizures. Mrs. R.'s seizure began in the foot region of the primary motor cortex, and as the seizure spread, more and more parts of her body became involved.

Seizures can have serious consequences: They can cause brain damage. Approximately 50 percent of patients with seizure disorders show evidence of damage to the hippocampus. The amount of damage is correlated with the number and severity of seizures the patient has had. Significant hippocampal damage can be caused by a single episode of **status epilepticus,** a condition in which the patient undergoes a series of seizures without regaining consciousness. The damage appears to be caused by an excessive release of glutamate during the seizure (Thompson et al., 1996).

Seizures have many causes. The most common cause is scarring, which may be produced by an injury, a stroke, or the irritating effect of a growing tumor. For injuries, the development of seizures may take a considerable amount of time. Often, a person who receives a head injury from an automobile accident will not start having seizures until several months later.

Various drugs and infections that cause a high fever can also produce seizures. In addition, seizures are commonly seen in alcohol or barbiturate addicts who suddenly stop taking the drug; the sudden release from the inhibiting effects of the alcohol or barbiturate leaves the brain in a hyperexcitable condition. In fact, this condition is a medical emergency, because it can be fatal.

Evidence suggests that NMDA receptors may be involved in the seizures caused by alcohol withdrawal. As you saw in Chapter 12, NMDA receptors are specialized glutamate receptors that control calcium channels. These channels open only when glutamate binds with the receptor *and* the membrane is depolarized. This double contingency is what seems to be responsible for at least one kind of synaptic modification involved in learning. Several studies have shown that alcohol blocks NMDA receptors (Gonzales, 1990). Perhaps, then, long-term suppression of NMDA receptors caused by chronic alcohol intake results in supersensitivity or "up-regulation," a compensatory mechanism produced by long-term inhibition of the receptors. When an alcoholic suddenly stops drinking, the NMDA receptors, which have been suppressed for so long, suddenly rebound. The increased activity causes seizures.

Seizure disorders are treated with anticonvulsant drugs, many of which work by increasing the effectiveness of inhibitory synapses. Most disorders respond well enough that the patient can lead a normal life. In a few instances, drugs provide little or no help. Sometimes, seizure foci remain so irritable that despite drug treatment, brain surgery is required. The surgeon removes the region of the brain surrounding the focus (almost always, the medial temporal lobe). Most patients recover well, with their seizures eliminated or greatly reduced in frequency. Mrs. R.'s treatment was a different matter; in her case, the removal of a meningioma eliminated the source of the irritation and ended her seizures. No brain tissue was removed.

■ CEREBROVASCULAR ACCIDENTS

You have already learned about the *effects* of cerebrovascular accidents, or *strokes*, in earlier chapters. For example, we saw that strokes can produce impairments in perception, emotional recognition and expression, memory, and language. This section will describe only their causes and treatments.

The incidence of strokes in the United States is approximately 550,000 per year. The likelihood of having a stroke is related to age; the probability doubles each decade after 45 years of age and reaches 1–2 percent per year by age 75 (Wolfe, Cobb, and D'Agostino, 1992). The two major types of strokes are *hemorrhagic* and *obstructive*. **Hemorrhagic strokes** are caused by bleeding within the brain, usually from a malformed blood vessel or from one weakened by high blood pressure. The blood that seeps out of the defective blood vessel accumulates within the brain, putting pressure on the surrounding brain tissue and damaging it. **Obstructive strokes—** those that plug up a blood vessel and prevent the flow of blood—can be caused by

Status epilepticus A condition in which a patient undergoes a series of seizures without regaining consciousness.

Hemorrhagic stroke A cerebrovascular accident caused by the rupture of a cerebral blood vessel.

Obstructive stroke A cerebrovascular accident caused by occlusion of a blood vessel.

thrombi or emboli. (Loss of blood blow to a region is called **ischemia,** from the Greek *ischein,* "to hold back" and *haima,* "blood.") A **thrombus** is a blood clot that forms in blood vessels, especially in places where their walls are already damaged. Sometimes, thrombi become so large that blood cannot flow through the vessel, causing a stroke. People who are susceptible to the formation of thrombi usually take a drug such as aspirin, which helps to prevent clot formation. An **embolus** is a piece of material that forms in one part of the vascular system, breaks off, and is carried through the bloodstream until it reaches an artery too small to pass through. It lodges there, damming the flow of blood through the rest of the vascular tree (the "branches" and "twigs" arising from the artery). Emboli can consist of a variety of materials, including bacterial debris from an infection in the lining of the heart or pieces broken off from a blood clot. As we will see in a later section, emboli can introduce a bacterial infection into the brain. (See *Figure 14.7.*)

Strokes produce permanent brain damage, but, depending on the size of the affected blood vessel, the amount of damage can vary from negligible to massive. If a hemorrhagic stroke is caused by high blood pressure, medication is given to reduce it. If one is caused by weak and malformed blood vessels, brain surgery may be used to seal off the faulty vessels to prevent another hemorrhage. If a thrombus was responsible for the stroke, anticoagulant drugs will be given to make the blood less likely to clot, reducing the likelihood of another stroke. If an embolus broke away from a bacterial infection, antibiotics will be given to suppress the infection.

What, exactly, causes the death of neurons when the blood supply to a region of the brain is interrupted? We might expect that the neurons simply starve to death because they lose their supply of glucose and oxygen to metabolize it. However, research indicates that the immediate cause of neuron death is the presence of excessive amounts of glutamate. In other words, the damage produced by loss of blood flow to a region of the brain is actually an excitotoxic lesion, just like one produced in a laboratory animal by the injection of a chemical such as kainic acid. (See Koroshetz and Moskowitz, 1996, for a review.)

When the blood supply to a region of the brain is interrupted, the oxygen and glucose in that region are quickly depleted. As a consequence, the sodium-potas-

Ischemia (*is kee mee uh*) The interruption of the blood supply to a region of the body.

Thrombus A blood clot that forms within a blood vessel, which may occlude it.

Embolus (*emm bo lus*) A piece of matter (such as a blood clot, fat, or bacterial debris) that dislodges from its site of origin and occludes an artery; in the brain an embolus can lead to a stroke.

(a)   (b)

FIGURE 14.7

Strokes. (a) Formation of thrombi and emboli. (b) An intracerebral hemorrhage.

sium transporters, which regulate the balance of ions inside and outside the cell, stop functioning. Neural membranes become depolarized, which causes the release of glutamate. The activation of glutamate receptors further increases the inflow of sodium ions and causes cells to absorb excessive amounts of calcium. (As we saw in Chapter 4, different types of glutamate receptors control different ion channels: NMDA receptors control calcium channels, and kainate and AMPA receptors control sodium channels.) The presence of excessive amounts of sodium and calcium within cells is toxic. The intracellular sodium causes the cells to absorb water and swell. The inflammation attracts microglia and activates them, causing them to become phagocytic. The phagocytic microglia begin destroying injured cells. Inflammation also attracts white blood cells, which can adhere to the walls of capillaries near the ischemic region and obstruct them. The presence of excessive amounts of calcium in the cells activates a variety of calcium-dependent enzymes, many of which destroy molecules that are vital for normal cell functioning. Finally, damaged mitochondria produce **free radicals**—molecules with unpaired electrons that act as powerful oxidizing agents. Free radicals are extremely toxic; they destroy nucleic acids, proteins, and fatty acids.

In recent years, researchers have sought ways to minimize the amount of brain damage caused by strokes. One approach has been to administer drugs that dissolve blood clots in an attempt to reestablish circulation to an ischemic brain region. This approach has met with some success. The NINDS rt-PA Study Group (1995) found that administration of a clot-dissolving drug called *rt-PA* (recombinant tissue plasminogen activator) 1.5 to 3 h after the onset of a stroke had clear benefits.

Another therapeutic approach has been to prevent the death of cells in the region that surrounds the ischemic region. Cells in this region live as long as several days but are eventually killed by inflammation, free radicals, and the effects of excessive glutamate release. Researchers are experimenting with anti-inflammatory agents, drugs that block glutamate receptors, chemicals that bind with free radicals and inactivate them, and drugs that stimulate inhibitory GABA receptors (Koroshetz and Moskowitz, 1996). Research with laboratory animals and preliminary clinical trials provide hope that such treatments may minimize the damage to the human brain caused by strokes.

Depending on the location of the brain damage, people who have strokes will receive physical therapy, and perhaps speech therapy, to help them recover from their disability. Several studies have shown that exercise and sensory stimulation can facil-

Free radical A molecule with unpaired electrons; acts as a powerful oxidizing agent; toxic to cells.

Research with both animals and humans has shown that exercise and sensory stimulation facilitate recovery of functions lost as a result of brain damage.

FIGURE 14.8

Effects of environmental stimulation on recovery from traumatic brain injury. Latency to reach the platform of a Morris milk maze as a function of days of training.

[Adapted from Hamm, R.J., Temple, M.D., O'Dell, D.M., Pike, B.R., and Lyeth, B.G. Journal of Neurotrauma, 1996, 13, 41–47.]

itate recovery from the effects of brain damage. For example, Taub et al. (1993) studied patients with strokes that impaired their ability to use one arm and hand. They forced the patients to use the impaired limb by putting the *unaffected* arm in a sling for fourteen days. This procedure produced long-term improvement in the patients' ability to use the affected arm. And in a laboratory study, Hamm et al. (1996) found that environmental stimulation facilitated recovery from traumatic brain injury similar to a concussion that might be caused by an automobile accident. After producing the brain injury, the investigators placed one group of rats in a complex environment that contained objects to explore. The other rats were placed in empty cages that contained only food and water. Ten days later, both groups were trained on the Morris milk maze. (As we saw in Chapter 12, learning this task involves relational memory, a relatively complex cognitive ability.) The environmental stimulation clearly facilitated the animals' recovery from the effects of the brain damage. (See *Figure 14.8.*)

INTERIM SUMMARY

Neurological disorders have many causes. Because we have learned much about the functions of the human brain from studying the behavior of people with various neurological disorders, you have already learned about many of them in previous chapters of this book. Brain tumors are caused by the uncontrolled growth of various types of cells *other than neurons*. They can be benign or malignant. Benign tumors are encapsulated and thus have a distinct border; when one is surgically removed, the surgeon has a good chance of getting all of it. Tumors produce brain damage by compression and, in the case of malignant tumors, infiltration.

Seizures are periodic episodes of abnormal electrical activity of the brain. Partial seizures are localized, beginning with a focus—usually, some scar tissue caused by previous damage or a tumor. When they begin, they often produce an aura, consisting of particular sensations or changes in mood. Simple partial seizures do not produce profound changes in consciousness; complex partial seizures do. Generalized seizures may or may not originate at a single focus, but they involve most of the brain. Some seizures involve motor activity; the most serious are the grand mal convulsions that accompany generalized seizures. The convulsions are caused by involvement of the motor cortex; the patient first shows a tonic phase, consisting of a few seconds of rigidity, and then a clonic phase, consisting of rhythmic jerking. Absence seizures, also called petit mal seizures, are common in children. They are characterized by periods of inattention and temporary loss of awareness. Seizures produced by abstinence after prolonged heavy intake of alcohol appear to be produced by supersensitivity (up-regulation) of NMDA receptors.

Cerebrovascular accidents damage parts of the brain through rupture of a blood vessel or occlusion (obstruction) of a blood vessel by a thrombus or embolus. A thrombus is a blood clot that forms within a blood vessel. An embolus is a piece of debris that is carried through the bloodstream and lodges in an artery. Emboli can arise from infections within the chambers of the heart or can consist of pieces of thrombi. The lack of blood flow appears to damage neurons primarily by stimulating a massive release of glutamate, which causes inflammation, phagocytosis by activated microglia, the production of free radicals, and activation of calcium-dependent enzymes. Potential treatments for stroke include administration of drugs that dissolve clots, reduce inflammation, block glutamate receptors, inactivate free radicals, or stimulate inhibitory GABA receptors. After a stroke has occurred, physical therapy can facilitate recovery and minimize a patient's deficits.

DISORDERS OF DEVELOPMENT

As you will see in this section, brain development can be affected adversely by the presence of toxic chemicals during pregnancy and by genetic abnormalities, both hereditary and nonhereditary. In some instances the result is mental retardation.

Toxic Chemicals

A common cause of mental retardation is the presence of toxins that impair fetal development during pregnancy. For example, if a woman contracts rubella (German measles) early in pregnancy, the toxic chemicals released by the virus interfere with the chemical signals that control normal development of the brain. Most women who receive good health care will be immunized for rubella to prevent them from contracting it during pregnancy.

In addition to the toxins produced by viruses, various drugs can adversely affect fetal development. For example, mental retardation can be caused by the ingestion of alcohol during pregnancy. Babies born to alcoholic women are typically smaller than average and develop more slowly. Many of them exhibit **fetal alcohol syndrome,** which is characterized by abnormal facial development and deficient brain development. Figure 14.9 shows photographs of the face of a child with fetal alcohol syndrome, of a rat fetus whose mother was fed alcohol during pregnancy, and of a normal rat fetus. As you can see, alcohol produces similar abnormalities in the offspring of both species. The facial abnormalities are relatively unimportant, of course. Much more serious are the abnormalities in the development of the brain. (See *Figure 14.9.*)

Recent research suggests that alcohol disrupts normal brain development by interfering with a **neural adhesion protein**—a protein that helps to guide the growth of neurons in the developing brain (Braun, 1996). Prenatal exposure to alcohol even appears to have direct effects on neural plasticity. Sutherland, McDonald, and Savage (1997) found that the offspring of female rats that were given moderate amounts of alcohol during pregnancy showed smaller amounts of long-term potentiation (described in Chapter 12).

Fetal alcohol syndrome A birth defect caused by ingestion of alcohol by a pregnant woman; includes characteristic facial anomalies and faulty brain development.

Neural adhesion protein A protein that plays a role in brain development; helps to guide the growth of neurons.

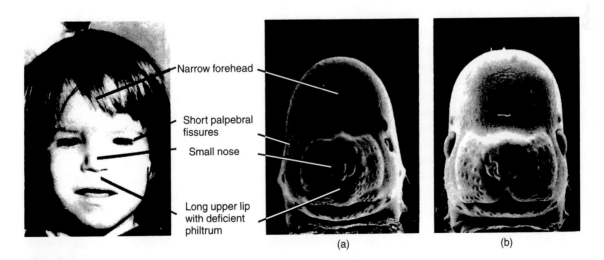

Narrow forehead

Short palpebral fissures

Small nose

Long upper lip with deficient philtrum

(a)

(b)

FIGURE 14.9

A child with fetal alcohol syndrome, along with magnified views of a rat fetus. (a) Fetus whose mother received alcohol during pregnancy. (b) Normal rat fetus.

[Photograph courtesy of Katherine K. Sulik.]

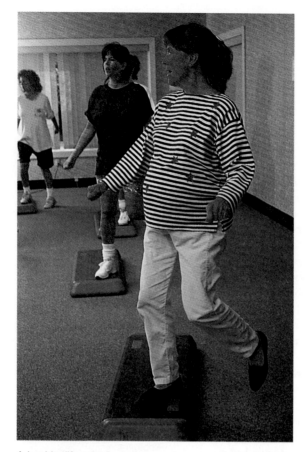

A healthy lifestyle, including good nutrition, exercise, and abstinence from alcohol or other drugs, provides the best environment for a fetus to develop in.

Phenylketonuria (PKU) (*fee nul kee ta new ree uh*) A hereditary disorder caused by the absence of an enzyme that converts the amino acid phenylalanine to tyrosine; the accumulation of phenylalanine causes brain damage unless a special diet is implemented soon after birth.

Pyridoxine dependency (*peer i dox een*) A metabolic disorder in which an infant requires larger-than-normal amounts of pyridoxine (vitamin B_6) to avoid neurological symptoms.

Galactosemia (*ga lak tow see mee uh*) An inherited metabolic disorder in which galactose (milk sugar) cannot easily be metabolized.

A woman need not be an alcoholic to impair the development of her offspring; some investigators believe that fetal alcohol syndrome can be caused by a single alcoholic "binge" during a critical period of fetal development. Now that we recognize the dangers of this syndrome, pregnant women are advised to abstain from alcohol (and from other drugs not specifically prescribed by their physician) while their bodies are engaged in the task of sustaining the development of another human being.

Inherited Metabolic Disorders

Several inherited "errors of metabolism" can cause brain damage or impair brain development. Normal functioning of cells requires intricate interactions among countless biochemical systems. As you know, these systems depend on enzymes, which are responsible for constructing or breaking down particular chemical compounds. Enzymes are proteins and thus are produced by mechanisms involving the chromosomes, which contain the recipes for their synthesis. "Errors of metabolism" refer to genetic abnormalities in which the recipe for a particular enzyme is in error, so the enzyme cannot be synthesized. If the enzyme is a critical one, the results can be very serious.

There are at least a hundred different inherited metabolic disorders that can affect the development of the brain. The most common and best-known is called **phenylketonuria (PKU).** This disease is caused by an inherited lack of an enzyme that converts phenylalanine (an amino acid) into tyrosine (another amino acid). Excessive amounts of phenylalanine in the blood interfere with the myelinization of neurons in the central nervous system. Much of the myelinization of the cerebral hemispheres takes place after birth. Thus, when an infant born with PKU receives foods containing phenylalanine, the amino acid accumulates and the brain fails to develop normally. The result is a severe mental retardation, with an average IQ of approximately 20 by six years of age.

Fortunately, PKU can be treated by putting the infant on a low-phenylalanine diet. The diet keeps the blood level of phenylalanine low, and myelinization of the central nervous system takes place normally. Once myelinization is complete, the dietary restraints can be relaxed, because a high level of phenylalanine no longer threatens brain development. During prenatal development, a fetus is protected by its mother's normal metabolism, which removes the phenylalanine from its circulation. However, if the *mother* has PKU, she must follow a strict diet during pregnancy or her infant will be born with brain damage. If she eats a normal diet, rich in phenylalanine, the high blood level of this compound will not damage her brain, but it will damage that of her fetus.

Diagnosing PKU immediately after birth is imperative so that the infant's brain is never exposed to high levels of phenylalanine. Consequently, many governments have passed laws that mandate a PKU test for all newborn babies. The test is inexpensive and accurate, and it has prevented many cases of mental retardation.

Other genetic errors of metabolism can be treated in similar fashion. For example, untreated **pyridoxine dependency** results in damage to cerebral white matter, to the thalamus, and to the cerebellum. It is treated by large doses of vitamin B_6. Another error of metabolism, **galactosemia,** is an inability to metabolize galactose, a sugar found in milk. If it is not treated, it, too, causes damage to cerebral white matter and to the cerebellum. The treatment is use of a milk substitute that does not contain galactose.

Some other inherited metabolic disorders cannot yet be treated successfully. For example, **Tay-Sachs disease,** which occurs mainly in children of Eastern European Jewish descent, causes the brain to swell and damage itself against the inside of the skull and against the folds of the dura mater than encase it. The neurological symptoms begin by four months of age and include an exaggerated startle response to sounds, listlessness, irritability, spasticity, seizures, dementia, and finally, death.

Tay-Sachs disease is one of several metabolic "storage" disorders. All cells contain sacs of material encased in membrane, called lysosomes ("dissolving bodies"). These sacs constitute the cell's rubbish removal system; they contain enzymes that break down waste substances that cells produce in the course of their normal activities. The broken-down waste products are then recycled (used by the cells again) or excreted. Metabolic storage disorders are genetic errors of metabolism in which one or more vital enzymes are missing. Particular kinds of waste products cannot be destroyed by the lysosomes, so they accumulate. The lysosomes get larger and larger, the cells get larger and larger, and eventually, the brain begins to swell and become damaged.

Researchers investigating hereditary errors of metabolism hope to prevent or treat these disorders in several ways. Some will be treated like PKU or galactosemia, by avoiding a constituent of the diet that cannot be tolerated. Others, such as pyridoxine dependency, will be treated by administering a substance that the body requires. Still others may be cured someday by the techniques of genetic engineering. Viruses infect cells by inserting their own genetic material into them and thus taking over the cells' genetic machinery, using it to reproduce themselves. Perhaps one day, researchers will develop special viruses that will "infect" an infant's cells with genetic information that is needed to produce the enzymes that the cells lack, leaving the rest of the cells' functions intact. Such viruses have already yielded useful results, such as the development of bacteria that produce human insulin. Someday, they may cure human genetic disorders as well.

Tay-Sachs disease A heritable, fatal, metabolic storage disorder; lack of enzymes in lysosomes causes accumulation of waste products and swelling of cells of the brain.

Down syndrome A disorder caused by the presence of an extra twenty-first chromosome, characterized by moderate to severe mental retardation and often by physical abnormalities.

Down Syndrome

Down syndrome is a congenital disorder that results in abnormal development of the brain, producing mental retardation in varying degrees. *Congenital* does not necessarily mean *hereditary;* it simply refers to a disorder that one is born with. Down syndrome is caused not by the inheritance of a faulty gene but by the possession of an extra twenty-first chromosome. The syndrome is closely associated with the mother's age; in most cases, something goes wrong with some of her ova, resulting in the presence of two (rather than one) twenty-first chromosomes. When fertilization occurs, the addition of the father's twenty-first chromosome makes three, rather than two. The extra chromosome presumably causes biochemical changes that impair normal brain development. The development of *amniocentesis,* a procedure whereby some fluid is withdrawn from a pregnant woman's uterus through a hypodermic syringe, has allowed physicians to identify fetal cells with chromosomal abnormalities and thus determine whether the fetus carries Down syndrome.

Down syndrome, described in 1866 by John Langdon Down, occurs in approximately 1 out of 700 births. An experienced observed can recognize people with this disorder; they have round heads, thick, protruding tongues that tend to keep the mouth open much of the time, stubby hands, short stature, low-set ears, and somewhat

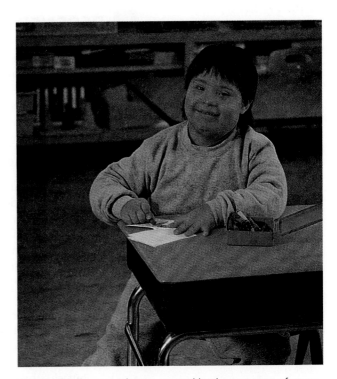

People with Down syndrome, caused by the presence of an extra 21st chromosome, are often only mildly retarded, and many of them can function well with only minimum supervision.

slanting eyelids. They are slow to learn to talk, but most do talk by age 5. The brain of a person with Down syndrome is approximately 10 percent lighter than that of a normal person, the convolutions (gyri and sulci) are simpler and smaller, the frontal lobes are small, and the superior temporal gyrus (the location of Wernicke's area) is thin. After age 30, the brain develops abnormal microscopic structures and begins to degenerate. Because this degeneration resembles that of Alzheimer's disease, it will be discussed in the next section.

Although the occurrence of any form of mental retardation is a tragedy, people with Down syndrome are often only moderately retarded. Given proper training, many of them can function well with only minimal supervision.

INTERIM SUMMARY

Developmental disorders can result in brain damage serious enough to cause mental retardation. During pregnancy, the fetus is especially sensitive to toxins, such as alcohol or chemicals produced by some viruses. Several inherited metabolic disorders can also impair brain development. For example, phenylketonuria is caused by the lack of an enzyme that converts phenylalanine into tyrosine. Brain damage can be averted by feeding the baby a diet low in phenylalanine, so early diagnosis is essential. Other inherited metabolic disorders include pyridoxine dependency, which can be treated by vitamin B_6, and galactosemia, which can be treated with a diet that does not contain milk sugar. Storage disorders, such as Tay-Sachs disease, are caused by the inability of cells to destroy waste products within the lysosomes, which causes the cells to swell and, eventually, die. So far, these disorders cannot be treated. Down syndrome is produced by the presence of an extra twenty-first chromosome. The brain development of people with Down syndrome is abnormal, and after age 30, their brains develop features similar to those of people with Alzheimer's disease.

DEGENERATIVE DISORDERS

Many disease processes—in particular, Parkinson's disease, Huntington's chorea, Alzheimer's disease, and multiple sclerosis—can cause degeneration of the cells of the brain. Some of these conditions injure particular kinds of cells, a fact that provides the hope that research will uncover the causes of the damage and find a way to halt it and prevent it from occurring in other people.

Parkinson's Disease

One of the most common degenerative neurological disorders, Parkinson's disease, is caused by degeneration of the nigrostriatal system—the dopamine-secreting neurons of the substantia nigra that send axons to the basal ganglia. The primary symptoms of Parkinson's disease are muscular rigidity, slowness of movement, a resting tremor, and postural instability. For example, once a person with Parkinson's disease is seated, he or she finds it difficult to arise. Once the person begins walking, he or she has difficulty stopping. Thus, a person with Parkinson's disease cannot easily pace back and forth across a room. Reaching for an object can be accurate, but the movement usually begins only after a considerable delay. Writing is slow and labored, and as it progresses, the letters get smaller and smaller. Postural movements are impaired. A normal person who is bumped while standing will quickly move to restore balance—for example, by taking a step in the direction of the impending fall or by reaching out with the arms to grasp onto a piece of furniture. However, a person with Parkinson's disease fails to do so and simply falls. A person with this disorder is even unlikely to put out his or her arms to break the fall.

Parkinson's disease also produces a resting tremor—vibratory movements of the arms and hands that diminish somewhat when the individual makes purposeful movements. The tremor is accompanied by rigidity; the joints appear stiff. However, the tremor and rigidity are not the cause of the slow movements. In fact, some patients with Parkinson's disease show extreme slowness of movements but little or no tremor.

Research has suggested that Parkinson's disease may be caused by toxins present in the environment, caused by faulty metabolism, or produced by unrecognized infectious disorders. As you saw in the Prologue and Epilogue of Chapter 4, the experience of several young people who took a contaminated drug led to research that found that various toxins can cause the degeneration of dopaminergic neurons. This research suggests that Parkinson's disease may be caused by toxins present in the environment. Fortunately, it also led to the discovery that an MAO inhibitor, deprenyl, is useful in treating the symptoms of Parkinson's disease and may even retard the progress of the neural degeneration.

Although most cases of Parkinson's disease do not appear to have genetic origins, researchers have discovered a particular mutation of a gene located on chromosome 4 that appears to produce this disorder (Polymeropoulos et al., 1996). If the normal functions of this gene can be discovered, we may receive some hints about the process that begins the degeneration of the nigrostriatal system.

As we saw in Chapter 4, the standard treatment for Parkinson's disease is L-DOPA, the precursor of dopamine. An increased level of L-DOPA in the brain causes a patient's remaining dopaminergic neurons to produce and secrete more dopamine and, for a time, alleviates the symptoms of the disease. But this compensation does not work indefinitely; eventually, the number of nigrostriatal dopaminergic neurons declines to such a low level that the symptoms become worse. In addition, high levels of L-DOPA produce side effects by acting on dopaminergic systems other than the nigrostriatal system. Some patients—especially those whose symptoms began when they were relatively young—become bedridden, scarcely able to move.

Neurosurgeons have been developing two stereotaxic procedures designed to alleviate the symptoms of Parkinson's disease that no longer respond to treatment with L-DOPA. The first one, transplantation of fetal tissue, attempts to reestablish the secretion of dopamine in the neostriatum. The tissue is obtained from the substantia nigra of aborted human fetuses and implanted into the caudate nucleus and putamen by means of stereotaxically guided needles. Although the procedure is still experimental, some good results have been obtained (Olanow, Kordower, and Freeman, 1996). As we saw in Chapter 5, PET scans have shown that fetal cells are able to grow in their new host and secrete dopamine, reducing the patient's symptoms.

Another procedure has a long history, but only recently have technological developments in imaging methods and electrophysiological techniques led to an increase in its popularity. The principal output of the basal ganglia comes from the **internal division of the globus pallidus (GP$_i$).** (The caudate nucleus, putamen, and globus pallidus are the three major components of the basal ganglia.) This output, which is directed through the thalamus to the motor cortex, is inhibitory. Furthermore, a decrease in the activity of the dopaminergic input to the caudate nucleus and putamen causes an *increase* in the activity of the GP$_i$. Thus, damage to the GP$_i$ might be expected to relieve the symptoms of Parkinson's disease. (See *Figure 14.10.*)

In the 1950s, Leksell and his colleagues performed pallidotomies (surgical destruction of the internal division of the globus pallidus) in patients with severe Parkinson's disease (Svennilson et al., 1960; Laitinen, Bergenheim, and Hariz, 1992). The surgery often reduced the rigidity and enhanced the patient's ability to move. Unfortunately, the surgery occasionally made the patient's symptoms worse and sometimes resulted in partial blindness. (The optic tract is located next to the GP$_i$.)

With the development of L-DOPA therapy in the late 1960s, pallidotomies were abandoned. However, it eventually became evident that L-DOPA worked for a limited

Internal division of the globus pallidus (GP$_i$) A division of the globus pallidus that provides inhibitory input to the motor cortex via the thalamus; sometimes stereotaxically lesioned to treat the symptoms of Parkinson's disease.

FIGURE **14.10**

The major connections of the basal ganglia and associated structures. Excitatory connections are shown as black lines; inhibitory connections are shown as red lines. Many connections, such as the inputs to the substantia nigra, are omitted for clarity. The internal division of the globus pallidus, the primary output of the basal ganglia and the target of stereotaxic surgery for Parkinson's disease, is outlined in gray.

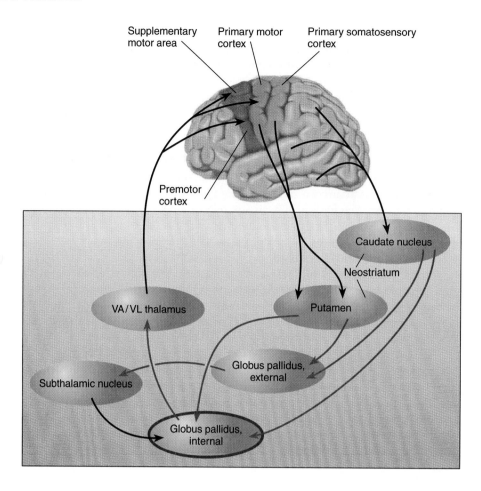

Huntington's chorea (*core ee uh*) An inherited disorder that causes degeneration of the basal ganglia; characterized by progressively more severe uncontrollable jerking movements, writhing movements, dementia, and finally, death.

time and that the symptoms of Parkinson's disease would eventually return. For that reason, in the 1990s, neurosurgeons again began experimenting with pallidotomies, first with laboratory animals and then with humans (Graybiel, 1996). This time, they used MRI scans to find the location of the GP_i and then inserted an electrode into the target region. They could then pass low-intensity, high-frequency stimulation through the electrode, thus temporarily disabling the region around its tip. If the patient's rigidity disappeared (obviously, the patient is awake during the surgery), then the electrode was in the right place. To make the lesion, the surgeon passes radiofrequency current of sufficient strength to heat and destroy the brain tissue. The results of this procedure have been so promising that several neurological teams have begun promoting its use in the treatment of relatively young patients whose symptoms no longer respond to L-DOPA. PET studies have found that after pallidotomy, the metabolic activity in the premotor and supplementary motor areas of the frontal lobes, normally depressed in patients with Parkinson's disease, returns to normal levels (Grafton et al., 1995), a result indicating that lesions of the GP_i do indeed release the motor cortex from inhibition.

Huntington's Chorea

Another basal ganglia disease, **Huntington's chorea,** is caused by degeneration of the caudate nucleus and putamen, especially of GABAergic and acetylcholinergic neurons. Whereas Parkinson's disease causes a poverty of movements, Huntington's chorea causes uncontrollable ones, especially jerky limb movements. (*Chorea* derives from the Greek *khoros*, meaning "dance.") The movements of Huntington's chorea look like fragments of purposeful movements but occur involuntarily. This disease is progressive and eventually causes death.

The symptoms of Huntington's chorea usually begin in the thirties and forties but can sometimes begin in the early twenties. The first signs of neural degeneration occur in the putamen, in a specific group of inhibitory neurons. Damage to these neurons removes some inhibitory control exerted on the premotor and supplementary motor areas of the frontal cortex. Loss of this control leads to involuntary movements.

Huntington's chorea is a hereditary disorder, caused by a dominant gene on chromosome 4. In fact, the gene has been located, and its defect has been identified as a repeated sequence of bases that code for the amino acid glutamine (Collaborative Research Group, 1993). This repeated sequence causes the gene product—a protein called *huntingtin*—to contain an elongated stretch of glutamine. Longer stretches of glutamine are associated with patients whose symptoms began at a younger age, a finding that strongly suggests that this abnormal portion of the huntingtin molecule is responsible for the disease.

Subsequent research discovered that other proteins interact with the elongated stretch of glutamine. Burke et al. (1996) found that GADPH, an enzyme that plays a critical role in glucose metabolism, interacts with huntingtin. Possibly, the abnormal huntingtin may somehow interfere with the action of GADPH and cause some cells to starve. Researchers in another laboratory (Li et al., 1995) discovered that huntingtin is associated with another protein found only in the brain, which they called HAP1 (huntingtin-associated protein 1). This team also discovered that HAP1 is found in neurons that contain nitric oxide synthase, the enzyme responsible for the production of nitric oxide (Li et al., 1996). As they noted, nitric oxide is extremely toxic, and the release of this chemical may cause the destruction of surrounding neurons. Further research will undoubtedly clarify the role of faulty huntingtin protein in the neuropathology of Huntington's chorea. Unfortunately, there is at present no treatment for the disorder.

Alzheimer's Disease

Several neurological disorders result in **dementia,** a deterioration of intellectual abilities resulting from an organic brain disorder. A common form of dementia is called **Alzheimer's disease,** which occurs in approximately 5 percent of the population above the age of sixty-five. It is characterized by progressive loss of memory and other mental functions. At first, the person may have difficulty remembering appointments and sometimes fails to think of words or people's names. As time passes, he or she shows increasing confusion, and increasing difficulty with tasks such as balancing a checkbook. The memory deficit most critically involves recent events, and it thus resembles the anterograde amnesia of Korsakoff's syndrome. If the person ventures outside alone, he or she is likely to get lost. Eventually, the person becomes bedridden, then becomes completely helpless, and finally, succumbs (Terry and Davies, 1980).

Alzheimer's disease produces severe degeneration of the hippocampus and neocortex, especially the association cortex of the frontal and temporal lobes. Figure 14.11 shows photographs of the brain of a patient with Alzheimer's disease and of a normal brain. You can see how much wider the sulci are in the patient's brain, especially in the frontal and temporal lobes, indicating substantial loss of cortical tissue. (See *Figure 14.11.*)

Earlier, I mentioned that the brains of patients with Down syndrome usually develop abnormal structures that are also seen in patients with Alzheimer's disease: *neuritic plaques* and *neurofibrillary tangles.* **Neuritic plaques** consist of a dense core of a protein known as **β amyloid,** surrounded by degenerating axons and dendrites, along with activated microglia and reactive astrocytes. Eventually, the phagocytic glial cells destroy the degenerating axons and dendrites, leaving only a core of β amyloid. The brains of Alzheimer's patients (and patients with Down syndrome) also contain

Dementia [*da men sha*] A loss of cognitive abilities such as memory, perception, verbal ability, and judgment; common causes are multiple strokes and Alzheimer's disease.

Alzheimer's disease A degenerative brain disorder of unknown origin; causes progressive memory loss, motor deficits, and eventual death.

Neuritic plaque An extracellular deposit containing a dense core of β amyloid protein surrounded by degenerating axons and dendrites and activated microglia and reactive astrocytes.

β amyloid [*amm i loyd*] A protein found in excessive amounts in the brains of patients with Alzheimer's disease.

(a)   (b)

FIGURE 1 4 . 1 1

Alzheimer's disease. (a) A lateral view of the right side of the brain of a person with Alzheimer's disease. (Rostral is to the right; dorsal is up.) Note that the sulci of the temporal lobe and parietal lobe are especially wide, indicating degeneration of the neocortex (*arrowheads*). (b) A lateral view of the right side of a normal brain.

(Photo of diseased brain courtesy of A. D'Agostino, Good Samaritan Hospital, Portland, Oregon; photo of normal brain © Dan McCoy/Rainbow.)

neurofibrillary tangles—dying neurons containing intracellular accumulations of twisted protein filaments that formerly served as the cells' internal skeleton. These tangles also contain amyloid. (See *Figure 14.12*.)

Many researchers believe that formation of neuritic plaques is caused by the production of a defective form of β amyloid. Normal β amyloid (sometimes called *short* β amyloid) consists of 40 amino acids. This protein is produced and secreted by cells (neurons and other cells) throughout life. Its function is not yet known. Several genetic mutations cause the production of a long form of β amyloid, consisting of 42 to 43 amino acids.

Research has shown that at least some forms of Alzheimer's disease appear to run in families and thus appear to be hereditary. Because the brains of people with Down syndrome (caused by an extra twenty-first chromosome) also contain deposits of amyloid, some investigators hypothesized that the twenty-first chromosome may be involved in the production of β amyloid and in Alzheimer's disease as well. In fact, St. George-Hyslop et al. (1987) found that this chromosome *does* contains a gene that produces the **beta amyloid precursor protein (APP).** APP consists of a long chain of amino acids that is cut apart by enzymes to produce β amyloid. The location of the cut determines whether the normal short form or the defective long form is produced. Since the discovery of the APP gene, several studies found specific mutations of the APP gene in cases of familial Alzheimer's disease (Martinez et al., 1993; Farlow et al., 1994). In addition, other studies found mutations of **presinilin** genes on chromosomes 1 and 14. The products of the APP genes and the presinilin genes all cause the defective long form of β amyloid to be produced, and all are associated with familial forms of Alzheimer's disease (Hardy, 1997).

Although these results suggest that the production of abnormal β amyloid plays an important role in the development of Alzheimer's disease, the fact is that most forms of Alzheimer's disease are *not* hereditary. What causes the accumulation of beta amyloid in these cases? The answer is

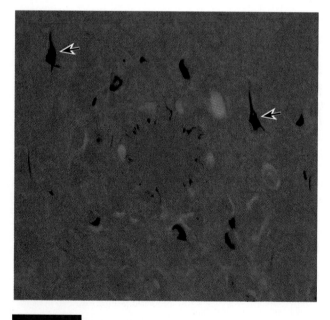

FIGURE 1 4 . 1 2

A photomicrograph of tissue from the brain of a patient who died of Alzheimer's disease. The mass in the center is a neuritic plaque, which consists of β amyloid protein surrounded by degenerating axons, dendrites, and cell bodies. Arrows indicate neurofibrillary tangles—dying neurons filled with protein filaments that formerly served as the cells' internal skeletons.

(Photo courtesy of D.J. Selkoe, Brigham and Women's Hospital, Boston.)

that we do not know, although some investigators have proposed that head injury, infections, excessive use of alcohol or other drugs, and exposure to toxic substances can trigger the formation of amyloid plaques. For example, examination of the brains of people who have sustained closed head injuries (including those that occur during prize fights) often reveal a widespread distribution of amyloid plaques. The finding that estrogen replacement therapy substantially reduces the risk of Alzheimer's disease in postmenopausal women indicates yet another link between physiological factors and the development of this disease (Henderson, 1997).

Another promising finding is the discovery that the immune system may contribute to the brain damage associated with Alzheimer's disease. Several studies have found that amyloid plaques contain substances characteristic of an immune reaction. As we saw, the plaques contain activated microglia and reactive astrocytes—phagocytic glial cells that perform functions similar to those of particular types of white blood cells (McGeer and Rogers, 1992; see *Figure 14.13*.). Some investigators believe that the microglia may even be responsible for the production of the deposits of beta amyloid (Wisniewski and Wegiel, 1992). Acting on observations that people who had been treated with anti-inflammatory drugs (for diseases such as rheumatoid arthritis or leprosy) seemed to have a particularly low rate of Alzheimer's disease, Rogers et al. (1993) administered an anti-inflammatory drug (indomethacin) or a placebo to 44 patients with mild to moderate symptoms of Alzheimer's disease. They found that the cognitive performance of the drug-treated patients improved by 1.3 percent over the six-month period, while that of the placebo patients declined by 8.4 percent. As Rogers noted, "We lost about 20 percent of our placebo patients because they went down hill behaviorally, so much that they wouldn't take medicine or sit for the test anymore . . . This didn't happen with the indomethacin patients" (Schnabel, 1993, p. 1719). As you might expect, these findings have stimulated further research, and drug companies are trying to develop even more effective anti-inflammatory drugs.

Multiple Sclerosis

Multiple sclerosis is an autoimmune demyelinating disease. At scattered locations within the central nervous system, myelin sheaths are attacked by the person's immune system, leaving behind hard patches of debris called *sclerotic plaques*. (See *Figure 14.14*.) The normal transmission of neural messages through the demyelinated axons is interrupted. Because the damage occurs in white matter located throughout the brain and spinal cord, a wide variety of neurological disorders is seen.

Multiple sclerosis afflicts women somewhat more frequently than men, and the disorder usually occurs in people in their late twenties or thirties. People who spend their childhood in places far from the equator are more

FIGURE 14.13

A neuritic plaque. The brown colors are β amyloid protein; the purple colors are reactive microglia, which are involved in inflammatory reactions.

(Courtesy of P.L. McGeer, University of British Columbia.)

Neurofibrillary tangle (*new row fib ri lair y*) A dying neuron containing intracellular accumulations of β amyloid and twisted protein filaments that formerly served as the cell's internal skeleton.

Beta amyloid precursor protein (APP) A protein produced and secreted by cells that serves as the precursor for β amyloid protein.

Presinilin (*pree sen ill in*) A protein produced by a faulty gene that causes β amyloid precursor protein to be converted to the abnormal short form; may be a cause of Alzheimer's disease.

FIGURE 14.14

A slice of a human brain of a person who had multiple sclerosis. The arrowheads point to sclerotic plaques in the white matter.

(Courtesy of A. D'Agostino, Good Samaritan Hospital, Portland, Oregon.)

likely to come down with the disease than those who live close to it. In addition, people born during the late winter and early spring are at higher risk. Hence, it is likely that some disease contracted during a childhood spent in a region in which the virus is prevalent causes the person's immune system to attack his or her own myelin. Perhaps a virus weakens the blood-brain barrier, allowing myelin protein into the general circulation and sensitizing the immune system to it, or perhaps the virus attaches itself to myelin. In any event, the process is a long-lived one, lasting for many decades.

Unfortunately, there is currently no specific treatment for multiple sclerosis. Because the symptoms of the disease are usually episodic—new or worsening symptoms followed by partial recovery—patients and their families often attribute the changes in the symptoms to whatever has happened recently. For example, if the patient has taken a new medication or gone on a new diet and the symptoms get worse, they will blame the symptoms on the medication or diet. Conversely, if the patient gets better, they will credit the medication or diet.

INTERIM SUMMARY

Parkinson's disease is caused by degeneration of dopamine-secreting neurons of the substantia nigra that send axons to the basal ganglia. Recent evidence suggests that the disease may be caused by toxic substances present in the environment. Alzheimer's disease, another degenerative disorder, involves much more of the brain; the disease process eventually destroys most of the hippocampus and cortical gray matter. The brains of affected individuals contain many amyloid plaques, which contain a core of amyloid protein surrounded by degenerating axons and dendrites. Some hereditary forms of Alzheimer's disease involve a defective gene for the amyloid precursor protein (APP). The degenerative process may involve the immune system; indeed, anti-inflammatory drugs may be useful in fighting this disorder. Multiple sclerosis, a demyelinating disease, is characterized by periodic attacks of neurological symptoms, usually with partial remission between attacks. The damage appears to be caused by the body's immune system, which attacks the protein contained in myelin.

DISORDERS CAUSED BY INFECTIOUS DISEASES

Several neurological disorders can be caused by infectious diseases, transmitted by bacteria, fungi or other parasites, or viruses. The most common are encephalitis and meningitis. **Encephalitis** is an infection that invades the entire brain. The most common cause of encephalitis is a virus that is transmitted by mosquitoes, who pick up the infectious agent from horses, birds, or rodents. The symptoms of acute encephalitis include fever, irritability, and nausea, often followed by convulsions, delirium, and signs of brain damage, such as aphasia or paralysis. Unfortunately, there is no specific treatment besides supportive care, and between 5 and 20 percent of cases are fatal; 20 percent of the survivors show some residual neurological symptoms.

Encephalitis can also be caused by the **herpes simplex virus,** which is the cause of cold sores (or "fever blisters") that most people develop in and around their mouth from time to time. Normally, the viruses live quietly in the *trigeminal nerve ganglia*—nodules on the fifth cranial nerve—that contain the cell bodies of somatosensory neurons that serve the face. The viruses proliferate periodically, traveling down to the ends of nerve fibers, where they cause sores to develop in mucous membrane. Unfortunately, they occasionally (but rarely) go the other way into the brain. Herpes encephalitis is a serious disease; the virus attacks the frontal and temporal lobes in particular and can severely damage them.

Encephalitis (*en seff a lye tis*) An inflammation of the brain; caused by bacteria, viruses, or toxic chemicals.

Herpes simplex virus A virus that normally causes cold sores near the lips but that can also cause brain damage.

Two other forms of viral encephalitis are probably already familiar to you: polio and rabies. **Acute anterior poliomyelitis** ("polio") is fortunately very rare in developed countries since the development of vaccines that immunize people against the disease. The virus causes specific damage to motor neurons of the brain and spinal cord: neurons in the primary motor cortex; in the motor nuclei of the thalamus, hypothalamus, and brain stem; in the cerebellum; and in the ventral horns of the gray matter of the spinal cord. Undoubtedly, these motor neurons contain some chemical substance that either attracts the virus or in some way makes the virus become lethal to them.

Rabies is caused by a virus that is passed from the saliva of an infected mammal directly into a person's flesh by means of a bite wound. The virus travels through peripheral nerves to the central nervous system and there causes severe damage. The symptoms include a short period of fever and headache, followed by anxiety, excessive movement and talking, difficulty in swallowing, movement disorders, difficulty in speaking, seizures, confusion, and, finally, death within two to seven days of the onset of the symptoms. The virus has a special affinity for cells in the cerebellum and hippocampus, and damage to the hippocampus probably accounts for the emotional changes that are seen in the early symptoms.

Fortunately, the incubation period for rabies lasts up to several months while the virus climbs through the peripheral nerves. (If the bite is received in the face or neck, the incubation time will be much shorter, because the virus has a smaller distance to travel before it reaches the brain.) During the incubation period, a person can receive a vaccine that will confer an immunity to the disease; the person's own immune system will destroy the virus before it reaches the brain.

Several infectious diseases cause brain damage even though they are not primarily diseases of the central nervous system. One such disease is acquired immune deficiency syndrome (AIDS). Records of autopsies have revealed that at least 75 percent of people who died of AIDS show evidence of brain damage (Levy and Bredesen, 1989). The brain damage often results in a syndrome called *AIDS dementia,* which is characterized by a loss of cognitive and motor functions. At first, the patients may become forgetful, they may think and reason more slowly, and they may have word-finding difficulties (anomia). Eventually, they may become almost mute. Motor deficits may begin with tremor and difficulty in making complex movement but then may progress so much that the patient becomes bedridden (Maj, 1990).

Evidence suggests that the cause of AIDS dementia may be the entry of excessive amounts of calcium into neurons. For several years, researchers have been puzzled by the fact that although AIDS certainly causes neural damage, neurons are not themselves infected by the HIV virus (the organism responsible for the disease). Lipton et al. (1990) found that the cause of neural death appears to be the entry of excessive amounts of calcium. (As we saw earlier, the death of neurons caused by seizures and by anoxia also involves the entry of excessive amounts of Ca^{2+}.) Lipton and his colleagues (Lipton, 1996, 1997) suggest that virus-infected astrocytes and white blood cells may be the cause of the calcium inflow. The infection causes these cells to secrete excitotoxic substances (including glutamate) that activate NMDA receptors. The investigators suggest that the drugs being developed to reduce the damage caused by strokes may also be useful in treating AIDS dementia.

Another category of infectious diseases of the brain actually involves inflammation of the meninges, the layers of connective tissue that surround the central nervous system. **Meningitis** can be caused by viruses or bacteria. The symptoms of all forms include headache, a stiff neck, and, depending on the severity of the disorder, convulsions, confusion or loss of consciousness, and sometimes death. The stiff neck is one of the most important symptoms. Neck movements cause the meninges to stretch; because they are inflamed, the stretch causes severe pain. Thus, the patient resists having his or her neck moved.

The most common form of viral meningitis usually does not cause significant brain damage. However, various forms of bacterial meningitis do. The usual causes

Acute anterior poliomyelitis A viral disease that destroys motor neurons of the brain and spinal cord.

Rabies A fatal viral disease that causes brain damage; usually transmitted through the bite of an infected animal.

Meningitis (*men in jy tis*) An inflammation of the meninges; can be caused by viruses or bacteria.

are spread of a middle-ear infection into the brain, introduction of an infection into the brain from a head injury, or the presence of emboli that have dislodged from a bacterial infection present in the chambers of the heart. Such an infection is often caused by unclean hypodermic needles; therefore, drug addicts are at particular risk for meningitis (as well as many other diseases). The inflammation of the meninges can damage the brain by interfering with circulation of blood or by blocking the flow of cerebrospinal fluid through the subarachnoid space, causing hydrocephalus. In addition, the cranial nerves are susceptible to damage. Fortunately, bacterial meningitis can usually be treated effectively with antibiotics. Of course, early diagnosis and prompt treatment are essential, because neither antibiotics nor any other known treatment can repair a damaged brain.

INTERIM SUMMARY

Infectious diseases can damage the brain. Encephalitis, usually caused by a virus, affects the entire brain. One form is caused by the herpes simplex virus, which infects the trigeminal nerve ganglia of most of the population. This virus tends to attack the frontal and temporal lobes. The polio virus attacks motor neurons in the brain and spinal cord, resulting in motor deficits or even paralysis. The rabies virus, acquired by an animal bite, travels through peripheral nerves and attacks the brain, particularly the cerebellum and hippocampus. An AIDS infection also produces brain damage, perhaps because infected white blood cells and astrocytes release excitotoxic chemicals that open calcium channels that permit a lethal dose of the ion to enter the cells of the brain. Meningitis is an infection of the meninges, caused by viruses or bacteria. The bacterial form, which is usually more serious, is generally caused by an ear infection, a head injury, or an embolus from a heart infection.

EPILOGUE

Seizure Surgery

Mrs. R.'s surgery was performed to remove a noncancerous brain tumor that, incidentally, produced seizures. As I mentioned in this chapter, neurosurgeons occasionally perform surgery specifically to remove brain tissue that contains a seizure focus. Such an operation, called *seizure surgery*, is performed only when drug therapy is unsuccessful.

Because seizure surgery often involves the removal of a substantial amount of brain tissue (usually, from one of the temporal lobes), we might expect it to cause behavioral deficits. But in most cases the reverse is true; people's performance on tests of neuropsychological functioning usually *increases*. How can the removal of brain tissue improve a person's performance?

The answer is provided by looking at what happens in the brain not *during* seizures but *between* them. The seizure focus—usually, a region of scar tissue—irritates the brain tissue surrounding it, causing increased neural activity that tends to spread to adjacent regions. Between seizures, this increased excitatory activity is held in check by a compensatory increase in inhibitory activity. That is, inhibitory neurons in the region surrounding the seizure focus become more active. (This phenomenon is known as *interictal inhibition*; *ictus* means "stroke" in Latin.) A seizure occurs when the excitation overcomes the inhibition.

The problem is that the compensatory inhibition does more than hold the excitation in check; it also sup-

presses the normal functions of a rather large region of brain tissue surrounding the seizure focus. Thus, even though the focus may be small, its effects are felt over a much larger area even between seizures. Removing the seizure focus and some surrounding brain tissue eliminates the source of the irritation and makes the compensatory inhibition unnecessary. Freed from interictal inhibition, the brain tissue located near the site of the former seizure focus can now function normally, and the patient's neuropsychological abilities will show an improvement.

As I mentioned in this chapter, seizures often occur after a head injury, but only after a delay of several months. The cause of the delay is related to some properties of neurons that make learning possible. Goddard (1967) implanted electrodes in the brains of rats and administered a brief, weak electrical stimulus once a day. At first, the stimulation produced no effects, but after several days the stimulation began to trigger small, short seizures. As days went by, the seizures became larger and longer until the animal was finally having full-blown clonic-tonic convulsions. Goddard called the phenomenon *kindling*, because it resembled the way a small fire can be kindled to start a larger one.

Kindling appears to be analogous to learning, and it presumably involves changes in synaptic strength like those seen in long-term potentiation. It can most easily be induced in the temporal lobe, which is the place where seizure foci are most likely to occur. The probable reason for the delayed occurrence of seizures after a head injury is that it takes time for kindling to occur. The irritation produced by the brain injury eventually causes increased synaptic strength in excitatory synapses located nearby.

Kindling has become an animal model of focal-seizure disorders, and it has proved useful in research on the causes and treatment of these disorders. For example, Silver, Shin, and McNamara (1991) produced seizure foci in rats through kindling and compared the effects of some commonly used medications on both seizures (the electrical events within the brain) and convulsions (the motor manifestations of the seizures). They found that one of the drugs they tested prevented the convulsions but left seizures intact, whereas another prevented both seizures and convulsions. Because each seizure is capable of producing some brain damage through overstimulation of neurons (especially those in the hippocampal formation, which become especially active during a seizure), the goal of medical treatment should be the elimination of seizures, not simply the convulsions that accompany them. Research with the animal model of kindling will undoubtedly contribute to the effective treatment of focal-seizure disorders.

KEY CONCEPTS

TUMORS

1. Brain tumors are uncontrolled growths of cells other than neurons within the skull that damage normal tissue by compression or infiltration.

SEIZURE DISORDERS

2. Seizures are periodic episodes of abnormal neural firing, which can produce a variety of symptoms. They usually originate from a focus, but some have no apparent source of localized irritation.

CEREBROVASCULAR ACCIDENTS

3. Cerebrovascular accidents, hemorrhagic or obstructive in nature, produce localized brain damage. The two most common sources of obstructive strokes are emboli and thrombi.

DISORDERS OF DEVELOPMENT

4. Developmental disorders can be caused by drugs or disease-produced toxins, or by chromosomal or genetic abnormalities.

DEGENERATIVE DISORDERS

5. Several degenerative disorders of the nervous system, including Parkinson's disease, Huntington's chorea, Alzheimer's disease, and multiple sclerosis, have received much attention from scientists in recent years.

DISORDERS CAUSED BY INFECTIOUS DISEASES

6. Infectious diseases, either viral or bacterial, can damage the brain. The two most important infections of the central nervous system are encephalitis and meningitis, but with the rise of the AIDS epidemic, AIDS dementia complex has become more common.

SUGGESTED READINGS

Adams, R.D., Victor, M., and Ropper, A.H. *Principles of Neurology*, 6th ed. New York: McGraw-Hill, 1997.

Feldman, R.S., Meyer, J.S., and Quenzer, L.F. *Principles of Neuropsychopharmacology*. Sunderland, MA: Sinauer Associates, 1997.

Mesulam, M.-M. *Principles of Behavioral Neurology*. Philadelphia: F.A. Davis, 1985.

15

Schizophrenia, the Affective Disorders, and the Anxiety Disorders

LEARNING OBJECTIVES

1. Describe the symptoms of schizophrenia and discuss evidence that indicates that some forms of schizophrenia are heritable.

2. Discuss drugs that alleviate or produce the positive symptoms of schizophrenia and discuss research on the dopamine hypothesis of schizophrenia.

3. Describe evidence that schizophrenia may result from brain damage or abnormal brain development.

4. Describe the two major affective disorders, their heritability, and their physiological treatments.

5. Summarize the monoamine hypothesis of depression and review evidence for brain abnormalities in people with affective disorders.

6. Explain the role of circadian rhythms in affective disorders: the effects of REM sleep deprivation and total sleep deprivation and the symptoms and treatment of seasonal affective disorder.

7. Describe the symptoms and possible causes of panic disorder.

8. Describe the symptoms and possible causes of obsessive-compulsive disorder.

Side Effects

Larry had become a permanent resident of the state hospital. His parents had originally hoped that treatment would help him enough so that he could live in a halfway house with a small group of other young men, but his condition was so serious that he required constant supervision. Larry had severe schizophrenia. The medication he was taking helped, but he still exhibited severe psychotic symptoms. In addition, he had begun showing signs of a neurological disorder that seemed to be getting worse.

Larry had always been a difficult child, shy and socially awkward. He had no real friends. During adolescence he became even more withdrawn and insisted that his parents and older sister keep out of his room. He stopped taking meals with the family, and he even bought a small refrigerator of his own for his room so that he could keep his own food, which he said he preferred to that "pesticide-contaminated" food his parents ate. His grades in school, which were never outstanding, got progressively worse, and when he was seventeen years old, he dropped out of high school.

Larry's parents recognized that something was seriously wrong with him. Their family physician suggested that he see a psychiatrist and gave them the name of a colleague that he respected, but Larry flatly refused to go. Within a year after he had quit high school, he became frankly psychotic. He heard voices talking to him, and sometimes his parents could hear him shouting for the voices to go away. He was convinced that his parents were trying to poison him, and he would eat only factory-sealed food that he had opened himself. Although he kept his body clean—sometimes he would stand in the shower

for an hour "purifying" himself—his room became frightfully messy. He insisted on keeping old cans and food packages because, he said, he needed to compare them with items his parents brought from the store to be sure they were not counterfeit.

One day, while Larry was in the shower purifying himself, his mother cleaned his room. She filled several large plastic garbage bags with the cans and packages and put them out for the trash collector. As she reentered the house, she heard a howling noise from upstairs. Larry had emerged from the shower and discovered that his room had been cleaned. When he saw his mother coming up the stairs, he screamed at her, cursed her savagely, and rushed down the stairs toward her. He hit her so hard that she flew through the air, landing heavily on the floor below. He wheeled around, ran up the stairs, and went into his room, slamming the door behind him.

An hour later, Larry's father discovered his wife unconscious at the foot of the stairs. She soon recovered from the mild concussion she had sustained, but Larry's parents realized that it was time for him to be put in custody. Because he had attacked his mother, a judge ordered that he be temporarily detained and, as a result of a psychiatric evaluation, had him committed to the state hospital. The diagnosis was "schizophrenia, paranoid type."

In the state hospital, Larry was given Thorazine (chlorpromazine), which helped considerably. For the first few weeks, he showed some symptoms commonly seen in Parkinson's disease—tremors, rigidity, a shuffling gait, and lack of facial expression—but these symptoms cleared up spontaneously, as his physician had predicted. The voices still talked to him

occasionally, but less often than before, and even then he could ignore them most of the time. His suspiciousness decreased, and he was willing to eat with the residents in the dining room. But he still obviously had paranoid delusions, and the psychiatric staff was unwilling to let him leave the hospital. For one thing, he refused to take his medication voluntarily. Once, after he had suffered a serious relapse, the staff discovered that he had only been pretending to swallow his pills and was later throwing them away. After that, they made sure that he swallowed them.

After several years, Larry began developing more serious neurological symptoms. He began pursing his lips and making puffing sounds, and later, he started grimacing, sticking his tongue out, and turning his head sharply to the left. The symptoms became so severe that they interfered with his ability to eat. His physician prescribed an additional drug, which reduced the symptoms considerably but did not eliminate them. As he explained to Larry's parents, "His neurological problems are caused by the medication that we are using to help with his psychiatric symptoms. These problems usually do not develop until a patient has taken the medication for many years, but Larry appears to be one of the unfortunate exceptions. If we take him off the medication, the neurological symptoms will get even worse. We could reduce the symptoms by giving him a higher dose of the medication, but then the problem would come back later, and it would be even worse. All we can do is try to treat the symptoms with another drug, as we have been doing. We really need a medication that helps treat schizophrenia without producing these tragic side effects."

Most of the discussion in this book has concentrated on the physiology of normal, adaptive behavior. The last two chapters summarize research on the nature and physiology of syndromes characterized by maladaptive behavior: mental disorders, autism, stress disorders, and drug abuse. The symptoms of mental disorders include deficient or inappropriate social behaviors; illogical, incoherent, or obsessional thoughts; inappropriate emotional responses, including depression, mania, or anxiety; and delusions and hallucinations. Research in recent years indicates that many of these symptoms are caused by abnormalities in the brain, both structural and biochemical.

Not too many years ago, some of the topics in these two chapters would not have been covered in a book concerned with the physiology of behavior. The anxiety disorders and autism were believed to be learned, primarily from parents who did a bad job raising their children. Although there was always at least some support for the suggestion that serious psychoses such as schizophrenia had a biological basis, other mental disorders were almost universally believed to be psychogenic in origin—that is, produced by "psychological" factors.

The tide has turned (or the pendulum has swung back, if you prefer that metaphor). Certainly, a person's family environment, social class, economic status, and similar factors affect the likelihood that he or she will develop a mental disorder and may help or hinder recovery. But physiological factors, including inherited ones and those that adversely affect development or damage the brain, play an important role, too.

◼ SCHIZOPHRENIA

Description

Schizophrenia afflicts approximately 1 percent of the world's population. Descriptions of symptoms in ancient writings indicate that the disorder has been around for thousands of years (Jeste et al., 1985). The major symptoms of schizophrenia are universal, and clinicians have developed criteria for reliably diagnosing the disorder in people of a wide variety of cultures (Flaum and Andreasen, 1990). *Schizophrenia* is probably the most misused psychological term in existence. The word literally means "split mind," but it does *not* imply a split or multiple personality. People often say that they "feel schizophrenic" about an issue when they really mean that they have mixed feelings about it. A person who sometimes wants to build a cabin in Alaska and live off the land and at other times wants to take over the family insurance business may be undecided, but he or she is not schizophrenic. The man who invented the term, Eugen Bleuler (1911/1950), intended it to refer to a break with reality caused by disorganization of the various functions of the mind, such that thoughts and feelings no longer worked together normally.

Schizophrenia is characterized by two categories of symptoms: positive and negative (Crow, 1980; Andreasen, 1995). **Positive symptoms** make themselves known by their presence. They include thought disorders, hallucinations, and delusions. A **thought disorder**—disorganized, irrational thinking—is probably the most important symptom of schizophrenia. Schizophrenics have great difficulty arranging their thoughts logically and sorting out plausible conclusions from absurd ones. In conversation they jump from one topic to another as new associations come up. Sometimes, they utter meaningless words or choose words for rhyme rather than for meaning. **Delusions** are beliefs that are obviously contrary to fact. Delusions of *persecution* are false beliefs that others are plotting and conspiring against oneself. Delusions of *grandeur* are false beliefs in one's power and importance, such as a conviction that one has godlike powers or has special knowledge that no one else possesses. Delusions of *control* are related to delusions of persecution; the person believes (for example) that

Schizophrenia A serious mental disorder characterized by disordered thoughts, delusions, hallucinations, and often bizarre behaviors.

Positive symptom A symptom of schizophrenia evident by its presence: delusions, hallucinations, or thought disorders.

Thought disorder Disorganized, irrational thinking.

Delusion A belief that is clearly in contradiction to reality.

he or she is being controlled by others through such means as radar or tiny radio receivers implanted in his or her brain.

The third positive symptom of schizophrenia is **hallucinations,** perceptions of stimuli that are not actually present. The most common schizophrenic hallucinations are auditory, but they can also involve any of the other senses. The typical schizophrenic hallucination consists of voices talking to the person. Sometimes, the voices order the person to do something; sometimes, they scold the person for his or her unworthiness; sometimes, they just utter meaningless phrases. Olfactory hallucinations are also fairly common; often they contribute to the delusion that others are trying to kill the person with poison gas. (See *Table 15.1.*)

In contrast to the positive symptoms, the **negative symptoms** of schizophrenia are known by the absence of normal behaviors: flattened emotional response, poverty of speech, lack of initiative and persistence, inability to experience pleasure, and social withdrawal. Negative symptoms are not specific to schizophrenia; they are seen in many neurological disorders that involve brain damage, especially to the frontal lobes. As we will see later in this chapter, evidence suggests that these two sets of symptoms result from different physiological disorders. Positive symptoms appear to involve excessive activity in some neural circuits that include dopamine as a neurotransmitter, and negative symptoms appear to be caused by brain damage. Some researchers believe that these two sets of symptoms involve a common set of underlying causes. (See *Table 15.1.*)

TABLE 15.1	Positive and Negative Symptoms of Schizophrenia	
Positive		**Negative**
Hallucinations		Flattened emotional response
Thought disorders		Poverty of speech
Delusions		Lack of initiative and persistence
Persecution		
Grandeur		Anhedonia (inability to experience pleasure)
Control		
		Social withdrawal

Heritability

One of the strongest pieces of evidence that schizophrenia is a biological disorder is that it appears to be heritable. Two approaches have established a link between schizophrenia and genes: adoption studies and twin studies. (The rationale for these approaches was discussed in Chapter 5.)

Kety et al. (1968) performed one of the earliest and best-known adoption studies. Kety and his colleagues identified a group of schizophrenic people who had been adopted when they were children. They found that the incidence of schizophrenia in the adopted families of the patients was exactly what would be expected in the general population. Thus, it did not appear that the patients became schizophrenic because they were raised in a family of schizophrenics. However, the investigators did find an unusually high incidence of schizophrenia in the patients' *biological* relatives (parents and siblings), even though the patients were not raised by and with them— and probably, in most cases, did not even know them. The results clearly favor the conclusion that a tendency to developing schizophrenia is heritable. A follow-up study of a larger population confirmed these results (Kety et al., 1994).

Twin studies have produced similar results (Gottesman and Shields, 1982; Tsuang, Gilbertson, and Faraone, 1991). According to these studies, the concordance rate for monozygotic twins is at least four times higher than the concordance rate for dizygotic twins, a finding that provides strong evidence that schizophrenia is a heritable trait.

If schizophrenia were a simple trait produced by a single gene, we would expect to see this disorder in at least 75 percent of the children of two schizophrenic parents if the gene were dominant. If it were recessive, *all* children of two schizophrenic parents should become schizophrenic. However, the actual incidence is less than 50 percent, which means either that several genes are involved or that having a "schizophrenia gene" imparts a *susceptibility* to develop schizophrenia, the disease itself being triggered by other factors.

Hallucination Perception of a nonexistent object or event.

Negative symptom A symptom of schizophrenia characterized by the absence of behaviors that are normally present: social withdrawal, lack of affect, and reduced motivation.

So far, researchers have not yet located a "schizophrenia gene," although several candidates have been found (Sherrington et al., 1988; Dawson and Murray, 1996; Silverman et al., 1996.) If susceptibility to schizophrenia is caused by a small number of genes, geneticists will undoubtedly succeed in finding them some day. Once they are found, other researchers will try to determine what role these genes play, which should provide useful information about the causes of schizophrenia.

Pharmacology of Schizophrenia: The Dopamine Hypothesis

Pharmacological evidence suggests that the positive symptoms of schizophrenia are caused by a biochemical disorder. The explanation that has accrued the most evidence is the *dopamine hypothesis,* which suggests that schizophrenia is caused by overactivity of dopaminergic synapses, probably those in the mesolimbic pathway, which projects from the ventral tegmental area to the nucleus accumbens and amygdala.

Effects of Dopamine Agonists and Antagonists

About 45 years ago, a French surgeon named Henri Laborit discovered that a drug used to prevent surgical shock seemed also to reduce anxiety (Snyder, 1974). A French drug company developed a related compound called **chlorpromazine,** which seemed to be even more effective. Chlorpromazine was tried on patients with a variety of mental disorders: mania, depression, anxiety, neuroses, and schizophrenia (Delay and Deniker, 1952a, 1952b). The drug was not very effective in treating neuroses or affective psychoses, but it had dramatic effects on schizophrenia.

The discovery of the antipsychotic effects of chlorpromazine profoundly altered the way in which physicians treated schizophrenic patients and made prolonged hospital stays unnecessary for many of them (the patients, that is). The efficacy of antipsychotic drugs has been established in many double-blind studies (Baldessarini, 1977). The drugs actually eliminate, or at least diminish, the patients' symptoms. The beneficial effects are not just a change in the patient's attitudes; the hallucinations and delusions go away or at least become less severe.

Since the discovery of chlorpromazine, many other drugs have been developed that relieve the positive symptoms of schizophrenia. These drugs were found to have one property in common: They block dopamine receptors. Another category of drugs has the opposite effect, namely, *production* of the positive symptoms of schizophrenia. The drugs that can produce these symptoms have one known pharmacological effect in common: They act as dopamine agonists. These drugs include amphetamine, cocaine, and methylphenidate (which block the reuptake of dopamine) and L-DOPA (which stimulates the synthesis of dopamine). The symptoms that these drugs produce can be alleviated with antipsychotic drugs, which further strengthens the argument that these drugs exert their therapeutic effects by blocking dopamine receptors.

How might we explain the apparent link between overactivity of dopaminergic synapses and the positive symptoms of schizophrenia? As we saw in Chapters 4 and 12, the most important systems of dopaminergic neurons begin in two midbrain nuclei, the substantia nigra and the ventral tegmental area. Most researchers believe that the mesolimbic pathway, which begins in the ventral tegmental area and ends in the nucleus accumbens and amygdala, is more likely to be involved in the symptoms of schizophrenia. The nigrostriatal pathway, whose axons project from the substantia nigra to the neostriatum (the caudate nucleus and putamen), plays an important role in movement and motor learning. (As you will recall, degeneration of the nigrostriatal pathway results in Parkinson's disease, the symptoms of which involve certain learning deficits as well as motor disorders.) Overactivity of the neurons of the nigrostriatal pathway produces involuntary movements but not the symptoms of schizophrenia.

Chlorpromazine A dopamine receptor blocker; a commonly prescribed antischizophrenic drug.

Why might overactivity of dopaminergic synapses in the nucleus accumbens and amygdala produce the symptoms of schizophrenia? As we saw in Chapter 12, the activity of dopaminergic synapses in the nucleus accumbens appears to be a vital link in the process of reinforcement. Drugs that act as agonists at these synapses (such as cocaine and amphetamine) strongly reinforce behavior; and if taken in large doses, they also produce the positive symptoms of schizophrenia. Perhaps the two effects of the drugs are related. If reinforcement mechanisms were activated at inappropriate times, then inappropriate behaviors—including delusional thoughts—might be reinforced. At one time or other, all of us have had some irrational thoughts, which we normally brush aside and forget. But if neural mechanisms of reinforcement became active while these thoughts were occurring, we would tend to take them more seriously. In time, full-fledged delusions might develop.

As Snyder (1974) notes, schizophrenics often report feelings of elation and euphoria at the beginning of a schizophrenic episode, when their symptoms flare up. Presumably, this euphoria is caused by hyperactivity of dopaminergic neurons involved in reinforcement. But the positive symptoms of schizophrenia also include disordered thinking and unpleasant, often terrifying delusions. The disordered thinking may be caused by disorganized attentional processes; the indiscriminate activity of the dopaminergic synapses in the nucleus accumbens makes it difficult for the patients to follow an orderly, rational thought sequence. Fibiger (1991) suggests that paranoid delusions may be caused by increased activity of the dopaminergic input to the amygdala. As we saw in Chapter 10, the central nucleus of the amygdala is involved with conditioned emotional responses elicited by aversive stimuli. The central nucleus receives a strong projection from the mesolimbic dopaminergic system, so Fibiger's suggestion is certainly plausible.

The Search for Abnormalities in Dopamine Transmission in the Brains of Schizophrenic Patients

Is there any evidence that dopaminergic activity in the brains of schizophrenic patients is, indeed, abnormal? Before I discuss the search for abnormalities, let's consider the possibilities. (These possibilities are based on what you learned about the pharmacology of neurons in Chapter 4.) First, too much dopamine might be released. This increased release could be caused by more activity of dopaminergic neurons, which itself could be a result of increased excitatory input to these neurons, decreased inhibitory input, or some change in the physiological properties of these neurons that makes them more sensitive to excitatory input. Another reason for increased dopamine release could be decreased numbers of dopamine autoreceptors, whose normal function is to prevent excessive release of the neurotransmitter. A second possibility could be that neurons that receive dopaminergic input are excessively sensitive to that input. For example, these postsynaptic neurons could contain more dopamine receptors, or some biochemical differences in the neurons could produce a greater response when the receptors are stimulated by the neurotransmitter. A third possibility could be that a slow reuptake process in dopaminergic terminals keeps molecules of dopamine in the synaptic cleft for an unusually long time, resulting in prolonged activation of the postsynaptic dopamine receptors. A possible cause of slow reuptake could be some deficit in the number or efficiency of dopamine transporter molecules. (See *Table 15.2*.)

Let's look at some of the evidence. One recent study found evidence that dopaminergic neurons may, indeed, release more dopamine. Laruelle et al. (1996) used a device similar to a PET scanner to estimate the release of dopamine caused by an intravenous injection of amphetamine. As we saw in Chapter 4, amphetamine stimulates the release of dopamine, apparently by causing the dopamine transporters that are present in the terminal buttons to run backward, pumping dopamine out rather than retrieving it after it has been released. Of course, this effect inhibits the reuptake of dopamine as well. Laruelle and his colleagues found

TABLE 15.2	Possible Causes of Increased Dopaminergic Transmission in the Brains of Schizophrenic Patients

INCREASED DOPAMINE RELEASE

More excitatory input to dopaminergic neurons

Less inhibitory input to dopaminergic neurons

Fewer or defective autoreceptors on dopaminergic neurons

INCREASED POSTSYNAPTIC RESPONSE TO DOPAMINE RELEASE

More postsynaptic dopamine receptors

More response in postsynaptic neuron to activation of dopamine receptors

PROLONGED ACTIVATION OF POSTSYNAPTIC RECEPTORS

Decreased reuptake of dopamine by dopaminergic terminal button

that the amphetamine caused the release of more dopamine in the striatum of schizophrenic patients. They also found that subjects with greater amounts of dopamine release showed greater increases in positive symptoms. (See *Figure 15.1.*)

The second possibility—that the brains of schizophrenic patients contain a greater number of dopamine receptors—has received much more attention. Because the earliest antipsychotic drugs appeared to work by blocking D_2 receptors, the earliest studies looked for increases in the numbers of these receptors in the brains of schizophrenics. Researchers have performed two types of analyses: postmortem

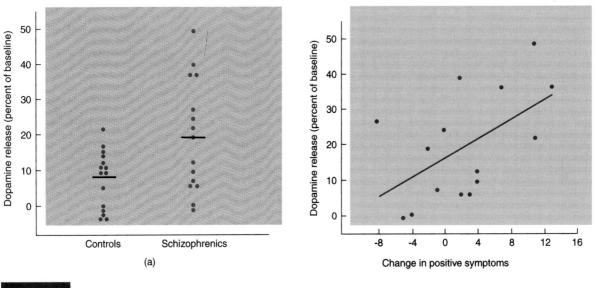

(a)

FIGURE 15.1

Results of the study by Laruelle et al. (1996). (a) Relative amount of dopamine released in response to amphetamine. (b) Relation between dopamine release and changes in positive symptoms of schizophrenic patients.

(Adapted from Laruelle, M., Abi-Dargham, A., Van Dyck, C.H., Gil, R., D'Souza, C.D., Erdos, J., McCance, E., Rosenblatt, W., Fingado, C., Zoghbi, S.S., Baldwin, R.M., Seibyl, J.P., Krystal, J.H., Charney, D.S., and Innis, R.B. Proceedings of the National Academy of Sciences, USA, 1996, 93, 9235–9240.)

measurements in the brains of deceased schizophrenic patients and PET scans after treatment with radioactive ligands for dopamine receptors. Unfortunately, the results have been mixed. Although some studies have found evidence for increased numbers of dopamine receptors, others have not; and some researchers suggest that the positive results may be caused by antipsychotic medication that the patients received (Wong et al., 1986; Jaskiw and Kleinman, 1988; Farde et al., 1990). In addition, most studies have focused on the neostriatum, a part of the basal ganglia that contains a high concentration of dopamine receptors. But the neostriatum is involved in motor control; why would excessive dopaminergic activity there cause schizophrenia?

The failure to obtain solid, unambiguous evidence that dopaminergic synapses are hyperactive in schizophrenic patients does not mean that the dopamine hypothesis should be abandoned. First, the early studies were probably looking in the wrong part of the brain. The neostriatum is large relative to the nucleus accumbens and amygdala, and it contains a very high concentration of dopamine receptors. Thus, it seemed like a logical place to look. But as we saw, the nucleus accumbens and the amygdala, not the neostriatum, are involved in functions that might be related to the positive symptoms of schizophrenia. Second, the early studies were probably concerned with the wrong type of receptors.

The older antipsychotic drugs certainly act as D_2 receptor antagonists, and they do have a strong effect in the neostriatum. This action undoubtedly accounts for the motor side effects that these drugs produce. (I will discuss this matter in the Epilogue.) But the affinity for D_2 receptors does not necessarily account for the ability of these drugs to relieve the symptoms of schizophrenia. **Clozapine,** a more recently developed drug, is a very effective antipsychotic medication, and its site of action is primarily on the nucleus accumbens, not the neostriatum (Kinon and Lieberman, 1996). In addition, it has little effect on D_2 receptors (Pickar, 1995). Instead, clozapine serves as a potent blocker of the recently discovered D_4 dopamine receptor; in fact, it has ten times more affinity for D_4 receptors than for D_2 receptors (Van Tol et al., 1991). Consequently, researchers are beginning to turn their attention to these receptors. They are also beginning to examine the possible role of another recently discovered dopamine receptor—the D_3 receptor—which is found in especially high concentrations in the human nucleus accumbens (Murray et al., 1994).

Two recent studies have found evidence for increased amounts of D_3 and D_4 dopamine receptors in the brains of deceased schizophrenics. Murray et al. (1995) found a twofold increase in the concentration of D_4 receptors in the nucleus accumbens. Gurevich et al. (1997) found a twofold increase in D_3 receptors in both the neostriatum and nucleus accumbens of schizophrenic patients. The patients had been drug free for at least one month before their deaths, so the increased concentration of D_3 receptors is unlikely to have been caused by medication. (See *Figure 15.2.*)

Although the recent discovery of the D_3 and D_4 dopamine receptors is stimulating research activity, it is still possible that nothing is wrong with dopaminergic neurons or dopamine receptors in the brains of patients with schizophrenia. Instead, the abnormality could lie elsewhere. As I mentioned earlier, overactivity of neurons that excite dopaminergic neurons or underactivity of neurons that inhibit them would both result in dopaminergic activation.

Clozapine An "atypical" antipsychotic drug; blocks D_4 receptors in the nucleus accumbens.

Receptor Density

High   Low

(a)   (b)   (c)

FIGURE 15.2

Pseudocolor images of concentrations of D_3 receptor binding in the human striatum. (a) Control subject. (b) Unmedicated schizophrenic patient. (c) Schizophrenic patient receiving antipsychotic medication. Cd = caudate nucleus, Pt = putamen, NA = nucleus accumbens.

(From Gurevich, E.V., Bordelon, Y., Shapiro, R.M., Arnold, S.E., Gur, R.E., and Joyce, J.N. Archives of General Psychiatry, 1997, 54, 225–232. Copyright 1997, American Medical Association.)

Schizophrenia as a Neurological Disorder

So far, I have been discussing the physiology of the positive symptoms of schizophrenia—principally, hallucinations, delusions, and thought disorders. These symptoms could very well be related to one of the known functions of dopaminergic neurons: reinforcement. But the negative symptoms of schizophrenia—flattened emotional response, poverty of speech, lack of initiative and persistence, inability to experience pleasure, and social withdrawal—are very different. Whereas the positive symptoms are unique to schizophrenia (and to amphetamine or cocaine psychosis), the negative symptoms are similar to those produced by brain damage caused by several different means. Many pieces of evidence suggest that the negative symptoms of schizophrenia are indeed a result of brain damage.

Evidence for Brain Damage in Schizophrenia

Although schizophrenia has traditionally been labeled a psychiatric disorder, most patients with schizophrenia exhibit neurological symptoms that suggest the presence of brain damage. These symptoms include catatonia; facial dyskinesias; unusually high or low rates of blinking; staring and avoidance of eye contact; absent blink reflex in response to a tap on the forehead; episodes of deviation of the eyes (especially to the right), accompanied by speech arrest; paroxysmal bursts of jerky eye movements; very poor visual pursuit of a smoothly moving object; inability to move the eyes without moving the head; poor pupillary light reactions; and continuous elevation of the brows, causing characteristic horizontal creasing of the forehead (Stevens, 1982). Although these symptoms can be caused by a variety of neuropathological conditions and hence are not unique to schizophrenia, their presence suggests that schizophrenia may be associated with brain damage of some kind.

Many studies have found evidence of brain damage in CT and MRI scans of schizophrenic patients. In one of the earliest studies, Weinberger and Wyatt (1982) obtained CT scans of eighty chronic schizophrenics and sixty-six normal controls of the same mean age (twenty-nine years). Without knowledge of the patients' diagnoses they measured the area of the lateral ventricles in the scan that cut through them at their largest extent, and they expressed this area relative to the area of brain tissue in the same scan. The relative ventricle size of the schizophrenic patients was more than twice as great as that of normal control subjects. (See *Figure 15.3.*) The most likely cause of the enlarged ventricles is loss of brain tissue; thus, the CT scans provide evidence that chronic schizophrenia is associated with brain damage.

Subsequent studies have found evidence for degeneration (or developmental abnormalities) in several parts of the brain. Abnormalities are commonly seen in the medial temporal lobes (Breier et al., 1992; Degreef et al., 1992; Bogerts et al., 1993), in the frontal lobes (Klausner et al., 1992; Raine et al., 1992; Turetsky et al., 1995), and in the medial diencephalon (Bornstein et al., 1992; D'Amato et al., 1992; Andreasen et al., 1994). In several of these studies, the severity of the brain abnormalities was correlated with the severity of the patients' negative symptoms.

Possible Causes of the Brain Damage

As we saw earlier, schizophrenia is a heritable disease, but its heritability is less than perfect. Why do fewer than half the children of parents with chronic schizophrenia become schizophrenic? Perhaps what is inherited is a defect that renders people susceptible to some environmental factors that adversely affect brain development or cause brain damage later in

FIGURE 15.3

Relative ventricular size in chronic schizophrenics and controls.

(From Weinberger, D.R., and Wyatt, R.J., in Schizophrenia as a Brain Disease, *edited by F.A. Henn and H.A. Nasrallah. New York: Oxford University Press, 1982. Reprinted with permission.)*

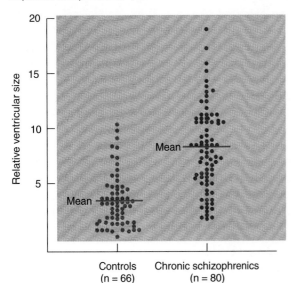

Controls
(n = 66)

Chronic schizophrenics
(n = 80)

life. According to this hypothesis, having a "schizophrenia gene" makes a person more likely to develop schizophrenia if exposed to these factors. In other words, schizophrenia is caused by an interaction between genetic and environmental factors. But as we shall see, the absence of a "schizophrenia gene" does not guarantee that a person will not develop schizophrenia; some cases of schizophrenia occur even in families with no history of schizophrenia or related mental illnesses. Let's look at the evidence concerning environmental factors that increase the risk of schizophrenia.

Epidemiological Studies. **Epidemiology** is the study of the distribution and causes of diseases in populations. Thus, epidemiological studies examine the relative frequency of diseases in groups of people in different environments and try to correlate the disease frequencies with factors that are present in these environments. Evidence from these studies indicates that the incidence of schizophrenia is related to several environmental factors: season of birth, viral epidemics, population density, latitude, and maternal stress. Let's examine each of these factors in turn.

Many studies have shown that people born during the late winter and early spring are more likely to develop schizophrenia—a phenomenon known as the **seasonality effect.** For example, Kendell and Adams (1991) studied the month of birth of over 13,000 schizophrenic patients born in Scotland between 1914 and 1960. They found that disproportionately more patients were born in February, March, April, and May. (See *Figure 15.4.*) These results have been confirmed by studies in several parts of the world, including Japan (Takei et al., 1995) and Taiwan (Tam and Sewell, 1995). In the southern hemisphere a disproportionate number of schizophrenic births also take place during late winter and early spring—during the months of August through December (McGrath, Welham, and Pemberton, 1995).

What factors might be responsible for the seasonality effect? One possibility is that pregnant women may be more likely to contract a viral illness during a critical phase of their infants' development. The brain development of their fetuses may be adversely affected either by a toxin produced by the virus or by the mother's antibodies against the virus. As Pallast et al. (1994) note, the winter flu season coincides with the second trimester of pregnancy of babies born in late winter and early spring. (As we shall see later, evidence suggests that critical aspects of brain development oc-

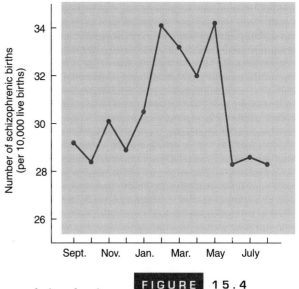

FIGURE 15.4

The seasonality effect. The graph shows the number of schizophrenic births per 10,000 live births.

(Based on data from Kendell, R.E., and Adams, W. British Journal of Psychiatry, 1991, 158, 758–763.)

Epidemiology The study of the distribution and causes of diseases in populations.

Seasonality effect The increased incidence of schizophrenia in people born during late winter and early spring.

Epidemiological studies have provided important information about the possible causes of schizophrenia. For example, the fact that schizophrenia is more prevalent in crowded urban areas with cold winter climates suggests that viral infections may play a role.

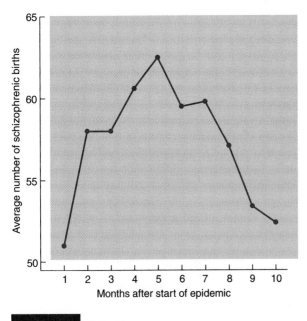

FIGURE 15.5

Average number of schizophrenic births in each of the ten months following an influenza epidemic in England and Wales between 1939 and 1960.

(Adapted from Sham, P.C., O'Callaghan, E., Takei, N., Murray, G.K., Hare, E.H., and Murray, R.M. British Journal of Psychiatry, 1992, 160, 461–466. Reprinted with permission.)

cur during the second trimester.) In fact, Kendell and Adams (1991) found that the relative number of schizophrenic births in late winter and early spring was especially high if the temperature was lower than normal during the previous autumn—a condition that keeps people indoors and favors the transmission of viral illnesses.

In a review of the relevant literature, Franzek and Beckmann (1996) noted that several studies have found that the seasonality effect occurs primarily in cities but is rarely found in the countryside. Because viruses are more readily transmitted in regions with high population densities, this finding is consistent with the hypothesis that at least one of the causes of the seasonality effect is exposure of pregnant women to viral illnesses during the second trimester.

If the viral hypothesis is true, then an increased incidence of schizophrenia should be seen in babies born a few months after an influenza epidemic, whatever the season. Several studies have observed just that. For example, a study of the offspring of women who were pregnant during an epidemic of type A2 influenza in Finland during 1957 showed an elevated incidence of schizophrenia (Mednick, Machon, and Huttunen, 1990). The increased incidence was seen only in the children of women who were in the second trimester of their pregnancy when the epidemic occurred. Another study (Sham et al., 1992) confirmed these findings in a study of infants born to mothers who were pregnant during several influenza epidemics in England and Wales between 1939 and 1960. As Figure 15.5 shows, the peak number of schizophrenic births occurred five months after the start of the epidemic, which means that the greatest susceptibility appears to occur during the second trimester of pregnancy. (See *Figure 15.5.*)

Several studies have reported that people born farther from the equator are more likely to develop schizophrenia. This phenomenon has been termed the **latitude effect.** For example, people born in northern Sweden or the northern United States are more likely to develop schizophrenia than are those born in the southern parts of these countries (Dalen, 1968; Torrey, Torrey, and Peterson, 1979). A similar phenomenon is seen in multiple sclerosis, an autoimmune disease that attacks the white matter of the central nervous system (Stevens, 1988). One possible explanation for the latitude effect is that the climate is colder in higher latitudes, and the decreased winter temperature might simply magnify the seasonality effect.

The final prenatal effect that I will mention may be independent of the ones I have described so far, or it may also involve viral infections. Huttunen and Niskanen (1978) reported a higher incidence of schizophrenia in the children born to women who learned that their husbands had been killed in combat during World War II. The stress of this news may have had direct effects on development of the women's fetuses, or it may have suppressed their immune systems, increasing the likelihood of their contracting a viral illness. As we will see in Chapter 16, stress has an inhibitory effect on the immune system.

Evidence for Abnormal Brain Development. So far, the evidence that I have cited concerning developmental factors in schizophrenia is epidemiological, having come from studies of populations, not individuals. Is there any direct evidence that abnormal prenatal development is associated with schizophrenia? The answer is yes; studies have reported both behavioral and anatomical evidence for developmental abnormalities. Walker and her colleagues (Walker, Savoie, and Davis, 1994; Walker, Lewine, and Neumann, 1996) obtained home movies from families with a schizophrenic child. They had independent observers examine the behavior of the children. In comparison with their normal siblings the children who subsequently became schizophrenic displayed more negative affect in their facial expressions and were more likely to show abnor-

Latitude effect The increased incidence of schizophrenia in people born far from the equator.

mal movements. (The rating were done blind; the observers did not know which children subsequently became schizophrenic.) These results are consistent with the hypothesis that the prenatal brain development of the children who became schizophrenic was not entirely normal.

As I mentioned earlier, some monozygotic twins are discordant for schizophrenia; that is, one of them develops schizophrenia and the other does not. Suddath et al. (1990) obtained evidence that differences in the structure of the brain may account for the discordance. The investigators examined MRI scans of monozygotic twins who were discordant for schizophrenia and found that in almost every case the twin with schizophrenia had larger lateral and third ventricles. In addition, the anterior hippocampus was smaller in the schizophrenic twins, and the total volume of the gray matter in the left temporal lobe was reduced. Figure 15.6 shows a set of MRI scans from a pair of twins; as you can see, the lateral ventricles are larger in the brain of the twin with schizophrenia. (See *Figure 15.6*.)

In the past, most researchers assumed that discordance for schizophrenia in monozygotic twins must be caused by differential exposure to some environmental factors after birth. Monozygotic twins not only are genetically identical, they also share the same intrauterine environment. Thus, because all prenatal factors should be identical, any differences must be a result of factors in the postnatal environment. However, some investigators have pointed out that the prenatal environment of monozygotic twins in *not* identical. In fact, there are two types of monozygotic twins: monochorionic and dichorionic. The formation of monozygotic twins occurs when the blastocyst (the developing organism) splits in two—when it clones itself. If twinning occurs before day 4, the two organisms develop independently, each forming its own placenta. (That is, the twins are *dichorionic*. The *chorion* is the outer layer of the blastocyst, which gives rise to the placenta.) If twinning occurs after day 4, the two organisms become *monochorionic*, sharing a single placenta. (See *Figure 15.7*.)

The placenta plays an extremely important role in prenatal development. It transports nutrients to the developing organism from the mother's circulation and transports waste products to her, which she metabolizes in her liver or excretes in her urine. It also constitutes the barrier through which toxins or infectious agents must

(a)   (b)

FIGURE 15.6

MRI scans of the brains of twins discordant for schizophrenia. The arrows point to the lateral ventricles. (a) Normal twin. (b) Twin with schizophrenia.

(Courtesy of D.R. Weinberger, National Institute of Mental Health, Saint Elizabeth's Hospital, Washington, D.C.)

FIGURE 15.7

Monozygotic twins. (a) Monochorionic twins, sharing a single placenta. (b) Dichorionic twins, each with its own placenta.

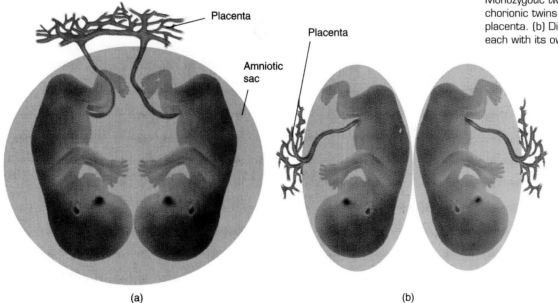

Placenta

Placenta

Amniotic sac

(a)   (b)

pass if they are to affect fetal development. The prenatal environments of mono-chorionic twins, who share a single placenta, are obviously more similar than those of dichorionic twins. Thus, we might expect that the concordance rates for schizo-phrenia of *monochorionic* monozygotic twins should be higher than those of *dichori-onic* monozygotic twins. And, as Davis, Phelps, and Bracha (1995) reported, they are. Davis and his colleagues examined sets of monozygotic twins who were concordant and discordant for schizophrenia. They used several indices to estimate whether a given pair was monochorionic or dichorionic. (For example, twins with mirror im-ages of physical features such as fingerprints, handedness, birthmarks, or hair swirls are more likely to be monochorionic.) The investigators estimated that the concor-dance rate for schizophrenia was 10.7 percent in the dichorionic twins and 60 per-cent in the monochorionic twins. These results provide strong evidence for an interaction between heredity and environment during prenatal development.

Bracha et al. (1992) also looked at the fingerprints of monozygotic twins who were concordant or discordant for schizophrenia, but for a different reason. As we saw, the migration of neurons into the cerebral cortex takes place during the second trimester of prenatal development. During this period, cells in the skin of the fin-gertips also migrate, forming the ridges that give us our fingerprints. (The central nervous system and the skin both originate from cells in the ectoderm, the outer em-bryonic layer.) Bracha and his colleagues reasoned that if something were interfer-ing with the brain development of one of the twins, it might show itself in the development of that individual's fingerprints, too. And they found exactly that. The fingerprints of the twins who were concordant for schizophrenia were nearly iden-tical, whereas the fingerprints of many of the discordant twins showed distinctive differences. A follow-up study looking at lines in twins' palms (which form at about the same time) confirmed these results (Davis and Bracha, 1996).

The evidence I have cited so far indicates that at least one cause—and perhaps the most important cause—of schizophrenia is disturbance of normal prenatal brain development. Presumably, genetic factors make some fetuses more sensitive to events that can disturb development. There is good evidence that obstetric compli-cations can also cause schizophrenia. In fact, several studies have found that if a schizophrenic person does not have relatives with a schizophrenic disorder, that per-son is more likely to have had a history of complications at or around the time of childbirth—and the person is more likely to develop the schizophrenic symptoms at an earlier age (Schwarzkopf et al., 1989; O'Callaghan, 1990; O'Callaghan et al., 1992.) Sometimes, brain damage received during adulthood can produce the symp-toms of schizophrenia. Buckley et al. (1993) found three such cases and reported that MRI scans revealed damage in the left temporal lobe. Thus, brain damage that is *not related to heredity* may also be a cause of schizophrenia.

In the interest of clarity and brevity, I have been selective in my review of research on schizophrenia. This puzzling and serious disorder has stimulated many ingenious hypotheses and much research. Some hypotheses have been proved wrong; others have not yet been adequately tested. Possibly, future research will find that all of these hypotheses (including the ones I have discussed) are incorrect, or one that I have not mentioned is correct. However, I am impressed with recent research, and I believe that we have real hope of finding the causes of schizophrenia in the near future. With the discovery of the causes we can hope for the discovery of methods of prevention.

INTERIM SUMMARY

Researchers have made considerable progress in the past few years in their study of the physiology of mental disorders, but many puzzles still remain. Schiz-ophrenia consists of positive and negative symptoms, the former involving the pres-ence of an unusual behavior and the latter involving the absence of a normal behavior. Because schizophrenia is at least somewhat heritable, it appears to have a biological basis. But evidence indicates that not all cases are caused by heredity, and some people who appear to carry a "schizophrenia gene" do not become schizophrenic.

The dopamine hypothesis—inspired by the findings that dopamine antagonists alleviate the positive symptoms of schizophrenia and that dopamine agonists increase or even produce them—is still dominant. This hypothesis states that the positive symptoms of schizophrenia are caused by hyperactivity of dopaminergic synapses. The involvement of dopamine in reinforcement could plausibly explain the positive effects of schizophrenia; inappropriately reinforced thoughts could persist and become delusions. Paranoid thoughts may be caused by dopaminergic activation of the central nucleus of the amygdala, a region involved in negative emotional responses. There is little evidence that an abnormally large amount of dopamine is released under resting conditions, but a PET study indicates that the administration of amphetamine causes a larger release of dopamine in the brains of schizophrenics. Studies suggest that the nucleus accumbens in the brains of schizophrenic patients may contain increased numbers of D_3 or D_4 dopamine receptors.

CT and MRI scans indicate that brain damage—especially in the frontal lobes, medial temporal lobes, and diencephalon—is associated with the negative symptoms of schizophrenia. Studies of the epidemiology of schizophrenia indicate that season of birth, viral epidemics during pregnancy, population density, latitude of birth, and prenatal stress all contribute to the occurrence of schizophrenia. In addition, home movies of very young children who later became schizophrenic indicate the early presence of abnormalities in movements and facial expressions. All these factors provide direct evidence of developmental abnormalities in the brains of schizophrenics. Further evidence is provided by the presence of an increased size of the third and lateral ventricles and a decreased size of the hippocampus in the schizophrenic member of monozygotic twins who are discordant for schizophrenia. The increased concordance rate of monochorionic monozygotic twins suggests that hereditary and prenatal environmental factors may interact. Finally, comparisons of the fingerprints and palm prints of twins who are concordant and discordant for schizophrenia provide evidence for factors that disturb prenatal development during the second trimester.

■ THOUGHT QUESTIONS

Suppose that a young schizophrenic woman insists on living in the streets and refuses to take antipsychotic medication. She is severely disturbed; she is undernourished and often takes intravenous drugs, which expose her to the risk of AIDS. Her parents have tried to get her to seek help, but she believes that they are plotting against her. Suppose further that we can predict with 90 percent accuracy that she will die within a few years. She is not violent, and she has never talked about committing suicide, so we cannot prove that her behavior constitutes an immediate threat to herself or to others. Should her parents be able to force her to receive treatment, or does she have an absolute right to be left alone, even if she is mentally ill?

■ MAJOR AFFECTIVE DISORDERS

Affect, as a noun, refers to feelings or emotions. Just as the primary symptom of schizophrenia is disordered thoughts, the **major affective disorders** (also called *mood disorders*) are characterized by disordered feelings.

Description

Feelings and emotions are essential parts of human existence; they represent our evaluation of the events in our lives. In a very real sense, feelings and emotions are

Major affective disorder A serious mood disorder; includes unipolar depression and bipolar disorder.

Normally, our feelings and emotions are tied to events that affect us. This woman shows the grief she feels from the death of her husband, a police officer.

what human life is all about. The emotional state of most of us reflects what is happening to us: Our feelings are tied to events in the real world, and they are usually the result of reasonable assessments of the importance these events have for our lives. But for some people, affect becomes divorced from reality. These people have feelings of extreme elation (*mania*) or despair (*depression*) that are not justified by events in their lives. For example, depression that accompanies the loss of a loved one is normal, but depression that becomes a way of life—and will not respond to the sympathetic effort of friends and relatives or even to psychotherapy—is pathological.

There are two principal types of major affective disorders. The first type is characterized by alternating periods of mania and depression—a condition called **bipolar disorder.** This disorder afflicts men and women in approximately equal numbers. Episodes of mania can last a few days or several months, but they usually take a few weeks to run their course. The episodes of depression that follow generally last three times as long as the mania. The second type is **unipolar depression,** or depression without mania. This depression may be continuous and unremitting or, more typically, may come in episodes. Unipolar depression strikes women two to three times more often than men. Mania without periods of depression sometimes occurs, but it is rare.

Severely depressed people usually feel extremely unworthy and have strong feelings of guilt. The affective disorders are dangerous; a person who suffers from a major affective disorder runs a considerable risk of death by suicide. According to Chen and Dilsaver (1996), 15.9 percent of people with unipolar depression and 29.2 percent of people with bipolar disorder attempt to commit suicide. Depressed people have very little energy, and they move and talk slowly, sometimes becoming almost torpid. At other times they may pace around restlessly and aimlessly. They may cry a lot. They are unable to experience pleasure; they lose their appetite for food and sex. Their sleep is disturbed; they usually have difficulty falling asleep and awaken early and find it difficult to get to sleep again. Even their body functions become depressed; they often become constipated, and secretion of saliva decreases.

Episodes of mania are characterized by a sense of euphoria that does not seem to be justified by circumstances. The diagnosis of mania is partly a matter of degree—one would not call exuberance and a zest for life pathological. People with mania usually exhibit nonstop speech and motor activity. They flit from topic to topic and often have delusions, but they lack the severe disorganization that is seen in schizophrenia. They are usually full of their own importance and often become angry or defensive if they are contradicted. Frequently, they go for long periods without sleep, working furiously on projects that are often unrealistic. (Sometimes, their work is fruitful; George Frideric Handel wrote *Messiah*, one of the masterpieces of choral music, during one of his periods of mania.)

Bipolar disorder A serious mood disorder characterized by cyclical periods of mania and depression.

Unipolar depression A serious mood disorder that consists of unremitting depression or periods of depression that do not alternate with periods of mania.

Heritability

The tendency to develop an affective disorder appears to be heritable. (See Moldin, Reich, and Rice, 1991, for a review.) For example, Rosenthal (1971) found that close relatives of people who suffer from affective psychoses are ten times more likely to develop these disorders than are people without afflicted relatives. Gershon et al. (1976) found that if one member of a set of monozygotic twins was afflicted with an affective disorder, the likelihood that the other twin was similarly afflicted was 69 percent. In contrast, the concordance rate for dizygotic twins was only 13 percent. Furthermore, the concordance rate for monozygotic twins appears to be the same whether the twins were raised together or apart (Price, 1968). The heritability of the affective disorders implies that they have a physiological basis.

Physiological Treatments

There are four effective biological treatments for depression: monoamine oxidase (MAO) inhibitors, drugs that inhibit the reuptake of norepinephrine and serotonin, electroconvulsive therapy (ECT), and sleep deprivation. (Sleep deprivation is discussed in a later section.) Bipolar disorder can be effectively treated by lithium salts. The fact that these disorders respond to medical treatment provides additional evidence that they have a physiological basis. Furthermore, the fact that lithium is very effective in treating bipolar affective disorders but not unipolar depression suggests that there is a fundamental difference between these two illnesses.

Before the 1950s there was no effective drug treatment for depression. In the late 1940s, clinicians noticed that some drugs that were used for treating tuberculosis seemed to elevate the patient's mood. Researchers subsequently found that a derivative of these drugs, iproniazid, reduced symptoms of psychotic depression (Crane, 1957). Iproniazid inhibits the activity of MAO, which destroys excess monoamine transmitter substances within terminal buttons. Thus, the drug increases the release of dopamine, norepinephrine, and serotonin. Other MAO inhibitors were soon discovered. Unfortunately, MAO inhibitors can have harmful side effects, so they must be used with caution.

Fortunately, another class of antidepressant drugs was soon discovered that did not produce such dangerous side effects: the **tricyclic antidepressants.** These drugs were found to inhibit the reuptake of 5-HT and norepinephrine by terminal buttons. By retarding reuptake, the drugs keep the neurotransmitter in contact with the postsynaptic receptors, thus prolonging the postsynaptic potentials. Thus, both the MAO inhibitors and the tricyclic antidepressant drugs are monoaminergic agonists.

Since the discovery of the tricyclic antidepressants, other drugs have been discovered that have similar effects. The most important of these are the **specific serotonin reuptake inhibitors (SSRI),** whose action is described by their name. One of them, fluoxetine (Prozac) is widely prescribed for its antidepressant properties and for its ability to reduce the symptoms of obsessive-compulsive disorder and social phobia. (Obsessive-compulsive disorder is described in the last section of this chapter.)

The third biological treatment for depression has an interesting history. Earlier in this century, a physician named von Meduna noted that psychotic patients who were also subject to epileptic seizures showed improvement immediately after each attack. He reasoned that the violent storm of neural activity in the brain that constitutes an epileptic seizure somehow improved the patients' mental condition. He developed a way to produce seizures by administering a drug, but the procedure was dangerous to the patient. In 1937, Ugo Cerletti, an Italian psychiatrist, developed a less dangerous method for producing seizures. He had previously learned that the local slaughterhouse applied a jolt of electricity to animals' heads to stun them before killing them. The electricity appeared to produce a seizure that resembled an epileptic attack. He decided to attempt to use electricity to induce a seizure more safely.

Cerletti tried the procedure on dogs and found that an electrical shock to the skull did produce a seizure and that the animals recovered with no apparent ill effects. He then used the procedure on humans and found it to be safer than the chemical treatment that had previously been used. As a result, **electroconvulsive therapy (ECT)** became a common treatment for mental illness. Before a person receives ECT, he or she is anesthetized and is given a drug similar to curare, which paralyzes the muscles, preventing injuries that might be produced by a convulsion. (Of course, the patient is attached to a respirator until the effects of this drug wear off.) Electrodes are placed on the patient's scalp (most often to the nonspeech-dominant hemisphere, to avoid

Tricyclic antidepressant A class of drugs used to treat depression; inhibits the reuptake of norepinephrine and serotonin; named for the molecular structure.

Specific serotonin reuptake inhibitor (SSRI) A drug that inhibits the reuptake of serotonin without affecting the reuptake of other neurotransmitters.

Electroconvulsive therapy (ECT) A brief electrical shock, applied to the head, that results in an electrical seizure; used therapeutically to alleviate severe depression.

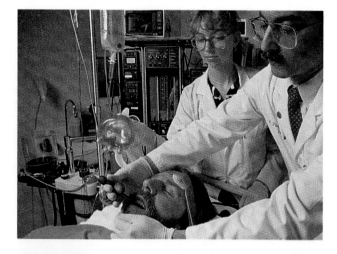

FIGURE **15.8**

A patient being prepared for electroconvulsive therapy.

(Will & Deni McIntyre/Photo Researchers, Inc.)

Lithium An element; lithium carbonate is used to treat bipolar disorder.

Carbamazepine A drug (trade name: Tegretol) that is used to treat seizures originating from a focus, generally in the medial temporal lobe.

Monoamine hypothesis A hypothesis that states that depression is caused by a low level of activity of one or more monoaminergic synapses.

damaging verbal memories), and a jolt of electricity triggers a seizure. Usually, a patient receives three treatments per week until maximum improvement is seen, which usually involves six to twelve treatments. The effectiveness of ECT has been established by placebo studies, in which some patients are anesthetized but not given shocks (Weiner and Krystal, 1994). Although ECT was originally used for a variety of disorders, including schizophrenia, we now know that its usefulness is limited to treatment of mania and depression. (See *Figure 15.8.*)

A depressed patient does not respond immediately to treatment with antidepressant drugs; improvement in symptoms is not usually seen before two to three weeks of drug treatment. In contrast, the effects of ECT are more rapid. A few seizures induced by ECT can often snap a person out of a deep depression within a few days. Although prolonged and excessive use of ECT causes brain damage, resulting in long-lasting impairments in memory (Squire, 1974), the judicious use of ECT during the interim period before antidepressant drugs become effective has undoubtedly saved the lives of some suicidal patients (Baldessarini, 1977). In addition, some severely depressed people are not helped by drug therapy; for them, occasional ECT is the only effective treatment.

The therapeutic effect of **lithium,** the drug used to treat bipolar affective disorders, is very rapid. This drug, which is administered in the form of lithium carbonate, is most effective in treating the manic phase of a bipolar affective disorder; once the mania is eliminated, depression usually does not follow (Gerbino, Oleshansky, and Gershon, 1978). Many clinicians and investigators have referred to lithium as psychiatry's wonder drug: It does not suppress normal feelings of emotions, but it leaves patients able to feel and express joy and sadness in response to events in their lives. Similarly, it does not impair intellectual processes; many patients have received the drug continuously for years without any apparent ill effects (Fieve, 1979). Between 70 and 80 percent of patients with bipolar disorder show a positive response to lithium within a week or two (Price and Heninger, 1994).

Investigators have not yet discovered the pharmacological effects of lithium that are responsible for its ability to eliminate mania. Some suggest that the drug stabilizes the population of certain classes of neurotransmitter receptors in the brain (especially serotonin receptors), thus preventing wide shifts in neural sensitivity. This effect may involve interference with the production of a class of second messengers—the chemical signals that link activation of metabotropic receptors with biochemical events within the cell (Atack, Broughton, and Pollack, 1995; Jope et al., 1996.)

Because some patients cannot tolerate the side effects of lithium, and because of the potential danger of overdose, researchers have been searching for alternative medications for bipolar disorder. One medication that has shown considerable promise is **carbamazepine** (Tegretol), a drug used to treat seizures that originate in the medial temporal lobes. Although carbamazepine is effective in treating the depressed phase of bipolar disorder, it effects on mania are more impressive (Post et al., 1984). (See *Figure 15.9*) In addition, it appears to help some bipolar patients who do not respond to treatment with lithium (Post, Weiss, and Chuang, 1992).

The Monoamine Hypothesis

The fact that depression can be treated effectively with MAO inhibitors and drugs that inhibit the reuptake of serotonin and norepinephrine suggested the **monoamine hypothesis:** Depression is caused by insufficient activity of monoaminergic neurons. Because the symptoms of depression do not respond to potent dopamine agonists such as amphetamine or cocaine, most investigators have focused their research efforts on the other two monoamines: norepinephrine and serotonin.

As we saw, the dopamine hypothesis of schizophrenia receives support from the fact that dopamine agonists can produce the symptoms of schizophrenia. Similarly, the monoamine hypothesis of depression receives support from the fact that depression can be caused by monoamine antagonists. Many hundreds of years ago, an alkaloid extract from *Rauwolfia serpentina,* a shrub of Southeast Asia, was found to be useful for treating snakebite, circulatory disorders, and insanity. Modern research has confirmed that the alkaloid, now called reserpine, has both an antipsychotic effect and a hypotensive effect (that is, it lowers blood pressure). The effect on blood pressure precludes its use in treating schizophrenia, but the drug is still occasionally used to treat patients with high blood pressure.

Reserpine has a serious side effect: It can cause depression. In fact, in the early years of its use as a hypotensive agent, up to 15 percent of the people who received it became depressed (Sachar and Baron, 1979). Reserpine interferes with the storage of monoamines in synaptic vesicles, reducing the amount of neurotransmitter released by the terminal buttons. Thus, the drug serves as a potent norepinephrine, dopamine, and serotonin antagonist. The pharmacological and behavioral effects of reserpine complement the pharmacological and behavioral effects of the drugs used to treat depression—MAO inhibitors and drugs that block the reuptake of norepinephrine and serotonin. That is, a monoamine antagonist produces depression, whereas monoamine agonists alleviate it.

Several studies have found that suicidal depression is related to decreased CSF levels of **5-HIAA** (5-hydroxyindoleacetic acid), a metabolite of serotonin that is produced when serotonin is destroyed by MAO. A decreased level of 5-HIAA implies that less 5-HT (serotonin) is being produced and released in the brain. Träskmann et al. (1981) found that CSF levels of 5-HIAA in people who had attempted suicide were significantly lower than those in controls. In a follow-up study of depressed and potentially suicidal patients, 20 percent of those with levels of 5-HIAA below the median subsequently killed themselves, whereas none of those with levels above the median committed suicide. More recent studies have confirmed these results (Roy, De Jong, and Linnoila, 1989).

Sedvall et al. (1980) analyzed the CSF of healthy, nondepressed volunteers. The families of subjects with unusually low levels of 5-HIAA were more likely to include people with depression. The results suggest that serotonin metabolism or release is genetically controlled and is linked to depression. Thus, these findings clearly support the monoamine hypothesis.

Delgado et al. (1990) used a different approach to study of the role of serotonin in depression—the **tryptophan depletion procedure.** They studied depressed patients who were receiving antidepressant medication and were currently feeling well. For one day, they had the patients eat a low-tryptophan diet (for example, salad, corn, cream cheese, and a gelatin dessert). Then the next day, the patients drank an amino acid "cocktail" that contained no tryptophan. The uptake of amino acids through the blood-brain barrier is accomplished by amino acid transporters. Because the patients' blood level of tryptophan was very low and that of the other amino acids was high, very little tryptophan found its way into the brain, and the level of tryptophan

FIGURE **15.9**

The effects of lithium carbonate and carbamazepine on symptoms of mania in patients with bipolar disorder.

(Adapted from Feldman, R.S., Meyer, J.S., and Quenzer, L.F. Principles of Neuropsychopharmacology. *Sunderland, MA: Sinauer Associates, 1997. After Post et al., 1984.)*

5-HIAA A breakdown product of the neurotransmitter serotonin (5-HT).

Tryptophan depletion procedure A procedure involving a low-tryptophan diet and a tryptophan-free amino acid "cocktail" that lowers brain tryptophan and consequently decreases the synthesis of 5-HT.

in the brain fell drastically. As you will recall, tryptophan is the precursor of 5-HT, or serotonin. Thus, the treatment lowered the level of serotonin in the brain.

Delgado and his colleagues found that the tryptophan depletion caused most of the patients to relapse back into depression. Then when they began eating a normal diet again, they recovered. These results strongly suggest that the therapeutic effect of at least some antidepressant drugs depends on the availability of serotonin in the brain.

Bremner et al. (1997) used a PET scanner to try to determine the brain regions involved in the relapse of depression caused by tryptophan depletion. To do so, they measured patients' regional cerebral metabolic rate before and after the patients drank a placebo or the amino acid "cocktail." They found that patients whose depression returned showed a decrease in brain metabolism in the dorsolateral prefrontal cortex, orbitofrontal cortex, and thalamus. Patients who did not relapse did not show these changes. These results are consistent with the general finding (discussed in Chapter 10) that the prefrontal cortex is involved in emotions.

Evidence for Brain Abnormalities

As we saw earlier in this chapter, many studies have found structural and biochemical abnormalities in the brains of schizophrenic patients. Some studies have reported abnormalities in patients with affective disorders, but the evidence is still inconclusive. A recent review by Soares and Mann (1997) noted that investigators have reported abnormalities in the prefrontal cortex, basal ganglia, hippocampus, thalamus, cerebellum, and temporal lobe. The most reliable findings were abnormalities in the prefrontal cortex, basal ganglia, and cerebellum of patients with unipolar depression and abnormalities of the cerebellum (and perhaps the temporal lobe) in those with bipolar disorder. Elkis et al. (1996) found evidence for a decreased amount of tissue in the prefrontal cortex of young patients with unipolar depression, which suggests the presence of a developmental abnormality or a degenerative process that occurs early in life.

Several imaging studies using PET or functional MRI have found evidence for increased regional metabolic activity in depressed patients. For example, Drevets et al. (1992) found an increase in the prefrontal cortex and the amygdala, and Wu et al. (1992) found an increase in the anterior cingulate cortex. Nobler et al. (1994) scanned patients before and after ECT treatment and found a reduction in the metabolic activity of the prefrontal cortex. In fact, the amount of reduction was correlated with a positive response to the treatment. (See *Figure 15.10*.)

As we saw earlier in this chapter, evidence indicates that schizophrenia can be produced by brain damage resulting from obstetric complications. Kinney et al. (1993) found that patients with bipolar disorder were more likely than their normal siblings to have a record of obstetric complications. The complications were mostly minor, so the authors suggest that they probably served as a contributing factor to the development of the disorder rather than the sole cause.

Role of Circadian Rhythms

One of the most prominent symptoms of depression is disordered sleep. The sleep of people with depression tends to be shallow; slow-wave delta sleep (stages 3 and 4) is reduced, and stage 1 is increased. Sleep is fragmented; people tend to waken frequently, especially to-

---

FIGURE **15.10**

Mean changes in cerebral blood flow after bilateral ECT. The largest reductions were seen in the prefrontal cortex of subjects whose symptoms improved after ECT (responders).

(From Nobler, M.S., Sackeim, H.A., Prohovnik, I., Moeller, J.R., Mukherjee, S., Schnur, D.B., Prudic, J., and Devanand, D.P. Archives of General Psychiatry, 1994, 51, 884–897. Copyright 1994, American Medical Association.)

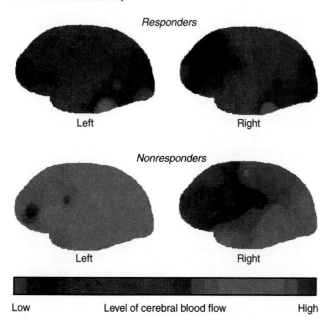

ward the morning. In addition, REM sleep occurs earlier, the first half of the night contains a higher proportion of REM periods, and REM sleep contains an increased number of rapid eye movements (Kupfer, 1976; Vogel et al., 1980). (See *Figure 15.11*.)

REM Sleep Deprivation

One of the most effective antidepressant treatments is sleep deprivation, either total or selective. Selective deprivation of REM sleep, accomplished by monitoring people's EEG and awakening them whenever they show signs of REM sleep, alleviates depression (Vogel et al., 1975; Vogel et al., 1990). The therapeutic effect, like that of the antidepressant medications, occurs slowly, over the course of several weeks. Some patients show long-term improvement even after the deprivation is discontinued; thus, it is a practical as well as an effective treatment. In addition, regardless of their specific pharmacological effects, other treatments for depression suppress REM sleep, delaying its onset and decreasing its duration. These facts suggest that some common mechanisms may affect both REM sleep and mood.

Scherschlicht et al. (1982) examined the effects of twenty antidepressant drugs on the sleep cycles of cats and found that all of them profoundly reduced REM sleep and most of them increased slow-wave sleep. In an extensive review of the literature, Vogel et al. (1990) found that all drugs that suppressed REM sleep (and produced a rebound effect when their administration was discontinued) acted as antidepressants. As a consequence, an increased amount of delta sleep occurs during the first pre-REM period. Kupfer et al. (1994) found that the effects of antidepressant drugs on sleep persisted throughout long-term treatment. (They observed patients for as long as three years.) These results suggest that the primary effect of antidepressant medication may be to suppress REM sleep, and the changes in mood may be a result of this suppression. However, some drugs that relieve the symptoms of depression (such as iprindole and trimipramine) do not suppress REM sleep. Thus, suppression of REM sleep cannot be the *only* way in which antidepressant drugs work.

Studies of families with a history of major depression also suggest a link between this disorder and abnormalities in REM sleep. For example, Giles, Roffwarg, and Rush (1987) found that first-degree relatives of people with depression are likely to show a short REM sleep latency, even if they have not yet had an episode of depression. Giles et al. (1988) found that the members of these families who had the lowest REM latency had the highest risk of subsequently becoming depressed. Abnormalities in REM sleep are seen early in life; Coble et al. (1988) found that newborn infants of mothers with a history of major depression showed patterns of REM sleep that were different from those of the infants of mothers without such a history.

Total Sleep Deprivation

Total sleep deprivation also has an antidepressant effect. Unlike specific deprivation of REM sleep, which takes several weeks to reduce depression, total sleep deprivation produces immediate effects (Wu and Bunney, 1990). Figure 15.12 shows the mood rating of a patient who stayed awake one night; as you can see, the depression was lifted by the sleep deprivation but returned the next day, after a normal night's sleep. (See *Figure 15.12*.)

Wu and Bunney suggest that during sleep a substance is produced that has a *depressogenic* effect. That is, the substance produces depression in a susceptible person. Presumably, this substance is produced in the brain and acts as a neuromodulator. During wak-

FIGURE 15.11

Patterns of the stages of sleep of a normal subject and of a patient with major depression. Note the reduced sleep latency, reduced REM latency, reduction in slow-wave sleep (stages 3 and 4), and general fragmentation of sleep (arrows) in the depressed patient.

(From Gillin, J.C., and Borbély, A.A. Trends in Neurosciences, 1985, 8, 537–542. Reprinted with permission.)

FIGURE 15.12

Changes in the depression rating of a depressed patient produced by a single night's total sleep deprivation.

(From Wu, J.C., and Bunney, W.E. American Journal of Psychiatry, Vol. 147, pp. 14–21, 1990. Copyright 1990, the American Psychiatric Association. Reprinted by permission.)

FIGURE 15.13

Mean mood rating of responding and nonresponding patients deprived of one night's sleep as a function of the time of day.

(From Wu, J.C., and Bunney, W.E. American Journal of Psychiatry, *Vol. 147, pp. 14–21, 1990. Copyright 1990, the American Psychiatric Association. Reprinted by permission.)*

ing, this substance is gradually metabolized and hence inactivated. Some of the evidence for this hypothesis is presented in Figure 15.13. The data are taken from eight different studies (cited by Wu and Bunney, 1990) and show self-ratings of depression of people who did and did not respond to sleep deprivation. (Total sleep deprivation improves the mood of patients with major depression approximately two-thirds of the time.) (See *Figure 15.13.*)

Why do only some people profit from sleep deprivation? This question has not yet been answered, but several studies have shown that it is possible to predict who will profit and who will not (Reinink et al., 1990; Riemann, Wiegand, and Berger, 1991; Haug, 1992). In general, depressed patients whose mood remains stable throughout the day will probably not benefit from sleep deprivation, whereas those whose mood fluctuates probably will. The patients who are most likely to respond are those who feel depressed in the morning but then gradually feel better as the day progresses. In these people sleep deprivation appears to prevent the depressogenic effects of sleep from taking place and simply permits the trend to continue. If you examine Figure 15.13, you can see that the responders were already feeling better by the end of the day. This improvement continued through the sleepless night and during the following day. The next night they were permitted to sleep normally, and their depression was back the following morning. As Wu and Bunney note, these data are consistent with the hypothesis that sleep produces a substance with a depressogenic effect. (See *Figure 15.13.*)

The antidepressant effects of REM sleep deprivation and that of total sleep deprivation appear to be different; one is slow and long-lasting, whereas the other is fast and short-lived. In addition, total sleep deprivation can even trigger an episode of mania in patients with bipolar disorder (Wehr, 1992). (Even nondepressed people often report feeling "high" after spending a night without sleep.) The fact that a person's mood can so quickly be altered suggests that it would be worthwhile to look for physiological changes before and after sleep deprivation to try to identify those that may play a role in the control of mood.

Although total sleep deprivation is not a practical method for treating depression (it is impossible to keep people awake indefinitely), several studies suggest that *partial* sleep deprivation can hasten the beneficial effects of antidepressant drugs (Szuba, Baxter, and Fairbanks, 1991; Leibenluft and Wehr, 1992). According to Szuba et al., the best method is to awaken patients at 2:00 A.M. and keep them awake until 9:00 P.M. Some investigators have found that *intermittent* total sleep deprivation (say, twice a week for four weeks) can have beneficial results (Papadimitriou et al., 1993).

Riemann et al. (1996) found that advancing the time of day that depressed patients sleep can prolong the beneficial effects of total sleep deprivation. Patients who slept between 5 P.M. and midnight after total sleep deprivation were less likely to relapse than were those who slept between 11 P.M. and 6 A.M. The early sleepers also showed a more normal distribution of REM sleep.

Seasonal Affective Disorder

Yet another phenomenon relates depression to sleep and waking—or, more specifically, to the mechanisms responsible for circadian rhythms. Some people become depressed during the winter season, when days are short and nights are long (Rosenthal et al., 1984). The symptoms of this form of depression, called **seasonal affective disorder,** are somewhat different from those of major depression; both forms include lethargy and sleep disturbances, but seasonal depression includes a craving for carbohydrate and an accompanying weight gain. (As you will recall, peo-

Seasonal affective disorder A mood disorder characterized by depression, lethargy, sleep disturbances, and craving for carbohydrates during the winter season when days are short.

ple with major depression tend to lose their appetite.) A much smaller percentage of the population becomes depressed during the summer, apparently because of the heat (Wehr, Sack, and Rosenthal, 1987). People with **summer depression** are more likely to sleep less, lose their appetite, and lose weight (Wehr et al., 1991).

Seasonal affective disorder can be treated by **phototherapy:** exposing people to bright light for several hours a day (Rosenthal et al., 1985; Stinson and Thompson, 1990). As you will recall, circadian rhythms of sleep and wakefulness are controlled by the activity of the suprachiasmatic nucleus of the hypothalamus. Light serves as a *zeitgeber;* that is, it synchronizes the activity of the biological clock to the day–night cycle. One possibility is that people with seasonal affective disorder require a stronger-than-normal zeitgeber to reset their biological clock. However, two studies found that light therapy had an antidepressant effect no matter what time of day it occurred (Wirz-Justice et al., 1993; Meesters et al., 1995). If the light were simply serving as a zeitgeber, we would expect different effects depending on the time of day the phototherapy occurred.

Phototherapy has even been found to help patients with unipolar depression. Neumeister et al. (1996) found that patients with unipolar depression who responded to total sleep deprivation were less likely to relapse later if they received phototherapy in the early morning and late afternoon. Patients who sat in front of a dim light (the placebo treatment) quickly relapsed.

Phototherapy appears to be a treatment without any adverse side effects besides a higher electric bill. According to a study by Wirz-Justice et al. (1996), even this side effect can be avoided. They found that a one-hour walk outside each morning reduced the symptoms of seasonal affective disorder. The investigators note that even on an overcast winter day, the early morning sky provides considerably more illumination than normal indoor artificial lighting, so a walk outside increases a person's exposure to light. (The exercise probably doesn't hurt, either.)

Seasonal affective disorder, which is provoked by the long nights and short days of winter, can be treated by daily exposure to bright lights.

INTERIM SUMMARY

The major affective disorders include bipolar affective disorder, with its cyclical episodes of mania and depression, and unipolar depression. Heritability studies suggest that genetic anomalies are at least partly responsible for these disorders. Depression can be successfully treated by MAO inhibitors, drugs that block the reuptake of norepinephrine and serotonin, electroconvulsive therapy, and sleep deprivation. Bipolar disorder can be successfully treated by lithium salts. Lithium appears to stabilize neural transmission, especially in serotonin-secreting neurons. It may do so by interfering with the production of a certain category of second messengers.

The therapeutic effect of noradrenergic and serotonergic agonists and the depressant effect of reserpine, a monoaminergic antagonist, suggested the monoamine hypothesis of depression. Several other lines of evidence support this hypothesis. Low levels of 5-HIAA (a serotonin metabolite) in the cerebrospinal fluid correlate with attempts at suicide. Depletion of tryptophan (the precursor of 5-HT) in the brain reverses the therapeutic effects of antidepressant medication, which lends further support to the conclusion that 5-HT plays a role in mood. Functional imaging studies suggest that depression involves a decrease in the dorsolateral prefrontal cortex, orbitofrontal cortex, and thalamus.

Summer depression A mood disorder characterized by depression, sleep disturbances, and loss of appetite.

Phototherapy Treatment of seasonal affective disorder by daily exposure to bright light.

Several studies have looked for abnormalities in the brains of depressed patients. In general, patients with unipolar depression show abnormalities in the prefrontal cortex, basal ganglia, and cerebellum, while patients with bipolar disorder show abnormalities in the cerebellum and (perhaps) temporal lobe.

Sleep disturbances are characteristic of affective disorders. In fact, total sleep deprivation rapidly (but temporarily) reduces depression in many people, and selective deprivation of REM sleep does so slowly (but more lastingly). In addition, almost all effective antidepressant treatments suppress REM sleep. Finally, a specific form of depression, seasonal affective disorder, can be treated by exposure to bright light, the zeitgeber that resets the biological clock. Clearly, the mood disorders are somehow linked to biological rhythms.

■ THOUGHT QUESTIONS

A television commentator, talking in particular about the suicide of a young pop star and in general about unhappy youth, asked with exasperation, "What would all these young people be doing if they had real problems like a Depression, World War II, or Vietnam?" People with severe depression often try to hide their pain because they fear others will scoff at them and say that they have nothing to feel unhappy about. If depression is caused by abnormal brain functioning, are these remarks justified? How would you feel if you were severely depressed and people close to you berated you for feeling so sad and told you to snap out of it and quit feeling sorry for yourself?

■ ANXIETY DISORDERS

As we saw earlier in this chapter, the affective disorders are characterized by unrealistic extremes of emotion: depression or elation (mania). The **anxiety disorders** are characterized by unrealistic, unfounded fear and anxiety. This section describes two of the anxiety disorders that appear to have biological causes: panic disorder and obsessive-compulsive disorder.

Panic Disorder

Description

People with **panic disorder** suffer from episodic attacks of acute anxiety—periods of acute and unremitting terror that grip them for variable lengths of time, from a few seconds to a few hours. The estimated incidence of panic disorder is between 1 and 2 percent of the population (Robbins et al., 1984). The disorder usually has its onset in young adulthood; it rarely begins after age thirty-five (Woodruff, Guze, and Clayton, 1972).

The basic symptoms of panic attack appear to be universal. For example, these symptoms are similar in residents of the United States, Puerto Rico, Germany, Lebanon, Korea, and New Zealand (Weissman et al., 1995). Panic attacks include many physical symptoms, such as shortness of breath, clammy sweat, irregularities in heartbeat, dizziness, faintness, and feelings of unreality. The victim of a panic attack often feels that he or she is going to die. Anxiety is a normal reaction to many stresses of life, and none of us is completely free from it. In fact, anxiety is undoubtedly useful in causing us to be more alert and to take important things seriously. However, the anxiety that we all feel from time to time is obviously different from the intense fear and terror experienced by a person gripped by a panic attack.

Between panic attacks, many people with panic disorder suffer from **anticipatory anxiety**—the fear that another panic attack will strike them. This anticipatory anxi-

Anxiety disorder A psychological disorder characterized by tension, overactivity of the autonomic nervous system, expectation of an impending disaster, and continuous vigilance for danger.

Panic disorder A disorder characterized by episodic periods of symptoms such as shortness of breath, irregularities in heartbeat, and other autonomic symptoms, accompanied by intense fear.

Anticipatory anxiety A fear of having a panic attack; may lead to the development of agoraphobia.

ety often leads to the development of a serious phobic disorder: **agoraphobia** (*agora* means "open space"). According to the American Psychiatric Association's official *Diagnostic and Statistical Manual IV*, agoraphobia associated with panic attacks is a fear of "being in places or situations from which escape might be difficult (or embarrassing) or in which help might not be available in the event of . . . a Panic Attack." Agoraphobia can be severely disabling; some people with this disorder have stayed inside their houses or apartments for years, afraid to venture outside. Although the incidence of panic disorder without agoraphobia is equal in men and women, women are twice as likely to develop panic disorder with agoraphobia (Bradwejn and Koszycki, 1994).

Possible Causes

Because the physical symptoms of panic attacks are so overwhelming, many patients reject the suggestion that they have a mental disorder, insisting that their problem is medical. In fact, a considerable amount of evidence suggests that panic disorder may have biological origins. First, the disorder appears to be hereditary; there is a higher concordance rate for the disorder between monozygotic twins than between dizygotic twins (Slater and Shields, 1969), and almost 30 percent of the first-degree relatives of a person with panic disorder also have panic disorder (Crowe et al., 1983). The pattern of panic disorder within a family tree suggests that the disorder is caused by a single, dominant gene (Crowe et al., 1987).

Panic attacks can be triggered in people with a history of panic disorder by a variety of conditions that activate the autonomic nervous system. These include injections of lactic acid (a by-product of muscular activity) or yohimbine (an α_2 adrenoreceptor antagonist), ingesting caffeine, and breathing air containing an elevated amount of carbon dioxide (Stein and Uhde, 1994). Lactic acid and breathing carbon dioxide both increase heart rate and rate of respiration, just as exercise does; yohimbine and caffeine have direct pharmacological effects on the nervous system.

Susceptibility to lactate-induced panic attacks appears to be at least partly heritable. Balon et al. (1989) infused forty-five normal subjects with sodium lactate and found that ten of them had panic attacks. The investigators obtained their subjects' family history, using an interviewer who did not know which subjects had had panic attacks. They found that over 24 percent of the relatives of the subjects with the panic attacks themselves had a history of anxiety disorders, compared with fewer than 8 percent in the nonresponders.

Anxiety disorders are usually treated by a combination of behavior therapy and a benzodiazepine. As we saw in Chapter 4, benzodiazepines have strong anxiolytic ("anxiety-dissolving") effects. The brain possesses benzodiazepine receptors, which are part of the $GABA_A$ receptor complex. When a benzodiazepine agonist binds with its receptor, it increases the sensitivity of the GABA binding site and produces an anxiolytic effect. On the other hand, when a benzodiazepine antagonist occupies the receptor site, it *reduces* the sensitivity of the GABA binding site and *increases* anxiety. Anxiety disorders, then, might be caused by a diminished number of benzodiazepine receptors or by the secretion of a neuromodulator that blocks the benzodiazepine binding site at the $GABA_A$ receptor.

As you read earlier in this chapter, serotonin appears to play a role in depression. Some evidence suggests that serotonin may play a role in anxiety disorders, too. Even though the symptoms of panic disorder and obsessive-compulsive disorder (described in the next section) are very different, drugs that serve as serotonin agonists (such as fluoxetine) have been successfully used to treat both disorders (Coplan, Gorman, and Klein, 1992). You will recall that short-term tryptophan depletion, caused by a low-tryptophan diet followed by the drinking of an amino acid "cocktail" that is deficient in tryptophan, rapidly increases the symptoms of depression in people with a history of unipolar depression. (The tryptophan depletion interferes with the synthesis of 5-HT.) Goddard et al. (1994) found that tryptophan depletion had no effects in

Agoraphobia A fear of being away from home or other protected places.

people with a history of panic disorder. These results have yet to be reconciled with the fact that serotonin agonists such as fluoxetine reduce the symptoms of panic disorder.

Obsessive-Compulsive Disorder

Description

As the name implies, people with an **obsessive-compulsive disorder** suffer from **obsessions**—thoughts that will not leave them—and **compulsions**—behaviors that they cannot keep from performing. Obsessions are seen in a variety of mental disorders, including schizophrenia. However, unlike schizophrenics, people with obsessive-compulsive disorder recognize that their thoughts and behaviors are senseless and desperately wish that they would go away. Compulsions often become more and more demanding until they interfere with people's careers and daily lives.

The incidence of obsessive-compulsive disorder is 1 to 2 percent. Females are slightly more likely than males to have this diagnosis. Like panic disorder, obsessive-compulsive disorder most commonly begins in young adulthood (Robbins et al., 1984). Cross-cultural studies find that the symptoms of this disorder are similar in various racial and ethnic groups (Akhtar et al., 1975; Khanna and Channabasavanna, 1987; Hinjo et al., 1989). People with this disorder are unlikely to marry, perhaps because of the common obsessional fear of dirt and contamination or because of the shame associated with the rituals they are compelled to perform, which causes them to avoid social contacts (Turner, Beidel, and Nathan, 1985).

Most compulsions fall into one of four categories: *counting, checking, cleaning,* and *avoidance.* For example, people might repeatedly check burners on the stove to see that they are off and windows and locks to be sure that they are locked. Davison and Neale (1974) reported the case of a woman who washed her hands more than five hundred times a day because she feared being contaminated by germs. The hand washing persisted even when her hands became covered with painful sores. Other people meticulously clean their apartment or endlessly wash, dry, and fold their clothes. Some become afraid to leave home because they fear contamination, and they refuse to touch other members of their family. If they do accidentally become "contaminated," they usually have lengthy purification rituals. (See *Table 15.3.*)

Some investigators believe that the compulsive behaviors seen in obsessive-compulsive disorder are forms of species-typical behaviors—for example, grooming, cleaning, and attention toward sources of potential danger—that are released from normal control mechanisms by a brain dysfunction (Wise and Rapoport, 1988). Fiske and Haslam (1997) suggest that the behaviors seen in obsessive-compulsive disorder are simply pathological examples of a natural behavioral tendency to develop and practice social rituals. For example, people perform cultural rituals to mark transitions or changes in social status, to diagnose or treat illnesses, to restore relationships with deities, or to ensure the success of hunting or planting. These rituals define the status of individuals and their relationships with other members of the society, and they provide comfort in knowing that the structure of the society approves the transition or change in status or is doing all it can to avert misfortune. Consider the following scenario (from Fiske and Haslam, 1997):

> Imagine that you are traveling in an unfamiliar country. Going out for a walk, you observe a man dressed in red, standing on a red mat in a red-painted gateway. . . . He utters the same prayer six times. He brings out six basins of water and meticulously arranges them in a symmetrical configuration in front of the gateway. Then he washes his hands six times in each of the six basins, using precisely the same motions each time. As he does this, he repeats the same phrase, occasionally tapping his right finger on his earlobe. Through your interpreter, you ask him what he is doing. He replies that there are dangerous polluting substances in the ground, . . . [and that] he must purify himself or something terrible will happen. He seems eager to tell you about his concerns. (p. 211)

Obsessive-compulsive disorder
A mental disorder characterized by obsessions and compulsions.

Obsession An unwanted thought or idea with which a person is preoccupied.

Compulsion The feeling that one is obliged to perform a behavior, even if one prefers not to do so.

TABLE 15.3 Reported Obsessions and Compulsions of Child and Adolescent Patients

Major Presenting Symptoms	Percent Reporting Symptom at Initial Interview
OBSESSION	
Concern or disgust with bodily wastes or secretions (urine, stool, saliva), dirt, germs, environmental toxins, etc.	43
Fear something terrible might happen (fire, death/illness of loved one, self, or others)	24
Concern or need for symmetry, order, or exactness	17
Scrupulosity (excessive praying or religious concerns out of keeping with patient's background)	13
Lucky/unlucky numbers	18
Forbidden or perverse sexual thoughts, images, or impulses	14
Intrusive nonsense sounds, words, or music	11
COMPULSION	
Excessive or ritualized hand washing, showering, bathing, toothbrushing, or grooming	85
Repeating rituals (going in/out of door, up/down from chair, etc.)	51
Checking doors, locks, stove, appliances, car brakes, etc.	46
Cleaning and other rituals to remove contact with contaminants	23
Touching	20
Ordering/arranging	17
Measures to prevent harm to self or others (e.g., hanging clothes a certain way)	16
Counting	18
Hoarding/collecting	11
Miscellaneous rituals (e.g., licking, spitting, special dress pattern)	26

Source: From Rapoport, J.L. *Journal of the American Medical Association,* 1988, *260,* 2888–2890.

Why is the man acting this way? Is he a priest following a sacred ritual, or does he have obsessive-compulsive disorder? Without knowing more about the spiritual rituals of the man's culture, we cannot say. Fiske and Haslam compared the features of obsessive-compulsive disorder and other psychological disorders in descriptions of rituals, work, or other activities in fifty-two cultures. They found that the features of obsessive-compulsive disorder (for example, observing lucky or unlucky numbers or colors with special significance, repeating activities, ordering or arranging things in specific configurations, or paying special attention to thresholds or entrances) were found in rituals in these cultures. The features of other psychological disorders were much less common. On the whole, the evidence suggests that the symptoms of obsessive-compulsive disorder represent an exaggeration of natural human tendencies.

Possible Causes

Evidence is beginning to accumulate suggesting that obsessive-compulsive disorder may have a genetic origin. Family studies have found that this disorder is associated with neurological disorders that appear during childhood (Pauls and Leckman, 1986; Pauls et al., 1986). One of them, **Tourette's syndrome,** is characterized by mus-

Tourette's syndrome A neurological disorder characterized by tics and involuntary vocalizations and sometimes by compulsive uttering of obscenities and repetition of the utterances of others.

cular and vocal tics: facial grimaces, squatting, pacing, twirling, barking, sniffing, coughing, grunting, or repeating specific words (especially vulgarities). Leonard et al. (1992a, 1992b) found that many patients with obsessive-compulsive disorder had tics and that many patients with Tourette's syndrome showed obsessions and compulsions. Both groups of investigators believe that the two disorders are produced by the same underlying causes, which may be the result of a single, dominant gene. It is not clear why some people with the faulty gene develop Tourette's syndrome early in childhood and others develop obsessive-compulsive disorder later in life.

As with schizophrenia, not all cases of obsessive-compulsive disorder have a genetic origin; the disorder sometimes occurs after brain damage caused by various means, such as birth trauma, encephalitis, and head trauma (Hollander et al., 1990; Berthier et al., 1996). In particular, the symptoms appear to be associated with damage to or dysfunction of the basal ganglia, cingulate gyrus, and prefrontal cortex (Giedd et al., 1995; Robinson et al., 1995).

Several investigators have found that obsessive-compulsive disorder sometimes accompanies Huntington's chorea and Sydenham's chorea, both of which involve degeneration of the basal ganglia (Swedo et al., 1989a; Cummings and Cunningham, 1992). **Sydenham's chorea** usually occurs in childhood or adolescence, after a group A β-hemolytic streptococcal infection (a "strep throat"). Like rheumatic fever (which usually involves the heart valves), Sydenham's chorea is an autoimmune disease, in which the patient's immune system attacks and damages certain tissues of the body—in this case, parts of the brain. Presumably, the obsessive and compulsive symptoms of Sydenham's chorea are caused by this damage. Husby et al. (1976) found evidence that the immune system of patients with Sydenham's chorea contained antibodies against proteins found in the subthalamic nucleus and parts of the basal ganglia.

Several studies using PET scans have found evidence of increased activity in the frontal lobes and cingulate gyrus (Baxter et al., 1989; Swedo et al., 1989b; Rubin et al., 1992; Lucey et al., 1997). Some studies have found evidence of decreased activity in the basal ganglia (consistent with the lesion studies I cited earlier), while others have reported an *increase*. Several studies have use functional imaging to measure regional brain activity of patients with obsessive-compulsive disorder before and after successful treatment with drugs or behavior therapy (Swedo et al., 1992; Rubin et al., 1995; Schwartz et al., 1996). In general, the improvements in a patient's symptoms were correlated with a reduction in the activity of the prefrontal cortex. These results provide especially strong evidence that the prefrontal cortex plays an important role in this disorder. And the fact that behavior therapy and drug therapy produced similar results is especially remarkable: It indicates that very different procedures may be bringing about physiological changes that alleviate a serious mental disorder.

Breiter et al. (1996) performed a particularly intriguing study with a group of patients with obsessive-compulsive disorder. They used functional MRI to measure their subjects' regional cerebral metabolism before and after having them hold some "contaminated" items. These items supposedly included tissue soaked in toilet water, plastic bags from contaminated waste barrels, and tissues into which someone had blown his nose. They also gave them some innocuous stimuli, including tissue soaked in clean water and new plastic bags. In fact, *all* the items the experimenters actually put in the subjects' hands were clean, but the switch was made out of the subjects' sight, so they believed that they were handling some items that were contaminated. Apparently, the act was convincing, because the subjects were quite disturbed by the "contaminated" objects. When the subjects were holding the "contaminated" items, the anterior cingulate cortex, the basal ganglia, the amygdala, and several regions of the prefrontal cortex showed increased activity. (You may be wondering how the experimenters induced the subjects to hold the "contaminated" items. I did, too, but the authors did not explain their methods of persuasion.)

Sydenham's chorea An autoimmune disease that attacks parts of the brain including the basal ganglia and produces involuntary movements and often the symptoms of obsessive-compulsive disorder.

As we saw in Chapter 10, the prefrontal cortex (particularly the orbitofrontal cortex) and the cingulate cortex are involved in emotional reactions, so it is not surprising to learn that they might be implicated in obsessive-compulsive disorder. In fact, some patients with severe obsessive-compulsive disorder have been successfully treated with surgical destruction of specific fiber bundles in the subcortical frontal lobe, including the cingulum bundle (which connects the prefrontal and cingulate cortex with the limbic cortex of the temporal lobe) and a region that contains fibers that connect the basal ganglia with the prefrontal cortex (Ballantine et al., 1987; Mindus, Rasmussen, and Lindquist, 1994). Of course, neurosurgery cannot be undone, so such procedures must be considered only as a last resort.

In one extraordinary case a patient performed his own psychosurgery. Solyom, Turnbull, and Wilensky (1987) reported the case of a young man with a serious obsessive-compulsive disorder whose ritual hand washing and other behaviors made it impossible for him to continue his schooling or lead a normal life. Finding that his life was no longer worthwhile, he decided to end it. He placed the muzzle of a .22-caliber rifle in his mouth and pulled the trigger. The bullet entered the base of the brain and damaged the frontal lobes. He survived and was amazed to find that his compulsions were gone. Fortunately, the damage did not disrupt his ability to make or execute plans; he went back to school and completed his education and now has a job. His IQ was unchanged. Ordinary surgery would have been less hazardous and messy, but it could hardly have been more successful.

By far, the most effective treatment of obsessive-compulsive disorder is drug therapy. To date, three effective drugs have been found: clomipramine, fluoxetine, and fluvoxamine. Although these drugs are also effective antidepressants, their antidepressant action does not seem to be related to their ability to relieve the symptoms of obsessive-compulsive disorder. For example, Leonard et al. (1989) compared the effects of clomipramine and desipramine (an antidepressant drug that does not affect the reuptake of serotonin) on the symptoms of children and adolescents with severe obsessive-compulsive disorder. For three weeks, all patients received a placebo. Then for five weeks, half of them received clomipramine (CMI) and the other half received desipramine (DMI) on a double-blind basis. At the end of that time the drugs were switched. As Figure 15.14 shows, CMI was a much more effective drug; in fact, when the patients were switched from CMI to DMI, their symptoms got worse. (See *Figure 15.14*.)

The importance of serotonergic activity in inhibiting compulsive behaviors is underscored by three interesting compulsions: trichotillomania, onychophagia, and acral lick dermatitis. *Trichotillomania* is compulsive hair pulling. People with this disorder (almost always females) often spend hours each night pulling hairs out one by one, sometimes eating them (Rapoport, 1991). *Onychophagia* is compulsive nail biting, which in its extreme can cause severe damage to the ends of the fingers. (For those who are sufficiently agile, toenail biting is not uncommon.) Double-blind studies have shown that both of these disorders can successfully be treated by clomipramine, the drug of choice for obsessive-compulsive disorder (Leonard et al., 1992).

Acral lick dermatitis is a disease of dogs, not humans. Some dogs will continuously lick at a part of their body, especially the wrist or ankle (called the *carpus* and the *hock*). The licking removes the hair and often erodes away the skin as well. The disorder seems to be genetic; it is seen almost ex-

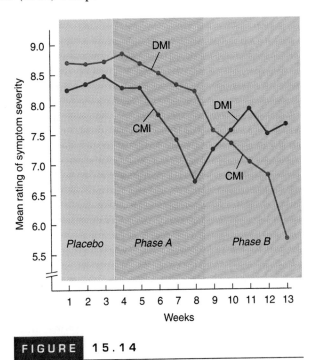

FIGURE 15.14

Mean rating of symptom severity of patients with obsessive-compulsive disorder treated with desipramine (DMI) or clomipramine (CMI).

(From Leonard, H.L., Swedo, S.E., Rapoport, J.L., Koby, E.V., Lenane, M.C., Cheslow, D.L., and Hamburger, S.D. Archives of General Psychiatry, 1989, 46, 1088–1092. Copyright 1989, American Medical Association.)

clusively in large breeds such as Great Danes, Labrador retrievers, and German shepherds, and it runs in families. A double-blind study found that clomipramine reduces this compulsive behavior (Rapoport, Ryland, and Kriete, 1992). At first, when I read the term "double-blind" in the report by Rapoport and her colleagues, I was amused to think that the investigators were careful not to let the dogs learn whether they were receiving clomipramine or a placebo. Then I realized that, of course, it was the dogs' owners who had to be kept in the dark.

INTERIM SUMMARY

The anxiety disorders severely disrupt some people's lives. People with panic disorder periodically have panic attacks, during which they experience intense symptoms of autonomic activity and often feel as if they are going to die. Frequently, panic attacks lead to the development of agoraphobia, an avoidance of being away from a safe place, such as home. Panic disorder is at least partly heritable, which suggests that it has biological causes.

Panic attacks can be triggered in many susceptible people by conditions that activate the autonomic nervous system, such as an caffeine, yohimbine, injection of lactate, or inhalation of air containing an elevated amount of carbon dioxide. Panic attacks can be alleviated by the administration of a benzodiazepine, a finding that suggests that the disorder may involve decreased numbers of benzodiazepine receptors or an inadequate secretion of an endogenous benzodiazepine agonist.

Obsessive-compulsive disorder is characterized by obsessions—unwanted thoughts—and compulsions—uncontrollable behaviors, especially those involving cleanliness and attention to danger. Some investigators believe that these behaviors represent overactivity of species-typical behavioral tendencies.

Obsessive-compulsive disorder has a heritable basis and is related to Tourette's syndrome, a neurological disorder characterized by tics and strange verbalizations. It can also be caused by brain damage at birth, encephalitis, and head injuries, especially when the basal ganglia are involved. PET scans indicate that people with obsessive-compulsive disorder tend to show increased glucose metabolism in the frontal lobes and cingulate gyrus, structures that are probably involved in emotional reactions. The destruction of the cingulum bundle, which links them with the anterior temporal lobe, reduces the symptoms, as do drugs such as clomipramine, which specifically block the reuptake of serotonin. Some investigators believe that clomipramine and related drugs alleviate the symptoms of obsessive-compulsive disorder by increasing the activity of serotonergic pathways that play an inhibitory role on species-typical behaviors. Three other compulsions, hair pulling, nail biting, and (in dogs) acral lick syndrome, are also suppressed by clomipramine.

THOUGHT QUESTIONS

Most reasonable people would agree that a person with mental disorders cannot be blamed for his or her thoughts and behaviors. Most of us would sympathize with someone whose life is disrupted by panic attacks or obsessions and compulsions, and we would not see their plight as a failure of willpower. After all, whether these disorders are caused by traumatic experiences or brain abnormalities (or both), the afflicted person has not chosen to be the way he or she is. But what about less dramatic examples: Should we blame people for their shyness or hostility or other maladaptive personality traits? If, as many psychologists believe, people's personality characteristics are largely determined by their heredity (and thus by the structure and chemistry of their brains), what are the implications for our concepts of "blame" and "personal responsibility"?

Tardive Dyskinesia

As a result of taking an antipsychotic medication, Larry, the schizophrenic man described in the Prologue, developed a neurological disorder called *tardive dyskinesia*. *Tardus* means "slow," and *dyskinesia* means "faulty movement"; thus, tardive dyskinesia is a late-developing movement disorder. (In Larry's case it actually came rather early.)

Tardive dyskinesia appears to be the opposite of Parkinson's disease. Whereas patients with Parkinson's disease have difficulty moving, patients with tardive dyskinesia are unable to stop moving. Indeed, dyskinesia commonly occurs when patients with Parkinson's disease receive too much L-DOPA. In schizophrenic patients, tardive dyskinesia is made *worse* by discontinuing the antipsychotic drug and is improved by increasing the dose. The symptoms are also intensified by dopamine agonists such as L-DOPA or amphetamine. Therefore, the disorder appears to be produced by an overstimulation of dopamine receptors. But if it is, why should it be originally caused by antipsychotic drugs, which are dopamine *antagonists*?

The answer seems to be provided by a phenomenon known as *supersensitivity*. Supersensitivity is a compensatory mechanism in which some types of receptors become more sensitive if they are inhibited for a period of time by a drug that blocks them. For tardive dyskinesia the relevant dopamine receptors are in the caudate nucleus, an important component of the motor system. (You will recall that Parkinson's disease is caused by degeneration of dopamine-secreting neurons that connect the substantia nigra with the caudate nucleus.) When these receptors are chronically blocked by an antipsychotic drug, they become supersensitive. In some cases the supersensitivity becomes so great that it overcompensates for the effects of the drug, causing the neurological symptoms to occur.

Fortunately, the wish expressed by Larry's physician has come true. Researchers *have* discovered a medication that treats the symptoms of schizophrenia without producing neurological side effects, and early indications suggest that tardive dyskinesia may become a thing of the past. Better yet, this drug, called *clozapine*, reduces the psychotic symptoms of many patients who are not significantly helped by the older antipsychotic drugs.

As you have learned in this chapter, most investigators believe that the therapeutic effects of antipsychotic drugs occur because the drugs block dopamine receptors in the nucleus accumbens and the prefrontal cortex. The fact that the drugs also block dopamine receptors in the caudate nucleus is unrelated to its therapeutic effects and, as you have seen, can produce neurological side effects. Thus, the ideal antipsychotic drug would inhibit dopaminergic transmission in the nucleus accumbens and prefrontal cortex but not in the caudate nucleus. And that, apparently, is just what clozapine does. Several studies using laboratory animals have shown that clozapine profoundly affects activity of the mesolimbic dopamine system without affecting the nigrostriatal dopamine system. For example, Chen, Paredes, and Gardner (1991) found that chronic daily treatment with clozapine reduced the release of dopamine (measured by means of microdialysis) in the nucleus accumbens but not in the caudate nucleus.

Clozapine does not appear to produce neurological side effects in human patients (Bruhwyler, Chleide, and Mercier, 1990). Although not enough time has elapsed to be sure what the drug's long-term effects will be, researchers hope that the drug will not produce tardive dyskinesia either. In addition, clozapine appears to be even more effective than other antipsychotic drugs in helping hard-to-treat patients. In a double-blind study, Kane et al. (1988) compared the effectiveness of clozapine and chlorpromazine (Thorazine, the drug Larry was taking) on 268 patients with severe schizophrenia and a proven history of poor response to antipsychotic medication. The study found that in six weeks of treatment, 30 percent of the clozapine-treated patients improved, compared with only 4 percent of the chlorpromazine-treated patients.

Clozapine is not yet routinely administered to all schizophrenic patients. For one thing, researchers discovered during early clinical trials that a small percentage of individuals taking the drug develop *agranulocytosis*, a life-threatening suppression of the production of white blood cells. Other antipsychotic drugs can cause agranulocytosis, but apparently the incidence of this disease is higher with clozapine. For this reason the white blood cell count of patients who receive the drug is carefully monitored.

The story is not over yet. The biochemical action of clozapine is different from that of other antipsychotic drugs, and researchers are working on the development of similar drugs that may prove to be even more effective in treating schizophrenia, produce no neurological side effects, and avoid the problem of agranulocytosis altogether.

KEY CONCEPTS

SCHIZOPHRENIA

1. Because a tendency to develop schizophrenia is heritable, biological factors may be important.
2. The effects of dopamine agonists and antagonists on the positive symptoms of schizophrenia give support to the dopamine hypothesis.
3. Because evidence of brain damage is found in people who display the negative symptoms of schizophrenia, some researchers believe that a pathological process, perhaps triggered by a virus, is responsible for schizophrenia.

MAJOR AFFECTIVE DISORDERS

4. The major affective disorders include major depression and bipolar disorder. Evidence suggests that both types are heritable.
5. The monoamine hypothesis was suggested by the findings that dopamine agonists and antagonists affect the symptoms of the affective disorders, and that depressed people tend to have a low level of a serotonin metabolite in their CSF.

6. The affective disorders are related to sleep disturbances and can be relieved by REM sleep deprivation or total sleep deprivation. In addition, some people suffer from seasonal affective disorder. Thus, affective disorders may be caused by malfunctions of the neural systems that regulate circadian rhythms.

ANXIETY DISORDERS

7. The two most serious anxiety disorders are panic disorder and obsessive-compulsive disorder. Both disorders appear to have a strong hereditary component.
8. Panic disorder is treated with benzodiazepines and may involve abnormalities in these receptors. It is also treated with serotonin agonists such as fluoxetine.
9. Obsessive-compulsive disorder may be related to the species-typical behaviors of grooming, cleaning, and attention to danger. It is treated with clomipramine, a serotonin agonist, which has inhibitory effects on these behaviors in laboratory animals.

SUGGESTED READINGS

Gershon, E.S., and Cloninger, C.R. *New Genetic Approaches to Mental Disorders*. Washington, DC: American Psychiatric Press, 1994.

Goodwin, D.W., and Guze, S.B. *Psychiatric Diagnosis*, 5th ed. New York: Oxford University Press, 1996.

Hollander, E. *Obsessive-Compulsive Related Disorders*. Washington, DC: American Psychiatric Press, 1993.

Mednick, S.A. *Fetal Neural Development and Adult Schizophrenia*. New York: Cambridge University Press, 1991.

Strange, P.G. *Brain Biochemistry and Brain Disorders*. Oxford, England: Oxford University Press, 1992.

Yudofsky, S.C., and Hales, R.E. *The American Psychiatric Press Textbook of Neuropsychiatry*. Washington, DC: American Psychiatric Press, 1997.

16

Autistic Disorder, Stress Disorders, and Drug Abuse

LEARNING OBJECTIVES

1. Describe the symptoms and possible causes of autism.

2. Describe the physiological responses to stress and their effects on health.

3. Discuss some of the long-term effects of stress, including posttraumatic stress disorder and cardiovascular disease, and describe the role of the coping response.

4. Discuss psychoneuroimmunology and the interactions between stress and the immune system.

5. Review the general characteristics and definitions of addiction.

6. Describe two common features of addictive drugs: positive and negative reinforcement.

7. Review the neural basis of the reinforcing effects and withdrawal effects of opiates.

8. Describe the behavioral and pharmacological effects of cocaine, amphetamine, and nicotine.

9. Describe the behavioral and pharmacological effects of alcohol, barbiturates, and cannabis.

10. Describe research on the role that heredity plays in addiction in humans.

11. Discuss methods of therapy for drug abuse.

A Sudden Craving

John was beginning to feel that perhaps he would be able to get his life back together. It looked like his drug habit was going to be licked. He had started taking drugs several years ago. At first, he had used them only on special occasions—mostly on weekends with his friends—but heroin proved to be his undoing. One of his acquaintances had introduced him to the needle, and he had found the rush so blissful that he couldn't wait a whole week for his next fix. Soon he was shooting up daily. Shortly after that, he lost his job and, to support his habit, began earning money through car theft and small-time drug dealing. As time went on, he needed more and more heroin at shorter and shorter intervals, which necessitated even more money. Eventually, he was arrested and convicted of selling heroin to an undercover agent.

The judge gave John the choice of prison or a drug rehabilitation program, and he chose the latter. Soon after starting the program, he realized that he was relieved to have been caught. Now that he was clean and could reflect on his life, he realized what would have become of him had he continued to take drugs. Withdrawal from heroin was not an experience he would want to live through again, but it turned out not to be as bad as he had feared. The counselors in his program told him to avoid his old neighborhood and to break contact with his old acquaintances, and he followed their advice. He had been clean for eight weeks, he had a job, and he had met a woman who really seemed sympathetic. He knew that he hadn't completely kicked his habit, because every now and then, despite

his best intentions, he found himself thinking about the wonderful glow that heroin provided him. But things were definitely looking up.

Then one day, while walking home from work, he turned a corner and saw a new poster plastered on the wall of a building. The poster, produced by an anti-drug agency, showed all sorts of drug paraphernalia in full color: glassine envelopes with white powder spilling out of them, syringes, needles, a spoon and candle used to heat and dissolve the drug. He was seized with a sudden, intense compulsion to take some heroin. He closed his eyes, trying to will the feeling away, but all he could feel was his churning stomach and his trembling limbs, and all he could think about was getting a fix. He hopped on a bus and went back to his old neighborhood.

Chapter 15 discussed mental disorders characterized by maladaptive emotions and thought processes. This chapter considers three more disorders with a physiological basis: autistic disorder, stress disorders, and drug abuse. Autistic disorder appears to be a hereditary disorder that affects development of the brain. Most autistic children show mental retardation, but some do not. However, all of them exhibit severe deficiencies in social behavior; some do not even seem to recognize the existence of people other than themselves.

Although we tend to think of stress disorders and drug abuse as the consequences of modern civilization, stress and drugs have probably been familiar to our species from its very beginnings. Modern research has shown that communal living in groups of nonhuman primates generates much stress—so much that some members die of stress-related illness. And our ancestors long ago discovered that eating or smoking certain plants (or drinking fermented fruit juice) had interesting effects on one's perception, mood, and behavior. Of course, the development of modern chemistry has enabled us to refine drugs found in plant tissue or produce chemicals that are not normally found in nature, and some of these drugs are much more potent (and potentially addictive) than those our ancestors encountered.

AUTISTIC DISORDER

Description

When a child is born, the parents normally expect to love and cherish it and to be loved and cherished in return. Unfortunately, approximately 4 in every 10,000 infants are born with a disorder that impairs their ability to return their parents' affection. The symptoms of **autistic disorder** include a failure to develop normal social relations with other people, impaired development of communicative ability, and lack of imaginative ability. The syndrome was named and characterized by Kanner (1943), who chose the term (*auto,* "self," *-ism,* "condition") to refer to the child's apparent self-absorption. The disorder afflicts boys three times more often than girls.

Infants with autistic disorder do not seem to care if they are held, or they may arch their backs when picked up, as if they do not want to be held. They do not look or smile at their caregivers. If they are ill, hurt, or tired, they will not look to someone else for comfort. As they get older, they do not enter into social relationships with other children and avoid eye contact with them. Their language development is abnormal or even nonexistent. They often echo what is said to them, and they may refer to themselves as others do—in the second or third person. For example, they may say, "You want some milk?" to mean "I want some milk." They may learn words and phrases by rote, but they fail to use them productively and creatively. Those who do acquire reasonably good language skills talk about their own preoccupations, without regard for other people's interests. They usually interpret other people's speech literally. For example, when an autistic person is asked, "Can you pass the salt?" he may simply say "Yes"— and not because he is trying to be funny or sarcastic.

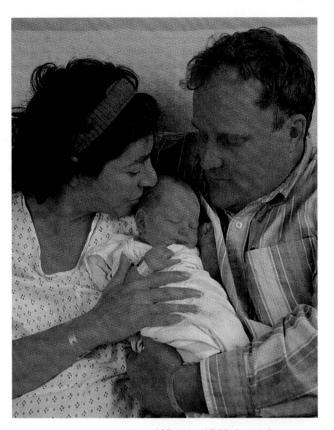

When a child is born, the parents normally expect to love and cherish it and to be loved and cherished in return.

Autistic people generally show abnormal interests and behaviors. For example, they may show stereotyped movements, such as flapping their hand back and forth or rocking back and forth. They may become obsessed with investigating objects, sniffing them, feeling their texture, or moving them back and forth. They may become attached to a particular object and insist on carrying it around with them. They may become preoccupied in lining up objects or in forming patterns with them, oblivious to everything else that is going on around them. They often insist on following precise routines and may become violently upset when they are hindered from doing so. They show no make-believe play and are uninterested in stories that involve fantasy. Although most autistic people are mentally retarded, not all are; and unlike most retarded people, they may be physically adept and graceful. Some have isolated skills, such as the ability to multiply two four-digit numbers very quickly, without apparent effort.

As you can see, autistic disorder includes affective, cognitive, and behavioral abnormalities. Frith, Morton, and Leslie (1991) suggest that the impaired socialization, communicative ability, and imagination that characterize autism stem from abnormalities in the brain that prevent the person from forming a "theory of mind." That is, the person is unable "to predict and explain the behavior of other humans in terms of their mental states" (p. 434). He or she just cannot see things from another person's point of view. As one autistic man complained, "Other people seem to have a special sense by which they can read other people's thoughts" (Rutter, 1983).

Frith and her colleagues cite an experiment of Baron-Cohen, Leslie, and Frith (1985), who administered the following test: Children were presented with a puppet show in which Sally put a marble in a basket and then left the room. The other puppet, Anne, took the marble out of the basket and put it in a box. When Sally returned, she wanted to play with the marble. Where will she look for it? (See *Figure 16.1.*) A normal four-year-old child will say, "In the basket," because he or she realizes that Sally

Autistic disorder A chronic disorder whose symptoms include failure to develop normal social relations with other people, impaired development of communicative ability, lack of imaginative ability, and repetitive, stereotyped movements.

FIGURE 16.1

A test of the ability of children to understand what another person might be thinking. Sally has a marble and puts it in a basket and leaves the room. Anne takes it out of the basket and puts it into the box. Sally returns and wants to play with her marble. Where will she look for it? Autistic children were more likely to say "in the box."

[Adapted from Frith, U., Morton, J., and Leslie, A.M. Trends in Neuroscience, 1991, 14, 433–438.]

does not know that Anne has moved it into the box. So will a retarded child with a mental age of five or six years. However, sixteen of twenty autistic children with a mean mental age of nine years said that Sally would look in the box. Apparently, they were unable to understand that people can hold beliefs different from their own.

Of course, this explanation does not account for all the symptoms of autism. For example, it does not explain why autistic children engage in stereotyped behaviors and seem to have a need for sameness in their environment. But it does suggest that a careful analysis of the syndrome may yield some hints about the underlying brain functions that are disrupted.

Possible Causes

When Kanner first described autism, he suggested that it was of biological origin; but not long afterward, influential clinicians argued that autism was learned. More precisely, it was taught—by cold, insensitive, distant, demanding, introverted parents. Bettelheim (1967) believed that autism was similar to the apathetic, withdrawn, and hopeless behavior seen in some of the survivors of the German concentration camps of World War II. You can imagine the guilt felt by parents who were told by a mental health professional that they were to blame for their child's pitiful condition. Some professionals saw the existence of autism as evidence for child abuse and advocated that autistic children be removed from their families and placed with foster parents.

Nowadays, researchers and mental health professionals almost universally believe that autism is caused by biological factors and that parents should be given help and sympathy, not blame. Careful studies have shown that the parents of autistic children are just as warm, sociable, and responsive as other parents (Cox et al., 1975). In addition, parents with one autistic child often raise one or more normal children. If the parents were at fault, we should expect *all* of their offspring to be autistic.

Heritability

Like all the mental disorders I have described so far, at least some forms of autism appear to be heritable. As we shall see, there appear to be *several* hereditary causes, as well as some nonhereditary ones. Between 2 and 3 percent of the siblings of people with autism are themselves autistic (Folstein and Piven, 1991; Bailey, 1993). That figure might seem low, but it is between 50 and 100 times the expected frequency of autism in the general population (4 cases per 10,000 people). As Jones and Szatmari (1988) note, many parents stop having children after an autistic child is born for fear of having another one with the same disorder; if they did not, the percentage of autistic siblings would be even larger.

The best evidence for genetic factors in autism comes from twin studies. These studies indicate that the concordance rate for monozygotic twins is as high as 96 percent, while the rate for dizygotic twins appears to be no higher than that for normal siblings (Folstein and Piven, 1991; Bailey et al., 1995). This difference is extremely large and indicates that autism is highly heritable. It also implies that autism is caused by a combination of several genes. Folstein and Piven also report that in the relatively few cases of monozygotic twins who are discordant for autism, the affected member was likely to have had a history of obstetric complications. This finding suggests that like schizophrenia and obsessive-compulsive disorder, autism can be caused by both hereditary and nonhereditary factors.

Investigators have suggested that autism is associated with some specific genetic disorders, such as phenylketonuria, Tourette's syndrome, and fragile X syndrome. **Phenylketonuria** (PKU) is caused by an inherited lack of an enzyme that converts phenylalanine (an amino acid) into tyrosine (another amino acid). Excessive amounts of phenylalanine in the blood interfere with the myelinization of neurons in the central nervous system, much of which takes place after birth. When PKU is diagnosed soon after birth, it can be treated by putting the infant on a low-phenylalanine diet. The diet keeps the blood level of phenylalanine low, and myelinization of the central nervous system takes place normally. However, if PKU is not diagnosed and an infant born with this disorder receives foods containing phenylalanine, the amino acid accumulates and the brain fails to develop normally. The result is a severe mental retardation—and, in some cases, autism (Lowe et al., 1980; Folstein and Rutter, 1988).

As we saw in Chapter 15, obsessive-compulsive disorder and Tourette's syndrome appear to be linked genetically. The same may be true for autism. As several investigators have noted, children with autism show obsessive interest in particular inanimate objects and engage in compulsive, stereotyped behaviors and rituals; thus, there is some similarity among the symptoms of these three disorders. Comings and Comings (1991) note that autistic patients and patients with Tourette's syndrome have the following symptoms in common: "attention deficits, babbling, echolalia, palilalia, echopraxia, facial grimacing, hand flicking, hyperactivity, inappropriate anger, obsessive-compulsive behaviors, onset in childhood, panic at minor environmental change, perseveration, poor control of speech volume, sniffing and smelling of objects, [and] stereotyped movements" (p. 180). (*Palilalia* is incessant repetition of words and phrases, and *echopraxia* is imitation of motions made by other people.) Comings and Comings also note that previous studies reported forty-one cases of autistic patients who subsequently developed Tourette's syndrome and described sixteen more such patients. Sverd (1991) reported ten additional patients with symptoms of both autism and Tourette's syndrome whose families contained relatives with Tourette's syndrome and related disorders. Two of these cases are listed in *Table 16.1*.

Brain Pathology

The fact that autism is highly heritable is presumptive evidence that the disorder is a result of structural or biochemical abnormalities in the brain. In addition, a variety of nongenetic pathological conditions can produce the symptoms of autism. For example, women who have contracted an infectious disease such as rubella (German measles) during pregnancy sometimes give birth to an autistic child (Chess, Fernandez, and Korn, 1971). Fernell, Gillberg, and Von Wendt (1991) found that 23 percent of children with infantile hydrocephalus showed autistic symptoms and that the severity of the hydrocephalus was correlated with the severity of the symptoms. Of course, hydrocephalus causes widespread brain damage, so this finding does not help us to decide what part of the brain might be involved in autism.

Studies by Miller and Strömland (1993) and Strömland et al. (1994) suggest that events that interfere with prenatal development early in pregnancy can increase the likelihood of autism. Thalidomide, a drug that was given to pregnant women in some countries during the 1960s to treat the symptoms of morning sickness, was later found to cause serious birth defects. Miller, Strömland, and their colleagues studied eighty-six people whose mothers had taken thalidomide during pregnancy and found that five of them were autistic. (This rate is 145 times higher than the rate of autism in the population as a whole.) All of the autistic people had been exposed to thalidomide between prenatal days 20 and 24. As Rodier et al. (1996) note, the only part of the central nervous system that forms at this time is the brain stem.

Researchers have found evidence for both structural and biochemical abnormalities in the brains of autistics, but so far, we cannot point to any single abnormality as the cause of the disorder. MRI scans and histological examination of the brains of deceased autistic patients have found evidence for abnormalities in the medial temporal

Phenylketonuria (*fee nul kee ta noo ree a*) A hereditary disorder caused by the absence of an enzyme that converts the amino acid phenylalanine to tyrosine; causes brain damage unless a special diet is implemented soon after birth.

TABLE 16.1	Symptoms and Family Histories of Two Patients with Autistic Disorder and Tourette's Syndrome		
Patient	**Autistic Symptoms**	**Tourette's Symptoms**	**Family History**
Case 6 Anna 4 years old	Poor eye contact. Disregarded people and ran into them as if they did not exist. Sometimes too attached to mother. Inconsistent response to verbal stimuli. Preferred solitary play. Echolalic, pronominal reversal. Unable to initiate and engage in conversation. Lined up toys. Flicks light switch on and off. Hand flapping. Covers ears when upset. Acute episode of agitation and aggressivity.	Onset age 3—eye blinking, facial tics, repetitive face touching and pushing hair from face, growling noises.	Father—eye blinking. Uncle—head tics. Grandfather—mouth stretches, eye twitches, delusional episode. Great aunt—facial grimaces. Delusions she is a world-class musician. Great uncle—claimed he controlled weather with a machine. Maternal uncle—socially awkward as adult, socially isolated as schoolboy. Uncle—fidgety, tapped fingers. Grandfather—socially awkward.
Case 7 Ronald 8 years old	Ignored people. Ran over children as if they did not exist. Poor eye contact. "Doesn't know how to address children and get into their circle." Brings up irrelevant topics "out of blue." No imaginative play. Used single words until age 3. Echolalic. Lined up toys. Markedly restricted interests and activities. Hyperactive.	Onset age 6—eye blinking, head jerks, shoulder shrugs, hand clapping, finger snapping, throat clearing, clucking noises.	Father—head jerks, shoulder shrugs, eye blinking. Doesn't work. Paternal uncle—throat clearing, head jerks, doesn't work. Paternal grandfather—strange, impulsive, fidgety.

Source: Adapted from Sverd, J. *American Journal of Medical Genetics,* 1991, *39,* 173–179.

FIGURE 16.2

Midsagittal MRI scans. The cerebellar vermis is shown in the lower right corner of each panel, outlined in white. (a) From a normal child. (b) and (c) From two children with Joubert syndrome, who also showed symptoms of autism. The vermis is completely lacking in (c).

(From Holroyd, S., Reiss, A.L., and Bryan, R.N. Biological Psychiatry, 1991, 29, 287–294. Reprinted with permission.)

lobe, the brain stem, and the cerebellum (DeLong, 1992; Happé and Frith, 1996). In a review of the literature, Courchesne (1991) concluded that the vermis of the cerebellum is less developed in cases of autism. In support of this conclusion, Holroyd, Reiss, and Bryan (1991) reported that *Joubert syndrome,* a genetic disorder that results in lack of development of the cerebellar vermis, produced symptoms of autism. Figure 16.2 shows midsagittal MRI scans of a normal subject and two patients with Joubert syndrome. As you can see, the vermis is absent or severely underdeveloped in the Joubert patients. (See *Figure 16.2.*) Although some studies failed to find cerebellar abnormalities in autistic patients, more recent ones support Courchesne's conclusion (Hashimoto et al., 1995; Haas et al., 1996). *Why* cerebellar abnormalities might produce the symptoms of autism is not at all clear. There is no evidence that damage to the cerebellum later in life—or damage to any other part of the brain, for that matter—causes pure autism (Happé and Frith, 1996). Thus, autism seems to be a result of some combination of brain abnormalities that occurs only during development.

(a) (b) (c)

INTERIM SUMMARY

Autistic disorder occurs in approximately 4 out of 10,000 infants. It is characterized by poor or absent social relations, communicative abilities, and imaginative abilities and the presence of repetitive, purposeless movements. Although autistics are usually, but not always, retarded, they may have a particular isolated talent. Some investigators believe that the most important cognitive deficit is the inability to imagine what others know or think about something and how they feel.

In the past, clinicians blamed parents for autism, but now it is generally accepted as a disorder with biological roots. Twin studies have shown that autism is highly heritable but that several genes are responsible for its development. It is often associated with Tourette's syndrome (as obsessive-compulsive disorder is) and can be caused by untreated phenylketonuria. Autism can also be caused by events that interfere with prenatal development, such as drugs or maternal infection with rubella and with hydrocephalus. MRI studies suggest that autism is associated with abnormalities in the medial temporal lobe, the brain stem, and the cerebellum.

STRESS DISORDERS

Aversive stimuli can harm people's health. Many of these harmful effects are produced not by the stimuli themselves but by our reactions to them. Walter Cannon, a famous physiologist, introduced the term **stress** to refer to the physiological reaction caused by the perception of aversive or threatening situations.

The word *stress* was borrowed from engineering, in which it refers to the action of physical forces on mechanical structures. The word can be a noun or a verb; and the noun can refer to situations or the individual's response to them. Because of this potential confusion, I will refer to "stressful" stimuli and situations as **stressors** and to the individual's reaction as a **stress response.** The word *stress* will refer to the general process (as in the title to this section).

The physiological responses that accompany the negative emotions prepare us to threaten rivals or fight them or to run away from dangerous situations. Walter Cannon introduced the phrase **fight-or-flight response** to refer to the physiological reactions that prepare us for the strenuous efforts required by fighting or running away. Normally, once we have bluffed or fought with an adversary or run away from a dangerous situation, the threat is over and our physiological condition can return to normal. The fact that the physiological responses may have adverse long-term effects on our health is unimportant as long as the responses are brief. But sometimes, the threatening situations are continuous rather than episodic, producing a more or less continuous stress response.

Physiology of the Stress Response

As we saw in Chapter 10, emotions consist of behavioral, autonomic, and endocrine responses. The latter two components, the autonomic and endocrine responses, are the ones that can have adverse effects on health. (Well, I guess the behavioral components can, too, if a person rashly gets into a fight with someone much bigger and stronger.) Because threatening situations generally call for vigorous activity, the autonomic and endocrine responses that accompany them are catabolic; that is, they help to mobilize the body's energy resources. The sympathetic branch of the autonomic nervous system is active, and the adrenal glands secrete epinephrine, norepinephrine, and steroid stress hormones. Because the effects of sympathetic activity are similar to those of the adrenal hormones, I will limit my discussion to the hormonal responses.

Stress A general, imprecise term that can refer either to a stress response or to a stressor (stressful situation).

Stressor A stimulus (or situation) that produces a stress response.

Stress response A physiological reaction caused by the perception of aversive or threatening situations.

Fight-or-flight response A species-typical response preparatory to fighting or fleeing; thought to be responsible for some of the deleterious effects of stressful situations on health.

Hypothalamus

Corticotropin-releasing factor (CRF)

ACTH (adrenocorticotrophic hormone)

Glucocorticoids

Adrenal cortex

Anterior pituitary gland

Neuron of sympathetic nervous system

Adrenal medulla

Epinephrine and norepinephrine

FIGURE 16.3

Control of the secretion of gluco-corticoids by the adrenal cortex and of catecholamines by the adrenal medulla.

Glucocorticoid (*glew ko kor ti koyd*) One of a group of hormones of the adrenal cortex that are important in protein and carbohydrate metabolism, secreted especially in times of stress.

Corticotropin-releasing factor (CRF) A hypothalamic hormone that stimulates the anterior pituitary gland to secrete ACTH (adrenocorticotropic hormone).

Adrenocorticotropic hormone (ACTH) (*a dree no kor ti ko trow pic*) A hormone released by the anterior pituitary gland in response to CRF; stimulates the adrenal cortex to produce glucocorticoids.

Epinephrine affects glucose metabolism, causing the nutrients stored in muscles to become available to provide energy for strenuous exercise. Along with norepinephrine, the hormone also increases blood flow to the muscles by increasing the output of the heart. In doing so, it also increases blood pressure, which, over the long term, contributes to cardiovascular disease.

Another stress-related hormone is *cortisol*, a steroid secreted by the adrenal cortex. Cortisol is called a **glucocorticoid** because it has profound effects on glucose metabolism. In addition, glucocorticoids help to break down protein and convert it to glucose, help to make fats available for energy, increase blood flow, and stimulate behavioral responsiveness, presumably by affecting the brain. They decrease the sensitivity of the gonads to luteinizing hormone (LH), which suppresses the secretion of the sex steroid hormones. In fact, Singer and Zumoff (1992) found that the blood level of testosterone in male hospital residents was severely depressed, presumably because of the stressful work schedule they are obliged to follow. Glucocorticoids have other physiological effects, too, some of which are only poorly understood. Almost every cell in the body contains glucocorticoid receptors, which means that few of them are unaffected by these hormones.

The secretion of glucocorticoids is controlled by neurons in the paraventricular nucleus of the hypothalamus (PVN). These neurons secrete a peptide called **corticotropin-releasing factor (CRF),** which stimulates the anterior pituitary gland to secrete **adrenocorticotropic hormone (ACTH).** ACTH enters the general circulation and stimulates the adrenal cortex to secrete glucocorticoids. (See *Figure 16.3.*)

CRF is also secreted within the brain, where it serves as a neuromodulator/neurotransmitter, especially in regions of the limbic system that are involved in emotional responses, such as the periaqueductal gray matter, the locus coeruleus, and the central nucleus of the amygdala. The behavioral effects produced by an injection of CRF into the brain are similar to those produced by aversive situations; thus, some elements of the stress response appear to be produced by the release of CRF by neurons in the brain. For example, intracerebroventricular injection of CRF decreases the amount of time a rat spends in the center of a large open chamber (Britton et al., 1982), it enhances the acquisition of a classically conditioned fear response (Cole and Koob, 1988), and it increases the startle response elicited by a sudden loud noise (Swerdlow et al., 1986). On the other hand, intracerebroventricular injection of a CRF antagonist *reduces* the anxiety caused by a variety of stressful situations (Kalin, Sherman, and Takahashi, 1988; Heinrichs et al., 1994; Skutella et al., 1994).

The secretion of glucocorticoids does more than help an animal to react to a stressful situation: It helps the animal to survive. If a rat's adrenal glands are removed, it becomes much more susceptible to the effects of stress. In fact, a stressful situation that a normal rat would take in its stride may kill one whose adrenal glands have been removed. And physicians know that if an adrenalectomized human is subjected to stressors, he or she must be given additional amounts of glucocorticoid (Tyrell and Baxter, 1981).

Health Effects of Long-Term Stress

Many studies of humans who have been subjected to stressful situations have found evidence of ill health. For example, survivors of concentration camps, who were obviously subjected to long-term stress, have generally poorer health later in life than other people of the same age (Cohen, 1953). Drivers of subway trains that injure or kill people are more likely to suffer from illnesses several months later (Theorell et al., 1992). Air traffic controllers—especially those who work at busy airports where the danger of collisions is greatest—show a greater incidence of high blood pressure, which gets worse as they grow older (Cobb and Rose, 1973). (See *Figure 16.4.*) They also are more likely to suffer from ulcers or diabetes.

A pioneer in the study of stress, Hans Selye, suggested that most of the harmful effects of stress were produced by the prolonged secretion of glucocorticoids (Selye, 1976). Although the short-term effects of glucocorticoids are essential, the long-term effects are damaging. These effects include increased blood pressure, damage to muscle tissue, steroid diabetes, infertility, inhibition of growth, inhibition of the inflammatory responses, and suppression of the immune system. High blood pressure can lead to heart attacks and stroke. Inhibition of growth in children who are subjected to prolonged stress prevents them from attaining their full height. Inhibition of the inflammatory response makes it more difficult for the body to heal itself after an injury, and suppression of the immune system makes an individual vulnerable to infections and (perhaps) cancer.

The adverse effects of stress on healing were demonstrated in a study by Kiecolt-Glaser et al. (1995), who performed punch biopsy wounds in the subjects' forearms, a harmless procedure used often in medical research. The subjects were people who were providing long-term care for relatives with Alzheimer's disease—a situation known to cause stress—and control subjects of the same approximate age and family income. The investigators found that healing of the wounds took significantly longer in the caregivers (48.7 days versus 39.3 days). (See *Figure 16.5.*)

Sapolsky and his colleagues have investigated one rather serious long-term effect of stress: brain damage. As you learned in Chapter 12, the hippocampal formation plays a crucial role in learning and memory, and evidence suggests that one of the causes of memory loss that occurs with aging is degeneration of this brain structure. Research with animals has shown that long-term exposure to glucocorticoids destroys neurons located in field CA1 of the hippocampal formation. The hormone appears to destroy the neurons by making them more susceptible to potentially harmful events, such as decreased blood flow, which often occurs as a result of the aging process. The primary effect of the hormone is to lower the ability of the neurons in the hippocampus to utilize glucose, so when the blood flow decreases, their metabolism falls and they begin to die (Sapolsky, 1986; Sapolsky, Krey, and McEwen, 1986). Perhaps, then, the stressors to which people are subjected throughout their lives increase the likelihood of memory problems as they grow older. In fact, Lupien et al. (1996) found that elderly people with elevated blood levels of glucocorticoids learned a maze more slowly than did those with normal levels.

Uno et al. (1989) found that if stress is intense enough, it can even cause brain damage in young primates. The investigators studied a colony of vervet monkeys housed in a primate center in Kenya. They found

 16.4

Incidence of hypertension in various age groups of air traffic controllers at high-stress and low-stress airports.

(Based on data from Cobb and Rose, 1973.)

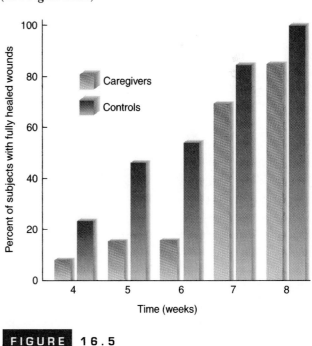

FIGURE 16.5

Percentage of caregivers and control subjects whose wounds had healed as a function of time after the biopsy was performed.

(Adapted from Kiecolt-Glaser, J.K., Marucha, P.T., Malarkey, W.B., Mercado, A.M., and Glaser, R. Lancet, 1995, 346, 1194–1196.)

(a)   (b)

FIGURE 16.6

Photomicrographs showing brain damage caused by stress. (a) Section through the hippocampus of a normal monkey. (b) Section through the hippocampus of a monkey of low social status subjected to stress. Compare the regions between the arrowheads, normally filled with large pyramidal cells.

(From Uno, H., Tarara, R., Else, J.G., Suleman, M.A., and Sapolsky, R.M. Journal of Neuroscience, 1989, 9, 1706–1711. Reprinted by permission of the Journal of Neuroscience.)

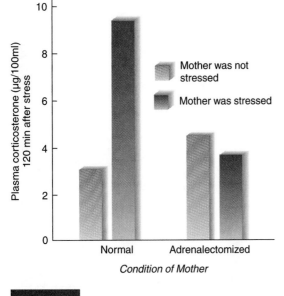

FIGURE 16.7

Effects of prenatal stress and glucocorticoid level on the stress response of adult rats. Adrenalectomy of the mother before she was subjected to stress prevented the development of an elevated stress response in the offspring during adulthood.

(Adapted from Barbazanges, A., Piazza, P.V., Le Moal, M., and Maccari, S. Journal of Neuroscience, 1996, 16, 3943–3949.)

that some monkeys died, apparently from stress. Vervet monkeys have a hierarchical society, and monkeys near the bottom of the hierarchy are picked on by the others; thus, they are almost continuously subjected to stress. (Ours is not the only species with social structures that cause a stress reaction in some of its members.) The deceased monkeys had gastric ulcers and enlarged adrenal glands, which are signs of chronic stress. And as Figure 16.6 shows, neurons in the CA1 field of their hippocampal formation were completely destroyed. (See *Figure 16.6*.) Severe stress appears to cause brain damage in humans as well; Jensen, Genefke, and Hyldebrandt (1982) found evidence of brain degeneration in CT scans of people who had been subjected to torture.

Even prenatal stress can affect behavior—presumably by affecting brain development. Takahashi, Turner, and Kalin (1992) found that rats whose mothers had been stressed reacted more strongly than did rats whose mothers had not been stressed when they were presented with stressful stimuli during adulthood.

The effects of prenatal stress, like the effects of stress in adulthood, appear to be mediated by the secretion of glucocorticoids. Barbazanges et al. (1996) subjected pregnant female rats to stress and later observed the effects of stress on their offspring in adulthood. They found that the prenatally stressed rats showed a prolonged secretion of glucocorticoids when they were subjected to restraint stress (placement in a small chamber). However, if the mothers' adrenal glands had been removed so that glucocorticoids could not be secreted during the stressful situation, their offspring reacted normally in adulthood. (The experimenters gave the adrenalectomized mothers controlled amounts of glucocorticoids to maintain them in good health.) (See *Figure 16.7*.)

Posttraumatic Stress Disorder

The aftermath of tragic and traumatic events such as those that accompany wars and natural disasters often includes psychological symptoms that persist long after the stressful events are

For many American veterans of the Vietnam war, this memorial symbolizes the grief they feel from the loss of their comrades and the horrors experienced during conflict. The experience of wars and other disasters can produce posttraumatic stress disorder in some participants.

over. According to the *DSM-IV*, **posttraumatic stress disorder** is caused by a situation in which a person "experienced, witnessed, or was confronted with an event or events that involved actual or threatened death or serious injury, or a threat to the physical integrity of self or others" that provoked a response that "involved intense fear, helplessness, or horror." The symptoms produced by such exposure include recurrent dreams or recollections of the event, feelings that the traumatic event is recurring ("flashback" episodes), and intense psychological distress. These dreams, recollections, or flashback episodes lead the person to avoid thinking about the traumatic event, which often results in diminished interest in social activities, feelings of detachment from others, suppressed emotional feelings, and a sense that the future is bleak and empty. Particular psychological symptoms include difficulty falling or staying asleep, irritability, outbursts of anger, difficulty in concentrating, and heightened reactions to sudden noises or movements.

Posttraumatic stress disorder can strike people at any age. Children may show particular symptoms that are not usually seen in adulthood, such as loss of recently acquired language skills or toilet training, and somatic complaints such as stomachaches and headaches. Usually, the symptoms begin immediately after the traumatic event, but they are sometimes delayed for several months or years.

Some studies suggest that preexisting personality factors may play a role in the development of posttraumatic stress disorder. For example, Mikulincer and Solomon (1988) studied Israeli soldiers who suffered a combat stress reaction during the 1982 war in Lebanon and found that those who tended to brood about their feelings were more likely to go on to develop posttraumatic stress disorder. The National Vietnam Veterans Readjustment Study carried out by the U.S. government found that four factors increased the likelihood that a soldier subjected to combat stress would develop posttraumatic stress disorder: being raised in a household with financial difficulty, having a history of drug abuse or dependency, having a history of affective disorders, and having a history of childhood behavior problems (Kulka et al., 1990). Because heredity plays an important role in shaping people's personality traits, we might expect that genetic factors might play some role in determining a person's susceptibility to developing posttraumatic stress disorder. In fact, twin studies indicate that they do (True et al., 1993).

As we saw earlier, prolonged exposure to glucocorticoids can cause brain damage, particularly in the hippocampus. At least two MRI studies have found evidence of hippocampal damage in veterans with combat-related posttraumatic stress disorder (Bremner et al., 1995; Gurvits et al., 1996). In the study by Gurvits et al., the vol-

Posttraumatic stress disorder
A psychological disorder caused by exposure to a situation of extreme danger and stress; symptoms include recurrent dreams or recollections; can interfere with social activities and produce a feeling of hopelessness.

ume of the hippocampal formation was reduced by over 20 percent, and the loss was proportional to the amount of combat exposure the veteran had experienced.

A PET study by Shin et al. (1997) investigated the effects of combat-related imagery on regional cerebral metabolism. The experimenters showed combat veterans with and without posttraumatic stress disorder pictures that showed innocuous items or combat-related items, such as body bags (the plastic bags in which soldiers killed in battle were placed). Then, while the subjects' heads were placed in the PET scanner, the experimenters read aloud sentences concerning the pictures the subjects had seen and asked them to imagine them. Imagining the combat-related pictures increased the activity in the anterior cingulate gyrus and right amygdala of the subjects with posttraumatic stress disorder, relative to control subjects. As we saw in Chapters 10 and 15, both of these brain regions are involved in reactions to situations that provoke anxiety and other negative emotional reactions.

Stress and Cardiovascular Disease

One of the most important causes of death is cardiovascular diseases—diseases of the heart and the blood vessels. Cardiovascular diseases can cause heart attacks and strokes. Heart attacks occur when the blood vessels that serve the heart become blocked; strokes involve the blood vessels in the brain. The two most important risk factors in cardiovascular disease are high blood pressure and a high level of cholesterol in the blood.

The degree to which people react to potential stressors may affect the likelihood that they will suffer from cardiovascular disease. For example, Wood et al. (1984) examined the blood pressure of people who had been subjected to a *cold pressor test* in 1934, when they were children. The cold pressor test reveals how people's blood pressure reacts to the stress caused by their hand being placed in a container of ice water for 1 minute. Wood and his colleagues found that 70 percent of the subjects who hyperreacted to cold pressor test when they were children had high blood pressure, compared with 19 percent of those who showed little reaction to the test.

A study with monkeys showed that individual differences in emotional reactivity are a risk factor for cardiovascular disease. Manuck et al. (1983, 1986) fed a high-cholesterol diet to a group of monkeys, which increases the likelihood of their developing coronary artery disease. They measured the animals' emotional reactivity by threatening to capture the animals. (Monkeys avoid contact with humans, and they perceive being captured as a stressful situation.) The animals that showed the strongest negative reactions eventually developed the highest rates of coronary artery disease. Presumably, these animals reacted more strongly to all types of stressors, and their reactions had detrimental effects on their health.

Apparently, at least some of the differences in emotional reactivity displayed by individual animals are caused by genetic differences in brain chemistry and function. Eilam et al. (1991) transplanted some tissue from the hypothalamus of genetically hypertensive rats into normal rats and found that the blood pressure of the recipient rats increased by an average of 31 percent. (Transplants of hypothalamic tissue from normotensive rats did not increase recipients' blood pressure.) (See *Figure 16.8.*)

The Coping Response

As we have seen, many of the harmful effects of long-term stress are caused by our own reactions—primarily the secretion of stress hormones. Some events that cause stress re-

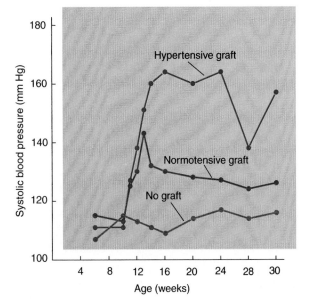

FIGURE 16.8

Systolic blood pressure in normal rats, rats with grafts of hypothalamic tissue from normal rats, and rats with grafts from genetically hypertensive rats.

(Adapted from Eilam, R., Malach, R., Bergmann, F., and Segal, M. Journal of Neuroscience, 1991, 11, 401–411.)

sponses, such as prolonged exertion or extreme cold, cause damage directly. These stressors will affect everyone; their severity will depend on each person's physical capacity. The effects of other stressors, such as situations that cause fear or anxiety, depend on people's perceptions and emotional reactivity. That is, because of individual differences in temperament or experience with a particular situation, some people may find a situation stressful and others may not. In these cases it is the perception that counts.

One of the most important variables that determine whether an aversive stimulus will cause a stress reaction is the degree to which the situation can be controlled. As we saw in Chapter 10, when an animal can learn a *coping response* that avoids contact with an aversive stimulus or decreases its severity, its emotional response will disappear. Weiss (1968) found that rats that learned to minimize (but not completely avoid) shocks by making a response whenever they heard a warning tone developed fewer stomach ulcers than did rats that had no control over the shocks. The effect was not caused by the pain itself, because both groups of animals received exactly the same number of shocks. Thus, being able to exert some control over an aversive situation reduces an animal's stress response. Humans react similarly. Situations that permit some control are less likely to produce signs of stress than those in which other people (or machines) control the situation (Gatchel, Baum, and Krantz, 1989). Perhaps this phenomenon explains why some people like to have a magic charm or other "security blanket" with them in stressful situations. Perhaps even the *illusion* of control can be reassuring.

We do not yet understand the neural mechanisms responsible for coping responses, but a study by Drugan et al. (1994) suggests that one of their effects may be the secretion of endogenous benzodiazepines. The experimenters trained rats in a task similar to the one used by Weiss (1968) that I just described. That is, all rats received shocks from time to time, but only the rats in the coping group could turn the shock off by making a response. As we just saw, the ability to make a coping response reduces stress. Drugan and his colleagues found that the level of endogenous benzodiazepines in the brain was higher in the animals in the coping group, compared with animals who rested in their home cages or those who had no control over the shock. As we saw in Chapter 4, endogenous benzodiazepines are neuromodulators produced in the brain that serve as ligands for binding sites on the $GABA_A$ receptor. They have the same anxiolytic effects as the benzodiazepine drugs such as Valium. (See *Figure 16.9.*)

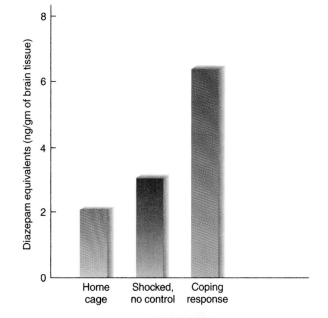

FIGURE 16.9

Mean levels of endogenous benzodiazepine receptor agonists in normal control rats, rats who were able to make a coping response, and rats who received inescapable shock.

(Adapted from Drugan, R.C., Basile, A.S., Ha, J.-.H., and Ferland, R.J. Brain Research, *1994, 661, 127–136.)*

Psychoneuroimmunology

As we have seen, long-term stress can be harmful to one's health and can even result in brain damage. The most important cause of these effects is elevated levels of glucocorticoids, but the high blood pressure caused by epinephrine and norepinephrine also plays a contributing role. In addition, the stress response can impair the functions of the immune system, which protects us from assault from viruses, microbes, fungi, and other types of parasites. Study of the interactions between the immune system and behavior (mediated by the nervous system, of course) is called **psychoneuroimmunology**. This relatively new field is described in the following subsection.

The Immune System

The immune system is one of the most complex systems of the body. Its function is to protect us from infection; and because infectious·organisms have developed de-

Psychoneuroimmunology The branch of neuroscience involved with interactions between environmental stimuli, the nervous system, and the immune system.

vious tricks through the process of evolution, our immune system has evolved devious tricks of its own. The description I provide here is abbreviated and simplified, but it presents some of the important elements of the system.

The immune system derives from white blood cells that develop in the bone marrow and in the thymus gland. Some of the cells roam through the blood or lymphatic system; others reside permanently in one place. The immune reaction occurs when the body is invaded by foreign organisms, including bacteria, fungi, and viruses. Two types of reactions occur: *nonspecific* and *specific*. One nonspecific reaction, called the *inflammatory reaction*, occurs early, in response to tissue damage produced by an invading organism. The damaged tissue secretes substances that increase the local blood circulation and make capillaries leak fluids, which causes the region to become inflamed. The secretions also attract phagocytic white blood cells that destroy both the invading cells and the debris produced by the breakdown of the body's own cells. Another nonspecific reaction occurs when a virus infects a cell. The infection causes the cell to release a peptide called *interferon*, which suppresses the ability of viruses to reproduce. In addition, **natural killer cells** continuously prowl through tissue; when they encounter a cell that has been infected by a virus or that has become transformed into a cancer cell, they engulf and destroy it. Thus, natural killer cells constitute one of our first defenses against the development of malignant tumors.

The immune system produces two types of specific immune reactions: *chemically mediated* and *cell-mediated*. Chemically mediated immune reactions involve antibodies. Infectious microorganisms have unique proteins on their surfaces, called **antigens.** These proteins identify the invaders to the immune system. Through exposure to the microorganisms, the immune system learns to recognize these proteins. (I will not try to explain the mechanism by which this learning takes place.) The result of this learning is the development of special lines of cells that produce specific **antibodies**—proteins that recognize antigens and help kill the invading microorganism. One type of antibody is released into the circulation by **B-lymphocytes,** which receive their name from the fact that they develop in bone marrow. These antibodies, called **immunoglobulins,** are chains of protein. Each type of immunoglobulin (there are five of them) is identical except for one end, which contains a unique receptor. A particular receptor binds with a particular antigen, just as a molecule of a hormone or neurotransmitter binds with its receptor. When the appropriate line of B-lymphocytes detects the presence of an invading bacterium, the cells release their antibodies, which bind with the antigens that are present on the surface of the invading microorganisms. The antigens either kill the invaders directly or attract other white blood cells, which then destroy them. (See *Figure 16.10a.*)

Natural killer cell A white blood cell that destroys cells infected by viruses.

Antigen A protein present on a microorganism that permits the immune system to recognize it as an invader.

Antibody A protein produced by a cell of the immune system that recognizes antigens present on invading microorganisms.

B-lymphocyte A white blood cell that originates in the bone marrow; part of the immune system.

Immunoglobulin An antibody released by B-lymphocytes that bind with antigens and help destroy invading microorganisms.

FIGURE 16.10

Immune reactions. (a) Chemically mediated reaction. The B-lymphocyte detects an antigen on a bacterium and releases a specific immunoglobulin. (b) Cell-mediated reaction. The T-lymphocyte detects an antigen on a bacterium and kills it directly or releases a chemical that attracts other white blood cells.

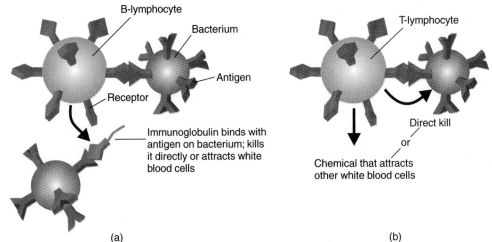

The other type of defense by the immune system, cell-mediated immune reactions, is produced by **T-lymphocytes,** which originally develop in the thymus gland. These cells also produce antibodies, but the antibodies remain attached to the outside of their membrane. T-lymphocytes primarily defend the body against fungi, viruses, and multicellular parasites. When antigens bind with their surface antibodies, the cells either directly kill the invaders or signal other white blood cells to come and kill them. (See *Figure 16.10b.*)

The reactions illustrated in Figure 16.10 are much simplified; actually, both chemically mediated and cell-mediated immune reactions involve several different types of cells. The communication between these cells is accomplished by **cytokines,** chemicals that stimulate cell division. The cytokines released by certain white blood cells when an invading microorganism is detected (principally *interleukin-1* and *interleukin-2*) cause other white blood cells to proliferate and direct an attack against the invader. The primary way in which glucocorticoids suppress specific immune responses is by interfering with the messages conveyed by the cytokines (Sapolsky, 1992).

Neural Control of the Immune System

As we will see in the next subsection, the stress response can increase the likelihood of infectious diseases. It may even affect the growth of cancers. What is the physiological explanation for these effects? One answer, probably the most important one, is that stress increases the secretion of glucocorticoids, and as we saw, these hormones directly suppress the activity of the immune system.

A direct relation between stress and the immune system was demonstrated by Kiecolt-Glaser et al. (1987). These investigators found that caregivers of family members with Alzheimer's disease, who certainly underwent considerable stress, showed weaker immune systems, based on several different laboratory tests. Bereavement, another source of stress, also suppresses the immune system. Schleifer et al. (1983) tested the husbands of women with breast cancer and found that their immune response was lower after their wives died. (See *Figure 16.11.*) Knapp et al. (1992) even found that when healthy subjects imagined themselves reliving unpleasant emotional experiences, the immune response measured in samples of their blood was decreased.

Several studies indicate that the suppression of the immune response by stress is largely mediated by glucocorticoids. For example, in a study with rats, Keller et al. (1983) found that the stress of inescapable shock decreased the number of lymphocytes (B-cells, T-cells, and natural killer cells) found in the blood. This effect was abolished by removal of the adrenal glands; thus, it appears to have been caused by the release of glucocorticoids triggered by the stress response.

Because the secretion of glucocorticoids is controlled by the brain (through its secretion of CRF), the brain is obviously responsible for the suppressing effect of these hormones on the immune system. Neurons in the central nucleus of the amygdala send axons to CRF-secreting neurons in the paraventricular nucleus of the hypothalamus; thus, we can reasonably expect that the mechanism responsible for negative emotional responses is also responsible for the stress response and the immunosuppression that accompanies it. Several studies have shown

T-lymphocyte A white blood cell that originates in the thymus gland; part of the immune system.

Cytokine (*site oh kine*) A category of chemicals released by certain white blood cells when they detect the presence of an invading microorganism; causes other white blood cells to proliferate and mount an attack against the invader.

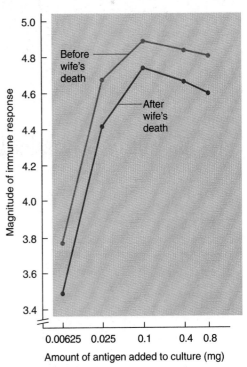

FIGURE 16.11

Stimulation of white blood cell (lymphocyte) production by an antigen in blood of husbands before and after their wives' death.

(Adapted from Schleifer, S.J., Keller, S.E., Camerino, M., Thornton, J.C., and Stein, M. Journal of the American Medical Association, 1983, 250, 374–377.)

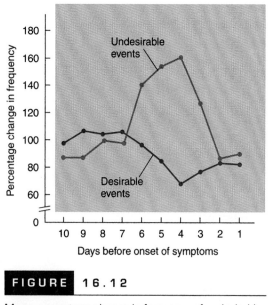

FIGURE 16.12

Mean percentage change in frequency of undesirable and desirable events during the ten-day period preceding the onset of symptoms of upper respiratory infections.

(Based on data from Stone, A.A., Reed, B.R., and Neale, J.M. Journal of Human Stress, 1987, 13, 70–74.)

FIGURE 16.13

Percent of subjects with colds as a function of an index of psychological stress.

(Adapted from Cohen, S., Tyrrell, D.A.J., and Smith, A.P. New England Journal of Medicine, 1991, 325, 606–612.)

that stress increases the activity of neurons in brain regions that have been shown to play a role in emotional responses, including the central nucleus of the amygdala and the PVN (Sharp et al., 1991; Imaki et al., 1992).

Stress and Infectious Diseases

Often, when a married person dies, his or her spouse dies soon afterward, frequently of an infection. In fact, a wide variety of stress-producing events in a person's life can increase the susceptibility to illness. For example, Glaser et al. (1987) found that medical students were more likely to contract acute infections and to show evidence of suppression of the immune system during the time that final examinations were given. In addition, autoimmune diseases often get worse when a person is subjected to stress, as Feigenbaum, Masi, and Kaplan (1979) found for rheumatoid arthritis. In a laboratory study, Rogers et al. (1980) found that when rats were stressed by handling them or exposing them to a cat, they developed a more severe case of an artificially induced autoimmune disease. Lehman et al. (1991) found that the incidence of diabetes in a strain of rats that are susceptible to this autoimmune disease was considerably higher when the animals were subjected to moderate chronic stress.

Stone, Reed, and Neale (1987) attempted to see whether stressful events in people's daily lives might predispose them to upper respiratory infection. If a person is exposed to a microorganism that might cause such a disease, the symptoms do not occur for several days; that is, there is an incubation period between exposure and signs of the actual illness. Thus, the authors reasoned that if stressful events suppressed the immune system, one might expect to see a higher likelihood of respiratory infections several days after such stress. To test their hypothesis, they asked volunteers to keep a daily record of desirable and undesirable events in their lives over a twelve-week period. The volunteers also kept a daily record of any discomfort or symptoms of illness.

The results were as predicted: During the three-to-five-day period just before showing symptoms of an upper respiratory infection, people experienced an increased number of undesirable events and a decreased number of desirable events in their lives. (See *Figure 16.12.*) Stone et al. (1987) suggest that the effect is caused by decreased production of a particular immunoglobulin that is present in the secretions of mucous membranes, including those in the nose, mouth, throat, and lungs. This immunoglobulin, IgA, serves as the first defense against infectious microorganisms that enter the nose or mouth. They found that IgA is associated with mood; when a subject is unhappy or depressed, levels of IgA are lower than normal. The results suggest that the stress caused by undesirable events may, by suppressing the production of IgA, lead to a rise in the likelihood of upper respiratory infections.

The results of the study by Stone and his colleagues were confirmed by an experiment by Cohen, Tyrrell, and Smith (1991). The investigators found that subjects who were given nasal drops containing cold viruses were much more likely to develop colds if they reported stressful experiences during the past year and if they said that they felt threatened, out of control, or overwhelmed by events. (See *Figure 16.13.*)

People's emotional reactions to aversive stimuli can harm their health. The stress response, which Cannon called the fight-or-flight response, is useful as a short-term response to threatening stimuli but is harmful in the long term. This response includes increased activity of the sympathetic branch of the autonomic nervous system and increased secretion of hormones by the adrenal gland: epinephrine, norepinephrine, and glucocorticoids.

Although increased levels of epinephrine and norepinephrine can raise blood pressure, most of the harm to health comes from glucocorticoids. Prolonged exposure to high levels of these hormones can increase blood pressure, damage muscle tissue, lead to infertility, inhibit growth, inhibit the inflammatory response, and suppress the immune system. It can also damage the hippocampus. Prenatal exposure to excessive levels of glucocorticoids (caused by maternal stress) causes developmental changes that appear to predispose animals to react more to stressful situations. Exposure to extreme stress can also have long-lasting effects; it can lead to the development of posttraumatic stress disorder.

Because the harm of most forms of stress comes from our own response to it, individual differences in personality variables can alter the effects of stressful situations. Research with twin studies indicates that heredity is one of the factors that determines an individual's response to stress. Another important variable is the ability to perform a coping response; being able to do so considerably reduces the aversive effects of stressful situations. One study suggests that performance of a coping response causes the release of endogenous benzodiazepines by neurons in the brain.

Psychoneuroimmunology is a relatively new field of study that investigates interactions between behavior and the immune system, mediated by the nervous system. The immune system consists of several types of white blood cells that produce both nonspecific and specific responses to invading microorganisms. The nonspecific responses include the inflammatory response, the antiviral effect of interferon, and the action of natural killer cells against viruses and cancer cells. The specific responses include chemically mediated and cell-mediated responses. Chemically mediated responses are carried out by B-lymphocytes, which release antibodies that bind with the antigens on microorganisms and kill them directly or target them for attack by other white blood cells. Cell-mediated responses are carried out by T-lymphocytes, whose antibodies remain attached to their membranes.

A wide variety of stressful situations have been shown to increase people's susceptibility to infectious diseases. The most important mechanism by which stress impairs immune function is the increased blood levels of glucocorticoids.

THOUGHT QUESTIONS

Researchers are puzzled by the fact that glucocorticoids suppress the immune system. Can you think of any potential benefits that come from the fact that our immune system is suppressed during times of danger and stress?

DRUG ABUSE

Drug addiction poses a serious problem to our species. Consider the disastrous effects caused by the abuse of one of our oldest drugs, alcohol: automobile accidents, fetal alcohol syndrome, cirrhosis of the liver, Korsakoff's syndrome, increased rate of heart disease, and increased rate of intracerebral hemorrhage. Smoking (addiction to nicotine) greatly increases the chances of dying of lung cancer, heart attack, and stroke; and women who smoke give birth to smaller, less healthy babies. Cocaine addiction can cause psychotic behavior, brain damage, and death from overdose; use of cocaine by pregnant women can result in the birth of babies with brain damage and consequent psychological problems; and competition for lucrative markets terrorizes neighborhoods, subverts political and judicial systems, and causes many deaths. The use of "designer drugs" exposes users to unknown dangers of untested and often contaminated products, as several people discovered when they acquired Parkinson's disease after taking a synthetic opiate tainted with a neurotoxin. Addicts who take their drugs intravenously run a serious risk of contracting AIDS. What makes these drugs so attractive to so many people?

The answer is that all of these substances stimulate brain mechanisms that are responsible for positive reinforcement. In addition, some of them reduce or eliminate unpleasant feelings, some of which are produced by the drugs themselves. The immediate consequences of these drugs are more powerful than the realization that in the long term, bad things will happen.

What Is Addiction?

The term *addiction* derives from the Latin word *addicere,* "to sentence." Someone who is addicted to a drug is, in a way, sentenced to a term of involuntary servitude, being obliged to fulfill the demands of his or her drug dependency.

A Little Background

Long ago, people discovered that many substances found in nature—primarily, leaves, seeds, and roots of plants but also some animal products—had medicinal qualities. They discovered herbs that helped to prevent infections, that promoted healing, that calmed an upset stomach, that reduced pain, or that helped to provide a night's sleep. They also discovered "recreational drugs"—drugs that produced pleasurable effects when eaten, drunk, or smoked. The most universal recreational drug, and perhaps the first one that our ancestors discovered, is ethyl alcohol. Yeast spores are present everywhere, and these microorganisms can feed on sugar solutions and produce alcohol as a by-product. Undoubtedly, people in many different parts of the world discovered the pleasurable effects of drinking liquids that had been left alone for a while, such as the juice that had accumulated in the bottom of a container of fruit. The juice may have become sour and bad-tasting because of the action of bacteria, but the effects of the alcohol encouraged people to experiment, which led to the development of a wide variety of fermented beverages.

Our ancestors also discovered other recreational drugs. Some of them were consumed only locally; others became so popular that their cultivation as commercial crops spread throughout the world. For example, Asians discovered the effects of the sap of the opium poppy and the beverage made from the leaves of the tea plant, East Indians discovered the effects of the smoke of cannabis, South Americans discovered the effects of chewing coca leaves and making a drink from coffee beans, and North Americans discovered the effects of the smoke of the tobacco plant. Many of the drugs they discovered served to protect the plants from animals (primarily insects) that ate them. Although the drugs were toxic in sufficient quantities, our ancestors learned how to take these drugs in quantities that would not make them ill—at least, not right away. The effects of these drugs on their brains kept them coming back for more.

Physical Versus Psychological Addiction

Some drugs have very potent reinforcing effects, which lead some people to abuse them or even to become addicted to them. Many people (psychologists, health professionals, and laypeople) believe that "true" addiction is caused by the unpleasant physiological effects that occur when an addict tries to stop taking the drug. For example, Eddy et al. (1965) defined *physical dependence* as "an adaptive state that manifests itself by intense physical disturbances when the administration of a drug is suspended" (p. 723). In contrast, they defined *psychic dependence* as a condition in which a drug produces "a feeling of satisfaction and a psychic drive that requires periodic or continuous administration of the drug to produce pleasure or to avoid discomfort" (p. 723). Most people regard the latter as less important than the former. But, as we shall see, the *reverse* is true.

For many years, heroin addiction has been considered as the prototype for all drug addictions. People who habitually take heroin become physically dependent on the drug; that is, they show *tolerance* and *withdrawal symptoms*. As we saw in Chapter 4, **tolerance** is the decreased sensitivity to a drug that comes from its continued use; the drug user must take larger and larger amounts of the drug for it to be effective. Once a person has taken an opiate regularly enough to develop tolerance, that person will suffer withdrawal symptoms if he or she stops taking the drug. **Withdrawal symptoms** are primarily the opposite of the effects of the drug itself. The effects of heroin—euphoria, constipation, and relaxation—lead to the withdrawal effects of dysphoria, cramping and diarrhea, and agitation.

Most investigators believe that tolerance is produced by the body's attempt to compensate for the unusual condition of heroin intoxication—a hypothesis that was first proposed by Himmelsbach (1943). The drug disturbs normal homeostatic mechanisms in the brain, and in reaction these mechanisms begin to produce effects opposite to those of the drug, partially compensating for the disturbance (Trujillo and Akil, 1991; Zukin et al., 1993). Because of these compensatory mechanisms, the user must take increasing amounts of heroin to achieve the effects that were produced when he or she first started taking the drug. They also account for the symptoms of withdrawal: When the person stops taking the drug, the compensatory mechanisms make themselves felt, unopposed by the action of the drug.

Heroin addiction has provided such a striking example of drug dependence that some authorities have concluded that "real" addiction does not occur unless a drug causes tolerance and withdrawal. Without doubt, withdrawal symptoms make it difficult for a person to stop taking heroin: They help to keep the person hooked. But withdrawal symptoms do not explain why a person becomes a heroin addict in the first place; that fact is explained by the drug's reinforcing effect. Certainly, people do not start taking heroin so that they will become physically dependent on it and feel miserable when they go without it. Instead, they begin taking it because it makes them feel good.

In the past, the preoccupation with "physical" drug dependence has led to the neglect of the addictive properties of some drugs. For example, some very potent drugs, including cocaine, do not produce physical dependency. That is, people who take the drug do not show tolerance; and if they stop, they do not show significant withdrawal symptoms. As a result, experts believed for many years that cocaine was a relatively innocuous drug, not in the same league as heroin. Obviously, they were wrong; cocaine is even more addictive than heroin.

Common Features of Addiction

What goes on physiologically to make a person dependent on a drug? This section describes some common features of addictive drugs—drugs that people often become dependent on. A later section describes the details of particular drugs.

Positive Reinforcement

Drugs that lead to dependency must first reinforce people's behavior. As we saw in Chapter 12, positive reinforcement refers to the effect that certain stimuli have on the behaviors that preceded them. If, in a particular situation, a behavior is regularly followed by an appetitive stimulus (one that the organism will tend to approach), then that behavior will become more frequent in that situation.

Tolerance The fact that increasingly large doses of drugs must be taken to achieve a particular effect; caused by compensatory mechanisms that oppose the effect of the drug.

Withdrawal symptoms The appearance of symptoms opposite to those produced by a drug when the drug is suddenly no longer taken; caused by the presence of compensatory mechanisms.

Role in Drug Abuse.   The effectiveness of a reinforcing stimulus is greatest if it occurs immediately after a response occurs. If the reinforcing stimulus is delayed, it becomes considerably less effective. The reason for this is found by examining the function of instrumental conditioning: learning about the consequences of our own behavior. Normally, causes and effects are closely related in time; we do something, and something happens, good or bad. The consequences of the actions teach us whether to repeat that action, and events that follow a response by more than a few seconds were probably not caused by that response.

An experiment by Logan (1965) illustrates the importance of the immediacy of reinforcement. Logan trained hungry rats to run through a simple maze in which a single passage led to two corridors. At the end of one corridor the rats would find a small piece of food. At the end of the other corridor they would receive much more food, but it would be delivered only after a delay. Although the most intelligent strategy would be to enter the second corridor and wait for the larger amount of food, the rats chose to take the small amount of food that was delivered right away. Immediacy of reinforcement took precedence over quantity.

This phenomenon explains why the most addictive drugs are those that have immediate effects. As we saw in Chapter 4, drug users prefer heroin to morphine not because heroin has a *different* effect, but because it has a more *rapid* effect. In fact, heroin is converted to morphine as soon as it reaches the brain. But because heroin is more lipid soluble, it passes through the blood-brain barrier more rapidly and its effects on the brain are felt sooner than those of morphine. The most potent reinforcement occurs when drugs produce sudden changes in the activity of the reinforcement mechanism; slow changes are much less reinforcing, and continuous activity may even be aversive. (As we will see later, the use of methadone for opiate addiction and the use of nicotine patches for tobacco addiction are based on this phenomenon.)

Neural Mechanisms.   As we saw in Chapter 12, all natural reinforcers that have been studied so far (such as food for a hungry animal, water for thirsty one, or sexual contact) have one physiological effect in common: They cause the release of dopamine in the nucleus accumbens (White, 1996). This effect is undoubtedly not the *only* effect of reinforcing stimuli, and even aversive stimuli can trigger the release of dopamine (Salamone, 1992). But even though there is much that we do not yet understand about the neural basis of reinforcement, the release of dopamine appears to be a *necessary* (but not *sufficient*) condition for reinforcement to take place.

Addictive drugs—including amphetamine, cocaine, opiates, nicotine, alcohol, PCP, and cannabis—trigger the release of dopamine in the nucleus accumbens, as measured by microdialysis (Di Chiara, 1995). Some drugs do so by increasing the activity of the dopaminergic neurons of the mesolimbic system, which originates in the ventral tegmental area and terminates in the nucleus accumbens (and some other forebrain regions). Other drugs inhibit the reuptake of dopamine by terminal buttons and hence facilitate the postsynaptic effects of dopamine. If the release of dopamine in the nucleus accumbens is prevented by damaging the mesolimbic neurons, most addictive drugs lose their reinforcing effects. The details of the ways in which particular drugs interact with the mesolimbic dopaminergic system are described later.

Negative Reinforcement

You probably have heard the old joke in which someone says that the reason he bangs his head against the wall is that "it feels so good when I stop." Of course, that joke is funny (well, mildly amusing) because we know that although no one would act that way, ceasing to bang our head against the wall is certainly better than continuing to do so. If someone else started hitting us on the head and we were able to do something to get them to stop, whatever it was that we did would certainly be reinforced.

A behavior that turns off (or reduces) an aversive stimulus will be reinforced. This phenomenon is known as **negative reinforcement,** and its usefulness is obvious. For example, consider the following scenario: A woman staying in a rented house cannot get to sleep because of the unpleasant screeching noise that the furnace makes. She goes to the basement to discover the source of the noise and finally kicks the side of the oil burner. The noise ceases. The next time the furnace screeches, she immediately goes to the basement and kicks the side of the oil burner. The unpleasant noise (the aversive stimulus) is terminated when the woman kicks the side of the oil burner (the response), so the response is reinforced.

It is worth pointing out that *negative reinforcement* should not be confused with *punishment.* Both phenomena involve aversive stimuli, but one makes a response more likely, while the other makes it less likely. For negative reinforcement to occur, the response must make the unpleasant stimulus end (or at least decrease). For punishment to occur, the response must *make the unpleasant stimulus occur.* For example, if a little boy touches a mousetrap and hurts his finger, he is unlikely to touch a mousetrap again. The painful stimulus *punishes* the behavior of touching the mousetrap.

As we saw earlier in this chapter, the withdrawal effects, which occur when a habitual user of a drug stops taking the drug, are unpleasant. Although positive reinforcement seems to be what provokes drug taking in the first place, reduction of withdrawal effects could certainly play a role in maintaining someone's drug addiction. The withdrawal effects are unpleasant, but as soon as the person takes some of the drug, these effects go away, producing negative reinforcement.

Negative reinforcement could also explain the acquisition of drug addictions under some conditions. If a person is suffering from some unpleasant feelings and then takes a drug that eliminates these feelings, the person's drug-taking behavior is likely to be reinforced. For example, alcohol can relieve feelings of anxiety. If a person finds herself in a situation that arouses anxiety, she may find that a drink or two makes her feel much better. In fact, people often anticipate this effect and begin drinking before the situation actually occurs.

Craving and Relapse

Why do drug addicts crave drugs? Why does this craving occur even after a long period of abstinence? Knowing the answers to these questions might help clinicians to devise therapies that will assist people in breaking their drug dependence once and for all.

Robinson and Berridge (1993) suggest that when an addictive drug activates the mesolimbic dopaminergic system, it gives *incentive salience* to stimuli present at that time. By this they mean that the stimuli associated with drug taking become exciting and motivating—a provocation to act. When a person with a history of drug abuse sees or thinks about these stimuli, he or she experiences craving—an impulse to take the drug. Note that this hypothesis does not imply that the craving is caused solely by an unpleasant feeling.

Evidence obtained from both humans and laboratory animals indicates that long-term drug abuse does, indeed, produce long-term changes. For example, Grant et al. (1996) used a PET scanner to measure regional metabolic activity of the brains of people with and without a history of cocaine abuse. The experimenters presented two types of stimuli: neutral and drug-related. The neutral stimuli included arts and crafts items such as a leather punch, a paintbrush, paint bottles, and clay and a videotape of a person handling some seashells. The drug-related stimuli included a glass pipe, a mirror, a razor blade, a straw, a pile of cocaine (yes, the real stuff), and a videotape of a people handling a white powder and sniffing and smoking it. The people with a history of cocaine abuse were told that after the experiment was over, they could sniff the pile of cocaine in front of them.

The PET scans revealed that the drug-related stimuli increased the activity of the dorsolateral prefrontal cortex, the amygdala, and the cerebellum, but only in sub-

Negative reinforcement The removal or reduction of an aversive stimulus that is contingent on a particular response, with an attendant increase in the frequency of that response.

(a)　　　　　(b)

High

Receptor density

Low

FIGURE 16.14

Concentration of D_3 dopamine receptors in the human ventral striatum, as measured by binding of 7-OH-DPAT. (a) Autoradiogram of the ventral striatum of a control subject. (b) Autoradiogram of the ventral striatum of a subject who died of a cocaine overdose. Cd = caudate nucleus, Pt = putamen, NA = nucleus accumbens. Note the increased concentration of D_3 receptors in the nucleus accumbens of the cocaine addict.

(From Figure 2, Staley, J.K., and Mash, D.C. Adaptive Increase in D3 Dopmine Receptors . . . , The Journal of Neuroscience, 1996, 16, 6100–6106.)

jects with a history of drug abuse. These stimuli also produced self-reports of craving in these subjects. The neutral stimuli had no effects on neural activity of subjects in either of the groups.

Several studies have suggested that long-term cocaine addiction may increase the sensitivity of D_3 dopamine receptors and that this increased sensitivity may be responsible for craving. D_3 receptors are found in brain regions that have been implicated in reinforcement—in particular, in the nucleus accumbens and other regions that receive information from the mesolimbic dopamine system (Levesque et al., 1992). This suggestion received support from a study by Staley and Mash (1996), who studied the brains of people who had died of cocaine overdoses. They found an increased density of dopamine D_3 receptors in the nucleus accumbens of these people, compared with the brains of people without a history of drug abuse. (See *Figure 16.14*.)

Commonly Abused Drugs

People have been known to abuse an enormous variety of drugs, including alcohol, barbiturates, opiates, tobacco, amphetamine, cocaine, cannabis, LSD, psilocybin, PCP, volatile solvents such as glues or even gasoline, ether, and nitrous oxide. The pleasure that children often derive from spinning themselves until they become dizzy may even be related to the effects of some of these drugs. Obviously, I cannot hope to discuss all these drugs in any depth and keep the chapter to a reasonable length, so I will restrict my discussion to the most important of them, in terms of popularity and potential for addiction. Some drugs, such as caffeine, are both popular and addictive, but because they do not normally cause intoxication, impair health, or interfere with productivity, I will not discuss them here. (Chapter 4 did discuss the behavioral effects and site of action of caffeine.) I will also not discuss the wide variety of hallocinogenic drugs such as LSD or PCP. Although some people enjoy the mind-altering effects of LSD, many people simply find them frightening; and in any event, LSD use does not normally lead to addiction. PCP (phencyclidine) acts as an inverse agonist at the NMDA receptor, which means that its effects overlap those of alcohol. Rather than devoting space to this drug, I have chosen to say more about alcohol, which is abused far more than any of the hallucinogenic drugs. If you would like to learn more about drugs other than the ones I discuss here, I suggest that you consult the books listed among the suggested readings at the end of this chapter.

Opiates

Opium, derived from a sticky resin produced by the opium poppy, has been eaten and smoked for centuries. Opiate addiction has several high personal and social costs. First, because heroin, the most commonly abused opiate, is an illegal drug, an addict becomes, by definition, a criminal. Second, because of tolerance, a person must take increasing amounts of the drug to achieve a "high." The habit thus becomes more and more expensive, and the person often turns to crime to obtain enough money to support his or her habit. Third, an opiate addict often uses unsanitary needles; at present, a substantial percentage of people who inject illicit drugs have been exposed in this way to hepatitis or the AIDS virus. Fourth, if the addict is a pregnant woman, her infant will also become dependent on the drug, which easily crosses the placental barrier. The infant must be given opiates right after being born and then weaned off the drug with gradually decreasing doses. Fifth, the uncertainty about the strength of a given batch of heroin makes it possible for a user to receive an unusually large dose of the drug, with possibly fatal consequences. In addition, dealers typically dilute pure heroin with various adulterants such as milk sugar, quinine, or talcum powder; and dealers are not known for taking scrupulous care with the quality and sterility of the substances they use. Some heroin-induced deaths have actually been reactions to the adulterants mixed with the drugs.

When an opiate is administered systemically, it stimulates opiate receptors located on neurons in various parts of the brain and produces a variety of effects, including analgesia, hypothermia (lowering of body temperature), sedation, and reinforcement. Opiate receptors in the periaqueductal gray matter are primarily responsible for the analgesia, those in the preoptic area are responsible for the hypothermia, and those in the mesencephalic reticular formation are responsible for the sedation. As we shall see, opiate receptors in the ventral tegmental area and the nucleus accumbens may play a role in the reinforcing effects of opiates, but other regions appear to be important, too.

As we saw earlier, reinforcing stimuli cause the release of dopamine in the nucleus accumbens. Injections of opiates are no exception to this general rule; Wise et al. (1995) found that the level of dopamine in the nucleus accumbens increased by 150 to 300 percent while a rat was pressing a lever that delivered intravenous injections of heroin. Rats will also press a lever that delivers injections of an opiate directly into the ventral tegmental area (Devine and Wise, 1994) or the nucleus accumbens Goeders, Lane, and Smith (1984). In other words, injections of opiates into both ends of the mesolimbic dopaminergic system are reinforcing. These findings suggest that the reinforcing effects of opiates are produced by activation of neurons of the mesolimbic system and release of dopamine in the nucleus accumbens.

Cocaine and Amphetamine

Cocaine and amphetamine have similar behavioral effects, because both act as potent dopamine agonists. However, their sites of action are different. Cocaine binds with and deactivates the dopamine transporter proteins, thus blocking the reuptake of dopamine after it is released by the terminal buttons. Amphetamine also inhibits the reuptake of dopamine, but its most important effect is to directly stimulate the release of dopamine from terminal buttons. Freebase cocaine ("crack"), a particularly potent form of the drug, is smoked and thus enters the blood supply of the lungs and reaches the brain very quickly. Because its effects are so potent and so rapid, it is probably the most effective reinforcer of all available drugs.

When people take cocaine, they become euphoric, active, and talkative. They say that they feel powerful and alert. Some of them become addicted to the drug, and obtaining it becomes an obsession to which they devote more and more time and money. As we saw in Chapter 15, long-term use of these drugs can produce symptoms that resemble those of paranoid schizophrenia. Laboratory animals, who will quickly learn to self-administer cocaine intravenously, also act excited and show intense exploratory activity. After receiving the drug for a day or two, rats start showing stereotyped movements, such as grooming, head bobbing, and persistent locomotion (Geary, 1987). If rats or monkeys are given continuous access to a lever that permits them to self-administer cocaine, they often self-inject so much cocaine that they die. In fact, Bozarth and Wise (1985) found that rats that self-administered cocaine were almost three times more likely to die than rats that self-administered heroin. (See *Figure 16.15*.)

Several studies have shown that intravenous injections of cocaine and amphetamine increase the concentration of dopamine in the nucleus accumbens, as measured by microdialysis

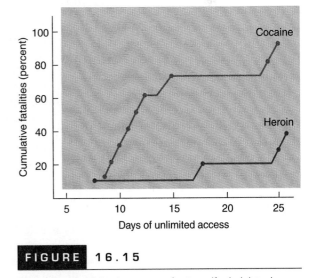

FIGURE 16.15

Cumulative fatalities in groups of rats self-administering cocaine or heroin.

(Adapted from Bozarth, M.A., and Wise, R.A. Journal of the American Medical Association, 1985, 254, 81–83. Reprinted with permission.)

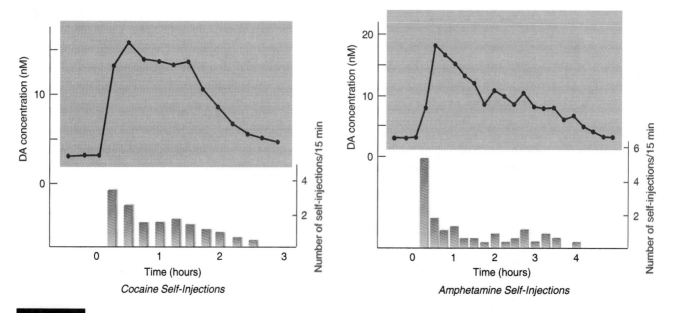

FIGURE 16.16

Dopamine concentration in the nucleus accumbens, measured by microdialysis, during self-administration of intravenous cocaine or amphetamine by rats.

(Adapted from Di Ciano, P., Coury, A., Depoortere, R.Y., Egilmez, Y., Lane, J.D., Emmett-Oglesby, M.W., Lepiane, F.G., Phillips, A.G., and Blaha, C.D. Behavioural Pharmacology, 1995, 6, 311–322.)

(Petit and Justice, 1989; Di Ciano et al., 1995; Wise et al., 1995). For example, Figure 16.16 shows data collected from rats who learned to press a lever that delivered intravenous injections of cocaine or amphetamine. The colored bars at the base of the graphs indicate the animals' responses, and the line graphs indicate the level of dopamine in the nucleus accumbens. (See *Figure 16.16*.)

Other lines of research indicate that the nucleus accumbens is a critical site for the reinforcing effects of cocaine and amphetamine. For example, rats will learn to press a lever that causes the injection of a small quantity of amphetamine directly into the nucleus accumbens (Hoebel et al., 1983; Phillips, Robbins, and Everitt, 1994). In addition, if drugs that block dopamine receptors are injected into the nucleus accumbens, cocaine loses much of its reinforcing effect (McGregor and Roberts, 1993; Caine et al., 1995). Finally, lesions of the nucleus accumbens or destruction of dopaminergic terminals there with a local injection of 6-HD interferes with the reinforcing effects of both cocaine and amphetamine (Caine and Koob, 1994).

Nicotine

Nicotine may seem rather tame in comparison to opiates, cocaine, and amphetamine. Nevertheless, nicotine is an addictive drug, and it undoubtedly accounts for more deaths than the so-called hard drugs. The combination of nicotine and other substances in tobacco smoke is carcinogenic and leads to cancer of the lungs, mouth, throat, and esophagus. The addictive potential of nicotine should not be underestimated; many people continue to smoke even when doing so causes serious health problems. For example, Sigmund Freud, whose theory of psychoanalysis stressed the importance of insight in changing one's behavior, was unable to stop smoking even after most of his jaw had been removed because of the cancer that this habit had caused (Brecher, 1972). He suffered severe pain and, as a physician, realized that he should have stopped smoking. He did not, and his cancer finally killed him.

Although executives of tobacco companies and others whose economic welfare is linked to the production and sale of tobacco products argue that smoking is a "habit" rather than an "addiction," evidence suggests that the behavior of people who regularly use tobacco resembles that of compulsive drug users. In a review of the literature, Stolerman and Jarvis (1995) note that smokers tend to smoke regularly or not at all; few can smoke just a little. Males smoke an average of seventeen cigarettes per day, while females smoke an average of fourteen. Nineteen out of twenty smokers smoke every day, and only 60 out of 3500 smokers questioned smoke fewer than five cigarettes per day. Forty percent of people continue to smoke after having had a laryngectomy (which is usually performed to treat throat cancer), more than 50 per-

Now that many employers prohibit smoking in the workplace, we have become accustomed to the sight of people standing outside a building, satisfying their nicotine addiction.

cent of heart attack survivors continue to smoke, and about 50 percent of people continue to smoke after submitting to surgery for lung cancer. Of those who attempt to quit smoking by enrolling in a special program, 20 percent manage to abstain for one year. The record is much poorer for those who try to quit on their own: One-third manage to stop for one day, one-fourth for one week, but only 4 percent manage to abstain for six months. It is difficult to reconcile these figures with the assertion that smoking is merely a "habit" that is pursued for the "pleasure" that it produces.

Ours is not the only species that is willing to self-administer nicotine; so will laboratory animals (Donny et al., 1995). Nicotine stimulates acetylcholine receptors, of course. It also increases the activity of dopaminergic neurons of the mesolimbic system, which contain these receptors (Mereu et al., 1987), and causes dopamine to be released in the nucleus accumbens (Damsma, Day, and Fibiger, 1989). Figure 16.17 shows the effects of two injections of nicotine or saline on the extracellular dopamine level of the nucleus accumbens, measured by microdialysis. (See *Figure 16.17.*)

Museo and Wise (1994) found that if a nicotinic agonist is injected directly into the ventral tegmental area when an animal is in a particular location, the animal will later show a preference for that location. (This phenomenon is called a **conditioned place preference,** and it indicates that the injection has a reinforcing effect.) Conversely, injecting a nicotinic antagonist directly into the ventral tegmental area will reduce the reinforcing effect of intravenous injections of nicotine (Corrigall, Coen, and Adamson, 1994). Thus, the reinforcing effect of nicotine appears to occur in the ventral tegmental area, on nicotinic receptors located on the dendrites of mesolimbic dopaminergic neurons.

Wise (1988) notes that because nicotine stimulates the tegmentostriatal dopaminergic system, smoking could potentially make it more difficult for a cocaine or heroin addict to stop taking the drug. As several studies with laboratory animals have shown, if self-administration of cocaine or heroin is extinguished through nonreinforcement, an injection of drugs that stimulate dopaminergic neurons can reinstate the responding. A similar "cross-priming" effect from cigarette smoking could potentially contribute to a relapse in people

Conditioned place preference
The learned preference for a location in which an organism encountered a reinforcing stimulus, such as food or a reinforcing drug.

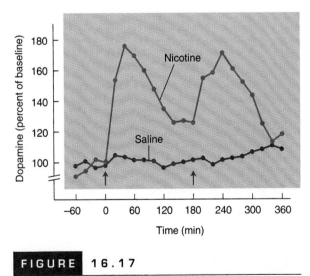

FIGURE 16.17

Changes in dopamine concentration in the nucleus accumbens, measured by microdialysis, in response to injections of nicotine or saline. The arrows indicate the time of the injections.

(Adapted from Damsma, G., Day, J., and Fibiger, H.C. European Journal of Pharmacology, 1989, 168, 363–368. Reprinted with permission.)

who are trying to abstain. (And because alcohol also stimulates dopaminergic neurons, drinking could present the same problem.)

Alcohol and Barbiturates

Alcohol has greater costs to society than any other drug. A large percentage of deaths and injuries caused by motor vehicle accidents are related to alcohol use, and alcohol contributes to violence and aggression. Chronic alcoholics often lose their jobs, their homes, and their families; and many die of cirrhosis of the liver, exposure, or diseases caused by poor living conditions and abuse of their bodies. As we saw in Chapter 14, women who drink during pregnancy run the risk of giving birth to babies with fetal alcohol syndrome, symptoms of which include malformation of the head and the brain. The leading cause of mental retardation in the Western world today is alcohol consumption by pregnant women (Abel and Sokol, 1986). Thus, understanding the physiological and behavioral effects of this drug is an important issue.

At low doses, alcohol produces mild euphoria and has an *anxiolytic* effect—that is, it reduces the discomfort of anxiety. At higher doses, it produces incoordination and sedation. In studies with laboratory animals the anxiolytic effects manifest themselves as a release from the punishing effects of aversive stimuli. For example, if an animal is given electric shocks whenever it makes a particular response (say, one that obtains food or water), it will stop doing so. However, if it is then given some alcohol, it will begin making the response again (Koob et al., 1984). This phenomenon explains why people often do things they normally would not when they have had too much to drink; the alcohol removes the inhibitory effect of social controls on their behavior.

Alcohol produces both positive and negative reinforcement. The positive reinforcement manifests itself as mild euphoria. As we saw earlier, *negative* reinforcement is caused by the termination of an aversive stimulus. If a person feels anxious and uncomfortable, then an anxiolytic drug that relieves this discomfort provides at least a temporary escape from an unpleasant situation. It is probably the unique combination of stimulating and anxiolytic effects—of positive and negative reinforcement—that makes alcohol so difficult for some people to resist.

Alcohol, like other addictive drugs, increases the activity of the dopaminergic neurons of the mesolimbic system and increases the release of dopamine in the nucleus accumbens as measured by microdialysis (Gessa et al., 1985; Imperato and Di Chiara, 1986). The release of dopamine appears to be related to the positive reinforcement that alcohol can produce. An injection of a dopamine antagonist directly into the nucleus accumbens decreases alcohol intake (Samson et al., 1993), as does the injection of a drug into the ventral tegmental area that decreases the activity of the dopaminergic neurons there (Hodge et al., 1993).

What is responsible for the sedative and anxiolytic effects of alcohol? In low to moderate doses, alcohol appears to have two major sites of action in the nervous system: NMDA receptors and GABA$_A$ receptors. Alcohol acts as an inverse agonist at NMDA receptors, interfering with the effects of glutamate. Like alcohol, NMDA antagonists produce sedative and anxiolytic effects and interfere with cognitive performance (Tabakoff and Hoffman, 1996). Also like alcohol, NMDA antagonists cause the release of dopamine in the nucleus accumbens (Imperato et al., 1990; Loscher, Annies, and Honack, 1991). Thus, NMDA receptors are at least partly responsible for both the positively and negatively reinforcing effects of alcohol.

In low doses, alcohol produces a mild euphoria and has an anxiolytic effect. For this reason, alcohol is a part of social occasions in many cultures.

As we saw in Chapter 12, NMDA receptors are involved in long-term potentiation, a phenomenon that plays an important role in learning. Thus, it will not surprise you to learn that alcohol, which antagonizes the action of glutamate at NMDA receptors, disrupts long-term potentiation and interferes with the spatial receptive fields of place cells in the hippocampus (Givens and McMahon, 1995; Matthews, Simson, and Best, 1996). Presumably, this effect at least partly accounts for the deleterious effects of alcohol on memory and other cognitive functions.

The second site of action of alcohol is the GABA_A receptor. Alcohol acts as an indirect agonist at these receptors, binding with one of the many binding sites and increasing the effectiveness of GABA in opening the chloride channel and producing inhibitory postsynaptic potentials. Suzdak et al. (1986) discovered a drug (Ro15-4513) that reverses alcohol intoxication by blocking the alcohol binding site on the GABA_A receptor. Figure 16.21 shows two rats that received injections of enough alcohol to make them pass out. The one facing us also received an injection of the alcohol antagonist and appears completely sober. (See *Figure 16.18.*)

This wonder drug is not likely to reach the market. Although the behavioral effects of alcohol are mediated by their action on GABA_A receptors and NMDA receptors, high doses of alcohol have other, potentially fatal effects on all cells of the body, including destabilization of cell membranes. Thus, people taking some of the alcohol antagonist could then go on to drink themselves to death without becoming drunk in the process. Drug companies naturally fear possible liability suits stemming from such occurrences.

Barbiturates have effects very similar to those of alcohol. In fact, both drugs act as indirect agonists on the GABA_A receptor (Maksay and Ticku, 1985). However, the binding sites for alcohol and barbiturates appear to be different; Ro15-4513, the alcohol antagonist, does not reverse the intoxicating effects of barbiturates (Suzdak et al., 1986). But because both drugs act on the same receptor, their effects are additive; if a person takes a moderate dose of alcohol and a moderate dose of a barbiturate, the effect can be fatal.

Cannabis

Another drug that people regularly self-administer—almost exclusively by smoking—is THC, the active ingredient in marijuana. As you learned in Chapter 4, THC receptors have been discovered, and their distribution in the brain has been mapped. The endogenous ligand for these receptors, anandamide, is a lipid. But we still do not know what situations trigger the release of anandamide or what functions this chemical serves. Incidentally, di Tomaso, Beltramo, and Piomelli (1996) discovered that chocolate contains three anandamidelike chemicals. Whether the existence of these chemicals is related to the great appeal that chocolate has for many people is not yet known. (I suppose that this is the place for a chocoholic joke.)

One thing we do now know about THC is that it, like other drugs with abuse potential, has an effect on dopaminergic neurons. Chen et al. (1990) injected rats with low doses of THC and measured the release of dopamine in the nucleus accumbens by means of microdialysis. Sure enough, they found that the injections caused the release of dopamine. (See *Figure 16.19.*)

As we saw in Chapter 4, the hippocampus contains a large concentration of THC receptors. Marijuana is known to affect

FIGURE 16.18

Effects of Ro15–4513, an alcohol antagonist. Both rats received an injection of alcohol, but the one facing us also received an injection of the alcohol antagonist.

(Photograph courtesy of Steven M. Paul, National Institute of Mental Health, Bethesda, Md.)

FIGURE 16.19

Changes in dopamine concentration in the nucleus accumbens, measured by microdialysis, in response to injections of THC or an inert placebo.

(Adapted from Chen, J., Paredes, W., Li, J., Smith, D., Lowinson, J., and Gardner, E.L. Psychopharmacology, 1990, 102, 156–162. Reprinted with permission.)

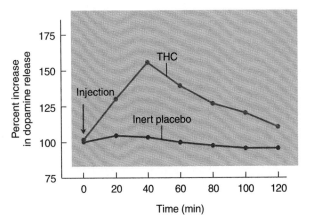

people's memory. Specifically, it impairs their ability to keep track of a particular topic; they frequently lose the thread of a conversation if they are momentarily distracted. Perhaps the drug does so by disrupting the normal functions of the hippocampus, which plays such an important role in memory.

Heredity and Drug Abuse

Not everyone is equally likely to become addicted to a drug. Many people manage to drink alcohol moderately, and even many users of potent drugs such as cocaine and heroin use them "recreationally" without becoming dependent on them. There are only two possible sources of individual differences in any characteristic: heredity and environment. Because this book considers the *physiology* of behavior, I will not discuss the role that environment plays in a person's susceptibility to the addicting effects of drugs. Obviously, environmental effects are important; people who are raised in a squalid environment without any real hope for a better life are more likely than other people to turn to drugs for some temporary euphoria and removal from the unpleasant world that surrounds them. But even in a given environment, poor or privileged, some people become addicts and some do not—and some of these behavioral differences are a result of genetic differences, as we will see in the following subsections.

Most of the research on the effects of heredity on addiction have been devoted to alcoholism. One of the reasons for this focus—aside from the importance of the problems caused by alcohol—is that almost everyone is exposed to alcohol. Most people drink alcohol sometime in their lives and thus have firsthand experience with its reinforcing effects. The same is not true for cocaine, heroin, and other drugs that have even more potent effects. In most countries, alcohol is freely and legally available in local shops, whereas cocaine and heroin must often be purchased in dangerous neighborhoods from unsavory dealers. From what we now know about the effects of addictive drugs on the nervous system, it seems likely that the results of studies on the heredity of alcoholism will apply to other types of drug addiction as well.

Before I begin my discussion of the genetics of alcohol abuse, I should mention that some investigators have recently begun studying the abuse of another freely available drug: nicotine (Gilbert and Gilbert, 1995; Heath et al., 1995). In general, studies have found that the heritability of smoking is just as strong as that of alcoholism. Smoking has also been shown to be related to some personal characteristics, including neurosis, social alienation, impulsiveness, sensation seeking, low conscientiousness, low socioeconomic status, and low achievement.

The Evidence

Alcohol consumption is not distributed equally across the population; in the United States, 10 percent of the people drink 50 percent of the alcohol (Heckler, 1983). The best evidence for an effect of heredity on susceptibility to alcoholism comes from two main sources: twin studies and cross-fostering studies. Monozygotic twins tend to resemble each other more closely than dizygotic twins in many ways, including the likelihood of alcohol abuse (Goodwin, 1979).

The second type of heritability study uses children who were adopted by nonrelatives when they were young. A study like this permits the investigator to estimate the effects of family environment as well as genetics. That is, one can examine the effects of being raised by an alcoholic parent, or having a biological parent who is an alcoholic, or both on the probability of becoming alcoholic. Such a study was carried out in Stockholm by Cloninger et al. (1981, 1985) and was replicated in Gothenburg, another Swedish city (Sigvardsson, Bohman, and Cloninger, 1996). Briefly, the studies found that heredity was much more important than family environment. But the story is not quite that simple.

In a review of the literature on alcohol abuse, Cloninger (1987) notes that many investigators have concluded that there are two principal types of alcoholics: those who cannot abstain but drink consistently and those who are able to go without drinking for long periods of time but are unable to control themselves once they start. (For convenience I will refer to these two groups as "steady drinkers" and "bingers.") Steady drinking is associated with antisocial personality disorder, which includes a lifelong history of impulsiveness, fighting, lying, and lack of remorse for antisocial acts. Binge drinking is associated with emotional dependence, behavioral rigidity, perfectionism, introversion, and guilt feelings about one's drinking behavior. Steady drinkers usually begin their alcohol consumption early in life, whereas binge drinkers begin much later. (See *Table 16.2*.)

Steady drinking is strongly influenced by heredity. The Stockholm adoption study found that men with fathers who were steady drinkers were almost seven times more likely to become steady drinkers themselves than were men whose fathers did not abuse alcohol. Family environment had no measurable effect; the boys began drinking whether or not the members of their adoptive family themselves drank heavily. Very few women become steady drinkers; the daughters of steady-drinking fathers instead tend to develop *somatization disorder*. People with this disorder chronically complain of symptoms for which no physiological cause can be found, leading them to seek medical care almost continuously. Thus, the genes that predispose a man to become a steady-drinking alcoholic (antisocial type) predispose a woman to develop somatization disorder. The reason for this interaction with gender is not known.

Binge drinking is influenced both by heredity and by environment. The Stockholm adoption study found that having a biological parent who was a binge drinker had little effect on the development of binge drinking unless the child was exposed to a family environment in which there was heavy drinking. The effect was seen in both males and females.

Possible Mechanisms

When we find an effect of heredity on behavior, we have good reason to suspect the existence of a biological difference. That is, genes affect behavior only by affecting the body. A susceptibility to alcoholism could conceivably be caused by differences in the ability to digest or metabolize alcohol or by differences in the structure or biochemistry of the brain. Most investigators believe that differences in brain physiology are more likely to play a role. Cloninger (1987) notes that many studies have shown that people with antisocial tendencies, which includes the group of steady drinkers, show a strong tendency to seek novelty and excitement. These people are disorderly and distractible (many have a history of hyperactivity as children) and show little restraint in their behavior. They tend not to fear dangerous situations or social disapproval. They are easily bored. On the other hand, binge drinkers tend to be anxious, emotionally dependent, sentimental, sensitive to social cues, cautious and apprehensive, fearful of novelty or change, rigid, and attentive to details. Their EEGs show little slow alpha activity, which is characteristic of a relaxed state (Propping, Kruger, and Mark, 1981). When they take alcohol, they report a pleasant relief of tension (Propping, Kruger, and Janah, 1980). Perhaps, as Cloninger suggests,

TABLE 16.2 Characteristic Features of Two Types of Alcoholism

Feature	TYPE OF ALCOHOLISM Steady	Binge
Usual age of onset (years)	Before 25	After 25
Spontaneous alcohol seeking (inability to abstain)	Frequent	Infrequent
Fighting and arrests when drinking	Frequent	Infrequent
Psychological dependence (loss of control)	Infrequent	Frequent
Guilt and fear about alcohol dependence	Infrequent	Frequent
Novelty seeking	High	Low
Harm avoidance	Low	High
Reward dependence	Low	High

Source: From Cloninger, C.R. *Science,* 1987, *236*, 410–416. Copyright 1987 by the American Association for the Advancement of Science.

these personality differences are a result of differences in the sensitivity of neural mechanisms involved in reinforcement, exploration, and punishment.

For example, steady drinkers may have an undersensitive punishment mechanism, which makes them unresponsive to danger and to social disapproval. They may also have an undersensitive reinforcement system, which leads them to seek more intense thrills (including those provided by alcohol) to experience pleasurable sensations. Thus, they seek the excitatory (dopamine-stimulating) effect of alcohol. Binge drinkers may have oversensitive punishment systems. Normally, they avoid drinking because of the guilt they experience afterward; but once they begin, and once the sedative effect begins, the alcohol-induced suppression of the punishment system makes it impossible for them to stop.

Therapy for Drug Abuse

There are many reasons for engaging in research on the physiology of drug abuse, including an academic interest in the nature of reinforcement and the pharmacology of psychoactive drugs. But most researchers entertain the hope that the results of their research will contribute to the development of ways to treat and (better yet) prevent drug abuse in members of our own species. As you well know, the incidence of drug abuse is far too high, so obviously, research has not yet solved the problem. However, real progress has been made.

The most common treatment for opiate addiction is methadone maintenance. Methadone is a potent opiate, just like morphine or heroin. If it were available in a form suitable for injection, it would be abused. (In fact, methadone clinics must control their stock of methadone carefully to prevent it from being stolen and sold to opiate abusers.) Methadone maintenance programs administer the drug to their patients in the form of a liquid, which they must drink in the presence of the personnel supervising this procedure. Because the oral route of administration increases the opiate level in the brain slowly, the drug does not produce a high, the way an injection of heroin will. In addition, because methadone is long-lasting, the patient's opiate receptors remain occupied for a long time, which means that an injection of heroin has little effect. Of course, a very large dose of heroin will displace methadone from opiate receptors and produce a "rush," so the method is not foolproof.

As we saw earlier, the reinforcing effects of cocaine and amphetamine are primarily a result of the sharply increased levels of dopamine that these drugs produce in the nucleus accumbens. Drugs that block dopamine receptors certainly block the reinforcing effects of cocaine and amphetamine, but they also produce dysphoria (an unpleasant feeling) and anhedonia (inability to experience pleasure). People will not tolerate the unpleasant feelings these drugs produce, so they are not useful treatments for cocaine and amphetamine abuse. Drugs that *stimulate* dopamine receptors can reduce a person's dependence on cocaine or amphetamine, but these drugs are just as addictive as the drugs they replace and have the same deleterious effects on health.

You may recall that several studies found that the increased sensitivity of D_3 dopamine receptors produced by chronic exposure to cocaine may be involved in the craving for cocaine experienced by people trying to break their dependency on cocaine. Some investigators suggest that drugs that block D_3 receptors may reduce this craving and thus be a useful adjunct to treatment of cocaine dependency (Staley and Mash, 1996).

An interesting approach to cocaine addiction is suggested by a study by Carrera et al. (1995), who conjugated cocaine to a foreign protein and managed to stimulate rats' immune systems to develop antibodies to cocaine. These "cocaine-immunized" rats were less sensitive to the activating effects of cocaine, and brain levels of cocaine in these animals were lower after an injection of the drug. As Leshner (1996) suggests, it might someday be possible to vaccinate cocaine abusers (or perhaps inject them with an antibody developed by genetic engineering) so that an injection of cocaine

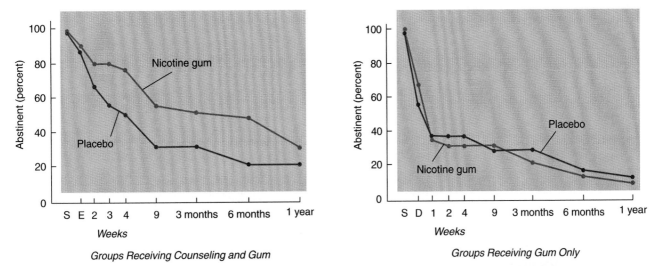

FIGURE 16.20

Percentage of smokers chewing nicotine gum alone or in conjunction with counseling who abstained from smoking.

(Adapted from Schneider, N.G., and Jarvik, M.E. NIDA Research Monographs, 1985, 53, 83–101.)

will not produce reinforcing effects. This treatment would have many advantages because (theoretically, at least) it would interfere only with the action of cocaine and not with the normal operations of people's reinforcement mechanisms. Thus, the treatment should not decrease their ability to experience normal pleasure.

A treatment similar to methadone maintenance has been used as an adjunct to treatment for nicotine addiction. For several years, chewing gum containing nicotine has been available by prescription, and more recently, transdermal patches that release nicotine through the skin have been marketed. Both methods maintain a sufficiently high level of nicotine in the brain to decrease a person's craving for nicotine. Once the habit of smoking has subsided, the dose of nicotine can be decreased to wean the person from the drug. Carefully controlled studies have shown that nicotine maintenance therapy, and not administration of a placebo, is useful in treatment for nicotine dependence (Stolerman and Jarvis, 1995). However, nicotine maintenance therapy is most effective if it is part of a counseling program. (See *Figure 16.20.*)

As we saw in Chapter 15, serotonin agonists have proved themselves useful in treatment of panic disorder and obsessive compulsive disorder (and related disorders such as hair pulling and nail biting). These drugs also appear to be useful in treating alcoholism; several double-blind studies have found that 5-HT reuptake blockers make it easier for alcoholics to abstain. For example, Naranjo et al. (1992) found that citalopram (a serotonin agonist) "decreased interest, desire, craving, and liking for alcohol" in alcoholics who were receiving treatment for their addiction. It appeared to do so by decreasing the reinforcing effects of alcohol.

Several studies have shown that opiate antagonists decrease the reinforcing value of alcohol in a variety of species, including our own (Altschuler, Phillips, and Feinhandler, 1980; Davidson, Swift, and Fitz, 1996; Reid, 1996). This finding suggests that the reinforcing effect of alcohol—at least in part—is produced by the secretion of endogenous opioids and the activation of opiate receptors in the brain. A study by Davidson, Swift, and Fitz (1996) clearly illustrates this effect. The investigators arranged a double-blind, placebo-controlled study with sixteen college-age men and women to investigate the effects of naltrexone on social drinkers. None of the participants were alcohol abusers, and pregnancy tests ensured that the women were not pregnant. They gathered around a table in a local restaurant/bar for three two-hour drinking sessions, two weeks apart. For several days before the meeting, they swallowed capsules that contained either naltrexone or an inert placebo. The results showed that naltrexone increased the latency to take the first sip and to take a second drink and that the blood alcohol levels of the naltrexone-treated participants were lower at the end of the session. In general, the people who had taken naltrex-

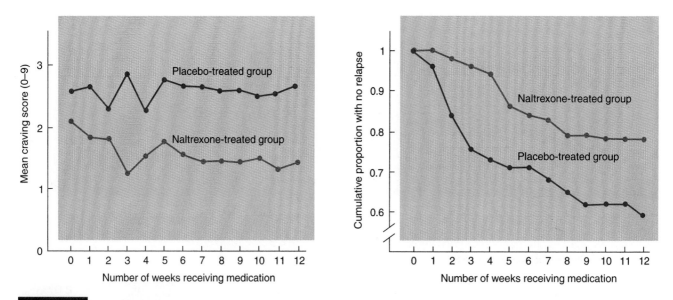

FIGURE 16.21

Mean craving score and proportion of patients who abstained from drinking while receiving naltrexone or a placebo.

[Adapted from O'Brien, C.P., Volpicelli, L.A., and Volpicelli, J.R. Alcohol, 1996, 13, 35–39.]

one found that their drinks did not taste very good—in fact, some of them asked for a different drink after taking the first sip.

These results are consistent with reports of the effectiveness of naltrexone as an adjunct to programs designed to treat alcohol abuse. For example, O'Brien, Volpicelli, and Volpicelli (1996) reported the results of two long-term programs using naltrexone along with more traditional behavioral treatments. Both programs found that administration of naltrexone significantly increased the likelihood of success. As Figure 16.21 shows, naltrexone decreased the participants' craving for alcohol and increased the number of participants who managed to abstain from alcohol. (See *Figure 16.21.*)

INTERIM SUMMARY

Addictive drugs are those whose reinforcing effects are so potent that some people who are exposed to them are unable to go for very long without taking them and their lives become organized around taking them. Originally, addictive drugs came from plants, which used them as a defense against insects or other animals that otherwise would eat them, but chemists have synthesized many other drugs that have even more potent effects. If a person regularly takes some addictive drugs (most notably, the opiates), the effects of the drug show tolerance, and the person must take increasing doses to achieve the same effect. If the person then stops taking the drug, withdrawal effects, opposite to the primary effects of the drug, will occur. However, withdrawal effects are not the cause of addiction—the abuse potential of a drug is related to its ability to reinforce drug-taking behavior.

Positive reinforcement occurs when a behavior is regularly followed by an appetitive stimulus—one that an organism will approach. All addictive drugs produce positive reinforcement; they reinforce drug-taking behavior. The faster a drug produces its effects, the more quickly dependence will be established. All addictive drugs stimulate the release of dopamine in the nucleus accumbens, a structure that plays an important role in reinforcement.

Negative reinforcement occurs when a behavior is followed by the reduction or termination of an aversive stimulus. If, because of a person's social situation or personality characteristics, he or she feels unhappy or anxious, a drug that reduces these feelings can reinforce drug-taking behavior by means of negative reinforcement. Also, the reduction of unpleasant withdrawal symptoms by a dose of the drug undoubtedly plays a role in maintaining drug addictions, but it is not the sole cause of craving.

Craving—the urge to take a drug to which one has become addicted—cannot be completely explained by withdrawal symptoms, because it can occur even after an addict has refrained from taking the drug for a long time. A PET study found that craving for cocaine increased the activity of the dorsolateral prefrontal cortex, the amygdala, and the cerebellum. Cocaine craving may be associated with increased numbers of D_3 dopamine receptors, and the brains of people with a history of cocaine abuse show increased density of D_3 receptors in the nucleus accumbens.

Opiates produce analgesia, hypothermia, sedation, and reinforcement. Opiate receptors in the periaqueductal gray matter are responsible for the analgesia, those in the preoptic area for the hypothermia, those in the mesencephalic reticular formation for the sedation, and those in the ventral tegmental area and nucleus accumbens at least partly for the reinforcement.

Cocaine inhibits the reuptake of dopamine by terminal buttons, and amphetamine causes the dopamine transporters in terminal buttons to run in reverse, releasing dopamine from terminal buttons. Besides producing alertness, activation, and positive reinforcement, cocaine and amphetamine can produce psychotic symptoms that resemble those of paranoid schizophrenia. The reinforcing effects of cocaine and amphetamine are mediated by an increase in dopamine in the nucleus accumbens.

The status of nicotine as a strongly addictive drug (for both humans and laboratory animals) was long ignored, primarily because it does not cause intoxication and because the ready availability of cigarettes and other tobacco products does not make it necessary for addicts to engage in illegal activities. However, the craving for nicotine is extremely motivating. Nicotine stimulates the release of mesolimbic dopaminergic neurons, and injection of nicotine into the ventral tegmental area is reinforcing.

Alcohol and barbiturates have similar (but not identical) effects. Alcohol has positively reinforcing effects and, through its anxiolytic action, has negatively reinforcing effects as well. It serves as an inverse agonist at NMDA receptors and an indirect agonist at $GABA_A$ receptors. It stimulates the release of dopamine in the nucleus accumbens.

The active ingredient in cannabis, THC, stimulates receptors whose natural ligand is anandamide. THC, like other addictive drugs, stimulates the release of dopamine in the nucleus accumbens.

Most people who are exposed to addictive drugs—even drugs with a high abuse potential—do not become addicts. Evidence suggests that the likelihood of addiction, especially to alcohol and nicotine, is strongly affected by heredity. There may be two types of alcoholism, one related to an antisocial, pleasure-seeking personality (steady drinkers) and another related to a repressed, anxiety-ridden personality (binge drinkers).

Although drug abuse is difficult to treat, researchers have developed several useful therapies. Methadone maintenance replaces addiction to heroin by addiction to an opiate that does not produce euphoric effects when administered orally. Similarly, nicotine-containing gum and transdermal patches help smokers combat their addiction. D_3 receptor antagonists show promise of helping people break an addiction to cocaine. The development of antibodies to cocaine in rats holds out the possibility that people may some day be immunized against the drug. Serotonin agonists show promise in decreasing craving for alcohol. However, the most effective pharmacological adjunct to treatment for alcoholism appears to be naltrexone, which blocks some of the drug's reinforcing effects.

A personal note: You are now at the end of the book (as you well know), and you have spent a considerable amount of time reading my words. While working on this book, I have tried to imagine myself talking to someone who is interested in learning something about the physiology of behavior. As I mentioned in the preface, writing is often a lonely activity, and the imaginary audience helped to keep me company. If you would like to turn this communication into a two-way conversation, write to me. My address is given at the end of the preface.

THOUGHT QUESTIONS

1. Although executives of tobacco companies have insisted that cigarettes are not addictive and assert that people smoke because of the pleasure the act gives them, research indicates that nicotine is, indeed, a potent addictive drug. Why do you think it took so long to recognize this fact?

2. In most countries, alcohol is legal and marijuana is not. In your opinion, why? What criteria would you use to decide whether a newly discovered drug should be legal or illegal? Danger to health? Effects on fetal development? Effects on behavior? Potential for dependence? If you applied these criteria to various substances in current use, would you have to change the legal status of any of them?

EPILOGUE
Classically Conditioned Craving

When a person takes heroin, the primary effects of the drug activate homeostatic compensatory mechanisms. These compensatory mechanisms are provided by neural circuits that oppose the effects of the drug. As Siegel (1978) has pointed out, the activation of these compensatory mechanisms is a response that can become classically conditioned to environmental stimuli that are present at the time the drug is taken. The stimuli associated with taking the drug—including the paraphernalia involved in preparing the solution of the drug, the syringe, the needle, the feel of the needle in a vein, and even the sight of companions who are usually present and the room in which the drug is taken—serve as conditional stimuli. The homeostatic compensatory responses provoked by the effects of the drug serve as the unconditional response, which becomes conditioned to the environmental stimuli. Thus, once classical

conditioning has taken place, the sight of the conditional stimuli will activate the compensatory mechanisms.

When John saw the poster, the sight of the drug paraphernalia acted as a conditional stimulus and elicited the conditional response the compensatory mechanism. Because he had not taken the drug, he felt only the effect of the compensatory mechanism: dysphoria, agitation, and a strong urge to relieve these symptoms and replace them with feelings of euphoria. He found the urge irresistible.

Experiments with laboratory animals have confirmed that this explanation is correct. For example, Siegel et al. (1982) gave rats daily doses of heroin—always in the same chamber—long enough for tolerance to develop. Then, on the test day, the experimenters gave the rats a large dose of the drug. Some of the animals received the drug in the familiar chamber, while others received it in a new environment. The investigators pre-

dicted that the animals receiving the drug in the familiar environment would have some protection from the drug overdose because the stimuli in that environment would produce a classically conditioned compensatory response. Their prediction was correct; almost all of the rats who received the overdose in the new environment died, compared with slightly more than half of the rats injected in the familiar environment. Siegel and his colleagues suggest that when human heroin addicts take the drug in an unfamiliar environment, they too run the risk of death from a drug overdose.

By the way, the story of John that I recounted in the Prologue is unlikely to occur nowadays. Because so many heroin addicts trying to break their habit have reported that the sight of drug paraphernalia made it difficult for them to abstain, the agencies trying to combat drug addiction have stopped preparing posters that feature them.

KEY CONCEPTS

AUTISTIC DISORDER

1. Autistic disorder is characterized by poor or absent social relations, communicative abilities, and imaginative abilities and the presence of repetitive, purposeless movements.
2. Although autism used to be blamed on poor parenting behavior, it is now recognized that the disorder is caused by hereditary factors or events that interfere with prenatal development.

STRESS DISORDERS

3. The stress response consists of the physiological components of an emotional response to threatening stimuli. The long-term effects of these responses, particularly of the secretion of the glucocorticoids, can damage a person's health.
4. The way people cope with stress can affect their physiological reaction, and thus their health.
5. Stress can suppress the immune system, primarily through the secretion of glucocorticoids, and therefore can make a person more susceptible to infections. Stress-related secretion of catecholamines may be a factor in the development of cardiovascular disease.

DRUG ABUSE

6. All addictive substances studied so far—including opiates, cocaine, amphetamine, nicotine, marijuana, and alcohol—have been shown to cause the release of dopamine in the nucleus accumbens.
7. Although chronic intake of opiates causes tolerance and leads to withdrawal symptoms, these phenomena are not responsible for addiction, which is caused by the ability of these drugs to activate dopaminergic mechanisms of reinforcement.
8. Alcohol intoxication appears to be caused by activation of a particular binding site on the $GABA_A$ receptor complex.
9. Research indicates that the susceptibility to alcoholism is strongly influenced by heredity. Binging and steady drinking appear to caused by different mechanisms.
10. Physiological therapy for drug addiction includes methadone for opiate addiction, nicotine chewing gum or skin patches for nicotine addiction, and serotonin agonists or naltrexone (an opiate receptor blocker) for alcoholism.

SUGGESTED READINGS

Ader, R., Felten, D.L., and Cohen, N. (eds.). *Psychoneuroimmunology,* 2nd ed. San Diego: Academic Press, 1991.

Bauman, M.L., and Kemper, T.L. *The Neurobiology of Autism.* Baltimore: Johns Hopkins University Press, 1994.

Brown, M.R., Koob, G.F., and Rivier, C. (eds.). *Stress: Neurobiology and Neuroendocrinology.* New York: Dekker, 1990.

Dietrich, R., and Erwin, V.G. *Pharmacological Effects of Ethanol on the Central Nervous System.* Boca Raton, FL: CRC Press, 1996.

Feldman. R.S., Meyer, J.S., and Quenzer, L.F. *Principles of Neuropsychopharmacology.* Sunderland, MA: Sinauer Associates, 1997.

Gershon, E.S., and Cloninger, C.R. *New Genetic Approaches to Mental Disorders.* Washington, DC: American Psychiatric Press, 1994.

Goodwin, D.W., and Guze, S.B. *Psychiatric Diagnosis,* 5th ed. New York: Oxford University Press, 1996.

Grilly, D.M. *Drugs and Human Behavior,* 2nd ed. Boston: Allyn and Bacon, 1989.

Winger, G., Hofmann, F.G., and Woods, J.H. *A Handbook on Drug and Alcohol Abuse: The Biomedical Aspects.* New York: Oxford University Press, 1992.

Yudofsky, S.C., and Hales, R.E. *The American Psychiatric Press Textbook of Neuropsychiatry.* Washington, DC: American Psychiatric Press, 1997.

REFERENCES

Abe, M., Saito, M., and Shimazu, T. Neuropeptide Y and norepinephrine injected into the paraventricular nucleus of the hypothalamus activate endocrine pancreas. *Biomedical Research,* 1989, *10,* 431–436.

Abel, E. L., and Sokol, R. J. Fetal alcohol syndrome is now a leading cause of mental retardation. *Lancet,* 1986, *2,* 1222.

Adams, D. B., Gold, A. R., and Burt, A. D. Rise in female-initiated sexual activity at ovulation and its suppression by oral contraceptives. *New England Journal of Medicine,* 1978, *299,* 1145–1150.

Adams, R. D. The anatomy of memory mechanisms in the human brain. In *The Pathology of Memory,* edited by G. A. Talland and N. C. Waugh. New York: Academic Press, 1969.

Adams, R. D., and Victor, M. *Principles of Neurology.* New York: McGraw-Hill, 1981.

Adey, W. R., Bors, E., and Porter, R. W. EEG sleep patterns after high cervical lesions in man. *Archives of Neurology,* 1968, *19,* 377–383.

Adieh, H. B., Mayer, A. D., and Rosenblatt, J. S. Effects of brain antiestrogen implants on maternal behavior and on postpartum estrus in pregnant rats. *Neuroendocrinology,* 1987, *46,* 522–531.

Adolphs, R., Tranel, D., Damasio, H., and Damasio, A. Impaired recognition of emotion in facial expressions following bilateral damage to the human amygdala. *Nature,* 1994, *372,* 669–672.

Adolphs, R., Tranel, D., Damasio, H., and Damasio, A. R. Fear and the human amygdala. *Journal of Neuroscience,* 1995, *15,* 5879–5891.

Advokat, C., and Kutlesic, V. Pharmacotherapy of the eating disorders: A commentary. *Neuroscience and Biobehavioral Reviews,* 1995, *19,* 59–66.

Akabayashi, A., Wahlestedt, C., Alexander, J. T., and Leibowitz, S. F. Specific inhibition of endogenous neuropeptide Y synthesis in arcuate nucleus by antisense oligonucleotides suppresses feeding behavior and insulin secretion. *Molecular Brain Research,* 1994, *21,* 55–61.

Akhtar, S., Wig, N., Pershad, D., and Varma, S. A phenomenological analysis of symptoms in obsessive compulsive disorder. *British Journal of Psychiatry,* 1975, *127,* 342–348.

Alam, M. N., McGinty, D., and Szymusiak, R. Neuronal discharge of preoptic anterior hypothalamic thermosensitive neurons: Relation to NREM sleep. *American Journal of Physiology: Regulatory, Integrative and Comparative Physiology,* 1995a, *269,* R1240–R1249.

Alam, M. N., Szymusiak, R., and McGinty, D. Local preoptic anterior hypothalamic warming alters spontaneous and evoked neuronal activity in the magno-cellular basal forebrain. *Brain Research,* 1995b, *696,* 221–230.

Aldrich, M. S. Narcolepsy. *Neurology,* 1992, *42,* 34–43.

Alexander, G. M., and Sherwin, B. B. Sex steroids, sexual behavior, and selective attention for erotic stimuli in women using oral contraceptives. *Psychoneuroendocrinology,* 1993, *18,* 91–102.

Alexander, G. M., Sherwin, B. B., Bancroft, J., and Davidson, D. W. Testosterone and sexual behavior in oral contraceptive users and nonusers: A prospective study. *Hormones and Behavior,* 1990, *24,* 388–402.

Alexander, M. P., and Albert, M. L. The anatomical basis of visual agnosia. In *Localization in Neuropsychology,* edited by A. Kertesz. New York: Academic Press, 1983.

Alexander, M. P., Fischer, R. S., and Friedman, R. Lesion localization in apractic agraphia. *Archives of Neurology,* 1992, *49,* 246–251.

Allen, L. S., and Gorski, R. A. Sexual orientation and the size of the anterior commissure in the human brain. *Proceedings of the National Academy of Sciences, USA,* 1992, *89,* 7199–7202.

Allison, D. B., Kaprio, J., Korkeila, M., Koskenvuo, M., Neale, M. C., and Hayakawa, K. The heritability of body mass index among an international sample of monozygotic twins reared apart. *International Journal of Obesity,* 1996, *20,* 501–506.

Altschuler, H. L., Phillips, P. E., and Feinhandler, D. A. Alterations of ethanol self-administration by naltrexone. *Life Sciences,* 1980, *26,* 679–688.

Anand, B. K., and Brobeck, J. R. Hypothalamic control of food intake in rats and cats. *Yale Journal of Biology and Medicine,* 1951, *24,* 123–140.

Andreasen, N. C. Symptoms, signs, and diagnosis of schizophrenia. *Lancet,* 1995, *346,* 477–481.

Andreasen, N. C., Arndt, S., Swayze, V., Cizadlo, T., Flaum, M., O'Leary, D., Ehrhardt, J. C., and Yuh, W. T. C. Thalamic abnormalities in schizophrenia visualized through magnetic resonance image averaging. *Science,* 1994, *266,* 294–298.

Angrilli, A., Mauri, A., Palomba, D., Flor, H., Birbaumer, N., Sartori, G., and Dipaola, F. Startle reflex and emotion modulation impairment after a right amygdala lesion. *Brain,* 1996, *119,* 1991–2000.

Anonymous. Effects of sexual activity on beard growth in man. *Nature,* 1970, *226,* 867–870.

Archer, J. Testosterone and aggression. *Journal of Offender Rehabilitation,* 1994, *5,* 3–25.

Arendt, J., Deacon, S., English, J., Hampton, S., and Morgan, L. Melatonin and adjustment to phase-shift. *Journal of Sleep Research,* 1995, *4,* 74–79.

Aroniadou, V. A., and Teyler, T. J. The role of NMDA receptors in long-term potentiation (LTP) and depression (LTD) in rat visual cortex. *Brain Research,* 1991, *562,* 136–143.

Aronson, B. D., Bell-Pedersen, D., Block, G. D., Bos, N. P. A., Dunlap, J. C., Eskin, A., Garceau, N. Y., Geusz, M. E., Johnson, K. A., Khalsa, S. B. S., Koster-Van Hoffen, G. C., Koumenis, C., Lee, T. M., LeSauter, J., Lindgren, K. M.,

Liu, Q., Loros, J. J., Michel, S. H., Mirmiran, M., Moore, R. Y., Ruby, N. F., Silver, R., Turek, F. W., and Zatz, M. Circadian rhythms. *Brain Research Reviews,* 1993, *18,* 315–333.

Aschoff, J. Circadian rhythms: General features and endocrinological aspects. In *Endocrine Rhythms,* edited by D. T. Krieger. New York: Raven Press, 1979.

Aston-Jones, G., and Bloom, F. E. Activity of norepinephrine-containing locus coeruleus neurons in behaving rats anticipates fluctuations in the sleep-waking cycle. *Journal of Neuroscience,* 1981, *1,* 876–886.

Atack, J. R., Broughton, H. B., and Pollack, S. J. Inositol monophosphatase: A putative target for Li$^+$ in the treatment of bipolar disorder. *Trends in Neurosciences,* 1995, *18,* 343–349.

Auer, R. N., Jensen, M. L., and Whishaw, I.Q. Neurobehavioral deficit due to ischemic brain damage limited to half of the CA1 section of the hippocampus. *Journal of Neuroscience,* 1989, *9,* 1641–1647.

Avenet, P., and Lindemann, B. Perspectives of taste reception. *Journal of Membrane Biology,* 1989, *112,* 1–8.

Bai, F. L., Yamano, M., Shiotani, Y., Emson, P. C., Smith, A. D., Powell, J. F., and Tohyama, M. An arcuato-paraventricular and -dorsomedial hypothalamic neuropeptide Y-containing system which lacks noradrenaline in the rat. *Brain Research,* 1985, *331,* 172–175.

Bailey, A. J. The biology of autism. *Psychological Medicine,* 1993, *23,* 7–11.

Bailey, A. J., Le Couteur, A., Gottesman, I., Bolton, P., Simonoff, E., Yuzda, E., and Rutter, M. Autism as a strongly genetic disorder: Evidence from a British twin study. *Psychological Medicine,* 1995, *25,* 63–77.

Bailey, J. M., and Pillard, R. C. A genetic study of male sexual orientation. *Archives of General Psychiatry,* 1991, *48,* 1089–1096.

Bailey, J. M., Pillard, R. C., Neale, M. C., and Agyei, Y. Heritable factors influence sexual orientation in women. *Archives of General Psychiatry,* 1993, *50,* 217–223.

Baizer, J. S., Ungerleider, L. G., and Desimone, R. Organization of visual inputs to the inferior temporal and posterior parietal cortex in macaques. *Journal of Neuroscience,* 1991, *11,* 168–190.

Baldessarini, R. J. *Chemotherapy in Psychiatry.* Cambridge, Mass.: Harvard University Press, 1977.

Balint, R. Seelenlahmung des "Schauens", optische Ataxie, raumliche Storung der Aufmerksamkeit. *Monatsschr. Psychiat. Neurol.,* 1909, *25,* 51–81.

Ballantine, H. T., Bouckoms, A. J., Thomas, E. K., and Giriunas, I. E. Treatment of psychiatric illness by stereotactic cingulotomy. *Biological Psychiatry,* 1987, *22,* 807–819.

Balon, R., Jordan, M., Pohl, R., and Yeragani, V. K. Family history of anxiety disorders in control subjects with lactate-induced panic attacks. *American Journal of Psychiatry*, 1989, *146*, 1304–1306.

Banks, W. A., Kastin, A. J., Huang, W. T., Jaspan, J. B., and Maness, L. M. Leptin enters the brain by a saturable system independent of insulin. *Peptides*, 1996, *17*, 305–311.

Baranyi, A., Szente, M. B., and Woody, C. D. Properties of associative long-lasting potentiation induced by cellular conditioning in the motor cortex of conscious cats. *Neuroscience*, 1991, *42*, 321–334.

Barbazanges, A., Piazza, P. V., Le Moal, M., and Maccari, S. Maternal glucocorticoid secretion mediates long-term effects of prenatal stress. *Journal of Neuroscience*, 1996, *16*, 3943–3949.

Barber, T. X. Responding to "hypnotic" suggestions: An introspective report. *American Journal of Clinical Hypnosis*, 1975, *18*, 6–22.

Barclay, C. D., Cutting, J. E., and Kozlowski, L. T. Temporal and spatial factors in gait perception that influence gender recognition. *Perception and Psychophysics*, 1978, *23*, 145–152.

Baron-Cohen, S., Leslie, A. M., and Frith, U. Does the autistic child have a "theory of mind"? *Cognition*, 1985, *21*, 37–46.

Bartness, T. J., Powers, J. B., Hastings, M. H., Bittman, E. L., and Goldman, B. D. The timed infusion paradigm for melatonin delivery: What has it taught us about the melatonin signal, its reception, and the photoperiodic control of seasonal responses? *Journal of Pineal Research*, 1993, *15*, 161–190.

Basbaum, A. I., and Fields, H. L. Endogenous pain control mechanisms: Review and hypothesis. *Annals of Neurology*, 1978, *4*, 451–462.

Basbaum, A. I., and Fields, H. L. Endogenous pain control systems: Brainstem spinal pathways and endorphin circuitry. *Annual Review of Neuroscience*, 1984, *7*, 309–338.

Bauer, R. H., and Fuster, J. M. Delayed-matching and delayed-response deficit from cooling dorsolateral prefrontal cortex in monkeys. *Journal of Comparative and Physiological Psychology*, 1976, *90*, 293–302.

Baxter, L. R., Schwartz, J. M., Mazziotta, J. C., Phelphs, M. E., Pahl, J. J., and Guze, B. H. Cerebral glucose metabolic rates in non-depressed obsessive compulsives. *American Journal of Psychiatry*, 1989, *145*, 1560–1563.

Baylis, G. C., Rolls, E. T., and Leonard, C. M. Selectivity between faces in the responses of a population of neurons in the cortex in the superior temporal sulcus of the monkey. *Brain Research*, 1985, *342*, 91–102.

Baylor, D. How photons start vision. *Proceedings of the National Academy of Sciences, USA*, 1996, *93*, 560–565.

Beamer, W., Bermant, G., and Clegg, M. Copulatory behavior of the ram, *Ovis aries*. II: Factors affecting copulatory satiety. *Animal Behavior*, 1969, *17*, 706–711.

Bean, N.J., and Conner, R. Central hormonal replacement and home-cage dominance in castrated rats. *Hormones and Behavior*, 1978, *11*, 100–109.

Bear, O., and Fedio, P. Qualitative analysis of interictal behavior in temporal lobe epilepsy. *Archives of Neurology*, 1977, *34*, 454–467.

Beauvois, M. F., and Dérouesné, J. Lexical or orthographic dysgraphia. *Brain*, 1981, *104*, 21–45.

Beauvois, M. F., and Dérouesné, J. Phonological alexia: Three dissociations. *Journal of Neurology, Neurosurgery and Psychiatry*, 1979, *42*, 1115–1124.

Bechara, A., Tranel, D., Damasio, H., Adolphs, R., Rockland, C., and Damasio, A. R. Double dissociation of conditioning and declarative knowledge relative to the amygdala and hippocampus in humans. *Science*, 1995, *269*, 1115–1118.

Beckstead, R. M., Morse, J. R., and Norgren, R. The nucleus of the solitary tract in the monkey: Projections to the thalamus and brainstem nuclei. *Journal of Comparative Neurology*, 1980, *190*, 259–282.

Beecher, H. K. *Measurement of Subjective Responses: Quantitative Effects of Drugs*. New York: Oxford University Press, 1959.

Beeman, E. A. The effect of male hormone on aggressive behavior in mice. *Physiological Zoology*, 1947, *20*, 373–405.

Behringer, R. R. The Müllerian inhibitor and mammalian sexual development. *Philosophical Transactions of the Royal Society of London B: Biological Sciences*, 1995, *350*, 285–288.

Beidler, L. M. Physiological properties of mammalian taste receptors. In *Taste and Smell in Vertebrates*, edited by G. E. W. Wolstenholme. London: J. & A. Churchill, 1970.

Bell, A. P., Weinberg, M. S., and Hammersmith, S. K. *Sexual Preference: Its Development in Men and Women*. Bloomington: Indiana University Press, 1981.

Benington, J. H., Kodali, S. K., and Heller, H. C. Stimulation of A1 adenosine receptors mimics the electroencephalographic effects of sleep deprivation. *Brain Research*, 1995, *692*, 79–85.

Benson, D. F., and Greenberg, J. Visual form agnosia. *Archives of Neurology*, 1969, *20*, 82–89.

Berger, B., Gaspar, P., and Verney, C. Dopaminergic innervation of the cerebral cortex: Unexpected differences between rodents and primates. *Trends in Neuroscience*, 1991, *14*, 21–27.

Bermant, G., and Davidson, J. M. *Biological Bases of Sexual Behavior*. New York: Harper & Row, 1974.

Berthier, M., Kulisevsky, J., Gironell, A., and Heras, J. A. Obsessive-compulsive disorder associated with brain lesions: Clinical phenomenology, cognitive function, and anatomic correlates. *Neurology*, 1996, *47*, 353–361.

Besson, J. M., Guilbaud, G., Abdelmoumene, M., and Chaouch, A. Physiologie de la nociception. *Journal of Physiology (Paris)*, 1982, *78*, 7–107.

Bettelheim, B. *The Empty Fortress*. New York: Free Press, 1967.

Bickford, P. C., Adams, C. E., Boyson, S. J., Curella, P., Gerhardt, G. A., Heron, C., Ivy, G. O., Lin, A. M. L. Y., Murphy, M. P., Poth, K., Wallace, D. R., Young, D. A., Zahniser, N. R., and Rose, G. M. Long-term treatment of male F344 rats with deprenyl: Assessment of effects on longevity, behavior, and brain function. *Neurobiology of Aging*, 1997, *18*, 309–318.

Bier, M. J., and McCarley, R. W. REM-enhancing effects of the adrenergic antagonist idazoxan infused into the medial pontine reticular formation of the freely moving cat. *Brain Research*, 1994, *634*, 333–338.

Binder, J. R., Rao, S. M., Hammeke, T. A., Yetkin, F. Z., Jesmanowicz, A., Bandettini, P. A., Wong, E. C., Estkowski, L. D., Goldstein, M. D., Haughton, V. M., and Hyde, J. S. Functional magnetic resonance imaging of human auditory cortex. *Annals of Neurology*, 1994, *35*, 662–672.

Bingman, V. P., and Mench, J. A. Homing behavior of hippocampus and parahippocampus lesioned pigeons following short-distance releases. *Behavioural Brain Research*, 1990, *40*, 227–238.

Bird, E., Cardone, C. C., and Contreras, R. J. Area postrema lesions disrupt food intake induced by cerebroventricular infusions of 5-thioglucose in the rat. *Brain Research*, 1983, *270*, 193–196.

Blaustein, J. D., and Olster, D. H. Gonadal steroid hormone receptors and social behaviors. In *Advances in Comparative and Environmental Physiology, Vol. 3*, edited by J. Balthazart. Berlin: Springer-Verlag, 1989.

Blest, A. D. The function of eyespot patterns in insects. *Behaviour*, 1957, *11*, 209–256.

Bleuler, E. Dementia Praecox of the Group of Schizophrenia. Translated by J. Zinkin. New York: International Universities Press, 1911/1950.

Bliss, T. V. P., and Lømo, T. Long-lasting potentiation of synaptic transmission in the dentate area of the anaesthetized rabbit following stimulation of the perforant path. *Journal of Physiology (London)*, 1973, *232*, 331–356.

Bloch, V., Hennevin, E., and Leconte, P. Interaction between post-trial reticular stimulation and subsequent paradoxical sleep in memory consolidation processes. In *Neurobiology of Sleep and Memory*, edited by R. R. Drucker-Colín and J. L. McGaugh. New York: Academic Press, 1977.

Blonder, L. X., Bowers, D., and Heilman, K. M. The role of the right hemisphere in emotional communication. *Brain*, 1991, *114*, 1115–1127.

Blumer, D., and Walker, A. E. The neural basis of sexual behavior. In *Psychiatric Aspects of Neurologic Disease*, edited by D. F. Benson and D. Blumer. New York: Grune & Stratton, 1975.

Bodner, M., Kroger, J., and Fuster, J. M. Auditory memory cells in dorsolateral prefrontal cortex. *NeuroReport*, 1996, *7*, 1905–1908.

Bogerts, B., Lieberman, J. A., Ashtari, M., Bilder, R. M., Degreef, G., Lerner, G., Johns, C., and Masiar, S. Hippocampus-amygdala volumes and psychopathology in chronic schizophrenia. *Biological Psychiatry*, 1993, *33*, 236–246.

Boller, F., and Dennis, M. *Auditory Comprehension: Clinical and Experimental Studies with the Token Test*. New York: Academic Press, 1979.

Bolton, R. F., Cornwall, J., and Phillipson, O. R. Collateral axons of cholinergic pontine neurones projecting to midline, mediodorsal and parafascicular thalamic nuclei in the rat. *Journal of Chemical Neuroanatomy*, 1993, *6*, 101–114.

Bon, C., Böhme, G. A., Doble, A., Stutzmann, J.-M., and Blanchard, J.-C. A role for nitric oxide in long-term potentiation. *European Journal of Neuroscience*, 1992, *4*, 420–424.

Bonnet, M. H., and Arand, D. L. We are chronically sleep deprived. *Sleep*, 1995, *18*, 908–911.

Born, R. T., and Tootell, R. B. H. Spatial frequency tuning of single units in macaque supragranular striate cortex. *Proceedings of the National Academy of Sciences, USA*, 1991, *88*, 7066–7070.

Bornstein, B., Stroka, H., and Munitz, H. Prosopagnosia with animal face agnosia. *Cortex*, 1969, *5*, 164–169.

Bornstein, R. A., Schwarzkopf, S. B., Olson, S. C., and Nasrallah, H. A. Third-ventricle enlargement and neuropsychological deficit in schizophrenia. *Biological Psychiatry*, 1992, *31*, 954–961.

Bottini, G., Corcoran, R., Sterzi, R., Paulesu, E., Schenone, P., Scarpa, P., Frackowiak, R. S. J., and Frith, C. D. The role of the right hemisphere in the interpretation of figurative aspects of language: A positron emission tomography activation study. *Brain*, 1994, *117*, 1241–1253.

Bouchard, C. Genetic factors in obesity. *Medical Clinics of North America*, 1989, *73*, 67–81.

Bouchard, C. Heredity and the path to overweight and obesity. *Medicine and Science of Sports Exercise*, 1991, *23*, 285–291.

Boulos, Z., Campbell, S. S., Lewy, A. J., Terman, M., Dijk, D. J., and Eastman, C. I. Light treatment for sleep disorders: Consensus report. 7: Jet-lag. *Journal of Biological Rhythms*, 1995, *10*, 167–176.

Bower, G. H., and Clark, M. C. Narrative stories as mediators for serial learning. *Psychonomic Science*, 1969, *14*, 181–182.

Bowers, D., and Heilman, K. M. A dissociation between the processing of affective and nonaffective faces. Paper presented at the meeting of the International Neuropsychological Society, Atlanta, 1981.

Bowers, D., Blonder, L. X., Feinberg, T., and Heilman, K. M. Differential impact of right and left hemisphere lesions on facial emotion and object imagery. *Brain*, 1991, *114*, 2593–2609.

Bowersox, S. S., Kaitin, K. I., and Dement, W. C. EEG spindle activity as a function of age: Relationship to sleep continuity. *Brain Research*, 1985, *63*, 526–539.

Boynton, R. M. *Human Color Vision.* New York: Holt, Rinehart and Winston, 1979.

Bozarth, M. A., and Wise, R. A. Toxicity associated with long-term intravenous heroin and cocaine self-administration in the rat. *Journal of the American Medical Association*, 1985, *254*, 81–83.

Bracha, H. S., Torrey, E. F., Gottesman, I. I., Bigelow, L. B., and Cunniff, C. Second-trimester markers of fetal size in schizophrenia: A study of monozygotic twins. *American Journal of Psychiatry*, 1992, *149*, 1355–1361.

Brackett, N. L., and Edwards, D. A. Medial preoptic connections with the midbrain tegmentum are essential for male sexual behavior. *Physiology and Behavior*, 1984, *32*, 79–84.

Bradbury, M. W. B. *The Concept of a Blood-Brain Barrier.* New York: John Wiley & Sons, 1979.

Bradwejn, J., and Koszycki, D. The cholecystokinin hypothesis of anxiety and panic disorder. *Annals of the New York Academy of Sciences*, 1994, *713*, 273–282.

Braun, A. R., Balkin, T. J., Wesensten, N.J., Gwadry, F., Carson, R. E., Varga, M., Baldwin, P., Belenky, G., and Herscovitch, P. Dissociated pattern of activity in visual cortices and their projections during human rapid eye movement sleep. *Science*, 1998, *279*, 91–95.

Braun, S. New experiments underscore warnings on maternal drinking. *Science*, 1996, *273*, 738–739.

Bray, G. A. Drug treatment of obesity. *American Journal of Clinical Nutrition*, 1992, *55*, 538S–544S.

Brecher, E. M. *Licit and Illicit Drugs.* Boston: Little, Brown & Co., 1972.

Breedlove, S. M. Sexual differentiation of the brain and behavior. In *Behavioral Endocrinology*, edited by J. B. Becker, S. M. Breedlove, and D. Crews. Cambridge, Mass.: MIT Press, 1992.

Breedlove, S. M. Sexual differentiation of the human nervous system. *Annual Review of Psychology*, 1994, *45*, 389–418.

Breier, A., Buchanan, R. W., Elkashef, A., Munson, R. C., Kirkpatrick, B., and Gellad, F. Brain morphology and schizophrenia: A magnetic resonance imaging study of limbic, prefrontal cortex, and caudate structures. *Archives of General Psychiatry*, 1992, *49*, 921–926.

Breisch, S. T., Žemlan, F. P., and Hoebel, B. G. Hyperphagia and obesity following serotonin depletion by intraventricular *p*-chlorphenylalanine. *Science*, 1976, *192*, 382–384.

Breiter, H. C., Rauch, S. L., Kwong, K. K., Baker, J. R., Weisskoff, R. M., Kennedy, D. N., Kendrick, A. D., Davis, T. L., Jiang, A. P., Cohen, M. S., Stern, C. E., Belliveau, J. W., Baer, L., O'Sullivan, R. L., Savage, C. R., Jenike, M. A., and Rosen, B. R. Functional magnetic resonance imaging of symptom provocation in obsessive-compulsive disorder. *Archives of General Psychiatry*, 1996, *53*, 595–606.

Bremner, J. D., Innis, R. B., Salomon, R. M., Staib, L. H., Ng, C. K., Miller, H. L., Bronen, R. A., Krystal, J. H., Duncan, J., Rich, D., Price, L. H., Malison, R., Dey, H., Soufer, R., and Charney, D. S. Positron emission tomography measurement of cerebral metabolic correlates of tryptophan depletion-induced depressive relapse. *Archives of General Psychiatry*, 1997, *54*, 364–374.

Bremner, J. D., Randall, P., Scott, T. M., Bronen, R. A., Seibyl, J. P., Southwick, S. M., Delaney, R. C., McCarthy, G., Charney, D. S., and Innis, R. B. MRI-based measurement of hippocampal volume in patients with combat-related posttraumatic stress disorder. *American Journal of Psychiatry*, 1995, *152*, 973–981.

Brickner, R. M. *The Intellectual Functions of the Frontal Lobe: A Study Based upon Observations of a Man after Partial Frontal Lobectomy.* New York: Macmillan, 1936.

Bridges, R. S. A quantitative analysis of the roles of dosage, sequence and duration of estradiol and progesterone exposure in the regulation of maternal behavior in the rat. *Endocrinology*, 1984, *114*, 930–940.

Bridges, R. S., and Ronsheim, P. M. Prolactin (PRL) regulation of maternal behavior in rats: Bromocriptine treatment delays and PRL promotes the rapid onset of behavior. *Endocrinology*, 1990, *126*, 837–848.

Britton, D. R., Koob, G. F., Rivier, J., and Vale, W. Intraventricular corticotropin-releasing factor enhances behavioral effects of novelty. *Life Sciences*, 1982, *31*, 363–367.

Broca, P. Remarques sur le siège de la faculté du langage articulé, suivies d'une observation d'aphemie (perte de la parole). *Bulletin de la Société Anatomique (Paris)*, 1861, *36*, 330–357.

Broussaud, D., di Pellegrino, G., and Wise, S. P. Frontal lobe mechanisms subserving vision-for-action versus vision-for-perception. *Behavioural Brain Research*, 1996, *72*, 1–15.

Brown, G. L., Ebert, M. H., Goyer, P. F., Jimerson, D. C., Klein, W. J., Bunney, W. E., and Goodwin, F. W. Aggression, suicide, and serotonin: Relationships to CSF amine metabolites. *American Journal of Psychiatry*, 1982, *139*, 741–746.

Brown, G. L., Goodwin, F. K., Ballenger, J. C., Goyer, P. F., and Major, L. F. Aggression in humans correlates with cerebrospinal fluid amine metabolites. *Psychiatry Research*, 1979, *1*, 131–139.

Brownell, H. H., Michel, D., Powelson, J., and Gardner, H. Surprise but not coherence: Sensitivity to verbal humor in right-hemisphere patients. *Brain and Language*, 1983, *18*, 20–27.

Brownell, H. H., Simpson, T. L., Bihrle, A. M., Potter, H. H., and Gardner, H. Appreciation of metaphoric alternative word meanings by left and right brain-damaged patients. *Neuropsychologia*, 1990, *28*, 173–184.

Bruce, H. M. A block to pregnancy in the mouse caused by proximity of strange males. *Journal of Reproduction and Fertility*, 1960a, *1*, 96–103.

Bruce, H. M. Further observations of pregnancy block in mice caused by proximity of strange males. *Journal of Reproduction and Fertility*, 1960b, *2*, 311–312.

Bruhwyler, J., Chleide, E., and Mercier, M. Clozapine: An atypical neuroleptic. *Neuroscience and Biobehavioral Reviews*, 1990, *14*, 357–363.

Bryden, M. P., and Ley, R. G. Right-hemispheric involvement in the perception and expression of emotion in normal humans. In *Neuropsychology of Human Emotion*, edited by K. M. Heilman and P. Satz. New York: Guilford Press, 1983.

Buchsbaum, M. S., Gillin, J. C., Wu, J., Hazlett, E., Sicotte, N., Dupont, R. M., and Bunney, W. E. Regional cerebral glucose metabolic rate in human sleep assessed by positron emission tomography. *Life Sciences*, 1989, *45*, 1349–1356.

Buck, L. B. Information coding in the vertebrate olfactory system. *Annual Review of Neuroscience*, 1996, *19*, 517–544.

Buck, L., and Axel, R. A novel multigene family may encode odorant receptors: A molecular basis for odor recognition. *Cell*, 1991, *65*, 175–187.

Buckley, P., Stack, J. P., Madigan, C., O'Callaghan, E., Larkin, C., Redmond, O., Ennis, J. T., and Waddington, J. L. Magnetic resonance imaging of schizophrenia-like psychoses associated with cerebral trauma: Clinicopathological correlates. *American Journal of Psychiatry*, 1993, *150*, 146–148.

Buggy, J., Hoffman, W. E., Phillips, M. I., Fisher, A. E., and Johnson, A. K. Osmosensitivity of rat third ventricle and interactions with angiotensin. *American Journal of Physiology*, 1979, *236*, R75–R82.

Burke, J. R., Enghild, J. J., Martin, M. E., Jou, Y. S., Myers, R. M., Roses, A. D., Vance, J. M., and Strittmatter, W. J. Huntington and DRPLA proteins selectively interact with the enzyme GAPDH. *Nature Medicine*, 1996, *2*, 347–335.

Burton, M. J., Rolls, E. T., and Mora, F. Effects of hunger on the responses of neurons in the lateral hypothalamus to the sight and taste of food. *Experimental Neurology*, 1976, *51*, 668–677.

Cabanac, M., and Lafrance, L. Facial consummatory responses in rats support the ponderostat hypothesis. *Physiology and Behavior*, 1991, *50*, 179–183.

Cador, M., Robbins, T. W., and Everitt, B. J. Involvement of the amygdala in stimulus-reward associations: Interaction with the ventral striatum. *Neuroscience*, 1989, *30*, 77–86.

Cahill, L., Babinsky, R., Markowitsch, H. J., and McGaugh, J. L. The amygdala and emotional memory. *Nature*, 1995, *377*, 295–296.

Cahill, L., Haier, R. J., Fallon, J., Alkire, M. T., Tang, C., Keator, D., Wu, J., and McGaugh, J. L. Amygdala activity at encoding correlated with long-term, free recall of emotional information. *Proceedings of the National Academy of Sciences, USA*, 1996, *93*, 8016–8021.

Cain, W. S. Olfaction. In *Stevens' Handbook of Experimental Psychology. Vol. 1. Perception and Motivation*, edited by R. C. Atkinson, R. J. Herrnstein, G. Lindzey, and R. D. Luce. New York: John Wiley & Sons, 1988.

Caine, S. B., and Koob, G. F. Effects of mesolimbic dopamine depletion on responding maintained by cocaine and food. *Journal of the Experimental Analysis of Behavior*, 1994, *61*, 213–221.

Caine, S. B., Heinrichs, S. C., Coffin, V. L., and Koob, G. F. Effects of the dopamine D-1 antagonist SCH 23390 microinjected into the accumbens, amygdala or striatum on cocaine self-administration in the rat. *Brain Research*, 1995, *692*, 47–56.

Calder, A. J., Young, A. W., Rowland, D., Perrett, D. I., Hodges, J. R., and Etcoff, N. L. Facial emotion recognition after bilateral amygdala damage: Differentially severe impairment of fear. *Cognitive Neuropsychology*, 1996, *13*, 699–745.

Calhoun, J. Population density and social pathology. *Scientific American*, 1962, *206*, 139–148.

Calingasan, N. Y., and Ritter, S. Lateral parabrachial subnucleus lesions abolish feeding induced by mercaptoacetate but not by 2-deoxy-D-glucose. *American Journal of Physiology*, 1993, *265*, R1168–R1178.

Callaway, C. W., Lydic, R., Baghdoyan, H. A., and Hobson, J. A. Pontogeniculoocipital waves: Spontaneous visual system activity during rapid eye movement sleep. *Cellular and Molecular Neurobiology*, 1987, *2*, 105–149.

Calvert, G. A., Bullmore, E. T., Brammer, M. J., Campbell, R., Williams, S. C. R., McGuire, P. K., Woodruff, P. W. R., Iversen, S. D., and David, A. S. Activation of auditory cortex during silent lipreading. *Science*, 1997, *276*, 593–596.

Campbell, R., De Gelder, B., and De Haan, E. The lateralization of lip-reading: A second look. *Neuropsychologia*, 1996, *34*, 1235–1240.

Campeau, S., Hayward, M. D., Hope, B. T., Rosen, J. B., Nestler, E. J., and Davis, M. Induction of the c-fos proto-oncogene in rat amygdala during unconditioned and conditioned fear. *Brain Research*, 1991, *565*, 349–352.

Campeau, S., Miserendino, M. J. D., and Davis, M. Intra-amygdala infusion of the N-methyl-D-aspartate receptor antagonist AP5 blocks acquisition but not expression of fear-potentiated startle to an auditory conditioned stimulus. *Behavioral Neuroscience*, 1992, *106*, 569–574.

Campfield, L. A., Smith, F. J., Guisez, Y., Devos, R., and Burn, P. Recombinant mouse ob protein: Evidence for a peripheral signal linking adiposity and central neural networks. *Science*, 1995, *269*, 546–549.

Cannon, W. B. The James-Lange theory of emotions: A critical examination and an alternative. *American Journal of Psychology*, 1927, *39*, 106–124.

Canteras, N. S., Simerly, R. B., and Swanson, L. W. Organization of projections from the medial nucleus of the amygdala: A PHA-L study in the rat. *Journal of Comparative Neurology*, 1995, *360*, 213–245.

Card, J. P., Riley, J. N., and Moore, R. Y. The suprachiasmatic hypothalamic nucleus: Ultrastructure of relations to optic chiasm. *Neuroscience Abstracts*, 1980, *6*, 758.

Carew, T. J. Development assembly of learning in *Aplysia*. *Trends in Neuroscience*, 1989, *12*, 389–394.

Caro, J. F., Kolaczynski, J. W., Nyce, M. R., Ohannesian, J. P., Opentanova, I., Goldman, W. H., Lynn, R. B., Zhang, P. L., Sinha, M. K., and Considine, R. V. Decreased cerebrospinal fluid/serum leptin ration in obesity: A possible mechanism for leptin resistance. *Lancet*, 1996, *348*, 159–161.

Carpenter, C. R. Sexual behavior of free ranging rhesus monkeys (*Macaca mulatta*). I: Specimens, procedures and behavioral characteristics of estrus. *Journal of Comparative Psychology*, 1942, *33*, 113–142.

Carrera, M. R., Ashley, J. A., Parsons, L. H., Wirsching, P., Koob, G. F., and Janda, K. D. Suppression of psychoactive effects of cocaine by active immunization. *Nature*, 1995, *378*, 727–730.

Carter, C. S. Hormonal influences on human sexual behavior. In *Behavioral Endocrinology*, edited by J. B. Becker, S. M. Breedlove, and D. Crews. Cambridge, Mass.: MIT Press, 1992.

Castles, A., and Coltheart, M. Varieties of developmental dyslexia. *Cognition*, 1993, *47*, 149–180.

Cavada, C., and Goldman-Rakic, P. S. Posterior parietal cortex in rhesus monkey. II: Evidence for segregated corticocortical networks linking sensory and limbic areas with the frontal lobe. *Journal of Comparative Neurology*, 1989, *287*, 422–445.

Chaudhari, N., Yang, H., Lamp, C., Delay, E., Cartford, C., Than, T., and Roper, S. The taste of monosodium glutamate: Membrane receptors in taste buds. *Journal of Neuroscience*, 1996, *16*, 3817–3826.

Chen, J., Paredes, W., and Gardner, E. L. Chronic treatment with clozapine selectively decreases basal dopamine release in nucleus accumbens but not in caudate-putamen as measured by in vivo brain microdialysis: Further evidence for depolarization block. *Neuroscience Letters*, 1991, *122*, 127–131.

Chen, J., Paredes, W., Li, J., Smith, D., Lowinson, J., and Gardner, E. L. Delta⁹-tetrahydrocannabinol produces naloxone-blockable enhancement of presynaptic basal dopamine efflux in nucleus accumbens of conscious, freely-moving rats as measured by intracerebral microdialysis. *Psychopharmacology*, 1990, *102*, 156–162.

Chen, W. R., Lee, S. H., Kato, K., Spencer, D. D., Shepherd, G. M., and Williamson, A. Long-term modifications of synaptic efficacy in the human inferior and middle temporal cortex. *Proceedings of the National Academy of Sciences, USA*, 1996, *93*, 8011–8015.

Chen, Y. W., and Dilsaver, S. C. Lifetime rates of suicide attempts among subjects with bipolar and unipolar disorders relative to subjects with other axis I disorders. *Biological Psychiatry*, 1996, *39*, 896–899.

Chess, S., Fernandez, F., and Korn, S. J. *Psychiatric Disorders of Children with Congenital Rubella*. New York: Brunner-Mazel, 1971.

Clark, J. T., Kalra, P. S., Crowley, W. R., and Kalra, S. P. Neuropeptide Y and human pancreatic polypeptide stimulates feeding behavior in rats. *Endocrinology*, 1984, *115*, 427–429.

Cloninger, C. R. Neurogenetic adaptive mechanisms in alcoholism. *Science*, 1987, *236*, 410–416.

Cloninger, C. R., Bohman, M., and Sigvardsson, S. Inheritance of alcohol abuse: Cross-fostering analysis of adopted men. *Archives of General Psychiatry*, 1981, *38*, 861–868.

Cloninger, C. R., Bohman, M., Sigvardsson, S., and von Knorring, A.-L. Psychopathology in adopted-out children of alcoholics: The Stockholm Adoption Study. *Recent Developments in Alcoholism*, 1985, *3*, 37–51.

Clugnet, M.-C., and LeDoux, J. E. Synaptic plasticity in fear conditioning circuits: Induction of LTP in the lateral nucleus of the amygdala by stimulation of the medial geniculate body. *Journal of Neuroscience*, 1990, *10*, 2818–2824.

Cobb, S., and Rose, R. M. Hypertension, peptic ulcer, and diabetes in air traffic controllers. *Journal of the American Medical Association*, 1973, *224*, 489–492.

Coble, P. A., Scher, M. S., Reynolds, C. F., Day, N. L., and Kupfer, D. J. Preliminary findings on the neonatal sleep of offspring of women with and without a prior history of affective disorder. *Sleep Research*, 1988, *16*, 120.

Coccaro, E. F. Neurotransmitter correlates of impulsive aggression in humans. *Annals of the New York Academy of Sciences*, 1996, *794*, 82–89.

Coccaro, E. F., Silverman, J. M., Klar, H. M., Horvath, T. B., and Siever, L. J. Familial correlates of reduced central serotonergic system function in patients with personality disorders. *Archives of General Psychiatry*, 1994, *51*, 318–324.

Cohen, E. A. *Human Behavior in the Concentration Camp*. New York: W. W. Norton, 1953.

Cohen, S., Tyrrell, D. A. J., and Smith, A. P. Psychological stress and susceptibility to the common cold. *New England Journal of Medicine*, 1991, *325*, 606–612.

Colditz, G. A. Economic costs of obesity. *American Journal of Clinical Nutrition*, 1992, *55*, 503S-507S.

Cole, B. J., and Koob, G. F. Propranolol antagonizes the enhanced conditioned fear produced by corticotropin releasing factor. *Journal of Pharmacology and Experimental Therapeutics*, 1988, *247*, 901–910.

Collaborative Research Group. A novel gene containing a trinucleotide repeat that is expanded and unstable on Huntington's disease chromosomes. *Cell*, 1993, *72*, 971–983.

Comings, D. E., and Comings, B. G. Clinical and genetic relationships between autism-pervasive developmental disorder and Tourette syndrome: A study of 19 cases. *American Journal of Medical Genetics*, 1991, *39*, 180–191.

Constantinidis, C., and Steinmetz, M. A. Neuronal activity in posterior parietal area 7a during the delay periods of a spatial memory task. *Journal of Neurophysiology*, 1996, *76*, 1352–1355.

Coover, G. D., Murison, R., and Jellestad, F. K. Subtotal lesions of the amygdala: The rostral central nucleus in passive avoidance and ulceration. *Physiology and Behavior*, 1992, *51*, 795–803.

Coplan, J. D., Gorman, J. M., and Klein, D. F. Serotonin related functions in panic-anxiety: A critical overview. *Neuropsychopharmacology*, 1992, *6*, 189–200.

Corkin, S., Sullivan, E. V., Twitchell, T. E., and Grove, E. The amnesic patient H. M.: Clinical observations and test performance 28 years after operation. *Society for Neuroscience Abstracts*, 1981, *7*, 235.

Cornelissen, P., Bradley, L., Fowler, S., and Stein, J. What children see affects how they read. *Developmental Medicine and Child Neurology*, 1991, *33*, 755–762.

Cornwall, J., Cooper, J. D., and Phillipson, O. T. Afferent and efferent connections of the laterodorsal tegmental nucleus in the rat. *Brain Research Bulletin*, 1990, *25*, 271–284.

Corrigall, W. A., Coen, K. M., and Adamson, K. L. Self-administered nicotine activates the mesolimbic dopamine system through the ventral tegmental area. *Brain Research*, 1994, *653*, 278–284.

Courchesne, E. Neuroanatomic imaging in autism. *Pediatrics*, 1991, *87*, 781–790.

Cowey, A., and Stoerig, P. The neurobiology of blindsight. *Trends in Neuroscience*, 1991, *14*, 140–145.

Cowley, J. J., and Brooksbank, B. W. L. Human exposure to putative pheromones and changes in aspects of social behaviour. *Journal of Steroid Biochemistry and Molecular Biology*, 1991, *39*, 647–659.

Cox, A., Rutter, M., Newman, S., and Bartak, L. A comparative study of infantile autism and specific developmental language disorders. I: Parental characteristics. *British Journal of Psychiatry*, 1975, *126*, 146–159.

Crane, G. E. Iproniazid (Marsilid) phosphate, a therapeutic agent for mental disorders and debilitating diseases. *Psychiatry Research Reports*, 1957, *8*, 142–152.

Crick, F., and Mitchison, G. The function of dream sleep. *Nature*, 1983, *304*, 111–114.

Crick, F., and Mitchison, G. REM sleep and neural nets. *Behavioural Brain Research*, 1995, *69*, 147–155.

Crow, T. J. A map of the rat mesencephalon for electrical self-stimulation. *Brain Research*, 1972, *36*, 265–273.

Crow, T. J. Positive and negative schizophrenic symptoms and the role of dopamine. *British Journal of Psychiatry*, 1980, *137*, 383–386.

Crowe, R. R., Noyes, R., Pauls, D. L., and Slymen, D. A family study of panic disorder. *Archives of General Psychiatry*, 1983, *40*, 1065–1069.

Crowe, R. R., Noyes, R., Wilson, A. F., Elston, R. C., and Ward, L. J. A linkage study of panic disorder. *Archives of General Psychiatry*, 1987, *44*, 933–937.

Cubelli, R. A selective deficit for writing vowels in acquired dysgraphia. *Nature*, 1991, *353*, 258–260.

Culebras, A., and Moore, J. T. Magnetic resonance findings in REM sleep behavior disorder. *Neurology*, 1989, *39*, 1519–1523.

Culotta, E., and Koshland, D. E. NO news is good news. *Science*, 1992, *258*, 1862–1865.

Cummings, J. L., and Cunningham, K. Obsessive-compulsive disorder in Huntington's disease. *Biological Psychiatry*, 1992, *31*, 263–270.

Currie, P. J., and Coscina, D. V. Regional hypothalamic differences in neuropeptide Y-induced feeding and energy substrate utilization. *Brain Research*, 1996, *737*, 238–242.

Dabbs, J. M., and Morris, R. Testosterone, social class, and antisocial behavior in a sample of 4,462 men. *Psychological Science*, 1990, *1*, 209–211.

Dabbs, J. M., Frady, R. L., Carr, T. S., and Besch, N. F. Saliva testosterone and criminal violence in young adult prison inmates. *Psychosomatic Medicine*, 1987, *49*, 174–182.

Dabbs, J. M., Ruback, J. M., Frady, R. L., and Hopper, C. H. Saliva testosterone and criminal violence among women. *Personality and Individual Differences*, 1988, *9*, 269–275.

Dacey, D. M. Circuitry for color coding in the primate retina. *Proceedings of the National Academy of Sciences, USA*, 1996, *93*, 582–588.

Dacey, D. M., Lee, B. B., Stafford, D. K., Pokorny, J., and Smith, V. C. Horizontal cells of the primate retina: Cone specificity without spectral opponency. *Science*, 1996, *271*, 656–659.

Dalen, P. Month of birth and schizophrenia. *Acta Psychiatrica Scandanivica*, 1968, *44* (Suppl.), 55–60.

Dallos, P. The active cochlea. *Journal of Neuroscience*, 1992, *12*, 4575–4585.

Damasio, A. R. Disorders of complex visual processing: Agnosias, achromatopsia, Balint's syndrome, and related difficulties of orientation and construction. In *Principles of Behavioral Neurology*, edited by M.-M. Mesulam. Philadelphia: F. A. Davis, 1985.

Damasio, A. R., and Damasio, H. The anatomic basis of pure alexia. *Neurology*, 1983, *33*, 1573–1583.

Damasio, A. R., and Damasio, H. Hemianopia, hemiachromatopsia, and the mechanisms of alexia. *Cortex*, 1986, *22*, 161–169.

Damasio, A. R., and Tranel, D. Knowing that "Colorado" goes with "Denver" does not imply knowledge that "Denver" *is* in "Colorado." *Behavioural Brain Research*, 1990, *40*, 193–200.

Damasio, A. R., and Tranel, D. Nouns and verbs are retrieved with differentially distributed neural systems. *Proceedings of the National Academy of Sciences, USA*, 1993, *90*, 4957–4960.

Damasio, A. R., Brandt, J. P., Tranel, D., and Damasio, H. Name dropping: Retrieval of proper or common nouns depends on different systems in left temporal cortex. *Society for Neuroscience Abstracts*, 1991, *17*, 4.

Damasio, A. R., Damasio, H., and Van Hoesen, G. W. Prosopagnosia: Anatomic basis and behavioral mechanisms. *Neurology*, 1982, *32*, 331–341.

Damasio, A. R., Yamada, T., Damasio, H., Corbett, J., and McKee, J. Central achromatopsia: Behavioral, anatomic, and physiologic aspects. *Neurology*, 1980, *30*, 1064–1071.

Damasio, H. Neuroimaging contributions to the understanding of aphasia. In *Handbook of Neuropsychology, Vol. 2*, edited by F. Boller and J. Grafman. Amsterdam: Elsevier, 1989.

Damasio, H., Eslinger, P., and Adams, H. P. Aphasia following basal ganglia lesions: New evidence. *Seminars in Neurology*, 1984, *4*, 151–161.

Damasio, H., Grabowski, T., Frank, R., Galaburda, A. M., and Damasio, A. R. The return of Phineas Gage: Clues about the brain from the skull of a famous patient. *Science*, 1994, *264*, 1102–1105.

D'Amato, T., Rochet, T., Dalery, J., Laurent, A., Chauchat, J.-H., Terra, J.-L., and Marie-Cardine, M. Relationship between symptoms rated with the Positive and Negative Syndrome Scale and brain measures in schizophrenia. *Psychiatry Research*, 1992, *44*, 55–62.

Damsma, G., Day, J., and Fibiger, H. C. Lack of tolerance to nicotine-induced dopamine release in the nucleus accumbens. *European Journal of Pharmacology*, 1989, *168*, 363–368.

Daniele, A., Giustolisi, L., Silveri, M. C., Colosimo, C., and Gainotti, G. Evidence for a possible neuroanatomical basis for lexical processing of nouns and verbs. *Neuropsychologia*, 1994, *32*, 1325–1341.

Darwin, C. *The Expression of the Emotions in Man and Animals*. Chicago: University of Chicago Press, 1872/1965.

Davidson, D., Swift, R., and Fitz, E. Naltrexone increases the latency to drink alcohol in social drinkers. *Alcoholism: Clinical and Experimental Research*, 1996, *20*, 732–739.

Davidson, J. M. Hormones and sexual behavior in the male. In *Neuroendocrinology*, edited by D. T. Krieger and J. C. Hughes. Sunderland, Mass.: Sinauer Associates, 1980.

Davis, J. D., and Campbell, C. S. Peripheral control of meal size in the rat: Effect of sham feeding on meal size and drinking rate. *Journal of Comparative and Physiological Psychology*, 1973, *83*, 379–387.

Davis, J. O., and Bracha, H. S. Famine and schizophrenia: First-trimester malnutrition or second-trimester beriberi? *Biological Psychiatry*, 1996, *40*, 1–3.

Davis, J. O., Phelps, J. A., and Bracha, H. S. Prenatal development of monozygotic twins and concordance for schizophrenia. *Schizophrenia Bulletin*, 1995, *21*, 357–366.

Davis, M. The role of the amygdala in fear and anxiety. *Annual Review of Neuroscience*, 1992a, *15*, 353–375.

Davis, M. The role of the amygdala in fear-potentiated startle: Implications for animal models of anxiety. *Trends in Pharmacological Sciences*, 1992b, *13*, 35–41.

Davison, G. C., and Neale, J. M. *Abnormal Psychology: An Experimental Clinical Approach*. New York: John Wiley & Sons, 1974.

Daw, N. W. Colour-coded ganglion cells in the goldfish retina: Extension of their receptive fields by means of new stimuli. *Journal of Physiology (London)*, 1968, *197*, 567–592.

Dawson, E., and Murray, R. Schizophrenia: A gene at 6p? *Current Biology*, 1996, *6*, 268–271.

Day, J., Damsma, G., and Fibiger, H. C. Cholinergic activity in the rat hippocampus, cortex and striatum correlates with locomotor activity: An in vivo microdialysis study. *Pharmacology, Biochemistry, and Behavior*, 1991, *38*, 723–729.

D'Cruz, O. F., Vaughn, B. V., Gold, S. H., and Greenwood, R. S. Symptomatic cataplexy in pontomedullary lesions. *Neurology*, 1994, *44*, 2189–2191.

Deacon, S., and Arendt, J. Adapting to phase shifts. I: An experimental model for jet lag and shift work. *Physiology and Behavior*, 1996, *59*, 665–673.

Dean, P. Effects of inferotemporal lesions on the behavior of monkeys. *Psychological Bulletin*, 1976, *83*, 41–71.

Debanne, D., Gähwiler, B. H., and Thompson, S. M. Asynchronous pre- and postsynaptic activity induces associative long-term depression in area CA1 of the rat hippocampus in vitro. *Proceedings of the National Academy of Sciences*, 1994, *91*, 1148–1152.

de Castro, J. M. Genetic influences on daily intake and meal patterns of humans. *Physiology and Behavior*, 1993, *53*, 777–782.

de Castro, J. M., and de Castro, E. S. Spontaneous meal patterns of humans: Influence of the presence of other people. *American Journal of Clinical Nutrition*, 1989, *50*, 237–247.

de Castro, J. M., McCormick, J., Pedersen, M., and Kreitzman, S. N. Spontaneous human meal patterns are related to preprandial factors regardless of natural environmental constraints. *Physiology and Behavior*, 1986, *38*, 25–29.

Degreef, G., Ashtari, M., Bogerts, B., Bilder, R. M., Jody, D. N., Alvir, J. M. J., and Lieberman, J. A. Volumes of ventricular system subdivisions measured from magnetic resonance images in first-episode schizophrenic patients. *Archives of General Psychiatry*, 1992, *49*, 531–537.

Dejerine, J. Contribution à l'étude anatomo-pathologique et clinique des différentes variétés de cécité verbale. *Comptes Rendus des Séances de la Société de Biologie et de Ses Filiales*, 1892, *4*, 61–90.

Delay, J., and Deniker, P. Le traitement des psychoses par une methode neurolytique derivée d'hibernothéraphie; le 4560 RP utilisée seul une cure prolongée et continuée. *Comptes Rendus Congrès des Médecins Aliénistes et Neurologistes de France et des Pays de Langue Française*, 1952a, *50*, 497–502.

Delay, J., and Deniker, P. 38 cas des psychoses traitées par la cure prolongée et continuée de 4560 RP. *Comptes Rendus Congrès des Médecins Aliénistes et Neurologistes de France et des Pays de Langue Française*, 1952b, *50*, 503–513.

Delgado, P. L., Charney, D. S., Price, L. H., Aghajanian, G. K., Landis, H., and Heninger, G. R. Serotonin function and the mechanism of antidepressant action: Reversal of antidepressant induced remission by rapid depletion of plasma tryptophan. *Archives of General Psychiatry*, 1990, *47*, 411–418.

DeLong, G. R. Autism, amnesia, hippocampus, and learning. *Neuroscience and Biobehavioral Reviews*, 1992, *16*, 63–70.

Dement, W. C. *Some Must Watch While Some Must Sleep*. San Francisco: W. H. Freeman, 1974.

Dement, W. C. The effect of dream deprivation. *Science*, 1960, *131*, 1705–1707.

Deol, M. S., and Gluecksohn-Waelsch, S. The role of inner hair cells in hearing. *Nature*, 1979, *278*, 250–252.

De Renzi, E., Perani, D., Carlesimo, G. A., Silveri, M. C., and Fazio, F. Prosopagnosia can be associated with damage confined to the right hemisphere: An MRI and PET study and a review of the literature. *Neuropsychologia*, 1994, *32*, 893–902.

Dérousné, J., and Beauvois, M.-F. Phonological processing in reading: Data from alexia. *Journal of Neurology, Neurosurgery, and Psychiatry*, 1979, *42*, 1125–1132.

Desimone, R., Albright, T. D., Gross, C. G., and Bruce, D. Stimulus-selective properties of inferior temporal neurons in the macaque. *Journal of Neuroscience*, 1984, *8*, 2051–2062.

Deutsch, J. A., and Gonzalez, M. F. Gastric nutrient content signals satiety. *Behavioral and Neural Biology*, 1980, *30*, 113–116.

De Valois, R. L., and De Valois, K. K. *Spatial Vision*. New York: Oxford University Press, 1988.

De Valois, R. L., Thorell, L. G., and Albrecht, D. G. Periodicity of striate-cortex-cell receptive fields. *Journal of the Optical Society of America*, 1985, *2*, 1115–1123.

Devane, W. A., Hanus, L., Breuer, A., Pertwee, R. G., Stevenson, L. A., Griffin, G., Gibson, D., Mandelbaum, A., Etinger, A., and Mechoulam, R. Isolation and structure of a brain constituent that binds to the cannabinoid receptor. *Science*, 1992, *258*, 1946–1949.

Devine, D. P., and Wise, R. A. Self-administration of morphine, DAMGO, and DPDPE into the ventral tegmental area of rats. *Journal of Neuroscience*, 1994, *14*, 1978–1984.

Di Chiara, G. The role of dopamine in drug abuse viewed from the perspective of its role in motivation. *Drug and Alcohol Dependency*, 1995, *38*, 95–137.

Di Ciano, P., Coury, A., Depoortere, R. Y., Egilmez, Y., Lane, J. D., Emmett-Oglesby, M. W., Lepiane, F. G., Phillips, A. G., and Blaha, C. D. Comparison of changes in extracellular dopamine concentrations in the nucleus accumbens during intravenous self-administration of cocaine or d-amphetamine. *Behavioural Pharmacology*, 1995, *6*, 311–322.

di Tomaso, E., Beltramo, M., and Piomelli, D. Brain cannabinoids in chocolate. *Nature*, 1996, *382*, 677–678.

Digiovanni, M., Dalessandro, G., Baldini, S., Cantalupi, D., and Bottacchi, E. Clinical and neuroradiological findings in a case of pure word deafness. *Italian Journal of Neurological Sciences*, 1992, *13*, 507–510.

Dijk, D. J., Boulos, Z., Eastman, C. I., Lewy, A. J., Campbell, S. S., and Terman, M. Light treatment for sleep disorders: Consensus report. 2: Basic properties of circadian physiology and sleep regulation. *Journal of Biological Rhythms*, 1995, *10*, 113–125.

Divac, I., Rosvold, H. E., and Szcwarcbart, M. K. Behavioral effects of selective ablation of the caudate nucleus. *Journal of Comparative and Physiological Psychology*, 1967, *63*, 184–190.

Dolan, R. P., and Schiller, P. H. Evidence for only depolarizing rod bipolar cells in the primate retina. *Visual Neuroscience*, 1989, *2*, 421–424.

Donny, E. C., Caggiula, A. R., Knopf, S., and Brown, C. Nicotine self-administration in rats. *Psychopharmacology*, 1995, *122*, 390–394.

Drevets, W. C., Videen, T. O., Price, J. L., Preskorn, S. H., Carmichael, S. T., and Raichle, M. E. A functional anatomical study of unipolar depression. *Journal of Neuroscience*, 1992, *12*, 3628–3641.

Dronkers, N. F. A new brain region for coordinating speech articulation. *Nature*, 1996, *384*, 159–161.

Drugan, R. C., Basile, A. S., Ha, J.-H., and Ferland, R. J. The protective effects of stress control may be mediated by increased brain levels of benzodiazepine receptor agonists. *Brain Research*, 1994, *661*, 127–136.

Dryden, S., Wang, Q., Frankish, H. M., Pickavance, L., and Williams, G. The serotonin (5-HT) antagonist methysergide increases neuropeptide-Y (NPY) synthesis and secretion in the hypothalamus of the rat. *Brain Research*, 1995, *699*, 12–18.

Duchenne, G.-B. *The Mechanism of Human Facial Expression*. Translated by R. A. Cuthbertson. Cambridge: Cambridge University Press, 1990. (Original work published 1862.)

Dunnett, S. B., Lane, D. M., and Winn, P. Ibotenic acid lesions of the lateral hypothalamus: Comparison with 6-hydroxydopamine-induced sensorimotor deficits. *Neuroscience*, 1985, *14*, 509–518.

Durie, D. J. Sleep in animals. In *Psychopharmacology of Sleep*, edited by D. Wheatley. New York: Raven Press, 1981.

Duvauchelle, C. L., and Ettenberg, A. Haloperidol attenuates conditioned place preferences produced by electrical stimulation of the medial prefrontal cortex. *Pharmacology, Biochemistry, and Behavior*, 1991, *38*, 645–650.

Eastman, C. I., Boulos, Z., Terman, M., Campbell, S. S., Dijk, D. J., and Lewy, A. J. Light treatment for sleep disorders: Consensus Report. 6: Shift work. *Journal of Biological Rhythms*, 1995, *10*, 157–164.

Eddy, N. B., Halbach, H., Isbell, H., and Seevers, M. H. Drug dependence: Its significance and characteristics. *Bulletin of the World Health Organization*, 1965, *32*, 721–733.

Eden, G. F., VanMeter, J. W., Rumsey, J. M., Maisog, J. M., Woods, R. P., and Zeffiro, T. A. Abnormal processing of visual motion in dyslexia revealed by functional brain imaging. *Nature*, 1996, *382*, 66–69.

Edwards, D. P., Purpura, K. P., and Kaplan, E. Contrast sensitivity and spatial-frequency response of primate cortical neurons in and around the cytochrome oxidase blobs. *Vision Research*, 1995, *35*, 1501–1523.

Ehrhardt, A. A., and Meyer-Bahlburg, H. F. L. Effects of prenatal sex hormones on gender-related behavior. *Science*, 1981, *211*, 1312–1318.

Eichenbaum, H., Otto, T., and Cohen, N. J. The hippocampus: What does it do? *Behavioral and Neural Biology*, 1992, *57*, 2–36.

Eichenbaum, H., Steward, C., and Morris, R. G. M. Hippocampal representation in spatial learning. *Journal of Neuroscience*, 1990, *10*, 331–339.

Eilam, R., Malach, R., Bergmann, F., and Segal, M. Hypertension induced by hypothalamic transplantation from genetically hypertensive to normotensive rats. *Journal of Neuroscience*, 1991, *11*, 401–411.

Ekman, P. *The Face of Man: Expressions of Universal Emotions in a New Guinea Village*. New York: Garland STPM Press, 1980.

Ekman, P. Facial expressions of emotion: An old controversy and new findings. *Philosophical Transactions of the Royal Society of London [B]*, 1992, *335*, 63–69.

Ekman, P., and Davidson, R. J. Voluntary smiling changes regional brain activity. *Psychological Science*, 1993, *4*, 342–345.

Ekman, P., and Friesen, W. V. Constants across cultures in the face and emotion. *Journal of Personality and Social Psychology*, 1971, *17*, 124–129.

El Mansari, M., Sakai, K., and Jouvet, M. Unitary characteristics of presumptive cholinergic tegmental neurons during the sleep-waking cycle in freely moving cats. *Experimental Brain Research*, 1989, *76*, 519–529.

Elias, M. Serum cortisol, testosterone and testosterone binding globulin responses to competitive fighting in human males. *Aggressive Behavior*, 1981, *7*, 215–224.

Elkis, H., Friedman, L., Buckley, P. F., Lee, H. S., Lys, C., Kaufman, B., and Meltzer, H. Y. Increased prefrontal sulcal prominence in relatively young patients with unipolar major depression. *Psychiatry Research: Neuroimaging*, 1996, *67*, 123–134.

Endoh, M., Maiese, K., and Wagner, J. A. Expression of the neural form of nitric oxide synthase by CA1 hippocampal neurons and other central nervous system neurons. *Neuroscience*, 1994, *63*, 679–689.

Erickson, J. C., Hollopeter, G., and Palmiter, R. D. Attenuation of the obesity syndrome of ob/ob mice by the loss of neuropeptide Y. *Science*, 1996, *274*, 1704–1707.

Ernulf, K. E., Innala, S. M., and Whitam, F. L. Biological explanation, psychological explanation, and tolerance of homosexuals: A cross-national analysis of beliefs and attitudes. *Psychological Reports*, 1989, *248*, 183–188.

Eslinger, P. J., and Damasio, A. R. Severe disturbance of higher cognition after bilateral frontal lobe ablation: Patient EVR. *Neurology*, 1985, *35*, 1731–1741.

Evans, J. J., Heggs, A. J., Antoun, N., and Hodges, J. R. Progressive prosopagnosia associated with selective right temporal lobe atrophy: A new syndrome? *Brain*, 1995, *118*, 1–13.

Everitt, B. J., Cador, M., and Robbins, T. W. Interactions between the amygdala and ventral striatum in stimulus-reward associations: Studies using a second-order schedule of sexual reinforcement. *Neuroscience*, 1989, *30*, 63–75.

Fanselow, M. S., and Kim, J. J. Acquisition of contextual Pavlovian fear conditioning is blocked by application of an NMDA receptor antagonist, D,L-2-amino-5-phosphonovaleric acid to the basolateral amygdala. *Behavioral Neuroscience*, 1994, *108*, 210–212.

Farde, L., Wiesel, F.-A., Stone-Elander, S., Halldin, C., Nördstrom, A.-L., Hall, H., and Sedvall, G. D2 dopamine receptors in neuroleptic-naive schizophrenic patients: A positron emission tomography study with [11C]raclopride. *Archives of General Psychiatry*, 1990, *47*, 213–219.

Farlow, M., Murrell, J., Ghetti, B., Unverzagt, F., Zeldenrust, S., and Benson, M. Clinical characteristics in a kindred with early-onset Alzheimers-disease and their linkage to a GT change at position-2149 of amyloid precursor protein gene. *Neurology*, 1994, *44*, 105–111.

Farris, T. W., Woolf, N. J., Oh, J. D., and Butcher, L. L. Reestablishment of laminar patterns of cortical acetylcholinesterase activity following axotomy of the medial cholinergic pathway in the adult rat. *Experimental Neurology*, 1993, *121*, 77–92.

Fava, M., Copeland, P. M., Schweiger, U., and Herzog, M. D. Neurochemical abnormalities of anorexia nervosa and bulimia nervosa. *American Journal of Psychiatry*, 1989, *146*, 963–971.

Feder, H. H. Estrous cyclicity in mammals. In *Neuroendocrinology of Reproduction*, edited by N. T. Adler. New York: Plenum Press, 1981.

Feigenbaum, S. L., Masi, A. T., and Kaplan, S. B. Prognosis in rheumatoid arthritis: A longitudinal study of newly diagnosed younger adult patients. *American Journal of Medicine*, 1979, *66*, 377–384.

Feigin, M. B., Sclafani, A., and Sunday, S. R. Species differences in polysaccharide and sugar taste preferences. *Neuroscience and Biobehavioral Reviews*, 1987, *11*, 231–240.

Feldman, R. S., Meyer, J. S., and Quenzer, L. F. Principles of Neuropsychopharmacology. Sunderland, Mass: Sinauer Associates, 1997.

Fernell, E., Gillberg, C., and Von Wendt, L. Autistic symptoms in children with infantile hydrocephalus. *Acta Paediatrica Scandanavica*, 1991, *80*, 451–457.

Fibiger, H. C. The dopamine hypothesis of schizophrenia and mood disorders: Contradictions and speculations. In *The Mesolimbic Dopamine System: From Motivation to Action*, edited by P. Willner and J. Scheel-Krüger. Chichester, England: John Wiley & Sons, 1991.

Fieve, R. R. The clinical effects of lithium treatment. *Trends in Neurosciences*, 1979, *2*, 66–68.

Fiez, J. A. Cerebellar contributions to cognition. *Neuron*, 1996, *16*, 13–15.

Filipek, P. A. Neurobiologic correlates of developmental dyslexia: How do dyslexics' brains differ from those of normal readers? *Journal of Child Neurology*, 1995, *10*, S62-S69.

Firestein, S., Zufall, F., and Shepherd, G. M. Single odor-sensitive channels in olfactory receptor neurons are also gated by cyclic nucleotides. *Journal of Neuroscience*, 1991, *11*, 3565–3572.

Fisher, C., Gross, J., and Zuch, J. Cycle of penile erection synchronous with dreaming (REM) sleep: Preliminary report. *Archives of General Psychiatry*, 1965, *12*, 29–45.

Fiske, A. P., and Haslam, N. Is obsessive-compulsive disorder a pathology of the human disposition to perform socially meaningful rituals? Evidence of similar content. *Journal of Nervous and Mental Disease*, 1997, *185*, 211–222.

Fitzpatrick, D., Itoh, K., and Diamond, I. T. The laminar organization of the lateral geniculate body and the striate cortex in the squirrel monkey *(Saimiri sciureus)*. *Journal of Neuroscience*, 1983, *3*, 673–702.

Fitzsimons, J. T., and Moore-Gillon, M. J. Drinking and antidiuresis in response to reductions in venous return in the dog: Neural and endocrine mechanisms. *Journal of Physiology (London)*, 1980, *308*, 403–416.

Flaum, M., and Andreasen, N. C. Diagnostic criteria for schizophrenia and related disorders: Options for DNS-IV. *Schizophrenia Bulletin*, 1990, *17*, 27–49.

Fleming, A., and Rosenblatt, J. S. Olfactory regulation of maternal behavior in rats. II: Effects of peripherally induced anosmia and lesions of the lateral olfactory tract in pup-induced virgins. *Journal of Comparative and Physiological Psychology*, 1974, *86*, 233–246.

Fleming, A., Vaccarino, F., and Luebke, C. Amygdaloid inhibition of maternal behavior in the nulliparous female rat. *Physiology and Behavior*, 1980, *25*, 731–745.

Fleming, A., Vaccarino, F., Tambosso, L., and Chee, P. Vomeronasal and olfactory system modulation of maternal behavior in the rat. *Science*, 1979, *203*, 372–374.

Fleming, A. S., and Sarker, J. Experience-hormone interactions and maternal behavior in rats. *Physiology and Behavior*, 1990, *47*, 1165–1173.

Fleming, A. S., Cheung, U., Myhal, N., and Kessler, Z. Effects of maternal hormones on "timidity" and attraction to pup-related odors in female rats. *Physiology and Behavior*, 1989, *46*, 449–453.

Fletcher, P. J., Currie, P. J., Chambers, J. W., and Coscina, D. V. Radiofrequency lesions of the PVN fail to modify the effects of serotonergic drugs on food intake. *Brain Research*, 1993, *630*, 1–9.

Flock, A. Physiological properties of sensory hairs in the ear. In *Psychophysics and Physiology of Hearing*, edited by E. F. Evans and J. P. Wilson. London: Academic Press, 1977.

Flood, J. F., and Morley, J. E. Increased food intake by neuropeptide Y is due to an increased motivation to eat. *Peptides*, 1991, *12*, 1329–1332.

Floody, O. R. Hormones and aggression in female mammals. In *Hormones and Aggressive Behavior*, edited by B. B. Svare. New York: Plenum Press, 1983.

Folstein, S. E., and Piven, J. Etiology of autism: Genetic influences. *Pediatrics*, 1991, *87*, 767–773.

Folstein, S. E., and Rutter, M. L. Autism: Familiar aggregation and genetic implications. *Journal of Autism and Developmental Disorders*, 1988, *18*, 3–30.

Franzek, E., and Beckmann, H. Gene-environment interaction in schizophrenia: Season-of-birth effect reveals etiologically different subgroups. *Psychopathology*, 1996, *29*, 14–26.

Friedman, M. I., and Bruno, J. P. Exchange of water during lactation. *Science*, 1976, *191*, 409–410.

Frith, U., Morton, J., and Leslie, A. M. The cognitive basis of a biological disorder: Autism. *Trends in Neuroscience*, 1991, *14*, 433–438.

Fulton, J. F. *Functional Localization in Relation to Frontal Lobotomy*. New York: Oxford University Press, 1949.

Fuster, J. M., and Jervey, J. P. Inferotemporal neurons distinguish and retain behaviorally relevant features of visual stimuli. *Science*, 1981, *212*, 952–955.

Gaffan, D., Gaffan, E. A., and Harrison, S. Disconnection of the amygdala from visual association cortex impairs visual reward-association learning in monkeys. *Journal of Neuroscience*, 1988, *9*, 3144–3150.

Galaburda, A. M., and Livingstone, M. Evidence for a magnocellular defect in developmental dyslexia. *Annals of the New York Academy of Science*, 1993, *682*, 70–82.

Gallassi, R., Morreale, A., Montagna, P., Cortelli, P., Avoni, P., Castellani, R., Gambetti, P., and Lugaresi, E. Fatal familial insomnia: Behavioral and cognitive features. *Neurology*, 1996, *46*, 935–939.

Gandelman, R., and Simon, N. G. Postpartum fighting in the rat: Nipple development and the presence of young. *Behavioral and Neural Biology*, 1980, *28*, 350–360.

Gardner, H., Brownell, H. H., Wapner, W., and Michelow, D. Missing the point: The role of the right hemisphere in the processing of complex linguistic materials. In *Cognitive Processing in the Right Hemisphere*, edited by E. Pericman. New York: Academic Press, 1983.

Gariano, R. F., and Groves, P. M. Burst firing induced in midbrain dopamine neurons by stimulation of the medial prefrontal and anterior cingulate cortices. *Brain Research*, 1988, *462*, 194–198.

Gatchel, R. J., Baum, A., and Krantz, D. S. *An Introduction to Health Psychology*, 2nd ed. New York: Newbery Award Records, 1989.

Gazzaniga, M. S. *The Bisected Brain*. New York: Appleton-Century-Crofts, 1970.

Gazzaniga, M. S., and LeDoux, J. E. *The Integrated Mind*. New York: Plenum Press, 1978.

Geary, N. Cocaine: Animal research studies. In *Cocaine Abuse: New Directions in Treatment and Research*, edited by H. I. Spitz and J. S. Rosecan. New York: Brunner-Mazel, 1987.

Gentilucci, M., and Rizzolatti, G. In *Vision and Action: The Control of Grasping*, edited by M. A. Goodale. Norwood, N.J.: Ablex, 1990.

George, M. S., Parekh, P. I., Rosinsky, N., Ketter, T. A., Kimbrell, T. A., Heilman, K. M., Herscovitch, P., and Post, R. M. Understanding emotional prosody activates right hemisphere regions. *Archives of Neurology*, 1996, *53*, 665–670.

Gerbino, L., Oleshansky, M., and Gershon, S. Clinical use and mode of action of lithium. In *Psychopharmacology: A Generation of Progress*, edited by M. A. Lipton, A. DiMascio, and K. F. Killam. New York: Raven Press, 1978.

Gerren, R., and Weinberger, N. M. Long term potentiation in the magnocellular medial geniculate nucleus of the anesthetized cat. *Brain Research*, 1983, *265*, 138–142.

Gershon, E. S., Bunney, W. E., Leckman, J., Van Eerdewegh, M., and DeBauche, B. The inheritance of affective disorders: A review of data and hypotheses. *Behavior Genetics*, 1976, *6*, 227–261.

Geschwind, N., Quadfasel, F. A., and Segarra, J. M. Isolation of the speech area. *Neuropsychologia*, 1968, *6*, 327–340.

Gessa, G. L., Muntoni, F., Collu, M., Vargiu, L., and Mereu, G. Low doses of ethanol activate dopaminergic neurons in the ventral tegmental area. *Brain Research*, 1985, *348*, 201–204.

Ghiraldi, L., and Svare, B. Unpublished observations cited in Svare, B. Recent advances in the study of female aggressive behavior in mice. In *House Mouse Aggression: A Model for Understanding the Evolution of Social Behavior*, edited by S. Parmigiani, D. Mainardi, and P. Brain. London: Gordon and Breach, 1989.

Gibbs, J., Young, R. C., and Smith, G. P. Cholecystokinin decreases food intake in rats. *Journal of Comparative and Physiological Psychology*, 1973, *84*, 488–495.

Gibbs, W. W. Gaining on fat. *Scientific American*, 1996, *275*, 88–94.

Giedd, J. N., Rapoport, J. L., Kruesi, M. J. P., Parker, C., Schapiro, M. B., Allen, A. J., Leonard, H. L., Kaysen, D., Dickstein, D. P., Marsh, W. L., Kozuch, P. L., Vaituzis, A. C., Hamburger, S. D., and Swedo, S. E. Sydenham's chorea: Magnetic resonance imaging of the basal ganglia. *Neurology*, 1995, *45*, 2199–2202.

Gilbert, D. G., and Gilbert, B. O. Personality, psychopathology, and nicotine response as mediators of the genetics of smoking. *Behavioral Genetics*, 1995, *25*, 133–148.

Giles, D. E., Biggs, M. M., Rush, A. J., and Roffwarg, H. P. Risk factors in families of unipolar depression. I: Psychiatric illness and reduced REM latency. *Journal of Affective Disorders*, 1988, *14*, 51–59.

Giles, D. E., Roffwarg, H. P., and Rush, A. J. REM latency concordance in depressed family members. *Biological Psychiatry*, 1987, *22*, 910–924.

Gillespie, P. G. Molecular machinery of auditory and vestibular transduction. *Current Opinion in Neurobiology*, 1995, *5*, 449–455.

Gillette, M. U., and McArthur, A. J. Circadian actions of melatonin at the suprachiasmatic nucleus. *Behavioural Brain Research*, 1995, *73*, 135–139.

Giordano, A. L., Siegel, H. I., and Rosenblatt, J. S. Nuclear estrogen receptor binding in the preoptic area and hypothalamus of pregnancy-terminated rats: Correlation with the onset of maternal behavior. *Neuroendocrinology*, 1989, *50*, 248–258.

Givens, B., and McMahon, K. Ethanol suppresses the induction of long-term potentiation in vivo. *Brain Research*, 1995, *688*, 27–33.

Glaser, R., Rice, J., Sheridan, J., Post, A., Fertel, R., Stout, J., Speicher, C. E., Kotur, M., and Kiecolt-Glaser, J. K. Stress-related immune suppression: Health implications. *Brain, Behavior, and Immunity*, 1987, *1*, 7–20.

Glaum, S. R., Hara, M., Bindokas, V. P., Lee, C. C., Polonsky, K. S., Bell, G. I., and Miller, R. J. Leptin, the obese gene product, rapidly modulates synaptic transmission in the hypothalamus. *Molecular Pharmacology*, 1996, *50*, 230–235.

Gloor, P., Olivier, A., Quesney, L. F., Andermann, F., and Horowitz, S. The role of the limbic system in experiential phenomena of temporal lobe epilepsy. *Annals of Neurology*, 1982, *12*, 129–144.

Goddard, A. W., Sholomskas, D. E., Walton, K. E., Augeri, F. M., Charney, D. S., Heninger, G. R., Goodman, W. K., and Price, L. H. Effects of tryptophan depletion in panic disorder. *Biological Psychiatry*, 1994, *36*, 775–777.

Goddard, G. V. Development of epileptic seizures through brain stimulation at low intensity. *Nature*, 1967, *214*, 1020–1021.

Goeders, N. E., Lane, J. D., and Smith, J. E. Self-administration of methionine enkephalin into the nucleus accumbens. *Pharmacology, Biochemistry, and Behavior*, 1984, *20*, 451–455.

Golden, P. L., MacCagnan, T. J., and Pardridge, W. M. Human blood-brain barrier leptin receptor: Binding and endocytosis in isolated human brain microvessels. *Journal of Clinical Investigation*, 1997, *99*, 14–18.

Gonzales, R. A. NMDA receptors excite alcohol research. *Trends in Pharmacological Science*, 1990, *11*, 137–139.

Goodale, M. A., and Milner, A. D. Separate visual pathways for perception and action. *Trends in Neuroscience*, 1992, *15*, 20–25.

Goodale, M. A., Meenan, J. P., Bülthoff, H. H., Nicolle, D. A., Murphy, K. H., and Racicot, C. I. Separate neural pathways for the visual analysis of object shape in perception and prehension. *Current Biology*, 1994, *4*, 604–610.

Goodglass, H. Agrammatism. In *Studies of Neurolinguistics*, edited by H. Whitaker and H. A. Whitaker. New York: Academic Press, 1976.

Goodwin, D. W. Alcoholism and heredity: A review and hypothesis. *Archives of General Psychiatry*, 1979, *36*, 57–61.

Gordon, H. W., and Sperry, R. Lateralization of olfactory perception in the surgically separated hemispheres in man. *Neuropsychologia*, 1969, *7*, 111–120.

Gorski, R. A., Gordon, J. H., Shryne, J. E., and Southam, A. M. Evidence for a morphological sex difference within the medial preoptic area of the rat brain. *Brain Research*, 1978, *148*, 333–346.

Gottesman, I. I., and Shields, J. *Schizophrenia: The Epigenetic Puzzle*. New York: Cambridge University Press, 1982.

Gouras, P. Identification of cone mechanisms in monkey ganglion cells. *Journal of Physiology (London)*, 1968, *199*, 533–538.

Goy, R. W., Bercovitch, F. B., and McBrair, M. C. Behavioral masculinization is independent of genital masculinization in prenatally androgenized female rhesus macaques. *Hormones and Behavior*, 1988, *22*, 552–571.

Grafton, S. T., Waters, C., Sutton, J., Lew, M. F., and Couldwell, W. Pallidotomy increases activity of motor association cortex in Parkinson's disease: A positron emission tomographic study. *Annals of Neurology*, 1995, *37*, 776–783.

Grant, S., London, E. D., Newlin, D. B., Villemagne, V. L., Liu, X., Contoreggi, C., Phillips, R. L., Kimes, A. S., and Margolin, A. Activation of memory circuits during cue-elicited cocaine craving. *Proceedings of the National Academy of Sciences, USA*, 1996, *93*, 12040–12045.

Grant, S. G. N., O'Dell, T. J., Karl, K. A., Stein, P. L., Soriano, P., and Kandel, E. R. Impaired long-term potentiation, spatial learning, and hippocampal development in *fyn* mutant mice. *Science*, 1992, *258*, 1903–1910.

Gray, C., Freeman, W. J., and Skinner, J. E. Chemical dependencies of learning in the rabbit olfactory bulb: Acquisition of the transient and spatial pattern change depends on norepinephrine. *Behavioral Neuroscience*, 1986, *100*, 585–596.

Graybiel, A. M. Basal ganglia: New therapeutic approaches to Parkinson's disease. *Current Biology*, 1996, *6*, 368–371.

Greenberg, D., Kava, R., Lewis, D. R., and Greenwood, M. R. C. Satiation following intraduodenal Intralipid preceded appearance of [^{14}C]-Intralipid in hepatic portal blood. *FASEB Journal*, 1991, *5*, A1451.

Greenberg, D., Smith, G. P., and Gibbs, J. Intraduodenal infusions of fats elicit satiety in the sham feeding rat. *American Journal of Physiology*, 1990, *259*, R110–R118.

Greenberg, R., and Pearlman, C. A. Cutting the REM nerve: An approach to the adaptive role of REM sleep. *Perspectives in Biology and Medicine*, 1974, *17*, 513–521.

Grigorenko, E. L., Wood, F. B., Meyer, M. S., Hart, L. A., Speed, W. C., Shuster, A., and Pauls, D. L. Susceptibility loci for distinct components of developmental dyslexia on chromosomes 6 and 15. *American Journal of Human Genetics*, 1997, *60*, 27–39.

Grill, H. J., and Kaplan, J. M. Caudal brainstem participates in the distributed neural control of feeding. In *Handbook of Behavioral Neurobiology. Vol. 10. Neurobiology of Food and Fluid Intake*, edited by E. Stricker. New York: Plenum Press, 1990.

Grill, H. J., Friedman, M. I., Norgren, R., Scalera, G., and Seeley, R. Parabrachial nucleus lesions impair feeding response elicited by 2,5-anhydro-D-mannitol. *American Journal of Physiology*, 1995, *268*, R676–R682.

Gross, C. G. Visual functions of inferotemporal cortex. In *Handbook of Sensory Physiology, Vol. 7: Central Processing of Visual Information*, edited by R. Jung. Berlin: Springer-Verlag, 1973.

Guerin, G. F., Goeders, N. E., Dworkin, S. I., and Smith, J. E. Intracranial self-administration of dopamine into the nucleus accumbens. *Society for Neuroscience Abstracts*, 1984, *10*, 1072.

Guilleminault, C., Wilson, R. A., and Dement, W. C. A study on cataplexy. *Archives of Neurology*, 1974, *31*, 255–261.

Gulevich, G., Dement, W. C., and Johnson, L. Psychiatric and EEG observations on a case of prolonged (264 hours) wakefulness. *Archives of General Psychiatry*, 1966, *15*, 29–35.

Gura, T. Obesity sheds its secrets. *Science*, 1997, *275*, 751–753.

Gurevich, E. V., Bordelon, Y., Shapiro, R. M., Arnold, S. E., Gur, R. E., and Joyce, J. N. Mesolimbic dopamine D_3 receptors and use of antipsychotics in patients with schizophrenia: A postmortem study. *Archives of General Psychiatry*, 1997, *54*, 225–232.

Gurvits, T. V., Shenton, M. E., Hokama, H., Ohta, H., Lasko, N. B., Gilbertson, M. W., Orr, S. P., Kikinis, R., Jolesz, F. A., McCarley, R. W., and Pitman, R. K. Magnetic resonance imaging study of hippocampal volume in chronic, combat-related posttraumatic stress disorder. *Biological Psychiatry*, 1996, *40*, 1091–1099.

Haas, R. H. Thiamin and the brain. *Annual Review of Nutrition*, 1988, *8*, 483–515.

Haas, R. H., Townsend, J., Courchesne, E., Lincoln, A. J., Schreibman, L., and Yeung-Courchesne, R. Neurologic abnormalities in infantile autism. *Journal of Child Neurology*, 1996, *11*, 84–92.

Hajak, G., Clarenbach, P., Fischer, W., Haase, W., Bandelow, B., Adler, L., and Ruther, E. Effects of hypnotics on sleep quality and daytime well-being: Data from a comparative multicentre study in outpatients with insomnia. *European Psychiatry*, 1995, *10*(Suppl. 3), 173S–179S.

Hakansson, M. L., Hulting, A. L., and Meister, B. Expression of leptin receptor messenger RNA in the hypothalamic arcuate nucleus: Relationship with NPY neurons. *Neuroreport*, 1996, *7*, 3087–3092.

Halaas, J. L., Gajiwala, K. D., Maffei, M., Cohen, S. L., Chait, B. T., Rabinowitz, D., Lallone, R. L., Burley, S. K., and Friedman, J. M. Weight-reducing effects of the plasma protein encoded by the obese gene. *Science*, 1995, *269*, 543–546.

Halgren, E. Walter, R. D., Cherlow, D. G., and Crandall, P. E. Mental phenomena evoked by electrical stimultion of the human hippocampal formation and amygdala. *Brain*, 1978, *101*, 83–117.

Halmi, K. A. Anorexia nervosa: Recent investigations. *Annual Review of Medicine*, 1978, *29*, 137–148.

Halmi, K. A., Eckert, E., LaDu, T. J., and Cohen, J. Anorexia nervose: Treatment efficacy of cyproheptadine and amitriptyline. *Archives of General Psychiatry*, 1986, *43*, 177–181.

Halpern, M. The organization and function of the vomeronasal system. *Annual Review of Neuroscience*, 1987, *10*, 325–362.

Hamm, R. J., Temple, M. D., O'Dell, D. M., Pike, B. R., and Lyeth, B. G. Exposure to environmental complexity promotes recovery of cognitive function after traumatic brain injury. *Journal of Neurotrauma*, 1996, *13*, 41–47.

Han, Y. C., Shaikh, M. B., and Siegel, A. Medial amygdaloid suppression of predatory attack behavior in the cat. 1: Role of a substance P pathway from the medial amygdala to the medial hypothalamus. *Brain Research*, 1996a, *716*, 59–71.

Han, Y. C., Shaikh, M. B., and Siegel, A. Medial amygdaloid suppression of predatory attack behavior in the cat. 2: Role of a GABAergic pathway from the medial to the lateral hypothalamus. *Brain Research*, 1996b, *716*, 72–83.

Happé, F., and Frith, U. The neuropsychology of autism. *Brain*, 1996, *119*, 1377–1400.

Hardy, J. Amyloid, the presinilins and Alzheimer's disease. *Trends in Neuroscience*, 1997, *4*, 154–159.

Harmon, L. D., and Julesz, B. Masking in visual recognition: Effects of two-dimensional filtered noise. *Science*, 1973, *180*, 1194–1197.

Harris, G. W., and Jacobsohn, D. Functional grafts of the anterior pituitary gland. *Proceedings of the Royal Society of London [B]*, 1951–1952, *139*, 263–267.

Hartline, H. K. The response of single optic nerve fibers of the vertebrate eye to illumination of the retina. *American Journal of Physiology*, 1938, *121*, 400–415.

Hashimoto, T., Tayama, M., Murakawa, K., Yoshimoto, T., Miyazaki, M., Harada, M., and Kuroda, Y. Development of the brainstem and cerebellum in autistic patients. *Journal of Autism and Developmental Disorders*, 1995, *25*, 1–18.

Haug, H.-J. Prediction of sleep deprivation outcome by diurnal variation of mood. *Biological Psychiatry*, 1992, *31*, 271–278.

Hauser, M. D. Right hemisphere dominance for the production of facial expression in monkeys. *Science*, 1993, *261*, 475–477.

Hawke, C. Castration and sex crimes. *American Journal of Mental Deficiency*, 1951, *55*, 220–226.

Haxby, J. V., Horwitz, B., Ungerleider, L. G., Maisog, J. M., Pietrini, P., and Grady, C. L. The functional organization of human extrastriate cortex: A PET-rCBF study of selective attention to faces and locations. *Journal of Neuroscience*, 1994, *14*, 6336–6353.

Hayaishi, O. Sleep-wake regulation by prostaglandins D2 and E2. *Journal of Biological Chemistry*, 1988, *263*, 14593–14596.

Heath, A. C., Madden, P. A. F., Slutske, W. S., and Martin, N. G. Personality and the inheritance of smoking behavior: A genetic perspective. *Behavioral Genetics*, 1995, *25*, 103–118.

Hebb, D. O. *The Organization of Behaviour.* New York: Wiley-Interscience, 1949.

Heckler, M. M. *Fifth Special Report to the U.S. Congress on Alcohol and Health.* Washington, D.C.: U.S. Government Printing Office, 1983.

Heffner, H. E., and Heffner, R. S. Role of primate auditory cortex in hearing. In *Comparative Perception. Vol. II. Complex Signals*, edited by W. C. Stebbins and M. A. Berkley. New York: John Wiley & Sons, 1990.

Heilman, K. M., Scholes, R., and Watson, R. T. Auditory affective agnosia: Disturbed comprehension of affective speech. *Journal of Neurology, Neurosurgery, and Psychiatry*, 1975, *38*, 69–72.

Heilman, K. M., Watson, R. T., and Bowers, D. Affective disorders associated with hemispheric disease. In *Neuropsychology of Human Emotion*, edited by K. M. Heilman and P. Satz. New York: Guilford Press, 1983.

Heimer, L., and Larsson, K. Impairment of mating behavior in male rats following lesions in the preoptic-anterior hypothalamic continuum. *Brain Research*, 1966/1967, *3*, 248–263.

Heinrichs, S. C., Menzaghi, F., Pich, E. M., Baldwin, H. A., Rassnick, S., Britton, K. T., and Koob, G. F. Anti-stress action of a corticotropin-releasing factor antagonist on behavioral reactivity to stressors of varying type and intensity. *Neuropsychopharmacology*, 1994, *11*, 179–186.

Hellhammer, D. H., Hubert, W., and Schurmeyer, T. Changes in saliva testosterone after psychological stimulation in men. *Psychoneuroendocrinology*, 1985, *10*, 77–81.

Henderson, W. W. The epidemiology of estrogen replacement therapy and Alzheimer's disease. *Neurology*, 1997, *48*, S27–S35.

Hendrickson, A. E., Wagoner, N., and Cowan, W. M. Autoradiographic and electron microscopic study of retino-hypothalamic connections. *Zeitschrift für Zellforschung und Mikroskopische Anatomie*, 1972, *125*, 1–26.

Henke, P. G. The telencephalic limbic system and experimental gastric pathology: A review. *Neuroscience and Biobehavioral Reviews*, 1982, *6*, 381–390.

Hennessey, A. C., Camak, L., Gordon, F., and Edwards, D. A. Connections between the pontine central gray and the ventromedial hypothalamus are essential for lordosis in female rats. *Behavioral Neuroscience*, 1990, *104*, 477–488.

Hering, E. *Outlines of a Theory of the Light Sense*, 1905. Translated by L. M. Hurvich and D. Jameson. Cambridge, Mass.: Harvard University Press, 1965.

Hernandez, L., and Hoebel, B. G. Feeding can enhance dopamine turnover in the prefrontal cortex. *Brain Research Bulletin*, 1990, *25*, 975–979.

Hetherington, A. W., and Ranson, S. W. Hypothalamic lesions and adiposity in the rat. *Anatomical Record*, 1942, *78*, 149–172.

Heuser, J. E. Synaptic vesicle exocytosis revealed in quick-frozen frog neuromuscular junctions treated with 4-aminopyridine and given a single electrical shock. In *Society for Neuroscience Symposia, Vol. II*, edited by W. M. Cowan and J. A. Ferrendelli. Bethesda, Md.: Society for Neuroscience, 1977.

Heuser, J. E., Reese, T. S., Dennis, M. J., Jan, Y., Jan, L., and Evans, L. Synaptic vesicle exocytosis captured by quick freezing and correlated with quantal transmitter release. *Journal of Cell Biology*, 1979, *81*, 275–300.

Heywood, C. A., Gaffan, D., and Cowey, A. Cerebral achromatopsia in monkeys. *European Journal of Neuroscience*, 1995, *7*, 1064–1073.

Hickok, G., Bellugi, U., and Klima, E. S. The neurobiology of sign language and its implications for the neural basis of language. *Nature*, 1996, *381*, 699–702.

Hickok, G., Klima, E., Kritchevsky, M., and Bellugi, U. A case of 'sign blindness' following left occipital damage in a deaf signer. *Neuropsychologia*, 1995, *33*, 1597–1601.

Higley, J. D., Mehlman, P. T., Higley, S. B., Fernald, B., Vickers, J., Lindell, S. G., Taub, D. M., Suomi, S. J., and Linnoila, M. Excessive mortaility in young free-ranging male nonhuman primates with low cerebrospinal fluid 5-hydroxyindoleacetic acid concentrations. *Archives of General Psychiatry*, 1996a, *53*, 537–543.

Higley, J. D., Mehlman, P. T., Poland, R. E., Taub, D. M., Vickers, J., Suomi, S. J., and Linnoila, M. CSF testosterone and 5-HIAA correlate with different types of aggressive behaviors. *Biological Psychiatry*, 1996b, *40*, 1067–1082.

Himmelsbach, C. K. Can the euphoric analgetic and physical dependence effects of drugs be separated? With reference to physical dependence. *Federation Proceedings*, 1943, *2*, 201–203.

Hinjo, S., Hirano, C., Murase, S., Kaneko, T., Sugiyama, T., Ohtaka, K., Aoyama, T., Takei, Y., Inoko, K., and Wakbayshai, S. Obsessive-compulsive symptoms in childhood and adolescence. *Acta Psychiatrica Scandanivica*, 1989, *80*, 83–91.

Hobson, J. A. *The Dreaming Brain.* New York: Basic Books, 1988.

Hodge, C. W., Haraguchi, M., Erickson, H., and Samson, H. H. Ventral tegmental microinjections of quinpirole decrease ethanol and sucrose-reinforced responding. *Alcohol: Clinical and Experimental Research*, 1993, *17*, 370–375.

Hodges, J. R., Patterson, K., Oxbury, S., and Funnell, E. Semantic dementia: Progressive fluent aphasia with temporal lobe atrophy. *Brain*, 1992, *115*, 1783–1806.

Hoebel, B. G., Monaco, A. P., Hernandez, L., Aulisi, E. F., Stanley, B. G., and Lenard, L. Self-injection of amphetamine directly into the brain. *Psychopharmacology*, 1983, *81*, 158–163.

Hofer, M. A., and Shair, H. N. Ultrasonic vocalization, laryngeal braking, and thermogenesis in rat pups: A reappraisal. *Behavioral Neuroscience*, 1993, *107*, 354–362.

Hohman, G. W. Some effects of spinal cord lesions on experienced emotional feelings. *Psychophysiology*, 1966, *3*, 143–156.

Hollander, E., Schiffman, E., Cohen, B., Rivera-Stein, M. A., Rosen, W., Gorman, J. M., Fyer, A. J., Papp, L., and Liebowitz, M. R. Signs of central nervous system dysfunction in obsessive-compulsive disorder. *Archives of General Psychiatry*, 1990, *47*, 27–32.

Holroyd, S., Reiss, A. L., and Bryan, R. N. Autistic features in Joubert syndrome: A genetic disorder with agenesis of the cerebellar vermis. *Biological Psychiatry*, 1991, *29*, 287–294.

Honda, T., and Semba, K. Serotonergic synaptic input to cholinergic neurons in the rat mesopontine tegmentum. *Brain Research*, 1994, *647*, 299–306.

Hopf, H. C., Mueller-Forell, W., and Hopf, N. J. Localization of emotional and volitional facial paresis. *Neurology*, 1992, *42*, 1918–1923.

Horne, J. Human slow wave sleep: A review and appraisal of recent findings, with implications for sleep functions, and psychiatric illness. *Experientia*, 1992, *48*, 941–954.

Horne, J. A. A review of the biological effects of total sleep deprivation in man. *Biological Psychology*, 1978, *7*, 55–102.

Horne, J. A. The effects of exercise on sleep. *Biological Psychology*, 1981, *12*, 241–291.

Horne, J. A. *Why We Sleep: The Functions of Sleep in Humans and Other Mammals.* Oxford, England: Oxford University Press, 1988.

Horne, J. A., and Harley, L. J. Human SWS following selective head heating during wakefulness. In *Sleep '88*, edited by J. Horne. New York: Gustav Fischer Verlag, 1989.

Horne, J. A., and Minard, A. Sleep and sleepiness following a behaviourally "active" day. *Ergonomics*, 1985, *28*, 567–575.

Horne, J. A., and Moore, V. J. Sleep effects of exercise with and without additional body cooling. *Electroencephalography and Clinical Neurophysiology*, 1985, *60*, 347–353.

Horowitz, R. M., and Gentili, B. Dihydrochalcone sweeteners. In *Symposium: Sweeteners*, edited by G. E. Inglett. Westport, Conn.: Avi Publishing, 1974.

Horton, J. C., and Hubel, D. H. Cytochrome oxidase stain preferentially labels intersection of ocular dominance and vertical orientation columns in macaque striate cortex. *Society for Neuroscience Abstracts*, 1980, *6*, 315.

Horvath, T. L., Naftolin, F., Leranth, C., Sahu, A., and Kalra, S. P. Morphological and pharmacological evidence for neuropeptide Y-galanin interaction in the rat hypothalamus. *Endocrinology*, 1996, *137*, 3069–3077.

Hosokawa, T., Rusakov, D. A., Bliss, T. V. P., and Fine, A. Repeated confocal imaging of individual dendritic spines in the living hippocampal slice: Evidence for changes in length and orientation associated with chemically induced LTP. *Journal of Neuroscience*, 1995, *15*, 5560–5573.

Houpt, T. A., Boulos, Z., and Moore-Ede, M. C. MidnightSun: Software for determining light exposure and phase-shifting schedules during global travel. *Physiology and Behavior*, 1996, *59*, 561–568.

Hubel, D. H., and Wiesel, T. N. Functional architecture of macaque monkey visual cortex. *Proceedings of the Royal Society of London*, 1977, *198*, 1–59.

Hubel, D. H., and Wiesel, T. N. Brain mechanisms of vision. *Scientific American*, 1979, *241*, 150–162.

Hublin, C. Narcolepsy: Current drug-treatment options. *CNS Drugs*, 1996, *5*, 426–436.

Hudspeth, A. J., and Gillespie, P. G. Pulling springs to tune transduction: Adaptation by hair cells. *Neuron*, 1994, *12*, 1–9.

Hughes, J., Smith, T. W., Kosterlitz, H. W., Fothergill, L. A., Morgan, B. A., and Moris, H. R. Identification of two related pentapeptides from the brain with potent opiate agonist activity. *Nature*, 1975, *258*, 577–579.

Humphrey, A. L., and Hendrickson, A. E. Radial zones of high metabolic activity in squirrel monkey striate cortex. *Society for Neuroscience Abstracts*, 1980, *6*, 315.

Humphreys, G. W., Donnelly, N., and Riddoch, M. J. Expression is computed separately from facial identity, and it is computed separately for moving and static faces: Neuropsychological evidence. *Neuropsychologia*, 1993, *31*, 173–181.

Hunterensor, M., Ousley, A., and Sehgal, A. Regulation of the *Drosophila* protein *Timeless* suggests a mechanism for resetting the circadian clock by light. *Cell*, 1996, *84*, 677–685.

Husby, G., Van De Rign, I., Zabriskie, J. B., Abdin, A. H., and Williams, R. C. Antibodies reacting with cytoplasm of subthalamic and caudate nuclei neurons in chorea and acute rheumatic fever. *Journal of Experimental Medicine*, 1976, *144*, 1094–1110.

Huttunen, M. O., and Niskanen, P. Prenatal loss of father and psychiatric disorders. *Archives of General Psychiatry*, 1978, *35*, 429–431.

Ibuka, N., and Kawamura, H. Loss of circadian rhythm in sleep-wakefulness cycle in the rat by suprachiasmatic nucleus lesions. *Brain Research*, 1975, *96*, 76–81.

Iggo, A., and Andres, K. H. Morphology of cutaneous receptors. *Annual Review of Neuroscience*, 1982, *5*, 1–32.

Ihnat, R., White, N. R., and Barfield, R. J. Pup's broadband vocalizations and maternal behavior in the rat. *Behavioral Processes*, 1995, *33*, 257–272.

Imaki, T., Shibasaki, T., Hotta, M., and Demura, H. Early induction of c-fos precedes increased expression of corticotropin-releasing factor messenger ribonucleic acid in the paraventricular nucleus after immobilization stress. *Endocrinology*, 1992, *131*, 240–246.

Imbeaud, S., Faure, E., Lamarre, I., Mattéi, M. G., di Clemente, N., Tizard, R., Carré-Eusèbe, D., Belville, C., Tragethon, L., Tonkin, C., et al. Insensitivity to anti-Müllerian hormone due to a mutation in the human anti-Müllerian hormone receptor. *Nature Genetics*, 1995, *11*, 382–388.

Imperato, A., and Di Chiara, G. Preferential stimulation of dopamine-release in the accumbens of freely moving rats by ethanol. *Journal of Pharmacology and Experimental Therapeutics*, 1986, *239*, 219–228.

Imperato, A., Scrocco, M. G., Bacchi, S., and Angelucci, L. NMDA receptors and in vivo dopamine release in the nucleus accumbens and caudatus. *European Journal of Pharmacology*, 1990, *187*, 555–556.

Ingelfinger, F. J. The late effects of total and subtotal gastrectomy. *New England Journal of Medicine*, 1944, *231*, 321–327.

Inoue, M., Koyanagi, T., Nakahara, H., Hara, K., Hori, E., and Nakano, H. Functional development of human eye movement in utero assessed quantitatively with real time ultrasound. *American Journal of Obstetrics and Gynecology*, 1986, *155*, 170–174.

Institute of Medicine. *Sleeping Pills, Insomnia, and Medical Practice*. Washington, D.C.: National Academy of Sciences, 1979.

Iwata, J., LeDoux, J. E., Meeley, M. P., Arneric, S., and Reis, D. J. Intrinsic neurons in the amygdaloid field projected to by the medial geniculate body mediate emotional responses conditioned to acoustic stimuli. *Brain Research*, 1986, *383*, 195–214.

Iwata, M. Kanji versus Kana: Neuropsychological correlates of the Japanese writing system. *Trends in Neurosciences*, 1984, *7*, 290–293.

Izard, C. E. *The Face of Emotion*. New York: Appleton-Century-Crofts, 1971.

Jacobs, B. L., and McGinty, D. J. Participation of the amygdala in complex stimulus recognition and behavioral inhibition: Evidence from unit studies. *Brain Research*, 1972, *36*, 431–436.

Jacobs, G. H. Primate photopigments and primate color vision. *Proceedings of the National Academy of Sciences, USA*, 1996, *93*, 577–581.

Jacobsen, C. F., Wolfe, J. B., and Jackson, T. A. An experimental analysis of the functions of the frontal association areas in primates. *Journal of Nervous and Mental Disorders*, 1935, *82*, 1–14.

Jakobson, L. S., Archibald, Y. M., Carey, D., and Goodale, M. A. A kinematic analysis of reaching and grasping movements in a patient recovering from optic ataxia. *Neuropsychologia*, 1991, *29*, 803–809.

James, W. What is an emotion? *Mind*, 1884, *9*, 188–205.

James, W. P. T., and Trayhurn, P. Thermogenesis and obesity. *British Medical Bulletin*, 1981, *27*, 43–48.

Jaramillo, F. Signal transduction in hair cells and its regulation by calcium. *Neuron*, 1995, *15*, 1227–1230.

Jaskiw, G., and Kleinman, J. Postmortem neurochemistry studies in schizophrenia. In *Schizophrenia: A Scientific Focus*, edited by S. C. Schulz and C. A. Tamminga. New York: Oxford University Press, 1988.

Jasper, J. H., and Tessier, J. Acetylcholine liberation from cerebral cortex during paradoxical (REM) sleep. *Science*, 1969, *172*, 601–602.

Jaynes, J. The problem of animate motion in the seventeenth century. *Journal of the History of Ideas*, 1970, *6*, 219–234.

Jeffcoate, W. J., Lincoln, N. B., Selby, C., and Herbert, M. Correlations between anxiety and serum prolactin in humans. *Journal of Psychosomatic Research*, 1986, *30*, 217–222.

Jensen, T., Genefke, I., and Hyldebrandt, N. Cerebral atrophy in young torture victims. *New England Journal of Medicine*, 1982, *307*, 1341.

Jeste, D. V., Del Carmen, R., Lohr, J. B., and Wyatt, R. J. Did schizophrenia exist before the eighteenth century? *Comprehensive Psychiatry*, 1985, *26*, 493–503.

Jewett, D.C., Cleary, J., Levine, A. S., Schaal, D. W., and Thompson, T. Effects of neuropeptide Y on food-reinforced behavior in satiated rats. *Pharmacology, Biochemistry, and Behavior*, 1992, *42*, 207–212.

Jiang, C. L., and Hunt, J. N. The relation between freely chosen meals and body habitus. *American Journal of Clinical Nutrition*, 1983, *38*, 32–40.

Johansson, G. Visual perception of biological motion and a model for its analysis. *Perception and Psychophysics*, 1973, *14*, 201–211.

Johnson, A. K., and Edwards, G. L. The neuroendocrinology of thirst: Afferent signaling and mechanisms of central integration. *Current Topics in Neuroendocrinology*, 1990, *10*, 149–190.

Johnson, M. K., Kim, J. K., and Risse, G. Do alcoholic Korsakoff's syndrome patients acquire affective reactions? *Journal of Experimental Psychology: Learning, Memory, and Cognition*, 1985, *11*, 22–36.

Johnson, S. W., and North, R. A. Opioids excite dopamine neurons by hyperpolarization of local interneurons. *Journal of Neuroscience*, 1992, *12*, 483–488.

Jones, B. E. Influence of the brainstem reticular formation, including intrinsic monoaminergic and cholinergic neurons, on forebrain mechanisms of sleep and waking. In *The Diencephalon and Sleep*, edited by M. Mancia and G. Marini. New York: Raven Press, 1990.

Jones, B. E., and Beaudet, A. Distribution of acetylcholine and catecholamine neurons in the cat brain stem studied by choline acetyltransferase and tyrosine hydroxylase immunohistochemistry. *Journal of Comparative Neurology*, 1987, *261*, 15–32.

Jones, D. T., and Reed, R. R. G_{olf}: An olfactory neuron specific-G protein involved in odorant signal transduction. *Science*, 1989, *244*, 790–795.

Jones, M. B., and Szatmari, P. Stoppage rules and genetic studies of autism. *Journal of Autism and Developmental Disorders*, 1988, *18*, 31–40.

Jones, S. S., Collins, K., and Hong, H.-W. An audience effect on smile production in 10-month-old infants. *Psychological Science*, 1991, *2*, 45–49.

Jope, R. S., Song, L., Li, P. P., Young, L. T., Kish, S. J., Pacheco, M. A., and Warsh, J. J. The phosphoinositide signal transduction system is impaired in bipolar affective disorder brain. *Journal of Neurochemistry*, 1996, *66*, 2402–2409.

Josso, N., Boussin, L., Knebelmann, B., Nihoul-Fekete, C., and Picard, J.-Y. Anti-Muellerian hormone and intersex states. *Trends in Endocrinology and Metabolism*, 1991, *2*, 227–233.

Jouvet, M. The role of monoamines and acetylcholine-containing neurons in the regulation of the sleep-waking cycle. *Ergebnisse der Physiologie*, 1972, *64*, 166–307.

Jouvet, M. Biochemical regulation of states of vigilance. *International Journal of Neurology*, 1975, *10*, 1–4, 141–157, 252–258.

Jouvet, M. Paradoxical sleep and the nature-nurture controversy. *Progress in Brain Research*, 1980, *53*, 331–346.

Kadekaro, M., Cohen, S., Terrell, M. L., Lekan, H., Gary, H., and Eisenberg, H. M. Independent activation of subfornical organ and hypothalamo-neurohypophysial system during administration of angiotensin II. *Peptides*, 1989, *10*, 423–429.

Kaga, K., Shindo, M., and Tanaka, Y. Central auditory information processing in patients with bilateral auditory cortex lesions. *Acta Otolaryngologica*, 1997, *532*, 77–82.

Kales, A., Scharf, M. B., Kales, J. D., and Soldatos, C. R. Rebound insomnia: A potential hazard following withdrawal of certain benzodiazepines. *Journal of the American Medical Association*, 1979, *241*, 1692–1695.

Kales, A., Tan, T.-L., Kollar, E. J., Naitoh, P., Preston, T. A., and Malmstrom, E. J. Sleep patterns following 205 hours of sleep deprivation. *Psychosomatic Medicine*, 1970, *32*, 189–200.

Kalin, N. H., Sherman, J. E., and Takahashi, L. K. Antagonism of endogenous CRG systems attenuates stress-induced freezing behavior in rats. *Brain Research*, 1988, *457*, 130–135.

Kanamori, N., Sakai, K., and Jouvet, M. Neuronal activity specific to paradoxical sleep in the ventromedial medullary reticular formation of unrestrained cats. *Brain Research*, 1980, *189*, 251–255.

Kane, J., Honigfeld, G., Singer, J., Meltzer, H., and the Clozaril Collaborative Study Group. Clozapine for the treatment-resistant schizophrenic: A double-blind comparison with chlorpromazine. *Archives of General Psychiatry*, 1988, *45*, 789–796.

Kanner, L. Autistic disturbances of affective contact. *The Nervous Child*, 1943, *2*, 217–250.

Kapp, B. S., Gallagher, M., Applegate, C. D., and Frysinger, R. C. The amygdala central nucleus: Contributions to conditioned cardiovascular responding during aversive Pavlovian conditioning in the rabbit. In *Conditioning: Representation of Involved Neural Functions*, edited by C. D. Woody. New York: Plenum Press, 1982.

Kapur, N., Thompson, S., Cook, P., Lang, D., and Brice, J. Anterograde but not retrograde memory loss following combined mammillary body and medial thalamic lesions. *Neuropsychologia*, 1996, *34*, 1–8.

Karacan, I., Salis, P. J., and Williams, R. L. The role of the sleep laboratory in diagnosis and treatment of impotence. In *Sleep Disorders: Diagnosis and Treatment*, edited by R. J. Williams and I. Karacan. New York: John Wiley & Sons, 1978.

Karacan, I., Williams, R. L., Finley, W. W., and Hursch, C. J. The effects of naps on nocturnal sleep: Influence on the need for stage 1 REM and stage 4 sleep. *Biological Psychiatry*, 1970, *2*, 391–399.

Karlson, P., and Luscher, M. "Pheromones": A new term for a class of biologically active substances. *Nature*, 1959, *183*, 55–56.

Karreman, M., and Moghaddam, B. The prefrontal cortex regulates the basal release of dopamine in the limbic striatum: An effect mediated by ventral tegmental area. *Journal of Neurochemistry*, 1996, *66*, 589–598.

Kartsounis, L. D., Rudge, P., and Stevens, J. M. Bilateral lesions of CA1 and CA2 fields of the hippocampus are sufficient to cause a severe amnesic syndrome in humans. *Journal of Neurology, Neurosurgery and Psychiatry*, 1995, *59*, 95–98.

Kasper, S., Rogers, S. L. B., Yancey, A., Schulz, P. M., Skwerer, R. G., and Rosenthal, N. E. Phototherapy in individuals with and without subsyndromal seasonal affective disorder. *Archives of General Psychiatry*, 1989a, *46*, 837–844.

Kasper, S., Wehr, T. A., Bartko, J. J., Gaist, P. A., and Rosenthal, N. E. Epidemiological findings of seasonal changes in mood and behavior: A telephone survey of Montgomery County, Maryland. *Archives of General Psychiatry*, 1989b, *46*, 823–833.

Katayama, Y., DeWitt, D. S., Becker, D. P., and Hayes, R. L. Behavioral evidence for cholinoceptive pontine inhibitory area: Descending control of spinal motor output and sensory input. *Brain Research*, 1986, *296*, 241–262.

Kattler, H., Dijk, D. J., and Borbély, A. A. Effect of unilateral somatosensory stimulation prior to sleep on the sleep EEG in humans. *Journal of Sleep Research*, 1994, *3*, 159–164.

Kavaliers, M. Brief exposure to a natural predator, the short-tailed weasel, induces benzodiazepine-sensitive analgesia in white-footed mice. *Physiology and Behavior*, 1985, *43*, 187–193.

Kawamura, M., Hirayama, K., and Yamamoto, H. Different interhemispheric transfer of kanji and kana writing evidenced by a case with left unilateral agraphia without apraxia. *Brain*, 1989, *112*, 1011–1018.

Kayama, Y., Ohta, M., and Jodo, E. Firing of "possibly" cholinergic neurons in the rat laterodorsal tegmental nucleus during sleep and wakefulness. *Brain Research*, 1992, *569*, 210–220.

Kaye, W. H. Neuropeptide abnormalities in anorexia nervosa. *Psychiatry Research*, 1996, *62*, 65–74.

Kaye, W. H., Berrettini, W., Gwirtsman, H., and George, D. T. Altered cerebrospinal fluid neuropeptide Y and peptide YY immunoreactivity in anorexia and bulimia nervosa. *Archives of General Psychiatry*, 1990, *47*, 548–556.

Keller, S. E., Weiss, J. M., Schleifer, S. J., Miller, N. E., and Stein, M. Stress-induced suppression of immunity in adrenalectomized rats. *Science*, 1983, *221*, 1301–1304.

Kelso, S. R., and Brown, T. H. Differential conditioning of associative synaptic enhancement in hippocampal brain slices. *Science*, 1986, *232*, 85–87.

Kelso, S. R., Ganong, A. H., and Brown, T. H. Hebbian synapses in hippocampus. *Proceedings of the National Academy of Sciences, USA*, 1986, *83*, 5326–5330.

Kendell, R. E., and Adams, W. Unexplained fluctuations in the risk for schizophrenia by month and year of birth. *British Journal of Psychiatry*, 1991, *158*, 758–763.

Kennard, C., Lawden, M., Morland, A. B., and Ruddock, K. H. Colour identification and colour constancy are impaired in a patient with incomplete achromatopsia associated with prestriate cortical lesions. *Proceedings of the Royal Society of London (B)*, 1995, *260*, 169–175.

Kennedy, S. H., and Goldbloom, D. S. Current perspectives on drug therapies for anorexia nervosa and bulimia nervosa. *Drugs*, 1991, *41*, 367–377.

Kertesz, A. Anatomy of jargon. In *Jargonaphasia*, edited by J. Brown. New York: Academic Press, 1981.

Kety, S. S., Rosenthal, D., Wender, P. H., and Schulsinger, K. F. The types and prevalence of mental illness in the biological and adoptive families of adopted schizophrenics. In *The Transmission of Schizophrenia*, edited by D. Rosenthal and S. S. Kety. New York: Pergamon Press, 1968.

Kety, S. S., Wender, P. H., Jacobsen, B., Ingraham, L. J., Jansson, L., Faber, B., and Kinney, D. K. Mental illness in the biological and adoptive relatives of schizophrenic adoptees: Replication of the Copenhagen Study in the rest of Denmark. *Archives of General Psychiatry*, 1994, *51*, 442–455.

Keverne, E. B., and de la Riva, C. Pheromones in mice: Reciprocal interactions between the nose and brain. *Nature*, 1982, *296*, 148–150.

Khanna, S., and Channabasavanna, S. Toward a classification of compulsions in obsessive compulsive neurosis. *Psychopathology*, 1987, *20*, 23–28.

Kiang, N. Y.-S. *Discharge Patterns of Single Fibers in the Cat's Auditory Nerve*. Cambridge, Mass.: MIT Press, 1965.

Kiecolt-Glaser, J. K., Glaser, R., Shuttleworth, E. C., Dyer, C. S., Ogrocki, P., and Speicher, C. E. Chronic stress and immunity in family caregivers of Alzheimer's disease victims. *Psychosomatic Medicine*, 1987, *49*, 523–535.

Kiecolt-Glaser, J. K., Marucha, P. T., Malarkey, W. B., Mercado, A. M., and Glaser, R. Slowing of wound healing by psychological stress. *Lancet*, 1995, *346*, 1194–1196.

Kihlstrom, J. F. Hypnosis. *Annual Review of Psychology*, 1985, *36*, 385–418.

Kinnamon, S. C., and Cummings, T. A. Chemosensory transduction mechanisms in taste. *Annual Review of Physiology*, 1992, *54*, 715–731.

Kinnamon, S. C., Dionne, V. E., and Beam, K. G. Apical localization of K^+ channels in taste cells provides the basis for sour taste transduction. *Proceedings of the National Academy of Sciences, USA*, 1988, *85*, 7023–7027.

Kinney, D. K., Yurgelun-Todd, D. A., Levy, D. L., Medoff, D., Lajonchere, C. M., and Radford-Paregol, M. Obstetrical complications in patients with bipolar disorder and their siblings. *Psychiatry Research*, 1993, *48*, 47–56.

Kinon, B. J., and Lieberman, J. A. Mechanisms of action of atypical antipsychotic drugs: A critical analysis. *Psychopharmacology*, 1996, *124*, 2–34.

Kinsey, A. C., Pomeroy, W. B., Martin, C. E., and Gebhard, P. H. *Sexual Behavior in the Human Female*. Philadelphia: Saunders, 1943.

Kinsley, C. H., Konen, C. M., Miele, L., Ghiraldi, L., and Svare, B. Intrauterine position modulates maternal behaviors in female mice. *Physiology and Behavior*, 1986, *36*, 793–799.

Kirkpatrick, B., Kim, J. W., and Insel, T. R. Limbic system fos expression associated with paternal behavior. *Brain Research*, 1994, *658*, 112–118.

Klausner, J. D., Sweeney, J. A., Deck, M. D. F., Haas, G. L., and Kelly, A. B. Clinical correlates of cerebral ventricular enlargement in schizophrenia. Further evidence for frontal lobe disease. *Journal of Nervous and Mental Disorders*, 1992, *180*, 407–412.

Kleitman, N. Basic rest-activity cycle—22 years later. *Sleep*, 1982, *4*, 311–317.

Kleitman, N. The nature of dreaming. In *The Nature of Sleep*, edited by G. E. W. Wolstenholme and M. O'Connor. London: J. & A. Churchill, 1961.

Knapp, P. H., Levy, E. M., Giorgi, R. G., Black, P. H., Fox, B. H., and Heeren, T. C. Short-term immunological effects of induced emotion. *Psychosomatic Medicine*, 1992, *54*, 133–148.

Knebelmann, B., Boussin, L., Guerrier, D., Legeai, L., Kahn, A., Josso, N., and Picard, J.-Y. Anti-Muellerian hormone Bruxelles: A nonsense mutation associated with the persistent Muellerian duct syndrome. *Proceedings of the National Academy of Sciences, USA*, 1991, *88*, 3767–3771.

Knefati, M., Somogyi, C., Kapas, L., Bourcier, T., and Krueger, J. M. Acidic fibroblast growth factor (FGF) but not basic FGF induces sleep and fever in rabbits. *American Journal of Physiology*, 1995, *269*, R87–R91.

Knoll, J. Sexual performance and longevity. *Experimental Gerontology*, 1997, *32*, 539–552.

Knoll, J., Dallo, J., and Yen, T. T. Striatal dopamine, sexual activity and lifespan: Longevity of rats treated with (-)deprenyl. *Life Sciences*, 1989, *45*, 525–531.

Knowlton, B. J., Mangels, J. A., and Squire, L. R. A neostriatal habit learning system in humans. *Science*, 1996, *273*, 1399–1402.

Kobatake, E., Tanaka, K., and Tamori, Y. Long-term learning changes the stimulus selectivity of cells in the inferotemporal cortex of adult monkeys. *Neuroscience Research*, 1992, *S17*, S237.

Kolvalzon, V. M., and Mukhametov, L. M. Temperature fluctuations of the dolphin brain corresponding to unihemispheric slow-wave sleep. *Journal of Evolutionary Biochemistry and Physiology*, 1982, *18*, 307–309.

Komisaruk, B. R., and Larsson, K. Suppression of a spinal and a cranial nerve reflex by vaginal or rectal probing in rats. *Brain Research*, 1971, *35*, 231–235.

Komisaruk, B. R., and Steinman, J. L. Genital stimulation as a trigger for neuroendocrine and behavioral control of reproduction. *Annals of the New York Academy of Sciences*, 1987, *474*, 64–75.

Koob, G. F., Thatcher-Britton, K., Britton, D., Roberts, D.C. S., and Bloom, F. E. Destruction of the locus coeruleus or the dorsal NE bundle does not alter the release of punished responding by ethanol and chlordiazepoxide. *Physiology and Behavior*, 1984, *33*, 479–485.

Koopman, P., Gubbay, J., Vivian, N., Goodfellow, P. N., and Lovell-Badge, R. Male development of chromosomally female mice transgenic for SRY. *Nature*, 1991, *351*, 117–121.

Koroshetz, W. J., and Moskowitz, M. A. Emerging treatments for stroke in humans. *Trends in Pharmacological Sciences*, 1996, *17*, 227–233.

Kovács, G., Vogels, R., and Orban, G. A. Selectivity of macaque inferior temporal neurons for partially occluded shapes. *Journal of Neuroscience*, 1995, *15*, 1984–1997.

Kovner, R., and Stamm, J. S. Disruption of short-term visual memory by electrical stimulation of inferotemporal cortex in the monkey. *Journal of Comparative and Physiological Psychology*, 1972, *81*, 163–172.

Kozlowski, L. T., and Cutting, J. E. Recognizing the sex of a walker from a dynamic point-light display. *Perception and Psychophysics*, 1977, *21*, 575–580.

Kral, J. G. Surgical treatment of obesity. *Medical Clinics of North America*, 1989, *73*, 251–264.

Kraly, F. S. Drinking elicited by eating. In *Progress in Psychobiology and Physiological Psychology*, *Vol. 14*, edited by A. N. Epstein and A. Morrison. New York: Academic Press, 1990.

Kramer, F. M., Jeffery, R. W., Forster, J. L., and Snell, M. K. Long-term follow-up of behavioral treatment for obesity: Patterns of weight regain among men and women. *International Journal of Obesity*, 1989, *13*, 123–136.

Kraut, R. E., and Johnston, R. Social and emotional messages of smiling: An ethological approach. *Journal of Personality and Social Psychology*, 1979, *37*, 1539–1553.

Krueger, J. M., and Majde, J. A. Cytokines and sleep. *International Archives of Allergy and Immunology*, 1995, *106*, 97–100.

Kuczmarski, R. J. Prevalence of overweight and weight gain in the United States. *American Journal of Clinical Nutrition*, 1992, *55*, 495S–502S.

Kuffler, S. W. Neurons in the retina: Organization, inhibition and excitation problems. *Cold Spring Harbor Symposium on Quantitative Biology*, 1952, *17*, 281–292.

Kuffler, S. W. Discharge patterns and functional organization of mammalian retina. *Journal of Neurophysiology*, 1953, *16*, 37–68.

Kulka, R. A., Schlenger, W. E., Fairbank, J. A., Hough, R. L., Jordan, B. K., Marmar, C. R., and Weiss, D. S. *Trauma and the Vietnam War Generation: Report of Findings from the National Vietnam Veterans Readjustment Study.* New York: Brunner/Mazel, 1990.

Kumar, K., Wyant, G. M., and Nath, R. Deep brain stimulation for control of intractable pain in humans, present and future: A ten-year follow-up. *Neurosurgery*, 1990, *26*, 774–782.

Kupfer, D. J. REM latency: A psychobiologic marker for primary depressive disease. *Biological Psychiatry*, 1976, *11*, 159–174.

Kupfer, D. J., Ehlers, C. L., Frank, E., Grochocinski, V. J., McEachran, A. B., and Buhari, A. Persistent effects of antidepressants: EEG sleep studies in depressed patients during maintenance treatment. *Biological Psychiatry*, 1994, *35*, 781–793.

Kurihara, K. Recent progress in taste receptor mechanisms. In *Umami: A Basic Taste*, edited by Y. Kawamura and M. R. Kare. New York: Dekker, 1987.

Kurihara, K., Katsuragi, Y., Matsuoka, I., Kashiwayanagi, M., Kumazawa, T., and Shoji, T. Receptor mechanisms of bitter substances. *Physiology and Behavior*, 1994, *56*, 1125–1132.

LaBar, K. S., LeDoux, J. E., Spencer, D. D., and Phelps, E. A. Impaired fear conditioning following unilateral temporal lobectomy in humans. *Journal of Neuroscience*, 1995, *15*, 6846–6855.

Laitinen, L. V., Bergenheim, A. T., and Hariz, M. I. Leksell's posteroventral pallidotomy in the treatment of Parkinson's disease. *Journal of Neurosurgery*, 1992, *76*, 53–61.

Lange, C. G. *Über Gemüthsbewegungen.* Leipzig, Germany: T. Thomas, 1887.

Langston, J. W., and Ballard, P. Parkinsonism induced by 1-methyl-4-phenyl-1,2,3,6-tetrahydropyridine (MPTP): Implications for treatment and the pathogenesis of Parkinson's disease. *Canadian Journal of Neurological Science*, 1984, *11*, 160–165.

Langston, J. W., Ballard, P., Tetrud, J., and Irwin, I. Chronic parkinsonism in humans due to a product of meperidine-analog synthesis. *Science*, 1983, *219*, 979–980.

Langston, J. W., Irwin, I., Langston, E. B., and Forno, L. S. Pargyline prevents MPTP-induced parkinsonism in primates. *Science*, 1984, *225*, 1480–1482.

Laruelle, M., Abi-Dargham, A., Van Dyck, C. H., Gil, R., D'Souza, C. D., Erdos, J., McCance, E., Rosenblatt, W., Fingado, C., Zoghbi, S. S., Baldwin, R. M., Seibyl, J. P., Krystal, J. H., Charney, D. S., and Innis, R. B. Single photon emission computerized tomography imaging of amphetamine-induced dopamine release in drug-free schizophrenic subjects. *Proceedings of the National Academy of Sciences, USA*, 1996, *93*, 9235–9240.

Laschet, U. Antiandrogen in the treatment of sex offenders: Mode of action and therapeutic outcome. In *Contemporary Sexual Behavior: Critical Issues in the 1970's*, edited by J. Zubin and J. Money. Baltimore: Johns Hopkins University Press, 1973.

Lavie, P., Pratt, H., Scharf, B., Peled, R., and Brown, J. Localized pontine lesion: Nearly total absence of REM sleep. *Neurology*, 1984, *34*, 1118–1120.

Lavond, D. G., Kim, J. J., and Thompson, R. F. Mammalian brain substrates of aversive classical conditioning. *Annual Review of Psychology*, 1993, *44*, 317–342.

Leblanc, R., Meyer, E., Bub, D., Zatorre, R. J., and Evans, A. C. Language localization with activation positron emission tomography scanning. *Neurosurgery*, 1992, *31*, 369–373.

LeDoux, J. E. Brain mechanisms of emotion and emotional learning. *Current Opinion in Neurobiology*, 1992, *2*, 191–197.

LeDoux, J. E. Emotion: Clues from the brain. *Annual Review of Psychology*, 1995, *46*, 209–235.

LeDoux, J. E., Iwata, J., Cicchetti, P., and Reis, D. J. Different projections of the central amygdaloid nucleus mediate autonomic and behavioral correlates of conditioned fear. *Journal of Neuroscience*, 1988, *8*, 2517–2529.

LeDoux, J. E., Iwata, J., Pearl, D., and Reis, D. J. Disruption of auditory but not visual learning by destruction of intrinsic neurons in the rat medial geniculate body. *Brain Research*, 1986, *371*, 395–399.

LeDoux, J. E., Sakaguchi, A., and Reis, D. J. Subcortical efferent projections of the medial geniculate nucleus mediate emotional responses conditioned to acoustic stimuli. *Journal of Neuroscience*, 1984, *4*, 683–698.

Lee, C., Parikh, V., Itsukaichi, T., Bae, K., and Edery, I. Resetting the *Drosophila* clock by photic regulation of PER and a PER-TIM complex. *Science*, 1996, *271*, 1740–1744.

Lehman, C. D., Rodin, J., McEwen, B., and Brinton, R. Impact of environmental stress on the expression of insulin-dependent diabetes mellitus. *Behavioral Neuroscience*, 1991, *105*, 241–245.

Lehman, M. N., and Winans, S. S. Vomeronasal and olfactory pathways to the amygdala controlling male hamster sexual behavior: Autoradiographic and behavioral analyses. *Brain Research*, 1982, *240*, 27–41.

Lehman, M. N., Silver, R., Gladstone, W. R., Kahn, R. M., Gibson, M., and Bittman, E. L. Circadian rhythmicity restored by neural transplant: Immunocytochemical characterization with the host brain. *Journal of Neuroscience*, 1987, *7*, 1626–1638.

Leibenluft, E., and Wehr, T. A. Is sleep deprivation useful in the treatment of depression? *American Journal of Psychiatry*, 1992, *149*, 159–168.

Leibowitz, S. F., Weiss, G. F., and Suh, J. S. Medial hypothalamic nuclei mediate serotonin's inhibitory effect on feeding behavior. *Pharmacology, Biochemistry, and Behavior*, 1990, *37*, 735–742.

Leon, M. Plasticity of olfactory output circuits related to early olfactory learning. *Trends in Neurosciences*, 1987, *10*, 434–438.

Leonard, C. M., Rolls, E. T., Wilson, F. A. W., and Baylis, G. C. Neurons in the amygdala of the monkey with responses selective for faces. *Behavioral Brain Research*, 1985, *15*, 159–176.

Leonard, C. S., Kerman, I., Blaha, G., Taveras, E., and Taylor, B. Interdigitation of nitric oxide synthase-, tyrosine hydroxylase-, and serotonin-containing neurons in and around the laterodorsal and pedunculopontine tegmental nuclei of the guinea pig. *Journal of Comparative Neurology*, 1995, *362*, 411–432.

Leonard, H. L., Lenane, M. C., Swedo, S. E., Rettew, D.C., and Rapoport, J. L. A double-blind comparison of clomipramine and desipramine treatment of severe onychophagia (nail biting). *Archives of General Psychiatry*, 1992, *48*, 821–827.

Leonard, H. L., Swedo, S. E., Rapoport, J. L., Koby, E. V., Lenane, M. C., Cheslow, D. L., and Hamburger, S. D. Treatment of obsessive-compulsive disorder with clomipramine and desipramine in children and adolescents: A double-blind crossover comparison. *Archives of General Psychiatry*, 1989, *46*, 1088–1092.

Leshner, A. I. Molecular mechanisms of cocaine addiction. *New England Journal of Medicine*, 1996, *335*, 128–129.

Lesser, R. Selective preservation of oral spelling without semantics in a case of multi-infarct dementia. *Cortex*, 1989, *25*, 239–250.

LeVay, S. A difference in hypothalamic structure between heterosexual and homosexual men. *Science*, 1991, *253*, 1034–1037.

Levesque, D., Diaz, J., Pilon, C., Martres, M. P., Giros, B., Souil, E., Schott, D., Morgat, J. L., Schwartz, J. C., and Sokoloff, P. Identification, characterization, and localization of the dopamine-D_3 receptor in rat brain using 7-(H-3)hydroxy-N,N-di-normal-propyl-2-aminotetralin. *Proceedings of the National Academy of Sciences, USA*, 1992, *89*, 8155–8159.

Levine, J. D., Gordon, N. C., and Fields, H. L. The role of endorphins in placebo analgesia. In *Advances in Pain Research and Therapy, Vol. 3*, edited by J. J. Bonica, J. C. Liebeskind, and D. Albe-Fessard. New York: Raven Press, 1979.

Levy, R. M., and Bredesen, D. E. Controversies in HIV-related central nervous system disease: Neuropsychological aspects of HIV-1 infection. In *AIDS Clinical Review 1989*, edited by P. Volberding, and M. A. Jacobson. New York: Marcel Dekker, 1989.

Lewin, R. Big first scored with nerve diseases. *Science*, 1989, *245*, 467–468.

Li, B.-H., Spector, A. C., and Rowland, N. E. Reversal of dexfenfluramine-induced anorexia and c-Fos/c-Jun expression by lesion in the lateral parabrachial nucleus. *Brain Research*, 1994, *640*, 255–267.

Li, X.-J., Li, S. H., Sharp, A. H., Nucifora, F. C., Schilling, G., Lanahan, A., Worley, P., Snyder, S. H., and Ross, C. A. A huntingtin-associated protein enriched in brain with implications for pathology. *Nature*, 1995, *378*, 392–402.

Li, X.-J., Sharp, A. H., Li, S.-H., Dawson, T. M., Snyder, S. H., and Ross, C. A. Huntingtin-associated protein (HAP1): Discrete neuronal localizations in the brain resemble those of neuronal nitric oxide synthase. *Proceedings of the National Academy of Sciences, USA*, 1996, *93*, 4839–4844.

Liao, D., Hessler, N. A., and Malinow, R. Activation of postsynaptically silent synapses during pairing-induced LTP in CA1 region of hippocampal slice. *Nature*, 1995, *375*, 400–404.

Lipton, S. A. Similarity of neuronal cell injury and death in AIDS dementia and focal cerebral ischemia: Potential treatment with NMDA open-channel blockers and nitric oxide–related species. *Brain Pathology*, 1996, *6*, 507–514.

Lipton, S. A. Neuropathogenesis of acquired immunodeficiency syndrome dementia. *Current Opinion in Neurology*, 1997, *10*, 247–253.

Lipton, S. A., Dreyer, E. B., Kaiser, P. K., and Offermann, J. T. HIV-1 coat protein neurotoxicity prevented by calcium channel antagonists. *Science*, 1990, *248*, 364–367.

Lisk, R. D., Pretlow, R. A., and Friedman, S. Hormonal stimulation necessary for elicitation of maternal nest-building in the mouse (*Mus musculus*). *Animal Behaviour*, 1969, *17*, 730–737.

Livingstone, M. S., and Hubel, D. H. Anatomy and physiology of a color system in the primate visual cortex. *Journal of Neuroscience*, 1984, *4*, 309–356.

Livingstone, M. S., and Hubel, D. H. Psychophysical evidence for separate channels for the perception of form, color, movement, and depth. *Journal of Neuroscience*, 1987, *7*, 3416–3468.

Livingstone, M. S., and Hubel, D. Segregation of form, color, movement, and depth: Anatomy, physiology, and perception. *Science*, 1988, *240*, 740–749.

Loeb, G. E. Cochlear prosthetics. *Annual Review of Neuroscience*, 1990, *13*, 357–371.

Loewenstein, W. R., and Mendelson, M. Components of receptor adaptation in a Pacinian corpuscle. *Journal of Physiology (London)*, 1965, *177*, 377–397.

Logan, F. A. Decision making by rats: Delay versus amount of reward. *Journal of Comparative and Physiological Psychology*, 1965, *59*, 1–12.

Logothetis, N. K., Pauls, J., and Poggio, T. Shape representation in the inferior temporal cortex of monkeys. *Current Biology*, 1995, *5*, 552–563.

Lømo, T. Frequency potentiation of excitatory synaptic activity in the dentate area of the hippocampal formation. *Acta Physiologica Scandinavica*, 1966, *68* (Suppl. 227), 128.

Loscher, W., Annies, R., and Honack, D. The N-methyl-D-aspartate receptor antagonist MK-801 induces increases in dopamine and serotonin metabolism in several brain regions of rats. *Neuroscience Letters*, 1991, *128*, 191–194.

Lowe, T. L., Tanaka, K., Seashore, M. R., Young, J. G., and Cohen, D. J. Detection of phenylketonuria in autistic and psychotic children. *Journal of the American Medical Association*, 1980, *243*, 126–128.

Lucey, J. V., Costa, D.C., Busatto, G., Pilowsky, L. S., Marks, I. M., Ell, P. J., and Kerwin, R. W. Caudate regional cerebral blood flow in obsessive-compulsive disorder, panic disorder and healthy controls on single photon emission computerised tomography. *Psychiatry Research: Neuroimaging*, 1997, *74*, 25–33.

Lupien, S., Lecours, A. R., Schwartz, G., Sharma, S., Hauger, R. L., Meaney, M. J., and Nair, N. P. V. Longitudinal study of basal cortisol levels in healthy elderly subjects: Evidence for subgroups. *Neurobiology of Aging*, 1996, *17*, 95–105.

Lydic, R., Baghdoyan, H. A., Hibbard, L., Bonyak, E. V., DeJoseph, M. R., and Hawkins, R. A. Regional brain glucose metabolism is altered during rapid eye movement sleep in the cat: A preliminary study. *Journal of Comparative Neurology*, 1991, *304*, 517–529.

Lynch, G., Larson, J., Kelso, S., Barrionuevo, G., and Schottler, F. Intracellular injections of EGTA block induction of long-term potentiation. *Nature*, 1984, *305*, 719–721.

Lynch, G., Larson, J., Staubli, U., and Granger, R. Variants of synaptic potentiation and different types of memory operations in hippocampus and related structures. In *Memory: Organization and Locus of Change*, edited by L. R. Squire, N. M. Weinberger, G. Lynch, and J. L. McGaugh. New York: Oxford University Press, 1991.

Lytton, W. W., and Brust, J. C. M. Direct dyslexia: Preserved oral reading of real words in Wernicke's aphasia. *Brain*, 1989, *112*, 583–594.

MacLean, H. E., Warne, G. L., and Zajac, J. D. Defects of androgen receptor function: From sex reversal to motor-neuron disease. *Molecular and Cellular Endocrinology*, 1995, *112*, 133–141.

MacLean, P. D. Psychosomatic disease and the "visceral brain": Recent developments bearing on the Papez theory of emotion. *Psychosomatic Medicine*, 1949, *11*, 338–353.

Maier, S. F., Drugan, R. C., and Grau, J. W. Controllability, coping behavior, and stress-induced analgesia in the rat. *Pain*, 1982, *12*, 47–56.

Maj, M. Organic mental disorders in HIV-1 infection. *AIDS*, 1990, *4*, 831–840.

Maksay, G., and Ticku, M. K. Dissociation of [^{35}S]t-butylbicyclophosphorothionate binding differentiates convulsant and depressant drugs that modulate GABAergic transmission. *Journal of Neurochemistry*, 1985, *44*, 480–486.

Malach, R., Reppas, J. B., Benson, R. R., Kwong, K. K., Jiang, H., Kennedy, W. A., Ledden, P. J., Brady, T. J., Rosen, B. R., and Tootell, R. B. H. Object-related activity revealed by functional magnetic resonance imaging in human occipital cortex. *Proceedings of the National Academy of Sciences, USA*, 1995, *92*, 8135–8139.

Mallow, G. K. The relationship between aggression and cycle stage in adult female rhesus monkeys (*Macaca mulatta*). *Dissertation Abstracts*, 1979, *39*, 3194.

Malsbury, C. W. Facilitation of male rat copulatory behavior by electrical stimulation of the medial preoptic area. *Physiology and Behavior*, 1971, *7*, 797–805.

Mann, M. A., Konen, C., and Svare, B. The role of progesterone in pregnancy-induced aggression in mice. *Hormones and Behavior*, 1984, *18*, 140–160.

Manning, L., and Campbell, R. Optic aphasia with spared action naming: A description and possible loci of impairment. *Neuropsychologia*, 1992, *30*, 587–592.

Manuck, S. B., Kaplan, J. R., and Clarkson, T. B. Behaviorally-induced heart rate reactivity and atherosclerosis in cynomolgus monkeys. *Psychosomatic Medicine*, 1983, *45*, 95–108.

Manuck, S. B., Kaplan, J. R., and Matthews, K. A. Behavioral antecedents of coronary heart disease and atherosclerosis. *Arteriosclerosis*, 1986, *6*, 1–14.

Maquet, P. Sleep function(s) and cerebral metabolism. *Behavioural Brain Research*, 1995, *69*, 75–83.

Maquet, P., Dive, D., Salmon, E., Sadzot, B., Franco, G., Poirrier, R., Von Frenckell, R., and Franck, G. Cerebral glucose utilization during sleep-wake cycle in man determined by positron emission tomography and [18F]2-fluoro-2-deoxy-D-glucose method. *Brain Research*, 1990, *513*, 136–143.

Maret, G., Testa, B., Jenner, P., El Tayar, N., and Carrupt, P.-A. The MPTP story: MAO activates tetrahydropyridine derivatives to toxins causing parkinsonism. *Drug Metabolism Reviews*, 1990, *22*, 291–232.

Margolin, D. I., and Goodman-Schulman, R. Oral and written spelling impairments. In *Cognitive Neuropsychology in Clinical Practice*, edited by D. I. Margolin. New York: Oxford University Press, 1992.

Margolin, D. I., and Walker, J. A. Personal communication, 1981.

Margolin, D. I., Marcel, A. J., and Carlson, N. R. Common mechanisms in dysnomia and post-semantic surface dyslexia: Processing deficits and selective attention. In *Surface Dyslexia: Neuropsychological and Cognitive Studies of Phonological Reading*, edited by M. Coltheart. London: Lawrence Erlbaum Associates, 1985.

Marrocco, R. T., Witte, E. A., and Davidson, M. C. Arousal systems. *Current Opinion in Neurobiology*, 1994, *4*, 166–170.

Marshall, J. C., and Newcombe, F. Patterns of paralexia: A psycholinguistic approach. *Journal of Psycholinguistic Research*, 1973, *2*, 175–199.

Martinez, M., Campion, D., Babron, M. C., and Clergetdarpous, F. Is a single mutation at the same socus responsible for all affected cases in a large Alzheimer pedigree (Fad4)? *Genetic Epidemiology*, 1993, *10*, 431–435.

Mas, M. Neurobiological correlates of masculine sexual behavior. *Neuroscience and Biobehavioral Reviews*, 1995, *19*, 261–277.

Mather, P., Nicolaïdis, S., and Booth, D. A. Compensatory and conditioned feeding responses to scheduled glucose infusions in the rat. *Nature*, 1978, *273*, 461–463.

Matsuda, L. A., Lolait, S. J., Brownstein, M. J., Young, A. C., and Bonner, T. I. Structure of a cannabinoid receptor and functional expression of the cloned cDNA. *Nature*, 1990, *346*, 561–564.

Matteo, S., and Rissman, E. F. Increased sexual activity during the midcycle portion of the human menstrual cycle. *Hormones and Behavior*, 1984, *18*, 249–255.

Matthews, D. B., Simson, P. E., and Best, P. J. Ethanol alters spatial processing of hippocampal place cells: A mechanism for impaired navigation when intoxicated. *Alcoholism: Clinical and Experimental Research*, 1996, *20*, 404–407.

Maunsell, J. H. R. Functional visual streams. *Current Opinion in Neurobiology*, 1992, *2*, 506–510.

Mawson, A. R. Anorexia nervosa and the regulation of intake: A review. *Psychological Medicine*, 1974, *4*, 289–308.

Mayer, D. J., and Liebeskind, J. C. Pain reduction by focal electrical stimulation of the brain: An anatomical and behavioral analysis. *Brain Research*, 1974, *68*, 73–93.

Mayer, D. J., Price, D. D., Rafii, A., and Barber, J. Acupuncture hypalgesia: Evidence for activation of a central control system as a mechanism of action. In *Advances in Pain Research and Therapy, Vol. 1*, edited by J. J. Bonica and D. Albe-Fessard. New York: Raven Press, 1976.

Mazur, A. Hormones, aggression, and dominance in humans. In *Hormones and Aggressive Behavior*, edited by B. B. Svare. New York: Plenum Press, 1983.

Mazur, A., and Lamb, T. Testosterone, status, and mood in human males. *Hormones and Behavior*, 1980, *14*, 236–246.

McCarley, R. W., and Hobson, J. A. The form of dreams and the biology of sleep. In *Handbook of Dreams: Research, Theory, and Applications*, edited by B. Wolman. New York: Van Nostrand Reinhold, 1979.

McCarthy, G., Blamire, A. M., Rothman, D. L., Gruetter, R., and Shulman, R. G. Echo-planar magnetic resonance imaging studies of frontal cortex activation during word generation in humans. *Proceedings of the National Academy of Sciences, USA*, 1993, *90*, 4952–4956.

McCarthy, R. A., and Warrington, E. K. *Cognitive Neuropsychology: A Clinical Introduction*. San Diego: Academic Press, 1990.

McCaul, K. D., Gladue, B. A., and Joppa, M. Winning, losing, mood, and testosterone. *Hormones and Behavior*, 1992, *26*, 486–504.

McClintock, M. K. Menstrual synchrony and suppression. *Nature*, 1971, *229*, 244–245.

McClintock, M. K., and Adler, N. T. The role of the female during copulation in wild and domestic Norway rats (*Rattus norvegicus*). *Behaviour*, 1978, *67*, 67–96.

McDonald, R. J., and White, N. M. A triple dissociation of memory systems: Hippocampus, amygdala, and dorsal striatum. *Behavioral Neuroscience*, 1993, *107*, 3–22.

McGeer, P. L., and Rogers, J. Anti-inflammatory agents as a therapeutic approach to Alzheimer's disease. *Neurology*, 1992, *42*, 447–449.

McGinty, D., Szymusiak, R., and Thomson, D. Preoptic/anterior hypothalamic warming increases EEG delta frequency activity within non-rapid eye movement sleep. *Brain Research*, 1994, *667*, 273–277.

McGinty, D. J., and Sterman, M. B. Sleep suppression after basal forebrain lesions in the cat. *Science*, 1968, *160*, 1253–1255.

McGrath, J., Welham, J., and Pemberton, M. Month of birth, hemisphere of birth and schizophrenia. *British Journal of Psychiatry*, 1995, *167*, 783–785.

McGregor, A., and Roberts, D. C. S. Dopaminergic antagonism within the nucleus accumbens or the amygdala produces differential effects on intravenous cocaine self-administration under fixed and progressive ratio schedules of reinforcement. *Brain Research*, 1993, *624*, 245–252.

McHugh, T. J., Blum, K. I., Tsien, J. Z., Tonegawa, S., and Wilson, M. A. Impaired hippocampal representation of space in CA1-specific NMDAR1 knockout mice. *Cell*, 1996, *87*, 1339–1349.

McIver, B., Connacher, A., Whittle, I., Baylis, P., and Thompson, C. Adipsic hypothalamic diabetes insipidus after clipping of anterior communicating artery aneurysm. *British Medical Journal*, 1991, *303*, 1465–1467.

McKenna, T. M., Weinberger, N. M., and Diamond, D. M. Responses of single auditory cortical neurons to tone sequences. *Brain Research*, 1989, *481*, 142–153.

Meddis, R., Pearson, A., and Langford, G. An extreme case of healthy insomnia. *Electroencephalography and Clinical Neurophysiology*, 1973, *35*, 213–214.

Mednick, S. A., Machon, R. A., and Huttunen, M. O. An update on the Helsinki influenza project. *Archives of General Psychiatry*, 1990, *47*, 292.

Meesters, Y., Jansen, J. H. C., Beersma, D. G. M., Bouhuys, A. L., and Van den Hoofdakker, R. H. Light therapy for seasonal affective disorder. The effects of timing. *British Journal of Psychiatry*, 1995, *166*, 607–612.

Mehlman, P. T., Higley, J. D., Faucher, I., Lilly, A. A., Taub, D. M., Vickers, J., Suomi, S. J., and Linnoila, M. Correlation of CSF 5-HIAA concentration with sociality and the timing of emigration in free-ranging primates. *American Journal of Psychiatry*, 1995, *152*, 907–913.

Meijer, J. H., and Rietveld, W. J. Neurophysiology of the suprachiasmatic circadian pacemaker in rodents. *Physiological Reviews*, 1989, *69*, 671–707.

Melander, T., Fuxe, K., Harfstrand, A., Eneroth, P., and Hökfelt, T. Effects of intraventricular injections of galanin on neuroendocrine functions in the male rat: Possible involvement of hypothalamic catecholamine neuronal systems. *Acta Physiologica Scandanavica*, 1987, *131*, 25–32.

Melzak, R. Phantom limbs. *Scientific American*, 1992, *266*(4), 120–126.

Menco, B. P. M., Bruch, R. C., Dau, B., and Danho, W. Ultrastructural localization of olfactory transduction components: The G protein subunit G_{olf} and type III adenylyl cyclase. *Neuron*, 1992, *8*, 441–453.

Mercer, J. G., Hoggard, N., Williams, L. M., Lawrence, C. B., Hannah, L. T., Morgan, P. J., and Trayhurn, P. Coexpression of leptin receptor and preproneuropeptide Y mRNA in arcuate nucleus of mouse hypothalamus. *Journal of Neuroendocrinology*, 1996, *8*, 733–735.

Meredith, M. Chronic recording of vomeronasal pump activation in awake behaving hamsters. *Physiology and Behavior*, 1994, *56*, 345–354.

Meredith, M., and O'Connell, R. J. Efferent control of stimulus access to the hamster vomeronasal organ. *Journal of Physiology*, 1979, *286*, 301–316.

Mereu, G., Yoon, K.-W. P., Boi, V., Gessa, G. L., Naes, L., and Westfall, T. C. Preferential stimulation of ventral tegmental area dopaminergic

neurons by nicotine. *European Journal of Pharmacology*, 1987, *141*, 395–400.

Mesulam, M.-M. Patterns in behavioral neuroanatomy: Association areas, the limbic system, and hemispheric specialization. In *Principles of Behavioral Neurology*, edited by M.-M. Mesulam. Philadelphia: F. A. Davis, 1985.

Mesulam, M.-M. Frontal cortex and behavior. *Annals of Neurology*, 1986, *19*, 320–325.

Meyer-Bahlburg, H. F. L. Psychoendocrine research on sexual orientation: Current status and future options. *Progress in Brain Research*, 1984, *63*, 375–398.

Mikulincer, M., and Solomon, Z. Attributional style and combat-related posttraumatic stress disorder. *Journal of Abnormal Psychology*, 1988, *97*, 308–313.

Miller, M. T., and Strömland, K. Thalidomide embryopathy: An insight into autism. *Teratology*, 1993, *47*, 387–388.

Miller, N. E. Understanding the use of animals in behavioral research: Some critical issues. *Annals of the New York Academy of Sciences*, 1983, *406*, 113–118.

Milner, A. D., Perrett, D. I., Johnston, R. S., and Benson, P. J. Perception and action in "visual form agnosia." *Brain*, 1991, *114*, 405–428.

Milner, B. Memory disturbance after bilateral hippocampal lesions. In *Cognitive Processes and the Brain*, edited by P. Milner and S. Glickman. Princeton, N.J.: Van Nostrand, 1965.

Milner, B. Memory and the temporal regions of the brain. In *Biology of Memory*, edited by K. H. Pribram and D. E. Broadbent. New York: Academic Press, 1970.

Milner, B., Corkin, S., and Teuber, H.-L. Further analysis of the hippocampal amnesic syndrome: 14-year follow-up study of H.M. *Neuropsychologia*, 1968, *6*, 317–338.

Minami, S., Kamegai, J., Sugihara, H., Suzuki, N., Higuchi, H., and Wakabayashi, I. Central glucoprivation evoked by administration of 2-deoxy-D-glucose induces expression of the c-fos gene in a subpopulation of neuropeptide Y neurons in the rat hypothalamus. *Molecular Brain Research*, 1995, *33*, 305–310.

Mindus, P., Rasmussen, S. A., and Lindquist, C. Neurosurgical treatment for refractory obsessive-compulsive disorder: Implications for understanding frontal lobe function. *Journal of Neuropsychiatry and Clinical Neurosciences*, 1994, *6*, 467–477.

Mishkin, M. Visual mechanisms beyond the striate cortex. In *Frontiers in Physiological Psychology*, edited by R. W. Russell. New York: Academic Press, 1966.

Mitchell, J. E. Psychopharmacology of eating disorders. *Annals of the New York Academy of Sciences*, 1989, *575*, 41–49.

Mitler, M. M. Evaluation of treatment with stimulants in narcolepsy. *Sleep*, 1994, *17*, S103–S106.

Moghaddam, B., and Bunney, B. S. Differential effect of cocaine on extracellular dopamine levels in rat medial prefrontal cortex and nucleus accumbens: Comparison to amphetamine. *Synapse*, 1989, *4*, 156–161.

Moldin, S. O., Reich, T., and Rice, J. P. Current perspectives on the genetics of unipolar depression. *Behavioral Genetics*, 1991, *21*, 211–242.

Mollon, J. D. "Tho' she kneel'd in that place where they grew...": The uses and origins of primate colour vision. *Journal of Experimental Biology*, 1989, *146*, 21–38.

Moltz, H., Lubin, M., Leon, M., and Numan, M. Hormonal induction of maternal behavior in the ovariectomized nulliparous rat. *Physiology and Behavior*, 1970, *5*, 1373–1377.

Money, J., and Ehrhardt, A. *Man & Woman, Boy & Girl.* Baltimore: Johns Hopkins University Press, 1972.

Money, J., Schwartz, M., and Lewis, V. G. Adult erotosexual status and fetal hormonal masculinization and demasculinization: 46,XX congenital virilizing adrenal hyperplasia and 46,XY androgen-insensitivity syndrome compared. *Psychoneuroendocrinology,* 1984, *9,* 405–414.

Moore, C. L. Interaction of species-typical environmental and hormonal factors in sexual differentiation of behavior. *Annals of the New York Academy of Sciences,* 1986, *474,* 108–119.

Moore, R. Y. Neural control of the pineal gland. *Behavioural Brain Research,* 1995, *73,* 125–130.

Moore, R. Y., and Eichler, V. B. Loss of a circadian adrenal corticosterone rhythm following suprachiasmatic lesions in the rat. *Brain Research,* 1972, *42,* 201–206.

Moore, R. Y., Card, J. P., and Riley, J. N. The suprachiasmatic hypothalamic nucleus: Neuronal ultrastructure. *Neuroscience Abstracts,* 1980, *6,* 758.

Morales, F. R., Boxer, P. A., and Chase, M. H. Behavioral state-specific inhibitory postsynaptic potentials impinge on cat lumbar motoneurons during active sleep. *Experimental Neurology,* 1987, *98,* 418–435.

Moran, T. H., Shnayder, L., Hostetler, A. M., and McHugh, P. R. Pylorectomy reduces the satiety action of cholecystokinin. *American Journal of Physiology,* 1989, *255,* R1059–R1063.

Morrell, M. J. Sexual dysfunction in epilepsy. *Epilepsia,* 1991, *32,* S38–S45.

Morrell, M. J., Sperling, M. R., Stecker, M., and Dichter, M. A. Sexual dysfunction in partial epilepsy: A deficit in physiologic sexual arousal. *Neurology,* 1994, *44,* 243–247.

Morris, J. S., Frith, C. D., Perrett, D. I., Rowland, D., Young, A. W., Calder, A. J., and Dolan, R. J. A differential neural response in the human amygdala to fearful and happy facial expressions. *Nature,* 1996, *383,* 812–815.

Morris, N. M., Udry, J. R., Khan-Dawood, F., and Dawood, M. Y. Marital sex frequency and midcycle female testosterone. *Archives of Sexual Behavior,* 1987, *16,* 27–37.

Morris, R. G. M., Garrud, P., Rawlins, J. N. P., and O'Keefe, J. Place navigation impaired in rats with hippocampal lesions. *Nature,* 1982, *297,* 681–683.

Moscovitch, M., and Olds, J. Asymmetries in emotional facial expressions and their possible relation to hemispheric specialization. *Neuropsychologia,* 1982, *20,* 71–81.

Moscovitch, M., Kapur, S., Koehler, S., and Houle, S. Distinct neural correlates of visual long-term memory for spatial location and object identity: A positron emission tomography study in humans. *Proceedings of the National Academy of Sciences, USA,* 1995, *92,* 3721–3725.

Mukhametov, L. M. Sleep in marine mammals. In *Sleep Mechanisms,* edited by A. A. Borbély and J. L. Valatx. Munich: Springer-Verlag, 1984.

Munro, J. F., Stewart, I. C., Seidelin, P. H., Mackenzie, H. S., and Dewhurst, N. E. Mechanical treatment for obesity. *Annals of the New York Academy of Sciences,* 1987, *499,* 305–312.

Murphy, P. J., Badia, P., Myers, B. L., Boecker, M. R., and Wright, K. P. Nonsteroidal anti-inflammatory drugs affect normal sleep patterns in humans. *Physiology and Behavior,* 1994, *55,* 1063–1066.

Murray, A. M., Hyde, T. M., Knable, M. B., Herman, M. M., Bigelow, L. B., Carter, J. M., Weinberger, D. R., and Kleinman, J. E. Distribution of putative D4 dopamine receptors in postmortem striatum from patients with schizophrenia. *Journal of Neuroscience,* 1995, *15,* 2186–2191.

Murray, A. M., Ryoo, H., Gurevich, E., and Joyce, J. N. Localization of dopamine D_3 receptors to mesolimbic and D_2 receptors to mesostriatal regions of human forebrain. *Proceedings of the National Academy of Sciences, USA,* 1994, *91,* 11271–11275.

Museo, G., and Wise, R. A. Place preference conditioning with ventral tegmental injections of cystine. *Life Sciences,* 1994, *55,* 1179–1186.

Myers, M. P., Wagner-Smith, K., Rotherfluh-Hilfiker, A., and Young, M. W. Light-induced degradation of TIMELESS and entrainment of the *Drosophila* circadian clock. *Science,* 1996, *271,* 1736–1740.

Myers, R. D., Wooten, M. H., Ames, C. D., and Nyce, J. W. Anorexic action of a new potential neuropeptide Y antagonist [D-Tyr27,36,D-Thr32]-NPY (27-36) infused into the hypothalamus of the rat. *Brain Research Bulletin,* 1995, *37,* 237–245.

Nadeau, S. E. Impaired grammar with normal fluency and phonology. *Brain,* 1988, *111,* 1111–1137.

Naeser, M. A., Palumbo, C. L., Helm-Estabrooks, N., Stiassny-Eder, D., and Albert, M. L. Severe nonfluency in aphasia: Role of the medial subcallosal fasciculus and other white matter pathways in recovery of spontaneous speech. *Brain,* 1989, *112,* 1–38.

Nafe, J. P., and Wagoner, K. S. The nature of pressure adaptation. *Journal of General Psychology,* 1941, *25,* 323–351.

Naito, K., Osama, H., Ueno, R., Hayaishi, O., Honda, K., and Inoue, S. Suppression of sleep by prostaglandin synthesis inhibitors in unrestrained rats. *Brain Research,* 1988, *453,* 329–336.

Nakahara, D., Ozaki, N., Miura, Y., Miura, H., and Nagatsu, T. Increased dopamine and serotonin metabolism in rat nucleus accumbens produced by intracranial self-stimulation of medial forebrain bundle as measured by in vivo microdialysis. *Brain Research,* 1989, *495,* 178–181.

Nakamura, T., and Gold, G. A cyclic nucleotide-gated conductance in olfactory receptor cilia. *Nature,* 1987, *325,* 442–444.

Naranjo, C. A., Poulos, C. X., Bremner, K. E., and Lanctot, K. L. Citalopram decreases desirability, liking, and consumption of alcohol in alcohol-dependent drinkers. *Clinical Pharmacology and Therapeutics,* 1992, *51,* 729–739.

Nathans, J., Piantanida, T. P., Eddy, R. L., Shows, T. B., and Hogness, D. S. Molecular genetics of inherited variation in human color vision. *Science,* 1986, *232,* 203–210.

Nauta, W. J. H. Hypothalamic regulation of sleep in rats: Experimental study. *Journal of Neurophysiology,* 1946, *9,* 285–316.

Nauta, W. J. H. Some efferent connections of the prefrontal cortex in the monkey. In *The Frontal Granular Cortex and Behavior,* edited by J. M. Warren and K. Akert. New York: McGraw-Hill, 1964.

Nef, P., Hermansborgmeyer, I., Artierespin, H., Beasley, L., Dionne, V. E., and Heinemann, S. F. Spatial pattern of receptor expression in the olfactory epithelium. *Proceedings of the National Academy of Sciences, USA,* 1992, *89,* 8948–8952.

Neumeister, A., Goessler, R., Lucht, M., Kapitany, T., Bamas, C., and Kasper, S. Bright light therapy stabilizes the antidepressant effect of partial sleep deprivation. *Biological Psychiatry,* 1996, *39,* 16–21.

Nichelli, P., Grafman, J., Pietrini, P., Clark, K., Lee, K. Y., and Miletich, R. Where the brain appreciates the moral of a story. *NeuroReport,* 1995, *6,* 2309–2313.

Nicholl, C. S., and Russell, R. M. Analysis of animal rights literature reveals the underlying motives of the movement: Ammunition for counter offensive by scientists. *Endocrinology,* 1990, *127,* 985–989.

Nicoll, R. A., Alger, B. E., and Nicoll, R. A. Enkephalin blocks inhibitory pathways in the vertebrate CNS. *Nature,* 1980, *287,* 22–25.

NINDS rt-PA Stroke Study Group. Tissue-plasminogen activator for acute ischemic stroke. *New England Journal of Medicine,* 1995, *333,* 1581–1587.

Nishino, S., Reid, M. S., Dement, W. C., and Mignot, E. Neuropharmacology and neurochemistry of canine narcolepsy. *Sleep,* 1994, *17,* S84–S92.

Nishino, S., Tafti, M., Reid, M. S., Shelton, J., Siegel, J. M., Dement, W. C., and Mignot, E. Muscle atonia is triggered by cholinergic stimulation of the basal forebrain: Implication for the pathophysiology of canine narcolepsy. *Journal of Neuroscience,* 1995, *15,* 4806–4814.

Nitz, D., Andersen, A., Fahringer, H., Nienhuis, R., Mignot, E., and Siegel, J. Altered distribution of cholinergic cells in the narcoleptic dog. *NeuroReport,* 1995, *6,* 1521–1524.

Nobler, M. S., Sackeim, H. A., Prohovnik, I., Moeller, J. R., Mukherjee, S., Schnur, D. B., Prudic, J., and Devanand, D. P. Regional cerebral blood flow in mood disorders. III: Treatment and clinical response. *Archives of General Psychiatry,* 1994, *51,* 884–897.

Noirot, E. Selective priming of maternal responses by auditory and olfactory cues from mouse pups. *Developmental Psychobiology,* 1972, *5,* 371–387.

Norgren, R., and Grill, H. Brain-stem control of ingestive behavior. In *The Physiological Mechanisms of Motivation,* edited by D. W. Pfaff. New York: Springer-Verlag, 1982.

Novin, D., VanderWeele, D. A., and Rezek, M. Hepatic-portal 2-deoxy-D-glucose infusion causes eating: Evidence for peripheral glucoreceptors. *Science,* 1973, *181,* 858–860.

Numan, M. Medial preoptic area and maternal behavior in the female rat. *Journal of Comparative and Physiological Psychology,* 1974, *87,* 746–759.

Numan, M., and Numan, M. J. Preoptic-brainstem connections and maternal behavior in rats. *Behavioral Neuroscience,* 1991, *105,* 1013–1029.

Numan, M., and Smith, H. G. Maternal behavior in rats: Evidence for the involvement of preoptic projections to the ventral tegmental area. *Behavioral Neuroscience,* 1984, *98,* 712–727.

Numan, M., Rosenblatt, J. S., and Komisaruk, B. R. Medial preoptic area and onset of maternal behavior in the rat. *Journal of Comparative and Physiological Psychology,* 1977, *91,* 146–164.

Nyby, J., Matochik, J. A., and Barfield, R. J. Intracranial androgenic and estrogenic stimulation of male-typical behaviors in house mice (*Mus domesticus*). *Hormones and Behavior,* 1992, *26,* 24–45.

Oaknin, S., Rodriguez del Castillo, A., Guerra, M., Battaner, E., and Mas, M. Change in forebrain Na,K-ATPase activity and serum hormone levels during sexual behavior in male rats. *Physiology and Behavior,* 1989, *45,* 407–410.

O'Brien, C. P., Volpicelli, L. A., and Volpicelli, J. R. Naltrexone in the treatment of alcoholism: A clinical review. *Alcohol*, 1996, *13*, 35–39.

O'Callaghan, E. Obstetric complicaitons, the putative familial-sporadic distinction, and tardive dyskinesia in schizophrenia. *British Journal of Psychiatry*, 1990, *157*, 578–584.

O'Callaghan, E., Gibson, T., Colohan, H. A., Buckley, P., Walshe, D. G., Larkin, C., and Waddington, J. L. Risk of schizophrenia in adults born after obstetric complications and their association with early onset of illness: A controlled study. *British Medical Journal*, 1992, *305*, 1256–1259.

O'Carroll, R., Shapiro, C., and Bancroft, J. Androgens, behavior and nocturnal erection in hypogonadal men: The effects of varying the replacement dose. *Clinical Endocrinology*, 1985, *23*, 527–538.

O'Connor, H. T., Richman, R. M., Steinbeck, K. S., and Caterson, I. D. Dexfenfluramine treatment of obesity: A double blind trial with post trial follow up. *International Journal of Obesity*, 1995, *19*, 181–189.

O'Dell, T. J., Hawkins, R. D., Kandel, E. R., and Arancio, O. Tests of the roles of two diffusible substances in long-term potentiation: Evidence for nitric oxide as a possible early retrograde messenger. *Proceedings of the National Academy of Sciences, USA*, 1991, *88*, 11285–11289.

Ogawa, S., Olazabal, U. E., Parhar, I. S., and Pfaff, D. W. Effects of intrahypothalamic administration of antisense DNA for progesterone receptor mRNA on reproductive behavior and progesterone receptor immunoreactivity in female rat. *Journal of Neuroscience*, 1994, *14*, 1766–1774.

O'Keefe, J., and Bouma, H. Complex sensory properties of certain amygdala units in the freely moving cat. *Experimental Neurology*, 1969, *23*, 384–398.

O'Keefe, J., and Dostrovsky, T. The hippocampus as a spatial map: Preliminary evidence from unit activity in the freely moving rat. *Brain Research*, 1971, *34*, 171–175.

Olanow, C. W., Kordower, J. H., and Freeman, T. B. Fetal nigral transplantation as a therapy for Parkinson's disease. *Trends in Neurosciences*, 1996, *19*, 102–109.

Olds, J. Commentary. In *Brain Stimulation and Motivation*, edited by E. S. Valenstein. Glenview, Ill.: Scott, Foresman, 1973.

Olds, M. E., and Fobes, J. L. The central basis of motivation: Intracranial self-stimulation studies. *Annual Review of Psychology*, 1981, *32*, 523–574.

O'Mara, S. M., Rolls, E. T., Berthoz, A., and Kesner, R. P. Neurons responding to whole-body motion in the primate hippocampus. *Journal of Neuroscience*, 1994, *14*, 6511–6523.

Owen, A. M., Milner, B., Petrides, M., and Evans, A. C. Memory for object features versus memory for object location: A positron-emission tomography study of encoding and retrieval processes. *Proceedings of the National Academy of Sciences, USA*, 1996, *93*, 9212–9217.

Oyachi, H., and Ohtsuka, K. Transcranial magnetic stimulation of the posterior parietal cortex degrades accuracy of memory-guided saccades in humans. *Investigative Ophthalmology and Visual Science*, 1995, *36*, 1441–1449.

Pallast, E. G. M., Jongbloet, P. H., Straatman, H. M., and Zeilhuis, G. A. Excess of seasonality of births among patients with schizophrenia and seasonal ovopathy. *Schizophrenia Bulletin*, 1994, *20*, 269–276.

Panksepp, J. Aggression elicited by electrical stimulation of the hypothalamus in albino rats. *Physiology and Behavior*, 1971, *6*, 321–329.

Papadimitriou, G. N., Christodoulou, G. N., Katsouyanni, K., and Stefanis, C. N. Therapy and prevention of affective illness by total sleep deprivation. *Journal of the Affective Disorders*, 1993, *27*, 107–116.

Papez, J. W. A proposed mechanism of emotion. *Archives of Neurology and Psychiatry*, 1937, *38*, 725–744.

Pascoe, J. P., and Kapp, B. S. Electrophysiological characteristics of amygdaloid central nucleus neurons during Pavlovian fear conditioning in the rabbit. *Behavioural Brain Research*, 1985, *16*, 117–133.

Passingham, R. Delayed matching after selective prefrontal lesions in monkeys (*Macaca mulatta*). *Brain Research*, 1975, *92*, 89–102.

Pattatucci, A. M. L., and Hamer, D. H. Development and familiality of sexual orientation in females. *Behavior Genetics*, 1995, *25*, 407–420.

Patterson, K., and Kay, J. A. How word-form dyslexics form words. Paper presented at the meeting of the British Psychological Society Conference on Reading, Exeter, England, 1980.

Pauls, D. L., and Leckman, J. F. The inheritance of Gilles de la Tourette's syndrome and associated behaviors. *New England Journal of Medicine*, 1986, *315*, 993–997.

Pauls, D. L., Towbin, K. E., Leckman, J. F., Zahner, G. E. P., and Cohen, D. J. Gilles de la Tourette's syndrome and obsessive-compulsive disorder. *Archives of General Psychiatry*, 1986, *43*, 1180–1182.

Peck, B. K., and Vanderwolf, C. H. Effects of raphe stimulation on hippocampal and neocortical activity and behaviour. *Brain Research*, 1991, *568*, 244–252.

Pelleymounter, M. A., Cullen, M. J., Baker, M. B., Hecht, R., Winters, D., Boone, T., and Collins, F. Effects of the obese gene product on body weight regulation in ob/ob mice. *Science*, 1995, *269*, 540–543.

Pennington, B. F., Gilger, J. W., Pauls, D., Smith, S. A., Smith, S. D., and DeFries, J. C. Evidence for major gene transmission of developmental dyslexia. *Journal of the American Medical Association*, 1991, *266*, 1527–1534.

Persky, H. Reproductive hormones, moods, and the menstrual cycle. In *Sex Differences in Behavior*, edited by R. C. Friedman, R. M. Richart, and R. L. Vande Wiele. New York: John Wiley & Sons, 1974.

Persky, H., Lief, H. I., Strauss, D., Miller, W. R., and O'Brien, C. P. Plasma testosterone level and sexual behavior of couples. *Archives of Sexual Behavior*, 1978, *7*, 157–173.

Pert, C. B., Snowman, A. M., and Snyder, S. H. Localization of opiate receptor binding in presynaptic membranes of rat brain. *Brain Research*, 1974, *70*, 184–188.

Petersen, S. E., Fox, P. T., Posner, M. I., Mintun, M., and Raichle, M. W. Positron emission tomographic studies of the cortical anatomy of single-word processing. *Nature*, 1988, *331*, 585–589.

Petersen, S. E., Fox, P. T., Snyder, A. Z., and Raichle, M. E. Activation of extrastriate and frontal cortical areas by visual words and word-like stimuli. *Science*, 1990, *249*, 1041–1044.

Petit, H. O., and Justice, J. B. Dopamine in the nucleus accumbens during cocaine self-administration as studied by in vivo microdialysis. *Pharmacology, Biochemistry and Behavior*, 1989, *23*, 899–904.

Petre-Quadens, O., and De Lee, C. Eye movement frequencies and related paradoxical sleep cycles: Developmental changes. *Chronobiologia*, 1974, *1*, 347–355.

Pfaff, D. W., and Keiner, M. Atlas of estradiol-concentrating cells in the central nervous system of the female rat. *Journal of Comparative Neurology*, 1973, *151*, 121–158.

Pfaff, D. W., and Sakuma, Y. Deficit in the lordosis reflex of female rats caused by lesions in the ventromedial nucleus of the hypothalamus. *Journal of Physiology*, 1979, *288*, 203–210.

Phillips, A. G., Coury, A., Fiorino, D., LePiane, F. G., Brown, E., and Fibiger, H. C. *Annals of the New York Academy of Sciences*, 1992, *654*, 199–206.

Phillips, D. P., and Farmer, M. E. Acquired word deafness, and the temporal grain of sound representation in the primary auditory cortex. *Behavioural Brain Research*, 1990, *40*, 85–94.

Phillips, G. D., Robbins, T. W., and Everitt, B. J. Bilateral intra-accumbens self-administration of d-amphetamine: Antagonism with intra-accumbens SCH-23390 and sulpiride. *Psychopharmacology*, 1994, *114*, 477–485.

Phillips, M. I., and Felix, D. Specific angiotensin II receptive neurons in the cat subfornical organ. *Brain Research*, 1976, *109*, 531–540.

Phillips, R. G., and LeDoux, J. E. Differential contribution of amygdala and hippocampus to cued and contextual fear conditioning. *Behavioral Neuroscience*, 1992, *106*, 274–285.

Pickar, D. Prospects for pharmacotherapy of schizophrenia. *Lancet*, 1995, *345*, 557–562.

Pickles, J. O., and Corey, D. P. Mechanoelectrical transduction by hair cells. *Trends in Neuroscience*, 1992, *15*, 254–259.

Pijl, S., and Schwartz, D. W. F. Intonation of musical intervals by deaf subjects stimulated with single bipolar cochlear implant electrodes. *Hearing Research*, 1995a, *89*, 203–211.

Pijl, S., and Schwartz, D. W. F. Melody recognition and musical interval perception by deaf subjects stimulated with electrical pulse trains through single cochlear implant electrodes. *Journal of the Acoustical Society of America*, 1995b, *98*, 886–895.

Pilleri, G. The blind Indus dolphin, *Platanista indi*. *Endeavours*, 1979, *3*, 48–56.

Pi-Sunyer, F. X. Health implications of obesity. *American Journal of Clinical Nutrition*, 1991, *53*, 1595S–1603S.

Pitkaenen, A., Stefanacci, L., Farb, C. R., Go, G.-G., LeDoux, J. E., and Amaral, D. G. Intrinsic connections of the rat amygdaloid complex: Projections originating in the lateral nucleus. *Journal of Comparative Neurology*, 1995, *356*, 288–310.

Pleim, E. T., and Barfield, R. J. Progesterone versus estrogen facilitation of female sexual behavior by intracranial administration to female rats. *Hormones and Behavior*, 1988, *22*, 150–159.

Poggio, G. F., and Poggio, T. The analysis of stereopsis. *Annual Review of Neuroscience*, 1984, *7*, 379–412.

Polymeropoulos, M. H., Higgins, J. J., Golbe, L. I., Johnson, W. G., Ide, S. E., Di Iorio, G., Sanges, G., Stenroos, E. S., Pho, L. T., Schaffer, A. A., Lazzarini, A. M., Nussbaum, R. L., and Duvoisin, R. C. Mapping of a gene for Parkinson's disease to chromosome 4q21-q23. *Science*, 1996, *274*, 1197–1199.

Portas, C. M., Thakkar, M., Rainnie, D., and McCarley, R. W. Microdialysis perfusion of 8-hydroxy-2-(di-n-propylamino)tetralin (8-OH-DPAT) in the dorsal raphe nucleus decreases serotonin release and increases rapid eye movement sleep in the freely moving cat. *Journal of Neuroscience*, 1996, *16*, 2820–2828.

Post, R. M., Ballenger, J. C., Uhde, T., and Bunney, W. Efficacy of carbamazepine in manic-depressive illness: Implications for underlying mechanisms. In *Neurobiology of Mood Disorders*, edited by R. M. Post and C. Ballenger. Baltimore: Williams and Wilkins, 1984.

Post, R. M., Weiss, S. R. B., and Chuang, D.-M. Mechanisms of action of anticonvulsants in affective disorders: Comparison with lithium. *Journal of Clinical Psychopharmacology*, 1992, *12*, 23s–35s.

Powers, J. B., and Winans, S. S. Vomeronasal organ: Critical role in mediating sexual behavior of the male hamster. *Science*, 1975, *187*, 961–963.

Preyer, S., Hemmert, W., Zenner, H. P., and Gummer, A. W. Abolition of the receptor potential response of isolated mammalian outer hair cells by hair-bundle treatment with elastase: A test of the tip-link hypothesis. *Hearing Research*, 1995, *89*, 187–193.

Price, J. The genetics of depressive behavior. *British Journal of Psychiatry*, 1968, *2*, 37–45.

Price, L. H., and Heninger, G. R. Drug therapy: Lithium in the treatment of mood disorders. *New England Journal of Medicine*, 1994, *331*, 591–598.

Price, R. A., and Gottesman, I. I. Body fat in identical twins reared apart: Roles for genes and environment. *Behavioral Genetics*, 1991, *21*, 1–7.

Pritchard, T. C., Hamilton, R. B., Morse, J. R., and Norgren, R. Projections of thalamic gustatory and lingual areas in the monkey, *Macaca fascicularis*. *Journal of Comparative Neurology*, 1986, *244*, 213–228.

Propping, P., Kruger, J., and Janah, A. Effect of alcohol on genetically determined variants of the normal electroencephalogram. *Psychiatry Research*, 1980, *2*, 85–98.

Propping, P., Kruger, J., and Mark, N. Genetic disposition to alcoholism: An EEG study in alcoholics and their relatives. *Human Genetics*, 1981, *59*, 51–59.

Quattrochi, J. J., Mamelak, A. N., Madison, R. D., Macklis, J. D., and Hobson, J. A. Mapping neuronal inputs to REM sleep induction sites with carbachol-fluorescent microspheres. *Science*, 1989, *245*, 984–986.

Quillen E. W., Keil, L. C., and Reid, I. A. Effects of baroreceptor denervation on endocrine and drinking responses to caval constriction in dogs. *American Journal of Physiology*, 1990, *259*, R618–R626.

Quirk, G. J., Repa, J. C., and LeDoux, J. E. Fear conditioning enhances short-latency auditory responses of lateral amygdala neurons: Parallel recordings in the freely behaving rat. *Neuron*, 1995, *15*, 1029–1039.

Raine, A., Lencz, T., Reynolds, G. P., Harrison, G., Sheard, C., Medley, I., Reynolds, L. M., and Cooper, J. E. An evaluation of structural and functional prefrontal deficits in schizophrenia: MRI and neuropsychological measures. *Psychiatry Research: Neuroimaging*, 1992, *45*, 123–137.

Raleigh, M. J., McGuire, M. T., Brammer, G. L., Pollack, D. B., and Yuwiler, A. Serotonergic mechanisms promote dominance acquisition in adult male vervet monkeys. *Brain Research*, 1991, *559*, 181–190.

Ralph, M. R., and Lehman, M. N. Transplantation: A new tool in the analysis of the mammalian hypothalamic circadian pacemaker. *Trends in Neuroscience*, 1991, *14*, 362–366.

Ramirez, I. Why do sugars taste good? *Neuroscience and Biobehavioral Reviews*, 1990, *14*, 125–134.

Rapoport, J. L. Recent advances in obsessive-compulsive disorder. *Neuropsychopharmacology*, 1991, *5*, 1–10.

Rapoport, J. L., Ryland, D. H., and Kriete, M. Drug treatment of canine acral lick: An animal model of obsessive-compulsive disorder. *Archives of General Psychiatry*, 1992, *49*, 517–521.

Rasmusson, D. D., Clow, K., and Szerb, J. C. Modification of neocortical acetylcholine release and electroencephalogram desynchronization due to brain stem stimulation by drugs applied to the basal forebrain. *Neuroscience*, 1994, *60*, 665–677.

Ratcliff, G., and Newcombe, F. Object recognition: Some deductions from the clinical evidence. In *Normality and Pathology in Cognitive Functions*, edited by A. W. Ellis. London: Academic Press, 1982.

Ratnasuriya, R. H., Eisler, I., Szmukler, G. I., and Russell, G. F. M. Anorexia nervosa: Outcome and prognostic factors after 20 years. *British Journal of Psychiatry*, 1991, *158*, 495–502.

Rauhofer, E. A., Smith, G. P., and Gibbs, J. Acute blockade of gastric emptying and meal size in rats. *Physiology and Behavior*, 1993, *54*, 881–884.

Rauschecker, J. P., Tian, B., and Hauser, M. Processing of complex sounds in the macaque nonprimary auditory cortex. *Science*, 1995, *268*, 111–114.

Ravussin, E., Valencia, M. E., Esparza, J., Bennett, P. H., and Schulz, L. O. Effects of a traditional lifestyle on obesity in Pima Indians. *Diabetes Care*, 1994, *17*, 1067–1074.

Raybin, J. B., and Detre, T. P. Sleep disorder and symptomatology among medical and nursing students. *Comprehensive Psychiatry*, 1969, *10*, 452–467.

Rechtschaffen, A., and Bergmann, B. M. Sleep deprivation in the rat by the disk-over-water method. *Behavioural Brain Research*, 1995, *69*, 55–63.

Rechtschaffen, A., Bergmann, B. M., Everson, C. A., Kushida, C. A., and Gilliland, M. A. Sleep deprivation in the rat. X: Integration and discussion of the findings. *Sleep*, 1989, *12*, 68–87.

Rechtschaffen, A., Gilliland, M. A., Bergmann, B. M., and Winter, J. B. Physiological correlates of prolonged sleep deprivation in rats. *Science*, 1983, *221*, 182–184.

Rechtschaffen, A., Wolpert, E. A., Dement, W. C., Mitchell, S. A., and Fisher, C. Nocturnal sleep of narcoleptics. *Electroencephalography and Clinical Neurophysiology*, 1963, *15*, 599–609.

Reid, L. D. Endogenous opioids and alcohol dependence: Opioid alkaloids and the propensity to drink alcoholic beverages. *Alcohol*, 1996, *13*, 5–11.

Reinink, E., Bouhuys, N., Wirz-Justice, A., and van den Hoofdakker, R. Prediction of the antidepressant response to total sleep deprivation by diurnal variation of mood. *Psychiatry Research*, 1990, *32*, 113–124.

Rempel-Clower, N. L., Zola, S. M., Squire, L. R., and Amaral, D. G. Three cases of enduring memory impairment after bilateral damage limited to the hippocampal formation. *Journal of Neuroscience*, 1996, *16*, 5233–5255.

Ressler, K. J., Sullivan, S. L., and Buck, L. A molecular dissection of spatial patterning in the olfactory system. *Current Opinion in Neurobiology*, 1994a, *4*, 588–596.

Ressler, K. J., Sullivan, S. L., and Buck, L. Information coding in the olfactory system: Evidence for a stereotyped and highly organized epitope map in the olfactory bulb. *Cell*, 1994b, *79*, 1245–1255.

Reynolds, D. V. Surgery in the rat during electrical analgesia induced by focal brain stimulation. *Science*, 1969, *164*, 444–445.

Rhees, R. W., Shryne, J. E., and Gorski, R. A. Onset of the hormone-sensitive perinatal period for sexual differentiation of the sexually dimorphic nucleus of the preoptic area in female rats. *Journal of Neurobiology*, 1990a, *21*, 781–786.

Rhees, R. W., Shryne, J. E., and Gorski, R. A. Termination of the hormone-sensitive period for differentiation of the sexually dimorphic nucleus of the preoptic area in male and female rats. *Developmental Brain Research*, 1990b, *52*, 17–23.

Riemann, D., Hohagen, F., Koenig, A., Schwarz, B., Gomille, J., Voderholzer, U., and Berger, M. Advanced vs normal sleep timing: Effects on depressed mood after response to sleep deprivation in patients with a major depressive disorder. *Journal of Affective Disorders*, 1996, *37*, 121–128.

Riemann, D., Wiegand, M., and Berger, M. Are there predictors for sleep deprivation response in depressive patients? *Biological Psychiatry*, 1991, *29*, 707–710.

Ritter, R. C., Brenner, L., and Yox, D. P. Participation of vagal sensory neurons in putative satiety signals from the upper gastrointestinal tract. In *Neuroanatomy and Physiology of Abdominal Vagal Afferents*, edited by S. Ritter, R. C. Ritter, and C. D. Barnes. Boca Raton, Fls.: CRC Press, 1992.

Ritter, R. C., Slusser, P. G., and Stone, S. Glucoreceptors controlling feeding and blood glucose: Location in the hindbrain. *Science*, 1981, *213*, 451–453.

Ritter, S., Dinh, T. T., and Friedman, M. I. Induction of Fos-like immunoreactivity (Fos-li) and stimulation of feeding by 2,5-anhydro-D-mannitol (2,5-AM) require the vagus nerve. *Brain Research*, 1994, *646*, 53–64.

Ritter, S., and Taylor, J. S. Capsaicin abolishes lipoprivic but not glucoprivic feeding in rats. *American Journal of Physiology*, 1989, *256*, R1232–R1239.

Ritter, S., and Taylor, J. S. Vagal sensory neurons are required for lipoprivic but not glucoprivic feeding in rats. *American Journal of Physiology*, 1990, *258*, R1395–R1401.

Rizzo, M., and Robin, D. A. Simultanagnosia: A defect of sustained attention yields insights on visual information processing. *Neurology*, 1990, *40*, 447–455.

Robbins, L. N., Helzer, J. E., Weissman, M. M., Orvaschel, H., Gruenberg, E., Burke, J. D., and Regier, D. A. Lifetime prevalence of specific psychiatric disorders in three sites. *Archives of General Psychiatry*, 1984, *41*, 949–958.

Robertson, G. S., Pfaus, J. G., Atkinson, L. J., Matsumura, H., Phillips, A. G., and Fibiger, H. C. Sexual behavior increases c-fos expression in the forebrain of the male rat. *Brain Research*, 1991, *564*, 352–357.

Robinson, D., Wu, H. W., Munne, R. A., Ashtan, M., Alvir, J. M. M., Lerner, G., Koreen, A., Cole, K., and Bogerts, B. Reduced caudate nucleus volume in obsessive-compulsive disorder. *Archives of General Psychiatry*, 1995, *52*, 393–398.

Robinson, T. E., and Berridge, K. C. The neural basis of drug craving: An incentive-sensitization theory of addiction. *Brain Research Reviews*, 1993, *18*, 247–291.

Rodier, P. M., Ingram, J. L., Tisdale, B., Nelson, S., and Romano, J. Embryological origin for autism: Developmental anomalies of the cranial nerve motor nuclei. *Journal of Comparative Neurology*, 1996, *370*, 247–261.

Roeltgen, D. P., Rothi, L. H., and Heilman, K. M. Linguistic semantic apraphia: A dissociation of the lexical spelling system from semantics. *Brain and Language*, 1986, *27*, 257–280.

Roffwarg, H. P., Muzio, J. N., and Dement, W. C. Ontogenetic development of human sleep-dream cycle. *Science*, 1966, *152*, 604–619.

Rogan, M. T., and LeDoux, J. E. LTP is accompanied by commensurate enhancement of auditory-evoked responses in a fear conditioning circuit. *Neuron*, 1995, *15*, 127–136.

Rogers, J., Kirby, L. C., Hempelman, S. R., Beery, D. L., McGeer, P. L., Kaszniak, A. W., Zalinshi, J., Cofield, M., Mansukhani, L., Willson, P., and Kogan, F. Clinical-trial of indomethacin in Alzheimers-disease. *Neurology*, 1993, *43*, 1609–1611.

Rogers, M. P., Trentham, D. E., McCune, W. J., Ginsberg, B. I., Rennke, H. G., Reike, P., and David, J. R. Effect of psychological stress on the induction of arthritis in rats. *Arthritis and Rheumatology*, 1980, *23*, 1337–1342.

Roland, P. E. Metabolic measurements of the working frontal cortex in man. *Trends in Neurosciences*, 1984, *7*, 430–435.

Rolls, E. T. Feeding and reward. In *The Neural Basis of Feeding and Reward*, edited by B. G. Hobel and D. Novin. Brunswick, Me.: Haer Institute, 1982.

Rolls, E. T. Neuronal activity related to the control of feeding. In *Neural and Humoral Controls of Food Intake*, edited by R. Ritter and S. Ritter. New York: Academic Press, 1986.

Rolls, E. T. Functions of the primate hippocampus in spatial processing and memory. In *Neurobiology of Comparative Cognition*, edited by D. S. Olton and R. P. Kesner. Hillsdale, N.J.: Lawrence Erlbaum Associates, 1989.

Rolls, E. T. A theory of hippocampal function in memory. *Hippocampus*, 1996, *6*, 601–620.

Rolls, E. T., and Baylis, G. C. Size and contrast have only small effects on the responses to faces of neurons in the cortex of the superior temporal sulcus of the monkey. *Experimental Brain Research*, 1986, *65*, 38–48.

Rolls, E. T., Yaxley, S., and Sienkiewicz, Z. J. Gustatory responses of single neurons in the orbitofrontal cortex of the macaque monkey. *Journal of Neurophysiology*, 1990, *64*, 1055–1066.

Rose, G. A., and Williams, R. T. Metabolic studies of large and small eaters. *British Journal of Nutrition*, 1961, *15*, 1–9.

Rose, J. D. Changes in hypothalamic neuronal function related to hormonal induction of lordosis in behaving hamsters. *Physiology and Behavior*, 1990, *47*, 1201–1212.

Roselli, C. E., Handa, R. J., and Resko, J. A. Quantitative distribution of nuclear androgen receptors in microdissected areas of the rat brain. *Neuroendocrinology*, 1989, *49*, 449–453.

Rosenblatt, J. S., and Aronson, L. R. The decline of sexual behavior in male cats after castration with special reference to the role of prior sexual experience. *Behaviour*, 1958a, *12*, 285–338.

Rosenblatt, J. S., and Aronson, L. R. The influence of experience on the behavioural effects of androgen in prepuberally castrated male cats. *Animal Behaviour*, 1958b, *6*, 171–182.

Rosenblatt, J. S., Hazelwood, S., and Poole, J. Maternal behavior in male rats: Effects of medial preoptic area lesions and presence of maternal aggression. *Hormones and Behavior*, 1996, *30*, 201–215.

Rosenthal, D. A program of research on heredity in schizophrenia. *Behavioral Science*, 1971, *16*, 191–201.

Rosenthal, N. E., Sack, D. A., Gillin, C., Lewy, A. J., Goodwin, F. K., Davenport, Y., Mueller, P. S., Newsome, D. A., and Wehr, T. A. Seasonal affective disorder: A description of the syndrome and preliminary findings with light therapy. *Archives of General Psychiatry*, 1984, *41*, 72–80.

Rosenthal, N. E., Sack, D. A., James, S. P., Parry, B. L., Mendelson, W. B., Tamarkin, L., and Wehr, T. A. Seasonal affective disorder and phototherapy. *Annals of the New York Academy of Sciences*, 1985, *453*, 260–269.

Rosewell, K. L., Siwicki, K. K., and Wise, P. M. A period (per)-like protein exhibits daily rhythmicity in the suprachiasmatic nuclei of the rat. *Brain Research*, 1994, *659*, 231–236.

Ross, E. D., Homan, R. W., and Buck, R. Differential hemispheric lateralization of primary and social emotions. *Neuropsychiatry, Neuropsychology, and Behavioral Neurology*, 1994, *7*, 1–19.

Rosser, A. E., and Keverne, E. B. The importance of central noradrenergic neurons in the formation of an olfactory memory in the prevention of pregnancy block. *Neuroscience*, 1985, *16*, 1141–1147.

Routtenberg, A. "Self-starvation" of rats living in activity wheels: Adaptation effects. *Journal of Comparative Psychology*, 1968, *66*, 234–238.

Routtenberg, A., and Malsbury, C. Brainstem pathways of reward. *Journal of Comparative and Physiological Psychology*, 1969, *68*, 22–30.

Roy, A., De Jong, J., and Linnoila, M. Cerebrospinal fluid monoamine metabolites and suicidal behavior in depressed patients. *Archives of General Psychiatry*, 1989, *46*, 609–612.

Rubin, B. S., and Barfield, R. J. Priming of estrous responsiveness by implants of 17B-estradiol in the ventromedial hypothalamic nucleus of female rats. *Endocrinology*, 1980, *106*, 504–509.

Rubin, R. T., Ananth, J., Villanueva-Meyer, J., Trajmar, P. G., and Mena, I. Regional [133]Xenon cerebral blood flow and cerebral ^{99m}Tc-HM-PAO uptake in patients with obsessive-compulsive disorder before and during treatment. *Biological Psychiatry*, 1995, *38*, 429–437.

Rubin, R. T., Villanueva-Meyer, J., Ananth, J., Trajmar, P. G., and Mena, I. Regional xenon 133 cerebral blood flow and cerebral technetium 99m HMPAO uptake in unmedicated patients with obsessive-compulsive disorder and matched normal control subjects: Determination by high-resolution single-photon emission computed tomography. *Archives of General Psychiatry*, 1992, *49*, 695–702.

Rudy, J. W., and Sutherland, R. J. Configural association theory and the hippocampal formation: An appraisal and reconfiguration. *Hippocampus*, 1995, *5*, 375–389.

Rusak, B., and Morin, L. P. Testicular responses to photoperiod are blocked by lesions of the suprachiasmatic nuclei in golden hamsters. *Biology of Reproduction*, 1976, *15*, 366–374.

Rusak, B., McNaughton, L., Robertson, H. A., and Hunt, S. P. Circadian variation in photic regulation of immediate-early gene mRNAs in rat suprachiasmatic nucleus cells. *Molecular Brain Research*, 1992, *14*, 124–130.

Rusak, B., Robertson, H. A., Wisden, W., and Hunt, S. P. Light pulses that shift rhythms induce gene expression in the suprachiasmatic nucleus. *Science*, 1990, *248*, 1237–1240.

Russchen, F. T., Amaral, D. G., and Price, J. L. The afferent connections of the substantia innominata in the monkey, *Macaca fascicularis*. *Journal of Comparative Neurology*, 1986, *242*, 1–27.

Russell, G. F. M., and Treasure, J. The modern history of anorexia nervosa: An interpretation of why the illness has changed. *Annals of the New York Academy of Sciences*, 1989, *575*, 13–30.

Russell, M. J. Human olfactory communication. *Nature*, 1976, *260*, 520–522.

Russell, M. J., Switz, G. M., and Thompson, K. Olfactory influences on the human menstrual cycle. Paper presented at the meeting of the American Association for the Advancement of Science, San Francisco, June 1977.

Rutter, M. Cognitive deficits in the pathogenesis of autism. *Journal of Child Psychology and Psychiatry*, 1983, *24*, 513–531.

Ryback, R. S., and Lewis, O. F. Effects of prolonged bed rest on EEG sleep patterns in young, healthy volunteers. *Electroencephalography and Clinical Neurophysiology*, 1971, *31*, 395–399.

Saayman, G. S. Aggressive behaviour in free-ranging chacma baboons (*Papio ursinus*). *Journal of Behavioral Science*, 1971, *1*, 77–83.

Sachar, E. J., and Baron, M. The biology of affective disorders. *Annual Review of Neuroscience*, 1979, *2*, 505–518.

Sackheim, H. A. Lateral asymmetry in bodily response to hypnotic suggestion. *Biological Psychiatry*, 1982, *17*, 437–447.

Sackheim, H. A., and Gur, R. C. Lateral asymmetry in intensity of emotional expression. *Neuropsychologia*, 1978, *16*, 473–482.

Sackheim, H. A., Paulus, D., and Weiman, A. L. Classroom seating and hypnotic susceptibility. *Journal of Abnormal Psychology*, 1979, *88*, 81–84.

Saffran, E. M., Marin, O. S. M., and Yeni-Komshian, G. H. An analysis of speech perception in word deafness. *Brain and Language*, 1976, *3*, 209–228.

Saffran, E. M., Schwartz, M. F., and Marin, O. S. M. Evidence from aphasia: Isolating the components of a production model. In *Language Production*, edited by B. Butterworth. London: Academic Press, 1980.

Sahu, A., Kalra, P. S., and Kalra, S. P. Food deprivation and ingestion induce reciprocal changes in neuropeptide Y concentrations in the paraventricular nucleus. *Peptides*, 1988, *9*, 83–86.

Saitoh, K., Maruyama, N., and Kudoh, M. Sustained response of auditory cortex units in the cat. In *Brain Mechanisms of Sensation*, edited by Y. Katsuki, R. Norgren, and M. Sato. New York: John Wiley & Sons, 1981.

Sakai, F., Meyer, J. S., Karacan, I., Derman, S., and Yamamoto, M. Normal human sleep: Regional cerebral haemodynamics. *Annals of Neurology*, 1979, *7*, 471–478.

Sakai, K. Some anatomical and physiological properties of pontomesencephalic tegmental neurons with special reference to the PGO waves and postural atonia during paradoxical sleep in the cat. In *The Reticular Formation Revisited*, edited by J. A. Hobson and M. A. Brazier. New York: Raven Press, 1980.

Sakai, K., and Jouvet, M. Brain stem PGO-on cells projecting directly to the cat dorsal lateral geniculate nucleus. *Brain Research*, 1980, *194*, 500–505.

Sakuma, Y., and Pfaff, D. W. Facilitation of female reproductive behavior from mesencephalic central grey in the rat. *American Journal of Physiology*, 1979a, *237*, R278–R284.

Sakuma, Y., and Pfaff, D. W. Mesencephalic mechanisms for integration of female reproductive behavior in the rat. *American Journal of Physiology*, 1979b, *237*, R285–R290.

Sakuma, Y., and Pfaff, D. W. Convergent effects of lordosis-relevant somatosensory and hypothalamic influences on central gray cells in the rat mesencephalon. *Experimental Neurology*, 1980a, *70*, 269–281.

Sakuma, Y., and Pfaff, D. W. Excitability of female rat central gray cells with medullary projections: Changes produced by hypothalamic stimulation and estrogen treatment. *Journal of Neurophysiology*, 1980b, *44*, 1012–1023.

Sakurai, Y., Sakai, K., Sakuta, M., and Iwata, M. Naming difficulties in alexia with agraphia for kanji after a left posterior inferior temporal lesion. *Journal of Neurology, Neurosurgery, and Psychiatry*, 1994, *57*, 609–613.

Salamone, J. D. Complex motor and sensorimotor function of striatal and accumbens dopamine: Involvement in instrumental behavior processes. *Psychopharmacology*, 1992, *107*, 160–174.

Saller, C. F., and Stricker, E. M. Hyperphagia and increased growth in rats after intraventricular injection of 5,7-dihydroxytryptamine. *Science*, 1976, *192*, 385–387.

Samson, H. H., Hodge, C. W., Tolliver, G. A., and Haraguchi, M. Effect of dopamine agonists and antagonists on ethanol reinforced behavior: The involvement of the nucleus accumbens. *Brain Research Bulletin*, 1993, *30*, 133–141.

Sananes, C. B., and Davis, M. N-methyl-D-aspartate lesions of the lateral and basolateral nuclei of the amygdala block fear-potentiated startle and shock sensitization of startle. *Behavioral Neuroscience*, 1992, *106*, 72–80.

Sanders, S. K., and Shekhar, A. Anxiolytic effects of chlordiazepoxide blocked by injection of $GABA_A$ and benzodiazepine receptor antagonists in the region of the anterior basolateral amygdala of rats. *Biological Psychiatry*, 1995, *37*, 473–476.

Sapolsky, R. Glucocorticoid toxicity in the hippocampus: Reversal by supplementation with brain fuels. *Journal of Neuroscience*, 1986, *6*, 2240–2244.

Sapolsky, R. M. Neuroendocrinology of the stress-response. In *Behavioral Endocrinology*, edited by J. B. Becker, S. M. Breedlove, and D. Crews. Cambridge, Mass.: MIT Press, 1992.

Sapolsky, R. M., Krey, L. C., and McEwen, B. S. The adrenocortical axis in the aged rat: Impaired sensitivity to both fast and delayed feedback inhibition. *Neurobiology of Aging*, 1986 *7*, 331–335.

Sassenrath, E. N., Powell, T. E., and Hendrickx, A. G. Perimenstrual aggression in groups of female rhesus monkeys. *Journal of Reproduction and Fertility*, 1973, *34*, 509–511.

Savander, V., Go, C. G., LeDoux, J. E., and Pitkaenen, A. Intrinsic connections of the rat amygdaloid complex: Projections originating in the basal nucleus. *Journal of Comparative Neurology*, 1995, *361*, 345–368.

Sawchenko, P. E., Gold, R. M., and Leibowitz, S. F. Evidence for vagal involvement in the eating elicited by adrenergic stimulation of the paraventricular nucleus. *Brain Research*, 1981, *225*, 249– 269.

Scammell, T. E., Price, K. J., and Sagar, S. M. Hyperthermia induces c-fos expression in the preoptic area. *Brain Research*, 1993, *618*, 303–307.

Schwartz, M. W., Peskind, E., Raskind, M., Boyko, E. J., and Porte, D. Cerebrospinal fluid leptin

levels: Relationship to plasma levels and to adiposity in humans. *Nature Medicine*, 1996, *2*, 589– 593.

Schenck, C. H., and Mahowald, M. W. Motor dyscontrol in narcolepsy: Rapid-eye-movement (REM) sleep without atonia and REM sleep behavior disorder. *Annals of Neurology*, 1992, *32*, 3–10.

Schenck, C. H., Bundlie, S. R., Ettinger, M. G., and Mahowald, M. W. Chronic behavioral disorders of human REM sleep: A new category of parasomnia. *Sleep*, 1986, *9*, 293–308.

Schenck, C. H., Garciarill, E., Segall, M., Noreen, H., and Mahowald, M. W. HLA class-II genes associated with REM-sleep behavior disorder. *Annals of Neurology*, 1996, *39*, 261–263.

Schenck, C. H., Hurwitz, T. D., and Mahowald, M. W. REM-sleep behavior disorder: An update on a series of 96 patients and a review of the world literature. *Journal of Sleep Research*, 1993, *2*, 224–231.

Scherschlicht, R., Polc, P., Schneeberger, J., Steiner, M., and Haefely, W. Selective suppression of rapid eye movement sleep (REMS) in cats by typical and atypical antidepressants. In *Typical and Atypical Antidepressants: Molecular Mechanisms*, edited by E. Costa and G. Racagni. New York: Raven Press, 1982.

Schiffman, S. S., Lockhead, E., and Maes, F. W. Amiloride reduces the taste intensity of Na^+ and Li^+ salts and sweeteners. *Proceedings of the National Academy of Sciences, USA*, 1983, *80*, 6136–6140.

Schiller, P. H. The ON and OFF channels of the visual system. *Trends in Neuroscience*, 1992, *15*, 86–92.

Schiller, P. H., and Malpeli, J. G. Properties and tectal projections of monkey retinal ganglion cells. *Journal of Neurophysiology*, 1977, *40*, 428–445.

Schiller, P. H., Sandell, J. H., and Maunsell, J. H. R. Functions of the ON and OFF channels of the visual system. *Nature*, 1986, *322*, 824–825.

Schleifer, S. J., Keller, S. E., Camerino, M., Thornton, J. C., and Stein, M. Suppression of lymphocyte stimulation following bereavement. *Journal of the American Medical Association*, 1983, *15*, 374–377.

Schnabel, J. New Alzheimer's therapy suggested. *Science*, 1993, *260*, 1719–1720.

Schneider, F., Gur, R. E., Alavi, A., Seligman, M. E. P., Mozley, L. H., Smith, R. J., Mozley, P. D., and Gur, R. C. Cerebral blood flow changes in limbic regions induced by unsolvable anagram tasks. *American Journal of Psychiatry*, 1996, *153*, 206–212.

Schwartz, M. F., Marin, O. S. M., and Saffran, E. M. Dissociations of language function in dementia: A case study. *Brain and Language*, 1979, *7*, 277–306.

Schwartz, M. F., Saffran, E. M., and Marin, O. S. M. The word order problem in agrammatism. I: Comprehension. *Brain and Language*, 1980, *10*, 249–262.

Schwartz, M. W., Peskind, E., Raskind, M., Boyko, E. J., and Porte, D. Cerebrospinal fluid leptin levels: Relationship to plasma levels and to adiposity in humans. *Nature Medicine*, 1996, *2*, 589–593.

Schwartz, W. J., and Gainer, H. Suprachiasmatic nucleus: Use of ^{14}C-labelled deoxyglucose uptake as a functional marker. *Science*, 1977, *197*, 1089–1091.

Schwarzkopf, S. B., Nasrallah, H. A., Olson, S. C., Coffman, J. A., and McLaughlin, J. A. Perinatal complications and genetic loading in schiz-

ophrenia: Preliminary findings. *Psychiatry Research*, 1989, *27*, 233–239.

Scott, S. K., Young, A. W., Calder, A. J., Hellawell, D. J., Aggleton, J. P., and Johnson, M. Impaired auditory recognition of fear and anger following bilateral amygdala lesions. *Nature*, 1997, *385*, 254–257.

Scott, T. R., and Plata-Salaman, C. R. Coding of taste quality. In *Smell and Taste in Health and Disease*, edited by T. N. Getchell. New York: Raven Press, 1991.

Scoville, W. B., and Milner, B. Loss of recent memory after bilateral hippocampal lesions. *Journal of Neurology, Neurosurgery and Psychiatry*, 1957, *20*, 11–21.

Sedvall, G., Fyrö, B., Gullberg, B., Nybäck, H., Wiesel, F.-A., and Wode-Helgodt, B. Relationship in healthy volunteers between concentrations of monoamine metabolites in cerebrospinal fluid and family history of psychiatric morbidity. *British Journal of Psychiatry*, 1980, *136*, 366–374.

Seeley, R. J., Kaplan, J. M., and Grill, H. J. Effect of occluding the pylorus on intraoral intake: A test of the gastric hypothesis of meal termination. *Physiology and Behavior*, 1995, *58*, 245–249.

Selye, H. *The Stress of Life*. New York: McGraw-Hill, 1976.

Semenza, C., and Zettin, M. Evidence from aphasia for the role of proper names as pure referring expressions. *Nature*, 1989, *342*, 678–679.

Sergent, J., and Signoret, J.-L. Functional and anatomical decomposition of face processing: Evidence from prosopagnosia and PET study of normal subjects. *Philosophical Transactions of the Royal Society of London [B]*, 1992, *335*, 55–62.

Sergent, J., and Villemure, J.-G. Prosopagnosia in a right hemispherectomized patient. *Brain*, 1989, *112*, 975–995.

Sforza, E., Montagna, P., Tinuper, P., Cortelli, P., Avoni, P., Ferrillo, F., Petersen, R., Gambetti, P., and Lagaresi, E. Sleep-wake cycle abnormalities in fatal familial insomnia: Evidence of the role of the thalamus in sleep regulation. *Electroencephalography and Clinical Neurophysiology*, 1995, *94*, 398–405.

Shallice, T. Phonological agraphia and the lexical route in writing. *Brain*, 1981, *104*, 413–429.

Sham, P. C., O'Callaghan, E., Takei, N., Murray, G. K., Hare, E. H., and Murray, R. M. Schizophrenia following pre-natal exposure to influenza epidemics between 1939 and 1960. *British Journal of Psychiatry*, 1992, *160*, 461–466.

Shapiro, L. E., Leonard, C. M., Sessions, C. E., Dewsbury, D. A., and Insel, T. R. Comparative neuroanatomy of the sexually dimorphic hypothalamus in monogamous and polygamous voles. *Brain Research*, 1991, *541*, 232–240.

Sharp, F. R., Sagar, S. M., Hicks, K., Lowenstein, D., and Hisanaga, K. C-fos mRNA, Fos, and Fos-related antigen induction by hypertonic saline and stress. *Journal of Neuroscience*, 1991, *11*, 2321–2331.

Shepherd, G. M. Discrimination of molecular signals by the olfactory receptor neuron. *Neuron*, 1994, *13*, 771–790.

Sher, A. E. Surgery for obstructive sleep apnea. *Progress in Clinical Biology Research*, 1990, *345*, 407–415.

Sherrington, R., Brynjolfsson, J., Petursson, H., Potter, M., Dudleston, K., Barraclough, B., Wasmuth, J., Dobbs, M., and Gurling, H. Localization of a susceptibility locus for schizophrenia on chromosome 5. *Nature,* 1988, *336,* 164–167.

Sherry, D. F., Jacobs, L. F., and Gaulin, S. J. C. Spatial memory and adaptive specialization of the hippocampus. *Trends in Neuroscience,* 1992, *15,* 298–303.

Sherwin, B. B. Sex hormones and psychological functioning in postmenopausal women. *Experimental Gerontology,* 1994, *29,* 423–430.

Sherwin, B. B., Gelfand, M. M., and Brender, W. Androgen enhances sexual motivation in females: A prospective, crossover study of sex steroid administration in the surgical menopause. *Psychosomatic Medicine,* 1985, *47,* 339–351.

Shimura, T., and Shimokochi, M. Involvement of the lateral mesencephalic tegmentum in copulatory behavior of male rats: Neuron activity in freely moving animals. *Neuroscience Research,* 1990, *9,* 173–183.

Shimura, T., Yamamoto, T., and Shimokochi, M. The medial preoptic area is involved in both sexual arousal and performance in male rats: Re-evaluation of neuron activity in freely moving animals. *Brain Research,* 1994, *640,* 215–222.

Shin, L. M., Kosslyn, S. M., McNally, R. J., Alpert, N. M., Thompson, W. L., Rauch, S. L., Macklin, M. L., and Pitman, R. K. Visual imagery and perception in posttraumatic stress disorder. *Archives of General Psychiatry,* 1997, *54,* 233–241.

Shindy, W. W., Posley, K. A., and Fuster, J. M. Reversible deficit in haptic delay tasks from cooling prefrontal cortex. *Cerebral Cortex,* 1994, *4,* 443–450.

Shipley, M. T., and Ennis, M. Functional organization of the olfactory system. *Journal of Neurobiology,* 1996, *30,* 123–176.

Sidman, M., Stoddard, L. T., and Mohr, J. P. Some additional quantitative observations of immediate memory in a patient with bilateral hippocampal lesions. *Neuropsychologia,* 1968, *6,* 245–254.

Siegel, J. M. Brainstem mechanisms generating REM sleep. In *Principles and Practice of Sleep Medicine,* edited by M. H. Kryger, T. Roth, and W. C. Dement. Philadelphia: W. B. Saunders, 1989.

Siegel, S. A Pavlovian conditioning analysis of morphine tolerance. In *Behavioral Tolerance: Research and Treatment Implications,* edited by N. A. Krasnegor. Washington, D.C.: NIDA Research Monographs, 1978.

Siegel, S., Hinson, R. E., Krank, M. D., and McCully, J. Heroin "overdose" death: Contribution of drug-associated environmental cues. *Science,* 1982, *216,* 436–437.

Sigvardsson, S., Bohman, M., and Cloninger, R. C. Replication of the Stockholm adoption study of alcoholism. *Archives of General Psychiatry,* 1996, *53,* 681–687.

Silva, A. J., Stevens, C. F., Tonegawa, S., and Wang, Y. Deficient hippocampal long-term potentiation in calcium-calmodulin kinase II mutant mice. *Science,* 1992, *257,* 201–206.

Silver, J. M., Shin, C., and McNamara, J. O. Antiepileptogenic effects of conventional anticonvulsants in the kindling model of epilepsy. *Annals of Neurology,* 1991, *29,* 356–363.

Silver, R., LeSauter, J., Tresco, P. A., and Lehman, M. N. A diffusible coupling signal from the transplanted suprachiasmatic nucleus controlling circadian locomotor rhythms. *Nature,* 1996, *382,* 810–813.

Silveri, M. C. Peripheral aspects of writing can be differentially affected by sensorial and attentional defect: Evidence from a patient with afferent dysgraphia and case dissociation. *Cortex,* 1996, *32,* 155–172.

Silveri, M. C., Leggio, M. G., and Molinari, M. The cerebellum contributes to linguistic production: A case of agrammatic speech following a right cerebellar lesion. *Neurology,* 1994, *44,* 2047–2050.

Silverman, J. M., Greenberg, D. A., Altstiel, L. D., Siever, L. J., Mohs, R. C., Smith, C. J., Zhou, G. L., Hollander, T. E., Yang, X. P., Kedache, M., Li, G., Zaccario, M. L., and Davis, K. L. Evidence of a locus for schizophrenia and related disorders on the short arm of chromosome 5 in a large pedigree. *American Journal of Medical Genetics,* 1996, *67,* 162–171.

Simpson, J. B., Epstein, A. N., and Camardo, J. S. The localization of dipsogenic receptors for angiotensin II in the subfornical organ. *Journal of Comparative and Physiological Psychology,* 1978, *92,* 581–608.

Sinclair, D. *Mechanisms of Cutaneous Sensation.* Oxford, England: Oxford University Press, 1981.

Singer, C., and Weiner, W. J. Male sexual dysfunction. *Neurologist,* 1996, *2,* 119–129.

Singer, F., and Zumoff, B. Subnormal serum testosterone levels in male internal medicine residents. *Steroids,* 1992, *57,* 86–89.

Sirigu, A., Duhamel, J.-R., and Poncet, M. The role of sensorimotor experience in object recognition. A case of multimodal agnosia. *Brain,* 1991, *114,* 2555–2573.

Sitaram, N., Moore, A. M., and Gillin, J. C. Experimental acceleration and slowing of REM ultradian rhythm by cholinergic agonist and antagonist. *Nature,* 1978, *274,* 490–492.

Skakkebaek, N. E., Bancroft, J., Davidson, D. W., and Warner, P. Androgen replacement with oral testosterone undecanoate in hypogonadal men: A double blind controlled study. *Clinical Endocrinology,* 1981, *14,* 49–61.

Skene, D. J., Deacon, S., and Arendt, J. Use of melatonin in circadian-rhythm disorders and following phase-shifts. *Acta Neurobiologiae Experimentalis,* 1996, *56,* 359–362.

Skutella, T., Criswell, H., Moy, S., Probst, J. C., Breese, G. R., Jirikowski, G. F., and Holsboer, F. Corticotropin-releasing hormone (CRH) antisense oligodeoxynucleotide induces anxiolytic effects in rat. *NeuroReport,* 1994, *5,* 2181–2185.

Slater, B., and Shields, J. Genetical aspects of anxiety. In *British Journal of Psychiatry Special Publication No. 3: Studies of Anxiety.* Ashford, Kent: Headley Bros., 1969.

Smith, C. Sleep states, memory processes and synaptic plasticity. *Behavioural Brain Research,* 1996, *78,* 49–56.

Smith, G. P., Gibbs, J., and Kulkosky, P. J. Relationships between brain-gut peptides and neurons in the control of food intake. In *The Neural Basis of Feeding and Reward,* edited by B. G. Hoebel and D. Novin. Brunswick, Maine: Haer Institute, 1982.

Smith, M. J. Sex determination: Turning on sex. *Current Biology,* 1994, *4,* 1003–1005.

Snyder, F. Towards an evolutionary theory of dreaming. *American Journal of Psychiatry,* 1966, *123,* 121–136.

Snyder, S. H. *Madness and the Brain.* New York: McGraw-Hill, 1974.

Soares, J. C., and Mann, J. J. The anatomy of mood disorders: Review of structural neuroimaging studies. *Biological Psychiatry,* 1997, *42,* 86–106.

Solyom, L., Turnbull, I. M., and Wilensky, M. A case of self-inflicted leucotomy. *British Journal of Psychiatry,* 1987, *151,* 855–857.

Sperry, R. W. Brain bisection and consciousness. In *Brain and Conscious Experience,* edited by J. Eccles. New York: Springer-Verlag, 1966.

Spiegler, B. J., and Mishkin, M. Evidence for the sequential participation of inferior temporal cortex and amygdala in the acquisition of stimulus-reward associations. *Behavioural Brain Research,* 1981, *3,* 303–317.

Squire, L. R. Stable impairment in remote memory following electroconvulsive therapy. *Neuropsychologia,* 1974, *13,* 51–58.

Squire, L. R. Memory and the hippocampus: A synthesis from findings with rats, monkeys, and humans. *Psychological Review,* 1992, *99,* 195–231.

Squire, L. R., Ojemann, J. G., Miezin, F. M., Petersen, S. E., Videen, T. O., and Raichle, M. E. Activation of the hippocampus in normal humans: A functional anatomical study of memory. *Proceedings of the National Academy of Sciences, USA,* 1992, *89,* 1837–1841.

Squire, L. R., Shimamura, A. P., and Amaral, D. G. Memory and the hippocampus. In *Neural Models of Plasticity: Experimental and Theoretical Approaches,* edited by J. H. Byrne and W. O. Berry. San Diego: Academic Press, 1989.

St. George-Hyslop, P. H., Tanzi, R. E., Polinsky, R. J., Haines, J. L., Nee, L., Watkins, P. C., Myers, R. H., Feldman, R. G., Pollen, D., Drachman, D., Growdon, J., Bruni, A., Foncin, J.-F., Salmon, D., Frommelt, P., Amaducci, L., Sorbi, S., Piacentini, S., Stewart, G. D., Hobbs, W. J., Conneally, P. M., and Gusella, J. F. The genetic defect causing familial Alzheimer's disease maps on chromosome 21. *Science,* 1987, *235,* 885–890.

Staley, J. K., and Mash, D. C. Adaptive increase in D3 dopamine receptors in the brain reward circuits of human cocaine fatalities. *Journal of Neuroscience,* 1996, *16,* 6100–6106.

Stallone, D., and Nicolaïdis, S. Increased food intake and carbohydrate preference in the rat following treatment with the serotonin antagonist metergoline. *Neuroscience Letters,* 1989, *102,* 319–324.

Stanley, B. G., Magdalin, W., and Leibowitz, S. F. A critical site for neuropeptide Y-induced eating lies in the caudolateral paraventricular/perifornical region of the hypothalamus. *Society for Neuroscience Abstracts,* 1989, *15,* 894.

Stanley, B. G., Magdalin, W., Seirafi, A., Thomas, W. J., and Leibowitz, S. F. The perifornical area: The major focus of (a) patchily distributed hypothalamic neuropeptide Y-sensitive feeding system(s). *Brain Research,* 1993b, *604,* 304–317.

Stanley, B. G., Willett V. L., Donias, H. W., Dee, M. G., and Duva, M. A. Lateral hypothalamic NMDA receptors and glutamate as physiological mediators of eating and weight control. *American Journal of Physiology: Regulatory, Integrative and Comparative Physiology,* 1996, *270,* R443– R449.

Stanton, P. K., and Sejnowski, T. J. Associative long-term depression in the hippocampus induced by Hebbian covariance. *Nature,* 1989, *339,* 215–218.

Starkey, S. J., Walker, M. P., Beresford, I. J. M., and Hagan, R. M. Modulation of the rat suprachiasmatic circadian clock by melatonin in-vitro. *NeuroReport,* 1995, *6,* 1947–1951.

Stein, J., and Walsh, V. To see but not to read: The magnocellular theory of dyslexia. *Trends in Neuroscience,* 1997, *20,* 147–152.

Stein, L., and Belluzzi, J. D. Cellular investigations of behavioral reinforcement. *Neuroscience and Biobehavioral Reviews,* 1989, *13,* 69–80.

Stein, M. B., and Uhde, T. W. The biology of anxiety disorders. In *American Psychiatric Press Textbook of Psychopharmacology*. Washington, D.C.: American Psychiatric Press, 1995.

Stellar, J. R., Kelley, A. E., and Corbett, D. Effects of peripheral and central dopamine blockade on lateral hypothalamic self-stimulation: Evidence for both reward and motor deficits. *Pharmacology, Biochemistry, and Behavior*, 1983, *18*, 433–442.

Stephan, F. K., and Nuñez, A. A. Elimination of circadian rhythms in drinking activity, sleep, and temperature by isolation of the suprachiasmatic nuclei. *Behavioral Biology*, 1977, *20*, 1–16.

Stephan, F. K., and Zucker, I. Circadian rhythms in drinking behavior and locomotor activity of rats are eliminated by hypothalamic lesion. *Proceedings of the National Academy of Sciences, USA*, 1972, *69*, 1583–1586.

Steriade, M. Basic mechanisms of sleep generation. *Neurology*, 1992, *42*(Suppl. 6), 9–18.

Steriade, M. Arousal: Revisiting the reticular activating system. *Science*, 1996, *272*, 225–226.

Steriade, M., Paré, D., Datta, S., Oakson, G., and Curr Dossi, R. Different cellular types in mesopontine cholinergic nuclei related to ponto-geniculo-occipital waves. *Journal of Neuroscience*, 1990, *8*, 2560–2579.

Sterman, M. B., and Clemente, C. D. Forebrain inhibitory mechanisms: Cortical synchronization induced by basal forebrain stimulation. *Experimental Neurology*, 1962a, *6*, 91–102.

Sterman, M. B., and Clemente, C. D. Forebrain inhibitory mechanisms: Sleep patterns induced by basal forebrain stimulation in the behaving cat. *Experimental Neurology*, 1962b, *6*, 103–117.

Sternbach, R. A. *Pain: A Psychophysiological Analysis*. New York: Academic Press, 1968.

Stevens, J. R. Neurology and neuropathology of schizophrenia. In *Schizophrenia as a Brain Disease*, edited by F. A. Henn and H. A. Nasrallah. New York: Oxford University Press, 1982.

Stevens, J. R. Schizophrenia and multiple sclerosis. *Schizophrenia Bulletin*, 1988, *14*, 231–241.

Stevens, S. S., and Newman, E. B. Localization of actual sources of sound. *American Journal of Psychology*, 1936, *48*, 297–306.

Stinson, D., and Thompson, C. Clinical experience with phototherapy. *Journal of the Affective Disorders*, 1990, *18*, 129–135.

Stolerman, I. P., and Jarvis, M. J. The scientific case that nicotine is addictive. *Psychopharmacology*, 1995, *117*, 2–10.

Stoll, S., Hafner, U., Pohl, O, and Muller, W. E. Age-related memory decline and longevity under treatment with Selegiline. *Life Sciences*, 1994, *55*, 2155–2163.

Stone, A. A., Reed, B. R., and Neale, J. M. Changes in daily event frequency precede episodes of physical symptoms. *Journal of Human Stress*, 1987, *13*, 70–74.

Stoyva, J., and Metcalf, D. Sleep patterns following chronic exposure to cholinesterase-inhibiting organophosphate compounds. *Psychophysiology*, 1968, *5*, 206.

Stricker, E. M., Swerdloff, A. F., and Zigmond, M. J. Intrahypothalamic injections of kainic acid produces feeding and drinking deficits in rats. *Brain Research*, 1978, *158*, 470–473.

Strömland, K., Nordin, V., Miller, M., Akerstrom, B., and Gillberg, C. Autism in thalidomide embryopathy: A population study. *Developmental Medicine and Child Neurology*, 1994, *36*, 351–356.

Stromswold, K., Kaplan, D., Alpert, N., and Rauch, S. Localization of syntactic comprehension by positron emission tomography. *Brain and Language*, 1996, *52*, 452–73.

Stunkard, A. J., Sørensen, T. I. A., Harris, C., Teasdale, T. W., Chakraborty, R., Schull, W. J., and Schulsinger, F. An adoption study of human obesity. *New England Journal of Medicine*, 1986, *314*, 193–198.

Sturgis, J. D., and Bridges, R. S. N-methyl-D-aspartic acid lesions of the medial preoptic area disrupt ongoing parental behavior in male rats. *Physiology and Behavior*, 1997, *62*, 305–310.

Sturup, G. K. Correctional treatment and the criminal sexual offender. *Canadian Journal of Correction*, 1961, *3*, 250–265.

Su, T.-P., Pagliaro, M., Schmidt, P. J., Pickar, D., Wolkowitz, O., and Rubinow, D. R. Neuropsychiatric effects of anabolic steroids in male normal volunteers. *Journal of the American Medical Association*, 1993, *269*, 2760–2764.

Suddath, R. L., Christison, G. W., Torrey, E. F., Casanova, M. F., and Weinberger, D. R. Anatomical abnormalities in the brains of monozygotic twins discordant for schizophrenia. *New England Journal of Medicine*, 1990, *322*, 789–794.

Sunderland, G. S., and Sclafani, A. Taste preferences of squirrel monkeys and bonnet macaques for polycose, maltose, and sucrose. *Physiology and Behavior*, 1988, *43*, 685–690.

Sutherland, R. J., and Rudy, J. W. Configural association theory: The role of the hippocampal formation in learning, memory, and amnesia. *Psychobiology*, 1989, *17*, 129–144.

Sutherland, R. J., McDonald, R. J., and Savage, D. D. Prenatal exposure to moderate levels of ethanol can have long-lasting effects on hippocampal synaptic plasticity in adult offspring. *Hippocampus*, 1997, *7*, 232–238.

Suzdak, P. D., Glowa, J. R., Crawley, J. N., Schwartz, R. D., Skolnick, P., and Paul, S. M. A selective imidazobenzodiazepine antagonist of ethanol in the rat. *Science*, 1986, *234*, 1243–1247.

Svare, B. Psychobiological determinants of maternal aggressive behavior. In *Aggressive Behavior: Genetic and Neural Approaches*, edited by E. C. Simmel, M. E. Hahn, and J. K. Walters. Hillsdale, N.J.: Lawrence Erlbaum Associates, 1983.

Svare, B. Recent advances in the study of female aggressive behavior in mice. In *House Mouse Aggression: A Model for Understanding the Evolution of Social Behavior*, edited by S. Parmigiani, D. Mainardi, and P. Brain. London: Gordon and Breach, 1989.

Svare, B., and Gandelman, R. Postpartum aggression in mice: The influence of suckling stimulation. *Hormones and Behavior*, 1976, *7*, 407–416.

Svare, B., Betteridge, C., Katz, D., and Samuels, O. Some situational and experiential determinants of maternal aggression in mice. *Physiology and Behavior*, 1981, *26*, 253–258.

Svare, B., Mann, M. A., Broida, J., and Michael, S. Maternal aggression exhibited by hypophysectomized parturient mice. *Hormones and Behavior*, 1982, *16*, 455–461.

Svennilson, E., Torvik, A., Lowe, R., and Leksell, L. Treatment of Parkinsonism by stereotactic thermolesions in the pallidal region. *Neurologica Scandanavica*, 1960, *35*, 358–377.

Sverd, J. Tourette syndrome and autistic disorder: A significant relationship. *American Journal of Medical Genetics*, 1991, *39*, 173–179.

Swaab, D. F., and Hofman, M. A. An enlarged suprachiasmatic nucleus in homosexual men. *Brain Research*, 1990, *537*, 141–148.

Swaab, D. F., and Hofman, M. A. Sexual differentiation of the human hypothalamus in relation to gender and sexual orientation. *Trends in Neuroscience*, 1995, *18*, 264–270.

Swanson, R. A. Physiologic coupling of glial glycogen metabolism to neuronal activity in brain. *Canadian Journal of Physiology and Pharmacology*, 1992, *70*, S138–S144.

Swanson, R. A., Morton, M. M., Sagar, S. M., and Sharp, F. R. Sensory stimulation induces local cerebral glycogenolysis: Demonstration by autoradiography. *Neuroscience*, 1992, *51*, 451–456.

Swedo, S. E., Pietrini, P., Leonard, H. L., Schapiro, M. B., Rettew, D.C., Goldberger, E. L., Rapoport, S. I., Rapoport, J. L., and Grady, C. L. Cerebral glucose metabolism in childhood-onset obsessive-compulsive disorder: Revisualization during pharmacotherapy. *Archives of General Psychiatry*, 1992, *49*, 690–694.

Swedo, S., Rapoport, J., Cheslow, D., Leonard, H., Ayoub, E., Hosier, D., and Wald, E. High prevalence of obsessive compulsive symptoms in patients with Sydenham's chorea. *American Journal of Psychiatry*, 1989a, *146*, 246–249.

Swedo, S. E., Schapiro, M. B., Grady, C. L., Cheslow, D. L., Leonard, H. L., Kumarn, A., Friedland, R., Rapoport, S. I., and Rapoport, J. L. Cerebral glucose metabolism in childhood-onset obsessive-compulsive disorder. *Archives of General Psychiatry*, 1989b, *46*, 518–523.

Sweet, W. H. Participant in brain stimulation in behaving subjects. Neurosciences Research Program Workshop, 1966.

Swerdlow, N. R., Geyer, M. A., Vale, W. W., and Koob, G. F. Corticotropin-releasing factor potentiates acoustic startle in rats: Blockade by chlordiazepoxide. *Psychopharmacology*, 1986, *88*, 147–152.

Szuba, M. P., Baxter, L. R., and Fairbanks, L. A. Effects of partial sleep deprivation on the diurnal variation of mood and motor activity in major depression. *Biological Psychiatry*, 1991, *30*, 817–829.

Szymusiak, R., and McGinty, D. Sleep suppression following kainic acid-induced lesions of the basal forebrain. *Experimental Neurology*, 1986, *94*, 598–614.

Tabakoff, B., and Hoffman, P. L. Alcohol addiction: An enigma among us. *Neuron*, 1996, *16*, 909–912.

Takahashi, L. K. Hormonal regulation of sociosexual behavior in female mammals. *Neuroscience and Biobehavioral Reviews*, 1990, *14*, 403–413.

Takahashi, L. K., Turner, J. G., and Kalin, N. H. Prenatal stress alters brain catecholaminergic activity and potentiates stress-induced behavior in adult rats. *Brain Research*, 1992, *574*, 131–137.

Takei, N., Sham, P. C., O'Callaghan, E., Glover, G., and Murray, R. M. Early risk factors in schizophrenia: Place and season of birth. *European Psychiatry*, 1995, *10*, 165–170.

Tam, W.-C. C., and Sewell, K. W. Seasonality of birth in schizophrenia in Taiwan. *Schizophrenia Bulletin*, 1995, *21*, 117–127.

Tanabe, T., Iino, M., Ooshima, Y., and Takagi, S. F. An olfactory area in the prefrontal lobe. *Brain Research*, 1974, *80*, 127–130.

Tanabe, T., Iino, M., and Takagi, S. G. Discrimination of odors in olfactory bulb, pyriform-amygdaloid areas, and orbitofrontal cortex of the monkey. *Journal of Neurophysiology*, 1975, *38*, 1284–1296.

Tanner, C. M. The role of environmental toxins in the aetiology of Parkinson's disease. *Trends in Neurosciences*, 1989, *12*, 49–54.

Taub, E., Miller, N. E., Novack, T. A., Cook, E. W., Fleming, W. C., Nepomuceno, C. S.,

Connell, J. S., and Crago, J. E. Technique to improve chronic motor deficit after stroke. *Archives of Physical Medicine and Rehabilitation*, 1993, *74*, 347–354.

Tei, H., Soma, Y., and Maruyama, S. Right unilateral agraphia following callosal infarction in a left-hander. *European Neurology*, 1994, *34*, 168–172.

Teitelbaum, P., and Epstein, A. N. The lateral hypothalamic syndrome: Recovery of feeding and drinking after lateral hypothalamic lesions. *Psychological Review*, 1962, *69*, 74–90.

Tempel, D. L., Leibowitz, K. J., and Leibowitz, S. F. Effects of PVN galanin on macronutrient selection. *Peptides*, 1988, *9*, 309–314.

Terenius, L., and Wahlström, A. Morphine-like ligand for opiate receptors in human CSF. *Life Sciences*, 1975, *16*, 1759–1764.

Terry, R. D., and Davies, P. Dementia of the Alzheimer type. *Annual Review of Neuroscience*, 1980, *3*, 77–96.

Tetel, M. J., Celentano, D. C., and Blaustein, J. D. Intraneuronal convergence of tactile and hormonal stimuli associated with female reproduction in rats. *Journal of Neuroendocrinology*, 1994, *6*, 211–216.

Tetel, M. J., Getzinger, M. J., and Blaustein, J. D. Fos expression in the rat brain following vaginal-cervical stimulation by mating and manual probing. *Journal of Neuroendocrinology*, 1993, *5*, 397–404.

Tetrud, J. W., and Langston, J. W. The effect of deprenyl (Selegiline) on the natural history of Parkinson's disease. *Science*, 1989, *245*, 519–522.

Theorell, T., Leymann, H., Jodko, M., Konarski, K., Norbeck, H. E., and Eneroth, P. "Person under train" incidents: Medical consequences for subway drivers. *Psychosomatic Medicine*, 1992, *54*, 480–488.

Thiels, E., Xie, X. P., Yeckel, M. F., Barrionuevo, G., and Berger, T. W. NMDA receptor-dependent LTD in different subfields of hippocampus in vivo and in vitro. *Hippocampus*, 1996, *6*, 43–51.

Thompson, L. T., and Best, P. J. Long-term stability of the place-field activity of single units recorded from the dorsal hippocampus of freely behaving rats. *Brain Research*, 1990, *509*, 299–308.

Thompson, S. M., Fortunato, C., McKinney, R. A., Müller, M., and Gähwiler, B. H. Mechanisms underlying the neuropathological consequences of epileptic activity in the rat hippocampus in vitro. *Journal of Comparative Neurology*, 1996, *372*, 515–528.

Thrasher, T. N. Role of forebrain circumventricular organs in body fluid blance. *Acta Physiologica Scandanavica*, 1989, *136 (Suppl. 583)*, 141–150.

Thrasher, T. N., and Keil, L. C. Regulation of drinking and vasopressin secretion: Role of organum vasculosum laminae terminalis. *American Journal of Physiology*, 1987, *253*, R108–R120.

Tordoff, M. G., and Friedman, M. I. Hepatic control of feeding: Effect of glucose, fructose, and mannitol. *American Journal of Physiology*, 1988, *254*, R969–R976.

Tordoff, M. G., Hopfenbeck, J., and Novin, D. Hepatic vagotomy (partial hepatic denervation) does not alter ingestive responses to metabolic challenges. *Physiology and Behavior*, 1982, *28*, 417–424.

Torrey, E. F., Torrey, B. B., and Peterson, M. R. Seasonality of schizophrenic births in the United States. *Archives of General Psychiatry*, 1979, *34*, 1065–1070.

Träskmann, L., Åsberg, M., Bertilsson, L., and Sjöstrand, L. Monoamine metabolites in CSF and suicidal behavior. *Archives of General Psychiatry*, 1981, *38*, 631–636.

True, W. R., Rice, J., Eisen, S. A., Heath, A. C., Goldberg, J., Lyons, M. J., and Nowak, J. A twin study of genetic and environmental contributions to liability for posttraumatic stress symptoms. *Archives of General Psychiatry*, 1993, *50*, 257–264.

Trujillo, K. A., and Akil, H. Opiate tolerance and dependence: Recent findings and synthesis. *New Biologist*, 1991, *3*, 915–923.

Trulson, M. E., and Jacobs, B. L. Raphe unit activity in freely moving cats: Correlation with level of behavioral arousal. *Brain Research*, 1979, *163*, 135–150.

Tsacopoulos, M., and Magistretti, P. J. Metabolic coupling between glia and neurons. *Journal of Neuroscience*, 1996, *16*, 877–885.

Tsien, J. Z., Huerta, P. T., and Tonegawa, S. The essential role of hippocampal CA1 NMDA receptor-dependent synaptic plasticity in spatial memory. *Cell*, 1996, *87*, 1327–1338.

Tsuang, M. T., Gilbertson, M. W., and Faraone, S. V. The genetics of schizophrenia: Current knowledge and future directions. *Schizophrenia Research*, 1991, *4*, 157–171.

Turetsky, B., Cowell, P. E., Gur, R. C., Grossman, R. I., Shtasel, D. L., and Gur, R. E. Frontal and temporal lobe brain volumes in schizophrenia: Relationship to symptoms and clinical subtype. *Archives of General Psychiatry*, 1995, *52*, 1061–1070.

Turner, S. M., Beidel, D. C., and Nathan, R. S. Biological factors in obsessive-compulsive disorders. *Psychological Bulletin*, 1985, *97*, 430–450.

Tyrell, J. B., and Baxter, J. D. Glucocorticoid therapy. In *Endocrinology and Metabolism*, edited by P. Felig, J. D. Baxter, A. E. Broadus, and L. A. Frohman. New York: McGraw-Hill, 1981.

Ungerleider, L. G., and Mishkin, M. Two cortical visual systems. In *Analysis of Visual Behavior*, edited by D. J. Ingle, M. A. Goodale, and R. J. W. Mansfield. Cambridge, Mass.: MIT Press, 1982.

Uno, H., Tarara, R., Else, J. G., Suleman, M. A., and Sapolsky, R. M. Hippocampal damage associated with prolonged and fatal stress in primates. *Journal of Neuroscience*, 1989, *9*, 1705–1711.

Valenstein, E. S. *Brain Control*. New York: John Wiley & Sons, 1973.

Valenstein, E. S. *Great and Desperate Cures: The Rise and Decline of Psychosurgery and Other Radical Treatments for Mental Illness*. New York: Basic Books, 1986.

van de Poll, N. E., Taminiau, M. S., Endert, E., and Louwerse, A. L. Gonadal steroid influence upon sexual and aggressive behavior of female rats. *International Journal of Neuroscience*, 1988, *41*, 271–286.

van der Lee, S., and Boot, L. M. Spontaneous pseudopregnancy in mice. *Acta Physiologica et Pharmacologica Néerlandica*, 1955, *4*, 442–444.

Van Essen, D. C., Anderson, C. H., and Felleman, D. J. Information processing in the primate visual system: An integrated systems perspective. *Science*, 1992, *255*, 419–423.

Van Tol, H. H. M., Bunzow, J. R., Hong-Chang, G., Sunahara, R. K., Seeman, P., Niznik, H. B., and Civelli, O. Cloning of the gene for a human dopamine D4 receptor with high affinity for the antipsychotic clozapine. *Nature*, 1991, *350*, 614–619.

Vandenbergh, J. G., Whitsett, J. M., and Lombardi, J. R. Partial isolation of a pheromone accelerating puberty in female mice. *Journal of Reproductive Fertility*, 1975, *43*, 515–523.

Vanderwolf, C. H. The electrocorticogam in relation to physiology and behavior: A new analysis. *Electroencephalography and Clinical Neurophysiology*, 1992, *82*, 165–175.

Vassar, R., Ngai, J., and Axel, R. Spatial segregation of odorant receptor expression in the mammalian olfactory epithelium. *Cell*, 1993, *74*, 309–318.

Vergnes, M., Depaulis, A., Boehrer, A., and Kempf, E. Selective increase of offensive behavior in the rat following intrahypothalamic 5,7-DHT-induced serotonin depletion. *Brain Research*, 1988, *29*, 85–91.

Verney, E. B. The antidiuretic hormone and the factors which determine its release. *Proceedings of the Royal Society of London [B]*, 1947, *135*, 25–106.

Victor, M., and Agamanolis, J. Amnesia due to lesions confined to the hippocampus: A clinical-pathological study. *Journal of Cognitive Neuroscience*, 1990, *2*, 246–257.

Voci, V. E., and Carlson, N. R. Enhancement of maternal behavior and nest behavior following systemic and diencephalic administration of prolactin and progesterone in the mouse. *Journal of Comparative and Physiological Psychology*, 1973, *83*, 388–393.

Vogel, G. W., Buffenstein, A., Minter, K., and Hennessey, A. Drug effects on REM sleep and on endogenous depression. *Neuroscience and Biobehavioral Reviews*, 1990, *14*, 49–63.

Vogel, G. W., Thurmond, A., Gibbons, P., Sloan, K., Boyd, M., and Walker, M. REM sleep reduction effects on depression syndromes. *Archives of General Psychiatry*, 1975, *32*, 765–777.

Vogel, G. W., Vogel, F., McAbee, R. S., and Thurmond, A. J. Improvement of depression by REM sleep deprivation: New findings and a theory. *Archives of General Psychiatry*, 1980, *37*, 247–253.

Volpe, B. T., LeDoux, J. E., and Gazzaniga, M. S. Information processing of visual stimuli in an extinguished field. *Nature*, 1979, *282*, 722.

vom Saal, F. S. Models of early hormonal effects on intrasex aggression in mice. In *Hormones and Aggressive Behavior*, edited by B. B. Svare. New York: Plenum Press, 1983.

vom Saal, F. S. Time-contingent change in infanticide and parental behavior induced by ejaculation in male mice. *Physiology and Behavior*, 1985, *34*, 7–15.

von Békésy, G. *Experiments in Hearing*. New York: McGraw-Hill, 1960.

Wahlestedt, C., Skagerberg, G., Edman, R., Heilig, M., Sundler, F., and Hakanson, R. Neuropeptide Y (NPY) in the area of the paraventricular nucleus activates the pituitary-adrenocortical axis in the rat. *Brain Research*, 1987, *417*, 33–38.

Walker, E. F., Lewine, R. R. J., and Neumann, C. Childhood behavioral characteristics and adult brain morphology in schizophrenia. *Schizophrenia Research*, 1996, *22*, 93–101.

Walker, E. F., Savoie, T., and Davis, D. Neuromotor precursors of schizophrenia. *Schizophrenia Bulletin*, 1994, *20*, 441–451.

Walker, P. A., and Meyer, W. J. Medroxyprogesterone acetate for paraphiliac sex offender. In *Violence and the Violent Individual*, edited by J. R. Hays, T. K. Roberts, and T. S. Solway. New York: SP Medical and Scientific Books, 1981.

Wallen, K. Desire and ability: Hormones and the regulation of female sexual behavior. *Neuroscience and Biobehavioral Reviews*, 1990, *14*, 233–241.

Wallen, K., Mann, D. R., Davis-DaSilva, M., Gaventa, S., Lovejoy, J. C., and Collins, D.C. Chronic gonadotropin-releasing hormone agonist treatment suppresses ovulation and sexual behavior in group-living female rhesus monkeys (*Macaca mulatta*). *Animal Behaviour*, 1986, *36*, 369–375.

Walsh, V., and Butler, S. R. The effects of visual cortex lesions on the perception of rotated shapes. *Behavioural Brain Research*, 1996, *76*, 127–142.

Walsh, V., Carden, D., Butler, S. R., and Kulikowski, J. J. The effects of V4 lesions on the visual abilities of macaques: Hue discrimination and color constancy. *Behavioural Brain Research*, 1993, *53*, 51–62.

Walters, E. E., and Kendler, K. S. Anorexia nervosa and anorexic-like syndromes in a population-based female twin sample. *American Journal of Psychiatry*, 1995, *152*, 64–71.

Wang, G., Tanaka, K., and Tanifuji, M. Optical imaging of functional organization in the monkey inferotemporal cortex. *Science*, 1996, *272*, 1665–1668.

Warrington, E. K., and James, M. Visual apperceptive agnosia: A clinico-anatomical study of three cases. *Cortex*, 1988, *24*, 1–32.

Warrington, E. K., and Shallice, T. Word-form dyslexia. *Brain*, 1980, *103*, 99–112.

Webb, W. B. *Sleep: The Gentle Tyrant*. Englewood Cliffs, N.J.: Prentice-Hall, 1975.

Webb, W. B. Some theories about sleep and their clinical implications. *Psychiatric Annals*, 1982, *11*, 415–422.

Webster, H. H., and Jones, B. E. Neurotoxic lesions of the dorsolateral pontomesencephalic tegmentum-cholinergic cell area in the cat. II: Effects upon sleep-waking states. *Brain Research*, 1988, *458*, 285–302.

Wehr, T. A. Improvement of depression and triggering of mania by sleep deprivation. *Journal of the American Medical Association*, 1992, *267*, 548–551.

Wehr, T. A., Giesen, H. A., Schulz, P. M., Anderson, J. L., Joseph-Vanderpool, J. R., Kelly, K., Kasper, S., and Rosenthal, N. E. Contrasts between symptoms of summer depression and winter depression. *Journal of the Affective Disorders*, 1991, *23*, 173–183.

Wehr, T. A., Sack, D. A., and Rosenthal, N. E. Seasonal affective disorder with summer depression and winter hypomania. *American Journal of Psychiatry*, 1987, *114*, 1602–1603.

Weinberger, D. R. Schizophrenia and the frontal lobe. *Trends in Neurosciences*, 1988, *11*, 367–370.

Weinberger, D. R., and Wyatt, R. J. Brain morphology in schizophrenia: *In vivo* studies. In *Schizophrenia as a Brain Disease*, edited by F. A. Henn and H. A. Nasrallah. New York: Oxford University Press, 1982.

Weiner, R. D., and Krystal, A. D. The present use of electroconvulsive therapy. *Annual Review of Medicine*, 1994, *45*, 273–281.

Weiskrantz, L. Residual vision in a scotoma: A follow-up study of "form" discrimination. *Brain*, 1987, *110*, 77–92.

Weiskrantz, L., Warrington, E. K., Sanders, M. D., and Marshall, J. Visual capacity in the hemianopic field following a restricted occipital ablation. *Brain*, 1974, *97*, 709–728.

Weiss, J. M. Effects of coping response on stress. *Journal of Comparative and Physiological Psychology*, 1968, *65*, 251–260.

Weissman, M. M., Canino, G. J., Greenwald, S., Joyce, P. R., Karam, E. G., Lee, C. K., Rubio-Stipec, M., Wells, J. E., Wickramaratne, P. J., and Wittchen, H. U. Current rates and symptom profiles of panic disorder in six cross-national studies. *Clinical Neuropharmacology*, 1995, *18*(Suppl. 2), S1–S6.

Weitzman, E. D. Sleep and its disorders. *Annual Review of Neuroscience*, 1981, *4*, 381–418.

Welsh, D. K., Logothetis, D. E., Meister, M., and Reppert, S. M. Individual neurons dissociated from rat suprachiasmatic nucleus express independently phased circadian firing rhythms. *Neuron*, 1995, *14*, 697–706.

Weltzin, T. E., Hsu, L. K. G., Pollice, C., and Kaye, W. H. Feeding patterns in bulimia nervosa. *Biological Psychiatry*, 1991, *30*, 1093–1110.

Wernicke, C. *Der Aphasische Symptomenkomplex*. Breslau, Prussia: Cohn & Weigert, 1874.

Westbrook, P. R. Treatment of sleep disordered breathing: Nasal continuous positive airway pressure (CPAP). *Progress in Clinical Biology Research*, 1990, *345*, 387–394.

Whipple, B., and Komisaruk, B. R. Analgesia produced in women by genital self-stimulation. *Journal of Sex Research*, 1988, *24*, 130–140.

White, F. J. Synaptic regulation of mesocorticolimbic dopamine neurons. *Annual Review of Neuroscience*, 1996, *19*, 405–436.

White, J. Autonomic discharge from stimulation of the hypothalamus in man. *Association for Research in Nervous and Mental Disorders*, 1940, *20*, 854–863.

Whitfield, I. C., and Evans, E. F. Responses of auditory cortical neurons to stimuli of changing frequency. *Journal of Neurophysiology*, 1965, *28*, 655–672.

Whitten, W. K. Occurrence of anestrus in mice caged in groups. *Journal of Endocrinology*, 1959, *18*, 102–107.

Wiener, S. I., Paul, C. A., and Eichenbaum, H. Spatial and behavioral correlates of hippocampal neuronal activity. *Journal of Neuroscience*, 1989, *9*, 2737–2763.

Wiesner, B. P., and Sheard, N. *Maternal Behaviour in the Rat*. London: Oliver and Brody, 1933.

Wilckens, T., Schweiger, U., and Pirke, K. M. Activation of 5-HT$_{1C}$-receptors suppresses excessive wheel running induced by semi-starvation in the rat. *Psychopharmacology (Berlin)*, 1992, *109*, 77–84.

Wilson, B. E., Meyer, G. E., Cleveland, J. C., and Weigle, D. S. Identification of candidate genes for a factor regulating body weight in primates. *American Journal of Physiology*, 1990, *259*, R1148–R1155.

Wilson, F. A. W., Scalaidhe, S. P. O., and Goldman-Rakic, P. S. Dissociation of object and spatial processing domains in primate prefrontal cortex. *Science*, 1993, *260*, 1955–1958.

Winans, S. S., and Powers, J. B. Olfactory and vomeronasal deafferentation of male hamsters: Histological and behavioral analyses. *Brain Research*, 1977, *126*, 325–344.

Winslow, J. T., and Miczek, J. A. Social status as determinants of alcohol effects on aggressive behavior in squirrel monkeys (*Saimiri sciureus*). *Psychopharmacology*, 1985, *85*, 167–172.

Winslow, J. T., Ellingoe, J., and Miczek, J. A. Effects of alcohol on aggressive behavior in squirrel monkeys: Influence of testosterone and social context. *Psychopharmacology*, 1988, *95*, 356–363.

Winter, P., and Funkenstein, H. The auditory cortex of the squirrel monkey: Neuronal discharge patterns to auditory stimuli. *Proceedings of the 3rd Congress of Primatology, Zurich*, 1971, *2*, 24–28.

Wirz-Justice, A., Graw, P., Kraeuchi, K., Gisin, B., Jochum, A., Arendt, J., Fisch, H.-U., Buddeberg, C., and Poeldinger, W. Light therapy in seasonal affective disorder is independent of time of day or circadian phase. *Archives of General Psychiatry*, 1993, *50*, 929–937.

Wirz-Justice, A., Graw, P., Kraeuchi, K., Sarrafzadeh, A., English, J., Arendt, J., and Sand, L. 'Natural' light treatment of seasonal affective disorder. *Journal of Affective Disorders*, 1996, *37*, 109–120.

Wise, R., Chollet, F., Hadar, U., Friston, K., Hoffner, E., and Frackowiak, R. Distribution of cortical neural networks involved in word comprehension and word retrieval. *Brain*, 1991, *114*, 1803–1817.

Wise, R. A. Psychomotor stimulant properties of addictive drugs. *Annals of the New York Academy of Sciences*, 1988, *537*, 228–234.

Wise, R. A., Leone, P., Rivest, R., and Leeb, K. Elevations of nucleus accumbens dopamine and DOPAC levels during intravenous heroin self-administration. *Synapse*, 1995, *21*, 140–148.

Wise, S. P., and Rapoport, J. L. Obsessive compulsive disorder: Is it a basal ganglia dysfunction? *Psychopharmacology Bulletin*, 1988, *24*, 380–384.

Wisniewski, H. M., and Wegiel, J. The role of perivascular and microglial cells in fibrillogenesis of β amyloid and PRP protein in Alzheimers disease and scrapie. *Research in Immunology*, 1992, *143*, 642–664.

Wolf, P. A., Cobb, J. L., and D'Agostino, R. B. In *Stroke*, edited by H. J. M. Barnett, B. M. Stein, J. P. Mohr, and F. M. Yatsu. New York: Churchill Livingstone, 1992.

Wolff, P. H., and Melngailis, I. Family patterns of developmental dyslexia: Clinical findings. *American Journal of Medical Genetics*, 1994, *54*, 122–131.

Wong, D. F., Wagner, H. N., Tune, L. E., Dannals, R. F., Pearlson, G. D., Links, J. M., Tamminga, C. A., Broussolle, E. P., Ravert, H. T., Wilson, A. A., Toung, J. K. T., Malat, J., Williams, J. A., O'Tuama, L. A., Snyder, S. H., Kuhar, M. J., and Gjedde, A. Positron emission tomography reveals elevated D$_2$ dopamine receptors in drug-naive schizophrenics. *Science*, 1986, *234*, 1558–1563.

Wong-Riley, M. Personal communication, 1978. Cited by Livingstone, M. S., and Hubel, D. H. Thalamic inputs to cytochrome oxidase-rich regions in monkey visual cortex. *Proceedings of the National Academy of Sciences, USA*, 1982, *79*, 6098–6101.

Wood, D. L., Sheps, S. G., Elveback, L. R., and Schirder, A. Cold pressor test as a predictor of hypertension. *Hypertension*, 1984, *6*, 301–306.

Wood, R. I., and Newman, S. W. Mating activates androgen receptor-containing neurons in chemosensory pathways of the male Syrian hamster brain. *Brain Research*, 1993, *614*, 65–77.

Woodruff, R. A., Guze, S. B., and Clayton, P. J. Anxiety neurosis among psychiatric outpatients. *Comprehensive Psychiatry*, 1972, *13*, 165–170.

Woodruff-Pak, D. S. Eyeblink classical conditioning in H. M.: Delay and trace paradigms. *Behavioral Neuroscience*, 1993, *107*, 911–925.

Woodworth, R. S., and Schlosberg, H. *Experimental Psychology.* New York: Holt, Rinehart and Winston, 1954.

Wooley, S. C., and Garner, D. M. Controversies in management: Should obesity be treated? Dietary treatments for obesity are ineffective. *British Medical Journal,* 1994, *309,* 655–656.

Wu, J. C., and Bunney, W. E. The biological basis of an antidepressant response to sleep deprivation and relapse: Review and hypothesis. *American Journal of Psychiatry,* 1990, *147,* 14–21.

Wu, J. C., Gillin, J. C., Buchsbaum, M. S., Hershey, T., Johnson, J. C., and Bunney, W. E. Effect of sleep deprivation on brain metabolism of depressed patients. *American Journal of Psychiatry,* 1992, *149,* 538–543.

Wysocki, C. J. Neurobehavioral evidence for the involvement of the vomeronasal system in mammalian reproduction. *Neuroscience and Biobehavioral Reviews,* 1979, *3,* 301–341.

Yadin, E., Thomas, E., Strickland, C. E., and Grishkat, H. L. Anxiolytic effects of benzodiazepines in amygdala-lesioned rats. *Psychopharmacology,* 1991, *103,* 473–479.

Yates, W. R., Perry, P., and Murray, S. Aggression and hostility in anabolic steroid users. *Biological Psychiatry,* 1992, *31,* 1232–1234.

Yettefti, K., Orsini, J. C., and Perrin, J. Characteristics of glycemia-sensitive neurons in the nucleus tractus solitarii: Possible involvement in nutritional regulation. *Physiology and Behavior,* 1997, *61,* 93–100

Yokota, T., Ishiai, S., Furukawa, T., and Tsukagoshi, H. Pure agraphia of kanji due to thrombosis of the Labbe vein. *Journal of Neurology, Neurosurgery, and Psychiatry,* 1990, *53,* 335–338.

Yost, W. A. Auditory image perception and analysis: The basis for hearing. *Hearing Research,* 1991, *56,* 8–18.

Young, A. W., Aggleton, J. P., Hellawell, D. J., Johnson, M., Broks, P., and Hanley, J. R. Face processing impairments after amygdalotomy. *Brain,* 1995, *118,* 15–24.

Zeki, S. The representation of colours in the cerebral cortex. *Nature,* 1980, *284,* 412–418.

Zeki, S. The visual image in mind and brain. *Scientific American,* 1992, *267*(3), 69–76.

Zeki, S., and Shipp, S. The functional logic of cortical connections. *Nature,* 1988, *335,* 311–317.

Zeki, S., Watson, J. D. G., Lueck, C. J., Friston, K. J., Kennard, C., and Frackowiak, R. S. A direct demonstration of functional specialization in human visual cortex. *Journal of Neuroscience,* 1991, *11,* 641–649.

Zeng, H. K., Qian, Z. W., Myers, M. P., and Rosbach, M. A light-entrainment mechanism for the *Drosophila* circadian clock. *Nature,* 1996, *380,* 129–135.

Zhang, C. Y., and Wong-Riley, M. T. T. Do nitric oxide synthase, NMDA receptor subunit R1 and cytochrome oxidase co-localize in the rat central nervous system? *Brain Research,* 1996, *729,* 205–215.

Zhou, F. C., Zhang, J. K., Lumeng, L., and Li, T. K. Mesolimbic dopamine system in alcohol-preferring rats. *Alcohol,* 1995, *12,* 403–412.

Zihl, J., Von Cramon, D., Mai, N., and Schmid, C. Disturbance of movement vision after bilateral posterior brain damage: Further evidence and follow up observations. *Brain,* 1991, *114,* 2235–2252.

Zola-Morgan, S., Squire, L. R., and Amaral, D. G. Human amnesia and the medial temporal region: Enduring memory impairment following a bilateral lesion limited to field CA1 of the hippocampus. *Journal of Neuroscience,* 1986, *6,* 2950–2967.

Zola-Morgan, S., Squire, L. R., Rempel, N. L., Clower, R. P., and Amaral, D. G. Enduring memory impairment in monkeys after ischemic damage to the hippocampus. *Journal of Neuroscience,* 1992, *12,* 2582–2596.

Zukin, S. R., Pellegrini-Giampietro, D. E., Knapp, C. M., and Tempel, A. Opioid receptor regulation. *Handbook of Experimental Pharmacology,* 1993, *104,* 107–123.

Zumpe, D., Bonsall, R. W., and Michael, R. P. Effects of the nonsteroidal aromatase inhibitor, fadrozole, on the sexual behavior of male cynomolgus monkeys *(Macaca fascicularis).* *Hormones and Behavior,* 1993, *27,* 200–215.

NAME INDEX

◼ SUBJECT INDEX

Note: Boldfaced page numbers indicate pages where terms are defined.